Cities of the United States

EIGHTH EDITION

Cities of the United States

EIGHTH EDITION

VOLUME 1

THE SOUTH

GALE
CENGAGE Learning·

Farmington Hills, Mich • San Francisco • New York • Waterville, Maine
Meriden, Conn • Mason, Ohio • Chicago

Cities of the United States, 8th edition

Project Editor: Jeffrey Muhr

Editorial: Kristin Key

Product Management: Leigh Ann Cusack

Intellectual Property Project Manager: Lynn Vagg

Composition and Electronic Prepress: Evi Seoud

Manufacturing: Rita Wimberley

Imaging: John Watkins

For product information and technology assistance, contact us at
Gale Customer Support, 1-800-877-4253.

For permission to use material from this text or product,
submit all requests online at **www.cengage.com/permissions.**
Further permissions questions can be emailed to
permissionrequest@cengage.com

Cover photographs reproduced by permission of Shutterstock, except for Denver, CO, Des Moines, IA and New Orleans, LA permission of Getty Images; Chicago, IL and New York, NY permission of Laurie Fundukian; and Denver, CO, and Anchorage, AK permission of Alamy. Banner art within text reproduced by permission of photos.com/Jupiterimages.

While every effort has been made to ensure the reliability of the information presented in this publication, Gale, Cengage Learning, does not guarantee the accuracy of the data contained herein. Gale accepts no payment for listing; and inclusion in the publication of any organization, agency, institution, publication, service, or individual does not imply endorsement of the editors or publisher. Errors brought to the attention of the publisher and verified to the satisfaction of the publisher will be corrected in future editions.

Gale
27500 Drake Rd.
Farmington Hills, MI 48331-3535

ISBN-13: 978-1-5730-2337-5 (4-vol. set)   ISBN-10: 1-5730-2337-X (4-vol. set)
ISBN-13: 978-1-5730-2339-9 (vol. 1)   ISBN-10: 1-5730-2339-6 (vol. 1)
ISBN-13: 978-1-5730-2340-5 (vol. 2)   ISBN-10: 1-5730-2340-X (vol. 2)
ISBN-13: 978-1-5730-2341-2 (vol. 3)   ISBN-10: 1-5730-2341-8 (vol. 3)
ISBN-13: 978-1-5730-2342-9 (vol. 4)   ISBN-10: 1-5730-2342-6 (vol. 4)

ISSN 0899-6075

This title is also available as an e-book.
ISBN-13: 978-1-5730-2343-6
ISBN-10: 1-5730-2343-4
Contact your Gale, Cengage Learning sales representative for ordering information.

Printed in Mexico
1 2 3 4 5 6 7 18 17 16 15 14

Contents

Contents

VOLUME 3—THE MIDWEST

Contents

VOLUME 4—THE NORTHEAST

Introduction

Cities of the United States (CUS) provides a one-stop source for all the vital information you need on 219 of America's top cities—those fastest-growing, as well as those with a particular historical, political, industrial, and/or commercial significance. Spanning the entire country, from Anaheim to Virginia Beach, each geographically-arranged volume of CUS brings together a wide range of comprehensive data. The volumes include: *The South; The West; The Midwest; and The Northeast.*

Within each volume, the city-specific profiles organize pertinent facts, data, and figures related to demographic, economic, cultural, geographic, social, and recreational conditions. Assembling myriad sources, CUS offers researchers, travelers, students, and media professionals a convenient resource for discovering each city's past, present, and future.

For this completely updated eighth edition, ten new cities have been added, providing even greater access to the country's growing urban centers. The new city profiles include:

- Bellevue, NE
- Dover, NH
- Essex, VT
- Idaho Falls, ID
- Joliet, IL
- Key West, FL
- Rogers, AR
- Taos, NM
- Telluride, CO
- Wellesley, MA

Key Features Unlock Vital Information

Cities of the United States offers a range of key features, allowing easy access to targeted information. Features include:

- Section headings—Comprehensive categories, which include **History, Geography and Climate, Population Profile, Municipal Government, Economy, Education, Research, Health Care, Recreation, Convention Facilities, Transportation,** and **Communications** (including city Web sites), make it easy to locate answers to specific questions.

- Combined facts and analysis—Fact-packed charts and detailed descriptions provide statistics and the rest of the story.

- "In Brief" fact sheets—One-page "at a glance" overviews provide the essential facts for each state and each city profiled.

- Economic information—Detailed updates about such topics as incentive programs, development projects, and largest employers help rate the business climate using criteria that matters to people.

- Directory information—Contact information at the end of many entry sections provides addresses, phone numbers, and email addresses for organizations, agencies, and institutions.

- Selected bibliography listings—Historical accounts, biographical works, and other print resources suggest titles to read if one wishes to learn more about a particular city.

- Web sites for vital city resources—Access points to URLs for information-rich sources, such as city government, visitors and convention bureaus, economic development agencies, libraries, schools, and newspapers provide researchers an opportunity to explore cities in more detail.

- Enlightening illustrations—Numerous photographs highlight points of interest.

- Handy indexing—A referencing guide not only to main city entries, but also to the hundreds of people and place names that fall within those main entries, leading a reader directly to the information they seek.

Designed For a Variety of Users

Whether you are a researcher, traveler, or executive on the move, *CUS* serves your needs. This is the reference long sought by a variety of users:

- Business people, market researchers, and other decision-makers will find the current data that helps them stay informed.

- People vacationing, conventioneering, or relocating will consult this source for questions they have about what's new, unique, or significant about where they are going.

- Students, media professionals, and researchers will discover their background work already completed.

Definitions of Key Statistical Resources

Following are explanations of key resources used for statistical data:

ACCRA (The Council for Community Economic Research; formerly the American Chamber of Commerce Researchers Association): The Cost of Living Index, produced quarterly, provides a useful and reasonably accurate measure of living cost differences among urban areas. Items on which the Index is based have been carefully chosen to reflect the different categories of consumer expenditures, such as groceries, housing, utilities, transportation, health care, and miscellaneous goods and services; taxes are excluded. Weights assigned to relative costs are based on government survey data on expenditure patterns for midmanagement households (typically the average professional worker's home, new construction with 2,400 square feet of living space). All items are priced in each place at a specified time and according to standardized specifications. Information regarding ACCRA and the Cost of Living Index can be found at www.accra.org. Please note that the ACCRA Cost of Living Index and ACCRA housing price information are reprinted by permission of ACCRA.

Metropolitan Statistical Area (MSA): The U.S. Office of Management and Budget (OMB) provides that each Metropolitan Statistical Area must include (a) at least one city with 50,000 or more inhabitants, or (b) a U.S. Census Bureau-defined urbanized area (of at least 50,000 inhabitants) and a total metropolitan population of at least 100,000 (75,000 in New England). The term was adopted in 1983. The term "metropolitan area" (MA) became effective in 1990. During the 2000 Census, the MSA standards were revised, establishing Core Based Statistical Areas (CBSAs). CBSAs may be either Metropolitan Statistical Areas or Micropolitan Statistical Areas. It is important to note that standards, and therefore content of 1990 Census MSAs, are not identical to 2000 Census MSA standards. Additional information regarding MSAs can be found at http://census.state.nc. us/glossary/msa.html.

FBI Crime Index Total: The total number of index offenses reported to the FBI during the year through its Uniform Crime Reporting Program. The FBI receives monthly and annual reports from law enforcement agencies throughout the country. City police, sheriffs, and state police file reports on the number of index offenses that become known to them. The FBI Crime Index offenses are: murder and non-negligent manslaughter; forcible rape; robbery; aggravated assault; burglary; larceny; motor vehicle theft; and arson.

Estimates of population: Between decennial censuses, the U.S. Bureau of the Census publishes estimates of the population using the decennial census data as benchmarks and data available from various agencies, both state and federal, including births and deaths, and school statistics, among other data.

Method of Compilation

The editors of *Cities of the United States* consulted numerous sources to secure the kinds of data most valuable. Each entry gathers together economic information culled in part from the U.S. Department of Labor/Bureau of Labor Statistics and state departments of labor and commerce, population figures derived from the U.S. Department of Commerce/ Bureau of the Census and from city and state agencies, educational and municipal government data supplied by local authorities, historical narrative based on a variety of accounts, and geographical and climatic profiles from the National Oceanic and Atmospheric Administration. Along with material supplied by chambers of commerce, convention and visitors bureaus, and other local sources, background information was drawn from periodicals and books chosen for their timeliness and accuracy. Through print resources, web sites, email contact, and/or phone calls with agency representatives, the information contained reflects current conditions.

Acknowledgments

The editors are grateful for the assistance provided by dozens of helpful chambers of commerce and convention and visitors bureau professionals, as well as municipal, library, and school employees for their invaluable generosity and expertise.

Comments and Suggestions Welcome

If you have questions, concerns, or comments about *Cities of the United States*, please contact the Project Editor:

Cities of the United States
Gale
27500 Drake Road
Farmington Hills, MI 48331
Phone: (248)699-4253
Toll-free: (800)347-GALE
Fax: (248)699-8075
URL: www.gale.cengage.com

Alabama

The State in Brief

Nickname: Heart of Dixie; Camellia State

Motto: We dare defend our rights

Flower: Camellia

Bird: Yellowhammer

Area: 52,420 square miles (2010; U.S. rank 30th)

Elevation: Ranges from sea level to 2,407 feet

Climate: Subtropical and humid; summers are long and hot, winters mild, rainfall abundant

Admitted to Union: December 14, 1819

Capital: Montgomery

Head Official: Robert Bentley (R) (until 2015)

Population

1990: 4,040,587
2000: 4,447,100
2010: 4,779,736
2012 estimate: 4,777,326
Percent change, 2000–2010: 7.5%
U.S. rank in 2012: 23rd
Percent of residents born in state: 70.2% (2012)
Density: 94.4 people per square mile (2010)
2012 FBI Crime Index Total: 190,571

Racial and Ethnic Characteristics (2012)

White: 3,321,318
Black or African American: 1,256,097
American Indian and Alaska Native: 26,166
Asian: 54,923
Native Hawaiian and Pacific Islander: 1,298
Hispanic or Latino (may be of any race): 182,268
Other: 117,524

Age Characteristics (2012)

Population under 5 years old: 305,091
Population 5 to 19 years old: 965,003
Percent of population 65 years and over: 13.9%
Median age: 37.8

Vital Statistics

Total number of births (2012–13): 58,858
Total number of deaths (2012–13): 48,922
AIDS cases reported through 2011: 10,596

Economy

Major industries: Paper products, agriculture, chemicals, textiles, lumber, wood, metals, electronics, automobiles, food processing
Unemployment rate (2012): 6.1%
Per capita income (2012): $23,587
Median household income (2012): $43,160
Percentage of persons below poverty level (2012): 18.1%
Income tax rate: 2.0% to 5.0%
Sales tax rate: 4.0%

Birmingham

■ The City in Brief

Founded: 1871 (chartered 1864)

Head Official: Mayor William A. Bell, Sr. (since 2010; current term expires 2017)

City Population
1990: 265,347
2000: 242,820
2010: 212,237
2012 estimate: 212,835
Percent change, 2000–2010: −12.6%
U.S. rank in 1990: 60th (State rank: 1st)
U.S. rank in 2000: 82nd (State rank: 1st)
U.S. rank in 2010: 97th (State rank: 1st)

Metropolitan Statistical Area Population
2000: 921,106
2010: 1,128,047
2012 estimate: 1,136,650
Percent change, 2000–2010: 22.5%
U.S. rank in 2000: 48th
U.S. rank in 2010: 49th

Area: 146.07 square miles

Elevation: 614 feet above sea level

Average Annual Temperatures: January, 43° F; July, 80° F; annual average 63° F

Average Annual Precipitation: 52.2 inches of rain; 2.1 inches of snow

Major Economic Sectors: steel, medical and banking industries, trade, finance, research, government

Unemployment Rate: 8.7% (2012)

Per Capita Income: $18,768

2012 FBI Crime Index Property: 14,788

Major Colleges and Universities: University of Alabama at Birmingham, Samford University, Birmingham-Southern College, Miles College

Daily Newspaper: *Birmingham News*

■ Introduction

Modern Birmingham calls itself the Magic City, but this young city, which was founded after the Civil War, has seen its days of adversity. Early in its history it suffered from epidemics, crime, and violence. It failed badly in two depressions and saw, in its darkest days, violent racial confrontations. After years of hard work on race relations, Birmingham gradually moved to such a state of racial equality that it was designated an All-America City in 1970 for its progress. Once dubbed the "Pittsburgh of the South," the city now employs the majority of its workers in service jobs. The arts continue to flourish, the city's medical research and treatment facilities are world class, and Birmingham ranks as one of the most important financial and banking centers in the southeastern United States. Residents attend plays, concerts, and sporting events in some of the finest facilities in the country, and they shop, eat, and relax in one of the Southeast's largest enclosed malls, the sparkling Riverchase Galleria. At the heart of the new Birmingham stands the city's symbol, a statue of Vulcan, Roman god of fire and the forge. To many, Birmingham seems to have been magically forged anew. In 2013 the National Civic League agreed again by naming Birmingham an All-America City.

■ Geography and Climate

Located 300 miles north of the Gulf of Mexico in north-central Alabama, Birmingham lies in the Jones Valley between a ridge of hills running from northeast to southwest and the Red Mountain Range, which runs in

Darryl Vest/Shutterstock.com

roughly the same direction. A hilly city, Birmingham stretches for about 15 miles along the valley. The hills northeast and north of the city are the foothills of the Appalachian Mountains. During winter, Birmingham experiences rather low minimum temperatures. Occasional very low temperatures prevent the growth of some vegetation that might usually be expected in a subtropical climate. Snow accumulation, however, is seldom heavy enough to cause problems. In summer, days are very warm; from April through October the daily highs are usually above 75° F, with lows seldom falling below 50° F. Most summer precipitation comes in the form of thunderstorms, especially in the month of July. In late summer and fall, Birmingham experiences occasional tropical storms and hurricanes due to its proximity to the Central Gulf Coast. Birmingham is located in Dixie Alley, a tornado alley that runs from northeast Texas to northern Alabama.

Area: 146.07 square miles

Elevation: 614 feet above sea level

Average Temperatures: January, 43° F; July, 80° F; annual average 63° F

Average Annual Precipitation: 52.2 inches of rain; 2.1 inches of snow

■ History

Steel-Making Potential Spurs Growth

The Cherokee, Choctaw, and Chickasaw tribes hunted in the Jones Valley long before the first European set foot there. The natives found a valley teeming with game and strikingly marked with giant outcroppings of red rock. John Jones and a group of pioneers came to the area in 1815 and established the village of Jonesboro, and in 1819 Jefferson County was formed. Over the next few decades the population of the area gradually increased, and the abundant red rock was found to be high-grade iron ore. By the time of the Civil War, two ore-reducing furnaces were operating for the Confederacy. They were destroyed by Wilson's Raiders in 1865, and development of the valley was virtually halted until 1871, when the Elyton Land Company, realizing the tremendous potential of the valley rich in not only iron ore, but also coal and limestone—the essential ingredients in steel making—founded and incorporated a city to be built at the junction of two major railroads. Thus Birmingham, named for the steel-producing city in England, came into being.

With the expansion of the railroads, what had once been farms and woods became a boomtown, its population growing from 1,200 people in 1871 to 4,000 people in 1873. By 1875, however, after a cholera epidemic and other setbacks, the city's population had dropped back to 1,200 people. Birmingham expanded again in 1880 when the Pratt mining operation began making coke. Two coke furnaces went into blast that year, and by 1885 the population was 25,000 people. Birmingham was growing, and it was beginning to experience some big-city problems, such as crime and disease (particularly typhoid, dysentery, and tuberculosis). The 1890s marked the founding of Birmingham-Southern College, the Mercy Home, and St. Vincent's Hospital, but it was also a decade torn by violence stemming from dangerous mine and foundry conditions and conflicts between union organizers and mine owners.

After January 1, 1900, when the first commercial shipment of steel was made, rolling mills and other factories producing finished steel products began operating in Birmingham. Labor troubles continued in the new century, and the city was plagued with corrupt government officials, vice, and gambling. But Birmingham was growing in positive ways as well. A new model town of Corey, planned by U.S. Steel, was developed by private business, and eight suburbs were incorporated into the city, doubling its population.

In October 1921, the city celebrated its fiftieth birthday with four days of festivities, including a visit by U.S. President Warren G. Harding and his wife. On a crest of prosperity that followed World War I, new apartment buildings, hotels, business facilities, and homes went up in Birmingham. During the 1920s, however, the secret white-supremacist organization, the Ku Klux Klan, gained considerable influence in the city; harassment, floggings, and unexplained violence against African Americans were unofficially tolerated by local authorities. As a one-industry town, Birmingham was devastated when the Great Depression of the 1930s reduced demand for iron and steel products; it quickly was deemed "the hardest hit city in the nation" by President Hoover's administration.

Birmingham was slow to recover from the Depression, although the federal government poured more than $350 million into the area in an attempt to stimulate the economy. The Works Progress Administration (WPA) tended to Birmingham's streets and parks, and among its projects was the restoration of the city's statue of Vulcan, the Roman god of the forge. The statue was removed from the fairgrounds and placed atop a pedestal on Red Mountain, where it still stands today. Gradually the city began to recover, and by the time World War II was declared in Europe, Birmingham's manufacturing plants were busy preparing for an all-out war effort.

City Meets Post-War Challenges

Following World War II, the economy of Birmingham continued to flourish. To help fill the need for economic diversification, two important institutions were brought to the city: the Medical School of the University of Alabama at Birmingham and the Alabama Research Institute. A development committee attracted more than one hundred new industries to the Birmingham area in the decade following World War II.

In spite of such diversification, however, Birmingham was still hard hit by a recession in 1957, and by 1960 the city was again struggling with unemployment. Along with economic woes, Birmingham was embroiled in civil rights conflicts in the 1950s and 1960s as it sought to avoid forced integration of public transport and facilities. In 1963 civil rights advocate Martin Luther King, Jr. began leading peaceful demonstrations in Birmingham. African American children joining in the protests were arrested by the thousands, and photographs from Birmingham of demonstrators being hosed down by police and attacked by police dogs were published worldwide. State police eventually were called in to help restore order. Tensions over the proposed full-scale integration of city classrooms erupted in more violence when a bomb exploded in the basement of a church, killing four young girls who were changing into their choir robes. Birmingham and the nation were shocked by the event, which convinced the city of the need for change and signaled the end of racial violence.

The 1970s proved to be the start of a new beginning for Birmingham. Birmingham was once again booming, as residential areas spread south and east, millions of feet of warehouse space were constructed, new shopping malls sprang up, and the downtown area was revitalized. Urban renewal efforts focused on the development of the University of Alabama at Birmingham, which helped position the city as a major medical and research center. Finally, the 1979 election of an African American educator as mayor ushered in a new era of racial harmony. One of Birmingham's darkest chapters ended in 2002 when jurors delivered a guilty verdict in the case of the 1963 church bombing that killed four African American girls.

In 2005 the Gulf Coast of Alabama and neighboring states were severely damaged by Hurricane Katrina. Some 112,866 Alabamans registered with the Federal Emergency Management Agency (FEMA) following the hurricane. Birmingham, like all cities and towns in Alabama, provided assistance to more than 40,000 displaced residents in areas where homes were destroyed.

With just more than one million residents in the metropolitan area, Birmingham is the largest city in Alabama. It has become a worldwide center for health care and boasts a large regional presence in finance, education, research, engineering, transportation, and distribution. The early part of the new century saw the city as a booming technological center, with a growing number of people employed in technology jobs. Its symphony, ballet, orchestra, and outstanding schools make it a leader in the arts. And, above all, Birmingham's residents have made integration work—in employment, education, recreation, and health care.

Historical Information: Birmingham Historical Society, One Sloss Quarters, Birmingham, AL 35222; telephone (205) 251-1880.

■ Population Profile

Metropolitan Statistical Area Population

1990: 839,945
2000: 921,106
2012 estimate: 1,136,650
Percent change, 2000–2010: 22.5%
U.S. rank in 2000: 48th
U.S. rank in 2010: 49th

City Residents

1990: 265,347
2000: 242,820
2010: 212,237
2012 estimate: 212,835
Percent change, 2000–2010: −12.6%
U.S. rank in 1990: 60th (State rank: 1st)
U.S. rank in 2000: 82nd (State rank: 1st)
U.S. rank in 2010: 97th (State rank: 1st)

Density: 1,453.0 people per square mile

Racial and ethnic characteristics

White: 47,736
Black or African American: 156,390
American Indian and Alaskan Native: 117
Asian: 2,715
Native Hawaiian and Other Pacific Islander: 132
Hispanic or Latino (may be of any race): 10,012
Other: 5,745

Percent of residents born in state: 79.5%

Age characteristics

Population under 5 years old: 16,128
Population 5 to 9 years old: 11,748
Population 10 to 14 years old: 12,577
Population 15 to 19 years old: 12,932
Population 20 to 24 years old: 18,351
Population 25 to 34 years old: 33,435
Population 35 to 44 years old: 26,135
Population 45 to 54 years old: 30,047
Population 55 to 59 years old: 13,817
Population 60 to 64 years old: 12,107
Population 65 to 74 years old: 13,216
Population 75 to 84 years old: 8,332
Population 85 years and over: 4,010
Median age: 35.4

Births (2010–11 Metropolitan Area)

Total number: 15,283

Deaths (2010–11 Metropolitan Area)

Total number: 10,862

Money income (2012)

Per capita income: $18,768

Median household income: $30,276
Total households: 87,407

Number of households with income of …

less than $10,000: 15,064
$10,000 to $14,999: 9,056
$15,000 to $24,999: 13,723
$25,000 to $34,999: 11,420
$35,000 to $49,999: 12,388
$50,000 to $74,999: 12,936
$75,000 to $99,999: 5,609
$100,000 to $149,999: 4,466
$150,000 to $199,999: 1,408
$200,000 or more: 1,337

Percent of families below poverty level: 31.4%

FBI Crime Index Property: 14,788

FBI Crime Index Violent: 3,237

■ Municipal Government

Birmingham is the county seat of Jefferson County. Birmingham operates under a mayor-council form of government. The mayor is elected at large every four years; the nine council members are also elected at large, but on a staggered basis in odd-numbered years. Birmingham was one of the nation's first cities to participate in an innovative program whereby citizens serve on boards, make economic decisions, and undertake various neighborhood projects. The Birmingham City Council is divided into nine committees, with three council members on each committee. Committee chairpersons are assigned by the president of the council. Each committee is responsible for hearing items that fall under its jurisdiction and then making recommendations to the council as a whole.

Head Official: Mayor William A. Bell, Sr. (since 2010; current term expires 2017)

Total Number of City Employees: 4,083 (2012)

City Information: City Hall, 710 N. 20th St., Birmingham, AL 35203; telephone (205) 254-2277

■ Economy

Major Industries and Commercial Activity

For many years Birmingham was a one-industry town, dependent on the iron and steel industry. While the steel industry no longer has the same prominence it once held in Birmingham, steel continues to play a key role in the economy. Several of the nation's largest steelmakers, including CMC Steel, U.S. Steel, McWane, and Nucor, all have a major presence in Birmingham. Nonetheless,

Birmingham's economy now relies more heavily on the medical and banking industries, as well as trade, finance, research, and government.

A magnet city for health care and medical research professionals, Birmingham boasts the University of Alabama Hospital, known throughout the nation for its research on the treatment of cardiovascular disease, diabetes, cancer, AIDS, and arthritis. St. Vincent's Health System, Baptist Health System, and Children's Health System (Children's of Alabama) are all major players in the Birmingham health-care market. Birmingham's Southern Research Institute, the largest nonprofit independent research laboratory in the Southeast, has gained national prominence.

As a leading national banking center, in 2013 Birmingham continued to serve as home to Regions Financial Corporation, a Fortune 500 company. Wells Fargo is a major employer for the metropolitan area.

So many auto-related companies have located to greater Birmingham that some residents call the area "Little Detroit." A half-hour southwest of Birmingham, in the town of Vance in Tuscaloosa County, Mercedes Drive leads to the first Mercedes-Benz auto plant ever built in North America. The Mercedes-Benz Vance plant, built in 1993, is also the first Mercedes-Benz passenger-car assembly plant outside Germany. State investments in auto production have led several auto-service production plants to open shop near Birmingham and in other areas of the state. These include BLG Logistics, Quality Sorting Service, TW-Fittings-NA, and WKW Erbsloh Automotive GmbH. Hyundai has a plant in Montgomery, and Honda operates one in Lincoln.

At the base of the expanding telecommunications industry is the city's status as one of two regional corporate headquarters of BellSouth Corporation, a subsidiary of AT&T, Inc. Birmingham is headquarters for the engineering and technical services of several power companies, including Alabama Power Company and Energen Corporation. With a plethora of Birmingham businesses working in international trade and warehousing and with the city's nearby waterways, Birmingham is a major distribution center. The city's proximity to the Warrior-Tombigbee River System, which connects to the Tennessee-Tombigbee Waterway, enables Birmingham to be a major shipper of general commodities.

Items and goods produced: cast iron pipe, transportation equipment (automotive, rail, and aircraft equipment), fabricated metal products, electronics, plastic products, office furniture, containers, paper products, and fire extinguishers

Incentive Programs–New and Existing Companies

Local programs: The City of Birmingham Office of Economic Development (OED) provides a wide variety of federal, state, and locally sponsored programs and activities, including financial assistance, employment training, business assistance and retention programs, and site-specific targeted economic development initiatives. Birmingham OED offers a number of financing programs, including SBA 7a Program, Birmingham Business Development Loan Program, EDA Revolving Loan Fund Program, Industrial Revenue Bond Financing, and Community Development Float Loans.

The OED operates a Foreign Trade Zone (FTZ) No. 98, which includes a general purpose zone located at the Birmingham International Airport and special purpose manufacturing subzones serving NAACO Industries and Mercedes-Benz USA. Through the FTZ program, companies that import component parts used in the production process may qualify for a reduction of tariff rates or delayed payment of tariffs.

The Birmingham Business Resource Center (BBRC) is a one-stop center for small business finance, loans, and related technical assistance. It brings together in one location a number of small business loan programs previously offered by the Office of Economic Development and area banks. The Birmingham Business Alliance (BBA) is a resource created in 2009 by the merger of Birmingham Regional Chamber of Commerce and the Metropolitan Development Board in order to focus on the economic growth of the entire seven-county Birmingham region. Birmingham's OED operates a business retention program with the BBA.

State programs: Alabama boasts a progressive state business environment as demonstrated by its comprehensive right-to-work laws, one-stop environmental permitting, and a positive state and local government attitude toward new and expanding business. Tax rates are competitive. The Alabama Capital Tax Credit Program offers income tax credit for new or expanding businesses that create new jobs. The state provides additional financing assistance through a number of programs, including the AlabamaSAVES Loan Program, Industrial Development Grant Program, Economic Development Revolving Loan Funds, Industrial Revenue Bonds, and Alabama Innovation Fund, to name a few.

Birmingham is one of three Alabama cities designated as state enterprise zones. The Alabama Enterprise Zone Program helps attract new business to Alabama with tax breaks to those operating in designated areas. Eligible new or expanding businesses located in the zone may qualify for state income or business privilege tax credits for new investments and for hiring new permanent employees who were formerly unemployed for at least 90 days.

Job training programs: The Alabama Industrial Development Training (AIDT) program provides a total delivery system for screening and selecting trainees and for designing and implementing training for any new or expanding manufacturers in the state of Alabama. The program provides a full range of customized technical training programs that are free to employers and trainees. AIDT supports several specialized training centers, including the Alabama Robotics Technology Park, Alabama Center for Advanced Woodworking Technology, Forest Product Development Center, and AIDT Maritime Training Center. Additional programs provide support for the telecommunications, aviation, automotive, and chemical industries, and other area manufacturers. Mobile training units are also used to go directly to the employer site to provide classroom and hands-on training. The Workforce Investment Act helps defer the costs of hiring and training new employees for private businesses.

Development Projects

In 2013, after two years of study and review, the city adopted a new 20-year strategic plan. As the name implies, the Birmingham Comprehensive Plan addresses a wide range of issues, including housing and community renewal, education, parks, transportation, and economic development. Under the topic of economy and jobs, the city seeks to expand on its strong position as a regional medical center. The city also plans to promote growth in the fields of life sciences research and advanced manufacturing. Officials believe that the tourist industry can be expanded by promoting the city's civil rights heritage. Sports tourism is also believed to have growth potential.

The plan addresses issue of workforce development with a call to provide high-quality career education and work experience programs in public schools and to promote career training services for adults. Better childcare and improved public transportation are included as items that support employment.

Plans to improve and expand the city's parks and green spaces are part of the overall vision as well. A key goal under the topic of green systems is to have a park or green space within walking distance of every resident. Sustainability and green energy fall under this topic as well. The new plan calls for conserving and protecting drinking water supplies and promoting green building designs and practices.

Another major topic of the comprehensive plan involves neighborhoods, housing, and community renewal. A primary goal is to make Birmingham a place where people of diverse socioeconomic and cultural backgrounds choose to live. One idea for achieving this goal is to create urban villages: compact, walkable, mixed-use neighborhood centers with easy access to public transit.

In private developments, a major renovation of one of downtown Birmingham's largest and most conspicuous vacant buildings, the Pizitz Building, began in 2010 but quickly stalled due to economic downturns. The project was renewed in 2013 as Bayer Properties sought to take advantage of the new statewide Alabama Historic Rehabilitation Historic Tax Credits. The building was constructed in 1908 as the flagship edifice for the major department store. The estimated $57 million facelift is set to include apartments, office space, a grocery store, and ground-floor retail space.

At the end of 2013, several additional renovation projects were in a lottery to receive Historic Tax Credits. When the fiscal year began on October 2013, there were so many applications for credits that the Alabama Historical Commission set up a lottery to determine the order in which projects would be reviewed. The lottery did not guarantee that the any project would be approved for tax credits, but project managers set to renovate or rebuild spaces in Birmingham hoped that early approval would work in their favor. The Federal reserve Bank of Atlanta (Birmingham), Redmont Hotel, Powell School, Avondale Fire Station No. 10, Thomas Jefferson Hotel, Brown Marx Tower, and the Florentine Building were potential recipients.

In 2013 city planners approved the design for a new intermodal terminal to serve Amtrak, Greyhound, and the Birmingham-Jefferson County Transit Authority. The existing copper-domed bus terminal and Amtrak station had become too small to accommodate the growing number of users. The initial plan to demolish the existing station was controversial. The station was built in 1999 with $4.5 million in federal funds, which prohibited destruction of the building without the city and county incurring federal penalties. However, city planners proved that the station could not accommodate expansion, negating potential fines from the federal government. About 80 percent of the cost for the new $30 million facility was to come from federal funds.

In 2012 REV Birmingham was established through the combined efforts of Operation New Birmingham and Main Street Birmingham. This public-private partnership has developed four primary project areas for revitalizing the city. REV City Center brings business owners and city officials together to create a sustainable business district. REV Neighborhoods works to organize merchants and encourage public-private revitalization partnerships in urban commercial districts. REV Business provides coaching and other resources to support small-business growth and innovation. REV Development identifies underutilized properties that can be revitalized or redeveloped, and works with private and nonprofit organizations to attract new businesses to those properties.

Economic Development Information: City of Birmingham Office of Economic Development, 710 20th Street North, Birmingham, AL 35203; telephone (205) 254-2799; fax (205) 254-7741. Birmingham Business Alliance, 505 20th Street North, Suite 200, Birmingham, AL 35203; telephone (205) 324-2100; fax (205) 324-2560. Alabama Department of Commerce, 401 Adams Avenue, P.O. Box 304106, Montgomery, AL 36130-4106; telephone (800) 248-0033; email contact@madeinalabama. com. Alabama Industrial Development Training, One Technology Court, Montgomery, AL 36116-3200;

telephone (334) 242-4158; fax (334) 242-0299. REV Birmingham, 505 20th Street North, Suite 150, Birmingham, AL 35203; telephone (205) 324-8797.

Commercial Shipping

Born at the junction of two railroads, and always an important transportation center, Birmingham today is served by an outstanding network of highways, extensive rail track, air-cargo facilities, and nearby navigable waterways. More than 100 truck lines, many with nationwide service, move goods and products for Birmingham companies.

The CSX and Burlington Northern Santa Fe railroad systems haul freight to and from the metropolitan area, where a multimodal system is located. Norfolk Southern opened the Birmingham Regional Intermodal terminal in 2012, in the unincorporated community of McCalla on the outskirts of Birmingham. This facility is a major hub in the Crescent Corridor project, a public-private partnership to create and maintain a rail corridor from New Orleans, Louisiana, to Newark, New Jersey.

Five cargo shippers offer services through Birmingham-Shuttlesworth International Airport. Birmingham's Airport Industrial Park is designated as a Foreign Trade Zone, a major asset in attracting additional business to the area. General commodities are transported economically on barges along the nearby Warrior-Tombigbee River System and the Tennessee-Tombigbee Waterway to other inland cities and through the Port of Mobile to foreign countries.

Labor Force and Employment Outlook

Birmingham's transformed economy is now less dependent on cyclical manufacturing and mining sectors and more on health and financial services. The following is a summary of data regarding the 2013 Birmingham labor force:

Size of civilian labor force: 99,569

Number of workers employed in . . .

   agriculture and mining: 404
   construction: 4,204
   manufacturing: 6,632
   wholesale trade: 1,978
   retail trade: 8,925
   transportation: 4,470
   information systems: 1,901
   finance: 6,147
   professional administration: 8,252
   education and social services: 22,270
   arts and leisure: 9,191
   other: 5,190
   public administration: 4,034

Average hourly earnings of production workers: $16

Unemployment rate: 8.7% (2012)

Employers

Largest regional employers (2013)	*Number of employees*
University of Alabama at Birmingham	23,000
Regions Financial Corporation	6,000
AT&T	5,750
St. Vincent's Health System	4,703
Honda Manufacturing of Alabama	4,500
City of Birmingham	4,083
Baptist Health System	4,000
Alabama Power Company	3,982
Children's Health System (Children's of Alabama)	3,652
Mercedes-Benz U.S. International	3,500
Blue Cross-Blue Shield of Alabama	3,000
BBVA Compass	2,804
Brookwood Medical Center	2,600
American Cast Iron Pipe Company	2,400
U.S. Steel-Fairfield Works	2,400

Cost of Living

Birmingham's cost of living, as well as its housing prices, are slightly below the national average.

The following is a summary of data regarding several key cost of living factors in the area.

2013 ACCRA Average House Price: $211,146

2013 ACCRA Cost of Living Index: 88

State income tax rate: 2.0% to 5.0%

State sales tax rate: 4.0%

Local income tax rate: 1.0%

Local sales tax rate: 6.0%

Property tax rate: $6.95 per every $100 of assessed value (2013)

Economic Information: City of Birmingham Office of Economic Development, 710 20th Street North, Birmingham, AL 35203; telephone (205) 254-2799; fax (205) 254-7741. Alabama Department of Commerce, 401 Adams Avenue, P.O. Box 304106, Montgomery, AL 36130-4106; telephone (800) 248-0033; email contact@ madeinalabama.com.

■ Education and Research

Elementary and Secondary Schools

In 2013 there were 49 schools in the Birmingham City School System. This number included 21 elementary schools, 11 middle schools, 9 K–8 schools, 7 high schools, and 1 alternative school. Birmingham City Schools employed approximately 3,100 individuals to serve the student population. Enrollment has been declining since the 1990s.

A capital improvement plan, funded by a one-cent Jefferson County sales tax, allowed for reconstruction and new construction of several facilities into the 2010s. The new Hudson K–8 School opened in August 2009. The Washington K–8 School opened in early 2010, along with Green Acres Middle School, which received major renovations and additions. Six new schools opened in 2011. Three new schools opened for the 2012–13 school year: Huffman High School, Hayes K–8 School, and Charles A. Brown Elementary School.

Seven career academies opened in August 2012. These programs are hosted at six public high schools: Carver, Huffman, Jackson-Olin, Parker, Wenonah and Woodlawn. The academies are designed for students who want a more career-focused program of study. Philips Academy and Ramsey High School provide a curriculum based on the International Baccalaureate program.

The school system offers specialized programs in English as a Second Language (ESL) and family literacy. In addition to programs for gifted students, Birmingham City Schools operate the Education Program for the Individual Child at EPIC Alternative Elementary School, with a population of 50 percent typical children and 50 percent children with developmental challenges; or 50 percent African American students and 50 percent white students; or 50 percent girls and 50 percent boys. EPIC schools aim to foster the individual student's sense of self-worth by helping students communicate and understand one another.

Birmingham is the home of the Alabama School of Fine Arts, one of only a few such schools in the country to offer intensive study in both academic areas and the arts for grades seven through twelve. Mikhail Baryshnikov once ranked the ballet school as one of the top three in the country. There are also several private and parochial schools in the greater Birmingham area, including John Carroll Catholic High School.

The following is a summary of data regarding the Birmingham City Schools.

Total enrollment: 25,914

Number of facilities

  total: 49
  elementary schools: 21
  junior high schools: 20
  high schools: 7
  other: 1

Student/teacher ratio: 16.08:1

Teacher salaries

  average (statewide): $48,282

Funding per pupil: $10,676

Public Schools Information: Birmingham City Schools, 2015 Park Place North, Birmingham, AL 35203; telephone (205) 231-4600.

Colleges and Universities

Eleven major institutions of higher learning are located in metropolitan Birmingham. They offer undergraduate and graduate degrees in such fields as engineering, business, education, medicine, nursing, pharmacy, religion, law, music, and liberal arts. The largest is the University of Alabama at Birmingham (UAB), with about 19,200 students. In 2012 the UAB School of Education was established as separate from the College of Arts and Sciences.

Samford University, a private institution affiliated with the Baptist State Convention, was listed as the third best Regional University–South in the *U.S. News & World Report* 2014 listing of Best Colleges.

Other Birmingham schools include Birmingham-Southern College, a four-year liberal arts school affiliated with the Methodist Church; Miles College; Bessemer State Technical College; Jefferson State Community College; University of Montevallo; Virginia College at Birmingham; Herzing College; Lawson State Community College; and ITT Technical Institute. Faulkner University (based in Montgomery) has an extension campus in Birmingham.

Libraries and Research Centers

The Birmingham Public Library (BPL) has 19 branches with a total collection of more than one million items, not including archival documents. The library's archival collection contains more than thirty million documents and 500,000 photographs pertaining to the City of Birmingham, the Episcopal Diocese of Alabama, the Civil Rights Movement in Alabama, and numerous organizations and institutions. In 2012 the Birmingham Public Library was named a Star Library by *Library Journal*. BPL is one of the nation's oldest federal depository libraries (established in 1895). It is also the only patent and trademark depository library in the state. BPL is part of the Jefferson County Library Cooperative, a system of forty public libraries with shared borrowing privileges.

More than twenty other libraries serve Birmingham; some of them are affiliated with educational institutions, while others are associated with religious groups or research centers. Their collections focus on such areas of interest as botany and horticulture, art, law, religion, regional history, engineering, genealogy, energy, science, medicine, and business.

In keeping with its status as a medical center for the Southeast, Birmingham is home to a large number of health-care research centers, most of which are supported by the University of Alabama at Birmingham (UAB). Major projects center on healthy aging, cancer, immunology, regenerative medicine, community health, cardiovascular disease, nanoscale materials and biointegration, and vision science, among others. UAB is a designated center for AIDS research, and its Spinal Cord Injury Care System is one of the few in the nation. In total, UAB sponsors 106 research centers, of which 21 have been designated university-wide interdisciplinary research centers.

The Southern Research Institute, with centers in Alabama, Maryland, and North Carolina, is nationally recognized for its virus studies, cancer research, and industrial research programs. Area research centers are active in other fields as well, including computers, education, labor, urban affairs, metallurgy, and electronics. The institute collaborates with UAB on a number of projects and initiatives, including the Alabama Drug Discovery Alliance and the Pulmonary Injury and Repair Center.

Public Library Information: Birmingham Public Library, 2100 Park Place, Birmingham, AL 35203; telephone (205) 226-3610.

■ Health Care

Internationally known as a medical center, Birmingham is a leader in the prevention and treatment of illness. The University of Alabama at Birmingham (UAB) is a leader in medical research and education.

The UAB Health System includes UAB Hospital, UAB Hospital–Highlands, Callahan Eye Hospital, Sprain Rehabilitation Center, Hazelrig-Salter Radiation Oncology, and UAB Women & Infants Center. The main campus of UAB Hospital is an 11-story, 1,046-bed facility with 37 operating suites, 4 intensive care units, and an emergency unit the size of a football field. Dozens of primary care and specialty care clinics also are sponsored by the UAB System, including Kirklin Clinic, one of the busiest outpatient clinics in the country with more than 600 physicians in 35 specialties. The clinic was designed by architect I. M. Pei. The UAB Comprehensive Cancer Center is one of 41 centers nationwide designated by the National Cancer Institute (NCI). It is the only NCI-designated comprehensive center in the six-state area that includes Alabama, Mississippi, Louisiana, Arkansas, South Carolina, and Georgia.

Many of the 17 hospitals in the area offer specialized care while providing a total of more than 6,000 beds. Health-care institutions other than those affiliated with the University of Alabama include hospitals operated by Baptist and Methodist churches, and others.

The Benjamin Russell Hospital for Children (Children's of Alabama), a private nonprofit pediatric hospital affiliated with the Department of Pediatric Medicine at the UAB School of Medicine, is one of the busiest pediatric medical centers in the United States. It is the third largest pediatric facility in the United States.

■ Recreation

Sightseeing

Visitors to Birmingham enjoy the variety of parks throughout the city, including the 90-acre Highland Park with its modern sports complex and golf course; Roebuck Park, known for its beautiful golf course and wooded grounds; Avondale, with an amphitheater, duck pond, and formal rose garden; East Lake, with more than 50 acres of freshwater; and Magnolia, known for its flowing fountains. Birmingham's Vulcan Park features a towering statue of Vulcan, the Roman god of fire and the forge, the city's symbol. Said to be the largest iron figure ever cast, it rises 55 feet above its pedestal to reach a total of 179 feet. This monument, a tribute to the iron industry in Birmingham, is unique in that it honors an industry rather than a person or event. A glass-enclosed elevator takes visitors to the statue's climate-controlled observation deck for an aerial view of the city.

One of the largest zoos in the Southeast, the Birmingham Zoo exhibits mammals, birds, and reptiles in near-natural surroundings within a 100-acre compound. Rare species such as Siberian tigers, white rhinoceroses, gorillas, and polar bears join exhibits of specimens from nations around the globe. The Social Animals Building is the latest example of a leading-edge zoo concept that groups animals in exhibits according to lifestyle characteristics rather than species. In 2005 the zoo celebrated its 50th year with the addition of an exhibit devoted to the urban, rural, and wild animals and environment of Alabama.

Across the street from the zoo are Birmingham's internationally known Botanical Gardens, which offer the visitor both indoor and outdoor plant displays of common and rare plants. Among its more than 67 acres of flowers and plants from around the world are an authentic Japanese garden and a rose garden featuring more than 2,000 blooming plants.

Birmingham's early history is preserved at the Arlington Antebellum Home and Gardens, a Greek Revival mansion built between 1845 and 1850, now restored to its original splendor and filled with period pieces. The home also hosts craft demonstrations and a variety of social functions.

At Ruffner Mountain Nature Center, a 1,000-acre nature preserve just five miles from the heart of the city center, 11 miles of hiking trails allow visitors to explore the nation's largest urban wilderness. The environmental education center offers a variety of changing exhibits and a gift shop. Free admission and free and fee-based programs are available for all ages. Thirty minutes south of the city, Oak Mountain State Park is Alabama's largest state park and offers 10,000 acres of mountains, forestland, and lakes with space for camping, hiking, biking, fishing, and horseback riding.

Arts and Culture

Birmingham is fast becoming a leading center for the arts in the Southeast, providing superb facilities, emphasizing arts education, and showcasing numerous performances and exhibits. The pride of Birmingham is the Birmingham-Jefferson Convention Complex, which occupies a seven-square-block area in the heart of the city. Presenting more than 600 events a year, the complex hosts meetings, conventions, sporting events, ballets, operas, plays, concerts, shows, and lectures. The complex's concert hall, called one of the finest facilities in the world, seats 3,000 people in an acoustically superior auditorium. Its theater seats more than 1,000 people and features a stage that can change from a proscenium opening to three other forms, depending on the performance. The theater plays host to the Alabama Symphony Orchestra, which offers both classical and pops performances. For young people interested in drama, the Birmingham Children's Theatre, which performs at the theater, has gained a national reputation.

The nonprofit Birmingham Music Cooperative is comprised of four member organizations and is dedicated to scheduling, fundraising, education, community outreach, and marketing efforts on behalf of its members, which include: the Birmingham Art Music Alliance, which features new music by local composers, community members, students, and professionals; the Birmingham Chamber Music Society, which performs in and around Birmingham; the Birmingham Music Club, which offers specialty performances by world-class performers and a strong outreach program; and Opera Birmingham, which stages full operas and recitals.

Birmingham is home to the Alabama Ballet, which performs on tour and in the city. The Alabama School of Fine Arts is famous for the quality of its young dancers. Southern Danceworks operates as Alabama's only modern dance company. The Birmingham Repertory Theatre, the Birmingham Festival Theatre, and the Terrific New Theatre (TNT) also stage dramatic offerings. The Alabama Jazz Hall of Fame has a permanent home downtown in the art deco Carver Theatre, and jazz is also performed by the Birmingham Heritage Band. The Alabama Theatre, a restored 1920s movie palace with a classic Wurlitzer organ, features concerts, plays, and recitals.

The University of Alabama at Birmingham hosts many cultural events. The Alys Robinson Stephens Performing Arts Center, located on the UAB campus, is part of a complex that includes a recital hall, a "black box" theater for student productions, and the Sirote Theater, where performances of the Alabama Shakespeare Festival are scheduled.

Birmingham's museums and galleries reflect its history, as well as the diverse interests of its residents. Located in the expanded Convention Complex, The Alabama Sports Hall of Fame Museum displays a host of articles relating to the sports history of the state, including plaques, trophies, uniforms, recordings, and films. Memorabilia such as Coach Paul "Bear" Bryant's cap and Pat Sullivan's Heisman trophy are housed in the museum.

The Birmingham Museum of Art holds a collection of 21,000 works of art. Said to be the largest municipally supported museum in the South, the museum features paintings and sculptures from many cultures and periods, including Pre-Colombian, Indian, and African. It is also noted for its collections of Wedgwood ceramics, Remington bronzes, and Oriental Art. The BMA complex includes a sculpture garden, a 350-seat auditorium, and a restaurant.

The Birmingham Civil Rights Institute houses exhibits that depict historical events pertaining to race relations from post–World War I to the present. The institute promotes research and discussion through its education program services. It was constructed across from the Sixteenth Street Baptist Church, where it is the focal point of a Civil Rights District that includes the church, an African American commercial neighborhood, the Fourth Avenue business district, and Kelly Ingram Park, site of many 1960s civil rights marches.

In 2013 a new bronze monument called Four Spirits was unveiled in Kelly Ingram Park as a memorial to Addie Mae Collins, Denise McNair, Cynthia Wesley, and Carole Robertson—the four girls killed in the Sixteenth Street Baptist Church bombing. The installation was one of many Birmingham events commemorating the 50th anniversary of the bombing. The life-size sculpture shows the girls on and around a bench. One of the girls releases six doves that represent the four girls and the two young black boys, Virgil Ware, 13, and Johnny Robinson, 16, who were killed in racially charged crimes that same day. The sculpture was created by Birmingham-born artist Elizabeth MacQueen.

Among Birmingham's other museums are the Alabama Museum of the Health Sciences, which contains items relating to the history of medicine; the Southern Museum of Flight, whose holdings include replicas of monoplanes and other items relating to the history of flight in Alabama; Meyer Planetarium, which gives programs on the stars and constellations; Bessemer Hall of History, which displays pioneer items, fossils, Civil War artifacts, and other unusual exhibits such as Adolph Hitler's typewriter; and the Sloss Furnaces National Historical Landmark, a combination museum and park where visitors can examine two blast furnaces and observe iron-making technology. The McWane Center in downtown Birmingham promotes scientific exploration for all ages. The 180,000-square-foot center features an IMAX Dome Theater, hands-on exhibits, educational programming, and permanent and traveling exhibits.

Festivals and Holidays

The city's annual Magic City Art Connection contemporary art festival takes place in April at Linn Park. The festival features music, dance, food and wine, and more than 200 juried art exhibitors. The Birmingham Civil Rights Institute sponsors an annual Juneteenth Culture Fest in June. The institute also sponsors many other educational and cultural events throughout the year. The young and growing Sidewalk Moving Picture Festival in August offers four days of independent film viewing at venues in Birmingham's downtown theater district.

The Alabama State Fair is held at the State Fairgrounds in Birmingham in September. Demonstrations, exhibitions, contests, and entertainment are presented along with items for display and sale. The annual Oktoberfest in September is sponsored by the FDSK German Culture Club at Das Haus. The Alabama Designer Craftsmen's Annual Fine Crafts Show in November is sponsored by Birmingham Botanical Gardens. November also brings the Fall FestivAle, sponsored by Free the Hops, an Alabama brewer's organization. Many residents kick off their Christmas season by attending the annual Christmas Parade and Tree Lighting, which includes musical entertainment. Other major celebrations include the Greek Food Festival and the Lebanese Food and Cultural Festival.

Sports for the Spectator

Birmingham has no major professional sports franchises. Nonetheless, often called "The Football Capital of the South," Birmingham enjoys a rich sports history. The legendary Paul "Bear" Bryant and Ralph "Shug" Jordan both coached football teams for many years at Birmingham's Legion Field Stadium, where the University of Alabama's Crimson Tide played its games to capacity crowds at Legion Field. Legion Field hosts the annual BBVA Compass Bowl, which features NCAA Division I football teams from the Southeastern Conference and American Athletic Conference.

Baseball fans go to Hoover Metropolitan Stadium from April to September to watch the Birmingham Barons, a Double A farm club of the Chicago White Sox. The Barons' former home and oldest American ballpark, Rickwood Field, offers visitors a glimpse into history with tours and games. Greyhound dogs race at the Birmingham Race Course, a track set on a 330-acre wooded site. The grandstand can accommodate 20,000 spectators who may also enjoy the clubhouse and private facilities.

The University of Alabama at Birmingham Blazers play at UAB Arena and the Birmingham-Jefferson Convention Complex. The Birmingham-Jefferson Convention Complex regularly hosts prestigious national basketball events and championships and is home to the Birmingham Steeldogs football team.

Sports for the Participant

The Birmingham Park and Recreation Board operates 124 public recreational facilities, which host 2 public golf courses, 16 swimming pools, more than 120 tennis courts, and 23 softball fields. Suburban communities also boast fine recreational opportunities. Marathoners can test their endurance in the annual Mercedes Marathon, or the city's 10K Vulcan Run. A large water and theme park in nearby Bessemer called Splash Adventure includes water sports, rides, auto racing, and skeet shooting.

The Barber Vintage Motorsports Park opened in 2003. It is home to the Honda Indy Grand Prix of Alabama. The racing facility and museum houses the Porsche Driving Experience school and hosts a variety of motorcycle and auto-racing events. Carved into the landscape, the state-of-the-art racetrack has no grandstands, with seating built into the surrounding hillside and offering good vantage points from most locations. The museum displays nearly 900 motorcycles and 45 cars, most from businessman George W. Barber Jr.'s own collection.

Fishing enthusiasts enjoy bass fishing in the area surrounding Birmingham, especially at Inland Lake, Lake Purdy, and in a bend in the Warrior River known as Locust Fork. Birmingham has been noted as one of the best places in the world for bass fishing by ESPN and *Bassmaster Magazine*. The city frequently hosts The Bassmaster Classic, the world championship of bass fishing.

Birmingham is famous for its beautiful golf courses. Its Oxmoor Valley Golf Course is one stop on the Robert Trent Jones Golf Trail, the largest golf-course construction project ever attempted with a total of 468 championship holes over 26 courses. According to *Golf* magazine, the course is "Alabama's equivalent of Disney World."

Railroad Park, opened in 2010, has become a popular spot for families. The 19-acre green space in downtown Birmingham covers a four-block stretch of Birmingham's Railroad Reservation, known as "Burlington North." The park includes an amphitheatre that can host 3,500 people, an artificial lake, flowers and vegetable gardens, playgrounds, trails and fitness stations, free Wi-Fi, a skateboarding park, and a covered space that houses offices, restrooms, a concession stand, and a catering kitchen.

Shopping and Dining

There are numerous shopping centers and malls in and around Birmingham, including Brook Highland Plaza and The Summit, which are located in Birmingham proper. One of the most exciting shopping centers in the Southeast is the Riverchase Galleria, located at the interchange of Interstate 459 and U.S. Highway 31, thirteen miles south of downtown Birmingham and in the center of the Riverchase community. The mall boasts the luxurious Wynfrey Hotel, an office tower, a ten-foot statue of blue herons in flight, the largest skylight in the country, and more than 200 stores.

Five Points South is an entertainment and shopping area on the south side that offers unique restaurants, bars, and specialty shops; it is the scene of a variety of festivals. The sights, sounds, and scents of an old-fashioned farmer's market are available at two Birmingham locations—the Jefferson County Truck Growers Association and Pepper Place Market. The Jefferson County market is open daily, year-round. The Pepper Place Market in the Lakeview Design District operates on Saturdays and offers fresh vegetables and flowers, baked goods, local organic produce, and cooking demonstrations by area chefs.

Birmingham residents are proud of their tradition of sumptuous dining coupled with southern hospitality. More than 600 restaurants dot the Birmingham area, from fast-food outlets to establishments specializing in ethnic cuisine and those featuring traditional southern barbecue: meat cooked slowly over coals and basted with savory sauce.

Visitor Information: Greater Birmingham Convention and Visitors Bureau, 2200 Ninth Avenue North, Birmingham, AL 35203; telephone (205) 458-8000. Visitor Information Centers are located on the lower level of the Birmingham International Airport, telephone (205) 458-8002, and at 1201 University Boulevard, telephone (205) 458-8001. For information on University of Alabama events, call (205) 934-0553. For weather information, call (205) 945-7000.

■ Convention Facilities

The Birmingham-Jefferson Convention Complex is located on seven square blocks in downtown Birmingham, only ten minutes from the airport. Its facilities include the Exhibition Hall, covering 220,000 square feet and featuring 74 meeting rooms to accommodate up to 1,200 participants; the 3,000-seat Concert Hall, one of the most acoustically effective structures in the country; the 1,000-seat Theatre, with a moveable stage that can be adjusted to suit differing performance requirements; and the Arena, which seats 19,000 people, making it one of the largest such facilities in the Southeast. Within the complex, the ten-story Medical Forum building contains classrooms, meeting space, commercial office suites, and an auditorium. The complex also features retail operations including the Alabama Sports Hall of Fame, and the adjoining 770-room Sheraton Birmingham hotel.

The historic art deco Boutwell Municipal Auditorium offers a main arena seating capacity of up to 6,000 people and an exhibition hall capacity of 1,000. About 20 minutes from the airport, the Bessemer Civic Center has a main hall that seats 1,600 people and additional meeting rooms for up to 300 people. Arthur's Conference Center has 2,560 square feet of meeting/banquet space that can be broken down into three smaller rooms. With a total of more than 14,000 hotel and motel rooms in the metropolitan area, Birmingham is ready to accommodate large and small groups.

Convention Information: Greater Birmingham Convention and Visitors Bureau, 2200 North Avenue North, Birmingham, AL 35203; telephone (800) 458-8085.

■ Transportation

Approaching the City

Seven commercial airlines operating at Birmingham-Shuttlesworth International Airport offer more than 140 daily flights to 37 cities. The airport is only ten minutes from downtown. Four interstate highways bring motorists into Birmingham: Interstates 20 and 59 connect from the east/northeast to the west/southwest; Interstate 65 from north to south; and Interstate 459, which bypasses the central city on the south. U.S. Highway 280 enters from the southeast, U.S. 31 from the north, U.S. 78 from the northwest, and U.S. 11 from the southwest and northeast. Amtrak offers daily passenger service to Birmingham from Mobile, New Orleans, and New York. Service to Los Angeles, Orlando, and New Orleans is provided three times per week. Greyhound also provides service to downtown Birmingham.

Traveling in the City

A hilly city, Birmingham lies in a valley running from northeast to southwest. The roads are laid out in a grid pattern; those that run roughly east–west are designated as numbered avenues, while those that run north–south are designated as numbered streets. The Birmingham-Jefferson County Transit Authority provides public transportation within the city of Birmingham. Nicknamed MAX—for Metro Area Express—the bus system provides regular city bus service and, in the downtown area, trolley-like vehicles called DART carry passengers from location to location throughout the central business district.

■ Communications

Newspapers and Magazines

Birmingham's only major daily newspaper is the *Birmingham News,* which is also the largest newspaper in Alabama. The *Birmingham Times* is a weekly paper that serves the city's African American community. Other newspapers in the city serve college students and various religious groups. Birmingham is also the home of the Southern Progress Corporation, which publishes magazines such as *Southern Living,* a monthly focusing on homes, cuisine, gardens, and recreation; and *Cooking Light,* one of the country's leading healthy lifestyle magazines. Other free alternative publications include *The Birmingham Weekly* (published every 10 days), *Birmingham Free Press* and *Black & White.* All of the city's newspapers have online components.

Television and Radio

As part of the Birmingham-Anniston-Tuscaloosa television market, the nation's 40th largest, Birmingham is served by eight television stations, of which four are affiliated with major commercial networks and one with public broadcasting. Additional stations are available via cable and satellite dish. The largest Roman Catholic media outlet in the world, EWTN, is headquartered in the Birmingham suburb of Irondale. The Birmingham metro area is served by more than 45 radio stations, which broadcast a wide range of programs, from gospel, country/western, and inspirational, to big band, jazz, news/talk, and rock. The Rick and Bubba show, syndicated to more than 25 stations primarily in the Southeast, originates from Birmingham's WZZK-FM.

Media Information: Birmingham News, PO Box 2553, Birmingham, AL 35202; telephone (205) 325-2444.

Birmingham Online

Alabama Department of Commerce. Available www.madeinalabama.com

Birmingham Business Alliance. Available www.birminghambusinessalliance.com

Birmingham City Schools. Available www.bhamcityschools.org

Birmingham Historical Society. Available www.bhistorical.org

Birmingham News. Available www.al.com/news

Birmingham Public Library. Available www.bplonline.org

Birmingham-Shuttlesworth International Airport. Available www.flybirmingham.com

City of Birmingham. Available www.informationbirmingham.com

City of Birmingham Office of Economic Development. Available http://www.informationbirmingham.com/oed/index.aspx

Greater Birmingham Convention and Visitors Bureau. Available www.birminghamal.org

BIBLIOGRAPHY

Currie, Stephen, *Birmingham Church Bombing* (Farmington Hills, MI: Lucent Books, 2006)

Fazio, Michael W, *Landscape of Transformations: Architecture and Birmingham, Alabama* (Knoxville: TN, University of Tennessee Press, 2010)

Hemphill, Paul, *Leaving Birmingham: Notes of a Native Son* (Tuscaloosa: University of Alabama Press, 2000)

McWhorter, Diane, *Carry Me Home: Birmingham, Alabama: The Climactic Battle of the Civil Rights Revolution* (New York: Simon & Schuster, 2001

Thome, T. K., *Last Chance for Justice: How Relentless Investigators Uncovered New Evidence Convicting the Birmingham Church Bombers* (Chicago: IL, Lawrence Hill Books, 2013)

Todd, Keith, *Birmingham Then and Now* (San Diego: CA, Thunder Bay Press, 2009)

Todd, Keith, *Insiders' Guide to Birmingham* (Guilford, CT: Insiders' Guides, 2011)

Huntsville

■ The City in Brief

Founded: 1805 (incorporated 1811)

Head Official: Mayor Tommy Battle (since 2008)

City Population
- 1990: 159,789
- 2000: 158,216
- 2010: 180,105
- 2012 estimate: 183,076
- Percent change, 2000–2010: 13.8%
- U.S. rank in 1990: 109th
- U.S. rank in 2000: 127th
- U.S. rank in 2010: 128th

Metropolitan Statistical Area Population
- 2000: 342,376
- 2010: 417,593
- 2012 estimate: 430,734
- Percent change, 2000–2010: 22%
- U.S. rank in 2000: 134th
- U.S. rank in 2010: 120th

Area: 202.73 square miles

Elevation: 600 feet above sea level

Average Annual Temperatures: January, 39° F; July, 80° F; annual average, 61° F

Average Annual Precipitation: 56.8 inches of rain; 2.8 inches of snow

Major Economic Sectors: government, aerospace and defense, vehicles, electronics, computer software and technology, telecommunications, retail

Unemployment Rate: 7.0% (2012)

Per Capita Income: $29,530

2012 FBI Crime Index Property: 9,261

Major Colleges and Universities: Alabama Agricultural and Mechanical University, University of Alabama in Huntsville, Oakwood University

Daily Newspaper: *The Huntsville Times*

■ Introduction

Huntsville is one of the Southeast's most interesting cities. It blends southern hospitality with innovative high-technology ventures and cultural diversity. After all, Huntsville is not nicknamed the "Rocket City" for nothing; technology, space, and defense industries have a major presence in Huntsville with the army's Redstone Arsenal, NASA's Marshall Space Flight Center, and Cummings Research Park. Huntsville is home to many *Fortune 500* company operations and offers a wide range of industries, such as aerospace technology, manufacturing, retail, and other professional services. The city also provides residents a variety of educational, recreational, and cultural opportunities. Huntsville is consistently named one of the best places to live and work by a number of national publications. A 200-year-old city, Huntsville can send those who seek its secrets to the moon and stars at the Space and Rocket Center, or back to the city's beginnings at Constitution Hall Village. Science or history, the city has it all.

■ Geography and Climate

Huntsville is located in the Tennessee River Valley. There are many mesas and large hills partially surrounding the city, associated with the Cumberland Plateau. Monte Sano ("Mountain of Health" in Italian), east of the city, is the most notable. Here, the 25th Alabama Battalion surrendered to Union troops on May 11, 1865. Other mountains include Round Top, Huntsville, and the

© Rob Hainer/Shutterstock.com

Green Mountains. Also, Wade Mountain lies to the north, Rainbow Mountain to the west, and Weeden and Madkin Mountains on Redstone Arsenal to the south. One can see Brindlee Mountain to the south across the Tennessee River. Like other regions of the Cumberland Plateau, Huntsville's land is karst in nature. Huntsville was founded around a karst spring, Big Spring, and there are many caves perforating the limestone bedrock beneath the city.

Huntsville experiences hot, humid summers and generally mild winters. Although most winters record some measurable snow, overall there is little significant snowfall. During the spring and fall, there may be tornadoes. Significant tornadoes occurred in 1974, 1989, and 1995. One of the largest tornado outbreaks in U.S. history hit the southeastern United States on April 27, 2011. The National Weather Service Huntsville Forecast Area experienced 39 tornadoes.

Area: 202.73 square miles

Elevation: 600 feet above sea level

Average Temperatures: January, 39° F; July, 80° F; annual average, 61° F

Average Annual Precipitation: 56.8 inches of rain; 2.8 inches of snow

■ History

Huntsville, the county seat of Madison County, was incorporated in 1811 in the far northern part of Alabama. Its history began earlier, however, as 1805 is recognized as the city's birth date. In that year, the city's namesake and first settler, John Hunt, arrived to settle the land around Big Spring, a karst spring. However, Hunt did not properly register his claim. The area was sold to the Georgian capitalist LeRoy Pope for $23 an acre. Pope named the town Twickenham to honor the home village of his distant kinsman, eighteenth-century English poet Alexander Pope. The people of the town later had the unpopular name changed back to Huntsville.

In 1819 Alabama became the 22nd state of the Union, and Huntsville was chosen as the first capital. It was here that the first state constitution was drafted, the first governor inaugurated, and the first legislature convened. It was only a temporary designation, however; the capital later moved to Cahaba, and eventually to Montgomery.

Many settlers from the east in the early nineteenth century bought land in the Tennessee Valley. Soon Huntsville became a frontier metropolis. Its growth came from the cotton and railroad industries—1,000 pounds of cotton per acre could regularly be harvested by farmers in the region. The high price of cotton spawned the growth of cotton merchants, bankers, and lawyers, and they operated out of offices on the west side of the square facing the courthouse, an area that became known as "Cotton Row." Huntsville's economy so depended upon cotton that the entire west side of town was reserved for cotton wagons and carts. Cotton was shipped down the Tennessee River to New Orleans. In 1831 the Indian Creek canal was opened from Hunt's Spring to Triana on the Tennessee River. In 1855 the Memphis and Charleston Railroad was completed, which made overland transportation much easier.

The Civil War

As the Civil War approached, Huntsville was initially opposed to secession, favoring compromise. But when President Lincoln called for an invasion of the South in 1861, Huntsville provided many men for the state's defense. The Fourth Alabama Infantry Regiment, led by Col. Egbert J. Jones of Huntsville, distinguished itself at the Battle of Manassas–Bull Run, the war's first major battle. The Fourth Alabama Infantry contained two Huntsville companies. These were the first Alabama troops to fight in the war, and they were present at the war's end when General Robert E. Lee surrendered to General Ulysses S. Grant at Appomattox in April 1865. Eight generals of the war were born in or near Huntsville, with four on each side. On April 11, 1862, Union troops led by General Ormsby M. Mitchell took the city by surprise. Mitchell seized the city to sever the Confederacy's rail communications. The Union troops used the city as a communications center for the remainder of the war, but guerrilla attacks harassed them. On May 11, 1865, the 25th Alabama Battalion was forced to surrender on Monte Sano.

Textile Center and Watercress Capital of the World

After the Civil War, with the completion of the Nashville, Chattanooga, and St. Louis Railway, industrialization in Huntsville took off. Northern and western capitalists invested in real estate, and cotton processing expanded. Huntsville became a center for cotton textile mills, such as the Lincoln and Merrimack mills. Many neighborhoods of present-day Huntsville were built to house the mill workers. The oldest textile mill in the state was the Huntsville Bell Factory, which began in 1809 and ceased operations in 1885. Lower pay gave Huntsville mills a competitive advantage over New England factories. Other economic mainstays were commerce, banking, nurseries, fruit orchards, and, later, watercress. Indeed, Huntsville became known as the Watercress Capital of the World because so much watercress from the region's cold springs was sold all over the East Coast, which had an appetite for the delicate leaves.

"Rocket City"

The Depression brought hard times to Huntsville's farmers and mill workers. There were a number of strikes in 1933–34, which led to walkouts and shutdowns in the textile industry. New Deal programs provided some relief, and with the establishment of the Tennessee Valley Authority (TVA), many power plants were built on the river. Such plants provided energy for large industrial initiatives and created a number of lakes, including the Guntersville lakes near Huntsville.

Huntsville played a large role in World War II. The Huntsville Arsenal, a chemical warfare plant, and the Redstone Ordnance Plant, which manufactured conventional artillery shells, were constructed on 40,000 acres of cotton land and swamps south of the Tennessee River. Thousands of workers poured into small-town Huntsville. When the war ended, the Huntsville Industrial Expansion Committee was formed to attract both large and small businesses to the region to capitalize on the trained labor force.

The Huntsville Arsenal closed in mid-1949 but later that year was merged with the Redstone Ordnance Plant to become the "Ordnance Guided Missile Center," the center of the Army's missile program. In 1950 under the direction of the German scientist Wernher von Braun, a team of rocket scientists came to Huntsville to work for the missile defense program. They developed the "Redstone Rocket," a surface-to-surface missile. Later, the Redstone Rocket was modified to become the Jupiter C. After the Soviet Union launched the first satellite into orbit in 1957, the United States scrambled to find a vehicle for the American Explorer I. It found one in Huntsville's Jupiter C. On January 31, 1958, the satellite launching was a success, and the National Aeronautics and Space Administration (NASA) was founded. In 1960 Redstone Arsenal was named Marshall Space Flight Center (MSFC) after Gen. George C. Marshall. Von Braun was named its director. The MSFC also developed the Saturn V rocket, which lifted America's astronauts to the moon during the Apollo program.

In 1970 the U.S. Space and Rocket Center was established in Huntsville. It became one of the most modern museums in the world, with 60 hands-on exhibits. Also, a Space Camp was established, where youth could discover what it took to become an astronaut. The army maintains training facilities for the North Atlantic Treaty Organization (NATO) and other allied military personnel at the Redstone Arsenal.

"Preserve America Community"

In 2007 Huntsville was recognized by First Lady Laura Bush as a Preserve America Community. Laura Bush noted that Huntsville's historical and cultural resources form an important part of the nation's heritage and should be preserved and enjoyed. With its rich history associated with landmarks in American culture, such as its significance in the United States' history in space technology, Huntsville continues to be a historic, all-American city. Nonetheless, Huntsville's transformation into a boomtown for business and technology in the South has continued to bode success for the city into the new century, often garnering attention as one of the best places to live and work. In 2012 a Gallup survey ranked Huntsville as the fourth Most Optimistic City in America. In 2013 *Forbes* magazine named Huntsville one of the 25 Best Places to Retire. *Livability* ranked Huntsville among its annual review of Top 100 Best Places to Live for 2014.

Historical Information: Madison County Commission, 100 Northside Square, Courthouse 700, Huntsville, AL 35801; telephone (256) 532-3492; fax (256) 532-6994.

■ Population Profile

Metropolitan Statistical Area Population

1990: 238,912
2000: 342,376
2012 estimate: 430,734
Percent change, 2000–2010: 22%
U.S. rank in 2000: 134th
U.S. rank in 2010: 120th

City Residents

1990: 159,789
2000: 158,216
2010: 180,105
2012 estimate: 183,076
Percent change, 2000–2010: 13.8%
U.S. rank in 1990: 109th
U.S. rank in 2000: 127th
U.S. rank in 2010: 128th

Density: 861.5 people per square mile

Racial and ethnic characteristics

White: 113,590
Black or African American: 58,439
American Indian and Alaskan Native: 527
Asian: 3,884
Native Hawaiian and Other Pacific Islander: 253
Hispanic or Latino (may be of any race): 10,009
Other: 6,383

Percent of residents born in state: 54.1%

Age characteristics

Population under 5 years old: 9,966
Population 5 to 9 years old: 12,994
Population 10 to 14 years old: 10,159
Population 15 to 19 years old: 12,778
Population 20 to 24 years old: 14,608
Population 25 to 34 years old: 26,858
Population 35 to 44 years old: 23,091
Population 45 to 54 years old: 26,802
Population 55 to 59 years old: 10,941
Population 60 to 64 years old: 8,818
Population 65 to 74 years old: 13,644
Population 75 to 84 years old: 8,802
Population 85 years and over: 3,615
Median age: 36.4

Births (2010–11 Metropolitan Area)

Total number: 5,152

Deaths (2010–11 Metropolitan Area)

Total number: 3,201

Money income (2012)

Per capita income: $29,530
Median household income: $46,821
Total households: 75,373

Number of households with income of . . .

less than $10,000: 7,167
$10,000 to $14,999: 5,048
$15,000 to $24,999: 8,784
$25,000 to $34,999: 8,333
$35,000 to $49,999: 9,929
$50,000 to $74,999: 11,888
$75,000 to $99,999: 8,005
$100,000 to $149,999: 9,324
$150,000 to $199,999: 3,638
$200,000 or more: 3,257

Percent of families below poverty level: 16.6%

FBI Crime Index Property: 9,261

FBI Crime Index Violent: 1,696

■ Municipal Government

The city of Huntsville is governed by a strong mayor-council form of government. The mayor is elected for a term of four years. He or she is chief executive and administrator of the city. The city council is made up of five council districts, established in 1988. Council members' terms are for four years with staggered terms: representatives of districts one and two run with the mayor, while representatives of districts three, four, and five run two years from that time.

Head Official: Mayor Tommy Battle (since 2008; current term expires 2016)

Total Number of City Employees: 2,206 (2013)

City Information: City of Huntsville, P.O. Box 308, Huntsville, AL 35804; telephone (256) 535-2489.

■ Economy

Major Industries and Commercial Activity

Since World War II, Huntsville has relied on its military and aerospace industries for economic well-being. However, new industries, such as the computer-related industries and the biotech industry, are emerging. Forty-seven Fortune 500 companies had operations in Huntsville/Madison County in 2013. The city promotes the establishment and retention of small businesses that strive to expand into tomorrow's large corporations. Among the city's 2013 accolades, *Business Facilities* magazine ranked Huntsville fourth in its survey of the best cities for growth potential. *Entrepreneur* magazine ranked the city as second in the South for computer programmers, and the Progressive Policy Institute named Huntsville/Madison Country fourth on its list of America's high-tech hotspots.

Aerospace and defense industries have the most significant economic impact on the Huntsville/Madison County area. Nearly every major U.S. aerospace corporation is represented in Huntsville, including Boeing, Northrup Grumman, and Lockheed Martin. Huntsville also plays a key role in the U.S. Army's technology development programs. Redstone Arsenal is home to more than sixty federal agencies and organizations employing about 31,500 people. Major tenants include the U.S. Army's Aviation and Missile Command; U.S. Army the Security Assistance Command; the U.S. Army Aviation and Missile Research, Development and Engineering Center; U.S. Army Garrison; U.S. Missile Defense Agency; NASA–Marshall Space Flight Center; the ATF National Center for Explosives Training & Research; and FBI Hazardous Devices School.

Founded in 1962, Cummings Research Park has expanded to become the second largest research park in the United States and fourth largest in the world. It began as a public-private initiative among the City of Huntsville, the University of Alabama in Huntsville Foundation, and Teledyne Brown Engineering. Cummings Research Park is one of the world's leading science and technology business parks, home to Fortune 500 companies, local and international high-tech enterprises, U.S. space and defense agencies, and competitive higher-education institutions. In 2013 Cummings Research Park hosted 300 companies employing 29,000 people.

Major telecommunications companies in Huntsville include SAIC, ADTRAN, Verizon, and DirecTV. Huntsville is a city of economic prosperity and resources for companies looking to relocate. Manufacturing companies continue to have a significant impact on the local economy, including Cinram International and Toyota Motor Manicuring Alabama.

Items and goods produced: aerospace and defense hardware and systems, vehicles, electronics, computer software and technology, copper tubing

Incentive Programs-New and Existing Companies

Local programs: The Chamber of Commerce of Huntsville-Madison County's Existing Industry Services program is designed to assist local companies on expansion plans in Huntsville-Madison County. Local incentives for new and existing businesses include property tax and sales tax abatements, corporate income tax capital credit, site grants, and the Tennessee Valley Authority (TVA) incentive program.

The AAMU Alabama A & M University (AAMU) Small Business Development Center provides free counseling to small businesses in a seven-county area.

State programs: Alabama boasts a progressive state business environment as demonstrated by its comprehensive right-to-work laws, one-stop environmental permitting, and a positive state and local government attitude toward new and expanding business. Tax rates are competitive. The Alabama Capital Tax Credit Program offers income tax credit for new or expanding businesses that create new jobs. The state provides additional financing assistance through a number of programs, including the AlabamaSAVES Loan Program, Industrial Development Grant Program, Economic Development Revolving Loan Funds, Industrial Revenue Bonds, and Alabama Innovation Fund, to name a few.

Job training programs: The Alabama Industrial Development Training (AIDT) program provides a total delivery system for screening and selecting trainees and for designing and implementing training for any new or expanding manufacturers in the state of Alabama. The program provides a full range of customized technical training programs that are free to employers and trainees. AIDT supports several specialized training centers, including the Alabama Robotics Technology Park, Alabama Center for Advanced Woodworking Technology, Forest Product Development Center, and AIDT Maritime Training Center. Additional programs provide support for the telecommunications, aviation, automotive, and chemical industries, and other area manufacturers. Mobile training units are also used to go directly to the employer site to provide classroom and hands-on training. The Workforce Investment Act helps defer the costs of hiring and training new employees for private businesses.

The AIDT-Huntsville Center is a 15,000-square-foot facility located near the Huntsville International Airport. With the high concentration of aerospace, machinery, automotive, engineering, and advanced information systems activity in the region, AIDT has joined with Huntsville businesses to create a successful model of worker training and assistance through the Huntsville Center. The Workforce Investment Act helps defer the costs of hiring and training new employees for private businesses.

Development Projects

As of 2013 there were several expansion and development projects underway by major companies in Huntsville. That year, Toyota announced it would invest a total of $150 million to boost machining capacity at its Huntsville engine plant. The company had already begun an $88 million expansion of assembly capacity of V6 engines. The company also plans to boost production of V8 and four-cylinder engines. This represents the company's fourth expansion project since 2003. The V6 expansion was scheduled for completion in 2014. Additional upgrades were scheduled for completion in 2015. Annual production capacity was set to increase from 500,000 to 750,000 engines.

The U.S. Army and Redstone Arsenal collaborated with Alabama developers to begin construction on Redstone Gateway, a planned 468-acre, mixed-use project to be comprised of approximately 4.6 million square feet of office, retail, and hospitality space once completed. Developers envision the park as an integrated business campus to serve Huntsville's next generation of businesses and their employees. About 1.2 million square feet of office space was to be constructed "behind the fence" of Redstone, meaning that it would be designed to adhere to anti-terrorist force protection standards. Construction began in 2010 and is expected to continue in three phases until about 2025.

The first tenants arrived in 2013, when Boeing relocated 500 employees to 1000 Redstone Gateway. Two additional buildings to accommodate an additional 900 Boeing employees were under construction. In 2013 Redstone Hospitality, LLC, announced plans to break ground in 2014 for a new Marriott TownPlace Suites hotel in Redstone Gateway. The hotel was to cover about 3.1 acres with 125 guest rooms, meeting rooms, a fitness and health facility, an indoor pool, and other amenities, and be built to fulfill Leadership in Energy and Environmental Design (LEED) Silver standards.

The Cummings Research Park constantly attracts investors and new developments. Wyle CAS Group completed an $18.75 million, 120,000-square-foot facility there in 2013. In October 2013 Davidson Technologies broke ground on a new $3.5 million, 22,000-square-foot building to accommodate up to 100 new employees. That month, HudsonAlpha Institute for Biotechnology welcomed CFD Research Corporation as the first tenants to its newly built 8,000-square-foot facility. HAIB is the cornerstone of a 150-acre biotech campus located in the park.

Bridge Street is a multi-phase $300-million mixed-use development in the research park, set ultimately to include approximately two million square feet of retail, restaurant, entertainment, office, hotel, and residential space. The Bridge Street Towne Center development is anchored by the Westin Hotels & Residences and Monaco Pictures movie theater; it also hosts some seventy upscale shops.

Phase II of Bridge Street partially opened in 2009 and consisted of retail, with Sports Authority as an anchor. In 2013 there was work on an expansion that would include a two-story flagship department store, 45,000 square feet of additional retail space, a large sit-down restaurant, and 900 new parking spaces.

In other commercial developments, the $100 million mixed-use Twickenham Square project broke ground in the medical district of downtown Huntsville in late 2012. The new development is located across from Huntsville Hospital and slated to be anchored by 246 loft apartments, a Publix supermarket, a 101-room Homewood Suites hotel, and a five-story office tower. Most major construction was scheduled for completion by late 2014.

Economic Development Information: Chamber of Commerce of Huntsville/Madison County, 225 Church Street, Huntsville, AL 35801; telephone (256) 535-2000; fax (256) 535-2015; email info@hsvchamber.org. City of Huntsville, P.O. Box 308, Huntsville, AL 35804; telephone (256) 535-2489.

Commercial Shipping

The area's strong interstate, rail, and air cargo infrastructure make for an ideal manufacturing location. The Port of Huntsville is an inland port that combines three major operating entities: the Huntsville International Airport, the International Intermodal Center, and the Jetplex Industrial Park.

The Huntsville International Airport has two parallel runways, one 10,000 feet and one 12,600 feet, with a 5,000-foot separation and one million square feet of cargo ramp space. The facility is equipped for Category I operations. This high-tech air cargo market is served by domestic and international all-cargo carriers. Weekly international nonstop service is available to Europe daily and three times per week to Mexico. Non-stop international cargo flights are available to Luxembourg, Hong Kong, Mexico City, and Sao Paulo. The airport is home to Foreign Trade Zone 83, as well as U.S. Customs.

The International Intermodal Center (IIC), located on the site of the Huntsville International Airport, is an innovative inland port facility. The IIC is a single hub location that specializes in a wide range of services including receiving, transferring, storing, and distributing air, rail, and highway cargo both domestically and internationally. An intermodal rail yard, complete with container handling and storage, is located adjacent to Huntsville International Airport (HSV) air cargo facilities.

Huntsville has two active commercial rail lines. The main line is run by Norfolk Southern. Another rail line is operated by Huntsville and Madison County Railroad Authority (HMCRA). The line connects to the Norfolk Southern line downtown and runs thirteen miles south, terminating at Norton Switch near Hobbs Island.

Huntsville is served by several U.S. highways, including 72, 231, and 431, and Interstate 565, an interstate highway spur that links the cities of Huntsville and Decatur to Interstate 65. Alabama Highway 53 also connects the city with Interstate 65 in Ardmore, Tennessee.

Labor Force and Employment Outlook

As the economy of the Huntsville area is made up mostly of technical, aerospace, manufacturing, and defense jobs and companies, it is often stated that Huntsville has more engineers per capita than anywhere else in the United States. In 2013 *CNNMoney.com* noted Huntsville as one of the nation's top ten places to find a job. That year *Entrepreneur* magazine ranked the city of Huntsville second in the South for computer programmers and one of the Top 25 Best U.S. Cities for Tech Startups. *Business Facilities* ranked Huntsville fourth in the nation for cities with the best economic growth potential.

Manufacturing jobs continue to grow as existing companies expand (such as Toyota). The number of jobs in research and development is expected to remain strong as well. In 2013, 20 companies in Huntsville/Madison County were listed on the *Inc 5000* Fastest Growing Companies list. These included Summit 7 Systems (technical solutions) and Five Stones Research.

The following is a summary of data regarding the 2012 Huntsville labor force:

Size of civilian labor force: 96,555

Number of workers employed in ...

agriculture and mining: 394
construction: 4,826
manufacturing: 9,283
wholesale trade: 1,403
retail trade: 9,401
transportation: 2,252
information systems: 2,170
finance: 3,760
professional administration: 14,903
education and social services: 17,506
arts and leisure: 8,956
other: 4,070
public administration: 6,429

Average hourly earnings of production workers: $15.99

Unemployment rate: 7.0% (2012)

Employers

Largest employers (Huntsville/Madison County 2013)

	Number of employees
U.S. Army/Redstone Arsenal	31,500
Huntsville Hospital System	7,129
NASA/Marshall Space Flight Center	6,000
Huntsville City Schools	3,079
The Boeing Company	2,600
Madison County Schools	2,389
SAIC (Science Applications International Corp.)	2,229
City of Huntsville	2,206
ADTRAN, Inc.	1,740
University of Alabama in Huntsville	1,675
CINRAM, Inc.	1,450
Sanmina–SCI Corporation	1,365
Qualitest	1,350
Intergraph Corporation	1,325

Cost of Living

The following is a summary of data regarding several key cost of living factors in the area.

2013 ACCRA Average House Price: $238,147

2013 ACCRA Cost of Living Index: 94

State income tax rate: 2.0% to 5.0%

State sales tax rate: 4.0%

Local income tax rate: None

Local sales tax rate: 4.0%

Property tax rate: $5.80 per every $100 of assessed value (2013)

Economic Information: Chamber of Commerce of Huntsville/Madison County, 225 Church Street, Huntsville, AL 35801; telephone (256) 535-2000; fax (256) 535-2015; email info@hsvchamber.org. City of Huntsville, P.O. Box 308, Huntsville, AL 35804; telephone (256) 535-2489.

■ Education and Research

Elementary and Secondary Schools

Schools were established in Huntsville in 1812. As of 2013, the Huntsville City School System consisted of 33 prekindergarten programs, 21 elementary schools, 8 middle schools, 7 high schools, and 5 Pre-K–8 schools.

In addition to the regular curriculum, the school district offers a variety of magnet programs, including creative and performing arts (Academy for Academics and Arts and Lee High School), engineering (Lee High School), law (Johnson High School), international baccalaureate (Columbia High School and Academy for Science and Foreign Language), and science and foreign languages (Academy for Science and Foreign Language). The system also hosts junior ROTC (Reserve Officers' Training Corps) programs for the U.S. Army, Air Force, and Marines.

The Huntsville Center of Technology provides skilled technical training for high school students and adults preparing for college or reentering the workforce. Beginning in fall 2013, all high school freshmen are required to take courses in career preparedness in order to graduate. Career fields include health science, plant science and agribusiness, engineering, robotics, business, information technology, biomedical sciences, cyber security, communications, culinary arts, and automotive technology, among others. Since each high school offers career preparedness courses in a different set of fields, transportation is provided for students interested in programs not hosted at their home school.

Several private, religiously affiliated, or independent schools are located in the Huntsville and Madison areas of north Alabama. These include Randolph School, Oakwood Academy, The Montessori School of Huntsville, Islamic Academy of Huntsville, and Grace Lutheran Academy. Holy Spirit Regional Catholic School in Huntsville was named a National Blue Ribbon School in 2013. Greengate School and Janice Mitchell Isbell Academy offer programs for students with learning differences, such as dyslexia.

The following is a summary of data regarding the Huntsville City Schools.

Total enrollment: 23,364

Number of facilities
    total: 41
    elementary schools: 21
    junior high schools: 13
    high schools: 7

Student/teacher ratio: 14.07:1

Teacher salaries
    average (statewide): $48,282

Funding per pupil: $9,610

Public Schools Information: Huntsville City Schools, 200 White Street, Huntsville, AL 35801; telephone (256) 428-6800.

Colleges and Universities

Alabama Agricultural and Mechanical University (Alabama A & M University) was established on December 16, 1875, as a land grant college. The university consists of four undergraduate colleges (Agricultural, Life, and Natural Sciences; Business and Public Affairs; Education, Humanities, and Behavioral Sciences; and Engineering, Technology, and Physical Sciences) and the School of Graduate Studies. The university offers more than 40 bachelor's programs, 23 master's programs, and 4 doctoral degrees. Undergraduate enrollment is nearly 5,000 students.

The University of Alabama in Huntsville (UAH) is organized into five colleges: business, engineering, liberal arts, nursing, and science. UAH is renowned for its engineering and science programs, such as astrophysics and atmospheric science. Total enrollment at UAH is about 7,700 students.

Oakwood University, founded in 1896, is a historically black college affiliated with the Seventh-Day Adventist Church. The university consists of the School of Arts and Sciences, the School of Business and Adult and Continuing Education, the School of Education and Social Sciences, the School of Nursing and Health Professions, and the School of Religion.

J. F. Drake State Technical College is a two-year college that trains individuals for employment in vocational, technical, and industrial pursuits. The college has five divisions: Business and Information Technology, Engineering Technology, Manufacturing and Applied Technology, Salon Management and Culinary Arts/Hospitality Services Management, and Health Sciences. The college benefits from being located in Huntsville, with its strong history of high technology and space industries.

Calhoun Community College is a two-year institution with its main campus in Decatur. However, it has two campuses in Huntsville—at Cummings Research Park and Redstone Arsenal. Virginia College in Huntsville is a career college offering several associate's and bachelor's degrees, along with master's degrees in business administration and criminal justice. Faulkner University (based in Montgomery) has an extension campus in Huntsville.

Libraries and Research Centers

The Huntsville-Madison County Public Library system was founded in 1818. It is Alabama's oldest continually operating library system. It has a Main Library on Monroe Street, plus eleven other branches and a bookmobile. The Main Library hosts the Subregional Library for the Blind and Physically Handicapped. This special library is part of the U.S. Library of Congress administered network serving persons who cannot use conventional printed materials. There are more than 530,000 volumes in the Main Library alone. The Main Library archives contain a wealth of historical resources, including displays of photographic collections and artifacts. The library has the state's highest circulation rate, and features daily public programs. The online catalog features a digital media zone for e-books and free music downloads.

In addition to the academic libraries of colleges and universities in the area, Huntsville is home to such special libraries as the library of the National Speleological Society, Redstone Scientific Information Center, and the Elbert Parsons Law Library.

The M. Louis Salmon Library at the University of Alabama in Huntsville has more than 412,000 books and subscriptions to 2,766 periodicals, along with collections of U.S. government documents, sound recordings, and microform and microfiche. The J.F. Drake Memorial Learning Resources Center at Alabama A & M University houses more than 256,000 volumes and 2,200 journals. It is a partial depository for government documents.

Huntsville has become a major regional center for high-tech research, with numerous companies and organizations contributing to research in aerospace, medical, biotechnology, and defense technologies. The University of Alabama in Huntsville sponsors nine major research centers. NASA and the Department of Defense are the university's largest research sponsors. The Research Institute of the University of Alabama in Huntsville sponsors applied research and engineering programs that meet the needs of the U.S. Department of Defense, NASA, and private industry partners. The Propulsion Research Center has gained national attention in the field of advanced propulsion technologies and their applications. Other research disciplines include applied optics, earth system science, information technology; management of science and technology, mechanical and aerospace engineering, modeling and simulation, nano-devices, space plasmas and astrophysics, structural biology, systems engineering, and robotics.

HudsonAlpha Institute for BioTechnology is the cornerstone of Cummings Research Park. Other companies located in the park include Auburn University Huntsville Research Center, CFD Research Corporation, Delta Research, and numerous others involved in research and development activities.

Heart Center Research, affiliated with Huntsville Hospital, is one of the largest non-university based research centers in the United States. Georgia Tech Research Institute also has a center in Huntsville that works on projects with the Missile Defense Agency.

Public Library Information: Huntsville-Madison County Public Library, 915 Monroe Street, Huntsville, AL 35801; telephone (256) 532-5940.

■ Health Care

Huntsville Hospital, established as an infirmary in 1895, includes the facilities of Huntsville Hospital, Huntsville Hospital for Women & Children, and the outpatient Huntsville Medical Mall. Huntsville Hospital is an 881-bed facility with a medical staff of more than 750 physicians supported by 7,000 hospital employees.

The 70-bed HealthSouth Rehabilitation Hospital of North Alabama in Huntsville provides care for a number of conditions including stroke, amputations, arthritis, brain Injury, hip fractures, joint replacement, multiple trauma, neurological disorders, and spinal cord injury. It is affiliated with Huntsville Hospital. Several other area hospitals are affiliated with Huntsville Hospital, including Madison Hospital, Athens-Limestone Hospital, Red Bay Hospital, Decatur general Hospital, and Lawrence Medical Center.

Huntsville Health Care Center is the city's oldest nursing and rehabilitative care center. In 2011 it was named Regional and National Center of the Year by Health Systems Management, Inc. Huntsville Emergency Medical Services provides care to more than 300,000 citizens across 800 square miles of Huntsville-Madison County. It is the state's only nationally accredited emergency medical service.

■ Recreation

Sightseeing

The Twickenham Historic District contains scores of outstanding nineteenth-century homes dating from as early as 1814. Early merchants, bankers, and attorneys built fashionable brick homes, many of which were seized by the Union Army during the Civil War. The occupation saved the houses from destruction. The Old Town district, north of the Square, contains many fine Victorian homes. Charming bungalows dominate the Five Points district. Madison's historic district dates from the mid-19th century.

Maple Hill Cemetery was established in 1818 on two acres of land purchased by the city from LeRoy Pope for $200. Today, Maple Hill Cemetery covers nearly 100 acres, in which between 80,000 and 100,000 people are buried. It is the oldest and largest cemetery in Alabama.

At Constitution Village, visitors can experience Alabama's rich history and become a part of the nineteenth century, as villagers dressed in period clothing lead groups through eight reconstructed Federal-style buildings. One can visit the site where forty-four delegates gathered to forge the way for Alabama's statehood in 1819. The Clay House, built in 1853, serves as a museum and art gallery. Harrison Brothers Hardware is the oldest continuously operating hardware store in Alabama, established in 1879 and located on the downtown square since 1897.

Burritt on the Mountain is a museum and historic park. The museum of regional history is housed in the mountaintop home of Dr. William Henry Burritt. The fourteen-room mansion was built in the shape of an X in the 1930s and is insulated with 2,200 bales of wheat straw. The Historic Park contains restored farm buildings, which interpret rural life from 1850 through 1900. Many nature trails wind through heavily wooded forest. The grounds offer a spectacular panoramic view of Huntsville and the Tennessee Valley. Concerts, plays, and art exhibits are frequently hosted on-site.

The U.S. Space and Rocket Center is the world's largest space attraction. It features many interactive exhibits surrounding Apollo, Mercury, and Space Shuttle spacecraft. Rockets developed in Huntsville range from the Army boosters that put America's first satellite and astronauts in orbit to NASA's Saturn V moon rocket and the Space Shuttle. At the U.S. Space and Rocket Center, one can stand under a "full stack"—the Space Shuttle, external tank, and two rocket boosters. Visitors can see the U.S. Space Camp Training Center and conduct simulated missions. They can experience three times the force of gravity in the G-Force Accelerator, maneuver through space aboard the Mission to Mars, and travel through space during shows in the Spacedome Imax Theater.

The Veterans Memorial Museum honors the accomplishments of American military men and women. The museum displays more than thirty historical military vehicles from World War I to the present, as well as tableaus, artifacts, and other memorabilia. It was designated as the State of Alabama Veterans Memorial Museum by the Alabama House of Representatives.

The Early Works Children's Museum is the South's largest hands-on history museum. Children can go back in time in the museum's rotunda, where exhibits bring to life Alabama's early history. They can hear stories from a talking tree, play a tune on giant-sized instruments, and build a house in the interactive architecture exhibit. Children also have an opportunity to try on clothes from the 1800s and milk a cow.

Sci-Quest is North Alabama's primary hands-on science center. More than 150 interactive exhibits await the young and young-at-heart. Exhibits include the Tornado Simulator, the Magnetic Pendulum, and Grossology, an exhibit of the human body. In addition to permanent and traveling exhibits, Sci-Quest offers education programs for children from age four through sixth grade. Presentations in 3-D are offered in the Immersive Reality Theater. The museum also has introduced a special Geeks' Night Out for adults (over 21), which offers science related-workshops and a chance to meet and mingle with like-minded science fans.

Harmony Park is a nature preserve of free-ranging exotic and endangered animals. Visitors remain in their cars on a two-mile route to see zebras, zebus, antelope, buffalo, a camel, ostriches, pythons, and crocodiles.

The Huntsville Botanical Garden is a beautiful 110-acre site with floral collections, woodland paths, and broad grassy meadows. The five-acre Central Corridor Garden features aquatic, perennial, and annual displays blooming from early spring through fall. Children of all ages love the G-scale trains that travel the Garden Railway. The Butterfly House features more than 50 species of native butterflies and is open May through September. Each year, more than 200,000 visitors enjoy special events such as the Spring Festival of Flowers, Scarecrow Trail, Galaxy of Lights, and summer concerts.

At Cathedral Caverns State Park, the large opening into the cavern measures 126 feet wide by 25 feet high. At the state park, visitors can explore Big Rock Canyon, Mystery River, Stalagmite Mountain, the Frozen Waterfall, and Goliath, a huge stalagmite column that reaches the ceiling of the cave some forty-five feet above.

Big Spring International Park is also a Huntsville area treasure that came to be in 1966 when the Japanese government planted approximately sixty cherry trees, and a Japanese general donated a red footbridge, which now spans a lagoon. Due to the NATO training program in Huntsville, other nations stationed there followed suit over the years, donating items such as the German sundial, a British park bench, Norwegian light beacon and fog bell, Swiss flag of roses, and other contributions.

Arts and Culture

The Huntsville Museum of Art is located in Big Spring International Park. More than 3,000 items are displayed in 13 galleries. The museum is also the home of the world's largest collection of Buccellati silver animals. Special traveling exhibits are shown throughout the year. The museum sponsors several art classes as well, and hosts a free Monday night concert series on an outdoor stage during the summer. Weeden House Museum and Garden, built in 1819, is the oldest building in Alabama still open to the public. The Weeden House Museum is noted for its entrance fanlight and collection of period furnishings. It was home to poet and artist Maria Howard Weeden.

Merrimack Hall Performing Arts Center includes a 300-seat, state-of-the-art performance hall, a 3,000-square-foot dance studio, and rehearsal and instructional spaces for musicians. The center offers classes in music, theater, and dance, master classes in all of the performing arts, summer camps, and several performances and productions each year.

The Broadway Theatre League puts on Broadway performances, programs for the entire family, and "star spotlights." Theatre Huntsville stages six to eight productions a year. The six main stage shows are presented in the 332-seat Von Braun Center Playhouse, a theater in the round. Theatre Huntsville also stages some performances, such as the popular *Shakespeare on the Mountain,* at other area venues.

The Renaissance Theatre seats eighty-five for performances ranging from Shakespeare to opera to Christmas programs. Fantasy Playhouse Children's Theater presents nine to ten performances of three regular season productions and an annual production of *A Christmas Carol* in the Von Braun Center Playhouse. The Fantasy Playhouse Children's Theater delights 12,000 people yearly.

The Huntsville Symphony Orchestra, directed by Gregory Vajda, presents a six-concert classical series, a three-concert pop series, and a four-concert Mainly Mozart Series at the Von Braun Center's Mark C. Smith Concert Hall. The Huntsville Community Chorus Association (HCCA), the area's oldest performing arts organization, began in 1946; its name changed from Trichoral to HCCA in 1950. This organization offers the best in choral music and musical theater. Musical entertainment is also provided by the Huntsville Chamber Music Guild and the Huntsville Traditional Music Association.

The Huntsville Ballet School and the Huntsville Ballet Company are housed in a building near Parkway Place; performances are held in the Von Braun Center's Mark C. Smith Concert Hall. Top guest dancers, such as the Hubbard Street Dance Chicago and the North Carolina Dance Theatre, are brought to town for performances as well. The ballet company's annual production of *The Nutcracker* is a local holiday tradition. The North Alabama Dance Center typically presents one public performance per year at the Von Braun Center.

Festivals and Holidays

The annual Northeast Alabama Craftsmen Association (NEACA) Craft Shows take place every March, September, and December at the Von Brown Center Exhibit Hall, with nearly every arts and craft category represented. In April, the Panoply Arts Festival, a Huntsville tradition for more than 25 years, is a three-day outdoor festival featuring presentations and demonstrations, while promoting and enhancing the arts.

In June the WEUP Black Arts Festival brings more than 165 performers to Alabama A & M University's campus; WEUP was Alabama's first black-owned and black-operated radio station, which took to the airwaves in 1958. Oktoberfest takes place in September, with vendors serving traditional German fare, as well as all-American hamburgers and hot dogs.

In October the Maple Hill Cemetery Stroll takes place; more than eighty Huntsville residents in period costumes represent notables from the past who are buried in the cemetery. They include five Alabama governors, characters from the Revolutionary and Civil Wars, a gypsy queen, renowned architect George Steele, artist Howard Weeden, and Tallulah Bankhead. In mid-November the Huntsville Botanical Garden is home to the Galaxy of Lights Walk Through Nights, where visitors can walk through a winter wonderland of holiday lights, enjoy the sounds of the season, and see real-life nursery rhyme characters, including Santa. The garden also hosts Galaxy of Lights Drive-Through, the largest holiday light show

in the Tennessee Valley. It is a family-oriented drive-through display featuring holiday themes, cartoon characters, and fantasy creations. In December the Twickenham District is aglow, with luminaries, trees, and front doors glimmering with holiday decorations; carolers also stroll through the streets.

Sports for the Spectator

Rocket City United makes Huntsville home to play in the National Premier Soccer League. The Huntsville Stars are a Southern League (Class AA) baseball team for the Milwaukee Brewers. The Huntsville Havoc is a Southern Professional Hockey League (SPHL) team. NASCAR-sanctioned stock car racing takes place at the Huntsville Speedway. The Dixie Derby Girls Roller Derby League is a member of the Women's Flat Track Roller Derby Association.

The Bulldogs are Alabama A & M University's NCAA Division I athletic teams. Men participate in soccer, golf, basketball, baseball, football, track and field, and tennis. Women field teams in basketball, bowling, cross country, track and field, volleyball, tennis, softball, and soccer. The University of Alabama in Huntsville athletic teams are the NCAA Division II Chargers. Men's teams include soccer, basketball, baseball, ice hockey, tennis, track, and cross country. Women's teams include softball, basketball, tennis, track, cross country, soccer, and volleyball.

Sports for the Participant

The Huntsville and Madison county area offers open space along scenic roadways to local pedestrians and bicyclists. Within the city limits, Huntsville offers many facilities for outdoor recreation. Huntsville has a total of 3,203 acres of parks; sixty-four parks are regularly cleaned and maintained. There are eleven city recreation centers. Golfers can tee off at the municipal golf course, or at five other public golf courses and two country club golf courses. There are 175 miles of bicycle pathways in the city, and three municipal swimming pools. Huntsville has thirty lighted municipal tennis courts for day or night play, and twenty-five courts for day use only. There are at least forty other public and private tennis courts available for use as well. The city also sponsors the Lydia Gold Skatepark, the Dog Spot (an off-leash play area), and a seasonal Everyone Can Play Splash Pad, designed to be accessible to children of all abilities. Major parks include Monte Sano State Park, a 2,000-acre area, and Big Spring International Park in downtown Huntsville.

Shopping and Dining

Downtown Huntsville's historic ambience makes it a pleasurable shopping and dining destination for residents and tourists alike. Harrison Brothers Hardware Store, Alabama's oldest operating hardware store, is filled with nostalgic hardware items, household gadgets, and local crafts. Numerous small shops can be found in the area. Madison Square Mall, a 1.1-million-square-foot shopping mall, is one of the largest retail shopping complexes in northern Alabama and south-central Tennessee. Anchored by Belk, JCPenney, and Sears, it has more than 120 specialty shops. There are several restaurants, including fast-food stops in the food court, and a movie theater. Shoppers can also find what they want at Parkway Place Mall, featuring Ann Taylor, Chico's, Hollister, and Williams-Sonoma. Parkway Place is 650,000 square feet anchored by Belk and Dillard's, with seventy other stores and a food court. Upscale shopping is offered at Bridge Street Towne Center, a mixed-use lifestyle center home to at least seventy stores and restaurants.

Downtown, the Huntsville Hilton, 1892 East Restaurant, and several other restaurants and nightspots offer great dining options. In Huntsville one can enjoy a large variety of cuisines, including Southern, Chinese, Thai, Korean, Japanese, Indian, Mexican, French, Greek, German, and Italian. There are also many seafood restaurants, steakhouses, and cafés.

Visitor Information: Huntsville/Madison County Convention & Visitors Bureau, 500 Church Street, Suite One, Huntsville, AL 35801; telephone (256) 551-2230; toll-free (800) 843-0468; fax (256) 551-2324; email info@huntsville.org.

■ Convention Facilities

Convention facilities are found in the Von Braun Center, which opened in 1975. The Von Braun Center has an arena capable of seating 9,000, a 1,955-seat concert hall, a 502-seat playhouse, and 150,000 square feet of convention space. The state-of-the-art South Hall provides more than 100,000 square feet of continuous space and 82,000 feet of column-free exhibit space, as well as its own 500-space covered parking garage, in addition to meeting rooms and a more than 20,000-square-foot lobby and pre-function area. The North Hall and East/West Hall provide an additional 50,000 square feet of flexible exhibit, meeting, and banquet space. Meeting rooms accommodate groups of all sizes.

Approximately 800 people can be accommodated at Sci-Quest science center. The Bertha Jones Conference Center at Alabama A & M University can accommodate 75 to 100 people; there are also other venues at the university that can accommodate up to 6,000 people standing up and 400–500 sitting down. Burritt on the Mountain has various rooms that can accommodate 100 people. Huntsville Botanical Garden can seat 80–100 people. Approximately 400 people can sit down in one large room at the Huntsville Depot Roundhouse. The Huntsville Museum of Art has various rooms for meetings, receptions, and other events. The Grand Hall can seat 200 for a theater-style presentation.

Convention Information Huntsville/Madison County Convention & Visitors Bureau, 500 Church Street, Suite One, Huntsville, AL 35801; telephone (256) 551-2230; toll-free (800) 843-0468; fax (256) 551-2324; email info@huntsville.org.

■ Transportation

Approaching the City

There are four major airlines providing passenger service out of Huntsville International Airport: American Airlines, Delta Airlines, United Airlines, and U.S. Airways. Non-stop service is offered to nine destinations. For those arriving by car, Huntsville is served by several U.S. Highways, including 72, 231, and 431, and an Interstate highway spur (Interstate 565) that links the two cities of Huntsville and Decatur to Interstate 65. Alabama Highway 53 also connects the city with Interstate 65 in Ardmore, Tennessee. Greyhound bus service is available.

Traveling in the City

The Huntsville Shuttle provides public transportation in the city with thirteen routes. Handi-Ride Paratransit Service for seniors and disabled citizens consists of fourteen vehicles. CommuteSmart Huntsville, a computerized service for working commuters, links commuters with potential carpooling companions.

■ Communications

Newspapers and Magazines

The Huntsville Times is Huntsville's only daily newspaper. It is the third largest newspaper in Alabama. A free online version is available online. *The Valley Planet* covers entertainment in the Huntsville region. It is published every three weeks on Thursday. The *Redstone Rocket* is a newspaper covering activities on Redstone Arsenal. *Speakin' Out News* is a weekly newspaper focused on African Americans. All three of these publications have online versions. *El Reportero* is a Spanish-language newspaper for North Alabama. A number of magazines are also based in the city; most serve specific business or religious interests. *Old Huntsville* is one of the most popular magazines in North Alabama; it combines a mixture of history, folklore, recipes, and memories.

Television and Radio

Four major television stations broadcast from Huntsville: affiliates of ABC, CBS, NBC, and Fox. Eleven AM and FM radio stations serve listeners in the area with a variety of formats.

Media Information: The Huntsville Times, 200 Westside Square, Suite 100, Huntsville, AL 35801; telephone (256) 532-4000; toll-free (800) 239-5271; email hsvnews@al.com.

Huntsville Online

Chamber of Commerce of Huntsville/Madison County, Alabama. Available www.huntsville alabamausa.com

City of Huntsville. Available www.huntsvilleal.gov

Huntsville City Schools. Available www.huntsville cityschools.org

Huntsville/Madison County Convention and Visitors Bureau. Available www.huntsville.org

Huntsville-Madison County Public Library. Available www.hmcpl.org

The Huntsville Times. Available www.al.com/ huntsvilletimes

BIBLIOGRAPHY

Hays, Paul A., *From Carnegie to Fort Book: The History of the Huntsville-Madison County Public Library* (West Conshohocken, PA: Infinity Publishing Co., 2005)

Kvach, John F., *Huntsville* (Mount Pleasant, SC: Arcadia Publishing, 2013)

Levin, Rob, ed., *One Sky, Countless Stars: A Photographic Portrait of Huntsville/Madison County* (Atlanta, GA: Riverbend Books, 2005)

Pruitt, Raneé G., *Eden of the South: A Chronology of Huntsville, Alabama, 1805–2005* (Huntsville, AL: Huntsville-Madison County Public Library, 2005)

Mobile

■ The City in Brief

Founded: 1702 (incorporated 1819)

Head Official: Mayor Sandy Stimpson (since 2013)

City Population
1990: 199,973
2000: 198,915
2010: 195,111
2012 estimate: 194,823
Percent change, 2000–2010: −1.9%
U.S. rank in 1990: 79th
U.S. rank in 2000: 105th (State rank: 3rd)
U.S. rank in 2010: 116th (State rank: 3rd)

Metropolitan Statistical Area Population
2000: 399,843
2010: 412,992
2012 estimate: 413,936
Percent change, 2000–2010: 3.3%
U.S. rank in 2000: 113th
U.S. rank in 2010: 124th

Area: 139.11 square miles

Elevation: 10 feet above sea level

Average Annual Temperatures: January, 51° F; July, 82° F; annual average, 68° F

Average Annual Precipitation: 66 inches

Major Economic Sectors: wholesale and retail trade, services, government, manufacturing

Unemployment Rate: 7.7% (2012)

Per Capita Income: $20,656

2012 FBI Crime Index Property: 12,103

Major Colleges and Universities: University of South Alabama, University of Mobile, Spring Hill College, Bishop State Community College

Daily Newspaper: *The Mobile Press-Register*

■ Introduction

Mobile is the oldest and third largest city in Alabama. It is also the state's only seaport, serving as a major industrial, shipping, and shipbuilding center. Located on the Mobile River at the head of the Gulf of Mexico's Mobile Bay, it was an important maritime site during the Civil War and both world wars. The area that is now Mobile was France's first Gulf Coast settlement, and except for St. Augustine, Florida, it is the oldest Latin town east of Mexico. Mobile's long-term French and Spanish heritage make it unique in Alabama and places the city among the elite urban centers of the South. Steeped in the heritage of a genuinely Southern past, Mobile continues to move forward as a truly modern city while benefitting from its industrial and port city past.

■ Geography and Climate

Mobile is located at the mouth of the Mobile River in southwest Alabama and stands at the head of Mobile Bay, thirty-one miles inland from where the bay meets the Gulf of Mexico. It is the seat of Mobile County. Mobile is one of the nation's wettest cities. Rainfall occurs fairly evenly throughout the year. Summers are hot and muggy; winters are mild. Mobile averages only twenty-one days each year at or below freezing temperatures. Average annual snowfall is less than half an inch. The city is occasionally threatened by hurricanes from the Gulf of Mexico and the West Indies. In 2004 Hurricane Ivan wreaked havoc on Mobile and surrounding areas. In August 2005 Mobile was hit again, this time by

Steven Frame/Shutterstock.com

Hurricane Katrina, which flooded the city's downtown. Tornadoes are another major concern for the area. On Christmas Day in 2012 a powerful twister swept through greater Mobile, causing damage in the Midtown area and cutting power to nearly 26,000 residents.

Area: 139.11 square miles

Elevation: 10 feet above sea level

Average Temperatures: January, 51° F; July, 82° F; annual average, 68° F

Average Annual Precipitation: 66 inches

■ History

French Establish First Settlement

Represented on maps as early as 1507, the Gulf of Mexico inlet now known as Mobile Bay was navigated by European seafarers in 1519 when ships under the command of Spanish Admiral Alonso Alvaraz de Pineda sought a safe harbor in which to undertake repairs. The bay area was not really explored, however, until 1558. It was included in the vast region claimed for France's King Louis XIV and

named Louisiana by French explorer Robert Cavelier de La Salle in 1682. France authorized two brothers, Pierre Le Moyne d'Iberville and Jean Baptiste Le Moyne de Bienville, to explore territories in Louisiana, and they arrived at the gulf inlet now called Mobile Bay in 1699.

The area was subsequently considered crucial to establishing French occupation of Louisiana, and the brothers were ordered to colonize the region, which was inhabited by the Mobile, or Maubila, tribe. In 1702 Bienville established Fort Louis de la Mobile—named to honor France's king and to acknowledge the native tribe—at Twenty-seven Mile Bluff on the banks of the Mobile River, just north of present-day Mobile. It was the first French town in the gulf region.

The settlement, which consisted of the log fort, Creole houses, a church, a hospital, a marketplace with shops, and a well, served as the capital of the vast Louisiana Territory. Women joined the community in 1704. When river flooding forced the colony to abandon Fort Louis de la Mobile in 1711, the settlement's 400 inhabitants moved downstream to a new site protected by a wooden fort at the river's mouth on Mobile Bay. During this era, pelts, furs, wax, and tallow were transported downriver to where the bay meets the gulf for transfer to oceangoing vessels. This settlement retained the name Mobile and remained the capital of the Louisiana Territory until New Orleans assumed that title in 1720. That same year, Mobile renamed its fort Fort Conde. A brick structure later replaced the original fort.

Mobile Becomes Part of the United States

Mobile continued to serve as an important center for diplomatic dealings with the neighboring tribal inhabitants. France ceded its territory east of the Mississippi River to Britain in 1763, and that year, taking possession of Fort Conde, the British renamed it Fort Charlotte. Two years later Mobile was the site of the Great Choctaw-Chickasaw Congress held among tribal leaders and British officials.

When Spain, at war with Britain, captured Mobile in 1779, the area traded in cotton and indigo and supported sawmills and brickyards. After two decades of Spanish rule, the region was returned to France, who sold the Louisiana Territory to the United States in 1803. It was not until after the War of 1812, however, that U.S. influence began to be felt in the region. The Bank of Mobile was established in 1818, Mobile was incorporated as a city shortly after Alabama attained statehood in 1819, and Fort Charlotte was dismantled in 1820.

Explosion Destroys City

Mobile's population by 1822 had reached nearly 3,000 people, a figure that subsequently quadrupled in less than two decades. As steamboats made upstream transportation possible, Mobile served as an important port for distributing goods brought in by oceangoing vessels as well as for exporting cotton and lumber. By the 1850s Mobile was the South's second largest cotton port, following New Orleans. Although tested by fires and yellow-fever epidemics, Mobile's prosperity by mid-century was secure. In 1861, recognizing the nation's deep political and social division, Alabama seceded from the United States as the Republic of Alabama and joined other Southern states to form the Confederacy.

Mobile was particularly valuable to the South because of its location on the Gulf of Mexico. The city maintained trade with Europe and the West Indies while constructing the first submarine used in warfare. But in 1864 during the Battle of Mobile Bay, Union forces, urged on by Admiral David Farragut's famous rallying cry, "Damn the torpedoes, full speed ahead!", defeated Confederate troops and captured southern strongholds around Mobile. Still, Mobile was the only major Southern port unoccupied by Yankee troops during the Civil War. At the war's end a tremendous ammunitions explosion in Mobile left massive destruction.

Mobile Emerges Triumphant

The city's post-Civil War recovery was aided by port-related activity; the shipping channel was deepened and shipbuilding increased. In the 1870s Mobile began serving as a major center for the importation of Brazilian coffee. Railroad expansion also contributed to Mobile's emergence as a major distribution center. At the beginning of the twentieth century, the city's port underwent further development and modernization, and in the 1920s the Alabama State Docks were conceived and realized as a means of providing and maintaining adequate port facilities. Mobile's shipbuilding contributed to war efforts during World War I, and during World War II the city's shipyards were packed with shifts of workers welding hulls for U.S. Navy ships.

While Mobile found itself weathering the violent racial tensions that swept the nation in the 1960s, the city was and is often the site of damaging tropical storms. Mobile sustained heavy losses after Hurricane Camille hit the Gulf Coast in 1969, destroying a total of $1.5 billion worth of property along the coast and claiming 250 lives in Mobile. Ten years later Hurricane Frederic was especially brutal for the city, with property damage in Mobile mounting to $1 billion. In 2004 Hurricane Ivan attacked the Gulf Coast, leaving Mobile another hefty bill.

In August 2005 Mobile was hit again, this time by Hurricane Katrina, which flooded the city's downtown, taking several lives. The storm surge recorded in Mobile Bay was 11.45 feet, nearly the highest ever recorded. (The previous record, from July 5, 1916, was 11.60 feet.) Downtown Mobile was flooded and a dusk-to-dawn curfew was imposed in the days after the storm. When the floodwaters subsided, Mobile had suffered little damage; people displaced by the storm from Louisiana and elsewhere in Alabama were able to relocate to Mobile. A total of twenty-four deaths likely related to Hurricane Katrina were recorded for Mobile and Baldwin counties.

In 2010 Mobile Bay was hit by a different type of disaster, which began with an explosion on the BP Deepwater Horizon oilrig about forty miles off the coast of Louisiana. The explosion occurred on April 20, 2010. For the next eighty-seven days, oil spilled into the Gulf at a rate of about 2.4 million gallons per day. By June, oil washed onto the shores of Alabama, Louisiana, Mississippi, and Florida. In total, about 4.9 million barrels of oil (206 million gallons) spilled into the Gulf of Mexico. Local economies were hit hard as fishing boats were forced to stay ashore, and tourists avoided Gulf beaches. Coastal habitats were devastated. Thousands of coastal birds and hundreds of sea turtles and dolphins were found dead or dying along affected areas.

The political and legal wrangling involved in securing funds for restoration projects continued into 2013. In November of that year, the state of Alabama received $12.6 million from the Gulf Environmental Benefit Fund, much of which was earmarked for projects to restore coastal habitats along Mobile Bay. The Mobile-based Mobile Baykeepers was one of the most prominent local organizations involved in restoration initiatives.

Historical Information: Historic Mobile Preservation Society, 300 Oakleigh Place, Mobile, AL 36604; telephone (251) 432-6161.

■ Population Profile

Metropolitan Statistical Area Population

1990: 476,923
2000: 399,843
2012 estimate: 413,936
Percent change, 2000–2010: 3.3%
U.S. rank in 2000: 113th
U.S. rank in 2010: 124th

City Residents

1990: 199,973
2000: 198,915
2010: 195,111
2012 estimate: 194,823
Percent change, 2000–2010: −1.9%
U.S. rank in 1990: 79th
U.S. rank in 2000: 105th (State rank: 3rd)
U.S. rank in 2010: 116th (State rank: 3rd)

Density: 1,402.6 people per square mile

Racial and ethnic characteristics

White: 85,239
Black or African American: 103,503
American Indian and Alaskan Native: 1,004
Asian: 2,417
Native Hawaiian and Other Pacific Islander: 44
Hispanic or Latino (may be of any race): 3,005
Other: 2,616

Percent of residents born in state: 74.2%

Age characteristics

Population under 5 years old: 13,519
Population 5 to 9 years old: 10,959
Population 10 to 14 years old: 12,852
Population 15 to 19 years old: 13,497
Population 20 to 24 years old: 16,845
Population 25 to 34 years old: 27,490
Population 35 to 44 years old: 22,031
Population 45 to 54 years old: 27,073
Population 55 to 59 years old: 12,436
Population 60 to 64 years old: 11,151
Population 65 to 74 years old: 14,586
Population 75 to 84 years old: 9,282
Population 85 years and over: 3,102
Median age: 36.2

Births (2010–11 Metropolitan Area)

Total number: 5,734

Deaths (2010–11 Metropolitan Area)

Total number: 4,069

Money income (2012)

Per capita income: $20,656
Median household income: $38,566
Total households: 76,621

Number of households with income of …

less than $10,000: 9,793
$10,000 to $14,999: 5,775
$15,000 to $24,999: 10,413
$25,000 to $34,999: 9,422
$35,000 to $49,999: 10,609
$50,000 to $74,999: 13,903
$75,000 to $99,999: 6,085
$100,000 to $149,999: 6,024
$150,000 to $199,999: 2,170
$200,000 or more: 2,427

Percent of families below poverty level: 23.2%

FBI Crime Index Property: 12,103

FBI Crime Index Violent: 1,314

■ Municipal Government

Mobile has a mayor-council form of government consisting of seven council members and one mayor. The mayor is elected at-large, while council members are elected for four-year terms from each of the seven city council districts.

Head Official: Mayor Sandy Stimpson (since 2013)

Total Number of City Employees: 2,323 (2013)

City Information: City of Mobile, PO Box 1827, Mobile, AL, 36633-1827; telephone (251) 208-7209.

■ Economy

Major Industries and Commercial Activity

The economy in Mobile and the greater Mobile Bay region is diverse, and there has been steady growth in several areas into the twenty-first century. Medicine and research, aerospace and aviation, retail trade, services, construction, and manufacturing are among Mobile's major businesses. Tourism has also found a place at the port.

The Port of Mobile is a significant factor in Mobile's economy. Its public deepwater terminals provide direct access to 1,500 miles of inland and intracoastal waterways, serving the Great Lakes, the Ohio and Tennessee river valleys (via the Tennessee-Tombigbee Waterway), and the Gulf of Mexico. From 2000 to 2010, Alabama's port grew from the fourteenth largest seaport in the United States to the ninth largest. The port sustains more than 127,500 direct and indirect jobs and has a statewide economic impact of about $7.92 billion.

While the city has seen growth in the areas of health care, banking, and research, manufacturing remains an important sector of the economy. German steelmaker

ThyssenKrupp operates a steel and stainless steel processing facility in Mobile. Outokumpu Stainless, another steel manufacturer, is also a major employer. UTC Aerospace Systems and Continental Motors are major aerospace manufacturers. Shipbuilding is an important industry in Mobile's economy. A number of chemical manufactures have operations in the Mobile Bay area, including Evonik, DuPont, and BASF Corporation.

Mobile has long been known for its shipbuilding facilities. Major shipbuilding and repair companies along the Port of Mobile include Austal USA, BAE Systems Southeast, C & G Boatworks, and Signal Ship Repair.

Items and goods produced: ships and ship-related items, steel, paper products, aircraft and aircraft engines, chemicals

Incentive Programs-New and Existing Companies

Local programs: The Mobile Area Chamber of Commerce serves as a regional economic development agency, coordinating with city, county, and private partners to provide assistance for new and expanding businesses. The Downtown Mobile Alliance supports redevelopment efforts in Downtown Mobile through marketing, advocacy, and the management of business improvement district services. Parts of Downtown Mobile may qualify for New Market Tax Credits administered by the state. These credits are designed for community development in low-income areas. Tax increment financing grant assistance may be available for qualifying economic development and redevelopment projects in Downtown Mobile.

State programs: Alabama boasts a progressive state business environment as demonstrated by its comprehensive right-to-work laws, one-stop environmental permitting, and a positive state and local government attitude toward new and expanding business. Tax rates are competitive. The Alabama Capital Tax Credit Program offers income tax credit for new or expanding businesses that create new jobs. The state provides additional financing assistance through a number of programs, including the AlabamaSAVES Loan Program, Industrial Development Grant Program, Economic Development Revolving Loan Funds, Industrial Revenue Bonds, and Alabama Innovation Fund, to name a few.

Mobile County is one of several Alabama counties designated as state enterprise zones. The Alabama Enterprise Zone Program helps attract new business to Alabama with tax breaks to those operating in designated areas. Eligible new or expanding businesses located in the zone may qualify for state income or business privilege tax credits for new investments and for hiring new permanent employees who were formerly unemployed for at least 90 days.

Job training programs: Mobile Works Inc. is a local partnership of business, education, labor, and community leaders, committed to providing regional businesses and local residents with access to quality training and job-search programs. The Alabama Industrial Development Training (AIDT) program provides a total delivery system for screening and selecting trainees, and for designing and implementing training for any new or expanding manufacturers in the state of Alabama. The program provides a full range of customized technical training programs that are free to employers and trainees. AIDT supports several specialized training centers, including the Alabama Robotics Technology Park, Alabama Center for Advanced Woodworking Technology, Forest Product Development Center, and AIDT Maritime Training Center (located in Mobile). The AIDT Center at Brookley Aeroplex offers training for the aviation, chemical, and telecommunications industries. Additional programs provide support for the telecommunications, aviation, automotive, and chemical industries, and other area manufacturers. Mobile training units are also used to go directly to the employer site to provide classroom and hands-on training.

The Mobile Area Chamber of Commerce's Center for Workforce Development (CWD) was launched in January 2000 in response to business community needs for better-trained workers. The CWD's purpose is to form strategic alliances in workforce development with the area's business, education, and community leaders. These alliances are designed to foster improvements in the quality of Mobile's workforce and ensure that the region remains competitive in a global economy.

The Workforce Investment Act helps defer the costs of hiring and training new employees for private businesses.

Development Projects

In 2012 the Mobile City Council adopted the New Plan for Mobile, a comprehensive local development plan to guide the city into 2020 and beyond. The plan focuses on four topic areas: urban design, neighborhood conservation, and public realm enhancements; economic development, market feasibility, business retention, and financial implementation; historical resources and cultural heritage; and transportation, parking, and infrastructure.

Many of the goals expressed in the plan rely on rethinking the city's land use policies. Instead of the use-based zoning system that dictates where certain types of businesses and residential areas can be developed, officials intend to implement a form-based code that focuses more on a building's layout in relationship to the surrounding environment. In particularly, city planners envision the development of mixed-use facilities to create pedestrian-friendly neighborhoods, where residents can easily walk to work, local shops, and entertainment venues.

Attracting new businesses to abandoned areas is a major part of the plan. A related idea involves creating historic districts for Oakdale and Maysville neighborhoods and renovating historic buildings for new business use. At the end of 2013, several Mobile renovation projects were in a lottery to receive Historic Tax Credits. When the fiscal year began in October 2013, there were so many applications for credits that the Alabama Historical Commission set up a lottery to determine the order in which projects would be reviewed. The lottery did not guarantee that the any project would be approved for tax credits, but project managers set to renovate or rebuild spaces in Mobile hoped that early approval would work in their favor. Hunter House, 951 Government Street, the DeBriar Building, and 408 Marine Street were potential recipients in 2013.

Brookley Aeroplex continues to attract new developments. The 1,650-acre industrial park is one of the largest of its kind on the Gulf Coast. In 2013 Airbus began construction of its new assembly facility for its A320 family of passenger jets. The $600 million facility was to employ 3,200 people during construction and create 1,000 permanent direct jobs. Safran Engineering Services, a major supplier for Airbus held its grand opening at the Aeroplex on the same day as the groundbreaking. With the addition of Airbus, *Business Facilities* magazine placed Mobile second on its annual listing of city's with the most economic growth potential.

Economic Development Information: Mobile Area Chamber of Commerce, 451 Government Street, Mobile, AL 36652; telephone (251) 433-6951; toll-free (800) 422-6951; fax (251) 432-1143; email info@mobilechamber.org. Alabama Department of Commerce, 401 Adams Avenue, P.O. Box 304106, Montgomery, AL 36130-4106; telephone (800) 248-0033; email contact@madeinalabama.com.

Commercial Shipping

The Port of Mobile is one of the largest deepwater ports in the United States. Covering 4,000 acres, the port has forty-one berths and four million square feet of open yards and warehousing. Mobile's importance as the center of a far-reaching distribution network is further enhanced by the Brookley Aeroplex, a designated Foreign Trade Zone. Brookley serves as a hub for cargo movement via air, water, rail and highway. Mobile Downtown Airport, on-site at Brookley Aeroplex, maintains an air cargo facility offering 48,000 square feet of sorting, distribution, and warehouse space.

There are about sixty-five motor freight carriers providing service in the Mobile area. Central Gulf Railroad is a rail-ship service that connects the Port of Mobile and Coatzacoalcos, Mexico. In addition, the Mobile rail market is served by five national Class I railroads with piggyback and containerized services.

Labor Force and Employment Outlook

Most of the local workforce is employed in service-based occupations. Wholesale and retail trade have the largest number of employees by industry sector. Transportation, warehousing, and utilities offer a significant number of jobs, a trend that is likely to continue as regional planners promote the area as a major distribution hub. Education, health care, and government organizations are among the top regional employers. Planners hope to increase the number of jobs in manufacturing, research and technology, and retail by recruiting new business and encouraging the expansion of existing companies.

The following is a summary of data regarding the 2012 Mobile labor force:

Size of civilian labor force: 91,746

Number of workers employed in . . .

agriculture and mining: 593
construction: 3,974
manufacturing: 6,669
wholesale trade: 1,935
retail trade: 10,842
transportation: 4,084
information systems: 1,569
finance: 4,380
professional administration: 8,661
education and social services: 21,178
arts and leisure: 8,670
other: 4,090
public administration: 3,030

Average hourly earnings of production workers: $18.27

Unemployment rate: 7.7% (2012)

Employers

Largest employers (2013)	*Number of employees*
Mobile County Public School System	7,283
University of South Alabama and USA Health System	5,151
Mobile Infirmary Health System	5,100
Austal	3,500
City of Mobile	2,323
Mobile County	1,603
ThyssenKrupp Steel	1,500
Providence Hospital	1,505
ST Aerospace Mobile	1,320
Springhill Memorial Hospital	1,200
BAE Systems Southeast Shipyards	1,057

Cost of Living

The following is a summary of data regarding several key cost of living factors in the area.

2013 ACCRA Average House Price: $231,890

2013 ACCRA Cost of Living Index: 91

State income tax rate: 2.0% to 5.0%

State sales tax rate: 4.0%

Local income tax rate: None

Local sales tax rate: 5.0%

Property tax rate: $6.35 per every $100 of assessed value (2013)

Economic Information: Mobile Area Chamber of Commerce, 451 Government Street, PO Box 2187, Mobile, AL 36652; telephone (251) 433-6951; fax (251) 432-1143; e-mail info@mobilechamber.org.

■ Education and Research

Elementary and Secondary Schools

The Mobile County Public School System is the oldest in the state and encompasses five separate school districts. The districts overlap, so that schools within the City of Mobile are not contained in one single district. The system educates more than 60,000 students and employs more than 3,600 teachers. In 2013 there were a total of 90 schools, which included 50 elementary schools, 15 middle schools, 12 high schools, and 6 magnet schools.

For the 2013–14 school year, four high schools hosted special career-based programs referred to as Signature Academies. These were the Academy of Teaching and Learning (Mary C. Montgomery High School), Health Career Access Program (Blount High School), Aviation and Aerospace Academy (B. C. Rain High School), and Manufacturing, Industry, and Technology Program (Citronelle High School).

The Mobile region also maintains a large parochial school system operated by the Catholic Archdiocese of Mobile. There are also a number of other religious and independent private schools in the area. The Alabama School of Mathematics and Science is a residential high school educating sophomores, juniors, and seniors in advanced studies of math, science, and technology. W. H. Council Traditional School (K–5) was named a National Blue Ribbon School in 2013.

The following is a summary of data regarding the Mobile County Public Schools.

Total enrollment: 62,016

Number of facilities

total: 90
elementary schools: 50
junior high schools: 15
high schools: 12
other: 13

Student/teacher ratio: 15.31:1

Teacher salaries

average (statewide): $48,282

Funding per pupil: $8,749

Public Schools Information: Mobile County Public Schools, 1 Magnum Pass, Mobile, AL 36618; telephone (251) 221-4000; fax (251) 693-8344.

Colleges and Universities

The University of South Alabama is a state school that offers several undergraduate and graduate degrees and enrolls more than 15,000 students in 10 colleges and schools, including the Mitchell College of Business, the College of Allied Health Professions, the Doctor of Pharmacy Program, and the School of Computing.

The University of Mobile, a private institution, is affiliated with the Southern Baptist Church. Divisions include the College of Arts and Sciences, the College of Christian Leadership, the School of Business, the School of Christian Ministries, the School of Education, the School of Nursing, the School of Music/Center for Performing Arts, the School of Worship Leadership, and the Center for Adult Programs. Numerous undergraduate programs are available, along with master's programs in business administration, education, Christian studies, marriage and family counseling, and nursing.

Spring Hill College is the third oldest Jesuit college in the country. It ranked among the top twenty Best Regional Universities–South in the 2014 *U.S. News and World Report* annual survey. A variety of undergraduate and master's programs are offered. Total enrollment in 2013 was about 1,328 students.

Mobile is also home to four campuses of Bishop State Community College and the Enterprise State Community College. Alabama Aviation Center at Mobile Faulkner University (based in Montgomery) has an extension campus in Mobile. Remington College also has a Mobile branch.

Libraries and Research Centers

The Mobile Public Library maintains ten branches, a bookmobile, and a collection of more than 400,000 volumes, as well as CDs, films, audio formats, and a growing number of e-books. Much of the material in the library's special collections focuses on regional history. These holdings are found at the Local History and Genealogy Services branch at 653 Government Street.

The system's specialized libraries in the area maintain holdings on fine arts, banking and finance, law, sports, and health sciences.

The University of South Alabama hosts five libraries. The Marx Library is the primary university-wide resource. Others include the Biomedical Library, the Mitchell College of Business Library, and the Doy Leale McCall Rare Book and Manuscript Library. An additional library is located on the Baldwin County Campus.

Research centers in the Mobile area include mineralization and primate research laboratories at the University of South Alabama, which also supports a Center for Business and Economic Research, Coastal Weather Research Center, Pheromone Center, Center for the Study of War and Memory, and Center for Hurricane Intensity and Landfall Investigation.

The University of South Alabama's Mitchell Cancer Institute (USAMCI) opened in 2008. The center is home to the first academic cancer research center in the Gulf Coast region, offering 125,000 square feet of research space, serving an estimated 2.5 million people in forty-two Gulf Coast counties of Alabama, Mississippi, and Florida.

On nearby Dauphin Island, twenty-two Alabama universities and colleges maintain a Sea Lab research complex for marine studies. Paper and pollution are among the subjects studied at the Erling Riis Research Laboratory.

Public Library Information: Mobile Public Library, 700 Government St., Mobile, AL 36602; telephone (251) 208-7073.

■ Health Care

The University of South Alabama Medical Center is an acute care facility that hosts the region's only Level I Trauma Center and the Regional Burn Center. Other specialty services are provided through the University of South Alabama's Heart Center, Comprehensive Sickle Cell Center, Epilepsy Monitoring Unit, Stroke Center, and Center for Weight Loss Surgery. The Mitchell Cancer Institute provides state-of-the art treatment options and promotes ongoing research.

The University of South Alabama health-care system also boasts the Children's and Women's Hospital, with sophisticated facilities and services. The Geri Moulton Children's Park on the grounds of this hospital provides space for children and their families to relax in a less clinical setting between treatments.

The Mobile Infirmary Medical Center is the state's largest not-for-profit hospital and includes cardiac and cancer services plus a rehabilitation hospital. Specialized care centers at Mobile Infirmary include the Bariatric Center of Excellence, cancer services, wound care, da Vinci robotic surgery, digestive health, Sleep Disorders

Center, and neuroendocrine tumor services, to name a few. Thomas Hospital in Fairhope and North Baldwin Infirmary are also part of the great Infirmary Health System.

Mobile's other hospitals include Providence Hospital and Springhill Medical Center. There are several outpatient primary care and specialty care clinics throughout the greater Mobile area, most of which are affiliated with the major hospitals.

■ Recreation

Sightseeing

Visitors to Mobile may want to stop at the Fort Conde Welcome Center in the Church Street East district. Built between 1724 and 1735, the brick fort was demolished 100 years later. The site was discovered during freeway excavations in the 1970s, and using original plans archived in France, the city undertook a partial reconstruction of the fort, which was dedicated in 1976. Today, a video presentation about Mobile and interactive video screens offer a glimpse of the many sightseeing opportunities that abound in this historic city. Visitors may tour Fort Conde accompanied by costumed guides who fire period muskets and cannons.

Mobile's colorful heritage has also been preserved in other historic districts. Near Fort Conde, the Conde-Charlotte Museum has been furnished in the various styles of Mobile's past eras. Among other historic sites in the Church Street East district are the Bishop Portier House, a Creole cottage from the 1830s, and townhouses dating from the 1850s and 1860s. The Oakleigh Garden historic district, a group of nineteenth-century Gulf Coast and Victorian cottages, centers around Oakleigh, an 1830s residence on 3.5 acres enhanced by azaleas and moss-covered oak trees.

Seven miles from Mobile Bay, near Spring Hill College, the Spring Hill historic district features mansions dating from the 1850s. The 1855 Bragg Mitchell Mansion on Spring Hill Avenue is a handsome antebellum mansion open to the public. The nine-block area known as De Tonti Square historic district consists of elegant townhouses, built in a variety of styles between 1840 and 1900, which are illuminated by the neighborhood's antique gas lights. The 1860 Italianate Richards-DAR House is splendidly furnished and boasts iron-lace porches and beautiful gardens. Included on the National Register of Historic Places are Mobile's Church Street Graveyard and Magnolia Cemetery, which contain headstones and funerary monuments from the earliest days of the area's history.

At Mobile's Battleship Alabama Memorial Park, the USS *Alabama*, the World War II submarine USS *Drum*, and the Aircraft Pavilion can be toured. The park also features a nature observatory. The Mobile Botanical

Gardens, adjacent to Langan Municipal Park, presents 100 acres of azaleas, camellias, magnolias, roses, and other native and exotic plants. Twenty miles south of Mobile, the 900-acre Bellingrath Gardens estate dazzles sightseers with sixty-five acres of landscaped flowers, trees, shrubs, and flowering bushes surrounding a luxurious home; 200 species of birds frequent the gardens.

Bayou La Batre, a fishing and shipbuilding community near Mobile, affords visitors many sightseeing opportunities, especially during the festivities connected with the annual blessing of the fleet. When Dauphin Island, two miles off the coast of Mobile County where Mobile Bay meets the Gulf of Mexico, was discovered by the Le Moyne brothers in 1699, it was found to be the site of burial grounds termed Indian shell mounds. The island also features Fort Gaines and lovely beaches. Fort Morgan on the tip of Gulf Shores Island is another remaining Confederate fort.

Arts and Culture

Among the community theater groups in Mobile are the Mobile Theatre Guild, the Joe Jefferson Players, and the Chickasaw Civic Theatre. Children's theater is presented by Mobile's Youth Theatre at the Playhouse in the Park. Mobile's colleges and universities also mount stage productions. Mobile audiences enjoy concerts sponsored by the Mobile Chamber Music Society at the Laidlaw Performing Arts Center and the Mobile Symphony Orchestra at the Saenger Theatre, under the direction of Scott Speck. The Mobile Symphony Youth Orchestra completed its first season in 2000–01 under the auspices of the Mobile Symphony. Mobile Opera performs at the Mobile Civic Center Theater under the direction of general director D. Scott Wright and artistic director Andy Anderson. Mobile Symphony and Mobile Opera share the Josephine Larkins Music Center, which they use for rehearsals, classes, teaching studios, and administrative offices. The Mobile Ballet brings exciting dance presentations to the Mobile Civic Center Theater; its dance school educates residents from toddlers to pre-professionals.

Mobile's municipal museum system maintains three facilities: the Museum of Mobile, Fort Conde, and the Phoenix Fire House Museum. The Museum of Mobile is located in Old City Hall, where it showcases furniture, silver, arms, ship models, documents, and historical records; its former location is slated to serve as a new Mardi Gras Museum. The Phoenix Fire House Museum is devoted to the city's fire fighting history. The Mobile Museum of Art is located west of downtown and houses a collection of more than 6,000 pieces spanning more than 2,000 years of culture, including paintings, prints, sculpture, lithographs, silver, quilts, porcelain, seventeenth- and eighteenth-century southern furnishings, and African art. The museum sponsors lectures, seminars and workshops, films, and musical performances throughout the year. The University of South Alabama opened an Archaeology Museum in 2012. The Gulf Coast Exploreum Science Center features exhibits that let visitors explore aquatic life and human science, and games and puzzles that demonstrate scientific concepts and stimulate problem-solving skills.

Festivals and Holidays

Mobile residents claim their city as the birthplace of Mardi Gras. The festive practices of Mardi Gras are thought to have been brought to the first Mobile settlement by its French colonists around 1700, and were later enhanced with traditions added by Spanish and subsequent settlers. Mobile's Mardi Gras today is observed with two weeks of balls, floats and parades, costumes, music from bands and minstrels, and pageantry. Mardi Gras is celebrated in Mobile with a variety of citywide events from late January through mid-February.

Also in late winter, Mobile celebrates its Azalea Trail Festival, when thirty-seven miles of azalea shrubs in bloom throughout Mobile are marked-out on two driving routes that afford trail followers a spectacular floral display. The festival also includes a 10-kilometer (6.21-mile) footrace, a historic homes tour, and other events. Another spring event is the Festival of Flowers on the campus of Spring Hill College. In June, contestants in the America's Junior Miss program compete in Mobile for college scholarships and other prizes.

Proximity to the Gulf of Mexico inspires summer events in and around Mobile. Among these is the Blessing of the Fleet in neighboring Bayou La Batre, where fishing boats are decorated for a water parade, arts and crafts are displayed, live crabs are raced, and seafood and gumbo are served in abundance. During the Alabama Deep Sea Fishing Rodeo held for a weekend on nearby Dauphin Island, anglers test their skills against each other and such prize fish as shark and blue marlin.

October's National Shrimp Festival in Gulf Shores promises seafood contests, a parade, an arts and crafts show, dancing, fireworks, boat racing, and a 10-kilometer (6.21-mile) footrace. Also in October, the Greater Gulf State Fair features exhibits of commercial, cultural, leisure, military, and agricultural interest. BayFest (October) brings in more than 200,000 guests to downtown Mobile to take in live music from more than 125 acts. BayFest offers continuous music for every taste, including country, classic rock, alternative, pop, jazz, R & B, rap, gospel, modern rock, and more.

Fall is also the time for the Mobile International Festival. Held in November, it showcases food and customs of more than thirty countries. Seasonal celebrations at Mobile's historic locations in December are followed by festivities surrounding January's Senior Bowl, an annual college football event that draws national attention.

Sports for the Spectator

Sports enthusiasts can view a wide range of sporting events in the Mobile area. Each January the nation's top college seniors meet in the city to play football in the prestigious Reese's Senior Bowl. The postseason competition, televised nationally, showcases upcoming talent and attracts scouts, coaches, and management representing professional football. Ladd-Peebles Stadium has been home to the Senior Bowl since 1951. The stadium also hosts the annual GoDaddy Bowl, which features opponents from the Mid-American Conference and Conference USA. Additionally, Ladd-Peebles Stadium is home for the University of South Alabama Jaguars football team. The Jaguars also compete in men's baseball and football; women's softball, volleyball, and soccer; and men's and women's basketball, cross country, tennis, and track and field.

The Mobile Bay Ladies Professional Golf Association (LPGA) Classic is held on the Robert Trent Jones Golf Trail at Magnolia Grove. Mobile's AA baseball team, the Mobile BayBears, entertain fans at Hank Aaron Stadium. The BayBears are affiliated with the Arizona Diamondbacks. The Mobile Bay Tornados are part of the American Basketball Association.

Sports for the Participant

The city of Mobile maintains eighty-five facilities that provide a variety of sports activities and opportunities. Langan Park's 720 acres surrounding a forty-acre lake offer golf, tennis, baseball, bicycling, paddle boating, and picnicking. Bowling alleys, skating rinks, swimming pools, and many tennis and basketball courts throughout Mobile add to the city's active life. Mobile's Magnolia Grove Golf Course is a stop on the Robert Trent Jones Golf Trail, the largest golf-course construction project ever attempted, with more than 450 holes among several courses throughout the state.

Mobile's residents and visitors can engage in many activities on or in adjacent water bodies. The city's proximity to the Gulf of Mexico is appreciated by bird watchers, who have an opportunity to view many migratory species crossing the gulf, as well as an abundance of local species. Sailing, windsurfing, canoeing, kayaking, waterskiing, swimming, and scuba diving are common on the area's rivers, Mobile Bay, and the Gulf of Mexico. The Gulf Yachting Association sponsors a variety of racing events around the Gulf Coast. At nearby Gulf State Park, 6,150 acres of park land include a two-mile stretch of sandy beach, a beachfront lodge, cabins, a campground, a swimming pool, two freshwater lakes for skiing, canoeing, sailing, and fishing, and facilities for tennis, cycling, and golf. Among the coastal area's other sites for sporting activities are Dauphin Island and Pleasure Island.

Fishing and hunting are also popular pursuits around Mobile. Freshwater fishing on such waterways as Dog River, Mobile River, the Tennessee-Tombigbee system, and the Tensaw River yield catches of bream, bass, and perch. Saltwater fishing from piers or banks on the Mobile Bay or the gulf brings in trout, flounder, and Spanish mackerel. Deep-sea fishing can be chartered in the Mobile area, yielding land sharks, snapper, amberjack, and sailfish. Hunters in the Mobile area bag waterfowl and game such as deer and wild turkey.

Shopping and Dining

Shopping venues in the Mobile area range from regional malls to specialty boutiques. A district of shops surrounds restored Fort Conde, and developments to the downtown waterfront area have brought about new entertainment, restaurant and shopping options. The Bel Air shopping mall also features a food court with a variety of ethnic and American foods. Mobile restaurants take full advantage of the area's abundant seafood, including gulf and bay shrimp, oysters, soft-shell crab, blue crab, red snapper, flounder, mullet, and trout. Among Mobile's other regional specialties are Creole and Cajun menus, Caribbean dishes such as West Indies salad, and traditional Southern fare such as catfish and barbecue. Ethnic dining is also available at establishments featuring European, Oriental, and Mexican menus.

Visitor Information: Mobile Area Chamber of Commerce, 451 Government Street, Mobile, AL 36652; telephone (800) 422-6951 or (251) 433-6951. Mobile Bay Convention and Visitors Bureau, PO Box 204, Mobile, AL 36601; telephone (800) 5-MOBILE or (251) 208-2000.

■ Convention Facilities

Downtown Mobile boasts the Mobile Civic Center Complex, which features a 10,000-seat arena with 80,000 square feet of exhibit space. There are also a 30,000-square-foot exposition hall, a 1,939-seat theater, and ample meeting rooms.

The Mobile Convention Center offers 100,000 square feet of exhibit space, 50,000 square feet of meeting and banquet space, and a 52,000-square-foot area for registration and receptions. The center is adjacent to the Adam's Mark Hotel. Among Mobile's other convention facilities are a dozen hotels, with meeting rooms for groups of 100–5,000 people. Saenger Theatre and Mitchell Center at the University of South Alabama also provide space for meetings and other gatherings.

Convention Information: Mobile Bay Convention and Visitors Bureau, PO Box 204, Mobile, AL 36601; telephone (800) 5-MOBILE or (251) 208-2000.

■ Transportation

Approaching the City

The Mobile Regional Airport is located approximately fourteen miles from downtown Mobile. Air travelers are served by Delta, United, American Airlines, and U.S. Airways. The Downtown Airport at Brookley Aeroplex is a general aviation airport favored by private and corporate planes for its proximity to downtown Mobile, which is only four minutes away by car. Motorists may reach Mobile via Interstates 10 and 65, and by U.S. highways 31, 43, 45, 90, and 98. An interstate spur connects Interstates 10 and 65 in downtown Mobile. In addition, several state roads lead into the city. There is a Greyhound station in Downtown Mobile.

Traveling in the City

The Mobile Metro Transit Authority, also known as "The Wave," operates twenty local bus routes to serve the area's transit needs. The Transit Authority also operates an electric-run trolley through downtown Mobile, Monday through Saturday. Known as the LoDa moda!, the trolley makes stops to downtown businesses, parks, hotels, and city buildings, and is free of charge.

■ Communications

Newspapers and Magazines

Mobile's only daily newspaper is *The Mobile Press-Register,* Alabama's oldest newspaper that dates back to 1813. *Lagniappe: Something Extra for Mobile* is an independent biweekly newspaper with a circulation of about 25,000. *Mobile Bay* is a premier lifestyle magazine for Mobile and Baldwin Counties.

Television and Radio

Mobile is served by three local television stations and receives broadcasts from other stations originating in Pensacola, Florida, and Huntsville, Alabama. There are several radio stations within close listening range of Mobile, some of which are in Florida and Mississippi. The two locally based radio stations are 92.1 FM WZEW and 105.5 FM WSNP Sports Radio.

Media Information: The *Mobile Press-Register,* PO Box 2488, Mobile, AL 36652; telephone (251) 219-5454.

Mobile Online

City of Mobile home page. Available www. cityofmobile.org

Historic Mobile Preservation Society. Available www.historicmobile.org

Lagniappe. Available www.lagniappemobile.com

Mobile Area Chamber of Commerce. Available www.mobilechamber.com

Mobile Bay Convention and Visitor's Bureau. Available www.mobile.org

Mobile County Public Schools. Available www. mcpss.com

Mobile Museum of Art. Available www. mobilemuseumofart.com

Mobile Press-Register. Available www.al.com/ press-register

Mobile Public Library. Available www.mplonline.org

BIBLIOGRAPHY

Bergeron, Arthur W., Jr., *Confederate Mobile* (Jackson, MS: University Press of Mississippi, 1991)

Burnett, Lonnie A., *Pen Makes a Good Sword: John Forsyth of the Mobile Register* (Tuscaloosa, AL: University of Alabama Press, 2006)

Parker, Elizabeth, *Haunted Mobile: Apparitions of the Azalea City* (Charleston, SC: Haunted America, 2009)

Pride, Richard A., *The Political Use of Racial Narratives: School Desegregation in Mobile, Alabama, 1954–97* (Urbana, IL: University of Illinois Press, 2002)

Sledge, John S., *The Pillared City: Greek Revival Mobile* (Athens, GA: University of Georgia Press, 2009)

Wilson, Edward O., *Why We Are Here: Mobile and the Spirit of a Southern City* (New York: Liveright Pub., 2012)

Montgomery

■ The City in Brief

Founded: 1819 (incorporated 1819)

Head Official: Mayor Todd Strange (since 2009)

City Population
> 1990: 187,106
> 2000: 201,568
> 2010: 205,764
> 2012 estimate: 205,285
> Percent change, 2000–2010: 2.1%
> U.S. rank in 1990: 84th
> U.S. rank in 2000: 100th (State rank: 2nd)
> U.S. rank in 2010: 102nd (State rank: 2nd)

Metropolitan Statistical Area Population
> 2000: 346,528
> 2010: 374,536
> 2012 estimate: 377,844
> Percent change, 2000–2010: 8.1%
> U.S. rank in 2000: 131st
> U.S. rank in 2010: 136th

Area: 156.57 square miles

Elevation: 240 feet above sea level

Average Annual Temperatures: January, 47° F; July, 82° F; annual average 65° F

Average Annual Precipitation: 52.7 inches

Major Economic Sectors: transportation and trade, government, manufacturing, health care, professional services

Unemployment Rate: 5.6% (2012)

Per Capita Income: $23,358

2012 FBI Crime Index Property: 12,058

Major Colleges and Universities: Alabama State University, Auburn University at Montgomery, Faulkner University, Amridge University, Troy University in Montgomery, Huntingdon College, Air University

Daily Newspaper: *The Montgomery Advertiser*

■ Introduction

The Alabama state capital of Montgomery has come a long way since its short-lived stint as the capital of the Confederate States of America. The city where Jefferson Davis was inaugurated as president of the Confederacy grew into the city where Dr. Martin Luther King, Jr., preached a message of peace and equality for all Americans, and a woman named Rosa Parks helped launch one of the most important events of the Civil Rights Movement, the Montgomery Bus Boycott. Several decades later, the city has grown into a diverse community where people from all walks of life come to live, work, and play. Montgomery boasts a diverse economy with a balance of government, manufacturing, trade, and professional services. The city is also blessed with beautiful parks and gardens, excellent schools, and first-class cultural institutions. Montgomery is proud of all it has to offer, but poised and ready to keep moving forward toward an even bigger and brighter future.

■ Geography and Climate

Montgomery is located in the state's south-central region and lies on the south bank of the Alabama River in a gently rolling area with fertile soil. It is the seat of Montgomery County and the state capital. The city is about 94 miles south of Birmingham and 173 miles north of Mobile. No topographical feature of the Montgomery area appreciably influences the local climate. Generally, the days from June through September show little

The State Capitol building in Montgomery. *Al Michaud/Getty Images*

change, with frequent afternoon rain showers that soon dissipate. Beginning in late August, the weather gets drier until the period of December through April, when there are great differences from day to day in the amount and intensity of rainfall. Droughts sometimes occur in spring, late summer, and early autumn. Differences between daytime and nighttime temperatures tend to be great in spring and autumn. While the occurrence of snow is a rarity, damaging tornadoes are not uncommon.

Area: 156.57 square miles

Elevation: 240 feet above sea level

Average Temperatures: January, 47° F; July, 82° F; annual average 65° F

Average Annual Precipitation: 52.7 inches

■ History

Early Days in Montgomery

Many centuries before Montgomery was founded, the land on which it sits was the site of two Indian towns called Ikanatchati and Towasa. Numerous mounds and burials sites have been uncovered there, proving it to have

been an area thickly settled by ancestors of the Creek people, the Alibamu Indians, from whom the state took its name. The first Europeans to visit the region were Hernando De Soto and his fellow Spanish explorers, who passed through the region in 1540. The first white inhabitant of the area was James McQueen, a Scottish trader, who arrived in 1716. The area remained sparsely inhabited until 1814, when Arthur Moore and his companions built cabins on local riverbanks. Three years later, the land was put up for sale and purchased by two groups of speculators.

General John Scott led a group of Georgians who built the town of Alabama but abandoned it when a second group of poor New Englanders founded a nearby town they called Philadelphia. Scott and his companions then built a new town they called East Alabama. Both groups began their settlements to make riches on future growth of the area. The rivalry between the two groups finally was settled in December 1819, when they merged the towns under the name Montgomery, Incorporated. The name was chosen to honor General Richard Montgomery, who had died in the Revolutionary War. Eleven days after Montgomery's founding, Alabama was admitted as a state. Three years earlier, Montgomery County had been named in honor of a local man, Major Lemuel P. Montgomery, who later lost his life when serving with U.S. president Andrew Jackson during a war with the Creek Indians.

Lafayette's Visit a Local Highlight

The year 1821 was important for Montgomery as the first steamboats reached the city, which was the northernmost point up the Missouri River to which large vessels from Mobile could travel. That same year, a stage line began to carry passengers eastward, and the newspaper the *Montgomery Republican* was founded.

From Montgomery's earliest days, cotton production was its most important local industry, with the first commercial cotton gin having been installed in the area at the beginning of the nineteenth century. Montgomery soon became an important port for shipping cotton from the region. Although the town was still small, it had two general stores whose owners accepted payment in either cotton or cash. The town also boasted a private school, a dancing school, a court whose docket showed more than one hundred cases, and a lively social calendar for wealthy residents. A grand ball held during the 1825 visit of distinguished Frenchman the Marquis de LaFayette was the highlight of the town's early history. About that time, the State Bank was founded, and real estate companies began to flourish as new settlers moved to the area.

Montgomery Becomes State Capital

In 1834 the state of Alabama voted to establish the Montgomery Railroad Company and build a rail route to West Point, Georgia. In time it became an important link in service between New York City and New Orleans. By 1840 Montgomery had a population of 2,179 residents. On January 30, 1846, the Alabama legislature announced that it had voted to move the capital from Tuscaloosa to Montgomery. The first legislative session in the new capital met in December 1847. In time, a Capitol building was erected under the direction of a Philadelphia, Pennsylvania architect. The first structure burned down in 1849 but was rebuilt in 1851 following the original plans.

Secession and Its Consequences

By the time of the Civil War, Alabamians were among the Southerners with the strongest anti-Northern sentiments. Their slave-based economy was made up of a triad of wealthy white planters, working class whites, and a large group of African American slaves who served at the whims of their masters. Wealthy planters were adamant about protecting the entrenched socio-economic structure and their accumulated wealth.

As whites' fears of change accelerated, it did not take long for secessionist movements to strengthen, and a Secession Convention met in Montgomery on January 6, 1861. On February 4, representatives of six seceding states assembled in Montgomery, which they chose as the provisional capital of the Confederate States of America. Five days later, Jefferson Davis was unanimously chosen

to serve as President of the Confederacy. A torchlight parade held on March 4 culminated in his inauguration. At that time, the population of the city stood at more than 8,850 citizens.

Montgomery's stint as capital of the Confederacy was short lived, however, when it became apparent that Virginia was to be the site of much of the early fighting. It then became necessary to shorten the line of communication between military headquarters and field officers. At the first Montgomery meeting of the Provisional Congress, representatives decided that the capital should be moved to Richmond, Virginia, within two months. Dedication to the Confederate cause remained strong, even when General James Wilson's federal raiders entered Montgomery in April 1865. Upon their arrival, local citizens burned more than 100,000 bales of cotton to prevent their falling into Union hands. In response, Union troops burned local small arms factories, railroad cars, and five steamboats.

Troubled Times Improve

The Reconstruction period following the end of the Civil War in 1865 was a time of hardships. Much of the wealth of local citizens had been wiped out, articles of common use were scarce, stores lay empty, and the means of traveling by steamer and railroad had been destroyed. A slow and painful economic and social recovery took place. By 1880 the population had grown to 16,713, and railroad expansion had helped local conditions to improve. Montgomery's geographic location and proximity to the most productive agricultural regions of the South, as well as the fact that it was the state capital, soon reconnected the city with other areas of the state and nation via roads and railways. By 1885 an intra-city electric trolley car system had been constructed.

In 1890 industrialists and financiers began to visit Montgomery in search of business sites. The first large lumber mill had been opened, and the local population stood at 21,883. In time, local textile and garment factories, cotton processing plants, and fertilizer plants were established.

First Half of Twentieth Century Brings Industrial Growth

The years between 1900 and 1940 saw steady industrial progress and local population growth from more than 30,000 to about 78,000 residents. Montgomery remained a focal point for cotton farmers, and livestock and dairy production became vital industries. In 1910 flight pioneers Orville and Wilbur Wright built an airfield in the city and opened a school of aviation. Later, during mid-century, Montgomery became a center for packing plants, furniture, construction, and chemical and food production.

During the 1940s African American citizens began to show their dissatisfaction with the restrictive "Jim

Crow" laws allowing discrimination, including the restriction of their voting rights. By the mid-1950s, the call for African American voter registration had greatly increased.

Desegregation and the Civil Rights Movement

In 1955 Montgomery saw a simple but historical event that was to influence the history of the United States. That year, a Montgomery woman named Rosa Parks was arrested for not yielding her bus seat to a white man. For the 381 days that followed, Montgomery African Americans boycotted the city's buses, making way for the December 1956 U.S. Supreme Court order for the desegregation of Montgomery buses.

The 1960s were a period of great upheaval in the United States and in the city of Montgomery. Supporters of the civil rights movement from the North and other areas of the South came to the city to support efforts by African Americans to gain civil rights, and Montgomery became the virtual headquarters of the civil rights movement. Groups of African Americans and whites, known as Freedom Riders, rode buses together throughout the South to protest segregation. On May 20, 1961, when a number of Freedom Riders arrived at the Montgomery bus station, they were beaten by local Ku Klux Klansmen, who were later tried and sentenced for their crimes.

In 1962 George Corley Wallace won the governorship of Alabama after a campaign based on his support for segregation. Standing on the state's Capitol steps, he made a famous speech championing segregation. The next year, Dr. Martin Luther King, Jr., came to Montgomery and preached against segregation.

In 1965 King led 25,000 demonstrators on a four-day march from Selma, Alabama, to Montgomery to seek voting rights for African Americans. When the 600 civil rights marchers reached the Edmund Pettus Bridge shortly after the walk began, they were attacked by local lawmen carrying clubs and using tear gas. The march continued only after a federal judge granted the protestors a court order protecting their right to march from Selma to Montgomery. Nearly 3,200 marchers set out for Montgomery, walking twelve miles a day and sleeping in fields. By the time they reached the capitol, their numbers had swelled to 25,000 people. Less than five months after the march, President Lyndon B. Johnson signed the Voting Rights Act of 1965, which represented a major victory for civil rights advocates.

In 1971 attorney Morris Dees founded the Southern Poverty Law Center in the city of Montgomery. The center promoted tolerance and took up the cause of poor people and minorities. It also helped sponsor construction of the local civil rights memorial. In 1991 a U.S. federal district judge furthered civil rights efforts when he ordered Alabama State University and other state institutions to hire more minority faculty and staff, and to make changes in their financial and admission policies.

The last decades of the 1900s brought many changes to the city of Montgomery. A new spirit of cooperation grew between its African American and white citizens, as did new industries, especially in the area of high technology. In addition, the establishment of Maxwell-Gunter Air Force Base further strengthened the local economy. By 1999 a wealth of new construction and the addition of Overlook Park—formerly a parking lot—marked the beginning of an extensive downtown renaissance.

In 2005 coastal areas of Alabama and neighboring states were severely damaged by Hurricane Katrina. Montgomery, along with cities and towns across Alabama, provided assistance to more than 40,000 displaced residents of areas where homes were destroyed. Montgomery was the site of the American Red Cross Disaster Relief effort for Alabama, and the city became a staging area for distribution of emergency personnel and supplies.

Throughout the first decade of the twenty-first century, the city invested more than $1 billion on development projects for Downtown Montgomery. Major projects included the new Riverwalk Stadium to house the city's minor league baseball team, the Montgomery Biscuits. The Riverwalk Amphitheater, a 5,000-seat open-air theater, drew crowds downtown for concerts, movies, and other live events. A new mixed-use development known as The Alley was built, with apartments, restaurants, shops, and entertainment venues, all designed to attract new residents as well as visitors. A boost to the tourist industry came with a major renovation of the Montgomery Convention Center, including the addition of the Renaissance Montgomery Hotel and Spa, and the Montgomery Performing Arts Center.

Into the 2010s, officials continued to work on plans to encourage development of a diverse economy, particularly by promoting projects to attract new companies, more tourists, and more permanent residents to the area.

Historical Information: Montgomery County Historical Society, 512 South Court Street, PO Box 1829, Montgomery, AL 36102; telephone (334) 264-1837; fax (334) 834-9292. Alabama Department of Archives and History, 624 Washington Ave., Montgomery, AL 36130; telephone (334) 242-4435.

■ Population Profile

Metropolitan Statistical Area Population

    1990: 292,517
    2000: 346,528
    2012 estimate: 377,844
    Percent change, 2000–2010: 8.1%
    U.S. rank in 2000: 131st
    U.S. rank in 2010: 136th

City Residents

1990: 187,106
2000: 201,568
2010: 205,764
2012 estimate: 205,285
Percent change, 2000–2010: 2.1%
U.S. rank in 1990: 84th
U.S. rank in 2000: 100th (State rank: 2nd)
U.S. rank in 2010: 102nd (State rank: 2nd)

Density: 1,289.5 people per square mile

Racial and ethnic characteristics

White: 78,369
Black or African American: 115,936
American Indian and Alaskan Native: 77
Asian: 4,977
Native Hawaiian and Other Pacific Islander: 96
Hispanic or Latino (may be of any race): 7,850
Other: 5,830

Percent of residents born in state: 71.4%

Age characteristics

Population under 5 years old: 14,806
Population 5 to 9 years old: 12,788
Population 10 to 14 years old: 15,046
Population 15 to 19 years old: 15,059
Population 20 to 24 years old: 17,060
Population 25 to 34 years old: 29,384
Population 35 to 44 years old: 26,465
Population 45 to 54 years old: 26,068
Population 55 to 59 years old: 13,623
Population 60 to 64 years old: 10,334
Population 65 to 74 years old: 13,816
Population 75 to 84 years old: 7,414
Population 85 years and over: 3,422
Median age: 34.6

Births (2010–11 Metropolitan Area)

Total number: 4,982

Deaths (2010–11 Metropolitan Area)

Total number: 3,276

Money income (2012)

Per capita income: $23,358
Median household income: $42,403
Total households: 79,764

Number of households with income of ...

less than $10,000: 8,477
$10,000 to $14,999: 6,359
$15,000 to $24,999: 10,115
$25,000 to $34,999: 8,203
$35,000 to $49,999: 12,567
$50,000 to $74,999: 13,791
$75,000 to $99,999: 7,743
$100,000 to $149,999: 7,970
$150,000 to $199,999: 2,193
$200,000 or more: 2,346

Percent of families below poverty level: 23.3%

FBI Crime Index Property: 12,058

FBI Crime Index Violent: 827

■ Municipal Government

Montgomery's municipal affairs are managed by a mayor-council form of government, with a nine-member city council and a mayor. Each is elected to a four-year term.

Head Official: Mayor Todd Strange (since 2009)

Total Number of City Employees: 2,500 (2013)

City Information: Mayor's Office, City of Montgomery, 103 North Perry Street, Montgomery, AL 36104; telephone (334) 241-2000; email mayor@ci.montgomery.al.us.

■ Economy

Major Industries and Commercial Activity

Montgomery has developed a diverse economy with a blend of services, trade, and industry. The City of Montgomery is the state capital and the seat of Montgomery County. It is also home to Maxwell-Gunter Air Force Base and Air University, the worldwide center for air force education. As a result, government and military operations anchor the local economy.

The city also plays a major role as a regional trade center, serving as a wholesale and distribution gateway to the entire Southeast. Montgomery's location in the center of a zone of rich black soil that stretches across Alabama makes it an important processing and shipping center for cotton, dairy, and other farm products. The city also boasts a large livestock market.

Manufacturing industries continue to grow in Montgomery. Major companies include Hyundai Motor Manufacturing Alabama, MOBIS Alabama, Koch Foods, Lear Corporation, and US Food Services. Finance, health care, education, information technology, and professional services are also important economic sectors. Civil War and Civil Rights tourism is a major part of Montgomery's history and economy.

Items and goods produced: automobiles and parts, water heaters, food and beverages, sportswear, paper and packaging products, pharmaceuticals

Incentive Programs-New and Existing Companies

Local programs: The Small Business Resource Center provides help to small businesses with everything from startup and counseling to non-conventional financing, training, recognition, and networking. An offshoot of the Montgomery Area Chamber of Commerce, the center also provides affordable space at below-market rates for startup entrepreneurs.

The City of Montgomery Department of Development was established in 2010 to provide focused development planning and assistance for mixed-use developments within the city. The department's Design Studio offers assistance for small businesses, including site selection, context studies, and site layout. The Montgomery Downtown Retail Pioneer Program offers a 1.75% sales tax credit for certain new retail businesses headquartered downtown that fulfill a daily retail need for residents. In 2013 the incentive was limited to grocery stores or other food markets.

State programs: Alabama boasts a progressive state business environment as demonstrated by its comprehensive right-to-work laws, one-stop environmental permitting, and a positive state and local government attitude toward new and expanding business. Tax rates are competitive. The Alabama Capital Tax Credit Program offers income tax credit for new or expanding businesses that create new jobs. The state provides additional financing assistance through a number of programs, including the AlabamaSAVES Loan Program, Industrial Development Grant Program, Economic Development Revolving Loan Funds, Industrial Revenue Bonds, and Alabama Innovation Fund, to name a few.

Montgomery is one of three Alabama cities designated a state enterprise zone. The Alabama Enterprise Zone Program helps attract new business to Alabama with tax breaks for those operating in designated areas. Eligible new or expanding businesses located in the zone may qualify for state income or business privilege tax credits for new investments, and for hiring new permanent employees formerly unemployed for at least 90 days.

Montgomery has been designated a general purpose foreign trade zone, which provides payment deferrals or cancellation for businesses in the zone. New or expanding businesses may also qualify for monetary grants to carry out site improvements.

Job training programs: The Alabama Industrial Development Training (AIDT) program provides a total delivery system for screening and selecting trainees and for designing and implementing training for any new or expanding manufacturers in the state of Alabama. The program provides a full range of customized technical training programs free to employers and trainees. AIDT supports several specialized training centers, including the Alabama Robotics Technology Park, Alabama Center for Advanced Woodworking Technology, Forest Product Development Center, and AIDT Maritime Training Center (located in Mobile). Additional programs provide support for the telecommunications, aviation,

automotive, and chemical industries, and other area manufacturers. Mobile training units go directly to employer sites to provide classroom and hands-on training. The Montgomery AIDT Center is the home office for AIDT.

Auburn University at Montgomery offers a variety of job training and employment services through its Center for Business, Alabama Training Institute, and Center for Advanced Technologies.

Development Projects

In 2011 the Montgomery Area Chamber of Commerce updated its own strategic development plan with the introduction of *Imagine a Greater Montgomery II: A Next Level Strategy*. Building on the strength and success of its previous five-year plan (2006–11), the chamber set four focus goals for development: achieve educational excellence and develop competitive regional talent; diversify economic growth; accelerate revitalization and improve quality of place; and build community capacity, engagement, and image.

In 2013 DENSO, a major global automotive supplier headquartered in Japan, announced plans to open a $2.2 million shipping plant warehouse in Montgomery. The warehouse is to serve as a distribution center for heating, ventilation, and air conditioning units, along with other parts, to DENSO's North American customers. In June 2013 DAS North America broke ground for a 300,000-square-foot facility in Montgomery. DAS supplies parts for Kia and Hyundai manufacturing facilities. With a $37 million capital investment, the company is expected to create 300 permanent jobs once the facility is complete.

In July 2013 Infinitus Energy broke ground on a technologically advanced $35 million waste recovery facility in Montgomery. The 81,992-square-foot facility is set to divert up to 85 percent of waste from city landfills, while recovering reusable cardboard, mixed paper, metals, aluminum cans, plastics, and wood.

In October 2013 Mims Management Group relocated its corporate headquarters to Montgomery, with a $17 million capital investment and fifty new jobs. Mims Management Group was founded by Montgomery native Daniel Mims. It is the parent company of Institutional Pharmacy Solutions and Northeast Pharmaceuticals Inc.

At the end of 2013, three Montgomery renovation projects seeking state-sponsored Historic Tax Credits were in a lottery for review. When the fiscal year began on October 2013, there were so many applications for credits that the Alabama Historical Commission set up a lottery to determine the order in which projects would be reviewed. The lottery did not guarantee that any project would be approved for tax credits, but project managers preparing to renovate or rebuild spaces in Montgomery hoped that early approval would work in their favor. The three projects up for review involved renovation and development of the Webber Building, Jefferson Davis Apartments, and Grove Court Apartments.

Economic Development Information: City of Montgomery Department of Development, One Dexter Plaza, Montgomery, AL 36104; telephone (334) 625-3737. Montgomery Area Chamber of Commerce, 41 Commerce Street, PO Box 79, Montgomery, AL 36101; telephone (334) 834-5200; fax: (334) 265-4745.

Commercial Shipping

CSX Transportation provides rail service through Montgomery, which hosts a CSX TRANSFLO terminal that facilitates the transfer of goods from rail to motor transport. There are about twenty local motor freight carriers in the Montgomery area. US Airways and Delta offer service out of Montgomery Regional Airport.

The Alabama River provides a nine-foot channel for barges to cross into the Gulf of Mexico through the port of Mobile. Alabama state docks in Mobile, accessible via waterway from Montgomery, offer 1000-ton capacity facilities inside a protected barge-turning basin. Barge transportation to the Great Lakes is available through the Tennessee-Tombigbee Waterway.

Labor Force and Employment Outlook

State, regional, and local government provide a substantial number of jobs in Montgomery, accounting for just over 25 percent of employment in 2013, according to the Alabama Department of Labor. Trade, transportation, utilities, and warehousing also provide a significant number of jobs. According to U.S. Department of Labor estimates, trade and transportation, manufacturing, education and health services, and leisure and hospitality were primary growth industries through 2013. Montgomery's leisure and hospitality industries also showed growth.

The following is a summary of data regarding the 2012 Montgomery labor force:

Size of civilian labor force: 96,787

Number of workers employed in . . .

    agriculture and mining: 338
    construction: 3,587
    manufacturing: 8,333
    wholesale trade: 1,996
    retail trade: 10,663
    transportation: 2,813
    information systems: 982
    finance: 5,129
    professional administration: 8,903
    education and social services: 18,779
    arts and leisure: 10,063
    other: 5,193
    public administration: 10,490

Average hourly earnings of production workers: $15.94

Unemployment rate: 5.6% (2012)

Employers

Largest employers (2013)	*Number of employees*
Maxwell-Gunter Air Force Base	12,280
State of Alabama	11,830
Montgomery Public Schools	4,524
Baptist Health	4,300
Hyundai Motor Manufacturing Alabama, LLC	3,100
Alfa Insurance Companies	2,568
City of Montgomery	2,500
Jackson Hospital & Clinic	1,300
MOBIS Alabama	1,221
Rheem Water Heaters	1,173

Cost of Living

The following is a summary of data regarding several key cost of living factors in the area.

2013 ACCRA Average House Price: $268,726

2013 ACCRA Cost of Living Index: 95

State income tax rate: 2.0% to 5.0%

State sales tax rate: 4.0%

Local income tax rate: None

Local sales tax rate: 6.0%

Property tax rate: $3.65 per every $100 of assessed value (2013)

Economic Information: Montgomery Area Chamber of Commerce, 41 Commerce Street, PO Box 79, Montgomery, AL 36101; telephone (334) 834-5200; fax (334) 265-4745.

■ Education and Research

Elementary and Secondary Schools

As of 2013 the Montgomery Public School System consisted of 53 schools, including 27 elementary schools, 9 traditional junior high and middle schools, 4 traditional high schools, 9 magnet schools that cover all grade levels, 3 alternative schools, and 1 special education center. There are programs for gifted students who perform above grade level. Magnet schools offer specialized programs, each with its own focus, including arts, technology, math, science, international studies, and advanced academics.

In 2013 Loveless Academic Magnet Program High School was ranked a gold-medal school, the seventh best public high school in the nation (first in Alabama), and the best magnet school in the nation by *U.S. News & World Report* in their annual survey. Brewbaker Technology Magnet High School was ranked eighth in Alabama.

The Children's Center of Montgomery is a non-profit organization serving Montgomery's severely disabled and special needs children. The center is funded in part by the county board of education and the State Department of Education, among others. Private schools in Montgomery include Alabama Christian Academy, The Montgomery Academy, Trinity Presbyterian School, East Montgomery Montessori School, Montgomery Catholic Preparatory School, and St. Jude Educational Institute.

The following is a summary of data regarding the Montgomery Public Schools.

Total enrollment: 31,316

Number of facilities

 total: 53
 elementary schools: 27
 junior high schools: 9
 high schools: 4
 other: 13

Student/teacher ratio: 15.1:1

Teacher salaries

 average (statewide): $48,282

Funding per pupil: $8,613

Public Schools Information: Montgomery Public Schools, 307 S. Decatur St., Montgomery, AL 36104; telephone (334) 223-6700.

Colleges and Universities

Montgomery is home to a variety of institutions of higher learning. Alabama State University, a historically black university, was founded as Lincoln School by nine former slaves. In 1874 it became the first state-supported educational institution for black students. In 1969 the institution became Alabama State University. Alabama State University enrolls more than 5,600 students and offers bachelor's degrees, master's programs, education specialist degrees, and doctoral programs. Notable among its programs are those in accounting, occupational therapy, health information management, and physical therapy.

Auburn University at Montgomery, a satellite campus of Auburn University, is known for its Center for Government and Public Affairs and its Center for Business and Economic Development. The main campus of Faulkner University, a Christian institution, is in Montgomery. The school offers more than forty majors from five colleges: Alabama Christian College of Arts and Sciences, College of Education, Harris College of Business and Executive Education, V. P. Black School of Biblical Studies, and Faulkner Law.

Huntingdon College is a United Methodist liberal arts college known for its unique Huntingdon Plan. This plan for all full-time students encompasses many areas including global awareness, critical thinking, strong writing, and hands-on learning as well as Judeo-Christian heritage and values.

The Trenholm State Technical College offers varied programs in technical, industrial, and service professions. South University–Montgomery offers several undergraduate and graduate programs, including master's degrees in business administration, criminal justice, and nursing.

Amridge University (formerly Southern Christian University) is an independent Christian college offering degree programs from four schools: the College of Business and Leadership, College of General Studies, School of Human Services, and the Turner School of Theology.

Adult students who work during the day are the special focus of Troy University's Montgomery campus. Students there earn associate, undergraduate, or graduate degrees while attending school exclusively at night and on weekends. Programs focus on business, education, arts, history, sciences, and social science; its graduate programs offer degrees in education, counseling, and business.

Thousands of military students come to Maxwell-Gunter Air Force Base to study at Air University, the primary professional training center for the U.S. Air Force. The university consists of several divisions and colleges. The Carl A. Spaatz Center for Officer Education includes four colleges: Air War College, Air Command and Staff College, Squadron Officer College, and International Officer School. The Ira C. Eaker Center for Professional Development includes the Commanders Professional Development School, USAF Personnel Professional Development School, Air Force Chaplain Corps College, and the National Security Space Institute. The LeMay Center for Doctrine Development and Education is also located at Maxwell.

Libraries and Research Centers

Montgomery has a variety of public and private libraries. Montgomery City-County Public Library has more than 600,000 volumes with a circulation in excess of 500,000 items each year. The system has eleven branches and a bookmobile service. The Alabama Supreme Court and State Law Library has 200,000 volumes on Alabama law and history. It is also one of the oldest U.S. government depository libraries in the state.

Maxwell-Gunter Air Force Base is home to the Air University Library, one of the largest federal libraries outside Washington D.C., and one of the largest military academic libraries in the world. The Maxwell-Gunter Community Libraries provide a wide range of services for military personnel, students, and their families stationed at the base.

The Lee Watkins Learning Center is the main library of Alabama State University. It is also home to the National Center for the Study of Civil Rights and African American Culture. The center houses a special oral history collection and a Jazz Music Library. The Nichols Main Library at Faulkner University houses more than 300,000 volumes and provides a wide array of theological and other academic research resources.

The Houghton Memorial Library at Huntingdon College is a United Methodist archive center for the Alabama-West Florida Conference. Troy University's Montgomery campus houses the award-winning Rosa Parks Library and Museum.

Baptist Medical Center, Central Alabama Veterans Health Care System, and Jackson Hospital & Clinic maintain medical libraries. Other libraries in the city include the Montgomery County Law Library, and the Montgomery Museum of Fine Arts Library.

Alabama State University hosts five major research centers: Center for Nanobiotechnology Research; Research Infrastructure and Minority Institutions; Center for Leadership and Public Policy; East Asian Institute for Business Research and Culture; and Urban Economic Research Development Center. The Center for Demographic Research at Auburn University at Montgomery conducts independent research on population topics.

Public Library Information: Montgomery City-County Public Library, 245 High St., PO Box 1950, Montgomery, AL 36102; telephone (334) 240-4300.

■ Health Care

The Baptist Health network operates not-for-profit clinics and hospitals throughout Montgomery. Baptist Medical Center East is a full-service hospital with a wide variety of services, such as emergency care, obstetrics, surgical services, laser surgery, nuclear medicine, outpatient addictive disease care, and wellness programs. Baptist Medical Center South is a 454-bed acute-care regional hospital known for its Center for Advanced Surgery and neonatal intensive care unit. Baptist Medical Center East is a 150-bed facility featuring 24-hour emergency services, a state-of-the-art labor and delivery center, Level II NICU, and an intensive care unit. Montgomery Cancer Center, one of the largest free-standing cancer centers in the nation, is part of the Baptist Health Network. Baptist Health also operates three

PriMed clinics throughout Montgomery, which are open every day for illnesses and minor emergencies.

Jackson Hospital encompasses a thirteen-city-block area. Specialties include the Advanced Spine Center, the Sleep Disorders Center, the Mom and Baby Center, McGough Oncology Center, the Stroke Center of Excellence, and a specialized Heart Center with state-of-the art surgical suites.

Additionally, active duty and retired military personnel may take advantage of the ambulatory care clinic at Maxwell Air Force Base, the 42nd Medical Group.

■ Recreation

Sightseeing

Many of Montgomery's most important tourist sites are located in the city's downtown and are within walking distance of one another. The Alabama State Capitol, built in 1850–51, is a National Historic Landmark and has been restored to its original design. At this site, Jefferson Davis was sworn in as president of the Confederacy and Martin Luther King, Jr., culminated the historic march through downtown Montgomery by calling for equality for all Americans.

The Civil Rights Memorial lists key events in the American civil rights movement, including the names of forty men, women, and children killed during the struggle. Nearby is Dexter Avenue King Memorial Baptist Church where Dr. Martin Luther King, Jr., issued many of his pleas for freedom. The church also served as the center of the famous 1955 bus boycott. The Dexter Parsonage Museum is the home where King and his family lived from 1954 to 1960.

Montgomery is also the home of the First White House of the Confederacy, where President Jefferson Davis and his family resided. The Alabama Judicial Building houses the state Supreme Court, the courts of criminal and civil appeals, and the state law library.

Old Alabama Town is a collection of restored homes and buildings from the nineteenth and early twentieth centuries, set in the heart of Montgomery's historic downtown. The site features a walking tour, live demonstrations, and a gift shop. Another popular tourist stop is the U.S. Air Force Heritage Museum, which houses the Air Force Enlisted Heritage Hall. The museum, on the grounds of Maxwell-Gunter Air Force Base, highlights important achievements of enlisted soldiers and the airplanes they used, as well as vintage military uniforms, historical photos, and paintings. The base occupies the site where, in 1910, Wilbur and Orville Wright opened the world's first flight training school.

Visitors are alerted to expect the unexpected at the over forty-acre Montgomery Zoo, which displays more than 500 animals from five continents living in a barrier-free setting lush with vegetation and crashing waterfalls.

One of the largest planetariums in the Southeast, the W. A. Gayle Planetarium allows visitors to view the sun, moon, planets, and stars projected on a fifty-foot domed ceiling.

Teague House (home to the Alabama Historical Commission) offers visitors a chance to observe one of the South's finest examples of late Greek Revival architecture, while the Murphy House antebellum mansion, which now houses the Montgomery Waterworks Board, is open for free tours. The *Harriott II* riverboat provides nautical tours of the city from its berth in historic Riverfront Park. For a unique experience, tourists can take a tram tour of the Hyundai Motor Manufacturing plant, where Hyundai engines are produced.

Downtown Montgomery along the Alabama River also offers exciting opportunities as part of the larger vision of revamping downtown. The Riverwalk development includes an amphitheater, a riverboat, and the Montgomery Biscuits baseball stadium. The area is three blocks from the convention center.

Arts and Culture

The 150-acre Wynton M. Blount Cultural Park plays host to two Montgomery Gems: the Montgomery Museum of Fine Arts and the Alabama Shakespeare Festival. The Montgomery Museum of Fine Arts' noted Blount Collection includes works by John Singer Sargent and Edward Hopper and spans 200 years of American art. The museum also displays collections of European art and offers an educational gallery called ARTWORKS, through which patrons can use their five senses to learn about works in the permanent collection and art in general.

The acclaimed Alabama Shakespeare Festival makes its home at the Carolyn Blount Theatre. The complex includes two separate theaters, the Festival Stage and the Octagon Stage. The Shakespeare Festival attracts more than 300,000 visitors annually. The park's Shakespeare Gardens hosts many events, including acoustic music concerts, lectures, and theatrical productions. The grounds are festooned with numerous lush plantings and an Elizabethan herb garden. Blount Cultural Park represents the largest single gift in the history of American arts philanthropy. The Alabama Artists Gallery features the work of the state's artists.

The F. Scott and Zelda Fitzgerald Museum is located in a former home of F. Scott Fitzgerald, author of *The Great Gatsby* and other American classics. It houses a large collection of photographs, possessions, partial manuscripts, and original correspondence between Fitzgerald and his wife Zelda, a fine artist.

Troy State University's Davis Theatre for the Performing Arts, which opened in 1930, is a renovated former movie palace that now hosts professional musicals, drama, chamber music, symphony concerts, dance, and

other performances. It is home to the Montgomery Symphony Orchestra, a community orchestra under the direction of Thomas Hinds. The symphony oversees a variety of educational programs as well as the Montgomery Youth Orchestra. The Montgomery Ballet, with artistic director Darren Christian McIntyre, also performs at the Davis Theatre. The company and affiliated dance school features performances of classics throughout the year. Faulkner University's Dinner Theatre is Montgomery's premier dinner theater venue.

Renowned country singer Hank Williams, Sr., is a son of Montgomery. The museum that bears his name features his 1952 Cadillac and other items, such as his clothing, piano, and band members' possessions. A life-size statue of the beloved singer stands across the street from the old city auditorium where many of his performances and his funeral took place.

Rosa L. Parks, the African American heroine who was the catalyst for the 1955 Montgomery bus boycott, is honored at Troy University's Rosa Parks Library and Museum, which opened in 2000. The 55,000-square-foot structure was built on the site where Mrs. Parks boarded the bus on which she refused to yield her seat. The interpretive museum is housed in the 7,000-square-foot first floor of the three-story building, which also houses the Troy State University Library. Permanent exhibits commemorating the civil rights movement are displayed, including a replica of the bus, original historical documents on loan from the City of Montgomery, and various sculptures. The Museum also contains a 2,200-square-foot, 103-seat multimedia auditorium.

The Alabama Cattleman's Association MOOseum tells the story of Alabama's agricultural history, focusing on the history of the cattle industry from the explorations of DeSoto to the present day. This museum also has interactive displays geared toward children.

The 34,406-square-foot Armory Learning Arts Center, a one-time National Guard Armory that underwent complete renovation in 1983, is home to the Arts Council of Montgomery. The council brings art, music, dance, and gymnastic instruction to the community. The center is the permanent home of the Alabama Dance Theatre, which presents both contemporary and classical dance performances, and twice a year presents major productions at the Davis Theatre. The Capri Theatre in Montgomery features art, foreign, and classic films.

Festivals and Holidays

Autumn is the season for many annual events on Montgomery's calendar. September brings the annual *Ballet & the Beasts,* a free performance of the Montgomery Ballet Company at Montgomery Zoo, and the Alabama Highland Games, sponsored by the Alabama Celtic Association. The Montgomery Symphony Orchestra bids summer adieu with "Broadway Under the Stars," a free performance at the Alabama

Shakespeare Festival grounds in September. October's calendar features the 10-day Alabama National Fair at the Alabama Agricultural Center (Garrett Coliseum). The Montgomery Zoo sponsors an annual Christmas Lights Festival in December.

March brings the Fitzgerald Museum Gala & Auction and the week-long Southeastern Livestock Exposition (SLE) Rodeo. In April, Auburn University at Montgomery presents an annual Global Cultural Festival, a free event featuring food, cultural performances, and exhibits from around the world. The Riverbend Brewfest and River Jam is a major food and music festival in May. The Montgomery Museum of Fine Arts holds its annual Flimp festival in May as well. In May 2013 Auburn University at Montgomery held its inaugural Montgomery Quidditch Tournament and Festival in conjunction with the Flimp Festival.

Culture blossoms in the summer air with July's free Montgomery Ballet Performance on the Green at Wynton M. Blount Cultural Park and the free Day of Late Summer performance by Alabama Dance Theatre. The National Center for the Study of Civil Rights and African American Culture at Alabama State University hosts the annual Black Film Festival in August. The Montgomery Dragon Boat Race and Festival takes place that same month.

Sports for the Spectator

As the home of Alabama State University, Auburn University at Montgomery, Troy State University's Montgomery campus, and other colleges, Montgomery offers a variety of football and baseball games and other college sports for fans to watch. The Montgomery Biscuits, the 2006 and 2007 AA Southern League baseball champions, make their home at Montgomery's Riverwalk Stadium. They are affiliated with the Tampa Bay Devil Rays. Montgomery Motorsports Park offers year-round drag racing and weekly events. November brings the Turkey Day Classic at Cramton Bowl, where the Alabama State University Hornets take on the Stillman College Tigers. Events kick off with the Turkey Day Classic Parade down Dexter Avenue. The Cramton Bowl was selected to host the first Camellia Bowl (2014), featuring college football teams from the Sun Belt and Mid-American conferences.

Sports for the Participant

Montgomery's Department of Parks and Recreation operates more than sixty parks and recreational facilities. Among the most popular are Buddy Watson Park, Oak Park, Riverfront Park, Overlook Park, Vaughn Road Park, and Woodmere Park. Tennis and softball facilities dot the parks, and arts, crafts, and fitness programming is available at The Armory Learning Arts Center on Madison Avenue. The Armory Gymnastics Center is a state-of-the-art center for specialized gymnastics training.

The Emory Folmar YMCA Soccer Complex hosts local leagues and sponsors regional and national tournaments.

The 26,000-square-foot Therapeutic Recreation Center on Augusta Street features a gymnasium, indoor and outdoor swimming pools, weight room, game room, locker rooms, meeting rooms, a kitchen, and tennis courts. There is also a greenhouse and fully accessible playground area. Lagoon Park Golf Course offers the year-round opportunity to play a 72-par championship course. Gateway Park features a nine-hole golf course.

Shopping and Dining

Montgomery is home to regional shopping malls and lifestyle centers with a mix of specialty shops and antique malls throughout. The Shoppes at EastChase feature an open-air main street with fountains, street lamps, lush landscaping, and upscale tenants. Eastdale Mall is another popular shopping site. The Eastbrook Flea Market and Antique Mall offers something a little different for the antique and bargain shopper. The Mulberry Shopping District has unique boutiques, antique shops, galleries, and restaurants. Fresh fruits, vegetables, and home-cooked specialties are for sale year-round at the State Farmers Market; the Montgomery Curb Market and Fairview Farmers Market are open seasonally.

Tourist-friendly Montgomery offers restaurants with a variety of cuisines from country to Cajun, Mexican, and Thai. Specialties include down-home Southern fare and just-caught seafood from the Gulf of Mexico. Other choices include Indian restaurants, an Australian steakhouse, Italian, Chinese, and the Farmers Market Café, which features fresh fruits and vegetables.

When it opened in nearby Prattville in August 2007, Bass Pro Shops Outdoor World, a 185,000-square-foot megastore, became a tourist destination. An estimated 10,000 shoppers visited the store on its opening day.

Visitor Information: Montgomery Area Chamber of Commerce Convention and Visitor Bureau, 300 Water Street, Montgomery, AL 36104; telephone (334) 262-0013; email tourism@montgomerychamber.com.

■ Convention Facilities

The Renaissance Montgomery Hotel and Spa at the Convention Center provides 73,000 square feet of meeting space, the 1,800-seat Montgomery Performing Arts Centre, and the 9,000-square-foot European-style spa. The entire hotel and convection complex provides 103,000 square feet of meeting space. In addition, Garrett Coliseum offers 31,000 square feet of meeting space and contains seating for 13,500, with an arena, barns, and parking facilities for 5,000 people.

Other convention and conference sites in Montgomery include the Embassy Suites Hotel and Convention

Center, the Hilton Garden Inn, and Auburn Montgomery Taylor Center.

Convention Information: Montgomery Area Chamber of Commerce Convention and Visitor Bureau, 300 Water Street, Montgomery, AL 36104; telephone (334) 262-0013; email tourism@montgomerychamber.com.

■ Transportation

Approaching the City

Montgomery Regional Airport is located six miles southwest of the city. It supports civilian use and provides facilities for the Alabama Army and Air National Guard. Air carriers serving Montgomery include American Eagle, Delta Connection, and US Airways. Daily flights travel to and from Atlanta, Dallas–Fort Worth, Memphis, and Charlotte.

Interstate 65, running north and south, and Interstate 85, running east and west, intersect in Montgomery. The two Interstates lead to Atlanta, Birmingham, Mobile, Huntsville, and Nashville. The city is also the southern terminus of Interstate 85. Montgomery is served by U.S. Highways 31, 80, 82, 231, and 331, all of which are connected by a four-lane perimeter road surrounding the city. Bus service to other parts of the region and the country is provided by Greyhound and Capital Trailways.

Traveling in the City

Major east–west streets include Fairview Avenue, Madison Avenue, and South Boulevard, while important north--south streets are Union and Perry streets and Norman Bridge Road. The Montgomery Area Transit System (MATS) is the local bus system providing service on seventeen fixed routes. MATS also provides a demand response service that allows riders to specify pick-up and drop-off locations, and the Lightning Route, a turn of the century replica trolley that circulates the historic downtown district.

■ Communications

Newspapers and Magazines

The *Montgomery Advertiser* is the city's only daily newspaper. The *Montgomery Independent* is published weekly. Several magazines focusing on hunting, fishing, farming, and agriculture are published in Montgomery. Monthly publications include the *Central Alabama Business Journal*, *Montgomery Living*, *Montgomery Parents*, and *Travel Host*.

Community Newspaper Holdings Inc., a leading publisher of local newspapers, is headquartered in Montgomery. The company publishes numerous daily newspapers and weekly publications in twenty-three states.

Television and Radio

There are eight licensed television stations in Montgomery and twenty-six licensed radio stations. Of the radio stations, twenty are FM stations offering jazz, country, religious, adult contemporary, and Top-40 formats, while six are AM stations that feature religious, talk, and sports programming.

Media Information: *The Montgomery Advertiser*, 200 Washington Street, Montgomery, AL 36104; telephone (334) 262-1611. *The Montgomery Independent*, 1810 West Fifth Street, Montgomery, AL 36106; telephone (334) 265-7320.

Montgomery Online

Alabama Shakespeare Festival. Available www.asf.net

City of Montgomery. Available www.montgomery.al.us

City of Montgomery Parks and Recreation. Available www.funinmontgomery.com

Maxwell-Gunter Air Force Base. Available www.maxwell.af.mil

Montgomery Adviser. Available www.montgomeryadvertiser.com

Montgomery Area Chamber of Commerce. Available www.montgomerychamber.com

Montgomery Area Chamber of Commerce Convention and Visitors Bureau. Available www.visitingmontgomery.com

Montgomery Biscuits baseball. Available www.biscuitsbaseball.com

Montgomery City-County Public Library. Available www.mccpl.lib.al.us/montgomery

Montgomery Public School System. Available www.mps.k12.al.us

BIBLIOGRAPHY

King, Martin Luther, Jr., *Stride toward Freedom: The Montgomery Story* (Boston, MA: Beacon Press, 2010)

Lewis, Wendy I. and Marty Ellis, *Montgomery: At the Forefront of a New Century* (Community, 1996)

Rogers, William Warren, *Confederate Home Front: Montgomery During the Civil War* (Tuscaloosa, AL: University of Alabama Press, 1999)

Theoharis, Jeanne, *The Rebellious Life of Mrs. Rosa Parks* (Boston, MA: Beacon Press, 2013)

Arkansas

The State in Brief

Nickname: Natural State

Motto: Regnat populus (The people rule)

Flower: Apple blossom

Bird: Mockingbird

Area: 53,179 square miles (2010; U.S. rank 29th)

Elevation: Ranges from 55 feet to 2,753 feet above sea level

Climate: Long hot summers, mild winters, ample rainfall

Admitted to Union: June 15, 1836

Capital: Little Rock

Head Official: Mike Beebe (D) (until 2015)

Population

1990: 2,350,725
2000: 2,673,398
2010: 2,915,918
2012 estimate: 2,916,372
Percent change, 2000–2010: 9.1%
U.S. rank in 2012: 32nd
Percent of residents born in state: 61.2% (2012)
Density: 56.0 people per square mile (2010)
2012 FBI Crime Index Total: 121,776

Racial and Ethnic Characteristics (2012)

White: 2,285,577
Black or African American: 453,062
American Indian and Alaska Native: 17,390
Asian: 35,744
Native Hawaiian and Pacific Islander: 5,516
Hispanic or Latino (may be of any race): 185,239
Other: 119,083

Age Characteristics (2012)

Population under 5 years old: 196,735
Population 5 to 19 years old: 597,449
Percent of population 65 years and over: 14.5%
Median age: 37.4

Vital Statistics

Total number of births (2012–13): 38,464
Total number of deaths (2012–13): 28,793
AIDS cases reported through 2011: 4,727

Economy

Major industries: Food products, agriculture, tourism, manufacturing
Unemployment rate (2012): 5.1%
Per capita income (2012): $22,007
Median household income (2012): $40,531
Percentage of persons below poverty level (2012): 18.7%
Income tax rate: 1.0% to 7.0%
Sales tax rate: 6.5%

Fort Smith

■ The City in Brief

Founded: 1817

Head Official: Mayor Sandy Sanders (since 2010; current term expires December 2014)

City Population
  1990: 73,511
  2000: 80,268
  2010: 86,209
  2012 estimate: 87,437
  Percent change, 2000–2010: 7.4%
  U.S. rank in 2000: 363rd (State rank: 2nd)
  U.S. rank in 2010: 345th (State rank: 2nd)

Metropolitan Statistical Area Population
  2000: 207,290
  2010: 298,592
  2012 estimate: 298,110
  Percent change, 2000–2010: 44%
  U.S. rank in 2000: 158th
  U.S. rank in 2010: 158th

Area: 52.94 square miles

Elevation: 449 feet above sea level

Average Annual Temperatures: January, 38° F; July, 82° F; annual average 61° F

Average Annual Precipitation: 41.8 total inches of precipitation; 6.3 inches of snow

Major Economic Sectors: manufacturing, including air conditioning systems, food products, pet food, and weapons products, transportation and shipping, healthcare services

Unemployment Rate: 4.0% (2012)

Per Capita Income: $20,846

2012 FBI Crime Index Property: 4,771

Major Colleges and Universities: University of Arkansas–Fort Smith, John Brown University, Webster University

Daily Newspaper: *Times Record*

■ Introduction

Located on the Arkansas River where the state of Arkansas meets Oklahoma, Fort Smith is the western gateway to Arkansas, and the state's second largest city. The former military fort was situated with great purpose in 1817 to separate warring native tribes, and its location continues to serve Fort Smith today as a manufacturing and tourism destination. The Arkansas River Valley separates the Ozark Plateau from the Ouachita Mountains, giving Fort Smith visitors and residents a smorgasbord of outdoor activities in which to participate. Fort Smith is known as the Wild West town of Arkansas, capitalizing on its history as a frontier military installation and the site of "Hanging" Judge Parker's notorious courtroom. During and just after the Civil War, former slaves and refugees from repressive regimes found a temporary home in Fort Smith and nearby Fort Chaffee in anticipation of a more democratic style of life. Today, Fort Smith remains a gateway to and from the West as a mecca for manufacturing businesses and a burgeoning tourist destination on its own merits.

■ Geography and Climate

Fort Smith is located on the Arkansas-Oklahoma border, where it is bisected by the Arkansas River and sandwiched between the Ouachita and Ozark national forests. Built on flats left by the meandering river, the city is level and green but enjoys easy access to mountains. Fort Smith sees the sun more than 200 days per year and experiences temperate weather during most months. The winters

The antebellum mansion of William Henry Harrison Clayton, Fort Smith, Arkansas. © *Andre Jenny/Alamy*

generally are mild, with less than seven inches of snow on average, while the summers are warm and often humid. Fort Smith sits at the edge of the reputed "Tornado Alley," and in spring of 1996 its downtown was devastated by a class F2 twister. (On the Fujita tornado damage scale, F1 is lowest and F5 highest.)

Area: 52.94 square miles

Elevation: 449 feet above sea level

Average Temperatures: January, 38° F; July, 82° F; annual average 61° F

Average Annual Precipitation: 41.8 total inches of precipitation; 6.3 inches of snow

■ History

The Fort That Wouldn't Die

The groundwork for Fort Smith's role in U.S. and Arkansas history was laid early and deep, as the native tribes that originally peopled the area during the Stone Age established communities in what later became valued and contested lands. Early inhabitants of western Arkansas have been characterized as "bluff dwellers" whose civilization dates back to 10,000 BC. The bluff dweller culture was absorbed into that of invading tribes, and by the time Spanish explorer Hernando de Soto ventured into Arkansas in 1541, the most numerous Arkansas residents were of the Quapaw tribe.

Other explorers followed, claiming the land in the name of their sponsoring country; in 1682 French explorer René Robert Cavelier de La Salle claimed the area for France as part of the Louisiana Territory. In Arkansas and back east, relocation of native peoples soon began as early European settlers required more land on which to live, hunt, and farm. The later 1700s saw an increasing mix of native tribes west of the Mississippi, not all of whom were on friendly terms. Closer proximity naturally resulted in heightened tensions and conflicts, endangering not just tribe members but also the increasing population of fur traders and pioneers employing the Arkansas River Valley as a funnel into the southwest. After Arkansas officially became part of the United States as the District of Arkansas in 1803, the federal government perceived a need to intervene in intertribal hostilities on the western edge of the burgeoning country. A new fort was established in 1817 on the banks of the Arkansas River where it meets the Poteau River, on a promontory of bluffs called Belle Point; the fort was named for General Thomas Smith of the federal garrison in St. Louis. For the next seven years, Fort Smith military personnel arbitrated clashes between the Osage and Cherokee tribes, negotiated treaties, and also patrolled U.S. borders contested by Spain.

The military presence in Arkansas allowed for an influx of settlers from the east, and a community began to grow up around Fort Smith. New businesses catered to soldiers with a drive to keep the installation occupied and thriving. Military forts of the time typically had a relatively brief lifespan as the western boundary of the United States continued to edge toward the Pacific. Indeed, the troops encamped at Fort Smith were relocated farther west in 1924; the fort retained its utility by serving as headquarters for the Western Choctaw Agency and also as the hub of enforcement for prohibition activities in that area. Location played a major role in Fort Smith's continued viability; the Arkansas River Valley provided easy access to the west where the fort and its surrounding community became the meeting point for many primary roads. The federal government and its military viewed Fort Smith increasingly as a strategic site based on access, and the fact that it was near but not encroaching upon a newly established Choctaw reservation in what had become known as Indian Territory. A new Fort Smith garrison was constructed in 1938, bringing with it an official town of the same name.

Fort Smith: A Stop on the "Trail of Tears"

The history of Fort Smith is inextricably interwoven with that of native peoples in the United States, from the fort's time as a peacekeeping entity to the part it played in the forced relocation of thousands of native tribes west of the Mississippi River. During Thomas Jefferson's tenure as president, American citizens sought more land and fewer conflicts with previous inhabitants of the eastern area. Jefferson's proposed solution was relocating eastern native tribes to a buffer zone between U.S. territory holdings and land claimed by European countries. Between 1816 and 1840, a number of eastern tribes ceded their land to the United States and voluntarily headed west to what is now Oklahoma. In 1830 President Andrew Jackson put into effect further plans for the relocation of eastern native peoples; the result was an exodus of more than 100,000 native men, women, and children on an arduous route that took them halfway across the country. There were several points of debarkation and multiple western routes used, but the "Trail of Tears" ultimately passed directly through the gateway community of Fort Smith. Military installations in the area assisted tribe members in rejoining their native communities, or held them temporarily while land assignments were made.

Fort Smith had come full circle. Its troops once again were keeping watch on a forced collective of age-old foes

and allies in a relatively concentrated area, more for purposes of protecting pioneers and California-bound prospectors of European descent than the tribes themselves. But then came a new kind of war.

Citizen Against Citizen: The Civil War at Fort Smith

In 1860 the state of Arkansas had a population of 435,450 people, 111,115 of whom were slaves of African descent, and 11,481 of whom were slaveholders of primarily European background. It appeared inevitable that when the Confederacy voted to secede from the Union in April 1861, Arkansas would join the Confederates; however, while more than 60,000 Arkansas residents joined rebel troops, at least 9,000 Anglos and more than 5,000 African Americans fought for the Union in a conflict that divided communities and families. Fort Smith was no exception—while it initially served in the war as a Confederate military installation and supply depot, Union troops took over the post on September 1, 1863.

Fort Smith's strategic location on intersecting rivers and roads made it both a valuable staging area as a Union outpost and a continuing target for the Confederate faithful holed up in surrounding mountains and Indian Territory. The garrison became, not for the last time in history, a refuge for besieged citizens aligned with the Union and suffered great deprivation when rebel troops ambushed supply sources. In 1865 Confederate leadership officially turned Arkansas, Texas, and Indian Territory over to the Union, and Fort Smith Confederates returned home to begin rebuilding the community's future.

Reconstruction, Retribution, and Reconciliation

Post-Civil War Reconstruction returned some states in the Union to a military form of government; consequently, Fort Smith became an outpost in the subdistrict of Arkansas, charged with enforcement of Reconstruction regulations and registration of freedmen. As a community, Fort Smith's function evolved slowly from military to administration of frontier justice, as a succession of tough judges presided on the bench and attempted to impose order on the populace. Judge Isaac Parker, the infamous "hanging judge," meted out sentences over a twenty-one-year period, ordering hundreds of defendants to jail and 160 men to "hang by the neck until you are dead, dead, dead!"

In 1896 Fort Smith ceased operations as a military outpost, and the community's focus became municipal growth while still sustaining the city's formative history. Reverberations from the Civil War continued as, in 1891, Jim Crow legislation segregated rail stations and kept the population divided literally and figuratively, until the issue of integration came to a head in 1957. In the interim, Arkansas weathered the Great Depression, accompanied as it was by crop-killing drought and the departure of many citizens from Fort Smith and Arkansas for what appeared to be greener pastures.

As the country began to rebound, Fort Smith established its identity as an industrial hub seated fortuitously at the nexus of two rivers leading to the Mississippi and an abundance of roadways radiating throughout the country. The former military installation served briefly as a relocation camp for Japanese and German U.S. citizens during World War II, but in 1975 and 1980 also provided shelter and transition for Vietnamese and Cuban refugees seeking asylum in the United States. Fort Smith's public school system now proudly embraces the diversity of its students just as the city embraces its history; adaptability and survival may be the best descriptors for the former Wild West town. Following its history of settling the "Wild West" and its law enforcement heritage, Fort Smith was selected by the U.S. Department of the Interior in 2007 as the location of the U.S. Marshals Museum. The proposed $50 million facility was slated to open in 2016.

Following national trends, employment in manufacturing declined in the early 2000s, with jobs in that sector going overseas. But tides are changing for Fort Smith. In 2010 *Forbes* magazine named Fort Smith the number-one city in America for cost of living, and the cost of living remained 14.7% below the national average through 2013. Also in 2013, Fort Smith won the number-two spot in *Forbes* for cost of doing business. (Shreveport, Louisiana, was first.) With consistently low costs of living and doing business, Fort Smith has worked to forge a new future, even as it recalls its past: *True West* magazine named it the number-one Western town in America in 2013.

Historical Information: Fort Smith Historical Society, PO Box 3676, Fort Smith, AR 72913; telephone (479) 452-2415.

■ Population Profile

Metropolitan Statistical Area Population
1990: 175,911
2000: 207,290
2012 estimate: 298,110
Percent change, 2000–2010: 44%
U.S. rank in 2000: 158th
U.S. rank in 2010: 158th

City Residents
1990: 73,511
2000: 80,268
2010: 86,209
2012 estimate: 87,437
Percent change, 2000–2010: 7.4%

U.S. rank in 2000: 363rd (State rank: 2nd)
U.S. rank in 2010: 345th (State rank: 2nd)

Density: 1,391.2 people per square mile

Racial and ethnic characteristics
White: 67,162
Black or African American: 7,562
American Indian and Alaskan Native: 1,910
Asian: 5,251
Native Hawaiian and Other Pacific Islander: 209
Hispanic or Latino (may be of any race): 14,543
Other: 5,343

Percent of residents born in state: 57.2%

Age characteristics
Population under 5 years old: 6,267
Population 5 to 9 years old: 7,207
Population 10 to 14 years old: 6,047
Population 15 to 19 years old: 6,187
Population 20 to 24 years old: 4,912
Population 25 to 34 years old: 13,011
Population 35 to 44 years old: 11,582
Population 45 to 54 years old: 11,679
Population 55 to 59 years old: 5,068
Population 60 to 64 years old: 3,956
Population 65 to 74 years old: 6,185
Population 75 to 84 years old: 3,782
Population 85 years and over: 1,554
Median age: 35.1

Births (2010–11 Metropolitan Area)
Total number: 3,932

Deaths (2010–11 Metropolitan Area)
Total number: 2,918

Money income (2012)
Per capita income: $20,846
Median household income: $36,792
Total households: 34,062

Number of households with income of ...
less than $10,000: 3,162
$10,000 to $14,999: 2,933
$15,000 to $24,999: 5,172
$25,000 to $34,999: 4,956
$35,000 to $49,999: 5,430
$50,000 to $74,999: 5,387
$75,000 to $99,999: 2,711
$100,000 to $149,999: 2,393
$150,000 to $199,999: 899
$200,000 or more: 1,019

Percent of families below poverty level: 25.7%

FBI Crime Index Property: 4,771

FBI Crime Index Violent: 687

■ Municipal Government

Fort Smith operates under a city administrator form of government in which the governing body is composed of a mayor and seven board directors. Four of the directors represent wards of the City of Fort Smith, while the mayor and the other three directors are elected by the broader population of the city. Terms of service are four years in duration, with off-set elections. The Board of Directors is chaired by the mayor and oversees matters of policy and budget. The mayor's role is, in part, as the ceremonial head of the city. The board employs a city administrator to oversee daily operations for the city. The mayor presides over the city board meetings, but does not have a vote. The mayor does have veto power and can break ties should they arise during board of director votes.

Head Official: Mayor Sandy Sanders (since 2010; current term expires December 31, 2014)

Total Number of City Employees: 922 (2012)

City Information: City of Fort Smith, 623 Garrison Avenue, Fort Smith, AR 72901; telephone (479) 784-2201; fax (479) 784-2430

■ Economy

Major Industries and Commercial Activity

Fort Smith is the manufacturing hub of Arkansas, with more goods produced in the vicinity than anywhere else in the state. National and international companies such as OK Industries, Arkansas Best, Gerber Foods, and Rheem Air Conditioning Products have facilities in Fort Smith and employ thousands of area workers. Recreation and tourism, particularly structured around the unique history of Fort Smith, is a growing industry. The pending construction of the U.S. Marshals Museum represented one of the biggest investments yet on that front. Like many communities across the nation, however, the recession took a toll on Fort Smith's economy and jobs in the latter half of the 2000s and into the early 2010s. Large companies based in Fort Smith, such as Arkansas Best, posted major losses in 2009 and 2010 and slipped from the *Fortune 500* list. Others, like the Whirlpool Corporation in 2012, closed their facilities entirely. Yet subsequent years brought a degree of recovery and stability, with many companies hiring again by 2013. The more than 100,000 square feet of warehouse space formerly occupied by Whirlpool was leased to Spartan Logistics in October 2013, offering the possibility of new jobs. Additionally, the friendly business climate attracted Walther Arms and Thermold Magazines, both weapons products manufacturers that relocated to Fort Smith in 2012 and 2013, respectively. Mars Petcare, a pet food manufacturer that began operations in Fort Smith in 2009, announced a $50 million expansion of its local facility

scheduled for completion in 2014. Old Dominion Freight Lines also was in the process of constructing a 65-bay terminal to serve regional clients.

Items and goods produced: air conditioning systems, food products, pet food, and weapons products

Incentive Programs-New and Existing Companies

Local programs: In conjunction with the Arkansas Economic Development Commission, Fort Smith offers a variety of investment and job creation incentives designed to attract and retain thriving businesses. Business retention teams conduct industry visits with major employers throughout the greater Fort Smith region. Business recruitment teams conduct recruitment visits to targeted industries in selected domestic and international regions to promote the greater Fort Smith region. The Chamber of Commerce works to promote similar development, initiating an "Invest in the Best" campaign in 2010 to fund recruitment efforts by the organization, and also spearheading efforts at regional collaboration.

State programs: The Arkansas Economic Development Commission (AEDC) offers a variety of tax incentives for the development of new businesses and expansion of existing businesses throughout the state. These include incentives in the categories of job creation, targeted businesses, research and development, non-profits, and tourism development.

The Arkansas Science and Technology Authority (ASTA) promotes scientific research, technology development, and business innovation in the state. To this end, it provides financial support for the transfer and development of innovative technology to an enterprise based in Arkansas. The authority offers a number of programs, including the Technology Transfer Assistance Grant Program, the Seed Capital Investment Program, the Technology Development Program, and the Centers for Applied Technology Program. Various tax credits and tax incentives are offered for businesses participating in qualified research and development programs.

A number of state-sponsored funding sources are available to qualified employers through the AEDC, ASTA, and the Arkansas Development Finance Authority (ADFA). These include the Arkansas Capital Access Program, the Venture Capital Investment Fund, ASTA Investment Fund, and industrial revenue bonds.

There are several special industrial location incentives offered by the State of Arkansas, including the Arkansas Enterprise Zone Program. Many other incentives offered by the state of Arkansas include corporate income tax credits, sales and use tax refunds, and the payment in lieu of taxes program. Information on many of these incentives is available through the Arkansas Department of Finance and Administration.

Start-up businesses can take advantage of several incentive packages, including Advantage Arkansas (an income tax credit program), Tax Back (refunds of sales and use taxes), and InvestArk (a sales and use tax credit program). Businesses in highly competitive categories such as manufacturing, agriculture and information technology may be eligible for incentive programs such as Create Rebate (payroll rebates) and the ArkPlus income tax credit program.

The State of Arkansas additionally provides specialized incentive programs to encourage development of specific components of a business (child care facilities, customized training, recycling) or to recruit particular industries to the area (motion picture companies, tourism businesses).

Job training programs: The Business and Industry Training Program sponsored by the Arkansas Economic Development Commission designs customized training programs to meet the specific needs of particular industries. Its emphasis is three-fold: recruiting workers, pre-employment training, and on-the-job training.

The Arkansas Construction Education Foundation Training Program offers classes and apprenticeship programs in Fort Smith and five other Arkansas locations. The University of Arkansas Fort Smith's Center for Business and Professional Development partners with local companies to develop skills of employees through customized training and other professional development opportunities, as well as consulting and strategic planning assistance.

Development Projects

With Community Development Block Grant (CDBG) funding, the City of Fort Smith addresses affordable housing issues, increases resources for the homeless, and attracts corporate expansion and relocations in the metropolitan area to grow employment opportunities for mid- and low-income community members. A number of Fort Smith's strategic action plan strategies seek to increase the income of workers in relation to their rental or mortgage burden, with tactics to include promotion of General Education Development (GED) programs that serve adults, encouragement of higher education for workers, and provision of quality childcare services that allow parents to work outside the home.

Downtown Fort Smith has experienced a renaissance in response to a growing tourism and convention market. The Fort Smith Downtown Development association has energized business recruitment to the area, including improvements to the Fort Smith Convention Center, the Riverfront Development, and Garrison Street. It also secured more than $700,000 in state and federal Historic Tax Credits to attract developers to dilapidated downtown buildings. Renovating existing buildings has supported efforts to focus downtown development that draws on Fort Smith's rich history. In 2012 alone, 16 new businesses opened in the downtown area, supported by $3 million in private investment. Development of the

riverfront area remained a joint effort by both the municipal government and the chamber of commerce.

Other major developments included the U.S. Marshals Museum. With an anticipated opening of 2016, the planned $50 million, 52,000 square-foot museum was to include some 10,000 square feet of historical artifacts to capture the past, present, and future roles of the nation's oldest federal law enforcement agency. Shortly before laying the building's cornerstone in 2013, the museum announced a slight relocation—about 2,000 feet north—to take advantage of a larger site made possible by the expansion of donated lands. The larger site offered more parking and landscaping options.

Lands of the former Fort Chaffee continued to undergo change in the 2010s. The Fort Chaffee Redevelopment Authority, created in 1997 after the base closed in 1995, received an allotment of 7,000 acres of former military lands for residential, commercial, and industrial development. (The other 65,000 acres of Fort Chaffee were leased by the federal government to the Arkansas National Guard.) Chaffee Crossing, as the development is known, has sought to preserve the local history of the fort while offering modern facilities, parks, homes, and business opportunities. Newcomers to Chaffee Crossing included business clients (Old Dominion Frieght Lines, Arvest Bank) as well as residential developers (Shire, Inc.). Property sales at Chaffee Crossing in 2012 topped 138 acres and $2.7 million in revenue. In 2012 the Fort Chaffee Redevelopment Authority was awarded the Base Redevelopment Project of the Year by the Association of Defense Communities.

Transportation projects throughout the greater Fort Smith region remained a focal point of development, with a strong emphasis on the extension of Interstate 49 through Chaffee Crossing and southward to U.S. Highway 71. In 2012 the city relocated several waterlines to make way for the road project, allowing construction to proceed on the final 1.5 miles of the 6-mile expansion, which neared completion in late 2013.

Economic Development Information: Fort Smith Regional Chamber of Commerce, 612 Garrison Avenue, Fort Smith, AR 72901; telephone (479) 783-3111

Commercial Shipping

Sited at the confluence of the Arkansas and Poteau Rivers, the city-owned Port of Fort Smith has experienced steady growth in tonnage, primarily composed of steel and scrap metal, passing through its terminal and on through the Mississippi River system. Proposed deepening of the Arkansas River system around the port offered the possibility of increased tonnage per vessel and thus lower transportation costs for products. Funding for the multimillion dollar project depended on federal support; it was not included in federal budgets for 2012 or 2013.

The port is served by both railroad and trucking companies. In general, local trucking companies have seen continued demand for service as they transport general commodities throughout the United States. Air freight services are also available through local companies and the Fort Smith Regional Airport, which serves an eight-county area.

Labor Force and Employment Outlook

With a strong base of manufacturing and excellent geographic location, Fort Smith has maintained its solid manufacturing base and evidenced resiliency despite economic challenges faced in the late 2000s and early 2010s. Mainstay local manufacturers such as Gerber Foods and Rheem Air Conditioning provide products for which there appears to be relatively stable demand, thereby minimizing employment fluctuations. Areas of growing employment have been tied to new or expanding businesses located in Chaffee Crossing, the redeveloped portion of the former Fort Chaffee. With a growing and involved local college in the University of Arkansas–Fort Smith—enrollment was expected to increase by 20 percent from 2013 to 2033—Fort Smith has seen increasing support for professional and business service professions. According to the U.S. Department of Labor, a long-term shift from goods-producing employment to service-producing activities was expected.

The following is a summary of data regarding the 2012 Fort Smith AR-OK Metropolitan Area labor force:

Size of civilian labor force: 41,012

Number of workers employed in . . .

agriculture and mining: 633
construction: 1,835
manufacturing: 7,433
wholesale trade: 1,199
retail trade: 4,564
transportation: 1,888
information systems: 527
finance: 1,629
professional administration: 2,291
education and social services: 9,253
arts and leisure: 3,970
other: 1,885
public administration: 1,152

Average hourly earnings of production workers: $14.21

Unemployment rate: 4.0% (2012)

Employers

Largest employers (2012)	*Number of employees*
Sparks Health System	2,400
Baldor Electric Company	2,393
OK Industries	1,800
Fort Smith Public Schools	1,783
St. Edward Mercy Medical Center	1,487
University of Arkansas–Forth Smith	951
Arkansas Best Corporation	936
City of Fort Smith	922
Rheem-Ruud	900
Golden Living/ Beverly Enterprises	800

Cost of Living

The following is a summary of data regarding several key cost of living factors in the area.

State income tax rate: 1.0% to 7.0%

State sales tax rate: 6.5%

Local income tax rate: None

Local sales tax rate: 3.25%

Property tax rate: 52.5 mills (2013)

Economic Information: Fort Smith Regional Chamber of Commerce, 612 Garrison Avenue, Fort Smith, AR 72901; telephone (479) 783-3111

■ Education and Research

Elementary and Secondary Schools

Public schools in Fort Smith are operated by Fort Smith Public Schools (FSPS). The district included 26 schools as of 2013, with 2 high schools, 4 junior high schools, 19 elementary schools, and 1 alternative learning center. The student population increased in the 2000s, with the most marked growth in non-English speaking and economically disadvantaged students. American College Test (ACT) scores of seniors in the district during the 2012–13 school year ranked above both state and national averages. Additionally, forty-four percent of Advanced Placement students received passing grades on year-end tests, exceeding the state average of thirty-four percent.

Art and music courses are well-supported in the district; piano keyboard labs, funded through the American Recovery and Reinvestment Act of 2009, were added in every elementary school for the start of the 2010–11 academic year. Other facilities in the district include an adult education center, a parent resource center, and a professional development and technology center.

Preschool, Head Start, and specialized programs are offered privately or through religious institutions.

Immaculate Conception Catholic School in Fort Smith was named a National Blue Ribbon School in 2013.

The following is a summary of data regarding the Fort Smith Public Schools.

Total enrollment: 14,107

Number of facilities

> total: 26
> elementary schools: 19
> junior high schools: 4
> high schools: 2
> other: 1

Student/teacher ratio: 15.5:1

Teacher salaries

> average (statewide): $47,700

Funding per pupil: $9,385

Public Schools Information: Fort Smith Public Schools, PO Box 1948, 3205 Jenny Lind, Fort Smith, AR 72902-1948; telephone (479) 785-2501.

Colleges and Universities

Institutions of higher education in Fort Smith offer a full array of academic opportunities including associate degrees, bachelor degrees, and master's degrees. The University of Arkansas–Fort Smith (UAFS) anchors the city's institutions of higher learning, supplemented by satellite campuses of John Brown University and Webster University. UAFS had an enrollment of 7,336 in 2013, with an anticipated increase to 9,000 students within twenty years. UAFS offers a range of educational degree programs, including technical certifications, certificates of proficiency, associate degrees, bachelor degrees in more than forty fields, and master's degrees. The university also has undertaken a push to grow on-campus residency, which increased from zero to thirteen percent between 2005 and 2013. While the university has navigated the limitations of its existing infrastructure, it also has supported renovations to make the campus more pedestrian and cyclist friendly, and boasts exceptional facilities such as the Baldor Technology Center and Pendergraft Health Sciences Center.

John Brown University (JBU), a private Christian institution, maintains an educational outreach center in Fort Smith. The center offers a bachelor's degree in organizational management through its Degree Completion Program. It also provides access to online degree programs for business administration and liberal arts.

Webster University has played a unique role in the local community. The school originally provided graduate-level classes to military personnel through the Joint Readiness Training Center associated with Fort Chaffee. In 2005 Webster University's campus moved to downtown Fort Smith. It offers master's degree programming in Human Resource Management and Business Administration locally, with additional advanced degree programs available online.

Libraries and Research Centers

Having the University of Arkansas–Fort Smith as a community partner allows Fort Smith residents to take advantage of its Boreham Library, with access to thousands of books, periodicals and databases; the Health Sciences program at UAFS also maintains a specialized library that benefits not only its students but residents working in the health-care sector.

The Fort Smith Public Libraries system is comprised of one main library and three branch libraries. The library hosts a specialized section for genealogical research. A law library is available at the Sebastian County Courthouse facility in Fort Smith. The Fort Smith Historical Society produces a journal and maintains archives of historical information regarding the city and its environs.

Public Library Information: Fort Smith Public Library, 3201 Rogers Avenue, Fort Smith, AR 72903; telephone (479) 783-0229.

■ Health Care

The greater metropolitan area that includes Fort Smith is served by a number of hospitals and clinics, with outpatient and specialty services provided by hundreds of organizations and individuals in private practice. The primary provider of health-care services locally is Sparks Regional Medical Center, established in Arkansas in 1887 by a local clergyman as St. John's Hospital. In the modern era, Sparks offers a range of outpatient and inpatient services, from preventive programs for diabetes and heart disease to rehabilitation for post-operative patients. The hospital's oncology unit is supported by a local cancer-care house for the comfort and convenience of cancer patients and their families. Sparks was designated a Level III Trauma Center by the Arkansas Department of Health in 2012; it opened a new ten-room surgical facility that same year.

Mercy Medical Center, an affiliate of the Sisters of Mercy health-care network, has served the Fort Smith community since 1905, providing acute care medical intervention to the metropolitan area. The 373-bed Fort Smith campus is one of more than 32 hospitals in the network that spans Arkansas, Missouri, Oklahoma, and Kansas. Specialties of the medical center include the Hembree Cancer Center, a neonatal intensive care unit, an ambulatory surgery center, and an inpatient hospice unit. Valley Behavioral Health System, formerly part of the Mercy system, acts as a stand-alone not-for-profit behavioral health provider of inpatient and outpatient services to adults, adolescents, and children.

Since 1974 Fort Smith's Area Health Education Center has served both as a local clinic and a family practice residency program. Its mission, supported by the Fort Smith Chamber of Commerce, is to improve supply and distribution of health-care professionals in Arkansas. The center has trained more than 170 family practice physicians, with a majority continuing to practice in the state.

■ Recreation

Sightseeing

The best way to get to know the city is to begin at the Fort Smith National Historical Site on the grounds of the old military installation. Here visitors can trace the history of the area from Wild West fort to "Trail of Tears" way station, to frontier justice courtroom. Fort Smith then continued its transformation, becoming a World War II relocation facility and later a refugee camp. In 1961 it became a National Historical Site and has been integrated into the modern city. Located at Fourth Street and Garrison Avenue, the urban park consists of maintained trails that lead guests past and through the remains of the two forts, a reconstruction of Judge Parker's infamous gallows, and a portion of the "Trail of Tears" along the Arkansas River. The Visitor Center at the Historical Site features displays that reflect on the fort's history from 1817 to 1871. The "Living the Legacy" educational program is a curriculum designed for grades two through five to make history come alive. The nearby Fort Smith Museum of History makes a convenient and logical follow-up stop.

The history tour of Fort Smith continues in the downtown area with the Belle Grove Historic District, a 22-square-block area added to the National Register of Historic Places in the early 1970s. Within the vicinity of Fifth, North H, Eighth, and North C streets are nearly 25 houses, some 130 years old, that have been restored along with the brick-paved streets. Architectural styles range from Romanesque, to Eastlake Victorian Renaissance, to Gothic Revival. The area contains a number of notable residences such as the Darby House, the Vaughn-Schaap House, and the Clayton House. No visit to downtown Fort Smith would be complete without a stop at Miss Laura's Visitor Center, allegedly the first former house of prostitution listed on the National Register of Historic Places. From there it's a short distance to The Hangman's House, the former residence of George Maledon, who carried out executions for Judge Isaac Parker for a number of years.

Tourists interested in transportation will enjoy the Fort Smith Trolley Museum, located downtown. The museum offers travelers who enjoy a leisurely pace the opportunity to tour the city on a restored 1926 trolley that makes a circuit from Garrison Street to the Fort Smith National Cemetery. On its route, the trolley stops at the Trolley Museum, which contains transportation-related artifacts.

The U.S. National Cemetery in Fort Smith, served by the trolley and within walking distance of downtown, provides its own silent commentary on the history of Fort Smith, with 10,000 gravesites dating from the establishment of the original fort. Confederate and Union soldiers both rest at the site, which was added to the National Register of Historic Places in 1999. Visitors can view the repositories of men hung at the order of Judge Isaac Parker as well as the grave of the infamous judge himself. Judge Parker's hanging legacy continues at the Oak Cemetery, which is also the final resting place of a number of deputy U.S. Marshals who worked with the judge.

In 2006 a family-friendly "retro" amusement park, West End Park, was created. This art deco attraction features a vintage carousel and Ferris wheel, as well as an antique railcar and classic double-decker bus. Evidencing the growing popularity of the park, the Ferris wheel set a city record for riders during festivities on July 4, 2013.

Fort Smith was set to open the U.S. Marshals Museum by 2016; the cornerstone of the 50,000-square-foot facility was placed in 2013. With 10,000 square feet of historical artifacts, the U.S. Marshals Museum is designed to evoke the past, present, and future roles of the nation's oldest federal law enforcement agency.

Arts and Culture

In January 2013 the Fort Smith Regional Art Museum opened on Rogers Avenue, in downtown Fort Smith. Previously, the Fort Smith Art Center, housed in the Vaughn-Schaap House in the Belle Grove Historic District, had served as the city's primary center for visual arts. Displays inside the Fort Smith Art Center included a permanent contemporary art show featuring local artists and monthly exhibits in a variety of media featuring local and national artists. The new Fort Smith Regional Art Museum was made possible in part by the donation of a 16,000-square-foot building from Arvest Bank in 2009. The Fort Smith Regional Art Museum retains the focus on local artists and offers receptions, lectures, and artist-led workshops in addition to its exhibitions.

Founded in 1979, the Western Arkansas Ballet Company not only offers lavish productions of well-known ballets but also operates a ballet academy. The Lorraine Cranford Summer Dance Workshop, named for the founder of Ballet Arkansas, began offering a week-long ballet camp featuring nationally known instructors in 2011. Productions often are performed in conjunction with performing arts departments of the Fort Smith Public Schools system or the University of Arkansas–Fort Smith. The Fort Smith Symphony is the city's professional orchestra, performing classical and popular music throughout the region since 1923.

Theater fans can take in a performance of "The Medicine Show on Hanging Day" at Miss Laura's Visitor Center, featuring Miss Laura and Hanging Judge Parker as characters. A more mainstream option might be provided by the all-volunteer Fort Smith Little Theater, which debuted in 1947 and is Arkansas's oldest continuously operating community theater. The players produce and perform an eclectic assortment of comedies, dramas, and musicals year-round.

The University of Arkansas at Fort Smith hosts a variety of cultural events throughout the year, including performances of vocal and instrumental music, operas, and plays.

Festivals and Holidays

Each May, Memorial Day weekend kicks off in Fort Smith with a Professional Rodeo Cowboys Association (PRCA) Rodeo parade that leads up to the Old Fort Days Rodeo and Barrel-Racing Futurity. Rated as one of the best rodeo events in the country, the competition runs for several weeks in May and provides a large pay-off for entrants in the Wild West contests. The Arkansas-Oklahoma State Fair in late September offers a similar flavor of down-home fun seasoned with history.

Another eclectic offering is the Riverfront Blues Festival, where for two days soulful music can be heard wafting over the Arkansas River. The Riverfront Blues Festival was named to the American Bus Association's "Top 100 Events in North America" list for 2014. Fort Smith's Festival on the Border began in 2011 and features musical performances to raise money for local and national charities.

Sports for the Spectator

University of Arkansas–Fort Smith athletic teams compete at the NCAA Division II level as part of the Heartland Conference. The athletic department houses a baseball team, a women's volleyball team, and men and women's squads for cross country, golf, and tennis.

Sports for the Participant

The Arkansas River is fed by smaller tributaries ideal for canoeing, kayaking, and whitewater rafting. Enthusiasts recommend the Mulberry River, the White River, Lee Creek, the Fourche River, and the slightly more distant Buffalo River. Abundant water in rivers and lakes makes the Fort Smith area an angler's paradise; top spots for fishing include the rivers, Lake Fort Smith, Blue Mountain Lake, Lake Shepherd Springs and a wealth of small bayous known only to locals.

Fort Smith is close enough for a day-trip to a variety of state parks with extensive trail systems. After a scenic drive south from Fort Smith, Queen Wilhelmina State Park offers a selection of trails with a variety of difficulty ratings. Nearby Blue Lake Mountain Trail is a beautiful and easy hike for trekkers of any ability. On Highway 10 to the east of Fort Smith, the Mount Magazine Trail is a bit more challenging with a payoff of breathtaking views. Mount Magazine State Park also offers more than 100 rock climbing routes that range from easy to a class 5.10 difficulty rating. The state parks include camping accommodations, as do the national forests in the Arkansas River Valley; the Ozark and Ouachita Mountain ranges are close enough for driving tours, overnight, or multi-day camping outings.

With more than 200 days of sunshine and temperate weather throughout much of the year, Fort Smith's golf courses are always open for business. The public course at Ben Geren Park has 27 holes, and there is a public 18-hole course at the Fort Smith Country Club, in operation since 1904. Other public courses in Fort Smith or nearby include The Links of Fort Smith (9 holes), Deer Trails Golf Course in Barling (9 holes), Vache-Grasse Course in Greenwood (18 holes), and Cedars Country Club in Van Buren (9 holes).

Shopping and Dining

The Historic Belle Grove District in downtown Fort Smith is home to specialty and antique stores, and is a central location for souvenir shopping. Central Mall Fort Smith houses stores selling a wide variety of wares including shoes, jewelry, clothing, books, cards, and foods. The newly constructed Fort Smith Pavilion, which was still adding merchants in 2013, includes more than twenty major retail businesses offering a variety of products.

Fort Smith visitors and residents can choose from more than 225 restaurants featuring a broad selection of ethnicities and tastes. Southern food and barbecue joints hold down a corner of the market, with more global fare represented by a menu of Mexican, Italian, Chinese and Thai eateries. Dining in Fort Smith covers all bases, from drive-through chain restaurants, to eat-with-your-fingers rib shacks, to fine bistro victuals. Lattes, espressos, mochas, and the occasional plain black coffee are served at local coffee shops and some restaurants.

Visitor Information: Fort Smith Convention & Visitors Bureau, 2 North B, Fort Smith, AR 72901; telephone (800) 637-1477 or (479)783-8888

■ Convention Facilities

Central to the Belle Grove Historic District, the U.S. National Cemetery, the Riverfront Park, and other downtown attractions is the Fort Smith Convention Center. The facility was completed in 2001 and features 40,000 feet of open space that can be subdivided, eight conference rooms, theater-style seating for up to 4,800 people, banquet-style seating for 2,100 people, room for 231 exhibit booths, and a performing arts theater that can seat an audience of up to 1,331 people.

Slightly north and east of the downtown Fort Smith area is Kay Rodgers Park, which hosts the annual Arkansas-Oklahoma State Fair and the Old Fort Rodeo and Barrel Racing Futurity. Kay Rodgers Park is home to the Expo Center, with 24,000 feet of meeting and exhibition space, Harper Stadium, and Hardin Arena. Harper Stadium is a covered open-air stadium that can seat 7,000–14,000 attendees for a variety of events. The smaller Hardin Arena includes space for as many as 345 barn stalls. Plentiful parking accommodates RVs and smaller vehicles.

Meeting rooms and pavilions can be reserved through the Parks and Recreation Commission of the City of Fort Smith.

■ Transportation

Approaching the City

The Fort Smith Regional Airport is located just south of the city limits and is served by American and Delta Airlines. In 2002 the airport completed a new terminal complex with improved accommodations for waiting passengers at a cost of $12.8 million, half of which came from federal funds. This effort was followed in 2005 by the opening of two new jet bridges that allow passengers to avoid inclement weather when boarding planes.

Vehicle traffic enters and exits Fort Smith via a network of roads, including Interstates 40 and 540, State Highway 22, and U.S. Highways 71 and 64. Razorback Cab service provides ground transportation; the airport also is served by several rental car companies. The 188th Fighter Wing of the Arkansas Air National Guard, Federal Express, TAC Air, and the Fort Smith Flying Club are other tenants of the airport.

Traveling in the City

Streets in the downtown area of Fort Smith are laid out in a grid pattern with somewhat of a northeastern orientation. U.S. Highways 64 and 71 and State Highway 22 intersect in the heart of Fort Smith, while Interstate 540 provides a bypass around the downtown area. The extension of Interstate 49 through Chaffee Crossing and southward to U.S. Highway 71 neared completion in late 2013. The Fort Smith Transit Department provides daytime and nighttime bus service to most parts of the city, and specialized services are available for community members and visitors with disabilities. The Fort Smith Trolley offers limited transportation between some downtown attractions.

■ Communications

Newspapers and Magazines

Fort Smith's local daily paper, the *Times Record*, is circulated throughout the Fort Smith metropolitan area and Sebastian County, and is owned by Stephens Media. A monthly magazine detailing local events, *Entertainment Fort Smith*, also is published locally. (It publishes a combined December-January issue.) *The Hispanos Unidos* is the city's local Hispanic newspaper. It is the main publication for the Spanish-language community in Fort Smith and northwest Arkansas.

Television and Radio

Fort Smith is served by television stations representing the major networks. Eight AM and ten FM radio stations broadcast in the Fort Smith metro area, running the gamut from alternative rock to talk radio.

Media Information: Times Record, 3600 Wheeler Avenue, Fort Smith, AR 72901; telephone (479) 785-7700

Fort Smith Online

City of Fort Smith. Available www.fortsmithar.gov
Fort Smith Convention and Visitors Bureau. Available www.fortsmith.org
Fort Smith National Historical Site. Available www.nps.gov/fosm
Fort Smith Public Library. Available www.fortsmithlibrary.org
Fort Smith Public Schools. Available www.fortsmithschools.org
Fort Smith Regional Chamber of Commerce. Available www.fschamber.com
Times Record. Available www.swtimes.com
The City Wire. Available www.thecitywire.com
Western Arkansas Planning and Development District. Available www.wapdd.org

BIBLIOGRAPHY

Bears, Edwin C. and Arrell M. Gibson, *Fort Smith: Little Gibraltar on the Arkansas, Second Edition* (University of Oklahoma Press, 1979)

Marr, Ron W. *Explorer's Guide Ozarks Including Branson, Springfield & Northwest Arkansas.* (Woodstock, VT: Countrymen Press, 2012)

Little Rock

■ The City in Brief

Founded: 1820 (incorporated 1835)

Head Official: Mayor Mark Stodola (since 2007; current term expires 2015)

City Population
    1990: 175,727
    2000: 183,133
    2010: 193,524
    2012 estimate: 196,530
    Percent change, 2000–2010: 5.7%
    U.S. rank in 1990: 96th (State rank: 1st)
    U.S. rank in 2000: 128th (State rank: 1st)
    U.S. rank in 2010: 117th (State rank: 1st)

Metropolitan Statistical Area Population
    2000: 583,845
    2010: 699,757
    2012 estimate: 715,210
    Percent change, 2000–2010: 19.9%
    U.S. rank in 2000: 77th
    U.S. rank in 2010: 74th

Area: 116 square miles

Elevation: Ranges from 300 feet to 630 feet above sea level

Average Annual Temperatures: January, 40° F; July, 82° F annual average 62° F

Average Annual Precipitation: 45.4 inches of rain; 5.1 inches of snow

Major Economic Sectors: government, health care, education, advanced manufacturing, services, trade and transportation

Unemployment Rate: 6.2% (2012)

Per Capita Income: $28,152

2012 FBI Crime Index Property: 15,804

Major Colleges and Universities: University of Arkansas at Little Rock, Philander Smith College, Arkansas Baptist College

Daily Newspaper: *Arkansas Democrat-Gazette*

■ Introduction

Located in the geographic center of Arkansas, Little Rock is also the state's undisputed historic, cultural, and economic hub. The capital since 1821 (when Arkansas was still just a territory) and the seat of Pulaski County, the largest city in Arkansas now acts as a key link between markets in the southwest and the southeast. The network of federal and state highways that pass through or near the city have brought it within 500 miles of ten major economic centers, and business and government leaders have worked to take advantage of this situation by bolstering the area's industrial base, expanding port facilities, and encouraging financial institutions to establish offices.

In other ways, too, Little Rock serves as a bridge between the "Old South" and the "New South." Nicknamed "The City of Roses" for its many gardens, Little Rock combines an old-fashioned, small-town ambiance with a modern dynamism that often turns to Dallas or Houston for inspiration. Historic sites documenting more than 150 years of Arkansas life are carefully preserved next to sparkling new skyscrapers. Little Rock is a city that honors its past while welcoming the future.

■ Geography and Climate

Centrally located on the Arkansas River on the dividing line between the Ouachita Mountains to the west and the flat lowlands of the Mississippi River valley to the east, Little Rock experiences all air mass types common to North America. Winters are mild, but periods of cold weather can

occur when arctic air moves in from the north. The city's proximity to the Gulf of Mexico results in summers that are often hot and humid. Precipitation is evenly distributed throughout the year, with the heaviest rain falling during the winter and early spring. Snowfall is almost nonexistent, but freezing rain is a possibility when cold air flow from the north meets up with the moist Gulf air.

Area: 116 square miles

Elevation: Ranges from 300 feet to 630 feet above sea level

Average Temperatures: January, 40° F; July, 82° F annual average 62° F

Average Annual Precipitation: 45.4 inches of rain; 5.1 inches of snow

■ History

Little Rock Named Territorial Capitol

The earliest inhabitants of the area that is now Little Rock were Stone Age people who—despite their lack of sophisticated tools, wagons, and domesticated animals—constructed huge earthen mounds that are still in existence. (Some of the most significant ones in the state are located just a short distance down the Arkansas River from Little Rock.) Used as public meeting places, living quarters, and burial chambers, these mounds have yielded numerous examples of pottery and other artifacts. Historians believe that the mound-builders' culture eventually was absorbed into that of more advanced and aggressive invaders.

In 1541, when Spain's Hernando de Soto became the first European to explore the territory, he and his party encountered a group of Indians who called themselves Quapaws or "downstream" people, a reference to the fact that they had migrated down the Mississippi River from Sioux lands in Missouri. It was estimated that approximately 7,000 Quapaws were then scattered throughout the region; by the time the French explorer René Robert Cavelier de La Salle claimed it as part of the Louisiana Territory in 1682, this number had dwindled to about 1,300 people, primarily due to disease and war.

The naming of Little Rock is said to have occurred in 1722 when another French explorer, Bernard de la Harpe, was leading a party up the Arkansas River from New Orleans and came upon two rock outcroppings, one large, one small, on opposite sides of the river. Local Indians had long used both rocks as landmarks; de la

Harpe presumably decided on the name "little rock" as a means of distinguishing the smaller outcropping from the larger bluff upstream, which he christened "French Rock."

Throughout the years when control of the region alternated between the Spanish and the French, few permanent settlements were established. Thus, at the time of the Louisiana Purchase in 1803, Arkansas was virtually uninhabited. Once the territory became part of the United States, however, increasing numbers of Americans were willing to move west of the Mississippi. The first white settler near the "little rock" is believed to have been William Lewis, a hunter. In July 1812 he built a small hut and planted a few pumpkin seeds so that he could file a homestead claim. In 1819 a land speculator from St. Louis named William Russell bought Lewis' claim, and by May 1820, he had staked out a town site. Later that same year, members of a rival faction laid out a second town site that they named Arkopolis. In 1821 Russell's Little Rock settlement was chosen as the capital of Arkansas Territory. When tensions between the two opposing groups touched off fears that the capital would be moved elsewhere, the speculators resolved their differences amicably, and the site was authoritatively named Little Rock.

Civil War Divides Citizens

Little Rock grew rather slowly after that, though it remained a boisterous frontier village for many years; it was officially chartered in 1831 and reincorporated in 1835. The 1830s also marked the beginning of cotton cultivation on a major scale, and it soon became the area's chief cash crop. Little Rock saw its importance as a distribution center increase as southbound steamboats loaded with cotton bales passed northbound boats carrying clothing, tools, and molasses from New Orleans.

A slave state with a large rural population of small farmers, Arkansas was drawn into national politics when it seceded from the Union in 1861 and began serving as a supply center for the Confederate Army. The state's sympathies were not entirely with the South, however; many citizens opposed secession, particularly those in the northern counties. When Little Rock was captured in 1863 and made headquarters for Union troops, the occupation was exceptional in its orderliness and cordiality.

Conservatives Rule for a Century

The postwar Reconstruction period in Arkansas was marked by financial ruin and political upheaval. Attempts to create a northern-style industrial economy failed, largely because the demands placed on the agrarian society were too great. Furthermore, disagreements between Republican liberals (who controlled the state government through a system of executive patronage) and mostly Democratic conservatives crippled efforts to

establish a more progressive regime. The conflict came to a head in 1874 with the so-called Brooks-Baxter War, when two rival politicians claimed the governorship of Arkansas. A legal battle ensued, and eventually the state constitution was rewritten to impose severe limits on the chief executive's power. Arkansas then entered a phase of conservative rule that endured for nearly a century.

After the turmoil of the Reconstruction period ended, Little Rock slowly began to broaden its economic base, especially in the areas of commerce and industry. The 1880s saw a great expansion in the state's railroad system, and the city's population soared to 25,874 people by 1890 (up from 12,000 people in 1870). During World War I, Little Rock became an army induction and training center with the opening of nearby Camp Pike, which was reactivated (as Camp Robinson) during World War II and again provided an influx of money and jobs in Little Rock.

In 1957 world attention was drawn to the Arkansas capital when Governor Orval E. Faubus and the Arkansas National Guard forcibly tried to prevent the integration of Little Rock Central High School. President Dwight D. Eisenhower responded by sending U.S. troops to the city with orders to enforce the integration and protect students. The incident left its mark, however; business and industrial developers were reluctant to locate to an area linked so closely in the public's mind with racism and segregation.

The 1960s brought sweeping changes to the South, and Little Rock for the most part abandoned the attitudes of the "Old South" to embrace a lifestyle compatible with that of the Sunbelt. The area's good climate and abundance of water and energy made it attractive to industry, and the 1970s and 1980s saw it recover some of the ground it lost in earlier years, as evidenced by employment and industrial growth.

Continued Growth of a Presidential City

The election of progressive Arkansas governor Bill Clinton to the U.S. presidency in 1992 placed a new focus on the city. The nation began associating Little Rock with the birthplace of its president rather than a center of racial strife. President Clinton facilitated this new focus, accepting the presidency on the steps of the Old State House in 1992 and celebrating his reelection in 1996 on its balcony. Even after his terms expired, Clinton continued the momentum of this presidential connection. In 2004 the William J. Clinton Presidential Center opened its doors, drawing the spotlight of national and international attention and tourism to Little Rock for years to come.

Into the 2010s, Little Rock focused on revamping its infrastructure, while continuing to attract new businesses. City-led projects demolished more than 100 unused houses and buildings in 2012 to make way for new development. Other initiatives sought to improve streets and street drainage. The city also aimed to hire dozens more police officers and firefighters to patrol and protect its growing population, while improving existing police and fire stations.

Historical Information: Arkansas History Commission, 1 Capitol Mall, Little Rock, AR 72201; telephone (501) 682-6900.

■ Population Profile

Metropolitan Statistical Area Population

1990: 513,026
2000: 583,845
2012 estimate: 715,210
Percent change, 2000–2010: 19.9%
U.S. rank in 2000: 77th
U.S. rank in 2010: 74th

City Residents

1990: 175,727
2000: 183,133
2010: 193,524
2012 estimate: 196,530
Percent change, 2000–2010: 5.7%
U.S. rank in 1990: 96th (State rank: 1st)
U.S. rank in 2000: 128th (State rank: 1st)
U.S. rank in 2010: 117th (State rank: 1st)

Density: 1,623.5 people per square mile

Racial and ethnic characteristics

White: 103,201
Black or African American: 82,170
American Indian and Alaskan Native: 1,036
Asian: 7,063
Native Hawaiian and Other Pacific Islander: 0
Hispanic or Latino (may be of any race): 12,854
Other: 3,060

Percent of residents born in state: 69.4%

Age characteristics

Population under 5 years old: 13,160
Population 5 to 9 years old: 11,969
Population 10 to 14 years old: 10,090
Population 15 to 19 years old: 13,403
Population 20 to 24 years old: 16,507
Population 25 to 34 years old: 29,334
Population 35 to 44 years old: 26,872
Population 45 to 54 years old: 25,369
Population 55 to 59 years old: 12,691
Population 60 to 64 years old: 12,172
Population 65 to 74 years old: 13,641
Population 75 to 84 years old: 7,283
Population 85 years and over: 4,039
Median age: 36.6

Births (2010–11 Metropolitan Area)

Total number: 9,610

Deaths (2010–11 Metropolitan Area)

Total number: 5,719

Money income (2012)

Per capita income: $28,152
Median household income: $45,267
Total households: 79,047

Number of households with income of . . .

less than $10,000: 8,534
$10,000 to $14,999: 4,748
$15,000 to $24,999: 10,620
$25,000 to $34,999: 8,771
$35,000 to $49,999: 9,947
$50,000 to $74,999: 12,974
$75,000 to $99,999: 8,273
$100,000 to $149,999: 8,113
$150,000 to $199,999: 3,623
$200,000 or more: 3,444

Percent of families below poverty level: 18.7%

FBI Crime Index Property: 15,804

FBI Crime Index Violent: 2,579

■ Municipal Government

Little Rock operates under a council and city manager form of government. In 2007 the mayor's position became full-time and was granted veto power, growing mayoral power but retaining the city manager position. A ten-member board of directors, elected on a non-partisan basis for staggered four-year terms, employs the manager to supervise daily operations of the city. Three board members are elected at-large, while the other seven represent each of the wards.

Head Official: Mayor Mark Stodola (since 2007; current term expires 2015); City Manager Bruce Moore

Total Number of City Employees: 2,423 (2012)

City Information: Little Rock City Government, 500 West Markham Street, Little Rock, AR 72201; telephone (501) 371-4510.

■ Economy

Major Industries and Commercial Activity

Little Rock is the state capital, the seat of Pulaski County, and home to a major U.S. Air Force base and U.S. National Guard training center. As a result, local, state, and federal government jobs are the undeniable anchor of the city's economy. However, revitalization of Little Rock has fueled its attraction of major corporations in more diverse industries, particularly advanced manufacturing and services. For example, Denmark-based company LM Wind Power manufactures wind blades in its Little Rock facility. Dassault Aircraft Services–Little Rock (a French company) supports a major completion center where Falcon jets are fitted with optional avionics and customized features as ordered by customers. Welspun Tubular LLC produces spiral-welded pipes for the oil and gas industry at its facility adjacent to Little Rock Port.

Skippy, the world's second most popular brand of peanut butter, is manufactured by Hormel Foods at its plant in Little Rock. Sage V Foods produces frozen and instant rice at its Little Rock Facility. Little Rock is the home base for several national and multinational companies and organizations. Two major communication companies—Allied Wireless Communications Corporation and the Fortune 500 Windstream Corporation—are headquartered in Little Rock. Dillard's, also a Fortune 500 based in Little Rock, is one of the city's top employers.

Because of its strategic location, Little Rock has long served as a center for trade. The Little Rock Port Industrial Park offers some of the finest facilities on the Arkansas River, enabling the city to promote itself not only as a distribution center for the state's agricultural products, but also for its increasing number of manufactured goods.

Finally, Little Rock has emerged as a major center for global nonprofit organizations. In addition to medical centers, the William J. Clinton Foundation, Heifer International, Winrock International, World Services for the Blind, and EAST Initiative are among the many nonprofits that make this city home.

In 2013 Little Rock ranked among the top-forty Best Places for Business and Careers according to *Forbes* magazine.

Items and goods produced: Peanut butter, rice, windmill blades, ceramic proppants, steel pipes, aircraft

Incentive Programs-New and Existing Companies

Local programs: The Little Rock Regional Chamber of commerce has a variety of programs to assist in business development and retention efforts. In partnership with the city government, the chamber conducts cost-benefit analyses and helps tailor incentive packages to specific industries. The Metro Little Rock Alliance represents a coalition of twelve counties in the greater Little Rock region and works to attract new businesses in several targeted industries, including biotechnology, aerospace, financial services, health care, non-profits, and manufacturing.

State programs: The Arkansas Economic Development Commission (AEDC) offers a variety of tax incentives for the development of new businesses and expansion of existing businesses throughout the state. These include incentives in the categories of job creation, targeted businesses, research and development, non-profits, and tourism development.

The Arkansas Science and Technology Authority (ASTA) promotes scientific research, technology development, and business innovation in the state. To this end, it provides financial support for the transfer and development of innovative technology to an enterprise based in Arkansas. The authority offers a number of programs, including the Technology Transfer Assistance Grant Program, the Seed Capital Investment Program, the Technology Development Program, and the Centers for Applied Technology Program. Various tax credits and tax incentives are offered for businesses participating in qualified research and development programs.

A number of state-sponsored funding sources are available to qualified employers through the AEDC, ASTA, and the Arkansas Development Finance Authority (ADFA). These include the Arkansas Capital Access Program, the Venture Capital Investment Fund, ASTA Investment Fund, and industrial revenue bonds.

There are several special industrial location incentives offered by the State of Arkansas, including the Arkansas Enterprise Zone Program. Many other incentives offered by the state of Arkansas include corporate income tax credits, sales and use tax refunds, and the payment in lieu of taxes program. Information on many of these incentives is available through the Arkansas Department of Finance and Administration.

Start-up businesses can take advantage of several incentive packages, including Advantage Arkansas (an income tax credit program), Tax Back (refunds of sales and use taxes), and InvestArk (a sales and use tax credit program). Businesses in highly competitive categories such as manufacturing, agriculture and information technology may be eligible for incentive programs such as Create Rebate (payroll rebates) and the ArkPlus income tax credit program.

The State of Arkansas additionally provides specialized incentive programs to encourage development of specific components of a business (child care facilities, customized training, recycling) or to recruit particular industries to the area (motion picture companies, tourism businesses).

Job training programs: The Business and Industry Training Program sponsored by the Arkansas Economic Development Commission designs customized training programs to meet the specific needs of particular industries. Its emphasis is threefold: recruiting workers, pre-employment training, and on-the-job training. The Existing Workforce Training Program (EWTP) provides financial assistance to companies for upgrading the skills of their existing workforce. Income tax credits are also available to companies who employ the EWTP.

Development Projects

Twelve counties, including Pulaski, united in 2003 to form the Central Arkansas Economic Development Alliance (CAEDA) to promote the region as an attractive location to new businesses. CAEDA changed its name to the Metro Little Rock Alliance in 2004 to incorporate "Little Rock" and improve the region's name recognition both nationally and internationally. The name change came as part of the adoption of the region's strategic plan. Funded by both private-sector companies and individual economic development agencies, the Metro Little Rock Alliance markets the region's workforce, low cost of doing business, central U.S. location, and transportation infrastructure.

In 2006 Heifer International dedicated a $17.5 million world headquarters in downtown Little Rock. In 2009 Caterpillar, one of the largest manufacturers of construction and mining equipment, announced a $140 million investment to locate its new North American motor grader production facility to North Little Rock. The plant began operations in June 2010, employing some 600 people.

An Internet fulfillment center for long-time employer Dillard's brought more than 300 jobs to the Little Rock area in 2011. Another thirty-five jobs were added in 2012 when All Weather Insulated announced the development of a new manufacturing facility at the Levi Strauss building in Little Rock. The facility opened in 2013 following an investment of $5.7 million.

A data analysis center for nGage Labs, base in Scottsdale, Arizona, was announced in October 2013 and was expected to provide at least thirty-five high-technology jobs. Along those lines in the public sector, the University of Arkansas at Little Rock announced the opening of the George W. Donaghey Emerging Analytics Center, which featured world-class technologies to support training in the growing industry of data analytics.

Dassault Aircraft Services–Little Rock, following the extension of its lease through 2040 at the Bill and Hillary Clinton National Airport, announced a $60 million expansion of its completion center located in Little Rock in 2013. Construction was slated to begin in 2014, with completion anticipated by 2016. The 250,000-square-foot increase in manufacturing space was to extend the company's total footprint at the facility to some 1.25 million square feet.

Partnerships with federal agencies, such as the U.S. Environmental Protection Agency and U.S. Department of Housing and Urban Development, have acquired funds for Little Rock to undertake sustainable and environmentally responsible development. Other funds for similarly green initiatives have come from state and county governments.

Economic Development Information: Little Rock Regional Chamber of Commerce, One Chamber Plaza, Little Rock, AR 72201; telephone (501) 374-2001; email chamber@littlerockchamber.com. Arkansas Economic Development Commission, 900 West Capitol Avenue, Little Rock, AR 72201; telephone 1-800-ARKANSAS.

Commercial Shipping

With its central location and accessibility to the Arkansas River, Little Rock is one of the major transportation centers of the South. The city's main asset is its port. The development of the Arkansas River into a year-round barge navigation route has meant that a city as far west as Tulsa, Oklahoma, has access to the Mississippi River, which in turn provides access to global markets through the international port at New Orleans, Louisiana. Consequently, a variety of products pass through the port, including forest products, bagged goods, steel coils and pipes, aluminum products, and such bulk products as rice, clay, bauxite, rock, fertilizer, and cement. Little Rock Port Terminal has a cargo lift capacity of 50 tons and bulk handling capacity of 200 tons per hour inbound and 350 tons per hour outbound. It also offers 157,000 square feet of warehouse space and 45,000 square feet of outside storage area.

The Little Rock Port Authority Railroad, operating on 12.2 miles of track since 1972, connects with the Union Pacific Railroad and the BNSF Railway. Each year it switches thousands of railroad cars and services a significant percentage of all cargo handled through the river terminal.

Little Rock Port Industrial Park is designated as a Foreign Trade Zone, enabling goods to be stored or processed without payment of customs duty until they are moved out of the zone and into normal domestic channels. Services in the Foreign Trade Zone are offered through a number of contract carrier barge lines, and include barge, rail, and truck terminals, as well as warehouse space and material handling equipment. Little Rock is also a U.S. Customs Port of Entry for both freight and passengers.

Dozens of franchised motor carriers in the metropolitan area provide regular service to points in each of the 48 contiguous states; ten major cities are within a day's drive. As of 2013, four carriers operated out of Little Rock Port. Air freight service, ranging from small package expediting to international freight forwarding, is readily available through ten airborne carriers based at Bill and Hillary Clinton National Airport.

Labor Force and Employment Outlook

Government accounts for a significant number of jobs in Little Rock. Little Rock Air Force Base employs about 4,500 active-duty and civilian personnel. Camp Joseph T. Robinson is the headquarters of the Arkansas National

Guard and Arkansas Air National Guard and home to the Lavern E. Weber Professional Education Center, the national training center for the Army National Guard.

Apart from the government, the leading employment industries in the Little Rock–North Little Rock–Conway area in 2012 were trade, transportation, and utilities; education and health services; and professional and business services. Within Little Rock itself, hospitals and medical service companies were among the largest employers. These include the University of Arkansas for Medical Sciences, Baptist Health, and Central Arkansas Veterans Healthcare System.

The following is a summary of data regarding the 2012 Little Rock–North Little Rock–Conway metropolitan area labor force:

Size of civilian labor force: 101,759

Number of workers employed in . . .

agriculture and mining: 257
construction: 3,046
manufacturing: 5,262
wholesale trade: 1,729
retail trade: 9,718
transportation: 3,472
information systems: 3,097
finance: 7,253
professional administration: 9,476
education and social services: 28,229
arts and leisure: 9,123
other: 4,032
public administration: 6,559

Average hourly earnings of production workers: $15.22

Unemployment rate: 6.2% (2012)

Employers

Largest employers in Pulaski County (2012) — *Number of employees*

Employer	Number of employees
University of Arkansas for Medical Sciences	8,500
Baptist Health	7,000
Little Rock Air Force Base	4,500
Acxiom	4,388
Little Rock School District	3,511
Central Arkansas Veterans Healthcare System	3,500
Entergy Arkansas	2,738
Pulaski County Special School District	2,700
AT&T	2,613
St. Vincent Health System	2,600
Arkansas Children's Hospital	2,470
City of Little Rock	2,423
Dillard's	2,400

Cost of Living

The following is a summary of data regarding several key cost of living factors in the area.

2013 ACCRA Average House Price: $274,267

2013 ACCRA Cost of Living Index: 98

State income tax rate: 1.0% to 7.0%

State sales tax rate: 6.5%

Local income tax rate: None

Local sales tax rate: 2.5%

Property tax rate: $7.01 for every $100 of assessed valuation (2013)

Economic Information: Little Rock Regional Chamber of Commerce, One Chamber Plaza, Little Rock, AR 72201; telephone (501) 374-2001; email chamber@littlerockchamber.com. Arkansas Economic Development Commission, 900 West Capitol Avenue, Little Rock, AR 72201; telephone 1-800-ARKANSAS.

■ Education and Research

Elementary and Secondary Schools

The Little Rock School District serves more than 25,000 students in 51 schools. Local schools are recognized for their multicultural diversity and high academic standards. The system adopted Common Core State Standards for the 2013–14 school year. The district's six designated magnet schools include Parkview Arts and Science Magnet High School, Mann Arts and Science Magnet Middle School, Booker Arts Magnet Elementary School, Carver Math and Science Magnet Elementary School, Gibbs Magnet Elementary School of Foreign Language and International Studies, and Williams Traditional Magnet Elementary School. In addition, eleven magnet programs are housed in traditional schools throughout the district.

A number of private and parochial schools also offer programs from pre-kindergarten through high school. These include the independent Pulaski Academy, The Cathedral School, Episcopal Collegiate School, and Lutheran High School. In addition, the city is home to two special facilities, the Arkansas School for the Blind and the Arkansas School for the Deaf.

The following is a summary of data regarding the Little Rock School District.

Total enrollment: 25,685

Number of facilities
total: 51
elementary schools: 30
junior high schools: 7
high schools: 5
other: 9

Student/teacher ratio: 14:1

Teacher salaries
average (statewide): $47,700

Funding per pupil: $12,244

Public Schools Information: Little Rock School District, 810 W. Markham Street, Little Rock, AR 72201; telephone (501) 447-1000.

Colleges and Universities

The University of Arkansas at Little Rock is by far the largest institution of higher learning in the city, enrolling more than 13,000 students. A branch of the main campus in Fayetteville, the Little Rock facility offers more than 100 programs of study. Medicine, nursing, health-related professions, and pharmacy are taught at a separate campus across town, the University of Arkansas for Medical Sciences. The university's William H. Bowen School of Law is located within walking distance from the judicial hub of downtown Little Rock. The University of Arkansas Clinton School of Public Service is also located in Little Rock.

Philander Smith College is a private four-year liberal arts college affiliated with the United Methodist Church and the United Negro College Fund. Philander Smith was founded in 1877 and was one of the Southwest's first African American colleges. Arkansas Baptist College, a historically black four-year liberal arts college founded in 1884 as the Minister's Institute, offers degrees in social sciences, business administration, theology, and liberal arts.

The Little Rock branch campus of Webster University, established in 1986, offers master's degrees in business administration, international business, business and organizational security management, management, health administration, environmental management, media communications, finance, and human resources management. The university provides special graduate-level programs for military personnel stationed at Little Rock Air Force Base. The Little Rock Center of John Brown University offers master's degrees in business and counseling.

Little Rock area residents also attend institutions in neighboring communities, including the University of Central Arkansas, Central Baptist College, Hendrix College, and Pulaski Technical College.

Libraries and Research Centers

The Central Arkansas Library System (CALS) serves Pulaski County and neighboring Perry County (with the exception of North Little Rock). Overall, there are sixteen branches within the system, including the Main Library and the Hillary Rodham Clinton Children's Library. The Richard C. Butler Center for Arkansas Studies within CALS promotes the study of Arkansas history though online resources and lesson plans for teachers. The system houses more that 850,000 volumes and has the largest research collection in the state.

Approximately two dozen special libraries also operate in Little Rock, most of them serving very specific medical or business needs. The Arkansas Arts Center/ Elizabeth Prewitt Taylor Memorial Library is a non-circulation research library that specializes in art, drama, and early American jazz.

The Ottenheimer Library at the University of Arkansas at Little Rock is the main university branch. Along with general resources for students, it contains special collections on Shakespeare and Elizabethan England (Meyer Collection); nineteenth-century literature and foreign languages (Rose Collection); and fiction, biography, philosophy, and history (Simon Collection). The D. W. Reynolds Library and Technical Center at Philander Smith College contains a special collection of African American fiction, biography and nonfiction, along with an impressive collection of museum-quality African America art.

The American Native Press Archives at the University of Arkansas at Little Rock, established in 1983 as a clearinghouse for information on American Indian and Alaska Native newspapers and periodicals, has evolved into one of the world's largest repositories of Native American expression. A joint effort of the Department of English and the Ottenheimer Library, it now archives products and materials of Native American literature, collects and documents the works of Native American writers, and constructs bibliographies of Native American writing and publishing. The archives, located in the Sequoyah National Research Center, also serve as a repository for the archives of the Native American Journalists Association and the Wordcraft Circle of Native Writers and Storytellers.

Little Rock is home to such special libraries as those operated by the Arkansas Geological Commission, the Arkansas History Commission and State Archives, and the Arkansas Supreme Court. It is also the seat of the Arkansas State Library, which serves as the information center for the state's libraries.

The William J. Clinton Presidential Library is the eleventh presidential library administered by the National Archives and Records Administration. The library archives contain 8 million pages of official records, 20 million emails, 2 million photographs, and 12,500 videotapes concerning the life and career of Bill Clinton.

The Arkansas Children's Hospital Research Institute in Little Rock conducts clinical research on a wide array of children's health concerns, including diabetes, birth defects, asthma, cancer, and childhood diseases. The Little Rock Geriatric Research, Education, and Clinical Center is affiliated with the Central Arkansas Veterans Health Care System of the U.S. Department of Veterans Affairs. While providing care to veterans, the center also conducts research on topics such as the cellular and molecular biology of aging; clinical nutrition, exercise, and metabolism in the elderly; and functional rehabilitation for the elderly.

The University of Arkansas for Medical Sciences (UAMS) is the cornerstone for medical research in Arkansas. The facility not only conducts research and development but also offers a business incubator program through UAMS BioVentures.

Public Library Information: Central Arkansas Library System, 100 Rock Street, Little Rock, AR 72201; telephone (501) 918-3000; email calsinfo@cals.org.

■ Health Care

Baptist Medical Center Little Rock is one of the largest local hospitals. The hospital houses the Bariatric Center, After Hours Pediatric Care Center, Cardiac Rehab Center, and Transplant Institute. The Hickingbotham Outpatient Center, Baptist Health Rehabilitative Institute, Baptist Health Eye Center, and Little Rock Diagnostic Clinic are located on the hospital campus.

St. Vincent's Infirmary is one of the city's oldest health-care institutions. It ranked first in Arkansas according to a *U.S. News & World Report* evaluation for 2014, with high performance in the specialty areas of cancer care, cardiology and health surgery, geriatrics, nephrology, neurology and neurosurgery, orthopedics, and urology. St. Vincent West in Little Rock is an outpatient facility housing the St. Vincent Family Clinic, St. Vincent Urgent Care, St. Vincent Sleep Disorders Center, and The Longevity Center.

The University of Arkansas for Medical Sciences is the state's only comprehensive academic health center. Founded in 1879 as a proprietary medical school by a group of eight physicians with twenty-two students, the institution is affiliated with the Arkansas Children's Hospital and the Central Arkansas Veterans Healthcare System. The hospital was ranked second in Arkansas by a 2014 *U.S. News & World Report* study, with high performance in the specialty areas of cancer care, nephrology, and urology.

Pinnacle Pointe Behavioral HealthCare is also located in Little Rock. It provides acute inpatient, outpatient, residential, and school-based treatment programs.

■ Recreation

Sightseeing

A good place to begin a tour of Little Rock is Riverfront Park, located directly on the riverfront in the center of the city. The park is the site of numerous fairs and festivals during the year, and it also offers visitors a place to relax or stroll along the promenade and read about the area's early history in an open-air pavilion. The "little rock," or *Le Petite Roche*, that gave the city its name is visible at the north end of Rock Street, adjacent to Riverfront Park.

Within walking distance of Riverfront Park is the Old State House, the original Arkansas state capitol building. This antebellum Greek Revival structure now houses a museum of Arkansas history that features changing exhibits of Victorian decorative arts and costumes, six period rooms, and items of state historical interest.

Many fine examples of antebellum and Victorian architecture are also on display in Quapaw Quarter, the oldest part of Little Rock. A number of homes have been restored and are listed in the National Register of Historic Places. The Villa Marre, a nineteenth-century Italianate Victorian home decorated with period furnishings, was featured in the television series *Designing Women* (1986–93). Visitors can drive or walk through this nine-square-mile area.

West of the downtown area is the Arkansas State Capitol, begun in 1899 and finished sixteen years later. The nation's only scaled replica of the U.S. Capitol in Washington, D.C., it is made of white limestone and marble and features a chandelier and six solid brass doors purchased from Tiffany's in New York City in 1908. South of downtown is the Governor's Mansion, a brick Georgian building completed in 1950 from materials gathered from older state properties. A double-iron filigree gate taken from the Confederate Soldiers' Home opens onto a circular drive fronting the mansion, which is surrounded by eight acres of lawn and gardens.

The Little Rock Zoo offers visitors the opportunity to observe more than 725 mammals, birds, reptiles, amphibians, and fish across more than thirty-three acres. The zoo participates in a variety of conservation efforts around the globe. In 2009 the Little Rock Zoo became one of five U.S. zoos to undertake the Language of Conservation project, which is based on a similar 2008 undertaking at New York's Central Park Zoo. The project involves the use of poetry to encourage visitors to think about wildlife conservation. Graphic installations were installed beginning in 2010.

Little Rock Central High School was designated a National Historic Site in 1998. Located at the intersection of Daisy L. Gatson Bates Drive and Park Street, the school commemorates the desegregation movement in the United States, particularly the nine African American students, known as the Little Rock Nine, who were escorted into the school by federal troops in 1957. Across the street, a visitor's center is located in a former Mobil gasoline station.

Arts and Culture

Robinson Center, located in the downtown area in Statehouse Plaza, is Little Rock's major performing arts facility. For decades, major Broadway shows, musical events, and ballets have been staged at Robinson Center. It is also the home of Ballet Arkansas, the Arkansas Symphony Orchestra, and Celebrity Attractions, a professional organization that offers a subscription season from September through May.

The Arkansas Arts Center is also an important location in the Little Rock arts scene. Based at the center is the Children's Theatre, where live performances are staged and where young people can receive theater training. The Arts Center houses six permanent galleries, a museum gift shop, and a restaurant. Classes in painting, drawing, photography, and dance are also offered.

Other theatrical organizations in Little Rock are the Arkansas Repertory Theater, known as The Rep, which brings professional shows to town from September through June; Wildwood Park for the Arts, which offers opera, cabaret, chamber performances, and festivals throughout the year; and Murry's Dinner Playhouse, presenting popular plays year-round.

Little Rock's museums and galleries offer visitors a view of Arkansas history and native crafts. The Museum of Discovery is an interactive children's museum originally established in 1927 as a museum of natural history and antiquities. Located in the River Market District's Museum Center, the museum underwent a complete renovation in 2011, closing for nine months as it transitioned fully from a collecting museum to a science center.

The Historic Arkansas Museum is the state's largest historic museum, and houses paintings, textiles, glassware, guns, furniture, jewelry, pottery, and other objects created by Arkansas artists over the past 200 years. It is located within walking distance of Riverfront Park and consists of a complex of more than a dozen antebellum buildings, some of which are on their original sites. Five homes (now museums) are of particular interest: Noland House, Woodruff House, Conway House, Hinderliter Tavern, and a log house.

The Dr. J. W. Wiggins Native American Art Collection is on display to the public at Sequoyah National Research Center. With more than 2,400 pieces, it is one of the most significant collections of contemporary Native American art. The research center also holds a collection of works by Choctaw artist Ronald Anderson, along with the Barry Lindley Collection (Inuit works),

the Jody and Mike Wahlig Collection (American Plains), and the J.T. Moncravie Osage Collection.

Other historical museums are the MacArthur Museum of Arkansas Military History; Old State House Museum of Arkansas History; and Ernie's Museum of Black Arkansans (EMOBA), the state's first African American history museum. Elsewhere in the city is the unique Esse Purse Museum, which looks at the role of women in history while noting the changing styles of this essential accessory.

The University of Arkansas at Little Rock features art galleries and a planetarium open to the public. The art galleries have changing exhibits of paintings, sculpture, graphics, arts and crafts, and photography, while the planetarium stages shows that cover astronomy, history, and science fiction.

The William J. Clinton Presidential Center and Park opened its doors in November 2004. This $165-million center is home to the William J. Clinton Presidential Library and Museum, housing millions of documents and artifacts relating to his administration. Sitting on twenty-six acres of park alongside the Arkansas River in downtown Little Rock, the center also hosts the University of Arkansas Clinton School of Public Service and offices of the Clinton Foundation.

Festivals and Holidays

Riverfest, celebrated in Riverfront Park every Memorial Day weekend, is Little Rock's biggest annual event and one of the largest music and arts festivals in the state. Attendees walk through the park, sampling ethnic foods and admiring the arts and crafts on display. There are also performances by musicians, including major stars, along with impromptu shows by jugglers, mimes, and magicians.

Also important to Little Rock is the Arkansas State Fair, held in October. Attended by 400,000 visitors, it features typical state fair events such as livestock judging and auctions, home arts competitions, rodeos, musical performances, motor sports, talent contests, and carnival rides, games, and amusements. In November the University of Arkansas at Little Rock hosts the annual International Celebration Week to promote awareness of national cultures and enhance cultural interactions among community members.

Martin Luther King, Jr., is honored every January with a parade, as is St. Patrick in March. The Quapaw Quarter Spring Tour of Historic Homes takes place each May, the same month that offers the Annual Territorial Fair at Historic Arkansas Museum, the Greek Food Festival, and the JamFest Heritage Festival at EMOBA. Music dominates the scene during June's Wildwood Festival of Music and Arts and the July 4th Pops on the River, an event of the Arkansas Symphony Orchestra. Each year the Museum of Discovery sponsors the Dino Dash and Discovery Fest. December features an annual

Christmas Frolic and Open House at the Historic Arkansas Museum.

Sports for the Spectator

The Arkansas Travelers arrived in Little Rock in 2007. The Class AA minor league team is a farm club of the Los Angeles Angels of Anaheim and plays at the Dickey-Stephens Park in North Little Rock. The University of Arkansas at Little Rock Trojans volleyball and men's and women's basketball teams play in the new state-of-the-art Jack Stephens Center. University of Arkansas at Little Rock baseball games are at Gary Hogan Field. I-30 Speedway hosts the annual Lucas Oil American Sprint Car Series.

Sports for the Participant

Located as it is on the Arkansas River, Little Rock offers anglers some of the best fishing of any city in the United States. Not far from the metropolitan area are many lakes, streams, and several state and national parks that also attract fans of sailing and other water sports. Local parks within a sixty-mile radius of Little Rock include: Petit Jean State Park, DeGray Lake Resort State Park, Lake Ouachita State Park, the Ouachita National Forest and Pinnacle Mountain State Park. The city maintains eleven major trails for hiking.

For those who prefer to stay within the city, Little Rock has more than fifty public parks and numerous recreation facilities, featuring such amenities as swimming pools, tennis courts, playgrounds, golf courses, and softball fields. Little Rock's best-known park is Riverfront Park, which boasts an amphitheater on the riverbank and an open-air pavilion as well as fountains and tree-lined walkways. War Memorial Park, one of the city's oldest, features the Little Rock Zoo, a fitness center, an 18-hole golf course, and the 53,000-seat War Memorial Stadium (football). Golfers can also tee-up at First Tee of Central Arkansas, Rabsamen Golf Course, and Hindman Park Golf Course.

Shopping and Dining

The River Market District, a $3-million development on President Clinton Avenue, offers a Farmer's Market plus restaurants and groceries in a scenic setting on the Arkansas River. The Promenade at Chenal is an open-air main street shopping district located in the Chenal Valley neighborhood. The mall features upscale shops and several restaurants. Park Plaza in Midtown has more than eighty stores.

The offerings of Little Rock's more than 300 restaurants range from down-home southern cooking (including ribs) to continental-style haute cuisine. Seafood and catfish abound at restaurants along the river, and ethnic specialties are available at a number of establishments in the metropolitan area.

Visitor Information: Little Rock Convention & Visitors Bureau, Markham and Broadway, Little Rock, AR 72201; telephone (501) 376-4781; toll-free (800) 844-4781.

■ Convention Facilities

With the development of Statehouse Plaza and its complex of meeting facilities and hotels, Little Rock has made a special effort to attract convention business. Situated along the Arkansas River, Statehouse Plaza is an eight-square-block area in downtown Little Rock that includes the Statehouse Convention Center, Robinson Center, and several major hotels, including the Peabody, Capital, and DoubleTree.

The Statehouse Convention Center features 220,000 square feet of meeting, reception, and exhibit space. The center is attached to the Little Rock Marriott Hotel, which offers additional meeting space along with more than 400 guest rooms. Down the street from the Statehouse Convention Center is the Robinson Center, which has a 14,867-square-foot exhibition hall that can hold nearly 800 people in the main room, with additional exhibition space and seating in other exhibition and meeting rooms.

The William J. Clinton Presidential Center provides 20,000 square feet of space for meeting, receptions, and other special events, with a full-service restaurant, Forty Two, onsite for catering. This center features two unique outdoor gathering spaces: The Scholars Garden and Clinton Presidential Park Bridge, the renovated Rock Island Railroad Bridge at the east end of the Arkansas River Trail.

Additional spaces for large groups are available at the Arkansas State Fairgrounds and Verizon Arena. Other area hotels and motels also provide meeting facilities for smaller groups.

Convention Information: Little Rock Convention & Visitors Bureau, Markham and Broadway, Little Rock, AR 72201; telephone (501) 376-4781; toll-free (800) 844-4781.

■ Transportation

Approaching the City

The Bill and Hillary Clinton National Airport is located within the city limits and is only three miles from downtown, thus making it one of the most convenient urban airports in the country. It is served by American Eagle, Delta, Southwest, United, US Airways, Frontier, and Allegiant. As of 2013, the airport had direct flights to thirteen U.S. cities. The airport handles about two million passengers each year and has facilities for private planes and corporate aircraft. A parking deck was added in 2001, and a $3-million renovation of the baggage claim wing was completed. Upgrades to the second level, including the concourse, were completed in the late 2000s.

For those approaching the city by car, access is made easy by the network of U.S. and state highways that intersect in the metropolitan area. Additionally, five U.S. Interstates—30, 40, 430, 440, and 630—facilitate Little Rock travelers.

Amtrak provides passenger service from Little Rock's restored Union Station to Chicago, St. Louis, Dallas, and San Antonio through its Texas Eagle service; connections to El Paso, Tucson, and Los Angeles are available. The city is also served by Greyhound and Jefferson passenger bus lines.

Traveling in the City

Little Rock is laid out in a basic grid pattern with streets numbered consecutively from the river to the edge of town. Interstates 630 and 30 bisect the city; freeway traffic is usually heavy. Bus service is provided by the municipally owned-and-operated Central Arkansas Transit (CAT). As of 2013, CAT's 59 buses operated on 22 fixed routes and 4 express routes.

Reborn after fifty-seven years, Little Rock's streetcars began rolling again in November 2004 and expanded service in 2007. Three replica vintage streetcars run along a 3.4-mile track that links major attractions between Little Rock and North Little Rock. Destinations include the Verizon Arena, the Statehouse Convention Center, River Market, Discovery Museum, Robinson Auditorium Concert Hall, Clinton Presidential Center, and Heifer International Headquarters.

■ Communications

Newspapers and Magazines

Little Rock has one major daily newspaper, the *Arkansas Democrat-Gazette,* a morning paper circulated statewide. The weekly publication *Arkansas Times* is a general lifestyle newspaper aiming to educate readers about news, politics, and entertainment in Arkansas, and *Arkansas Business* has served readers on a weekly basis since 1984. Several magazines are also based in the city;

most serve specific business, lifestyle, or religious interests.

Television and Radio

Twelve television stations broadcast from Little Rock. Twenty-one FM radio stations serve listeners in the area with a wide variety of formats, in an addition to ten AM stations.

Media Information: *Arkansas Democrat-Gazette,* 121 East Capitol Avenue, Little Rock, AR 72201; telephone (501) 378-3400.

Little Rock Online

Arkansas Democrat-Gazette. Available www. arkansasonline.com

Arkansas Department of Economic Development. Available www.arkansasedc.com

Arkansas History Commission. Available www.ark-ives.com

City of Little Rock. Available www.littlerock.org

Little Rock Convention & Visitors Bureau. Available www.littlerock.com

Little Rock Parks and Recreation. Available www. littlerock.org/parksrecreation

Little Rock Regional Chamber of Commerce. Available www.littlerockchamber.com

Little Rock School District. Available www.lrsd.org

University of Arkansas at Little Rock. Available www.ualr.edu

William J. Clinton Presidential Center. Available www.clintonpresidentialcenter.org

BIBLIOGRAPHY

Anderson, Karen, *Little Rock: Race and Resistance at Central High School* (Princeton, NJ: Princeton University Press, 2010)

Jacoway, Elizabeth, *Turn Away Thy Son: Little Rock, The Crisis That Shocked the Nation* (New York: Free Press, 2007)

Kirk, John A., *Redefining the Color Line: Black Activism in Little Rock, Arkansas, 1940–1970* (Gainesville, FL: University Press of Florida, 2002)

Rush, Kimberly Reynolds, *Historic Photos of Little Rock* (Nashville, TN: Turner Publishing Company, 2009)

Rogers

■ The City in Brief

Founded: May 1, 1881 (incorporated June 6, 1881)

Head Official: Mayor Greg Hines (since 2011)

City Population
> 1990: 24,692
> 2000: 38,829
> 2010: 55,964
> 2012 estimate: 58,895
> Percent change, 2000–2010: 44.1%
> U.S. rank in 2010: 624th

Metropolitan Statistical Area Population
> 2000: 347,045
> 2010: 463,204
> 2012 estimate: 482,013
> Percent change, 2000–2010: 33.5%
> U.S. rank in 2000: 130th
> U.S. rank in 2010: 109th

Area: 37.94 square miles

Elevation: 1,371 feet above sea level

Average Annual Temperatures: January, 35.0° F; July, 78.0° F; annual average, 57.3° F

Average Annual Precipitation: Rainfall, 40–45 inches; snowfall, 6–12 inches; annual average, 44.6 inches

Major Economic Sectors: Food-related industries, health care, retail

Unemployment Rate: 3.7% (2012)

Per Capita Income: $23,909

2012 FBI Crime Index Property: 2,091

Major Colleges and Universities: Bryan University, University of Arkansas Global Campus, John Brown University Rogers Center

Daily Newspaper: *Rogers Morning News, Arkansas-Democrat Gazette*

■ Introduction

The suburb of Rogers is part of the Fayetteville–Springdale–Rogers Metropolitan Statistical Area (MSA), which is among the fastest growing areas in the nation. Despite setbacks during a 2007–09 nationwide recession, the city of Rogers continues to grow and thrive. Public schools rank highly in national surveys, and job growth in the MSA was steady in the early 2010s. In 2011 the MSA was ranked fifth in *Forbes* Best Cities for Jobs survey. In both 2010 and 2011, Rogers ranked tenth in the *CNN Money* Best Places to Live survey in the small cities category.

■ Geography and Climate

Rogers is located in Benton County, in the Ozarks Region of northwest Arkansas. The city is about 20 miles north of Fayetteville and less than 8 miles southeast of Bentonville, the county seat. Lake Atalanta was created in 1936 by the Works Progress Administration, and Beaver Lake was created in 1966 as one of the first impoundments along the White River system of Arkansas and Missouri. Rogers enjoys warm summers and moderate winters. The greatest amount of precipitation occurs in spring, typically in May and June.

Area: 37.94 square miles

Elevation: 1,371 feet above sea level

Average Temperatures: January, 35.0° F; July, 78.0° F; annual average, 57.3° F

Average Annual Precipitation: Rainfall, 40–45 inches; snowfall, 6–12 inches; annual average, 44.6 inches

© David R. Frazier Photolibrary, Inc. / Alamy

■ History

The first settlers came to Rogers around 1830. They were primarily subsistence farmers, but tobacco soon became a major cash crop. In 1857 John Butterfield organized the Overland Mail Company and tapped Callahan's Tavern (in northeast Rogers) as a stop along the Butterfield Overland Mail Route. This brought more settlers and businesses into the area. However, the route from Tipton, Missouri, to California closed at the start of the Civil War, since it passed through Confederate territories.

Rogers gained its place on the map on May 10, 1881, when it became a stop along the St. Louis–San Francisco Railway. The town was named for Captain Charles Warrington Rogers, general manager of the railway. The town was incorporated on June 6, 1881, with about 600 residents.

Acres of apple orchards surrounded Rogers, making the town a major center for trade in apples and apple products. By the end of the 1920s, the industry had declined considerably as orchards fell prey to insects, disease, and bad weather. It was about this time that poultry production became more prominent in the local economy. From the mid-1950s to the early 2000s, the poultry industry grew steadily. In 2013 Tyson Foods and Ozark Mountain Poultry were among the top employers.

Historical Information: Rogers Historical Museum, 322 South Second Street; telephone, (479) 621-1154; email museum@rogersarkansas.com.

■ Population Profile

Metropolitan Statistical Area Population
2000: 347,045
2012 estimate: 482,013
Percent change, 2000–2010: 33.5%
U.S. rank in 2000: 130th
U.S. rank in 2010: 109th

City Residents
1990: 24,692
2000: 38,829
2010: 55,964
2012 estimate: 58,895
Percent change, 2000–2010: 44.1%
U.S. rank in 2010: 624th

Density: 1,114.8 people per square mile

Racial and ethnic characteristics
White: 48,615
Black or African American: 636

American Indian and Alaskan Native: 643
Asian: 1,562
Native Hawaiian and Other Pacific Islander: 0
Hispanic or Latino (may be of any race): 17,807
Other: 6,180

Percent of residents born in state: 35.6%

Age characteristics

Population under 5 years old: 5,449
Population 5 to 9 years old: 5,047
Population 10 to 14 years old: 4,035
Population 15 to 19 years old: 4,561
Population 20 to 24 years old: 4,185
Population 25 to 34 years old: 9,146
Population 35 to 44 years old: 7,799
Population 45 to 54 years old: 7,258
Population 55 to 59 years old: 2,398
Population 60 to 64 years old: 2,424
Population 65 to 74 years old: 2,782
Population 75 to 84 years old: 1,460
Population 85 years and over: 1,092
Median age: 31.2

Births (2010–11 Metropolitan Area)

Total number: 6,877

Deaths (2010–11 Metropolitan Area)

Total number: 3,061

Money income (2012)

Per capita income: $23,909
Median household income: $52,308
Total households: 19,280

Number of households with income of ...

less than $10,000: 1,023
$10,000 to $14,999: 1,017
$15,000 to $24,999: 1,821
$25,000 to $34,999: 1,823
$35,000 to $49,999: 3,127
$50,000 to $74,999: 4,228
$75,000 to $99,999: 2,363
$100,000 to $149,999: 2,306
$150,000 to $199,999: 755
$200,000 or more: 817

Percent of families below poverty level: 14.9%

FBI Crime Index Property: 2,091

FBI Crime Index Violent: 202

■ Municipal Government

Rogers has a mayor-council form of government. The mayor is elected to a four-year term. The eight-members of the Rogers City Council represent four city wards, with two per ward. Council members are elected to two-year terms. The council meets on the second and fourth Tuesdays of each month. A city clerk, city judge, and city attorney also are elected to four-year terms.

Head Official: Mayor Greg Hines (since 2011)

Total Number of City Employees: 350 (2013 est.)

City Information: Rogers City Hall, 301 W. Chestnut, Rogers, Arkansas 72756; telephone: (479) 621-1117.

■ Economy

Major Industries and Commercial Activity

Poultry production is one of the most important industries in Rogers. While the headquarters for Tyson Foods, Inc., is located in nearby Springdale, a poultry production plant, distribution center, and frozen foods production facility are located in Rogers. The company is one of the top employers in the city. Ozark Mountain Poultry opened in Rogers in 2000 and has become a major employer as well.

Sam Walton opened his first Wal-Mart store in Rogers on July 2, 1962. The company headquarters is in nearby Bentonville, but the claims center and retail stores located in Rogers provide a significant number of local jobs.

Other top employers in Rogers include Rogers Public Schools, Mercy Health System of NWA, Pinnacle Healthcare, Crossland Construction, and Glad Manufacturing.

Items and goods produced: poultry and frozen food products, plastic bags, cutting tools, aluminum wheels, telephone and communications equipment, airguns

Incentive Programs-New and Existing Companies

Local programs: The Small Business Council of the Rogers-Lowell Area Chamber of Commerce offers a variety of resources to help potential business owners. A Minority Business Development Program also has been launched to encourage diversity in business ownership and employment. State programs

State programs: The Arkansas Economic Development Commission (AEDC) offers a variety of tax incentives for the development of new businesses and expansion of existing businesses throughout the state. These include incentives in the categories of job creation, targeted businesses, research and development, non-profits, and tourism development.

The Arkansas Science and Technology Authority (ASTA) promotes scientific research, technology development, and business innovation in the state. To this end, it provides financial support for the transfer and development of innovative technology to an enterprise based in Arkansas. The authority offers a number of programs, including the Technology Transfer Assistance Grant Program, the Seed Capital Investment Program, the Technology Development Program, and the Centers for Applied Technology Program. Various tax credits and tax incentives are offered for businesses participating in qualified research and development programs.

A number of state-sponsored funding sources are available to qualified employers through the AEDC, ASTA, and the Arkansas Development Finance Authority (ADFA). These include the Arkansas Capital Access Program, the Venture Capital Investment Fund, ASTA Investment Fund, and industrial revenue bonds.

There are several special industrial location incentives offered by the State of Arkansas, including the Arkansas Enterprise Zone Program. Many other incentives offered by the state of Arkansas include corporate income tax credits, sales and use tax refunds, and the payment in lieu of taxes program. Information on many of these incentives is available through the Arkansas Department of Finance and Administration.

Start-up businesses can take advantage of several incentive packages, including Advantage Arkansas (an income tax credit program), Tax Back (refunds of sales and use taxes), and InvestArk (a sales and use tax credit program). Businesses in highly competitive categories such as manufacturing, agriculture and information technology may be eligible for incentive programs such as Create Rebate (payroll rebates) and the ArkPlus income tax credit program.

The State of Arkansas additionally provides specialized incentive programs to encourage development of specific components of a business (child care facilities, customized training, recycling) or to recruit particular industries to the area (motion picture companies, tourism businesses).

Job training programs: The Rogers-Lowell Area Chamber of Commerce works closely with the regional Northwest Arkansas Council and area colleges and universities to provide job training resources for local industries.

The Business and Industry Training Program sponsored by the Arkansas Economic Development Commission designs customized training programs to meet the specific needs of particular industries. Its emphasis is threefold: recruiting workers, pre-employment training, and on-the-job training.

Development Projects

Rogers partners with nearby Lowell to plan regional economic development projects through the Rogers-Lowell Area Chamber of Commerce. As part of the Vision 2025 strategic plan, Rogers officials have identified nine priority areas: local street improvements; community

appearance and beautification; parks, facilities, and green space; advancement of downtown Rogers; workforce recruitment and retention; trails, bike trails and community connectivity; proposed arena/community gathering place; engagement of emerging leadership; and public school district promotion. A major regional project will include a connection of Highway 265 from Fayetteville through Lowell to Rogers. Main Street Rogers is an independent nonprofit organization working to revitalize and promote the Downtown Rogers Historic District.

Economic Development Information: Main Street Rogers, 301 W. Chestnut St., Rogers, AR 72756; telephone: (479) 936-5487; fax (479) 631-2767. Rogers-Lowell Area Chamber of Commerce, 317 W. Walnut, Rogers, AR 72756; telephone (479) 636-1240; toll-free: (800) 364-1240; fax: (479) 636-5485; email info@rogerslowell.com.

Commercial Shipping

The Arkansas and Missouri Railroad Co. provides freight service for Northwest Arkansas. The railroad operates between Monett, Missouri, and Fort Smith, Arkansas (south of Rogers). The Kansas City Southern Railway has a north–south line that passes through Siloam Springs (southwest of Rogers).

The Port of Fort Smith is located at the confluence of the Arkansas and Poteau Rivers. This port lies on the McClellan-Kerr Arkansas River Navigation System, which accesses the Mississippi River and the Gulf of Mexico. The port is served by the Arkansas-Missouri Railroad and via Interstate 540 from Rogers. Several commercial motor carriers operate in and around Rogers.

Labor Force and Employment Outlook

The Arkansas Department of Workforce Services ranks educational services; professional, scientific, and technical services; ambulatory health care services, food services; and truck transportation as the top five growth industries for the Northwest Arkansas Workforce Investment Area through 2018, based on net growth in employment. The construction and health and education services industries are expected to show the greatest percentage of job growth through 2020.

Size of civilian labor force: 28,716

Number of workers employed in . . .

agriculture and mining: 130
construction: 1,828
manufacturing: 4,525
wholesale trade: 757
retail trade: 6,330
transportation: 1,013
information systems: 355
finance: 1,205
professional administration: 2,882

education and social services: 3,387
arts and leisure: 2,906
other: 1,169
public administration: 363

Average hourly earnings of production workers: $13.93

Unemployment rate: 3.7% (2012)

Employers

Largest employers (2013)	Number of employees
Tyson Foods, Inc.	2,398
Rogers Public Schools	1,926
Wal-Mart Stores, Inc.	1,543
Mercy Health System of NWA	1,400
Crossland Construction	700
Rogers Tool Works	700
Ozark Mountain Poultry	641
Glad Manufacturing	600
Superior Industries International	520

Cost of Living

The following is a summary of data regarding several key cost of living factors in the area.

2013 ACCRA Average House Price: $230,680

2013 ACCRA Cost of Living Index: 87

State income tax rate: 1.0% to 7.0%

State sales tax rate: 6.5%

Local income tax rate: None

Local sales tax rate: 2%

Property tax rate: 52.7 mills (2013)

■ Education and Research

Elementary and Secondary Schools

Rogers Public Schools operates 15 elementary schools, 4 middle schools, 3 high schools, and an alternative school. The district serves more than 14,000 students. In 2012 Russell D. Jones Elementary School was named a National Blue Ribbon School. Bellview Elementary School earned the same honor in 2011. Both Rogers Heritage High School and Rogers High School were recognized as Silver Medal Schools in the 2013 *U.S. News*

& World Report Best High Schools rankings. Rogers Heritage was ranked as the third best high school in Arkansas, while Rogers High was listed as seventh best in the state. Rogers New Technology High School is part of the nationwide New Tech Network that focuses on project-based learning in innovative learning environments. Private and parochial schools in Rogers include the Benton County School of the Arts (K–12), St. Vincent de Paul Catholic School (K–8), Shiloh Christian School (PK–1), and Providence Academy (K–12).

The following is a summary of data regarding Rogers Public Schools.

Total enrollment: 14,340

Number of facilities
total: 23
elementary schools: 15
junior high schools: 4
high schools: 3
other: 1

Student/teacher ratio: 16.38:1

Teacher salaries
average (statewide): $47,700

Funding per pupil: $8,412

Public Schools Information: Rogers Public Schools, 500 W. Walnut, Rogers, AR 72756; telephone (479) 636-3910; fax (479) 631-3504.

Colleges and Universities

The Adult Education Center of Northwest Arkansas Community College is located in Rogers. Bryan University offers diploma programs and associate's degrees in various fields of study. The Global Campus of the University of Arkansas has a location in Rogers offering a limited number of undergraduate courses. The John Brown University Rogers Center offers undergraduate degree completion programs in liberal arts, business administration, and organizational management. Master's degrees are offered in business administration, education, and counseling fields. The University of Phoenix Northwest Arkansas Learning Center also is located in Rogers.

Libraries and Research Centers

The Rogers Public Library (est. 1904) houses a collection of more than 140,000 books, videos, magazines, and recordings, including a growing number of e-books and audio books. Patrons may also borrow books from other local public libraries in Bentonville, Fayetteville, and Springdale. More than 50 computers with Internet access are available for the public. The Rogers Historical Museum Research Library holds about 4,000 articles, books, research manuscripts, maps, and cemetery and obituary records, along with more than 15,000 historic photographs on local topics.

Public Library Information: Rogers Public Library, 711 S. Dixieland Road, Rogers, AR 72758; telephone (479) 621-1152.

■ Health Care

Mercy Hospital Northwest Arkansas is the primary health-care facility located in Rogers. Several major health-care facilities are located nearby in Bentonville, Lowell, and Fayetteville. Mercy Hospital Northwest Arkansas is a Catholic, not-for-profit hospital that is part of the national Sisters of Mercy Health System. The main Medical Campus is a 350,000-square-foot center with 200 beds. The Mercy Physicians Plaza hosts the Mercy Heart and Vascular Center, Mercy Wellness Center, Mercy Institute of Gastroenterology, Rogers Medical Center, Mercy Women's Health, and the Mercy Sleep Center.

Health Care Information: Mercy Medical Center, 2710 Rife Medical Lane, Rogers, AR 72758; telephone (479) 338-8000.

■ Recreation

Sightseeing

Tourists can get a feel for the city by spending an afternoon Historic Downtown Rogers. Unique locally owned shops, art galleries, and restaurants are interspersed with other local businesses. The original building that housed Wal-Mart Store #1 is located at 719 W. Walnut Street, just outside of downtown Rogers.

Arts and Culture

Several art and cultural institutions are located in downtown Rogers. Admission is free at the Rogers Historical Museum. The Rogers Daisy Airgun Museum features the world's largest collection of antique airguns and honors the Daisy Manufacturing Company, based in Rogers since 1958. Theater buffs can see a production of the Rogers Little Theater group at Victory Theater in downtown Rogers.

Festivals and Holidays

From April through October, Frisco Park hosts Pickin' in the Park, free Saturday night concerts featuring local musicians. The annual Frisco Festival in August draws residents to Historic Downtown Rogers for a weekend of street dances, music, food, car shows, and other family-friendly events sponsored by local businesses. On the first Saturday of October, the city sponsors the NWA International Festival to encourage diversity by showcasing cultures from around the world. Representatives from more than 50 countries participate in the event. The annual Goblin Parade takes place in downtown Rogers every October, as young residents trick-or-treat at local businesses. The annual Rogers Christmas Parade, complete with a visit from Santa, takes place on the first Monday in December.

Sports for the Spectator

Pinnacle Country Club in Rogers hosts the annual Wal-Mart Northwest Arkansas Championship, a 54-hole tournament on the Ladies Professional Golf Association Tour. Rogers Regional Sports Center opened in 2013 to host the 32nd Annual Snowball Classic Softball Tournament (January), the oldest winter softball tournament in the central United States. The new complex features six ball fields and is expected to sponsor numerous regional tournaments in the coming years. Fans of Double-A minor league baseball can watch the Northwest Arkansas Naturals at Arvest Ballpark in nearby Springdale. Rogers residents root for the University of Arkansas Razorbacks at Donald W. Reynolds Razorback Stadium (football), Bud Walton Arena (men's and women's basketball), and Baum Stadium at George Cole Field (baseball), all in Fayetteville. Parsons Stadium in Springdale is home to the annual Rodeo of the Ozarks.

Sports for the Participant

Outdoor enthusiasts can find plenty of opportunities for hiking, fishing, boating, swimming, scuba diving, and camping at Beaver Lake, located about 10 minutes from downtown Rogers. The Hobbs State Park–Conservation Area lies on the southern shore of the lake. The city maintains 15 parks, a skateboard and splash park, 26 athletic fields, and a 22-mile greenways and trails system. Dock Wheeler Park hosts the largest softball program in the state. There are five golf courses.

Shopping and Dining

Pinnacle Hills Promenade Mall is a popular site for shopping, dining, and entertainment. Cabela's, a major retailer of hunting, fishing, and outdoor gear, opened its first Arkansas store next to the mall in 2012. The Shoppes at Pinnacle Hills, located across from the John Q. Hammons Conference Center, is another popular site for upscale shopping and dining. Both large and small national retail stores are featured at Scottsdale Center. Historic Downtown Rogers offers a variety of shopping, dining, and entertainment venues with local flair. Other major sites in Rogers include Frisco Station Mall, Tuscany Square Shopping Center, Kingston Centre, and Pleasant Crossing Center.

Visitor Information: Rogers Arkansas Convention & Visitors Bureau, 317 W. Walnut St., Rogers, Arkansas 72756; telephone (800) 364-1240; fax (479) 636-5485.

■ Convention Facilities

John Q. Hammons Convention Center is attached to the Embassy Suites Northwest Arkansas Hotel, Spa & Convention Center in Rogers. The facility offers 80,000 square feet of event space capable of hosting 42 separate events simultaneously. Conference space is also available at University of Arkansas Global Campus in Rogers.

Convention Information: Rogers Arkansas Convention & Visitors Bureau, 317 W. Walnut St., Rogers, Arkansas 72756; telephone (800) 364-1240; fax (479) 636-5485.

■ Transportation

Approaching the City

By air, the easiest route into Rogers is through the Northwest Arkansas Regional Airport (XNA) in Bentonville. Roads into and around Rogers include U.S. Route 62, U.S. Route 71, and Arkansas Highway 12. Rogers Municipal Airport–Carter Field provides services for charter flights and private planes.

Traveling in the City

Ozark regional transit has one fixed bus route that serves Rogers. NWA Taxi Cab Service also is available in the city.

■ Communications

Newspapers and Magazines

The *Rogers Morning News* and the *Arkansas-Democrat Gazette* are the primary local newspapers.

Television and Radio

Rogers residents receive broadcasts from major affiliates out of Fayetteville, Bentonville, and other neighboring cities.

Media Information: *Rogers Morning News*, 313 South 2nd Street, Rogers, AR 72756; telephone (479) 636-4411.

Rogers Online

City of Rogers. www.rogersarkansas.com
Northwest Arkansas Council. www.nwacouncil.org
Rogers Arkansas Convention & Visitors Bureau. www.visitrogersarkansas.com
Rogers-Lowell Area Chamber of Commerce. www.rogerslowell.com
Rogers/NWA Online. www.nwaonline.com/metro/rogers
Rogers Public Library. www.rogerspubliclibrary.org
Rogers Public Schools. www.rogers.schoolfusion.us

BIBLIOGRAPHY

Marr, Ron W. *Explorer's Guide Ozarks Including Branson, Springfield & Northwest Arkansas.* (Woodstock, VT: Countrymen Press, 2012)

Delaware

The State in Brief

Nickname: First State; Diamond State

Motto: Liberty and independence

Flower: Peach blossom

Bird: Blue hen chicken

Area: 2,489 square miles (2010; U.S. rank 49th)

Elevation: Ranges from sea level to 440 feet above sea level

Climate: Temperate, with mild winters and hot summers

Admitted to Union: December 7, 1787

Capital: Dover

Head Official: Jack Markell (D) (until 2017)

Population

1990: 666,000
2000: 783,600
2010: 897,934
2012 estimate: 900,131
Percent change, 2000–2010: 14.6%
U.S. rank in 2012: 45th
Percent of residents born in state: 45.5% (2012)
Density: 460.8 people per square mile (2010)
2012 FBI Crime Index Total: 35,659

Racial and Ethnic Characteristics (2012)

White: 634,259
Black or African American: 192,629
American Indian and Alaska Native: 2,877
Asian: 29,177
Native Hawaiian and Pacific Islander: 377
Hispanic or Latino (may be of any race): 73,230
Other: 40,812

Age Characteristics (2012)

Population under 5 years old: 56,062
Population 5 to 19 years old: 176,992
Percent of population 65 years and over: 14.5%
Median age: 38.7

Vital Statistics

Total number of births (2012–13): 11,286
Total number of deaths (2012–13): 8,025
AIDS cases reported through 2011: 4,337

Economy

Major industries: Chemicals, agriculture, manufacturing, business and financial services
Unemployment rate (2012): 5.4%
Per capita income (2012): $29,733
Median household income (2012): $60,119
Percentage of persons below poverty level (2012): 11.5%
Income tax rate: 2.2% to 6.95%
Sales tax rate: None

Dover

■ The City in Brief

Founded: 1683; incorporated 1829

Head Official: Mayor Carleton E. Carey, Sr. (since 2007; current term expires 2014)

City Population
  1990: 27,630
  2000: 32,135
  2010: 36,047
  2012 estimate: 36,643
  Percent change, 2000–2010: 12.2%

Metropolitan Statistical Area Population
  2000: 126,697
  2010: 162,310
  2012 estimate: 167,626
  Percent change, 2000–2010: 28.1%
  U.S. rank in 2000: 279th
  U.S. rank in 2010: 250th

Area: 22.7 square miles

Elevation: 36 feet above sea level

Average Annual Temperatures: 55° F

Average Annual Precipitation: 44.14 inches

Major Economic Sectors: foodstuffs, apparel and personal product manufacturing, other manufacturing, military

Unemployment Rate: 6.2% (2012)

Per Capita Income: $20,743

2012 FBI Crime Index Property: 2,189

Major Colleges and Universities: Delaware State University, Wilmington University

Daily Newspaper: *Delaware State News*

■ Introduction

Dover is the capital of Delaware and the seat of Kent County. The city, which dates back to the 1600s, is acclaimed for its lovely tree-lined streets, preserved town green, and impressive Georgian and Victorian architecture. Long a center of government, business, and agriculture, Dover has become a tourist mecca as visitors come to enjoy the city's historical offerings, tax-free shopping, and the excitement of slots, NASCAR racing, and harness racing that takes place at Dover Downs. The city was named after Dover in England and is the site of Dover Air Force Base.

■ Geography and Climate

Dover is located in central Delaware on the St. Jones River on the Delmarva peninsula. The river forms the Silver Lake Reservoir that lies just north of the downtown area. The city is approximately 40 miles south of Wilmington. The rather flat area has a moderate climate with four distinct seasons. Summer has many warm days with hot, humid periods and mild nights. Surface winds generally blow from the northwest except in June when southerly winds prevail. From May through September winds blow from the southwest.

Area: 22.7 square miles

Elevation: 36 feet above sea level

Average Temperatures: 55° F

Average Annual Precipitation: 44.14 inches

■ History

Dover Becomes State Capital

At the time of the arrival of the first white men, the Lenape Indians lived along the banks of the Delaware River. The land where Dover now stands was part of a much larger grant called Zwaanendael (Valley of the

Legislative building at state capitol in Dover. © *Stock Connection Blue / Alamy*

Swans), where a group of Dutch patrons attempting to colonize it were killed by the local tribe in 1631. William Penn chartered Kent County, and Penn ordered his surveyors to lay out a town in 1683. In 1697, a court house was built at the site, but it was not until 1717 that Dover was plotted around a central green. By that time, most of the Native Americans had been forced to relocate elsewhere. Craftsmen and artisans such as cabinet makers, shoemakers, carpenters, tailors, and hatters shared the green with government officials and residents, as well as several inns and taverns. An Act of Assembly in 1742 provided for the establishment of a market square, and the 1751 census estimated the population of Kent County to be 1,320 families. In 1777, Dover became the capital of Delaware, largely because it was deemed safer from attack than the old capital, New Castle. Ten years later, in a Dover tavern, a Delaware convention ratified the Federal Constitution. Because it was the first to ratify, Delaware became known as "the first state" and enjoys the highest level of seniority at ceremonial events.

From the 1720s to the 1770s the construction of many fine homes took place throughout Dover and the surrounding countryside, many of which still survive today. During the Revolutionary War, the famous Delaware militia marched to join Washington's main army. One regiment earned the nickname "The Blue Hens' Chickens" because of the spirited fighting cocks that Delaware men carried with them to war, a name which was .

In 1784 Thomas Coke and Francis Asbury, ordained ministers of the new religious movement known as Methodism, came to the area from England to serve as superintendents for the denomination in the United States. Thomas Coke was soon appointed as the first bishop of the Methodist Episcopal Church in America and the area around Dover became known as the "Cradle of Methodism in America."

The city of Dover was incorporated in 1829 and has remained one of the nation's smallest state capitals. During the eighteenth century, Kent County was an important agricultural area, providing grain, fruit, and vegetables to the Continental army. However, worn out by generations of poor farming practices, Kent County's soil became far less productive during the Federal period. By the time of the Civil War, the soil had recovered and agriculture became stronger than ever. Farmers introduced fertilizer and employed scientific methods to graft peach trees. The extension of the Delaware Railroad line to Dover in 1855 enabled Kent County farmers to reach a national market. Just the year before, two men by the names of Richardson and Roberts had opened a canning company to process local products, and other canneries soon followed. Eventually, canning became Dover and Kent County's principal industry.

During the Civil War period in the mid-nineteenth century, every possible attitude toward the Confederate conflict had adherents in Dover, from those who passionately supported the federal government, to those who were willing to fight to maintain the Southern way of life. Federal troops entered the area during the 1862 and 1864 elections to guard the polls from violence.

A Century of Development

During the post Civil-War era, Dover continued to grow. Electricity was introduced to the city and building boom added the post office, a Roman Catholic Church, and a new Kent County court house. The year 1873 marked the opening of the Wilmington Conference Academy, now Wesley College.

U.S. Route 13, also known as the Dupont Highway, was completed in 1924, marking the beginning of commercial development in the area. In 1933, Capitol Square was laid out and the Legislative Hall became the home of the State's General Assembly. The creation of the capitol complex, paid for out of lottery funds, along with the expansion of City Plaza, lent a handsome setting for Dover's Georgian and Victorian architecture. The first non-agricultural major industry to locate in Dover was International Latex, now known as Playtex, which opened its first operation in 1937 and continues to be an important employer in the community.

In 1941, the U.S. government established the Dover Air Force Base at the site of the city's new airport facilities. The site served as a rocket research center as well as a pilot training center. After World War II, several large manufacturing companies began moving into the area. From 1960 to 1970, the city annexed over 8,000 acres of land into its jurisdiction, primarily for residential purposes. Further development of U.S. Route 13 and Route 8 through the 1980s and 1990s provided another boost for commercial development.

Dover has maintained its unique balance between the small-town, all-American feel and economic prosperity. Dover and the First State continue to be of national importance, as the home state of vice president and former U.S. Senator Joe Biden. Dover Air Force Base provides great stability as a top employer, along with prominent manufacturers such as Playtex. NASCAR racing and slots gambling at Dover Downs make the area a hotbed of tourist activity. Tourists are also drawn in by Delaware's tax-free shopping, and many businesses have expanded their presence in Dover due to the state's progressive corporation laws, low cost of incorporation, and tax benefits. Dover is also the location of the Delaware Court of Chancery, widely recognized as the nation's preeminent forum for the determination of disputes involving the thousands of businesses incorporated in Dover, regardless if they operate elsewhere. Its unique competence in and exposure to issues of business law are unmatched and are a major benefit to the companies incorporated there.

Historical Information: Delaware Public Archives, 121 Martin Luther King Jr. Blvd North, Dover, DE 19901; telephone (302) 744-5000; email aarchives@ state.de.us.

■ Population Profile

Metropolitan Statistical Area Population

2000: 126,697
2010: 162,310
2012 estimate: 167,626
Percent change, 2000–2010: 28.1%
U.S. rank in 2000: 279th
U.S. rank in 2010: 250th

City Residents

1990: 27,630
2000: 32,135
2010: 36,047
2012 estimate: 36,643
Percent change, 2000–2010: 12.2%

Density: 912.7 people per square mile

Racial and ethnic characteristics

White: 17,855
Black or African American: 15,662
American Indian and Alaskan Native: 101
Asian: 1,050
Native Hawaiian and Other Pacific Islander: 131
Hispanic or Latino (may be of any race): 2,448
Other: 1,844

Percent of residents born in state: 36.1%

Age characteristics

Population under 5 years old: 2,377
Population 5 to 9 years old: 2,152
Population 10 to 14 years old: 2,264
Population 15 to 19 years old: 3,948
Population 20 to 24 years old: 4,673
Population 25 to 34 years old: 4,629
Population 35 to 44 years old: 3,964
Population 45 to 54 years old: 3,966
Population 55 to 59 years old: 1,968
Population 60 to 64 years old: 1,604
Population 65 to 74 years old: 2,623
Population 75 to 84 years old: 1,722
Population 85 years and over: 753
Median age: 30.5

Births (2010–11 Metropolitan Area)

Total number: 2,214

Deaths (2010–11 Metropolitan Area)

Total number: 1,406

Money income (2012)

Per capita income: $20,743
Median household income: $43,902
Total households: 12,398

Number of households with income of . . .

less than $10,000: 1,202
$10,000 to $14,999: 1,079
$15,000 to $24,999: 1,132
$25,000 to $34,999: 1,436
$35,000 to $49,999: 1,794
$50,000 to $74,999: 2,646
$75,000 to $99,999: 1,380
$100,000 to $149,999: 1,368
$150,000 to $199,999: 215
$200,000 or more: 146

Percent of families below poverty level: 19.6%

FBI Crime Index Property: 2,189

FBI Crime Index Violent: 280

■ Municipal Government

Dover operates with a council-manager form of government. The mayor and nine council members are elected by non-partisan votes and each serve two-year terms. Eight council members are elected from four districts and serve staggered terms. One council member and the mayor are elected at large.

Head Official: Mayor Carleton E. Carey, Sr. (since 2007; current term expires 2014)

Total Number of City Employees: 350 (2013)

City Information: City of Dover, City Hall, 15 East Loockerman Street, Dover, DE 19903-0475; telephone (302) 736-7004.

■ Economy

Major Industries and Commercial Activity

Dover is a center of government, commerce, and industry for Central Delaware. Since the early 1980s, the number of farms in the area has decreased. Agricultural trade and support industries such as farm machinery, fertilizers, and grain elevators have continued to play significant roles in the economy. The city is home to Kraft Foods, which produces gelatin, pudding desserts, rice, and other food items at its more than one-million-square-foot facility in Dover. Foods and food items produced in Dover include soft drinks, dairy products, corn, wheat, fruits and vegetables, and dry and canned goods.

Dover Air Force Base has a substantial economic impact on the local economy totaling more than $466 million per year as of 2013. The base operates the largest aerial port facility on the East Coast and serves as a focal point for military cargo movement to Europe and the Middle East. Its mechanized-computerized cargo handling arrangement makes possible the processing of up to 1,200 tons of cargo during a 24-hour period. In 2013 Dover Air Force Base had a workforce of 6,400 people, 1,000 of whom were civilians.

Procter & Gamble's Dover plant produces disposable wet wipe paper products at a 546,000-square-foot site it acquired in 1996. Playtex Apparel, Inc. and Playtex Products, Inc. manufacture and distribute intimate apparel as well as personal care items. Major manufacturers include PPG Industries, which produces paint products, and Hirsh Industries, a leading manufacturer of consumer durables such as file cabinets. Dover also has a hand in the defense industry. ILC is a major producer of fabrics and clothing for military and aerospace uses. Best known for being the primary producers of space suits, like those produced for Project Apollo in the 1960s, ILC is also one of the largest suppliers of gas masks to the military. While those businesses have thrived, other Dover staples have left the area in the late 2000s. Dow Reichhold Inc. closed their operations in 2008. Sunroc Corporation, producers of water coolers and drinking fountains, closed its operations in 2010. A Georgia-Pacific packaging facility closed in 2013.

Delaware State University, Delaware Technical and Community College, and Wesley College are considered to be major employers in education. In health care and social services, top employers include Bayhealth Medical Center, Silver Lake Center (eldercare), and Westminster Village (retirement community).

Tourism is another important industry in Dover and Kent County. Due to the well known absence of sales tax, visitors from nearby states such as New York and New Jersey come quite often. The addition of slot machines at the horse racing tracks in Dover (Dover Downs), Harrington, and Wilmington brings in even more visitors. Two weekends a year, NASCAR stock car races held at Dover International Speedway temporarily makes Dover the largest city in Delaware, attracting over 100,000 visitors. Among NASCAR enthusiasts, the track has earned the nickname of "The Monster Mile."

Items and goods produced: foodstuffs, paper products, personal care products, apparel, aeronautical gear

Incentive Programs-New and Existing Companies

Local programs: The Central Delaware Chamber of Commerce offers existing businesses consulting assistance and counseling services by retired executives, and also provides resources for small businesses. Downtown Dover Redevelopment Incentives are offered by the city that may include a 10-year property tax abatement and a waiver of some permit fees. The Downtown Dover Partnership also offers loans and grants for some projects. The Central Delaware Economic Development Council assists companies with basic information, building and

site selection, and dealing with local and state government agencies. The Kent County branch of the Delaware Small Business and Technology Development Center is located at Delaware State University.

State programs: The state of Delaware has no general sales tax and no personal property or inventory tax. Real property taxes are among the lowest in the nation, and some investment and holding companies may receive exemptions on corporate income tax. The Delaware Strategic Fund provides low-interest loans and grants to businesses to support job creation, relocaion, expansion, and Brownfield redevelopment. The Delaware Capital Access Program is a private-public match program to encourage small-business lending by banks by offering portfolio insurance. Also in support of small businesses, the state has dedicated $12.1 million designed to provide nascent companies with access to low-interest loans. A Rural Irrigation Program operated by the state is a revolving loan fund for Delaware's farmers. Grants are also available for companies pursing innovative technology research that might bring new jobs or revenue into the state. The Downtown Delaware resource center provides resources to support redevelopment in historic downtown areas throughout the state.

Job training programs: The Delaware Economic Development Office custom designs and operates training programs on a shared or no-cost basis to be determined individually. Programs are administered through the Delaware Workforce Development Center. Delaware Technical and Community College provides start-up and upgrading programs tailored to the needs of new and existing industries. Apprenticeship training is available at Polytech School District's Adult Education program.

Development Projects

A new main library opened in 2012 at a cost of $21 million. The new library opened after 17 months of construction. The 46,000-square-foot building included a dedicated space for children's programming, an outdoor performance area, meeting rooms, and a job center. The previous main library, built in 1961, closed following the opening of the new main branch. The city completed renovations to facilities at Noble's Pond in 2013.

In 2012 Kraft Foods announced a $10 million expansion to its one-million-square-foot manufacturing facility in Dover. The project completed in 2013 and added 29 full-time jobs to the local economy. A number of smaller businesses opened in 2013, including Acorn Books, Anytime Fitness, A to Z Cycles, Frankfurt Bakery, Bayard Pharmacy, and Classic Cakes, among others.

Accomplishments by the Downtown Dover Partnership during the 2010s included a Community Development Block Grant for a Youth Employment Program, a USDA Rural Development Grant for training and marketing projects, purchase and sale of several downtown properties, and extended leases with the Inner City Cultural League and Dover Interfaith Housing Coalition, both with properies in downtown Dover.

Economic Development Information: Central Delaware Economic Development Council, Suite 2-B, 9 Lookerman Street, P.O. Box 576, Dover, DE 19903; telephone (800) 624-2522. Delaware Economic Development Office, 99 Kings Hwy., Dover, DE 19901; telephone (302) 739-4271; fax (302) 739-5749. Downtown Dover Development Corporation, 101 West Loockerman Street, Suite 1A, Downtown Dover, DE 19904; telephone (302) 678-2940.

Commercial Shipping

The Port of Wilmington, 40 miles north, provides direct access to Interstate 495, and both Norfolk Southern and CSX railroads serve the terminal with rail sidings viable at most warehouse facilities at the port. In the late 1990s, the port expanded its docking area to handle both larger ships and a greater number of ships. Motor freight services are available.

Labor Force and Employment Outlook

Kent County boasts an available and trainable labor force and a pool of skilled labor with an excellent work ethic. Between 1970 and 2000, the county's labor force more than doubled while the number of new companies increased by more than 10 percent in a decade. During the 2000s,employment grew much less. Nonetheless, the Dover area has attempted to be a place for innovation and entrepreneurship. Garrison Oak Technology Park and Kent County Aero Park continue to provide potential for significant future job growth in manufacturing, research and development, and high-technology industry. In addition, research conducted at various business incubators on the campus of Delaware State University could provide additional future job and company growth potential.

The following is a summary of data regarding the 2012 Dover labor force:

Size of civilian labor force: 16,156

Number of workers employed in . . .

    agriculture and mining: 45
    construction: 469
    manufacturing: 817
    wholesale trade: 237
    retail trade: 1,804
    transportation: 528
    information systems: 264
    finance: 572
    professional administration: 906
    education and social services: 4,882
    arts and leisure: 1,628
    other: 474
    public administration: 1,380

Average hourly earnings of production workers: $16.72

Unemployment rate: 6.2% (2012)

Employers

Largest employers (2012)	*Number of employees*
Dover Air Force Base	6,400
State of Delaware	4,500
Bayhealth Medical Center	3,123
Dover Downs Co., Inc.	1,495
Dover Mall LP	1,000
Delaware State University	958
Capital School District	881
Kraft Foods Inc.	604
Energizer Personal Care (Playtex Products)	496
City of Dover	405

Cost of Living

The following is a summary of data regarding several key cost of living factors in the area.

2013 ACCRA Average House Price: $236,400

2013 ACCRA Cost of Living Index: 104

State income tax rate: 2.2% to 6.95%

State sales tax rate: None

Local income tax rate: None

Local sales tax rate: None

Property tax rate: $2.0259 per $100 of assessed valuation (2012)

Economic Information: Central Delaware Chamber of Commerce, 435 N. Dupont Hwy, Dover, DE 19901; telephone (302) 678-0892; fax (302) 678-0189.

■ Education and Research

Elementary and Secondary Schools

The Capital Area School District serves most students in Dover; some are also served by Caesar Rodney School District. The Capital School District offers gifted programs in elementary and secondary schools, language arts and mathematics programs, and a school with multiage grouping. There are 12 public schools in the district. In 2013 Allen Frear Elementary School was named a National Blue Ribbon School of Excellence by the U.S. Department of Education. Handicapped children are served by the Kent County Community School. The Caesar Rodney School District has a few schools in Dover, including the Dover Air Force Base Middle School. This school is unique in that it is run by the local school district and not by the Department of Defense, unlike most military base schools.

There are several private schools in Dover, including Catholic and Amish elementary schools.

The following is a summary of data regarding the Capital School District.

Total enrollment: 6,321

Number of facilities

total: 12
elementary schools: 7
junior high schools: 2
high schools: 1
other: 2

Student/teacher ratio: 14.3:1

Teacher salaries

average (statewide): $57,934

Funding per pupil: $12,999

Public Schools Information: Capital School District, 198 Commerce Way, Dover, DE 19904; telephone (302) 672-1500.

Colleges and Universities

Delaware State University, with an enrollment of about 4,300 students, was founded in 1890 as a college for African Americans. It is the second largest university in the state behind the University of Delaware, offering a variety of bachelor, master, and doctorate degree programs within its five colleges. It is affiliated with the United Methodist Church. Bachelor's and master's degree programs are available through Wilmington University, which has sites at Dover Air Force Base and just north of Dover Downs. It has eight locations throughout Delaware, as well as five in New Jersey and one in Maryland. Diversified technical associate degree programs, diploma programs, and certificate and special interest programs are offered at the Delaware Technical and Community College's (DTCC) four locations. The other campuses are in Georgetown, Stanton, and Wilmington. The University of Delaware maintains an extension site in Dover that offers an associate's degree program in arts.

Libraries and Research Centers

The Dover Public Library opened a new, $21 million main library in 2012. It has more than 100,000 volumes and provides access to more than 30 online research databases, including archives of major newspapers.

Services include reference materials and aids, book talks, and seasonal and children's programs. The Kent County Library, also located in Dover, sponsors local programming and maintains a bookmobile.

The Dover Air Force Base maintains a library containing nearly 30,000 volumes focusing on the United States Air Force and various military topics, with special collections on Transition Assistance. Besides being the site of the Delaware Division of Libraries State Library, Dover is home to the state's Department of Transportation Library, the Delaware Public Archives, and libraries of the Delaware Department of Public Instruction, the Delaware State House Museum, the Legislative Council Library, and the State's Law Library. The State Library of Delaware provides special services to people who are blind, physically handicapped, or homebound.

The William C. Jason Library of Delaware State University has over 300,000 volumes and 1,300 serial subscriptions. The Parker Library at Wesley College shares library privileges with all the public libraries in Kent and Sussex counties and all Delaware technical libraries.

The Applied Mathematics Research Center at Delaware State University was established in 2003 with funding from the Department of Defense. Other research departments at the University include the Delaware Center for Scientific and Applied Computation, the Applied Optics Center, and the Delaware Center for Enterprise Development.

Founded in the 1950s, the National Council on Agricultural Life and Labor Research Fund (NCALL Research) provides housing counseling services along with studies on safe and sanitary rural housing, particularly for farm workers.

The St. Jones Estuarine Research Reserve offers group tours and free general admission to its environmental research center that features a variety of programs and nature trails along with canoe and boat trips as it strives to promote the general public's knowledge of estuaries.

Public Library Information: Dover Public Library, 35 Loockerman Plaza Dover, DE 19901; telephone (302) 736-7030.

■ Health Care

The medical needs of Dover's residents are met at the city's Bayhealth Medical Center, a 310-bed general medical and surgical hospital that offers a variety of services including in-patient and outpatient care, neonatal special care, coronary care, same-day surgery, a modern imaging department, respiratory care, a cancer center, neurodiagnostics, and a 24-hour emergency department. Bayhealth admitted more than 17,000 patients in 2013, and its emergency room treated in excess of 77,000 patients. *U.S. News & World Report* ranked the hospital second in the state in its 2013–14 rankings, with the center receiving high-performing marks for its pulmonology care.

■ Recreation

Sightseeing

A good place to begin exploring Dover is the Delaware State Visitor Center on Federal Street in the downtown area, which offers maps, brochures, and information. The center also features changing exhibits about the area. Many historic structures are clustered downtown around the Green, with buildings ranging from those built in Colonial times to the Victorian period. Once the site of early fairs and markets, today the Green hosts political rallies, public events, and civic celebrations. Although the building itself was demolished in 1830, visitors can still visit the Golden Fleece Tavern site where Delaware representatives ratified the U.S. Constitution.

At one end of the Green stands the Old State House, where the General Assembly met from 1777 until 1934, which was restored in 1976. That body now meets in the Legislative Hall, which displays paintings of former governors and war heroes. Nearby are the Colonel John Haslet Armory and the refurbished Richardson & Robbins canning plant, which now houses the Department of Natural Resources and other state offices. At Christ's Church there is a monument to Caesar Rodney (1729–84), a signer of the Declaration of Independence and an esteemed patriot and local leader. Perhaps the quaintest building on the Green is the tiny Old Post Office, believed to be the city's first. The Delaware Museum of Small Town Life and the Delaware Archaeology Museum, together known as the Meeting House Galleries, occupy a 1790 Presbyterian Church and an 1880 Sunday school building on Meeting House Square, about three blocks from the Green. The archaeological exhibit focuses on Native Americans and the Main Street exhibit on typical small town life.

Thousands of people each year travel to the Air Mobility Command Museum at Dover Air Force Base, which houses a growing collection of vintage planes and artifacts that reflect the evolution, history, and varied missions of military airlift and tanker aircraft. Special emphasis is placed on the history of Dover AFB since its beginnings in 1941. Housed in a restored World War II hangar that was once the home of the Army Air Force Rocket Test Center, the museum is a registered National Historic Site. There is a large outside airpark, a commemorative garden, and an excellent spot to watch airfield operations.

The history of 200 years of farm life is exhibited at the Delaware Agricultural Museum and Village, which opened in 1980 and features 10,000 objects, and a re-created nineteenth-century village.

Nipper, the famous RCA Victor canine symbol, is the star of the Johnson Victrola Museum, which traces the history of the Victor Talking Machine Company, later known as RCA. The museum is a replica of a 1920s Victrola dealer's store.

Arts and Culture

Dover has a number of interesting historical and art museums. The Hall of Records, which houses the Division of Historical and Cultural Affairs, contains the Royal Charter that Charles II gave to the Duke of York for the land that is now Delaware. The Biggs Museum of American Art, which opened in 1993 and was founded by Sewell C. Biggs, features 24 galleries of decorative arts.

Originally founded in 1904, the 600-seat Schwartz Center for the Arts is the home of the Dover Symphony Orchestra, a non-profit community orchestra that performs four times a year. Originally named The Dover Opera House, the building was renamed The Capital Theater in 1923. After decades of success, it fell into disrepair and the building was closed in 1982. Spurred on by a statewide fundraising effort, the dilapidated facility was revived in 2001 after an $8.3 million restoration. The Schwartz Center also presents comedy shows, music, dance, live theater, and film festivals. A community partnership with nearby Wilmington's Grand Opera House, local universities, and other arts organizations seeks to maximize usage of the center.

Theater and dance troupes are among the entertainment at the Delaware State University Education and Humanities Theatre along with an art gallery on the campus grounds. On a smaller scale, the Wesley College Chapel plays host to a wide array of performances.

The Dover Art League's Art Center offers classes, a series of exhibits, and a children's summer arts camp.

Arts and Culture Information: Greater Dover Arts Council, PO Box 475, Dover, DE 19903-0475; telephone (302)7 36-7050. Kent County and Greater Dover, Delaware Convention and Visitors Bureau, 435 North DuPont Highway, Dover, DE 19901; telephone (800) 233-KENT or (302) 734-4888.

Festivals and Holidays

A festive parade and dancing around the maypole mark the opening of the Dover Days Festival (also known as Old Dover Days), a celebration with music, arts and crafts, and a showcase of local homes and gardens that takes place over the first weekend in May. June brings a variety of music at the June Jam and the annual Spring and Summer Concert Series on the Green along with the African American Heritage Festival at Mirror Lake. A fireworks display at the Capitol Square tops off the annual Fourth of July Celebration, and later in the month the Delaware State Fair in Harrington spotlights top-name music stars, auto racing, a rodeo, and demolition derbies. Fairgoers flock to the animal and agricultural exhibits and the gigantic midway offering amusement rides and name entertainment.

Each October is the Governor's Annual Fall Festival at Woodburn. The holiday season is welcomed by the Delaware Hospice Festival of Trees, the Caroling on the Green event, and the Governor's Annual Christmas Open House at Woodburn. February's Winter Festival takes place at Delaware State University.

Sports for the Spectator

Dover does not field any teams in major league sports but does offer the excitement of horse- and auto- racing. Dover Downs and nearby Dover International Speedway, while two separate organizations, is said to be the only area in the country that accommodates both horse racing and auto racing, on two separate tracks. Each sport attracts hundreds of thousands of fans annually. The first weekend in June is the time for the NASCAR Sprint Cup Series race, while May features both a NASCAR Nationwide Series event and a NASCAR Camping World Truck Series race. Live harness racing is presented during November and December.

Sports for the Participant

Dover's Silver Lake, one of four lakes in Kent County, offers picnicking, boating, and fishing on 182 acres. The city has 24 other parks that provide a variety of features including historic monuments, children's playground equipment, and fishing piers. Short drives to Delaware Bay and the Atlantic Ocean provide opportunities for swimming, water skiing, and other water-related activities. Public golf courses are available and tennis courts can be found at school and college grounds.

Schutte Park is located on the west side of town and takes up 57 acres to house its softball/baseball and hockey/soccer fields along with ample space for picnic pavilion rentals. The Parks and Recreation Department expanded the park in 2008 with the John W. Pitts Recreation Center, a 19,000-square-foot, multi-million dollar project. The indoor center hosts adults and youth sports leagues, as well as fitness classes.

The Amish Country Bike Tour is sponsored in part by the city each year on the first Saturday after Labor Day. Bike routes are mapped to take riders through the farmlands and small settlements that dot the Kent County landscape. Stops for food and live music are available.

About 10 miles north of Dover is the Bombay Hook National Wildlife Refuge in Smyrna where visitors can view migratory shorebirds and waterfowl via hiking and driving tours of the 16,000 acres of marshes, ponds, fields, and forest.

Shopping and Dining

Tax-free shopping attracts people from all over the region to Dover's stores. Main Street Dover boasts many specialty shops located in unique buildings. Curbside

horses and buggies from nearby Amish towns are a common site at the legendary Spence's Bazaar on New Street, where bargain hunters peruse everything from housewares to antique furniture. The Dover Mall features many national chain stores.

With approximately 220 eateries, Kent County has claimed to have the highest amount of restaurants per capita in the United States. Dover and the surrounding area boast a wide variety of dining establishments, featuring everything from traditional Southern fare to foods of many nations including Thai, Chinese, Indian, Mongolian, Mexican, and Italian. Seafood places and casual American eateries also abound. A variety of fine dining can be found as well.

Visitor Information: Kent County and Greater Dover, Delaware Convention and Visitors Bureau, 435 North DuPont Highway, Dover, DE 19901; telephone (800) 233-KENT or (302) 734-4888.

■ Convention Facilities

An 18,000-square-foot ballroom is available at the Dover Downs Hotel & Casino, and can be divided into three separate areas for events such as stand-up receptions, sit-down dinners, and tradeshows. Further, the hotel provides six corporate meeting rooms and three smaller hospitality suites. Military and veterans groups can reserve meeting rooms for 30 to 200 people at the Air Mobility Command Museum on Dover Air Force Base. Delaware State University has a meeting space to accommodate 3,000 people. Wesley College and Delaware technical and Community College offer spaces for smaller groups.

The Sheraton Dover Hotel and Conference Center was the primary conference site in the city. The center offered 21,000 square feet of exhibition space, a ballroom that could accommodate 1,500 for dinner, and 22 meeting rooms, as well as 156 hotel rooms. In 2013 Delaware State University signed a 15-year lease agreement for the facility, with students moving into the former hotel rooms. The university had the option to buy the property after two years.

Convention Information: Kent County and Greater Dover, Delaware Convention and Visitors Bureau, 435 North DuPont Highway, Dover, DE 19901; telephone (800) 233-KENT or (302) 734-4888. Dover Downs Hotel & Casino, 1131 North DuPont Highway, Dover DE 19901; telephone (800) 711-5882 or (302) 674-4600.

■ Transportation

Approaching the City

For many years, metropolitan Dover was a bottleneck, especially on the weekends, with visitors traveling to and from the Atlantic beaches. Relief arrived with the opening of a $100 million bypass around the city on Route 1. Carolina Trailways offers bus service to the city. The closest Amtrak rail service is available at Wilmington and the closest major airport is in Philadelphia.

Traveling in the City

U.S. Highways 13 and 113 run north and south in Dover and connect to Delaware Route 1. State highway 8 is the main east–west passage. Central Delaware Transit offers a state-run, fixed-route bus system that operates around the city. Carolina Trailways and Blue Diamond offer bus services in the city and around the county. Historic attractions around the Green are accessible on foot.

■ Communications

Newspapers and Magazines

Dover's daily newspaper is the *Delaware State News*. The *Dover Post* is its weekly newspaper. Wilmington's *The News Journal* is also read in Dover.

Television and Radio

Major commercial television stations received in the area are broadcast from other cities. Marquee Broadcasting, Inc., maintains a station in Dover. Two AM radio stations (WDOV and WRJE) and eight FM stations are broadcast out of Dover.

Media Information: *Delaware State News,* 110 Galaxy Drive, Dover, DE 19903; telephone (302) 674-3600.

Dover Online

Capital School District. Available www.capital.k12.de.us

Central Delaware Chamber of Commerce. Available www.cdcc.net

City of Dover home page. Available www.cityofdover.com

Delaware Economic Development Office. Available www.dedo.delaware.gov

Delaware Online. Available www.delawareonline.com

Dover Air Force Base. Available www.dover.af.mil

Dover Post. Available www.doverpost.com

Delaware Historical Society. Available www.hsd.org

Kent County and Greater Dover, Delaware Convention and Visitors Bureau. Available www.visitdover.com

BIBLIOGRAPHY

Jackson, James B, *The Golden Fleece Tavern: The Birthplace of the First State* (Dover, DE: Friends of Old Dover, 1987)

Slavin, Timothy A., *Dover: Images of America* (Mount Pleasant, SC: Arcadia Publishing, 2003)

Walls, Bruce, *Tales of Old Dover* (Decatur, IL: Spectator Books, 1977)

Wilmington

■ The City in Brief

Founded: 1638 (chartered 1739)

Head Official: Mayor Dennis P. Williams (since 2013)

City Population
1990: 71,529
2000: 72,664
2010: 70,851
2012 estimate: 71,289
Percent change, 2000–2010: −2.5%
U.S. rank in 1990: 311th (State rank: 1st)
U.S. rank in 2000: 417th (State rank: 1st)
U.S. rank in 2010: 456th (State rank: 1st)

Metropolitan Statistical Area Population
2000: 5,687,147
2010: 5,965,343
2012 estimate: 6,018,800
Percent change, 2000–2010: 4.9%
U.S. rank in 2000: 6th
U.S. rank in 2010: 5th

Area: 10.8 square miles

Elevation: Approximately 74 feet above sea level

Average Annual Temperatures: 54.0° F

Average Annual Precipitation: 40.25 inches; 19.9 inches of snow

Major Economic Sectors: pharmaceuticals, finance, manufacturing, wholesale and retail trade

Unemployment Rate: 8.0% (2012)

Per Capita Income: $25,987

2012 FBI Crime Index Property: 3,824

Major Colleges and Universities: University of Delaware, Widener University

Daily Newspaper: *The News-Journal*

■ Introduction

After years of living in Philadelphia's shadow, Wilmington has emerged as a national banking center. Beginning with the du Pont family enterprises, the city has been a leading industrial and shipping hub since the nineteenth century. A diversified labor force and low corporate tax burden has made Wilmington extremely attractive to new businesses. In addition, Delaware's largest city is strategically located between New York City, Philadelphia, Baltimore, and Washington D.C. Although situated in the most densely populated area of the northeast, Wilmington is a very livable city. Because of its small size, it enjoys the advantages of a large metropolitan area while escaping the disadvantages, such as major traffic congestion, noise pollution, and smog. City residents profit from a comparatively low cost of living and cultural perquisites inherent in an area that boasts two of the country's top museums and bills itself as the "Corporate Capital of the World."

■ Geography and Climate

Wilmington is located in the northeast corner of Delaware, on the western bank of the Delaware River where the Christina River joins Brandywine Creek. The city is part of the Atlantic Coastal Plain, which combines flat, low land at sea level with gentle, rolling hills that extend northward into Pennsylvania. The Delaware River forms the city's eastern border with the Atlantic Ocean beyond; Chesapeake Bay lies to the southwest. These large water masses determine the city's climate. Summers are warm and humid, and winters are generally mild. During the summer, relative humidity is about 75 percent

John Greim/LOOP IMAGES

and fog is frequent throughout the year. Most winter precipitation falls as rain or sleet. Rainfall is heaviest in summer when it comes in the form of thunderstorms. Hurricanes moving northward along the Atlantic Coast occasionally cause heavy rainfall, but winds seldom reach hurricane force in Wilmington. Strong easterly and southeasterly winds sometimes cause high tides in the Delaware River, resulting in flooding of lowlands and damage to riverfront properties.

Area: 10.8 square miles

Elevation: Approximately 74 feet above sea level

Average Temperatures: 54.0° F

Average Annual Precipitation: 40.25 inches; 19.9 inches of snow

■ History

Lenni-Lenape Indians lived in the Wilmington area long before Europeans and Africans arrived on Delaware's shores. "Lenni" means pure or original and "Lenape" means the people. Their control extended north into Pennsylvania and south to the Potomac; their customs and traditions resembled those of their neighbors, the Nanticokes and the Powhatans of Virginia. European settlers first encountered this tribe of "peacemakers" in the early seventeenth century.

Various Countries Possess Early Colony

Wilmington was the first permanent Old World settlement in the entire Delaware Valley. In March 1638, a Swedish expedition led by Peter Minuit entered Delaware Bay. They sailed up the river and entered the Minquas Kill (today's Christina River). Going two miles inland, they cast anchor opposite a natural stone wharf. Here at "The Rocks"-which are still visible today at the foot of Seventh Street-Minuit stepped ashore and made a treaty with the Lenni-Lenapes. The land he purchased was dubbed New Sweden and Swedish soldiers soon began constructing a fort they named after their queen, Christina. Inside the fort they built the first log cabins in America. Before the ship left in June, the 24 original Swedes, Finns, Dutch, and German settlers were joined by Anthoni, "The Black Swede," a freedman from the Caribbean. All 25 were alive and well two years later when the ship returned. In all, Sweden sent 12 expeditions to the new world, but the fledgling colony received little support from Queen Christina and in 1656 was overtaken by the Dutch. Peter Stuyvesant, the Governor of New Amsterdam, laid siege to the tiny colony and ultimately the Swedes surrendered.

In 1664, as a result of a war between Holland and England, the colony along the Delaware was brought under English rule. Then, in 1681, William Penn received a grant from England's King Charles II for the largest tract ever given a commoner. "Penn's Woods," or Pennsylvania, was intended to be a haven for members of the Society of Friends, or Quakers. For the next fifty years, Penn and Lord Baltimore would vie for ownership of the three counties of New Castle, Kent, and Sussex. As Pennsylvania added western counties, Delaware demanded home rule, and in 1704 the counties were granted their own assembly with Pennsylvania and Delaware sharing the same crown-appointed governor.

Around 1730, a large tract of land in what is now Wilmington was deeded to a man named Thomas Willing, who called the tiny settlement Willingtown. Willingtown was a farming community of 15 to 20 houses when prosperous Quakers began to arrive in 1735. Immediately they began investing in property and, simultaneously, the town began to grow. At this time there was no formal government; therefore, decisions were made by consent of all the townspeople. Then, in 1739, England's King George II granted a charter addressed to "the People of Wilmington;" the king is thought to have arbitrarily named the town after his friend Spencer Compton, Earl of Wilmington. The first election held under the borough charter took place on September 8, 1740. This same year the first vessel built for foreign trade, the *Wilmington,* sailed for Jamaica. A brisk shipping trade continued to benefit local merchants despite wars and privateers. Industries such as brick-making, pottery, tanning, and flour-milling (at mills along the Brandywine) began to flourish.

Wilmington in Revolutionary Times

The summer of 1777 found the community of Wilmington in the center of the struggle for American independence from England. George Washington established Revolutionary army headquarters in Wilmington, as did General Anthony Wayne. After the British took Wilmington, following the Battle of Brandywine, the town became a British camp. The Presbyterian Meeting House was used as a prison and residents' houses were requisitioned to care for the wounded. Wilmingtonians did not see the last of British troops until the end of October 1777.

An economic slump followed the war, but soon Wilmington had a fleet of ships engaged in coastal, as well as European, trade. Many Irish passed through the Port of Wilmington at this time, as well as French refugees from Santo Domingo. Scarcely had these immigrants settled when hundreds more poured in from Philadelphia, where yellow fever was rampant. Until the epidemic, Wilmington

merchants had depended on Philadelphia banks for financial support. Suddenly isolated from their neighbor, they realized the need for economic self-sufficiency and founded the Bank of Delaware in 1795.

Economic Development Marks Nineteenth Century

Between the close of the Revolution and the War of 1812, Wilmington's population increased to 5,000, the town spread westward, and streets were widened to accommodate the flow of traffic. Five turnpikes built between 1808 and 1815 greatly increased Wilmington's trade. Steamboats ran regularly between the town and Philadelphia, as did stagecoaches carrying passengers and freight. One of the earliest railroads in the United States, the Newcastle & Frenchtown Railway, opened in 1831, and soon after came the Wilmington & Susquehanna. By 1831 Wilmington's population had grown so large that leading citizens petitioned the legislature to incorporate the town as a city. The charter was granted in 1832 and city officials were elected.

From 1832 until the Civil War, new enterprises sprang up on the shores of the Christina River, supplementing those already prospering along the Brandywine. Shipbuilding, paper milling, and the manufacture of machine tools, iron, railroad cars, and cotton joined the earlier industries of flour milling and leather tanning. As new industries developed, the population grew. In 1860 there were 21,250 residents in the city; in 1920 there were 110,168.

Wilmington in the Twentieth Century

World War I kept all available industrial plants working full time; blast furnaces and shipyards operated round-the-clock. The conflict brought immense trade to E. I. du Pont de Nemours and Company, which had been producing gun powder in the area since 1802. After the war du Pont moved away from explosives to manufacture materials such as Nylon, Dacron, Orlon, and Cellophane. When other chemical companies moved into the region, Wilmington became known as "The Chemical Capital of the World." This industrial expansion brought great wealth to the area, and in the decades following World War II, a large increase in population.

Like many American cities, Wilmington has seen a steady flow of residents leave the city for the suburbs. The exodus of the middle class left the city to the urban poor, particularly to blacks and the elderly, creating new problems. Racial violence that broke out in the wake of Martin Luther King Jr.'s assassination on April 4, 1968, required heavy patrol by the National Guard for many months.

A shift in economy began in 1981 with the Financial Center Development Act. The act liberalized many laws governing banking operations with the state. Subsequent state legislation was directed to attracting international finance and insurance companies. Through the 1990s, several banking and financial services organizations moved to the state and to Wilmington to take advantage of this pleasant economic climate. With a liberal tax structure, many *Fortune* 500 companies decided to incorporate in or near Wilmington, bringing the city yet another nickname, the "Corporate Capital."

Since the mid-1990s more than $1 billion, much of it in private funds, has been invested in major downtown redevelopment projects. The MBNA complex, now home to Bank of America, who bought MBNA, undertook a $32 million renovation of the former Daniel L. Herrmann Courthouse and consists of seven buildings alone. Other bank and insurance headquarters have found their home in downtown Delaware, such as Barclays Bank and American Life Insurance Company. In 2002 the huge former Delaware Trust Building, which had been destroyed by fire, was converted to the Residences at Rodney Square, a 278-unit luxury apartment complex.

The revitalization of downtown buildings and new housing construction and the redevelopment of the Christina Riverfront continue to be priorities for the city and state governments. The revitalization of the central business area continues to stimulate increased interest in Wilmington. Revitalization efforts include new restaurants, the construction of a live performance theater, a baseball stadium, the Chase Center, a 1.7-mile Riverwalk along the riverfront, and the installation of a steel-rail trolley connecting the riverfront with the business area. The city's first children's museum opened in 2010, also along the Riverfront.

While several banks continued to expand operations in Wilmington, a welcome sign of recovery after a financial crisis and nationwide recession in the late 2000s, the future of the city's manufacturing industries remained uncertain. After a General Motors plant closed in 2009, Fisker Automotive, a maker of hybrid vehicles, agreed to take over the facility. Despite major federal and state subsidies, the troubled company never produced a vehicle, filing for bankruptcy in 2013. Still, the city's location near major cities along the eastern seaboard and the lucrative Port of Wilmington were constants that would continue to lure new industries for years to come.

Historical Information: Delaware Historical Society Library, 505 Market Street, Wilmington DE 19801; telephone (302) 655-7161.

■ Population Profile

Metropolitan Statistical Area Population

2000: 5,687,147
2010: 5,965,343
2012 estimate: 6,018,800

Percent change, 2000–2010: 4.9%
U.S. rank in 2000: 6th
U.S. rank in 2010: 5th

City Residents

1990: 71,529
2000: 72,664
2010: 70,851
2012 estimate: 71,289
Percent change, 2000–2010: −2.5%
U.S. rank in 1990: 311th (State rank: 1st)
U.S. rank in 2000: 417th (State rank: 1st)
U.S. rank in 2010: 456th (State rank: 1st)

Density: 6,497.6 people per square mile

Racial and ethnic characteristics

White: 26,947
Black or African American: 39,561
American Indian and Alaskan Native: 102
Asian: 806
Native Hawaiian and Other Pacific Islander: 0
Hispanic or Latino (may be of any race): 11,044
Other: 3,873

Percent of residents born in state: 53.2%

Age characteristics

Population under 5 years old: 5,129
Population 5 to 9 years old: 4,391
Population 10 to 14 years old: 4,534
Population 15 to 19 years old: 4,775
Population 20 to 24 years old: 4,912
Population 25 to 34 years old: 12,172
Population 35 to 44 years old: 8,836
Population 45 to 54 years old: 9,327
Population 55 to 59 years old: 4,291
Population 60 to 64 years old: 3,815
Population 65 to 74 years old: 4,814
Population 75 to 84 years old: 2,828
Population 85 years and over: 1,465
Median age: 34.7

Births (2010–11 Metropolitan Area)

Total number: 74,382

Deaths (2010–11 Metropolitan Area)

Total number: 51,613

Money income (2012)

Per capita income: $25,987
Median household income: $37,167
Total households: 29,045

Number of households with income of ...

less than $10,000: 3,571
$10,000 to $14,999: 2,420
$15,000 to $24,999: 4,331

$25,000 to $34,999: 3,606
$35,000 to $49,999: 3,422
$50,000 to $74,999: 4,344
$75,000 to $99,999: 2,786
$100,000 to $149,999: 2,695
$150,000 to $199,999: 843
$200,000 or more: 1,027

Percent of families below poverty level: 25.8%

FBI Crime Index Property: 3,824

FBI Crime Index Violent: 1,228

■ Municipal Government

Wilmington, the New Castle County seat, has a mayor-council form of government. Elected to a four-year term, the mayor is the city's chief administrator. Like the mayor, Wilmington's 13 city council members are elected for four-year terms every presidential election year. There are eight council members representing city districts and four members-at-large.

Head Official: Mayor Dennis P. Williams (since 2013)

Total Number of City Employees: 1,120 (2012)

City Information: City of Wilmington, 800 North French Street, Wilmington, DE 19801; telephone (302) 576-2489.

■ Economy

Major Industries and Commercial Activity

Delaware is a national corporate center, and more than half of the *Fortune* 500 charter their operations in the city because of the state's favorable corporate franchise tax laws and nationally recognized Court of Chancery. Major industries in Wilmington include banking, chemicals, pharmaceuticals, imports and exports, and tourism and hospitality. DuPont, its largest and most historical company, was ranked 72th on the *Fortune* 500 list in 2013. The Wilmington/Newark metropolitan area is home to some of the world's most prominent chemical, pharmaceutical, and technology companies, including, in addition to DuPont, AstraZeneca and W. L. Gore and Associates. The Delaware Technology Park in Newark has hosted more than 75 technology-driven businesses, including 25 that have matured and "graduated" from the park as of 2013.

Many banks are located in Wilmington. However, banking was shaken by a nationwide recession in the late 2000s, caused by a financial crisis. MBNA Bank, once the area's largest employer with more than 11,000 workers, was bought by Bank of America in 2006. Bank of America continued to be a major employer in the area. American Life Insurance Company's world headquarters is an impressive anchor in the city's developing Christina Gateway, a commercial center encompassing the eastern sector to the waterfront. Blue Cross-Blue Shield also has headquarters in the downtown area.

In 2010 student lending giant Sallie Mae announced it would move its headquarters from Virginia to Wilmington. That same year, Delaware was also able to attract Fisker Automotive to buy and retool the shuttered former General Motors auto assembly plant, which closed in 2009. However, Fisker suffered a number of setbacks, ranging from a curtailment of federal funds to the bankruptcy of a battery supplier to flooding caused by 2012's Hurricane Sandy. The company filed for bankruptcy in 2013 without producing a single, despite some $21.5 million in loans from the state.

The Port of Wilmington has a major impact on both the local and state economies. The port is the top seaport in North America for fresh fruit, banana, and juice concentrate imports. This full-service deepwater port welcomes over 400 vessels each year and handles over 5 million tons of cargo. Car carriers that acll on Wilmington's port include Hoegh Autoliners, Liberty Global, Alliance Navigation, Mitsui O.S.K. Lines, and ARC. Other products received at the port include steel, forest products, petroleum, and bulk materials.

Tax-free shopping and historical attractions are the big draws for tourists.

Items and goods produced: chemicals, medical apparatus, pharmaceuticals

Incentive Programs-New and Existing Companies

Local programs: Wilmington provides strong incentives to businesses in the city. Among the city incentives is a micro loan program that offers loans to entrepreneurs located in the city that are establishing for-profit businesses and plan to use funds for working capital or acquisition of materials. In particular, new businesses must demonstrate that they will benefit low- or moderate-income residents. The program also has a training component that helps new business owners development plans related to business finance and other technical aspects of managing a business. The Disadvantage Enterprise Program directs city contracting and subcontracting opportunities toward qualifying businesses that are majority owned and operated by one or more socially or economically disadvantaged individuals. The city's Minority Business Enterprise Office supports both new and expanding businesses in Wilmington with micro loans, training, and other support services.

State programs: The state of Delaware has no general sales tax and no personal property or inventory tax. Real property taxes are among the lowest in the nation, and some investment and holding companies may receive exemptions on corporate income tax. The Delaware Strategic Fund provides low-interest loans and grants to businesses to support job creation, relocation, expansion, and Brownfield redevelopment. The Delaware Capital Access Program is a private-public match program to encourage small-business lending by banks by offering portfolio insurance. Also in support of small businesses, the state has dedicated $12.1 million designed to provide nascent companies with access to low-interest loans. A Rural Irrigation Program operated by the state is a revolving loan fund for Delaware's farmers. Grants are also available for companies pursing innovative technology research that might bring new jobs or revenue into the state. The Downtown Delaware resource center provides resources to support redevelopment in historic downtown areas throughout the state.

Job training programs: The Delaware Economic Development Office custom designs and operates training programs on a shared or no-cost basis to be determined individually. Programs are administered through the Delaware Workforce Development Center. Training contracts may be arranged with colleges, vocational schools, specialized training centers, and independent agencies that provide business, industrial, and service-related instruction.

Development Projects

Wilmington Delaware is in the midst of a renaissance with the redevelopment of the Riverfront and historic Market Street districts. Major real estate investments in concert with public funding have transformed the city of Wilmington's Riverfront into a vibrant and exciting place to conduct business, as evidenced by the major corporate investments of Barclays Bank, Capital One 360, and AAA Mid-Atlantic. Some of the amenities to the riverfront include access to casual and fine dining, access to mass transit and even a day care facility. Between 1997 and 2013, more than $1 billion has been invested in riverfront development.

In an additional development along Wilmington's waterfront area, plans for a $37 million Westin Hotel were announced in 2012, with an expected opening in 2014. Nearby, a $20 million Penn Cinema Riverfront & IMAX broke ground in 2012 and was open by 2013.

Contributing to the economic health of the downtown and Wilmington Riverfront regions has been the presence of Wilmington Station. The rail station received more than $35 million renovations, which completed in 2011. Funds came from the American Recovery and Reinvestment Act, the Delaware Department of Transportation, and Amtrak. Major repairs to the brick exterior were completed, as was a total remodeling of the interior of the station. As of 2013, the station handled more than 700,000 passengers annually.

In 2012 Citi opened an office in Wilmington that employed 145 people, with the expectation to ultimately employ some 260. The prior year, the Delaware Economic Development Office had awarded Citi a $3 million grant to support the expansion of its presence in the state, some $2.5 million of which went to supporting the new jobs. Between 2007 and 2010, Citi had provided the state with $43.4 million in Community Development Investments and $2 million in grants to non-profit entities.

Masley Glove Company, which designs gloves primarily for the U.S. military, relocated to Wilmington in 2013.

Economic Development Information: Wilmington Renaissance Corporation, 100 West 10th St, Suite 206, Wilmington, DE 19801; telephone (302) 656-2909. Wilmington Economic Development Corporation, Community Service Building, 100 West 10th Street, Suite 706, Wilmington, DE; telephone (302) 571-9088.

Commercial Shipping

The flow of goods in and out of Wilmington is facilitated by its network of interstate highways and air and rail freight service. Perhaps the city's greatest economic asset, the state-owned Port of Wilmington lies at the mouth of the Christina River, only 65 miles from Atlantic Ocean shipping lanes. Incoming cargo, such as fresh fruit, concentrated juice, vehicles, lumber, and steel can be dispatched directly from ships to freight cars, trucks, and lighter carriers, saving handling costs and speeding delivery. The port has been designated a Free Trade Zone, offering customs benefits that are attractive to international trade. The port's discharging facilities include two 46-ton container cranes that can handle 35 containers an hour. Rail access to the port is available through Norfolk Southern and CSX.

The interstate highways that pass through Wilmington give truckers direct access to one-third of the nation's consumers; more than 60 common and contract carriers operate in the metropolitan area..

The New Castle County Airport offers worldwide cargo services with an unusually fast and efficient ground delivery system. Repair and maintenance services, leasing and storage facilities for commercial and corporate aircraft are also available. Also within a short commute of Wilmington are both Philadelphia International Airport and Dover Air Force Base. Additionally, the smaller public-use airports of New Garden, Brandywine, and Spitfire are within 20 miles of downtown Wilmington.

Labor Force and Employment Outlook

Wilmington offers businesses a diverse labor force with a diverse mixture of blue- and white-collar workers. Financial services and the chemical industries remain major elements of Wilmington's economy, although banking was hard hit by a nationwide recession and financial crises of the late 2000s. Government is also highly present in Wilmington, despite the fact that Dover is the capital city. Many state offices and employees one would normally expect to find in the state capital, including the headquarters of the Office of the Attorney General, are actually in Wilmington.

The following is a summary of data regarding the 2012 Wilmington labor force:

Size of civilian labor force: 34,701

Number of workers employed in . . .

agriculture and mining: 220
construction: 997
manufacturing: 1,861
wholesale trade: 413
retail trade: 2,895
transportation: 1,125
information systems: 899
finance: 4,326
professional administration: 3,399
education and social services: 7,838
arts and leisure: 2,839
other: 1,337
public administration: 1,936

Average hourly earnings of production workers: $20.94

Unemployment rate: 8.0% (2012)

Employers

Largest employers (2012)	*Number of employees*
State of Delaware	13,000
Christiania Care Health Services	10,400
E.I. Du Pont Nemours & Company	8,100
Bank of America (MBNA)	7,100
Wal-mart Stores, Inc.	4,700
AstraZeneca, Inc.	4,500
University of Delaware	4,000
A. I. Dupont Institute	2,821
Christina School District	2,300
The Y of Delaware	2,300

Cost of Living

In comparison with other eastern seaboard cities such as Philadelphia and New York, Wilmington boasts of relatively low living costs, particularly those associated with housing.

The following is a summary of data regarding several key cost of living factors in the area.

2013 ACCRA Average House Price: $319,933

2013 ACCRA Cost of Living Index: 110

State income tax rate: 2.2% to 6.95%

State sales tax rate: None

Local income tax rate: 1.25%

Local sales tax rate: None

Property tax rate: $1.7670 per $100 of assessed valuation (2013)

Economic Information: Delaware Department of Labor, Wilmington Office, 4425 North Market Street, Wilmington, DE 19802; telephone (302) 761-8085.

■ Education and Research

Elementary and Secondary Schools

In 1976 the New Castle County School District was reorganized and divided into four separate districts: Brandywine, Red Clay Consolidated, Christina, and Colonial. Each district encompasses some part of Wilmington, along with other suburban communities, and each elects a seven-member board of education to govern its elementary and secondary schools. The New Castle County Vo-Tech School District provides vocational training for area students. The Christina, Brandywine, and Colonial districts all offer special programs for gifted students. Christina offers programs including the Delaware Autism Program and the state's school for visually-impaired and hearing-impaired persons. Tally Middle School and Mount Pleasant High School in the Brandywine district offer students an International Baccalaureate Program. Red clay has special mentoring programs.

There are several charter schools in the city as well. The Charter School of Wilmington, founded in 1996, is sponsored by a group of companies that include Bell Atlantic, DuPont, Delmarva Power, Medical Center of Delaware, and Zeneca, Inc. The school was named a 2013 National Blue Ribbon School of Excellence by the U.S. Department of Education. Cab Calloway School of the Arts, founded in 1992, matches traditional learning with an arts curriculum.

In addition to the public school system, there are over 50 private schools, both religious (Catholic and Jewish) and independent. The Cathedral Choir School of Delaware and the Music School of Delaware in Wilmington are notable for music education.

The following is a summary of data regarding the Christina School District.

Total enrollment: 17,190

Number of facilities

   total: 29
   elementary schools: 19
   junior high schools: 4
   high schools: 3
   other: 3

Student/teacher ratio: 14.4:1

Teacher salaries

   average (statewide): $57,934

Funding per pupil: $14,915

Public Schools Information: Christina School District, 600 N. Lombard Street, Wilmington, DE 19801; telephone 302 552-2600.

Colleges and Universities

Much of the growth in post-secondary education in Wilmington was the result of an aggressive recruitment strategy by the Wilmington Renaissance Corporation, which called for the creation of a university campus district near Market Street. Together these efforts brought over 7,000 students to downtown Wilmington. Both Delaware State University and Drexel University opened satellite campuses on Market Street in the 2000s. In addition, the Delaware College of Art and Design, Delaware's only professional art and design school, opened in 1997; and Springfield College also launched a center for human services near downtown. Delaware Technical and Community College also has an extension site in Wilmington. The Delaware Campus of Widener University School of Law is in North Wilmington. This campus also houses the Legal Education Institute.

Other major accredited institutions in the Wilmington metropolitan region include the University of Delaware (Newark, DE), West Chester University of Pennsylvania (West Chester, PA), Wilmington University (New Castle, DE), and Goldey-Beacom College (Pike Creek Valley, DE).

Libraries and Research Centers

The Wilmington Public Library system consists of the Wilmington and North Wilmington branches. Founded in 1788, the library houses more than 335,000 volumes, as well as a special collection on Delaware history, film and record collections, and an African American Collection of books, videos, and audio cassettes. Woodlawn Library, part of the New Castle County system, has a collection of about 50,000 volumes and shares a campus with a small park. Brandywine Hundred, Kirkwood, and Elsemere libraries are also part of the county system.

Wilmington is also home to numerous special libraries. Among them are the Delaware Academy of Medicine's Lewis B. Flinn Library, devoted to consumer health; the Delaware Art Museum's Helen Farr Sloan Library & Archives; the Widener Law Library; E. I. du Pont de Nemours and Company Law Library; Hagley Museum and Library; and the Historical Society of Delaware Library. Research centers located in Wilmington include the Delaware Biotechnology Institute, a public-private partnership doing scientific research that is helping to develop Delaware's growing life sciences industry. In addition, five state-sponsored Advanced Technology Centers provide research and development in the areas of laser optics, semiconductors, and advanced materials. Alfred I. du Pont Institute of the Nemours Foundation performs research in pediatric orthopedics, cytogenetics, and microbial genetics.

Public Library Information: Wilmington Public Library, One Customs House Building, 704 King St., 3rd Floor, Wilmington, DE 19801; telephone (302) 571-7400.

■ Health Care

Two of Delaware's largest medical facilities, Christiana Care Health System and the Alfred I. du Pont Institute, are located in Wilmington. Christiana Care comprises Christiana Hospital (in Newark), Eugene du Pont Preventive Medicine and Rehabilitation Institute, Riverside Transitional Care, and Wilmington Hospital. The center is a teaching hospital affiliated with Thomas Jefferson University, the University of Delaware, and Delaware Technical and Community College. Christiana was named the top hospital in Delaware for 2013–14 by *U.S. News & World Report* and was ranked 38th nationally for its gynecological care.

Since 1940, the Alfred I. du Pont Institute has treated children who suffer from crippling diseases. Today it is a multispecialty pediatric center researching problems in neurology, genetics, developmental medicine, plastic surgery and sports medicine. The Nemours Alfred I. duPont Hospital for Children, a 192-bed facility, was ranked as one of the top children's hospitals in the nation in 2013–14 by *U.S. News & World Report*. It was nationally ranked in eight specialties, including fifth overall in orthopedics.

Wilmington's other medical facilities include St. Francis Hospital, the only Catholic hospital in Delaware, and the Wilmington Veteran's Administration Medical Center.

■ Recreation

Sightseeing

From the eighteenth-century homes in Wilmington Square to the country estates along the Brandywine, Wilmington's attractions are rich in history. Prominent among them is the legacy of one family. The du Ponts, who did so much to shape the city's economy, have also had a pervasive influence on its cultural life.

One of the du Pont's greatest contributions is Nemours Mansion and Gardens, the 300-acre estate of Alfred I. du Pont, who designed the mansion in the style of a Louis XVI chateau and filled it with European art works. Its 77 rooms are furnished with antique furniture, oriental rugs, tapestries, and outstanding paintings dating to the fifteenth century. Outside, formal gardens extend a third of a mile from the main vista of the mansion. Ten miles north is Longwood Gardens, the 1,050-acre horticultural masterpiece of Pierre Samuel du Pont. In spring, summer, and fall, visitors enjoy more than 350 acres of outdoor gardens, fountain displays, fireworks, theatrical productions, and concerts. During the winter months the main attraction is a group of heated conservatories that shelter many rare and exotic plants. Gardening enthusiasts can also experience naturalistic garden designs and native plants at their best at the Mt. Cuba Center, the former estate of Mr. and Mrs. Lammot Copeland du Pont, in nearby Greenville.

Historic Wilmington can be glimpsed at several locations in the area. Fort Christina State Park is the site of the original fort the Swedes built when they landed in 1638. Today visitors see a monument to that expedition by Swedish sculptor Carl Milles and the kind of log cabin that would have been built by an early settler. Next to the park is the Tall Ship *Kalmar Nyckel,* a full-size recreation of the ornate, armed ship that brought the early settlers here. The 139-foot ship is Delaware's sea- going Ambassador of Good Will. Erected in 1698, Holy Trinity Church (also known as Old Swedes Church) is the oldest church in the United States that stands as originally built and is still used for regular worship. Once of Swedish Lutheran affiliation, it has been used for Episcopal services since 1791. Formerly the center of Wilmington's social and political life, Old Town Hall (1798) serves as a museum, while a beautiful Art Deco building across the street houses the Delaware Historical Society's Museum offices and Research Library. Visitors can view exhibits pertaining to Delaware history at the Delaware History Museum, part of the complex. Rockwood Mansion, built in 1851 by Quaker merchant Joseph Shipley, serves as an outstanding example of rural Gothic architecture; the English-style country house and gardens are now administered by New Castle County's Department of Parks and Recreation. The mansion's furnishings include decorative arts and archives from the seventeenth to the early twentieth centuries. At Wilmington Square are four beautiful eighteenth-century houses, moved to the site in 1976, which are now used for meeting and office space by the Delaware Historical Society.

Wilmington residents enjoy a total of more than 550 acres of park land, almost 200 acres of which comprise Brandywine Park. Designed by Frederick Law Olmsted, who created New York City's Central Park, Brandywine provides a setting of natural beauty only 10 minutes from downtown Wilmington. Brandywine Zoo houses many exotic species of animals from North and South America and Africa. A focal point of Wilmington's waterfront attractions is the Port of Wilmington at the end of Christina and Terminal avenues. Visitors are invited to witness the day-to-day operations of one of the nation's busiest ports. Approximately four miles upstream, running from the Amtrak Station to the Shipyard Shops/ Frawley Stadium/Chase Center, is the Riverwalk with many Christina River attractions. The Christina Riverboat Company offers lunch, dinner, moonlight, and specialty cruises on a three-mile boat ride down the Christina Riverfront.

Other notable historic and architectural sites include the historic, renovated Wilmington Train Station, the African Union First Colored Methodist Protestant Church, the Quaker Meeting House, the Wilmington Club, and I. M. Pei building. Visitors may also enjoy taking a relaxing stroll through a few of the city's historic neighborhoods, such as Brandywine Village, Little Italy, Quaker Hill, and the Ships Tavern District.

Arts and Culture

The cultural tastes of Wilmington's benefactors are reflected in sites throughout the area, while widespread patronage sustains local artists and arts organizations. The Delaware Division of the Arts, headquartered in Wilmington, is the mentor to many of the city's cultural groups. It directly supports monthly exhibitions of the visual arts and publishes a directory of visual artists.

Theater, dance, and music productions figure prominently in the city's cultural life. Highlighting Wilmington's downtown renewal efforts is the 1,100-seat Grand Opera House. The Grand Opera House is one of the finest examples of cast-iron architecture in America. Built in 1871, the meticulously restored theater serves as the home the City Theater Company, the Contemporary Stage Company (summer theater), First State Ballet Theatre, the Delaware Symphony Orchestra, and Opera Delaware. The Delaware Symphony Orchestra is a professional symphony orchestra that performs more than 40 classical, pops, and chamber concerts each year, as well as touring engagements. One of the city's oldest arts companies, Opera Delaware performs two annual fully-staged productions with complete orchestra plus a Family Opera Theater production each spring. The Opera House also hosts stand-up comedians, jazz concerts, and world culture events on its 100-event annual schedule. The Baby Grand, the Opera House's small stage, seats about 300.

The 400-seat Delaware Theatre Company, founded in 1979, offers a series of plays in its Christina Riverfront location from November to April. Six professional first-run Broadway shows and an acclaimed children's series are staged regularly from September to May at the 1,200-

seat DuPont Theater in the Hotel du Pont. The DuPont Theater is also the setting each December for a lavish production of the "Nutcracker Ballet" performed by the Wilmington Ballet Academy of the Dance. Other theater groups include the Wilmington Drama League, the New Candlelight Theater, and Three Little Bakers Dinner Theatre.

Like so many other attractions in the area, several of Wilmington's major museums and galleries are linked to the du Pont family. Henry Francis du Pont spent a lifetime collecting the finest American furniture and decorative arts made or used between 1640 and 1840. At Winterthur Museum, Garden, and Library the furniture of Duncan Phyfe, the silver of Paul Revere, and room furnishings from all over the eastern seaboard are displayed in 200 period settings, from a New England kitchen to a Georgia Empire-style dining room. Three new galleries have been built adjacent to the existing museum. Surrounding the museum are 200 landscaped acres, reminiscent of an eighteenth-century English park, and Chandler Woods. The Enchanted Woods Children's Garden is there.

Eleuthere I. du Pont, discovering that high-quality black powder (gunpowder) was a scarce commodity in eighteenth-century America, began an industry that grew into one of the world's largest corporations. At Hagley Museum on the Brandywine the life of the nineteenth-century mill worker has been recreated. As visitors stroll along the banks of the river, they see a restored operating wooden water wheel, turbine-powered roll wheels, a vintage steam engine, a stone quarry, a machine shop, and a hydroelectric plant. Overlooking the powder yards is Eleutherian Mills, the Georgian-style country home built by E. I. du Pont in 1803. The Hagley Library is one of the finest repositories of industrial and manufacturing history in the United States.

The Delaware Museum of Natural History reflects the interests of its founder, John du Pont. Visitors encounter examples of Delaware flora and fauna. They can also walk across Australia's Great Barrier Reef, view an African waterhole, and enter the Hall of Birds, which features a 27-pound bird egg. In addition, the museum houses one of the world's finest shell collections, a scale model of the International Space Station, and a permanent dinosaur exhibit.

The Delaware Art Museum completed an expansion and renovation project in 2005 to update the facility with a new facade, additional exhibit and conference space, outdoor gardens for sculptural displays, and improved handicap access. A world-class institution, the Museum hosts a 12,000 piece collection of traditional and contemporary paintings, sculpture, photography, and crafts that represent some of the finest American art from 1840 to the present, and includes the largest collection of Pre-Raphaelite paintings outside the United Kingdom. The Delaware Center for Contemporary Arts opened at the Riverfront in 2000. It houses seven art galleries, 26 artist studios, an auditorium, a classroom, and a gift shop. The Christina Cultural Arts Center, originally designed as a community center for Polish and Swedish families, now hosts multicultural events and performances throughout the year. The Delaware Children's Museum opened in 2010 along the city's Riverfront, focusing on math, science, and technology. Previously, Wilmington was one of the nation's largest cities without a children's museum.

The Wilmington area's other museums include the Brandywine River Museum, which houses three generations of Wyeth family paintings as well as works by Howard Pyle, Maxfield Parrish, and many other American artists. The Delaware Center for Horticulture is located on DuPont Street. The Rockwood Museum, a nineteenth-century country estate, features decorative arts from the seventeenth through nineteenth centuries, and the George Reed II House & Garden in Historic New Castle is a fine example of Georgian architecture.

The Chase Center opened in 1998 as a major part of the redevelopment of the Christina Riverfront. This 25,000-square-foot exhibition center's first exhibition was Nicholas & Alexandra: The Last Imperial Family of Czarist Russia. The exhibit attracted more than 500,000 people during its six-month run. The Delaware Sports Museum and Hall of Fame is also located on the Riverfront. One popular out-of-town attraction includes the Biggs Museum of American Art in Dover. For military history buffs, the Air Mobility Command Museum, also in Dover, houses some of the most unique and distinguished military flying machines of the past 50 years.

Festivals and Holidays

In May, Wilmington Flower Market is a week-long celebration, followed in June by the Greek Festival at Holy Trinity Church. June is also the month when thousands flock to Wilmington's Little Italy (the area surrounding St. Anthony of Padua Church) for the annual St. Anthony's Italian Festival. Independence Day is celebrated with an annual event on the Riverfront. Also in July, Rockwood Museum's Old-Fashioned Ice Cream Festival is a family favorite. In fall comes the Brandywine Festival of the Arts, when more than 250 artists from around the country exhibit their works along the riverbank. Visitors can find paintings, sculpture, jewelry, and crafts, or partake in an afternoon auction each day of the festival while they enjoy the scenic beauty of Brandywine Park. The August Quarterly is considered to be the oldest continually held African American festival in the nation. The focus of the festival is on religious revival and freedom with several local churches providing gospel music and youth performances. The Riverfront Blues Festival and the Peoples' Festival, a tribute to Bob Marley, are also held in August. September is the month for the Polish Festival at St. Hedwig's Church, and the

Hispanic Festival. The annual Halloween Loop costume party draws thousands of people each year. Many local museums host special Christmas events, including a Christmas at Rockwood, a Yuletide Tour at Winterthur, and a holiday Candlelight Tour at Hagley Mills Museum. The Saint Lucia Celebration, the Swedish festival of Lights, is hosted at Old Swedes Church.

Sports for the Spectator

The Wilmington Blue Rocks, a Single-A minor league team affiliated with the Kansas City Royals, plays at the 6,532 seat Daniels S. Frawley Stadium on Madison Street. Racing enthusiasts in Wilmington enjoy Delaware Park Horse Racing and Slots, which hosts daytime thoroughbred racing from April to September at one of the nation's most picturesque sporting facilities. A different kind of racing draws Wilmingtonians to the Winterthur Point-to-Point on the first Sunday in May. Five amateur steeplechases are the main event, preceded by pony races and a parade of horse-drawn coaches and carriages. The DuPont Country Club has hosted a number of Ladies Professional Golf Association events. The massively popular NASCAR auto racing circuit makes three stops annually nearby at the Dover International Speedway. Blue Diamond Park in New Castle features Motocross, BMX, and ATV racing. The Wilmington Rowing Center sponsors an annual regatta.

Sports for the Participant

Wilmington residents have easy access to more than 4,500 acres of county park land. Those who prefer to ride their own horses are invited to try the equestrian trails at Bellevue State Park on the former estate of William du Pont. The park's nearly 300 acres offer bridle trails, indoor and outdoor equestrian tracks, a fishing pond, a fitness track, and the Bellevue Tennis Center. Rockford Park offers tennis courts, a baseball field, a special dog run area, and snow-sledding hills. The Rockford Tower is open for visitors to make their way to the top. The Wilmington Municipal Golf Course is managed by the city and offers 18 holes of championship golf, in addition to the area's many other public and private courses. Delaware's largest freshwater marsh is in Brandywine State Park, making it a favorite with birdwatchers. Avid fishermen reel in crappie, bluegill, and rock bass here. The park offers 12 miles of hiking and equestrian trails, as well as canoeing on Brandywine Creek. Rolling meadows and woodlands also make this a winter favorite for cross-country skiers. Wilmington has three YMCAs and a downtown racquetball facility. The Caesar Rodney Half Marathon and 5K Run takes place in the city in March.

Shopping and Dining

Because there is no sales tax in Delaware, retailing is strong in Wilmington. The enclaves of Trolley Square, Historic New Castle, Hockessin, Little Italy, Newark, Centreville, and Kennett Square in Pennsylvania, offer one-of-a-kind shops and boutiques. Market Street Mall offers specialty shops, restaurants, and cafes in the heart of Wilmington's central business district. Christiana Mall (south of Wilmington, along Interstate 95) features four major anchor stores and more than 130 shops. Concord Mall, on Concord Pike, has more than 90 specialty shops. Three art galleries featuring hand-made crafts and fine art from around the country are within a half-hour drive of each other: The André Harvey Studio, Creations Fine Woodworking Gallery, and Sommerville Manning Gallery.

Fine dining is the norm for Wilmington's upscale, metropolitan population. City restaurants feature everything from Chesapeake Bay blue crabs to Japanese tempura. Many of the area's colonial inns and taverns are still serving guests. Fresh seafood and steaks are the norm at the waterside restaurants along Riverfront Wilmington. Mediterranean and Italian fare can be found at Wilmington's Little Italy neighborhood. Trolley Square has sidewalk cafes, cozy bistros, and lively pubs. For a taste of history, visitors and locals go to the colonial taverns in nearby historic New Castle.

Rodney Square and Little Italy have farmers markets open from May or June through October. The Trolley Square Farmer's Market is only open on Fridays in September.

Visitor Information: Greater Wilmington Convention and Visitors Bureau, 100 West 10th Street, Suite 20, Wilmington, DE 19801; telephone (800) 489-6664. Wilmington Renaissance Corporation, 100 West 10th St, Suite 206, Wilmington, DE 19801; telephone (302) 656-2909.

■ Convention Facilities

The Wilmington area offers meeting planners more than 4,000 rooms plus meeting facilities that range from intimate country getaways to large world-class conference centers accommodating 1,000 people in a single room. The area's largest event and convention venue is the Chase Center on the Riverfront, which offers more than 60,000 square feet of exhibit and meeting space, including an additional 45,000 square feet added in 2005. Convenient to major airports, hotels, Interstate 95, and Amtrak, the center has boardrooms, meeting rooms, ballrooms, state-of-the-art audio-visual, and more than 2,400 parking spaces.

New Castle County boasts more than 40 hotels that specialize in small- and medium-sized conferences and meetings plus 400 restaurants, all set in the beautiful Brandywine Valley with its vistas made famous by three generations of Wyeths. One of the larger venues is Clayton Hall Conference Center at the

University of Delaware, which offers state-of-the-art amenities accommodating intimate gatherings to 1,500-person conclaves. The Hampton Inn & Suites Chadds Ford in nearby Glenn Mills, Pennsylvania, offers almost 15,000 square feet made up of 13 well-lit meeting/banquet rooms, including a state-of-the-art auditorium with built-in AV and seating for up to 200 people. The Hotel du Pont is a historic property that includes 30 meeting rooms, five in the self-contained Executive Conference Center, and 11 rooms in a state-of-the-art High Tech Conference Center. Also located within the Hotel du Pont is the multipurpose 1,200-seat Du Pont Theater, available for meetings. Unique meeting sites in Wilmington include the Delaware Art Museum, Delaware Museum of Natural History, and the Grand Opera House.

Convention Information: Greater Wilmington Convention and Visitors Bureau, 100 West 10th Street, Suite 20, Wilmington, DE 19801; telephone (800) 489-6664.

■ Transportation

Approaching the City

Wilmington is only 30 minutes from Philadelphia International Airport, a major hub, making the city easy to reach by plane. Door-to-door limousine service is available to all parts of the city. Wilmington-Philadelphia Airport, about 10 minutes from downtown Wilmington in New Castle, provides commercial service through Frontier airlines to Atlanta, Chicago, Denver, Detroit, Fort Myers, Orlando, and Tampa.

Located in the middle of the heavily traveled northeast corridor, Wilmington is also convenient to reach by car. Interstate 95, the major north–south route from Maine to Florida, cuts through the western portion of the city. The Wilmington Bypass, Interstate 495, connects Interstate 95 with downtown and offers easy access to the Port of Wilmington. Travelers arriving on the New Jersey Turnpike from points north cross the Delaware River and enter Wilmington on Interstate 295. In addition to the interstate highway system, U.S. routes 13, 40, 41, and 202 allow access to the city. With the completion of limited access Delaware Route 1, the largest project in the history of the Delaware Department of Transportation, central and south Delaware to the Maryland border are now connected to Interstate 95.

Wilmington's Amtrak Station provides passenger service with connections to all major points. Travelers arriving from New York, Philadelphia, Baltimore, or Washington, D.C., can take the high speed Acela Express as well as conventional Amtrak and SEPTA (commuter) trains. The station is a five-minute walk to downtown stores and hotels and has facilities for both long-term and short-term parking. More than 700,000 passengers pass through the station annually.

Traveling in the City

Because of Wilmington's small size, residents enjoy minimal levels of traffic congestion, noise pollution, and smog. If they choose, they can drive from the heart of downtown to the open spaces of the "chateau country" in fifteen minutes. A number of well-traveled routes carry commuters to the central business district from the densely populated suburbs. Well over 10,000 parking spaces in the downtown area allow for easy access to offices, restaurants, shops, and entertainment centers. To promote individual and business use of carpooling, vanpooling and bus service, Delaware's Commuter Service Administration has developed a free, computerized matching service including auto-geocoding for more than 17,000 streets in New Castle County. The Wilmington Wayfinding Project has added over 100 signs throughout the city to direct visitors to major locations and attractions.

Another alternative for city residents is public transportation. The Delaware Authority for Regional Transit (DART) operates bus routes through Wilmington and its suburbs. DART accommodated 12.8 million passenger trips in 2012. The Delaware Administration for Specialized Transit (DAST) provides lift-equipped buses for the elderly and the handicapped. The Southeastern Pennsylvania Transportation Authority (SEPTA) runs several daily trains between Wilmington and Philadelphia.

■ Communications

Newspapers and Magazines

The News Journal is the primary newspaper serving Wilmington as well as the state of Delaware. Other Wilmington-based publications include: *Delaware Today,* a general-interest monthly magazine; *The Dialog,* published by the Catholic Press of Wilmington; *Delaware Medical Journal;* and the online *New Castle Business Ledger.*

Television and Radio

Four television stations originate in Wilmington: WHYY, Inc., Local Media TV Philadelphia, LLC, Ion Media Philadelphia License, Inc., and Word of God Fellowship, Inc. Wilmington viewers receive most programs from stations located in Philadelphia and other cities in Pennsylvania and New Jersey. The same is true of radio broadcasts; the city is home to four AM stations and three FM stations but is considered part of a market that also encompasses eastern Pennsylvania (including Philadelphia) and northern New Jersey.

Media Information: The News Journal, P.O. Box 15505, Wilmington, DE 19850; telephone (302) 324-2500.

Wilmington Online

Brandywine School District. Available www.brandy wineschools.org

Christina School District. Available www.chris tinak12.org

City of Wilmington. Available www.ci.wilmington. de.us

Delaware Department of Labor. Available www. delawareworks.com

Delaware Office of Economic Development. Available www.dedo.delaware.gov

The News Journal. Available www.delawareonline. com

New Castle County Chamber of Commerce. Available www.nccedc.com

Red Clay Consolidated School District. Available www.edline.net/pages/RedClay

Wilmington Convention and Visitors Bureau. Available www.visitwilmingtonde.com

Wilmington Public Library. Available wilmington. lib.de.us

Wilmington Renaissance Corporation. Available www.bigideaswilmington.com

BIBLIOGRAPHY

Chance, Elbert, *The Blue Rocks, Past and Present: Wilmington's Baseball Team* (Wilmington, DE: Cedar Tree Books, 2000)

Espenshade, Christopher T., *William Hare: Master Potter of Wilmington, Delaware, 1839–1885* (Dover, DE: Delaware Heritage Press, 2011)

Lincoln, Anna T., *Wilmington, Delaware: Three Centuries under Four Flags, 1609-1937* (Kennikat Press, 1977)

Thompson, Priscilla, and Sally O'Byrne, *Wilmington's Waterfront* (Charleston, SC: Arcadia Publishing, 1999)

Florida

The State in Brief

Nickname: Sunshine State

Motto: In God we trust

Flower: Orange blossom

Bird: Mockingbird

Area: 65,758 square miles (2010; U.S. rank 22nd)

Elevation: Ranges from sea level to 345 feet above sea level

Climate: Humid with abundant sunshine; ranges from subtropical to tropical

Admitted to Union: March 3, 1845

Capital: Tallahassee

Head Official: Rick Scott (R) (until 2015)

Population

1990: 12,938,000
2000: 15,982,378
2010: 18,801,310
2012 estimate: 18,885,152
Percent change, 2000–2010: 17.6%
U.S. rank in 2012: 4th
Percent of residents born in state: 35.0% (2012)
Density: 350.6 people per square mile (2010)
2012 FBI Crime Index Total: 727,075

Racial and Ethnic Characteristics (2012)

White: 14,438,364
Black or African American: 3,005,551
American Indian and Alaska Native: 58,119
Asian: 464,587
Native Hawaiian and Pacific Islander: 11,575
Hispanic or Latino (may be of any race): 4,247,427
Other: 906,956

Age Characteristics (2012)

Population under 5 years old: 1,076,198
Population 5 to 19 years old: 3,427,199
Percent of population 65 years and over: 17.5%
Median age: 40.8

Vital Statistics

Total number of births (2012–13): 215,542
Total number of deaths (2012–13): 182,121
AIDS cases reported through 2011: 126,839

Economy

Major industries: Agriculture, tourism, manufacturing, services, trade, government
Unemployment rate (2012): 6.8%
Per capita income (2012): $26,451
Median household income (2012): $47,309
Percentage of persons below poverty level (2012): 15.6%
Income tax rate: None
Sales tax rate: 6.0%

Jacksonville

■ The City in Brief

Founded: 1816 (incorporated 1832)

Head Official: Mayor John Peyton (R) (since 2003; term expires June 2011)

City Population
- 1990: 635,230
- 2000: 735,617
- 2010: 821,784
- 2012 estimate: 836,507
- Percent change, 2000–2010: 11.7%
- U.S. rank in 1990: 15th (State rank: 1st)
- U.S. rank in 2000: 20th (State rank: 1st)
- U.S. rank in 2010: 11th (State rank: 1st)

Metropolitan Statistical Area Population
- 2000: 1,122,750
- 2010: 1,345,596
- 2012 estimate: 1,377,850
- Percent change, 2000–2010: 19.8%
- U.S. rank in 2000: 45th
- U.S. rank in 2010: 40th

Area: 758 square miles

Elevation: ranges from sea level to 71 feet

Average Annual Temperatures: 68.0° F

Average Annual Precipitation: 51.3 inches

Major Economic Sectors: Financial services, health care, aviation and aerospace, advanced manufacturing, information technology

Unemployment Rate: 7.3% (2012)

Per Capita Income: $23,282

2012 FBI Crime Index Property: 34,674

Major Colleges and Universities: University of North Florida, Jacksonville University, Florida State College at Jacksonville, Flagler College, Edward Waters College, Florida Coastal School of Law,

Daily Newspaper: *Florida Times-Union*

■ Introduction

Jacksonville is a cosmopolitan riverside city and the major city in northeast Florida, which is known as the First Coast because of its long history. Jacksonville is close to miles of beautiful Atlantic coastline, and tourists are also drawn by the city's sunny climate, recreational activities, culture, bustling downtown, and such sites as a restored Civil War fortress, America's oldest city (nearby St. Augustine), and the many sites reflecting the area's rich African American cultural heritage. Jacksonville's location also has made it a major transportation and distribution center, and it is headquarters for the *Fortune* 500 company CSX. To live up to its heritage and maximize the return on its location, Jacksonville pushed hard for downtown development during the 2000s and 2010s, investing hundreds of millions infrastructure to support private development and attract residents to new downtown residential structures.

■ Geography and Climate

Jacksonville is located in the northeast corner of Florida on the banks of the St. Johns River, adjacent to the Atlantic Ocean. The Napoleon Bonaparte Broward Bridge (popularly known as the Dames Point Bridge) over the St. Johns River, was named in honor of the man who served as governor of Florida from 1905 to 1909. The bridge, with towers that reach 470 feet above the water, is the second longest concrete cable-stayed bridge in the Western Hemisphere.

Downtown Jacksonville, FL marina on the St. John's River. © *LBarnwell/Alamy*

The city has four distinct seasons: cool in spring and fall, mild in winter, and warm in summer with plenty of sunshine year round. There was only one serious hurricane in the twentieth century (Hurricane Dora in 1964) as natural phenomena form a weather shield for the area.

Area: 758 square miles

Elevation: ranges from sea level to 71 feet

Average Temperatures: 68.0° F

Average Annual Precipitation: 51.3 inches

■ History

Town Founded on River Site

Historians hold that the Timucua tribe lived on the site of today's Jacksonville since before the year 2000 B.C. The first documented European visitors to the area were a group of French Huguenots, led by Rene de Laudonniere, who sailed into the mouth of the St. Johns River in 1562. They soon founded Fort Caroline (on the river north of the present downtown), which was captured by the Spanish

during a bloody massacre in 1565. The Florida region became a territory of the United States in 1821, following a 300-year period of battles between Spain, France, and Great Britain. That same year Georgia plantation owner Isaiah D. Hart moved to the narrowest spot of the St. Johns River known as "Cowford," where cows were transported by ferry across the river. On this site in 1822 Hart laid out the plans for the town of Jacksonville, which he named after General Andrew Jackson, provisional governor of the Florida Territory who later became president. The small community of 100 people was chartered as a town and elected its first mayor in 1832. In 1845 Florida became a state. By 1859 when Jacksonville was chartered as a city, it had become the state's major port, exporting both timber goods and cotton.

Jacksonville During the Latter Nineteenth Century

Jacksonville was not part of the Confederacy during the time of the Civil War (1861-1865); however, both sides fought for the land and the Union Army occupied the city on four different occasions. Following the battle of Olustee, which took place in the city, wounded Union soldiers were brought to Jacksonville's homes and churches, some of which were converted to military hospitals. Union forces destroyed the city but it was quickly rebuilt.

During the second half of the nineteenth century, Jacksonville had a population of about 7,500 permanent residents and drew more than 75,000 tourists annually. Jacksonville began to grow and prosper during the 1870s with the development of its lumber and shipping industries. Like many other east Florida coastal areas, Jacksonville's beach communities became established with the development of the railway system. A group of Jacksonville businessmen united in the late 1800s to construct a rail system that ended at the beach east of town. In time deluxe hotels were built, beach property was sold, and in 1888 the first direct railroad service between the city and the North was established. That same year, 427 people were killed by a yellow fever epidemic that assailed the city.

Fire Causes Large-Scale Destruction

By 1900 the city had a population approaching 30,000 people. The new century dawned with the Great Fire of 1901 when embers from a stove ignited materials at the Cleveland Fiber Factory. Before it was extinguished, the fire had destroyed nearly 2,400 buildings, decimated 146 city blocks, killed 7 people, left 10,000 people homeless, and destroyed $15 million worth of property. Fortunately, the city was once again quickly rebuilt and the population grew to more than 91,000 people by 1920.

Briefly a Film Center; Industry Revives

Jacksonville was an important site for the early development of the film industry, and Florida's first motion picture studios opened there in 1908. The warm weather year round and the low cost of labor and housing boosted this development, which continued until the early 1920s, when the industry moved to California.

The population of Jacksonville stood at more than 173,000 people by 1940. Mayport Naval Base and two naval air stations were built in the city during the Second World War (1941-1945). Suburban sprawl during the 1950s resulted in a loss of population for the city, while the county population grew. In 1968 the city and Duval County consolidated, and Jacksonville grew in the rankings of U.S. cities by size from sixty-first to twenty-second.

In the period of the 1960s and 1970s local focus was directed toward industrial diversification and development of the city's port facilities. Redevelopment efforts transformed the downtown area, and new service industries, especially finance and insurance, were booming as the city entered the twenty-first century.

Rebuilding Downtown

Jacksonville expanded into a new direction when it was awarded a team franchise by the National Football League in 1993. The Jacksonville Jaguars draw thousands of fans to the downtown area on a regular basis, adding lifeblood to the local businesses. This newfound football momentum sharply increased when the city hosted Super Bowl XXXIX in February 2005, the smallest market ever to do so.

Downtown development and redevelopment remained the city's focus through the 2000s and 2010s. Like many sprawling metropolitan areas, Jacksonville has sought to recapture population concentration in the downtown area. Growth in the aerospace industry, exemplified by Flightstar Aircraft Services and Northrup Grumman's expansions in 2013, exemplified the type of high-tech development the city sought.

Historical Information: Jacksonville Historical Society, 317 A. Philip Randolph Blvd., Jacksonville, FL 32202-2217; telephone (904) 665-0064.

■ Population Profile

Metropolitan Statistical Area Population

2000: 1,122,750
2010: 1,345,596
2012 estimate: 1,377,850
Percent change, 2000–2010: 19.8%
U.S. rank in 2000: 45th
U.S. rank in 2010: 40th

City Residents

1990: 635,230
2000: 735,617
2010: 821,784
2012 estimate: 836,507
Percent change, 2000–2010: 11.7%
U.S. rank in 1990: 15th (State rank: 1st)
U.S. rank in 2000: 20th (State rank: 1st)
U.S. rank in 2010: 11th (State rank: 1st)

Density: 1,100.1 people per square mile

Racial and ethnic characteristics

White: 505,082
Black or African American: 250,500
American Indian and Alaskan Native: 2,467
Asian: 37,272
Native Hawaiian and Other Pacific Islander: 1,058
Hispanic or Latino (may be of any race): 68,794
Other: 40,128

Percent of residents born in state: 49.9%

Age characteristics

Population under 5 years old: 58,879
Population 5 to 9 years old: 59,579
Population 10 to 14 years old: 46,320
Population 15 to 19 years old: 51,725
Population 20 to 24 years old: 65,898

Population 25 to 34 years old: 128,873
Population 35 to 44 years old: 108,592
Population 45 to 54 years old: 117,549
Population 55 to 59 years old: 53,473
Population 60 to 64 years old: 47,401
Population 65 to 74 years old: 56,335
Population 75 to 84 years old: 27,986
Population 85 years and over: 13,897
Median age: 35.5

Births (2010–11 Metropolitan Area)

Total number: 17,601

Deaths (2010–11 Metropolitan Area)

Total number: 10,910

Money income (2012)

Per capita income: $23,282
Median household income: $45,577
Total households: 310,528

Number of households with income of . . .

less than $10,000: 27,975
$10,000 to $14,999: 19,127
$15,000 to $24,999: 37,482
$25,000 to $34,999: 36,063
$35,000 to $49,999: 45,835
$50,000 to $74,999: 57,735
$75,000 to $99,999: 35,475
$100,000 to $149,999: 33,727
$150,000 to $199,999: 9,066
$200,000 or more: 8,043

Percent of families below poverty level: 17.7%

FBI Crime Index Property: 34,674

FBI Crime Index Violent: 5,189

■ Municipal Government

The city of Jacksonville and Duval County voted in 1968 to establish a consolidated government designed to use all community resources in solving problems that affect the entire county area. The city's strong-mayor form of government is divided into 14 districts of nearly equal population, each of which is represented by a council member. Five additional council members represent the entire community as a whole. These 19 council members are the legislative body of Jacksonville, and are elected to four-year terms.

In May of each year the Council elects a president and vice president, who serve one-year terms beginning July 1.

Head Official: Mayor John Peyton (R) (since 2003; term expires June 2011)

Total Number of City Employees: 5,823 (2014)

City Information: City of Jacksonville, 117 W. Duval St., Jacksonville, FL 32202; telephone (904)630-CITY (2489).

■ Economy

Major Industries and Commercial Activity

With its diverse economic base, young, energetic population, and high quality of life, Jacksonville experienced substantial growth during the latter decades of the twentieth century. The early years of the twenty-first century supported continued growth, but Jacksonville, like most U.S. cities, experience a slowdown during a national recession in the late 2000s before growth returned in the early 2010s.

The city is a transportation hub, with a deepwater port that ranks among the top-two vehicle-handling ports in the nation. The Jacksonville Port Authority (JAXPORT) owns and operates three public marine terminals and one passenger cruise terminal. Jacksonville is served by three airports, three seaports, a highway system that links the city to three major interstates, and a rail system served by three railroads—CSX, Norfolk Southern, and Florida East Coast. CSX is based in Jacksonville. Three important naval air stations within the city limits and Kings Bay Submarine Base nearby in Georgia give Jacksonville one of the largest military presences in the country.

Pulp and paper mills play substantial roles in the local economy, and Georgia Pacific Corp. and Smurfit-Stone Container Corp. are two of the area's largest manufacturers. Construction equipment and building materials is another key segment of the Jacksonville economy, with Ring Power Corporation, USG Corporation, and Vulcan Materials Company among the top employers in the region. Other large manufacturers are Northrop Grumman (aircraft), Anheuser-Busch (beer), Vistakon (optical products), Swisher International Inc. (cigars and smokeless tobacco), Medtronic Xomed (surgical products), and Dura Automotive Systems Inc. (automotive components). Saft, a world leader in the design, development, and manufacture of renewable energy storage, broke ground on a Jacksonville manufacturing facility for lithium-ion cells and batteries that opened in 2011 with an annual sales capacity of $300 million.

Aviation is a natural fit to Jacksonville. Thousands of naval personnel exit the military every year in Jacksonville, and most remain in northeast Florida, supplying the area with a rich resource of aviation skills and related technical experience. Aviation-related training programs in the Jacksonville area include Florida Community College of Jacksonville's Aviation Center of Excellence, located at the Cecil Commerce Center, which is also home to one of four airports in Jacksonville. The city experienced a boom in the aviation industry in the early 2000s. Flightstar Aircraft Services announced a $30.5 million expansion in 2013, and Northrup Grumman filed plans for a new $80 million facility in nearby St. Augustine.

Items and goods produced: aircraft, machinery, paper and paper products, building products, beer, soft drinks, tobacco, and optical and surgical products

Incentive Programs-New and Existing Companies

Local programs: The Jacksonville Regional Chamber of Commerce maintains close relationships with the City of Jacksonville, the Jacksonville Economic Development Commission, the Jacksonville Port Authority, and the more than 3,000 local businesses that are Chamber members. The businesses that have located or expanded in Jacksonville cite the many city and state incentives that are available, the support of city and business leaders, and the fact that the consolidated city-county government allows for faster permitting and less bureaucratic red tape overall.

The JAXUSA Partnership is Jacksonville and Northeast Florida's regional economic development initiative. A private nonprofit, the partnership works in partnership with the Jacksonville Regional Chamber of Commerce, the Jacksonville Economic Development Commission, JEA (public utilities), the counties of the region (Baker, Clay, Duval, Flagler, Nassau, Putnam and St. Johns), WorkSource, the Jacksonville Port and Aviation Authoritys, the Jacksonville Transportation Authority, and private sector corporations. Investment dollars are channeled into business recruitment, existing business services, education and workforce preparation, and special economic initiatives.

The Northwest Jacksonville Development Fund makes available grants or loans for infrastructure improvements, facade renovation, and purchase of land or buildings. Several tax credits for development in the downtown area are offered by the local govenrment, including job tax credits, sales tax refunds, and property tax credits.

State programs: Enterprise Florida is a partnership between Florida's government and business leaders and is the principal economic development organization for the state of Florida. Enterprise Florida's mission is to increase economic opportunities for all Floridians by supporting the creation of quality jobs, a well-trained workforce, and globally competitive businesses. It pursues this mission in cooperation with its statewide network of economic development partners. Among the incentive programs managed at the state level is the Economic Development Transportation Fund, which helps fund the cost of transportation projects, such as access roads and road widening, required for the establishment, expansion, or retention of businesses in Florida. The state's Qualified

Target Industry Tax Refund is similar to a Miami-Dade program that rewards the creation of jobs in certain industries.

Florida has a favorable tax climate, with benefits such as no corporate income tax on limited partnerships, no sales tax on purchases of raw materials incorporated in a final product for resale, and no personal state income tax. The state also offers various sales and use tax exemptions for machinery and equipment purchase, electric energy, research and development, and other aspects of doing business in the area.

Job training programs: Florida is a statewide, business-led workforce policy board that partners with the Florida Department of Economic Opportunity and regional workforce boards. The 24 regional boards have primary responsibility for direct services through a statewide network of One-Stop Career systems. One-Stop Career Centers are the central elements of the One-Stop system that provide integrated services to employers, workers, and jobseekers. Two are located in Jacksonville. CareerSource Florida administers two training grant initiatives to assist both employers and job seekers. Quick Response Training (QRT) Grants provide funding for customized training to new or expanding businesses. Incumbent Worker Training (IWT) Grants provide funding for programs that help existing full-time employees upgrade their skills.

Development Projects

Downtown Vision, Inc. (DVI), a not-for-profit organization designed to bolster the downtown community and promote it as an ideal venue for business and tourism, was established in 2000. Its initiatives include programs to make the downtown area clean and safe, to market the area through television programs, radio spots, and publications, to tackle transportation and parking issues, and retain and attract business. Between 2000 and 2012, more than $1.7 billion in development took place downtown, with an additional $586 million of active construction projects and $567 million of proposed developments.

In 2012 construction completed on a new Duval County Courthouse. The 800,000-square-foot facility was built at a cost of $350 million. Three major transportation projects were completed between 2007 and 2011. The bridge span of Mathews Bridge was completed in 2007 for nearly $13 million; a 10-phase, $148 million interchange reconstruction at the intersection of Interstates 95 and 10 completed in 2011; and repainting and repairs to the Hart Bridge ended in 2011 after a $26 million investment. These projects were completed by the Florida Department of Transportation.

Municipal intiatives included a mix of streetscape improvements in the city totaled more than $2.1 million in 2012 alone and focused on making areas more pedestrian friendly. More utilitarian projects included $5 million to improve stormwater systems and drainage along city streets, work undertaken in 2011. The Jacksonville Transportation Authority has proposed development of a $182 million transportation center for the city. Portions of the facility achieved design approval in 2011, although initial proposals dated to 2000.

In private developments, Baptist Medical Center completed a $27.5 million surgical wing in 2010, adding 19,000 square feet of post-surgical recovery rooms. It then built a new $200 million East Wing of its Baptist Hospital during 2012 and 2013. A proposal for a mixed use facility in the former Marble Bank Trio buildings had attracted $70 million of investment by 2012. Many residential and mixed use projects were in various stages of development during 2013.

Economic Development Information: Jacksonville Regional Chamber of Commerce, 3 Independent Dr., Jacksonville, FL 32202; telephone (904) 366-6600; info@myjaxchamber.com. Downtown Vision, Inc., 214 N. Hogan St., Ste. 120, Jacksonville, FL 32202; telephone (904) 634-0303; fax (904) 634-8988.

Commercial Shipping

The hub of seven major roadways—Interstates 10, 95, and 295, and U.S. Highways 1, 17, 90, and 301—Jacksonville has a straight shipping line to the Midwest, West, and Northeast. It is served by numerous trucking lines, three major railroads, and Jacksonville International Airport. One of the largest deepwater ports in the south Atlantic, the Jacksonville Port Authority manages three public marine terminals and one passenger cruise terminal. In 2011 Jacksonville's Port achieved its 11th consecutive year of record revenue and was second in the United States for vehicle handling, first for vehicle exports.

Labor Force and Employment Outlook

Jacksonville is an attractive site for expanding companies, in part because of its abundance of workers due to in-migration, natural growth, a strong military presence, and the area's educational institutions. Relocating businesses have been drawn to the area's quality of life, its sunshine, and its sports, recreational, and cultural opportunities, as well as the region's emphasis on well-planned growth. Jacksonville has more than 75 regional career academies that align with the city's target industries and provides hundreds of paid internships annually to the rising workforce. The school system promotes career academies and a focus in science, math, and technology courses to help prepare the local workforce.

The following is a summary of data regarding the Jacksonville labor force:

Size of civilian labor force: 424,579

Number of workers employed in . . .

agriculture and mining: 1,419
construction: 19,665

manufacturing: 22,108
wholesale trade: 9,335
retail trade: 47,160
transportation: 26,433
information systems: 5,913
finance: 43,316
professional administration: 42,190
education and social services: 76,567
arts and leisure: 38,109
other: 17,850
public administration: 21,009

Average hourly earnings of production workers: $15.82

Unemployment rate: 7.3% (2012)

Employers

Largest employers (2012)	Number of employees
Naval Air Station Jacksonville	25,240
Duval County Public Schools	14,480
Naval Station Mayport	9,000
City of Jacksonville	8,820
Baptist Health	8,270
Bank of America Merrill Lynch	8,000
Florida Blue	6,500
Mayo Clinic Jacksonville	4,970
Citi	4,200
J P Morgan Chase	4,200

Cost of Living

The following is a summary of data regarding several key cost of living factors in the area.

2013 ACCRA Average House Price: $210,329

2013 ACCRA Cost of Living Index: 93

State income tax rate: None

State sales tax rate: 6.0%

Local income tax rate: None

Local sales tax rate: 1.0%

Property tax rate: $19.1927 per $1,000 (2013)

Economic Information: Jacksonville Regional Chamber of Commerce, 3 Independent Dr., Jacksonville, FL 32202; telephone (904) 366-6600; info@myjaxchamber.com.

■ Education and Research

Elementary and Secondary Schools

Duval County Public Schools is one of the nation's largest school systems, serving more than 120,000 students. According to 2012 rankings by the *Washington Post,* Duval County included eight of the nation's top 300 high schools. Advanced International Certificate of Education Programs are available at four high schools, and Advanced Placement courses are offered at 10. The Early College Program serves four high-school campuses, and International Baccalaureate diplomas are awarded at awarded at four high schools. The school system also offers career academies to prepare students for work in local industries that are current or future targets of economic development. Special programs are available for the more than 400 students that are teen parents, hospitalized or homebounds, or are prekindergarten students with disabilities. McKay scholarships allow special-needs students to transfer to other public schools in the district.

The city has more than 100 private schools as well as 21 charter schools, which enrolled more than 6,000 students in 2013.

The following is a summary of data regarding the Duval County Public Schools.

Total enrollment: 123,997

Number of facilities

    total: 162
    elementary schools: 104
    junior high schools: 28
    high schools: 19
    other: 11

Student/teacher ratio: 15.51:1

Teacher salaries

    average (statewide): $46,702

Funding per pupil: $8,987

Public Schools Information: Duval County Public Schools, 1701 Prudential Dr., Jacksonville, FL 32207; telephone (904) 390-2000.

Colleges and Universities

The University of North Florida in Jacksonville enrolls more than 16,000 students in undergraduate and graduate courses. It offers strong undergraduate degree programs in business, health-care professions, communications, and psychology. *U.S. News & World Report* ranked the college among the top 60 regional universities in 2014. Also ranked by *U.S. News & World Report* was Jacksonville University, a private institution that placed 62 in the publication's listing. Health professions were by far the most popular degree programs, followed by business, management, and marketing tracts. Florida State College at Jacksonville offers more than 100 degree programs and technical certificates across 11 schools of study. Flagler College is a small private institution rated highly for its academic rigor and enrolls under 3,000 students annually. Edward Waters College is private, historically black college. Florida Coastal School of Law is a fully accredited institution providing law degrees to students from 46 different U.S. states.

Libraries and Research Centers

The Jacksonville Public Library serves residents of Duval County include the main library and 20 regional, community, or neighborhood branches. The library provides services that include books by mail, talking books, and special needs library services. There were nearly 600,000 library card holders as of 2012 using the library's collection of some 2.8 million books, periodicals, DVDs, CDs, and other materials. Total circulation was 8.4 million, spread among 4.6 million unique library visitors. Circulation of electronic materials totaled nearly 200,000. Special collections are devoted to Floridiana, African American history and culture, the Holocaust, music, and genealogy.

There are more than a dozen other libraries in the city. Some are affiliated with higher educational institutions, while others are associated with religious groups, research centers, or the U.S. Navy. Their collections focus on such areas as art, science, health care delivery, law, business, education, and liberal arts.

Public Library Information: Jacksonville Public Libraries, 303 North Laura Street, Jacksonville, FL 32202; telephone (904) 630-2665.

■ Health Care

Six major hospitals serve the Jacksonville area. The city is also home to a branch of the renowned Mayo Clinic, which provides medical diagnosis, treatment, and surgery in more than 50 specialties. Opened in 1986, the Jacksonville facility was the first extension of Mayo Clinic of Rochester, Minnesota. From 1987 until 2008, patients of the Mayo Clinic who needed hospitalization were admitted to nearby St. Luke's Hospital. In 2008 the 214-bed Mayo Clinic Hospital opened in Jacksonville, bringing the Mayo Clinic's inpatient and outpatient services together in one facility.

According to *U.S. News & World Report,* the Mayo Clinic in Jacksonville was tied for the top rating in the city along with Baptist Medical Center. Baptist Medical Center has an 844-bed general medical and surgical facility and was nationally ranked by *U.S. News & World Report* for its care in diabetes and endocrinology.

Shands Jacksonville Medical Center has 620 beds and also serves as a teaching hospital. Memorial Hospital, with 425 beds, admitted about 22,000 patients in 2013. St. Vincent's Medical Center is a general medical and surgical hospital with 501 beds; St. Luke's Hospital has 221 beds.

■ Recreation

Sightseeing

The hub of Florida's First Coast has much to offer visitors with its theaters, museums, art galleries, riverboat cruises, beautiful fountains, outstanding musical events, and historic sites.

Jacksonville's miles of beautiful wide beach area has three main sections: Atlantic Beach, Neptune Beach, and Jacksonville Beach. The Jacksonville Beach Pier is a place known for fishing and people-watching; artifacts, paintings, and lighthouse models are the focus at the American Lighthouse and Maritime Museum in Jacksonville Beach. The beach's Seawalk Pavilion features music concerts at its 2,000-seat open-air auditorium. The Pablo Historical Park, a few blocks off the beach, preserves the area's railroad history with a nineteenth-century station master's house, a railroad depot, and a 1911 vintage steam locomotive. Since 1996, the 40-car auto ferry *Jean Ribault* has been ferrying vessels across the St. Johns River between historic Fort George Island and the fishing village of Mayport, home of a large commercial shrimp fleet. Mayport Naval Air Station, one of the nation's largest navy ship facilities, is located in this charming community. Favorite beach area recreation and camping sites are the Kathryn Abbey Hanna State Park with 450 acres of picnic areas, salt and freshwater fishing, and Little Talbot Island State Park beach and campground.

Jacksonville's downtown area is centered on the shores of the St. Johns River. On the north bank of the river is Jacksonville Landing, a festive marketplace featuring fine dining, boutiques, and an open courtyard that frequently offers entertainment. Across the river on the Southbank is the Riverwalk. Its wooden boardwalk, lined with shops, restaurants, and outdoor vendors, extends for more than a mile along the river, allowing visitors a wonderful view of the city's skyline. At the end of the Riverwalk is Friendship Park, the site of the city's iconic fountain. The fountain, which began operation in 1965, originally fired water as high as 10 stories over the park and was illuminated at night. A renovation in 2000 cost $1.3 million for computer-controlled light towers, new pump equipment, and upgrades to the basin and sidewalks. A $3.1 million renovation to add grassy areas, more seating, new sidewalks and lighting, and refurbish the pumps, pipes, and electrical systems completed in 2011.

The Jacksonville Zoological Gardens, located on the city's north side, house more than 2,000 animals and 1,000 species of plants. An African veldt (an open grazing area typical of southern Africa) has been recreated and visitors can experience it firsthand on a wood boardwalk. The African Loop exhibit, as it is known, allows visitors to stroll along a 1,400-foot boardwalk and observe animals in the expansive habitat. Other exhibits include Monsoon Asia, Australian Adventure, and Range of the Jaguar.

Tours that display all the steps of the beer-making process are available at the Anheuser-Busch Brewery. The World Golf Village (in nearby St. Augustine) is home to the World Golf Hall of Fame, a PGA Tour Academy, and an IMAX theater.

The Fort Caroline National Memorial is the site of the first Protestant settlement in the United States. Established in 1564, the site overlooks the St. Johns River and includes a replica of the original fort. Located on Fort George Island, the 1792 Zephaniah Kingsley Plantation contains the remains of slave quarters. Nature walks are available at the Nature Trails at the University of North Florida, the only state university in the country located in a protected wildlife area. Self-guided and expert-guided walking tours of historical areas around the city are well worth the exploration.

Located 25 miles from the city, Fernandina Beach is a 300-year-old town that was once a haven for pirates and smugglers and today features many restored buildings and eighteenth-century homes. A half-hour south of Jacksonville by car is the nation's oldest city, St. Augustine. A walk along the recently restored St. George Street, with its authentic Spanish-Colonial homes and quaint shops, provides a view of more than 400 years of American history.

Camp Milton Historic Preserve, named for Florida's Civil War governor, John Milton, is a 124-acre park that features an educational center, boardwalk, interpretive hiking trails, and a tree sanctuary.

Arts and Culture

From musical theater to contemporary drama, the arts are alive and well in Jacksonville. This is partly due to the Cultural Council of Greater Jacksonville, which keeps the spotlight on the arts and encourages public and private partnerships to increase arts funding.

The Jacksonville Symphony Orchestra (JSO), founded in 1949, is one of the premier orchestras of the Southeast. JSO offers classical performances with world-class guest artists at Robert E. Jacoby Symphony Hall at the Times-Union Center for the Performing Arts, the only true orchestra hall in Florida. The Florida Community College at Jacksonville Artists Series brings top quality national and international entertainers to the Florida Theatre at Times-Union Center for the Performing Arts. The Alhambra Dinner Theatre has been producing professional Broadway style shows since 1967 and is one of the few remaining dinner theaters in North America.

Jacksonville's museums and galleries reflect the diverse historical and cultural interests of its residents. The Museum of Science and History features wonderful exhibits showing the history of the area, science and health demonstrations, and nature studies. An indoor playground at the museum and the adjacent Bryan Gooding Planetarium bring fun to young and old alike. The Museum of Contemporary Art Jacksonville, on the city's south side, houses five galleries with nearly 800 works of art and features a collection of pre-Columbian artifacts as well as exhibits of painting, sculpture, and photography. Its adjacent outdoor sculpture garden is a famous place for picnicking. The Karpeles Manuscript Library Museum, located in the restored former First Church of Christ Scientist, is one of seven in the nation that exists to display the historical manuscript collection of David and Marsha Karpeles. Surrounded by two acres of beautiful English and Italian waterfront gardens in Riverside, the Cummer Museum of Art and Gardens is the largest museum in northeast Florida. Its permanent collection of more than 4,000 objects includes works from prehistoric, medieval, Renaissance, Baroque, Rococo, 19th Century Impressionist, and modern art eras. The Ritz Theatre houses the LaVilla Museum, displaying a permanent collection of African American history. The Jacksonville Maritime Heritage Center is dedicated to artwork and large-scale models of maritime-related events and objects from the history of Jacksonville and the First Coast. The Mandarin Museum and Historical Society includes the garden of author Harriet Beecher Stowe, who wintered there, and the Beaches Museum and History Center chronicles area development and devastation caused by natural disasters, especially hurricanes.

Festivals and Holidays

The Jacksonville Jazz Festival is the city's best-known annual event. This three-day celebration takes place in the spring, and draws classic and contemporary jazz and blues celebrities and includes the Great American Jazz Piano Competition. The Jacksonville Beach Summer Jazz series is geared toward families, with ocean-side concerts at Sea Walk Pavilion in June and July. Other music festivals include the Springing the Blues Festival for three days each April.

The World of Nations Celebration provides locals and visitors access to culinary traditions of more than 30 countries and also showcases international traditions and attire. Isle of Eight Flags Shrimp Festival in May includes everything from mock pirate invasions to shrimp boat races to various preparations of shrimp. The Great Atlantic Seafood and Music Festival in March combines music, food, and crafts.

October includes the Jacksonville Film Festival, known as Jax Film Fest, which celebrated its 10th anniversary in 2012. In the early 1900s, Jacksonville was a fixture of the film industry; while it has since declined, the three-day festival recalls the importance of the industry in the city's early history and also references contemporary efforts to revive it.

Sports for the Spectator

More than 70,000 avid fans flock to watch the Jaguars of the National Football League, who play home games on Sundays from September to January at EverBank Field. The arena is also the site of two annual college event games: the TaxSlayer.com Gator Bowl, and the University of Florida vs. University of Georgia contest. Jacksonville Veterans Memorial Arena, built on the site of the former Jacksonville Coliseum in 2003. The Jacksonville Suns are a Double-A affiliate of the Miami Marlins. And play games at the Baseball Grounds of Jacksonville, and the Jacksonville Giants play in the American Basketball Association.

Athletic enthusiasts in Jacksonville also enjoy March's Players Championship, which attracts 150,000 spectators to Sawgrass Resort, the toughest course on the Professional Golfers Association tour. The AT&T Greater Jacksonville Kingfish Tournament & Festival in July draws nearly 50,000 people. The 42-mile Rudder Club Mug Race in May attracts both local and Olympic sailors for the longest river sailboat race in the world.

Sports for the Participant

Jacksonville is home to one of the largest urban park systems in the nation. Residents and visitors enjoy more than 82,000 acres of land that extends from the rivers to the beaches. Nearly 60 miles of free beaches avail themselves to boating, sailing, surfing, fishing, and swimming. Playgrounds, tennis courts, picnic areas, about 70 golf courses, and dozens of public pools offer more choices.

The Fort Clinch State Park, a restored Civil War fort built in 1847, has picnic grounds, beaches, and an ocean fishing pier. Adventure Landing features two miniature golf courses, batting cages, a go-cart track, an uphill water coaster, and Shipwreck Island water park. Hikers enjoy the trails at Timucuan Ecological Historic Preserve.

Shopping and Dining

Jacksonville is a shopper's delight, offering interesting shops downtown and arty shops along the beaches. Jacksonville Landing offers a festive marketplace atmosphere, with novelty and gift shops, name-brand apparel, antiques, toys, and locally made accessories along with entertainment venues. The Avenues mall on the Southside and Regency Square Mall in Arlington each offer more than 100 nationally known retailers, as does St. Johns Town Center. Artisans sell their goods at the Riverside Arts Market and Avonlea Antique Mall. Riverside-Avondale, one of the country's largest National Register of Historic Districts, is a charming place to stroll, shop, and dine. San Marco Square, in the style of St. Mark's Square in Venice, offers an open-air produce market, restaurants, and boutiques, together with a water fountain, bronze lions, and a gazebo.

Local fish camps and waterside restaurants with their fresh seafood fare add to the pleasure of dining in Jacksonville. Southern barbecue is also a tradition. A delectable selection of ethnic foods from Japanese to Greek to Indian or Tex-Mex are offered by the city's many casual and upscale restaurants downtown or at suburban or beach locations.

Visitor Information: Visit Jacksonville and the Beaches, 208 N. Laura St., Ste. 102, Jacksonville, FL 32202 Jacksonville, FL 32202; telephone (904) 798-9111; toll-free (800) 733-2668.

■ Convention Facilities

The Prime F. Osborn III Convention Center, formerly the Jacksonville Railroad Terminal, boasts 265,000 square feet of space, including a 5,000-square-foot kitchen. The 1919 Neoclassical Revival railway terminal boasts a fully restored 10,000-square-foot ballroom (the Grand Lobby) and 22 meeting rooms. The convention center is connected to a nearby hotel by the Automated Skyway Express. The refurbished Times-Union Center for the Performing Arts includes a 3,000-seat concert theater, a 600-seat theater, and an 1,800-seat symphony hall. The refurbished Jacksonville Veterans Memorial Arena multipurpose facility accommodates 10,000 people for meetings. Other meeting facilities are the restored Florida Theatre, Conference Center at The Avenues, and the Adam W. Herbert University Center at the University of North Florida, a full-service conference and meeting facility.

Convention Information: Visit Jacksonville and the Beaches, 208 N. Laura St., Ste. 102, Jacksonville, FL 32202 Jacksonville, FL 32202; telephone (904) 798-9111; toll-free (800) 733-2668.

■ Transportation

Approaching the City

Jacksonville International Airport is only minutes from the central business district. The airport served a total of 5.2 million passengers in 2012, with 87,448 total takeoffs and landings. In addition to its international airport, Jacksonville has two general aviation facilities, Craig Airport and Herlong Airport, which facilitate travel by private or corporate aircraft. Amtrak offers passenger rail service.

Drivers approach Jacksonville via three major interstate highways that lead to the city—Interstates 10, 95 and 295); U.S. Highways 1, 17, 90, and 301 also traverse

the city. Beltways built around the city and main arteries linked to key locations make all parts of Jacksonville easily accessible.

Traveling in the City

The St. Johns River bisects the city and traveling across one or several bridges is commonplace. Seven bridges span the river within Duval County and the Intracoastal Waterway, and the area's many tributaries are crossed by dozens of small bridges. Local bus transportation is provided by the Jacksonville Transportation Authority (JTA). The bus system operates 56 routes that travel 8.5 million miles annually with 320 buses. All buses are equipped with bicycle racks, and a paratransit service provides door-to-door transportation for the disabled, elderly, and disadvantaged. The downtown area is also served by JTA's Automated Skyway Express, a monorail system.

■ Communications

Newspapers and Magazines

Jacksonville's major daily (morning) paper is the *Florida Times-Union* and had an average weekday circulation of nearly 90,000 in 2013. The *Jacksonville Business Journal* and the *Financial News and Daily Record* are the area's business publications. Other weekly newspapers are *The Florida Star,* serving the black community, and the *Florida Baptist Witness.* Newspapers published in Jacksonville Beach include the semiweekly *Beaches Leader.* *Jacksonville Magazine* is a monthly publication devoted to the city's attractions, community resources, and recreational opportunities.

Television and Radio

Jacksonville is served by 16 local television stations, including regional stations of major networks and public broadcasting. There are 29 licensed radio stations in Jacksonville. Of these, 17 are FM stations offering jazz, country, religious, adult contemporary, and Top 40 formats, while there are 12 AM stations that feature religious, talk, and sports programming.

Media Information: *Florida Times-Union,* 1 Riverside Ave., PO Box 1949, Jacksonville, FL 32231; telephone (904) 359-4111.

Jacksonville Online

City of Jacksonville home page. Available www.coj. net

Downtown Jacksonville, Inc. Available www.downtownjacksonville.org

Duval County Public Schools. Available www. duvalschools.org

Enterprise Florida. Available www.eflorida.com

Florida Times-Union. Available jacksonville.com

Jacksonville Historical Society. Available jaxhistory.com

Mayo Clinic Jacksonville. Available www.mayoclinic.org/jacksonville

Visit Jacksonville. Available www.visitjacksonville.com

BIBLIOGRAPHY

Bean, Shawn C., The First Hollywood: Florida and the Golden Age of Silent Filmmaking (Gainesville: University Press of Florida, 2008)

Buker, George E., *Jacksonville: Riverport-Seaport* (Columbia, SC: University of South Carolina Press, 1992)

Crooks, James B., *Jacksonville After the Fire, 1901-1919: A New South City* (Jacksonville, FL: University of North Florida Press, 1991)

Hyman, Ann, and Mascusi, Ron, eds., *Jacksonville Greets the 20th Century: The Pictorial Legacy of Leah Mary Cox* (Gainesville: University Press of Florida, 2002)

Jacksonville Historical Society, *Jacksonville in Vintage Postcards: Between the Great Fire and the Great War* (Mount Pleasant, SC: Arcadia Publishing, 2001)

O'Connor, Mallory McCane, Florida's American Heritage River: Images from the St. Johns Region (Gainesville: University Press of Florida, 2009)

Key West

■ The City in Brief

Founded: January 8, 1828

Head Official: Mayor Craig Cates (since 2009); City Manager Bob Vitas (Since 2012)

City Population
- 1990: 24,832
- 2000: 25,478
- 2010: 24,649
- 2012 estimate: 24,870
- Percent change, 2000–2010: −3.3%

Micropolitan Area Statistical Population
- 2000: 79,589
- 2010: 73,090
- 2012 estimate: 74,809
- Percent change, 2000–2010: −8.2%
- U.S. rank in 2000: Not available
- U.S. rank in 2010: 477th

Area: 6 square miles

Elevation: 18 feet above sea level

Average Annual Temperatures: January, 69.0° F; August, 85.0° F; annual average 78.0° F

Average Annual Precipitation: 40 inches

Major Economic Sectors: Tourism, fishing

Unemployment Rate: 3.8% (2012)

Per Capita Income: $31,710

2012 FBI Crime Index Property: 1,546

Major Colleges and Universities: Florida Keys Community College, Leo University

Daily Newspaper: *The Key West Citizen*

■ Introduction

More than 2.7 million visitors travel to Key West each year. While the Caribbean-island atmosphere is a major draw, the city has a variety of historic and cultural attractions as well. Once a stop for pirates, by the early 20th century the tiny island became a favored retreat for men such as Ernest Hemingway and Harry S. Truman. Island culture reflects a unique blend of Cuban, Afro-Caribbean, and American influences. Tourism is by far the most important industry for the island and the entire Florida Keys region. However, fishing continues to play a significant economic role. Key West is the seat of Monroe County and home to Naval Air Station Key West.

■ Geography and Climate

The small island of Key West is the southernmost city in the continental United States. It is one of about 1,700 islands in the archipelago known as the Florida Keys. These coral and limestone islands extend in a southwest arc from the southern point of Florida. The island of Key West is about 4 miles long and 1.5 miles wide. It lies some 130 miles from Miami; Cuba lies about 106 miles to the south. The Atlantic Ocean is to the east, and the Gulf of Mexico is to the west. Key West is the seat of Monroe County, which encompasses all of the Florida Keys and portions of the Everglades National Park and Big Cypress National Preserve on the southwest Florida mainland. The climate is subtropical, creating an environment more like the Caribbean islands than the Florida mainland. Many of the tropical plants found on the island—including coconut palm, hibiscus, and the famous Key lime tree—are introduced species that thrive in the warm, humid weather.

There are two seasons. The wet season extends from June through October, and the dry season runs from November through May. August is the warmest month. The dry season brings cooler temperatures. Though the

© Robert Harding Picture Library Ltd / Alamy

official Atlantic hurricane season is from June through November, the worst storms often appear from August through October.

Area: 6 square miles

Elevation: 18 feet above sea level

Average Temperatures: January, 69.0° F; August, 85.0° F; annual average 78.0° F

Average Annual Precipitation: 40 inches

■ History

The earliest known inhabitants of the Florida Keys were the Calusa, Native Americans of southwest Florida that survived primarily as fishermen. The first Europeans to come to the Florida Keys were Spanish explorers. One of the most prominent was Ponce de Leon, who traveled around the keys in 1513 searching for the elusive fountain of youth. The Spanish government claimed the islands that year. Key West originally was named Cayo Hueso (Bone Island) by other Spanish explorers who reportedly found bones on the island during early trips.

For nearly three centuries, European settlers steered clear of the island, which was known as a resting stop for pirates. In 1815 the Spanish government granted the island to Juan Pablo Salas, an army officer. Salas sold Key West to American businessman John Simonton in 1822. That year, Lieutenant Matthew C. Perry was sent to establish an American naval presence. He was followed by Commodore David Porter, who established a naval base from which to launch a campaign against pirates. The City of Key West was incorporated as the Monroe Country seat in 1828.

For several years, the primary industries of the island were fishing (particularly sponges and spiny lobster), salvaging shipwrecks (usually caused by storms), and cigar manufacturing. The presence of the U.S. Navy kept Key West under Union control during the Civil War, despite the fact that many residents were sympathetic to the Confederate cause.

Key West was nearly destroyed by a hurricane in 1935. Reconstruction included the new Overseas Highway (1938) that connected the keys to mainland Florida.

The warm climate and generally laid-back atmosphere of the island drew many famous visitors in the early 20th century. Harry S. Truman visited several times and stayed in a former officer's house, soon known as the Little White House. Other famous visitors included Ernest Hemingway, James Audubon, and Tennessee Williams. These visits inspired a thriving tourist industry.

Trouble brewed in 1982 when the U.S. Border Patrol set up a roadblock on the Overseas Highway at the mainland to search for narcotics and illegal immigrants. In response, the City of Key West staged a mock secession from the United States on April 23, 1982, and declared itself the Conch Republic. The roadblock was soon removed. An annual festival commemorating these events is one of many festivities that drew more than 2.7 million visitors to Key West in 2012.

■ Population Profile

Micropolitan Area Statistical Population

2000: 79,589
2010: 73,090
2012 estimate: 74,809
Percent change, 2000–2010: −8.2%
U.S. rank in 2000: Not available
U.S. rank in 2010: 477th

City Residents

1990: 24,832
2000: 25,478
2010: 24,649
2012 estimate: 24,870
Percent change, 2000–2010: −3.3%

Density: 4,411.8 people per square mile

Racial and ethnic characteristics

White: 21,533
Black or African American: 2,344
American Indian and Alaskan Native: 220
Asian: 366
Native Hawaiian and Other Pacific Islander: 8
Hispanic or Latino (may be of any race): 4,633
Other: 399

Percent of residents born in state: 31.1%

Age characteristics

Population under 5 years old: 1,345
Population 5 to 9 years old: 845
Population 10 to 14 years old: 1,005
Population 15 to 19 years old: 700
Population 20 to 24 years old: 2,104
Population 25 to 34 years old: 3,942
Population 35 to 44 years old: 3,945
Population 45 to 54 years old: 4,661
Population 55 to 59 years old: 1,569
Population 60 to 64 years old: 1,747
Population 65 to 74 years old: 1,601
Population 75 to 84 years old: 862
Population 85 years and over: 544
Median age: 40.2

Births (2010–11 Micropolitan Area)

Total number: 694

Deaths (2010–11 Micropolitan Area)

Total number: 632

Money income (2012)

Per capita income: $31,710
Median household income: $51,891
Total households: 9,412

Number of households with income of …

less than $10,000: 538
$10,000 to $14,999: 353
$15,000 to $24,999: 939
$25,000 to $34,999: 1,119
$35,000 to $49,999: 1,490
$50,000 to $74,999: 1,936
$75,000 to $99,999: 1,065
$100,000 to $149,999: 1,187
$150,000 to $199,999: 319
$200,000 or more: 466

Percent of families below poverty level: 11.8%

FBI Crime Index Property: 1,546

FBI Crime Index Violent: 208

■ Municipal Government

Key West has a commission-manager government that consists of seven commissioners, six of whom are elected from single member districts. The mayor oversees the commission and is elected at large for a term of two years. He or she may not serve for more than a total of eight years. District commissioners are elected for a term of four years and may not serve for more than a total of twelve years. The city manager, appointed by the commission, serves as the chief executive and administrative officer of the city.

Head Officials: Mayor Craig Cates (since 2009, reelected for 2013–15 term); City Manager Bob Vitas (since 2012)

Total Number of City Employees: 464

City Information: City of Key West City Hall, 3126 Flagler Avenue, Key West, FL 33040; telephone (305) 809-3844; fax (305) 809-3771.

■ Economy

Major Industries and Commercial Activity

Tourism is by far the most important industry for Key West and Monroe County. Key West receives more than 2.7 million tourists each year. Fishing has a significant impact on the local economy. Over 80 percent of the spiny lobster harvested in the state of Florida is caught in Monroe County. Government services, education, and health services are also significant to the local economy.

Items and goods produced: Seafood

Incentive Programs-New and Existing Companies

Local programs: Local businesses may be eligible for funding and other assistance through the Caroline Street Corridor and Bahama Village Community Redevelopment Agency. Florida's Community Redevelopment Agencies (CRA) are public organizations that work to improve a specific area (called a Community Redevelopment District) through redevelopment and economic investment. The Key West Small Business Development Center (SBDC), located at Florida Keys Community College, is part of the statewide Florida SBDC Network. At the center, certified business analysts offer one-on-one consulting to help potential business owners with business plans, marketing plans, market research, feasibility studies, loan proposals, accounting systems, and strategic plans.

State programs: Enterprise Florida is a partnership between Florida's government and business leaders and is the principal economic development organization for the state of Florida. Enterprise Florida's mission is to increase economic opportunities for all Floridians by supporting the creation of quality jobs, a well-trained workforce, and globally competitive businesses. It pursues this mission in cooperation with its statewide network of economic development partners. Among the incentive programs managed at the state level is the Economic Development Transportation Fund, which helps fund the cost of transportation projects, such as access roads and road widening, required for the establishment, expansion, or retention of businesses in Florida. The state's Qualified Target Industry Tax Refund is similar to a Miami-Dade program that rewards the creation of jobs in certain industries.

Florida has a favorable tax climate, with benefits such as no corporate income tax on limited partnerships, no sales tax on purchases of raw materials incorporated in a final product for resale, and no personal state income tax. The state also offers various sales and use tax exemptions for machinery and equipment purchase, electric energy, research and development, and other aspects of doing business in the area.

Job training programs: The Florida Department of Economic Opportunity provides policy, planning, and oversight for job training programs funded under the federal Workforce Investment Act, along with vocational training, adult education, employment placement, and other workforce programs administered by a variety of state and local agencies. Regional workforce development boards operate under charters approved by the Workforce Development Board.

Workforce Florida is a statewide, business-led workforce policy board that partners with the Florida Department of Economic Opportunity and regional workforce boards. The 24 regional boards have primary responsibility for direct services through a statewide network of One-Stop Career systems. One-Stop Career Centers are the central elements of the One-Stop system that provide integrated services to employers, workers, and jobseekers. The Key West One-Stop Career Center is operated through the South Florida Workforce Investment Board in Region 23 (Miami-Dade and Monroe Counties). Workforce Florida administers two training grant initiatives to assist both employers and job seekers. Quick Response Training (QRT) Grants provide funding for customized training to new or expanding businesses. Incumbent Worker Training (IWT) Grants provide funding for programs that help existing full-time employees upgrade their skills.

Development Projects

The Tourist Development Council of Monroe County works to promote tourism to the area and to ensure long-term sustainable growth in the industry. The Comprehensive Planning Team is a committee of the Growth Management Committee charged with defining and implementing countywide development goals. In 2013 the team was working to update the county's comprehensive plan by setting goals through the year 2030.

The City of Key West initiated a five-year capital improvements program in 2012 that includes projects to restore waterfront areas and update the transit system. One major project was renovating the former Glynn Archer Elementary School building into the new Key West City Hall. The Garrison Bight and Key West Bight were targeted for repairs and improvements as part of the program, which extends to 2017.

Economic Development Information: City of Key West City Hall, 3126 Flagler Avenue, Key West, FL 33040; telephone (305) 809-3844; fax (305) 809-3771. Monroe County Tourist Development Council, 1201 White Street, Suite 102, Key West, FL, 33040; telephone (305) 296-1552, (800) 648-5510; fax (305) 296-0788. Enterprise Florida, 800 N. Magnolia Ave. Suite 1100, Orlando, FL 32803; telephone (407) 956-5600; fax (407) 956-5599.

Commercial Shipping

Freight facilities are available at the Port of Key West and Key West International Airport. Ground shipments come in and out of the Florida Keys along U.S. Route 1.

Labor Force and Employment Outlook

Naval Air Station (NAS) Key West is the largest employer in Monroe County with nearly 3,000 personnel, including civilian support and contractors. NAS Key West hosts the Joint Interagency Task Force South, U.S. Coast Guard, and U.S. Army Special Forces Underwater Training School. The county and municipal governments employ nearly 1,000 people. Tourism and tourist related industries draw the greatest number of local workers. More than 40% of the county workforce is employed in the leisure and hospitality industry. The tourist industry is expected to remain strong as local development councils continue to implement long-term plans to make Key West a year-round tourist destination.

Size of civilian labor force: 14,580

Number of workers employed in . . .

agriculture and mining: 65
construction: 886
manufacturing: 201
wholesale trade: 191
retail trade: 1,649
transportation: 1,251
information systems: 176
finance: 939
professional administration: 1,026
education and social services: 1,434
arts and leisure: 4,218
other: 382
public administration: 1,238

Average hourly earnings of production workers: $Not available

Unemployment rate: 3.8% (2012)

Employers

Largest employers (Monroe County, 2012)

	Number of employees
U.S. Armed Services	2,931
Monroe County Schools	1,047
Ocean Reef Club	904
Monroe County Sheriff's Office	592
Monroe County Government	531
Lower Keys Medical Center	486
City of Key West	464
Historic Tours of America	300
Waldorf Astoria Resorts (Casa Marina/Reach Resort)	275
Florida Keys Aqueduct Authority	255

Cost of Living

The following is a summary of data regarding several key cost of living factors in the area.

State income tax rate: None

State sales tax rate: 6.0%

Local income tax rate: None

Local sales tax rate: 1.5%

Property tax rate: 10.53450 mills (2013)

Economic Information: Key West Chamber of Commerce, 510 Greene Street, 1st Floor, Key West, Florida 33040; telephone (305) 294-2587; fax (305) 294-7806; email info@keywestchamber.org.

■ Education and Research

Elementary and Secondary Schools

Key West is served by the Monroe County School District, with administrative offices in Key West. The school system includes a mix of traditional, Montessori, alternative, and charter schools. In Key West there are two traditional elementary schools and one traditional high school. Key West Collegiate School is a charter high school. Academic Connections for Excellence covers grades 6 through 12. Key West Montessori and Horace O'Bryant School are K–8 facilities. The Sigsbee Charter School at Key West Naval Air Station has elementary and middle school programs. Keys Center Academy is an alternative school for at-risk students. The Monroe County School District also sponsors Head Start and adult education programs. The Basilica School of Saint Mary Star of the Sea is a private, pre-K–8 Catholic school.

The following is a summary of data regarding Monroe County Schools.

Total enrollment: 8,356

Number of facilities
total: 18
elementary schools: 5
junior high schools: 2
high schools: 3
other: 8

Student/teacher ratio: 13.7:1

Teacher salaries
average (statewide): $Not available

Funding per pupil: $12,126

Public Schools Information: Monroe County School District, 241 Trumbo Road, Key West, FL 33040; telephone (305) 293-1400; fax (305) 293-1407.

Colleges and Universities

Students at Florida Keys Community College (FKCC) can earn an associate in arts degree, or an associate in science degree in the following fields: computer programming, computer information technology, diving business and technology, business administration, marine engineering, marine environmental technology, or nursing. Vocational programs in law enforcement are also available, along with certificate programs in a limited number of fields, including marine propulsion, small business management, and emergency medical technician basics. The main FKCC campus in Key West has one residence hall—Lagoon Landing—for students from other keys. Students may also attend classes at the Middle Keys Center in Marathon and the Upper Keys Center in Tavernier.

The Key West Education Center of Saint Leo University is located at Key West Naval Air Station and offers both on-site and distance learning options. Saint Leo is a Catholic liberal arts college based in Tampa that offers more than 40 academic programs, including associate's, bachelor's, and master's degree programs.

Hodges University (with main campuses in Fort Myers and Naples) operates a learning site on the campus of Florida Keys Community College. The school offers associate's, bachelor's, and master's degrees in several different fields.

Libraries and Research Centers

The headquarters branch of the Monroe County Library is located in Key West. Four additional branches are located in Big Pine, Marathon, Key Largo, and Islamorada. The Florida History Department at the Key West branch features a collection of oral histories recorded by the Key West Women's Club in the 1970s. Computer stations with free Internet access are located at all branches. An interlibrary loan program allows local residents to borrow books from participating libraries on the Florida mainland. Visitors to any of the Florida Keys can obtain a library card for a fee. Visitors can participate in the library's free paperback exchange program without obtaining borrowing privileges.

Public Library Information: Monroe County Public Library, 700 Fleming Street, Key West, FL 33040; telephone (305) 292-3595; fax (305) 295-3626.

■ Health Care

Lower Keys Medical Center is a full-service, 167-bed, acute care medical facility with a 24-hour emergency room, laboratory, radiology services, and medical transport helicopter. The facility provides a full range of primary care and inpatient and outpatient services. The facility also has a dedicated Heart Care Center and Wound Healing Center. It is the only hospital in the Florida Keys that offers labor and delivery services. The dePoo Medical Building is a behavioral center operated as part of the Lower Keys Medical Center. Medical detox programs are among many of the behavior health services offered.

The Naval Branch Health Clinic Key West provides outpatient health care for active duty military, their families, and other eligible beneficiaries.

Health Care Information: Lower Keys Medical Center, 5900 College Rd., Key West, FL 33040; telephone (305) 294-5531.

■ Recreation

Sightseeing

While many visitors prefer to spend time on the water, there are many things to see and do on land as well. The Harry Truman Little White House is open for tours. Originally built for a naval officer, it eventually became Truman's home away from home. Ernest Hemingway lived and wrote in Key West from 1931 to 1961. His home on Whitehead Street is now a museum of his life and work. The Audubon House and Gardens displays a collection of original Audubon art and images. Exhibits recount the naturalist's 1832 visit to Key West, during which he discovered and drew 22 species of birds that were included in his book *Birds of America*.

Nature lovers also enjoy the Key West Tropical Forest and Botanical Garden, and the Key West Butterfly and Nature Conservancy. History buffs have access to the Key West Shipwreck Treasures Museum, Flager Station Overseas Railway Museum, and Mel Fisher Maritime Museum. The Florida Keys Eco-Discovery center is a family-friendly site hosted by the Florida Keys National Marine Sanctuary. It features numerous interactive exhibits on plants and animals native to the keys. A walk through the Bahama Village neighborhood gives visitors a glimpse of the Afro-Caribbean influence on island culture. Sightseeing tours are offered by boat, trolley, and seaplane. Dolphin encounters and fishing charters are popular.

Arts and Culture

The Waterfront Playhouse has been noted as one of the best professional theaters in Florida by *Florida Monthly Magazine*. Tennessee Williams Theater is a major venue for musical and theatrical productions presented by touring groups and companies. The 2013–14 season included performances by Clint Black, the Oak Ridge Boys, STOMP, South Florida Symphony Orchestra, and the Mamma Mia National Tour.

The Key West Art & Historical Society maintains three museums, with a combined collection of more than 25,000 objects related to the people, places, and history of the area. The Custom House Museum was built in 1891. It serves as headquarters for the historical society and features two floors of exhibits from the society's collection of artifacts. The Lighthouse Tower and Keeper's Quarters has exhibits on various keepers of the light and an 1846 hurricane. Fort East Martello displays an eclectic collection of relics from the Civil War, exhibits on the wrecking and cigar-manufacturing industries, the unique folk art of Mario Sanchez, and metal sculptures by Stanley Papio.

There are dozens of art galleries in Key West featuring a variety of folk art and contemporary works in various forms, including paintings, prints, photographs, pottery, jewelry, woodcarvings, glass, sculpture, and textiles.

Festivals and Holidays

The Sunset Celebration is a nightly arts festival at the Mallory Square Dock. Throughout the year, a wide variety of street performers entertain locals and visitors as they wait to watch the sunset over the Gulf. Local artists and crafters set up stalls to exhibit and sell their works. Performers and artists usually set up a few hours before sunset. The annual Florida Keys Seafood Festival is sponsored by Florida Key's Commercial Fishermen's Association to promote the county's second-largest industry. The Conch Republic Independence Celebration each April celebrates the brief secession of Key West from the United States in 1982.

Hemingway Days is a weeklong festival in July celebrating the life and work of Ernest Hemingway through a series of serious and lighthearted events. Literary events include book readings and the announcement of winners for the annual Lorian Hemingway Short Story Competition. There is also a Hemingway Look-Alike Competition and a tame version of the Running of the Bulls. The annual Key West Marlin Tournament is held in conjunction with Hemingway Days.

The Fantasy Fest in October features ten days of street fairs, parties, parades, and other events sponsored by local businesses. Revelers and performers don costumes for the annual Royal Coronation Ball and the Fantasy Fest Parade, two of the most popular events. The annual Bahama Village Goombay Festival usually marks the beginning of the Fantasy Fest, but stands alone as a two-day cultural festival celebrating Afro-Caribbean heritage. The Key West "Bight" Before Christmas Festival is a series of events that stretch from Thanksgiving through New Year's Eve. These events include the annual Lighting of Harbor Walk and the Hometown Holiday Parade.

Sports for the Spectator

The annual Schooner Wharf Minimal Regatta in May draws large crowds each year. The competition is fierce among boaters who create their own crafts from plywood and duct tape.

Sports for the Participant

Visitors and residents can participate in nearly every type of water sport, including fishing, snorkeling, scuba diving, parasailing, jet skiing, water skiing, kayaking, wind surfing, and sailing. The most popular beach areas are Smathers Beach, Simonton Beach, and Rest Beach. Several companies provide guides and boats for those seeking the best fishing spots.

Key West Golf Club features an 18-hole, par-70 championship course designed by golf legend Rees Jones. Clayton Sterling Complex sponsors a popular youth baseball league on four fields. Rose Hernandez Softball Field hosts youth softball teams, while Wickers Sports Complex hosts men's softball. Wickers also has a youth football program.

Shopping and Dining

Numerous shops, galleries, restaurants, nightclubs, and other notable sites are located along Duval Street in downtown Key West, including the popular Hard Rock Cafe Key West. The historic seaport area at Key West Bight also features many unique and noteworthy shops and restaurants. At either location, treasure hunters can find everything from unique crafts made by local artists to fine art and jewelry.

Visitor Information: Monroe County Tourist Development Council, 1201 White Street, Suite 102, Key West, FL, 33040; telephone (305) 296-1552, (800) 648-5510; fax (305) 296-0788.

■ Convention Facilities

Several hotels and resorts provide space for meetings and special events. Facilities are available for groups between 40 and 450 people. The largest meeting facilities are located at the Key West Marriott Beachside Hotel.

Convention Information: Monroe County Tourist Development Council, 1201 White Street, Suite 102, Key West, FL, 33040; telephone (305) 296-1552, (800) 648-5510; fax (305) 296-0788.

■ Transportation

Approaching the City

Key West International Airport receives connecting flights from several major cities in Florida. There are shuttle services available to Key West for travelers arriving at Miami International Airport or Fort Lauderdale–Hollywood International Airport. Amtrak takes passengers as far as Fort Lauderdale. The main road in is U.S. Route 1, which begins at mile marker 0 in Key West and extends to Fort Kent, Maine. The stretch over the keys is nicknamed the Overseas Highway. The Port of Key West is a port of call for several cruise lines. Many marinas on Key West welcome private boats. Key West Express operates a year-round ferry service between Fort Myers Beach and the Key West Bright Ferry Terminal in the seaport district.

Traveling in the City

Walking is the preferred mode of transportation on the small island. There are several rental shops providing bicycles and motor scooters for visitors who want a quicker way to get from place to place. Trolleys, taxis, tour trains, and pedi-cabs also are available. Key West Transit provides convenient bus service around the island and to several locations along the lower keys. Seven-day and thirty-one-day bus passes are available at discounted rates.

■ Communications

Newspapers and Magazines

The Key West Citizen is the only daily newspaper from the Florida Keys. It is owned by Cooke Communications, LLC, which also publishes the *Florida Keys Free Press* (weekly), *Paradise* (a weekly entertainment magazine), *Southernmost Flyer* (a weekly for the military community), *Keys Style* (a monthly magazine), and *The Menu* (a quarterly restaurant guide).

Television and Radio

WCAY-CD (Key TV) is an independent television station in Key West, owned by Beach TV Properties in Panama City, Florida. WGEN-TV is a Spanish language station that broadcasts locally as an affiliate of MundoFox. WKIZ (1500 AM) provides local news. Major television and radio broadcasts are rebroadcast from the Miami-Ft. Lauderdale area.

Media Information: *The Key West Citizen*, 3420 Northside Drive, Key West, FL 33040, telephone (305) 292-7777; fax (305) 294-0768.

Key West Online

City of Key West. www.keywestcity.com

The Florida Keys and Key West, Monroe County Tourist Development Council. http://www.fla-keys.com

Key West Chamber of Commerce. www.keywestchamber.org

The Key West Citizen online. http://keysnews.com

Monroe Country Public Library. www.keyslibraries.org

BIBLIOGRAPHY

Epstein, Bob, *A History of Fishing in the Florida Keys.* (Charleston, SC: The History Press, 2013)

Kerstein, Robert J, *Key West on the Edge: Inventing the Conch Republic* (Gainesville, FL: University Press of Florida, 2012)

Malone, Laura, *Key West* (Berkeley, CA: Avalon Travel, 2011)

Miami

■ The City in Brief

Founded: 1836 (incorporated 1896)

Head Official: City Mayor Tomas P. Regalado (R) (since 2009; term expires 2017); County Mayor Carlos Gimenez (since 2011; current term expires 2015)

City Population

> 1990: 358,648
> 2000: 362,470
> 2010: 399,457
> 2012 estimate: 413,864
> Percent change, 2000–2010: 10.2%
> U.S. rank in 1990: 46th (State rank: 2nd)
> U.S. rank in 2000: 56th (State rank: 2nd)
> U.S. rank in 2010: 44th (State rank: 2nd)

Metropolitan Statistical Area Population

> 2000: 5,007,564
> 2010: 5,564,635
> 2012 estimate: 5,762,717
> Percent change, 2000–2010: 11.1%
> U.S. rank in 2000: 6th
> U.S. rank in 2010: 8th

Area: 36 square miles

Elevation: 12 feet above sea level

Average Annual Temperatures: 76.7° F

Average Annual Precipitation: 58.53 inches

Major Economic Sectors: tourism, trade, banking, manufacturing

Unemployment Rate: 7.7% (2012)

Per Capita Income: $20,671

2012 FBI Crime Index Property: 22,271

Major Colleges and Universities: University of Miami, Miami-Dade Community College, Florida International University, Barry University, St. Thomas University

Daily Newspaper: *Miami Herald; Diario Las Americas; El Nuevo Herald*

■ Introduction

Described as the "only great city of the world that started as a fantasy," Miami, with its subtropical climate, naturally protected harbor, and spectacular beaches, has traditionally been a haven for tourists and retirees. Since the late 1980s, however, the city has sustained unprecedented growth and, while transforming its image, has emerged as a center of international finance and commerce and as a regional center for Latin American and Haitian art. An unincorporated village shortly before the turn of the twentieth century, Miami boasts a metropolitan area that includes a large unincorporated area and 35 incorporated areas or municipalities, all of which make up Miami-Dade County. Greater Miami offers a diversity of lifestyles and attractions to both residents and visitors in a variety of small towns and cities such as Coconut Grove, Miami Beach, South Beach, Coral Gables, Bal Harbour, Bal Harbour, and Hialeah. With easy access to other parts of the country, Miami has developed into one of America's major transportation hubs, both by air and by sea. Tourism, Miami's most important economic sector, has turned it into a year-round city that offers something for everyone.

■ Geography and Climate

Located at the mouth of the Miami River on the lower east coast of Florida, Miami is bordered on the east by Biscayne Bay, an arm of the Atlantic Ocean. Farther east, the islands of Key Biscayne and Miami Beach shelter the bay from the Atlantic Ocean, thus providing Miami with a naturally protected harbor. Once pine and palmetto

© Richard Cavalleri/Shutterstock.com

flatlands, the Miami area boasts sandy beaches in its coastal areas and gives way to sparsely wooded outlying areas. A man-made canal connects the city to Lake Okeechobee, located 90 miles northwest of Miami.

Miami's year-round semi-tropical climate is free of extremes in temperature, with a long, warm summer and abundant rainfall followed by a mild, dry winter. Summer humidity levels—usually in the 86 to 89 percent range during the day—make Miami the second most humid city in the United States. Hurricanes occasionally affect the area in September and October; tornadoes are rare. Waterspouts are sometimes sighted from the beaches in the summer, but significant damage seldom occurs.

Area: 36 square miles

Elevation: 12 feet above sea level

Average Temperatures: 76.7° F

Average Annual Precipitation: 58.53 inches

■ History

Early Settlement Attempts Create Conflict

South Florida was settled more than four thousand years ago by primitive people who had established a thriving culture by the time Spanish explorers led by Ponce de Leon arrived in 1513. The principal native tribe in the region that is now Miami-Dade County was the Calusa (renamed Tequesta by de Leon), whose members built villages along the Miami River. The name Miami comes from the Calusa word "Mayami," meaning "Big Water." Tequesta-or Chequescha-their village on the north bank of the river, became the site of the future city of Miami.

Spanish conquistadors, attracted by the mild climate, abundant food sources, and fresh water supply-and by tales of gold and other riches-made repeated attempts to colonize the Miami region during the early sixteenth century but were met with hostility from the Calusas. Nevertheless, by the early 1700s, less than two hundred years after the arrival of the Spanish, most of the native population of south Florida had disappeared. European diseases like smallpox had severely reduced their numbers, as did inter-tribal wars. The few Calusas who remained were threatened by invading Creek and Seminole Indians, and in 1711 many fled to Havana, Cuba.

Spain, never really successful in settling the Miami region, supported France against the British during the French and Indian War, and as a result lost Florida to the victorious British in 1763. In 1783, after the American Revolution, Florida briefly reverted to Spanish possession, but in 1821 Spain ceded Florida to the United

States for $5 million. Over the next two decades, settlers moving into the Biscayne Bay area encountered conflict with the Seminoles living there. In 1836, as part of an effort to quell the angry Seminoles, the U.S. Army took over Fort Dallas-originally a naval post at the mouth of the Miami River. In 1842, after numerous skirmishes, the remaining Seminoles were driven into the Everglades swamp, a region so unfit for human habitation that the government did not challenge their occupation of it. Seven years later a permanent structure was built at Fort Dallas from which the army could monitor the Seminoles.

While other outposts in Florida flourished after the final Seminole conflict, Miami and Dade County suffered. Farming had become impossible and settlers drifted to other locales. By 1860 the name Miami no longer appeared in public records. The Civil War barely touched the few people who lived in the isolated Miami River settlement; in fact, it was assumed by those in prosperous north Florida towns that the southern region was uninhabited. Although stragglers, deserters, and freed slaves passed through Miami after the war, few settled there.

The City Attracts Entrepreneurs

In the 1870s investors and developers from the Midwest moved into the area, claiming old titles and buying land. Among them was Julia Tuttle, the wealthy widow of a Cleveland businessman, who enjoyed life in Miami and saw potential for a resort community there. She persuaded Henry Flagler to extend his Florida East Coast Railroad into the wilderness beyond Palm Beach. On April 15, 1896, Flagler brought his railroad into Miami and also began to develop the town, which was incorporated in 1896. Other entrepreneurs followed, and Miami grew from a village with a population of 343 people to a flourishing resort. Miami Beach was founded in 1915.

After World War I, improved highways gave greater access from the north and triggered an unprecedented building boom. In 1920 the city's population was 30,000 people; by 1925 real estate speculation swelled the population to 200,000 people. A year later the boom had collapsed, but it had laid the basis for future development in office buildings, hotels, housing, and a network of streets and roads. A hurricane in 1926 killed 243 people and caused damage estimated at $1.4 billion in 1990 dollars. Miami's phenomenal growth slowed.

World War II brought a second boom to Miami. Soldiers replaced tourists, and after the war servicemen who had trained in the city returned to make their homes there. This second boom has continued without significant interruption to the present. It was given impetus in the 1960s with the migration of more than 178,000 refugees from Communist Cuba. The Cuban migration transformed Miami into an international city, strengthening existing ties with the Caribbean and South America.

Today the city is bilingual; Spanish-speaking employees work at most businesses, and downtown shops post signs in both English and Spanish. Still, racial tensions persisted. For example, an incident of alleged police brutality toward an African American caused major rioting in 1980. And African Americans staged a tourism boycott resulting from the snubbing by county commissioners of former South African President Nelson Mandela during his visit to Miami in 1990.

End of Century Sees Political Turmoil, Reform Efforts

Capitalizing on its multinational character, Miami moved during the 1980s and 1990s into the forefront of world commerce and finance. Hundreds of thousands of European visitors discovered Miami Beach, popularizing the Art Deco hotels and adding to the city's cosmopolitan flair. But in the wake of racial and ethnic tensions, some highly publicized murders of foreign tourists, and Hurricane Andrew in 1992, at least 100,000 non-Hispanic whites fled the Greater Miami area between 1990 and 1996, leaving a city that was the only large U.S. city with a Hispanic majority.

The city struggled in the late twentieth century to balance the needs of its mostly poor citizens with the need for business development. In spite of its glamorous image, Miami was the nation's fourth poorest city. In 1997, faced with a $68 million budget shortfall, Miami became the first city in Florida to have an oversight board appointed by the state. City voters rejected a plan to dissolve Miami as separate entity and merge it with the county, though county voters approved to change the name of Dade County to Miami-Dade County. This name change did little to help Miami, whose problems had become more than financial. The 2000 incident involving Elian Gonzalez, a five-year-old Cuban boy who survived a shipwreck to arrive in the United States only to be returned to Cuba by the U.S. government, deepened ethnic tensions between Miami's Cuban and non-Cuban population. By the turn of the century, corruption in the city government and a number of controversial police shootings brought about scrutiny by the U.S. Department of Justice.

A Radical with a Business Vision

Desperate for a positive change, disenchanted voters shook up Miami's government by electing Manuel A. Diaz mayor in 2001. Diaz, a lawyer who had never held elected office, immediately and radically restructured the government. Modeling it on a private-sector organization, he eliminated some departments and consolidated others, and incorporated a vertical structure consisting of such positions as a Chief Executive Officer and Chief Financial Officer. Business processes were rewritten at each employee and government level, and a new emphasis was placed on accountability, training, and timely service to citizens. A number of programs were developed and implemented to boost the local economy and improve the quality of life for Miami's residents and visitors. By 2004, only three years after the city was nearly bankrupt and its bonds were junk grade, Wall Street gave its bonds an A+ rating, the highest in Miami's history. Diaz's remarkable results in such a short time earned him the Urban Innovator of the Year Award by the Manhattan Institute. In 2009, Diaz was prevented from running for reelection by the city's term limits.

A nationwide recession in the late 2000s shuttered many of the city's banks and cooled the real estate market. While the financial sector recovered slowly, the real estate industry recovered more rapidly, with significant growth having returned by the early 2010s. The fast pace of downtown developments—sometimes referred to as the "return of the cranes"—was a positive economic sign for the city. Resorts World Miami's $3.1 billion downtown development, scheduled to open in 2015, was the most ambitious bet yet on the city's future economic growth.

Historical Information: Historical Museum of Southern Florida, 101 W. Flagler St., Miami, FL 33130; telephone (305) 375-1492; email e.info@historymiami.org.

■ Population Profile

Metropolitan Statistical Area Population

2000: 5,007,564
2010: 5,564,635
2012 estimate: 5,762,717
Percent change, 2000–2010: 11.1%
U.S. rank in 2000: 6th
U.S. rank in 2010: 8th

City Residents

1990: 358,648
2000: 362,470
2010: 399,457
2012 estimate: 413,864
Percent change, 2000–2010: 10.2%
U.S. rank in 1990: 46th (State rank: 2nd)
U.S. rank in 2000: 56th (State rank: 2nd)
U.S. rank in 2010: 44th (State rank: 2nd)

Density: 11,135.9 people per square mile

Racial and ethnic characteristics

White: 313,496
Black or African American: 82,688
American Indian and Alaskan Native: 557
Asian: 4,652
Native Hawaiian and Other Pacific Islander: 0
Hispanic or Latino (may be of any race): 283,107
Other: 12,471

Percent of residents born in state: 29%

Age characteristics

Population under 5 years old: 24,740
Population 5 to 9 years old: 21,613
Population 10 to 14 years old: 20,612
Population 15 to 19 years old: 18,763
Population 20 to 24 years old: 25,197
Population 25 to 34 years old: 73,340
Population 35 to 44 years old: 59,677
Population 45 to 54 years old: 57,884
Population 55 to 59 years old: 24,619
Population 60 to 64 years old: 22,663
Population 65 to 74 years old: 30,924
Population 75 to 84 years old: 23,430
Population 85 years and over: 10,402
Median age: 38.8

Births (2010–11 Metropolitan Area)

Total number: 65,977

Deaths (2010–11 Metropolitan Area)

Total number: 45,537

Money income (2012)

Per capita income: $20,671
Median household income: $28,935
Total households: 149,591

Number of households with income of . . .

less than $10,000: 26,836
$10,000 to $14,999: 15,685
$15,000 to $24,999: 24,367
$25,000 to $34,999: 18,574
$35,000 to $49,999: 18,947
$50,000 to $74,999: 18,941
$75,000 to $99,999: 9,020
$100,000 to $149,999: 8,704
$150,000 to $199,999: 3,948
$200,000 or more: 4,569

Percent of families below poverty level: 31.5%

FBI Crime Index Property: 22,271

FBI Crime Index Violent: 4,856

■ Municipal Government

Miami's system of government is two-tiered: municipal and county. At the municipal level are a city mayor, five commissioners, and a city manager. The Miami-Dade County, or metropolitan government, consists of an executive mayor, a county manager, and 13 county commissioners, each of whom represents a district and serves a four-year term. The county government administers issues that affect the greater metropolitan area, such as transportation and pollution control.

Head Officials: City Mayor Tomas P. Regalado (R) (since 2009; term expires 2017); County Mayor Carlos Gimenez (since 2011; current term expires 2015)

Total Number of City Employees: 3,630 (2012)

City Information: City Mayor's Office, 3500 Pan American Dr., Miami, FL 33133; telephone (305)250-5300; fax (305)854-4001; email tregalado@miamigov.com. County Mayor's Office, Stephen Clark Center, 111 NW 1st St., 29th Fl., Miami, FL 33128; telephone (305)375-5071; fax (305)375-1274; email mayor@miamidade.gov

■ Economy

Major Industries and Commercial Activity

For most of Miami's history, its economy has been based on tourism. In fact, it was not so long ago that the city came to life only during the winter months when tourists from cold northern regions flocked to its beaches, hotels, and resorts. That phenomenon is no longer the case, as tourists visit the region throughout the year, infusing the local economy with revenue for such expenses as hotel rooms, restaurants, shopping, transportation, and attractions.

While tourism continues to be the principal industry in Miami, the city's economy has become more diversified. Trade is increasingly vital to the economy. Its close proximity to Latin America and the Caribbean make it the center of international trade with those areas. Because many companies choose to establish their Latin American headquarters in southern Florida, Miami-Dade County is known as the "Gateway to the Americas." More than 1,000 multinational corporations have operations in the region.

The city's international trade infrastructure is vast and varied. Among airports in the United States, Miami International Airport is the principal passenger and cargo transit point between the United States and Latin America. In 2012 the annual economic impact of the airport was estimated at $32.8 billion, contributing more than one-quarter-million jobs directly and indirectly to the local economy, or nearly one out of every four jobs. The Port of Miami is one of the busiest containerized ports in the United States. The World Trade Center Miami is Florida's oldest international organization, and assists member companies to introduce and expand their international presence. Miami was home to more than 70 foreign consulates in 2013 and the operations of 1,100 multinational corporations, both of which supported international trade exceeding $100 billion. Two free trade zones exist in Greater Miami, the Homestead Free Zone and the Miami Free Zone, one of the world's largest privately owned and operated zones.

Until a nationwide recession in 2009, which included a collapse of the financial industry, banking

was another growing segment of the economy. In 2007 there were 59 commercial banks and 11 thrift institutions doing business in the Miami area, with combined deposits of $38.8 billion. Overall, Miami has one of the largest concentrations of domestic and international banks on the East Coast south of New York. Following the recession, the banking landscape changed somewhat in Miami. Twenty-three Florida banks failed in 2009 and fifteen failed in 2010. Bank failures in Florida and across the nation slowed in 2012, but Florida still ranked second nationally (behind Georgia) for most bank failures during the previous five years.

The real estate market was similarly affected. From the late 1990s until 2005, the Miami-Dade area was one the nation's hottest real estate markets. By 2006 the real estate market in Miami-Dade County and neighboring Broward County had cooled and foreclosures grew sharply. In the first half of 2007, foreclosures in the two counties had increased by some 300 percent. Shortly thereafter, the market began to stabilize, aided by incentives and support from the federal government. By 2013 analysts reported that the Miami area once again ranked highly among all U.S. real estate markets, with homes selling more quickly and for more money during 2013.

Two companies headquartered in Miami appeared on the 2012 *Fortune* 500 list. These were World Fuel Services, ranked 85th, and Ryder System, a trucking company ranked 407th.

Items and goods produced: apparel, textiles, books and magazines, pharmaceuticals, medical and diagnostic testing equipment, plastics, aluminum products, furniture, light manufactured goods, transportation equipment, cement, electronic components, agricultural products such as tomatoes, beans, avocadoes, and citrus fruits

Incentive Programs-New and Existing Companies

Local programs: The Beacon Council is the agency responsible for recruiting new businesses to Miami-Dade County in an effort to create new jobs. The Council's many free services include site identification; labor recruitment and training; business data and economic research; packaging local, state, and federal business incentives; and import/export assistance. The Council promotes the many advantages of doing business in Miami-Dade County, including a number of business incentive programs and a favorable tax structure. Business location incentives at the local level include Empowerment Zone and Enterprise Zone opportunities, each of which offers tax or wage credits to businesses based on the number of new jobs created. The Miami-Dade County Targeted Jobs Incentive Fund is available to companies that are on the list of industries identified by the county as desirable additions to the local economy.

The Urban Jobs Tax Credit Program provides up to a $1,000 tax credit per new job, with a minimum of 20 jobs, for new companies, or 10 new jobs for existing companies. Areas where the credit is valid are determined by the city.

State programs: Enterprise Florida is a partnership between Florida's government and business leaders and is the principal economic development organization for the state of Florida. Enterprise Florida's mission is to increase economic opportunities for all Floridians by supporting the creation of quality jobs, a well-trained workforce, and globally competitive businesses. It pursues this mission in cooperation with its statewide network of economic development partners. Among the incentive programs managed at the state level is the Economic Development Transportation Fund, which helps fund the cost of transportation projects, such as access roads and road widening, required for the establishment, expansion, or retention of businesses in Florida. The state's Qualified Target Industry Tax Refund is similar to a Miami-Dade program that rewards the creation of jobs in certain industries.

Florida has a favorable tax climate, with benefits such as no corporate income tax on limited partnerships, no sales tax on purchases of raw materials incorporated in a final product for resale, and no personal state income tax. The state also offers various sales and use tax exemptions for machinery and equipment purchase, electric energy, research and development, and other aspects of doing business in the area.

Job training programs: Florida is a statewide, business-led workforce policy board that partners with the Florida Department of Economic Opportunity and regional workforce boards. The 24 regional boards have primary responsibility for direct services through a statewide network of One-Stop Career systems. One-Stop Career Centers are the central elements of the One-Stop system that provide integrated services to employers, workers, and jobseekers. CareerSource Florida administers two training grant initiatives to assist both employers and job seekers. Quick Response Training (QRT) Grants provide funding for customized training to new or expanding businesses. Incumbent Worker Training (IWT) Grants provide funding for programs that help existing full-time employees upgrade their skills. Training services are provided by several local colleges, including Miami-Dade College, Florida International University, the Miami-Dade County Public Schools System, and other vocational or technical centers.

Development Projects

Resorts World Miami is a 13.9-acre complex scheduled for completion in 2015. One of the largest development projects ever undertaken in the state of Florida, it was estimated to cover 10 million square feet at a cost of $3.1 billion. The plan included a 700,000-square-foot convention center and a 200,000-square-foot ballroom marketed as the largest in the nation. Other aspects of the facility included 250,000 square feet of luxury retail, 50 restaurants, and 5,200 hotel rooms. Construction alone was expected to employ some 15,000 people, and the facility's general operations were anticipated to employ 30,000. The sprawling Resorts World complex was to anchor an urban village that would also link some of the area's main attractions: American Airlines Arena, Bayside Marketplace, and Bayfront Park.

Many of Miami's largest private development projects were for new high-rise luxury condominiums. These included the Brickell House, begun in 2012 and under construction through 2013. The 46-floor, $170 million building was to contain nearly 400 residential units. A 32-floor, 300-residence structure began construction in 2013 and was also to include a restaurant and office space on the bottom level. A 55-floor, $400 luxury facility broke ground in July 2013 and was to include 192 residential units.

Minor projects by the county's parks and recreation department transformed empty lots on 117th street into Gratigny Plateau Park, established greenways along Brickell Promenade, refurbished an inner-city baseball field at Arcola Park, and revamped the Tamiami Park Recreation Center.

The city's guiding master plan, effective through 2025, prioritized redevelopment of streets and increasing of greenways, promotion of transit and regional connectivity, better usage of the city's waterfront areas, and cultivation of the city's identity as a business and cultural hub.

Economic Development Information: City of Miami: Economic Initiatives, 444 SW 2nd Ave., 5th Floor, Miami, FL 33130; telephone (305) 416-1435; fax (305) 416-2156; email amj@miamigov.com. The Beacon Council, 80 SW 8th St., Ste. 2400, Miami, FL 33130; telephone (305) 579-1300; fax (305) 375-0271; email info@beaconcouncil.com.

Commercial Shipping

Miami is a major commercial shipping center. One reason is due to Miami International Airport (MIA). MIA is a domestic and international trade hub, and a primary commerce link between North and South America. In 2012 the airport ranked first among all U.S. airports in international freight, and third in total freight. It also ranked third for combined freight and mail. Among all airports worldwide, it stood in ninth place for international freight. Its trade support infrastructure includes a Cargo Clearance Center that provides 24-hour service by close to 300 inspectors from the U.S. Customs Service, Department of Agriculture, Fish and Wildlife Service, and Food and Drug Administration.

The Port of Miami is the world's largest cruise port. It is also a busy cargo port, handling 900,000 twenty-foot equivalent units in 2012. The Enforcement Link to Mobile Operations (ELMO) project, introduced in 2012, expedited inspection times for cargo passing through the port. The Miami Free Zone's principal function is importing for domestic U.S. consumption. Fifteen minutes from the seaport and five minutes from the airport, the free zone is one of the largest duty-free zones in the United States. Major freight railroads serving Miami consist of two Class I railroads, CSX and Norfolk Southern, and the Florida East Coast, a regional carrier.

Labor Force and Employment Outlook

The Miami-Dade County labor force is Florida's largest and most comprehensive. The region's labor advantages include a large and diverse pool of Spanish-speaking and bilingual workers who contribute to Miami's expansion as a headquarters of international operations.

The following is a summary of data regarding the 2012 Miami labor force:

Size of civilian labor force: 205,874

Number of workers employed in . . .

    agriculture and mining: 719
    construction: 17,208
    manufacturing: 7,910
    wholesale trade: 6,707
    retail trade: 20,335
    transportation: 11,069
    information systems: 3,782
    finance: 11,329
    professional administration: 21,954
    education and social services: 30,314
    arts and leisure: 24,031
    other: 15,871
    public administration: 4,767

Average hourly earnings of production workers: $13.98

Unemployment rate: 7.7% (2012)

Employers

Largest employers (2013)	*Number of employees*
Miami-Dade County Public Schools	48,571
Miami-Dade County	29,000
U.S. Federal Government	19,500
State of Florida	17,100
University of Miami	16,000
Baptist Health South Florida	13,376
Public Health Trust/ Jackson Memorial Hospital	12,571
Publix Supermarkets	10,800
American Airlines	9,000
Florida International University	8,000

Cost of Living

While not as high as the cost of living in New York, Boston, Los Angeles, or Washington, D.C., Miami's cost of living was still above the national average, with a 2013 study by the Economic Policy Institute estimating that income needed to be more than twice that of the federal poverty line in order to sustain a modest living standard.

The following is a summary of data regarding several key cost of living factors in the area.

2013 ACCRA Average House Price: $313,975

2013 ACCRA Cost of Living Index: 107

State income tax rate: None

State sales tax rate: 6.0%

Local income tax rate: None

Local sales tax rate: 1.0%

Property tax rate: $22.6515 per $1,000 of assessed property value (2013)

Economic Information: The Beacon Council, 80 SW 8th Street, Suite 2400, Miami, FL 33130; telephone (305)579-1300; fax (305)375-0271; email info@beacon-council.com

■ Education and Research

Elementary and Secondary Schools

Like all public schools in the state of Florida, the public elementary and secondary schools of Miami are part of a county-wide district. Miami-Dade County Public Schools are administered by a partisan nine-member elected school board that appoints a superintendent. The district operates one of the largest magnet school systems in the nation, offering specialized fields of study in such areas as mathematics, science, and technology; gifted education; international education; Montessori; visual and performing arts; communications and humanities; and careers and professions. Additionally, 145 charter schools operated within the school district as of 2013. A November 2013 bond issue passed authorizing $1.2 billion for Miami-Dade County Public Schools to undertake facility renovations, update technology, replace existing schools, expand student capacity, and enhance facility safety.

Miami-Dade County has about 300 private schools.

The following is a summary of data regarding the Miami-Dade County Public Schools.

Total enrollment: 347,366

Number of facilities
  total: 337
  elementary schools: 173
  junior high schools: 100
  high schools: 57
  other: 7

Student/teacher ratio: 16.39:1

Teacher salaries
  average (statewide): $46,702

Funding per pupil: $9,059

Public Schools Information: Miami-Dade County Public Schools, 1450 N.E. Second Avenue, Miami, FL 33132; telephone (305) 995-1000.

Colleges and Universities

Florida International University, which enrolls more than 46,000 students, is the largest four-year university in South Florida. In addition to its undergraduate programs, it has a college of law, education, and business administration for graduate degree programs, in addition to others. The University of Miami is a private university noted for its business school. In 2014 the University of Miami was ranked 47th nationally by *U.S. News & World Report*. The university enrolls about 16,000 students annually, with most majoring in business-related programs, followed by biological or biomedical sciences. Miami Dade College offers two-year and four-year degrees to more than 175,000 students at its seven campuses. Barry University and St. Thomas University are both affiliated with the Roman Catholic Church; Florida Memorial University is affiliated with American Baptist Churches in the USA. A satellite campus is operated by Trinity International University (Illinois) in Davie, Florida. The school is affiliated with the Evangelical Free Church of America. The Miami International University of Art & Design offers associate, bachelor's, and master's degrees.

Libraries and Research Centers

In addition to its main branch in downtown Miami, the Miami-Dade Public Library System operates 48 branches. The library also operates four bookmobiles and offers access to over 1,500 public computers. Its entire collection numbers more than 3.5 million volumes. In addition, the library also holds numerous newspapers, magazines, films, records, tapes, sheet music, and photographs. The Main Library serves as a resource center for the system and provides information via seven subject departments: art, business, languages, music, science, urban affairs, and genealogy. Special collections are held in the Florida Room, the Foundations Center Regional Collection, and the U.S. and State Documents department; special interests include Florida and foreign languages, particularly Spanish. The library sponsors a wide array of educational and culturally enriching programs and exhibitions. A budget shortfall in 2013–14 threatened a number of library branches for the 2014–15 fiscal year, with significant layoffs and branch closures under serious consideration.

Miami is home to a number of special libraries, including the University of Miami, which houses more than 2.5 million volumes. The library at the Wolfsonian Museum features a collection of about 60,000 books and other materials focusing on industrial arts, design, and architecture. The Wolfsonian's research and study center traces the interconnections of European culture with other cultures. Numerous other research centers are affiliated with academic institutions, conducting research activities in such fields as medicine, energy, marine science, economics, Latin America and the Caribbean, the environment, and aging.

Public Library Information: Miami-Dade Public Library System, 101 W. Flagler St., Miami, FL 33130; telephone (305) 375-2665.

■ Health Care

Miami-Dade County has one of largest concentrations of medical facilities in the state. These facilities provide comprehensive human and social services through an array of programs that includes emergency assistance, mental health care, substance abuse treatment and prevention, homeless shelter, veteran services, and other traditional social services.

Miami's Jackson Health System includes the University of Miami–Jackson Memorial Medical Center, considered one of the best hospitals in the United States. It is also Miami-Dade County's only public hospital. The medical center has some 1,637 beds with more than 64,000 admissions annually, as of 2013. It is also a teaching hospital and is accredited by the Commission on Accreditation of Rehabilitation Facilities. The center is the flagship institute for several other area facilities, including University of Miami Hospital and Clinics, Holtz Children's Hospital (located at the medical center), Bascom Palmer Eye Institute at the University of Miami, and the University of Miami Sylvester Cancer Center. With the only Level I trauma center in the Miami-Dade area, Jackson Health System's Ryder Trauma Center is one of the busiest in the United States. In 2014 *U.S. News & World Report* ranked the University of Miami–Jackson Memorial Medical Center first nationally for ophthalmology; the hospital was a high-performing hospital in six other fields. For pediatric care, Holtz Children's Hospital was ranked nationally in six specialties.

Baptist Hospital of Miami owns several facilities in the area and is highly regarded for the quality of its patient care. The main hospital has 672 beds and admits more than 38,000 patients annually. South Miami Hospital, with 357 beds, and Mount Sinai Medical Center, with 666 beds, also provide a full range of care to area patients. The Cleveland Clinic, based in Ohio, has a facility in Weston, Florida—Cleveland Clinic Florida—with 155 beds; it admits more than 10,000 patients annually and performs 10,000 surgeries while also attending to 30,000 emergency-room patients.

■ Recreation

Sightseeing

Visitors to Miami will find a variety of activities, from an adventure-filled day at a nature park to a nostalgic stroll through a historic district. The city's principal attraction is Miami Seaquarium, south Florida's largest tropical aquarium. Seaquarium features performing dolphins, killer whales and sea lions, in addition to thousands of other sea creatures in display tanks, as well as tropical gardens and a wildlife sanctuary. Another popular family-oriented wildlife/nature park is Monkey Jungle, where hundreds of monkeys, gorillas, and trained chimpanzees swing freely through a natural rain forest. Chimpanzees perform daily. Similar to Monkey Jungle, Jungle Island and Parrot Jungle present more than 1,000 tropical birds that fly free. Featured are trained birds that perform daily in 20-minute shows. Located between downtown Miami and South Beach, Parrot Jungle includes an Everglades exhibit, children's area with petting zoo, animal barn, playground and water play areas, baby bird and plant nurseries, picnic pavilions, food court, a theater, two amphitheaters, jungle trails, and aviaries.

Perhaps the ultimate wildlife experience can be found at Zoo Miami. This cageless zoo is set on approximately 327 developed acres of natural habitats, where more than 500 species of the world's animals roam on islands separated from visitors by moats. Among those are 40 endangered species. Also available for visitors are more than 1,000 species of trees, palms, and other plants, and hundreds of orchids maintained by the Eastern Airlines Orchid Society.

The Miami area maintains some of the nation's most beautiful tropical gardens. Fairchild Tropical Botanical Garden, in nearby Coral Gables, is one of the finest botanical gardens in the continental United States. It features paths that wind through a rain forest, sunken gardens, a rare plant house, and 11 lakes displaying a wide variety of tropical vegetation. When the gardens sustained massive damage from Hurricane Andrew in 1992,

scientists from around the globe gathered to begin to help restore this world-class botanical paradise. Wings of the Tropics, a conservatory filled with tropical butterflies and flowering nectar plants, opened in 2012.

Miami has preserved much of its rich past and embraced its social and ethnic diversity. A 30-block strip called Calle Ocho showcases Miami's Cuban culture in restaurants, nightclubs, sidewalk coffee shops, parks, cigar factories, and boutiques. The Art Deco District in Miami Beach contains more than 800 buildings designed in the Art Deco architecture and pastel colors of the 1930s. Another reminder of the past is Vizcaya Museum & Gardens, an Italian Renaissance-style palace with beautiful formal gardens overlooking Biscayne Bay. Vizcaya, which was built by James Deering, the founder of International Harvester, houses a collection of fifteenth- to early nineteenth-century European art.

Arts and Culture

The primary venues for concerts and theatrical performances in Miami are the Gusman Center for the Performing Arts, the Jackie Gleason Theater of the Performing Arts, and the Miami-Dade County Auditorium. The Gusman Center, an ornate Baroque-style theater, has been transformed from a 1920s movie palace into an elegant stage for the performing arts. The Miami-Dade County Auditorium, featuring Art Deco revival decor, is a performance site for many local and international artists. The Florida Shakespeare Theater performs in a new space in the Historic Biltmore Hotel. The Miami Light Project, which performs artistic works such as musicals, stand-up comedy, and dance, performs in various locations. The Adrienne Arsht Center for the Peforming Arts of Miami-Dade County was completed in 2006 after five years and $472 million of construction, with funding coming from both public and private sources. It is a venue for the Florida Grand Opera, Miami City Ballet, and the New World Symphony. The New World Symphony seeks to prepare young, highly gifted graduates of distinguished music programs for placement in top-ranked orchestras around the world.

Several Miami-area museums and galleries reflect the city's varied culture. The Pérez Art Museum Miami, which opened in December 2013, was a $200 million, 200,000-square-foot waterfront facility that focused on contemporary art of the twentieth and twenty-first centuries. The Bass Museum of Art in the heart of the Art Deco district in Miami Beach houses a permanent collection of Old Masters, sculptures, textiles and period furniture. Other art museums in the region include the Jewish Museum of Florida, the Museum of Contemporary Art, the Lowe Museum of Art, and World Erotic Art Museum. The Wolfsonian boasts a collection that includes ceramics, glass, books, and furniture. Also instrumental in Miami's cultural life is the Art in Public Places program, one of the earliest of its kind, which has commissioned more than 650 works in the Metro-Dade area.

The Museum of HistoryMiami has exhibitions and collections that tell of the area's rich past and also connect it to the contemporary city and region. In 2011 the museum became part of the Smithsonian Institution Affiliations Program, which provides the facility with collaboration opportunities and collection-sharing with Smithsonian museums. Other historical museums include the 1891 Barnacle State Historic Site in Coconut Grove, Coral Gables' restored 1920s Merrick House, and the Holocaust Memorial.

Arts and Culture Information: Greater Miami Convention and Visitors Bureau, 701 Brickell Ave., Ste. 2700, Miami, FL 33131; telephone (305) 539-3000.

Festivals and Holidays

Miami hosts countless festivals and fairs throughout the year. Many reflect the city's rich cultural heritage. The Hispanic Heritage Festival features art, theater, dance, Latin folklore, and cuisine. The nation's largest Hispanic festival is Carnaval Miami, featuring salsa, brilliant costumes, and Cuban delicacies. It culminates in an all-day block party in the heart of Little Havana, the Calle Ocho Festival, which earned the title of the world's largest street party because it spans 23 city blocks. Cowbells, whistles, and washboard bands salute summer's Miami/Bahamas Goombay Festival, which celebrates Bahamian culture.

Art festivals abound. One of the largest and most prestigious is Art Basel Miami Beach. This fair, sister to the world famous Art Basel Switzerland, debuted in December 2002 and is now one of the most successful art fairs in North America. January's annual Art Deco Weekend in South Miami Beach features tours of the historic Art Deco district, site of more than 800 buildings from the 1920s and 1930s, and includes an antique car show, a costume ball, films, and lectures. Other art events include the Coconut Grove Arts Festival, a three-day event held in February, as well as the Miami Beach Festival of the Arts, and the South Miami Art Festival. Film festivals are just as common. The Miami International Film Festival showcases films from the United States, South America, Europe, the near East, and Australia that might not otherwise be seen in this country. Other festivals spotlight Jewish, gay and lesbian, Brazilian, African American, and Italian films.

The Orange Bowl Festival centers on the Discover Orange Bowl football game on New Year's night. This festival, which has been held annually since 1933, includes the King Orange Jamboree and sports tournaments for children and adults. The season of Lent is kicked off with the Greater Miami Mardi Gras celebration. The South Beach Wine & Food Festival is ranked as one of the nation's top ten wine events and features a partnership with the Food Network cable television station. More than 100 rides and 50,000 exhibits are featured at the Miami-Dade County Fair and Exposition, an 18-day event held in the spring.

Sports for the Spectator

Miami offers a variety of spectator sports at both the professional and collegiate level. The Miami Dolphins of the National Football League play their home games in Sun Life Stadium. Marlins park, home of Major League Baseball's Florida Marlins, opened in 2012 and seats 37,000 fans. The AmericanAirlines Arena houses the professional basketball team the Miami Heat, who play from November through April. The Florida Panthers of the National Hockey League play from October through April at the BB&T Center in neighboring Broward County.

The city of Miami is the site of the Discover Orange Bowl, which features the annual New Year's Day football game between two top-ranked collegiate teams. The University of Miami Hurricanes play their home basketball games at Sun Life Stadium, while the Florida International University Golden Panthers play on Alfonso Field at FIU Stadium.

Other popular spectator sports in the Miami area are horse and auto racing. Calder Race Course in Miami offers thoroughbred racing, while the Homestead-Miami Speedway is a magnet for auto-racing enthusiasts. Those interested in other sports can choose among golf tournaments, greyhound races, horse shows, regattas, soccer matches, and tennis tournaments such as the Sony Open.

Sports for the Participant

A complete range of outdoor activities is available year-round in Miami at numerous public and private facilities. Miami-Dade County Parks, Recreation, and Open Spaces Department operates six golf courses, with many more public and private courses available to visitors . Tennis courts for day and evening play are located in many parks and recreation areas throughout Miami and the county; in addition, most hotels have their own tennis facilities.

The extensive public park system in the Miami area includes 260 parks across nearly 13,000 acres of land and is the third largest county park system in the nation. Two national parks, Everglades and Biscayne, are also in the Miami area. Among the recreational activities that can be pursued in Miami's parks are picnicking, canoeing, boating, hiking, camping, fishing, swimming, basketball, softball, handball, racquetball, vita course trails, and 80 miles of Class I bike trails.

Water sports are pursued with great enthusiasm in Miami's ocean and bay. Most local dive shops offer lessons, certification courses, and dive trips for scuba and skin diving. Among the favorite diving spots are Haulover

Park and Biscayne National Park. For surfing one can go to Haulover Beach in Sunny Isles and South Pointe in South Miami Beach. A popular place for windsurfing is Hobie Beach in Key Biscayne. Waterskiing schools, jumps, towing services, and ski boat rentals can be found along beaches and causeways throughout the Miami area. Many beach hotels also offer water sports equipment rental.

Fishing is another favorite pastime. A freshwater fishing license, obtainable at bait and tackle stores, is required for anyone between the ages of 15 and 65 years. The Florida Game and Fresh Water Commission publishes guides to fishing regions. In the Miami area the popular spots are Tamiami Canal, from west Miami along U.S. Highway 41, which is noted for pan fish and bass; and Thompson Park fishing camp, a 270-acre campground near Hialeah, with three catch-and-release fishing lakes available only to campers. No license is required for saltwater fishing, but minimum size and bag limits apply. Fishing piers are located at Haulover Park, Baker's Haulover Cut, and South Pointe. Full-service charter boats and party boats for deep sea fishing are available at area marinas. Annual events include the Mayor's Cup Billfish and Miami Billfish tournaments.

Shopping and Dining

In keeping with its international image, Miami offers a cosmopolitan shopping experience. Every kind of shopping facility is available in the area, from indoor and outdoor malls to elegant specialty boutiques. Virtually all famous high-end retailers and designers, have a presence in the area.

Aventura Mall, located in the northern portion of Miami-Dade County, is the largest super-regional mall in south Florida, with 2.7 million feet of retail space and anchored by Nordstrom, Bloomingdale's, Macy's, JCPenney, and Sears. It contains more than 300 upscale shops and restaurants, as well as a 24-screen movie theater. The Village of Merrick Park features roughly 100 stores and restaurants in a natural environment complete with landscaped fountains, tropical foliage, and serene gardens. In Little Havana ethnic shops offer a variety of exotic items, from Cuban coffee and rum-soaked pastries to mantillas and furniture. The Falls, located on the southern edge of the city and anchored by Bloomingdale's and Macy's, sets its more than 100 shops among covered walkways, footbridges, and waterfalls. Bloomingdale's and Macy's planned an additional set of stores at the Miami Worldcenter downtown, scheduled to open in 2016 after adding a combined 425,000 square feet of shopping space to the city. In Coconut Grove, CocoWalk shopping district resembles a European village. Bal Harbour Shops are in Miami Beach in an area called the Rodeo Drive of the South because of their exclusive stores and designer boutiques. Lincoln Road Mall, located in the Art Deco District of Miami Beach, was

the first pedestrian-only shopping street in the United States. In trendy South Miami, The Shops at Sunset Place, an entertainment-shopping complex, has waterfalls, fountains, a grand staircase, and 35-foot Banyan trees.

Dadeland Mall features 185 specialty stores. Biscayne Bay's open-air Bayside Marketplace, on 20 acres of waterfront property at the north end of Bayside Park, has more than 120 shops that offer merchandise not ordinarily found in regional shopping areas. Just west of Miami Beach is the Miami Design District, comprised of interior design showrooms, and home furnishings and furniture stores that are open to the public.

With its expanding role in international trade, cuisine from every culture as well as local specialties can be found in a wide variety of dining establishments in Miami. Dining in the Miami Beach area offers plenty of beachside eateries with casual fare. Not surprisingly, the downtown area features high-end restaurants, many with a Latin influence and others, such as sushi restaurants, taking advantage of the city's proximity to the sea. Enhancing the ethnic diversity of Miami's dining possibilities are the more than 30 restaurants, supper clubs, and cafeterias in Little Havana.

Visitor Information: Greater Miami Convention and Visitors Bureau, 701 Brickell Ave., Ste. 2700, Miami, FL 33131; telephone (305) 539-3000.

■ Convention Facilities

Generous hotel space and a warm climate, coupled with a diverse range of available leisure activities, make the city an ideal spot for business mixed with pleasure. However, the city has long lacked a major convention facility to attract potential business clients. Resorts World Miami, a 13.9-acre complex scheduled for completion in 2015, was expected to fill that gap. One of the largest development projects ever undertaken in the state of Florida, the plan included a 700,000-square-foot convention center and a 200,000-square-foot ballroom marketed as the largest in the nation. Other aspects of the facility included 5,200 hotel rooms.

Existing facilities include the Miami Convention and Conference Center, located on the Miami River in the heart of the business and financial district. It offers meeting facilities for up to 42,000 people. The Hyatt Regency Miami is adjacent to the center, and also offers convention facilities, bringing the total meeting space to some 100,000 square feet, including a 5,000-seat auditorium. The James L. Knight International Center can seat up to 4,646 people plus 16,000 square feet of exhibition space. It also has a fully professional sound system.

The Miami Beach Convention Center, which spans four city blocks and sits adjacent to the Jackie Gleason

Theatre, offers more than one million square feet of meeting space and hosts the city's largest conventions. In 2009 the Center's management implemented an environmental program to counteract the environmental footprint of such a large space.

For groups ranging in size from 20 to 1,350 people, other downtown meeting sites can be found in numerous hotels. Some resort hotels located in Miami offer meeting facilities along with a variety of activities, including health clubs and water sports; similarly, some resort hotels located in nearby Coconut Grove, Key Biscayne, and Coral Gables also accommodate large and small meeting groups. Miami Beach, too, offers a number of hotels with meeting facilities, of which the best known are the Fontainebleau, Eden Roc Miami Beach, and Doral, popular for decades as tourist resorts.

Convention Information: Greater Miami Convention and Visitors Bureau, 701 Brickell Ave., Ste. 2700, Miami, FL 33131; telephone (305) 539-3000.

■ Transportation

Approaching the City

Visitors arriving by plane stop at the Miami International Airport, an ultramodern facility only seven miles from downtown and served by some 89 carriers. MIA is the one of the busiest in the world and had the second highest international passenger traffic in the country as of 2012. A terminal expansion of the airport was expected to complete in 2014. The Metropolitan Miami-Dade County Aviation Department also maintains four general aviation facilities that handle corporate aircraft flights. The Port of Miami is the world's busiest cruise port, with six new ships docking at the port in 2013 alone. Amtrak provides passenger rail service into and out of the city. A 65-mile commuter rail system, Tri-Rail, links downtown Miami to Fort Lauderdale and Palm Beach, and to Miami International Airport.

The major north–south expressways into Miami are Interstate 95, the Palmetto Expressway (also called State Road 826), and the Florida Turnpike. Main east–west routes are Interstate 195, the Dolphin Expressway (State Road 836), the Airport Expressway (State Road 112), the Tamiami Trail (U.S. Highway 4, which is also Southwest Eighth Street), and the Miami Beach Causeways (MacArthur, Venetian, Julia Tuttle, and 79th Street). Other east–west thoroughfares are the Bal Harbour (Broad Street), Sunny Isles (State Road 826) and William Lehman Causeways.

Traveling in the City

Miami is laid out in a grid pattern organized around a downtown intersection of Miami Avenue (east–west) and Flagler Street (north–south), which divides the city into four quadrants. For ease in getting around, visitors have only to remember that "streets," "lanes," and "terraces" run east and west, while "avenues," "courts," and "places" run north and south.

Miami's Metrorail and Metrobus systems are operated by the MetroDade Transportation Administration. A tourist attraction in its own right, Metrorail carries passengers in air conditioned, stainless steel trains on an elevated railway over a 25-mile route from south of the city to north Miami-Dade. It provides connections to all major areas of the city, with 23 stops one-mile apart. With the completion of the downtown Metromover, Miami-Dade County became the first community in the world to have a people mover connected to a rail system. The Metromover is a free service that is made up of individual motorized cars running atop a 4.4-mile elevated track, looping around the downtown and connecting to the Metrorail. Interconnecting with the Metrorail and the Metromover is the fleet of buses known as Metrobus, which runs almost 365 days per year. The 800 buses in the system travel 29 million miles across 95 routes annually.

Bus, boat, and even helicopter tours are a relaxing way to see Miami and its environs. Comprehensive tour service is provided by numerous tour companies that feature half- and full-day bus or trolley excursions in and around Miami. For those who would like to experience the full effect of the city's skyline, several cruise lines in Miami Beach offer luncheon and moonlight boat excursions.

■ Communications

Newspapers and Magazines

Miami's major daily newspaper, the morning *Miami Herald,* is supplemented by two Spanish-language dailies, *Diario Las Americas* and *El Nuevo Herald,* which is published by the *Herald.* The *Daily Business Review* serves the city's legal and business communities. *The Miami Times* is an African American community newspaper. *Miami Today* is a weekly newspaper aimed at upper management. The *Miami New Times* is an alternative news and arts weekly.

Television and Radio

Miami is served by 28 local television stations, including affiliates of major networks and public broadcasting. There are 25 radio stations within close listening range to residents of the Miami area. Of these, 13 are licensed FM stations offering jazz, Spanish, country, religious, and pop music formats, while there are 12 licensed AM stations that feature religious, talk, Spanish/Caribbean, and sports programming. Radio programming from surrounding areas is available in Miami.

Media Information: The Miami Herald, 3511 NW 91 Ave., Miami, FL 33172; telephone (800) 843-4372.

Miami Online

The Beacon Council. Available www.beaconcouncil.com

City of Miami home page. Available www.miamigov.com

Diario las Americas. Available www.diariolasamericas.com

El Nuevo Herald. Available www.elnuevoherald.com

Enterprise Florida. Available www.eflorida.com

History Miami. Available www.historymiami.org

Greater Miami Chamber of Commerce. Available www.miamichamber.com

Greater Miami Convention and Visitors Bureau. Available www.miamiandbeaches.com

Jackson Health System. Available www.jacksonhealth.org

Miami-Dade County home page. Available miamidade.gov

Miami-Dade County Public Schools. Available www.dadeschools.net

Miami-Dade Public Library System. Available www.mdpls.org

Miami Department of Economic Initiatives. Available www.ci.miami.fl.us/economicdevelopment

The Miami Herald. Available www.miamiherald.com

BIBLIOGRAPHY

Bramson, Seth, *Miami: The Magic City* (Charleston, SC: Arcadia, 2007)

Dunlop, Beth, *National Trust Guide to Miami and South Florida: America's Guide for Architecture and History Travelers* (New York: John Wiley & Sons, 2007)

Giller, Norman M., *Designing the Good Life: Norman M. Giller and the development of Miami Modernism* (Gainesville, FL: University of Florida Press, 2007)

Lynn, Catherine. *Marion Manley: Miami's First Woman Architect.* Athens: University of Georgia Press, 2010.

Miller, Mark, *Miami and the Keys* (Washington, DC: National Geographic Society, 1999)

Muir, Helen, *Miami, U.S.A.* (Miami, FL: Pickering Press, 1990)

Parks, Arva Moore, and Carolyn Klepser, *Miami Then & Now* (Berkeley, CA: Thunder Bay Press, 2003)

Portes, Alejandro, and Alex Stepick, *City on the Edge: The Transformation of Miami* (Berkeley, CA: University of California Press, 1993)

Shulman, Allan T., et al. *Miami Architecture: an AIA Guide Featuring Downtown, the Beaches, and Coconut Grove.* (Gainesville: University Press of Florida, 2010).

Orlando

■ The City in Brief

Founded: 1857 (incorporated 1875)

Head Official: Mayor Buddy Dyer (since 2003)

City Population
>1990: 164,674
>2000: 185,951
>2010: 238,300
>2012 estimate: 249,525
>Percent change, 2000–2010: 28.2%
>U.S. rank in 1990: 104th (State rank: 6th)
>U.S. rank in 2000: 122nd (State rank: 6th)
>U.S. rank in 2010: 79th (State rank: 5th)

Metropolitan Statistical Area Population
>2000: 1,644,561
>2010: 2,134,411
>2012 estimate: 2,223,674
>Percent change, 2000–2010: 29.8%
>U.S. rank in 2000: 30th
>U.S. rank in 2010: 26th

Area: 94 square miles

Elevation: 127 feet above sea level (average)

Average Annual Temperatures: 72.8° F

Average Annual Precipitation: 48.35 inches

Major Economic Sectors: tourism, health care and education services, advanced manufacturing, aviation and aerospace, digital media, agritechnology, research and development, transportation and distribution, business and financial services

Unemployment Rate: 8.4% (2012)

Per Capita Income: $25,254

2012 FBI Crime Index Property: 16,304

Major Colleges and Universities: University of Central Florida, Rollins College

Daily Newspaper: *Orlando Sentinel*

■ Introduction

Orlando is located in the heart of Central Florida, home to a thriving tourism industry. Residents and tourists are attracted to the city's lakes, palm trees, and citrus groves. Major attractions such as Universal Orlando and Universal Studios Florida attract millions of visitors to the area annually. But tourism isn't the only force at work; manufacturers and distributors, airlines, and technology companies have relocated to the sunny city. Industries such as life science research and development, film production, military training and simulation, transportation, and medical technology ventures are adding to Orlando's growing local economy.

■ Geography and Climate

Orlando is the seat of Orange County, though its metropolitan area also includes portions of Seminole, Lake, and Osceola counties. Located approximately 150 miles from the Florida–Georgia border, in an area surrounded by numerous citrus growers and 1,200 lakes, Orlando lies about 50 miles from the Atlantic to the east, 75 miles from the Gulf Coast to the west, and about 375 miles from the tip of the Florida Keys. Abundant sunshine and warm temperatures are the norm. Daily temperatures range from the low 70s to the mid 80s from October to May, and nighttime lows average from the low 50s to the mid 60s, with occasional freezes in between December and February. From May through September the daily average highs are in the upper 80s to mid 90s, and lows average from the upper 60s to mid 70s. Prevailing winds are southerly at nine miles per hour. The summers are

© Songquan Deng/Shutterstock.com

humid and thundershowers occur frequently in the afternoon.

Area: 94 square miles

Elevation: 127 feet above sea level (average)

Average Temperatures: 72.8° F

Average Annual Precipitation: 48.35 inches

■ History

City Built Around Fort

Orlando, once known as The Phenomenal City, has experienced phenomenal change since the arrival of European settlers in 1835. At that time, the region was inhabited by the Seminole tribe of Native Americans. Historians believe that the Seminoles, whose named is said to mean "wild and separate," inhabited the Central Florida region for 6,000 to 12,000 years. The Second Seminole War, which spanned the period from 1835 to 1842, began when disagreements arose between the natives and the American settlers on such issues as land, cattle, and slaves. In the years following the war the

natives moved away, leaving the pioneers who built their town around Fort Gatlin. Until 1845 Orange County, of which the city of Orlando is the county seat, was known as Mosquito County. Tradition holds that Orlando was named after Orlando Reeves, an American soldier on sentinel duty for a scouting party. While Reeves' companion slept, a native approached disguised as a rolling log. Reeves, seeing what was occurring, fired his gun, woke the other soldiers, and saved them from peril. However, Reeves himself succumbed to an arrow shot by the native. Prior to receiving the name Orlando in 1857, the town was known as Jernigan, after Aaron Jernigan, a settler from Georgia. The first post office was established in 1850.

Citrus Industry Spurs Development

Prior to the 1880s, the two biggest industries in central Florida were cattle breeding and cotton growing. During the 1880s some of the pioneers started growing citrus trees. The growth of Orlando in size and prosperity was associated with the need for better transportation to citrus markets on the part of citrus growers. The city had its first rail lines by 1881, and during the 1880s and 1890s there was an influx of new fruit growers. By 1886 the city's streets were lined with office buildings, churches, hotels, and schools, and tourists from the north began to spend summers in the area.

Disaster struck in 1894 when a three-day freeze destroyed nearly all the citrus trees in Orange County. The freeze had a devastating effect on the community, which suffered losses of an estimated $100 million. Packing plants closed, banks closed, people lost their jobs, and it was 15 years before Orlando fully recovered.

City Attains Major Status

Between 1910 and 1920 the population of Orlando doubled, and the city was transformed from a rural citrus growing area to a major city. During the 1920s a great building boom aided in Orlando's continuing prosperity, evidenced by the opening of the Orlando Public Library in 1923 and the Municipal Auditorium in 1926. During the Great Depression of the 1930s, the federal government's Works Progress Administration programs aided in the upgrading of the Municipal Airport, the building of a new football stadium at Tinker Field, and park development, and by 1944 many new jobs had been created.

Another building boom followed World War II, and new suburbs, new roadways, and new shopping centers were built. In 1956 the forerunner of the Lockheed Martin company began operations, becoming the largest employer in Central Florida. Gradually many more companies and workers followed. In 1968 Florida Technological University (now called the University of Central Florida opened its doors. That same year marked the beginning of the Orlando Naval Training Center.

City Becomes World-Class Tourist Site

The development of Walt Disney World in 1971 in nearby Buena Vista spurred a construction boom that included apartment buildings, hotels and motels, banks, commercial shopping areas, and tourist-related businesses. The city's Municipal Justice Building was erected in 1972 and SeaWorld of Florida followed in 1973. Tourism increased, thanks to tourist sites such as Universal Orlando, which opened in 1990. To the dismay of many local people, what had once been a sleepy backwater town was rapidly becoming a world class tourist mecca. The town of Orlando was recognized as one of the world's most popular vacation sites.

The economic climate during the 1990s and 2000s was marked by diversification. The tools and technologies that were once geared toward military services were applied to the business sector, and the region developed into a high technology corridor. Industries like software, simulation, digital media, and biotechnology began to boom, fueling further growth and development. Tourism is still the city's primary industry, but Orlando has also developed a reputation for high-tech businesses and industries both related and unrelated to the entertainment industry. Medical research is a rapidly developing industry in the area.

Historical Information: Orange County Regional History Center, 65 E. Central Blvd., Orlando, FL 32801; telephone (407) 836-8500; toll-free (800) 965-2030.

■ Population Profile

Metropolitan Statistical Area Population
2000: 1,644,561
2010: 2,134,411
2012 estimate: 2,223,674
Percent change, 2000–2010: 29.8%
U.S. rank in 2000: 30th
U.S. rank in 2010: 26th

City Residents
1990: 164,674
2000: 185,951
2010: 238,300
2012 estimate: 249,525
Percent change, 2000–2010: 28.2%
U.S. rank in 1990: 104th (State rank: 6th)
U.S. rank in 2000: 122nd (State rank: 6th)
U.S. rank in 2010: 79th (State rank: 5th)

Density: 2,327.3 people per square mile

Racial and ethnic characteristics
White: 142,314
Black or African American: 77,311
American Indian and Alaskan Native: 394
Asian: 7,653
Native Hawaiian and Other Pacific Islander: 36
Hispanic or Latino (may be of any race): 68,873
Other: 21,817

Percent of residents born in state: 39%

Age characteristics
Population under 5 years old: 18,166
Population 5 to 9 years old: 16,885
Population 10 to 14 years old: 15,240
Population 15 to 19 years old: 12,398
Population 20 to 24 years old: 22,457
Population 25 to 34 years old: 50,169
Population 35 to 44 years old: 41,323
Population 45 to 54 years old: 29,112
Population 55 to 59 years old: 11,415
Population 60 to 64 years old: 9,318
Population 65 to 74 years old: 13,003
Population 75 to 84 years old: 7,167
Population 85 years and over: 2,872
Median age: 32.4

Births (2010–11 Metropolitan Area)
Total number: 26,060

Deaths (2010–11 Metropolitan Area)

Total number: 14,503

Money income (2012)

Per capita income: $25,254
Median household income: $41,266
Total households: 98,916

Number of households with income of …

less than $10,000: 8,148
$10,000 to $14,999: 7,144
$15,000 to $24,999: 14,095
$25,000 to $34,999: 12,691
$35,000 to $49,999: 15,871
$50,000 to $74,999: 18,983
$75,000 to $99,999: 8,036
$100,000 to $149,999: 8,187
$150,000 to $199,999: 2,610
$200,000 or more: 3,151

Percent of families below poverty level: 20.0%

FBI Crime Index Property: 16,304

FBI Crime Index Violent: 2,508

■ Municipal Government

The city of Orlando has a mayor and six commissioners, all of whom are elected to four-year terms. The mayor is the full-time chief executive officer of the city and presides over all city council meetings. The city council must confirm all mayoral appointments of department heads. The six city commissioners are elected on a nonpartisan basis by district.

Head Official: Mayor Buddy Dyer (since 2003)

Total Number of City Employees: 3,059 (2013)

City Information: Orlando City Hall, P.O. Box 4990, Orlando, FL 32802-4990; telephone (407) 246-2121.

■ Economy

Major Industries and Commercial Activity

Orlando is known around the world for its major entertainment attractions in the area, especially Walt Disney World and Epcot (in nearby Lake Buena Vista), and Universal Orlando. However, behind the scenes of the area's tourism and entertainment industry is a dynamic and diversified economy that has expanded enormously. Among its most important industry clusters are advanced manufacturing, life sciences, digital media, aviation and aerospace, agritechnology, optics and photonics, and digital media.

The aviation and aerospace industry has had a foothold in the Orlando area for decades. The flight training industry was drawn to the area's favorable year-round climate, and military air bases were established in World War II. Since then, with a number of international and regional airports and thriving high technology expertise, the area has given rise to companies providing aircraft and ground support services; Signature Flight Support, one of the largest such companies in the world, is based in Orlando. One of the world's most advanced flight training schools, FlightSafety International, is located in the area. Lockheed Martin and Siemens, both major defense contractors, have a strong presence in metro Orlando.

The influx of technology-related companies to the area has made Orlando one of the fastest growing high-technology centers in the nation. The metro area has one of the country's largest concentrations of modeling, simulation, and training (MS&T) businesses, research centers, and educational facilities. The MS&T sector, which has its roots in military services, provides applications in such diverse fields as homeland security, emergency services, entertainment, information and medical technologies, optics and photonics, and transportation. Another strong segment of the high-technology industry is software. This field, another offshoot of military applications, focuses on financial services and includes other areas like utilities, billing, higher education, multimedia, animation, and military training. Companies engaged in life sciences, digital media, and health-care companies are all expanding. Notable firms include the videogame maker Electronic Arts Tiburon; the digital animation studios of Premise Entertainment and Two Door Productions; and a top-rated research center, Sanford-Burnham Medical Research Institute.

Also benefiting from the area's specialization in high technology is the field of advanced manufacturing. Companies involved in this field provide high-tech parts for a broad range of products and applications, such as power generation systems, wireless communications, computers, medical imaging, instruments and control, and automotive systems.

In addition to advanced manufacturing, Orlando is a prime locale for other types of manufacturing, warehousing, and distribution. New manufacturers have been attracted in part by Orlando's efficient air service, low cost of doing business, growing work force, and high quality of life. Plastics is a key subsector, with Tupperware Corporation leading the field. Other important manufacturing segments include metal fabrication and parts, infrastructure materials, defense, power plant systems, microelectronics, and laser equipment. As for distribution, Metro Orlando is one of the world's few quadramodal transportation centers, with the ability to transport goods via land, air, sea, and space.

The area's network of interstate highways, its international and regional airports, and its proximity to the Kennedy Space Center and the Port of Tampa combine to give Orlando a distribution advantage over other areas. Such items as restaurant equipment, health-care products, auto parts, and consumer electronics are all stored in the area's modern warehouses.

Orlando's fertile farmlands, regional health-care system, and expertise in photonics and MS&T have also given rise to a strong biotechnology industry in such areas as research, clinical trials, agricultural sciences, and medical training. This vibrant field has applications in industrial food ingredients, plant reproduction, bioterrorism defense, medical products, and modeling systems for laboratories.

Items and goods produced: military electronics and missiles, food and beverages, plastics, motors and engine components, concrete, electronic components, medical equipment, film and video productions

Incentive Programs-New and Existing Companies

Local programs: The Metro Orlando Economic Development Commission attracts new business investment by marketing the Orlando region worldwide as a top location for business. It also works with local companies to assist them with expansion plans and other business concerns. Its key services and support range from relocation and expansion expertise to export counsel to long-term planning with its community partners. Orange County commissioners aggressively provide inducements, such as tax credits and refunds for developing jobs and properties in targeted areas, to companies that will have a significant impact on the economy. The city of Orlando also offers incentives to new or expanding businesses, including tax credits, assistance with development fees, and discounts on film production costs.

The University of Central Florida's Business Incubation Program, founded in 1999, has helped hundreds of emerging companies generate revenue and create more than 3,300 new jobs in Central Florida. The Business Incubation Program represents collaboration between the University of Central Florida, the Florida High Tech Corridor Council, Orange, Osceola, Seminole and Volusia Counties, and the cities of Apopka, Kissimmee, Orlando, St. Cloud, and Winter Springs. The UCF Business Incubator at Central Florida Research Park serves Orlando.

State programs: Enterprise Florida is a partnership between Florida's government and business leaders and is the principal economic development organization for the state of Florida. Enterprise Florida's mission is to increase economic opportunities for all Floridians by supporting the creation of quality jobs, a well-trained workforce, and globally competitive businesses. It pursues this mission in cooperation with its statewide network of economic development partners. Among the incentive programs

managed at the state level is the Economic Development Transportation Fund, which helps fund the cost of transportation projects, such as access roads and road widening, required for the establishment, expansion, or retention of businesses in Florida. The state's Qualified Target Industry Tax Refund is similar to a Miami-Dade program that rewards the creation of jobs in certain industries.

Florida has a favorable tax climate, with benefits such as no corporate income tax on limited partnerships, no sales tax on purchases of raw materials incorporated in a final product for resale, and no personal state income tax. The state also offers various sales and use tax exemptions for machinery and equipment purchase, electric energy, research and development, and other aspects of doing business in the area.

Job training programs: Florida is a statewide, business-led workforce policy board that collaborates with the Florida Department of Economic Opportunity and regional workforce boards. The 24 regional boards have primary responsibility for direct services through a statewide network of One-Stop Career systems. One-Stop Career Centers are the central elements of the One-Stop system that provide integrated services to employers, workers, and jobseekers. CareerSource Florida administers two training grant initiatives to assist both employers and job seekers. Quick Response Training (QRT) Grants provide funding for customized training to new or expanding businesses. Incumbent Worker Training (IWT) Grants provide funding for programs that help existing full-time employees upgrade their skills.

CareerSource Central Florida, representing Metro Orlando, is the regional arm of CareerSource Florida Inc., an agency charged with administering the state's workforce policy, programs, and services. Quick Response Training is a state-administered program that provides funding for customized training for new or expanding businesses, while Incumbent Worker Training serves existing businesses.

The University of Central Florida offers programs specifically designed to train students for major target industries. Other regional schools, such as Valencia Community College and Seminole Community College, offer degrees in industry-related fields.

Development Projects

In 2013 Siemens Energy opened a new, state-of-the-art wind turbine training facility in Orlando. The $7 million, 40,000-square-foot facility created 50 jobs. That year, Sedgwick Claims Management Services, Inc., a provider of innovative, technology-enabled claims and productivity management solutions, announced plans to open a 30,000-square-foot call center in Orlando with a capital investment of $1.2 million. The new center will create 225 new jobs. MarJam Supply Company, a construction supply company, announced it would build a new location in Orlando with a capital investment of $1.6 million. The global cargo logistics provider, National Air Cargo Holdings, Inc., relocated its headquarters from Michigan to Orlando in 2013. The company planned to create up to 105 new jobs through 2015 with a capital investment of $875,000 in the region.

Development continues at Orlando's Lake Nona Medical City, a 650-acre health and life sciences park designed as a premier location for medical care, research, and education. Eight new companies set up shop at Lake Nona in 2013. DaVita Rx, LLC, a full-service pharmacy specializing in renal care, opened a new facility with an $8.7 million capital investment and intentions to create 100 new jobs through 2015. Mazor Robotics, Inc., an Israeli developer of innovative surgical robots and complementary products placed their U.S. headquarters at Lake Nona, with 20 employees and plans to create 34 new jobs through 2016. Catalyst Rx, a full-service pharmacy benefit manager, planned to create 300 jobs at their Lake Nona facility through 2016. The Profil Institute for Clinical Excellence, a center for clinical research in diabetes and obesity, opened its first East Coast location in collaboration with Florida Hospital. Other companies opening in Lake Nona included Prime Therapeutics, BeneCard PBF, AcariaHealth, and Axium Healthcare Pharmacy, Inc.

The revitalization of Downtown Orlando continued throughout 2013 as well. One major project involved expansion of the LYMMO transit system. Demolition of the former Amway Arena began to clear the way for the first phase in the new Creative Village development. City planners envision Creative Village as a 68-acre urban neighborhood that will be home to college facilities, high-tech, digital media and creative companies, and a diverse mix of students, employees, and residents. Work continued on the Dr. Phillips Center for the Performing Arts, which was expected to open for the 2014–15 season. The new center will include three theaters (Walt Disney Theater, Acoustical Theater, and the Alexi and Jim Pugh Theater), an outdoor plaza and performance space, rehearsal rooms, administrative offices, and an educational facility. The city's old Mercado shopping village is being transformed into the I-Drive Live retail, dining, and entertainment development, which will feature a 425-foot observation wheel called the Orlando Eye, a 25,000-square-foot Madam Tussauds wax museum, and 25,000-square-foot Sea Life Aquarium. The new attractions were scheduled to open in 2014.

City and county officials are working with the Florida Department of transportation on the SunRail commuter rail transit project that will run along 61 miles of existing freight rail tracks through a four-county area (Orange, Seminole, Volusia, and Osceola). The first phase of SunRail will link DeBary to Orlando.

Economic Development Information: Metro Orlando Economic Development Commission, 301 E. Pine St.,
Ste. 900, Orlando, FL 32801; telephone (407) 422-7159; fax (407) 425-6428; email info@orlandoedc.com.

Commercial Shipping

With global shipping opportunities via air, land, sea, and space, metropolitan Orlando is one of the world's few quadramodal transportation centers. Orlando International Airport is the third-largest airport in the United States for domestic origin and destination. It offers non-stop service to 81 domestic cities and 34 international destinations. The airport is also the site of Foreign Trade Zone #42. Orlando is also served by six regional airports, of which Orlando Sanford International Airport (Sanford, Florida) is the largest. Orlando Sanford is also the site of Foreign Trade Zone #250. These zones permit foreign goods to be stored or processed without import duty.

The city also benefits from Florida's deregulation of the trucking industry within its borders. Many shippers report rates of 10 percent or less than the national average. Orlando is served by some 60 motor freight carriers, with Interstates 4 and 95 providing access to many areas throughout the state and the Southeast. Freight rail service is provided by CSX Transportation and Florida Central Railroad transport cargo. CSX Intermodal has a terminal located in Orlando. Orlando's nearest navigable waterways are at Port of Sanford, 20 miles away; Port Canaveral, 50 miles away; and Port of Tampa, 70 miles away. The nearby Kennedy Space Center offers deep water ports as well as launch facilities.

Labor Force and Employment Outlook

In 2013 the leisure and hospitality industry accounted for the highest percentage of jobs (20 percent of all jobs) for the Orland metropolitan statistical area. Professional and business services was the next highest employment industry, followed by education and health services, retail trade, and government. Leisure and hospitality also had the greatest percentage job growth from 2012 to 2013 at about 4.6 percent.

In Orlando proper, the largest leisure and hospitality employers included Universal Orlando, Sea World Parks and Entertainment, Hilton Hotels, and Westgate Resorts. Other large employers include Orlando Health, Lockheed Martin, Siemens, and the University of Central Florida.

The following is a summary of data regarding the 2013 Orlando labor force:

Size of civilian labor force: 142,609

Number of workers employed in . . .
agriculture and mining: 276
construction: 6,531
manufacturing: 5,022
wholesale trade: 2,889
retail trade: 15,189

transportation: 6,996
information systems: 2,640
finance: 9,544
professional administration: 18,989
education and social services: 23,836
arts and leisure: 25,005
other: 5,424
public administration: 3,887

Average hourly earnings of production workers: $14.94

Unemployment rate: 8.4% (2012)

Employers

Largest employers (2013)	*Number of employees*
Universal Orlando	16,000
Orlando Health	15,810
University of Central Florida	10,388
Hilton Hotels	9,595
Lockheed Martin	6,470
Darden Restaurants	6,277
Sea World Parks and Entertainment	6,022
Westgate Resorts	5,323
Siemens	4,395

Cost of Living

The cost of living in metro Orlando was 2.1 percent above the national average as of 2013, after falling below the national average during the late 2000s.

The following is a summary of data regarding several key cost of living factors in the area.

State income tax rate: None

State sales tax rate: 6.0%

Local income tax rate: None

Local sales tax rate: 0.5%

Property tax rate: $20.1498 per $1,000 of assessed property value (2013)

Economic Information: Metro Orlando Economic Development Commission, 301 E. Pine St., Ste. 900, Orlando, FL 32801; telephone (407) 422-7159; fax (407) 425-6428; email info@orlandoedc.com.

■ Education and Research

Elementary and Secondary Schools

Orange County Public Schools is one of the largest districts in the nation. The district offers pre-kindergarten classes during the regular school year and during the summer. All high schools offer some advanced placement and honors courses. Magnet programs are available in all high schools and some elementary schools in such areas aviation/aerospace, language, fine arts, science, economics, medicine, law, finance, animal science, and international studies. Programs are available for students who are physically or emotionally handicapped, learning disabled, speech and language or hearing impaired, autistic, or visually impaired. Occupational and physical therapy programs are also available. Gifted education programs are offered at elementary, middle, and high school level. There are 32 charter schools in the district.

There are several independent and faith-based private schools in Orlando. The Catholic Diocese of Orlando has 15 schools in the region.

The following is a summary of data regarding the Orange County Public Schools.

Total enrollment: 176,008

Number of facilities

total: 184
elementary schools: 123
junior high schools: 38
high schools: 19
other: 4

Student/teacher ratio: 15.84:1

Teacher salaries

average (statewide): $46,702

Funding per pupil: $8,317

Public Schools Information: Orange County Public Schools, 445 W. Amelia St., Orlando, FL 32801; telephone (407) 317-3200.

Colleges and Universities

The University of Central Florida (UCF) is the largest institution of higher learning in the Orlando area and the second largest university in the nation, with a total enrollment of some 60,000 students. UCF is a public state university based in Orlando with three regional campuses. The university offers undergraduate, graduate, and specialist programs in business, education, engineering, health sciences, nursing, and in high-technology areas such as aviation and aerospace, biotechnology, and computer modeling, simulation and training.

Ana G. Menendez University–Orlando is a unique dual-language institution where classes are held in both Spanish and English in order to develop bilingual leaders. The university offers a variety of bachelor's degrees, as well as MBAs with specializations in accounting, finance, management, and human resources. Polytechnic University of Puerto Rico, Orlando Campus is a private, non-profit institution that offers bachelor's and master's degrees in engineering and business administration. Adventist University of Health Sciences works in partnership with Florida Hospital to train students in allied health and nursing fields. Bachelor's degrees are available in nursing and radiologic sciences. Associate's degrees are available in fields such as diagnostic medical sonography, nuclear medicine, and occupational therapy.

Valencia Community College, with over 28,000 students, has six campuses (four in Orlando) and offers university parallel and career training programs. Keiser University Orlando provides training in the fields of business, criminal justice, and nursing.

Libraries and Research Centers

The Orange County Library System consists of the Orlando Public Library and 14 branches. The system houses approximately two million books, e-books, periodicals, DVDs, CDs, art reproductions, slides, and maps. Its special collections include the Walt Disney World Collection, the Florida Collection, the Genealogy Collection (the largest in the Southeast), and state documents.

The University of Central Florida Libraries has a collection of more than 2.4 million volumes, including 624,000 e-books. In addition, the libraries keep 43,000 serial subscriptions, of which 40,500 are in electronic format. The library owns about 3.1 million microforms and 51,500 media titles in various formats. UCF is a partial depository for both United States and Florida government publications. Special collections include the Bryant West Indies Collection, Floridiana Collection, the Wagar and Scott Simpkinson Space Collections, and Carey Hand Funeral Home Records.

The Learning Resource Center and the Robert Arthur Williams Library of Adventist University of Health Sciences contains outstanding collections of print and video information in nursing and allied health fields.

The University of Central Florida is a major research university. Research and training facilities sponsored by the school include the Materials Characterization Facility (MCF), Institute for Simulation and Training (IST), Space Education and Research Center, Florida Solar Energy Center, BioMolecular Science Center, and Center for Research and Education in Optics and Lasers (CREOL).

Located adjacent to the University of Central Florida is the Central Florida Research Park, one of the top science parks in the world. The park is a joint venture between the university and Orange County to promote relations between industry and the university. Consisting of more than 1,000 acres, it is occupied by more than 125 companies in the fields of simulation and training, lasers, optical filters, behavioral sciences, diagnostic test equipment, and oceanographic equipment. One of the park's major tenants is the Naval Air Warfare Center Training Systems Division, the world's leading simulation center for military training. Other tenants include Aegis Technologies, Center for Drug Discovery and Diagnostics, Morgan

research Corporation, Northrop Grumman, U.S. Army Research Institute–Simulator Systems Research Unit, and Wyle Laboratories.

The Sanford-Burnham Medical Research Institute is a non-profit public-benefit corporation with faculties in Orlando and San Diego California. The institute has established major research programs in cancer, neurodegeneration, diabetes, and infectious, inflammatory, and childhood diseases. The institute is widely known for its work in stem cell research and drug discovery technologies.

Public Library Information: Orange County Library System, 101 E. Central Blvd., Orlando, FL 32801; telephone (407) 835-7323.

■ Health Care

Florida Hospital, based in Orlando, is a private, not-for-profit network of 22 campuses throughout the state. It is part of the greater Adventist Health System. For 2014 it was ranked as the best hospital in Florida by *U.S. News & World Report.* It was ranked 10th in the nation in the field of gynecology. The two main campuses in Orlando proper are the Florida Hospital East Orlando and Florida Hospital Orlando, the latter of which is the flagship of the system. Treating more than one million patients each year, Florida Hospital is one of the busiest in the United States. It is noted for its programs in cardiology, cancer, women's medicine, diabetes, orthopedics, and rehabilitation.

Another nonprofit, Orlando Regional Medical Center is an 808-bed tertiary hospital in downtown Orlando that is the flagship center for Orlando Health. Specialties include trauma, cardiovascular services, orthopedics, neurosciences, internal medicine, and minimally invasive bariatric surgery. This center is home to Central Florida's only Level I trauma center. Additional Orlando Health centers in Orlando proper include the Arnold Palmer Hospital for Children, the Winnie Palmer Hospital for Women and Babies, Dr. P. Phillips Hospital, and the M. D. Anderson Cancer Center Orlando.

The Nemours Children's Hospital and Pediatric Health Campus is a nationally recognized center for pediatric subspecialties. The clinic serves children from the greater Orlando area as well as around the United States and the world. The Orlando VA Medical Center was scheduled to open at Lake Nona Medical City in 2014.

■ Recreation

Sightseeing

The greater Orlando area has many attractions, particularly its theme parks, which attract visitors from all over the world. New rides and exhibits are unveiled every year at Walt Disney World's four parks in nearby Buena Vista: the Magic Kingdom, with its seven themed lands; Epcot, which provides journeys to Future World and to the World Showcase; Disney's Hollywood Studios, where spectators can experience actual movie and television production; and Animal Kingdom, Disney World's largest attraction at 500 acres. Universal Orlando features the Islands of Adventure and Universal Studios Florida, a high-technology movie-themed attraction with more than 40 rides, shows, shops, and restaurants, both of which rank just below the Disney parks in annual attendance. The newest addition to Universal's theme park came in 2010 with the opening of The Wizarding World of Harry Potter. This collection of rides is based on the popular J. K. Rowling *Harry Potter* novels.

Gatorland offers the chance to observe thousands of alligators, birds, and animals; its alligator breeding marsh was seen in the movie *Indiana Jones and the Temple of Doom*. Shamu the Killer Whale is the focus at SeaWorld Orlando marine life park. SeaWorld's Aquatica waterpark opened in 2008. The park has two wave pools, water slides, raft rides, and lazy rivers, and exotic animals that visitors can meet close up.

A view of Florida's floral splendor is the attraction at Harry P. Leu Gardens, featuring the largest formal rose garden in Florida. Also on display are 50 acres of camellias, as well as palm, bamboo, herb, vegetable, and butterfly gardens.

Arts and Culture

Once known primarily for sunshine and oranges, Orlando is developing its arts and cultural profile as the city continues to grow. Major performances are offered throughout the year by the Orlando Ballet and Orlando Philharmonic Orchestra. In 2013 these groups performed at the Bob Carr Performing Arts Centre, while eagerly anticipating the fall 2014 opening of their new home of the Dr. Phillips Center for the Performing Arts.

Among the region's other musical groups are the Florida Symphony Youth Orchestra, whose members range from the third grade through college sophomore, and the Bach Festival Society, both located in Winter Park. Orlando Loch Haven Park, a 45-acre cultural oasis, is home to some of Florida's finest facilities for the arts, sciences, and humanities. Among them is the Orlando Museum of Art, considered one of the South's finest museums. It offers permanent collections of nineteenth- and twentieth-century American, pre-Columbian, and African art, as well as summer art camp and studio classes. Also in the park is the 207,000-square-foot Orlando Science Center, one of the largest facilities of its kind in the Southeast, and the Mennello Museum of American Art, Florida's only museum devoted solely to displaying vernacular work. Loch Haven is also the site of the Orlando Repertory Theatre, Orlando Shakespeare Theater, Orlando Fire Museum, and the Orlando Garden Club.

An authentic 1926 firehouse complete with antique trucks and Central Florida artifacts from pre-history,

pioneer times, and the Victorian era are on view at the Orange County Regional History Center.

Festivals and Holidays

Fun and frolic abound at a variety of special events that attract residents and visitors alike in Greater Orlando. February brings the Valentine's Stroll at the Harry P. Leu Gardens and the Bands, Brew, and BBQ Festival at SeaWorld. The Central Florida Fair, which is approaching its centennial, is held in the spring. April brings the Orlando Cabaret Festival, a two-week celebration of comedy and musical performances, and the Fiesta Medina, Orlando's longest running Latin community festival. The Orlando Shakespeare Theater presents Shakespearean works performed by professional actors at the Lake Eola Amphitheater in April. It is followed by the Orlando International Fringe Theatre Festival in May, featuring more than 300 performing artists and theatrical troupes. Orlando celebrates Independence Day with Fireworks at the Fountain, a free fireworks display and laser show at Lake Eola Park. Halloween is celebrated at a number of local venues including Universal Studios Florida, where the celebration lasts for 14 days. The lighting of Orlando's Great American Christmas Tree in early December ushers in the holiday season.

Sports for the Spectator

The wildly popular Orlando Magic National Basketball Association team plays its home games at the Amway Center from November through April. The Amway is also home to the Orlando Predators, who play arena football from April through August and the Orlando Solar Bears of the ECHL (East Coast Hockey League).

Football fans can catch the Russell Athletic Bowl in December, and then ring in the new year with the Capital One Bowl, a college contest held on New Year's Day at the Florida Citrus Bowl Stadium. This stadium is also home to University of Central Florida Knights football games, the Superbowl of Motorsports, and the AMA Supercross Series. Golf enthusiasts can enjoy the Arnold Palmer Invitational and the Tavistock Cup in March and the Children's Miracle Network Classic in November.

Sports for the Participant

Metro Orlando is a golf and tennis mecca with numerous golf courses and tennis courts. RDV Sportsplex Athletic Club features a full-service fitness center with a variety of group classes and programs throughout the year. The club's training center once held the practice court of the Orlando Magic. This center now houses the Parisi Speed School, where thousands of world-class athletes have come to reach their potential. RDV Sportsplex also features programs for swimming, tennis, and basketball.

Hundreds of freshwater lakes offer a paradise for boating enthusiasts and swimmers. More than 100 camp-grounds and thousands of acres of national forest are available to hunters and campers. Orlando itself has 83 parks, 17 park and recreation centers, and 2 recreation centers for seniors. The city sponsors seven Afterschool All-Stars programs that provide afterschool activities at local middle schools, five days per week.

Shopping and Dining

Orlando provides a delightful array of combination shopping/entertainment experiences. The Florida Mall, anchored by Saks Fifth Avenue, Macy's, Dillard's, and Nordstrom, is central Florida's largest shopping center. The Mall at Millenia, also located in Orlando, offers dozens of specialty retailers as well as Neiman Marcus, Bloomingdale's, and Macy's. Located across from the Orange County Convention Center, Pointe Orlando is an open-air complex that features more than 60 retailers, restaurants, and entertainment facilities. The Church Street Station has more than 50 shops and restaurants in a Victorian atmosphere. Discount shoppers may find treasures among the 119 shops at Orlando Premium Outlets.

Orlando offers a wide array of dining experiences from fast-food and family restaurants, to lavish fine-dining establishments and novelty eateries. The region's 4,400 restaurants can satisfy any palate, from sushi to steak and pasta to grits. A unique specialty is gator tail or gator nuggets. The pleasant weather permits many outdoor dining settings, as well as meals aboard a paddle wheel steamer. American, Indian, Italian, Chinese, Continental, Japanese, and Mediterranean cuisine are available in greater Orlando.

Visitor Information: Visit Orlando, 6700 Forum Dr., Ste. 100, Orlando, FL; 32821; telephone (407) 363-5872; toll-free (800) 972-3304; fax (407) 370-5000.

■ Convention Facilities

As befits a city with a reputation as an exciting destination with plenty to do, Orlando is popular with meeting planners. Greater Orlando is capable of accommodating meetings and expositions both large and small. The Orange County Convention Center, located just south of the city has more than two million square feet of exhibit space and 74 meeting rooms with an additional 62,000 square feet of space in the Valencia Room. Several large resort hotels provide meeting rooms and space for exhibitions, banquets, and reception. The largest are Rosen Shingle Creek and Orlando World Center Marriott. Others include Hilton Orlando and the Florida Hotel and Conference Center. The combined meeting space in Orlando area hotels adds up to more than one million square feet. Orlando offers hotel rooms with accommodations ranging from budget hotels to lavish themed resorts.

Convention Information: Visit Orlando, 6700 Forum Dr., Ste. 100, Orlando, FL; 32821; telephone (407) 363-5872; toll-free (800) 972-3304; fax (407) 370-5000.

■ Transportation

Approaching the City

Orlando International Airport offers non-stop service to and from 81 domestic cities, and 34 international destinations. In nearby Sanford, Orlando Sanford International Airport offers scheduled domestic and scheduled/charter international service from several airlines. Other airports serving the Orlando area include Orlando Executive Airport, Kissimmee Gateway Airport, and Leesburg International Airport.

For drivers, two major limited-access highway systems bisect Central Florida, the crossroads of the state's highway network. Interstate Highway 4 runs east and west across Florida from Daytona Beach, and Interstate 95 runs from Tampa to the Atlantic coast. Florida's Turnpike runs south to Miami and north to join Interstate 95. Greyhound Lines offers interstate and intrastate bus service to and from Orlando. There are four Amtrak stations in the Orlando area. For those Amtrak passengers wishing to take their automobiles with them, the Auto Train can be boarded at nearby Sanford.

Traveling in the City

State Road 408 (East–West Expressway) expedites traffic through Orlando. The Martin Andersen Bee Line Expressway (State Road 528) provides direct access to JFK Space Center, Port Canaveral, and the Atlantic Coast beaches. Other highways serving the city include U.S. Highway 441, which runs east and west, U.S. Highways 17, 92, and 27, which run north and south, as well as numerous state roadways. State Road 417 (Central Florida GreeneWay) has been named one of the nation's top 10 roads by the American Automobile Association.

LYNX, the Central Florida Regional Transportation Authority, operates buses that serve Orange County and adjoining Seminole and Osceola counties. Free service in downtown Orlando is provided on a three-mile, dedicated-lane transit system called LYMMO. LYNX also supports a Road Ranger roadside assistance program on Interstate 4 in cooperation with State Farm for stranded motorists. Through the LYNX Vanpool Program, groups of 6 to 12 people can form their own carpools by designating a primary driver and qualifying for use of a LYNX van. Members pay for fuel and tolls and a monthly fee that includes the use of the van and all maintenance and insurance for the vehicle.

To revolutionize travel in and out of the city, a commuter transit SunRail is under construction. The 61-mile transit will run along existing freight rail tracks stretching through a four-county area (Orange, Seminole, Volusia, and Osceola).

■ Communications

Newspapers and Magazines

Orlando's daily (morning) newspaper is the *Orlando Sentinel.* *The Orlando Times* is a weekly newspaper focusing on the African American community, while the *Orlando Business Journal* speaks to the business community. *Orlando Weekly* is a weekly alternative newspaper covering news and entertainment in central Florida. Several magazines are published in Orlando, including *Orlando Family Magazine.*

Television and Radio

Orlando is served by 18 local television stations, including major broadcast affiliates, public television, and religious channels. There are 17 AM and FM radio stations licensed for broadcasts out of Orlando. Additional stations are received from neighboring communities.

Media Information: *Orlando Sentinel,* 633 North Orange Avenue, Orlando, FL 32801-1349; telephone (407) 420-5000.

Orlando Online

City of Orlando's home page. Available www.ci.orlando.fl.us

Metro Orlando Economic Development Commission. Available www.orlandoedc.com

Orange County Library System. Available www.ocls.info

Orange County Public Schools. Available www.ocps.net

Orange County Regional History Center. Available www.thehistorycenter.org

Visit Orlando. Available www.visitorlando.com

Orlando Sentinel. Available www.orlandosentinel.com

BIBLIOGRAPHY

McCain, Joan, *Orlando: The City Beautiful* (Orlando, FL: Tribune Publishers, 1991)

Monaghan, Kelly, *Universal Orlando: The Ultimate Guide to the Ultimate Theme Park Adventure,* 6th ed. (Branford, CT: Intrepid Traveler, 2007)

Snow, Michelle, *Walt Disney World & Orlando For Dummies*(New York, NY: Wiley Publishing Inc., 2004)

St. Petersburg

■ The City in Brief

Founded: 1887 (incorporated 1893)

Head Official: Mayor Rick Kriseman (since 2014)

City Population
>1990: 240,318
>2000: 248,232
>2010: 244,769
>2012 estimate: 246,533
>Percent change, 2000–2010: −1.4%
>U.S. rank in 1990: 65th (State rank: 4th)
>U.S. rank in 2000: 79th (State rank: 4th)
>U.S. rank in 2010: 76th (State rank: 4th)

Metropolitan Statistical Area Population
>2000: 2,395,997
>2010: 2,783,243
>2012 estimate: 2,842,878
>Percent change, 2000–2010: 16.2%
>U.S. rank in 2000: 21st
>U.S. rank in 2010: 19th

Area: 60 square miles

Elevation: Ranges from sea level to 60 feet above sea level

Average Annual Temperatures: 73.1° F

Average Annual Precipitation: 44.77 inches

Major Economic Sectors: tourism, financial services, manufacturing, medical technology, health and education services, information technology, marine sciences, professional and business services

Unemployment Rate: 7.0% (2012)

Per Capita Income: $28,312

2012 FBI Crime Index Property: 12,451

Major Colleges and Universities: University of South Florida, St. Petersburg College, Eckerd College, Stetson University College of Law

Daily Newspaper: *Tampa Bay Times*, *Tampa Tribune*, *Pinellas Edition*

■ Introduction

The Sunshine City of St. Petersburg is so confident of its good weather that one of the local papers once had a tradition of giving away that day's edition anytime the sun did not shine. Surrounded by water and beaches on three sides and 234 miles of coastline, the city has drawn generations of winter sun seekers, many of whom return to retire. St. Petersburg has a booming local economy, especially in tourism, health care, and professional services. Moreover, St. Pete, as it is frequently referred to, was the birthplace of spring training for several major league baseball teams in 1914; today Tropicana Field is home to the region's own team, the Tampa Bay Rays. Part of the larger Tampa Bay area that also includes the major cities of Tampa and Clearwater, St. Petersburg is connected directly to a string of small Gulf-of-Mexico beach communities across the Intracoastal Waterway. With continued development in business, residential, and tourist areas, the city has become a premier destination to work, live, and play. In 2013 Livability.com listed St. Petersburg in its annual ranking of the top 100 best places to live.

■ Geography and Climate

St. Petersburg is situated on the Pinellas Peninsula in southernmost Pinellas County and is the largest of the county's municipalities. It is surrounded by the Gulf of Mexico to the west and Tampa Bay to the east. To the north, the city borders Clearwater. The 345 miles of shoreline around the peninsula include the resort communities of Clearwater Beach, Dunedin, Indian

Photo courtesy of the city of St. Petersburg

Rocks Beach, Redington/Belleair Beach, Madeira Beach, St. Petersburg, St. Pete Beach, Safety Harbor, Tarpon Springs, and Treasure Island. The Sunshine Skyway Bridge spans Tampa Bay to connect St. Petersburg with Manatee County to the south. More than 20 barrier islands buffer the Pinellas Peninsula from the Gulf of Mexico, resulting in a calm surf ideal for family water activities. The area's semitropical climate includes the summer thunderstorm season running from June through September, with frequent afternoon rains. St. Petersburg has one of the highest relative humidity rates in the country at 70 percent, a distinction it shares with neighboring Tampa. Nevertheless, the "Sunshine City" holds a Guinness World Record for the most consecutive days of sunshine—768 days beginning in 1967—and boasts an average 361 days of sunshine per year.

Area: 60 square miles

Elevation: Ranges from sea level to 60 feet above sea level

Average Temperatures: 73.1° F

Average Annual Precipitation: 44.77 inches

■ History

Railroad Line Leads to City's Founding

Like much of Florida, the Tampa Bay area had been settled by Native Americans for generations before the first white explorer arrived. The region was visited in 1513 when Ponce de Leon of Spain anchored near Mullet Bay to clean barnacles from his ships. His party was greeted with a violent reception from the Timucuan tribe and de Leon retreated. Eight years later, de Leon returned, suffered an arrow wound, and again fled, this time to Cuba, where he died of his injury. A statue of de Leon stands in the city's Waterfront Park today. Seven years after de Leon's disaster, another Spanish explorer, Panfile de Narvaez, landed in St. Petersburg on Good Friday of 1528. He, too, had notoriously bad relations with Native Americans, and following some preliminary explorations, Narvaez died in a storm while leaving the region.

The first modern settler to remain in the area was John Constantine Williams of Detroit, Michigan, where his father was the first mayor. Williams, like many who would come after him, moved to Florida for his health. An asthma sufferer, Williams bought thousands of acres in

St. Petersburg, but lived in Tampa until an 1887 yellow fever epidemic there drove him across the bay.

Williams transferred part of his land to Russian exile Peter Demens and in return Demens extended his Orange Belt Railroad from Sanford, Florida, west to Tarpon Springs and then south along the Gulf coast to Williams's settlement. As part of the deal, Williams agreed to let the railway man name the settlement. Demens called it St. Petersburg after his Russian birthplace. When the railroad made its first run in 1888, the population of St. Petersburg numbered 30 people. Even with the new rail line, the population reached only 273 people two years later. Williams, who died in 1892, the same year St. Petersburg was incorporated, built the first big resort in the city at the corner of Central Avenue and Second Street. Called The Detroit, the hotel still stands today. Originally part of Hillsborough County, Pinellas County seceded in 1912 to become a separate county.

Tourism soon followed. By 1909 the first direct train arrived from New York City. The next year, Lew Brown, publisher of *The Independent* newspaper, began his tradition of giving away that day's papers anytime the sun did not appear-a promise that was kept until the paper closed in the 1980s. Giveaways averaged just four a year, and according to the *Guinness Book of World Records,* the longest stretch of sunshine was 768 days in a row.

Early Baseball Days

Professional baseball's spring training had first come to Florida as early as 1888 in Jacksonville, but it was civic boosters in St. Petersburg who made Grapefruit League action an institution. The city's first game was played on February 27, 1914. The hosting St. Louis Browns lost to the Chicago Cubs, who were training in Tampa and made the trip by steamboat across Tampa Bay. Al Lang, a former Pittsburgh, Pennsylvania, launderer, moved to St. Petersburg in 1909 and soon became mayor. Lang, a baseball fan, enticed the Philadelphia Phillies to St. Petersburg in 1915. When Philadelphia got off to a rousing start back north for the regular season, St. Petersburg's good spring weather got much of the credit. City leaders later named their baseball stadium after Lang.

Real Estate Boom Collapses

Improved roads, increased automobile travel, and the search for warm weather helped make St. Petersburg one of the first Florida cities to live through the real estate boom of the 1920s. The city counted 14 residents in 1920 and 50,000 residents just five years later. The boom years left a legacy of landmarks built in the Mediterranean Revival style that today remain as a graceful reminder of the city's past.

However, the first boom did not last. By the Great Depression of the 1930s, all nine of the city's banks had collapsed, script was used instead of U.S. currency, and the population dropped back down to 40,000 people. Signs posted at the edge of the city warned newcomers against moving in.

On New Year's Day in 1914, commercial aviation was inaugurated in St. Petersburg, or, more precisely, in the waters just offshore. Pilot Tony Jannus flew a lone passenger (St. Petersburg's mayor), who had paid $400 for the honor, from the yacht basin in St. Petersburg to the foot of Lee Street in Tampa. The flight, on the wooden *Benoist XIV* airboat, took 23 minutes, and 3,000 spectators cheered its arrival. The St. Petersburg-Tampa Airboat Line survived for a year before interest flagged.

Foul weather has altered the area on several occasions. In 1843, four decades before the Detroiter Williams arrived, Antonio Maximo set up a fishing camp at the southernmost tip of the Pinellas peninsula. However, five years later, a hurricane wiped out his holdings and Maximo disappeared. Much later, the hurricane of 1921 brought 106-mile-per-hour winds and more than 6 inches of rain in one 24-hour period, washing ships up to a half mile inland. The city's main pier was destroyed.

Modern Development Extends to Gulf Beaches

Despite these weather-related problems, development continued. Ten major hotels were built in the first half of the 1920s. More important, bridges were extended to the Gulf beaches, which are separated from St. Petersburg proper by the Intracoastal Waterway. Then, in late 1924, the Gandy Bridge, connecting St. Petersburg to Tampa, was opened, eliminating dependence on unreliable ferry schedules or what could be a day-long train ride around Old Tampa Bay to the city of Tampa. When tourist-dependent St. Petersburg suffered because of gas rationing during World War II, the U.S. Air Corps filled the void by stationing many of its troops in the area's big hotels. The resorts returned to civilian use after the war. During the post-war years, a second bridge spanning Tampa Bay was added and the Sunshine Skyway linking St. Petersburg to communities to the south was built in 1954. The original bridge collapsed in 1980 from a ship collision and was replaced in 1987 with the largest cable suspension bridge in the Western Hemisphere, rising 19 stories above Tampa Bay.

In the 1960s the city moved to shift its image from a retirement haven to a prime spot for investment and business growth. Besides tourism, the fields of health care, manufacturing, high technology, marine sciences, and electronics were emerging to lead St. Petersburg into its future. The 1970s brought concerns for environmental preservation, which led the city to develop the largest reclaimed water system in the nation.

In the 1980s the city began to take a closer look at redevelopment and revitalization of its downtown neighborhoods, including the urban core known as

Midtown. In two decades, over $1.6 billion was invested in construction projects. Into the 2010s, development in this area continued, particularly with a trend for mixed-use facilities incorporating retail, office, and residential spaces.

Historical Information: St. Petersburg Museum of History, 335 Second Ave., NE, St. Petersburg, FL 33701; telephone (727) 894-1052.

■ Population Profile

Metropolitan Statistical Area Population

2000: 2,395,997
2010: 2,783,243
2012 estimate: 2,842,878
Percent change, 2000–2010: 16.2%
U.S. rank in 2000: 21st
U.S. rank in 2010: 19th

City Residents

1990: 240,318
2000: 248,232
2010: 244,769
2012 estimate: 246,533
Percent change, 2000–2010: −1.4%
U.S. rank in 1990: 65th (State rank: 4th)
U.S. rank in 2000: 79th (State rank: 4th)
U.S. rank in 2010: 76th (State rank: 4th)

Density: 3,964.4 people per square mile

Racial and ethnic characteristics

White: 169,944
Black or African American: 60,839
American Indian and Alaskan Native: 832
Asian: 7,368
Native Hawaiian and Other Pacific Islander: 121
Hispanic or Latino (may be of any race): 20,734
Other: 7,429

Percent of residents born in state: 40.7%

Age characteristics

Population under 5 years old: 13,229
Population 5 to 9 years old: 11,497
Population 10 to 14 years old: 11,687
Population 15 to 19 years old: 14,013
Population 20 to 24 years old: 18,757
Population 25 to 34 years old: 32,112
Population 35 to 44 years old: 32,026
Population 45 to 54 years old: 36,280
Population 55 to 59 years old: 18,716
Population 60 to 64 years old: 16,078
Population 65 to 74 years old: 23,587
Population 75 to 84 years old: 12,375

Population 85 years and over: 6,176
Median age: 41.7

Births (2010–11 Metropolitan Area)

Total number: 30,923

Deaths (2010–11 Metropolitan Area)

Total number: 28,605

Money income (2012)

Per capita income: $28,312
Median household income: $43,886
Total households: 104,131

Number of households with income of . . .

less than $10,000: 9,483
$10,000 to $14,999: 7,011
$15,000 to $24,999: 12,315
$25,000 to $34,999: 13,060
$35,000 to $49,999: 16,068
$50,000 to $74,999: 19,591
$75,000 to $99,999: 10,063
$100,000 to $149,999: 9,415
$150,000 to $199,999: 3,397
$200,000 or more: 3,728

Percent of families below poverty level: 17.2%

FBI Crime Index Property: 12,451

FBI Crime Index Violent: 2,239

■ Municipal Government

St. Petersburg has a strong mayor-council form of government, which combines a mayor with an eight-member elected council. Council members are elected from single-member districts. The mayor and council members serve four-year terms. The mayor is responsible for the day-to-day affairs of the city, while the council looks after city policy, city budget, and mayoral appointments of other city officials.

Head Official: Mayor Rick Kriseman (since 2014)

Total Number of City Employees: 3,628 (2013)

City Information: City of St. Petersburg, 175 Fifth Street North, St. Petersburg, FL 33701; telephone (727) 893-7111.

■ Economy

Major Industries and Commercial Activity

St. Petersburg's economy has traditionally been fueled by tourism. As the most popular destination city along Florida's west coast, the city attracts millions of national and international visitors annually. Yet the city's economy is more diverse. In recent years the city has identified eight business clusters that have shown continued potential for economic growth. These are medical technologies and life sciences; financial services; marine and environmental sciences; information technologies; manufacturing; arts, culture, events, and tourism; and professional and business services.

Medical technologies and life sciences is the top business cluster for the city. The area's research hospitals make it a logical site for medical technology firms. About 53 percent of all medical device manufacturing companies in Florida's High Tech Corridor are based in Pinellas County. Notable health and medical technologies companies in St. Petersburg include Bayfront Medical Center, St. Petersburg General Hospital, and Claro Scientific.

Not only does the city and extending area serve as a base for many financial companies, these companies in turn stimulate growth in other industries by providing the financial resources for development and expansion. Raymond James Financial has its headquarters in St. Petersburg. Two other financial firms, Fidelity National Financial—a *Fortune* 500 company in 2013—and Franklin Templeton Investments, are also among the major companies with offices in the area.

Manufacturing companies are attracted to the region's transportation infrastructure. Pinellas County ranks second in the state for manufacturing employment. Jabil Circuit, another *Fortune* 500 company, manufactures semiconductors and is headquartered in the city.

Similarly, information technology companies have taken advantage of partnerships with local universities and colleges. St. Petersburg is home to numerous small- and medium-sized software and Web development enterprises. While Pinellas County is Florida's second smallest county geographically, it has 3.8 high-tech companies per square mile.

The city's proximity to Tampa Bay and the Gulf of Mexico make it a prime spot for marine science. In fact, it is the largest marine science community in the Southeast. This segment in the economy is augmented by local research facilities, including the Florida Institute of Oceanography, the U.S. Geological Survey St. Petersburg Coastal and Marine Science Center, and the University of South Florida's College of Marine Science.

Items and goods produced: computer and office equipment, electronic components, computer components, plastic products, medical devices, pharmaceuticals, fiber optic cable

Incentive Programs-New and Existing Companies

Local programs: The city of St. Petersburg administers various programs to assist business start-up, expansion, and relocation. New and existing business owners can seek support through The Greenhouse (formerly the Business Assistance Center) and the Small Business Development Center at the University of South Florida St. Petersburg. The St. Petersburg Certified Development Corporation offers loans of up to $100,000 for qualified businesses owned by veterans, minorities, or women. The city helps manufacturing or industrial plants, health-care facilities and public-works projects to obtain financing below the conventional borrowing rates through industrial revenue bonds. An ad-valorem tax exemption is available whereby eligible property owners are exempt from city and county taxes on approved renovation of historic properties for 10 years. Both the City of St. Petersburg and Pinellas County provide job-creation incentives. The city-based incentive requires that a company add 500 new jobs paying at least 115 percent of average county wages. For the county-based incentive, companies must add 200 new high paying jobs.

State programs: Enterprise Florida is a partnership between Florida's government and business leaders and is the principal economic development organization for the state of Florida. Enterprise Florida's mission is to increase economic opportunities for all Floridians by supporting the creation of quality jobs, a well-trained workforce, and globally competitive businesses. It pursues this mission in cooperation with its statewide network of economic development partners. Among the incentive programs managed at the state level is the Economic Development Transportation Fund, which helps fund the cost of transportation projects, such as access roads and road widening, required for the establishment, expansion, or retention of businesses in Florida. The state's Qualified Target Industry Tax Refund is similar to a Miami-Dade program that rewards the creation of jobs in certain industries.

Florida has a favorable tax climate, with benefits such as no corporate income tax on limited partnerships, no sales tax on purchases of raw materials incorporated in a final product for resale, and no personal state income tax. The state also offers various sales and use tax exemptions for machinery and equipment purchase, electric energy, research and development, and other aspects of doing business in the area.

Job training programs: Florida is a statewide, business-led workforce policy board that collaborates with the Florida Department of Economic Opportunity and regional workforce boards. The 24 regional boards have primary responsibility for direct services through a statewide network of One-Stop Career systems. One-Stop Career Centers are the central elements of the One-Stop system that provide integrated services to employers, workers, and jobseekers. CareerSource Florida administers two training grant initiatives to assist both employers and job seekers. Quick Response Training (QRT) Grants provide funding for customized training to new or expanding businesses. Incumbent Worker Training (IWT)

Grants provide funding for programs that help existing full-time employees upgrade their skills.

WorkNet Pinellas is the local branch of CareerSource Florida. This location provides employment services—including assessment, education, and training—to employers and job seekers throughout the county. Among its training services are the Quick Response Training Program, which provides customized employee training grants to new and expanding businesses, and Incumbent Worker Training, which offers customized training to existing companies in need of training for incumbent employees. The Industry Services Training Program provides basic employee training, consulting, and technical assistance through the Pinellas County School Board. The Success Training & Retention Services program extends intensive skills and development training to inexperienced, unemployed, or underemployed job seekers. The HB-1 Technical Skills Training Grant Program was designed to fill the gap in skills between U.S. technology employees and those entering the U.S. workforce via HB-1 visas. The Entrepreneurial Academy provides business training to new business owners or those who are planning to establish a business.

Development Projects

In 2013 Triad Retail Media moved its headquarters from Tampa to a larger, expandable facility in St. Petersburg. The company develops online marketing campaigns for companies such as eBay and Wal-Mart. The new 65,000-square-foot facility at 100 Carillon Parkway includes video and photography studios. Also in 2013 Trader Joe's announced a new store would be added in St. Petersburg. In August 2013 All Children's Hospital made a land swap deal with the city to acquire a 1.5-acre spot downtown for a new 250,000-square-foot medical tower. In exchange, the hospital will give the city a 2.5-acre plot at Fourth Street S. and 11th avenue, which will be developed into a new park as part of the city's Pinellas Trail expansion.

Publix Shopping Center closed at the end of 2013 for redevelopment, with a grand reopening scheduled for late 2014. Another anticipated project for late 2014 was the Broadmoor YMCA expansion. The new $6.6 million YMCA was designed to contain a health and wellness center, group exercise and spin classrooms, a full gymnasium, locker rooms, an outdoor sports field, a preschool center, and a cafe. Construction began on a new Calypso Rum Bar and Island Grill restaurant for downtown in October 2013. Also in October, city officials announced plans to develop a 1.5-mile stretch along 34th Street South as the new Skyway Marina District. The district plan includes the addition of dining, shopping, and recreation venues. The area will be designed as a pedestrian and bike-friendly area, with improved public transportation to and from the district as well. The development plans were expected to come before the city council for full approval sometime in 2014.

In 2013 an ongoing concern for many residents and local business owners was the fate of St. Petersburg Pier. Built in 1973, the inverted pyramid structure featured shopping, restaurants, galleries, live musical entertainment, an aquarium, and an art gallery. The Pier closed in May 2013 as city officials made plans to demolish the structures and rebuild. However, later that year city residents voted to reject the new designs submitted by Maltzan Architecture. The fate of the development project was left unknown at the end of 2013.

Economic Development Information: City of St. Petersburg Economic Development Department, P.O. Box 2842, St. Petersburg, FL, 33731; telephone (727) 893-7100; toll-free (800) 874-9026; fax (727) 892-5465. St. Petersburg Area Chamber of Commerce, 100 Second Avenue North, Ste 150, St. Petersburg, FL 33701; telephone (727) 821-4069; fax (727) 895-6326.

Commercial Shipping

The Port of Tampa and Port of Manatee serve Pinellas County's commercial shipping needs. Port of Tampa, a crucial link between the United States and Central and South America, is the largest port in the Southeast and one of the nation's largest by tonnage handled. Port Manatee, one of the state's busiest, is the closest of the area's deepwater ports to the Gulf of Mexico. Both ports provide custom house brokers, freight forwarding, and other services. St. Petersburg also has a port of entry, though it is a nonoperating or landlord port managed by the city. The port is part of a Free Trade Zone.

Three airports—Tampa International, St. Petersburg-Clearwater International, and Albert Whitted—serve the area, with Tampa International Airport being the largest. Albert Whitted Airport is owned and operated by the City of St. Petersburg. The 110-acre facility handles approximately 80,000 general aviation aircraft operations annually and is the home base to an estimated 185 aircraft. Freight is shipped by rail via CSX.

Labor Force and Employment Outlook

According to reports from the U.S. Bureau of Labor Statistics, the largest number of jobs in St. Petersburg metropolitan area in 2013 were in the trade, transportation, and utilities industry. Professional and business services also provided a substantial number of jobs, followed by education and health services, government, and leisure and hospitality.

The following is a summary of data regarding the 2012 St. Petersburg labor force:

Size of civilian labor force: 131,850

Number of workers employed in...

    agriculture and mining: 580
    construction: 5,348
    manufacturing: 7,894

wholesale trade: 3,134
retail trade: 15,652
transportation: 4,438
information systems: 2,241
finance: 11,257
professional administration: 14,532
education and social services: 27,607
arts and leisure: 14,067
other: 5,230
public administration: 4,316

Average hourly earnings of production workers: $14.92

Unemployment rate: 7.0% (2012)

Employers

*Largest private employers
(2013)*   *Number of employees*

Home Shopping Network	2,800
Raymond James Financial	2,600
Bright House Networks	2,000
Fidelity Information Services	1,800
Jabil Circuit Inc.	1,600
Ceridian Benefits Services	1,000
Progress Energy Florida	1,000
Transamerica Life Insurance	900
Franklin Templeton Investments	900
PSCU Financial Services, Inc.	850

Cost of Living

The following is a summary of data regarding several key cost of living factors in the area.

2013 ACCRA Average House Price: $233,125

2013 ACCRA Cost of Living Index: 93

State income tax rate: None

State sales tax rate: 6.0%

Local income tax rate: None

Local sales tax rate: 1.0%

Property tax rate: 21.4636 mills (2013)

Economic Information: City of St. Petersburg Economic Development Department, P.O. Box 2842, St. Petersburg, FL, 33731; telephone (727) 893-7100; toll-free (800) 874-9026; fax (727) 892-5465. St. Petersburg Area Chamber of Commerce, 100 Second Avenue North, Ste 150, St. Petersburg, FL 33701; telephone (727) 821-4069; fax (727) 895-6326.

■ Education and Research

Elementary and Secondary Schools

Pinellas County Schools is the seventh largest district in Florida and one of the largest in the nation. More than 100,000 students are enrolled at 140 public schools. The school district has nine Centers of Excellence with career/technical high school programs. Career academies offer high school instruction in academic subjects based on such industries or occupations as veterinary science, automobiles, architecture, and business technology. High school magnet programs include two International Baccalaureate programs, two arts centers, a criminal justice program, and a program for students interested in the medical field. Magnet programs are also offered at elementary and middle school levels. The system supports 12 charter schools. Programs for gifted students as well as the learning disabled are available. The district has two dropout prevention programs for students in fifth through eighth grade.

There are several independent and parochial schools in St. Petersburg and the surrounding metropolitan area. These include Admiral Farragut Academy, Shorecrest Preparatory School, St. Petersburg Catholic High Schools, and Gulfcoast Seventh-Day Adventist School.

The following is a summary of data regarding the Pinellas County Public Schools.

Total enrollment: 104,001

Number of facilities
total: 140
elementary schools: 74
junior high schools: 21
high schools: 17
other: 28

Student/teacher ratio: 14.34:1

Teacher salaries
average (statewide): $46,702

Funding per pupil: $9,063

Public Schools Information: Pinellas County Schools, 301 Fourth St. SW, Largo, FL 33770; telephone (727) 588-6000.

Colleges and Universities

The University of South Florida (USF) St. Petersburg has a total undergraduate enrollment of more than 4,900 students and offers 35 degree programs in three schools: College of Arts and Sciences, College of Business, and College of Education. Seventeen master's degree programs are also available. The largest academic programs are biology, psychology, accounting, education, environmental science, criminology, English, journalism, interdisciplinary social science, and finance. The USF College of Marine Science is also located in St. Petersburg. It has an annual enrollment of about 100 students working on graduate degrees and participating in the school's extensive research programs.

Eckerd College is a private liberal arts college known for its programs in marine science, environmental studies, international relations and global affairs, creative writing, and management. The school features a popular study abroad program and offers bachelor's programs in 38 majors.

The St. Petersburg College, formerly the state's oldest two-year college, is now a four-year college and is one of the nation's leaders in number of associate degrees awarded. The school has 10 campus sites throughout the county, four of which are located in St. Petersburg proper. The Downtown St. Petersburg location offers early morning and evening class schedules to accommodate local workers. The Allstate Center campus is home to the Southeastern Public Safety Institute, which offers degrees and certificates in such fields as criminal justice, crime science technology, law enforcement, and fire science technology.

St. Petersburg is also home to the Poynter Institute, a journalism school that has substantial control in Times Publishing Company, publisher of the *Tampa Bay Times*. The Pinellas Technical Education Center offers a number of technical programs at its St. Petersburg campus.

Libraries and Research Centers

The St. Petersburg Public Library System contains nearly a half million general subject titles, plus special collections of Florida history, genealogy, more than 1,000 periodical subscriptions, and back issues of local newspapers. In addition to the main library, there are six branches throughout the city, including the West Community Library at St. Petersburg College. The resources of 14 other local libraries, all members of the Pinellas Public Library Cooperative (PPLC), are also available to residents through interlibrary loans. The PPLC maintains the regional Pinellas Talking Book Library, which features audio books, books in Braille, and large-print books and magazines.

The USF College of Marine Science collaborates with numerous private and government organizations to conduct research in biological, chemical, geological, and physical oceanography, along with marine resource assessment. It is home to the Knight Oceanographic Research Center, which is a collaborative effort of Florida public and private universities and conducts research in

such fields as ocean currents, endangered species, beach erosion, water quality, tourism, and shipping.

Other marine research facilities include the Florida Institute of Oceanography, the U.S. Geological Survey St. Petersburg Coastal and Marine Science Center, and SRI International. The Tampa Bay Research Institute, which studies viruses and molecular genetics, is also located in the city.

Public Library Information: St. Petersburg Public Library System, Main Library, 3745 9th Ave, N., St. Petersburg, FL 33713; telephone (727) 893-7724.

■ Health Care

The city of St. Petersburg has seven major hospitals, including Bayfront Health St. Petersburg and St. Anthony's Hospital. St. Anthony's Hospital, located downtown, has earned a reputation for excellence in the fields of general surgery, orthopedics, cancer treatment, diabetes management, and neurology. St. Anthony's sponsors the Minimally Invasive Skull Base Center, one of the few centers in the nation that offers a specialized program for tumors of the skull base and orbit.

Bayfront Health St. Petersburg is a 480-bed private teaching hospital affiliated with the University of South Florida. The hospital provides comprehensive services in trauma and emergency care, orthopedics, obstetrics and gynecology, cardiology, neurosciences, primary care, and rehabilitation treatments. Bayfront Health is accredited as a Level II trauma center, a Level III regional perinatal intensive care center, comprehensive stroke center, chest pain center, Level IV epilepsy center, and certified hip and knee replacement center. Bayflite, the largest hospital-based flight program in the southeastern United States, is also hosted at Bayfront Health. This program brings lifesaving trauma care to thousands in a 17-county region. The Bayfront Baby Place, Bayfront Family Health Center, Bayfront Medical Plaza, Bayfront Rejuvenations, Bayfront St. Pete Same Day Surgery Center, Bayfront Wound Care and Hyperbaric Center, and James Heart Center are all located within St. Petersburg proper to offer an extended range of medical services through the Bayfront system.

All Children's Hospital is a 259-bed teaching hospital affiliated with Johns Hopkins Medicine. The main St. Petersburg campus also houses the Child Development and Rehabilitation Center, the Pediatric Emergency Center, and the Outpatient Care Center (which also contains Ronald McDonald House). Other major medical centers include Edward White Hospital, Northside Hospital and Heart Institute, St. Petersburg General Hospital, and the Bay Pines VA Healthcare System.

■ Recreation

Sightseeing

At Sunken Gardens, a city-owned, century-old botanical park, more than 50,000 plants and flowers bloom on four acres that also contain a subtropical forest, butterfly garden, trails, waterways, and flamingos. An adjacent historic building was renovated to include the Great Explorations Children's Museum and restaurants. Weedon Island Preserve Cultural and Natural History Center is found on 3,164 acres of historic parkland featuring a boardwalk, hiking trails, and a 45-foot-high observation tower.

Jim Healey & Jack Lake Baseball Boulevard stretches between Al Lang Stadium to Tropicana Field. Along the way, a series of home plate-shaped plaques tell the history of baseball in the city. The Tampa Bay Walk of Fame outside of Tropicana Field honors sports legends from the 11-county Tampa Bay metro area. Tropicana Field also contains the Ted Williams Museum & Hitters Hall of Fame.

Arts and Culture

The American Stage Theatre Company, a professional not-for-profit organization, presents a variety of productions in addition to its annual American Stage in the Park offerings. St. Petersburg Little Theatre is Florida's oldest continually operated community theater. The Palladium Theater at St. Petersburg College offers a variety of musical programs throughout the year, featuring all forms of music from jazz and blues to opera. The nationally known Florida Orchestra performs classics and pop favorites at the Duke Energy Center for the Arts' Mahaffey Theater, bringing in guest performers and conductors in addition to its own musicians. Concerts and sporting events are also held at the downtown Coliseum.

St. Petersburg boasts the world's largest collection of the works of the Spanish surrealist artist Salvador Dali. In a dramatic waterfront setting, Dali's sculptures, paintings, and other works, dating from 1914 forward, are discussed during regularly scheduled tours at the Salvador Dali Museum. The St. Petersburg Museum of Fine Arts, the only comprehensive art collection on the state's west coast, owns more than 4,000 pieces of European, American, Oriental, and pre-Columbian art, including works by Paul Cezanne, Paul Gauguin, Claude Monet, and Pierre-Auguste Renoir.

The St. Petersburg Museum of History features exhibits of Florida and St. Petersburg history and a Flight #1 wing housing a full-scale replica of the historic *Benoist XIV* airboat, which flew the world's first scheduled commercial airline trip in 1914. The Florida Holocaust Museum in St. Petersburg honors the memory of the millions of innocent men, women, and children who suffered or died in the Holocaust. Exhibits include artifacts, memorabilia, letters by camp prisoners, and an original boxcar from Nazi-occupied Poland.

The Science Center of Pinellas County, located in St. Petersburg, offers seven acres of exhibits, many hands-on, as well as a planetarium, observatory, 600-gallon marine touch tank, adoptable animal room, Laser Odyssey Theater, and exhibits relating to Native American and African American pioneers. The planetarium and observatory at St. Petersburg College presents star shows from September through April.

The Morean Arts Center has a 6,000-square-foot gallery dedicated to the works of the glass blowing artist Dale Chihuly. The Morean Arts Center is the oldest visual arts organization in Pinellas County. Founded as the Art Club of St. Petersburg, the organization has provided art exhibitions and classes since 1917.

Festivals and Holidays

St. Petersburg celebrates the birthday of Martin Luther King Jr. each January with the National MLK Drum Major for Justice Parade, one of the nation's largest civic parades and festival of bands. The Festivals of Speed take place in April, featuring exotic cars, boats, and bikes from the past 100 years. The Mainsail Arts Festival in April is considered one of the best fine art shows in the nation. Earth Day and Arbor Day are celebrated with the Green Thumb Festival, which features tree and plant sales, a plant diagnostic clinic, flower shows, and a children's plant fair.

The Tampa Bay Caribbean Carnival celebrates the islands' traditional food and soca, calypso, and reggae music. American Stage in the Park, also known as Shakespeare in the Park, presents the works of Shakespeare at Demen's Landing by the city's professional theater group.

More than 50 authors convene annually for the Festival of Reading at the University of South Florida in Saint Petersburg in October. Writers of all genres, including several children's authors, participate in the annual festival to sign books, read excerpts from their books, and answer questions. The annual St. Petersburg Science Festival takes place in October, in conjunction with MarineQuest, the annual open house of the Florida Fish and Wildlife Conservation Commissions Fish and Wildlife Research Institute.

Snowfest, held on the first Saturday in December, features a toboggan slide, reindeer races, an art tent, cookie decorating, and more. The First Night celebration, held on New Year's Eve, offers alcohol-free family activities in dozens of venues throughout downtown St. Petersburg.

Sports for the Spectator

Baseball is big in the St. Petersburg area. Major League Baseball's Tampa Bay Rays are based in St. Petersburg and play at the city's domed Tropicana Field. Spring training brings three other Major League teams to the area, the

Philadelphia Phillies to Clearwater, the Toronto Blue Jays to Dunedin, and the New York Yankees to Tampa.

World-class auto racing arrived in the city in 2003 with the first annual Firestone Grand Prix of St. Petersburg. The event takes place over three days in the spring on a waterfront circuit that incorporates part of a runway at Albert Whitted Municipal Airport. The Showtime Speedway, located near the St. Petersburg/Clearwater Airport, hosts stock car racing every Saturday night. Greyhound racing is a big draw during the January-to-June season at Derby Lane; more than one million fans flock to the track to watch the races and dine in the Derby Club restaurant. Each spring brings the Regata del Sol al Sol, an annual 456-mile yacht race from St. Petersburg to Isla Mujeres, Mexico. Powerboat racing is the attraction in the St. Petersburg Offshore Super Series held each June, featuring 35–40 powerboats competing on a 5-mile race course.

For sports fans who are willing to travel a short way, Tampa is the home of the National Football League's Tampa Bay Buccaneers, the National Hockey League's Tampa Bay Lightning, and the Tampa Bay Storm, a championship arena football team.

Sports for the Participant

St. Petersburg's sunny climate means year-round outdoor activities for the sports-minded. The city boasts that it spends more per capita on its parks and recreation programs than any other city in the country. Anglers can harvest more than 300 species of fish in the Gulf of Mexico, Tampa Bay, and area lakes. Charters are available from boat captains along many piers, but shore-bound fishermen can still try their luck at Fort De Soto Park. Among the many annual fishing tournaments is the competitive Suncoast Tarpon Roundup, held every summer from May through July.

The Pinellas Trail runs 47 miles from Tarpon Springs to St. Petersburg along an abandoned CSX railroad right-of-way, linking parks, scenic coastal areas, and neighborhoods for bicyclists, pedestrians, and in-line skaters. St. Anthony's Triathlon, one of the nation's top triathlons in terms of prize money, attracts over 4,000 athletes who compete each April in swimming, biking, and running events. Two Meek and Mighty Triathlons, with shorter distances, are offered the same weekend for young and older amateur participants.

The city maintains over 150 parks, with more than 100 picnic areas, 77 playgrounds, 76 tennis courts, 33 football and soccer fields, 30 basketball courts, 24 baseball and softball fields, 9 volleyball courts, 6 dog parks, 2 skate parks, a sprayground, and a Jai-Alai court. Sixteen recreation centers provide sports, fitness, and arts activities for children and adults. Twenty-one boat ramps are available at nine parks. There are nine public pools and five city beaches. Golf enthusiasts may choose from three municipal courses, including Mangrove Bay Golf Course. The St. Petersburg Shuffleboard Club is the world's oldest and largest shuffleboard club and is the site of the National Shuffleboard Hall of Fame.

Fort De Soto Park, with a beach ranked among the top 10 in the country, stretches across five islands (or keys) at the south end of the peninsula. Open from sunrise to sunset, the park offers opportunities for bird watching, picnicking, swimming, biking, fishing, in-line skating, and camping on 900 acres on the Gulf of Mexico. The actual fort, on Mullet Key, was intended for coastal defense during the Spanish-American War, but construction was not completed until after hostilities ended. The guns at Fort De Soto, facing south, have never been fired in battle.

On the south side of the city, Boyd Hill Nature Park is a precious oasis—245 acres of unspoiled land-with over 3 miles of trails and boardwalks that lead visitors through hardwood hammocks, sand pine scrub, pine flatwoods, willow marsh, and lakeshore. On the other side of town, 400-acre Sawgrass Lake Park offers a one-mile elevated nature trail through marshland. Private operators offer boat tours on waterways around and through the city.

Shopping and Dining

St. Petersburg combines shopping opportunities at regional malls and charming downtown settings. Tyrone Square Mall features 170 specialty stores and three on-site restaurants. There are more than two dozen art galleries downtown. Stylish Beach Drive has recently been joined by the revived Central Avenue district to offer even more restaurant, shopping, art gallery, and entertainment choices. The Shops at St. Pete entertainment and retail complex offers a wide variety of shopping and dining establishments. The two-story, open-air shopping center is a mix of Florida contemporary and traditional Mediterranean architectural styles with stucco-faced buildings and wrought iron touches.

Dining in St. Petersburg ranges from fresh seafood restaurants with scenic waterfront views to ethnic cuisines from Europe, Asia, Latin America, and the Caribbean. Favorite local dishes include paella Valenciana, a dish featuring shellfish, chicken, vegetables and rice; smoked local mullett; and locally caught grouper either blackened, baked, broiled, or fried. The greater Suncoast area provides a choice of more than 1,500 restaurants.

Visitor Information: St. Petersburg/Clearwater Area Convention & Visitors Bureau, 3805 58th Street North, Suite 2-200, Clearwater, FL 33760; telephone (727) 464-7200; toll-free (877) 352-3224.

■ Convention Facilities

Large meeting spaces are available in St. Petersburg at Tropicana Field, Duke Energy Center for the Arts-Mahaffey Theater, and The Coliseum (a historic 1924 ballroom setting). St. Petersburg's resort hotels, both large and small, can handle conventions, meetings, and other events, with five housing a large amount of meeting space; St. Petersburg Bayfront Hilton and the Renaissance Vinoy Resort have the largest single meeting rooms, measuring 7,221 and 6,724 square feet, respectively. Unusual settings for meetings and receptions include beaches, museums, and cruise ships.

Convention Information: St. Petersburg/Clearwater Area Convention & Visitors Bureau, 3805 58th Street North, Suite 2-200, Clearwater, FL 33760; telephone (727) 464-7200; toll-free (877) 352-3224.

■ Transportation

Approaching the City

Most visitors arrive at the larger Tampa International Airport, a 30- to 45-minute drive away. Others find their way through the St. Petersburg-Clearwater International Airport. The Albert Whitted Airport, situated on the waterfront in downtown St. Petersburg, serves corporate aircraft, private pilots, and helicopters. The Port of Tampa accommodates international cruise ships.

Most southbound drivers to St. Petersburg pass through Tampa and over Old Tampa Bay. Interstate 275, which runs through the city, connects to both Interstates 4 and 75 in Tampa. U.S. Highway 19 connects St. Petersburg to the rest of Pinellas County to the north. The Sunshine Skyway bridge, at the terminus of Interstate 275, spans the mouth of Tampa Bay to join St. Petersburg with Manatee County, including the cities of Bradenton and Sarasota to the south. There is a Greyhound Station at Dr. Martin Luther King Jr. Street. Amtrak brings passengers to the Pinellas Park Square station in Clearwater.

Traveling in the City

St. Petersburg is laid out in an easy-to-navigate grid pattern with streets running north to south and avenues running east to west. Interstate 275 and U.S. Highway 19 are the two major north–south arteries. Central Avenue cuts through downtown and runs out to the beaches on the Gulf coast. Public bus transportation is operated by Pinellas Suncoast Transit Authority (PSTA), which operates 40 routes. The Suncoast Beach Trolleys begin at Park Street Terminal in downtown Clearwater and travel through to 75th Avenue and Gulf Boulevard, hitting all major beach communities. The Downtown Looper trolley takes visitors around the city with 13 stops. Locals are encouraged to take advantage of the city's growing network of bike trails.

■ Communications

Newspapers and Magazines

The Pulitzer Prize-winning *St. Petersburg Times,* a morning paper, was renamed the *Tampa Bay Times* in 2012. Times Publishing Company, which owns the *Tampa Bay Times,* also publishes *Florida Trend* magazine, a monthly publication published circulated statewide that focuses on business and finance in the state. The *St. Petersburg Tribune* is a local edition of the *Tampa Tribune. Neighborhood News* is a St. Petersburg weekly.

Television and Radio

There are two television stations broadcasting from St. Petersburg—CW and CBS. Six other stations operate from Tampa, including network affiliates, two public stations, and the nationwide Home Shopping Network. Cable television is available to residential subscribers. There are four FM and three AM radio stations based in St. Petersburg, with other stations serving the area from Tampa, Clearwater, and Sarasota.

Media Information: Tampa Bay Times, 490 First Avenue South, St. Petersburg, FL 33701; telephone (727) 893-8111.

St. Petersburg Online

City of St. Petersburg home page. Available www. stpete.org

Pinellas County Schools. Available www.pcsb.org

St. Petersburg Area Chamber of Commerce. Available www.stpete.com

St. Petersburg-Clearwater Area Convention and Visitors Bureau. Available www.visitstpeteclearwater.com.

St. Petersburg Museum of History. Available www. spmoh.com.

St. Petersburg Public Library System. Available www.splibraries.org

Tampa Bay Times. Available www.tampabay.com

Tampa Tribune. Available www.tbo.com

BIBLIOGRAPHY

Anderson, Anne W., *Insider's Guide to the Greater Tampa Bay Area including Tampa, St. Petersburg, and Clearwater* (Insiders' Guides Inc., 2009)

Arsenault, Raymond, *St. Petersburg and the Florida Dream, 1888–1950* (Norfolk: University Press of Florida, 1996)

Ayers, R. Wayne, *St. Petersburg: The Sunshine City* (Mount Pleasant, SC: Arcadia Publishing, 2001)

Byrd, Alan, *Florida Spring Training: Your Guide to Touring the Grapefruit League, 3rd ed.* (Branford, CT: Intrepid Traveler, 2007)

Rooks, Sandra W., *St. Petersburg Florida (Black America Series)* (Mount Pleasant, SC: Arcadia Publishing, 2003)

Wilson, Jon, *The Golden Era in St. Petersburg: Postwar Prosperity in the Sunshine City* (Charleston, SC: The History Press, 2013)

Tallahassee

■ The City in Brief

Founded: 1824 (incorporated 1825)

Head Official: Mayor John Marks (since 2003)

City Population

    1990: 124,773
    2000: 150,624
    2010: 181,376
    2012 estimate: 186,977
    Percent change, 2000–2010: 20.4%
    U.S. rank in 1990: 146th (State rank: 8th)
    U.S. rank in 2000: 135th (State rank: 8th)
    U.S. rank in 2010: 125th (State rank: 7th)

Metropolitan Statistical Area Population

    2000: 320,304
    2010: 367,413
    2012 estimate: 376,331
    Percent change, 2000–2010: 14.7%
    U.S. rank in 2000: 141st
    U.S. rank in 2010: 137th

Area: 96 square miles

Elevation: 150 feet above sea level

Average Annual Temperatures: 68.0° F

Average Annual Precipitation: 63.21 inches

Major Economic Sectors: government, health and education services, trade and transportation

Unemployment Rate: 7.8% (2012)

Per Capita Income: $22,399

2012 FBI Crime Index Property: 8,617

Major Colleges and Universities: Florida State University, Florida A & M University, Tallahassee Community College

Daily Newspaper: *Tallahassee Democrat*

■ Introduction

As the state capital, the city is a center of both government and education for the state of Florida. Tallahassee shares little of what brings many tourists to Florida, besides its weather. With no beaches, bays, oceanfront high-rises, cruise ship terminals, or theme parks, a slower pace seems to resound in Tallahassee, which is more a town of Old South charm than that of booming tourism. Tallahassee, which means "old fields" in the Apalachee Indian language, has a youthful vitality that seems to draw many to the area to learn, work, play, and stay. In 2013 Livability.com placed Tallahassee on its list of top 100 best places to live.

■ Geography and Climate

Nestled among the rolling hills of northwest Florida, Tallahassee is located in a region of the Florida panhandle known as the Big Bend. The city is less than 20 miles south of the Georgia state line and 25 miles north of the Gulf of Mexico, 178 miles west of Jacksonville, and 200 miles east of Pensacola. Its hilly terrain abounds with lakes, forests, and gardens. Tallahassee is sometimes referred to as the "City of Seven Hills" from the seven historic roads leading uphill on the approach to the capitol. Tallahassee has a mild, moist climate with four distinct seasons, including subtropical summers with frequent thunderstorms, and 90 days with above 90 degree temperatures annually. Winters are often rainy with less sunshine than in summer and occasional below freezing days. High winds occur most frequently in late winter and early spring, and full-blown hurricanes directly hit about every 17 years.

Area: 96 square miles

Elevation: 150 feet above sea level

© Ian Dagnall/Alamy

Average Temperatures: 68.0° F

Average Annual Precipitation: 63.21 inches

■ History

Early Settlements of Tallahassee

As long ago as 10,000 B.C., Native Americans lived in the Red Hills of Tallahassee where they constructed temple mounds on the shores of what is now Lake Jackson (six of the mounds are preserved at Lake Jackson Mounds State Archaeological Site). Prior to the coming of the Europeans, Tallahassee had gained importance as a village of more than 30,000 people. The Apalachee tribes, who lived there from about 500 B.C. through the 1600s, were farmers. They developed impressive works of pottery, which were traded as far away as the Great Lakes. Remains of their communities can be observed at the city's Museum of Florida History.

Although the Spanish explorer Narvaez visited the region in 1628, the first important exploration by Europeans took place in 1539, when Hernando de Soto and hundreds of Spanish settlers and soldiers came and held the first Christmas celebration in the New World. By 1607, almost wiped out by diseases brought by the Europeans, many of the Apalachee left, earning the area the name Tallahassee, or "old fields." The Apalachee who remained accepted the Christian faith, and nearly twenty missions were established in what later became Leon County. In 1704, after almost a century of peaceful co-existence, both the Spanish and the Apalachee were forced to flee from the area after an attack by Colonel James Moore of South Carolina and his Creek allies.

In 1739, encouraged by the Spaniards, who wanted to restore their foothold in the area, members of the Seminole tribe established towns and nearby farms. In 1763, the Tallahassee area became a British possession when Spain ceded Florida to England in exchange for Cuba. The Spaniards again took charge of the area in 1783. General Andrew Jackson, soon to become governor of West Florida, banished the Seminoles in 1818, who by then were demonstrating resistance to growing American influence.

Tallahassee Becomes Territorial, Then State Capital

The U.S. Territory of Florida was established in 1821, and the Territorial Legislature decided to found its new capital mid-way between St. Augustine and Pensacola, at the site of present-day Tallahassee. The area quickly gained a reputation as a rather lawless place where gunfire and knife duels were not uncommon. To bring law and order to the citizenry, the Tallahassee Police Department was established. Within a short time, a plantation economy developed around Tallahassee, which became part of the agricultural central region of Florida. Territorial Governor William P. DuVal laid out the city in 1824. By 1837 a rail line connected Tallahassee with its Gulf of Mexico port, St. Marks, and Tallahassee had become the commercial and social center for the region.

Early settlers faced difficult times with Indian attacks, a yellow fever epidemic, bank failures, hurricanes, and a terrible downtown fire. Despite these obstacles, by 1845 Tallahassee had become the capital of Florida, with government playing an ever more important role in the city's development.

The City in the Civil War

In 1861 as part of the Confederacy, Florida seceded from the Union and Tallahassee was one of the sites where important battles were fought. Defended only by old men and young boys, the city was able to stave off a Union attack in 1865 at the Battle of Natural Bridge in southeast Leon County, the only Confederate capital east of the Mississippi to avoid capture.

Union leader Edward M. McCook took over governance of the city in 1865, and on May 20 read the Emancipation Proclamation freeing the slaves. While some African Americans moved to the city, most remained in rural areas working as tenant farmers.

Education began to attain prominence in Tallahassee around the mid-nineteenth century. In 1851 the West Florida Seminary was established; it later became the Florida State College for Women and today it is Florida State University. The Florida Agricultural and Mechanical University was founded in 1884, the state's first institution for African Americans.

Post Civil War, Twentieth-Century Developments

Wealthy Northerners discovered the area in the 1870s and 1880s, and former cotton estates were bought up and turned into hunting retreats. Prompted by the concerns of plantation owners over the potential loss of the native quail population, Tall Timbers Research Station was established in the 1920s, and soon became an international groundbreaker in the study of ecological issues. In 1929 Dale Mabry Air Field opened, and commercial aviation was first brought to the area. During the 1930s nearly 100 new buildings were constructed in Tallahassee and Leon County as a result of Franklin Roosevelt's New Deal programs.

By the twentieth century, government and education had replaced agriculture as the chief industries in Tallahassee. During the early part of the century, hotels

and boarding houses developed to accommodate the growing number of legislators in the city. In an effort at beautification, hundreds of oaks and dogwood trees were planted. During the decade of the 1940s Tallahassee grew by nearly two-thirds, going from a population of nearly 32,000 people to a population of 52,000 people.

By the 1960s the dogwood had become the symbol of Tallahassee, and an annual parade and celebration called Springtime Tallahassee was initiated. The 1960s also saw the integration of the city's schools and the founding of Tallahassee Community College. A new Capital Complex was constructed and dedicated in 1978, and Tallahassee's new civic center opened in 1981.

Tallahassee's 1999 designation by the National Civic League as an All America City (AAC) was described by Mayor Scott Maddox as "clearly one of the most exciting things to ever happen to Tallahassee . . . . [It] verifies what we've known for so long-that we have one of the greatest cities in all of America." The Tallahassee Boys' Choir was one of the community projects that led to the AAC honor; the others were the Community Human Services Partnership, a joint human services funding program from the city, Leon County, and the United Way, and Kleman Plaza, a cornerstone of downtown development and revitalization. In the 2000s, Tallahassee's Go Green initiative won the city numerous awards and national recognition for environmental stewardship and sustainability.

Since 1980, the city has witnessed a tremendous increase in annexation activity with nearly 75 additional square miles having been added during this time, swelling the size of Tallahassee to over 103 square miles by 2009. The population continues to grow steadily as well. From 1980 to 2000 the population grew from 113,583 to 150,624. In 2010 the population was at 181,376.

Historical Information: Tallahassee Historical Society, P.O. Box 3713, Tallahassee, Florida 32315-3713. State Archives of Florida, Florida Department of State, R.A. Gray Building, 500 Bronough St., Tallahassee FL 32399-0250; telephone (850) 245-6700.

■ Population Profile

Metropolitan Statistical Area Population

2000: 320,304
2010: 367,413
2012 estimate: 376,331
Percent change, 2000–2010: 14.7%
U.S. rank in 2000: 141st
U.S. rank in 2010: 137th

City Residents

1990: 124,773
2000: 150,624
2010: 181,376

2012 estimate: 186,977
Percent change, 2000–2010: 20.4%
U.S. rank in 1990: 146th (State rank: 8th)
U.S. rank in 2000: 135th (State rank: 8th)
U.S. rank in 2010: 125th (State rank: 7th)

Density: 1,809.3 people per square mile

Racial and ethnic characteristics

White: 107,303
Black or African American: 64,337
American Indian and Alaskan Native: 355
Asian: 7,351
Native Hawaiian and Other Pacific Islander: 0
Hispanic or Latino (may be of any race): 13,066
Other: 7,631

Percent of residents born in state: 55.3%

Age characteristics

Population under 5 years old: 9,303
Population 5 to 9 years old: 9,549
Population 10 to 14 years old: 7,713
Population 15 to 19 years old: 21,070
Population 20 to 24 years old: 41,318
Population 25 to 34 years old: 31,527
Population 35 to 44 years old: 19,230
Population 45 to 54 years old: 17,701
Population 55 to 59 years old: 8,101
Population 60 to 64 years old: 5,862
Population 65 to 74 years old: 8,607
Population 75 to 84 years old: 4,629
Population 85 years and over: 2,367
Median age: 26.2

Births (2010–11 Metropolitan Area)

Total number: 4,159

Deaths (2010–11 Metropolitan Area)

Total number: 2,371

Money income (2012)

Per capita income: $22,399
Median household income: $38,865
Total households: 72,525

Number of households with income of . . .

less than $10,000: 12,629
$10,000 to $14,999: 5,101
$15,000 to $24,999: 8,477
$25,000 to $34,999: 7,659
$35,000 to $49,999: 10,529
$50,000 to $74,999: 10,635
$75,000 to $99,999: 6,146
$100,000 to $149,999: 6,762
$150,000 to $199,999: 2,476
$200,000 or more: 2,111

Percent of families below poverty level: 32.2%

FBI Crime Index Property: 8,617

FBI Crime Index Violent: 1,582

■ Municipal Government

Tallahassee has had a council-manager form of government since 1919, with a mayor and four commissioners elected at large who serve staggered four-year terms. The city commission appoints the city manager who oversees most city departments and administers the daily operation of the city.

Head Official: Mayor John Marks (since 2003)

Total Number of City Employees: 2,736 (2013)

City Information: City of Tallahassee, City Commission, 300 South Adams Street, Tallahassee, FL 32201; telephone (850) 891-8181.

■ Economy

Major Industries and Commercial Activity

Government is the central focus of Tallahassee's economy, although education, health care, and trade and transportation are significant industries as well. As Florida's seat of state government, Tallahassee is home to more than 2,000 registered lobbyists and more than 300 professional and business organizations.

Top players in the Capital Region health-care industry include Tallahassee Memorial HealthCare and Capital Regional Medical Center. With educational partners such as Florida A&M University and Florida State University, the health care and educational services industries have sparked growth in research and development.

Institutions such as Innovation Park-Tallahassee, affiliated with Florida A&M University and Florida State University, place Tallahassee on the cutting edge of technology. Regional planners have take steps to further promote growth in renewable energy and clean technology. The Capital Region is also home to several aerospace and defense companies, such as General Dynamics Land Systems and Datamaxx Group.

Items and goods produced: pulpwood, pine extracts, insecticides, pre-stressed concrete, lumber, feed

Incentive Programs-New and Existing Companies

Local programs: The Economic Development Council of Tallahassee/Leon County works toward promoting a diversified economy that continues to grow and create more jobs and business opportunities for both new and existing industries. The City of Tallahassee has several economic development programs available to eligible businesses and/or property owners. Many of the programs offer specific incentives and funding, while others are planning tools designed to promote economic development; some of the incentives are available only in specific areas, while others are available throughout the City. The City of Tallahassee/Leon County Targeted Business Program offers incentives to new and existing businesses that create value-added jobs and promote the sale of goods and services outside the local economy. The level of rebate is based on the number of jobs created, the percentage of higher paying jobs, the level of capital investment, location within a targeted area, and environmental sensitivity in the design. The Tallahassee Urban Job Tax Credit Program provides state tax credits of between $1,000 and $1,500 per new employee for eligible businesses that locate or expand operations within the designated area.

State programs: Enterprise Florida is a partnership between Florida's government and business leaders and is the principal economic development organization for the state of Florida. Enterprise Florida's mission is to increase economic opportunities for all Floridians by supporting the creation of quality jobs, a well-trained workforce, and globally competitive businesses. It pursues this mission in cooperation with its statewide network of economic development partners. Among the incentive programs managed at the state level is the Economic Development Transportation Fund, which helps fund the cost of transportation projects, such as access roads and road widening, required for the establishment, expansion, or retention of businesses in Florida. The state's Qualified Target Industry Tax Refund is similar to a Miami-Dade program that rewards the creation of jobs in certain industries.

Florida has a favorable tax climate, with benefits such as no corporate income tax on limited partnerships, no sales tax on purchases of raw materials incorporated in a final product for resale, and no personal state income tax. The state also offers various sales and use tax exemptions for machinery and equipment purchase, electric energy, research and development, and other aspects of doing business in the area.

Job training programs: Florida is a statewide, business-led workforce policy board that collaborates with the Florida Department of Economic Opportunity and regional workforce boards. The 24 regional boards have primary responsibility for direct services through a statewide network of One-Stop Career systems. One-Stop Career Centers are the central elements of the One-Stop system that provide integrated services to employers, workers, and jobseekers. CareerSource Florida administers two training grant initiatives to assist both employers and job seekers. Quick Response Training (QRT) Grants provide funding for customized training to new or expanding businesses. Incumbent Worker Training (IWT) Grants provide funding for programs that help existing full-time employees upgrade their skills.

The CareerSource One-Stop Career Centers in Tallahassee include the Workforce Plus Center for Business & Employer Services and Workforce Plus Leon.

Development Projects

The Economic Development Council of Tallahassee/Leon County has identified six targeted industry sectors that already have a strong foothold in the Capital Region and show great growth potential. These are renewable energy and environment (clean tech); aviation, aerospace, defense, and national security; health services and human performance enhancement; information technology; research and engineering; and transportation and logistics.

In 2013 the New York law firm Kaye Scholer announced the opening of a new Tallahassee office that was expected to bring 100 high-paying jobs to the city. Tallahassee Regional Airport began the final phase of its runway reconstruction project in January 2014. The project included the extension of one existing runway and modifications to all existing runways in order to comply with FAA safety guidelines. Additional upgrades and additions were made to terminal facilities, as officials hope to provide quicker, more efficient service to travelers, thus boosting the image, passenger numbers, and profits of the airport.

In December 2013 the Leon County Commission announced plans to consider the development of a new convention center hotel complex. Preliminary plans include construction of a world-class basketball facility, a convention center hotel adjacent to the existing Trumbull Conference Center and a new home for the Florida State University College of Business. Preliminary estimates for the cost of such a project were set at about $260 million, with $24 million drawn from county tax revenue.

Economic Development Information: The Economic Development Council of Tallahassee/Leon County, Inc., 800 E. Park Avenue, Tallahassee, FL 32301; telephone (850) 224-8116, fax (850) 425-1056. City of Tallahassee Economic and Community Development Department, 435 North Macomb Street, Tallahassee, FL 32301; telephone (850) 891-6500.

Commercial Shipping

Tallahassee is served by more than 10 motor freight carriers, as well as several package delivery services. Delta Cargo maintains a warehouse at the Tallahassee Regional Airport to provide air cargo service. DHL and FedEx also maintain air cargo operations at the airport.

Labor Force and Employment Outlook

The government sector is by far the largest employment industry in Tallahassee. According to reports from the

U.S. Bureau of Labor Statistics, Tallahassee had more than 61,000 local, state, and federal government employees at the end of 2013. The trade, transportation, and utilities industry also provided a significant number of jobs, though the individual companies have a moderate number of employees. Several of the top employers for 2013 represented the health and education services industry, including Florida State University, Leon County Schools, Florida A&M University, and Tallahassee Memorial HealthCare.

The following is a summary of data regarding the 2012 Tallahassee labor force:

Size of civilian labor force: 101,391

Number of workers employed in . . .

    agriculture and mining: 56
    construction: 2,733
    manufacturing: 1,910
    wholesale trade: 1,296
    retail trade: 12,055
    transportation: 2,042
    information systems: 1,331
    finance: 4,301
    professional administration: 11,306
    education and social services: 23,268
    arts and leisure: 11,902
    other: 4,320
    public administration: 11,637

Average hourly earnings of production workers: $14.28

Unemployment rate: 7.8% (2012)

Employers

Largest regional employers (2013)	*Number of employees*
State of Florida	24,599
Florida State University	6,119
Leon County Schools	4,550
Tallahassee Memorial HealthCare	3,190
City of Tallahassee	2,736
Publix Supermarket	2,102
Florida A&M University	1,923
Leon County	1,919
Walmart Stores	1,300
Tallahassee Community College	1,144
Capital regional Medical Center	867
ACS	800
Capital City Bank Group	502
Capital Health Plan	425

Cost of Living

The following is a summary of data regarding several key cost of living factors in the area.

State income tax rate: None

State sales tax rate: 6.0%

Local income tax rate: None

Local sales tax rate: 1.5%

Property tax rate: $20.9004 per $1,000 of assessed valuation (2013)

Economic Information: The Economic Development Council of Tallahassee/Leon County, Inc., 800 E. Park Avenue, Tallahassee, FL 32301; telephone (850) 224-8116, fax (850) 425-1056. City of Tallahassee Economic and Community Development Department, 435 North Macomb Street, Tallahassee, FL 32301; telephone (850) 891-6500.

■ Education and Research

Elementary and Secondary Schools

The Leon County School District offers programs in education for the gifted, physically and emotionally handicapped, and homebound, as well as programs in vocational education, special education, adult job preparation, and adult general education. SAIL (School for Arts and Innovative Learning) is a magnet school for high school students. The district supports five charter schools and the LCS Virtual School. Leon County Schools Adult and Community Education is the primary provider of adult education classes.

The following is a summary of data regarding the Leon County Public Schools.

Total enrollment: 33,326

Number of facilities
    total: 50
    elementary schools: 24
    junior high schools: 8
    high schools: 6
    other: 12

Student/teacher ratio: 15.95:1

Teacher salaries
    average (statewide): $46,702

Funding per pupil: $8,423

Public Schools Information: Leon County Schools, 2757 W. Pensacola St., Tallahassee, FL 32304; telephone (850) 487-7100.

Colleges and Universities

Florida State University offer more than 275 undergraduate, graduate, doctoral, professional and specialist degree programs in 16 colleges. Top programs include arts (dance, film, music, and theatre), physics, chemistry, political science, psychology, criminology, public administration, library science, information, human sciences, business, and law.

Florida A&M University (FAMU) was founded in 1888 as a primarily African American institution. It has about 11,000 students annually. The university offers 54 bachelor's degrees, 28 master's degrees, 3 professional degrees, and 12 doctoral degrees. The most popular undergraduate programs include architecture, journalism, computer information sciences, and psychology. Top graduate programs include pharmaceutical sciences, physical therapy, engineering, physics, applied social sciences, business, and sociology.

Tallahassee Community College serves more than 14,000 students, most of whom are in the Associate in Arts College and University Transfer program, allowing students to complete the first two years of a bachelor's degree before transferring to one of many Florida state colleges and universities. Keiser University Tallahassee, a private college, provides associate and bachelor degree programs in such fields as criminal justice, business administration and culinary arts. Embry-Riddle Aeronautical University has a Tallahassee campus offering undergraduate and graduate degrees in aviation and aeronautical programs.

Libraries and Research Centers

The LeRoy Collins Leon County Public Library System maintains seven branches housing some 530,000 volumes, along with numerous audio books, CDs, DVDs, and magazines. Computer stations with Internet access are available at each branch. Special features include the Job and Career Accelerator programs for job seekers and the Small Business Center at the Main Library.

The city of Tallahassee boasts more than 40 special and research libraries affiliated with educational institutions, state agencies, and private companies. Governmental libraries cover such subjects as environmental protection, agriculture, commerce, legal affairs, transportation, medical services, and public service.

The State Library of Florida houses a book collection of more than 312,000 volumes on public administration and government, social sciences, education, library and information science, and business and computer applications. The Florida Collection in the Dorothy Dodd Room contains 60,000 items, including books, manuscripts, maps, memorabilia, and periodicals. The State Documents Collection contains more than 140,000 documents, and the Federal Documents collection has more than 150,000 items; the library is a selective federal depository library for documents that relate to the interests and concerns of Floridians.

Innovation Park of Tallahassee has become a major research hub for North Florida. The park is managed by the Leon County Research and Development Authority, in partnership with Florida State University, Florida A&M University, Tallahassee Community College, and several governmental and industrial sector representatives.

Research centers affiliated with Florida State University (FSU) cover such topics as European politics, aquatic research, biomedical toxicology, environmental hazards, marine biology, neuroscience, communication science, computing, weather, insurance, management, real estate, population studies, and education. FSU's 330,000-square-foot National High Magnetic Field Laboratory in Innovation Park is the largest and highest powered facility of its kind in the world for scientific research and engineering. The High-Performance Materials Institute at FSU develops advanced composite materials for a variety of industries. Researchers at Florida A&M University study areas such as anti-inflammatory drugs, space life sciences, computers, transit, and child development.

Other research centers in the city include Tall Timbers Research Station and Land Conservancy, dedicated to protecting wildlands and preserving natural habitats; the Dyslexia Research Institute; and institutions that study conflict resolution, government, taxation, family services, and archeology.

Public Library Information: LeRoy Collins Leon County Public Library, 200 West Park Avenue, Tallahassee, FL 32301; telephone (850) 606-2665.

■ Health Care

Tallahassee is served by two local hospitals plus walk-in clinics and a mental health center. Tallahassee Memorial HealthCare (TMH) is a 772-bed acute-care hospital that provides open-heart surgery and cardiac transplantation, renal dialysis, laser surgery, and lithotripsy. Other services include a community cancer treatment center, neurological intensive care services, a psychiatric center, and the area's only neonatal high-risk nursery. TMH has the only accredited community hospital cancer program in the areas and the only state-designated level II trauma center. Special health centers with TMH include A Woman's Place (Women's Pavilion), Tallahassee Memorial Cancer Center, Memory Disorder Clinic, The Recovery Center, and Parkinson's Center.

Capital Regional Medical Center is a fully accredited, acute care hospital serving the residents of North Florida and South Georgia. Surgical specialties include a heart surgery program and orthopedic, urological, and neuro-surgery centers. Other services include a full range of outpatient services, specialized intensive care units, radiology, respiratory care, physical therapy, a Wound Care Center, Family Center, and a hyperbaric oxygen chamber. The emergency services at the main campus include an Express ER program to attend to minor injuries and a special Senior Care ER.

Big Bend Hospice offers compassionate in-home care to people with terminal illnesses, with several satellite offices in Northern Florida. Hospice House, a homelike residence for patients who cannot remain at home through the end of their illness, offers short-term crisis care.

■ Recreation

Sightseeing

Tallahassee offers the visitor a handsome vista of rolling hills, abundant trees, and an interesting variety of Southern architectural styles. The downtown district was formed according to the plan of William DuVal, governor of the Florida Territory. The major symbols of the state of Florida's government are its Old and New Capitol Buildings. The old Greek Revival-style 1845 building was expanded in 1902, with the addition of grand porticoes and a majestic dome. The New Capitol erected in 1978 is an example of the new classicism style. A fifth-floor observation deck allows visitors to watch the legislature in session.

Within the Park Avenue Historic District, visitors can stroll along streets lined with graceful ante-bellum and turn-of-the-century homes, explore the Old City Cemetery, and enjoy the newly renovated city parks. The district's historic Knott House Museum is known as the "house that rhymes," for the poems attached to its Victorian era furnishings. The Calhoun Street Historic District, once termed "gold dust street" because of its wealthy residents, is home to the 1856 Brokaw-McDougall House and Gardens.

Other historic houses worth noting are the Governor's Mansion, patterned after Andrew Jackson's The Hermitage, and the Antebellum home of the LeMoyne Center for the Visual Arts, listed on the National Register of Historic Places. Free tours are offered on the grounds of the Goodwood Museum and Gardens. Fine crystal, porcelain, and period furniture are among the collections of the Pebble Hill Plantation, which features gardens, a kennel, a firehouse, a log cabin schoolhouse, and a cemetery. Nearby Alfred B. Maclay Gardens State Park displays flowers and shrubs in a setting of reflecting pools, bubbling fountains, and a natural lake.

Driving tours along the lush, 95 miles of moss-draped canopy roads of the region (so named for their arching live oaks overhead) include the Native Trail tour, which focuses on architectural history; the Cotton Trail, which traces the impact of the area's cotton trade; and the Quail Trail Tour, which highlights the ante-bellum hunting estates that dot the landscape.

Animals such as red wolves, Florida panthers, and alligators thrive on the 52 acres of the Tallahassee Museum, which offers a nature center, an 1880s farm, child friendly exhibits, and special events throughout the year. The National High Magnetic Field Laboratory on the Florida State University campus offers tours of its state-of-the-art facility where such high-tech procedures as magnetic resonance imaging and tests with semi-conductors and super-conductors are performed. The Tallahassee Antique Car Museum has an extensive collection of rare cars and collectible memorabilia.

Arts and Culture

The Donald L. Tucker Civic Center at Florida State University plays host to touring Broadway shows during its main September-through-March season. The renowned Florida State University (FSU) School of Theatre offers productions at its three facilities: the Richard G. Fallon Theatre, The Lab Theatre, and the Augusta Conradi Studio Theatre. The university's School of Music presents more than 450 concerts, recitals, and opera performances annually. FSU's Ruby Diamond Concert Hall plays host to the Tallahassee Symphony Orchestra, whose season, which includes four Classic Concerts, two Casual Concerts and a Young People's Concert, runs from September to May. The Tallahassee Ballet Company, also housed at FSU's Ruby Diamond Concert Hall, presents three major performances annually and provides ballet lessons for the community. Florida A&M University hosts a variety of concerts in the Foster-Tanner Fine Arts Center recital hall. Theatre Tallahassee produces a variety of traditional offerings as well as its avant-garde "Coffeehouse Productions."

The Museum of Florida History allows visitors to climb aboard a reconstructed steamboat, examine sunken treasures, and march to a Civil War musical beat. The Mission San Luis, site of the only reconstructed Spanish mission in Florida and a Native American village, offers ongoing excavations, exhibits, and living history demon-strations. Florida State University Museum of Fine Arts has a permanent collection of more than 5,000 objects ranging from pre-Columbian pottery to contemporary prints. Special collections include the Chezem African Collection, the Cranbrook Print Collection, and the Cressman Collection of ornamental glass.

Festivals and Holidays

Seven Days of Opening Nights is a weeklong February festival featuring art, dance, music, film, and performances.

Tallahassee welcomes spring with March's Jazz and Blues Festival at the Tallahassee Museum, and the Springtime Tallahassee celebration, spanning dates in March and April. A parade kicks off the spring events, which include six stages of entertainment and more than 250 food and craft vendors. The FSU Flying High Circus stages shows in Tallahassee during the first two weekends in April before moving to Callaway Gardens in Georgia for the summer.

The Florida African Dance Festival in June features dancers and drummers from around the world. July events include the area's largest fireworks display on Independence Day at Tom Brown Park, and the Swamp Stomp at the Tallahassee Museum, featuring guitar music in all its variety.

The crafts and culture of the Seminole, Miccosukee, Creek, and Choctaw are the focus of the Native American Heritage Festival each September. The TFFxFAME (formerly the Tallahassee Film Festival) presents an annual festival in the fall, but also sponsors music, art, and film events throughout the year. In order to keep the Spanish-speaking culture alive in Tallahassee, the North Florida Hispanic Association hosts a yearly Hispanic festival in October. Autumn is also the time for the North Florida Fair with its livestock shows, performances, and carnival rides, and the Halloween Howl at the Tallahassee Museum with its ghost stories and trick or treating on a circa-1800s farm. The joys and lights of Christmas brighten up December's Winter Festival downtown and the Knott House Museum Candlelight Tour.

Sports for the Spectator

Although Tallahassee does not field any professional teams, watching college sporting events is very popular—so popular, in fact, that the city sponsors Downtown Get Downs, high-spirited, themed block parties, on most Friday nights preceding college home football games. The free events feature food vendors, live entertainment, arts and crafts, and more. Football, baseball, and other intercollegiate sports are played by the Florida State Seminoles and Florida A&M Rattlers.

The Tallahassee Sports Council is involved in hosting multisport and community partnership events, such as the NCAA basketball and tennis championships and the Sunshine State Games. The Sports Council also serves as agent to such local sports entities as the Tallahassee Soccer Association.

The Red Hills International Horse Trials is a nationally recognized equestrian competition in March featuring Olympic riders competing in dressage, cross country, and stadium jumping.

Sports for the Participant

The city has more than 2,700 acres of parkland. The popular St. Marks Trail, extending from Tallahassee south to the coast, is available to cyclists, skaters, hikers, and equestrians. A stretch of parks in the downtown area spans some five blocks. Several ocean beaches are less than 70 miles away, and Tallahassee has its own freshwater beaches. Lake Hall at Alfred B. Maclay Gardens State Park and Lake Bradford offer public beach access, swimming, boating, fishing, and other water sports. Golfers can enjoy the city's Jake Gaither Golf Course and Hilamen Park Golf Course, as well as award-winning private courses. Three centers provide lighted tennis courts. Numerous lakes are available for freshwater fishing including Lake Jackson, Lake Talquin, Lake Iamonia, and Lake Miccosukee. The city also maintains 11 swimming pools, 30 fitness trails, 7 gymnasiums, and 86 athletic fields.

Shopping and Dining

Downtown Tallahassee wide variety of shopping experiences. The All Saints and College Town Districts are the most popular sites for modern fashions. Governor's Square is home to over 100 stores and restaurants, anchored by four full-line department stores, and a 500-seat food court. Bradley's County Store is renowned for homemade sausage and Southern goods and is on the National Register of Historic Places.

Restaurant offerings in the city range from the international cuisines of France, Italy, and Thailand to seafood in all its variety, classic American cooking, and steak and barbecues.

Visitor Information: Visit Tallahassee, 106 East Jefferson Street; telephone (850) 606-2305; toll-free (800) 628-2866.

■ Convention Facilities

As the government center for the state of Florida, Tallahassee is the preferred location for most gatherings of Florida professionals. Tallahassee has more than 5,300 rooms in more than 50 hotels and motels. The Donald L. Tucker Civic Center at Florida State University is the main convention site in the city, with a 13,800-seat arena, and 52,000 square feet of meeting, dining, and exhibition space. The Augustus B. Turnbull III Florida State Conference Center and the Tallahassee Community College Capitol Center can accommodate small conferences. Out of the ordinary meeting areas include the North Florida Fairgrounds and the Wakulla Springs Lodge and Conference Center. Historic Dorothy B. Oven Park, part of the Lafayette Land Grant awarded to General Marquis de Lafayette in 1824 by the United States Congress, has a Main House that is available to the public for rental use for seminars, meetings, weddings, memorials, and receptions.

Convention Information: Visit Tallahassee, 106 East Jefferson Street; telephone (850) 606-2305; toll-free (800) 628-2866.

■ Transportation

Approaching the City

A number of interstate and state highways converge in Tallahassee including U.S. highways 27, 90, 319, as well as state highways 20 and 363. Greyhound Bus Lines also serves the city. The Tallahassee Regional Airport, which is served by four major airlines, is located five miles southwest of downtown. The airport serves more than 800,000 passengers each year. Greyhound has a station in Tallahassee.

Traveling in the City

StarMetro, an extensive public transit system, offers 14 weekday routes, 11 Saturday routes, 7 night and Sunday routes, university shuttles, and Dial-A-Ride elderly and disabled services. There is a modern transfer facility at C.K. Steele Plaza. Traveling downtown becomes a fun event on The Old Town Trolley, with its brass fittings and cable-car gong. City officials are working to make the city more bicycle friendly.

■ Communications

Newspapers and Magazines

The *Tallahassee Democrat* is the city's daily newspaper. The *Capital Outlook* is an African American weekly, while *Cultura Latina* is a bilingual magazine marketed for the Hispanic community. The *Florida Bar News*, the *FSView & Florida Flambeau,* and other legal and college newspapers are published in the city. All of these publications have online editions.

Journals on engineering, agriculture, and the funeral industry are also published in Tallahassee. *Tallahassee Magazine,* a bimonthly, is the region's only full-color lifestyle publication. It features award-winning writing on the people and business of the area, and carries a dining guide and calendar of events.

Television and Radio

Tallahassee has nine licensed television stations, including NBC and ABC affiliates. Other stations are received from neighboring cities. Eighteen AM and FM radio stations are licensed for broadcasts from Tallahassee.

Media Information: *Tallahassee Democrat,* 277 N. Magnolia Drive, Tallahassee, Florida, 32301; telephone (850) 599-2100.

Tallahassee Online

City of Tallahassee home page. Available www. talgov.com

Economic Development Council of Tallahassee/ Leon County. Available taledc.com/

Leon County home page. Available cms.leon countyfl.gov/

Leon County Schools. Available www.leon.k12.fl.us

Leroy Collins Leon County Public Library. Available www.leoncountyfl.gov/library/

Tallahassee Chamber of Commerce. Available www. talchamber.com

Tallahassee Democrat. Available www.tallahassee. com

Visit Tallahassee. Available www.visittallahassee.com

BIBLIOGRAPHY

Molloy, Johnny, *Best easy day hikes, Tallahassee* (Guilford, CT: Falcon, 2011)

Paisley, Clifton, *The Red Hills of Florida, 1528-1865* (Tuscaloosa, AL: University of Alabama Press, 1989)

Rabby, Glenda Alice, *The Pain and the Promise: The Struggle for Civil Rights in Tallahassee, Florida* (Athens, GA: University of Georgia Press, 1999)

Tampa

■ The City in Brief

Founded: 1824 (incorporated 1887)

Head Official: Mayor Pam Iorio (NP) (since April 2003; term expires March 2011)

City Population
> 1990: 280,015
> 2000: 303,447
> 2010: 335,709
> 2012 estimate: 347,650
> Percent change, 2000–2010: 10.6%
> U.S. rank in 1990: 55th (State rank: 3rd)
> U.S. rank in 2000: 57th (State rank: 3rd)
> U.S. rank in 2010: 55th (State rank: 3rd)

Metropolitan Statistical Area Population
> 2000: 2,395,997
> 2010: 2,783,243
> 2012 estimate: 2,842,878
> Percent change, 2000–2010: 16.2%
> U.S. rank in 2000: 21st
> U.S. rank in 2010: 19th

Area: 112.1 square miles

Elevation: Ranges from sea level to about 48 feet above sea level

Average Annual Temperatures: 73.1° F

Average Annual Precipitation: 44.77 inches

Major Economic Sectors: wholesale and retail trade, services, government

Unemployment Rate: 7.7% (2012)

Per Capita Income: $28,819

2012 FBI Crime Index Property: 9,947

Major Colleges and Universities: University of South Florida, University of Tampa, St. Petersburg College

Daily Newspaper: *The Tampa Tribune; St. Petersburg Times*

■ Introduction

Tampa is Florida's third most populous city, and its chief treasure is its diversity. The city today combines elements of the Italian, Spanish, Indian, Cuban, and African American cultures that reflect its historical development and give Tampa a cosmopolitan flair. Its warm, sunny weather, Gulf Coast location, abundant labor supply, and spirit of cooperation between the public and private sectors have made it a very attractive choice for companies wishing to expand or relocate. The influx of new businesses and residents has in turn revitalized the city, sparking a multibillion-dollar construction and renovation boom that combines the best of old Tampa with dynamic new structures to better serve the growing community. International firms are finding the seven-county Tampa Bay region ideal for their U.S. headquarters or manufacturing facilities. Tampa is proud of its accomplishments and excited about the future.

■ Geography and Climate

Located midway down Florida's west coast, about 25 miles east of the Gulf of Mexico, Tampa is bordered on the south and west by the Hillsborough and Old Tampa bays. Downtown is divided by the winding Hillsborough River, which originates northeast of the city and empties into Hillsborough Bay. The city's year-round semitropical climate is free from many of the extremes found elsewhere. Its most remarkable feature is the summer thunderstorm season. On an average of 90 days from June through September, late afternoon thundershowers

© Aerial Archives/Alamy

sweep across the area, making Tampa one of the stormiest cities in the United States and giving the city the distinction of being the "Lightning Capital of North America."

Area: 112.1 square miles

Elevation: Ranges from sea level to about 48 feet above sea level

Average Temperatures: 73.1° F

Average Annual Precipitation: 44.77 inches

■ History

First Established Settlement Called Fort Brooke

When Spanish explorers first arrived in the Tampa Bay region in 1528, they encountered a native civilization that had flourished there for at least 3,500 years. Several different tribes dominated the Gulf Coast, including the Tocobaga, the Timucua, the Apalachee, and the Caloosa (also spelled Calusa). It was a Caloosa village called *Tanpa* (a name meaning "stick of fire") that eventually became known to the Spanish as Tampa. Annihilated by

an onslaught of European diseases against which they had no immunity, the various Tampa Bay tribes had all but vanished by 1700. Raiding parties comprised of English colonists from the north and members of other Indian tribes destroyed the few remaining settlements. Desolate and uninhabited, the Tampa Bay region was held briefly by the British in the late 1700s, then once again became a Spanish possession after the American Revolution. In 1821, Spain ceded the Florida territory to the United States for $5 million.

By this time, northern Florida had become a haven for displaced Seminole Indians and runaway black slaves from nearby southern states. Because white settlers were eager to move into the region and grow cotton, the federal government decided to relocate the Indians further south, around Tampa Bay. A fort was established on the eastern shore of the Hillsborough River to house the soldiers sent there to keep an eye on the angry Seminoles. Erected in 1824 and named Fort Brooke (after the army colonel in command), it was the first permanent, modern settlement on the site of present-day Tampa.

Area's Economy Rollercoasters

The 1830s and 1840s were marked by repeated violent conflicts between the Seminoles and white soldiers and settlers. Although Tampa emerged from the so-called Second Seminole War (1835-1842) as a fledgling town rather than just a frontier outpost, it subsequently endured a variety of setbacks, including further skirmishes with the Seminoles, yellow fever epidemics, and, in 1848, a hurricane-generated tidal wave that leveled the village.

In the 1850s a rebuilt Tampa expanded, and by 1855 it had grown enough to incorporate as a city. After the Third Seminole War (1855-1858) saw most of the Indian population removed to Oklahoma, the town experienced a boom of sorts. An extremely lucrative beef trade with Cuba flourished, as did the related activities of shipping and shipbuilding. During and after the Civil War, however, Tampa, like much of the rest of the South, suffered economic ruin, compounded throughout the 1860s and 1870s by periodic outbreaks of yellow fever.

The 1880s ushered in a dramatic turnaround for the dying city-the discovery of rich phosphate deposits nearby and, more important, the coming of Henry Bradley Plant's Jacksonville, Tampa & Key West Railroad company. Potential new settlers streamed into the city in search of business opportunities. One of these was Cuban cigar manufacturer Vicente Martinez Ybor, who left Key West in 1885 to establish his operations in Tampa; within just a few years, cigars had become the city's trademark, as well as its chief industry. The city was a point of embarkation for soldiers sent to Cuba in the Spanish-American War.

The next fifty years were marked by continued economic growth for Tampa. At the turn of the century, subzero temperatures forced farmers in the northern part of the state to relocate farther south, Tampa became the new center for the expanding citrus industry. World War I led to a demand for ships that kept Tampa's docks humming with activity. During the early 1920s, land speculators and tourists from the North flocked to the state and gave rise to a building boom in Tampa and the surrounding area. Even after the rest of the Florida real estate market collapsed in 1926, Tampa managed to hold its own. But, like much of the rest of the country, Tampa suffered severe economic setbacks during the Depression of the 1930s. Its number-one industry, cigar manufacturing, went into a sharp decline as product demand decreased and more and more factories became automated; never again would cigar manufacturing figure as prominently in the city's economic makeup.

Downtown Experiences Decline and Rebirth

The growing American involvement in World War II proved to be the stimulus Tampa's paralyzed economy needed. Thousands of troops were stationed in and around the city, and government contracts again revived the shipbuilding industry. But in the 1950s and 1960s Tampa lost residents and businesses to the suburbs, and the downtown area quickly deteriorated. During the early 1970s, government and business united to revive the

ailing downtown area and change Tampa's image. After a rocky and unfocused start in the 1960s, Tampa's urban renewal program emerged in the 1970s and 1980s as a carefully and professionally planned alternative to the earlier spontaneous approach. Downtown soon became the site of new office buildings, stores, stadiums, convention centers, and condominiums, and the local economy flourished. The city and the surrounding region saw a boom in business expansions and relocations in the 1990s that is only picking up speed today. Today, Tampa proclaims itself a city "where the good life gets better every day"-an urban area on the threshold of changes that will assure it of a vital role in the country's future.

Historical Information: Tampa Bay History Center, 225 South Franklin Street, Tampa, FL 33602-5329; telephone (813)228-0097; email info@tampabayhistory center.org

■ Population Profile

Metropolitan Statistical Area Population
2000: 2,395,997
2010: 2,783,243
2012 estimate: 2,842,878
Percent change, 2000–2010: 16.2%
U.S. rank in 2000: 21st
U.S. rank in 2010: 19th

City Residents
1990: 280,015
2000: 303,447
2010: 335,709
2012 estimate: 347,650
Percent change, 2000–2010: 10.6%
U.S. rank in 1990: 55th (State rank: 3rd)
U.S. rank in 2000: 57th (State rank: 3rd)
U.S. rank in 2010: 55th (State rank: 3rd)

Density: 2,960.2 people per square mile

Racial and ethnic characteristics
White: 225,771
Black or African American: 86,746
American Indian and Alaskan Native: 624
Asian: 13,124
Native Hawaiian and Other Pacific Islander: 126
Hispanic or Latino (may be of any race): 82,055
Other: 21,259

Percent of residents born in state: 42.5%

Age characteristics
Population under 5 years old: 21,695
Population 5 to 9 years old: 21,181
Population 10 to 14 years old: 22,296

Population 15 to 19 years old: 25,797
Population 20 to 24 years old: 29,003
Population 25 to 34 years old: 56,569
Population 35 to 44 years old: 46,610
Population 45 to 54 years old: 49,612
Population 55 to 59 years old: 19,804
Population 60 to 64 years old: 17,113
Population 65 to 74 years old: 19,959
Population 75 to 84 years old: 12,827
Population 85 years and over: 5,184
Median age: 34.4

Births (2010–11 Metropolitan Area)

Total number: 30,923

Deaths (2010–11 Metropolitan Area)

Total number: 28,605

Money income (2012)

Per capita income: $28,819
Median household income: $41,524
Total households: 135,990

Number of households with income of …

less than $10,000: 16,182
$10,000 to $14,999: 9,620
$15,000 to $24,999: 17,497
$25,000 to $34,999: 16,099
$35,000 to $49,999: 18,120
$50,000 to $74,999: 21,642
$75,000 to $99,999: 11,598
$100,000 to $149,999: 12,542
$150,000 to $199,999: 5,183
$200,000 or more: 7,507

Percent of families below poverty level: 22.7%

FBI Crime Index Property: 9,947

FBI Crime Index Violent: 2,162

■ Municipal Government

Tampa, the Hillsborough County seat, adopted a nonpartisan mayor-council form of government in 1945. Elections are held every four years, at which time city residents choose the mayor and seven council members. Tampa's only incorporated suburb is Temple Terrace; Plant City is in eastern Hillsborough County.

Head Official: Mayor Pam Iorio (NP) (since April 2003; term expires March 2011)

Total Number of City Employees: 4,084 (2009)

City Information: City of Tampa, 306 E. Jackson St., Tampa, FL 33602; telephone (813)274-8211.

■ Economy

Major Industries and Commercial Activity

Early in the twentieth century, Tampa was unquestionably a one-industry town. From the late 1880s through the 1930s, cigar manufacturing and related activities-primarily box construction and lithography-dominated the economy. Several hundred competing firms annually turned out well over 100 million hand-rolled examples of the city's best-known product.

The current story of Tampa, however, is quite different. Though still known for its cigars (now made with tobacco from sources other than Cuba), Tampa branched out to become the industrial, commercial, and financial hub of Florida's west coast; a third of the state's entire population, in fact, lives within a two-hour drive of the city.

Part of what has made Tampa's future so promising is its diversified economic base. The push to diversify first came after World War II, when the emphasis was on fostering the growth of heavy industry. But in the late 1970s, as the traditional stability and profitability of heavy industry seemed threatened, a movement began to make Tampa appealing to a wide variety of businesses, especially those that were more service-related and office-oriented. Since then, the city has been touted as an ideal location for companies in search of regional headquarters, for insurance companies, banking and other financial firms, and for various high-technology industries. The business world has responded with enthusiasm. Looking toward the future, city developers are aggressively seeking to expand into aerospace and medical technology and international trade and to attract additional electronics and financial firms. Today, Tampa is a center not only for cigars and tourism, but also for agriculture, food processing, electronics and other high-technology fields, health care and related industries, and finance.

To those who know Tampa only as a vacation spot, it may come as a surprise to learn that the city is a thriving agribusiness center. Hillsborough County markets an abundance of citrus fruit, beef cattle, dairy products, eggs, vegetables, ornamental plants and flowers, and tropical fish. As a result, many agriculture-related industries have been attracted to the area, including food processing firms; feed, fertilizer, and insecticide companies; and paper and metal container manufacturers. Yuengling operates a major brewery in Tampa.

Tampa has attained the status of a foreign trade zone, an area where goods can be unloaded for repacking, storage, or transshipment without being subject to import duties. International firms are finding the seven-county Tampa Bay region ideal for their U.S. headquarters or manufacturing facilities. As of 2009, 394 foreign-owned companies from 34 nations in 18 industries were present in the region.

Although Tampa's economy is strong, the city is not immune to the ups and downs of the marketplace. The bursting of the US housing bubble in 2006 affected

Tampa's housing sector. Foreclosures and high home-owner vacancy rates during 2007 through 2009 have led to home price declines and low levels of new home construction. Residential permits for new housing in Hillsborough County fell 19.4 percent in 2008 and 43.6 percent in 2009.

Items and goods produced: cigars, electronic equipment, medical equipment, beer, paint, cigars, fabricated steel, fertilizers, citrus products, livestock, processed shrimp, decorative plants, and flowers

Incentive Programs-New and Existing Companies

The Tampa Hillsborough Economic Development Corporation is Hillsborough County's primary business recruitment and retention economic development team in partnership with Hillsborough County and Tampa, Temple Terrace, Plant City, and private investors. Its primary mission is to create jobs that pay above-average wages and to broaden the tax base by generating new, sustainable capital investment.

In 2007, *Expansion Management Magazine* ranked Hillsborough County in the top 20 of more than 3,000 counties in the United States for recruitment and attraction. A 2010 KPMG study ranked Tampa as the most competitive large city in the United States when it comes to business operating costs. *Moody's Economy.com* describes Tampa as Florida's financial services capital. Tampa is among the nation's "most-wired" cities and is one of the top ten for security-cleared professional jobs requiring technical, computer and engineering skills, a background in international affairs, intelligence and foreign languages.

Local programs: The Tampa Bay Black Business Investment Corporation and the Hispanic Business Incentive Fund sponsor loans for deserving businesses. Tampa has a number of Enterprise Zones and areas designated as Community Redevelopment Areas, which qualify for many state-sponsored tax incentives. The City of Tampa operates the Brownfields Assessment Grant Program to assist four Community Redevelopment Areas of the city in assessment and reuse planning for potentially contaminated properties. A façade improvement program is available for commercial properties in the same four areas. Another local program offers grants relating to construction of facilities to provide neighborhood amenities.

State programs: Enterprise Florida is a partnership between Florida's government and business leaders and is the principal economic development organization for the state of Florida. Enterprise Florida's mission is to increase economic opportunities for all Floridians by supporting the creation of quality jobs, a well-trained workforce, and globally competitive businesses. It pursues this mission in cooperation with its statewide network of economic development partners. Among the incentive programs

managed at the state level is the Economic Development Transportation Fund, which helps fund the cost of transportation projects, such as access roads and road widening, required for the establishment, expansion, or retention of businesses in Florida. The state's Qualified Target Industry Tax Refund is similar to a Miami-Dade program that rewards the creation of jobs in certain industries.

Florida has a favorable tax climate, with benefits such as no corporate income tax on limited partnerships, no sales tax on purchases of raw materials incorporated in a final product for resale, and no personal state income tax. The state also offers various sales and use tax exemptions for machinery and equipment purchase, electric energy, research and development, and other aspects of doing business in the area.

Job training programs: Florida is a statewide, business-led workforce policy board that collaborates with the Florida Department of Economic Opportunity and regional workforce boards. The 24 regional boards have primary responsibility for direct services through a statewide network of One-Stop Career systems. One-Stop Career Centers are the central elements of the One-Stop system that provide integrated services to employers, workers, and jobseekers. CareerSource Florida administers two training grant initiatives to assist both employers and job seekers. Quick Response Training (QRT) Grants provide funding for customized training to new or expanding businesses. Incumbent Worker Training (IWT) Grants provide funding for programs that help existing full-time employees upgrade their skills.

The local CareerSource Florida centers are administered through Tampa Bay Workforce Alliance. They include the Workforce Tampa Career Center and the Workforce Brandon Career Center.

Development Projects

As of late 2010, the $110 million 40th Street Corridor Enhancement Project was nearly complete. In five phases, the 40th Street project was created to enhance a 4.2 mile stretch of 40th Street from Hillsborough Avenue north to Fowler Avenue. In December 2008, segment B was completed, including a new four-lane bridge. When all phases of the project are complete, it will include roadway lighting, bike lanes, a drainage system, and landscaped medians.

The Riverwalk project along the Hillsborough River originated in 1975; however plans for the walkway were delayed for many years. The Riverwalk became a top priority with Mayor Pam Iorio's administration. As of 2009, all 2.2 miles of Riverwalk in the Phase I plan were either completed, under construction, in design, or committed to by a developer. Another announcement in early 2005 was the state allocation of $283 million to provide direct truck access from the Port of Tampa to Interstate 4 via the Lee Roy Selmon Crosstown

Expressway. When completed, the highway will be able to safely filter truck traffic away from Tampa's historic Ybor City district and into and out of the Port of Tampa. The $390 million connector project is a coordinated effort between the Florida Department of Transportation (FDOT), Florida's Turnpike, and the Tampa-Hillsborough Expressway Authority (THCEA). The project completion date in 2013 coincides with anticipated completion of a third set of locks for the Panama Canal that will enable pass-through of very large cargo ships, ensuring cargo and container increases for the Port of Tampa when the expanded canal is fully operational in 2014.

Construction continues on the expanded Curtis Hixon Waterfront Park. Soon to be Tampa's premier gathering place, the new Curtis Hixon Waterfront Park will be home to the new Tampa Museum of Art and the new Glazer Children's Museum.

Tampa's health care facilities are also undergoing expansion and renovation. St. Joseph's Hospitals/South Florida Baptist Hospital includes four hospitals in the Tampa Bay area: St. Joseph's Hospital, St. Joseph's Women's Hospital, St. Joseph's Children's Hospital of Tampa, and South Florida Baptist Hospital. A fifth hospital, St. Joseph's Hospital-North, opened in 2010, the first new hospital in the area in 30 years. In 2010-11 *U.S. News & World Report* included Tampa General Hospital (near downtown on Davis Islands) on its list of the nation's top 50 hospitals in six areas of specialization: orthopedics, diabetes and endocrinology, geriatrics, urology, heart and heart surgery, and kidney disorders.

Economic Development Information: Greater Tampa Chamber of Commerce, PO Box 420, Tampa, FL 33601; telephone (813)228-7777 or (800)298-2672; email info@tampachamber.com.

Commercial Shipping

Tampa's economy benefits greatly from Tampa International Airport. In addition to being one of the nation's busiest airports in terms of passenger traffic, the airport is also a major air cargo hub. In 2009 the airport handled some 175.7 million tons of cargo and 13 million tons of mail. The CSX railway system also links Tampa to the south and east, and nearby interstate and state highways provide convenient delivery and receiving routes for the 41 motor freight lines operating in the city. Its greatest asset, however, is its port-the 19th largest (by tonnage in 2008) in the country and the largest in the state of Florida-handling some 40 million tons of cargo annually.

The closest U.S. maritime center to the Panama Canal, the Port of Tampa serves as a gateway to Latin America. It is also home to one of the world's largest shrimp fleets and features modern shipbuilding and ship repair facilities. As the result of a federally-funded harbor-deepening project, super cargo ships have gained access to the port. The Tampa-Hillsborough International

Affairs Commission maintains an office in the Port of Tampa headquarters building. The port's director is charged with establishing the Tampa metropolitan area as a center for international commerce and tourism for west central Florida. In 2008, the Port of Tampa began plans for a container terminal expansion costing some $70-100 million.

Labor Force and Employment Outlook

The steady migration into the Tampa-Hillsborough County area has resulted in an increasingly younger population and work force. In the period May 2006 through May 2007, nonagricultural employment in the area rose by 1.1 percent, adding some 14,100 jobs. Of that increase, 49 percent was accounted for by the education/health services and leisure/hospitality services sectors.

The following is a summary of data regarding the 2009 Tampa-St. Petersburg-Clearwater FL Metro Area labor force:

Size of civilian labor force: 178,483

Number of workers employed in . . .

agriculture and mining: 387
construction: 7,951
manufacturing: 7,251
wholesale trade: 4,517
retail trade: 17,614
transportation: 6,267
information systems: 4,175
finance: 15,402
professional administration: 23,557
education and social services: 35,855
arts and leisure: 18,433
other: 7,521
public administration: 6,401

Average hourly earnings of production workers: $14.92

Unemployment rate: 7.7% (2012)

Employers

Largest employers (2013)	*Number of employees*
Hillsborough County School District	24,692
Hillsborough County Government	10,502
Tampa International Airport	7,500
Verizon Communications	7,000
MacDill Air Force Base	6,656

University of South	
Florida	6,000
Tampa General	
Hospital	5,842
Publix Supermarkets	4,984
Veterans	
Administration	
Hospital	4,529
City of Tampa	4,502
St. Joseph's Hospital	4,273
H. Lee Moffit	
Cancer Center	3,725
Bank of America	3,679

Cost of Living

Compared to American cities of similar size and other Florida cities such as Miami, Fort Lauderdale, West Palm Beach, and Sarasota, Tampa enjoys a low cost of living. The cost of living was just 1.1 percent above the national average in 2013.

The following is a summary of data regarding several key cost of living factors in the area.

2013 ACCRA Average House Price: $233,125

2013 ACCRA Cost of Living Index: 93

State income tax rate: None

State sales tax rate: 6.0%

Local income tax rate: None

Local sales tax rate: 1.0%

Property tax rate: $21.31650 per $1,000 of assessed valuation (2013)

Economic Information: Greater Tampa Chamber of Commerce, PO Box 420, Tampa, FL 33601; telephone (813)228-7777 or (800)298-2672; email info@tampa chamber.com.

■ Education and Research

Elementary and Secondary Schools

Like all public schools in the state, the public elementary and secondary schools of Tampa are part of a county-wide district. The Hillsborough district is the eighth largest in the country, and ranks sixth in the United States by the number of National Board certified teachers. The system is administered by a nonpartisan, seven-member school board that appoints a superintendent. The district manages 43 charter schools, which span a range of grades.

There are some 140 private and parochial schools that also operate in Hillsborough County. These range from institutions that stress achievement-oriented college preparatory courses to those that emphasize basic education combined with strict religious training.

The following is a summary of data regarding the Hillsborough County Public Schools.

Total enrollment: 194,525

Number of facilities

total: 266
elementary schools: 142
junior high schools: 46
high schools: 27
other: 51

Student/teacher ratio: 14.44:1

Teacher salaries

average (statewide): $46,702

Funding per pupil: $8,761

Public Schools Information: Hillsborough County Public Schools, 901 E. Kennedy Blvd., PO Box 3408, Tampa, FL 33601-3408; telephone (813)272-4000.

Colleges and Universities

There are some 19 institutions of higher learning with campuses in or near the Hillsborough County/Tampa area (includes nearby St. Petersburg). These include traditional four-year and two-year colleges and universities, as well as religious, technical, and business schools. The University of South Florida is the largest of these. Other two and four-year colleges and universities include the University of Tampa, a private medium-sized school offering both undergraduate and post-graduate degrees, Florida College, and Hillsborough Community College. The Art Institute of Tampa (a branch of the Miami International University of Art and Design), National-Louis University, and the International Academy of Design and Technology are also in the city. ITT Technical Institute, primarily a two-year institution that also awards bachelor's degrees in electronics engineering technology, also has a campus in Tampa.

Libraries and Research Centers

In addition to its main branch in the downtown area (the John F. Germany Library), the Tampa-Hillsborough County Public Library system has 26 branches. The newest branch, the 40,000-square-foot SouthShore Regional Library, opened in 2006. The Tampa-Hillsborough County Public Library collection numbers over 8.7 million books, plus numerous films, records, talking books, magazines, newspapers, maps, photographs, and art reproductions. The system also operated two mobile units. Many of the system's libraries were refurbished and expanded in the early 2000s. Tampa is home to some 20 public or private research centers, a number of which were affiliated with or located on the University of South Florida (USF) campus. In addition, there are also 14 bioscience organizations in the Tampa area, as well as some 49 bioscience-related companies.

Public Library Information: John F. Germany Library, 900 N. Ashley, Tampa, FL 33602; telephone (813)273-3652; fax (813)272-5640

■ Health Care

Tampa is home to some 13 major hospitals and medical centers. These include two children's hospitals, a Veterans Administration hospital, and a teaching hospital centered on the University of South Florida's (USF) College of Medicine, College of Nursing, and College of Public Health, all of which are under the USF Health system banner. Other hospitals and medical centers include the university's H. Lee Moffitt Cancer Center and Research Institute, which operates a 162-bed hospital. Tampa General Hospital is the area's largest single hospital, with 877 licensed beds. It serves as the regional referral center in such fields as burn treatment, neonatal and pediatric care, and poison control. In 2010, St. Joseph's Women's Hospital began construction on a $75 million expansion. Its new 125,000 square foot building will house the St. Joseph's Children's Hospital's Neonatal ICU with 64 NICU private suites, the Shimberg Breast Center, and other specialty services for women and newborns.

The University Community Health System operates four hospitals throughout Tampa with a combined total of 963 beds. The system's new Pepin Heart Hospital and Dr. Kiran C. Patel Research Institute began operations in April 2006.

■ Recreation

Sightseeing

Visitors to Tampa can pursue a wide variety of activities, from the thrills of a day at a popular theme park to the quiet beauty of a leisurely walk along a waterfront boulevard. The city's premier attraction-and the state's second busiest, after Walt Disney World in Orlando-is Busch Gardens, a 335-acre entertainment center, jungle garden, and open zoo in which several thousand animals roam free on a simulated African veldt. Open 365 days a year, the park has rides, live shows (some starring animals and birds), shops, and games, all linked by a nineteenth-century African theme-and all only a few minutes north of downtown. Next to Busch Gardens is Adventure Island, another family-oriented theme park centered around water-related activities, including flumes, a pool that produces five-foot waves, and several giant slides. More than 10,000 aquatic plants and animals, representing

1,340 species from around the world, are on display at the Florida Aquarium. The Aquarium's popular Swim with the Fishes exhibit, in which visitors can actually experience the thrill of scuba diving on a Florida coral reef, has been duplicated by the Aquarium's new Dive with the Sharks exhibit. In addition, the Aquarium's Explore-A-Shore is a 2.2 acre play and discovery zone just for kids.

Tampa's Lowry Park Zoo includes shows, interactive exhibits, children's play areas, and rides. In 2004, the first section of the new Safari Africa exhibit opened. Lowry Park Zoo has been rated "Number 1 Family-Friendly Zoo in the U.S." by *Child Magazine*.

Plant Hall, the administration building of the University of Tampa, originally opened in 1891 as the opulent Tampa Bay Hotel. Entrepreneur Henry B. Plant's pet project, the 511-room palatial structure cost $3 million and defied categorization with its eclectic blend of Moorish, Near Eastern, and Byzantine architectural styles. Never a commercial success, the hotel was deeded to the city in 1904, and for the next twenty-five years, it was the site of various social events. The University of Tampa, in need of room to expand, took over the Tampa Bay Hotel during the 1930s. Today, it is probably the city's most recognized landmark.

More than any other major Florida city, Tampa has retained much of its Latin flavor. Ybor City, Tampa's Latin Quarter, is a National Register Historic District and, as such, is one of the city's most architecturally intact neighborhoods. The area developed around two cigar factories built in the mid-1880s by Cubans forced from their homeland by Spanish oppression. It soon became a center for Cuban revolutionary activity, even serving for a time as a home to Jose Marti, a writer, poet, and patriot considered the George Washington of Cuba. Today, the former Ybor Cigar Factory goes by the name of Ybor Square; it houses shops, boutiques, and restaurants. Other historic buildings in the Ybor City area include the El Pasaje Hotel, formerly a private club for Ybor City notables who hosted visitors such as Teddy Roosevelt and Winston Churchill; the Ritz Theatre; and the Ferlita Bakery, now the home of the Ybor City State Museum.

Some of Tampa's most interesting sights are best explored on foot. From the 4.5-mile sidewalk along Bayshore Boulevard, one of the longest continuous walkways in the world, the casual stroller can marvel at the striking mansions on one side and a sweeping view of the bay and the city's skyline on the other. The residential neighborhoods of Hyde Park (adjacent to Bayshore Boulevard) and Davis Islands are also ideally suited for walking tours.

Bus tours and boat tours of Tampa are especially carefree ways to see the city and its surroundings. Though they originate in St. Petersburg, the Gray Line Bus Tours can be boarded in Tampa at the Greyhound and Trailways terminals.

Arts and Culture

In 1967 the Florida State legislature created the Arts Council of Tampa to coordinate and promote the performing and visual arts in the Tampa region. Today, renamed the Arts Council of Hillsborough County, the council is actively involved in developing and administering school programs in dance, visual arts, music, poetry, creative writing, and theater; providing grants services to individual artists and arts organizations; scheduling events; and operating the Tampa Theatre, an ornate movie palace of the 1920s that has been restored to its former grandeur to serve film buffs, as well as fans of dance, music, and drama.

The Tampa Bay Performing Arts Center is a multipurpose facility located at the northern edge of downtown on a nine-acre riverfront site. It is a joint public-private venture designed to accommodate many different kinds of performances, and the largest performing arts complex south of New York City's Kennedy Center. Its five theaters and its rehearsal studio are used by local arts groups, touring drama companies, country music artists, and for the Center's own presentations.

Tampa is home to a variety of performing groups. American Stage, Stageworks, and the Alley Cat Players present seasons of drama, cabaret, classics and comedies. The University of South Florida and the University of Tampa both have theater training programs for actors, directors, and designers. Other local groups include the Carollwood Players community theater, and the Bits 'n Pieces Puppet Theater, which produces children's classics featuring giant puppets, as well as conventional actors. The Kuumba Dancers and Drummers teach and perform traditional dances and rhythms of a variety of African cultures. At the University of South Florida, the dance department is housed in a state-of-the-art studio and theater, teaching and performing forms of dance from jazz to ballet to modern. Music is presented by the Florida Orchestra, which is based in the three west coast cities of Tampa, St. Petersburg and Clearwater. It performs over 150 concerts each year from the Fall through the Spring. Musical entertainment is also provided by the Master Chorale, Tampa Oratorio, and myriad smaller community and college groups. Lights On Tampa, a biennial program providing unique platforms for cutting-edge contemporary art and ideas within the public realm, has been recognized by Americans for the Arts as one of the 50 most exemplary programs in the past 50 years.

Several museums and galleries are based in Tampa. Among them are the Museum of Science and Industry, which offers hands-on displays and demonstrations of a scientific and technological nature pertaining specifically to Florida's weather, environment, agriculture, and industry. The Tampa Museum of Art features changing art exhibitions from across the country and houses the Southeast's largest and most significant permanent collection of Classical Art of Ancient Greece and Rome.

The Henry B. Plant Museum features Victorian furniture and art objects in settings similar to those that would have greeted Tampa Bay Hotel guests in the late 1800s. The Ybor City State Museum provides an overview of the cigar industry and its history in Tampa, as well as information about the area's Latin community. Situated on the campus of the University of South Florida are two of the area's best contemporary art facilities. The Contemporary Art Museum has in its collection some of the finest of the world's modern artists, and organizes exhibitions of contemporary art to tour the United States and Europe. Graphicstudio, an experimental printmaking facility, has hosted such notables as Robert Rauschenberg, James Rosenquist, Jim Dine, and Miriam Shapiro. Kids City delights youngsters aged two to twelve with indoor, hands-on exhibits set in a realistic outdoor miniature village.

Other Tampa art facilities include the Florida Center for Contemporary Art, the state's only alternative artist's gallery, which highlights new work by emerging and established artists throughout Florida. The Lee Scarfone Gallery, the University of Tampa's fine arts college teaching gallery, exhibits works by students and faculty as well as artists of regional and national renown. Tampa has many fine galleries, and one of the highlights of the gallery season is a special event called Gallery HOP, an evening when all of the galleries are open and buses transport thousands of viewers on tours of the varied display sites around the city.

Arts & Culture Information: Arts Council of Hillsborough County., 1000 N. Ashley Drive, #105, Tampa, FL 33602; telephone (813)276-8250.

Festivals and Holidays

The Gasparilla Pirate Fest, on the last Saturday in January and dating back to 1904, is a noisy and colorful Mardi Gras-like festival that takes place in the downtown waterfront area. Named in honor of Jose Gaspar, Tampa's legendary "patron pirate," the Gasparilla invasion calls for a group of more than 700 costumed pirates (usually some of the city's most prominent business and social leaders) to sail into Tampa harbor on a three-masted schooner (complete with cannons and flying a Jolly Roger flag), capture the city, and kidnap the mayor. They then parade along Bayshore Boulevard accompanied by lavish floral floats and marching bands. Other activities held during Gasparilla Week include world-class distance runs, a children's parade, and a bicycle race. The festival ends with Fiesta Day in Ybor City, a day-long party of dancing in the streets, free Spanish bean soup, sidewalk artists, and a torchlight parade during which the pirates make their final appearance of the year.

In February, the Florida State Fair opens its annual twelve-day run. The largest fair of its kind south of the Mason-Dixon Line, the Florida State Fair features traditional agricultural exhibits and demonstrations, items for display and for sale, food, rides, auto races, shows, and contests, all spread out on a 301-acre site beside seven lakes.

Other Tampa celebrations include the Gasparilla Festival of the Arts, the Winter Equestrian Festival, the outrageous Guavaween Halloween festival, The Hillsborough County Fair, the Tampa-Hillsborough County Storytelling Festival, and a variety of ethnic festivals. First Night is a New Year's Eve festival to celebrate the arts.

Sports for the Spectator

The Tampa sporting scene has changed drastically in recent years with the addition of new stadiums and teams. The region's major league baseball team, the Tampa Bay Rays, play at St. Petersburg's Tropicana Field. The Bay Area has four other major professional sports teams: the Tampa Bay Buccaneers of the National Football League (NFL), the Tampa Bay Lightning of the National Hockey League (NHL), the Tampa Bay Storm of the Arena Football League (AFL), and FC Tampa Bay of the US Soccer Federation. The Tampa Bay Lightning won the Stanley Cup in 2004. The Buccaneers won Super Bowl XXXVII in 2003 and play at the 66,321-seat Raymond James Stadium, the only NFL stadium with a theme-park element-a cannon-firing pirate ship located at one end of the playing field in Buccaneer Cove. The state-of-the-art St. Pete Times Forum is home to both the Lightning and the Storm.

The New York Yankees' major league team uses Legends Field, modeled after the original Yankee Stadium in New York, for spring training. The Tampa Yankees, a Yankees' minor league team, play each year from April through September at Legends Field.

Horse racing and dog racing are popular spectator sports in the Tampa area. The renovated Tampa Bay Downs (located about fifteen miles west of the city) is the only thoroughbred track on Florida's west coast. The Tampa Greyhound Track, open since 1933, is one of the most popular in the United States. Located north of downtown, it is open year round. Top professional and amateur golfers compete each year in the Outback Steakhouse Pro Am which is played at the Tournament Players Club.

Collegiate athletic events of all kinds are regularly scheduled at the University of South Florida and the University of Tampa. Tampa hosts NCAA football's Outback Bowl in January. Golf and tennis tournaments, wrestling and boxing matches, equestrian shows, and automobile and boat races are also held on a regular basis in and around the city.

Sports for the Participant

With its warm climate, proximity to the water, and numerous public and private facilities, Tampa is ideal for those who enjoy golf, tennis, swimming, canoeing and boating, fishing, and other sports on a year-round basis.

Golf is especially popular. Tampa has dozens of public courses, but several other local semiprivate clubs allow greens fee players. For tennis enthusiasts, the city has more than a thousand public and private tennis courts. The Tampa recreation department also maintains racquetball courts, basketball courts, shuffleboard courts, recreation centers, gym facilities, playgrounds and community centers, a softball complex, and more than a hundred other fields. For those who prefer less strenuous forms of relaxation, the city alone has 146 parks; other parks and wilderness areas are located nearby. Just to the northeast of the city is the Hillsborough River State Park, which is ideal for those who enjoy picnicking, camping, canoeing, fishing, and hiking.

Much of the sports activity in Tampa occurs in or on the water. The city maintains 14 swimming pools, including one handicapped facility and one supplied with water from a natural spring; and four beaches. Picnic Island, a park located near where Teddy Roosevelt and the Rough Riders camped during the Spanish-American War, offers swimming, boating, and fishing. Ben T. Davis Municipal Beach, only fifteen minutes from downtown on the Courtney Campbell Causeway, is popular with swimmers as well as with windsurfers and catamaran sailors.

Both saltwater and freshwater fishing are excellent in the Tampa Bay area. A license is required for saltwater fishing. Good spots are everywhere-off bridges and piers and even downtown off Davis Islands or Bayshore Boulevard. Deep-sea charters are also readily available for those who would rather venture out into the gulf. Tarpon, cobia, kingfish, sea trout, mackerel, blue-tailed redfish, and bass are among the many varieties in abundance.

Shopping and Dining

A wide variety of retail establishments flourish in and around Tampa, from large regional malls featuring nationally known stores to small specialty shops promoting goods of a more local nature. International Plaza, adjacent to Tampa International Airport, has four department stores and over 200 specialty shops, as well as an open-air village of fine restaurants and small boutiques. Citrus Park Town Center Mall offers over 120 upscale shops and a 20-screen movie theater. Central Ybor caters to those seeking a more unusual shopping experience. Capitalizing on its status as a historic landmark in an ethnic neighborhood, Ybor leans more toward antique stores and gift shops with a Latin American focus. Near downtown Tampa is Old Hyde Park Village, which offers more than 60 shops plus restaurants and movie theaters in a historic outdoor setting.

Ranging in type from typical fast food fare to specialties served in elegant or unique settings, Tampa's many restaurants offer diners many choices. Fresh seafood (from the Gulf of Mexico) and Cuban cuisine (including thick, crusty bread and black bean soup) are local favorites.

Visitor Information: Tampa Bay Convention and Visitors Bureau., 401 E. Jackson Street, #2100, Tampa, FL 33602; telephone (813)223-1111; fax (813)223-6616.

■ Convention Facilities

Tampa's $140 million Tampa Convention Center complex is located near Harbour Island. It contains approximately 200,000 square feet of exhibition space, a 36,000-square-foot ballroom, 36 breakout rooms with a total of 42,000 square feet, and more than 80,000 square feet of prefunction space. It is located near 11 major hotels.

The Sun Dome at the University of South Florida, a large multipurpose facility, can accommodate about 11,000 people for concerts, lectures, trade shows, banquets, and large conventions.

For those seeking facilities for groups ranging in size from 10 to 2,500 people, Tampa has much to offer. Among the choices are the Egypt Temple Shrine, a well-equipped hall for banquets and more entertainment-oriented functions. The Florida State Fair's Expo Park Hall also offers indoor and outdoor facilities. Spacious and convenient meeting areas for smaller groups are also available at nearly 50 hotels and resorts in Tampa, many of them recently renovated.

Convention Information: Tampa Bay Convention and Visitors Bureau., 401 E. Jackson Street, #2100, Tampa, FL 33602; telephone (813)223-1111; fax (813) 223-6616.

■ Transportation

Approaching the City

The Tampa International Airport (TIA) is the city's main airport. A modern facility it is located 12 miles from downtown, and was designed to be user-friendly for passengers leaving or arriving in Tampa. It was the first airport in the country to use a people-mover system to transport passengers from remote buildings to terminals. TIA is also one of the busiest airports in the United States. In 2009, the airport handled almost 17 million passengers, and was served by 22 airlines. A second, smaller facility, the Peter O. Knight Airport, is located on Davis Islands. It serves Tampa's general aviation traffic and executive aircraft, and even has a seaplane basin and ramp. Charters and flight instruction are also available.

The major direct routes linking Tampa are Interstate 75 from the north or south (which becomes Interstate 275 as it passes through the city), Interstate 4 from the northeast (which merges with Interstate 275 downtown), State Road 60 from the southeast, and U.S. Highway 41

(a coastal road also known as the Tamiami Trail) from the south. U.S. Highways 41 and 301 roughly parallel Interstate 75 on the west and east, respectively.

Passenger rail service by Amtrak connects Tampa to Miami, Orlando, Jacksonville, Washington, D.C., and New York City. The city is also served by four cruise lines: Carnival, Celebrity, Holland American, and Royal Caribbean. The Port of Tampa's cruise industry handled 767,760 passengers and 178 cruise ship sailings in 2008. One of the most popular departure ports for western Caribbean cruises, Tampa also offers year-round cruises to Cozumel, Costa Maya, and Vancouver.

Traveling in the City

Allowing for constraints imposed by certain geographic features, Tampa is laid out in a basic grid pattern. Florida Avenue divides east from west, and John F. Kennedy Boulevard and Frank Adamo Drive (State Road 60) divide north from south.

Public transportation in the Tampa area is provided by the Hillsborough Area Regional Transit Authority, or as it is more commonly known, HARTline. Although Tampa's mass transit system is primarily bus-based, a 2.4 mile-long trolley line is operated. Known as the TECO Line System, it connects Tampa's downtown, Channelside, and Ybor City areas. Neighboring Pinellas County also operates a public transit system that connects Tampa with St. Petersburg and Clearwater.

■ Communications

Newspapers and Magazines

Tampa's major daily newspaper is *The Tampa Tribune,* a morning publication. Residents also read the *St. Petersburg Times.* A weekly alternative paper, *Creative Loafing Tampa* serves the Tampa, St. Petersburg, and Clearwater region. Tampa's magazine that focuses on lifestyles, local events, shopping, dining, books, films, and entertainment is *Tampa Bay Metro Magazine.*

Television and Radio

Tampa is served by six local television stations, four commercial stations and two public television stations. However, because of Tampa's close proximity to St. Petersburg and Clearwater, television stations from those cities are also received in Tampa. Additional stations are also available via cable and satellite. There are 43 radio stations within close listening range to residents of the Tampa area. Of these, 24 are FM stations offering jazz, country, religious, adult contemporary, public radio, and Top 40 formats, while there are 19 AM stations that feature religious, talk, Spanish language, and sports programming.

Media Information: *The Tampa Tribune,* 200 S. Parker St., Box 191, Tampa, FL 33601; telephone (813) 259-7711; email readerservice@tampatrib.com

Tampa Online

Central Florida Development Council. Available www.cfdc.org

City of Tampa home page. Available www.tampagov.net

Greater Tampa Chamber of Commerce. Available www.tampachamber.com

Hillsborough County Public Schools. Available www.sdhc.k12.fl.us

Tampa Bay Convention and Visitors Bureau. Available www.gotampa.com

Tampa Bay History Center. Available www.tampabayhistorycenter.org

Tampa Bay Library Consortium. Available www.tblc.org

Tampa-Hillsborough County Public Library System. Available www.thpl.org

Tampa Tribune. Available www.tampatrib.com

BIBLIOGRAPHY

Anderson, Anne W., *Insider's Guide to the Greater Tampa Bay Area including Tampa, St. Petersburg, and Clearwater* (Insiders' Guides Inc., 2009)

Byrd, Alan, *Florida Spring Training: Your Guide to Touring the Grapefruit League, 3rd ed.* (Branford, CT: Intrepid Traveler, 2007)

Knetsch, Joe, *Florida in the Spanish-American War* (Charleston, SC: History Press, 2011)

Georgia

The State in Brief

Nickname: Empire State of the South; Peach State

Motto: Wisdom, justice, and moderation

Flower: Cherokee rose

Bird: Brown thrasher

Area: 59,425 square miles (2010; U.S. rank 24th)

Elevation: Ranges from sea level to 4,784 feet above sea level

Climate: Long, hot summers and short, mild winters

Admitted to Union: January 2, 1788

Capital: Atlanta

Head Official: Nathan Deal (R) (until 2015)

Population

1990: 6,478,000
2000: 8,186,453
2010: 9,687,653
2012 estimate: 9,714,569
Percent change, 2000–2010: 18.3%
U.S. rank in 2012: 9th
Percent of residents born in state: 55.3% (2012)
Density: 168.4 people per square mile (2010)
2012 FBI Crime Index Total: 375,920

Racial and Ethnic Characteristics (2012)

White: 5,903,173
Black or African American: 2,970,481
American Indian and Alaska Native: 24,937
Asian: 318,530
Native Hawaiian and Pacific Islander: 4,498
Hispanic or Latino (may be of any race): 853,602
Other: 492,950

Age Characteristics (2012)

Population under 5 years old: 685,245
Population 5 to 19 years old: 2,096,806
Percent of population 65 years and over: 10.8%
Median age: 35.4

Vital Statistics

Total number of births (2012–13): 132,184
Total number of deaths (2012–13): 73,288
AIDS cases reported through 2011: 42,068

Economy

Major industries: Trade, manufacturing, food manufacturing, services
Unemployment rate (2012): 6.8%
Per capita income (2012): $25,309
Median household income (2012): $49,604
Percentage of persons below poverty level (2012): 17.4%
Income tax rate: 1.0% to 6.0%
Sales tax rate: 4.0%

Atlanta

■ The City in Brief

Founded: circa 1837 (incorporated as Marthasville, 1843; reincorporated 1847)

Head Official: Mayor Kasim Reed (D) (since 2010; term expires 2014)

City Population
1990: 393,929
2000: 416,474
2010: 420,003
2012 estimate: 443,768
Percent change, 2000–2010: 0.8%
U.S. rank in 1990: 36th (State rank: 1st)
U.S. rank in 2000: 48th (State rank: 1st)
U.S. rank in 2010: 40th (State rank: 1st)

Metropolitan Statistical Area Population
2000: 4,112,198
2010: 5,268,860
2012 estimate: 5,442,113
Percent change, 2000–2010: 28.1%
U.S. rank in 2000: 11th
U.S. rank in 2010: 9th

Area: 132 square miles

Elevation: 1,010 feet above sea level

Average Annual Temperatures: 64.2° F

Average Annual Precipitation: 50.77 inches

Major Economic Sectors: machinery, electricity, transportation, food and beverages, printing, publishing, textiles, apparel, furniture, telecommunications hardware, plastics, chemicals, automobiles

Unemployment Rate: 8.1% (2012)

Per Capita Income: $35,829

2012 FBI Crime Index Property: 28,554

Major Colleges and Universities: Georgia State University, Georgia Institute of Technology, Emory University, Clark Atlanta University, Morehouse College, Spelman College, Interdenominational Theological Seminary

Daily Newspaper: *Atlanta Journal-Constitution*

■ Introduction

Georgia's capital and largest city, Atlanta is a major financial, transportation, and cultural force in the South and nationally, and the focus of a metropolitan statistical area that covers more than 8,000 square miles and includes more than 100 municipalities. People from all over the country, joined by immigrants from other lands, have flocked to Atlanta, which offers Old South graciousness blended with an ambitious zest for expansion and dominance Ted Turner, communications mogul and one of the city's well-known citizens, has declared that Atlanta has "absolutely everything going for it—climate, location, great transportation, easy air access, and a government that's both cooperative and supportive." This is a judgment widely shared by both residents and visitors. While area growth stagnated during a national recession in the late 2000s, worsened by a greater-than-average decline in home prices, growth returned steadily in the 2010s. Two massive development projects—new stadiums for the Atlanta Braves and Atlanta Falcons—were set to become the metropolitan area's newest monuments in 2017, a fitting legacy for the host of the 1996 Summer Olympics.

■ Geography and Climate

Located in the foothills of the southern Appalachians in the north-central part of the state, Atlanta has a mild

© Sean Pavone/Shutterstock.com

climate that rotates through all four seasons. July is the warmest month on average, with the highest temperature recorded in 2012 at 106 degrees Fahrenheit. January is the coolest month on average, with the lowest recorded temperature at -9 degrees Fahrenheit in 1899. The Chattahoochee River forms the northwestern boundary of the city. Stone Mountain can be seen on the eastern side of the city. The city is the seat of Fulton County. The city's elevation and relative closeness to the Gulf of Mexico and the Atlantic Ocean moderate the summer heat; mountains to the north retard the southward movement of polar air masses, thereby providing mild winters. Most precipitation falls in the form of rain, with the heaviest concentration in March. Snowfall is negligible, though a snowstorm of about four inches occurs about every five years. Tornado activity is also fairly frequent in the area. Atlanta has had major issues with droughts, which makes water a limited resource.

Area: 132 square miles

Elevation: 1,010 feet above sea level

Average Temperatures: 64.2° F

Average Annual Precipitation: 50.77 inches

■ History

City Develops as Trade Center

Until the early nineteenth century, the site near the Chattahoochee River where Atlanta is located (originally named the "Standing Peach Tree" for a peach tree on a small hill about seven miles away) was virgin territory sparsely occupied by Creek and Cherokee Native American tribes. The first permanent white settlers arrived in the area during the War of 1812, when a small fort was built near the Cherokee village of Standing Peachtree. After the war, the land around the fort was slowly settled by farmers from northern Georgia, the Carolinas, and Virginia. Then, in the late 1830s, the Western & Atlantic Railroad was constructed connecting the Chattahoochee River with the town of Chattanooga to the north. The area thus became an important trade center and a village soon developed at the southern end of the railroad. Initially called Terminus (after the word for the engineer's final stake), the village was chartered as Marthasville in 1843 in honor of the governor's daughter, then renamed Atlanta in 1845 and reincorporated in 1847.

By the end of the 1850s, the population of Atlanta had grown to 10,000 people (up from approximately 2,500 people in 1847) and the city had undergone extensive industrial development to become a railway hub, a vital trade link between North and South. Retaining the rough-and-tumble spirit of a frontier town, Atlanta had also progressed as a center of civilization and culture. When the Civil War broke out, Atlanta ceased trade with the North and was established as a Confederate military post. Because of its railroads and factories the city was a prime target, and it was bombarded by Union forces in July 1864.

The Battle of Atlanta was fierce. For a time Southern troops were able to defend the city, but military and civilian casualties from enemy shells and typhoid fever were high. The battle lost, the mayor, James Calhoun, and a few citizens surrendered on September 2, 1864. The fall of Atlanta was catastrophic. All civilians were evacuated and 90 percent of the structures in the city were destroyed by the Union troops under General William T. Sherman as they marched toward Georgia's Atlantic coast. Reconstruction began almost immediately after Sherman's army departed. Slowed by smallpox epidemics in 1865 and 1866 that forced the building of a temporary hospital, efforts to rebuild the city were nevertheless successful, and in 1868 Atlanta became the state capital (officially confirmed in 1877).

Atlanta Becomes a Major City

Expansion and growth continued through the nineteenth century and into the early decades of the twentieth, though the city was beset by periodic racial conflict. By 1920 the population of Atlanta had reached 200,000 people. The Great Depression brought more hard times, as it did throughout the country, but the city rose to meet the challenge of World War II. The transportation hub for the Southeast, Atlanta was one of the most important cities in the war effort.

After the war came renewed expansion in manufacturing, as well as a vital role in aviation. Having been a railroad center for most of its history, Atlanta was by the 1950s also the busiest and most important airline center in the South. In recent decades both the economy and cultural life have flourished, with Atlanta emerging as the major city of the "New South." Racial tensions were not as pronounced in Atlanta throughout the 1960s as desegregation took place in the public schools and city businesses and restaurants. However, citizens found a new spirit of cooperation and teamwork in the political process by becoming the first major city in the South to elect an African American mayor, Maynard Jackson, in 1973. Atlanta gained momentum in growth and prosperity throughout the 1970s and 1980s and gained a national spotlight by hosting the National Democratic Convention in 1988. Atlanta was the focus of world attention when it hosted the 1996 Centennial Summer Olympic Games. By most media accounts, the city had distinguished itself as world class and an economic leader.

Like many areas in the Sun Belt, the Atlanta region has seen explosive growth since the 1970s, with a dramatic 38.9 percent growth of the metropolitan area's population between 1990 and 2000 and an additional 28.1 percent growth between 2000 and 2010. This growth has stemmed from Atlanta's status as a major business center and transportation hub. The local economy has been bolstered by the Hartsfield-Jackson Atlanta International Airport, the busiest passenger airport in the world, which enjoyed an expansion of its international wing that opened in 2012. Consumer goods find easy transport in the highly successful rail system. Since the 1996 Olympic Games, Atlanta's strength as a business community has been frequently reflected in its regular distinction as one of the top-five cities with the most *Fortune 500* headquarters. A national recession in the late 2000s disrupted Atlanta's economy, especially its overheated housing market, but growth returned in the 2010s, with expectations of reaching pre-recession employment levels by the middle of the decade.

Unlike most major cities, metropolitan Atlanta does not have major natural boundaries, such as an ocean, lakes, or mountains, which might normally constrain growth. While this has been beneficial to the growth of the area, it has also garnered attention as an archetype for cities experiencing rapid growth and resultant urban sprawl. With its attention on commerce, much of the city's green space has been developed, and Atlanta has ranked in the bottom among cities of similar density in the area of park land per capita. Traffic congestion and air pollution have also made a mark in Atlanta. In 2007 the American Lung Association ranked Atlanta among the highest levels of air particle pollution in the United States; however, improvements dropped Atlanta to 18th in the association's 2013 rankings. Managing urban and suburban growth, and its effect on air quality, ease of transportation, and downtown development, remained a central concern guiding governmental policies and popular interest throughout the 2010s.

Despite its modern skyline, Atlanta maintains a sense of Southern charm in the midst of metropolitan living. The area has offered vibrant arts scene along with beautiful parks and exciting activities. Many tourists are drawn to the historical significance of the area, including its Civil War landmarks. This mix of history, tourism, and business opportunities has provided the boundless prosperity that the area has enjoyed and expects to enjoy in the future.

Historical Information: Atlanta History Center, 130 W. Paces Ferry Rd. NW, Atlanta, GA 30305-1366; telephone (404) 814-4000.

■ Population Profile

Metropolitan Statistical Area Population

2000: 4,112,198
2010: 5,268,860
2012 estimate: 5,442,113

Percent change, 2000–2010: 28.1%
U.S. rank in 2000: 11th
U.S. rank in 2010: 9th

City Residents

1990: 393,929
2000: 416,474
2010: 420,003
2012 estimate: 443,768
Percent change, 2000–2010: 0.8%
U.S. rank in 1990: 36th (State rank: 1st)
U.S. rank in 2000: 48th (State rank: 1st)
U.S. rank in 2010: 40th (State rank: 1st)

Density: 3,154.3 people per square mile

Racial and ethnic characteristics

White: 173,766
Black or African American: 237,154
American Indian and Alaskan Native: 1,351
Asian: 17,449
Native Hawaiian and Other Pacific Islander: 308
Hispanic or Latino (may be of any race): 23,322
Other: 13,740

Percent of residents born in state: 52.9%

Age characteristics

Population under 5 years old: 28,578
Population 5 to 9 years old: 20,021
Population 10 to 14 years old: 22,147
Population 15 to 19 years old: 29,582
Population 20 to 24 years old: 47,552
Population 25 to 34 years old: 90,393
Population 35 to 44 years old: 67,190
Population 45 to 54 years old: 51,260
Population 55 to 59 years old: 22,855
Population 60 to 64 years old: 21,756
Population 65 to 74 years old: 23,841
Population 75 to 84 years old: 12,881
Population 85 years and over: 5,712
Median age: 33.1

Births (2010–11 Metropolitan Area)

Total number: 74,174

Deaths (2010–11 Metropolitan Area)

Total number: 31,266

Money income (2012)

Per capita income: $35,829
Median household income: $44,784
Total households: 177,215

Number of households with income of ...

less than $10,000: 26,248
$10,000 to $14,999: 11,883
$15,000 to $24,999: 19,286
$25,000 to $34,999: 17,499
$35,000 to $49,999: 19,286
$50,000 to $74,999: 27,234
$75,000 to $99,999: 15,485
$100,000 to $149,999: 18,142
$150,000 to $199,999: 8,444
$200,000 or more: 13,708

Percent of families below poverty level: 26.0%

FBI Crime Index Property: 28,554

FBI Crime Index Violent: 6,027

■ Municipal Government

Atlanta, the Fulton County seat, is governed by a mayor and a 15-member city council that is managed by an additional council president. There are 12 members elected by district and three elected at large. The mayor is chief executive officer and oversees administration of city government.

Head Official: Mayor Kasim Reed (D) (since 2010; term expires 2014)

Total Number of City Employees: 8,323 (2013)

City Information: City of Atlanta, Office of Communications, 55 Trinity Ave., Suite 2500, Atlanta, GA 30303; telephone (404) 330-6004; fax (404) 658-6893.

■ Economy

Major Industries and Commercial Activity

Atlanta has become a leading world center of business and trade. Atlanta contains some of the world's largest headquarters of some of the world's most well recognized companies, such as The Coca Cola Company, Georgia-Pacific, AT&T Mobility, Cable News Network, Delta Air Lines, The Home Depot, and Turner Broadcasting. In all, Atlanta was home to 14 *Fortune* 500 companies as of 2012, ranking third among all cities, outpaced only by New York, New York, and Houston, Texas. A total of 26 companies were ranked among the *Fortune* 1000. These companies combined to produce $321.2 billion in annual revenues. Two additional *Fortune* 500 companies, Aflac and Mohawk Industries, were located nearby but outside the metropolitan area.

Atlanta's business-friendly environment also has drawn the attention of companies looking to relocate. In 2010, two *Fortune 500* companies relocated their headquarters to the area: First Data from Colorado, and National Cash Register (NCR) from Ohio. This environment has also uplifted local area companies, such as Aaron's, Global Payments, and Carter's, who all broke into the *Fortune 1000* for the first time in 2010. In 2013 PulteGroup, the nation's largest homebuilder, announced it was relocating from Detroit to Atlanta.

While the Coca-Cola Company wields considerable influence in Atlanta—much of it in areas outside its immediate manufacturing concerns—no single industry or firm truly dominates the local economy. Delta Air Lines operates one of the largest hub airports in the nation and employed 27,000 throughout the metropolitan area as of 2013. There is also a sizable financial sector. SunTrust Banks, one of the nation's largest banks, is headquartered in the city. Government regulation has a hand in Atlanta, home of the Centers for Disease Control and Prevention (CDC), a Nuclear Regulatory Commission regional headquarters, and a Federal Reserve Bank district headquarters. Finally, Atlanta is known as a major cable television programming hub, where the Turner Broadcasting System and Cox Enterprises call home. Industry focus areas in 2013 were bioscience and health information technology, clean technology, and advanced manufacturing, among others.

Meanwhile, the auto manufacturing industry has suffered as Ford Motors and General Motors shut down plants in 2006 and 2008. Not all was lost, however, as Korean automaker Kia opened a plant in 2009 in West Point. It continued to hire more employees through 2013 and also attracted a motor parts manufacturer, Hyundai Dymos, to the area to build transmissions, axles, and seats. Porportionally, the housing industry suffered more in Atlanta than in many other large cities, a factor that held back economic growth and tempered the construction industry through the early 2010s.

Other problems could loom for Atlanta businesses and residents, however. The sprawling metropolis historically has suffered droughts that affect the area's water supply significantly. Seventy-five percent of the area's water comes from reservoirs at Lake Lanier and Lake Allatoona. Alabama and Florida both have claimed rights to the lake's water for commercial usage; in the ensuing legal batter, a 2009 ruling in favor of the challenging states was overturned in 2011 and upheld when the U.S. Supreme Court declined to hear the case in in 2012. National Congressional representatives for respective states were considering alternative options through 2013, with Atlanta officials and business leaders considering nine-figure investments to development a sustainable solution for Atlanta's water supply.

Items and goods produced: machinery, electricity, transportation, food and beverages, printing, publishing, textiles, apparel, furniture, telecommunications hardware, plastics, chemicals, automobiles

Incentive Programs-New and Existing Companies

Georgia has the reputation for being a strong pro-business state. Many new companies have relocated to metro Atlanta and have either built new facilities or converted vacant office space. The various local and state business incentives offered have encouraged these company moves as well as expansions of local firms.

Local programs: Atlanta has an array of programs designed to attract new businesses to the area. Loan programs include the New Markets Catalyst Fund, a revolving loan porgram to support small-business lending in depressed communities; Small Business Loan, which focuses on small, minority-, and female-owned businesses; Business Improvement Loan Fund, providing loans for targeted business districts when business owners do not qualify for market-rate loans; The Phoenix Fund, for small- and medium-sized companies; New Market Tax Credits, offering below-market-rate loans; and Opportunity Loan Fund, providing gap financing for businesses that create at least five new jobs in Atlanta.

Tax credits include the Landmark Historic Property Tax Abatement Program, to preserve historic Atlanta properties; Atlanta Neighborhood Development Partnership Programs & Loans Funds, which gives eligible business owners financial support to develop mixed-income housing; Fulton County/City of Atlanta Land Bank Authority, empowered to extinguish tax liens and resell tax-foreclosed properties; and Tax Allocation Districts, areas with incentives for business development to support public improvement projects.

State programs: Georgia has business-friendly tax laws; the state does not use the unitary tax method, but instead taxes businesses only on income apportioned to Georgia. A Job Tax Credit offers employers that create jobs in Geogria up to $4,000 in income-tax deductions per job. Georgia's Opportunity Zones, defined as redevelopment or revitalization targets, provide Job Tax Credits for the creation of as few as two jobs. Less developed census tracts also provide Job Tax Credits, as do military zones. Tax credits also hinge on the average wage of job created and the size of the project—designated "Mega Project Tax Credits" allow large employers who create at least 1,800 jobs to claim a tax credit of $5,250 for as many as 4,500 employees. One-stop permitting, enterprise zones, and foreign trade zones also support economic development in Georgia. Georgia's fourth-lowest unionization rate nationally and status as a right-to-work state also draws employers.

Job training programs: The Georgia Department of Technical and Adult Education administers the Georgia Quick Start program, offering job-specific training programs through a large network of college, university, and satellite campus sites within the state. By developing and implementing high quality customized training programs and materials, Quick Start assists the company in obtaining a trained work force ready to begin as soon as the company opens for business. The HOPE Scholarship program funds Georgia students' college tuition if they meet academic targets during high school. In addition, metro Atlanta's colleges and universities provide a continuing supply of educated and ready-to-work graduates.

Development Projects

The staging of the 1996 Centennial Olympic Games in Atlanta had a tremendous impact on development. More than $2 billion was spent on new construction, sporting arenas, entertainment venues, and beautification projects in preparation for the games. Another $100 million went to hotel renovations and expansions. The downtown area received the lion's share of improvements as the city furthered its goal of becoming world class. Buildings were leveled and 21 acres were cleared to create the $57 million Centennial Olympic Park, which now serves as the centerpiece of downtown Atlanta.

Expansion and development of attractions and event spaces has become an important part of economic development. The Georgia Aquarium, one of the largest in the world, completed in 2005 with the support of a $250 million donation from Bernie Marcus, founder of Atlanta-based Home Depot. A new World of Coca-Cola opened nearby two years later in 2007. Cobb Galleria opened a multipurpose performing arts center in 2007 that includes meeting spaces and food and beverage capabilities.

Cobb County successfully courted another major tenant—the Atlanta Braves—in 2013. The Braves, who played at Turner Field, the converted track and field stadium from the 1996 Olympics, announced in late 2013 that they would be moving from the venue to a new stadium in Cobb County in 2017. Disputes with Fulton County over renovations and parking led the team to plan a move from Turner Field after just two decades of residence. Cobb County officials lured the Braves with $450 million in public support to construct a new stadium and surrounding area. The planned 42,000-seat stadium was estimated to cost $672 million. Turner Field was to be demolished after the Braves' final season there in 2016.

The Braves departure from the downtown area was in contrast to plans for a new retractable-roof stadium for the city's National Football League franchise, the Atlanta Falcons. A 71,000-seat, $1.2-billion facility was to be completed in 2017. Atlanta funded the massive project through an extension of a hotel-motel tax expected to contribute $200 million, or 17 percent of the stadium's cost. Additional city funded was expected to contribute hundreds of millions to maintain the stadium during the first 30 years of its existence, the lease term agreed upon with the Falcons. The remaining 83 percent of stadium construction was to be funded through a combination of personal seat licenses by season ticket holders, the National Football League, and the football franchise.

Developments in museums are in the works for Atlanta. In 2007 the mayor announced plans for the creation of the Center For Civil and Human Rights in the city. The center was to offer information of the contributions of Atlantans and Georgians in the Civil Rights

movement and house the Martin Luther King Jr. Collection currently at Morehouse College. The project, adjacent to the World of Coca Cola and Georgia Aquarium, was expected to open in 2014. In 2012 Legoland Discovery Centre opened to visitors with a 35,000 square foot facility, which includes a replica of the Atlanta skyline made from 250,000 legos. The College Football Hall of Fame planned to open a new facility in Atlanta in 2014.

In 2012 a new international terminal at Hartsfield-Jackson International Airport opened, allowing passengers to access the landside without having to use an automated people mover. The $1.4 million facility was funded through $1 billion in municipal bonds as well as $400 million in private investment from airlines. It included 1.2 million square feet of terminal and concourse space and added 12 new gates to the airport, as well as additional security and parking areas.

Overall, Atlanta ranked as one of the top economic development areas in the country in 2012. While Georgia placed first among states in the southeast and sixth in the nation, Atlanta was named fourth among all U.S. cities.

Economic Development Information: Metro Atlanta Chamber of Commerce, 235 Andrew Young International Blvd. NW, Atlanta, GA 30303; telephone (404) 880-9000. Invest Atlanta: Atlanta's Development Authority, 133 Peachtree Street NE, Suite 2900, Atlanta, GA 30303 (440) 880-4100.

Commercial Shipping

An extensive array of air, rail, and truck connections makes Atlanta a city with a robust cargo industry. Hartsfield-Jackson Atlanta International Airport is the main focus of activity, with three main air cargo complexes, a perishables complex, and a USDA inspection station serving 19 cargo airlines as of 2012. Warehouse space for cargo totals 1.3 million square feet and supports parking for 28 aircraft. A Foreign Trade Zone located near the airport at the Atlanta Tradeport provides companies with an opportunity to delay, reduce, or eliminate customs duty on imported items, while the U.S. Customs Service Model Inland Port is a highly computerized center designed to expedite quick clearance for international.

The railroad, for so long crucial to Atlanta's well-being, continues to serve the city through two major systems, CSX and Norfolk Southern, which operate more than 100 freight trains in and out of the city daily. There are more than 100 motor freight carriers in Atlanta. Such commercial shipping capabilities have made Atlanta one of the largest inland ports in the world.

Labor Force and Employment Outlook

Atlanta enjoys an expanding labor pool derived from the surrounding counties and from people coming to the city from other parts of the country and the world. Skilled laborers are more than willing to relocate to Atlanta. The presence of several institutes of higher education also contributes to a fairly well-educated resident workforce. Employment growth recovered from a recession in the late 2000s, with the city adding 37,000 jobs in 2012 and 53,000 in 2013. Still, employment was not expected to reach pre-recession levels until 2016. In 2013 the fastest growing jobs were in business and professional services, followed by leisure and hospitality, and manufacturing. *Forbes* ranked Atlanta the "Best City for New College Grads in 2013."

The following is a summary of data regarding the 2012 Atlanta labor force:

Size of civilian labor force: 234,136

Number of workers employed in ...

  agriculture and mining: 515
  construction: 6,629
  manufacturing: 10,162
  wholesale trade: 5,354
  retail trade: 19,688
  transportation: 11,983
  information systems: 8,512
  finance: 15,067
  professional administration: 40,073
  education and social services: 42,767
  arts and leisure: 22,818
  other: 8,746
  public administration: 8,514

Average hourly earnings of production workers: $15.40

Unemployment rate: 8.1% (2012)

Employers

Largest employers (2012)	*Number of employees*
Allied Barton Security Services	4,205
International Business Machine Corporation	3,769
The Coca-Cola Company	3,608
Turner Broadcasting System, Inc.	2,000
Cable News Network	1,889
Air Service Corporation	1,665
Accenture LLP	1,555
AT&T Services, Inc.	1,247
Georgia-Pacific Corporation	1,170
Tenet Health System, Inc.	1,164

Cost of Living

Atlanta's cost of living figures, while high for the South, compare favorably with those of other major metropolitan areas in the United States.

The following is a summary of data regarding several key cost of living factors in the area.

2013 ACCRA Average House Price: $236,057

2013 ACCRA Cost of Living Index: 96

State income tax rate: 1.0% to 6.0%

State sales tax rate: 4.0%

Local income tax rate: None

Local sales tax rate: 4.0%

Property tax rate: $44.435 per $1,000 of assessed valuation (2013)

Economic Information: Metro Atlanta Chamber of Commerce, 235 Andrew Young International Blvd. NW, Atlanta, GA 30303; telephone (404) 880-9000. Invest Atlanta: Atlanta's Development Authority, 133 Peachtree Street NE, Suite 2900, Atlanta, GA 30303 (440) 880-4100.

■ Education and Research

Elementary and Secondary Schools

The Atlanta Public Schools system serves the city of Atlanta, as well as unincorporated portions of Fulton and DeKalb Counties. The school system graduated 1,972 students in 2013, who collectively earned more than $100 million in scholarships and grants from colleges and universities. Nearly 75 percent of the study body was eligible for free or reduced lunches; the computer-to-student ratio was 1:2. Atlanta Public Schools operates 13 charter schools.

In the state of Georgia, any student who graduates from high school with at least a 3.0 grade point average is eligible for free college tuition at any of the state's colleges or universities. The program is called the HOPE (Helping Outstanding Pupils Educationally) Scholarship and is funded by the Georgia lottery. For fiscal year 2013–14, HOPE Scholarship grants exceeded $228 million dollars and were distributed to more than 148,000 students.

More than 200 private schools also operate in the Atlanta area, ranging from residential preparatory institutions to church-affiliated programs. A number of private schools offer foreign language curriculums. These include Saturday schools that offer instruction in German, Arabic, Chinese, and Japanese. There is also a full-time Japanese school in Atlanta.

The following is a summary of data regarding the Atlanta Public Schools.

Total enrollment: 49,796

Number of facilities

total: 105
elementary schools: 53
junior high schools: 14
high schools: 21
other: 17

Student/teacher ratio: 13.5:1

Teacher salaries

average (statewide): $53,906

Funding per pupil: $13,631

Public Schools Information: Atlanta Public Schools, Administrative Office, 130 Trinity Ave., Atlanta, GA 30303; telephone (404) 802-3500.

Colleges and Universities

Metropolitan Atlanta is home to more than 20 accredited post-secondary institutions, including several of the most prestigious in the United States. They feature more than 300 programs of study and offer a variety of associate and undergraduate degrees, as well as graduate degrees in such fields as medicine, law, and theology. The two largest public universities are Georgia State University and the Georgia Institute of Technology, the latter of which is famous for its research programs in dozens of different high-technology disciplines. Georgia Tech's research expenditures reached nearly $690 million in 2012, placing it among the top-10 in the nation among universities without a medical school. Emory University, a nationally prominent private research institution, is consistently ranked in the top 20 schools naIntionally by *US News & World Report.* External research funding at Emory exceeded $500 million in 2013.

The Atlanta University Center Consortium is the largest consortium of private African American colleges in the nation. The center is comprised of four colleges: Clark Atlanta University, Morehouse College, Spelman College, and Morehouse School of Medicine. Other notable facilities in Atlanta include: Mercer University's Cecil B. Day Campus, its Stetson School of Business and Economics, and its Southern School of Pharmacy; Oglethorpe University; and Agnes Scott College, a women's liberal arts college affiliated with the Presbyterian Church. Atlanta Technical College was named "America's Best Community College" by *Washington Monthly* in 2007 and received the Perdue Award for Technical Education from the Technical College System of Georgia in 2012. The metropolitan area also has large public two-year and four-year colleges to serve students, including Clayton State University and several schools that offer specialized vocational and religious instruction. The University of Georgia, with more than 35,000 students, is located about 70 miles northeast of Atlanta's city center.

Libraries and Research Centers

In addition to a modern central library located downtown, the Atlanta-Fulton Public Library System operates 33 branches throughout the city and Fulton and DeKalb counties, as well as a bookmobile. As of 2013, there were more than 509,000 library card holders. The system's holdings include more than 2.5 million items, including periodicals, and a large collection of compact discs, records, and audio- and videotapes. Coinciding with the library system's centennial anniversary, the Central Library completed major renovations in 2002 and includes a modern, fully equipped instructional learning center. The Auburn Avenue Research Library, part of the public library system, is devoted to collecting materials on African American history and culture. Among Atlanta's several outstanding historical research libraries is the Jimmy Carter Library and Museum, dedicated to the former president. Georgia Tech's Library and Information Center circulates more than 100,000 books annually to students and employs some 125 trained faculty and staff; Emory University Libraries include the Goizueta Business Library and a Manuscript, Archives, and Rare Book Library. Other campus libraries in Atlanta house special collections of material; many are open to the public for in-house reading and research. Morehouse College houses the Martin Luther King Jr. Collection, which contains 1,100 books from King's personal library, in addition to many handwritten notes and other items of historical importance.

Nearly 150 research centers are based in Atlanta. Georgia Institute of Technology hosts a large number of them, including the Advanced Technology Development Center, Mid-America Earthquake Center, Fusion Research Center, and Georgia Tech Institute for Electronics and Nanotechnology. Emory University hosts many research centers, including the Center for AIDS Research, Influenza Pathogenesis & Immunology Research Center, and Winship Cancer Institute. Other topics under investigation at local research centers are wide ranging; among them are health care, computers and software, bioengineering, economics, mining, biotechnology, business, women's studies, electronics, energy, and pharmacology.

Atlanta boasts four research centers of international renown. The U.S. Centers for Disease Control and Prevention studies some of the world's deadliest diseases in maximum security laboratories. The Yerkes Regional Primate Research Center is the oldest continuously operated center for research on the biological and behavioral characteristics of nonhuman primates. Affiliated with Emory University and founded in 1982 by former President Jimmy Carter and his wife, Rosalynn, The Carter Center focuses on global environmental, agricultural, economic, and public health concerns; its Task Force for Child Survival and Development addresses issues of immunization, malnutrition, disease control, and child advocacy.

In 2010, Georgia State University's Andrew Young School of Policy Studies landed the Census Bureau's Atlanta Research Data Center, a high-level business, social, and health statistical data warehouse, placing the region among an exclusive number of locations to house this type of information.

Public Library Information: Atlanta-Fulton Central Library, 1 Margaret Mitchell Square, Atlanta, GA 30303; telephone (404) 730-1700.

■ Health Care

A regional as well as a national leader in health care, the Atlanta metropolitan area is home to more than 60 hospitals supporting 40,000 medical personnel and more than 10,000 beds. Twelve hospitals are located in the city proper. One of the major full-service institutions is Grady Memorial Hospital, used as a teaching hospital by the medical schools of both Emory University and More-house College. It is the only Level 1 trauma center within a 100-mile radius of Atlanta. Grady has operated a separate, state-of-the-art care facility for HIV and AIDS patients since 1994. Emory University Hospital has been on the "America's Best Hospitals" list annually compiled by *U.S. News & World Report* for more than 20 years. For 2013–14, the hospital achieved national rankings in five fields: cancer, cardiology and heart surgery, neurology and neurosurgery, ophthalmology, and psychiatry. That same year, Atlanta's Shepard Center ranked 10th in the magazine's list of top rehabilitation centers. Other institutions in the city include Georgia Baptist Healthcare System, Piedmont Healthcare, and the Atlanta Medical Center. Atlanta also serves as the home of the Centers for Disease Control and Prevention, which includes the region's federal Public Health Service.

■ Recreation

Sightseeing

The Atlanta area offers extraordinarily rich opportunities for leisure, pleasure, and culture. A popular site within the city is Grant Park, which includes scenic walking paths; the Zoo Atlanta featuring a Giant Panda exhibit; and some Civil War fortifications. The Civil War Museum on park grounds houses the famous Cyclorama, a huge three-dimensional panoramic painting of the Battle of Atlanta. Visitors sit on a revolving platform to view the work, the impact heightened by sound and light effects as

well as a narration that explains the scene. Open since 1893, it is dubbed "The Longest Running Show in the Country." Various Civil War battle sites, parks, cemeteries, and memorials are also scattered throughout the city and are accessible to visitors.

Georgia Aquarium, opened in 2005, features more than 55,000 animals, including enormous whale sharks in its 6.3 million gallon Ocean Voyager exhibit. The World of Coca-Cola moved to its new location near the Georgia Aquarium in 2007. The 75,000-square-foot center houses a collection of exhibits and more than 1,000 articles commemorating the history of Atlanta's most famous product. Visitors can stop at various serving stations throughout the center to sample Coke products from around the world.

Also within the city is the Georgia State Capitol. Built in 1889 and patterned after the Capitol in Washington, D.C., it has a dome plated with gold mined in northern Georgia. Besides serving as the meeting place for the state's General Assembly, the Capitol is home to the Georgia State Museum. Another popular attraction is the CNN Center, the news and entertainment center of Turner Broadcasting's global headquarters, which offers tours, shops, and restaurants.

Underground Atlanta is an "adult playground" of bars, restaurants, and shops in the heart of the city's downtown. Every New Year's it plays host to the "Peach Drop" with music, fireworks, and an 800-pound peach resembling New York's Times Square ball. The Martin Luther King Jr. National Historic Site near Underground Atlanta honors the slain civil rights leader, a native of Atlanta. The entire area was renovated to give a sense of the neighborhood as it was during King's lifetime. The district encompasses King's childhood home, the Ebenezer Baptist Church (where he preached), and, adjacent to the church, his tomb. The district includes a visitors' center that tells the story of the civil rights movement and King's role in the movement. Nearby is the Martin Luther King Jr. Center for Nonviolent Social Change that draws about 650,000 visitors annually.

Outside Atlanta are several other notable attractions. The most popular is Stone Mountain, located about 20 miles east of downtown. The world's largest mass of exposed granite, the treeless dome stands more than 800 feet above the surrounding plain and measures approximately 5 miles in circumference. On the mountain's north face are carved colossal figures of Robert E. Lee, Jefferson Davis, and General Stonewall Jackson. Work began in 1923, but after several design changes it was not declared completed until 1972. A 3,200-acre park fans out from the base of the mountain, featuring a lake and recreational facilities for dozens of sports and other outdoor activities such as waterslides, golf, and tennis along with laser shows and a riverboat. Also within the park is Magnolia Hall, an authentic antebellum plantation house moved from another Georgia location and restored to its former elegance. Some 20 miles north of Atlanta is

Kennesaw Mountain National Battlefield Park, which also combines history and recreation. The site of several major Civil War battles, the Kennesaw Mountain area now boasts a museum and some fortifications along with hiking trails and picnic grounds.

For those seeking pure entertainment, Six Flags Over Georgia is located about 12 miles west of the city. The 331-acre family-oriented theme park features more than 100 rides, musical shows, and other attractions. During the summer months, thousands of visitors make it one of the busiest parks in the area. Six Flags White Water offers a variety of water-related activities such as giant slides, raft rides, and body flumes.

For nature-lovers, the Fernbank Science Center has trails, natural history exhibits, and one of the largest planetariums in the nation. The Fernbank Museum of Natural History offers 160,000 square feet of space providing dinosaur and wildlife exhibits and an IMAX theater. The Atlanta Botanical Garden, located as part of Piedmont Park, is also a favorite stop for those wishing to enjoy its vegetable, herb, rose, and oriental plantings. The Botanical Garden also includes a children's garden and a conservatory with rare and endangered plants from rainforests and deserts. The Atlanta Preservation Center offers a number of walking tours through Atlanta neighborhoods.

Arts and Culture

Atlanta has a vital theater, dance, and music community that profits from the area's fine facilities and the generous patronage of its businesses and interested citizens. Integral to Atlanta's cultural life is the Woodruff Arts Center, consisting of the Alliance Theatre, the Atlanta Symphony Orchestra, the High Museum of Art, and Young Audiences of Atlanta. In 2005 the High Museum completed a major expansion project that doubled the size of the existing museum with the inclusion of three new buildings in the Woodruff Arts Center Campus. The permanent collection of the High Museum included more than 13,000 works of art as of 2013, and the museum enjoys an ongoing relationship with the Louvre Museum of Paris. Additional entertainment is provided by numerous other professional and amateur groups based in Atlanta, including Atlanta Ballet (the oldest regional ballet company in the United States, originating in 1929), the Atlanta Shakespeare Company, and the Georgia Ensemble Theatre. Since 1978, The Center of Puppetry Arts, with a collection of more than 4,500 items, is said to be the only facility in the country devoted solely to puppetry and features three performance series, workshops, and a museum.

The Cobb Energy Performing Arts Centre in northwest Atlanta opened in September 2007. The 2,750-seat theater hosts Broadway shows, ballets, concerts, educational shows, opera, corporate meetings and events. The facility also includes a 10,000-square-foot ballroom and 1,000 parking spaces. Another major center is the Callanwolde Fine Arts Center, located in a 1920s-era Gothic-Tudor-style mansion. The center accommodates 4,000 students annually with various arts classes, and offers a range of concerts, recitals, and exhibits. Local colleges and universities also sponsor a wide variety of performing arts programs in theater, dance, and music.

Atlanta's museums and galleries cater to many different interests. State and local history are on view at the Atlanta History Center, whose main attractions are the Swan House, a former private residence that typifies the milieu of a wealthy Atlanta family during the 1930s; Tullie Smith House, a restored 1835 farm house that illustrates how early Georgia farmers lived and worked; the Margaret Mitchell House, the home of the Pulitzer Prize–winning author of *Gone With the Wind*; and several gardens. The Atlanta History Center also house exhibitions commemorating the 1996 Centennial Olympic Games and golf great Bobby Jones.

Other museums in the city include the Wren's Nest, a Victorian mansion that was named a National Historic Landmark in 1962 and was home to Joel Chandler Harris, creator of the Uncle Remus stories, and now displays original furnishings, books, and memorabilia; the Governor's Mansion, a modern structure built in Greek Revival style and housing nineteenth-century furnishings; the Fernbank Museum of Natural History, whose exhibits include A Walk Through Time in Georgia; and the William Breman Jewish Heritage Museum, a 50,000-square-foot facility that opened in 1996 and has exhibits dating to 1733, when Jews first settled in Georgia, along with a Holocaust gallery. Self-guided tours of several downtown art galleries are generally offered the first Thursday of every month throughout the year.

The Center For Civil and Human Rights was under construction during 2013, with an antcipated opening in spring 2014. The College Football Hall of Fame was also expected to open in 2014, with more than 94,000 square feet of exhibits and located adjacent to the Georgia World Congress Center and Centennial Olympic Park. The new College Football Hall of Fame was to replace an existing facility in Indiana.

Festivals and Holidays

Two of Atlanta's biggest celebrations are the Dogwood Festival, held every spring for more than 75 years, and the Arts Festival, a staple on the fall calendar. The Dogwood Festival coincides with the blooming of dogwood trees in the area in April; events include a parade, tours, garden competitions, arts and crafts displays, canine competition, and musical performances. From April through September, Centennial Olympic Park hosts a series of Wednesday night concerts known as Wednesday Wind Down. A variety of music includes jazz and reggae. Held in downtown Atlanta, the Arts Festival is a week-long affair that attracts nearly more than 200 local and national artists across twelve artistic mediums. The spring includes two long running festivals, the Atlanta Jazz Festival and the Decatur Arts Festival.

Among Atlanta's other annual events include the Atlanta Summer Beer Fest and Virginia Highland Summerfest. The Peachtree Road Race, a 10-K run held annually since 1970 during the July 4th holiday, is the nation's second largest 10-K race, with more than 60,000 registered runners and more than 150,000 spectators. The National Black Arts Festival, held in late June and early July at the Woodruff Arts Center focusing on dance, music, and art; the Stone Mountain Highland Games and Scottish Festival, an October celebration since 1973 that brings international travelers to the region; and December's Chick-fil-A Bowl, which featues college football opponents from the Southeastern Conference and Atlantic Coast Conference.

Sports for the Spectator

Fans of sports of all kinds can usually find their favorite form of action somewhere in Atlanta, the sports capital of the South. The city is home to many professional franchises: the Falcons, a National Football League team; baseball's National League team, the Braves of Major League Baseball; the Hawks, a National Basketball Association team; and the Dream, a Women's National Basketball Association team. Both the Falcons and Braves were scheduled to move from their respective homes, the Georgia Dome and Turner Field, in 2017 following major metropolitan development proejcts. The Hawks face their rivals at the $219 million Philips Arena, which opened in September 1999. The final PGA Tour event in the golfing season features the nearby East Lake Golf Club. The Atlanta Thrashers, a National Hockey League team, left Atlanta for Winnipeg, Canada, following the 2011 season.

Since 1934 Atlanta has been home to the nation's largest recreational tennis league, Atlanta Lawn and Tennis Association (ALTA), with more than 81,000 members. Stone Mountain Tennis Center, which seats about 2,000 people around two center courts and has an 8,000-seat stadium, played host to the 1996 Centennial Olympic Tennis. The city also hosts many collegiate competitions in these same sports, among them the annual NCAA Division I football Chick-fil-A Bowl (formerly the Peach Bowl), and NCAA basketball tournament contests, including the Final Four in 2013.

Auto racing buffs have two tracks to choose from just outside the metropolitan area. Atlanta Motor Speedway, about 25 miles south of the city, features NASCAR and other events. Forty-five miles north of the city is Road Atlanta, site of road-course racing events—including Grand Prix Atlanata—that draw top international drivers and thousands of spectators. The Atlanta Steeplechase is the area's major horse show, held at Kingston Downs.

The Atlanta Silverbacks are the city's men's professional soccer team and are part of the North American Soccer League. The Atlanta Silverbacks Women were founded in 2007 and play in the United Soccer Leagues W-League. The Association of Volleyball Professionals hosts events in Atlanta.

Sports for the Participant

Atlanta's physical setting and mild climate combine to make the city and its environs ideal for outdoor activities of all types. Running is an especially popular local sport; the Atlanta Track Club is one of the largest in the country and it sponsors a number of annual events, including the Peachtree Road Race 10-K and the Atlanta Women's 5-K. Golfers may choose from more 100 courses and a host of new luxury golf communities growing up outside the city, while tennis players can visit any one of more than 200 courts.

Water sports enthusiasts can take advantage of the facilities along the Chattahoochee River to go canoeing, rafting, fishing, and camping. Within an hour's drive of the city are Lake Lanier and Lake Allatoona, both man-made lakes surrounded by recreation areas that encompass beaches, golf courses, horseback riding trails, and other amenities. Hiking trails at nearby Stone Mountain Park features a 1.2-mile path that leads to the top of the granite mass and a 5-mile trail around the base. Snow Mountain, opened in November 2007, features a wintertime snow park for tubing.

The Peachtree Center Athletic Club brings a number of activities to the downtown area such as aquatics, racquetball, pilates, squash, and group fitness. Path trails throughout the city offer special pathways for pedestrian, cyclists, and rollerbladers throughout the city. Other sports complexes include the Tom Lowe Shooting Grounds (formerly Wolf Creek Shooting Complex), the Stone Mountain Tennis Complex, and the Arena at Gwinnett Center. There are 13 outdoor public pools for summer swims and four natatoriums.

Shopping and Dining

Atlanta's modern shopping facilities draw consumers to the city from throughout the entire region. More than a dozen malls and outlet centers ring the metropolitan area. Lenox Square, in the Buckhead neighborhood, and nearby Phipps Plaza, offer exclusive shops such as Neiman Marcus, Macy's, and Bloomingdale's along with antique stores. Downtown, the Mall at Peachtree Center offers shopping in the heart of the city, while other shopping opportunities await at Underground Atlanta. Opened since 1999 just north of Atlanta is the Mall of Georgia, anchored by JCPenney's, Dillard's, Macy's, Nordstrom, and Belk, and supplemented by more than 225 additional stores; its restaurants offer cuisines ranging from traditional Southern food to upscale and ethnic delicacies. The mall's decor incorporates the five regions of Georgia and their histories. Ten miles south of the city is the State Farmer's Market, a gigantic retail and wholesale center where visitors have the opportunity to buy fresh fruit, vegetables, eggs, meats, plants, shrubs, and flowers. Throughout the downtown area there are many mixed-use developments offering shopping and dining opportunities, including Atlantic Station, which has more than 50 unique retailers and more than 20 restaurants.

Atlanta diners have hundreds of restaurants to choose from, and traditional Southern cooking (catfish, hushpuppies, ham and redeye gravy, barbecue, fried chicken, and Brunswick stew) and soul food are widely available. Atlanta's growth as a center of international business has made haute cuisine and ethnic specialties extremely popular alternatives to traditional southern fare. The legendary fast-food restaurant, The Varsity, has been serving Atlanta customers since 1928 in its two-story building downtown; it had eight sister locations as of 2013.

Visitor Information: Atlanta Convention and Visitors Bureau; 233 Peachtree Street, NE; Suite 1400; Atlanta, GA 30303; telephone (404) 521-6600.

■ Convention Facilities

Easy access to the city, a good public transportation system, an abundance of hotel rooms, and a mild climate have combined to make Atlanta one of the leading convention centers in the United States, by most accounts ranking just behind Chicago and Orlando. Atlanta's major convention facilities are the Georgia World Congress Center, which contains 1.4 million square feet of exhibit space, including the 1,740-seat Sidney Marcus Auditorium and the 33,000-square-foot Thomas B. Murphy Ballroom, as well as 103 meeting rooms; and Philips Arena, which offers an 18,000-seat and 17,000-square-foot facility for meetings, athletic events, and concerts. The Georgia Dome, the home of the Atlanta Falcons through 2016, was scheduled to be domlished after the completion of a new, retractable-roof facility slated to open in 2017 adjacent to the Georgia Dome. These facilities are linked by the Georgia International Plaza, a gathering place featuring fountains and outdoor sculpture. The Georgia International Convention Center near the airport has 400,000 square feet of flexible meeting space. Three buildings connected by elevated walkways comprise AmericasMart, a permanent wholesale market which provides space for exhibiters and trade shows. The Boisfeuillet Jones Atlanta Civic Center provides a 5,800 square-foot ballroom and a 4,600-seat theater. Cobb Galleria Centre offers 144,000 square feet of exhibit space and in an 88-acre complex. Gwinnett Center offers 80 acres of southern views about 30 minutes north of downtown Atlanta. The center offers a 13,000-seat arena, 50,000 square-foot exhibit hall, 23 meeting rooms, and a 21,600 square-foot ballroom.

Atlanta also boasts dozens of smaller, more intimate meeting facilities, some of them in unusual settings. Among them are the Woodruff Arts Center, High Museum of Art, Fox Theatre (a renovated "movie palace" built in 1929), Academy of Medicine, Martin Luther King Jr. Center for Non-Violent Social Change, Callanwolde Fien Arts Center (formerly a private residence), and Houston Mill House (a country estate). Other facilities are available at many of the city's hotels.

Convention Information:

Atlanta Convention and Visitors Bureau; 233 Peachtree Street, NE; Suite 1400; Atlanta, GA 30303; telephone (404) 521-6600. Georgia Department of Economic Development, 75 Fifth Street, NW, Suite 1200, Atlanta, GA 30308; telephone (404) 962-4000.

■ Transportation

Approaching the City

Often referred to as Atlanta's number-one economic asset, Hartsfield-Jackson Atlanta International Airport has been distinguished as "the world's busiest passenger airport," serving more than 95 million passengers annually. The huge, ultramodern facility is only 10 miles from downtown and is served by more than 17 mainline carriers that fly non-stop or one-stop to more than 200 national and international destinations. The airport's six terminals are connected by an automated underground train system. In 2012 a new $1.4 million international terminal opened, allowing passengers to access the landside without having to use an automated people mover. There are 20 general airports in the area serving private and corporate aircraft.

Three major interstates—75 (Northwest Express), 85 (Northeast Express), and 20—route traffic into and out of Atlanta, making it one of the leading interstate highways centers in the nation. Interstate 285, known as the Perimeter or Atlanta Bypass, forms a loop around the city.

Amtrak provides passenger rail service to Atlanta; travelers can go west to New Orleans (via Birmingham, Alabama) or east to Washington, D.C. (via Charlotte, North Carolina). Greyhound has buses into and out of the city each day at the Amtrak station.

Traveling in the City

Cars are the mode of choice for most Atlantans, making it one of the most congested cities in the United States, with some of the longest commute times. The city is encircled by Interstate 285. Atlanta can present a challenge to drivers for several reasons. For instance, the city is not laid out in a grid pattern, so there are few rectangular blocks or square intersections. Five main streets converge downtown in an area known as Five Points; these streets divide the city roughly into geographic quadrants (northeast, northwest, southeast, and southwest). Further complicating matters is the fact that more than 30 avenues, lanes, drives, and other thoroughfares in Atlanta contain the word "Peachtree," but only Peachtree *Street* is truly a main road.

Public transportation in Atlanta is operated by the train- and bus-based Metropolitan Atlanta Rapid Transit Authority, or MARTA, which offers 200 bus routes with 44 stations. Bus and rail cars are handicapped accessible. In addition, 48 miles of rail track make up the four subway system lines. Atlanta's subway system, operated by MARTA, is one of the busiest subway systems in the country. As of 2012, the average total daily ridership for the system (both bus and rail) was about 430,000 passengers, with total usage that year amounting to nearly 135 million unlinked passenger trips..

■ Communications

Newspapers and Magazines

Cox Enterprises publishes more than a dozen daily newspapers in the United States, including the major daily, the *Atlanta Journal-Constitution*. The *Atlanta Journal-Constitution* reached more than 230,000 readers each weekday and more than 650,000 on Sunday as of 2013. The *Atlanta Voice* and *Atlanta Daily World* serve Atlanta's African American community. There are many other weeklies, including *Atlanta Business Chronicle* and *Mundo Hispanico,* a Hispanic-oriented paper published since 1979. Many other daily, weekly, and biweekly newspapers are circulated throughout the metropolitan area, most of them focusing on county and community news, consumer affairs, and business topics. *Atlanta Magazine* and *Atlanta Homes & Lifestyles* cover life in the city. Many other monthly magazines based in Atlanta target at specific business, medical, educational, and hobbyist markets. Regional bureaus of national and international broadcast and print news sources operate offices in the city, including the Associated Press and *The Wall Street Journal.*

Television and Radio

According to Nielsen Media Research, Atlanta was the ninth largest market in television broadcasting in 2013 and, according to Arbitron that same year, ninth in radio broadcasting as well. Metropolitan Atlanta had more than 2.3 million television households, and the third largest cable television service provider in the United States, Cox Communications of Cox Enterprises, makes Atlanta home. There were 20 licensed television stations broadcasting from the Atlanta area in 2013, including major network affiliates, public, and independent stations. Cable service is also available, with CNN, TNT, Headline News, The Weather Channel, and The Cartoon Network all based in Atlanta. In the 1970s, Atlanta became a national media force when entrepreneur Ted Turner launched his independent "superstation," WTBS-TV Superstation and the Cable News Network (CNN), viewed by cable television subscribers across the United States. Turner Broadcasting System merged with Time Warner in the 1990s to create one of the largest media

empires in the world. As for radio, 12 AM and 15 FM licensed stations broadcast from Atlanta, offering news, public service programming, and a variety of musical formats to metropolitan listeners. Four colleges operate radio stations, as well as the local public school district. WSB AM, the flagship station of Cox Radio, was the first broadcast station in the South. The nationally syndicated Neal Boortz and Clark Howard shows are broadcast from WSB AM. Atlanta is also where Sean Hannity and Ryan Seacrest got their start in radio.

Media Information: *The Atlanta Journal-Constitution,* 223 Perimeter Center Pkwy, Atlanta, GA 30346; telephone (800) 933-9771. *Atlanta Magazine,* 260 Peachtree St., Ste. 300, Atlanta, GA 30303; telephone (404) 527-5500; fax (404) 527-5575.

Atlanta Online

Atlanta Convention and Visitors Bureau. Available www.atlanta.net

Atlanta Daily World. Available www.AtlantaDailyWorld.com

Atlanta Development Authority. Available www.investatlanta.com

Atlanta-Fulton County Library System. Available www.afplweb.com

Atlanta History Center. Available www.atlantahistorycenter.org

Atlanta Journal-Constitution. Available www.ajc.com

The Atlanta Nation (daily internet newspaper). Available www.atlantanation.com

Atlanta Public Schools. Available www.atlanta.k12.ga.us

City of Atlanta home page. Available www.atlantaga.gov

Central Atlanta Progress. Available www.atlantadowntown.com

Fulton County home page. Available www.co.fulton.ga.us

Georgia Department of Economic Development. Available www.georgia.org

Metro Atlanta Chamber of Commerce. Available www.metroatlantachamber.com

BIBLIOGRAPHY

Kyi, Tonya Llody, *Atlanta* (New York: Midpoint Trade Books, 2012)

Link, William A., *Atlanta, Cradle of the New South: Race and Remembering in the Civil War's Aftermath.* (Chapel Hill: University of North Carolina Press, 2013)

Mitchell, Margaret, *Gone with the Wind.* (New York: Macmillan, 1936)

Van Wieren, Pete, *Of Mikes and Men: A Lifetime of Braves Baseball* (Chicago: Triumph Books, 2010)

Willard, Fred, *Down on Ponce: A Novel* (Atlanta, GA: Longstreet Press, 1997)

Marietta

■ The City in Brief

Founded: 1834 (incorporated 1852)

Head Official: Mayor Steve Tumlin (R) (since 2010; term expires 2018)

City Population
- 1990: 44,129
- 2000: 58,748
- 2010: 56,579
- 2012 estimate: 57,564
- Percent change, 2000–2010: −3.7%
- U.S. rank in 1990: 582nd (State rank: 13th)
- U.S. rank in 2000: 557th (State rank: 13th)
- U.S. rank in 2010: 613th (State rank: 13th)

Metropolitan Statistical Area Population
- 2000: 4,112,198
- 2010: 5,268,860
- 2012 estimate: 5,442,113
- Percent change, 2000–2010: 28.1%
- U.S. rank in 2000: 11th
- U.S. rank in 2010: 9th

Area: 21.95 square miles

Elevation: 1,128 feet above sea level

Average Annual Temperatures: 61.2° F

Average Annual Precipitation: 48.61 inches

Major Economic Sectors: wholesale and retail trade, aircraft, food and beverage products, services, education, government

Unemployment Rate: 7.6% (2012)

Per Capita Income: $24,770

2012 FBI Crime Index Property: 2,548

Major Colleges and Universities: Southern Polytechnic State University, Chattahoochee Technical College

Daily Newspaper: *Marietta Daily Journal; Atlanta Journal-Constitution*

■ Introduction

Marietta, located in Cobb County approximately 20 miles from Atlanta, is part of the vast exurban community northwest of the city. Cobb County likes to market the area's recreational attractions by referring to itself as "the very best of Atlanta." While the city is not bereft of beautiful historic landmarks, Mariettans spend hundreds of thousands of dollars sowing seeds and planting trees and shrubs to promote beautification throughout the city. The town square, bleached-white gazebos, and antebellum mansions give Marietta the misty feeling of the Old South. Nonetheless, southern charm intersects business, as investment in infrastructure and demolition of old, unused buildings has brought jobs and development to the area since the 1970s. Cobb County invested more in infrastructure—including water, sewer, road, and other utilities—between 1970 and 1990 than any other county in Georgia, and during that period more houses were built in the county than anywhere else in the state. The influx of new residents even resulted in the popular use of the new pronunciation of the city's name, MARRY-etta, rather than the traditional May-RETT-a. Plans for the Atlanta Braves to build a new stadium in Cobb County for 2017 were to reconfigure slightly the geography of Atlanta, tieing Marietta and other northwest suburbs more closely to the city center.

■ Geography and Climate

Marietta is located about 15 miles northwest of Atlanta, along the Chattahoochee River. The city is bordered by

Photo by Johnny Walker. Courtesy of the City of Marietta.

Lake Allatoona to the northwest, while its southern boundary lies south of Interstate 20. The North Georgia Mountains are to the north. Marietta is the seat of Cobb County, which is also made up of the cities of Acworth, Austell, Kennesaw, Powder Springs, and Smyrna. About 78 percent of Cobb County's population lives in unincorporated areas. Citizens enjoy four seasons featuring a mild climate where winters seldom go below the 30s, and summer highs can reach into the 90s.

Area: 21.95 square miles

Elevation: 1,128 feet above sea level

Average Temperatures: 61.2° F

Average Annual Precipitation: 48.61 inches

■ History

Europeans Take Over Indian Lands

For many years, Cobb County was the home of the Creek tribe, descendants of the Mississippian tribes that inhabited the northwest section of Georgia from approximately 800 A.D. The Creeks were driven south of the Chattahoochee River by the Cherokees in the early

1800s. Cobb County was still part of the Cherokee Indian Territory when Marietta's earliest European settlers came. They began to arrive in the early 1830s from other parts of Georgia, when they won land lotteries used to allocate the Indian lands. Other early migrants, most of English and Scotch-Irish descent, traveled south to Georgia through the Mid-Atlantic States. The Cherokee land had been divided into 40-acre gold and 160-acre farm tracts with most of Cobb County originally settled by gold-seekers and people looking for good farmland. Despite several treaties to protect the rights of the Cherokees, in 1835 these Native Americans were forced to move west, and the whites moved in for good. Although some of the Native Americans left voluntarily, more than 17,000 were relocated by the federal government to Oklahoma by way of the infamous Trail of Tears. Traces of its Native American heritage remain in Cobb County in place names such as Sweetwater, Allatoona, and Kennesaw. Some of the Indian trails were widened to accommodate wagons, which in time brought in more settlers and launched trade in the county.

Early History of Marietta

By 1833, nearly 100 people had settled in the area of Marietta, chosen as a town site in part because of the springs located near the present town square. The county

224

was named in honor of Judge Thomas Willis Cobb, who was a Georgia Congressman, U.S. Senator, and later a judge of the Ocmulgee Circuit of the Superior Court. The city of Marietta was named for his wife. Marietta's first courthouse, a single room log cabin, was built in 1834. By the mid 1830s, several river ferries began operating to transport people, wagons, and livestock across the Chattahoochee. Marietta was also selected as a home base for Colonel Stephen Long of the U.S. Army Corps of Engineers, who was chosen to head the Western & Atlantic Railroad project.

In the mid-1840s, Marietta had more than 1,500 residents. By the next decade, it was a popular resort town for people from "the low country," who were attracted in part by the mild climate and the alleged therapeutic powers of local spring water. The state-owned Western & Atlantic Railroad began runs in 1845 and was completed in May 1850, providing access to a ready market for farmers and manufacturers and reducing the costs of conveying merchandise. Cities and towns sprang up along major rail lines running through Cobb County. In 1852 Marietta's formal incorporation took place. From 1850 to 1861, Marietta was considered a carefree town and was once described as "the fastest town in Georgia." During this period, businesses included tailor shops, warehouses, grocery stores, general stores, carriage and wagon shops, a tin and gunsmith shop, a bakery, professional services, and other small businesses.

Civil War Brings Destruction

On April 11, 1862, the first disruptive effects of the Civil War were felt by the city's people when a group of 22 undercover Union agents arrived. After staying overnight at Kennesaw House, a former hotel, which still stands west of the town square, the agents boarded the W & A Railroad northbound train at the Marietta Station. At Big Shanty (now Kennesaw), the Union spies took control of the train. They were later caught by "Andrew's Raiders" after a now-famous locomotive chase with the backward pursuing "The Texas" overtaking "The General" near Ringgold, Georgia. The hard times of the War Between the States culminated with the Union occupation of the city on July 3, 1864, following battles around Kennesaw Mountain. During that time, the courthouse and all county records were destroyed when General Sherman's troops burned every public building on Marietta's town square.

Prosperity Slowly Returns in Post-War Period

After the Civil War, recovery was slow for Marietta as for the rest of the South. Over time, however, the city began to prosper as new businesses moved in, and an 1860s account reveals that the city once again was beginning to attract visitors. In the 1870s, a new jail and courthouse were built, and summer tourists were honored at a reception in the city square. County finances gradually

were improving, but the blackened ruin of the county courthouse remained as a reminder of the "War of Northern Aggression," as it was termed in the South, until the construction of a new building began in 1872. Industrialization came to the Marietta area in the late nineteenth century, gradually overtaking agriculture as the major factor in the county's economy over the next half century. The Marietta Bank (now called First National Bank of Cobb County) opened in 1888, and a paper mill, two chair and two marble companies, a textile mill, and a machine works sparked the economic recovery. By 1899, street lights illuminated the town, a local telephone company was operating, and there was a railroad depot in downtown Marietta. Still, the rural parts of Cobb County endured low cotton prices for years. In 1900 as many as 56 percent of the county's farmers paid rent as tenants with typical fees amounting to a fourth of their cotton crop along with a third of their corn. By 1905 an electric railway operated between Marietta and Atlanta, spawning residential development as Cobb County residents commuted to jobs in Atlanta.

Schools were established early in Marietta, and the city set up its independent school system in 1892. In 1919 the city organized the first Parent-Teacher Association (PTA) in the county. (In fact, The National PTA was founded in Washington, D.C. by Alice McLellan Birney (1858-1907), a former Marietta resident.)

Early construction of highways was concentrated in Marietta from 1917 to 1921, and the county began a federally-subsidized road program at that same time. Old Highway 41 was paved in 1926, allowing ready access between Marietta and Atlanta and encouraging trade.

Aircraft Industry Aids Recovery

Cobb County's economy remained dependent on agriculture until 1940 when manufactured goods produced amounted to twice the value of agricultural products. Hard times took over during the Great Depression of the 1930s, and World War II played a part in the recovery. In 1941, Rickenbacker Field (now Dobbins Air Force Base) was built south of Marietta along with the adjoining 200-acre Bell Aircraft Plant. During World War II, B-29s were produced at the plant and employment reached 28,000 people. With the local population able to supply only a small part of the work force for the large plant, newcomers poured in, necessitating the construction of new housing projects. About that time a 45-acre complex was built and named Larry Bell Park, in honor of the President of Bell Aircraft Corporation. The plant closed in 1946, but reopened in 1951 as the Lockheed-Georgia Company. Some of the aircraft produced there include B-47s, C-130s, C-141s, C-5As, C-5Bs, and the Jetstar. Employment at the plant of the Bell Aircraft Corporation, Georgia's largest employer at that time, reached more than 31,000 people by the 1960s.

Businesses and the real estate industry burgeoned when thousands of people moved to Cobb County and the Greater Atlanta area. Construction of Interstate 75 through the county in the 1950s increased the impact of tourism and brought outside investments for industry and housing. During the following years major developments included the opening of the first major office parks in the 1960s, the opening of Cumberland Mall in 1973, the opening of the first major hotels and shopping malls and the establishment of the Cobb Convention and Visitors Bureau in the 1980s, and the construction of the $47 million Galleria Convention Centre in 1992.

Entering the twenty-first century as an "All-America City," Marietta has tried to continue the tradition of maintaining historic value while maintaining economic value. While the end of the 2000s proved to be a difficult economic time for the metropolitan area and the nation, Marietta's retained some stability from the presence of its air force base and major defense contractor Lockheed Martin. Successful passage of a $68 million bond in 2013 to demolish unused buildings signaled optimism among residents that economic hardships of the past were behind them, with new business developments ahead.

Historical Information: Cobb County Public Library System, Central Library, 266 Roswell St., Marietta, GA 30060; telephone (770) 528-2320. City of Marietta, 205 Lawrence St., Marietta, GA 30060; telephone (770) 794-5502. Marietta Museum of History, 1 Depot Street, Suite 200, Marietta, GA 30060; telephone (770) 794-5710.

■ Population Profile

Metropolitan Statistical Area Population

2000: 4,112,198
2010: 5,268,860
2012 estimate: 5,442,113
Percent change, 2000–2010: 28.1%
U.S. rank in 2000: 11th
U.S. rank in 2010: 9th

City Residents

1990: 44,129
2000: 58,748
2010: 56,579
2012 estimate: 57,564
Percent change, 2000–2010: −3.7%
U.S. rank in 1990: 582nd (State rank: 13th)
U.S. rank in 2000: 557th (State rank: 13th)
U.S. rank in 2010: 613th (State rank: 13th)

Density: 2,173.0 people per square mile

Racial and ethnic characteristics

White: 32,035
Black or African American: 18,091

American Indian and Alaskan Native: 96
Asian: 1,664
Native Hawaiian and Other Pacific Islander: 0
Hispanic or Latino (may be of any race): 12,240
Other: 5,678

Percent of residents born in state: 38.3%

Age characteristics

Population under 5 years old: 4,675
Population 5 to 9 years old: 3,172
Population 10 to 14 years old: 3,534
Population 15 to 19 years old: 3,158
Population 20 to 24 years old: 4,874
Population 25 to 34 years old: 10,253
Population 35 to 44 years old: 9,202
Population 45 to 54 years old: 7,737
Population 55 to 59 years old: 2,944
Population 60 to 64 years old: 2,270
Population 65 to 74 years old: 3,033
Population 75 to 84 years old: 1,959
Population 85 years and over: 753
Median age: 34.3

Births (2010–11 Metropolitan Area)

Total number: 74,174

Deaths (2010–11 Metropolitan Area)

Total number: 31,266

Money income (2012)

Per capita income: $24,770
Median household income: $42,135
Total households: 23,034

Number of households with income of . . .

less than $10,000: 2,349
$10,000 to $14,999: 1,307
$15,000 to $24,999: 2,628
$25,000 to $34,999: 3,474
$35,000 to $49,999: 3,379
$50,000 to $74,999: 3,569
$75,000 to $99,999: 2,347
$100,000 to $149,999: 2,476
$150,000 to $199,999: 769
$200,000 or more: 736

Percent of families below poverty level: 20.7%

FBI Crime Index Property: 2,548

FBI Crime Index Violent: 474

■ Municipal Government

Marietta is organized of under a form of government that includes a mayor, council, and city manager. The city is governed by a mayor elected at-large and a seven-member city council (one from each ward) whose members serve four-year terms, for an unlimited number of terms. Day-to-day administration is handled by the city manager, the city's chief executive officer, who is appointed by the city council. The council-manager relationship is compared to that of a board of directors and CEO in a private company.

Head Official: Mayor Steve Tumlin (R) (since 2010; term expires 2018)

Total Number of City Employees: 796 (2014)

City Information: City of Marietta, 205 Lawrence St., Marietta, GA 30060; telephone (770) 794-5526.

■ Economy

Major Industries and Commercial Activity

Dobbins Air Reserve Base on the south side of town and a Lockheed Martin manufacturing plant are among the major industries in the city. The company's Marietta location is home to the C-130 Hercules transport and the F-22 Raptor air dominance fighter. The Marietta site is also responsible for the avionics and engine modernization programs for the C-5 Galaxy strategic transport, as well as P-3 Orion program operations, including the new wing production line. The plant also handles center-wing assembly for the F-34 Lightning II. Marietta offers strong advantages in terms of low costs for building and leasing, as well as a moderate cost of living. Other major industries in Marietta, as of 2013, included Atlanta Beverage, Coca-Cola Bottling, Southern Ice Cream, Tip Top Poultry, and Wellstar Health Systems. Educational institutions such as Chattahoochee Technical Collge, Southern Polytechnic State University, and Marietta City Schools.

Marietta is part of Cobb County, and, further, part of the greater Atlanta metro area. As a result, economic activities of the metro area have a great influence on the city. Cobb County itself has a diverse business base that encompasses manufacturing and distribution, administrative headquarters operations, service industries, and retailers. The booming service economy and the large migration of Northern companies into the South have formed a new class of entrepreneurs. Marietta and Cobb County compete with cities such as Nashville, Birmingham, Charlotte, Dallas, and Fairfax, Virginia, for the attention of relocating businesses. Cobb County has the advantages of relatively low property taxes, as well as the diversity and availability of site and buildings. Cobb County is a vital center for commerce, with increasingly more office, retail, and industrial space available.

Items and goods produced: aerospace equipment, aircraft parts, medical devices, food and beverage products, zippers, chemicals telecommunications equipment

Incentive Programs-New and Existing Companies

Local programs: The Cobb Chamber of Commerce works to maintain a healthy economy by bringing business and industry to the area and helping established firms grow. Through six Area Councils in the Cumberland, East Cobb, Marietta, North Cobb, Smyrna, and South Cobb areas, the Cobb Chamber unifies and advocates for Cobb's business community. Each council is represented on the Cobb Chamber Board of Directors and promotes grassroots actions. The Cobb Chamber handles administration for the Development Authority of Cobb County and the Cumberland Community Improvement District, which supports the Cumberland Transportation Network. The City of Marietta also works in cooperation with the Development Authority of Marietta and the Downtown Marietta Development Authority to offer business development incentives.

Census tract 303 in Marietta was designated a Military Zone by the state of Georgia in 2011, making businesses in the area eligible for up a $3,500 employee tax credit for two full-time employees during the first five years of employment. Marietta also provides tax incentives for developments in its GreenTech Corridor, as well as discounted discounted utility rates for refurbishing of unused buildings.

Financial loan assistance comes to eligible businesses from the Marietta Growth Fund, which supports small-business lending. The loan program seeks businessest that will create jobs for low- and moderate-income residents. The city government partners with the local chamber, as well as county and state officials, to support expansion of existing businesses.

State programs: Georgia has business-friendly tax laws; the state does not use the unitary tax method, but instead taxes businesses only on income apportioned to Georgia. A Job Tax Credit offers employers that create jobs in Georgia up to $4,000 in income-tax deductions per job. Georgia's Opportunity Zones, defined as redevelopment or revitalization targets, provide Job Tax Credits for the creation of as few as two jobs. Less developed census tracts also provide Job Tax Credits, as do military zones. Tax credits also hinge on the average wage of job created and the size of the project—designated "Mega Project Tax Credits" allow large employers who create at least 1,800 jobs to claim a tax credit of $5,250 for as many as 4,500 employees. One-stop permitting, enterprise zones, and foreign trade zones also support economic development in Georgia. Georgia's fourth-lowest unionization rate nationally and status as a right-to-work state also draws employers.

Job training programs: The Georgia Department of Technical and Adult Education administers the Georgia Quick Start program, offering job-specific training programs through a large network of college, university, and satellite campus sites within the state. By developing and implementing high quality customized training programs and materials, Quick Start assists the company in obtaining a trained work force ready to begin as soon as the company opens for business. The HOPE Scholarship program funds Georgia students' college tuition if they meet academic targets during high school. Chattahoochee Technical College is the state's largest technical college and provides job training for certain industries, including eco-friendly industrial activities.

Development Projects

While early 2000s development within the city focused on renovation or new construction of commercial and housing units to replace vacant lots with more attractive sites for businesses and residents, this type of development waned in the late 2000s due to a nationwide recession. Some of these projects resumed in the early 2010s. As of 2013, The Marietta Redevelopment Corporation, had undertaken development projects to create roughly 860 housing units, add 193,000 square feet of office and retail space, and 13 acres of greenspace.

In private development, office space at the Atlanta Northern Traction Company building, a roughly 40,000-square-foot facility, had finalized site selection near the downtown area by 2013. A mixed-use subdivision known as Magnet at Historic Marietta began construction in 2013 and was to includea four-phase development of craftsman-inspired single-family homes. Marietta Walk was a planned development for 58 townhomes and 18 single-family homes, with a second phase of development to potentially include an additional 45 condominiums and 50,000 square feet of office and retail space. Projects completed by 2013 included Marietta Mills Lofts, Village at Frasier Park, and Emerson Hill Townhomes.

Marietta voters approved a $68 million bond for redevelopment of the Franklin Road corridor in 2013. Most money was slated to demolish decrepit buildings, which in turn was expected to spur private business investment.

The Atlanta Braves agreed to move from their Fulton County home at Turner Field to a new stadium in Cobb County—but not in Marietta—beginning in 2017. The expansive development associated with the stadium, pegged at more than $600 million, brought Marietta closer to one of Atlanta's major attractions. Cobb County residents were expected to fund several hundred million dollars of stadium development through a reallocation and increase in local taxes.

Economic Development Information: Cobb Chamber of Commerce, 240 Interstate N Pkwy SE, Atlanta, GA 30339; telephone (770) 980-2000. City of Marietta, 205 Lawrence St., Marietta, GA 30060; telephone (770) 794-5502.

Commercial Shipping

CSX offers rail service through Marietta (to Chattanooga). For motor freight, Marietta and Cobb County are part of the Atlanta Commercial Zone, with 11 interstate and 50 inter/intrastate terminals, and 23 local terminals. General aviation aircraft are served by McCollum Field, a county airport that can handle operations of small jets and other craft weighing less than 33,000 pounds. The airport has a 4,600-foot bituminous runway and offers aircraft tiedown, airframe and power plant repair, a hangar, and lighted runway. The Hartsfield-Jackson Atlanta International Airport, the busiest in the world, is conveniently nearby. Hartsfield-Jackson Atlanta International Airport is the main focus of activity, with three main air cargo complexes, a perishables complex, and a USDA inspection station serving 19 cargo airlines as of 2012. Warehouse space for cargo totals 1.3 million square feet and supports parking for 28 aircraft. A Foreign Trade Zone located near the airport at the Atlanta Tradeport provides companies with an opportunity to delay, reduce, or eliminate customs duty on imported items, while the U.S. Customs Service Model Inland Port is a highly computerized center designed to expedite quick clearance for international.

Labor Force and Employment Outlook

Low unemployment levels and some of the lowest property tax levels in metro Atlanta continue to assist Marietta and Cobb County in their attractiveness to businesses and residents. Service producing industries have typically offered the largest number of employment opportunities. As of 2013, Cobb County was the second most educated county in the state and fifteenth in the nation, with more than half the workforce holding at last a bachelor's degree.

The following is a summary of data regarding the 2012 Marietta labor force:

Size of civilian labor force: 34,295

Number of workers employed in . . .

    agriculture and mining: 88
    construction: 2,664
    manufacturing: 2,872
    wholesale trade: 398
    retail trade: 2,754
    transportation: 1,729
    information systems: 1,074
    finance: 1,996
    professional administration: 5,504
    education and social services: 6,030
    arts and leisure: 3,016
    other: 1,339
    public administration: 1,120

Average hourly earnings of production workers: $15.40

Unemployment rate: 7.6% (2012)

Employers

Largest employers (2012)	Number of employees
Lockheed Martin	7,000
WellStar Kennestone Hospital	4,664
YKK Corporation of America	2,400
Alere	1,981
Columbian Chemical Company	1,300
Marietta City Schools	1,157
Cobb County Board of Education	1,060
C.W. Matthews Contracting, Inc.	961
Cobb County Government	900
Dobbisn Air Reserve Base	800

Cost of Living

The following is a summary of data regarding several key cost of living factors in the area.

2013 ACCRA Average House Price: $285,700

2013 ACCRA Cost of Living Index: 99

State income tax rate: 1.0% to 6.0%

State sales tax rate: 4.0%

Local income tax rate: None

Local sales tax rate: 2.0%

Property tax rate: $31.453 per $1,000 of assessed valuation (2013)

Economic Information: Cobb Chamber of Commerce, 240 Interstate N Pkwy SE, Atlanta, GA 30339; telephone (770) 980-2000.

■ Education and Research

Elementary and Secondary Schools

There are two school districts in Marietta, the Marietta City School District and the Cobb County School District. Residents of the City of Marietta attend the Marietta City School District, and residents that live in Marietta but not within the city limits attend schools in the Cobb County School District. Marietta City School District became one of the state's first charter systems in 2008. Marietta High School was named to the annual list of best high schools by *U.S. News & World Report* in

2013, ranked 27th in Georgia and in the top 1,500 nationally. The national Digital School Districts Survey, administered by the Center for Digital Education, gave Marietta City Schools the top honor for mid-sized school districts, and listed the system among the top 10 nationally for Technology Know-How in 2013.

Since 1995 Marietta High School has offered an International Baccalaureate Program (IB), and, with the addition of an IB elementary program in 2007 and middle school program in 2008, the school system became one of the few in the nation to offer the full IB K–12 program. In addition, Marietta offers a comprehensive program for exceptional and gifted children in elementary, middle, and high school. The system offers special education programs, reading recovery classes, and a program called Project Key aimed at pre-school handicapped children. Marietta Center for Advanced Academics, the city's first magnet school, opened in 2005 and was named a 2013 National Blue Ribbon School of Excellence by the U.S. Department of Education. Here, the science, technology, engineering and mathematics (STEM) program is offered for grades six to eight. In 2013 the school system renewed its accreditation, first achieved in 2007, with the Southern Association of Colleges and Schools Council on Accreditation and School Improvement. It is the highest rating offered by the association.

Several private schools, both church-affiliated and nonsectarian, are located in the area.

The following is a summary of data regarding the Marietta City Schools.

Total enrollment: 8056

Number of facilities
total: 12
elementary schools: 8
junior high schools: 2
high schools: 1
other: 1

Student/teacher ratio: 13.82:1

Teacher salaries
average (statewide): $53,906

Funding per pupil: $10,829

Public Schools Information: Marietta City Schools, 250 Howard St., Marietta, GA 30060; telephone (770) 422-3500; fax (770) 425-4095.

Colleges and Universities

Marietta is home to Southern Polytechnic State University. Founded in 1948 and located on 203 acres within the city, it offers abou 5,500 students associate degree transfer programs and 45 undergraduate majors in its bachelor's degree programs, including 14 areas of engineering technology and related fields, as well as master's degree programs in all five academic schools: Architecture and Construction Management; Computing and Software Engineering; Engineering Technology and Management; Arts and Sciences; and Engineering.

In 2009 Chattahoochee, North Metro, and Appalachian Technical colleges merged to become Chattahoochee Technical College, the largest technical college in the state of Georgia. The college has eight area locations, including its main campus in Marietta. It enrolled more than 17,000 students in 2012, with more than one quarter over the age of 30, and employed 194 full-time faculty and 344 part-time faculty. The college provides 75 associate degree, diploma, and technical certificate programs covering business sciences, computer sciences and engineering technology, health sciences, personal and public services, and technical studies.

Life University provides 11 bachelor's degree programs, two associate degree programs, and features a School of Chiropractic. The Lincoln College of Technology, a career training school offering many two-year programs, has a campus in Marietta, as does the similar Georgia Highalnds College. Kennesaw State University, with about 18,000 students, offers a broad selection of undergraduate majors as well as graduate programs in business administration and education in nearby Kennesaw, Georgia.

Libraries and Research Centers

The Cobb County Public Library System, one of the largest in the state, is comprised of a 64,000-square-foot main library in Marietta and 16 branches. The main branch contains more than 300,000 items, with some 15,000 focusing on local history and genealogy, displayed in the Georgia Room. A central feature of the Cobb County Library System is access to GALILEO, an award-winning initiative of the University System of Georgia. This web-based system allows Georgia citizens access to multiple information resources, including more than 70 databases and 3,000 journal and magazine titles in full text. GALILEO can be accessed from home with a free password provided by the library.

Special libraries in Marietta include Lockheed's comprehensive Technical Information Center and Southern Polytechnic State University's science and engineering library. Research centers located in Marietta include the U.S. Army Corps of Engineers' South Atlantic Division Laboratory, which tests soil and water quality among other activities, and the Marietta Eye Clinic, which conducts clinical research as part of its mission.

Public Library Information: Cobb County Public Library, Central Library, 266 Roswell St., Marietta, GA 30060; telephone (770) 528-2320.

■ Health Care

The Cobb County region supports four large hospitals; Marietta's largest is WellStar Kennestone Hospital with 580 beds. The hospital was ranked by *U.S. News & World Report* as the best hospital in the Piedmont region and sixth in the Atlanta metropolitan area for 2013–14. Its highest performing speciality was orthopedics. Kennestone has made treatment of minor illness and injuries more convenient to residents through its seven urgent care centers located throughout the area, including one in Marietta. Tranquility at Kennesaw Mountain, located in Marietta, is a community hospice operated by WellStar. Atherton Place, an independent and personal care living facility on the main campus, serves senior citizens, while Health Place, is WellStar's 40,000-square-foot fitness center and is open to the public, specializing in cardiac rehabilitation. WellStar Windy Hill Hospital in Marietta offers specialized care for long-term recovery. Tower Road Healthcare and Rehabilitation Center in Marietta accommodates residents in its postacute rehabilitation center. The Marietta Health and Rehab Center provides short- or long-term 24-hour care and rehabilitation for patients.

Dozens of facilities in nearby Atlanta, most within 20 miles, offer some of the highest rated medical facilities in the country.

■ Recreation

Sightseeing

As home to six historic districts, some on the National Register of Historic Places, Marietta is known for its historic charm and architecture. The first stop to make on a visit to Marietta is at the Welcome Center to pick up tour maps. The center itself is a sight to see, located in a renovated 1898 train station right off Marietta Square. The revitalized square is the heart of the city, serving as an entertainment site with several popular nightspots and restaurants. The focal point of the square is Glover Park, where winding brick paths lead to a majestic, three-tiered fountain, to an ornate Victorian gazebo, and to a scaled-down replica of "The General," a celebrated Civil War locomotive, where children can climb, slide, and pretend. The park is the location for frequent special events, festivals and concerts.

A walking tour of the downtown features at least 100 homes and buildings that span the period from antebellum to Victorian and evoke the sentiment and beauty of days gone by. The William Root House, one of the city's oldest residences, houses a museum depicting life in Cobb County during the 1840s and is open from Tuesdays to Saturdays. Other structures include classic Victorian, Queen Anne, Greek Revival, and Plantation Plain-style residences. The 1854 Greek classic style First Presbyterian Church, St. James Episcopal Church, and the 1866 Zion Baptist Church are part of the Historic District's walking tour. Other buildings of note include former general stores, a "Breakfast House" hotel, and a former hardware store.

Marietta City Cemetery was established in the 1830s and houses the gravesites of many of the city's earilest and most prominent residents. Marietta Confederate Cemetery, located next to the city cemetery, dates to 1863 when a plantation owner donated a tract of land to bury 20 soldiers who died in a train accident; it ultimately included more than 3,000 soldiers, with at least one from every Confederate state. It is the largest Confederate cemetery south of Richmond, Virginia. Marietta National Cemetery contains graves of more than 17,000 Union and Confederate soldiers; many were casualties of the Battle of Kennesaw Mountain, and 3,000 gravesites remain unknown.

Not far from the center of town, Kennesaw Mountain National Battlefield Park, a Civil War fortress, provides miles of wood trails, original earthworks and cannons that stand as silent witnesses to the decisive battle in which Confederate troops, vastly outnumbered, defended Kennesaw Mountain in a bloody effort to block Sherman's March to Atlanta. Visitors can learn about the battle that took place and view exhibits depicting the harsh conditions soldiers endured in the front ranks. Visitors may also walk on the grounds and view the family cemetery of the Kolb Farm, a significant battle site during the Civil War.

Well worth a visit is the Concord Covered Bridge, one of the few remaining covered bridges in operation, nestled on Nickajack Creek alongside historic Ruff's Mill. Built in 1872 is part of a historic district that also features nineteenth century homes and the Concord Woolen Mills. Another interesting spot is home to the remains of the nineteenth-century Marietta Manufacturing Mill on the banks of the Sope Creek.

The Aurora, a horse-drawn 1879 Silsby Steamer, is on display at the Marietta Fire Museum. It has been fully renovated and is said to be the best-restored engine of its kind in the world. The Southern Museum, since 2001 a part of the prestigiuos Smithsonian Affiliations Program, provides a close-up look at the "General," a steam locomotive that caused quite a stir in 1862 when Union soldiers known as Andrew's Raiders hijacked it and sped northwest to damage the line and seal off Chattanooga in the Civil War campaign. Marietta also features a Gone With the Wind Museum: Scarlett on the Square that opened in 2003 and maintains a wide variety of memorabilia from the classic book and movie. Located within the historic Kennesaw House is the Marietta Museum of History that displays such items as Civil War uniforms and a local photography collection.

No visit to Marietta would be complete without paying respects to the "Big Chicken," a local landmark. In 1963 a Marietta restaurateur wanted a focal point for his eatery and commissioned a Georgia Tech student to create a plucky, triangular-shaped fowl, complete with eyes that rolled, a beak that snapped open and shut, and a comb that dipped in the breeze. At one point, a hydraulic lift made the bird operational, but for the most part it stands as a silent object of wonder for foreign visitors who have declared it to be "so American" and an important element of Marietta folklore. It eventually became a franchise restaurant of Kentucky Fried Chicken. The Big Chicken has inspired the Gran Poulet, an art festival featuring fowl-inspired works of every description.

Arts and Culture

The best in professional live theater, both contemporary and classical, is offered Out of Box Theatre and Next Stage Theatre Company, both of which occupied the historic 225-seat Theatre in the Square on Marietta Square until 2012, when they left for smaller venues. Classical music concerts are offered by the Cobb Symphony, established in 1951. Georgia Ballet performs regularly at the Cobb County Civic Center. The long vacant Strand Theater in Marietta Square has been the site of restoration, with a grand reopening in 2009, in the hopes of offering yet another venue for film and live performances and events. Once a major motion picture house in the 1930s, the renovated Strand is home to the Atlanta Lyric Theatre, Marietta's musical performing group.

The Marietta-Cobb Museum of Art is located just off the Square. The museum's permanent exhibit is the only metropolitan Atlanta museum to focus on nineteenth and twentieth century American art. Workshops, lectures, poetry readings, special art showings and children's activities are also provided. The museum is housed in Marietta's original U.S. Post Office and a museum dedicated to the buildings history is within the art museum. Art lovers can also visit the Mable House Arts Center in southern Cobb County. Smyrna's Lillie Glassblowers allows spectators to watch as liquid crystal is transformed into exquisite designs for artistic and scientific purposes.

Festivals and Holidays

Annual events in Marietta involve a wide variety of activities. The last weekend in April brings the Taste of Marietta food festival. In spring, Cobb Landmarks and Historical Society sponsors Through the Garden Gate, a spring tour of gardens in the city. An annual Easter Egg Hunt is held at Laurel Park. In May arts, crafts, and food concessions fill Glover Park at the May-Retta Daze Arts and Crafts Festival. Summer brings the Glover Park Concert Series, a variety of musical presentations that extend through June, July, and August. The Fourth of July celebration starts the day with a parade and is filled with food and completed by fireworks at dusk. Labor Day Weekend's Art in the Park at Marietta Square showcases local artists' paintings, photography and pottery in Glover Park.

September ushers in Marietta Streetfest, formerly Marietta Antique Street Festival, established in 1992, which draws more than 50 antiques dealers from across the state. Late September's North Georgia State Fair at Miller Park features carnival rides, top name entertainment, contests, and special attractions. In October Marietta Square becomes the site of the Harvest Square Arts and Crafts Festival, featuring a special program called Halloween Happenings with carnival games and activites for children 12 and younger. December brings The Marietta Pilgrimage: A Christmas Home Tour, featuring six private historic homes decorated for the holidays. Audiences enjoy the holiday excitement of the Georgia Ballet's performances of *The Nutcracker* at Cobb County Civic Center. Each spring the city celebrates Founders' Day, when the City Square is decked out for a weekend festival, the highlight of which is an antique show.

Sports for the Spectator

Al Bishop Softball Complex is the site of numerous national/regional softball tournaments on its five lighted playing fields. While Marietta does not have a professional team of its own, Marietta's professional sports fans have an exciting series of events to choose from by making the fifteen-mile trip to nearby Atlanta, home to several professional franchises, from football to hockey. The Atlanta Braves announced in 2013 that they would relocate to Cobb County in a new stadium beginning in 2017, bringing the team within a few miles of the Marietta city limits..

Sports for the Participant

The Cobb County Parks, Recreation, & Cultural Affairs Department, one of the largest in the Southeast, operates 44 facilities over 1,350 developed acres. Tennis, swimming, softball, gymnastics, and soccer are offered, as are arts and crafts classes and informational programs. Marietta has an impressive network of 18 municipal parks, most fully equipped with playground facilities, athletic fields and tennis courts. The tiny quarter-acre Monarch Park is the site of a butterfly garden. Wildwood Park offers a beautiful 28-acre site of nature and jogging trails. At the site of the former Marietta Country Club, the Marietta City Club opened as Cobb County's first public Professional Golfer's Association standard golf course on 126 acres and a professional shop.

Visitors to Kennesaw Mountain National Battlefield Park enjoy five marked hiking trails, the longest of which extends for sixteen miles. Laurel Park has a jogging trail, basketball court, picnic facilities, 13 tennis courts, and a sand volleyball court on 25 acres. The Chattahoochee River National Recreation Area consists of more than 1,700 acres in four parks along the waterway. Concessionaires rent canoes, rafts, or kayaks at various points along the river so that water buffs can experience the river's whitewater thrills firsthand. The Lake Allatoona Reservoir, which boasts a 330-acre lake and 124 land-acres, is ideal for fishing, boating, swimming, camping,

hiking, and picnicking. In the town of Acworth, Acworth Beach and Lake Acworth offer swimming, fishing, picnicking, and sunbathing.

Shopping and Dining

Cobb County offers shoppers a variety of options from the corner store to huge regional shopping malls like Cumberland Mall and Town Center at Cobb, each with more than one million square feet. Marietta is the home of Providence Square shopping center, with more than 20 stores and restaurants. Quaint shops surrounding Marietta Square offer art, fine china, jewelry, clothing, and novelty items. There are several antique shops in the city. For those who want to enjoy the South's weather while they shop, they can head to Vinings Jubilee, a tree-lined district of upscale retail, quaint shops, award-winning restaurants, day spas and unique boutiques. Other shopping areas include Marietta Trade Center, The Avenue West Cobb, Town and Country Shopping Center, Merchants Walk, and Akers Mill Shopping Center. The Church Street Market provides foods native to the area along with quaint home and garden products.

Southern cuisine, featuring such treats as baked squash casserole or turnip greens, or palate-tempting fare served in classic plantation style, makes for memorable dining experiences. A variety of ethnic cuisines, including Japanese, Mexican, Slovakian, Australian, Italian, Chinese, and standard American and continental fare are available at the many eateries that proliferate the area.

Visitor Information: Cobb County Convention and Visitors Bureau, 1 Galleria Parkway SE, Atlanta, GA 30339; telephone 678-303-2622. City of Marietta, 205 Lawrence St., Marietta, GA 30060; telephone (770) 794-5526. Marietta Welcome Center & Visitors Bureau, 4 Depot St., Marietta, GA 30060; telephone (770) 429-1115.

■ Convention Facilities

The nearby Cobb Galleria Centre provides 320,000 square feet of meeting and exhibit space. The $40 million facility offers a 144,000-square-foot exhibit/arena space; a 25,000-square-foot ballroom; nearly 24,000 square feet of registration/pre-function space, and 20 meeting rooms ranging from 528 to 1,750 square feet. Connected to the center is the Renaissance Atlanta Waverly Hotel & Convention Center with 27 meeting rooms and 60,000 square feet of meeting space and 522 deluxe hotel suites. Marietta offers 30 hotels and motels in a variety of price ranges. Dozens more are available in the surrounding Cobb County area.

Within the city itself is the Hilton Atlanta/Marietta Hotel & Conference Center, which has 25,000 square feet of meeting space, including a 6,500-square-foot ballroom. Other meeting spaces are available at the Marietta-Cobb Museum of Art and the Marietta Gone With the Wind Museum. Laurel Park offers space for special events.

Convention Information: Cobb County Convention and Visitors Bureau, 1 Galleria Parkway SE, Atlanta, GA 30339; telephone 678-303-2622. City of Marietta, 205 Lawrence St., Marietta, GA 30060; telephone (770) 794-5526. Marietta Welcome Center & Visitors Bureau, 4 Depot St., Marietta, GA 30060; telephone (770) 429-1115.

■ Transportation

Approaching the City

Atlanta's Hartsfield-Jackson Atlanta International Airport serves the greater metro area, including Marietta. Some 17 mainline airlines served Hartsfield-Jackson in 2013, with direct or one-stop flights to some 200 domestic and international destinations. Cobb County is bisected by Interstate 75 and U.S. Highway 41/Cobb Parkway. It is bordered on the east by Atlanta's perimeter highway, Interstate 285, and the Chattahoochee River, and on the south by Interstate 20. North of Marietta, Interstate 75, which heads northwest to Chattanooga, branches off with Interstate 575, a connection that leads to U.S. highways in northeast Georgia.

Traveling in the City

Cumberland Transportation Network and Cobb Community Transit offer alternative ways to get around and connect Cobb County with Atlanta and the MARTA (Metropolitan Atlanta Rapid Transit Authority) rapid transit system. The construction of a new stadium for the Atlanta Braves in Cobb County, to be completed by 2017, gave rise to the possibility of extending MARTA lines more deeply into the area.

■ Communications

Newspapers and Magazines

Marietta's daily newspapers are the *Marietta Daily Journal* and *The Atlanta Journal-Constitution* (an Atlantan publication). *Marietta.com* is the city's online magazine and city guide. In the county, *East Cobber* is published weekly. Several magazines are published in Marietta, including the monthly *Our Town* and *North American Whitetail Magazine,* published eight times per year.

Television and Radio

Cobb County has access to eight local television stations, all but one from Atlanta. Two AM and two FM stations broadcast from Marietta. Cable services are available. WGHR at Southern Polytechnic State University broadcasts from within the city. Marietta benefits from Atlantan radio programming.

Media Information: Marietta Daily Journal, 580 Fairground St. SE, Marietta, GA 30060; telephone (770) 795-5000. *The Atlanta Journal-Constitution,* 223 Perimeter Center Pkwy, Atlanta, GA 30346; telephone (800) 933-9771.

Marietta Online

City of Marietta home page. Available www. mariettaga.gov

Cobb Chamber of Commerce. Available www. cobbchamber.org

Cobb County School District. Available www.cobb. k12.ga.us

Cobb County Convention & Visitors Bureau. Available www.travelcobb.org

Cobb County Public Library. Available www. cobbcat.org

Marietta City Schools. Available www.marietta-city. org

Marietta Daily Journal. Available www.mdjonline. com

Marietta Welcome and Visitors Bureau. Available www.mariettasquare.com

BIBLIOGRAPHY

Lassiter, Patrice Shelton, *Generations of Black Life in Kennesaw & Marietta, Georgia* (Charleston, SC: Arcadia Pub., c1999)

Savannah

■ The City in Brief

Founded: 1733 (chartered 1789)

Head Official: Edna Branch Jackson (since 2012; current term expires 2016)

City Population
 1990: 137,560
 2000: 131,510
 2010: 136,286
 2012 estimate: 142,010
 Percent change, 2000–2010: 3.6%
 U.S. rank in 1990: 129th
 U.S. rank in 2000: 182nd (State rank: 6th)
 U.S. rank in 2010: 181st (State rank: 4th)

Metropolitan Statistical Area Population
 2000: 293,000
 2010: 347,611
 2012 estimate: 361,941
 Percent change, 2000–2010: 18.6%
 U.S. rank in 2000: 150th
 U.S. rank in 2010: 145th

Area: 75 square miles

Elevation: approximately 46 feet above sea level

Average Annual Temperatures: 66.4° F

Average Annual Precipitation: 49 inches

Major Economic Sectors: services, wholesale and retail trade, government, manufacturing, tourism, military, health care, and port operations

Unemployment Rate: 6.1% (2012)

Per Capita Income: $18,173

2012 FBI Crime Index Property: 8,325

Major Colleges and Universities: Savannah State University, Armstrong Atlantic State University, Savannah Technical Institute, Savannah College of Art and Design

Daily Newspaper: *Savannah Morning News*; *Statesboro Herald*

■ Introduction

Once named as "The most beautiful city in North America" by Paris's famed *Le Monde* newspaper, Savannah has continued to develop into a premier destination for both tourists and businesses. Visitors in growing numbers flock to experience the city's mild climate, old world charm and atmosphere, moderately priced accommodations, and unique historic downtown district. One of the largest ports in the nation, the Port of Savannah continued to drive business and provide jobs vital to the area economy through the 2010s. Its vast and inexpensive warehousing facilities, as well as the city's prime location for moving goods into or away from the port, has continued to draw expansions of existing companies and new business arrivals to the area. Savannah is listed consistently as a top retirement location, and is lauded for its southern architectural charms and mix of historic relevance and modern economic drivers.

■ Geography and Climate

Savannah is located on the Georgia–South Carolina border where the Savannah River and the Atlantic Ocean are the natural boundaries of both the city and the state. In its semi-tropical location, Savannah usually has warm, and frequently hot, humid weather throughout the year. The city is set on the coastal plain and is surrounded by flat and low marshland to the north and east, and higher land, rising as high as 51 feet above sea level to the south and west. About half of the land to the west and south is clear of trees; the other half is woods, much of which lies

Jerry Driendl/Getty Images

in swamp. The intercoastal waterway runs down the Savannah coast, as do numerous rivers and inlets. There are seven months in which the average temperature is 70 degrees or higher. Summer temperatures are moderated by frequent afternoon showers. Average snowfall is less than one-half inch per month in winter.

Area: 75 square miles

Elevation: approximately 46 feet above sea level

Average Temperatures: 66.4° F

Average Annual Precipitation: 49 inches

■ History

City Designed by British Colonist

On February 12, 1733, James E. Oglethorpe and 114 colonists from Gravesend, England, arrived at Yamacraw Bluff on the Savannah River to found America's thirteenth colony, Georgia. Many of the new settlers were poor. Their purpose was to increase imperial trade and navigation along the coastal waterway and to establish a protective buffer between Spanish Florida and the northern English colonies during the Spanish War. It is said that Oglethorpe had four rules for his new community:no slaves, no Roman Catholics, no strong drink, and no lawyers. The name Savannah is said to have derived either from the Sawana people who inhabited the region or from a Shawnee word for the Savannah River.

Oglethorpe designed the basic layout of Savannah into blocks of five symmetrical 60-by-90-foot lots. Included in his plan were 24 public squares (21 of which are still in existence). They were intended to serve both as public meetings places and as areas where citizens could camp out and fortify themselves against attack from natives, Spaniards (who ruled Florida), and even marauding pirates. Thus Savannah became America's first planned city. This system of public squares was intended as central areas of fortification, as well as social areas for the colonists.

Immigrants from around the world were attracted to Oglethorpe's city. By the time the American Revolution started, the population of Savannah exceeded 3,000, making it the twentieth largest town in the American colonies.

Savannah During the Revolution

During the Revolutionary War, Savannah was taken by colonial insurgents. The following year, in 1778, the British recaptured the city. In 1779 the American army was unsuccessful in its attempts to retake the city. Finally, in 1782, the British left the city to return to England. Savannah was the chief city and capital of the Georgia colony until after the war ended in 1783.

Cotton Dominates Economy

From the outset, Savannah was an important seaport. In 1755 James Habersham and Francis Harris organized the first import-export businesses of the colony with the selling of cattle products. Before the American Revolution, the products of agriculture and trade with the Indians were sent back to England. At one time, diked rice paddies almost surrounded the city. Savannah prospered, and many of its historic homes were built. When the scourge of yellow fever swept through the city in 1820, the rice culture was abandoned and cotton became the dominant crop. For nearly a century, trading in the Cotton Exchange on Savannah's waterfront set world cotton prices. Cotton farming was greatly expanded following Eli Whitney's invention of the cotton gin, an event that took place near Savannah in 1793. Shortly thereafter, cotton shipments from the area soared to more than two million bales annually.

Marine History Events

Transportation history was made in 1819 when the SS <i>Savannah</i> became the first steamship to cross an ocean, traveling from Savannah to Liverpool, England. Later, in 1834, the shift from sail to steam was furthered when the country's first all-iron vessel, the <i>John Randolph,</i> was built, owned, and operated in Savannah.

The City During the Civil War and Beyond

Savannah, which had a large free African American population before the Civil War, suffered from the Union navy's coastal blockade during the war. The city was captured by General William T. Sherman in 1864 after the citizens surrendered rather than risk total destruction of Savannah (as had already happened in Atlanta). As a result, Sherman sent a famous message to President Abraham Lincoln in which he said:"I beg to present to you as a Christmas gift, the city of Savannah with 140 heavy guns and plenty of ammunition and also about 25,000 bales of cotton."

The capture of Savannah brought on rampant vandalism. Throughout the reconstruction period (1865-1877) and beyond, the city went through hard times. Nevertheless, the first art museum in the Southeast, Telfair Academy of Arts And Sciences, was opened in 1886. Still, it is said that the city's civic pride did not revive until the early 1900s, when the National Park Services restored nearby Fort Pulaski. This revival inspired a group of Savannah citizens to begin restoration efforts. In March 1912, Savannah citizen Juliette Gordon Low formed the first Girl Scout troop in the nation and later her birthplace was made into the national Girl Scout museum and national program center. World War I and its aftermath put restoration efforts on hold. The years following the war were harsh ones for Savannah. The boll weevil wiped out cotton crops and the city fell into a decline. Many of its beautiful structures fell into disrepair.

Some say it was the proposal to demolish the 1815 Davenport House that galvanized the city. In 1955 city residents created the Historic Savannah Foundation with the purpose of restoring old buildings in the city's original town center. Many sites in and around Savannah received the National Historic Landmark designation in 1966 and the city has been heralded as a masterpiece in urban planning. A multimillion-dollar riverfront revitalization in 1977 peaked the restoration efforts. The historic district encompasses more than 2,300 architecturally and historically significant buildings in its 2.5-square-mile area. Restoration and preservation of these buildings continues to the present day. Restoration efforts have also included the existing City Market, including adaptive reuse of historic warehouses.

Throughout the 1980s and 1990s, Savannah began developing into a hot spot for tourism. In 1996, Savannah was host of the sailing competitions during the Summer Olympics held in Atlanta, Georgia. Construction of the $83 million waterfront complex of the Savannah International Trade and Convention Center was completed in May 2000 on Hutchinson Island. The island also boasts a 409-room Westin Savannah Harbor Golf Resort, featuring a Greenbrier spa and a world-class, 18-hole Troon golf course.

Between 1990 and 2007, the container tonnage moved at the port rose steadily at an annual rate of 10 percent or more. In 2008 when there was almost no rise at all for the first time in 13 years, the effects of a national recession reached Savannah's port, as the international exchange of goods declined. Within a few years, however, the increase in port activity resumed, and Savannah retained its rating as the second busiest U.S. port through 2012, trailing on Los Angeles. The success of existing business that utilized the port facilities encouraged expansion, and brought new businesses into the region.

Tourism remained steady and strong into the 2010s. What Savannah has—that most cities do not—is its historical relevance as a romantic place people want to see. As noted in the <i>New York Times,</i> "Certain things about Savannah never change. It remains one of America's loveliest cities, organized around a grid of 21 squares, where children play, couples wed, and, in the evenings, lone saxophonists deliver a jazz soundtrack."

Historical Information: Georgia Historical Society, 501 Whitaker Street, Savannah, GA 31401; telephone (912) 651-2125; fax (912) 651-2831. Visit Savannah, 101 East Bay Street, Savannah, GA 31401; telephone (912) 644-6400.

■ Population Profile

Metropolitan Statistical Area Population

2000: 293,000
2010: 347,611
2012 estimate: 361,941
Percent change, 2000–2010: 18.6%
U.S. rank in 2000: 150th
U.S. rank in 2010: 145th

City Residents

1990: 137,560
2000: 131,510
2010: 136,286
2012 estimate: 142,010
Percent change, 2000–2010: 3.6%
U.S. rank in 1990: 129th
U.S. rank in 2000: 182nd (State rank: 6th)
U.S. rank in 2010: 181st (State rank: 4th)

Density: 1,321.2 people per square mile

Racial and ethnic characteristics

White: 54,817
Black or African American: 79,663
American Indian and Alaskan Native: 567
Asian: 2,874
Native Hawaiian and Other Pacific Islander: 144
Hispanic or Latino (may be of any race): 7,940
Other: 3,945

Percent of residents born in state: 61.8%

Age characteristics

Population under 5 years old: 11,079
Population 5 to 9 years old: 8,816
Population 10 to 14 years old: 7,777
Population 15 to 19 years old: 9,670
Population 20 to 24 years old: 17,114
Population 25 to 34 years old: 25,215
Population 35 to 44 years old: 14,632
Population 45 to 54 years old: 16,608
Population 55 to 59 years old: 6,869
Population 60 to 64 years old: 6,851
Population 65 to 74 years old: 9,371
Population 75 to 84 years old: 4,983
Population 85 years and over: 3,025
Median age: 31.0

Births (2010–11 Metropolitan Area)

Total number: 5,044

Deaths (2010–11 Metropolitan Area)

Total number: 2,715

Money income (2012)

Per capita income: $18,173
Median household income: $34,832
Total households: 51,445

Number of households with income of ...

less than $10,000: 6,952
$10,000 to $14,999: 4,901
$15,000 to $24,999: 7,125
$25,000 to $34,999: 6,862
$35,000 to $49,999: 7,760
$50,000 to $74,999: 9,455
$75,000 to $99,999: 3,844
$100,000 to $149,999: 2,920
$150,000 to $199,999: 966
$200,000 or more: 660

Percent of families below poverty level: 27.4%

FBI Crime Index Property: 8,325

FBI Crime Index Violent: 878

■ Municipal Government

Savannah has operated under the council-manager form of government since 1954. The city has an elected mayor, eight aldermen, and an appointed city manager. Elections are held every four years. There are six alders representing geographic districts and two elected at large, as is the mayor. Savannah is in Chatham County.

Head Official: Edna Branch Jackson (since 2012; current term expires 2016)

Total Number of City Employees: 2,500 (2012)

City Information: City of Savannah, P.O. Box 1027, Savannah, GA 31402; telephone (912) 651-6410 (Public Information Office).

■ Economy

Major Industries and Commercial Activity

Savannah has an economy consisting of manufacturing, port and transportation, tourism, military and government, and creative and technical businesses.

Manufacturing is diverse with products including paper and forest products, corporate jets, construction equipment, food processing, and chemicals. The largest plants include Gulfstream Aerospace, an executive jet aircraft manufacturer; International Paper, the largest producer of paper for paper bags in the United States; and Derst Baking Company, which makes bread, rolls, and cakes. Georgia Pacific, a leading manufacturer of tissue, pulp, paper, packaging, and building products, is headquartered in Savannah. JCB, the third largest producer of construction equipment in the world, built its North American headquarters in Savannah in 2000.

The Georgia Ports Authority maintains the largest single container terminal in North America at Savannah, which was the second busiest in the United States in 2012, trailing only Los Angeles. More than four-million square feet of warehouse space is available within 30 miles of the port, and the surrounding area provides access to two major interstate highways. Port ships come and go to more than 150 countries around the world, with just over half of port cargo loaded as exports as of 2012. Several private and public warehouses in the area make use of port services, including large facilities of major corporations such as Target, Lowes, IKEA and Heineken USA. The Savannah Airport Commission operates a Foreign Trade Zone that includes the Savannah Port Authority Industrial Park, among other areas.

Meanwhile, tourism proves to be one of the largest economic drivers of the Savannah economy. Even during a nationwide recession in the late 2000s, the number of visitors and their direct spending impact remained about the same. Savannah hosted more than 50 million visitors between 2000 and 2010. More than 12 million visitors came to Savannah in 2011, including 6.8 million for overnight visits. Visitor spending totaled $1.94 billion. The city's attractiveness as a visitor destination is enhanced by its charming historic district, accommodations, and accessibility. Savannah has the added distinction of being one of America's most haunted cities, a major draw for tourists. With its pleasant weather, the tourism industry operates year-round. In addition, tourism has given visitors the invitation to become residents.

The military plays an important role in the economic health of the city as well. There are more than 27,000 active military personnel, contractors and civilian support staff working within the Savannah metropolitan statistical area. The U.S. Army's Third Infantry Division (Mechanized) is housed at Fort Stewart, 40 miles from Savannah. Hunter Army Airfield, part of the army complex, is located in Savannah. The strong presence of military personnel and their dependants has a major impact on the extra demand for retail and food service as well as other services, with the total annual economic impact estimated at $1.53 billion as of 2012.

There are more than 300 creative and technical firms located in Savannah. The Creative Coast, an organization formed by the city of Savannah and the Savannah Economic Development Authority, works to encourage continued growth in this sector, which promises to bring businesses with leading-edge technologies into the area.

Items and goods produced: paper and paper products, sugar, dental instruments, jet aircraft, aerospace equipment, flatbed trailers, refrigerated and freight vans, chemical solutions, food processing, color pigments

Incentive Programs-New and Existing Companies

Local programs: The Savannah Economic Development Authority (SEDA) is the business solicitation organization in the City of Savannah and Chatham County. It assists companies interested in relocating to, or expanding in, the Savannah area at no cost to the client. The Coastal Area District Development Authority, established as a not-for-profit in 1972, extends loans to area businesses at long-term, below-market fixed rates. The Business Retention Action Team partners with other area organizations to assist businesses in tasks ranging from job training to governmental lobbying. Tax incentives include a job tax credit, special headquarters tax credit, and child care tax credit; tax exemptions are available for qualifying businesses and include exemptions from property and inventory taxes, as well as sales taxes for manufacturing machinery.

State programs: Georgia has business-friendly tax laws; the state does not use the unitary tax method, but instead taxes businesses only on income apportioned to Georgia. A Job Tax Credit offers employers that create jobs in Georgia up to $4,000 in income-tax deductions per job. Georgia's Opportunity Zones, defined as redevelopment or revitalization targets, provide Job Tax Credits for the creation of as few as two jobs. Less developed census tracts also provide Job Tax Credits, as do military zones. Tax credits also hinge on the average wage of job created and the size of the project—designated "Mega Project Tax Credits" allow large employers who create at least 1,800 jobs to claim a tax credit of $5,250 for as many as 4,500 employees. One-stop permitting, enterprise zones, and foreign trade zones also support economic development in Georgia. Georgia's fourth-lowest unionization rate nationally and status as a right-to-work state also draws employers.

Job training programs: The Georgia Department of Technical and Adult Education administers the Georgia Quick Start program, offering job-specific training programs through a large network of college, university, and satellite campus sites within the state. By developing and implementing high quality customized training programs and materials, Quick Start assists the company in obtaining a trained work force ready to begin as soon as the company opens for business. The HOPE Scholarship program funds Georgia students' college tuition if they meet academic targets during high school. Chattahoochee Technical College is the state's largest technical college and provides job training for certain industries, including eco-friendly industrial activities.

Several local workforce development and training programs provide students educational and technical skills through apprenticeships, internships and professional development programs. Savannah Technical College provides certificates of credit to give employees a general understanding of the skills needed for work in manufacturing, warehouse and distribution, leadership, and customer service.

Development Projects

Savannah is unique in having a large tract of waterfront land open for development and located close to the central business and historic districts. Since the late 1990s, the Savannah Economic Development Authority has put considerable effort into development of the Crossroads Business Park; Dollar Tree completed a $20 million, 400,000-square-foot extension of its existing space there in 2013. Great Dane trucking company announced in 2013 that it was moving its local corporate headquarters and innovation campus to a facility at Crossroads Business Park. The $15 million facility was expected to be completed in early 2015. After closing its Savannah manufacturing facility in 2008, Great Dane reopened a new 450,000-square-foot facility in nearby Statesboro in 2012. Several other businesses, including Gulfstream Aerospace, planned or completed expansions at Crossroads Business Park in 2012 and 2013.

The Savannah River Landing project, a 54-acre, $800 million mixed-use development adjacent to President Street and General McIntosh Boulevard proposed in the early 2000s, remained stalled in 2013 as private investors wrangled over financial responsibilities and final plans. Designed to be an extension of Savannah's historic district, the Savannah River Landing was to incorporate parks, squares and tree-lined streets, eventually including 2 hotels, 150,000 square feet of office space, 200,000 square feet of retail space, condominiums, town houses, and riverfront estates. However, until ownership and plans were finalized, the exact nature of development remained uncertain.

Mitsubishi Power Systems constructed a $325 million gas turbine manufacturing and service facility in several phases beginning in 2011. The 500,000-square-foot facility, known as the Savannah Machinery Works, employed 500 people and spread across 166 acres in Pooler, Georgia.

Savannah College of Art and Design began a 1.74-acre site development called One West Victory in 2013. The project intended to redevelop two late nineteenth-century buildings into 114 student apartments, a restaurant, study hall, and student lounge, as well as a 218-space parking deck. All 124,000 square feet were to be LEED-certified for their environmentally conscious design.

Groundbreaking for the Outlet Mall of Georgia in Pooler, near Savannah, occurred in September 2013. The location next to Interstate 95 is passed by 25 million drivers annually and features more than 1,800 existing hotel rooms. The outlet mall was expected to open in 2015 at a cost of $200 million.

Economic Development Information: Savannah Economic Development Authority, 131 Hutchinson Island Road, 4th Floor, Savannah, GA 31421; telephone (912) 447-8450 or (800) 673-7388; fax (912) 447-8455; email moreinfo@seda.org.

Commercial Shipping

Savannah is one of the southeast's leading seaports and cargo hubs. Shipping activity is focused on the Port of Savannah, which is supported by two railroads, CSX and Norfolk Southern, and two interstate highways, as well as Savannah/Hilton Head International Airport. The Foreign Trade Zone is generally owned and operated by the airport, with the port and others operating within it. The port has also been designated as a part of this Foreign Trade Zone to encourage international commerce, as have several other area sites. The airport moved 7,595 tons of cargo in 2012, below peak totals above 10,000 tons achieved in 2006 and 2007.

The Port of Savannah has two deepwater terminals: Garden City terminal and Ocean Terminal. The second busiest U.S. container port as of 2012, the Port of Savannah handles 40 percent of all U.S. containerized poultry exports. Because of its location on the coast, the port serves as a major distribution point to and from a 26-state region, which services 75 percent of the country. The port has access to incoming products from eastern and southeast Asia, India, the Middle East, and the Mediterranean basin. Efforts to expand the port's depth from 42- to 47-feet received federal approval in 2013, and $231 million in state funding, but still awaited an additional $400 million of federal support.

Labor Force and Employment Outlook

Georgia is a right-to-work state. Labor costs in Georgia are low and union activity is minimal. Savannah-area colleges and universities generate nearly 7,000 graduates annually, with many trained in sought-after fields related to computers, engineering, and economics. The large military population at Fort Stewart and Hunter Army Airfield provides a ready workforce of trained military veterans entering the civilian world, as well as their nonmilitary dependents.

The following is a summary of data regarding the 2012 Savannah labor force:

Size of civilian labor force: 65,520

Number of workers employed in . . .

    agriculture and mining: 115
    construction: 2,483
    manufacturing: 3,616

wholesale trade: 1,193
retail trade: 7,892
transportation: 3,350
information systems: 776
finance: 2,552
professional administration: 5,023
education and social services: 13,137
arts and leisure: 10,564
other: 2,704
public administration: 4,293

Average hourly earnings of production workers: $20.39

Unemployment rate: 6.1% (2012)

Employers

Largest employers (2012)	*Number of employees*
Gulfstream Aerospace	7,300
Fort Stewart/Hunter Army Airfield	4,719
Memorial Health University Medical Center	4,643
Savannah/Chatham County Board of Education	4,600
St. Joseph's/Candler Health System	3,170
Wal-Mart	2,935
City of Savannah	2,500
Savannah College of Art and Design	1,750
Chatham County	1,500
Georgia-Pacific Savannah River Mill	1,200

Cost of Living

Savannah is a relatively inexpensive town in which to live and do business—the cost of living was 2.9 percent below the national average in 2013.

The following is a summary of data regarding several key cost of living factors in the area.

2013 ACCRA Average House Price: $196,486

2013 ACCRA Cost of Living Index: 91

State income tax rate: 1.0% to 6.0%

State sales tax rate: 4.0%

Local income tax rate: None

Local sales tax rate: 3.0%

Property tax rate: $30.389 per $1,000 of assessed valuation (2013)

Economic Information: Savannah Economic Development Authority, 131 Hutchinson Island Road, 4th Floor, Savannah, GA 31421; telephone (912) 447-8450 or (800) 673-7388; fax (912) 447-8455; email moreinfo@seda.org. Savannah Area Chamber of Commerce, 101 East Bay Street, Savannah, GA 31401; telephone 912-644-6400.

■ Education and Research

Elementary and Secondary Schools

The Savannah-Chatham County Public School System features a number of special programs for students from K–12. The Savannah-Chatham County Public Schools Academy Programs offer students the opportunity to pursue specialized courses of study. Courses of study include math, technology, and design—offered as early as elementary school—and visual and performing arts. International Baccalaureate programs are available beginning in elementary school and continuing through high school.

The Oatland Island Wildlife Center of Savannah, operated by the school district, serves thousands of students from school systems throughout the southeastern United States. It is located just east of Savannah on a marsh island and features a two-mile nature trail through maritime forest, salt marsh, and freshwater wetlands. Along the trail, visitors can observe native animals, such as Florida panthers, Eastern timber wolves, and alligators, in their natural habitat.

An early college program has been designed to offer students advanced studies and credits through classes taught by faculty members of Savannah State University and Savannah Technical College. Coastal Georgia Comprehensive Academy offers vocational programs for students with special needs. In the state of Georgia, any student who graduates from high school with at least a 3.0 grade-point average is eligible for free college tuition at any of the state's colleges or universities. The program is called the HOPE (Helping Outstanding Pupils Educationally) Scholarship and is funded by the Georgia lottery. For fiscal year 2013–14, Hope Scholarship grants exceeded $228 million dollars and were distributed to more than 148,000 students.

Among Savannah's many private schools, St. Andrew's School was honored in 2013 by the *Washington Post* as one of the nation's most challenging schools, the second consecutive year the institution received the honor. It was the only school in the state to receive such recognition.

The following is a summary of data regarding the Chatham County Public Schools.

Total enrollment: 35,246

Number of facilities

  total: 64
  elementary schools: 27
  junior high schools: 16
  high schools: 10
  other: 11

Student/teacher ratio: 13.05:1

Teacher salaries

  average (statewide): $53,906

Funding per pupil: $9,666

Public Schools Information: Savannah-Chatham County Public School System, 208 Bull Street, Savannah, GA 31401; telephone (912) 395-5600.

Colleges and Universities

A variety of colleges and universities offer bachelor's, master's, professional, and doctorate degree programs in Savannah. The main campuses of Savannah State University, Savannah College of Art and Design, Armstrong Atlantic State University, and South University are the major degree-awarding universities. In 2008 Mercer University of Macon, Georgia, began a four-year doctor of medicine program at the Memorial University Medical Center. Other schools include Georgia Tech Savannah and a satellite campus of Georgia Southern University known as the Coastal Georgia Center. Two technical institutions, Savannah Technical College and the Skidaway Institute of Oceanography, call Savannah home.

Better known as SCAD, Savannah College of Art and Design offers bachelor and master of fine arts degrees as well as the master of arts and master of architecture. SCAD has become one of the largest art and design schools in the country, whose students often garner accolades and recognition in the art world. *DesignIntelligence* named SCAD the nation's top school for architecture, design, and interior design in 2014.

Savannah State University, part of the University System of Georgia and touting itself as the oldest public historically black university in Georgia, enrolls more than 4,000 students and offers bachelor's degrees through its colleges of business administration, liberal arts and social sciences, science and technology, and teacher education. Master's degrees can be earned in business administration, public administration, urban studies and planning, and social work. Armstrong Atlantic State University enrolls about 7,000 students and offers undergraduate degree programs in arts and sciences, health professions, education, and science and technology. Graduate degree programs numbered 18 as of 2013, with most focused in education and health. South University offers degrees from its schools of creative arts, nursing and health, business and information technology, and legal and criminal justice. Savannah Technical College offers job training and skills in

more than 50 certificate, professional, diploma, and associate degree programs and has five area campuses.

A variety of schools maintain satellite campuses in Savannah. Georgia Southern University in Statesboro, 50 miles from Savannah, offers undergraduate and graduate programs through its Coastal Georgia Center, in addition to year-round classes focusing on basic computer schools and professional development. The Embry-Riddle Aeronautical University's Savannah Center is located on the Hunter Army Airfield and offers courses in aviation-related fields. Columbia College at the Hunter Army Airfield offers associate's and bachelor's degree programs to military personnel and working adults. Online as well as campus-based courses are offered at Saint Leo University's Savannah Education Center. Georgia Tech Savannah, best known for applied research, has been considered a leading university for technology transfer.

Libraries and Research Centers

Savannah's Live Oak Public Libraries serve Chatham, Effingham, and Liberty counties. It has 17 branches in addition to the main Bull Street building, and a bookmobile. The library has more than 500,000 volumes and makes available thousands of periodicals, records, cassettes, compact discs and videocassettes, CD-ROM resources, and special collections on local history. The library also offers access to state-of-the-art computerized indexes, on-line information services, and the Internet. Annually, the library circulates nearly 2 million materials and logs 670,000 computer sessions by patrons. A special Business Resource Center, located at the Southwest Chatham branch, is available to assist those interested in opening their own business. Other libraries in the area include college-related and medical libraries, a municipal research library, the Georgia Historical Society Library, the Catholic Diocese of Savannah Office of Archives, the Chatham County Law Library, the John McGowan Library at Skidaway Institute, and a U.S. Army Corps of Engineers technical library.

Marine research is conducted at the University of Georgia and at Skidaway Institute of Oceanography. At Herty Foundation Research and Development Center, fibrous materials are studied. Management of the facility was transferred to Georgia Southern University in 2012 to take advantage of collaborations between the center and the university. The Cyber Security Research Institute at Armstrong Research Institute conducts training and research on cyber security to serve both businesses and governmental agencies. The Department of Energy's Savannah River National Laboratory and Savannah River Ecology Laboratory are science and technology centers. Faculty from Georgia Tech Savannah are involved in research projects with industry and government agencies.

Public Library Information: Live Oak Public Libraries, 2002 Bull Street, Savannah, GA 31401; telephone (912) 652-3600.

■ Health Care

Savannah is the health-care hub of a 35-county area encompassing coastal Georgia and parts of South Carolina. The Memorial Health University Medical Center, with 622 beds, has a special pediatric care facility and is the area's only Level 1 trauma center. It operates the Savannah campus of Mercer University's School of Medicine. The Curtis and Elizabeth Anderson Cancer Institute at Memorial specializes in research and comprehensive care. In 2013 Memorial was named to the Georgia Hospital Association' Partnership for Health and Accountability Core Measures Honor Roll, Presidential Category, for its exceptional patient outcomes.

St. Joseph's/Candler Health System is a private, faith-based non-profit hospital focusing on innovative programs in early detection and prevention. With 285 beds, St. Joseph's Hospital is a leader in heart care services, and orthopedics and neurology. Candler Hospital is Georgia's first hospital (first chartered in 1804) and the second oldest continuously operating hospital in the United States. Candler Hospital offers primary care, outpatient, and women's and children's services. The hospital system was ranked 13th in Georgia by U.S. News & World Report for 2013–14, with high performing specialties listed as ear, nose, and throat and gynecology. The system is affiliated with Emory University Health-Care and the H. Lee Moffitt Cancer Center and Research Institute in Tampa, Florida.

Other health facilities located in Savannah include: Georgia Regional Hospital at Savannah, an inpatient psychiatric facility; Coastal Harbor Health System, providing residential psychiatric treatment for children and adolescents; Select Specialty Hospital for acute long-term care; and, Willingway Hospital, a recognized leader in the treatment of alcoholism and drug dependency.

■ Recreation

Sightseeing

Visitors are attracted to Savannah for many reasons, especially the opportunity to tour the city's beautiful Historic District, the country's largest historic urban landmark district. Downtown Savannah is known for the 22 park-like squares that make up its landmark historic district. In 2010 one of the three "lost" squares, Ellis, was reclaimed and restored after razing the parking garage that scarred the neighborhood; two other squares are "lost," destroyed in the course of urban development. Most squares are named in honor or a person or historical event, and contain monuments, memorials, statutes, plaques, and other artistic elements. Nearby, the Savannah Victorian Historic District invites visitors to walking tours of beautiful homes and architecture.

The Savannah Visitors Center, located at the former Central of Georgia Railroad Station, itself a national historic landmark and oldest standing antebellum rail facility in America, offers helpful brochures, maps, and publications. Walking, driving, and carriage tours of the city are also available. The nearby Roundhouse Complex contains the oldest and most complete railroad repair shop in the United States.

Tours of the Historic Landmark District include six different neighborhoods and views of garden-like public squares and hundreds of restored eighteenth- and nineteenth-century buildings with ornate ironwork, gingerbread trim, and picturesque fountains. (About seven houses are open as museums.) Highlights of the district include the Owens-Thomas House, circa 1816–19, which was designed by John Jay and considered to be the finest example of Regency architecture in America; the Davenport House Museum, built between 1815 and 1820, a fine example of Federal architecture and period decorative arts; and the Juliette Gordon Low Birthplace, which is restored and furnished to depict the 1870s and was the city's first National Historic Landmark.

Interesting churches in the district are the First African Baptist Church (1861), the oldest African American congregation in the United States; the 1890 Wesley Monumental United Methodist Church; Temple Mickve Israel, the third oldest synagogue in the United States; Christ Episcopal Church (1838), which was the first church established in the colony; and the Cathedral of St. John the Baptist, the oldest Roman Catholic congregation in the state, founded in 1700 by French colonists.

The Cotton and Naval Stores Exchange (1886) was the center of commerce when Savannah was the world's foremost cotton port; it opened for tours in 2010. Other interesting civic sites include the U.S. Customs House (1852); the 1905 City Hall; Colonial Park Cemetery, the second oldest burial ground (1750–1853) for colonists; and Bonaventure Cemetery, resting place of many local residents, made famous by the publication of *Midnight in the Garden of Good and Evil*. The recently restored City Market features City Market Art Center, shops, restaurants, and taverns. Particularly scenic streets include Factor's Walk, known for iron bridges and cobblestones; Riverfront Street, with restaurants, pubs, and shops housed in old cotton warehouses; Gaston Street, distinguished by its stately old homes; and Oglethorpe Avenue, a fashionable residential street. Beauty abounds at Emmett Park, with its Harbor Light and fountain, and at Forsyth Park, with its beautiful azalea blooms, Confederate monument, and restored fountain. There are about 30 companies offering haunted tourism, featuring ghost tours and evening lantern walks that share the myths and legends of the town as well as the factual history.

The city of Savannah has many other interesting attractions outside the Historic District. Bethesda Academy, originally the Bethesda Orphan House and Academy, is located on the Isle of Hope and is the oldest continuously operated home for boys in America. Its

William H. Ford Sr. Museum and Visitors Center houses items connected with Bethesda's history dating back to the 1700s and reopened following renovations in 2013. The Massie Heritage Center is the only remaining original building of Georgia's oldest chartered school system. The University of Georgia Marine Education Center and Aquarium, 10 miles southeast of the city on Skidaway Island, features an aquarium exhibit of marine life found in Georgia's waters.

Old Fort Jackson, the oldest remaining brickwork fort in Georgia, and the Savannah History Museum at the Visitors Center offer artifacts and exhibits from the eighteenth and nineteenth centuries. Fort Pulaski National Monument, 15 miles east of Savannah; Fort McAllister State Historic Park, 22 miles south; and Tybee Island Light Station and Museum provide exhibits concerning the Civil War period. The Tybee Island Lighthouse, guardian of the Savannah River since 1736, offers tours. The Ships of the Sea Maritime Museum presents a large collection of models and maritime memorabilia representing man's 2,000-year quest to conquer the seas. Trustees Garden Village was the site of the first public agricultural experimental garden in America. It is now a residential area and home of the famous Pirates' House (1759) frequented by seamen and pirates alike. The Georgia State Railroad Museum offers a glimpse of the oldest and most complete pre-Civil War railroad repair facility in the country. The Mighty Eighth Air Force Museum in Pooler honors the sacrifices made during and after World War II by the largest air strike force in history, which was formed in Savannah in 1942. The Ralph Gilbert Mark Civil Rights Museum tells the story of Savannah's role in the movement.

Arts and Culture

With its splendid squares and parks, elegant architecture, and lush vegetation, Savannah creates a studio and stage artscape for its performing and visual arts. The Telfair Academy of Arts and Sciences was one of the South's first public museums. The Historic Savannah Theatre, which gave its first performance in 1818, performs a season of live drama plus a summer musical. The Savannah Philharmonic Orchestra runs a September–May concert season and often performs in conjunction with the community-run Philharmonic Chorus. The Lucas Theatre for the Arts opened in 1921 and shows classic and popular films. Various entertainments are offered at the Savannah Civic Center throughout the year. The Savannah Civic Center also offers an additional 500 events annually, from entertainment to sports to cultural events.

There are more than 25 art galleries in downtown Savannah. City Market Art Center features two city blocks of studios for about 35 artists to display and sell their work in the neighboring galleries. Opened in 1885 as the first public art museum in the Southeast, the Telfair Museum of Art in the historic district is Savannah's premier art museum. The handsome William Jay-designed mansion features American painting and art of the eighteenth and nineteenth centuries, as well as the 1818 Octagon Room, dining room, and the restored 1886 rotunda gallery. The museum was named the 2012 "Best of Savannah" winner by *Savannah Magazine*.

The King-Tisdell Cottage museum in the historic district is dedicated to preserving aspects of African American culture and heritage and displays documents, furniture, and art objects of the 1890s. The Great Savannah Races Museum profiles early automobile races in the city, including the first American Grand Prix. The Savannah Children's Museum is an all-outdoor interactive museum that teaches children through play. Built in 2012, it is the city's first children's museum; a second phase of development with an indoor area was in the planning and fundraising stages during 2013.

Arts and Culture Information: Visit Savannah, 101 East Bay Street, Savannah, GA 31401; telephone (912) 644-6400.

Festivals and Holidays

Savannah is host to more than 200 festivals and events annually. During the first two weeks in February, the Georgia Heritage Celebration's Colonial Faire and Muster, sponsored by the Historic Savannah Foundation, celebrates the state's colonial history. The Black Heritage Festival, held the second week in February, is a series of events featuring the cultural and artistic contributions of African Americans. The Savannah Irish Festival is held in February at the Civic Center Area in the Historic District. Sheep to Shawl Festival at Oatland Island in early March provides the opportunity to watch the annual shearing of the sheep and the processing and hand weaving of the wool.

The St. Patrick's Day Parade is Savannah's biggest event and the second largest St. Patrick's Day celebration in the country. More than one-quarter of a million people participate in this event, which began in the early 1800s. Savannah Music Festival, Georgia's largest music arts festival, is a 15-day fest featuring concerts in downtown venues and includes international talent in blues, jazz, and classical music. The Savannah Tour of Homes and Gardens offers self-guided walking tours of private homes in six historic neighborhoods over four days in late March. An ecumenical Easter Sunrise service is a Tybee Island tradition.

The Savannah Shakespeare Festival, SCAD's International Festival, Savannah Scottish Games, and Tybee Island Beach Bum Parade round out the list of activities in May. June offers the Savannah Asian Festival. Picnics, music, arts, food, and fireworks at sites around the city help residents and visitors hail the Fourth of July holiday.

City Market and Forsyth Park are the sites for the week-long Savannah Jazz Festival in September. National, regional, and local jazz stars assist in the workshops, jazz seminars, and other events. Oktoberfest is held early in the month of October and features German food, imported beer, arts, and entertainment along River Street. Greek music and food aromas fill the air three days in mid-October at the Savannah Greek Festival. The Savannah Film Festival, sponsored by SCAD, features films and videos from around the world. The Savannah Harbor Boat Parade of Lights Cruise at the end of November, featuring a fireworks extravaganza and tree lighting, kicks off the Savannah Harbor Holiday Series. Christmas in Savannah offers a Christmas parade, tours of historic homes, Civil War reenactments, and other events.

Sports for the Spectator

Historic Grayson Stadium, opened 1926, is the site of the home games of the Class A South Atlantic League Savannah Sand Gnats, a farm team of Major League Baseball's New York Mets. Grayson Stadium boasts of fielding such legendary players as Babe Ruth, Jackie Robinson, and Shoeless Joe Jackson. Armstrong Atlantic State University, Savannah State University, and Savannah College of Art and Design field teams in such sports as football, basketball, baseball, softball, and volleyball. The Martin Luther King Arena of the Savannah Civic Center hosts wrestling, truck shows, and Disney on Ice tours. The Liberty Mutual Legends of Golf tournament, a PGA Champions Tour spot, is played on Hutchinson Island in late April. The St. Patrick's Day Rugby Tournament features the Savannah Shamrocks Rugby Club along with more than 75 visiting teams, making it one of the nation's largest rugby tournaments. The Greater Savannah Sports Council actively promotes the city as a site for major amateur sporting events.

Sports for the Participant

Savannah's warm weather allows participation in outdoor activities year round. Savannah offers excellent facilities for jogging, tennis, golf, swimming, boating, and other water sports. The city had 46 public recreational neighborhood parks as of 2013, including facilities with recreation centers, swimming pools, athletic fields, basketball courts, and tennis courts. In addition to the The Club at Savannah Harbor golf course, located within city limits, dozens of golf courses are located in the surrounding area, with nearby Hilton Head South Carolina offering some of the best courses in the nation. For boating, fishing and swimming enthusiasts, Savannah offers seven marinas locally that provide access to 420 miles of navigable waters and 87,000 acres of tidal marshland, as well as the intercoastal waterway. Nearby Tybee Island, formerly known as Savannah Beach, provides access to the beautiful oceanfront. Several companies offer deep-sea charter fishing tours, dolphin tours, and kayak and other boat rentals. The Critz Tybee Run Fest offers distances from a one-mile fun run to a full 26.2-mile marathon. The Enmark Savannah River Bridge Run in December is a 10-K race that crosses Talmadge Memorial Bridge over the Savannah River twice.

Shopping and Dining

Savannah offers numerous choices for enthusiastic shoppers, including two traditional enclosed malls, as well as large shopping centers, boutiques, antique shops, flea markets, and restored warehouse complexes. A wide variety of specialty shops can be found around the Historic District at Factors Walk, River Street, Broughton Street, and City Market. Oglethorpe Mall in midtown offers more than 100 other stores. Savannah Mall on the south side has four major department stores and an indoor carousel. Savannah Festival Factory Outlet Center offers brand name merchandise at substantial savings. The Outlet Mall of Georgia in Pooler, near Savannah, was expected to open in 2015 at a cost of $200 million. River Street's nineteenth-century warehouses have been converted into shops, restaurants, and nightclubs.

Savannah is a city renowned for its hospitality. While the city offers a wide choice of dining establishments, visitors are particularly delighted by the "down-home southern cookin'" for which the area is famous. The diverse land and water of the region produces catfish and chicken for frying, hush puppies, grits, sweet potatoes for pie, collards and turnip greens, okra, scallions, dried peas, ham and turkey for smoking, meat for barbecuing, peanuts for boiling, white butter beans, white and yellow turnips, cornmeal for bread, tomatoes, oysters, crab for crabcakes, and shrimp. In addition to this sort of delectable fare, the city's many restaurants offer the cuisines of China, Japan, Italy, and Greece, as well as continental dishes. Well-known restaurants in the Historic District include the Moon River Brewing Company, the only brew pub in the city; Clary's Café, made famous by *Midnight in the Garden of Good and Evil*; Elizabeth on 37th, known for its Southern cuisine, and The Olde Pink House, a fine-dining seafood establishment.

Visitor Information: Visit Savannah, 101 East Bay Street, Savannah, GA 31401; telephone (912) 644-6400.

■ Convention Facilities

The $83 million Savannah International Trade & Convention Center is the centerpiece of a remarkable renaissance blending the best of the Old and New South into a unique meetings destination. Located in the "Historic Meeting District," the state-of-the-art, 330,000-square-foot complex features 100,000 square feet of customizable exhibit space with impressive vistas of Savannah's bustling waterfront. An additional 50,000 square feet of prime meeting space accommodates large general sessions to small private retreats. Highly flexible, these first-class facilities include the 25,000-square-foot Grand Ballroom, a variety of 13 meeting rooms, 4 executive-class boardrooms, and a 367-seat auditorium. Several downtown area hotels offer event space.

The Savannah Civic Center also offers several auditoriums and ballroom areas for meetings and events. The Martin Luther King Arena at the Civic Center is often used for conventions and trade shows. The arena has seating for up to 9,600, and the exhibit hall can accommodate 400. The Johnny Mercer Theatre seats up to 2,506 and has one of the largest prosceniums in the Southeast.

Convention Information: Visit Savannah, 101 East Bay Street, Savannah, GA 31401; telephone (912) 644-6400. Savannah International Trade and Convention Center, One International Drive, Savannah, GA 31402-0248; telephone (912) 447-4000. Savannah Civic Center, 301 W. Oglethorpe Ave., Savannah, GA; telephone (912) 651-6550.

■ Transportation

Approaching the City

Savannah/Hilton Head International Airport, located 12 miles west of the city, is served by American Airlines, Delta, jetBlue, United, and US Airways. The airport served 4,416 passengers per day in 2012, with an average of 248 takeoffs and landings. Roughly half of the commercial flights were operated by Delta. Savannah Aviation, a charter service, is also located at the facility. Savannah is reached by automobile on Interstate 95 (north–south,) which links Savannah with other cities along the East Coast, and Interstate 16 (east–west) via Interstate 75 from Atlanta. Amtrak provides rail service through Savannah between New York, Miami, and Tampa. Greyhound provides intercity bus transportation and charter service.

Traveling in the City

Interstate 95 runs just west of Savannah, and Interstate 16 comes from the west and stops at the city's center. The city's historic district is 10 miles east of the intersection of Interstates 95 and 16. U.S. Highway 80 from Tybee Island and the Atlantic Ocean, 17 miles away, crosses the city going east and west, and U.S. Highway 17 bisects the northwest quadrant of the city, coming from the north. Chatham Area Transit (CAT) provides local bus service and wheelchair-accessible free shuttle service from downtown hotels, inns, and the visitor's center to the Historic District and other attractions. As of 2013, it averaged nearly 12,000 riders daily. Taxi companies serve all parts of the city. Savannah Belles Ferry offers service to Hutchinson Island from downtown and is operated by CAT.

■ Communications

Newspapers and Magazines

Savannah's major daily newspaper is the *Savannah Morning News*. The *Statesboro Herald*, originating from nearby Statesboro, Georgia, is also available in the city six days a week. The *Savannah Daily News* is operated by Coastal Empire News and provides news in the Savannah and Brunswick, Georgia, metropolitan areas by aggregating daily news from six area websites. Local weeklies include the arts-centered *Connect Savannah*. *The Savannah Tribune* and *Savannah Herald* focuses on the city's African American community. *The Savannah Jewish News* is published 10 times per year. *Savannah Magazine* is also published in Savannah.

Television and Radio

Eight television stations broadcast from Savannah, including one public broadcasting station, WVAN. Savannah's 5 AM and 11 FM stations cover a wide variety of formats including talk and public radio, classical, jazz, rock, religious, and adult contemporary.

Media Information: Savannah Morning News, PO Box 1088, Savannah, GA 31402; telephone (912) 236-9511.

Savannah Online

Chatham County home page. Available www.chathamcounty.org

City of Savannah government home page. Available www.savannahga.gov

Georgia Historical Society. Available www.georgiahistory.com

Georgia Labor Market Explorer. Available explorer.dol.state.ga.us

Live Oak Public Libraries. Available www.liveoakpl.org

Savannah Area Chamber of Commerce. Available www.savannahchamber.com

Visit Savannah. Available www.visitsavannah.com

Savannah-Chatham County Public Schools. Available www.savannah.chatham.k12.ga.us

Savannah Economic Development Authority. Available www.seda.org

Savannah International Trade & Convention Center. Available www.savtcc.com

Savannah Morning News. Available www.savannahnow.com

BIBLIOGRAPHY

Berendt, John, *Midnight in the Garden of Good and Evil* (New York: Vintage Books, 1999)

Jakes, John, *Savannah or A Gift for Mr. Lincoln* (Dutton Books, 2004)

Morekis, Jim, *Moon Spotlight Savannah and the Georgia Coast,* 2nd ed. (Avalon Travel Publishing, 2010)

Price, Eugenia, *Savannah* (Nashville: Turner, 2013)

Zepke, Terrance, *Ghosts of Savannah* (Sarasota: Pineapple Press, Inc., 2012)

Kentucky

The State in Brief

Nickname: Bluegrass State

Motto: United we stand, divided we fall

Flower: Goldenrod

Bird: Cardinal

Area: 40,408 square miles (2010; U.S. rank 37th)

Elevation: Ranges from 257 feet to 4,145 feet above sea level

Climate: Temperate, with plentiful rainfall; occasional winter temperature extremes in the mountains

Admitted to Union: June 1, 1792

Capital: Frankfort

Head Official: Steven L. Beshear (D) (until 2015)

Population

1990: 3,685,296
2000: 4,041,769
2010: 4,339,367
2012 estimate: 4,340,167
Percent change, 2000–2010: 7.4%
U.S. rank in 2012: 26th
Percent of residents born in state: 70.2% (2012)
Density: 109.9 people per square mile (2010)
2012 FBI Crime Index Total: 121,578

Racial and Ethnic Characteristics (2012)

White: 3,823,344
Black or African American: 339,228
American Indian and Alaska Native: 8,607
Asian: 49,681
Native Hawaiian and Pacific Islander: 2,370
Hispanic or Latino (may be of any race): 131,039
Other: 116,937

Age Characteristics (2012)

Population under 5 years old: 280,640
Population 5 to 19 years old: 862,070
Percent of population 65 years and over: 13.4%
Median age: 38.0

Vital Statistics

Total number of births (2012–13): 54,554
Total number of deaths (2012–13): 41,881
AIDS cases reported through 2011: 5,867

Economy

Major industries: Food products, agriculture, energy, trade, manufacturing
Unemployment rate (2012): 5.7%
Per capita income (2012): $23,210
Median household income (2012): $42,610
Percentage of persons below poverty level (2012): 18.6%
Income tax rate: 2.0% to 6.0%
Sales tax rate: 6.0%

Bowling Green

■ The City in Brief

Founded: 1798

Head Official: Mayor Bruce Wilkerson (since 2011)

City Population
> 1990: 40,641
> 2000: 49,528
> 2010: 58,067
> 2012 estimate: 59,707
> Percent change, 2000–2010: 17.2%
> U.S. rank in 2010: 591st

Metropolitan Statistical Area Population
> 2000: 104,166
> 2010: 125,953
> 2012 estimate: 128,016
> Percent change, 2000–2010: 20.9%
> U.S. rank in 2000: 325th
> U.S. rank in 2010: 327th

Area: 38.5 square miles

Elevation: 547 feet above sea level

Average Annual Temperatures: 59.1° F

Average Annual Precipitation: 48.86 inches of rain; 3.0 inches of snow

Major Economic Sectors: Manufacturing, distribution and logistics, government, educational services

Unemployment Rate: 7.6% (2012)

Per Capita Income: $19,414

2012 FBI Crime Index Property: 3,025

Major Colleges and Universities: Western Kentucky University

Daily Newspaper: *Bowling Green Daily News*

■ Introduction

Bowling Green is one of Kentucky's largest cities by population. Within an hour's drive from the major cities of Nashville, Tennessee, and Louisville, Bowling Green has focused on retaining its manufacturing base while encouraging entrepreneurship. With Bowling Green's General Motors Assembly Plant, home of the Chevrolet Corvette, as a manufacturing anchor, the city has become known for its automotive industry, which also includes several automotive parts and supply companies. However, the city has also expanded its reach as a regional center for health care and educational services.

■ Geography and Climate

Located amid grassy plateaus of South Central Kentucky, Bowling Green is the seat of Warren County. The region is dotted with many small bodies of water that surround the nearby Barren River, which is the largest body. Bowling Green has four distinct seasons, and while the region endures few extremes of weather, it is subject to unexpected changes in temperature of relatively short duration. Precipitation is relatively constant year around. However, the region is subject to infrequent, but disastrous, flooding.

Area: 38.5 square miles

Elevation: 547 feet above sea level

Average Temperatures: 59.1° F

Average Annual Precipitation: 48.86 inches of rain; 3.0 inches of snow

■ History

A band of explorers called "long hunters" passed through the Kentucky Wilderness in 1775, carving their names on trees to signal their passage. They reached a land full of rivers, streams, forests, atop rolling but rugged hills.

Bowling Green Area Convention and Visitors Bureau.

A settler named Robert Moore soon built a homestead along a large spring that would become the city of Bowling Green. Around the same time, the Revolutionary War raged on. In 1792 the Kentucky territory became the 15th state in the union.

A petition of behalf of new residents of the area caused a General Assembly to make Warren County an establishment in 1797 in honor of Dr. Joseph Warren, who fought in the Battle of Bunker Hill. A year later, Robert Moore and his brother George donated more than 30 acres of land to create a town around newly constructed buildings. At the first county commissioners meeting in early 1798, pioneers named the town Bolin Green, after Bowling Green Square in New York City where patriots had melted a statue of King George III and instead made bullets during the American Revolution. The new town consisted of stores, a single tavern, and simple houses, with the oldest building being The Mariah Moore House erected in 1818.

The commercialized city rises

Bowling Green continued to expand its commercial capabilities, and formed the Bank of the Commonwealth in 1821. The first newspaper was published in the late 1820s called the Spirit of the Times. A doctor's office, a private boys' school, a Masonic lodge, and a handful of churches followed. When it came to transportation to nearby cities, stagecoach lines became the connection between Bowling Green and Louisville, Nashville, and Hopkinsville. Flatboats transported food and other goods south to New Orleans. Improvements in infrastructure followed with stock companies lending money to improve the railroad and river systems, locks, and dams, so the paddle wheel and steamboats could easily transport passengers up and down the Barren River. Bowling Green's solid foundation and continuing advancements made it a vibrant economy and nice place to live.

Businesses continued to spring up all about town in the 1840s. The Thomas Quigley building drug store at the corner of Main and State streets opened its doors, followed by the Marshall House Jewelry store in 1847. Steamboat trips to Louisville, picnics at Beech Bend, and visits to the mysterious Mammoth Cave were all ways residents entertained themselves. A wool factory, candle factory, iron foundry, and flour mills were built to manufacture local goods. In 1859 the Louisville and Nashville Railroad connected Bowling Green to northern and southern cities. This transportation route was particularly important as the nation moved toward the Civil War. In 1861 Confederate forces moved, making Bowling Green a temporary capital of Confederate Kentucky. A few months later, however, the

Confederates left as news came that Union forces had taken key strongholds to the north.

After the war and into the 1900s, the city enjoyed steady growth. A number of colleges for men and women were established in the city, including Western Kentucky State Normal School (now Western Kentucky University), which was established in 1906. As the manufacturing industry developed, the population boomed. The completion of Interstate 65 in the late 1960s made it even easier for new businesses and residents to make Bowling Green their home. By the end of 1970, the city was larger than Ashland and Newport.

In 1980 General Motors Corporation chose Bowling Green as the site for their Corvette assembly plant. Several automotive parts and supplies companies came in behind them, making the automotive industry an anchor for the local economy. Over the next few decades, the population continued to grow steadily. In 1990 the population was estimated at about 40,641. That number grew to 49,296 in 2000 and then to 58,067 in 2010. In the early twenty-first century, a downtown renaissance began under the leadership of the Downtown Redevelopment Authority. The city continued to welcome new businesses, while expanding the city's reach as a center for culture and education. Development projects included construction of Riverwalk Park, Circus Square, the Fountain Square Market, and the Southern Kentucky Performing Arts Center.

Historical Information: Kentucky Museum, Western Kentucky University Libraries, 1444 Kentucky Street, Bowling Green, KY 42101; telephone (270) 745-2592.

■ Population Profile

Metropolitan Statistical Area Population

2000: 104,166
2010: 125,953
2012 estimate: 128,016
Percent change, 2000–2010: 20.9%
U.S. rank in 2000: 325th
U.S. rank in 2010: 327th

City Residents

1990: 40,641
2000: 49,528
2010: 58,067
2012 estimate: 59,707
Percent change, 2000–2010: 17.2%
U.S. rank in 2010: 591st

Density: 1,730.3 people per square mile

Racial and ethnic characteristics

White: 43,717
Black or African American: 8,925
American Indian and Alaskan Native: 27
Asian: 2,435
Native Hawaiian and Other Pacific Islander: 17
Hispanic or Latino (may be of any race): 3,939
Other: 4,586

Percent of residents born in state: 56.6%

Age characteristics

Population under 5 years old: 3,907
Population 5 to 9 years old: 2,944
Population 10 to 14 years old: 3,573
Population 15 to 19 years old: 6,121
Population 20 to 24 years old: 10,441
Population 25 to 34 years old: 8,989
Population 35 to 44 years old: 6,249
Population 45 to 54 years old: 6,134
Population 55 to 59 years old: 3,034
Population 60 to 64 years old: 2,058
Population 65 to 74 years old: 3,102
Population 75 to 84 years old: 2,020
Population 85 years and over: 1,135
Median age: 27.4

Births (2010–11 Micropolitan Area)

Total number: 868

Deaths (2010–11 Micropolitan Area)

Total number: 622

Money income (2012)

Per capita income: $19,414
Median household income: $31,272
Total households: 23,219

Number of households with income of ...

less than $10,000: 3,294
$10,000 to $14,999: 2,715
$15,000 to $24,999: 3,570
$25,000 to $34,999: 3,312
$35,000 to $49,999: 3,188
$50,000 to $74,999: 3,270
$75,000 to $99,999: 1,857
$100,000 to $149,999: 1,279
$150,000 to $199,999: 394
$200,000 or more: 340

Percent of families below poverty level: 29.4%

FBI Crime Index Property: 3,025

FBI Crime Index Violent: 189

■ Municipal Government

Bowling Green's city-manager form of government was established in 1969. The city manager oversees daily operations and carries out directives of the Board of Commissioners, which acts as the legislative branch of the city government. The Board of Commissioners consists of the mayor, who serves a four-year term, and four elected commissioners, who each serve two-year terms. In 2013 the city manager was Kevin DeFabbo.

Head Official: Mayor Bruce Wilkerson (since 2011)

Total Number of City Employees: 730 (2013)

City Information: City of Bowling Green, 1001 College Street, Bowling Green, KY 42101; telephone (270) 393-3000.

■ Economy

Major Industries and Commercial Activity

Manufacturing still plays a significant role in the local economy. Bowling Green is most notable for its economic strength in the automobile industry. General Motors maintains an assembly plant in Bowling Green that produces the famous Chevy Corvette. Several automotive parts and supplies companies are located in Bowling Green as well, including Kobe Aluminum Automotive Products and Shiloh Industries. Holley Performance Products produces carburetors, fuel pumps, and other performance parts. In addition, BADA Hennessy Industries manufactures steel weights for cars and trucks. Trace Die Cast supplies the automotive industry with high-quality aluminum die castings. Other major manufacturers in Bowling Green include Alpha, Inc., (plastic packaging), Bilstein Group (strip steel), Berry Plastics, and Bowling Green Metalforming.

Distribution and logistics is an important sector for the economy of south-central Kentucky, which is home to companies such as Sun Products Corporation, the Fruit of the Loom Distribution Center, and the Tractor Supply Co. Distribution Center. Food processing companies located in the region include the Kroger Company Country Oven Bakery, T. Marzetti, Company, and J. M. Smuckers.

Educational services and government are also significant sectors in the economy.

Items and goods produced: automobiles, automotive and industrial parts, aluminum alloys, steel weights, aluminum die casting, food and beverages, plastics

Incentive Programs-New and Existing Companies

Local programs: Assistance for new and expanding business is available through the City of Bowling Green, and the Bowling Green Area Chamber of Commerce. The City of Bowling Green offers a Job Development Incentive Program for companies creating new jobs that produce a minimum of $10,000 in city withholding tax annually. Community Development Block Grants and a low-interest Bowling Green Revolving Loan Fund are also available.

State programs: The state of Kentucky offers an extensive array of incentives for business start-up and expansion. The Kentucky Economic Development Finance Authority (KEDFA) of the Kentucky Cabinet for Economic Development oversees a wide variety of programs and services available to businesses, including existing businesses, newly locating companies, start-ups, small and minority businesses, and many others. Small businesses may benefit from the Kentucky Small Business Credit Initiative, which supports participating lenders in efforts to finance businesses that typically fall outside of standard lending guidelines. Small businesses involved in manufacturing, agribusiness, or service and technology may qualify for the Small Business Loan Program, which provides loans between $15,000 and $100,000 for a term of 10 years. The Kentucky Small Business Tax Credit provides credits for eligible businesses with 50 or fewer full-time employees who create one or more jobs while investing at least $5,000 in qualifying equipment or technology.

The Kentucky Business Investment Program offers income tax credits for new and existing agribusinesses, regional and national headquarters, manufacturing companies, and non-retail service- or technology-related companies. New or expanding businesses involved in service or technology, manufacturing, or tourism can apply for assistance through the Kentucky Enterprise Initiative Act, which provides sales and use tax refunds for building and construction materials or equipment used for research and development and data processing. The Kentucky Economic Development Direct Loan Program offers below-market interest rates for businesses involved in agribusiness, tourism, industrial ventures, or the service industry.

Some special incentives are available for high-tech companies, including the High-Tech Investment/Construction Pools, which provide funds for commercialization of a product, process, or innovation. The KEDFA also offers a matching funds program for Phase 1 and Phase 2 federal small business innovation research and small business technology transfer awards received by Kentucky businesses. A special Kentucky New Energy ventures Fund has been established to assist in the development of commercialization of alternative fuels and renewable energy. Companies providing large investments in renewable and alternative energy facilities may be eligible for a variety of negotiated incentives through the Incentives for Energy Independence Act.

Agribusiness companies may be legible for assistance through the Kentucky Agricultural Development Fund or the Kentucky Agricultural Finance Corporation. Businesses involved in tourism may qualify for the recovery of development costs through the Tourism Development Act, which is administered through the Kentucky Tourism, Arts, and Heritage Cabinet.

Job training programs: Workforce training assistance is provided through the Bluegrass State Skills Corporation (BSSC) of the Kentucky Cabinet for Economic Development. The BSSC Grant-in-Aid program provides grants for training of workers in new and expanding businesses and continuing training for workers in existing companies. The Skills Training Investment Credit program offers state tax credits for approved training programs.

The Kentucky Office of Employment and Training, a branch of the Kentucky Department of Workforce Investment, provides training assistance under the Workforce Investment Act. The Bowling Green Area Career Center serves Warren County.

Customized employee training programs are available through the Kentucky Community and Technical College System. In the Bowling Green area, these services are provided through the main campus of Southcentral Kentucky Community and Technical College, the Transpark Center, and the Kentucky Advanced Technology Institute.

Development Projects

In 2013 the Austria-based plastic packaging company Alpha, Inc., announced plans to expand its manufacturing operations in Bowling Green. The $22.4 million investment was expected to create 72 new jobs. Alpha produces packaging for items such as beverages, motor oils, and cleaning supplies. Also in 2013 the German-based Bilstein Group announced plans to establish a production plant in Kentucky Transpark. An investment of $120 million was expected to create about 150 new jobs. Bilstein North America produces cold-rolled strip steel products.

Economic Development Information: Bowling Green Area Chamber of Commerce, 701 College Street, P.O. Box 51, Bowling Green, KY 42102; telephone (270) 781-3200; fax (270) 843-0458.

Commercial Shipping

An hour northeast from Nashville, Tennessee, and two hours south of Lexington, Kentucky, Bowling Green enjoys a central location with available land for establishment of distribution facilities. The two most accessible methods of transportation are by road or air. Easy access to Interstate 65 makes motor carry to Louisville available, with Interstate 64 heading to Lexington from there. The Nashville International Airport is Bowling Green's closest hub for commercial air travel. L and N Railroad travels through Bowling Green, as well as the R. J. Corman Railroad, which has only a short line through Warren County.

Labor Force and Employment Outlook

According to the U.S. Bureau of Labor Statistics, government was the largest non-farm employment sector in Bowling Green (by number of employees) in 2013. Trade, transportation, and utilities was the second-largest employment sector, followed by education and health services and manufacturing.

The following is a summary of data regarding the 2012 Bowling Green labor force:

Size of civilian labor force: 31,569

Number of workers employed in . . .

agriculture and mining: 109
construction: 1,305
manufacturing: 3,913
wholesale trade: 523
retail trade: 4,206
transportation: 1,293
information systems: 627
finance: 836
professional administration: 1,920
education and social services: 7,345
arts and leisure: 4,004
other: 1,042
public administration: 467

Average hourly earnings of production workers: $14.69

Unemployment rate: 7.6% (2012)

Employers

Largest employers (2013)	*Number of employees*
Commonwealth Health Corporation	2,250
Western Kentucky University	1,578
Warren County Board of Education	1,896
General Motors Corvette Plant	1,035
Holley Performance Products	950
DESA International	800
City of Bowling Green	730
Tristar Greenview Regional Hospital	610
Eagle Industries	600
Fruit of the Loom	600
Houchens Industries	534
Huish Detergents	500
Bowling Green Board of Education	492

Cost of Living

The cost of living in Bowling Green was just over 88 percent of the national average in 2013, making it an attractive and affordable place to live and work.

The following is a summary of data regarding several key cost of living factors in the area.

2013 ACCRA Average House Price: $244,133

2013 ACCRA Cost of Living Index: 93

State income tax rate: 2.0% to 6.0%

State sales tax rate: 6.0%

Local income tax rate: 1.85%

Local sales tax rate: None

Property tax rate: ranges from $1.1139 to $1.7099 per $100 of assessed value (2013)

Economic Information: Bowling Green Area Chamber of Commerce, 701 College Street, P.O. Box 51, Bowling Green, KY 42102; telephone (270) 781-3200; fax (270) 843-0458.

■ Education and Research

Elementary and Secondary Schools

Warren County encompasses many public schools and independent schools. Warren County Public Schools has 24 schools, of which 21 are located within Bowling Green. Bowling Green Independent School District has eight schools, including Bowling Green High School, which was ranked among the top 3 percent of high schools nationwide by the *Washington Post* and as one of the top 10 schools in Kentucky by *U.S. News & World Report* in 2012. The new Dishman-McGinnis Elementary School was set to open in August 2014.

Other area schools include Anchored Christian School, Bowling Green Christian Academy, Foundation Christian Academy, Holy Trinity Lutheran School, Old Union School, and St. Joseph Interparochial School.

The following is a summary of data regarding the Bowling Green Independent School District.

Total enrollment: 3,877

Number of facilities

    total: 29
    elementary schools: 18
    junior high schools: 5
    high schools: 5
    other: 1

Student/teacher ratio: 16.02:1

Teacher salaries

    average (statewide): $50,038

Funding per pupil: $9,854

Public Schools Information: Bowling Green Independent School District, 1211 Center Street, Bowling Green, KY 42101; telephone (270) 746-2200. Warren County Public Schools, 303 Lovers Lane, Bowling Green, KY 42103; telephone (270) 781-5150.

Colleges and Universities

Western Kentucky University (WKU), home of the Hilltoppers sports teams, was established in 1906 by the Commonwealth of Kentucky. The school sits on College Heights, the highest point in south-central Kentucky, and overlooks the Barren River valley. WKU has a student population of more than 21,000.

Southcentral Kentucky Community and Technical College has three campuses in Bowling Green; the main campus is on Morgantown Road. The Kentucky Advanced Technology Institute (KATI) campus has programs that focus on business administrative systems, computer and information technologies, medical information technology, and office systems technology. The Transpark Center campus offers programs in computerized manufacturing and machining technology and engineering technology.

Libraries and Research Centers

Warren County Public Library has a Main Library, three branch libraries (Bob Kirby Branch, Graham Drive Community, and Smith Grove Branch), and a bookmobile (called the Mobile Branch) that carries 6,000 library materials throughout the county. The library hosts speakers, book signings, and a variety of programs from free computer training classes to programs for babies through adults.

The main branch of Western Kentucky University Libraries is the Helm-Cravens Library on the Bowling Green campus. The Educational Resource Center, Special Collections Library, and Visual and Performing Arts Library are also located on the main campus. Regional branches are located in Glasgow, Elizabethtown, and Owensboro.

Western Kentucky University supports several research centers and institutes through the Applied Research and Technology Program. These include the Advanced Materials Institute, Agriculture Research and Education Complex, Astrophysics and Space Science Institute, Biotechnology Center, Hoffman Environmental Research Center, and the Social Science Research Center. The WKU Nondestructive Analysis Center (WKU NOVA) is home to a large chamber scanning electron microscope (LC-SEM), making WKU the only university in North America to have such a device.

Public Library Information: Warren County Public Library, 1225 State St., Bowling Green, KY 42101; telephone (270) 781-4882; fax (270) 781-3699.

■ Health Care

Bowling Green has two hospitals. TriStar Greenview Regional Hospital, a 211-bed acute care facility, provides a full-range of services, including emergency services and the latest technologies in surgical and cardiac care. The Sarah Cannon Cancer Center at Tristar Regional is part of one of the nation's largest regional community-based cancer treatment and research programs.

The 490-bed Medical Center at Bowling Green is a branch of the Commonwealth Health Corporation. It has several affiliated health-care facilities to provide patients the services they need without having to go far from home. The Medical Center itself received full Cycle III accreditation in 2010 to perform percutaneous coronary intervention (PCI). The procedure involves the use of cardiac catheterization to treat narrowed coronary arteries of the heart. The Medical Center is the only hospital in south-central Kentucky to receive this accreditation by the review committee of the Society for Chest Pain Centers. The Heart Institute at the Medical Center offers the region's only comprehensive cardiac program including open-heart surgery. The Commonwealth Regional Specialty Hospital, which is a long-term acute care hospital affiliated with the Medical Center, treats patients who require constant treatment for chronic problems.

■ Recreation

Sightseeing

The National Corvette Museum, which features more than 75 cars and prototypes, opened an educational driving simulator theater in 2010 to teach responsible driving habits. The General Motors Corvette Assembly Plant, built in 1981, offers tours that follow the one-mile assembly-line process of creating the famed sports car.

Beech Bend Amusement Park and Splash Lagoon offers more than 40 rides and is home to the Sea Dragon ride, purchased from pop music icon Michael Jackson's Neverland home in California and moved to Bowling Green in 2009. In addition to the Sea Dragon, Beech Bend's twisting wooden roller coaster, the Kentucky Rumbler, is a popular attraction. Tiki Island at Splash Lagoon features the 275,000-gallon Surf's Up Wave Pool, Lazy River, and the Ragin' Rapids water slides.

Aviation Heritage Park stands as a memorial to south-central Kentucky pilots. The park features military aircraft as well as exhibits on the pilots. Barren River Imaginative Museum of Science has more than 50 exhibits, including a mini-tornado and electrostatic generator.

Historic places to visit include the Historic Railpark and Train Museum that features a two-story museum and 450-foot exhibit display track with six historical cars and a Post Office Car commissioned nearly a century ago. The historic Riverview at Hobson Grove is a pre-Civil War home of Atwood Gaines Hobson and Juliet van Meter Hobson. During the war, the Italianate architectural home was used as a magazine for weapons when Bowling Green was a confederate stronghold.

Arts and Culture

The Capitol Arts Center located in the historic Fountain Square Park in downtown Bowling Green is under the management of the Southern Kentucky Performing Arts Center, Inc. (SKyPAC). The Capitol is home to the SKyPac Education and Gallery Department, Houchens Gallery, and Mezzanine Gallery. It is also a host theater for touring and local theater and musical groups, including the SKyPac Youth Theater and Orchestra Kentucky of Bowling Green. The Phoenix Public Theatre of Kentucky, a nonprofit organization, is a company for local and nearby residents of all ages.

Other music organizations in the area include the Symphony at WKU, featuring musicians from Western Kentucky University and the community, and the Southern Kentucky Blues Society. Each summer, downtown's Fountain Square Park brings in artists for Concerts in the Park that are held during afternoons and evenings.

Festivals and Holidays

Seasonal events in Bowling Green include the Duncan Hines Festival, an annual baking festival held during the summer and named for the local Duncan Hines Baking conglomerate. It is hosted by the Bowling Green Junior Woman's Club, which began such events as The Adventures of Good Baking Contest. The Bowling Green International Festival is held on the last Saturday in September every year in Circus Square Park. The festival highlights different countries and cultures with crafts, dancing, and music representing all parts of the world.

Sports for the Spectator

The Bowling Green Hot Rods, named to recognize Bowling Green's automotive identity, is the city's minor league baseball team. They are a Midwest League Class A farm team for the Tampa Bay Rays. The Hot Rods play at the state-of-the-art 4,500-seat Bowling Green Ballpark, which was completed in 2009.

The Western Kentucky University men's Hilltoppers and women's Lady Toppers are the major college teams in the area. The Hilltoppers have eight men's sports teams, including a men's basketball program that is among the most winning Division I teams in the United States. The Lady Toppers have nine sports teams, including soccer and volleyball. Teams play at the 7,500-seat E. A. Diddle Arena on Western Kentucky University's campus.

The Beech Bend raceway is a place to watch and participate in drag and stock car racing on Saturday nights.

Sports for the Participant

Bowling Green boasts an array of opportunities for amateur athletes. Golfers can visit CrossWinds Golf Course, the Golf Course at Riverview, or Paul Walker Golf Course. The city maintains 18 parks, three recreation centers, a skate park, and disc golf course. Men's softball, Bowling Green West Little League, soccer, basketball, and volleyball are offered at select parks and recreation centers. Tennis lessons are offered at Kereiakes Park. In the summer months, people can swim at the Russell Sims Aquatic Center, which holds a zero-depth entry 50-meter pool, two water slides, and splash playground. The center is open to the public Memorial Day through Labor Day. Bowling Green has been recognized as a Bicycle-Friendly Community by the League of American Bicyclists. Several bike routes have been mapped throughout the city, ranging from beginner-level, safe pathways for parents and children to advanced rides for those who can navigate through heavy street traffic.

Shopping and Dining

For shopping needs, visitors and residents can shop at the more than 100 specialty stores at Greenwood Mall, which is anchored by department stores Macy's, Sears, JCPenney, and Dillard's. The mall sits conveniently near Interstate 65, allowing easy access to shopping, dining at one of five restaurants, or seeing a movie at the Regal Cinema.

In addition to the mall, shoppers may visit the unique stores downtown at Fountain Square. Flea Land of Bowling Green and Vette City Antique Mall and Flea Market are places to find furniture, collectibles, and other interesting trinkets.

Bowling Green also boasts a wide variety of restaurants, ranging from franchises to unique and historical settings. In Fountain Square Park, Micki's on Main offers gumbo, sandwiches, and Cajun fare, while adjoining 440 Main offers seafood along with hearty favorites such as artichoke and cheese fritters, and jambalaya. Mariah's in downtown is located in the city's oldest brick house, which is on the National Register of Historic Homes.

Visitor Information: Bowling Green Area Convention and Visitors Bureau, 352 Three Springs Rd., Bowling Green, KY 42104; telephone: (800) 326-7465; fax: (270) 842-2104.

■ Convention Facilities

The Sloan Convention Center is Bowling Green's largest event and meeting facility. The 60,000-square-foot center has 35,500 square feet of meeting and exhibit space. The grand ballroom consists of 19,500 square feet, but can be divided into four small ballrooms for receptions, theater-style presentations, round-table set ups, and classroom style space. In addition, the center has six breakout meeting rooms. With state-of-the-art audio-visual equipment,

catering and nearby activities such as the CrossWinds Golf Course next door, the Sloan Convention Center is the best site in Bowling Green for large-scale events. The nearby Courtyard by Marriott and Hilton Garden Inn, both across the street, together have 2,225 square feet of meeting space, and the Holiday Inn University Plaza Hotel, which connects to the convention center, has more than 4,500 square feet of additional meeting space.

Besides Sloan, other facilities in the area include the Carroll Knicely Conference Center near Western Kentucky University's campus. It consists of class-rooms, auditoriums, and computer lab and reception rooms that can hold from 20 to 1,100 people depending on the room. The facility can accommodate weddings, receptions, banquets, dinners, and class and family reunions.

Convention Information: Bowling Green Area Convention and Visitors Bureau, 352 Three Springs Rd., Bowling Green, KY 42104; telephone: (800) 326-7465; fax: (270) 842-2104.

■ Transportation

Approaching the City

Bowling Green's closest international airport is the Nashville International Airport, located 61 miles southwest and an hour from Bowling Green's city center. The airport is served by seven major airlines. The nearest regional airport used for domestic flights is Bowling Green-Warren County Regional Airport. Louisville International Airport is two hours north of Bowling Green.

When arriving by car, visitors can approach coming south on Interstate 65. Visitors can also travel using Greyhound Bus Lines.

Traveling in the City

GO BG Transit operates five bus routes to different destinations within city limits. Riders can easily get to major spots such as Fountain Square Park, Greenwood Mall, Western Kentucky University, and more. Service runs from 7:00 a.m. to 6:00 p.m. Monday through Friday. On the second Saturday of every month, the transit runs a shopping shuttle to transport riders to local shopping centers. ADA Complementary Paratransit is available for disabled residents. Hours are the same as GO BG Transit, and the buses go door-to-door to pick up and drop off riders. Disabled riders must qualify to be eligible for this service.

■ Communications

Newspapers and Magazines

The *Bowling Green Daily News* is Bowling Green's major daily newspaper. Other publications based in Bowling

Green include *SOKY Happenings*, *College Heights Herald* (Western Kentucky University student newspaper), and *The Amplifier*, south-central Kentucky's monthly entertainment guide.

Television and Radio

There are six licensed television stations broadcasting from Bowling Green, including affiliates of NBC and ABC and a public broadcasting network operated at Western Kentucky University. Viewers can also watch stations based in nearby cities. There are eight licensed radio stations broadcasting from Bowling Green.

Media Information: *Bowling Green Daily News*, 813 College Street, P.O. Box 90012, Bowling Green, KY 42101; telephone (270) 781-1700.

Bowling Green Online

Bowling Green Area Chamber of Commerce. Available www.bgchamber.com

Bowling Green Area Convention and Visitors Bureau. Available www.visitbgky.com

Bowling Green Daily News. Available www.bgdailynews.com

Bowling Green Independent School District. Available www.b-g.k12.ky.us

City of Bowling Green. Available www.bgky.org.

Warren County Public Library. Available www.warrenpl.org.

BIBLIOGRAPHY

Benford, Tom, *Corvette* (St. Paul: MBI Publishing Company and Motorbooks, 2007)

Frankfort

■ The City in Brief

Founded: 1786 (chartered 1786)

Head Official: Mayor William May (since 2013)

City Population
- 1990: 25,968
- 2000: 27,741
- 2010: 25,527
- 2012 estimate: 27,420
- Percent change, 2000–2010: −8.0%

Micropolitan Statistical Area Population
- 2000: 66,798
- 2010: 70,706
- 2012 estimate: 70,326
- Percent change, 2000–2010: 5.9%
- U.S. rank in 2000: 975th
- U.S. rank in 2010: 484th

Area: 15 square miles

Elevation: 510 feet above sea level

Average Annual Temperatures: 55.1° F

Average Annual Precipitation: 49.09 inches total precipitation; 7.3 inches of snow

Major Economic Sectors: government, trade and transportation, professional services, education and health services, manufacturing

Unemployment Rate: 6.2% (2012)

Per Capita Income: $22,533

2012 FBI Crime Index Property: 1,267

Major Colleges and Universities: Kentucky State University

Daily Newspaper: *The State Journal*

■ Introduction

Walking around one of the nation's oldest and smallest state capitals, it becomes clear that what Frankfort lacks in size it makes up for in charm. The pristine Kentucky River winds through the city, where cultural treasures and architecture have endured the test of time. It's no wonder Frankfort is frequently listed in polls measuring top small metropolitan cities in which to live. It's the perfect mixture of small-town living and access to big-city amenities.

■ Geography and Climate

Frankfort, county seat of Franklin County, is located in a beautiful valley in the Bluegrass region of Kentucky. The city lies within an hour's drive of the major metropolitan areas of Louisville (to the west) and Lexington (to the east), with Cincinnati less than a two hour-drive to the north. The city sits on an alluvial plain between the Kentucky River and 150-foot-high steep bluffs, on an S-loop in the river 60 miles above its mouth. The river divides the city into north and south sides, which are connected by bridges. The Bluegrass terrain is rocky and gently rolling, and the land is well suited to agriculture. Disastrous flooding of the Kentucky River at Frankfort has occurred at intervals through history: in 1937, 1972, 1974, 1976, 1997, 1989, 2002, and 2010.

Area: 15 square miles

Elevation: 510 feet above sea level

Average Temperatures: 55.1° F

Average Annual Precipitation: 49.09 inches total precipitation; 7.3 inches of snow

Kentucky: Frankfort

The State Capitol building in Frankfort. © James Blank

■ History

Easterners Hear of Garden of Eden in Kentucky

Before Europeans first began to explore the area where Frankfort now stands, the land was heavily forested and teeming with wild game. Shawnee, Delaware, and Cherokee hunting parties followed migrating herds of buffalo, deer, and elk across the Kentucky River near present-day Frankfort. The tribes frequently fought among themselves to control the hunting grounds of Kentucky. In the mid-eighteenth century, backwoodsmen in Pennsylvania, Virginia, and the Carolinas began to feel overcrowded; they complained of land shortages, falling supplies of wild game, and depleted soil, and they cast their eyes on the lush land of Kentucky. In 1751 North Carolina backwoodsman Christopher Gist may have been the first white man to set eyes on the beautiful valley in which Frankfort now lies, but he was forced to leave after learning that Frenchmen and their Indian allies occupied the area (then claimed by France).

Frontiersman John Finlay built a log cabin in the area in about 1752, but his hunting and trading—and any further white settlement—were interrupted by the outbreak of the French and Indian War in 1754. The British won that war, but King George's Proclamation of 1763 then prohibited white settlement of the area. It was not until 1769 that Finley was able to return; he brought with him legendary frontiersman Daniel Boone and four other men intent on hunting and exploration.

Boone, Finley, and other so-called Long Hunters (named for the long periods of time they spent hunting) inflamed the public back East with their stories about the rich land of Kentucky and the opportunities it offered to get rich quick. In 1773 Governor John Murray of Virginia, better known as Lord Dunmore, sent survey parties to Kentucky (then a Virginia county), including one led by Robert McAfee. McAfee and his group surveyed and laid claim to 600 acres of land in and around Frankfort. More settlers poured westward, the Natives reacted with hostility, and in 1774 Lord Dunmore's War erupted. The war ended with the defeat

262

CITIES OF THE UNITED STATES, EIGHTH EDITION

of the Indians and the signing of a peace treaty in the spring of 1775, at about the same time the battle of Lexington and Concord ushered in the American Revolution.

Town Rises, Prospers on Banks of Kentucky River

Land speculators took advantage of the distractions of wartime and laid claim to vast areas of Kentucky. Meanwhile, McAfee's doubtful claim to the area around Frankfort lapsed, lawsuits were filed, and in 1786 General James Wilkinson, a fellow soldier and friend of George Washington, found himself in possession, at a very cheap price, of most of what is now the downtown district of Frankfort (north of the Kentucky River). Wilkinson set to work organizing a town. He chose the name Frankfort to honor the memory of a man named Stephen Frank, a Jewish pioneer who had been shot by Indians, possibly near a river crossing known as Frank's Ford. Streets were laid out and named in honor of Wilkinson, his wife (Ann), his friends from the Revolutionary War, and even for some Spanish friends (Wilkinson was said to be a secret agent of the Spanish government, and it was rumored that he planned to make Kentucky a Spanish colony). Wilkinson built the second house in Frankfort, a log cabin, but his wife refused to live in the crude structure. The house became a tavern that over the years hosted such celebrities as Aaron Burr, the Marquis de Lafayette, and Henry Clay.

Land speculators and pioneers flocked to Frankfort; they cleared land for farms and built houses. By the late 1780s, a church and schoolhouse had been built, and large quantities of tobacco were growing on farms around Frankfort. While the town did not grow as quickly as Wilkinson had envisioned and he decided not to live there himself, he saw that there was money to be made, and in 1791 he built a tobacco warehouse on his Frankfort land. In 1792 Frankfort was named the capitol of the recently admitted state of Kentucky. Up until the last raid took place in 1794, Frankfort settlers were kept busy fending off hostile Indians; thereafter, the tobacco business thrived and salt pork, animal skins, and hemp joined the economic mix, followed by livestock and lumbering. By 1800 Frankfort was the second largest town in Kentucky after Lexington, with a population of 628. A library opened in 1814; several beautiful and elegant homes and churches were built, some of which are still standing; and the central business district began to expand.

The Lexington and Ohio railroad came to town in 1835, and soon Frankfort began to prosper as a manufacturing center. The population grew from 4,755 people in 1860 to 5,396 people in 1874; by 1900, the population was 9,487 people. Residents processed wood from the huge timberlands of Kentucky and produced cotton goods, carriages, paper, lumber, and distilled liquors, including the corn liquor for which the state became famous.

Politics, War, and the Modern City

Lexington and Louisville had vied to be Kentucky's capital, and when Frankfort's capitol building burned twice, in 1815 and 1824, the two cities challenged the rebuilding in Frankfort. Each time, the structure was rebuilt. The presence of government has flavored the social life and affected the economy of the town. National political figures such as Henry Clay, U.S. senators John J. Crittenden and John G. Carlisle, and Supreme Court Justice John M. Harlan trained in Frankfort. Nineteenth-century visitors to Frankfort, expecting to encounter backwoodsmen in the legislature, reported astonishment at the eloquence of Kentucky orators.

Kentucky was officially a part of the Union during America's Civil War, but many of its citizens were slave owners and Southern sympathizers. The peace of Frankfort was disturbed in 1862 when General Bragg's Confederate Forces seized the city and set up a Confederate State Government. Before the first session met, Yankee guns began firing on the town and the Southerners withdrew. The years following the Civil War saw the development of a modern city on the Kentucky. A school system developed, and by 1900 a movement began urging legislators to fund and construct a modern Capitol. In June 1910 citizens throughout Kentucky gathered to witness the formal dedication of architect Frank Mills Andrews's masterpiece, the Beaux Arts design Kentucky State Capitol.

The early twentieth century brought more disturbances to the peace of Frankfort, punctuated by some periods of prosperity. The city dealt with the assassination of Governor William Goebel during a hotly contested election in 1900, as well as outbreaks of racial violence, a legacy of Civil War days, when more than a third of the town's residents were slaves. The Prohibition era brought a decline in the distilling industry and thus in agricultural production. The Great Depression and a severe drought in the 1930s led to hardship and a decline in population. Further misery came when the Ohio River flooded in 1937, engulfing basements and lifting small homes and businesses off their foundations. Estimated damage was $5 million. However, beginning in 1935, the New Deal stimulated a growth in government employment and the beginning of a housing boom. By the time World War II ended, the city, which had changed little since the turn of the century, stood poised to enter its greatest era of growth.

Frankfort experienced a population explosion between 1940 and 1970, from 11,492 residents to 21,356 residents. Demand for housing skyrocketed and farmland rapidly disappeared to make way for subdivisions. Frankfort tripled in size as suburbs were annexed by the city. Realizing the need for a more formal style of government to suit its larger size, in 1956 Frankfort voters approved the manager-commission form of government. Frankfort's infrastructure was modernized and roads were improved, resulting in the move of manufacturing industries to the suburbs, leaving a concentration of government workers downtown. Gradually, the small and compact city, with its charming blend of architectural styles developed over more than a century, expanded into a sprawling city characterized by a more uniform, less ornamental style of construction. Commercial strips grew where homes once stood; shopping centers sprang up on the outskirts of town, further reducing the importance of downtown Frankfort as a retail center.

The 1960s and 1970s saw considerable downtown building activity, with modern high rises replacing slums but also displacing many African American residents. Capital Plaza, a convention center that became the home of Kentucky State University Thoroughbreds basketball, and the Federal Building created a new skyline for Frankfort.

The city experienced a severe tornado in 1974 that caused millions of dollars in damage. Four years later, in December 1978, the Kentucky River rose to 48.5 feet, breaking the 1937 record by almost a foot. This time the damage exceeded $14.5 million and brought home the need for flood control, a challenge that Frankfort leaders were still grappling with when another disastrous flood occurred in 1997. In 2002 there was yet another flood, but its effects were not as devastating. The city's fifth-highest flood to date occurred in May 2010 when the Kentucky River reached 42.84 feet.

Historical Information: Kentucky Historical Society at the Thomas D. Clark Center for Kentucky History, 100 West Broadway, Frankfort, KY 40601; telephone (502) 564-1792.

■ Population Profile

Micropolitan Statistical Area Population

2000: 66,798
2010: 70,706
2012 estimate: 70,326
Percent change, 2000–2010: 5.9%
U.S. rank in 2000: 975th
U.S. rank in 2010: 484th

City Residents

1990: 25,968
2000: 27,741
2010: 25,527
2012 estimate: 27,420
Percent change, 2000–2010: −8.0%

Density: 1,783 people per square mile

Racial and ethnic characteristics

White: 20,335
Black or African American: 4,640
American Indian and Alaskan Native: 27

Asian: 453
Native Hawaiian and Other Pacific Islander: 0
Hispanic or Latino (may be of any race): 1,048
Other: 1,965

Percent of residents born in state: 69.9%

Age characteristics

Population under 5 years old: 1,712
Population 5 to 9 years old: 1,341
Population 10 to 14 years old: 1,593
Population 15 to 19 years old: 2,024
Population 20 to 24 years old: 2,168
Population 25 to 34 years old: 3,875
Population 35 to 44 years old: 3,960
Population 45 to 54 years old: 3,304
Population 55 to 59 years old: 2,157
Population 60 to 64 years old: 1,489
Population 65 to 74 years old: 2,170
Population 75 to 84 years old: 1,158
Population 85 years and over: 469
Median age: 37.3

Births (2010–11 Micropolitan Area)

Total number: 868

Deaths (2010–11 Micropolitan Area)

Total number: 622

Money income (2012)

Per capita income: $22,533
Median household income: $38,651
Total households: 12,233

Number of households with income of ...

less than $10,000: 1,347
$10,000 to $14,999: 669
$15,000 to $24,999: 1,526
$25,000 to $34,999: 1,604
$35,000 to $49,999: 2,649
$50,000 to $74,999: 1,857
$75,000 to $99,999: 1,186
$100,000 to $149,999: 1,093
$150,000 to $199,999: 239
$200,000 or more: 63

Percent of families below poverty level: 23.1%

FBI Crime Index Property: 1,267

FBI Crime Index Violent: 132

■ Municipal Government

Frankfort is governed through the commission-manager form of government. The four members of the city commission are elected to two-year terms, and the mayor is elected to a four-year term. The city manager is responsible for the day-to-day operations of the city, while the mayor and commissioners make policy decisions and enact ordinances. In 2013 Tim Zisoff was the city manager.

Head Official: Mayor William May (since 2013)

Total Number of City Employees: At least 200 (2013 est.)

City Information: City of Frankfort, 315 West Second St. Frankfort, KY 40601; telephone (502) 875-8500; email info@frankfort.ky.gov.

■ Economy

Major Industries and Commercial Activity

State government and private professional service firms doing business with the state have had a stabilizing effect on the area's economy. Educational and health-care services also play a significant role in the local economy. Major local manufacturers produce automotive wheels and stamped automotive parts, automotive wire products, as well as air brake components, pipes, and oil valves for the heating industry. Other local industries make tool and die products, pallets and wood furniture, and fabrics. World-famous Kentucky bourbon is also produced locally. Frankfort serves as a trading center for mid-Kentucky.

Items and goods produced: automotive parts, thermoplastics, construction products, machinery, alcoholic beverages

Incentive Programs-New and Existing Companies

Local programs: The Kentucky Capital Development Corporation (KCDC) offers assistance to new and existing businesses with site development support, providing local funds to help offset costs such as grading, road construction, and utility extensions. It also makes available recaptured grant funds to businesses to help them purchase and lease machinery and equipment. Downtown Frankfort, Inc., offers assistance with retail and office location information in the city's historic downtown. The Frankfort Area Chamber of Commerce also provides assistance for new and existing businesses.

State programs: The state of Kentucky offers an extensive array of incentives for business start-up and expansion. The Kentucky Economic Development Finance Authority (KEDFA) of the Kentucky Cabinet for Economic Development oversees a wide variety of programs and services available to businesses, including existing businesses, newly locating companies, start-ups, small and minority businesses, and many others. Small businesses may benefit from the

Kentucky Small Business Credit Initiative, which supports participating lenders in efforts to finance businesses that typically fall outside of standard lending guidelines. Small businesses involved in manufacturing, agribusiness, or service and technology may qualify for the Small Business Loan Program, which provides loans between $15,000 and $100,000 for a term of 10 years. The Kentucky Small Business Tax Credit provides credits for eligible businesses with 50 or fewer full-time employees who create one or more jobs while investing at least $5,000 in qualifying equipment or technology.

The Kentucky Business Investment Program offers income tax credits for new and existing agribusinesses, regional and national headquarters, manufacturing companies, and non-retail service- or technology-related companies. New or expanding businesses involved in service or technology, manufacturing, or tourism can apply for assistance through the Kentucky Enterprise Initiative Act, which provides sales and use tax refunds for building and construction materials or equipment used for research and development and data processing. The Kentucky Economic Development Direct Loan Program offers below-market interest rates for businesses involved in agribusiness, tourism, industrial ventures, or the service industry.

Some special incentives are available for high-tech companies, including the High-Tech Investment/Construction Pools, which provide funds for commercialization of a product, process, or innovation. The KEDFA also offers a matching funds program for Phase 1 and Phase 2 federal small business innovation research and small business technology transfer awards received by Kentucky businesses. A special Kentucky New Energy ventures Fund has been established to assist in the development of commercialization of alternative fuels and renewable energy. Companies providing large investments in renewable and alternative energy facilities may be eligible for a variety of negotiated incentives through the Incentives for Energy Independence Act.

Agribusiness companies may be legible for assistance through the Kentucky Agricultural Development Fund or the Kentucky Agricultural Finance Corporation. Businesses involved in tourism may qualify for the recovery of development costs through the Tourism Development Act, which is administered through the Kentucky Tourism, Arts, and Heritage Cabinet.

Job training programs: Workforce training assistance is provided through the Bluegrass State Skills Corporation (BSSC) of the Kentucky Cabinet for Economic Development. The BSSC Grant-in-Aid program provides grants for training of workers in new and expanding businesses and continuing training for workers in existing companies. The Skills Training Investment Credit program offers state tax credits for approved training programs. The Kentucky Office of Employment and Training, a branch of the Kentucky Department of Workforce Investment, provides training assistance under the Workforce Investment Act. The main branch of the Kentucky Division of Workforce and Employment Services is located in Frankfort.

Customized employee training programs are available through the Kentucky Community and Technical College System. In the Frankfort metropolitan area, these services are provided through the Lawrenceburg Campus of Bluegrass Community and Technical College.

Development Projects

In 2013 Hayashi Telempu North America announced plans to establish a manufacturing center in Frankfort. The Japanese-based company, which produces automotive interior parts, planned to redevelop an existing 60,000-sqaure-foot facility on Fortune Drive. The $10.7 million investment was expected to create more than 100 new jobs. Also in 2013, Mitsui Knzoku Caltalysts America announced it would move into an existing facility in Frankfort to establish a manufacturing plant for its automobile and motorcycle catalytic converters. With a $19.5 million investment, the company expects to create at least 50 new jobs.

Economic Development Information: Kentucky Capital Development Corporation, 109 Consumer Lane, Frankfort, KY 40601; telephone (502) 226-5611; Fax (502) 226-6634. Downtown Frankfort, Inc., 100 Capital Ave., Frankfort, KY 40601; telephone (502) 223-2261, fax (502)352-2806.

Commercial Shipping

Frankfort does not have its own airport, but Blue Grass Airport in nearby Lexington serves the city's commercial shipping needs, offering national and international transport and a U.S Customs cargo inspection area. There are several trucking companies within the greater Frankfort area.

Labor Force and Employment Outlook

Since Frankfort is the state capital and county seat, the state, county, and municipal governments employ a significant number of people. Professional services, particularly those related to government operations, also draw a large number of employees. Health-care and educational services provide significant employment opportunities as well.

The following is a summary of data regarding the 2012 Frankfort labor force:

Size of civilian labor force: 13,668

Number of workers employed in . . .

agriculture and mining: 19
construction: 696
manufacturing: 1,208
wholesale trade: 26
retail trade: 1,392

transportation: 375
information systems: 91
finance: 466
professional administration: 875
education and social services: 1,828
arts and leisure: 2,315
other: 429
public administration: 2,573

Average hourly earnings of production workers: $Not available

Unemployment rate: 6.2% (2012)

Employers

Largest employers (2013)	*Number of employees*
Monoplast of North America	760
Frankfort Regional Medical Center	650
Buffalo Trace Distillery	318
Topy America	250
HP Enterprise Services	165
Meritor Inc	150
Greenheck Fan Corp.	129

Cost of Living

Within an easy drive of big city amenities in Louisville and Lexington, Frankfort retains a small-town feel with small-town living expenses.

The following is a summary of data regarding several key cost of living factors in the area.

State income tax rate: 2.0% to 6.0%

State sales tax rate: 6.0%

Local income tax rate: 1.95%

Local sales tax rate: None

Property tax rate: .2090 per $100 assessed value of real estate (2013)

Economic Information: Frankfort Area Chamber of Commerce, 100 Capitol Ave., Frankfort, KY 40601; telephone (502) 223-8261; fax (502) 223-5942.

■ Education and Research

Elementary and Secondary Schools

The Frankfort Independent School District consists of three schools: Second Street School (primary and middle grades), Frankfort High School, and the Capital City

Prep (a nontraditional/alternative school). Frankfort High School offers 11 advanced placements courses, a science career pathway, an aviation career pathway, and a consumer science career pathway. Franklin County Public Schools consists of seven elementary schools, two middle schools, and four high schools: Franklin County High School, Western Hills High School, Franklin County Career and Technical Center, and The Academy (for at-risk youth). The Franklin County Career and Technical Center provides training in automotive technology, carpentry, health science, information technology, pre-engineering, and welding.

Frankfort and Franklin County are also home to a number of private and religious primary and middle schools, including Capital Day School (pre-K–8), which focuses on accelerated learning with a traditional approach, and Good Shepherd School (pre-K–8)

The following is a summary of data regarding the Frankfort Independent School District.

Total enrollment: 799

Number of facilities

    total: 16

    elementary schools: 8

    junior high schools: 2

    high schools: 5

    other: 1

Student/teacher ratio: 11.58:1

Teacher salaries

    average (statewide): $50,038

Funding per pupil: $11,682

Public Schools Information: Frankfort Independent School District, 959 Leestown Lane, Frankfort, KY 40601; telephone (502) 875-8661; fax (502) 875-8663. Franklin County Public Schools, 916 East Main St., Frankfort, KY 40601; telephone (502) 695-6700, fax (502) 695-6708.

Colleges and Universities

Kentucky State University consists of the College of Arts and Sciences; College of Agriculture, Food Science, and Sustainable Systems; College of Business and Computer Science, College of Professional Studies, and the Whitney Young School of Honors and Liberal Studies. The university offers a range of associate's and bachelor's degree, along with master's degrees in public administration, aquaculture and aquatic sciences, computer science, business administration, and special education. Pre-law students can also earn credits as interns in the State Office of the Attorney General. Once strictly an African American institution, the student body is now racially mixed. Enrollment is about 2,000 students per year.

Libraries and Research Centers

With one building and two bookmobiles, the Paul Sawyier Public Library serves Frankfort and Franklin County. An interlibrary loan program gives residents access to resources from participating libraries throughout the state. The library's collection of books, e-books, magazines, newspapers, art prints, and audiovisual materials numbers more than 116,000. The library has focused reading programs for children from one year to adolescence.

Students at Kentucky State University Paul G. Blazer Library have access to numerous print, audio, and online resources. Students also have access to materials from more than dozen different colleges and universities through an interlibrary loan program.

The Martin F. Schmidt Research Library at the Kentucky Historical Society's Thomas D. Clark Center for Kentucky History houses more than 90,000 books, 9,000 oral history interviews, 15,000 reels of microfilm, including some of nineteenth-century newspapers, and thousands of historical photographs. The Kentucky Historical Society also maintains the Civil Rights Movement in Kentucky Online Digital Media Database, which contains audio and video interviews and more than 10,000 pages of electronic transcripts.

The Kentucky Department for Libraries and Archives provides state research facilities and governmental records. This department also oversees the Kentucky Talking Book Library of audio and Braille materials that are available to the public. The Kentucky Military Records and Research Branch houses archives of the Kentucky Department of Military Affairs going back to 1791. The archives of the Center of Excellence for the Study of African Americans (CESKAA) at Kentucky State University include images, manuscript collections, and oral histories of African American Kentuckians, as well as the Fletcher collection on African American theater.

The KSU Aquaculture Research Center seeks to meet future world food demands through research on more than 15 varieties of farmed fish. The KSU Cooperative Extension Program manages a 203-acre research and demonstration farm, which includes a field laboratory and a greenhouse for agricultural research and community education.

Public Library Information: Paul Sawyier Public Library, 319 Wapping St., Frankfort, KY 40601; telephone (502) 352-2665, fax (502) 227-2250.

■ Health Care

Frankfort Regional Medical Center (FRMC), a 173-bed acute care facility, features a team approach and a full-range of emergency care, maternity services, diagnostic imaging, and intensive care. The medical center provides outpatient service and treatment programs for substance abuse, as well as psychiatric care. The Franklin Medical Pavilion for primary care and outpatient care is adjacent to the hospital. The FRMC Center for Women's Health provides medical care for all phases of a woman's life, and the Breast Care Center provides diagnostic and biopsy services for early detection of cancers and other breast diseases.

■ Recreation

Sightseeing

The Frankfort/Franklin County Tourist and Convention Commission's Visitors Center, located five blocks from the Kentucky statehouse, offers maps and information about local sites. Two good places to get a feeling for the personalities that formed Frankfort's history are the Corner in Celebrities Historic District, which is actually one square block behind Wilkinson Street in the north part of town, and the Frankfort Cemetery, located on a high cliff overlooking the city. Dozens of famous Kentuckians have lived on and near the Corner. Historic residences open to the public include Orlando Brown House, a Greek Revival home designed by architect Gideon Shryock; and the adjacent Liberty Hall, built in 1796 in the Federalist style by John Brown, Orlando Brown's brother and Kentucky's first U.S. Senator.

The Frankfort Cemetery is dominated by the marble marker over the graves of Daniel and Rebecca Boone; it is carved with scenes from the lives of the pioneer couple. The cemetery is also the final resting place of 17 Kentucky governors. Another notable site to visit is the Kentucky Vietnam Veterans Memorial, a large 65-foot-tall monument that acts as a giant sundial and is engraved with 1,100 names, including 23 missing in action.

The 1910 Kentucky State Capitol's Beaux Arts design features 70 Ionic columns, decorative murals, and sculptures of Kentucky dignitaries, as well as the First Lady Doll Collection. Tourists throw coins for good luck at the floral clock that is located on the west lawn of the capitol grounds. Next to the capitol and overlooking the Kentucky River, the Governor's Mansion, built of native limestone, was modeled after France's Petit Trianon, Marie Antoinette's summer villa. The Greek Revival Old State Capitol, which served as the seat of state government from 1830 to 1910, features a self-supporting staircase held together by precision and pressure. These state buildings are open for tours. Another outstanding local site is the 1910 prairie-style Ziegler-Brockman House, designed by Frank Lloyd Wright.

Nature lovers will find native flora and fauna at the Kentucky Department of Fish & Wildlife's Salato Wildlife Education Center in Frankfort. Bird watchers will be particularly interested in the Clyde E. Buckley Wildlife Sanctuary and Audubon Center, a 374-acre haven with hiking trails, a bird blind, and a nature center operated by the National Audubon Society.

Kentucky is famous for its bourbon, and visitors may tour the Woodford Reserve Distillery, which dates back to 1812, to see how it is produced. Guides lead tourists to see the bulb-shaped stills, huge fermenting vats, and a warehouse where the charred white oak barrels are stored. Bottling into the distillery's unique-shaped bottles still is accomplished by hand. The Buffalo Trace Distillery, first to ever ship bourbon down the Mississippi River and winner of more than 200 awards, offers tours weekdays and Saturdays.

Arts and Culture

The Grand Theatre: Frankfort's Center for the Arts, presents a variety of programs throughout the year, including local and touring musical groups, classic films, plays, and other performing art events. The Bluegrass Theatre Guild performs at the Grand Theatre and other venues. The Capital City Chorale is a community group that performs at different venues throughout the city. The Capital Art Guild promotes public knowledge of the visual arts via exhibits, technique demonstrations, art classes, and community art projects.

The Thomas D. Clark Center for Kentucky History displays the survey notes penned by Daniel Boone as he helped map the new frontier. Also on display are early civil rights documents. Visitors may take a journey along Kentucky's timeline, from the rustic life of early pioneer times through modern life. The center, which houses a gift shop as well as the state museum and research library, presents educational programs and special events. It features the Hall of Governors of Kentucky, and a permanent exhibit gallery showcasing *A Kentucky Journey*, which tells the state's story, and a changing exhibit gallery spotlighting the artifacts of the Kentucky Historical Society.

Displays of weapons, uniforms, flags, and other memorabilia at the Kentucky Military History Museum honor the service of the state militia, state guard, and other volunteer military organizations. The museum is located in the 1850 Old State Arsenal, a brick Gothic Revival castle on a cliff overlooking the Kentucky River.

The Center of Excellence for Study of Kentucky African Americans (CESKAA) at Kentucky State University sponsors a number of exhibits and displays throughout the year. They include an annual *Many Cultures, One Art* quilt exhibit, a Civil War symposium, a forum on the Great Black Jockeys, and other special events.

Festivals and Holidays

The festival season begins with the Governor's Downtown Derby Celebration in May, featuring guided tours of the Capitol building and gardens, along with food, entertainment, and activities for children. The Kentucky Herb Festival takes also takes place in May. It offers lectures on gardening and music, and hosts an outdoor herbal luncheon. The first full weekend in June brings the Capital Expo Arts & Crafts Festival, three days of arts and crafts, live entertainment, an antique car show, hot air balloon rides, and fireworks. June also brings Boone Day, the Kentucky Historical Society's annual symposium to commemorate Daniel Boone's first observance of Kentucky. July's Franklin County Fair & Horse Show features antiques, a flower and doll show, a demolition derby, a gospel sing, a beauty contest, and children' events. Also in July, Frankfort teams with other central Kentucky cities to host the week-long Central Kentucky Civil War Heritage Trail.

In September, the state's diverse job, ethnic, and family traditions are celebrated at the Kentucky Folklife Festival downtown. The Great Pumpkin Festival features the Black Cat 5K run, a haunted house, hayrides, and a costume parade down Main Street. The Candlelight Tour of downtown takes place in November. An evening of food, music, and shopping kicks off the holiday season. Also in November, the Kentucky Book Fair draws more than 100 authors of national and worldwide renown. The city rings in December with a parade, tree lighting ceremony, caroling, and viewing the wares of more than 100 craft exhibitors.

Sports for the Spectator

The Kentucky State University sports teams are Division II competitors in the National Collegiate Athletic Association (NCAA). KSU is affiliated with the Southern Intercollegiate Athletic Conference (SIAC) and competes for conference championships in all sports. Men's Thorobreds teams include basketball, football, baseball, cross country, track, and golf. Football games are played at the university's Alumni Stadium. Many of the indoor sports, including basketball, are played at the William Exum Center on campus. The Thorobrettes women's teams include basketball, softball, cross country and track, and volleyball.

Frankfort Convention Center hosts several annual basketball tournaments, including the annual Touchstone Energy All "A" Classic, a statewide basketball tournament for the smallest 131 high schools in Kentucky. Others include the Mid-South Conference Basketball Tournament, the Kentucky Intercollegiate Athletic Conference Final Four Basketball Tournament, and the NAIA Division I Women's Basketball National Championship.

Sports for the Participant

The Frankfort Parks and Recreation Department maintains nine parks with facilities available for tennis, baseball and softball, football, basketball, soccer, gold, disc golf, biking, and swimming, along with hiking and picnicking. The 150-acre Capitol View Park is a favorite site for sports enthusiasts. Lakeview Park features a nine-hole golf course and a skate park.

Shopping and Dining

On downtown Frankfort's tree-lined streets, shops offer such items as art pieces, gifts, clothing, books, antiques, and model trains. Shaded under flowering trees, St. Clair Street features an old-fashioned general store as well as boutiques. Visitors flock to Rebecca Ruth Candy shop on the East Side of town to buy bourbon-flavored sweets made on the same curved marble bar top where the secret recipe was developed more than 70 years ago. The city's major mall is Franklin Square, which features a department store, music, clothing, and gift shops, as well as cinemas and restaurants. Completely Kentucky offers a wide range of food and gift items that were all made within the state.

Dining choices in Frankfort run the gamut from home-style and barbecue, to ethnic varieties including Thai, Chinese, Mexican, Irish, and Italian, to seafood and steak. Cajun cooking is the draw at Rick's White Light Diner, while Jim's Seafood specializes in catfish, trout, and fried banana peppers.

Visitor Information: Frankfort/Franklin County Tourist & Convention Commission, 100 Capitol Ave., Frankfort, KY 40601; telephone (502) 875-8687; toll-free (800) 960-7200.

■ Convention Facilities

Nestled along the Kentucky River within short walking distance of downtown's shops and restaurants, the Frankfort Convention Center adjoining Capital Plaza seats 5,365 people in arena seating, 5,047 people for concerts, and 800 people for banquets. The adjacent Capital Plaza Hotel is equipped with an additional 8,000 square feet of meeting/convention space offered in 10 flexible meeting rooms. In addition to extensive audio-visual equipment, the hotel offers expert catering services and award-winning banquet menus.

Convention Information: Frankfort Convention Center, 405 Mero St., Frankfort, KY 40601; telephone (502) 564-5335.

■ Transportation

Approaching the City

Air travelers to Frankfort usually arrive at Lexington's Blue Grass Airport, 25 miles east of downtown Frankfort (a trip of about 35 minutes), then take a taxi to the city. Greyhound offers bus service into Frankfort.

Traveling in the City

Frankfort is laid out in grid patterns in sections north and south of the Kentucky River. The north side includes the older residential section, the Old Capitol, and the downtown business section; its major north-south thoroughfare is Wilkinson Boulevard, named for the city's founder. The Kentucky State Capitol is located in the mostly residential south section. Public transport is offered by the Frankfort Transit System, which runs three fixed weekday routes covering all major shopping centers, hospital, senior centers, and most state office buildings. There is one Saturday route.

■ Communications

Newspapers and Magazines

The State Journal is Frankfort's daily newspaper. Magazines published in Frankfort include *Kentucky Bench & Bar Magazine,* and *Kentucky Afield.*

Television and Radio

NBC, CBS, ABC, and Fox television affiliates broadcast from Lexington and Louisville. Cable television service is provided by the Frankfort Plant Board. There are eight FM and two AM licensed radio stations in Frankfort.

Media Information: *The State Journal,* 1216 Wilkinson Blvd, Frankfort, KY 40601; telephone (502)227-4556; fax (502) 227-2831.

Frankfort Online

Welcome to Frankfort. Available www.frankfort.ky. gov

Frankfort Area Chamber of Commerce. Available www.frankfortky.info

Frankfort Convention Center. Available www. frankfortconventioncenter.com

Frankfort/Franklin County Tourist and Convention Commission. Available www.visitfrankfort.com

Frankfort Regional Medical Center. Available www. frankfortregional.com

Frankfort Independent Schools. Available www. frankfort.k12.ky.us

Kentucky Cabinet for Economic Development. Available www.thinkkentucky.com

Kentucky Historical Society. Available www.history. ky.gov

Kentucky State University. Available www.kysu.edu

Paul Sawyier Public Library. Available www.pspl.org

BIBLIOGRAPHY

Hervey, Amanda, *Kentucky A to Z* (Frankfort, KY: Kentucky Monthly, 2012)

Kramer, Carl E., *Capital on the Kentucky: A Two Hundred Year History of Frankfort & Franklin County* (Frankfort, KY: Historic Frankfort, Inc., 1986)

Wallace, James C. and Gene Burch, *Frankfort: Capital of Kentucky* (Louisville, KY: Merrick Printing Co., 1994)

Lexington

■ The City in Brief

Founded: 1775 (incorporated 1781)

Head Official: Mayor Jim Gray (since 2011)

City Population
1990: 225,366
2000: 260,512
2010: 295,803
2012 estimate: 305,489
Percent change, 2000–2010: 13.5%
U.S. rank in 1990: 70th (State rank: 2nd)
U.S. rank in 2000: 70th (State rank: 1st)
U.S. rank in 2010: 63rd (State rank: 2nd)

Metropolitan Statistical Area Population
2000: 408,326
2010: 472,099
2012 estimate: 485,023
Percent change, 2000–2010: 15.6%
U.S. rank in 2000: 109th
U.S. rank in 2010: 106th

Area: 284.5 square miles (Lexington-Fayette)

Elevation: Approximately 966 feet above sea level

Average Annual Temperatures: 54.9° F

Average Annual Precipitation: 44.6 inches

Major Economic Sectors: government, health and educational services, business and professional services, manufacturing

Unemployment Rate: 5.4% (2012)

Per Capita Income: $28,502

2012 FBI Crime Index Property: 13,399

Major Colleges and Universities: University of Kentucky, Transylvania University

Daily Newspaper: *Lexington Herald-Leader*

■ Introduction

In the heart of the nation's Bluegrass Country, Lexington, Kentucky, is a city that has artfully blended history, horses, culture, and industry to create a uniquely desirable quality of life. With its graciously restored downtown buildings complementing its modern office and convention facilities, Lexington exemplifies the benefits of a successful public-private partnership. In 1974 the city merged its government with Fayette County to streamline services. The efficient consolidation became known as Lexington-Fayette County Urban County Government. A spirit of cooperation propels the community toward its goals of excellence in education as well as economic growth. Lexington was once known as the Athens of the West because many early artists, poets, and architects settled in the region; each left a sense of his or her own style. In 2012 *Business Week* named Lexington among the 50 best cities in America. In 2013 *Forbes* ranked the city as the seventh best place to retire.

■ Geography and Climate

Located on the lush, grassy plateaus of Kentucky's central Bluegrass Country at the edge of the Cumberland Gap, Lexington is the county seat of Fayette County. The fertile region is dotted with numerous small creeks that run to the nearby Kentucky River. The largest bodies of water in the area are the reservoirs of the Kentucky American Water Company.

Lexington has four distinct seasons, and while the region endures few extremes of weather, it is subject to unexpected changes in temperature of relatively short duration. Precipitation is fairly constant year round, with an average of three to four inches per month. September

Henryk Sadura/Shutterstock.com

and October in Lexington are considered the most agreeable months of the year.

Area: 284.5 square miles (Lexington-Fayette)

Elevation: Approximately 966 feet above sea level

Average Temperatures: 54.9° F

Average Annual Precipitation: 44.6 inches

■ History

Permanent Community Established in 1779

Pioneer Daniel Boone was one of the first white men to explore the territory known today as the Bluegrass Country. The births of the United States and the city of Lexington occurred at nearly the same moment in history. In June 1775 a small band of pioneers who were camped in the bluegrass amid buffalo and Native American trails received word of the battle of Lexington, Massachusetts, that marked the beginning of the American Revolution. In a spirit of adventure and independence, the pioneers named their campsite for the historic conflict. Development of a permanent settlement was postponed for four years when several members of the patriotic group departed to enlist in the Continental Army. Hostile natives also discouraged pioneer incursion into this wilderness. Neighboring pioneer villages were plagued by the often violent resistance of the natives and many believed this opposition was incited and encouraged by the British.

The present-day state of Kentucky was, at that time, part of the far-flung properties of Virginia, visited only by hunters, surveyors, and explorers. In 1779 a party of settlers journeyed to Lexington from nearby Harrodsburg and erected several cabins and a stockade in an effort at establishing a permanent community. In 1780 the Virginia Assembly divided its sprawling Kentucky District into three counties—Lincoln, Jefferson, and Fayette (named for the Revolutionary War hero, French General Mortier de Lafayette). The following year Lexington incorporated, became county seat of Fayette County, and was granted township status.

City Develops as Trading Center

The popular and fertile Bluegrass Country quickly attracted settlers from Virginia, North Carolina, Maryland, and Pennsylvania. Within two decades, Lexington, with 1,800 citizens, was the largest town in western America. A thriving community of stores, taverns, hotels, and industries grew steadily in the protective curve of the Kentucky River, and Lexington became known as a major supply center linking east to west. Stores kept their shelves stocked with goods carted overland from Philadelphia and Baltimore and paid eastern merchants with hides, skins, furs, homemade linens, beef, ham, lard, and lumber. The development of farming added whiskey, tobacco, and hemp to the list of products exported to eager merchants to the east, west, and south.

Local Horse Industry Gets Its Start

Local fascination with the breeding, rearing, training, and racing of thoroughbred horses has always been an important element of life in the Bluegrass Country. The limestone soil, rich bluegrass, and mild climate combined to make the area prime horse country. The town's first race course was established shortly after 1788, when civic leaders banned the sport on downtown streets. Thoroughbreds, trotters, and saddle horses brought from Virginia and the Carolinas joined breeding stallions from England and Arabia during the early 1800s, and another industry was launched.

In 1787 the flourishing Lexington community expanded its communication and education services. John Bradford's printing press produced the state's first newspaper, the *Kentucky Gazette*. Log cabin schools gave way to a succession of private and semi-public schools, and a group of persuasive Lexington businessmen convinced the trustees of Transylvania College to relocate from Danville. The college established law and medical departments, attracted students from throughout the South, and added immeasurably to the prestige of the frontier town.

City Falters Economically Then Rallies

The Commonwealth of Kentucky split from Virginia in 1792 and was admitted as the 15th state in the Union. Lexington was its temporary capital and enjoyed considerable status as a seat of higher learning and an industrial center until shortly after the turn of the century, when the success of the steamboat gave the rival city of Louisville, located on the Ohio River, a distinct advantage. Development faltered in Lexington with the rise of the river cities, and by the time railroads established a much-needed link to the Ohio River, the economic damage was already evident in the unemployment rate, the number of declared bankruptcies, and the declining population.

Lexington's civic and business leaders then began to steer the town away from its fading industrial economy and encourage an emphasis on culture and education instead. Tax dollars were diverted toward promotion and support of the arts and the growth of Transylvania University. Gradually, the frontier town gained a reputation as the "Athens of the West," and Transylvania was referred to by many as the "Harvard of the West." A measure of Lexington's success can be seen in rival Louisville's unsuccessful attempt, during the 1830s, to lure Transylvania's medical school to that town.

Although the state officially declared itself neutral, the Civil War pitted neighbor against neighbor within Kentucky. While their traditions were southern, many political and industrial influences were of the North. During the war years, the horse racing industry was suspended, but progress was made in other areas. The University of Kentucky was established at Lexington in 1865 and thrives today, attracting students, researchers, and athletes. Horseracing experienced a resurgence after the war, and as the popularity of cigarettes grew among soldiers during the Civil and World Wars, tobacco farming became a major industry in the Lexington area.

Present-Day City in Growth Spurt

Modern Lexington's economy is still firmly based in horses, cattle, burley tobacco, and of course, the academic community of the University of Kentucky. During recent times, downtown Lexington has been revitalized by a surge of growth and new development, especially in the corporate service sectors of the economy; yet, through the work of such organizations as the Lexington Downtown Development Authority, the city has been diligent in preserving its roots through renovation and preservation of many of its historic buildings and neighborhoods. Called "the city in the park" because of its location in the middle of hundreds of beautiful, park-like horse farms, Lexington offers a charming blend of big-city amenities and small-town friendliness. In fact, Lexington was the first city in the country to create an urban service boundary to protect the surrounding countryside. Before, after, and between meeting sessions at the modern Lexington Center convention complex, visitors find plenty to see and do. History, art, and culture are all within easy and safe walking distance and include beautiful historic office buildings, churches, and homes; many of Lexington's finest restaurants, specialty shops and galleries; and major performance and sports arenas. Lexington is part of a metropolitan statistical area comprised of Bourbon, Clark, Fayette, Jessamine, Madison, Scott, and Woodford counties.

Historical Information: The Blue Grass Trust for Historic Preservation, 253 Market Street, Lexington, KY 40507; telephone (859) 253-0362; fax (859) 259-9210.

■ Population Profile

Metropolitan Statistical Area Population

    2000: 408,326
    2010: 472,099
    2012 estimate: 485,023
    Percent change, 2000–2010: 15.6%
    U.S. rank in 2000: 109th
    U.S. rank in 2010: 106th

City Residents

    1990: 225,366
    2000: 260,512

2010: 295,803
2012 estimate: 305,489
Percent change, 2000–2010: 13.5%
U.S. rank in 1990: 70th (State rank: 2nd)
U.S. rank in 2000: 70th (State rank: 1st)
U.S. rank in 2010: 63rd (State rank: 2nd)

Density: 1,042.8 people per square mile

Racial and ethnic characteristics

White: 235,352
Black or African American: 42,816
American Indian and Alaskan Native: 511
Asian: 10,493
Native Hawaiian and Other Pacific Islander: 45
Hispanic or Latino (may be of any race): 21,319
Other: 16,272

Percent of residents born in state: 60.1%

Age characteristics

Population under 5 years old: 19,384
Population 5 to 9 years old: 17,508
Population 10 to 14 years old: 17,986
Population 15 to 19 years old: 20,447
Population 20 to 24 years old: 34,480
Population 25 to 34 years old: 48,420
Population 35 to 44 years old: 40,871
Population 45 to 54 years old: 38,611
Population 55 to 59 years old: 17,362
Population 60 to 64 years old: 16,717
Population 65 to 74 years old: 19,070
Population 75 to 84 years old: 10,326
Population 85 years and over: 4,307
Median age: 34.0

Births (2010–11 Metropolitan Area)

Total number: 6,288

Deaths (2010–11 Metropolitan Area)

Total number: 3,373

Money income (2012)

Per capita income: $28,502
Median household income: $47,785
Total households: 122,046

Number of households with income of ...

less than $10,000: 11,531
$10,000 to $14,999: 7,893
$15,000 to $24,999: 13,633
$25,000 to $34,999: 13,241
$35,000 to $49,999: 17,037
$50,000 to $74,999: 20,499
$75,000 to $99,999: 13,597
$100,000 to $149,999: 14,498
$150,000 to $199,999: 4,947
$200,000 or more: 5,170

Percent of families below poverty level: 18.5%

FBI Crime Index Property: 13,399

FBI Crime Index Violent: 1,066

■ Municipal Government

On January 1, 1974, Lexington and Fayette County made Kentucky history by merging their governments into a single system. Called the Lexington-Fayette County Urban County Government, the consolidation was the result of nearly four years of study and eliminated many duplicate services as well as the need for two separate property taxes. The government is administered by the mayor and a 15-member urban county council. Twelve members of the council are district members and three are at-large members. The district members are elected for two-year terms and may serve up to six consecutive terms. The at-large members are elected for four-year terms and may serve up to three consecutive terms. The at-large member who receives the most votes in the general election is appointed as the vice mayor.

Head Official: Mayor Jim Gray (since 2011)

Total Number of City Employees: 2,699 (2013)

City Information: Lexington-Fayette Urban County Government, 200 E. Main St, Lexington, KY 40507; telephone (859) 425-2255; toll-free (888) 987-8111.

■ Economy

Major Industries and Commercial Activity

Horses are a billion-dollar industry in the Bluegrass Country. Home to more than 450 horse farms, Lexington is surrounded by the greatest concentration of thoroughbred horse farms in the world. Rich limestone soil, lush grasses, and a moderate climate combine to create an ideal spot for the raising, breeding, and training of horses. The Bluegrass Country is the birthplace of the state's native breed—the American Saddlebred—and a center for the breeding of the Standardbred.

While horse breeding is the area's big business, horse racing is probably its claim to fame. The local economy greatly benefits from tourists who come from around the world in large numbers. Keeneland Race Course and the Red Mile attract horse-lovers, experts, and gamblers from around the world. Kentucky Horse Park, a 1,224-acre park built on a former thoroughbred stud farm, is a major attraction.

Agriculture also benefits from the mineral-rich land. Kentucky is one of the leading producers of burley tobacco in the United States, with Lexington-Fayette County producing the largest crop. Corn, soybeans, alfalfa hay, wheat, and barley are also produced in the area, and Lexington is a major market for beef cattle as well. Lexington's central location within Kentucky and the United States is attractive to manufacturers, distributors, and business interests.

However, while the city and state of Kentucky fervently protect and promote the region's strong agricultural and horse-country identity, they also are attempting to keep pace with economic trends. As a result, Lexington has emerged as a leading American city in economic growth. A concerted effort has been made to diversify the area's economy toward more manufacturing and high-technology ventures. Educational and health services has become a strong and growing sector of the economy. In fact, into the early 2000s and 2010s, the combined service sectors outpaced manufacturing in employment and wages.

Industry analysts forecast continued progress for Lexington, targeting the area for both population growth and economic development in the twenty-first century. They predict particular strides in the areas of finance, insurance, and real estate, while community leaders continue to encourage the growth of high technology industries and plan marketing strategies to capitalize on tourism.

Items and goods produced: horses, corn, soybeans, alfalfa hay, wheat, metal products, bourbon, peanut butter, industrial valves, furniture, tobacco products, construction equipment

Incentive Programs-New and Existing Companies

Local programs: Commerce Lexington, also known as the Greater Lexington Chamber of Commerce, provides a variety of services for businesses thinking of starting up or relocating in greater Lexington, including site selection services and a Minority Business Development Program. Some businesses might qualify for financial assistance through the Access Loan Program, a cooperative venture between Commerce Lexington and local banks.

State programs: The state of Kentucky offers an extensive array of incentives for business start-up and expansion. The Kentucky Economic Development Finance Authority (KEDFA) of the Kentucky Cabinet for Economic Development oversees a wide variety of programs and services available to businesses, including existing businesses, newly locating companies, start-ups, small and minority businesses, and many others. Small businesses may benefit from the Kentucky Small Business Credit Initiative, which supports participating lenders in efforts to finance businesses that typically fall outside of standard lending guidelines. Small businesses involved in manufacturing, agribusiness, or service and technology

may qualify for the Small Business Loan Program, which provides loans between $15,000 and $100,000 for a term of 10 years. The Kentucky Small Business Tax Credit provides credits for eligible businesses with 50 or fewer full-time employees who create one or more jobs while investing at least $5,000 in qualifying equipment or technology.

The Kentucky Business Investment Program offers income tax credits for new and existing agribusinesses, regional and national headquarters, manufacturing companies, and non-retail service- or technology-related companies. New or expanding businesses involved in service or technology, manufacturing, or tourism can apply for assistance through the Kentucky Enterprise Initiative Act, which provides sales and use tax refunds for building and construction materials or equipment used for research and development and data processing. The Kentucky Economic Development Direct Loan Program offers below-market interest rates for businesses involved in agribusiness, tourism, industrial ventures, or the service industry.

Some special incentives are available for high-tech companies, including the High-Tech Investment/Construction Pools, which provide funds for commercialization of a product, process, or innovation. The KEDFA also offers a matching funds program for Phase 1 and Phase 2 federal small business innovation research and small business technology transfer awards received by Kentucky businesses. A special Kentucky New Energy ventures Fund has been established to assist in the development of commercialization of alternative fuels and renewable energy. Companies providing large investments in renewable and alternative energy facilities may be eligible for a variety of negotiated incentives through the Incentives for Energy Independence Act.

Agribusiness companies may be legible for assistance through the Kentucky Agricultural Development Fund or the Kentucky Agricultural Finance Corporation. Businesses involved in tourism may qualify for the recovery of development costs through the Tourism Development Act, which is administered through the Kentucky Tourism, Arts, and Heritage Cabinet.

Job training programs: Workforce training assistance is provided through the Bluegrass State Skills Corporation (BSSC) of the Kentucky Cabinet for Economic Development. The BSSC Grant-in-Aid program provides grants for training of workers in new and expanding businesses and continuing training for workers in existing companies. The Skills Training Investment Credit program offers state tax credits for approved training programs.

The Kentucky Office of Employment and Training, a branch of the Kentucky Department of Workforce Investment, provides training assistance under the Workforce Investment Act. The Lexington Area Career Center serves Fayette and Jessamine Counties.

Customized employee training programs are available through the Kentucky Community and Technical College System. In Lexington, these services are provided through the Cooper, Newtown, and Leestown campuses of Bluegrass Community and Technical College. The Kentucky Small Business Development Center at the University of Kentucky offers a wide range of technical assistance and consulting services for businesses.

Development Projects

For the twenty-first century, Lexington continues to work toward diversifying the local economy, while maintaining a strong manufacturing foundation. Toward that end, Commerce Lexington has identified seven strategic target areas on which to focus their development efforts. These are advanced manufacturing, animal sciences, business and professional services, clean technology, life sciences, software and information technology, and visitor industries.

According to reports from Commerce Lexington, during the six-year period 2007–12 a total of 14,477 jobs were created as a result of the 42 new businesses and 125 business expansions in Lexington and the Central Kentucky region that Commerce Lexington's economic development programs serve. In 2013 Commerce Lexington and the Strides Ahead Foundation launched the FULL STRIDE five-year strategic development initiative focused on job growth. At the time of the kick-off celebration, the capital funds campaign for the project had reached about 61 percent of the $4 million dollar goal.

In 2013 several new technology companies announced plans to move to Lexington. These included Bauer Labs, Directed Energy Inc., Hitron Technologies, Mercury Data Systems, New Global Systems for Intelligent Transportation Management, Nicolalde Research and Development, NOHMs Technologies, Science Tomorrow, and Twin Star TDS. Together these companies pledged a total investment of $7.5 million and the creation of about 190 new jobs.

Also in 2013, Tiffany & Company announced plans to expand its facility in Commerce Lexington's Blue Grass Business Park. The company was to add 75 new employees with a capital investment of $2 million. That same year, Tempur-Pedic celebrated the grand opening of its new global headquarters in Coldstream Research Campus. Hummingbird Nano announced plans to expand its Coldstream facility, and the J.M. Smucker Company announced plans to expand its Jif peanut butter production facility with an investment of more than $44 million in new equipment, building improvements, and new construction.

Economic Development Information: Commerce Lexington, 330 E. Main St., Suite 205, Lexington, KY 40507; telephone (859) 254-4447; email: info@locatein-lexington.com.

Commercial Shipping

Lexington lies at the center of a 31-state distribution zone. Easy access to two major interstate systems makes motor carrier service readily available. Since Toyota Motor Manufacturing chose to locate its award-winning Camry/Avalon/Venza manufacturing plant just 14 miles north of Lexington, the Interstate 75 and Interstate 64 corridors have come to be known as America's Auto Axis, reflecting the profusion of automotive suppliers that have located near enough to meet just-in-time inventory requirements for the Toyota, Saturn, Nissan, Honda, Ford, and Corvette plants located within the immediate area. There are numerous motor freight providers in the Lexington-Fayette County area.

RJ Corman rail has local terminals that connect to CSX and Norfolk Southern lines. An intermodal terminal is in nearby Georgetown. Lexington Bluegrass Airport (LEX) is a major international hub; numerous air cargo companies maintain facilities there as well. The airport hosts a U.S. Customs Service Office. There are also full-service international airports in nearby Louisville and Cincinnati.

Labor Force and Employment Outlook

Analysts rate Lexington high on the scale of available, quality labor. The University of Kentucky and 11 other nearby accredited colleges produce an ample supply of management-level workers, a particular concern of corporate and high technology businesses seeking to locate in the Bluegrass Country. Analysts also describe the area as having an abundance of clerical, skilled, semi-skilled, and unskilled workers. In 2013 *Forbes* magazine ranked Lexington as seventh in the nation in its survey of best mid-sized cities for jobs.

According to the U.S. Bureau of Labor Statistics, the government sector had the greatest number of employees in 2013. However, the combined number of service jobs, including educational and health services and business and professional services, was greater. Trade, transportation, and utilities followed government for the greatest number of jobs in a single sector. From 2012 to 2013, professional and business services showed the highest employment growth rate, followed by leisure and hospitality.

The following is a summary of data regarding the 2012 Lexington labor force:

Size of civilian labor force: 167,788

Number of workers employed in . . .
  agriculture and mining: 3,520
  construction: 6,519
  manufacturing: 12,797
  wholesale trade: 3,670
  retail trade: 16,436
  transportation: 4,836
  information systems: 3,176
  finance: 8,427

professional administration: 16,306
education and social services: 46,687
arts and leisure: 17,285
other: 7,330
public administration: 5,979

Average hourly earnings of production workers: $15.31

Unemployment rate: 5.4% (2012)

Employers

Largest employers (2013)	*Number of employees*
University of Kentucky	14,000
Fayette County Public Schools	5,374
Transportation Cabinet of Kentucky	4,500
Kentucky Health and Family Services Cabinet	3,610
KentuckyOne Health	3,000
Lexington-Fayette County Urban County Government	2,699
Lexmark International	2656
Xerox	2,530
Baptist Healthcare System	2,496
Wal-Mart	2,027

Cost of Living

The following is a summary of data regarding several key cost of living factors in the area.

2013 ACCRA Average House Price: $213,879

2013 ACCRA Cost of Living Index: 88

State income tax rate: 2.0% to 6.0%

State sales tax rate: 6.0%

Local income tax rate: 2.25%

Local sales tax rate: None

Property tax rate: ranges from $.0150 to $1.1637 per $100 of assessed value (2013)

Economic Information: Commerce Lexington, 330 E. Main St., Suite 205, Lexington, KY 40507; telephone (859) 254-4447; email info@locateinlexington.com.

■ Education and Research

Elementary and Secondary Schools

Historically known as an educational center in the South, Lexington has maintained its concern with providing excellence in education. The Fayette County Public School System was established when the Lexington and Fayette County Boards of Education merged in 1967. The district is managed by a five-member elected board and an appointed superintendent. All elementary and select high schools in the district have English as a Second Language programs available. More than 40,000 students are enrolled. The system sponsors 19 magnet programs and other specialized programs, including the Academy of Information Technology and StationArts, both at Bryan Station High; a pre-engineering curriculum at Lafayette High and Leestown Middle; an International Baccalaureate program at Tates Creek High; JROTC at Bryan Station and Henry Clay; the Carter G. Woodson Academy, and STEAM Academy.

East Side Technical Center, Locust Trace AgriScience Farm, and Southside Technical Center High offer occupational training for high school students. Juniors and seniors can apply for the Entrepreneur Leadership Institute. This summer program is hosted by Commerce Lexington to help prepare students for a future in the business world.

In addition to the public school system, Lexington has more than 30 private schools. These include Sayre School, Sphinx Academy, Lexington Montessori, Saints Peter and Paul Regional Catholic School, and Blue Grass Baptist School.

The following is a summary of data regarding the Fayette County Public Schools.

Total enrollment: 37,819

Number of facilities

total: 63
elementary schools: 35
junior high schools: 12
high schools: 5
other: 11

Student/teacher ratio: 14.53:1

Teacher salaries

average (statewide): $50,038

Funding per pupil: $10,382

Public Schools Information: Fayette County Public Schools, 701 E. Main St., Lexington, KY 40502; telephone (859) 381-4100.

Colleges and Universities

Lexington is the home of the University of Kentucky (UK), which was established in 1865 and enrolls more than 28,000 students. UK is home to 16 major colleges including schools of medicine, law, engineering, arts and sciences, and business. The Carnegie Foundation ranks UK as a Research I university, making it the only institution in Kentucky with such recognition.

Transylvania University is a small four-year institution affiliated with the Christian Church; it was established in 1780 and enrolls more than 1,000 students. It is one of the oldest colleges west of the Allegheny Mountains. Bluegrass Community and Technical College is part of the Kentucky Community and Technical College System. This public two-year degree granting institution offers career training in business, allied health, and technical education. Three of the school's six campuses are located in Lexington. Lexington is also home to the college's North American Racing Academy at Thoroughbred Training Center, a professional jockey school. More than 14,200 students are enrolled.

Within a 40-mile radius are Eastern Kentucky University and seven other colleges: Asbury, Berea, Centre, Georgetown, Kentucky State, Midway, and Southeastern Christian College. Together they award undergraduate and advanced degrees in a full range of fields, including medicine, law, engineering, economics, architecture, and library science. The city is also home to the Lexington Theological Seminary and the Kentucky Campus of Asbury Seminary. Several vocational and business schools are in the area as well.

Libraries and Research Centers

Lexington Public Library's collection includes more than 600,000 book volumes, plus e-books, magazines, films, audio- and videotapes, filmstrips, microfiche and microfilm, and art reproductions. The library system includes the Central Branch on East Main Street, plus five branch libraries. The library houses a collection of early Kentucky newspapers and books and the Lexington Urban County Documents Collection.

The University of Kentucky Libraries hold more than 3.4 million book volumes and numerous special collections, including Appalachiana and government documents. Other Lexington-area libraries include those associated with academic institutions, hospitals, museums, religious organizations, and corporations. The unique Keeneland Library is devoted to thoroughbred horse racing and contains some 15,000 books and journals, along with 250,000 photographic negatives, and thousands of newspaper articles. It also maintains the entire archive of the *Daily Racing Form* newspaper.

Most of the research centers in Lexington are affiliated with the University of Kentucky. They conduct research activities in such fields as life sciences, social and cultural studies, private and public policy and affairs, physical sciences, engineering, tobacco production, and multi-disciplinary programs. The Kentucky Rural Health Works Program, an offshoot of the school's agricultural

college, seeks to help rural Kentucky communities make informed decisions in the development of their health facilities. The University of Kentucky Coldstream Research Campus is dedicated to the development of knowledge-based firms. Once a prominent bluegrass horse farm, Coldstream provides a synergetic research camp environment for science and technology-focused businesses, and University of Kentucky faculty, staff, and students. Other subjects of research facilities include horses, asphalt, energy (particularly coal), and tobacco. The Kentucky Center for Public Issues focuses on matters of concern to the general public.

Public Library Information: Lexington Public Library, 140 E. Main St., Lexington, KY 40507; telephone (859) 231-5500.

■ Health Care

Lexington offers a wide choice of quality medical treatment facilities to its residents. Area facilities include several cardiac rehabilitation centers and medical research centers. One of the largest hospitals in Lexington is St. Joseph Hospital, a 433-bed full-service hospital affiliated with KentuckyOne Health. UK Albert B. Chandler Hospitals (Pavilions A and H), Kentucky Children's Hospital, and UK Good Samaritan are part of the University of Kentucky Health System. The main medical campus also features the Makenna David Pediatric Emergency Center. Both KentuckyOne Health and UK Health System provide primary care and outpatient medical centers throughout the city.

Other facilities include Cardinal Hill Rehabilitation Hospital, Central Baptist Hospital, Ridge Behavioral Health System, Shriners Hospitals for Children, and the Veterans Administration Medical Center.

■ Recreation

Sightseeing

Many sights in the Lexington area are points of historic interest. The Lexington History Museum (free admission) is housed in the beautiful old Fayette County Courthouse (circa 1900). Exhibits include a timeline of the area's history, a photographic study of Lexington's African American community and a special display of the IBM Selectric Typewriter, once produced locally. Perryville Battlefield in nearby Perryville, Kentucky, is the site of Kentucky's bloodiest and most important Civil War battle. The battle marked a fatal loss of the initiative for the South. Each October, the battle is re-enacted; throughout the year, living history activities with costumed interpreters are available.

Henry Clay's 20-room mansion, Ashland, is furnished with Clay family heirlooms and set on 20 acres of woodland and formal gardens. The Hunt-Morgan House is a Federal-style home built in 1814 for Kentucky's first millionaire, John Wesley Hunt; it was also the boyhood home of Lexington's first mayor, Charlton Hunt, Confederate General John Hunt Morgan, and geneticist and Nobel Prize winner Thomas Hunt Morgan. The restored house features a collection of Civil War memorabilia, early nineteenth-century paintings, a garden, and a courtyard. Built in 1802, the Mary Todd Lincoln House is the former first lady's childhood home. The Georgian-style building contains displays of personal articles that once belonged to the Todd-Lincoln families, including part of Mary's Meissen china collection.

The Lexington Cemetery is nationally recognized as one of America's most beautiful arboretums and is listed in the National Register of Historic Places for landscape design. The cemetery was chartered in 1848 and features landscaped grounds, two lakes, and monuments to such Kentucky greats as statesman Henry Clay, Confederate General John Hunt Morgan, the Mary Todd Lincoln family, and author James Lane Allen. An elegant Greek Revival mansion built in 1847 is the center of the 10-acre Waveland State Shrine, named for the acres of wind-blown bluegrass that once surrounded the historical complex. The home is furnished in nineteenth-century style and is surrounded by servant's quarters, a country store, gardens, an orchard, and a craft shop.

Pope Villa, designed in 1810–11 by architect Benjamin Henry Latrobe for Senator John and Eliza Pope, is a suburban villa in the neoclassical style. The villa is a perfect square, with a domed, circular rotunda in the center of the second story. Transylvania University was founded in 1780, the first college west of the Alleghenies, and features the Old Morrison Hall, built in 1833, and Patterson Cabin, built by Lexington's pioneer founder Robert Patterson. Another notable building in Lexington is Loundon House, a unique castellated Gothic Villa that serves as the headquarters and gallery space of the Lexington Art League.

Nature can be enjoyed at Lexington-area attractions such as the University of Kentucky Landscape Garden Center, a collection of plants, flowers, and herbs. Raven Run Nature Sanctuary, a 726-acre park dedicated to the preservation of the Kentucky River Palisades, features more than 400 species of wildflowers and a seven-mile network of hiking trails.

One of Lexington's best-known attractions is Kentucky Horse Park, a 1,224-acre tribute to the animal that makes the area famous. The park features a larger-than-life-size statue of the champion racehorse Man O'War and famed Secretariat. More than 30 breeds of horses, from racing thoroughbreds to miniature ponies; twin theaters, and the International Museum of the Horse, which traces the history of horses. Special events include horse shows, rodeos, polo matches, and national competitions involving horses and their riders or trainers.

Arts and Culture

Lexington was an acknowledged center for art and culture as early as the mid-1800s, earning the nickname Athens of the West. The commitment to culture continues today. LexArts supports arts organizations, artists, and educational institutions throughout Lexington and Central Kentucky. LexArts operates two facilities in downtown Lexington, ArtsPlace and the Downtown Arts Center. ArtsPlace is a working center for individual and group activities in the visual and performing arts and features the juried work of Kentucky artists in its gallery, as well as free performances that range from classical music to jazz and from ballet to modern dance. The four-story building contains studios, a rehearsal and performance hall, and offices for numerous cultural groups; it is adjacent to the Lexington Opera House, where many of its organizations stage their presentations.

Some of the groups housed at ArtsPlace are Bluegrass Printmakers Cooperative, the Center for Old Music in the New World, the Central Kentucky Youth Orchestras, the Lexington Ballet Company, the Lexington Chamber Chorale, and the Lexington Philharmonic Orchestra. The Lexington Philharmonic performs popular and classical concerts at the Otis A. Singletary Center for the Arts at the University of Kentucky. The seasons of Lexington's performing arts groups generally run September through May; in summer, Shakespeare in the Park presents free outdoor performances.

Other musical groups in Lexington include the Guitar Society of Lexington-Central Kentucky, a non-profit arts organization that promotes and fosters awareness of the guitar as an instrument of classical music and sponsors several concerts annually; the University Artist Series, which annually sponsors a season of musical performances; and the Lexington Singers, a choral group of more than 180 singers who perform several holiday, pops, and classical concerts annually. The Lexington Singers has four children's choirs, divided by skill level for children grades one through eight.

The Living Arts and Science Center, which is housed in the restored Kinkead House mansion, encourages artistic expression and learning. Cinema buffs view new and classic films at the renovated Italian Renaissance style Kentucky Theater.

Lexington-area museums display a wide variety of art and artifacts. The Headley-Whitney Museum contains the unique artifacts and reflects the interests of Lexington artist George Headley. The museum consists of three buildings and features a shell grotto, a jewel room filled with miniatures fashioned from precious gems and metals, an Oriental gallery, an art library, and other changing exhibits. The Explorium of Lexington provides interactive exhibits for children from 1 to 12 years old. Special galleries focus on the environment, human growth, local history, play, foreign travel, and science.

At the University of Kentucky Art Museum, a collection of fourteenth- through twentieth-century European, American, African, and Pre-Columbian art is on display. Tracing the culture and development of Kentucky man from the Paleoindians to the Shawnee, the William S. Webb Museum of Anthropology at the University of Kentucky features textiles, kinship art, and religion. The Mitchell Fine Arts Center at Transylvania University houses the Morlan Gallery and a rare collection of scientific apparatus.

The American Saddlebred Museum at the Kentucky Horse Park offers a multimedia theater presentation and a touch-screen interactive video photo file of world champion horses. The Kentucky Horse Park also features the International Museum of the Horse. The Aviation Museum of Kentucky features restored historic aircraft.

Festivals and Holidays

Seasonal events in Lexington include the LexArts Weekend in February, a St. Patrick's Day parade in March, a Festival of the Bluegrass in June, a weeklong July Fourth celebration, a Woodland Arts Fair in August, the Lexington Roots and Heritage Festival in September, and the Southern Lights Holiday Festival in November and December, which includes a downtown Christmas Parade. Downtown Lexington hosts an annual Mayfest that features more than 100 artists, traditional Maypole dances, strolling entertainment, and tours of historic Gratz Park, where the event takes place.

Sports for the Spectator

The Keeneland Race Course is the scene of fine thoroughbred racing during April and October. The beautifully landscaped course was established in 1936 on Keene family property, which was part of a 1783 land grant from patriot Patrick Henry, a cousin of the family. Steeped in the gentile tradition of the Old South, the track even provides ladies with parasols when the sun is reflecting off the copper roof. The highlight of the spring meet is the Blue Grass Stakes, the last major race before the Kentucky Derby (held in Louisville but simulcast and celebrated wholeheartedly in Lexington). Horse sales are scheduled four times annually in a world-famous pavilion; facilities include a private clubhouse, a grandstand that accommodates 5,000 people, and stables for 1,200 horses.

The Red Mile harness track, built in 1875, is the second-oldest harness track in the world. It has the reputation of being the fastest track in the world because more world records have been set at this one-mile, red-clay track than at any other. Racing meets are held here in the spring, summer, and fall, with the Kentucky Futurity, the final jewel in trotting's Triple Crown, held in October. The Junior League Horse Show, the nation's largest outdoor Saddlebred show, is held at the Red Mile in July of each year. The Lexington Polo Club holds

matches from June through October at the Kentucky Horse Park.

There are dozens of horse shows around town and at the Kentucky Horse Park throughout the year, including the Rolex Kentucky Three-Day Event in April that is the only four-star event of its kind. Other highlights include the July's Junior League Horse Show, the nation's largest outdoor saddlebred show.

The Lexington Legends play at the state-of-the-art Whitaker Bank Ballpark. The $13.5 million ballpark seats nearly 7,000 and features more than 20 luxury suites as well as two lawn areas where fans can picnic as they watch the game.

The University of Kentucky (UK) competes in a wide variety of Division I collegiate sports. The Wildcats basketball team plays at Rupp Arena and has won more NCAA championships than any program in history and is arguably, next to horseracing, the overriding sports passion in the Bluegrass State. The UK football team also plays in the top-tier Southeastern Conference; games are played at Commonwealth Stadium. Memorial Coliseum is the site of the University of Kentucky Lady Cats games.

Sports for the Participant

Lexington sees its beautiful countryside as both an attraction and an enhancement to its way of life, and the city has long sought to protect and preserve green space. More than 100 parks comprising 4,000 acres serve citizens and visitors with a variety of services, facilities, and programs, including ballfields, summer playground programs, cultural activities, fitness trails, golf courses, swimming pools, and city-wide special events and contests. Special parks include McConnell Springs, a 26-acre natural pocket within an industrial area; Shillito Park, which contains softball, baseball, soccer, and football fields, tennis courts, a fitness trail with exercise stations, and picnic shelters; Jacobson Park, which features a lake stocked with fish for anglers, a marina with pedal boats, a nature center, and an amphitheater; Masterson Station Park, the site of unique, comprehensive equestrian programs including clinics, lectures, and horseback riding lessons; and Raven Run Nature Sanctuary, which contains rare wildflowers, hiking trails, and picnicking facilities in a beautiful, informal setting.

Lexington's moderate climate offers plenty of incentive and opportunities for outdoor recreation, and when the temperatures dip low enough, residents can be found cross-country skiing, sledding, or ice skating in the parks and surrounding countryside. Lexington Ice Center is open year-round for day and night sessions of skating lessons and hockey games.

Golf is an option throughout all but the coldest months. A number of public and semi-private courses are available to golfers, including such Pete Dye–designed layouts as Kearney Hill Golf Links and Peninsula Golf

Resort, as well as the Gay Brewer, Jr. Course at Picadome, Lakeside Golf Course, and Meadowbrook Golf Course.

The city also maintains two skate parks, three disc golf courses, and four dog parks.

Shopping and Dining

Lexington has more than a dozen major shopping centers, including modern indoor malls that feature both large department stores and smaller specialty shops. Turfland Mall has department stores and retail shops, and Fayette Mall has more than 120 stores, making it the largest shopping mall in Lexington. The Shops at Lexington Center is convenient to downtown and the convention center. The city also offers plenty of boutique and specialty shopping areas. Clay Avenue Shops are a collection of stores in a former turn-of-the-century residential neighborhood. Victorian Square and Dudley Square are historic, renovated areas in the downtown with restaurants, fashions, and Kentucky/Appalachian handicrafts.

Chevy Chase Village is a thriving and eclectic mix of shops near the University of Kentucky. The Kentucky Store on Victorian Square has Kentucky souvenirs. Festival Market is a specialty food, retail, and entertainment center adjacent to Victorian Square. Lexington Farmers' Market is held every Saturday on West Vine Street, each Tuesday and Thursday at Maxwell and South Broadway, and on Sundays on Southland Drive and Hamburg. In the winter the market moves indoors to Victorian Square on Saturdays. It features fruits and vegetables, herbs, flowers, jams and jellies, honey, Kentucky specialties, and more. The J. Peterman Company, based in Lexington, operates a store in the city. Lexington is legendary for antique hunters. There are three antique malls within the city limits, and more than 200 shops in the surrounding area.

Cuisines from around the world can be had in Lexington in myriad restaurants that range from casual to fine dining. Mid-south regional food specialties found in Lexington include the Kentucky Hot Brown sandwich, Derby Pie, catfish, country ham, southern fried chicken, spoonbread, hushpuppies, and chess pie. Some of the more popular restaurants serving up Bluegrass fare include Café Jennifer at the Woodlands, any of several Ramsey's Diner restaurants around town, or deSha's in Victorian Square, which is famous for serving cream-style cornbread with honey butter. For fine dining, patrons visit Jonathan at Gratz Park or Le Deauville in the Historic District, among others. Lygnah's Irish Pub near the University of Kentucky campus was commended for its burgers in *Southern Living* magazine. Alfalfa has vegetarian fare.

Visitor Information: Lexington Convention and Visitor's Bureau, 250 West Main Street, Lexington, KY 40507-1513; telephone (859) 233-1221; toll-free (800) 848-1224.

■ Convention Facilities

Lexington Center, an 11-acre downtown complex, is the city's largest convention facility. The center includes Rupp Arena, which can be configured to accommodate seating requirements ranging from 3,500 to 23,000 people. The adjacent Lexington Convention Center has 130,000 square feet of banquet, exhibition, and meeting space. The Lexington Opera House is also part of the complex and is available for meeting and convention trade in addition to its full schedule of performing arts events. The Hyatt Regency and Hilton Lexington hotels are connected to the center by skywalks. The hotels offer more than 700 guest rooms, and an additional 46,000 square feet of exhibit space adjacent to meeting rooms. Meeting space is available in several unusual and historic settings near downtown, including ArtsPlace, Bell House, and the Bodley-Bullock House. Also connected to the convention center is Triangle Park, with cascading fountains and acres of flowering pear trees. Shopping and a specialty food court are available at the Shops at Lexington Center collection.

Lexington contains more than 6,000 rooms in its more than 50 hotels and motels. Most of the major chains are represented and offer ballrooms, conference rooms, or meeting rooms. The city prides itself on being able to handle conventions of nearly every size and type.

Convention Information: Lexington Convention and Visitor's Bureau, 250 West Main Street, Lexington, KY 40507-1513; telephone (859) 233-1221; toll-free (800) 848-1224.

■ Transportation

Approaching the City

Lexington's modern airport, Blue Grass Airport, is about five miles west of the city and 10 minutes from the heart of downtown. It is served by five major airlines, providing 13 non-stop destinations and offering more than 85 flights daily. The airport serves more than one million passengers each year. For those arriving by car, Lexington is conveniently located along the juncture of two interstate highways: Interstate 75 approaches from the north and south, while Interstate 64 approaches from the east and west. Blue Grass Parkway, a four-lane toll road, provides access to western Kentucky via U.S. Highway 60, and Mountain Parkway can be reached via Interstate 64. Kentucky Route 4, New Circle Road—a four-lane beltway—completely encircles the city. Greyhound travels into Lexington.

Traveling in the City

Lexington Transit Authority (LexTran) provides transportation options to visitors and area residents, including the LexTran bus system and LexVan vanpool ridesharing for commuters. Buses are wheelchair accessible, and bicycle racks are available. A free trolley service in the downtown area completes a circular route in 20 minutes. The city's Transit Authority created a Transit Center, which provides more than 700 handicapped-accessible parking spaces for the downtown.

■ Communications

Newspapers and Magazines

The *Lexington Herald-Leader* is Lexington's major daily newspaper. Several other specialty publications are based in Lexington, including *The Blood-Horse, Horseman and Fair World,* and *Kentucky Kernel,* which is the student daily newspaper of University of Kentucky.

Television and Radio

There are four licensed television stations in Lexington, including ABC, NBC, and CBS affiliate stations. In addition, the region's viewers can tune in stations originating in nearby cities. The local cable television provider is Insight Communications. There are 12 licensed radio stations broadcasting from Lexington, offering music, sports, and news.

Media Information: Lexington Herald-Leader, 100 Midland Avenue, Lexington, KY 40508-1999; telephone (859)231-3100; toll-free (800) 274-7355.

Lexington Online

Commerce Lexington. Available www.lexchamber.com

Downtown Lexington Corporation. Available www.downtownlex.com

Fayette County Public Schools. Available www.fcps.net

Lexington Downtown Development Authority. Available www.lexingtondda.com

Lexington-Fayette Urban County Government. Available www.lexingtonky.gov

Lexington Herald-Leader. Available www.kentucky.com

Lexington Convention and Visitors Bureau. Available www.visitlex.com

Lexington Public Library. Available www.lexpublib.org

BIBLIOGRAPHY

Scaggs, Deirdre A., *Women in Lexington* (Charleston, SC: Arcadia, 2005)

Raitz, Karl B., *Kentucky's Frontier Highway: Historical Landscapes along the Maysville Road* (Lexington, KY: University Press of Kentucky, 2012)

Wright, John D., Jr., *Heart of the Bluegrass* (Lexington, KY: Lexington-Fayette, 1982)

Louisville

■ The City in Brief

Founded: 1778 (incorporated 1828)

Head Official: Mayor Greg Fischer (R) (since 2011)

City Population
- 1990: 269,555
- 2000: 256,231
- 2010: 597,337
- 2012 estimate: 605,108
- Percent change, 2000–2010: 133.1%
- U.S. rank in 1990: 58th
- U.S. rank in 2000: 69th (State rank: 2nd)
- U.S. rank in 2010: 27th (State rank: 1st)

Metropolitan Statistical Area Population
- 2000: 1,025,598
- 2010: 1,283,566
- 2012 estimate: 1,302,457
- Percent change, 2000–2010: 25.2%
- U.S. rank in 2000: 43rd
- U.S. rank in 2010: 42nd

Area: 66.65 square miles

Elevation: 488 feet above sea level

Average Annual Temperatures: 56.9° F

Average Annual Precipitation: 44.54 inches

Major Economic Sectors: Trade, transportation, and utilities; professional and business services, educational and health services, government, manufacturing

Unemployment Rate: 7.2% (2012)

Per Capita Income: $24,554

2012 FBI Crime Index Property: 28,606

Major Colleges and Universities: University of Louisville, Bellarmine College, Spalding University

Daily Newspaper: *Courier-Journal*

■ Introduction

Noted for the Kentucky Derby, mint juleps, and Southern charm, Louisville preserves the best of the past while adjusting to the future. The city's economy is in transition, combining a reliance on traditional industries with redevelopment to attract new business enterprises. The face of the city has been changed by a downtown renaissance fueled by $2 billion in public and private investment, which supported the development of the 4th Street Live! entertainment district. Other new downtown attractions include the KFC Yum! Center Waterfront Arena, a basketball and all-purpose arena that overlooks the Ohio River and the Muhammad Ali Center. The metropolitan area spans seven counties in Kentucky and Indiana and boasts the advantages of both urban and rural living. New green initiatives, supported by government agencies and private enterprise, illustrate Louisville's interest in moving forward. More than just the home of the Kentucky Derby, Louisville remains a city proud of its legacy and committed to the future.

■ Geography and Climate

Louisville is located on the south bank of the Ohio River, about 377 miles above its confluence with the Mississippi River. Beargrass Creek and its south fork divide the city into two sectors with different types of topography. Louisville's eastern portion, with an elevation of 565 feet, is hilly, while the western part, lying in the flood plain of the Ohio River, is flat, with an average elevation of 465 feet. The climate is variable because of the city's position in mid-altitudes and in the interior of the continent; in

both winter and summer there are hot and cold spells of brief duration. On the average, winters are moderately cold and summers are very warm.

Area: 66.65 square miles

Elevation: 488 feet above sea level

Average Temperatures: 56.9° F

Average Annual Precipitation: 44.54 inches

■ History

Canal Completion Spurs City's Development

One historian has noted that chances of a settlement being established where Louisville now stands—adjacent to the Falls of the Ohio on a plain along the Ohio River—for a long time appeared unlikely because of treacherous rapids that had forced many prospective Native American, French, and Spanish settlers to turn back. In 1773 Thomas Bullitt was sent with a small surveying party to the site to plan a town, but they remained for less than a year. Then, in 1778, Colonel George Rogers Clark, accompanied by 120 soldiers and 20 families, established the first permanent settlement on nearby Corn Island, a

land mass in the Ohio River that has since been worn away by water. The following year Clark and his party moved to a fort on the mainland that served as a base for supplying Clark's expeditions into the Northwest Territory. This settlement, on the site of what is now 12th Street, was officially designated a town by the Virginia legislature in 1780 and named in honor of France's King Louis XVI for French service against the British during the American Revolution. A year later, Clark again moved his group and built Fort Nelson at the foot of present-day 7th Street.

Louisville, incorporated as a city in 1828, became an important river port because of its location on the Ohio River, a main artery for westward expansion. The economy profited greatly from the portaging of goods around the falls, but the advent of steamboats from New Orleans made it apparent that the falls were a barrier to development. In 1830 the Louisville & Portland Canal was completed, thus providing a water bypass around the falls and opening the way for increased river traffic from Pittsburgh to New Orleans.

Cultural and Economic Growth Continues

By the mid-nineteenth century Louisville was a prosperous industrial center and had begun to thrive culturally, its citizens surprising European visitors with their sophistication and cultivated tastes. As part of the New Orleans commercial empire, Louisville attracted two new groups of people who were to make permanent contributions to the life of the city—the French from New Orleans and the Germans from Pittsburgh.

During the Civil War the city served as an important Union supply depot, but the conflicting loyalties among its residents reflected the often bitter division between pro-Union and pro-Confederate sentiments that existed throughout the state of Kentucky. After the war Louisville was forced to adjust to the collapse of the southern plantation economy; new merchandising methods were initiated and railroad links were established with other major cities in the South.

The city continued to grow, and by 1900 the population had surpassed 200,000 people. During the 1920s a building boom brought skyscrapers to Louisville's silhouette, and in 1925 an electrical power plant was constructed at the Falls of the Ohio. The city was relatively untouched by the depression, as the tobacco trade and manufacturing maintained their normal levels; federal job programs during the 1930s helped to alleviate unemployment. In the winter of 1937, the Ohio River flooded and devastated the city, but by the summer of that same year Louisville was able to resume its usual way of life through rehabilitation loans and Red Cross assistance.

The city has undergone extensive redevelopment and revitalization with completion of many projects including Riverfront Plaza and Belvedere, 4th Street Live!, Glassworks, the Kentucky Center for African American Heritage, KFC Yum! Center Waterfront Arena, and the Muhammad Ali Center. A direct link to the past has been retained with the restoration of old buildings that are being used as museums, theaters, shops, and restaurants. The challenge for the twenty-first century was to solidify downtown Louisville as a place where people wanted to live and work.

Historical Information: Louisville Free Public Library, 301 York Street, Louisville, KY 40203; telephone (502) 574-1611.

■ Population Profile

Metropolitan Statistical Area Population
2000: 1,025,598
2010: 1,283,566
2012 estimate: 1,302,457
Percent change, 2000–2010: 25.2%
U.S. rank in 2000: 43rd
U.S. rank in 2010: 42nd

City Residents
1990: 269,555
2000: 256,231

2010: 597,337
2012 estimate: 605,108
Percent change, 2000–2010: 133.1%
U.S. rank in 1990: 58th
U.S. rank in 2000: 69th (State rank: 2nd)
U.S. rank in 2010: 27th (State rank: 1st)

Density: 1,836.6 people per square mile

Racial and ethnic characteristics
White: 430,659
Black or African American: 138,894
American Indian and Alaskan Native: 543
Asian: 13,352
Native Hawaiian and Other Pacific Islander: 208
Hispanic or Latino (may be of any race): 29,391
Other: 21,452

Percent of residents born in state: 70.2%

Age characteristics
Population under 5 years old: 40,673
Population 5 to 9 years old: 35,620
Population 10 to 14 years old: 40,521
Population 15 to 19 years old: 38,711
Population 20 to 24 years old: 42,154
Population 25 to 34 years old: 87,604
Population 35 to 44 years old: 76,713
Population 45 to 54 years old: 86,988
Population 55 to 59 years old: 41,922
Population 60 to 64 years old: 35,784
Population 65 to 74 years old: 41,031
Population 75 to 84 years old: 26,354
Population 85 years and over: 11,033
Median age: 37.3

Births (2010–11 Metropolitan Area)
Total number: 16,542

Deaths (2010–11 Metropolitan Area)
Total number: 11,142

Money income (2012)
Per capita income: $24,554
Median household income: $42,609
Total households: 242,395

Number of households with income of …
less than $10,000: 23,944
$10,000 to $14,999: 16,984
$15,000 to $24,999: 31,498
$25,000 to $34,999: 28,661
$35,000 to $49,999: 35,645
$50,000 to $74,999: 41,912
$75,000 to $99,999: 24,796
$100,000 to $149,999: 23,894
$150,000 to $199,999: 7,179
$200,000 or more: 7,882

Percent of families below poverty level: 19.3%

FBI Crime Index Property: 28,606

FBI Crime Index Violent: 3,989

■ Municipal Government

In 2003 Louisville became the first major metropolitan city in three decades to merge its city and county governments. The Louisville-Jefferson County Metro Government, dubbed "Louisville Metro," is led by a 26-member Metro Council. Members are elected by district to serve staggered, four-year terms. The mayor operates as the city's chief executive.

Head Official: Mayor Greg Fischer (R) (since 2011)

Total Number of City Employees: approximately 6,105 (2012)

City Information: Louisville Metro Hall, 527 W. Jefferson, Louisville, KY 40202; telephone (502)574-2003

■ Economy

Major Industries and Commercial Activity

The geography of Louisville, specifically its river accessibility, central location, and mild climate have contributed to its importance as a center for industry and commerce. The city has traditionally been a manufacturing center for durable goods including appliances, cars, and trucks. However, the area's economy has diversified, bringing with it more skilled and high-tech employment opportunities.

Trade, transportation, and utilities is one of the largest economic sectors in the Louisville-Jefferson County area. Some of the largest logistics, warehousing, and distribution companies in the area are UPS Supply Chain Solutions, Verst Group Logistics, and Derby Industries.

There is a fairly strong manufacturing sector in Louisville. Ford Motor Company produces the Escape at its Louisville manufacturing plant, which has been open since 1955 and covers more than three million square feet. Manufacturing plants for GE Appliance and Lighting and Brown-Forman Co. are also located in Louisville.

The services sector is the leading economic sector in the region. Tourism is the third largest service industry in Jefferson County. Travelers spend approximately $1.2 billion a year in the county. About 26,000 jobs are supported by the tourism industry in Jefferson County. Greater Louisville is also an important center for local, state, and federal government agencies. The Kentucky Air National Guard is headquartered at the Louisville International Airport's Standiford field, the U.S. Defense Department operates the Defense Mapping Agency, the Department of Veterans Affairs operates a veterans hospital in the area, and the U.S. Corp of Engineers maintains the McAlpine Locks and Dam.

The Louisville area is headquarters to some of the nation's top companies, including companies Yum! Brands Inc., which includes KFC (formerly Kentucky Fried Chicken), Pizza Hut, and Taco Bell; Kindred Healthcare; and Humana Inc. One of the better-known industries based in Louisville is Hillerich & Bradsby, makers of the famous Louisville Slugger baseball bat. The headquarters for Presbyterian Church (USA) and the American Printing House for the Blind, the official source of texts for the visually impaired, are also in the city. Other major companies in the area include Charter Communications (cable TV), Brown-Forman Co., Norton Healthcare, KentuckyOne Health, Republic Bancorp, and First Financial Services Corp.

Items and goods produced: Automobiles and trucks, home appliances, lighting systems, alcoholic beverages, pork products, aluminum foil, plastics, poultry

Incentive Programs-New and Existing Companies

Local programs: Greater Louisville Inc., The Metro Chamber of Commerce, is the agency responsible for working with new and existing businesses to create jobs and capital investment in Louisville. It was formed by the merger of the Greater Louisville Economic Development Partnership and the Louisville Chamber of Commerce. In addition to low taxes and low costs of doing business, Louisville offers a variety of financial incentives. Among them is the Manufacturing Tax Moratorium, which offers new or expanding manufacturing operations a five-year moratorium on all assessed property and real estate taxes, and the Property Tax Assessment and reassessment Moratorium. The Louisville Metro Brownfields Loan Program provides financing for economic development in older industrial areas of the city.

Several financing programs are available through the Metropolitan Business Development Corporation. These include the Louisville Agribusiness Loan, Small and Disadvantaged Business Loan, Accessibility Loan, and the Brownfield Cleanup Loan Program.

Greater Louisville's Foreign Trade Zone is located within Clark Maritime Center, Eastpoint Business Center, Jefferson Riverport International, and the Greater Louisville Technological Park.

State programs: The state of Kentucky offers an extensive array of incentives for business start-up and expansion. The Kentucky Economic Development Finance Authority (KEDFA) of the Kentucky Cabinet for Economic Development oversees a wide variety of programs and services available to businesses, including existing businesses, newly locating companies, start-ups, small and minority businesses, and many others. Small businesses may benefit from the Kentucky Small Business Credit Initiative, which supports participating lenders in efforts to finance businesses that typically fall outside of standard lending guidelines. Small businesses involved in manufacturing, agribusiness, or service and technology may qualify for the Small Business Loan Program, which provides loans between $15,000 and $100,000 for a term of 10 years. The Kentucky Small Business Tax Credit provides credits for eligible businesses with 50 or fewer full-time employees who create one or more jobs while investing at least $5,000 in qualifying equipment or technology.

The Kentucky Business Investment Program offers income tax credits for new and existing agribusinesses, regional and national headquarters, manufacturing companies, and non-retail service- or technology-related companies. New or expanding businesses involved in service or technology, manufacturing, or tourism can apply for assistance through the Kentucky Enterprise Initiative Act, which provides sales and use tax refunds for building and construction materials or equipment used for research and development and data processing. The Kentucky Economic Development Direct Loan Program offers below-market interest rates for businesses involved in agribusiness, tourism, industrial ventures, or the service industry.

Some special incentives are available for high-tech companies, including the High-Tech Investment/Construction Pools, which provide funds for commercialization of a product, process, or innovation. The KEDFA also offers a matching funds program for Phase 1 and Phase 2 federal small business innovation research and small business technology transfer awards received by Kentucky businesses. A special Kentucky New Energy ventures Fund has been established to assist in the development of commercialization of alternative fuels and renewable energy. Companies providing large investments in renewable and alternative energy facilities may be eligible for a variety of negotiated incentives through the Incentives for Energy Independence Act.

Agribusiness companies may be legible for assistance through the Kentucky Agricultural Development Fund or the Kentucky Agricultural Finance Corporation. Businesses involved in tourism may qualify for the recovery of development costs through the Tourism Development Act, which is administered through the Kentucky Tourism, Arts, and Heritage Cabinet.

Job training programs: Workforce training assistance is provided through the Bluegrass State Skills Corporation (BSSC) of the Kentucky Cabinet for Economic Development. The BSSC Grant-in-Aid program provides grants for training of workers in new and expanding businesses and continuing training for workers in existing companies.

The Skills Training Investment Credit program offers state tax credits for approved training programs.

The Kentucky Office of Employment and Training, a branch of the Kentucky Department of Workforce Investment, provides training assistance under the Workforce Investment Act. The Louisville Area Career Center serves Jefferson, Henry, Oldham, Shelby, Spencer, Trimble, and Bullitt Counties.

Customized employee training programs are available through the Kentucky Community and Technical College System. In Louisville, these services are provided through the Jefferson Technical Campus, the Downtown Campus, and the Southwest Campus of Jefferson Community and Technical College.

The unique partnership of the University of Louisville, Jefferson Community and Technical College, and UPS established the Metropolitan College. The college addresses workforce needs by providing special curricula and work-friendly class schedules that cater to the needs of UPS Worldport part-time employees who work at night, enabling them to study for technical certifications, two-year, or four-year degrees. The program not only offers free education, but it also helps decrease the turnover rate for newly hired employees.

Development Projects

Greater Louisville officials have identified 10 niche industries with potential for growth and have begun work to attract new and expanding businesses from these industries to Louisville. The target niche industries are advanced manufacturing, lifelong wellness and aging care, craft distilling, logistics, automotive, food and beverage, franchises, health enterprises, life sciences, and pharmacy supply chain.

In 2013 the Scotland-based First State Investments International Inc., a privately owned investment manager, announced plans to open a Louisville office to provide administrative support for its global operations. Their plans moved one step closer to reality in December 2013 when the Kentucky Economic Development Finance Authority approved their application for up to $500,000 in tax incentives for up to 10 years. If the project moves forward, the company expects to invest $2 million in its Louisville office, creating 19 jobs with an average wage, including benefits, of $79 per hour.

In 2013 the city announced that six new specialty retail establishments would be added to South Fourth Street, including Art Eatables, a small-batch bourbon truffle shop; The Leading Man, a men's clothing store; and Les Filles Louisville, an artisan jewelry and accessories shop. That year the city also announced plans for a new Aloft hotel in the heart of downtown Louisville. The $22 million, eight-story boutique hotel was to be developed by the Poe Companies and managed by White Lodging. It planned to feature 175 guest rooms and suites and 2,800 square feet of meeting space.

In September 2013 construction began on the new Hilton Garden Inn Downtown at Clay Commons. The eight-story, 121,700-square-foot building was to have 162 guest rooms and an open-air rooftop restaurant and bar. Also, eBay Enterprise announced plans to invest $45 million in a reconstruction project to join two newly purchased buildings into one new facility. The expansion effort included the creation of 150 new full-time jobs.

Economic Development Information: Greater Louisville Inc., 614 West Main Street, Suite 6000, Louisville, KY 40202; telephone (502) 625-0000; email info@ greaterlousiville.com.

Commercial Shipping

Louisville's economy is served by dozens of motor carriers that provide efficient, one-day access to major domestic markets via Interstates 65, 64, and 71. CSX and Norfolk Southern Railroad systems connect the city with major markets in the United States, Canada, and Mexico. Louisville is the international air-freight hub for United Parcel Service; UPS Worldport offers next-day air service to 200 markets, including China, Europe, and Russia. Another important component in the local economy is the Port of Louisville, which handles an average of seven million tons of cargo yearly.

Labor Force and Employment Outlook

According to the U.S. Bureau of Labor Statistics, the largest employment sector in the Lousiville-Jefferson County area in 2013 was trade, transportation, and utilities. However, the combined service sectors, including health and educational services, professional and business services, and other services, accounted for a much larger number of jobs. Humana Inc., Norton Healthcare, and KentuckyOne Health were among the top employers. The government sector was also a significant employer, as was manufacturing. The top manufacturing employers for the region include Ford Motor Company, GE Appliance and Lighting, and Brown-Forman Co.

The following is a summary of data regarding the 2012 Louisville labor force:

Size of civilian labor force: 309,970

Number of workers employed in . . .

agriculture and mining: 678
construction: 12,476
manufacturing: 30,008
wholesale trade: 8,547
retail trade: 27,650
transportation: 22,695
information systems: 7,008
finance: 20,730
professional administration: 26,012
education and social services: 67,200
arts and leisure: 26,981
other: 14,003
public administration: 8,533

Average hourly earnings of production workers: $17.2

Unemployment rate: 7.2% (2012)

Employers

Largest private-sector employers (2013)	*Number of employees*
United Parcel Service Inc	20,047
Humana Inc.	11,235
Norton Healthcare	9,666
KentuckyOne Health Inc.	8,893
Ford Motor Co.	8,512
GE Appliances and Lighting.	6,000
Kroger Co.	5,152
Baptist Healthcare System	4,854
Catholic Archdiocese of Louisville	2,345
LG&E and KU Energy.2,131	
Kindred Healthcare	2,130

Cost of Living

Costs are lower than might be expected in a metropolitan area of Louisville's size, due in part to the fact that the population is spread out over seven largely rural counties in Kentucky and Indiana.

The following is a summary of data regarding several key cost of living factors in the area.

2013 ACCRA Average House Price: $232,494

2013 ACCRA Cost of Living Index: 91

State income tax rate: 2.0% to 6.0%

State sales tax rate: 6.0%

Local income tax rate: 2.20%

Local sales tax rate: None

Property tax rate: $36.6600 per $1,000 of assessed value (2013)

Economic Information: Greater Louisville Inc., 614 West Main Street, Suite 6000, Louisville, KY 40202; telephone (502) 625-0000; email: info@greaterlousiville. com.

■ Education and Research

Elementary and Secondary Schools

Jefferson County Public Schools is one of the largest districts in the country. The district has more than 100,000 students in 172 schools and learning centers. There are more than 6,400 teachers. The school system offers students a variety of optional programs including advanced programs for gifted students; career/technological programs for middle school students; magnet programs; strict, traditional school curriculums; trade schools; and special programs for handicapped students. The county is home to the Gheens Academy of Curricular Excellence and Instructional Leadership, a national model for teacher training.

There are several private schools in area as well. These include Academy for Individual Excellence, Louisville Collegiate School, Kentucky Country Day School, Summit Academy of Greater Louisville, The DePaul School, Walden School, and Waldorf School of Louisville. There are numerous Catholic schools supported by the Archdiocese of Louisville.

The following is a summary of data regarding the Jefferson County Public Schools.

Total enrollment: 97,331

Number of facilities

total: 172

elementary schools: 89

junior high schools: 23

high schools: 19

other: 41

Student/teacher ratio: 15.85:1

Teacher salaries

average (statewide): $50,038

Funding per pupil: $10,989

Public Schools Information: Jefferson County Public Schools, VanHoose Education Center, 3332 Newburg Rd., Louisville, KY 40218; telephone (502) 485-3011.

Colleges and Universities

The University of Louisville has an average enrollment of more than 21,000 students in 12 colleges and schools, including the Speed School of Engineering, the Brandeis School of Law, and the Kent School of Social Work. Bellarmine College offers master's degrees in business administration, education, applied information technology, and nursing, in addition to more than 50 undergraduate degrees. Spalding University is an independent liberal arts college that was founded by the Sisters of Charity of Nazareth. It offers associate's, bachelor's, and master's degrees in several fields, along

with doctorates in leadership education and psychology. Sullivan University is the state's largest independent four-year institution, with programs in eight schools and colleges, including the National Center for Hospitality Studies, the Institute for Legal Studies, and the College of Health Sciences. Three branches of Jefferson Community and Technical College are located in Louisville.

Libraries and Research Centers

The main branch of the Louisville Free Public Library is located downtown, with 17 other branches and a bookmobile. The library circulates more than four million books, videos, DVDs, and CDs. The library collection includes a Kentucky History and Kentucky Author Collection. It is a Federal Depository library for government documents.

The University of Louisville Libraries has more than two million volumes, with special collections on astronomy, mathematics, and Irish literature. The W. L. Lyons Brown Library at Bellarmine University is home to the Thomas Merton Center, which features a special collection of research materials on the life and work of the Trappist monk. The Filson Historical Society has one of the country's leading research collections for genealogy.

More than 30 research centers are located in Louisville; some are affiliated with local colleges and hospitals, and others concentrate on such fields as genealogy, health, engineering, law, crime prevention, and alcoholic beverage production. The Donald E. Baxter, M.D. Biomedical Research Building is part of the University of Louisville School of Medicine and one of the cornerstones for attracting research scientists to its Health Sciences Center. The university's transplantation research program received international acclaim when it performed the second successful hand transplant in the world.

Public Library Information: Louisville Free Public Library, 301 York Street, Louisville, KY 40203; telephone (502) 574-1611.

■ Health Care

Baptist Hospital East is part of the Baptist Healthcare System. The hospital offers a comprehensive range of services in multiple specialty areas, including cancer care, heart care, mother and baby care, minimally invasive surgery, neuroscience services, orthopedic services, a sleep center and women's care, among others. Special departments include Baptist Sports Medicine, the Center for Pain Management, and the Post-Polio Syndrome Clinic. Baptist Express Care is a network of drop-in clinics based in local Wal-Mart stores throughout the city.

University of Louisville Hospital is affiliated with KentuckyOne Health and offers a full range of medical services. Special care centers include the James Graham Brown Cancer Center, the Stroke Center, the only Level

I trauma center in the region, the Center for Women and Infants, and the Comprehensive Epilepsy Center. KentuckyOne also manages Jewish Hospital and Sts. Mary and Elizabeth Hospital, among others in the region.

Norton Health Care operates five hospitals in Louisville, including Norton Brownsboro Hospital. Norton Hospital, Norton Suburban Hospital, Norton Audubon Hospital, and the Kosair Children's Hospital.

■ Recreation

Sightseeing

Louisville offers a variety of recreational activities, from a leisurely steamboat excursion on the Ohio River to a fun-filled day at a theme park. The city retains a flavor of the past with its historic Main Street, a restored district that features one of the largest collections of cast-iron buildings in the United States. Many homes have also been restored; regular tours are offered to visitors who wish to experience a taste of life as it was in the eighteenth and nineteenth centuries. Among the most popular residences are Locust Grove, the last home of Louisville founder George Rogers Clark; Farnsley-Moreman Landing, a nineteenth-century Kentucky "I" house with a two-story Greek Revival portico; the Farmington Historic Site, which features octagonal rooms; the Brennan House, the last remaining private home in downtown Louisville; the Culbertson mansion, an example of Second Empire architecture; and the Whitehall House and Gardens, a classic Revival antebellum mansion on 10 acres. The Thomas Edison Butchertown House/Museum, a shotgun cottage, contains a collection of Edison inventions.

Tours are available at the 1871 Spalding University Mansion and at Conrad-Caldwell House, a completely renovated 1895 home in Old Louisville, a neighborhood of elegant nineteenth-century mansions. The Filson Historical Society is headquartered in a 1900s home and features artifacts, manuscripts, portraiture, special collections, and a library for historical and genealogical research. The Kentucky Center for African American Heritage tells the story of African Americans in Kentucky. The Zachary Taylor National Cemetery and Monument honors the dead of many wars, and the Cave Hill Cemetery and Arboretum is a historic 297-acre cemetery and botanical garden.

Animal lovers can visit the Louisville Zoo, which displays more than 1,300 animals in a park-like setting. The zoo showcases a gorilla forest habitat, bear habitat, and Glacier Run, a 108,000 gallon saltwater home to harbor seals and California sea lions. The Louisville Nature Center is an urban oasis where visitors can enjoy more than 150 species of birds, wild animals and flower-decked trails.

Several local industries provide tours of their facilities. Among them are Jim Beam American Outpost,

located about 25 miles south of the city; Hillerich & Bradsby, makers of the Louisville Slugger baseball bat; and Louisville Stoneware Company, where visitors can paint their own pottery. The American Printing House for the Blind and Callahan Museum, which creates products and services for the blind and visually impaired, offers plant and museum tours. Horse-drawn carriages ride past historical sites, and public excursions on the Ohio River aboard the *Belle of Louisville, Spirit of Jefferson,* and *Star of Louisville* can also be arranged.

Arts and Culture

The performing and visual arts flourish in Louisville, the first city to create a community fund for the arts. The Kentucky Center for the Performing Arts has four theaters that stage a variety of performances ranging from symphony, opera, and ballet to children's theater, a Broadway series, and country music. The center is home to the Louisville Orchestra, Kentucky Opera, Louisville Ballet, Stage One, and PNC Bank Broadway Across America–Louisville. It also hosts community theaters and special Kentucky Center Presents performances.

The Louisville Visual Art Association (LVAA) is a nonprofit, artist-oriented organization dedicated to the creation and appreciation of visual art in all media. The downtown LVAA center offers art classes for talented elementary and high school students; it also hosts year-round exhibitions and special events such as jazz concerts and the Boat Race Party during Derby Week. The Louisville Glassworks galleries feature artists from around the world, as well as glass blowing workshops and classes. The Mellwood Arts and Entertainment Center features 200 artist studios, specialty retail shops, galleries (including a three-story tenant art gallery), teaching studios, office space, rehearsal space for theater groups and dancers, and entertainment space.

Housed in a historic landmark built in 1837, the Tony-Award-winning Actors Theatre of Louisville is internationally known for the annual Humana Festival of New American Plays, one of the world's most important showcases for aspiring playwrights; other theater groups include Kentucky Shakespeare Festival, Bunbury Theatre, and Broadway at Iroquois. Stage One Family Theatre presents productions throughout the year at The Kentucky Center.

The museums and galleries of Louisville highlight much that is unique to the city and the region. For example, the Kentucky Derby Museum is the world's largest equine museum, offering hands-on computerized simulated racing, a 360-degree audio-visual presentation about the Kentucky Derby, and a live thoroughbred exhibit. The Louisville Slugger Museum showcases the famous bat and the history of the family that created it.

Among the museums dedicated to science and technology is the Kentucky Science Center, which features hands-on exhibits and an aerospace collection as well as an

IMAX theater. The Portland Museum features a light and sound show that carries viewers back to nineteenth-century Louisville. Located on the University of Louisville campus, Gheens Science Hall and Rauch Memorial Planetarium offer multimedia astronomy presentations.

Festivals and Holidays

Louisville's major annual events calendar is full, beginning in February with the National Farm Machinery Show and Tractor Pull Championships, one of the nation's most popular and best-attended functions of its kind. In April and May the city hosts the Kentucky Derby Festival offering 70 events. Held in conjunction with the running of the Kentucky Derby, it is one of the country's largest civic celebrations. The Great Steamboat Race and the Great Balloon Race are two of the more popular Derby events. The Cherokee Triangle Art Fair also occurs in April. May is the month for the Kentucky Reggae Festival.

The Waterside Independence Festival takes place over Independence Day weekend. July also brings Shakespeare in the Park, the Coca-Cola Operation Brightside Volleyball Classic, and the Kentucky Music Weekend Bluegrass Festival. The Kentucky State Fair runs for 10 days beginning in mid-August. The Corn Island Storytelling Festival is in September. The Louisville Irish Fest, Bluegrass Balloon Festival, and the Captain's Quarters Regatta are also held this month.

October is the month for the St. James Court Art Show, the Louisville Jaycees Oktoberfest, and the Halloween Party at the Louisville Zoo. The year ends with Christmas in the City, a Victorian Christmas celebration involving street vendors, carolers, and house tours. The Mayor's Midnight Special on New Year's Eve is an outdoor family party.

Sports for the Spectator

Louisville's best-known sporting event is the Kentucky Derby. For racing fans, Louisville offers two horse-racing tracks, Churchill Downs (for thoroughbred racing) and Louisville Downs (for harness racing). Churchill Downs' spring racing dates are April through June; fall racing takes place in October and November. Louisville Downs features nighttime races in early spring, summer, and fall. Churchill Downs features a similar event called Downs After Dark which consists of 11 races. The event runs on select evenings from June until November.

Louisville's $26 million, 13,000-seat Louisville Slugger Field is home to the Louisville Bats, a Triple-A affiliate of the Cincinnati Reds. The University of Louisville fields highly regarded football and basketball teams; the Cardinals play football at Papa John's Cardinal Stadium.

Sports for the Participant

Louisville public parks contain more than 200 tennis courts, a number of 9-hole and 18-hole golf courses, and some 15 swimming pools. Many lakes in the metropolitan area's parks are stocked for fishing, and some parks located along the Ohio River provide access to river fishing. Water sports are also a favorite pastime on the river during the summer. The Louisville Extreme Park offers skateboarding, in-line skating and biking on 40,000 square feet of concrete surface. Bicycling is a popular sport in Kentucky, and each fall the Louisville Bicycle Club sponsors the My Old Kentucky Home Bicycle Tour, a two-day event that draws more than 400 cyclists.

Shopping and Dining

Louisville offers a wide variety of retail establishments in more than 100 shopping centers, including enclosed malls and several neighborhood shopping areas. The Oxmoor Center features 110 specialty stores and three department stores. Jefferson Mall is a regional shopping center located near the airport. Main and Market Streets between 5th and 9th is the primary downtown shopping area. Antique shops, galleries and unique boutiques are plentiful in the Bardstown Road, Frankfort Avenue areas, and Chenoweth Lane in St. Matthews.

Dining in Louisville can range from a casual meal at a fast-food establishment or a family treat at an ethnic cafe to an elegant event at a gourmet restaurant. Foods that have made Louisville famous are burgoo, originally a game stew made with squirrel, venison, or opossum—but now more likely to contain a blend of pork, beef, mutton, and chicken—in a spicy tomato sauce with a mixture of vegetables that might include cabbage, peppers, and potatoes; the Hot Brown, a layered sandwich of country ham, turkey, bacon, tomatoes, and cheese served bubbling hot; and the Benedictine, a delicate sandwich incorporating cream cheese and chopped cucumber.

Visitor Information: Louisville Convention and Visitors Bureau, 401 W. Main St., Suite 2300, Louisville, KY 40202; toll-free (888) 568-4784.

■ Convention Facilities

The dual appeal of a vital urban climate steeped in history makes Louisville an ideal place for large and small meetings. Louisville's largest meeting facility is the Kentucky International Convention Center. The facility's 300,000 square feet include a 360-seat theater, a 30,000-square-foot ballroom, and 52 meeting rooms. The center is located in the heart of downtown and connected by skywalks to the Hyatt Regency Hotel and two parking garages. Another downtown facility is the all-purpose Louisville Gardens, located in the shopping district. The Gardens can accommodate groups ranging from 100 to 6,000 people.

The Convention Center's sister facility, the Kentucky Exposition Center, is located just two minutes from

Louisville International Airport. It is one of the world's largest multipurpose buildings on one floor. Offering 30 acres and 1 million square feet of space, together with paved parking for 1,200 cars, it is within easy driving distance of hotels and motels. Its indoor arena, Freedom Hall, seats 19,000 people. The six-building complex hosts more than 500 events, including the annual Kentucky State Fair, the National Farm Machinery Show, and the North American International Livestock Exposition, and attracts four million people each year. Its multipurpose building, Broadbent Arena, is the site of tractor pulls, basketball tournaments, and graduation ceremonies, while Cardinal Stadium hosts sporting events concerts and stage presentations.

Unique meeting space is available on the *Belle of Louisville*, a 1914 paddlewheel steamboat; the *Belle* hosts receptions for up to 750 people from April through October, or seated dinners for some 300 people from November through December. *Spirit of Jefferson*, a sternwheeler excursion boat built in 1963, also hosts chartered cruises and features two indoor climate-controlled decks to accommodate 150 people.

Hotel space in Louisville is plentiful-approximately 17,000 rooms are available in the metropolitan area. More than 3,000 hotel rooms are located downtown, with most within walking distance of the Kentucky International Convention Center. The Louisville Marriott Downtown, adjacent to the Convention Center, boasts 616 rooms and 50,000 square feet of meeting space. The 1,300-room Galt House Hotel completed a $60 million renovation in 2008. Other area hotels include the 392-room Hyatt Regency Louisville, the 321-room Seelbach Hilton, and the 140-room Courtyard by Marriott Louisville Downtown.

Convention Information: Louisville Convention and Visitors Bureau, 401 W. Main St., Suite 2300, Louisville, KY 40202; toll-free (888) 568-4784.

■ Transportation

Approaching the City

Louisville International Airport is located 10 minutes from downtown and enjoys easy access to interstate highways. The airport was served by six major carriers in 2013: AirTran, American Airlines, Delta, Southwest, United, and US Airways. That year, it offered non-stop service to 24 destinations, including 8 of the 10 busiest U.S. airports. A second, smaller airport at Bowman Field provides a variety of local and state aviation services.

Louisville is at the center of three major interstates: Interstate 65 from the north or south, Interstate 64 from the east or west, and Interstate 71 from the northeast. U.S. Highway 60 (Broadway) intersects the city east and west.

Traveling in the City

Louisville is laid out on a grid pattern slightly tilted on the east–west axis. Broadway (U.S. Highway 60) divides the city north from south, and Second Street divides east from west.

The Transit Authority of River City (TARC) provides the city's bus-based mass transit system. The service area covers the Louisville metropolitan area as well as Jefferson, Oldham, and Bullitt Counties; it also includes Floyd and Clark Counties in Southern Indiana, with the state of Indiana contributing to TARC's funding.

■ Communications

Newspapers and Magazines

Louisville's major daily newspaper is the *Courier-Journal* (morning). Its weekday circulation averaged just over 130,000 as of 2013. *The Voice Tribune* is a weekly business newspaper. *Louisville Business First* and a number of special-interest magazines are also based in Louisville, including the weekly *Leo (The Louisville Eccentric Observer)*, *The Louisville Defender*, and the monthly lifestyle publication *Louisville Magazine*. Other publications serve readers involved in the building trades, agriculture, computers, and religion.

Television and Radio

Louisville is served by 11 television stations. Eight AM and 10 FM radio stations broadcast a variety of musical formats plus news and talk.

Media Information: Louisville Courier-Journal, 525 West Broadway, Louisville, KY 40201-7431; telephone (502) 582-4011.

Louisville Online

City of Louisville Home Page. Available www.louisvilleky.gov

Greater Louisville Convention and Visitors Bureau. Available www.gotolouisville.com

Greater Louisville Inc. (Metro Chamber of Commerce). Available www.greaterlouisville.com

Jefferson County Public Schools. Available www.jefferson.k12.ky.us

Louisville Free Public Library. Available www.lfpl.org

BIBLIOGRAPHY

Luhan, Gregory A., *The Louisville Guide* (New York: Princeton Architectural Press, 2004)

Von Borries, Philip, *The Louisville Baseball Almanac* (Charleston, SC: History Press, 2010)

Wright, George C., *Life Behind a Veil: Blacks in Louisville, Kentucky 1865–1930* (Baton Rouge, LA: Louisiana State University Press, 1985)

Louisiana

The State in Brief

Nickname: Pelican State

Motto: Union, justice, and confidence

Flower: Magnolia

Bird: Eastern brown pelican

Area: 52,378 square miles (2010; U.S. rank 31st)

Elevation: Ranges from eight feet below sea level to 535 feet above sea level

Climate: Subtropical and humid, with long, hot summers and short, mild winters

Admitted to Union: April 30, 1812

Capital: Baton Rouge

Head Official: Bobby Jindal (R) (until 2016)

Population

1990: 4,220,164
2000: 4,468,976
2010: 4,533,372
2012 estimate: 4,529,605
Percent change, 2000–2010: 1.4%
U.S. rank in 2012: 25th
Percent of residents born in state: 78.5% (2012)
Density: 104.9 people per square mile (2010)
2012 FBI Crime Index Total: 185,804

Racial and Ethnic Characteristics (2012)

White: 2,856,883
Black or African American: 1,450,992
American Indian and Alaska Native: 28,702
Asian: 71,460
Native Hawaiian and Pacific Islander: 1,826
Hispanic or Latino (may be of any race): 192,582
Other: 119,742

Age Characteristics (2012)

Population under 5 years old: 313,009
Population 5 to 19 years old: 934,427
Percent of population 65 years and over: 12.4%
Median age: 35.9

Vital Statistics

Total number of births (2012–13): 61,703
Total number of deaths (2012–13): 42,002
AIDS cases reported through 2011: 22,242

Economy

Major industries: Chemicals, energy, trade, manufacturing, tourism
Unemployment rate (2012): 5.2%
Per capita income (2012): $24,264
Median household income (2012): $44,673
Percentage of persons below poverty level (2012): 18.7%
Income tax rate: 2.0% to 6.0%
Sales tax rate: 4.0%

Baton Rouge

■ The City in Brief

Founded: 1719 (incorporated 1817)

Head Official: Mayor Melvin "Kip" Holden (since 2005; term expires 2017)

City Population
>1990: 219,531
>2000: 227,818
>2010: 229,493
>2012 estimate: 230,040
>Percent change, 2000–2010: 0.7%
>U.S. rank in 1990: 73rd (State rank: 2nd)
>U.S. rank in 2000: 85th (State rank: 2nd)
>U.S. rank in 2010: 85th (State rank: 2nd)

Metropolitan Statistical Area Population
>2000: 705,973
>2010: 802,484
>2012 estimate: 815,298
>Percent change, 2000–2010: 13.7%
>U.S. rank in 2000: 66th
>U.S. rank in 2010: 65th

Area: 76.84 square miles

Elevation: 83 feet above sea level

Average Annual Temperatures: 67° F

Average Annual Precipitation: 63.08 inches of rain; 0.2 inches of snow

Major Economic Sectors: petrochemical and general manufacturing, agribusiness, health care, government, transportation, film production

Unemployment Rate: 6.0% (2012)

Per Capita Income: $23,903

2012 FBI Crime Index Property: 12,059

Major Colleges and Universities: Louisiana State University, Southern University

Daily Newspaper: *The Advocate*

■ Introduction

Baton Rouge, the state capital of Louisiana and the county seat of Baton Rouge Parish, has been described as "a happy blend of Cajun *joie de vivre* and progressive American know-how" and seeks to give all visitors a taste of "authentic Louisiana at every turn." Situated on the Mississippi River in the heart of the state, the city is an important center in the Sun Belt market. The city, the second largest in the state, is becoming one of the fastest growing in the South. The moderate year-round temperatures and a relaxed environment make Baton Rouge a desirable place for residents and visitors alike. Baton Rouge's population exploded after Hurricane Katrina in 2005 as it absorbed the aftermath of the evacuation; more predictable population growth has followed. Petrochemical companies continued to pace the economy into the 2010s, though Baton Rouge enjoyed remarkable diversity that exploited all the region's economic assets—location, natural resources, state government power, and university expertise.

■ Geography and Climate

Baton Rouge is the third most southern capital city geographically in the continental United States, after Austin, Texas, and Tallahassee, Florida. Baton Rouge is the state capital and the seat of East Baton Rouge Parish. Baton Rouge is about 75 miles north of the Gulf of Mexico and 70 miles northwest of New Orleans. The city and its eight surrounding parishes are known collectively as the "Capital Region." Located in southeast Louisiana, the city rests on the east bank of the Mississippi River at

Pattie Steib/BigStockPhoto.com

the first series of bluffs north of the river delta's coastal plain. Baton Rouge's proximity to the coastline exposes the metropolitan region to hurricanes. However, the bluffs generally protect the city's residents from hurricanes, subsequent flooding, or other natural disasters. In addition to this natural barrier, the city has built a levee system stretching from the bluff southward to protect the riverfront and low-lying agricultural areas. The city's subtropical climate is free of extremes in temperature, except for occasional brief winter cold spells. Precipitation is ample throughout the year. Snow is rare.

Area: 76.84 square miles

Elevation: 83 feet above sea level

Average Temperatures: 67° F

Average Annual Precipitation: 63.08 inches of rain; 0.2 inches of snow

■ History

French Settlers Found City

The second largest city in Louisiana, Baton Rouge was established as a military post by the French in 1719. The present name of the city, however, dates back to 1699, when French explorers noted a blood-stained cypress tree stripped of its bark that marked the boundary between Houma and Bayou Goula tribal hunting grounds. They called the tree "le baton rouge," or red stick. The native name for the site had been Istrouma. From evidence found along the Mississippi, Comite, and Amite rivers, and in three native mounds remaining in the city, archaeologists have been able to date habitation of the Baton Rouge area to 8000 B.C.

Capital City Grows Steadily

Since European settlement, Baton Rouge has functioned under seven governing bodies: France, England, Spain, Louisiana, the Florida Republic, the Confederate States, and the United States. In the mid-1700s when French-speaking settlers of Acadia, Canada's maritime regions, were driven into exile by British forces, many took up residence in rural Louisiana. Popularly known as Cajuns, descendants of the Acadians maintained a separate culture that immeasurably enriched the Baton Rouge area. Incorporated in 1817, Baton Rouge became Louisiana's state capital in 1849. During the first half of the nineteenth century the city grew steadily as the result of steamboat trade and transportation; at the outbreak of the Civil War the population was 5,500 people. The war halted economic progress but did not actually touch the town until it was occupied by Union forces in 1862.

In August of that year, the Third Battle of Baton Rouge was fought at Port Hudson, less than 25 miles north of the city. Six thousand Confederate troops were ultimately defeated by 18,000 Union soldiers in one of the longest sieges in American military history.

Petrochemical Industry Develops

During the war, the state capital had been moved to Shreveport, but it was returned to Baton Rouge in 1880. By the beginning of the twentieth century, the town had undergone significant industrial development as a result of its strategic location for the production of petroleum, natural gas, and salt. In 1909 the Standard Oil Company built a facility that proved to be a lure for other petrochemical firms. Throughout World War II, these plants increased production for the war effort and contributed to the growth of the city. Accelerated growth brought problems in how the city would continue to provide services for a larger number of residents in and around the city. In 1947 residents approved a plan to consolidate the city and parish governments. The plan went into effect on January 1, 1949.

In the 1950s and 1960s, with the construction and development of the Port of Greater Baton Rouge, the city experienced a boom in the petrochemical industry, causing the city to expand even more away from the river and threatening to strand the historic downtown area. City planning authorities began to address this concern most directly in the 1980s and 1990s by initiating a wide variety of development projects in the downtown area. Between the 1980s and the first decade of the new century, over $1 billion was invested in development projects, such as a $370 million Capitol Park project that included renovation and new construction of offices, retail space, and parking facilities. Petrochemical facilities around Baton Rouge are plentiful, contributing to 17 billion gallons of gasoline generated each year, and billions in revenue for the state.

Post Hurricane Katrina

Baton Rouge experienced a dramatic and unexpected boom in August 2005 when Hurricane Katrina hit New Orleans. At about 80 miles away, Baton Rouge suffered only minor wind damage and inconvenient power outages. But within days the population of Baton Rouge doubled as evacuees from New Orleans began to arrive. While many evacuees stayed only for a short time, reports indicated that the population of Baton Rouge had increased anywhere between 50,000 and 100,000 people in the two years since the hurricane, meeting pre-Katrina estimates of the city's population for 2030. The dramatic change caused problems in traffic, public safety, and educational services. City officials began to expect that many of these new residents would stay long term. In response, city residents approved a $500 million road construction plan funded by sales tax revenues and hired about 100 additional police officers. As part of regional post Katrina rebuilding efforts, the city was also designated as part of the Gulf Opportunity Zone (GO Zone), which covers most of the southern region of the state. Special economic incentives developed by state and local authorities have assisted in the renovation or new development of businesses within the GO Zone.

While dealing with the economic and managerial issues of the post Katrina population surge, the city had to deal with a hurricane of their own. In August 2008, Hurricane Gustav's arrival made it the worst hurricane to directly affect the Baton Rouge area. Damage was mostly caused by wind, shutting down the city for five days. Power was not restored to all residents for three weeks. Debris clean up went on for four months. Baton Rouge's vulnerability drove some companies out of the city, such as Blue Cross and Blue Shield, which had a backup crisis headquarters in the city destroyed by the storm. Meanwhile, other companies continued to believe in the city's future. The city continues to be home to The Shaw Group, a *Fortune 500* company as of 2013, and in 2009 Albemarle Corporation, a *Fortune* 1000 company, moved its corporate offices to the city, adding to the city's chemicals industry. Existing chemical companies, including behemoths ExxonMobil, Shell, and Dow, all expanded operations in the city during 2012–13.

Historical Information: Foundation for Historical Louisiana, 502 North Blvd., Baton Rouge, LA, 70802; telephone (225) 387-2464. Baton Rouge Genealogical and Historical Society, PO Box 80565, Southeast Station, Baton Rouge, LA 70898-0565. Louisiana Genealogical and Historical Society, PO Box 82060, Baton Rouge, LA 70884-2060. Louisiana State Archives, Secretary of State Building, 3851 Essen Lane, Baton Rouge, LA 70809-2137; telephone (225) 922-1000.

■ Population Profile

Metropolitan Statistical Area Population
2000: 705,973
2010: 802,484
2012 estimate: 815,298
Percent change, 2000–2010: 13.7%
U.S. rank in 2000: 66th
U.S. rank in 2010: 65th

City Residents
1990: 219,531
2000: 227,818
2010: 229,493
2012 estimate: 230,040
Percent change, 2000–2010: 0.7%
U.S. rank in 1990: 73rd (State rank: 2nd)

U.S. rank in 2000: 85th (State rank: 2nd)
U.S. rank in 2010: 85th (State rank: 2nd)

Density: 2,982.5 people per square mile

Racial and ethnic characteristics

White: 88,624
Black or African American: 127,558
American Indian and Alaskan Native: 624
Asian: 7,794
Native Hawaiian and Other Pacific Islander: 0
Hispanic or Latino (may be of any race): 5,785
Other: 5,440

Percent of residents born in state: 77.7%

Age characteristics

Population under 5 years old: 13,181
Population 5 to 9 years old: 12,657
Population 10 to 14 years old: 13,546
Population 15 to 19 years old: 18,426
Population 20 to 24 years old: 33,551
Population 25 to 34 years old: 35,767
Population 35 to 44 years old: 23,044
Population 45 to 54 years old: 27,418
Population 55 to 59 years old: 15,332
Population 60 to 64 years old: 10,393
Population 65 to 74 years old: 14,472
Population 75 to 84 years old: 8,516
Population 85 years and over: 3,737
Median age: 31.0

Births (2010–11 Metropolitan Area)

Total number: 11,349

Deaths (2010–11 Metropolitan Area)

Total number: 6,240

Money income (2012)

Per capita income: $23,903
Median household income: $37,419
Total households: 87,336

Number of households with income of ...

less than $10,000: 11,280
$10,000 to $14,999: 6,995
$15,000 to $24,999: 12,798
$25,000 to $34,999: 10,226
$35,000 to $49,999: 11,892
$50,000 to $74,999: 12,828
$75,000 to $99,999: 8,279
$100,000 to $149,999: 7,365
$150,000 to $199,999: 2,939
$200,000 or more: 2,734

Percent of families below poverty level: 24.9%

FBI Crime Index Property: 12,059

FBI Crime Index Violent: 2,507

■ Municipal Government

The City of Baton Rouge and the Parish of East Baton Rouge have a consolidated government, the first consolidation of a county and city government in the United States, administered by a mayor-president and a 12-member East Baton Rouge Parish Metropolitan Council, with one member elected for each of 12 districts. The mayor-president and all council members are elected at the same time to four-year terms, with a limit of three consecutive terms.

Head Official: Mayor Melvin "Kip" Holden (since 2005; term expires 2017)

Total Number of City Employees: 4,384 (2012)

City Information: City of Baton Rouge, 222 Saint Louis St., Baton Rouge, LA 70802; telephone: (225) 389-3123; fax (225) 389-3127.

■ Economy

Major Industries and Commercial Activity

Baton Rouge is a major petrochemical, industrial, medical, and research center of the American South. The diverse economic climate also allows older industries, such as the seafood industry, to thrive, while new industries gain solid ground. Some 20,000 businesses operated in the area as of 2013. Baton Rouge was ranked among the top 20 cities in the United States for Best Cities for Information Jobs and America's Engineering Hubs by *Forbes* in 2013. The two honors were among more than 20 received by the city from major publications during 2012 and 2013.

The state is generally rich with resources, especially petroleum and natural gas. In the greater Baton Rouge area, a natural resources basin exists which gives industries inexpensive access to the natural resources of gas, oil, water, timberland, sulfur, salt, and other raw materials. Forest products are Baton Rouge's leading commodity, including such products as woodpulp, linerboard, flitches, logs, plywood, lumber, milk carton stock, newsprint, and other paper products. Louisiana is among the nation's largest producers of cotton, sugar cane, yams, rice, and pecans.

Louisiana's petrochemical industry manufactures one quarter of America's petrochemicals. The Baton Rouge area is home to large operations of very well-known companies. The ExxonMobil refinery in Baton Rouge has a capacity of just over 500,000 barrels per day of crude oil and manufactures about 10 billion pounds of petrochemicals annually. ExxonMobil also operates a 118-acre plastics plant in the city. Meanwhile, Dow Chemical operates a 1,500-acre facility in nearby Iberville and West Baton Rouge parishes, employing more than 3,000 people. Shell also has a chemical facility in the area that manufactures chemicals used to make personal care products, such as soaps, shampoos, and household cleaners. BASF, another world leader in chemicals, also has a site near the Dow facility.

In addition to its natural resources, the city's location makes it ideal for general manufacturing and transportation. Baton Rouge is home to the farthest inland port on the Mississippi River that can accommodate ocean-going tankers and cargo carriers. As a result, the port and shipping industries have a major impact on the Baton Rouge economy. Ships transfer their cargo at Baton Rouge onto rails and pipelines going east and west, or barges travelling north. The Port of Greater Baton Rouge is one of the 10 largest ports in the nation, equipped to handle both ocean-going vessels and river barges. A 45-foot channel on the lower Mississippi River carves out 3,000 feet of continuous deep-water ship berthing space, establishing the region as one of the nation's most attractive locations for large-scale industrial development. The region served by the port thrives on the large industrial and chemical complexes, as well as agricultural interests, along the 85 miles of the Mississippi River in the port's jurisdiction. The port generates $118 million in total tax revenues within a four-parish area each year.

Targeted industries in 2013 were chemicals and new energy production, fabricated structural metals, software design, technical research and consulting, and advanced shared services. While chemicals and new energy production and advanced shared services were current industries targeted for long-term expansion, fabricated structural materials were a relatively new sector targeted for the near- or mid-term, and software design and technical research were long-term goals. Top foreign direct investment partners included the United Kingdom, Germany, and Canada.

Emerging sectors included health care, film production, and emerging fuels. Health-care development focused primarily on research, especially the Pennington Biomedical Research Center. After the Louisiana Motion Picture Incentive Program of 2002, the state experienced a 600 percent increase in film production in just one year. With the addition of Louisiana Film Tax Credit and the Digital Media Tax Incentive Program in 2005, the Capitol Region hoped to inspire new growth in the film and video gaming industries.

Items and goods produced: petrochemicals, plastics, wood, paper products, seafood, agricultural products

Incentive Programs-New and Existing Companies

Local programs: The East Baton Rouge Quality Jobs program offers local tax abatement for companies bringing new revenue from payroll into East Baton Rouge Parish. Abatements last for up to 10 years and cover property taxes associated with the new investment. New business investments must create at least 100 jobs and exceed the average regional industry wage. Developments must also be financed through Industrial Development Bonds to qualify. The East Baton Rouge Enterprise Zone Program rebates some local sales taxes on construction materials and equipment. For retail businesses to qualify, they must be located in certain targeted census tracts. Tax rebates are 1.9 percent. As of 2013, many small- and medium-sized businesses were still eligible for Gulf Opportunity Zone (GO Zone) and Renewal Community Tax Credit programs. The Louisiana Business and Technology Center at Louisiana State University is a small business incubator for technology companies. The Downtown Development District offers special incentives for restoration of historic buildings and general façade improvements.

State programs: Louisiana has pledged itself to broaden its business base through liberal development incentives and loan programs. The Louisiana Quality Jobs Act offers a tax rebate of up to 6 percent of payroll paid each year for 10 years to new companies in selected industries or those that have at least 75 percent of sales out-of-the-state. A rebate on state sales/use tax is also available on construction materials, machinery, and equipment. The Enterprise Zone Program offers some companies a $2,500 tax credit for every new permanent job created during the first five years of operation as well as a sales/use tax rebate on select equipment. An Industrial Property Tax Exemption Program offers 10-year abatements for some new and expanding manufacturers. A Research and Development Credit provides tax credits up to 40 percent for companies that can also claim federal income tax credit for research. The Louisiana Motion Picture Investor Tax Credit offers a 30 percent credit for investments of $300,000 and up. An additional Digital Interactive Media and Software Development Incentive offers a 35 percent tax credit. Restoration Tax Abatement Program provides a five-year deferred assessment on renovations and improvements. The Federal Historic Rehabilitation Tax Credit provides a 20 percent tax credit for rehabilitations expenses to a certified historic structure. Designation of a historic site allows it to access a tax credit up to $25,000 per structure during renovation. The Louisiana FastStart program offers incentives for outside companies choosing to locate in Louisiana, and the Industrial Tax Exemption Program is available for existing and new manufacturing operations.

Job training programs: The Louisiana Department of Education offers a Quickstart Program through which specialized training programs are developed for new and expanding businesses that will provide at least 10 new jobs. Training is offered either at a neutral site or at the company facility. The Job Training Partnership Act assists industries in choosing applicants, provides customized training for specific occupational skills and reimburses industry up to 50 percent for wages paid. Other opportunities are available through the Louisiana Department of Labor.

An Incumbent Worker Training Program is offered at the Baton Rouge Community College in cooperation with the Louisiana Department of Labor and local businesses for the continued education and training of the workforce. Job skills training is also being offered to support the film, music, and entertainment business.

Development Projects

In 2012, ExxonMobil announced plans to spend $215 to expand an existing chemical plant in Baton Rouge, as well as a lubricants facility in Port Allen, located in West Baton Rouge Parish. The expansion was expected to create 45 new jobs and nearly 400 indirect jobs. The latest project was the capstone on nearly $1 billion of investment by ExxonMobil in Louisiana between 2009 and 2012. Completion was expected in 2014. Also in the petro-chemical industry, Shell announced a new gas-to-liquids facility in Ascension Parish in 2013. The $12.5-billion facility was to create 740 jobs. Dow Chemical planned a $1.06-billion expansion of its rubber production in 2013 as well. Further, Shintech revealed plans for a $500 million expansion on its chemical plants, aimed for completion by 2015.

In 2013 Honeywell decided to expand its four Louisiana production sites at a cost of $208 million. Two of the sites are located in Baton Rouge, with the others in Shreveport and Geismar. Honeywell's Performance Materials and Technology facilities are involved in chemical and new energy production. Jogler, a manufacturer of liquid level gauges, announced its relocation to Baton Rouge from Houston in 2013, with plans for a $1.1 million facility expected to create 60 jobs. The 20,000-square-foot facility was to manufacture sight flow indicators, magnetic level indicators, and level controls as well.

An IBM Services Center with 800 new jobs in Baton Rouge was announced in 2013. To accommodate the new positions, IBM was constructing a $55 mixed-use facility. In addition to the business-related facilities, the 11-story building—located along the Mississippi River—was to include 95 apartments and 9 townhomes.

Active capital improvement projects by the city were budgeted at $35.9 million for 2014, with all major projects focused on road improvements, and none totaling more than $6.3 million. In 2013 the city completed nearly $70 million of similar improvement projects. Improvements to the city's sewer system, overseen by the federal Environmental Protection Agency, were carried out beginning in 2002 with an expected completion date of 2018. A library improvement program has been funded through a property tax increase lasting from 2005 until 2015. Fairwood Library Branch opened in 2013. A $12 million terminal expansion and renovation project at the Baton Rouge

Metropolitan Airport lasted from 2011 until 2013. A $2 million generator was to be installed in 2014 to protect the airport from potential power outages caused by natural disasters or terrorist attacks.

The city's Plan Baton Rouge Master Plan has guided downtown development seeking to make the area more attractive both for residents and visitors. Construction of North Boulevard Town Square completed its first phase in 2012. Also part of the plan, the redesign of Galvez Plaza completed in 2013. Construction on Repentance Park also completed in 2013. City Hall Plaza and downtown greenway projects remained in the planning phases in 2014.

Economic Development Information: City of Baton Rouge, 222 Saint Louis St., Baton Rouge, LA 70802; telephone: (225) 389-3123; fax (225) 389-3127. Baton Rouge Area Chamber of Commerce, 564 Laurel Street, Baton Rouge, LA 70801-1808; telephone (225) 381-7125.

Commercial Shipping

The Port of Greater Baton Rouge, one of the largest deep-water ports in the United States, links the city to markets throughout the world and ranked within the top 13 in the nation as of 2013. Nearly 50 percent of all American markets are accessible by barge through the Mississippi Inland Waterway System. The port has a bulk coke handling facility handling more than one million tons of green and calcine coke annually. As of 2013, the port generated more than 20,000 jobs with an estimated payroll of $119 million. The terminal handles chemicals such as acids and glycol-based products. The port is served by three railroads: Union Pacific, Illinois Central/Canadian National Railway, and the Kansas City Southern Railroad.

A system of interstate highways permits access to and from Baton Rouge for more than 40 common motor carriers that ship a broad range of materials through the area. More than 50 barge and steamship companies offer services to the interior of the United States. The Baton Rouge Metropolitan Airport has Foreign Trade Zone status. The airport has a modern cargo facility with 63,000 square feet of space.

Labor Force and Employment Outlook

The passage of a right-to-work law has made Louisiana an attractive state for employers. In Baton Rouge, a wide variety of educational programs are available for workers; the workforce, in both professional and skilled labor fields, is fairly well educated. The employment base is diverse, with most job growth in 2013 coming in construction and business and professional services. Five sectors—hospitality, professional and business services, construction, education and health services, and trade, transportation, and utilities—employed between 9 and 18 percent of the population, highlighting the diversity of the area's economy.

The following is a summary of data regarding the 2012 Baton Rouge area labor force:

Size of civilian labor force: 120,263

Number of workers employed in...

agriculture and mining: 1,170
construction: 7,806
manufacturing: 5,785
wholesale trade: 2,374
retail trade: 12,406
transportation: 3,056
information systems: 2,346
finance: 5,912
professional administration: 11,779
education and social services: 28,779
arts and leisure: 14,796
other: 5,376
public administration: 5,692

Average hourly earnings of production workers: $22.94

Unemployment rate: 6.0% (2012)

Employers

Largest employers (Metropolitan area, 2012)

	Number of employees
Louisiana State Government	13,628
Turner Industries	9,671
East Baton Rouge Parish School System	5,995
Louisiana State University	5,600
Baton Rouge City-Parish Government	4,384
Exxon Mobil Chemical Co.	4,275
The Shaw Group	4,243
Our Lady of the Lake Medical Center	4,009
Performance Contractors	3,500
Baton Rouge General Medical Center	3,000

Cost of Living

The cost of living in Baton Rouge is near the national average, checking in at 1.0 percent above the national average as of 2013.

The following is a summary of data regarding several key cost of living factors in the area.

2013 ACCRA Average House Price: $256,667

2013 ACCRA Cost of Living Index: 92

State income tax rate: 2.0% to 6.0%

State sales tax rate: 4.0%

Local income tax rate: None

Local sales tax rate: 5.0%

Property tax rate: $105.698 per $1,000 of assessed valuation; residential property is assessed at 10% of fair market value (2013)

Economic Information: Baton Rouge Area Chamber of Commerce, 564 Laurel Street, Baton Rouge, LA 70801-1808; telephone (225) 381-7125.

■ Education and Research

Elementary and Secondary Schools

Public elementary and secondary schools in Baton Rouge are part of the East Baton Rouge Parish school system, administered by an 11-member school board that appoints a superintendent. The system offers specialized programs for gifted students as well as arts education, English as a second language, magnet, Montessori, college preparatory, and vocational programming. Exceptional Student programs are available for challenged students up to 22 years old. The district also managed seven charter schools as of 2013–14.

Several parochial and private schools also operate in the Baton Rouge area. Most Blessed Sacrament School, operated by the Diocese of Baton Rouge, was named a National Blue Ribbon School of Excellence in 2013 by the U.S. Department of Education.

The following is a summary of data regarding the East Baton Rouge Parish Schools.

Total enrollment: 42,723

Number of facilities

total: 76
elementary schools: 46
junior high schools: 13
high schools: 14
other: 3

Student/teacher ratio: 13.21:1

Teacher salaries

average (statewide): $49,634

Funding per pupil: $12,612

Public Schools Information: East Baton Rouge Parish School System, 1050 S. Foster Drive, Baton Rouge, LA 70806; telephone (225) 922-5400.

Colleges and Universities

Baton Rouge is home to two major universities, Louisiana State University (LSU) and Southern University and A&M College (SUBR). LSU, with more than 30,000 students, offers undergraduate programs in about 70 fields and advanced degrees in more than 120 fields, including law and medicine. LSU was ranked 135th among national universities by *U.S. News & World Report* in 2013. SUBR, with more than 10,000 students, is the largest African American university system in the nation. Its nursing program is among the top-10 producers nationwide of African American nurses.

Baton Rouge Community College was established in 1995 and enrolls at least 7,000 students. It is an open-admission two-year college offering dozens of associate's degrees and certificates across five divisions. Industrial training programs are available at several post secondary vocational-technical schools in greater Baton Rouge, including the Baton Rouge Regional Technical Institute. Louisiana Technical College has six locations in the Baton Rouge area. Our Lady of the Lake College is an independent Catholic college that offers bachelor's degrees in nursing, health sciences, humanities, behavioral sciences, and arts and sciences, as well as master's degrees in nursing and anesthesiology. Enrollment at Our Lady of the Lake College is about 1,800 students. Other independent programs are located in the city. Southeastern Louisiana University School of Nursing is located in the city's medical district, offering traditional bachelors and masters degree programs, as well as other nursing certifications. Tulane University has a satellite medical school in Baton Rouge.

Libraries and Research Centers

In addition to its main library in Baton Rouge, the East Baton Rouge Parish Library operates 13 branches. The Fairwood branch opened in 2013. The total library collection includes more than one million volumes, plus magazines, newspapers, films, cassette tapes, compact discs, videos, talking books, and art reproductions. Special collections include materials on Louisiana and Baton Rouge history, a Black Heritage collection, and Braille books for children. Baton Rouge residents also have access to libraries at Louisiana State University and Southern University and to several governmental libraries. The State Library of Louisiana is located in the city, providing Louisianans access to more than 11 million items through its collection and electronic resources, combined with a statewide online lending network of public libraries.

Dozens of research centers are located in the Baton Rouge area. Many of them are affiliated with local universities and conduct research in such fields as agriculture, mining, and environmental studies. Key LSU research institutes include the Pennington Biomedical Research Center, which houses the largest

academically based nutrition research center in the world, and SUBR's Center for Coastal Zone Assessment and Remote Sensing, which works in partnership with NASA's Stennis Space Center. Other LSU research programs include the Center for Advanced Microstructures and Devices, the Hazardous Waste Research Center, the National Ports and Waterways Institute, and the Institute for Recyclable Materials. SUBR sponsors the Center for Energy and Environmental Studies and the Center for Small Farm Research.

Research facilities in the private sector include the ExxonMobil R&D Laboratories, Albemarle Technical Center, and West Paine Laboratories. Public-sector programs include the USDA's Honey Bee Breeding, Genetics, and Physiology Research Center.

Public Library Information: East Baton Rouge Parish Library, 7711 Goodwood Blvd., Baton Rouge, LA 70806-7699; telephone (225) 231-3700.

■ Health Care

Baton Rouge General Medical Center (BRGMC) has two locations in the city. BRGMC has become particularly well-known for advances in cancer care through the Pennington Cancer Center and cardiac care through the Womack Heart Center. BRGMC also offers a Level III Regional Neonatal Intensive Care Unit and the region's only burn center. The 226-bed Woman's Hospital specializes in care for mothers and newborns but offers services to women of all ages. Earl K. Long Medical Center was the teaching arm of LSU's Medical School, as well as part of the state's charity hospital system. The center closed in 2013, with medical students and their patients moving to Our Lady of the Lake Medical Center, which has both inpatient and outpatient services and is also well-known for treatment in heart diseases. Summit Hospital is located southeast of Baton Rouge.

■ Recreation

Sightseeing

Baton Rouge seeks to give visitors a taste of Louisiana at every turn. Visitors can do this by building and taking one of the visitors' bureau's culture trails. Trendy lifestyle centers mix with old world plantations and swamps. Visitors might want to start any sightseeing ventures at the Capitol Park Welcome Center on River Road. From there, a walking tour leads to such historic buildings as the Pentagon Barracks, St. James Episcopal Church, and the Washington Fire House No. 1. History has also been preserved in the Old State Capitol, built in 1849, featuring ornate architecture and gardens. Other points of interest are the New State Capitol, at 34 stories the tallest capitol building in the nation; the Old Governor's

Mansion; and the New Governor's Mansion. A visitor can experience the city's past by touring the elegant plantations in the area, or exploring some of its "haunted" sites. Among the most beautifully restored plantations are Poche Plantation, Magnolia Mound, Oak Alley, and Myrtles. Even the university's architecture is a thing of beauty. With red-tiled rooftops, stucco buildings, and moss-draped trees, Louisiana State University was listed as one of the nation's 20 most beautiful campuses in Thomas Gaines' *The Campus as a Work of Art.*

Baton Rouge features one of the country's finest zoos, the initial funding for which came from children collecting pennies. Its natural habitat exhibits contain more than 1,800 animals and birds. Otter Pond offers above- and below-water views of a naturalistic otter habitat.

Swamp tours by airboat are available at Cypress Flats, Bluebonnet Swamp and Nature Center, and at other locations around the city. Baton Rouge's riverfront can be toured on a riverboat and the Atchafalaya Swamp can be toured by boat. Bus and boat tours are also available through various charter companies that offer services ranging from brief excursions in the city to overnight trips through Cajun country. Baton Rouge is about a 1.5-hour drive from the French Quarter in New Orleans..

Casino gambling and live entertainment are available at the Belle of Baton Rouge, Hollywood Casino, and L'Auberge Casino Hotel.

Arts and Culture

Baton Rouge is a culturally vital city. A renewed interest in the arts beginning in the late 1980s resulted in large part from the construction of performing arts facilities in the 12,000-seat Baton Rouge River Center and the designation of the Arts Council of Greater Baton Rouge as the official arts agency. Opened in 2005, the 125,500-square-foot Shaw Center for the Arts houses the Louisiana State University (LSU) Museum of Art, the 325-seat Manship Theatre, rehearsal halls, LSU School of Art galleries and classrooms, and retail space. The Louisiana State Museum opened nearby in 2006.

Theater, dance, and music are available to Baton Rouge's audiences of all tastes. Housed in The Baton Rouge River Center, the Baton Rouge Symphony Orchestra offers a full season of orchestral programming. The Opera Louisiane and the Baton Rouge Ballet Theatre also reside and perform in The Baton Rouge River Center; the ballet performs classical and modern works. The Baton Rouge Little Theater is the area's most successful community theater. Among other groups integral to the cultural life of Baton Rouge are the music and drama departments at Louisiana State University (LSU) and Southern University.

Museums and galleries in Baton Rouge also offer variety. At the Louisiana Art and Science Museum visitors may see a renovated railroad station featuring restored cars dating from 1883 to 1940, the Discovery Depot for young children, the Lindy Boggs Space Station and Mission Control, and the Pennington Planetarium and ExxonMobil Space Theater. Historical Baton Rouge firefighting equipment and memorabilia are featured at the Old Bogan Fire Station. A complex of more than twenty buildings reproducing life on a nineteenth-century Louisiana plantation awaits visitors to the LSU Rural Life Museum. The LSU campus also offers and art museum and an art gallery, a natural science museum, historic Indian Mounds, and other interesting attractions.

The Old Arsenal Museum offers a tour of an old powder magazine. The Enchanted Mansion exhibits rare and unusual dolls. Baton Rouge's USS *Kidd* World War II destroyer and the Louisiana Naval War Memorial is one of the area's top attractions.

Festivals and Holidays

February (or March) brings Baton Rouge's best known special event, Mardi Gras, with its Krewe of Mystique Parade and other events. Also in February, the LSU Livestock Show and Championship Rodeo show place at the Parker Agricultural Center on the LSU campus. The annual Red Stick International Animation Festival in April merges technology with art and offers workshops, screenings, and lectures for students, industry professionals, and families looking for fun. The Art Melt in July features works by local artists. Other Baton Rouge celebrations are the Baton Rouge Blues Week and FestForAll, both in April, the Jambalaya Festival in Gonzales in May, 4th of July Freedom Fest, the Louisiana Ballooning Foundation Balloon Championship in August, and the Greater Baton Rouge State Fair in October.

Sports for the Spectator

Baton Rouge is home to the Louisiana State University Tigers, the Lady Tigers, and the Southern University Jaguars. The LSU sports complex, site of Division I NCAA football, basketball, and track competition, is rated among the best in the country. Tigers Stadium is the site of Tiger football games and the legendary pre-game tailgate parties. Pete Maravich Assembly Center is home to Tiger basketball. Southern's refurbished A. W. Mumford Stadium hosts Jaguar football. The F. G. Clark Activity Center at Southern University hosts Southwestern Athletic Conference basketball. Australian rules football also has a mark in the city with the Baton Rouge Tigers, who began playing in 2004. The city is also home to the Baton Rouge Rugby Club, which competes in the Deep South Rugby Union as a Division II team. The Baton Rouge Capitals began play as a United Soccer League Premier Development League team in 2007. The team plays in Olympia Stadium.

Sports for the Participant

BREC, the Recreation and Park Commission for the Parish of East Baton Rouge, maintains and operates 184 neighborhood parks with a broad array of facilities and programming. Facilities include 190 public tennis courts, 184 city parks, 75 recreational centers, 8 swimming pools, 7 public golf courses, and even an amusement water park. Facilities in the parks include a theatre and cultural center at Independence Park; Cohn Arboretum on Foster Road and the Highland Observatory on Highland Road. Facilities for BMX, archery, rugby, mountain biking, tennis, and other athletic pursuits are also available. Among the private sports facilities in Baton Rouge is the Country Club of Louisiana, which features an 18-hole Jack Nicklaus golf course, 10 outdoor and 3 indoor tennis courts, and a swimming pool.

Shopping and Dining

According to the Baton Rouge Convention and Visitors Bureau, the visitor who has only one free afternoon to spend in Baton Rouge should spend it at the Perkins Road Historic Merchants District, which has been compared to New Orleans's Magazine Street shopping area. The visitor will find a dozen charming shops and galleries and four restaurants featuring local cuisine, hamburgers and crawfish pies, and possibly the best Italian food in town. Downtown Baton Rouge offers shopping opportunities for those interested in fine art, gifts, designer furnishings, stained glass, and other novelties. The Main Street Market at Fifth and Main features about 20 vendors offering food and gifts for sale. The Red Stick Farmer's Market is also located downtown, open on Saturday mornings. The Mall of Louisiana offers more than 150 quality stores on two levels. The Cortana Mall has four major department stores. Baton Rouge offers unique shopping at several locations, including The Royal Standard on Perkins Road, where more than two dozen merchants offer international wares.

Baton Rouge's numerous restaurants satisfy any dining taste, from fast food to gourmet continental, served in casual or elegant settings. Specialties include Cajun and Creole cooking and fresh seafood from the Gulf of Mexico. One notable location is Mike Anderson's Seafood Restaurant, originally opened in 1975 by the LSU All-American football player.

Visitor Information: Baton Rouge Area Convention and Visitors Bureau, 359 Third Street, Baton Rouge, LA 70801; telephone (800) LA-ROUGE.

Convention Facilities

The principal convention facility in Baton Rouge is the Baton Rouge River Center, located downtown on the banks of the Mississippi River. The Baton Rouge River Center is within walking distance of hotels, restaurants, shops, and major attractions. The entire complex is comprised of three main facilities: the Arena, the

Exhibition Hall and the Theater for Performing Arts. The River Center Arena is a 10,000-seat arena, with 30,000 square feet of exhibition space and more than 7,000 square feet of meeting space. The 70,000 square-foot Exhibition Hall can be combined with the arena to create more than 100,000 square-feet of contiguous exhibit space. The River Center hosts events such as concerts, conventions, sporting events, trade shows and theater productions. The Sheraton Baton Rouge Convention Center Hotel offers 14,000 square feet of meeting space along with 300 guest rooms.

Among other meeting facilities in Baton Rouge are the Pete Maravich Assembly Center and Student Union, both located on the campus of Louisiana State University, and F. G. Clark Activity Center and Smith-Brown Memorial Union, both on the Southern University campus. Several local hotels offer small group meeting spaces and banquet facilities.

Convention Information: Baton Rouge Area Convention and Visitors Bureau, 359 Third Street, Baton Rouge, LA 70801; telephone (800) LA-ROUGE.

Transportation

Approaching the City

Located off Interstate 110 approximately five miles north of downtown Baton Rouge, the Baton Rouge Metropolitan Airport is served by Delta, American, United, and U. S. Airways. The facility, which underwent renovations during the 2000s and into the 2010s, provides nonstop flights to Atlanta, Dallas, Houston, Memphis, and Charlotte, with connecting service also available through major southern cities.

The major highway routes into Baton Rouge by car or bus are the east–west Interstates 10 and 12 and the north–south interstates 55 and 61. Interstate 10, which runs across the continent from Jacksonville to Los Angeles, gives the motorist a fine view of Baton Rouge. Interstate 55 connects the city with points as far north as Chicago. Greyhound Bus Lines also has a terminal downtown.

Following Hurricane Katrina in 2005, traffic congestion in Baton Rouge worsened significantly, as many coastal residents moved at least temporarily to the city. Millions of dollars of federal money expanded Interstate 10 around Baton Rouge to six lanes, resulting in a 38 percent drop in traffic congestion between 2012 and 2013, according to the INRIX Gridlock Index.

Traveling in the City

Baton Rouge is laid out on a grid pattern, with streets in the northern half of the city intersecting at right angles; in the southern half, however, streets run diagonally. Florida Boulevard divides north from south; east is divided from west by the Acadian Throughway. Public bus service in the city is provided by Capitol Area Transit System

(CATS), which offers 22 different routes. Paratransit service is available on demand. Charter bus services are also available.

■ Communications

Newspapers and Magazines

Baton Rouge's major daily newspaper is *The Advocate*. The paper was purchased by New Orleans businessman John Georges in 2013. *The Baton Rouge Post* is available online. Scholarly or literary magazines published in Baton Rouge include the *The Southern Review*, as well as a variety of publications by the various universities and colleges. In addition, magazines on engineering, agriculture, the oil industry, library science, business, and pharmacy are published in the city.

Television and Radio

Baton Rouge has 13 television stations, including major network affiliates and public broadcasting. Additional television stations are based in surrounding communities, and cable and satellite service is available. In addition, 6 AM and 13 FM radio stations broadcast from Baton Rouge, including one station from Baton Rouge Magnet High School.

Media Information: The Advocate, Capital City Press LLC, 7290 Bluebonnet Blvd, Baton Rouge, LA 70810; telephone (800) 960-6397.

Baton Rouge Online

The Advocate. Available theadvocate.com

Baton Rouge Area Chamber of Commerce. Available www.brac.org

Baton Rouge Area Convention and Visitors Bureau. Available www.visitbatonrouge.com

The Baton Rouge Post. Available www. batonrougepost.com

City of Baton Rouge–Parish of East Baton Rouge home page. Available www.brgov.com

East Baton Rouge Parish School System. Available www.ebrschools.org

Louisiana State Archives. Available www.sos. louisiana.gov

The State Library of Louisiana. Available www.state. lib.la.us

BIBLIOGRAPHY

East, Charles, *Baton Rouge, A Civil War Album.* (Baton Rouge, LA: East, 1977)

Field, Martha Reinhard Smallwood, *Louisiana Voyages: The Travel Writings of Catharine Cole* (Jackson, MS: University Press of Mississippi, 2006)

Guarisco, Tom, Above Baton Rouge: A Pilot's View Then and Now (Baton Rouge: Louisiana State University Press, 2009)

Phillips, Faye. *The History of West Baton Rouge Parish: People, Places, Progress.* (St. Louis, MO: Reedy Press, 2012)

New Orleans

■ The City in Brief

Founded: 1718 (incorporated 1805)

Head Official: Mayor Mitchell J. Landrieu (since 2010; term expires 2014)

City Population
> 1990: 496,938
> 2000: 484,674
> 2010: 343,829
> 2012 estimate: 369,250
> Percent change, 2000–2010: −29.1%
> U.S. rank in 1990: 24th (State rank: 1st)
> U.S. rank in 2000: 38th (State rank: 1st)
> U.S. rank in 2010: 52nd (State rank: 1st)

Metropolitan Statistical Area Population
> 2000: 1,316,510
> 2010: 1,167,764
> 2012 estimate: 1,205,374
> Percent change, 2000–2010: −11.3%
> U.S. rank in 2000: 38th
> U.S. rank in 2010: 46th

Area: 181 square miles

Elevation: Ranges from 5 feet below sea level to 15 feet above sea level

Average Annual Temperatures: 68.8° F

Average Annual Precipitation: 64.16 inches

Major Economic Sectors: entertainment, tourism and hotels, construction, financial services, oil and gas, maritime/transportation, shipbuilding and aerospace

Unemployment Rate: 7.3% (2012)

Per Capita Income: $25,697

2012 FBI Crime Index Property: 13,689

Major Colleges and Universities: University of New Orleans, Tulane University, Louisiana State University School of Medicine, Southeastern Louisiana University, Loyola University Xavier University, Dillard University

Daily Newspaper: *The Times-Picayune*

■ Introduction

New Orleans would not exist without the port, the Mississippi River, and the city's prime location on the Gulf of Mexico. Its roots are deep in the saturated soils of the delta; its history is a pageant of canoes, rafts, paddlewheels, and barges from mid-America converging with sails and steamships from around the world. Despite the devastating physical effects of Hurricane Katrina in 2005 and the psychological impact of the BP Oil Spill in the Gulf in 2010, the people of New Orleans have rallied behind their city to rebuild not only the structures and services, but the character that has made the "the Big Easy" a famous tourist destination. While work to fully restore the city's schools, hospitals, and homes remained ongoing into the 2010s, the city has taken recovery in stride, and the vast majority of tourist sites and attractions have been restored and businesses rebuilt. The city's international seaport has direct water connections to half the United States and continues to support the local economy. The city has worked tirelessly to move forward from the series of challenges it faced during the 2000s, but it also has reencountered the city's historic struggles: establishing a high-quality local education system, eradicating poverty, and rebranding the city as more than just a tourist destination priorities.

■ Geography and Climate

With miles of waterfront in three directions, New Orleans is partly peninsular. The heart of the city spreads around a

Bourbon Street, French Quarter, New Orleans, LA. *Don Klumpp/Getty Images*

curve of the Mississippi River—source of the nickname "Crescent City"—while edging Lake Pontchartrain on the north. Lake Pontchartrain connects to Lake Borgne, a broad opening to the Gulf of Mexico. Lakes, marshlands, and bayous extend from the city in all directions. A massive levee system protects the city from river flooding and tidal surges.

Louisiana is divided into parishes rather than counties; New Orleans itself occupies the entirety of Orleans Parish, while metropolitan New Orleans extends west into St. Charles, St. John, and St. James; south into Jefferson, Plaquemines, and St. Bernard Parishes; and north into St. Tammany Parish, and into other parishes as well.

A humid, semi-tropical climate in New Orleans is kept from extremes by surrounding waters. While snowfall is negligible, rain occurs throughout the year. Waterspouts caused by small tornadoes are frequently seen on nearby lakes.

The city essentially lies in a geographic bowl that rests an average of six feet below sea level. This has made the city vulnerable to frequent flooding from the Mississippi and Lake Pontchartrain and to violent hurricanes and tropical storms that come into the Gulf. One of the world's most extensive levee systems was first constructed for New Orleans by the U.S. Army Corps of

Engineers through the initiative of the Mississippi River Commission in 1879. These levees were primarily built with flood protection in mind. While some upgrades had been made to system, the structures could not withstand the flood surge of Hurricane Katrina, the Category 3 storm that hit the city in August 2005. The newly rebuilt levee system has thus far passed the tests of lesser storms.

Area: 181 square miles

Elevation: Ranges from 5 feet below sea level to 15 feet above sea level

Average Temperatures: 68.8° F

Average Annual Precipitation: 64.16 inches

■ History

French Settlers Leave Their Mark

The first Europeans known to travel past the site of New Orleans were followers of Hernando Cortez, a Spanish soldier of fortune who died on the banks of the Mississippi River in 1543. In 1682 the French explorer Robert Cavelier de La Salle, led an expedition from

Canada that traced the Mississippi, called "Father of Waters," as far as the Gulf of Mexico, and boldly claimed all land between the Alleghenies and Rockies for his sovereign, France's Louis XIV. La Salle was assassinated before he could direct the building of a settlement in the land he called "Louisiane." In 1718 Jean Baptiste Le Moyne, Sieur de Bienville, a founder of outposts in what are now Biloxi, Mississippi, and Mobile, Alabama, placed a cross at a point where the Mississippi curved near Lake Pontchartrain to mark the site for a new settlement. The proposed town was named for Phillipe, Duc d'Orleans, who was governing France during Louis XV's childhood.

To establish a population in the new settlement, France sent prisoners, slaves, and bonded servants. An unscrupulous speculator, John Law, beguiled the Duc d'Orleans into giving him a 25-year charter to exploit the new territory and managed to lure a few Europeans across the seas with tales of nearby gold. The men who arrived found only a village of cypress huts and criminals surrounded by swamp, disease, and hostile Native American tribes. Under threat of a revolt, France then sent "wives" for the colonists: about ninety women from Paris jails, a wild group chaperoned by Ursuline nuns until they were married. Later, poor girls of good reputation were also recruited to bring the settlement a core of respectability, but by then the ribald side of New Orleans's lifestyle had been established. Swamp conditions were hard on its inhabitants, yet the settlement grew into a French crown colony and soon served as territorial capital.

Origins of Creoles and Cajuns

In 1762 New Orleans citizens suddenly found themselves subjects of Charles III of Spain; France's Louis XV had paid a debt to his Spanish cousin by giving away Louisiana. The thoroughly French colony drove out the Spanish commissioner sent to govern them. In the summer of 1763, about 22 Spanish warships and 3,000 troops arrived to restore order and install another governor, this time without provoking open opposition. Descendants of these early French-Spanish colonial times are known as Creoles. French-speaking families also began emigrating from Canada's maritime region, Acadia-now Nova Scotia and New Brunswick-to flee British occupation. Referred to as Acadians, and eventually Cajuns, they found sanctuary in New Orleans and in the bayous of the wide Mississippi Delta not far from the city.

In 1788 and 1794 devastating fires destroyed most of the buildings in New Orleans's French Quarter, or Vieux Carre (Old Square); these were replaced by structures of a decidedly Spanish nature. About the same time a process for making granulated sugar made sugar cane an important cash crop in a market soon dominated by cotton. Thousands of refugees from Haiti arrived during the Haitian revolution of 1791 to 1804. When Spain transferred Louisiana back to France in 1803, the U.S. President Thomas Jefferson adroitly bought the

territory for $15 million. New Orleans was incorporated two years later. Louisiana became a state in 1812. The city was unsuccessfully attacked in 1815 (Battle of New Orleans) by British forces during the War of 1812.

The years following the Louisiana Purchase saw rapid development and swift growth in the city's slave and free population. United States and foreign interests invested in the expanding port and immigration increased.

City Boasts Multicultural Neighborhoods

Americans settling in nearby Faubourg Ste. Marie, the present business district, developed a suburb very different in nature from the old French Quarter. Other individualistic neighborhoods developed, including the Irish Channel, a rowdy waterfront area; Bucktown, a one-street fishing village on the shore of Lake Pontchartrain in Jefferson Parish; and the wealthy residential Garden District.

The city's prosperity depended heavily on slave labor, however, and economic threats to this trade made New Orleans intensely pro-Confederate in the Civil War. After the war, reconstruction in New Orleans was hampered by rivalry between ethnic and economic factions, yet eventually, the city emerged as a railroad and shipping center. New Orleans survived a yellow fever and cholera outbreak in 1853 in which nearly 11,000 people died, a malaria outbreak in 1871, a yellow fever outbreak in 1878 in which more than 4,000 people died, a severe hurricane in 1915, and an influenza epidemic in 1918 in which 35,000 people died statewide.

Jazz, considered to be a uniquely American music idiom, developed in New Orleans at the beginning of the twentieth century while the city continued to celebrate its cultural origins with the phenomenally successful Mardi Gras and world-renowned cuisine. Tourists began to flock to the city to experience its heralded celebrations and unique neighborhoods. While crime troubled the city in later years of the twentieth century-a blight the city has continued to fight against-New Orleans fiercely protects its legendary heritage. Eighteenth- and nineteenth-century buildings nestle in the shadow of sleek modern towers, convention centers, and shopping facilities, part of the mix of business, history, and good times that characterizes the city's charm.

Hurricane Katrina

At the beginning of the twenty-first century, a downtown rebirth was on the minds of city planners. But all plans came to a tragic halt on August 29, 2005 when Hurricane Katrina landed in the city and one of the worst natural disasters in U.S. history began to unfold. Evacuation plans were set in motion in anticipation of the storm, but nearly 150,000 people were still in the city when the storm made landfall. The next day, waters from the storm surge broke through the city levees. About 80 percent of the city was soon underwater at depths of up to 20 feet. Many residents were taken to shelters in the Louisiana

Superdome and the New Orleans Convention Center, but were later transferred to temporary shelters in neighboring regions, such as the Houston Astrodome. Then on September 23, Hurricane Rita brought yet another surge, causing a new breach in a repaired levee and once again flooding areas that workers were trying to clear. Nearly 1,900 people died and many more were left homeless. The initial response from the Federal Emergency Management Agency (FEMA) of the Department of Homeland Security was criticized as too slow and inadequate for the needs of so many left devastated.

Post-Katrina

In 2010 an explosion on an oil rig in the Gulf of Mexico, near the Mississippi River delta, caused a wellhead to leak—a leak that would flow for three months. The spill caused extensive damage to marine and wildlife habitats as well as the Gulf's fishing and tourism industries. The spill had a major impact on nearby New Orleans, which not only had to deal with the environmental impacts, but also became the central location for a plethora of lawsuits against the facility's operators and owners.

By 2012, $14 billion dollars had been spent by the Army Corps of Engineers to rebuild the levee system around the city. Some criticized the work as a mere patchwork for a system that requires total renovation; only future storms could decisively argue the point, and the system succeeding in its first test, the relatively weak Hurricane Isaac in 2012. By that same year, an estimated 76 percent of the city's pre-Katrina population had returned, as had an estimated 90 percent of the metropolitan area.

Historical Information: The Williams Research Center, Historic New Orleans Collection, 410 Chartres Street, New Orleans, LA 70130; telephone (504) 598-7171.

■ Population Profile

Metropolitan Statistical Area Population

2000: 1,316,510
2010: 1,167,764
2012 estimate: 1,205,374
Percent change, 2000–2010: −11.3%
U.S. rank in 2000: 38th
U.S. rank in 2010: 46th

City Residents

1990: 496,938
2000: 484,674
2010: 343,829
2012 estimate: 369,250
Percent change, 2000–2010: −29.1%
U.S. rank in 1990: 24th (State rank: 1st)

U.S. rank in 2000: 38th (State rank: 1st)
U.S. rank in 2010: 52nd (State rank: 1st)

Density: 2,029.4 people per square mile

Racial and ethnic characteristics

White: 125,220
Black or African American: 220,735
American Indian and Alaskan Native: 1,235
Asian: 10,775
Native Hawaiian and Other Pacific Islander: 0
Hispanic or Latino (may be of any race): 19,657
Other: 11,285

Percent of residents born in state: 72.2%

Age characteristics

Population under 5 years old: 24,486
Population 5 to 9 years old: 21,430
Population 10 to 14 years old: 21,575
Population 15 to 19 years old: 23,621
Population 20 to 24 years old: 29,463
Population 25 to 34 years old: 64,997
Population 35 to 44 years old: 45,506
Population 45 to 54 years old: 49,292
Population 55 to 59 years old: 24,641
Population 60 to 64 years old: 22,175
Population 65 to 74 years old: 24,060
Population 75 to 84 years old: 11,571
Population 85 years and over: 6,433
Median age: 34.8

Births (2010–11 Metropolitan Area)

Total number: 15,558

Deaths (2010–11 Metropolitan Area)

Total number: 9,928

Money income (2012)

Per capita income: $25,697
Median household income: $36,004
Total households: 146,018

Number of households with income of ...

less than $10,000: 23,742
$10,000 to $14,999: 12,045
$15,000 to $24,999: 19,454
$25,000 to $34,999: 16,308
$35,000 to $49,999: 18,531
$50,000 to $74,999: 20,329
$75,000 to $99,999: 12,879
$100,000 to $149,999: 12,169
$150,000 to $199,999: 4,544
$200,000 or more: 6,017

Percent of families below poverty level: 28.5%

FBI Crime Index Property: 13,689

FBI Crime Index Violent: 2,958

■ Municipal Government

New Orleans operates under a mayor-council form of government; the mayor is elected for a four-year term, as is the seven-member city council. Five council members represent single-member districts and two council members are elected at-large. The council approves a budget put forth by the mayor; the council regulates utilities and has the final say in zoning matters.

Head Official: Mayor Mitchell J. Landrieu (since 2010; term expires 2014)

Total Number of City Employees: 4,312 (2013)

City Information: City of New Orleans, 1300 Perdido St., New Orleans, LA 70112; telephone (504) 658-4000.

■ Economy

Major Industries and Commercial Activity

The New Orleans economy is dominated by four major sectors: oil/gas and related activities, tourism, the port and ship/boat building, and aerospace manufacturing. The presence of universities, hospitals, legal, accounting and other professional services, together with key installations of the U.S. Navy and other military operations in the region added further to its diversified economic base.

Economic actively was impacted immensely by Hurricane Katrina in 2005, the Deepwater Horizon oil spill in 2010, and a nationwide recession that plagued the country for several intervening years. Many of these jobs have returned, albeit slowly. Louisiana has relied more heavily on tourism to carry it through the hard times. The city's magnetic French Quarter, America's largest Mardi Gras festival, and riverboat gambling established New Orleans as a tourist mecca. *Travel + Leisure* magazine named New Orleans among the five best cities in the world in 2012. The French Quarter was largely undamaged by Katrina; and the Mardi Gras Festival and New Orleans Jazz Festival returned to the city the year after the storm. The city has continued to attract major conventions, corporate meetings, and major sports events into the 2010s. The city has even bid to host the 2024 Summer Olympic Games.

Some of New Orleans's largest private employers are shipbuilding firms, where workers build and repair vessels for the U.S. Navy, merchant fleets, and cruise ship lines. Lockheed Martin, manufacturers of aerospace components for NASA space projects, uses a large work force at its New Orleans operations. The facility features one of the world's largest manufacturing plants—43 acres under one roof—and a port with deep-water access for the transportation of large space structures.

The economy has diversified into such varied fields as health services, aerospace, and research and technology.

The New Orleans region is also a major transportation hub and a leader in production of crude oil and natural gas processing facilities. At the peak of the 2010 oil spill, more than 50,000 barrels were flowing and lost each day, having a direct impact on the industry in New Orleans.

As growth returned to the city, so did the accolades. Since 2011 New Orleans has been named among the top-eight cities for relocation, top-three for information technology growth, and top city for "America's Biggest Brain Magnets," all by *Forbes* magazine; the top metropolitan area for economic recovery by the Brookings Institution; and second largest boomtown in the United States by *Bloomberg News*. Emerging industries included bioinnovation, creative digital media, and sustainable industries.

Items and goods produced: ships, petrochemical products, foods, stone, clay and glass products

Incentive Programs-New and Existing Companies

Local programs: New Orleans has several local initiatives designed to spur business growth. Its Fresh Food Retailer Initiative sought to increase access to fresh foods for underserved communities within the city limits by providing direct financial assistance to retail businesses. Assistance included forgivable and low-interest loans to supermarkets, grocery stores, and others. New Orleans applied a $7 million Disaster Community Development Block Grant to the program, which is matched by the Hope Enterprise Corporation. New Orleans's Small Business Assistance Fund includes a partnership with NewCorp, Inc., to support new and existing businesses. The $2 million fund offers loans at 8 percent interest to both profit and not-for-profit businesses, ranging from $10,000 to $100,000. The loan term extends up to 84 months. Also to support small businesses, New Orleans companies have access to the Goldman Sachs "10,000 Small Businesses" fund, which is a $500 million investment to support small businesses and job growth in the United States. The Restoration Tax Abatement Program provides five-year property tax abatement for the expansion, restoration, improvement, or development of existing commercial structures and owner-occupied residences. The Quality Jobs tax allows businesses in targeted industries to receive tax rebates in the form of a 5–6 percent cash rebate of annual gross payroll for 10 years for creating new jobs.

State programs: Louisiana has pledged itself to broaden its business base through liberal development incentives and loan programs. The Louisiana Quality Jobs Act offers a tax rebate of up to 6 percent of payroll paid each year for 10 years to new companies in selected industries or those that have at least 75 percent of sales out-of-the-state. A rebate on state sales/use tax is also available on construction materials, machinery, and equipment. The Enterprise Zone Program offers some companies a

$2,500 tax credit for every new permanent job created during the first five years of operation as well as a sales/use tax rebate on select equipment. An Industrial Property Tax Exemption Program offers 10-year abatements for some new and expanding manufacturers. A Research and Development Credit provides tax credits up to 40 percent for companies that can also claim federal income tax credit for research. The Louisiana Motion Picture Investor Tax Credit offers a 30 percent credit for investments of $300,000 and up. An additional Digital Interactive Media and Software Development Incentive offers a 35 percent tax credit. Restoration Tax Abatement Program provides a five-year deferred assessment on renovations and improvements. The Federal Historic Rehabilitation Tax Credit provides a 20 percent tax credit for rehabilitations expenses to a certified historic structure. Designation of a historic site allows it to access a tax credit up to $25,000 per structure during renovation. The Louisiana FastStart program offers incentives for outside companies choosing to locate in Louisiana, and the Industrial Tax Exemption Program is available for existing and new manufacturing operations.

Job training programs: The Louisiana Department of Education offers a Quickstart Program through which specialized training programs are developed for new and expanding businesses that will provide at least 10 new jobs. Training is offered either at a neutral site or at the company facility. The Job Training Partnership Act assists industries in choosing applicants, provides customized training for specific occupational skills and reimburses industry up to 50 percent for wages paid. Other opportunities are available through the Louisiana Department of Labor.

The New Orleans Job Corps Center is a no-cost education and career technical training program through the U.S. Department of Labor for people ages 16 to 24. Career training is available in carpentry, medical assistantship, culinary arts, electrical work, health occupations technology, and medical office support. YouthWork offers employment and on-the-job training to people ages 14 to 21. NOLA YouthWorks also has a summer program.

Development Projects

In the aftermath of Hurricane Katrina, billions of federal dollars flowed into New Orleans to support development projects that repaired and rebuilt massive swaths of the city's landscape. Repairs to the city's levee system alone totaled some $14 billion. By 2012 and 2013, however, Katrina-related development projects had mostly completed, with new developments moving the city forward rather than simply bringing it back to the status quo.

In 2013 Domain Companies announced that it had secured financing and begun construction on a $200 million development in downtown New Orleans known as South Market District. The mixed-use transit-oriented development initially was to include 209 luxury apartments and 22,000 square feet of retail space. Restaurants

and entertainment venues were also to be included. The South Market District included four blocks in the historic downtown New Orleans area along Girod Street, from Loyola Avenue to Baronne Street. Total development was to add 600 apartments and 170,000 square feet of retail space.

Eight new schools opened in 2012, following another seven that opened the year prior. The major undertaking, which included 17 new constructions and 13 significant renovations, began in 2008 and had a total estimated cost of $1.8 billion. The final completion date was set for 2016–17. Widening of the Huey P. Long Bridge completed in 2013 after seven years at $1.2 billion of investment. The widening created three 11-foot-wide lanes in each direction; previously, there were two 9-foot-wide lanes flowing both ways.

The U.S. Department of Veterans Affairs was building a new hospital on 30-acres in mid-city New Orleans. With 200-beds the $995 million hospital was expected to open in 2014 and four years of construction. The Federal Government was also in the process of constructing a $750 million Federal City, which was to become the new home of the Marine Corps Reserve, housing residential and commercial space as well as thousands of military offices.

City projects slated for 2014 totaled some $73.5 million of investments. The largest project was a new criminal evidence and processing complex, estimated at $14.5 million. Other major initiatives were $12.7 million municipal yacht harbor repairs, $8.7 million for the second phase of the Behrman Soccer Complex, and $8.3 million for the first phase of remediation and stabilization of the Municipal Auditorium. The city also planned to spend $6.5 million on interior renovations to the criminal district courts.

Some phases of expansion for the National World War II Museum completed in 2012, with the project ongoing through 2016 at a cost of $320 million.

Economic Development Information: Greater New Orleans, Inc., 365 Canal Street, Suite 2300, New Orleans, LA 70130; telephone (504) 527-6900.

Commercial Shipping

The Port of South Louisiana (LaPlace) regularly leads the nation—and the rest of the Western Hemisphere—in cargo tonnage, and the ports of New Orleans, Baton Rouge, and Plaquemines typically place among the top 10. The Port of New Orleans, the largest inland port in the United States, is a hub of national and international transportation. It is connected to a network of 19,000 miles of inland waterways consisting of the Mississippi River, its tributaries, and other systems. More than 4,000 ship calls are made at the region's deepwater ports every year. French explorers were the first to identify the Mississippi river mouth region as an important port location that was connected by waterways to a vast section of interior territory. American traders and farmers floated their goods downstream to New Orleans and, after 1812, steamboats transported upriver commodities that ocean-going vessels landed at New Orleans. The modern history of the Port of New Orleans, however, began in 1896 when the Louisiana state legislature created a state agency to serve as port authority. In 1925 the Inner Harbor Navigational Canal was built to connect the Mississippi River and Lake Pontchartrain. Also known as the Industrial Canal, it serves as the mouth of the Mississippi River-Gulf Outlet, built in the 1960s as a route to the Gulf of Mexico that is more than 40 miles shorter than the Mississippi River route.

Seventy percent of the nation's waterways drain through the Port of New Orleans, which operates a Foreign Trade Zone, where foreign and domestic goods can be stored and processed without being subject to U.S. customs and regulations. Commercial vessels and ship tonnage entering and leaving the area make the Port of New Orleans one of the world's busiest harbors, with imports and exports serving the iron and steel, manufacturing, agricultural, and petrochemical industries. Port-related activities involve shipbuilding and repair, grain elevators, coal terminals, warehouses, and distribution facilities, as well as steamship agencies, importers and exporters, international banks, transportation services, and foreign consular or trade offices. The port is also a departure point for a variety of pleasure cruises to Caribbean destinations and for upriver riverboat and paddlewheel cruises.

With the strategic benefits of both a major international port and one of the few double-track Mississippi River crossings, the city is served by six of the seven Class I railroads in North America: Union Pacific Railroad, BNSF Railway, Norfolk Southern Railway, Kansas City Southern Railway, CSX Transportation and Canadian National Railway. The New Orleans Public Belt Railroad provides interchange services between the railroads.

Labor Force and Employment Outlook

In a bold and sweeping move, regional business leaders closed the books on their 140 year old regional chamber and its economic development arm MetroVison, to take on a five-year plan to generate 30,000 new jobs and $1 billion in new payroll. Recognizing that the most relevant issue for the region is a stalled economy, leaders created Greater New Orleans, Inc. to be the new, streamlined organization to implement best-practice strategies to achieve these measurable objectives.

The following is a summary of data regarding the 2012 New Orleans labor force:

Size of civilian labor force: 179,434

Number of workers employed in . . .
    agriculture and mining: 2,375
    construction: 9,423
    manufacturing: 6,169
    wholesale trade: 2,766
    retail trade: 14,644
    transportation: 7,541
    information systems: 3,032
    finance: 7,835
    professional administration: 18,191
    education and social services: 41,175
    arts and leisure: 27,558
    other: 7,138
    public administration: 8,508

Average hourly earnings of production workers: $20.78

Unemployment rate: 7.3% (2012)

Employers

Largest employers (2012)	*Number of employees*
Louisiana State University Health	7,000
Northrup Grumman Ship Systems	6,000
Tulane University	5,000
U.S. Post Office	4,000
University of New Orleans	3,114
North Oaks Health System	2,700
Harrah's New Orleans Casino	2,700
New Orleans Police Supt	2,185
St. Tammany Parish Sheriff	2,000
NASA Michoud	2,000

Cost of Living

The following is a summary of data regarding several key cost of living factors in the area.

2013 ACCRA Average House Price: $286,242

2013 ACCRA Cost of Living Index: 97

State income tax rate: 2.0% to 6.0%

State sales tax rate: 4.0%

Local income tax rate: None

Local sales tax rate: 5.0%

Property tax rate: $147.06 to 148.15 per $1,000 of assessed valuation; residential property is assessed at 10% of fair market value (2013)

Economic Information: Greater New Orleans, Inc., 365 Canal Street, Suite 2300, New Orleans, LA 70130; telephone (504) 527-6900.

■ Education and Research

Elementary and Secondary Schools

The school system in New Orleans has undergone major reconstruction efforts in the wake of Hurricane Katrina. After the storm, a majority of the city's schools, some 64, were turned over to the Louisiana Department of Education as part of the new Recovery School District (RSD). The RSD was originally created in 2003 to assist underperforming schools by managing them directly or turning them into charter schools. Charter schools have been the primary means of governing RSD schools. (Not all RSD schools are in New Orleans.) The Orleans Parish School Board directly ran or oversaw the remainder as charter schools. Overall, about 80 percent of New Orleans public school students attended charter schools in 2013. Due to new construction and ongoing reorganization of the school system, breakdown of the system by type of school was unavailable.

The following is a summary of data regarding the Recovery School District.

Total enrollment: 9,234

Number of facilities
total: 84 (2013 est.)

Student/teacher ratio: 13.03:1

Teacher salaries
average (statewide): $49,634

Funding per pupil: $17,221

Public Schools Information: Recovery School District, 1641 Poland Avenue, New Orleans, LA 70117; telephone (504)872-0600. New Orleans Public Schools, 3520 General DeGaulle Dr., New Orleans, LA 70114; telephone (504) 304-3520.

Colleges and Universities

Tulane University, founded in 1834 as the Medical College of Louisiana, is one of the nation's leading independent research universities. Through 10 academic divisions, the university offers degrees in architecture, medicine, public health, business, law, liberal arts, tropical medicine, the sciences and engineering, and social work. In 2013 total enrollment was about 13,500. *U.S. News & World Report* ranked Tulane 52nd among all national universities in 2013. The University of New Orleans, with nearly 50 areas of study and more than 40 degree programs, had a total enrollment of 10,071 in 2013.

Loyola University New Orleans is one of the leading Jesuit colleges and universities in the United States and was ranked the 9th best college regionally by *U.S. News & World Report* in 2013. Total enrollment is approximately 5,000 students. Loyola offers some 60 programs for undergraduate students in the Colleges of Humanities and Natural Sciences, Social Sciences, Business, and Music and Fine Arts.

Dillard University is one of the oldest predominantly African American institutions in the country and was a founding member of the United Negro College Fund. The school had an undergraduate enrollment of just over 1,300 in 2013 and was ranked among the top Tier 2 liberal arts colleges according to *U.S. News & World Report* in 2013. Xavier University of Louisiana, established in 1925, is the nation's only historically African American and Catholic universities. It is particularly well-known for its College of Pharmacy (est. 1927). The premed program at Xavier is considered by some to be a national model of quality. In 2013 enrollment was reported at about 3,178.

Other institutes of higher learning in New Orleans include the Louisiana State University School of Medicine, offering medical and dental education; Our Lady of Holy Cross College; New Orleans Baptist Theological Seminary; and a branch of Southern Louisiana University, as well as several two-year colleges and vocational-technical schools.

Libraries and Research Centers

Hurricane Katrina caused severe damage to 8 of the 12 branches of the New Orleans Public Library System, but all had reopened by 2013. During the rebuild, a bookmobile service was established in 2006 to continue services to some areas while branches were rebuilt. Grants to provide interim library services came from the Bill & Melinda Gates Foundation, and money from the Carnegie Corporation of New York supported reconstruction and restocking efforts. More than three million volumes were donated to the New Orleans Public Library in the storm's aftermath. Due to a lack of adequate storage space, the system has had to ask potential donors to hold on to books until proper facilities were available, or to simply send monetary donations.

The New Orleans Public Library maintains the New Orleans City Archives as well as The Louisiana Division located on the third floor of the Main Library. The materials housed in the Louisiana Division/City Archives suffered no damage from Katrina. The Division collects, through purchase and gift, all types of printed, manuscript, graphic, and oral resources relating to the study of Louisiana and its citizens. Other areas of interest include the Mississippi River, the Gulf of Mexico, and the South. Included are books by or about Louisianians; city, regional, and state documents; manuscripts, maps, newspapers, periodicals, microfilms, photographs, slides, motion pictures, sound recordings, video tapes, postcards, and ephemera of every sort. The Genealogy Collection contains books, periodicals, microfilms, and CD-ROMs with emphasis on the Southeast United States, Nova Scotia, France, and Spain. The library also hosts a literacy program and a new African American Resource Center.

The University of Tulane has several special library collections, with W. R. Hogan Archive of New Orleans Jazz being one of the most well-known. The main Howard-Tilton Memorial Library at Tulane University houses the Latin American Library and the Maxwell Music Library. The Rudolph Matas Library is located in the School of Medicine. The Special Collections Division in Jones Hall includes the Southeastern Architectural Archive, University Archives, Rare Books and Manuscripts, and the Louisiana Collection. The Amistad Research Center at Tulane University pursues research and maintains a library and archives in such subject areas as African American history and culture, ethnic minorities of the United States, civil rights, abolitionism, and Protestant denominations.

The Louisiana State Museum Historical Center library maintains a collection of French and Spanish colonial documents, eighteenth- and nineteenth-century maps, and nineteenth-century personal manuscripts. A 20,000-volume library at the World Trade Center of New Orleans collects works on import and export trade, travel, international relations, economics, and transportation.

Tulane is a leading national research university with nearly 20 research programs in such diverse topics as AIDS, politics, Mesoamerican ecology, and Latin America. Tulane research centers include the Roger Thayer Stone Center for Latin American Studies, the Middle American Research Institute, the Tulane/Xavier Center for Bioenvironmental Research, the Murphy Institute, the Tulane Cancer Center, the Tulane Center for Stem Cell Research and Regenerative Medicine, and the Newcomb College Center for Research on Women.

Louisiana State University Medical Center conducts research on a variety of medical topics, such as oncology, cystic fibrosis, human development, hearing, eye diseases, and arteriosclerosis. The Louisiana Business and Technology Center at LSU in Baton Rouge has been considered one of the top technology incubators in the United States.

The Audubon Nature Institute's Center for Research of Endangered Species conducts research programs on reproductive physiology, endocrinology, genetics, embryo transfer, and others in hopes of ensuring survival of endangered species.

Public Library Information: New Orleans Public Library, 219 Loyola Avenue, New Orleans, LA 70112; telephone (504) 529-7323.

■ Health Care

Before Hurricane Katrina, the city was internationally known as a center for medical care and research with approximately 5,200 staffed beds, and 1,800 medical and surgical specialists, serving the health-care needs of a multistate area as well as Latin America and other foreign countries. Katrina threw the city into a health-care crisis, with most health services shutting down just as the population needed them the most. University Hospital, the city's primary trauma center, reopened in February 2007 with a limited number of beds and reduced services. Services at the Veterans Hospital were shut down with patients referred to clinics outside of the city. A new Veterans Administration hospital was slated to open in 2014.

As of 2013 the top-ranked hospital in the city was Ochsner Medical Center, which was nationally ranked in eight specialties and included a 771-bed general medicine and surgical hospital. Tulane Medical Center includes 235 beds and some 630 physicians. Tulane also operates a hospital in Metairie and 25 clinics in the area. Louisiana State University's medical facilities in New Orleans were still in flux in 2013, recovering from extensive damage caused by Hurricane Katrina. In 2013 the university operated an interim public hospital and clinic in the area, while five major facilities, including the flagship University Hospital, remained closed. Many patients were referred to other facilities in nearby areas.

In total, there were 44 hospitals in the New Orleans in 2013, including Touro Infirmary and Children's Hospital in Orleans Parish, East Jefferson Medical Center and Clinic, Tulane-Lakeside Hospital, Ochsner Clinic Foundation and Hospital, Kenner Regional Medical Center and Omega Hospital in East Jefferson Parish, and West Jefferson Medical Center.

The Louisiana Cancer Research Center opened in 2013 downtown through the combined efforts of Louisiana State, Tulane, and Xavier Universities. The Tulane Cancer Center offers comprehensive screening and treatment programs. The Tulane Center for Abdominal Transplant, part of the Tulane University Hospital and Clinic, specializes in the treatment of all diseases involving the liver, pancreas, and kidneys. Terminally ill patients and their families are also served by the Hospice of Greater New Orleans.

■ Recreation

Sightseeing

While Hurricane Katrina caused extensive damage in the city, the spirit of hospitality was not destroyed. Tourism has been a big industry for the city and post-Katrina reconstruction of major tourist sites and attractions began almost immediately after the storm cleared. While many smaller restaurants and entertainment spots may have closed their doors completely, many others have been added in the rebirth of the city. The most prominent attractions, such as shopping, dining, and entertainment in the French Quarter and the annual Mardi Gras celebration, are still available, offering the same sights, sounds, and tastes that have made New Orleans a place to remember.

Visitors can tour New Orleans by bus, boat, seaplane, streetcar, or horse-drawn carriage, whether seeking a general-interest excursion or a specialized trip. Points of interest include Cajun country; picturesque homes, plantations, and gardens; and historic sites. Self-guided driving and walking tours are also available in the city. The Blue Diamond Collection Tours offer three-hour Catastrophe Tours with narration that includes the history of the city, how it was built, and what happened when and where during Hurricane Katrina.

New Orlean's City Park is 1,300 acres for visitors to see. Larger than New York City's Central Park, it is among the top-10 oldest, largest, and most visited urban public parks in the United States. It is home to the world's largest collection of mature live oak trees, some older than 600 years. New Orleans's French Quarter is one of America's most famous neighborhoods and an 85-block national historic landmark containing individually historic buildings. Park rangers in Jean Lafitte National Historic Park offer free walking tours that begin at the park information center. A living slice of history, the French Quarter, also known as Vieux Carré ("Old Square" in French), is home to people from all walks of life. Compared to other parts of the city, the French Quarter was minimally affected by the hurricanes in 2005. This resilient neighborhood's intriguing architecture is mainly Spanish, dating from the late 1700s after two fires destroyed nearly all of the city's French buildings. Visits to the French Quarter usually begin in Jackson Square, originally a municipal drill field and parade ground known as the "Place d'Armes." Painters and musicians hone their arts in the square while pigeons flock around the famed equestrian statue of General Andrew Jackson. The square is dominated by St. Louis Cathedral, built in 1794 and remodeled in 1850. Next door, the Cabildo, the one-time Spanish government building where Jefferson's Louisiana Purchase agreement was signed, houses French Emperor Napoleon Bonaparte's death mask and a collection of folk art. Visitors can also walk down Bourbon Street, the most famous of French Quarter streets and a tourist hotspot famous for its many drinking establishments.

A section of the Mississippi River levee adjacent to Jackson Square serves as a promenade. Renamed the Moon Walk when renovated, it offers a scenic view of the river. The Woldenburg Riverfront Park, stretching from Canal Street to the Moonwalk, gives direct access to the Mississippi River. Elsewhere in the French Quarter landmarks such as the Old Ursuline Convent—the oldest recorded building in the Mississippi Valley and now restored as Archbishop Antoine Blanc Memorial—and Preservation Hall—the city's most famous jazz club where pioneers of the idiom still perform nightly—join with

antique shops, confectioneries, Bourbon Street jazz clubs, world-famous restaurants, historic homes, art galleries, sidewalk cafes, and outdoor markets to make the French Quarter New Orleans's top tourism drawing card.

The Audubon Nature Institute comprises several attractions throughout New Orleans. Its Audubon Zoo displays more than 2,000 animals in natural habitats. The Audubon Zoo is one of five U.S. zoos to undertake the "Language of Conservation" project, which involves the use of poetry to inspire visitors to think about wildlife conservation. Part of the zoo, the spectacular Aquarium of the Americas displays exhibits of 530 species of fish, birds, and reptiles. Adjacent to the Aquarium is the Entergy IMAX Theater.

New Orleans's varied neighborhoods, central business district, and surrounding areas provide a wide range of other attractions as well. City Park, one of the largest municipal parks in the country, showcases an 18-foot sundial, a carousel, a children's story land, and a miniature train, as well as points of historic interest. Construction began on the fortifications at Fort Pike Commemorative Area in 1818 and the buildings were used in various capacities until after the Civil War; now a 125-acre park surrounds the fort.

In the business district, sights include the Civic Center, which anchors a complex of state and city buildings around an attractive plaza. Creole cottages and shotgun houses dominate the scene in many New Orleans neighborhoods. Both have a murky ancestry. The Creole cottage, two rooms wide and two or more rooms deep under a generous pitched roof with a front overhang or gallery, is thought to have evolved from various European and Caribbean forms. The shotgun house is one room wide and two, three or four rooms deep under a continuous gable roof. As legend has it, the name was suggested by the fact that because the rooms and doors line up, one can fire a shotgun through the house without hitting anything.

Among the area's picturesque and historic sites is the Longue Vue House and Gardens, a classical Greek Revival mansion with eight acres of meticulously tended grounds showcasing a spectacular Spanish Court. Conveying residents and visitors past antebellum homes, the St. Charles Avenue Streetcar Line is listed on the National Register of Historic Places and represents the nation's only surviving historic streetcar system. All 35 electric cars were manufactured by the Brill & Perley Thomas Company between 1922 and 1924 and are still in use. The Riverfront Line connects the cultural and commercial developments along the riverfront. In the Garden District, a New Orleans neighborhood registered with the Historic Landmarks Commission, stately nineteenth-century homes line wide streets.

Because the high water table restricts burials in New Orleans to above-ground edifices, the city's old cemeteries (called "cities of the dead") are often sought out for their unusual beauty. Following the Spanish custom of using vaults, the walls of the cemetery are lined with vaults; some tombs look like miniature homes, complete with iron fence, lining rows within the cemetery that resembled streets. There are more than 40 cemeteries in the metropolitan New Orleans area. Metairie Cemetery is thought by many to be the most beautiful as well as the most unique cemetery, not only in New Orleans, but anywhere in the world, featuring architecture styles from around the world.

Crossing 24 miles of open water between Jefferson and St. Tammany parishes, the Lake Pontchartrain Causeway is the world's longest overwater highway bridge; other drives along area waterfronts and bayou country afford scenic views as well. The NASA Michoud Assembly Facility, Fairgrounds and Jefferson Downs racetracks, the Pitot House Museum, and the Chalmette National Historical Park are among the many other points of interest in and around New Orleans.

Arts and Culture

New Orleans enjoys an extensive cultural life, full of music, theater, and historical artistry. However, flood-waters from Katrina and Rita infiltrated and shut down many theaters throughout the city. Meanwhile, tourist traffic reached historic lows in the years since the storms, a nationwide economic downturn took hold of the country, and, as a result, an across-the-board tightening in government arts funding had a major impact on the arts in the city.

Broadway productions and movies were staged at the Saenger Theatre, on the National Register of Historic Places. Significantly damaged by the flooding from Katrina, the theater reopened in 2013. Le Petit Theatre du Vieux Carré offers community theater on two stages housed in historic architecture. Le Petit Theatre was established in 1916 and has been recognized as one of the leading community theaters in the nation. During the 2004–05 season, Le Petit Theatre began construction for a million-dollar orchestra pit, new stage, and fly loft—the stage had been unchanged since 1922. Katrina flooded the near-complete construction, closing the theater until 2010.

The New Orleans Cultural Center with its Municipal Auditorium and Theater of the Performing Arts hosts ballets, operas, and concerts. University theaters, dinner theaters, the Contemporary Arts Center, and other area stages also mount various performing arts productions. With a repertoire that ranges from classical to popular music, the Louisiana Philharmonic Orchestra (LPO) is one of the best known orchestras in the region. The Orpheum Theater in New Orleans, the home of the LPO, was severely damaged by Katrina, and as a result the LPO performed its concert season at six different venues throughout the city. As of 2013 the Orpheum was for sale for the third time in eight years, with investors frustrated by a failure to make progress on restoration.

The New Orleans Opera Association features renowned guest soloists in its full productions, while concerts by chamber groups spotlight music for smaller groups. Various university and church organizations also offer musical performances in the New Orleans area, while at nightspots around the city listeners can find rhythm and blues, rock and roll, reggae, Cajun, and country music performed by national and local talent.

But music in New Orleans means just one thing to many residents and visitors: jazz. In the late nineteenth and early twentieth centuries, African American musicians evolved a style of music that fused African American rhythms and improvisatory methods with European musical styles and the syncopated St. Louis-based piano music known as ragtime. This blend formed the basis for a musical idiom heard in Storyville—New Orleans's brothel district—as well as in parades and at parties, picnics, and funerals. Gradually the new style of musical expression, called jazz, began to take hold outside the city's African American community; the first jazz record-ing was made in 1917 by a white New Orleans group called the Original Dixieland Jazz Band. Many consider jazz to have come of age with the trumpet genius of Louis Armstrong, a New Orleans native whose music is familiar worldwide and whose statue graces New Orleans's Armstrong Park.

Venues for traditional Dixieland include Preservation Hall, Dixieland Hall, and the New Orleans Jazz Club. Despite having to close several performance buildings in the wake of Katrina, groups like the Preservation Hall Jazz Band continued touring. In 2006 the Preservation Hall Jazz Band was awarded the National Medal of Arts, and the group celebrated its 50th anniversary on tour in 2011. Equally distinctive is Cajun music, dominated by the sound of the fiddle and accordion. Traditional straight-ahead jazz such as Armstrong played is the predominant style heard in present-day New Orleans nightclubs, on Bourbon Street in the French Quarter, and elsewhere across the birthplace of jazz.

The oldest and largest museum in the state is the Louisiana State Museum (LSM), an eight-building historic complex in the French Quarter, New Orleans. The old New Orleans Mint building, which housed the LSM exhibits on jazz and the Mardi Gras Carnival, suffered damage from Hurricane Katrina but reopened in 2007. The LSM presents folk art and traveling exhibi-tions as well. The Confederate Museum, the oldest museum in New Orleans, preserves Civil War flags, uniforms, weapons, currency, and other mementos. The Louisiana Children's Museum presents hands-on exhi-bits, puppet workshops, and storytelling, and includes one of the few interactive math exhibits in a children's museum.

At the New Orleans Historic Voodoo Museum in the French Quarter, occult displays and the Witchcraft Shop merge a part of old and modern New Orleans. Marie Laveau's grave in St. Louis Cemetery #1 is visited and meticulously maintained by legions of followers, who still place offerings there, including food or various symbols of Voodoo. One ritual that still lives on is the marking of her tomb with chalk in the shape of a cross or an X. The New Orleans Pharmacy Museum preserves antique remedies and apothecary equipment in an 1823 pharmacy building.

The prestigious New Orleans Museum of Art exhibits works ranging from Renaissance to avant-garde. The Contemporary Arts Center has three galleries and two theaters. It features art exhibits, as well as music, drama, and videotapes in its facility. The Sydney and Walda Besthoff Sculpture Garden adjacent to the New Orleans Museum of Art in City Park features 42 extraordinary sculptures installed among 100-year-old oaks, mature pines, magnolias and camellias. The sculptures, valued in excess of $25 million, include works by world-renowned twentieth-century artists as Henry Moore, George Rickey, Jacques Lipchitz, and George Segal. The Besthoff Sculpture Garden is open to the public without charge. There are about 150 other art galleries in the city where local, national, and international artists show their work throughout the year. The Ogden Museum of Southern Art, prompted by the devastation of Hurricane Katrina, has offered several special exhibits including, *Come Hell and High Water: Portraits of Hurricane Katrina Survivors*, *New Housing Prototypes for New Orleans,* and *Louisiana Story: A Photographic Journey.*

The National World War II Museum opened in 2000 in New Orleans. Initially, it was known as the National D-Day Museum, but an official designation by the U.S. Congress changed its name to the present one in 2003. The museum includes artifacts and exhibits from D-Day at Normandy, Home Front and the Pacific; Solomon Victory Theater, which shows *Beyond All Boundaries*; Stage Door Cantoon; John E. Kushner Restoration Pavilion; and the American Sector restaurant and Soda Shop. Some of these exhibits were part of the 10-year, $320 million expansion to quadruple the museum's size and tell the complete story of the war. All phases of the project were set to finish in 2016.

Scenes of New Orleans history are on display at the Musée Conti Wax Museum. House museums, such as the Gallier House in the French Quarter, carefully restored to its mid-nineteenth-century elegance, are available for tours.

Festivals and Holidays

The most famous of all celebrations in New Orleans—and perhaps in the nation—is Mardi Gras. Rooted in the Roman Catholic liturgical calendar, Mardi Gras season begins on January 6, or Twelfth Night. Parades, private balls, and parties continue through Mardi Gras Day, the day before Ash Wednesday, which signifies the beginning of the six-week period of Lent that precedes Easter.

Carnival celebrations culminate in rollicking street revelry, formal masked balls, and ritualistic torchlight parades featuring elaborate floats, dancing, lavish costumes, and merriment that infects visitors and residents alike.

The Sugar Bowl, a major American college football game, on New Years' Day is the oldest annual sporting event in New Orleans and one of the oldest in the country; besides football, festivities include tennis, yachting, and other events. In spring the New Orleans Jazz and Heritage Festival is an extravaganza attracting thousands of musicians, craftsmen, and chefs to New Orleans for 10 days of concerts, displays, and revelry featuring blues, gospel, ragtime, Cajun, swing, folk, and jazz performances. During the seven-day Spring Fiesta, plantations, courtyards, and private homes throughout New Orleans can be viewed on special tours. In July, the city hosts Carnaval Latino, the Gulf South's most elaborate Hispanic Festival. The ESSENCE Music Festival, one of the largest African American festivals in the country, returned to New Orleans in 2007 after a one year absence. From April to October various food festivals in the New Orleans area highlight crawfish, catfish, crab, andouille sausage, strawberries, gumbo, and other delicacies. The French Quarter Festival, one such food fest, usually takes place in April. New Orleans Christmas is a series of special events spanning the month of December. The city administration supports a nonprofit group, French Quarter Festivals, Inc., that coordinates free, public festivals in the city.

Sports for the Spectator

The Louisiana Superdome, reopened post-Katrina in 2006, is home to the National Football League's New Orleans Saints, the 2009 Super Bowl champions. The Superdome has hosted the Super Bowl a record seven times, including in 2013. The annual Sugar Bowl, one of the top college football bowl games, and Tulane University's football contests are also played there. The Zephyrs, a Triple-A affiliate of the Miami Marlins, play minor-league baseball at Zephyr Field. The New Orleans Arena is home to the Arena Football League's New Orleans VooDoo and the National Basketball Association's New Orleans Pelicans, known as the Hornets until 2013. The city is also home to the Big Easy Rollergirls, an all-female flat track roller derby team, and the New Orleans Mojo, a women's football team. Consecutive racing schedules at Jefferson Downs and the Fairgrounds racetracks fill the equestrian calendar. Sports spectators can also see tennis tournaments and golf's Zurich Classic of New Orleans. In nearby Slidell, the Bayou Liberty Pirogue Races test the skill of boaters skippering dugout canoes known as pirogues. The Ted Gormely Stadium in City Park, hosting local high school football games, is a state-of-the-art sports facility that hosted the 1992 Olympic Track & Field Triad.

Sports for the Participant

New Orleans's 1,300-acre City Park suffered more than $40 million in damage from Hurricane Katrina, but city officials and federal government assistance continued to work to finance and implement repairs through 2013. Larger than New York City's Central Park, it is among the top-10 largest and most visited urban public parks in the United States. The park offers picnic shelters, golf courses, driving range, soccer fields, softball fields, a botanical garden, boating, fishing, and even horse stables. The City Park / Pepsi Tennis Center, one of the top municipal tennis facilities in the country, has 16 hard courts and 10 clay courts. The Tennis Center hosts the annual City Park Grand Slam Tennis Tournament and in the past has hosted professional events. Boating and fishing events at City Park returned to the park in 2009. Horseback riding in the park is possible through the Equest Farm, which offers riding lessons and party packages as well.

For runners, the city annually hosts the Rock 'n' Roll Mardi Gras Marathon and the 10-K Crescent City Classic road race. Popular water sports such as wind surfing, sailing, and boating are possible year-round on New Orleans–area lakes and through the region's lush bayous and marshlands. The delta has always been a prime area for deep-water and freshwater fishing, crawfishing, crabbing, and shrimping, in addition to seasonal duck and deer hunting.

Shopping and Dining

Canal Street has historically been a center in New Orleans for department stores and specialty shops, and the locale continues its tradition with such retail and office developments as One Canal Place and the nearby Riverwalk, which features not only shops but restaurants, cafes, bars, and magnificent views of the Mississippi River. At once-famous Jax Brewery, now a marketplace, shops, entertainment, and Louisiana food specialties lure visitors. In the French Quarter, handicraft, antique, and candy stores draw buyers from around the country. Accessible via the St. Charles Street streetcar, Magazine Street's clusters of small shops begin in the Garden District and extend for more than three miles of antique shops and art galleries.

For more than 160 years the long, narrow French Market across from Jackson Square in the French Quarter has furnished area cooks with exotic spices, fresh produce, and cheeses at stalls encompassing coffee houses and craft shops as well. Shops retailing health food, books, brassware, perfume, and other specialty items are also popular among visiting and resident consumers.

New Orleans, dubbed the nation's culinary capital, considers cooking and dining to be art forms. There are more than 800 restaurants open in the metropolitan area (not counting fast food and chain restaurants). Local chefs excel in variety while specializing in unique Cajun and Creole cuisines. Creole cooking, originally the region's urban gastronomic style, combines several elements: the French provincial talent for incorporating a wide variety of ingredients into its repertoire, the Spanish taste for zest, the Choctaw affinity for herbs and spices, the African understanding of slow cooking, the American Southern tradition, and subsequent ethnic infusions. Creole cuisine is perhaps best exemplified by its complex sauces with Mediterranean and Caribbean inflections. Cajun cuisine, on the other hand, originally the region's rural cooking style, is more robust and savory and is typified by such dishes as boudin, a smoky pork sausage; crawfish etouffe, a tomato-based stew of small lobster-like crustaceans served over rice; boiled crawfish liberally seasoned with cayenne pepper; or blackened redfish, a highly seasoned fillet of fish charred in a hot skillet.

Cajun and Creole elements are combined in the cuisine of present-day New Orleans, and diners can find numerous local specialties: jambalaya, a spicy blend of shrimp, ham, tomatoes, vegetables, and rice; andouille, a salty sausage; gumbo, from an African word meaning okra, now signifying a thick soup; red beans and rice, traditionally a washday recipe featuring kidney beans; dirty rice, pan-fried leftover rice cooked with giblets, spices, and onions; mirliton, a vegetable pear cooked like squash; plantains, large starchy bananas served as a side dish; seafood, from oysters Rockefeller and shrimp Creole to boiled crab and broiled pompano; and the po' boy, a fried sandwich on crusty French bread typically featuring oysters but possibly instead featuring roast beef, crab, or shrimp. Diners in New Orleans are likely to encounter eggplant, avocados, yams, and mangoes in the regional cuisine as well. Sweet offerings typical of the Crescent City include pecan pralines, bread or rice pudding with caramel or whiskey sauce, and beignets-square, fried doughnuts sprinkled with powdered sugar. Coffee in New Orleans is brewed strong and sometimes blended with roasted chicory root or chocolate, and it can be served as cafe au lait-half hot milk-or cafe brulot-mixed with spices, orange peel, and liqueurs and set aflame. Residents and visitors alike find dining in New Orleans to be an event in itself.

Visitor Information: The New Orleans Metropolitan Convention and Visitors Bureau, 2020 St. Charles Avenue, New Orleans, LA 70130; telephone (504) 566-5011 or (800) 672-6124.

■ Convention Facilities

New Orleans is home to one of America's most popular meeting venues, the Ernest M. Morial Convention Center, located on the Mississippi River in the heart of the business district and within easy walking distance of the French Quarter. The center underwent a $60 million interior makeover after Hurricane Katrina, completed in 2009. The center offers 1.1 million square feet of contiguous exhibit space in 12 divisible exhibit halls, 140 meeting rooms, and a 4,000 seat auditorium. The convention center also has an adjacent business center. The center consistently places among the top 10 hosts of the largest number of conventions and tradeshows.

The enormous Louisiana Superdome seats a maximum of 72,003 people and offers 166,180 square feet of unobstructed convention floor space in the main arena. Four main ballrooms and 26 reception rooms are available. Post-Katrina renovations included the four 20,000-square-foot club rooms. Situated in the northwest corner of the business district, the Superdome is close to government offices and hotels. The New Orleans Arena, adjacent to the Superdome, seats up to 17,000 in its main arena and also offers three club lounge areas for smaller meetings and receptions.

The John A. Alario Sr. Event Center and the Alario Center Festival Grounds, located at the Bayou Segnette Sports Complex, offers a 2,200-seat Main Arena, 21,840 square feet of column-free exhibit space, and 10 acres of outdoor exhibit or festival space.

On the north side of the French Quarter, the Municipal Auditorium was the city's fourth largest convention center but was severely flooded by Hurricane Katrina and remained closed through 2013. Additional exhibit space and meeting rooms for large gatherings can be found at the Pontchartrain Center, which includes the Belle Grove Plantation Ballroom, and at local universities. Smaller groups of 200 to 300 people, however, often seek out New Orleans's unique atmosphere for gatherings in such unusual settings as the Storyville Jazz Hall and the New Orleans Paddlewheels Creole Queen—at the International Cruise Terminal—or in Terrell House, a guest home lavishly furnished in Victorian antiques.

Convention Information: The New Orleans Metropolitan Convention and Visitors Bureau, 2020 St. Charles Avenue, New Orleans, LA 70130; telephone (504) 566-5011 or (800) 672-6124.

■ Transportation

Approaching the City

The Louis Armstrong New Orleans International Airport (identified by "MSY," standing for Moisant Stock Yards), which is located west of the city in Kenner, provides full service for more than 3.5 million people annually. Delta and Southwest Airlines combined to account for more than half of all flights. Private planes and corporate and charter flights often prefer to use Lakefront Airport, on the Lake Pontchartrain coast near the central business district. Military and commercial flights also use the Lakefront Airport.

Interstates 59 and 55 and U.S. Highway 61 approach New Orleans from the north, while Interstate 10 (the Pontchartrain Expressway) and U.S. Highway 90 carry east–west drivers into the city. Long term plans call for Interstate 49 to reach New Orleans, extending access to Lafayette, and construction was underway in 2013. Auto ferries cross the Mississippi at various locations. Overnight Amtrak trains from and to Chicago, Memphis, Atlanta, New York, Los Angeles, and Orlando arrive at and depart from the Union Passenger Railroad Terminal. The Port of New Orleans facilitates the inclusion of New Orleans as a port of call for commercial pleasure cruises in the Gulf of Mexico.

Traveling in the City

The city of New Orleans is served by Interstates 10, 510, and 610. The city is also known for its many bridges, particularly the Crescent City Connection, the Twin Span Bridge, and Lake Pontchartrain Causeway. At 24 miles, the Lake Pontchartrain Causeway is among the top-five longest bridges in the world. The New Orleans Regional Transit Authority in New Orleans operates an extensive bus system connecting most areas of the city. In the downtown business district, a shuttle traverses a route that connects the city's three largest convention facilities with major hotels and with the French Quarter. Visitors often include a ride on the historic electric streetcar along the St. Charles Streetcar Line as a part of their New Orleans experience, while the Riverfront Streetcar Line transports visitors to cultural and shopping destinations in that district. The city's flat landscape, simple street grid, and mild weather have made it popular for both bicycle and pedestrian transportation.

■ Communications

Newspapers and Magazines

The Times-Picayune is the city's leading daily newspaper and had a weekday circulation of more than 150,000 as of 2013. Other periodicals originating from New Orleans are: the weekly *Gambit*, covering local politics, dining and entertainment; *OffBeat*, a free monthly music and entertainment magazine; and, *Louisiana Weekly*, covering the African American community. The weekly *New Orleans City Business* and *New Orleans Magazine* (published out of Metairie) are available at most city newsstands. *Clarion Herald* is the monthly Catholic magazine published through the Archdiocese of New Orleans. The University papers include the *Loyola Maroon*, the *Tulane Hullabaloo*, and the *Xavier Herald*.

Television and Radio

Fourteen television stations broadcast in New Orleans, including affiliates of major national networks and public broadcasting. Talk shows, gospel music, news, religion, and contemporary music head the programming of more than 10 licensed AM and 13 FM stations in New Orleans. Clear Channel Radio is responsible for seven stations and Entercom Broadcasting hosts six stations.

Media Information: *New Orleans Time-Picayune,* 3800 Howard Ave., New Orleans, LA 70125; telephone (800) 925-0000.

New Orleans Online

City of New Orleans Home Page. Available http://www.nola.gov/

New Orleans Chamber of Commerce. Available www.neworleanschamber.org

New Orleans Metropolitan Convention and Visitors Bureau. Available www.neworleanscvb.com

New Orleans Public Library. Available nutrias.org

New Orleans Public Schools. Available www.nops.k12.la.us

Recovery School District. Available www.nolapublicschools.net

BIBLIOGRAPHY

Birch, Eugenie L. and Susan M. Wachter, eds., *Rebuilding Urban Places after Disaster: Lessons from Hurricane Katrina*(Philadelphia, PA: University of Pennsylvania Press, 2006)

Kanon, Tom, *Tennesseans at War, 1812–15: Andrew Jackson, the Creek War, and the Battle of New Orleans* (Tuscaloosa, AL: University of Alabama Press, 2014)

Klingman, John P., *New in New Orleans Architecture* (Gretna, LA: Pelican Pub. Co., 2012)

Savage, James A., *Jim Garrison's Bourbon Street Brawl: The Making of a First Amendment Milestone* (Lafayette: University of Louisiana at Lafayette Press, 2010)

Sexton, Richard, *New Orleans: Elegance and Decadence* (San Francisco, CA: Chronicle Books, 1993)

Young, Andrew, *An Easy Burden: The Civil Rights Movement and the Transformation of America* (New York: HarperCollins, 1996)

Shreveport

■ The City in Brief

Founded: 1836 (incorporated, 1839)

Head Official: Mayor Cedric B. Glover (since 2006; term expires 2014)

City Population
1990: 198,525
2000: 200,145
2010: 199,311
2012 estimate: 201,878
Percent change, 2000–2010: −0.4%
U.S. rank in 1990: 79th
U.S. rank in 2000: 88th
U.S. rank in 2010: 108th

Metropolitan Statistical Area Population
2000: 392,302
2010: 398,604
2012 estimate: 406,253
Percent change, 2000–2010: 1.6%
U.S. rank in 2000: 122nd
U.S. rank in 2010: 130th

Area: 117.8 square miles

Elevation: 209 feet above sea level

Average Annual Temperatures: January, 46.4° F; July, 83.4° F; annual average, 65.7° F

Average Annual Precipitation: 51.30 inches of rain; 1.5 inches of snow

Major Economic Sectors: Government, health care, hospitality, gambling, manufacturing, retail, military, customer service, film

Unemployment Rate: 5.7% (2012)

Per Capita Income: $23,794

2012 FBI Crime Index Property: 9,862

Major Colleges and Universities: Louisiana State University Shreveport, Centenary College, Louisiana Technical College, Bossier Parish Community College

Daily Newspaper: *The Shreveport Times, The Shreveport Sun, Bossier Press Tribune*

■ Introduction

Greater Shreveport is both a historic city and a modern metropolis. While it is the third largest city in the state, Shreveport is second only to New Orleans among Louisiana cities in terms of historic landmarks. Shreveport is the commercial and cultural center of the "Ark-La-Tex" or "Texarkana," the area where Arkansas, Louisiana, and Texas meet. Many people in the community refer to the two cities of Shreveport and Bossier City as "Shreveport-Bossier." Located in northwest Louisiana, Shreveport and its surrounding area offers residents and visitors much to enjoy in their leisure time, with festivals to attend year-round on Festival Plaza and throughout the city. The state of Louisiana is regarded by many as a sportsman's paradise, and Shreveport is no exception, as the city is surrounded by lakes and the Red River. Riverboat casinos, along with fishing and waterskiing, have spurred growth in tourism. The cost of living is low, the climate is mild, and access to high-quality health care is readily available, making the Shreveport area attractive to retirees. Many veterans formerly stationed at Barksdale Air Force Base settle permanently in northwest Louisiana after retirement. Economic development in both the film industry and natural gas drilling cooled after high expectations in the early 2000s, but construction of a massive steel manufacturing facility was set to invigorate manufacturing through the 2010s and into the 2020s.

Anne Rippy/Getty Images

■ Geography and Climate

Shreveport sits in the northwest corner of Louisiana, a five-hour drive north from New Orleans and a mere 20 miles east of the Texas border. Shreveport lies at a low elevation just across the Red River from Bossier City, Louisiana. Outside the bounds of the city proper are pine forests, cotton fields, and wetlands. The low elevation area is referred to as Shreveport-Bossier or Ark-La-Tex, which reflects its proximity to the states of Arkansas and Texas. Shreveport experiences hot summers, with temperatures averaging in the 80s, and chillier winters, with temperatures averaging around 40 degrees. The climate is largely temperate, though it does share some of the humid subtropical characteristics of other Southern cities. Severe thunderstorms, heavy rain, hail, damaging winds, and tornadoes occur in the area during the spring and summer months. Winters, however, are mild.

Area: 117.8 square miles

Elevation: 209 feet above sea level

Average Temperatures: January, 46.4° F; July, 83.4° F; annual average, 65.7° F

Average Annual Precipitation: 51.30 inches of rain; 1.5 inches of snow

■ History

In 1682 the French explorer Robert Cavelier de La Salle led an expedition from Canada that traced the Mississippi, called "Father of Waters," as far as the Gulf of Mexico, and boldly claimed all land between the Alleghenies and Rockies for his sovereign, France's Louis XIV. La Salle was assassinated before he could direct the building of a settlement in the region he called "Louisiane." Shreveport itself wasn't founded until almost 150 years later.

The Caddo Indians farmed the region that now includes Shreveport. Because the Red River was blocked for 180 miles by a build-up of debris, known as the "Great Raft," white explorers did not encounter the Caddo Indians and the Caddos lived peacefully in isolation. The Osage orange tree, native to the region and commonly referred to as *bois de arc*, was important to the Caddo; they made bows, which they traded with other tribes, from its strong, flexible wood.

The Caddo Indians signed the Treaty of Cession of 1835 and sold their lands to the U.S. government. In 1836 a parcel of the Caddo Indian lands was sold to the Shreve Town Company, formed by a group of eight businessmen for the purpose of establishing a town. One year later, they established the village of Shreve Town.

Clearing the Red River

Shreve Town was named in honor of Captain Henry Miller Shreve, a steamboat captain. Under his leadership the U.S. Army Corps of Engineers had cleared the Red River, which was previously not navigable because it was blocked by debris for about 180 miles. Once the engineers had cleared the river, commerce and exploration along its length was possible. Shreveport was ideally situated near the Texas Trail, the land route to the independent Republic of Texas. Until the end of 1836 Shreve Town was the westernmost town in the United States.

In 1838 a new parish, Caddo Parish, was created out of Natchitoches Parish, and on March 20, 1839, Shreve Town was officially incorporated as Shreveport. Shreveport was designated the parish seat on October 6, 1840; it remains the parish seat today. The original town had eight streets running east-west from the Red River. These streets were crossed by another eight streets running north-south. This configuration of city blocks remains the modern city's center.

The last surrender of Confederate forces occurred here on June 6, 1865. Following the economic depression of the Civil War era, Caddo Parish found renewed prosperity with the Oil Boom of the early 1900s. Oil derricks dotting the countryside of North Caddo Parish serve as a reminder of the thriving oil well drilling industry that gave rise to communities such as Oil City and the Caddo Lake region of Louisiana. This "black gold" prosperity lasted from around 1904 to 1914.

The Red River remained an important trading artery for much of the nineteenth century. However, by 1914 river traffic had declined thanks to the rise of the railroad. The sharp decrease in river traffic had allowed a build-up of silt, making navigation impossible. The river didn't become navigable again until the 1990s.

Boomtown

The first major industry to take hold in the area was agriculture. Lumber and manufacturing also were important to the city's development. But it was not until after the discovery of oil in 1906 that Shreveport truly became a boomtown.

The first offshore oil well in the world was at Shreveport's Caddo Lake. Oil continued to be an important part of the economic fabric in Shreveport until the 1980s, when the entire oil industry suffered a downturn. Shreveport was particularly hard hit. Several large area businesses closed, and the city's population decreased. However, the advent of the riverboat gambling industry in the late 1990s allowed Shreveport to recoup some of its losses and become known as a tourist destination.

Barksdale Air Force Base was the largest air force base in the nation when it was built in the 1930s. It was an integral facility for the U.S. during World War II and continued to play an important economic role throughout the twentieth century. In the mid-twentieth century, The Louisiana Hayride, broadcast from Shreveport, was a launching pad for a number of musical stars, including Hank Williams, Johnny Cash, Kitty Wells, George Jones and Elvis Presley.

In 2005 Shreveport remained largely unscathed by Hurricane Katrina, which devastated large swaths of the state of Louisiana; however, the region immediately opened its doors to more than 20,000 evacuees from New Orleans and other affected areas. Likewise, the 2010 oil spill largely left Shreveport unaffected, unlike the Gulf portions of the state. The exodus from New Orleans offered the city a brief boost in its film industry as projects relocated to Shreveport. The most dramatic event in the late decade was the discovery of Haynesville Shale as a potential major shale gas resource in 2008. The rock formation underneath the Shreveport area is estimated to be one of the largest natural gas fields in the contiguous 48 states. However, a decline in natural gas prices in the late 2000s and early 2010s cooled investments and tempered economic prospects. The 2013 announcement of a new steel manufacturing facility offered the possibility of lasting good news—and nearly 700 new jobs.

Historical Information: Special Collections, Louisiana State University in Shreveport, One University Place, Shreveport, LA 71115; telephone (318) 797-5378.

■ Population Profile

Metropolitan Statistical Area Population
2000: 392,302
2010: 398,604
2012 estimate: 406,253
Percent change, 2000–2010: 1.6%
U.S. rank in 2000: 122nd
U.S. rank in 2010: 130th

City Residents
1990: 198,525
2000: 200,145
2010: 199,311
2012 estimate: 201,878
Percent change, 2000–2010: −0.4%
U.S. rank in 1990: 79th
U.S. rank in 2000: 88th
U.S. rank in 2010: 108th

Density: 1,891.4 people per square mile

Racial and ethnic characteristics
White: 84,900
Black or African American: 109,836
American Indian and Alaskan Native: 402
Asian: 3,229
Native Hawaiian and Other Pacific Islander: 55

Hispanic or Latino (may be of any race): 6,139
Other: 3,456

Percent of residents born in state: 76.6%

Age characteristics

Population under 5 years old: 14,260
Population 5 to 9 years old: 12,971
Population 10 to 14 years old: 14,434
Population 15 to 19 years old: 12,714
Population 20 to 24 years old: 15,318
Population 25 to 34 years old: 31,124
Population 35 to 44 years old: 22,553
Population 45 to 54 years old: 26,480
Population 55 to 59 years old: 14,793
Population 60 to 64 years old: 10,298
Population 65 to 74 years old: 14,155
Population 75 to 84 years old: 8,314
Population 85 years and over: 4,464
Median age: 35.0

Births (2010–11 Metropolitan Area)

Total number: 5,822

Deaths (2010–11 Metropolitan Area)

Total number: 3,778

Money income (2012)

Per capita income: $23,794
Median household income: $37,531
Total households: 78,212

Number of households with income of . . .

less than $10,000: 8,625
$10,000 to $14,999: 6,155
$15,000 to $24,999: 11,682
$25,000 to $34,999: 10,336
$35,000 to $49,999: 10,766
$50,000 to $74,999: 11,291
$75,000 to $99,999: 7,070
$100,000 to $149,999: 7,245
$150,000 to $199,999: 2,456
$200,000 or more: 2,586

Percent of families below poverty level: 21.8%

FBI Crime Index Property: 9,862

FBI Crime Index Violent: 1,550

■ Municipal Government

Shreveport, part of Caddo Parish, operates under a mayor-council form of government. The council is composed of seven members, each of whom is elected from a separate district of the city. The mayor, who functions as the city executive, serves a term of four years. The mayor may attend city council meetings and express opinions but cannot vote or force a vote on any matter.

Head Official: Mayor Cedric B. Glover (since 2006; term expires 2014)

Total Number of City Employees: 2,782 (2013)

City Information: City of Shreveport, 505 Travis Street, Shreveport, LA 71107; telephone (318) 673-5010.

■ Economy

Major Industries and Commercial Activity

Shreveport was once a major player in United States oil business and at one time could boast Standard Oil of Louisiana as a locally based company. The Louisiana branch was later absorbed by Standard Oil of New Jersey. So while oil dominated much of the Gulf area, Shreveport has had to rely on other industries. Government and health care are the two largest industries in the area, accounting for eight of the top nine employers in the region. The Willis-Knighton Health System alone contributes some $1.8 billion annually to the local economy.

Other major industries in Shreveport include hospitality and entertainment, which center mainly on the city's casino business. As of 2013, local casinos generated more than $200 million in gross revenue and employed 9,000 people annually. The city receives in excess of $13 million in tax revenue from gambling each year.

Manufacturing, retail, the military, and customer service also play a role in the local economy. Barksdale Air Force Base is a major employer in the Shreveport-Bossier region; it is one of only two remaining sites in the United States that flies B-52 bombers. Northwest Louisiana is also an important region for the timber industry, thanks to the long growing season and favorable climate. Agribusiness includes cotton, the top-produced row crop, and poultry, the main animal good. Northwest Louisiana is known for its bee colonies, and the pollination industry pumps a reported annual $400 million into the economy. Fruit crops like blueberries and peaches are grown seasonally.

In 2008 excitement grew over a bedrock of shale, the Haynesville Shale, discovered in the Shreveport area. Development peaked in 2010, when more than 190 drilling rigs operated in the area, and residents received as much as $30,000 per acre for drilling rights to their land. As the price of natural gas declined, so too did the efforts of natural gas drillers. While energy remained a potential economic driver for the future, only about 40 drilling rigs remained in the area as of 2013.

In the 2000s, Shreveport's film industry boomed, and the city was included as part of "Hollywood South," a nickname given to Louisiana as it grew in fame as the third largest film industry in the country, next to California and New York. In 2005–06 the industry generated $300 million in film production budgets, and in 2010 it totaled $182 million. However, by 2013 that figure had slipped to just $70. Much of the industry's boom during the late 2000s was attributed to the unavailability of other Louisiana locations, notably New Orleans, in the wake of Hurricane Katrina in 2005.

Shreveport was home to Shreveport Operations, a General Motors plant. The plant, which produced large vehicles like the Hummer and GMC Colorado, closed in 2012.

Items and goods produced: paper and wood products, agriproducts, injection moldings, aluminum shelters, automotive parts, fixtures and cabinets, packaging materials, noise barriers

Incentive Programs-New and Existing Companies

Local programs: Permit fees for City Codes and Ordinances are waived in the Downtown Development Area for those companies rehabilitating buildings constructed prior to 1960. The city's economic development loan program offers low-interest rate loans to for-profit companies if they can prove that their undertaking will stimulate job growth, retain existing jobs, provide management training and increase general business activity for low- to moderate-income households. The downtown area offers the DSDC Low-Interest Loan Program, a financial incentive to provide rehabilitation funds to property owners and small businesses in downtown Shreveport. The downtown area also offers a Façade Rebate program, Programming Mini Grants to encourage downtown events and festivals, and a Historic Restoration Grants matching funds for 5–50 percent of qualified costs.

State programs: Louisiana has pledged itself to broaden its business base through liberal development incentives and loan programs. The Louisiana Quality Jobs Act offers a tax rebate of up to 6 percent of payroll paid each year for 10 years to new companies in selected industries or those that have at least 75 percent of sales out-of-the-state. A rebate on state sales/use tax is also available on construction materials, machinery, and equipment. The Enterprise Zone Program offers some companies a $2,500 tax credit for every new permanent job created during the first five years of operation as well as a sales/use tax rebate on select equipment. An Industrial Property Tax Exemption Program offers 10-year abatements for some new and expanding manufacturers. A Research and Development Credit provides tax credits up to 40 percent for companies that can also claim federal income tax credit for research. The Louisiana Motion Picture Investor Tax Credit offers a 30 percent credit for investments of $300,000 and up. An additional Digital

Interactive Media and Software Development Incentive offers a 35 percent tax credit. Restoration Tax Abatement Program provides a five-year deferred assessment on renovations and improvements. The Federal Historic Rehabilitation Tax Credit provides a 20 percent tax credit for rehabilitations expenses to a certified historic structure. Designation of a historic site allows it to access a tax credit up to $25,000 per structure during renovation. The Louisiana FastStart program offers incentives for outside companies choosing to locate in Louisiana, and the Industrial Tax Exemption Program is available for existing and new manufacturing operations.

Job training programs: The Louisiana Department of Education offers a Quickstart Program through which specialized training programs are developed for new and expanding businesses that will provide at least 10 new jobs. Training is offered either at a neutral site or at the company facility. The Job Training Partnership Act assists industries in choosing applicants, provides customized training for specific occupational skills and reimburses industry up to 50 percent for wages paid. Other opportunities are available through the Louisiana Department of Labor.

Development Projects

In the mid-1990s, riverboat gambling began in casinos on the Red River, a development that spurred growth in the economically stagnant city. It also encouraged redevelopment near the riverfront and in the downtown area, which has continued to the present day.

In 2013 Benteler International began the first phase of a $975 million steel manufacturing project at the Port of Caddo-Bossier, located in Shreveport. The manufacturing facility, eventually expected to create nearly 700 jobs, was expected to open its first phase in 2015, with a second phase complete by 2020. The final project was slated to cover 1.35 million square feet and 330 acres. To locate the facility in the area, the German-based company was offered an incentive package worth more than $70 million by the state government. Local development agencies contributed an additional $11.6 million in infrastructure improvements in areas surrounding the facility.

Paper bag manufacturing Ronpak opened a facility and corporate headquarters in Shreveport in 2013. The $16.8 million manufacturing facility in Shreveport located the company more closely to a major purchaser in Dallas, Texas. The company employed 109 individuals, with plans to double employment in the coming years. Another manufacturing company, Libbey Inc., also announced investment in Shreveport in 2013. The company planned a $20 million facility for glass manufacturing, in addition to a segment devoted to research in glassmaking technology. Libbey already had a presence in Shreveport, employing some 500 citizens, and the new plant was expected to add an additional 70 direct and 75 indirect jobs.

Municipal development projects to facilities in 2013 totaled just over $48 million. Most projects were small and included improvements and maintenance to fire stations, city hall, bus stations, and parking areas. The largest project devoted $8.4 million to developments in the city's downtown Festival Plaza; the project received an equivalent amount of funding in 2012. Municipal transportation projects received $54.2 million in financial support for 2013; improvements to water supply and existing infrastructure were budgeted $95.1 million, with sewer system projects receiving an additional $127.3 million. Some projects devoted to infrastructure improvements received financial support at both state and federal levels.

Construction on a 36-mile segment of Interstate 49, leading from the Arkansas border to Shreveport, was expected to complete in 2016 at a cost of $670; portions of the new interstate segment were open in 2013.

Economic Development Information: Greater Shreveport Chamber of Commerce, 400 Edwards St., Shreveport, LA 71101; telephone (318) 677-2500.

Commercial Shipping

Shreveport is located next to the Red River and the Port of Caddo-Bossier, which makes it a strategic location for manufacturers seeking to ship throughout the South and Midwest. It is a hub for motor freight delivery, since the area has convenient access to Interstate 20 (east–west) and Interstate 49 (north–south), which connects Shreveport to Interstate 10 (east–west) in south Louisiana. The Shreveport Regional Airport is served by several air cargo carriers and handlers, including FedEx, Express, UPS, Empire Airlines, and Integrated Airline Services, and handles an average of more than five million pounds of cargo annually. A United States Customs Port of Entry is located at the airport.

The Port of Caddo-Bossier has two Class 1 rail lines, although only Union Pacific is available at the port complex. Three port-owned locomotives provide railcar switching services, and more than 20,000 square feet of rail storage is available.

Labor Force and Employment Outlook

As of 2013, Shreveport was experiencing employment gains in information, services, and mining and logging. Declines were felt in government, professional and business services, manufacturing, and construction sectors. While the loss of a General Motors manufacturing facility in 2012 negatively impacted the area's job outlook, the pending construction of the Benteler steel facility was reason for optimism in the manufacturing sector. Other industries, such as film and natural gas drilling, were significant but inconsistent employers, with the scope of their long-term employment impact uncertain through 2013.

The following is a summary of data regarding the 2013 Shreveport-Bossier City labor force:

Size of civilian labor force: 96,441

Number of workers employed in . . .

    agriculture and mining: 2,675
    construction: 4,633
    manufacturing: 4,779
    wholesale trade: 2,345
    retail trade: 9,376
    transportation: 4,436
    information systems: 1,718
    finance: 3,769
    professional administration: 7,207
    education and social services: 26,067
    arts and leisure: 12,810
    other: 4,662
    public administration: 3,588

Average hourly earnings of production workers: $17.61

Unemployment rate: 5.7% (2012)

Employers

Largest employers (2013)	*Number of employees*
State of Louisiana	13,522
Barksdale Air Force Base	9,423
Caddo Parish School Board	6,289
LSU Health Sciences Center	5,902
Willis-Knighton Health Systems	4,306
Harrah's Horseshoe Casino/Louisiana Downs	3,332
City of Shreveport	2,782
Bossier Parish School Board	2,633
Christus Schumpert Health System	2,074
U.S. Support Company	1,952

Cost of Living

The cost of living in Shreveport was slightly below the national average as of 2013.

The following is a summary of data regarding several key cost of living factors in the area.

2013 ACCRA Average House Price: $282,040

2013 ACCRA Cost of Living Index: 93

State income tax rate: 2.0% to 6.0%

State sales tax rate: 4.0%

Local income tax rate: None

Local sales tax rate: 4.55%

Property tax rate: $130.71 per $1,000 of assessed valuation; residential property is assessed at 10% of fair market value (2013)

Economic Information: Greater Shreveport Chamber of Commerce, 400 Edwards St., Shreveport, LA 71101; telephone (318) 677-2500.

■ Education and Research

Elementary and Secondary Schools

Shreveport is served by Caddo Parish Public Schools. As of 2013, the school system had earner nine Blue Ribbon Schools of Excellence from the U. S. Department of Education. The system has a number of charter and magnet programs, including the largest JROTC unit in the nation at Huntington High School, and earned a Certificate of Excellence in Financial Reporting.

There were 17 private schools in the greater Shreveport region in 2013, enrolling about 5,300 students.

The following is a summary of data regarding the Caddo Parish Schools.

Total enrollment: 41,894

Number of facilities

total: 70
elementary schools: 42
junior high schools: 12
high schools: 6
other: 10

Student/teacher ratio: 14.49:1

Teacher salaries

average (statewide): $49,634

Funding per pupil: $10,823

Public Schools Information: Caddo Public Schools, 1961 Midway Ave., PO Box 32000, Shreveport, LA 71130-2000; telephone (318) 603-6300.

Colleges and Universities

Shreveport is home to Louisiana State University in Shreveport, a branch of the state system, which had an enrollment of 4,124 students in 2013. The university has a local economic impact on the city estimated at more than $46 million annually. Between 2008 and 2013,

faculty of the university generated more than $20 million in research grants. The LSU Health Shreveport is the only medical school in northern Louisiana and also offers graduate degrees in Biochemistry and Molecular Biology; Cellular Biology and Anatomy; Microbiology and Immunology; Molecular and Cellular Physiology; and Pharmacology, Toxicology and Neuroscience.

Centenary College of Louisiana, founded in 1825, is the oldest chartered liberal arts college west of the Mississippi River. The school is affiliated with the United Methodist Church and enrolls about 700 undergraduates. In 2013 *U.S. News & World Report* named it among the top 170 national liberal arts colleges. Other Shreveport area institutions of higher learning include Louisiana Technical College, Shreveport-Bossier Campus; Southern University at Shreveport; Bossier Parish Community College; Embry-Riddle Aeronautical University at Barksdale Air Force Base; Grambling State University; and Northwestern State University of Louisiana.

Libraries and Research Centers

The Shreve Memorial Library, which serves Caddo parish, was founded in 1923. It is the largest public library system in Louisiana, and consists of twelve full-time branches, nine part-time branches, and one bookmobile for delivery of books. Annual circulation averages more than one million volumes.

The Noel Memorial Library at LSU Shreveport is home to an Archives and Special Collections section with a wealth of unique material pertaining to the history of Northwest Louisiana, in addition to the Noel Collection of rare books. The library's collection totaled more than 250,000 volumes, 2,000 journals, and 300 online databases as of 2013.

The Biomedical Research Foundation of Northwest Louisiana is a 10-story research facility with 56 wet labs and a Positron Emission Tomography (PET) Imaging Center. The Consortium for Education, Research and Technology (CERT) is a partnership promoting collaboration projects among campuses of northern Louisiana's post-secondary institutions. InterTech, a $12.2 million research incubator, is a two-story, 60,000-square-foot facility where clients, mostly pharmaceutical companies, share $500,000 worth of equipment in a core laboratory.

Public Library Information: Shreve Memorial Library Main Branch, 424 Texas Street, P.O. Box 21523, Shreveport, LA 71101-3522; telephone (318) 226-5897; fax (318) 226-4780.

■ Health Care

The Willis-Knighton Medical Center was ranked the second-best hospital in Louisiana in 2013–14 by *U.S. News & World Report,* with high-performing marks in 11 categories. The hospital has 902 beds and admits more than 35,000 patients annually. The Shriner's Hospital for Children specializes in the treatment of bone, joint, and muscle problems in children, part of a network of 22 pediatric nonprofit hospitals across the country that provide specialty care at no charge. The Interim Louisiana State University Public Hospital has 502 beds. It also includes a teaching hospital associated with the School of Medicine. Smaller hospitals include the WK Bossier Health Center and Christus Health Shreveport-Bossier. The Overton Brooks VA Medical Center serves more than 130,000 veterans in the Ark-La-Tex area. LifeCare Hospitals, Inc., provides long-term acute care at its facility with 130 beds.

■ Recreation

Sightseeing

Shreveport's main tourist draw is as a destination spot for gamblers. Shreveport and neighboring Bossier City are home to six riverboat casinos: Boomtown Casino & Hotel, El Dorado Resort Casino, Horseshoe Casino & Hotel, Margaritaville Resort Casino, DiamondJacks Casino and Resort, and Sam's Town Hotel & Gambling Hall. Harrah's Louisiana Downs, primarily a horse racing venue, also hosts gambling. For the tourist seeking another sort of thrill, Shreveport also boasts the Yogie & Friends Exotic Cat Sanctuary, which is the state's only sanctuary for large, exotic cats such as lions, cougars, and tigers. Another popular tourist activity is a trip on the Red River with the "Spirit of the Red" River Cruise. The Gardens of the American Rose Center lies on 118 acres and is the headquarters for the American Rose Society.

The Pioneer Heritage Center, part of LSU Shreveport, is a unique combination of academic resource and tourist destination. It includes seven plantation structures, such as the Thrasher House; Caspiana House (the big house from Caspiana Plantation); a detached kitchen; a log single-pen blacksmith shop; a doctor's office; and a commissary.

The city is home to a variety of historic churches from the mid- to late 1800s, from Baptist churches to Methodist churches to Jewish congregations. In addition, there are also a number of museums in the Shreveport-Bossier area. The Ark-La-Tex Antique and Classic Vehicle Museum has more than 40 classic and antique cars on display, while the Barksdale Global Power Museum displays authentic uniforms, dioramas and aircraft dating back to World War I. Sci-Port: Louisiana's Science Center has more than 290 science, space science, technology, and math exhibits, as well as an IMAX theater. The Barnwell Garden and Art Center is both a botanical conservancy and an art museum. In Bossier, the collection at the Touchstone Wildlife and Art Museum has more than 1,000 mounted animals from around the world, in addition to American Indian artifacts and memorabilia from the Civil War and World Wars I and II.

Other area museums include the Stephens African-American Museum, the Caddo Pine Island Oil and Historical Society Museum, the Dorcheat Historical Association Museum, the Vivian Railroad Station Museum, Southern University Museum of Art, Red River Crossroads Museum, Spring Street Historical Museum, Shreveport Water Works Museum, and the Bossier Parish Library Historical Center.

Arts and Culture

Shreveport is home to a large number of cultural institutions for a city its size. The Strand Theatre, built in 1925, stands as the official state theatre of Louisiana. The theatre is listed on the National Register of Historic Places, and has been listed in *USA Weekend* and the *AMC Magazine* as one of the "Top 5 Glitziest Theatres for Live Performance" nationwide. It plays host to Broadway shows, comedy performances, and concerts. The River City Repertory Theatre, which lifted the curtain on its first performance at the Strand Theatre in 2006, is the first professional theater company in the northern Louisiana area. Louisiana Dance Theatre is the resident dance company of Louisiana Dance Foundation, and specializes in ballet performances. The Shreveport Metropolitan Ballet begins each season with Fall for Dance, a free performance given in conjunction with other local dance groups. LSU Shreveport's theatre department has operated Swine Palace, a non-profit professional theatre, since 1992. The Shreveport Opera has been bringing librettos to northern Louisiana since the late 1940s. The Shreveport Symphony Orchestra, which began around the same time, broadcasts all major concerts on Red River Radio, the regional public radio network that reaches 50,000 listeners each week.

Several amateur theater groups also make their home in Shreveport. The East Bank Community Theatre and the Shreveport Little Theatre provide a local home for amateur actors. The Shreveport Gilbert & Sullivan Society specializes in staging musicals by the composers from whom they draw their name. Peter Pan Players was the region's first children's theater company.

The students at the Hurley School of Music, part of Centenary College, give several concerts and recitals a semester. Also housed at Centenary College is the Marjorie Lyons Playhouse, where students in the Department of Theatre and Dance perform.

For the art lover, Shreveport area galleries include the East Bank Gallery, Louisiana State University in Shreveport Gallery, and Meadows Museum of Art at Centenary College, and R. W. Norton Art Gallery.

Festivals and Holidays

Shreveport prides itself on being a festival center, and its unique local culture is reflected in several of its many annual celebrations. Many of the area's seasonal and cultural celebrations are held in Festival Plaza, a three-block corridor developed by the city to facilitate their culture. The Gusher Days festival in Gladewater celebrates the heritage of the area's history in the oil industry. In the spring, the Louisiana Film Festival, an independent film festival, is held annually at Centenary College.

Mardi Gras is, of course, a huge occasion for celebration everywhere in Louisiana, and Shreveport is no exception. Several area Krewes (private clubs), including Asclepius, Centaur, Highland, Janus, Les Femmes Mystique, and Apollo host parades. The James Burton International Guitar Festival, which features a variety of local and national guitarists, draws visitors to the city each year when it is held each April.

Also in April are the Scottish Tartan Festival and the American Rose Center Spring Bloom Celebration. Later that month, the best artwork of students from Caddo and Bossier Parish Schools is exhibited at the Convention Center as part of ArtBreak. The Poke Salad Festival in May features a parade and celebration of poke salad, a celebrated local dish. Over Memorial Day, Shreveport's Cajun heritage is celebrated with Mudbug Madness, featuring boiled crawfish, Cajun/Creole food, music, and crafts. During the summer, the fun continues with Let the Good Times Roll!, the largest African-American music and arts festival in north Louisiana. Riverblast, held annually on the banks of the Red River, occurs during the July Fourth holiday.

Fall kicks off with the Super Derby Festival, held annually for 10 days in September. In addition to the central event, a three-year-old thoroughbred horse race, it includes fireworks, a golf tournament, and a "wiener-dog race" featuring dachshunds. Just before Halloween, there's the Pumpkin Shine on Line, with seasonal fun for the whole family. Also in October is the Monterey Days Festival, which focuses on local crafts and food. The annual autumnal celebration and largest outdoor festival in northern Louisiana, the Red River Revel Arts Festival is an eight-day celebration of local arts, food, and shopping. The State Fair of Louisiana is held just outside Shreveport at the Hirsch Memorial Coliseum each year for two weeks at the end of October and beginning of November, and has done so since 1906. It includes a carnival, livestock exhibitions, cooking demonstrations, and competitions in divisions of everything from BB Guns to photography. Also in November, the Highland Jazz & Blues Festival is held annually, celebrating Louisiana's tradition of music.

The holiday season is a busy one for festivals in Shreveport. At Christmas, event-goers have their pick of Holiday in Dixie, Christmas on Caddo, and Holiday Trail of Lights.

Sports for the Spectator

Shreveport is not home to any major league professional teams, and despite a rich history of minor league sports, contemporary Shreveport has struggled to maintain its franchises. Baseball has a particularly tumultuous past;

baseball teams in Shreveport went through 15 name changes and nearly as many different leagues between 1895 and 2011. The Shreveport-Bossier Captains, an independent minor league team, played in the South Division of the American Association but were sold to an owner in Laredo, Texas, in 2011, leaving the city without a team. The Bossier-Shreveport Mudbugs won the Central Hockey League title in 2011, then ceased operations. Bossier City Battle Wings, an Arena Football League 2 team, last played in 2010.

The Shreveport Rugby Football Club, a member of USA Rugby, was founded in 1977 and is considered the oldest continuously competing sport team in Shreveport. The Aftershock of the Independent Women's Football League play in Independence Stadium.

On the collegiate front, the LSU Shreveport Pilots play in the Gulf Coast Athletics Conference as part of the NAIA (National Association of Intercollegiate Athletics). They field teams in baseball, women's tennis, and men's and women's basketball. The AdvoCare V100 Bowl is an NCAA post-season football bowl game that typically features teams of the Atlantic Coast Conference and Southern Conference. It has been a Shreveport tradition since 1976 and takes place each year at Independence Stadium.

Nearby Bossier City is home to one of the three horse tracks in the state, Harrah's Louisiana Downs. Harrah's Louisiana Downs is a popular spot for horse racing enthusiasts. A variety of stakes races are run on its John Franks Turf Course. Even more popular in Shreveport than horse racing, however, is car racing. There are at least four sites in the metro area, including the Ark-La-Tex Speedway, for stock car racing.

Sports for the Participant

There are ample opportunities for the athletically inclined to enjoy Shreveport. Shreveport has two municipal golf courses, Huntington Golf Course and Querbes Golf Course, both 18 holes. Several additional golf courses are located nearby. There are three tennis centers. Interstate Skateboard Park is a popular spot for younger Shreveport residents. S'port Port Indoor Soccer facility hosts soccer camps and leagues year round.

The local enthusiasm for car racing isn't just confined to the stands; instead, many Shreveport residents enjoy themselves at the Bayou Cajun Raceway, a go-kart facility, and the Red River Raceway, which specializes in drag racing.

For the outdoor enthusiast, there is Bayou Dorcheat Preserve, with more than 40 acres of protected land. Caddo Lake and Lake Bistineau are popular year-round fishing spots; so is Cross Lake, located on the west side of Shreveport, which also provides the city water supply. The Walter B. Jacobs Memorial Nature Park is a 160-acre nature park that includes a pine-oak-hickory forest and five miles of nature trails.

Other area parks, administered by the City and Parish Parks system, include the Arthur Ray Teague Parkway Park, C. Bickham Dickson Park, and Riverfront Park.

Shopping and Dining

There are several popular shopping sites in Shreveport, including the Louisiana Boardwalk, a 550,000 square foot complex, which is one of the largest outlet, dining, and entertainment destinations in Louisiana. The Line Avenue District is a five-mile stretch of antique shops and unique specialty shops, while Southeast Shreveport is home to chains like White House Black Market, Belk, and World Market. Mall St. Vincent in Shreveport and Pierre Bossier Mall in Bossier City are the area's most prominent malls.

Restaurant Row on Line Avenue is known as the heart of Shreveport cuisine. Excellent Cajun and Creole cooking is easy to find; area specialties include country-fried steak and potatoes, fried catfish, seafood gumbo, and even alligator for the more adventurous palate. Higher end establishments include Anthony's Steak & Seafood and the Texas Street Steakhouse, while local favorites like Noble Savage Tavern and Southern Maid Donuts are a bit easier on the wallet. Ethnic restaurants from a variety of world cuisines are also easy to find in Shreveport.

Visitor Information: Shreveport-Bossier City Convention & Tourist Bureau, 629 Spring Street, Shreveport, LA 71101-3645; telephone toll-free (888) 458-4748.

■ Convention Facilities

The Shreveport Convention Center reopened in 2006 after a large renovation project that created a main hall with more than 95,000 square feet of exhibit space, 10 individual meeting rooms, a large boardroom, and full-service amenities. A 313-room Hilton Hotel next to the Convention Center opened in 2007. Just across the river, the CenturyLink Center in Bossier City provides 34,000 square feet of space for meetings, trade shows, and conventions.

Convention Information: Shreveport Convention Center, 400 Caddo Street, Shreveport, LA 71101; telephone (318) 841-4000.

■ Transportation

Approaching the City

Shreveport is served by two main airports, the Shreveport Regional Airport and the Downtown Shreveport Airport. The Shreveport Regional Airport was served by four airlines in 2013: Allegiant, American, Delta, and United. A $7.5 million cargo terminal opened in 2009, an anchor for the city's AeroPark Industrial Park. The airport has nonstop flights to Las Vegas, Dallas–Fort Worth, Atlanta, Houston, and Denver. The Downtown Shreveport

Airport mainly houses corporate and private aircraft, in addition to aircraft maintenance providers and the Southern University Shreveport airframe and power plant mechanics certification school. The facility boasts a 5,018-foot runway.

Shreveport has convenient access to Interstate 20 (east–west) and Interstate 49 (north–south), which connects Shreveport to Interstate 10 (east–west) in south Louisiana.

Traveling in the City

SporTran, Shreveport's regional transportation system, has a fleet of more than 50 buses that run seven days a week. In addition, vans operate a demand-response paratransit system seven days a week. The Shreveport highway system has a cross-hair and loop freeway system surrounding the city. The Inner Loop Freeway, also known as Louisiana Highway 3132 on the south side, surrounds the downtown. The Bert Kouns Industrial Loop, also known as Louisiana Highway 526, circles further south and intersects Interstate 49.

■ Communications

Newspapers and Magazines

The main newspaper in the Shreveport-Bossier area is the daily, *The Shreveport Times.* Other papers include the weekly *The Shreveport Sun.* While Bossier City is also served by the *Shreveport Times,* area residents also have access to the daily *Bossier Press-Tribune,* published three times per week. Nearby Webster Parish is served by the *Minden Press-Herald. SB Magazine,* published monthly in Shreveport, contains interviews with local figures in addition to features on business, politics, and sports. Other alternative publications include *Forum News* and *City Lights.* The Barksdale Air Force Base publishes the weekly *Barksdale Warrior.* Two times a year, the North Louisiana Historical Association publishes their journal, *North Louisiana History.*

Television and Radio

Major cable and satellite television companies serve the Shreveport area and nearby Bossier City. Ten television stations broadcast from within the Shreveport city limits, in addition to 6 AM and 11 FM radio stations available in the region.

Media Information: The Shreveport Times, 222 Lake St., Shreveport, LA 71101; telephone (318) 459-3200.

Shreveport Online

Caddo Public Schools. Available www.caddo.k12.la.us

City of Shreveport Home Page. Available www.shreveportla.gov

Shreve Memorial Library. Available www.shreve-lib.org

Shreveport-Bossier Convention and Tourist Bureau. Available www.shreveport-bossier.org

Shreveport Chamber of Commerce. Available www. shreveportchamber.org

BIBLIOGRAPHY

Kennedy, Richard S., ed., *Literary New Orleans: Essays & Meditations* (Baton Rouge, LA: Louisiana State University Press, 1992)

Lornell , Kip, and Tracey E. W. Laird, eds., *Shreveport Sounds in Black and White* (Jackson: University Press of Mississippi, 2008)

Palombo, Bernadette J., et al., *Wicked Shreveport* (Charleston, SC: History Press, 2012)

Young, Andrew, *An Easy Burden: The Civil Rights Movement and the Transformation of America* (New York: HarperCollins, 1996)

Maryland

The State in Brief

Nickname: Old Line State, Free State

Motto: Fatti maschii, parole femine (Manly deeds, womanly words)

Flower: Black-eyed susan

Bird: Baltimore oriole

Area: 12,406 square miles (2010; U.S. rank 42nd)

Elevation: Ranges from sea level to 3,360 feet above sea level

Climate: Temperate, with mild winters and hot summers; cooler in mountains

Admitted to Union: April 28, 1788

Capital: Annapolis

Head Official: Martin O'Malley (D) (until 2015)

Population

1990: 4,781,468
2000: 5,296,486
2010: 5,773,552
2012 estimate: 5,785,496
Percent change, 2000–2010: 9.0%
U.S. rank in 2012: 19th
Percent of residents born in state: 47.5% (2012)
Density: 594.8 people per square mile (2010)
2012 FBI Crime Index Total: 190,086

Racial and Ethnic Characteristics (2012)

White: 3,408,049
Black or African American: 1,700,174
American Indian and Alaska Native: 17,323
Asian: 323,363
Native Hawaiian and Pacific Islander: 2,419
Hispanic or Latino (may be of any race): 472,285
Other: 334,168

Age Characteristics (2012)

Population under 5 years old: 365,258
Population 5 to 19 years old: 1,149,656
Percent of population 65 years and over: 12.4%
Median age: 37.9

Vital Statistics

Total number of births (2012–13): 73,240
Total number of deaths (2012–13): 46,205
AIDS cases reported through 2011: 38,418

Economy

Major industries: Manufacturing, defense, food processing, fishing, tourism
Unemployment rate (2012): 5.4%
Per capita income (2012): $36,056
Median household income (2012): $72,999
Percentage of persons below poverty level (2012): 9.4%
Income tax rate: 2.0% to 5.75%
Sales tax rate: 6.0%

Annapolis

■ The City in Brief

Founded: 1649 (chartered 1708)

Head Official: Mayor Mike Pantelides (since 2013; current term expires 2017)

City Population
- 1990: 33,195
- 2000: 35,876
- 2010: 38,394
- 2012 estimate: 38,577
- Percent change, 2000–2010: 7.0%

Metropolitan Statistical Area Population
- 2000: 2,552,994
- 2010: 2,710,489
- 2012 estimate: 2,753,149
- Percent change, 2000–2010: 6.2%
- U.S. rank in 2000: 19th
- U.S. rank in 2010: 20th

Area: 7.2 square miles

Elevation: 92 feet above sea level

Average Annual Temperatures: 85.2° F

Average Annual Precipitation: 39.03 inches of rain; 14.4 inches of snow

Major Economic Sectors: Government, maritime industries, tourism, military manufacturing, food and beverage products, industrial manufacturing, telecommunications

Unemployment Rate: 4.7% (2012)

Per Capita Income: $41,045

2012 FBI Crime Index Property: 1,042

Major Colleges and Universities: U.S. Naval Academy, St. John's College, Anne Arundel Community College

Daily Newspaper: *The Capital*

■ Introduction

Annapolis is a cosmopolitan American city with a small-town atmosphere, and is a city of many faces. It has been named one of America's Prettiest Towns and celebrated itself as self-proclaimed "most romantic city in America" in 2010. But it is also known for more than just its beauty. For more than 350 years it has played an integral part in national affairs. The city has long been the site of the U.S. Naval Academy, and marine activities remain a vital part of community life. Despite being home to high-tech industries, vast health-care complexes, and modern businesses, the city has managed to maintain its seventeenth-century charm. Visitors can enjoy the more than three centuries of American architecture on display there.

■ Geography and Climate

Annapolis is located in central Maryland on the south bank of the Severn River, near the mouth of the Chesapeake Bay. It is 27 miles south-southeast of Baltimore and 27 miles east of Washington, D.C. The lowest land in Annapolis is near sea level at the City Dock, and the level climbs to 92 feet between Bay Ridge Avenue and Forest Drive. Excluding the U.S. Naval Academy, the city has 17 miles of waterfront.

Annapolis has a temperate mid-latitude climate with warm, humid summers and mild winters. The weather during spring and autumn is generally pleasant. There are no pronounced wet and dry seasons, but summer often brings sudden heavy showers, damaging winds, and lightning. Breezes from the Chesapeake Bay and nearby creeks moderate the city's temperature. Regional rainfall averages slightly more than 39 inches annually, while snowfall averages below 15 inches per year.

Annapolis Harbor. *Kenneth Wiedemann/StockPhoto.com*

Area: 7.2 square miles

Elevation: 92 feet above sea level

Average Temperatures: 85.2° F

Average Annual Precipitation: 39.03 inches of rain; 14.4 inches of snow

■ History

Early Settlement

Before white settlers arrived in Maryland, the Algonquin and other Native American tribes occupied the region. By the time Annapolis was settled in 1649, the Algonquins were gone from the area, forced out by raiding parties of the Susquehannock tribe.

The original white settlement of the area near Annapolis was at Greenbury Point, although the land is now mostly covered by the Severn River. In the middle of the seventeenth century, Puritans living in Virginia were threatened with severe punishments by the Anglican Royal Governor if they did not conform to the worship of the Anglican church. Then Cecil Calvert, the second Lord Baltimore, offered the Pilgrims generous land grants, freedom of worship, and trading privileges if they

agreed to move to Maryland, which he wanted to have settled. In 1649 they started a community on a site at the mouth of the Severn River on the western shore of Chesapeake Bay.

The Puritans named their new settlement Providence. In 1650, Lord Baltimore, the overseer of the colony, granted a charter to the county that surrounded Providence. He named it Anne Arundel County after his beloved wife, Anne Arundel, who had died shortly before at the age of thirty-four. But the Puritans refused to sign an oath of allegiance to Lord Baltimore, in part because he was a Roman Catholic. In 1655 he sent the St. Mary's militia, headed by Governor William Stone, to force the Puritans into submission. A battle between the two groups took place on March 25, 1655. The Puritans won the conflict, which was the first battle between Englishmen on the North American continent. Eventually, Maryland became a royal colony. The capital was moved farther north in 1694 to the site of present-day Annapolis. By that time, for reasons unknown, the Puritan settlement of Providence had all but disappeared.

Development of Annapolis

Over time a small community began to develop on the peninsula that is the site of present-day Annapolis. It was known as Anne Arundel Town, taking its name from the county. The settlement grew and by the late 1600s the population of the province had reached nearly 25,000 residents. People started to object that the then-capital, St. Mary's, was too far away from where the majority of the people lived.

Royal Governor Francis Nicholson decided a more centrally located capital was needed and chose the site of what is now Annapolis. He named the new capital Annapolis in honor of Princess Anne, who became queen of England in 1702. It was Nicholson who determined that the city be built on a grand baroque street plan much like the great capitals of Europe. Streets were designed to radiate from a circle that was to contain the capitol. In a second circle was built an Anglican church. Residential areas were built for the prosperous families, for artisans, and for working men and their families. In 1696, Nicholson granted a charter to King William's School, which was built in Annapolis's center.

During the second half of the seventeenth century, the people of colonial Anne Arundel County had violent encounters with the Algonquins and other tribes along the shores of the Magothy River. The Indians staged raids there to try to protect their tribe and their lands from colonists, who often used devious methods to take advantage of them. Eventually the colonists won out.

Annapolis Prospers

In time Annapolis became the political, social, cultural, and economic hub of Maryland. The city gained its charter in 1708. Annapolis and Anne Arundel County continued to grow into a major shipping port. By the last third of the 1700s, the only town in Maryland to rival Annapolis as a shipping center was Baltimore.

Those were prosperous times for some. With the help of the fertile soil and a slave economy, plantation owners and wealthier citizens were able to furnish their houses with luxury items from Europe. Young ladies and gentlemen wore elegant clothing and attended fancy balls at various large homes.

During the years shortly before the start of the Revolutionary War, and even during wartime, citizens of Annapolis enjoyed racing, dancing, and gambling. Luckily for Annapolitans, the Revolutionary War and the wars of the nineteenth century bypassed the area. During the war's later years, French volunteer Marquis de Lafayette helped enliven the city's social scene.

Site of Annapolis Convention

From 1783 to August 1784, Annapolis served as the United States' first peacetime national capital. There in 1783 General George Washington resigned from the Continental Army. The next year, the Treaty of Paris ending the American Revolution was ratified there. In 1786 the city served as the seat of the Annapolis Convention, at which delegates from five states met to discuss proposed changes to the Articles of Confederation by which the country was then run.

During this period slavery played a large role in the economy. Alex Haley, the late author of the world-famous account of his family entitled *Roots*, was able to trace back the arrival of his ancestors, who had been kidnapped from Africa, to the Annapolis City Dock. Although Maryland was formally a slave state, many of its citizens opposed the institution. Archaeologists have found that there was a large, free African American population in the area before the Civil War.

From Post-Revolution to Civil War Times

After the Revolutionary War, Baltimore forged ahead of Annapolis as a center of commerce. However, in 1808, Fort Severn was built on Windmill Point to prevent the British from attacking Annapolis during the War of 1812. (Soldiers inhabited the fort until 1845. Then the post was transferred to the U.S. Navy, becoming the U.S. Naval Academy in 1850.)

As early as 1800 Annapolis had developed into a city of stately residences and public buildings patterned on those in London, England. Members of local high society enjoyed such diversions as fox hunts and racing meets. During the Civil War years most Annapolitans sympathized with the South but did not engage in acts of violence. At that time, facilities at the Naval Academy and St. John's College were used to house injured soldiers.

Agriculture and Tourism

Until well into the nineteenth century, Anne Arundel County remained agrarian, with tobacco the main crop. Other important crops were wheat, corn, and fruit. Seafood such as oysters and crab were also a mainstay of the local diet. The addition of steamboats to the local scene after the Civil War brought many visitors to the area, as vacationers fled to the shore to leave behind the heat of the larger cities. This prompted the growth of resorts, beaches, yacht clubs, and summer communities.

In the 1880s the railroad brought a period of development in the area. By 1890 the population of the city had reached 7,604 people. Crops were shipped to markets in Washington, D.C., Philadelphia, and beyond.

The City in the Twentieth Century

During the twentieth century, the area continued to develop, due to such factors as the growth of the state government, the presence of U.S. Navy and Coast Guard facilities, the completion of a bridge to the Delmarva peninsula, and the development of Baltimore-Washington International Airport. Today, Annapolis remains a thriving naval and government center. It has enjoyed the benefits of having its own developing local high-tech firms, while also serving as a commuter community for nearby Washington D.C. and Baltimore.

Historical Information: Maryland Historical Society, 201 West Monument St., Baltimore, MD 21201; telephone (410) 685-3750. Anne Arundel County Historical Society, P.O. Box 385, Linthicum, MD 21090-0385; telephone (410) 760-9679.

■ Population Profile

Metropolitan Statistical Area Population

2000: 2,552,994
2010: 2,710,489
2012 estimate: 2,753,149
Percent change, 2000–2010: 6.2%
U.S. rank in 2000: 19th
U.S. rank in 2010: 20th

City Residents

1990: 33,195
2000: 35,876
2010: 38,394
2012 estimate: 38,577
Percent change, 2000–2010: 7.0%

Density: 5,344.4 people per square mile

Racial and ethnic characteristics

White: 23,526
Black or African American: 10,367
American Indian and Alaskan Native: 0
Asian: 885
Native Hawaiian and Other Pacific Islander: 0
Hispanic or Latino (may be of any race): 6,488
Other: 3,799

Percent of residents born in state: 42.1%

Age characteristics

Population under 5 years old: 3,067
Population 5 to 9 years old: 2,610
Population 10 to 14 years old: 974
Population 15 to 19 years old: 1,732
Population 20 to 24 years old: 3,019
Population 25 to 34 years old: 6,932
Population 35 to 44 years old: 5,030
Population 45 to 54 years old: 4,902
Population 55 to 59 years old: 2,478
Population 60 to 64 years old: 2,749
Population 65 to 74 years old: 3,124
Population 75 to 84 years old: 1,148
Population 85 years and over: 812
Median age: 36.9

Births (2010–11 Metropolitan Area)

Total number: 33,729

Deaths (2010–11 Metropolitan Area)

Total number: 22,788

Money income (2012)

Per capita income: $41,045
Median household income: $71,082
Total households: 16,136

Number of households with income of . . .

less than $10,000: 1,051
$10,000 to $14,999: 460
$15,000 to $24,999: 1,389
$25,000 to $34,999: 833
$35,000 to $49,999: 1,730
$50,000 to $74,999: 3,108
$75,000 to $99,999: 2,215
$100,000 to $149,999: 2,795
$150,000 to $199,999: 1,151
$200,000 or more: 1,404

Percent of families below poverty level: 12.5%

FBI Crime Index Property: 1,042

FBI Crime Index Violent: 177

■ Municipal Government

Annapolis is the capital of Maryland and the seat of Anne Arundel County. The Annapolis city council includes eight aldermen, who serve four-year terms and the mayor, who presides at meetings. Each alderman represents one of eight wards, or geographical areas, of the city. The mayor serves full-time as the chief executive officer of the city and may serve two consecutive four-year terms.

Head Official: Mayor Mike Pantelides (since 2013; current term expires 2017)

Total Number of City Employees: 537 (2012)

City Information: Mayor's Office, City of Annapolis, Annapolis City Hall, 160 Duke of Gloucester Street, Annapolis, MD 21401; telephone (410) 263-7997; email mayor@annapolis.gov

■ Economy

Major Industries and Commercial Activity

The government sector—the State Capital, Anne Arundel County Seat, Fort George G. Meade, and the United States Naval Academy—maritime industries, and tourism are some of Annapolis and Anne Arundel County's major economic components.

Government-related industry provides more than 10,000 individuals with jobs in the public administration field across the region. The largest employer in the state of Maryland, Fort George G. Meade, located in Anne Arundel County, consists of more than 56,000 service members, civilian employees, and contractors. Its expanded labor force Fort Meade supports efforts of many federal agencies, such as the National Security Agency, Defense Media Activity, Defense Information Systems Agency, Defense Courier Service, and U.S. Cyber Command. Operations of a number of now-closed military bases have been centralized at Fort Meade.

Annapolis is home to nearly 15 percent of all the maritime businesses in Maryland. Since the 1960s, Annapolis has been known as the place for buying and selling of boats. A city-sponsored survey of the industry reported in 2008 that about 24 percent of the city's maritime industry was boat building, while 21 percent was excursion or sightseeing, 19 percent boat dealers, and the remainder made up of marinas, merchandising, and boat repair. Employment in the industry was estimated around 1,700. A nationwide recession stymied the industry during the late 2000s, as it depends heavily on expenditures of disposable income.

Tourism, also a thriving industry in Annapolis and Anne Arundel County, employs about 23,000 residents countywide, and tourists spent some $3.4 billion in 2013.

The Anne Arundel Medical Center, a major private sector employer in the county, also provides jobs for more than 5,000 full and part-time employees. It completed a $424 million expansion project in 2011. Other important private companies in Anne Arundel County in 2013 were ARINC, Booz Allen & Hamilton, CSC, General Dynamics, and Northrop Grumman. That year, there were some 14,735 area businesses.

Items and goods produced: radar and electronics equipment, undersea warfare equipment, seafood processing, small boats, concrete products, plastic, beverages

Incentive Programs-New and Existing Companies

Local programs: The Anne Arundel Economic Development Corporation (AAEDC) provides loans of up to $300,000 to county-based or new companies seeking a county presence. Loans are made through the Arundel Business Loan Fund in the form of direct loans and Small Business Administration guaranteed loans. The Business Corridor Investment Loan Program (BCIP) is set up to encourage economic activity in four pilot project areas in Anne Arundel County and Annapolis revitalization districts. The BCIP offers qualified business owners zero interest loans of up to $35,000 for improvements to the exterior and interior of their business. Job creation tax credits and community revitalization tax credits are also available.

The City of Annapolis offers small businesses a sprinkler cost assistance program and incentives in its designated arts and entertainment district.

State programs: The Maryland Industrial Development Financing Authority (MIDFA) provides financing assistance for capital assets and working capital to small- and mid-sized businesses that demonstrate a significant economic impact. This assistance includes programs that insure loans made by financial institutions up to 80 percent and not exceeding $2.5 million; taxable bond financing; tax-exempt bond financing for non-profit organizations and manufacturing facilities; and linked deposits that provide loans below market rates to qualified small businesses in rural areas with high unemployment rates. The Maryland Small Business Development Financing Authority (MSBDFA) provides financing for small businesses through a variety of programs, including a contract financing program, an equity participation investment program, a long-term guaranty program, and a surety bonding program.

Major incentive programs include Job Creation Tax Credits amounting to the lesser of $1,000 or 2.5 percent of annual wages for each qualifying permanent job; Cybersecurity Investment tax credits, to attract start-up companies in the area; Enterprise Zone credits, One Maryland tax credits for business location in distressed counties; Research and Development tax credits to refund research expenditures; Biotechnology tax credits; Brownfields tax credits; BRAC Zones credits for infrastructure improvements; Cellulosic Ethanol credits to refund research and development expenditures; and Security Clearance credits to refund expenses associated with meeting security requirements of defense projects.

The Maryland Economic Development Assistance Authority and Fund provides direct loans to certain industries in certain regions. The Maryland Venture Fund is a nationally recognized model for seed and early-stage investing. Target industries include technology companies involved in software, communications, cybersecurity, and life science ventures. Funds for other venture firms are distributed through InvestMaryland. A number of loan programs for agricultural businesses are available, as are Community Development Block Grants.

Job training programs: Maryland's Credit Connections program is a specialized training program for commercial bankers intended to increase lending in the state, grow credit ratings of state companies, and lessen risk assumed by lenders. The program was launched in 2010 in association with the Federal Reserve Bank of Richmond. The state's Partnership for Workforce Quality is a business development grant program to improve the competitiveness of small and mid-sized manufacturing and technology companies. It provides matching grants for training of existing employees. Workforce Investment Boards located throughout the state offer training funds. For Annapolis, the regional board is the Anne Arundel Workforce Development Corporation. Anne Arundel Community College offers business training programs in computers, management and leadership, communication, and customer service. The University of Maryland provides training specialists to review, analyze, and recommend safety training programs.

Development Projects

Anne Arundel Medical Center completed a $424 million emergency room, expanding its area facilities. The new emergency room included a new pediatrics emergency department. A project that involved three years of construction, the completed facility featured two waiting rooms, eight triage bays, blood draw stations, and new treatment rooms. The pediatric emergency wing included sixteen inpatient beds, eliminating the need to transfer patients out of the emergency department after admission. The building was LEED certified for its environmentally conscious design.

City infrastructure projects during 2013 included a new water treatment plant, which was the largest public construction project in the city's history. The $35 million facility replaced the 1929 plant that was in need of replacement. The new water treatment plant was capable of processing four million gallons of water per day and was located next to the old facility. Most of the funding came from a low-interest state loan; the remainder was a combination green-building grant and city bond issue. Minor city projects included streetscape improvements such as curb, signpost, and streetlight repainting. Flood mitigation projects for fiscal year 2014 were slated to receive $7.5 million in funding.

Economic Development Information: Annapolis Economic Development Corporation, 200 Westgate Circle, Annapolis, MD 21401; telephone (410) 280-2712; email info@annapolisedc.org. Anne Arundel Economic Development Corporation, 2660 Riva Road, Suite 200, Annapolis, MD 21401; telephone (410) 222-7410, fax (410)222-7415; email info@aaedc.org

Commercial Shipping

Freight carriage is provided by the CSX Transportation and Norfolk Southern. More than 100 motor freight common carriers serve Anne Arundel County. The international Port of Baltimore is nearby, providing easy access to a major port for water transportation. To take advantage of its proximity to the port, Anne Arundel County has invested in the local transportation infrastructure by upgrading and expanding its highway, commuter, and light rail system.

Labor Force and Employment Outlook

Maryland's is among the best educated and highly skilled work forces in the nation. Over 300 of Anne Arundel's businesses having 100 or more workers. In total, the county's 14,735 businesses employ 239,839 citizens.

The following is a summary of data regarding the 2012 Annapolis labor force:

Size of civilian labor force: 22,262

Number of workers employed in . . .

agriculture and mining: 22
construction: 1,186
manufacturing: 855
wholesale trade: 298
retail trade: 1,987
transportation: 373
information systems: 547
finance: 1,176
professional administration: 3,528
education and social services: 4,281
arts and leisure: 2,829
other: 1,358
public administration: 2,392

Average hourly earnings of production workers: $Not available

Unemployment rate: 4.7% (2012)

Employers

Largest employers (2012)	Number of employees
United States Naval Academy	2,340
Verizon Maryland	844
TeleCommunication Systems, Inc.	650
Constellation Energy Group	500
ARC of the Central Chesapeake Region	360
Giant Food–Forest Drive	250
Towne Park LTD	250
Ledo Pizza System, Inc.	200
United Association of Journeymen & Apprentices	200
St. John's College	197

Cost of Living

The following is a summary of data regarding several key cost of living factors in the area.

State income tax rate: 2.0% to 5.75%

State sales tax rate: 6.0%

Local income tax rate: 2.56%

Local sales tax rate: None

Property tax rate: $1.136 per $100 of assessed value (2013)

Economic Information: Annapolis and Anne Arundel County Chamber of Commerce, 49 Old Solomons Island Road, Suite 204, Annapolis, MD 21401; telephone (410) 266-3960; fax (410) 266-8270; email info@aaaccc.org.

■ Education and Research

Elementary and Secondary Schools

Annapolis students attend the Anne Arundel County Public Schools. In addition to basic academic subjects, the school system offers classes in computer education, music, art, health, physical education, foreign languages, library media, and technology. It also boasts a special gifted and talented program. As of 2013, some 87 percent of graduating seniors in the district pursued post-secondary education, winning scholarships worth more than $540 million. Test scores in the district in both math and reading exceeded state averages. The district also claimed 12 National Blue Ribbon Schools of Excellence and 16 Maryland Blue Ribbon Schools of Excellence throughout its history.

The city is also served by a number of private and parochial schools, including the Annapolis Area Christian School, the Aleph Bet Jewish Day School, the Chesapeake Montessori School, the Key School, and Saint Anne's Day School.

The following is a summary of data regarding the Anne Arundel County Public Schools.

Total enrollment: 75,481

Number of facilities

    total: 125
    elementary schools: 83
    junior high schools: 19
    high schools: 12
    other: 11

Student/teacher ratio: 14.8:1

Teacher salaries

    average (statewide): $65,113

Funding per pupil: $13,019

Public Schools Information: Anne Arundel County Public Schools, 2644 Riva Rd., Annapolis, MD 21401; telephone (410) 222-5000.

Colleges and Universities

The United States Naval Academy in downtown Annapolis, founded in 1845, provides undergraduate education for the members of the U.S. Navy. On its more than 338-acre campus, the institution admits about 1,220 students from every state and several foreign countries each year, for a total enrollment of 4,536. The academy offers a core curriculum of required courses as well as a choice of 24 major fields of study. The Brigade of Midshipmen, as the student body is known, undergoes a rigorous academic program and intense physical training to prepare them for being commissioned as ensigns in the Navy or second lieutenants in the Marine Corps. *U.S. News & World Report* ranked the institution 12th among national liberal arts colleges in 2013.

Annapolis is also home to St. John's College, the third oldest college in the nation and a National Historic Landmark. The co-educational, four-year liberal arts institution has an enrollment of about 450 to 475 undergraduates with about 82 percent of students living on campus, and offers bachelor and master of arts degrees. It has a second campus in Santa Fe, New Mexico. Rather than employing typical college classes and lectures, St. John's instructors teach primarily by way of seminars, tutorials, and laboratories. St. John's students follow a curriculum that is based on in-depth reading of the major works of Western thought.

Annapolis is also served by the University of Maryland's University College, which provides undergraduate and graduate courses at its Annapolis Center. In addition, Anne Arundel Community College, a public two-year college, enrolled approximately 53,000 students in 2,800 credit and noncredit courses annually as of 2013, with courses available at its main campus and more than 90 county locations including schools, churches, and senior centers.

Libraries and Research Centers

The Anne Arundel County Public Library, founded in 1921, has its headquarters in Annapolis. Its 15 county-wide library branches contain more than one million items and employ 300 part- or full-time workers. In addition to popular materials and information services, the library provides story time programs, special business and health collections, a bookmobile, and services for disabled persons and adult new readers. Public Internet access is available at all branches.

The U.S. Naval Academy's Nimitz Library houses a vast number of books in its general collections and boasts a variety of special collections that focus on naval history, naval and military science, and science and technology. The U.S. Navy Library focuses on energy research and materials and environmental control.

Other libraries in the city include the Maryland State Archives Library, the Maryland State Law Library, the Maryland Department of Legislative Services Library, St. John's College Library, the Anne Arundel Medical Center Library, and the Environmental Protection Agency Office of Analytical Services Library.

A number of research institutes make their home in Annapolis. The Historic Annapolis Foundation Research Center has special subject interests in architecture, city planning, urban design, and local and state history. The

Smithsonian Environmental Research Center is located near Annapolis in Edgewater, Maryland.

Public Library Information: Anne Arundel County Public Library, 5 Harry S. Truman Pkwy., Annapolis, MD 21401; telephone (410) 222-7371.

■ Health Care

Annapolis is served by the city's Anne Arundel Medical Center (AAMC), which treats patients at its location at the Carl A. Brunetto Medical Park. The Medical Center, which provides 401 licensed beds, served more than 76,000 emergency room patients and admitted more than 25,000 as of 2013. The hospital completed a more than $400 million construction project for a new emergency department in 2011. The Clatanoff Pavilion offers a variety of women's health care services, including obstetrics and gynecology services, maternity suites, and a critical care nursery. The Donner Pavilion houses the DeCesaris Cancer Institute, a state-of-the-art cancer treatment center. Patients needing same-day surgery are treated at the Edwards Surgical Pavilion, where more than 600 surgeries are performed every month. The Sajak Pavilion includes the hospital's Breast Center, focusing on the needs of breast cancer patients, as well as other medical and administrative offices such as Anne Arundel Diagnostics, the Diabetes Center, and the AAMC Foundation. The Medical Park also makes available critical care treatment, outpatient surgery, and health education. In October 2010, Anne Arundel Health System opened a new Community Health Center in 2011 to serve uninsured and under-insured residents.

■ Recreation

Sightseeing

Chosen by *National Geographic Adventure* magazine as one of the country's top waterfront towns, charming Annapolis boasts more surviving colonial buildings than any city in the country, and the entire downtown is a registered National Historic Landmark. Annapolis is a great city to tour on foot with its unusual street layout in the center city—there are two major circles with streets spoking around them. Sightseers can observe an attractive mix of Colonial, Federal, and Victorian architecture, especially in the National Historic Landmark District. Visitors can also observe the comings and goings of yachts at the waterfront and explore over 500 miles of shoreline peppered with historic Chesapeake Bay lighthouses.

The focal point of sightseeing in Annapolis is the Maryland State House with its unique narrow dome, which is topped by an unusual tower and observation deck. Built in 1779, it is the oldest capital building in the United States that has been in continuous use. The old Senate Chamber was the site of the meetings of the Continental Congress during 1783–84 and also functioned as the U.S. capitol. It was here that George Washington resigned his position as commander-in-chief of the Continental Army in 1784. Just a few weeks later, the building was the site of the signing of the Treaty of Paris that ended the Revolutionary War. Tours of the building are offered daily.

From the State House visitors can see the colorful streets featuring houses and shops from different periods and in various styles as they wander down to the Riverfront and Market Square, a popular tourist spot. City Dock, which underwent construction in 2007 and 2008, is the only remaining pre-Revolutionary seaport in the country.

Annapolis provides tours of a number of interesting private residences. The Banneker-Douglass Museum, set in the first African Methodist Episcopal Church of Annapolis, dates from 1803. It houses the Douglass Museum of African American Life and History. The Charles Carroll House, with its terraced gardens, is also open for visitors. It was the home of the only Roman Catholic to sign the Declaration of Independence.

Tours of the Chase-Lloyd House, with its large and magnificent facade, allow visitors to view its prized interior woodwork, furniture from three centuries, and a dramatic arched triple window. The brick Hammond-Harwood House, the Georgian masterpiece work of famed architect William Buckland, contains unique wood-carved trim and an authentic period garden. The William Paca House and Garden was the home of a three-term Maryland Governor and signer of the Declaration of Independence. The Georgian mansion, built in the 1760s, has a carved entrance and formal rooms and stands as another fine example of William Buckland's design skills. Another residence, called The Barracks, is a typical dwelling of a colonial tradesman and is furnished to depict the life of a Revolutionary War soldier.

Tours are available of the magnificent grounds of the U.S. Naval Academy, often referred to as "the Yard," where highlights of the history of the American Navy are represented by statues, artifacts, paintings, and ships. Memorial Hall honors Academy graduates who were killed in action. The Lejeune Physical Education Center contains the Athletic Hall of Fame. Among other highlights of a visit to the academy grounds are the U.S. Naval Academy Museum, the crypt of naval hero John Paul Jones, and the 600-year-old Liberty Tree, the site where in 1652 the early settlers made peace with the local Susquehannock Indians.

Arts and Culture

Annapolis is home to excellent museums and performing arts groups. The Historic Annapolis Museum, once called History Quest, reopened in October 2010 with a six-by-six foot model of eighteenth century Annapolis as its spectacular focal point. The museum also features cutouts of famous people who have visited Annapolis, such as Michelle Obama and Mark Twain. The Maryland Federation of Art maintains the Circle Gallery, Maryland's oldest artistic-run gallery, which provides juried exhibitions by regional artists. The Elizabeth Myers Mitchell Art Gallery at St. John's College features art shows, gallery talks, and tours. Also noteworthy is the Annapolis Maritime Museum which preserves over 400 years of maritime history.

Local residents and visitors enjoy performances by the Annapolis Chorale, a 180-member chorus; the Annapolis Opera, which presents one full opera each year plus special events such as vocal competitions and children's operas; and the Annapolis Symphony Orchestra, which features a family series, a classic series, and a pops series, plus an annual gala event, the Symphony Orchestra Ball, and the annual free Summer Series concert. The Ballet Theatre of Maryland, the state's largest professional ballet company, offers a mix of classical and modern ballet. Patrons can take a variety of classes from pottery to puppetry at the Maryland Hall for the Creative Arts. Other local arts groups include the Annapolis Summer Garden Theatre, featuring Broadway and Shakespearean productions under the stars; the Colonial Players of Annapolis theater group; the Talent Machine Company, a children's theater group; and Them Eastport Oyster Boys, who provide a comical musical history of the area.

Festivals and Holidays

September brings the Anne Arundel County Fair and the Maryland Seafood Festival, both of which provide many opportunities for food and fun. October's highlights are the U.S. Sailboat Show and Powerboat Show. Candlelight tours through historic homes and public buildings and the Lights on the Bay holiday displays herald the arrival of the holiday season. December features include the Lights Parade of decorated sailboats and First Night Annapolis, a New Year's Eve celebration of jugglers, dancers, and choirs. January is enlivened by the Annapolis Heritage Antique Show. The City Dock is the site of April's Bay Bridge Boat Show.

June kicks off summer activities with the Annapolis Arts, Crafts, and Wine Festival. Summer activities also include the Star-Spangled Celebration and Fourth of July fireworks. August's Kunta Kinte Heritage Festival at St. John's College commemorates the landing of the ancestors of Alex Haley, the author of *Roots*, the book and television series that tell the story of Haley's family who were slaves in America. Also in August, the Annapolis Rotary Club Crab Feast is the world's largest event of its kind. The Maryland Renaissance Festival takes place in an English village setting with ten stages and a jousting arena and continues through October.

Sports for the Spectator

Annapolis calls itself the Sailing Capital of the World. Sailboat racing is a popular sport and enthusiastic fans can watch water events such as regattas, boat festivals, and races. The Chesapeake Bay Yacht Racing Association provides information on the racing scene. April typically brought the Marlborough Hunt Races in which horses raced around a three-mile track; the event was cancelled in 2013 for the third consecutive year, although fans and organizers continued to work to revive the event. Sports fans can enjoy athletic events at the U.S. Naval Academy including men's football, basketball, and lacrosse, among others, as well as nine women's sports. The Northrop Grumman Military Bowl features two college football teams from NCAA Division I.

Sports for the Participant

Annapolis provides endless opportunities for yachting and water sports. The Annapolis Department of Recreation and Parks maintains more than 30 neighborhood parks on some 200 acres, including street-end or "pocket" parks; they have basketball courts, ball fields, tennis courts, playgrounds, and boating facilities. The department offers a variety of programs including athletic tournaments, arts and crafts, and fun runs. Truxtun Park features the Moyer Community Recreation Center and offers outdoor activities on 70 acres, including a pool, tennis courts, basketball courts, outdoor playing fields, and a multi-purpose facility. The Arundel Olympic Swim Center has a 50-meter pool, wading pool, poolside spa, and diving boards. Residents can also enjoy the county's parks, sports leagues, fitness and self-defense classes, and other activities.

Shopping and Dining

The city is served by Westfield Annapolis Shopping Mall, which features more than 240 specialty stores and restaurants, including anchors Nordstrom, JCPenney, Sears, Macy's, and Lord and Taylor. Other malls include the Annapolis Harbour Center, a 290,000-square-foot retail center. The city's downtown has a variety of exclusive gift and specialty shops, galleries, antique shops, and jewelry stores. The city is also served by the Eastport and Forest Plaza shopping areas.

Annapolis has a fine array of restaurants. Although many of them specialize in seafood, there are also Mexican, French, Mediterranean, Chinese, Italian, Irish, and Japanese dining spots to enjoy. The Treaty of Paris Restaurant offers fine dining in a lovely eighteenth-century dining room. The 49 West Cafe is a European-style cafe, wine bar, and gallery, providing light gourmet fare in a relaxed atmosphere filled with art, music, books, and newspapers.

Visitor Information: Annapolis & Anne Arundel County Conference & Visitors Bureau, 26 West St., Annapolis, MD 21401; telephone (888) 302-2852.

■ Convention Facilities

The Historic Inns of Annapolis's Governor Calvert House provides 51 guest rooms, a ballroom and atrium, and a conference center for small to medium-sized events. Governor's Hall can handle a banquet for 200 people or a reception for 400 people, as well as offering theater-style seating for 250 people. The Loews Annapolis Hotel offers more than 18,000 square feet of flexible meeting space and can accommodate groups of up to 1,000 people. The Annapolis Marriott Waterfront Hotel offers 8,200 square feet of meeting space including ballrooms, boardrooms, and outdoor spaces. The Chesapeake Ballroom has 3,850 square feet of space and can accommodate 500 people for a reception.

Convention Information: Annapolis & Anne Arundel County Conference & Visitors Bureau, 26 West St., Annapolis, MD 21401; telephone (888) 302-2852.

■ Transportation

Approaching the City

Major highways to Annapolis include U.S. Highway 50/301 (Interstate 595) and Maryland Route 2/170/450. U.S. Highway 50/301 passes on the city's west side and continues eastward over the Bay Bridge. Coming from the north, Interstate 97 exits onto Route 50/301 just west of the city. Coming from the South, Maryland Route 2 enters the city in the Parole area, and U.S. Route 301 comes northward and joins U.S. Route 50 west of the city.

The closest major airport to Annapolis is Baltimore-Washington International, about 18 miles northwest of downtown, which has 13 airlines with non-stop flights to dozens of domestic destinations and seven international destinations, including London. Air travelers can proceed from the airport to Annapolis via light rail, passenger trains, limo, van, or taxi service.

The Maryland Transit Administration (MTA) operates several bus routes and light rail to Washington and nearby suburbs. Carolina Trailways operates limited bus service through nearby Baltimore and Glen Burnie, and Greyhound also provides bus service. Amtrak offers rail service to Baltimore's Penn Station, and Union Station in Washington, D.C.

Traveling in the City

Annapolis's main east–west thoroughfare is West Street, also known as Route 50. Radiating northwest and southeast from downtown's Church Circle is Duke of Gloucester Street. College Avenue runs northeast from the circle.

Annapolis Transit has seven bus routes that serving stops throughout the city and the Eastern Shore area. There are also commuter shuttles from downtown to nearby Kent Island and to the Navy-Marine Corps Memorial Stadium. Gasoline-powered trolleys run within the central business district. Local waterways are served by the Annapolis Water Taxi, which can be picked up at the waterfront. Bicycles are a welcomed form of transportation in Annapolis. The city offers several designated bike routes that use a combination of grade-separated trails and city streets. The city announced a master bicycling plan in 2012 intended to earn the League of American Bicyclists' rating of the city as a Bronze-level Bicycle Friendly Community, with the goal of achieving recognition as a Silver-level Community by 2016. Helmet use is encouraged for bicycle riders in the city, and visitors to the U.S. Naval Academy are required to wear helmets there.

■ Communications

Newspapers and Magazines

The Capital is Annapolis's daily paper. The city's local magazine is called *Inside Annapolis.*

Other locally published magazines include *Chesapeake Bay Magazine,* a boating publication; *Chesapeake Family,* a consumer parenting magazine; the *Maryland Register,* which focuses on public administration and law; *Municipal Maryland,* a publication of the Maryland Municipal League aimed at elected and appointed Maryland city officials; the Naval Institute's *Proceedings,* a magazine on naval and maritime news; and alumni magazines of the local colleges.

Television and Radio

The city is served by numerous commercial and public television stations from metropolitan Washington, D.C., and Baltimore; there is also a public station broadcast from Annapolis. Annapolis area radio stations include FM stations W260BM of Hope Christian Church and WLZL of CBS Radio, and AM stations WNAV, an adult contemporary station, and WYRE. The U.S. Naval Academy broadcasts on station WRNV, while Anne Arundel Community College is served by station WACC.

Media Information: Capital Gazette Newspapers, 2000 Capital Drive, Annapolis, MD 21401; telephone (410) 268-5000.

Annapolis Online

Annapolis and Anne Arundel County Chamber of Commerce. Available www.annapolischamber.com

Annapolis and Anne Arundel County Conference & Visitors Bureau. Available www.visitannapolis.org

Anne Arundel County Public Library. Available www.aacpl.net

Anne Arundel Economic Development Corporation. Available www.aaedc.org

Anne Arundel Medical Center. Available www.aahs.org

The Capital newspaper. Available www.
    capitalgazette.com
City of Annapolis. Available www.ci.annapolis.md.us

BIBLIOGRAPHY

Eshelman, Ralph E., *A Travel Guide to the War of 1812
    in the Chesapeake: Eighteen Tours in Maryland,*
Virginia, and the District of Columbia (Baltimore,
    MD: Johns Hopkins University Press, 2011)

Risjord, Norman K., *Builders of Annapolis: Character
    and Enterprise in a Colonial Capital* (Baltimore, MD:
    Maryland Historical Society, 1997)

Baltimore

■ The City in Brief

Founded: 1696 (incorporated 1797)

Head Official: Mayor Stephanie Rawlings-Blake (D) (since 2010)

City Population

    1990: 736,014
    2000: 651,154
    2010: 620,961
    2012 estimate: 621,342
    Percent change, 2000–2010: −4.6%
    U.S. rank in 1990: 12th (State rank: 1st)
    U.S. rank in 2000: 23rd (State rank: 1st)
    U.S. rank in 2010: 21st (State rank: 1st)

Metropolitan Statistical Area Population

    2000: 2,552,994
    2010: 2,710,489
    2012 estimate: 2,753,149
    Percent change, 2000–2010: 6.2%
    U.S. rank in 2000: 19th
    U.S. rank in 2010: 20th

Area: 80.8 square miles

Elevation: 148 feet above sea level

Average Annual Temperatures: 54.6° F

Average Annual Precipitation: 41.94 inches (20.8 inches of snow)

Major Economic Sectors: Manufacturing, including metals, chemicals, and apparel; maritime industries, aerospace, food processing, health care, information technology

Unemployment Rate: 8.6% (2012)

Per Capita Income: $23,457

2012 FBI Crime Index Property: 29,149

Major Colleges and Universities: Johns Hopkins University, Peabody Institute, University of Baltimore, University of Maryland at Baltimore, Morgan State University

Daily Newspaper: *The Baltimore Sun*

■ Introduction

Baltimore's fortuitous location on the northern Chesapeake Bay has been at the heart of its social and economic development. Farther inland than other eastern seaports, the city is convenient to landlocked areas. Water-related industry quickly developed around Baltimore harbor, and when tracks for the nation's first railroad were laid there in 1829, the thriving port city increased both its accessibility to other cities and its attractiveness to immigrants and investors. Through careful city planning and cooperation between public and private investors, Baltimore has entered the ranks of America's "comeback cities" in recent years. Its educational system is on an upswing, with standardized test scores and graduation rates on the rise. It has increased its sustainability through eco-friendly transportation initiatives and green building standards. And its downtown business district has been transformed into a mecca of sparkling new hotels, retail centers, and office buildings. But despite its movement towards high-technology polish, Baltimore has not carelessly tossed aside its traditional working-class image. Many of its urban renewal programs focus on the preservation or renovation of historical buildings and neighborhoods amidst new construction. For example, its wildly popular Oriole Park at Camden Yards offers state-of-the-art amenities in a turn-of-the-century style baseball stadium. Likewise, completion of renovations on the centuries-old Port of Baltimore in 2012 symbolized the city's bridge between old and new, and served as a reminder as to why Baltimore has been dubbed the "charmed city."

Laura Stone/Shutterstock.com

■ Geography and Climate

Located on the Mid-Atlantic coast, Baltimore was built at the mouth of the Patapsco River, which empties directly into the Chesapeake Bay. The city is protected from harsh weather variations year-round by the Chesapeake Bay and Atlantic Ocean to the east and the Appalachian Mountains due west. Freezing temperatures generally do not occur after mid-April or before the end of October, allowing the area approximately 195 frost-free days. Precipitation tends to be equally distributed throughout the year, but the greatest amounts accrue during summer and early fall-the thunderstorm and hurricane seasons, respectively. Since snow is often mixed with rain and sleet due to Baltimore's relatively mild winter temperatures, freezing rain is considered a greater hazard to motorists and pedestrians than the infrequent snowfall that remains on the ground more than several days.

Area: 80.8 square miles

Elevation: 148 feet above sea level

Average Temperatures: 54.6° F

Average Annual Precipitation: 41.94 inches (20.8 inches of snow)

■ History

City Founded on Tobacco-Centered Economy

The geology at the mouth of the Patapsco River determined the location of Baltimore. The area lies on a fall line where hard rocks of the piedmont meet the coastal plains of the tidewater region. A large, natural harbor had formed, and streams coursing from the north and west toward the Patapsco fall line had tremendous velocity. This made them ideal sites for water-driven mills. Additionally attractive to early settlers were the plentiful forests, fertile countryside, and moderate climate that was ideal for agriculture.

In 1632, England's King Charles I gave George Calvert (Lord Baltimore) a vast area in colonial America that became Baltimore County in 1659. During the 1660s the Maryland General Assembly appointed commissioners who granted land patents and development privileges to enterprising colonists. Although the Piscataway and Susquehannock tribes originally lived in neighboring regions, tribal competition and the onslaught of colonial diseases dissipated all but a few hundred of the Native Americans in Maryland by 1700.

The sandy plains bordering the Chesapeake Bay were ideal for growing tobacco, and a tobacco-based economy quickly developed in pre-Revolutionary Maryland. An area of 550 acres, formerly known as "Cole's Harbor," was sold to Baltimore landowners Daniel and Charles Carroll in 1696; they sold a parcel of this land in one-acre lots for development. These lots became Baltimore Town, which grew quickly in both size and trade. By 1742 regular tobacco shipments were leaving Baltimore harbor for Europe.

Radical Politics Gain Popularity

Productive mills had also sprung up along the northwestern tributaries of the Patapsco; the market for locally-milled flour and grain was primarily directed toward the British slave and sugar colonies in the West Indies. This trade was cut off at the outset of the American Revolution, a loss that cost Baltimore. The loss was partly mitigated when Congress authorized private citizens to arm and equip their own vessels for war in 1776; privateering became a growth industry in Baltimore, since the city had become an important center for shipbuilding. Anti-British activities in the city during this era earned Baltimore a reputation for radical politicking that lasted through the nineteenth century. Baltimore was the meeting place of the Continental Congress after the British occupied Philadelphia in 1777.

City Prospers During Reconstruction

After the Revolutionary War, Baltimore, incorporated in 1797, resumed its commercial success by exporting grain, particularly to South America. A slump in maritime trade prompted the building of America's first public railroad in Baltimore in 1828, thus linking the city to other parts of the country and expanding commercial possibilities. During the Civil War, Maryland remained Unionist but Baltimore was split. Trade was cut off with the South and badly hurt with the North, but Baltimore managed to profit as a military depot. The city recovered rapidly from the physical and economic damages of the war, embarking during the reconstruction era on the period of its greatest prosperity.

Renewal Follows Destruction

In 1904 Baltimore was struck by a fire that had started in a cotton warehouse and soon spread to destroy more than 2,000 buildings. This calamity initiated improvements in the streets and the harbor and the construction of a sewer system that was considered one of the most modern of its time. The city again prospered during World War I, its economy remained relatively untouched by the 1930s Depression, and Baltimore continued to flourish as a military supply center during World War II.

Baltimore's urban renewal began in 1947, when inner city decay was so extensive that more than 45,000 homes were considered substandard. A rigorous construction and rehabilitation program reduced this number to 25,000 by 1954. In 1955 public and private cooperation resulted in

the formation of the Greater Baltimore Committee, a group of influential businessmen who worked with municipal agencies to develop civic programs. Extensive neighborhood revitalization and development were undertaken in the 1970s and 1980s. Projects included the construction of shops and restaurants in Harbor Place, the Maryland Science Center, the National Aquarium, the American Visionary Art Museum and the construction of a rapid transit line to the suburbs. Waterfront development carried on in the 1990s and into the new millennium, with many old neighborhoods experiencing a growth in popularity.

The 1990s were also a time of sharp population declines. Like many of the older, urban areas of the northeast, Baltimore faced an exodus to the suburbs and lost 11.5 percent of its population. However, by the 2000s and into the 2010s, Baltimore's urban population began to return to the city. Hand in hand, businesses have relocated to Baltimore's downtown and their employees have moved in along with them. Baltimore's proximity to U.S. defense institutions in and around Washington, D.C., has made it a growing hub for cybersecurity firms seeking billion-dollar government contracts.

Historical Information: Maryland Historical Society, 201 West Monument St., Baltimore, MD 21201; telephone (410) 685-3750. Jewish Museum of Maryland, 15 Lloyd Street, Baltimore, MD 21202; telephone (410) 732-6400; email info@jewishmuseummd.org.

■ Population Profile

Metropolitan Statistical Area Population

2000: 2,552,994
2010: 2,710,489
2012 estimate: 2,753,149
Percent change, 2000–2010: 6.2%
U.S. rank in 2000: 19th
U.S. rank in 2010: 20th

City Residents

1990: 736,014
2000: 651,154
2010: 620,961
2012 estimate: 621,342
Percent change, 2000–2010: −4.6%
U.S. rank in 1990: 12th (State rank: 1st)
U.S. rank in 2000: 23rd (State rank: 1st)
U.S. rank in 2010: 21st (State rank: 1st)

Density: 7,671.5 people per square mile

Racial and ethnic characteristics

White: 187,742
Black or African American: 394,998
American Indian and Alaskan Native: 1,862
Asian: 15,757

Native Hawaiian and Other Pacific Islander: 46
Hispanic or Latino (may be of any race): 27,571
Other: 20,937

Percent of residents born in state: 68.4%

Age characteristics

Population under 5 years old: 42,221
Population 5 to 9 years old: 37,939
Population 10 to 14 years old: 33,315
Population 15 to 19 years old: 39,519
Population 20 to 24 years old: 54,750
Population 25 to 34 years old: 109,063
Population 35 to 44 years old: 73,869
Population 45 to 54 years old: 84,051
Population 55 to 59 years old: 38,039
Population 60 to 64 years old: 34,654
Population 65 to 74 years old: 40,597
Population 75 to 84 years old: 23,431
Population 85 years and over: 9,894
Median age: 34.2

Births (2010–11 Metropolitan Area)

Total number: 33,729

Deaths (2010–11 Metropolitan Area)

Total number: 22,788

Money income (2012)

Per capita income: $23,457
Median household income: $39,788
Total households: 240,575

Number of households with income of ...

less than $10,000: 33,912
$10,000 to $14,999: 19,068
$15,000 to $24,999: 30,317
$25,000 to $34,999: 26,202
$35,000 to $49,999: 32,433
$50,000 to $74,999: 41,426
$75,000 to $99,999: 21,582
$100,000 to $149,999: 21,298
$150,000 to $199,999: 7,716
$200,000 or more: 6,621

Percent of families below poverty level: 25.2%

FBI Crime Index Property: 29,149

FBI Crime Index Violent: 8,789

■ Municipal Government

Baltimore is the only city in the state of Maryland not located within a county. It is governed by a mayor and a fifteen-member city council who are elected to four-year terms.

Head Official: Mayor Stephanie Rawlings-Blake (D) (since 2010)

Total Number of City Employees: 15,124 (2012)

City Information: City Hall, 100 N. Holliday St., Baltimore, MD 21202; telephone (410)396-3835; fax (410)576-9425

■ Economy

Major Industries and Commercial Activity

Baltimore's heritage as a strategically located East Coast port is drawn upon by its developers today. The city's revived downtown and central location among major East Coast cities has made it increasingly attractive to new or expanding businesses. The blue-collar tradition exemplified by Bethlehem Steel's ranking as top employer in the 1980s has been replaced by jobs in the service sector in fields such as law, finance, medicine, hospitality, entertainment, maritime commerce and health, and a workforce that has grown to include one of the highest concentrations of residents with advanced degrees in the nation. Baltimore is a major shipping and receiving center for coal, grain, iron, steel, and copper. Baltimore also remains a center for shipbuilding.

Into the 2010s, the importance of cybersecurity grew the information technology industry in Baltimore. More than 13,000 cybersecurity jobs were available in Baltimore as of 2013, with that number expected to increase, mostly as a result of demand from government entities. The total value of government contracts for information security jobs was expected to top $14 billion by 2017.

Baltimore is an established center of medicine and biosciences. It is a national headquarters for advanced medical treatment and research with two pioneering teaching hospitals, Johns Hopkins Hospital and the University of Maryland Medical Center. As of 2013, Johns Hopkins had been ranked the top hospital in the United States in 22 of the past 23 years. (It placed second in 2012–13). The Baltimore area is the research center for the mapping of the human genome and its resulting commercial applications.

Year after year, Greater Baltimore ranks among the nation's top 20 markets in key retail categories. Tourism, spurred on by the opening or expansion of downtown attractions, has boosted construction, and the success of the Inner Harbor renovation has lured city residents back downtown. Tourism in Baltimore brings increased revenues each year, with increased hotel occupancy rates, convention-related spending, overall air travel to the city, increased tax revenues and growth in the number of leisure and hospitality jobs. In 2011, Baltimore hosted 22.3 million visitors from across the United States that spent $4.75 billion for both business and pleasure.

Items and goods produced: steel pipe; plate, sheet, and tin mill products; ships and ship-related products; aerospace equipment; sugar and processed foods; copper and oil refining; chemicals; clothing

Incentive Programs-New and Existing Companies

Local programs: The Economic Alliance of Greater Baltimore helps businesses to access the broad range of competitive incentives offered by the State of Maryland and local jurisdictions. The Baltimore Development Corporation provides several incentives. A Micro Revolving Loan Fund supports mall businesses with financing to meet operation needs and for capital purchases ranging from furniture to machinery and equipment. A Brownfield Tax Credit offers a five-year tax credit for redevelopment of a vacant or underutilized industrial or commercial property, especially those properties that are or appear to be environmentally contaminated. Façade improvements are support with grants from the Baltimore Development Corporation as well. Payment in Lieu of Taxes (PILOTs) are available through the city, as is Tax Increment Financing (TIFs).

State programs: The Maryland Industrial Development Financing Authority (MIDFA) provides financing assistance for capital assets and working capital to small- and mid-sized businesses that demonstrate a significant economic impact. This assistance includes programs that insure loans made by financial institutions up to 80 percent and not exceeding $2.5 million; taxable bond financing; tax-exempt bond financing for non-profit organizations and manufacturing facilities; and linked deposits that provide loans below market rates to qualified small businesses in rural areas with high unemployment rates. The Maryland Small Business Development Financing Authority (MSBDFA) provides financing for small businesses through a variety of programs, including a contract financing program, an equity participation investment program, a long-term guaranty program, and a surety bonding program.

Major incentive programs include Job Creation Tax Credits amounting to the lesser of $1,000 or 2.5 percent of annual wages for each qualifying permanent job; Cybersecurity Investment tax credits, to attract start-up companies in the area; Enterprise Zone credits, One Maryland tax credits for business location in distressed counties; Research and Development tax credits to refund research expenditures; Biotechnology tax credits; Brownfields tax credits; BRAC Zones credits for infrastructure improvements; Cellulosic Ethanol credits to refund research and development expenditures; and Security Clearance credits to refund expenses associated with meeting security requirements of defense projects.

The Maryland Economic Development Assistance Authority and Fund provides direct loans to certain industries in certain regions. The Maryland Venture Fund is a nationally recognized model for seed and early-stage investing. Target industries include technology companies involved in software, communications, cybersecurity, and life science ventures. Funds for other venture firms are distributed through InvestMaryland. A number of loan programs for agricultural businesses are available, as are Community Development Block Grants.

Job training and recruitment programs:

Maryland's Credit Connections program is a specialized training program for commercial bankers intended to increase lending in the state, grow credit ratings of state companies, and lessen risk assumed by lenders. The program was launched in 2010 in association with the Federal Reserve Bank of Richmond. The state's Partnership for Workforce Quality is a business development grant program to improve the competitiveness of small and mid-sized manufacturing and technology companies. It provides matching grants for training of existing employees. Workforce Investment Boards located throughout the state offer training funds.

Development Projects

By 2013, more than $1 billion had been spent on the Westside Initiative, which incorporates the redevelopment of 100 square blocks and links the finance district to the University of Maryland's graduate and medical schools. The public-private partnership, first approved in 1999, included an array of completed, ongoing, and planned projects. An $80 million mixed-use facility undertaken by Bank of America and Centerpoint LLC included 400 apartments, 30,000 square feet of street-level retail space, and a 250-seat live performance theater completed its final phase in 2012. Other projects included Zenith Apartments, Hampton Inn at Camden Yards, Baltimore Hilton Convention Center Hotel, Hippodrome Theatre, Bromo Seltzer Art Tower, Lexington Market, and many more.

The East Baltimore Development Project was founded in 2003 to relocate families from some of the city's most blighted neighborhoods. By 2013, the program had relocated 584 families and cleared 31 acres of dilapidated residential buildings. It also opened a Science and Technology Park at Johns Hopkins for biotechnology tenants in 2008, created 220 residential units in 2009, and opened a new elementary school in the area that same year. The project is non-profit public-private partnership that hinges on leveraging Johns Hopkins as an economic driver. The total project included 2,100 units of mixed-income homeownership, 1.7 million square feet of life sciences research and office space, and a seven-acre community learning campus that included an early childhood center in addition to the aforementioned school. There has been some criticism of the $1.8 billion, 88-acre project and its long-term viability, which has been staunchly refuted by project managers.

In 2012 the Port of Baltimore and Ports America Chesapeake completed a $1.3 billion project to allow the port to handle super-Panamax ships, the world's largest cargo vessels. This offered the ports a competitive advantage against most ports along the U.S. Atlantic coast.

Exelon Corporation was building a new headquarters at Harbor Point in Baltimore as of 2013, with construction expected to complete in 2015. The final facility was expected to contain 550,000 square feet of office space and 50,000 square feet of retail. The projected cost was $200 million. Various hotel, retail, and residential projects under construction in downtown Baltimore as of 2013 totaled $590 million. An additional $1.44 billion had been pledged to future projects.

Economic Development Information: Economic Alliance of Greater Baltimore, 1 East Pratt Street, Suite 200, Baltimore, MD 21202; telephone (410) 468-0100 or (888) 298-4322, fax (410)468-3383. Baltimore Development Corporation, 36 South Charles Street, Baltimore, MD 21201-3015; telephone (410) 837-9305; fax (410) 837-6363.

Commercial Shipping

Baltimore-Washington International Airport is a major cargo carrier for the mid-Atlantic region. CSX and Norfolk Southern railroad systems service industry throughout the Baltimore area. Several major interstate highways run through Baltimore; Interstate 95 links Baltimore with major cities from New England to Florida, and Interstate 70 connects it with the Midwest. More than 100 trucking lines also accommodate the Baltimore area.

The most significant mover of goods in the area is the Port of Baltimore, one of the largest and busiest deepwater ports in the nation. It completed a more than $1 billion expansion in 2012 to handle the world's largest cargo ships. One hundred fifty miles closer to key Midwestern markets than any other Atlantic Coast port, the Port of Baltimore has lower transportation costs between its marine terminals and inland points of cargo origin or destination. Baltimore also benefits by having two access routes to its port: from the north through the Chesapeake & Delaware Canal, and from the south up the Chesapeake Bay.

Labor Force and Employment Outlook

Baltimore was once the second largest point of entry for immigrants into the United States. Just as the city's demographic profile has changed over the years, so have its primary employment opportunities. Jobs in manufacturing, long in decline along with most U.S. cities, have been replaced by opportunities in health care, education, information technology, and financial services. Many of Baltimore's residents have moved back into the downtown area—population increased 14 percent between 2000 and 2013—meaning that many companies have also centered their operations downtown. An estimated 77 percent of residents had graduated from high school, with just over one quarter holding a bachelor's degree or higher.

The following is a summary of data regarding the 2012 Baltimore labor force:

Size of civilian labor force: 311,906

Number of workers employed in . . .

    agriculture and mining: 323
    construction: 13,798
    manufacturing: 13,861
    wholesale trade: 4,611
    retail trade: 24,304
    transportation: 13,620
    information systems: 5,275
    finance: 14,873
    professional administration: 30,111
    education and social services: 80,936
    arts and leisure: 24,072
    other: 13,098
    public administration: 24,976

Average hourly earnings of production workers: $17.61

Unemployment rate: 8.6% (2012)

Employers

Largest employers (2012)	*Number of employees*
State of Baltimore	38,349
City of Baltimore and Schools	27,029
Johns Hopkins University	22,000
Johns Hopkins Hospital and Health System	18,090
Federal Government	10,088
University of Maryland Medical System	9,423
University System of Maryland	8,900
MedStar Health	6,010
LifeBridge Health	5,213
Mercy Health Services	3,738
Constellation Energy/BGE	3,116
St. Agnes HealthCare	2,833
Kennedy Krieger Institute	2,449

Cost of Living

When it comes to buying groceries, paying a mortgage or hopping on a subway, Baltimore is one of the most affordable of all East Coast cities. Still, its cost of living was more than 13 percent above the national average in 2013.

The following is a summary of data regarding several key cost of living factors in the area.

2013 ACCRA Average House Price: $456,223

2013 ACCRA Cost of Living Index: 116

State income tax rate: 2.0% to 6.25%

State sales tax rate: 6.0%

Local income tax rate: 3.05%

Local sales tax rate: None

Property tax rate: $2.248 per $100.00 assessed value (2013)

Economic Information: Economic Alliance of Greater Baltimore, 1 East Pratt Street, Suite 200, Baltimore, MD 21202; telephone (410) 468-0100 or (888) 298-4322, fax (410)468-3383.

■ Education and Research

Elementary and Secondary Schools

Baltimore City Public Schools serve the largest number of low-income and special-needs students in the state of Maryland. As of 2013–14 some 84 percent of students qualified as low income. Historically, Baltimore's public schools have struggled to create an effective educational environment for its children in the face of disastrous financial problems. The system's Master Plan, updated for each new school year, is part of a city-state partnership aimed at reforming the troubled system by focusing on student assessment, program evaluation, institutional research, and shared planning and accountability.

Significant progress has been made. In 2013 the Maryland Model for School Readiness Report noted that 77.6 percent of kindergartners were "fully ready," a ninth consecutive annual increase in the measure. Between 2004 and 2013, reading and math performance at the middle school level have both risen by more than 20 percentage point, up to 67.9 percent and 58.9 percent respectively. At the high school level, 85.9 percent of students who entered high school in 2008–09 had either graduated or were still working toward their degree, reflecting a decrease in the dropout rate. City schools' 2013–14 plan included implementation of the national Common Core State Standards, an expansion of teacher evaluation, and a 21st Century Buildings Plan aimed at improving and modernizing facilities. Among the cities schools are 31 charter schools.

Some 200 private and parochial schools also operate in the Baltimore area.

The following is a summary of data regarding the Baltimore City Public Schools.

Total enrollment: 83,800

Number of facilities
　total: 195
　elementary schools: 131
　junior high schools: 26
　high schools: 31
　other: 7

Student/teacher ratio: 14.6:1

Teacher salaries
　average (statewide): $65,113

Funding per pupil: $15,483

Public Schools Information: Baltimore City Public School System, 200 East North Avenue, Baltimore, MD 21202; telephone (443) 984-2000.

Colleges and Universities

Of the approximately 30 colleges and universities located in the Baltimore metropolitan area, nearly half are within city limits. Towson University, the oldest four-year college in Maryland and the largest in the Baltimore area, offers bachelor's, master's, and doctoral degrees in more than 100 fields. Considered one of Baltimore's outstanding assets, Johns Hopkins University boasts a world-renowned medical school and an affiliation with a prestigious music conservatory, the Peabody Institute. In 2006, the university also began offering free tuition to qualified Baltimore Public City School graduates through its Baltimore Scholars Program. Loyola College offers a joint program in medical technology with Baltimore's Mercy Medical Center. Its Sellinger School of Business and Management has been named among *Princeton Review's* top business schools for five consecutive years, from 2010 through 2014. The University of Baltimore, a state-supported institution, awards upper-division, graduate, and law degrees. One of five campus units of the University of Maryland, the University of Maryland at Baltimore offers professional programs in health and medical fields, social work, and law, as well as undergraduate degrees in a variety of fields. At Morgan State University students can earn master's degrees in 30 fields and doctoral degrees in 14. Coppin State University benefits from a cooperative program with local industries and offers both bachelor's and master's degree programs.

The Baltimore area's other large academic institutions include University of Maryland, Baltimore County, the U.S. Naval Academy, the Maryland Center for Career and Technology Education Studies, the Ner Israel Rabbinical College, Notre Dame of Maryland University, the Maryland Institute College of Art, Anne Arundel Community College in Arnold, Harford Community College in Bel Air, McDaniel College in Westminster, Howard Community College, and Carroll Community College.

Libraries and Research Centers

Baltimore's public library system, The Enoch Pratt Free Library, is one of the oldest free public library systems in the United States, with 21 branches, a bookmobile, and a Central Library that also serves as the state Library Resource Center. The Central Library includes 1.9 million books, pamphlets, and tapes; 1.05 million U.S. government documents; 600,000 magazines, newspapers, and microform books; 11,000 periodicals; and more than 21,000 DVDs and videos, among other materials. The library also offers special collections which include African American materials, the works of Baltimore authors H. L. Mencken and Edgar Allan Poe, and the Maryland Department, which holds extensive books, periodicals, and other documents on all aspects of life in the state of Maryland and its cities.

Ten nationally-recognized research universities are also located in Greater Baltimore, along with John Hopkins University, which is the largest recipient of research-funding of any university in the United States, receiving some $1.88 billion in 2012. Research activities at centers affiliated with Johns Hopkins University focus on such subject areas as biophysics, Alzheimer's Disease, STDs, inherited diseases and other maladies, alternatives to animal testing, communications, and mass spectrometry. The University of Maryland at Baltimore also supports medical research work through its Biotechnology Institute. The Space Telescope Science Institute, the principal scientific element of the NASA Hubble Space Telescope Project, is based in Baltimore.

Public Library Information: Enoch Pratt Free Library, 400 Cathedral St., Baltimore, MD 21201; telephone (410) 396-5430.

■ Health Care

At least thirty accredited hospitals offering a wide range of general and specialized services and more than 70,000 healthcare professionals are located within the Baltimore city limits. Cardiac rehabilitation units, hospice programs, extensive psychiatric and drug rehabilitation programs, and neonatal intensive care are among the special services available in various Baltimore hospitals. In addition to the many fine teaching hospitals throughout the city, Baltimore's institutions include two world-class medical

schools: the Johns Hopkins University School of Medicine and the University of Maryland School of Medicine.

Johns Hopkins Hospital, affiliated with the university, has been ranked first in the nation by *U.S. News & World Report* for 22 of 23 years as of 2013. (It ranked second in 2012.) It is one of the most advanced and prestigious hospitals in the world. It is ranked first by *U.S. News & World Report* in five medical specialties: Ear, Nose & Throat; Geriatrics; Neurology and Neurosurgery; Urology; and Rheumatology; it is ranked among the top six in 10 other categories. The Sidney Kimmel Comprehensive Cancer Center at Johns Hopkins provides the most advanced cancer care in the country. The Johns Hopkins Bayview Medical Center's Burn Center is a recognized program for the treatment of burn injuries. Another of Baltimore's teaching hospitals, the University of Maryland Medical System, boasts a shock trauma center that was one of the first of its kind, and its University of Maryland Medical Center was ranked nationally in five different specialty programs by *U.S. News & World Report* in 2013. Sinai Hospital of Baltimore is one of the city's largest and most completely equipped hospitals, with 456 beds. Another teaching facility, Union Memorial Hospital, is known for its work in sports medicine and was ranked nationally by *U.S. News & World Report* in 2013 for its care in orthopedics; Maryland General Hospital is also a teaching hospital. Other Baltimore hospitals are Bon Secours Hospital serving West Baltimore, and Mercy Medical Center.

Baltimore is also home to Health Care for the Homeless (HCH), which celebrated its 25th anniversary in 2010 with the opening of a new facility. HCH provides health care, advocacy, and education to adults and children experiencing homelessness.

■ Recreation

Sightseeing

With its extensively developed waterfront, overhead skywalks, and numerous plazas and promenades, downtown Baltimore is ideally geared to the pedestrian tourist. Many visitors begin their tour of the city at Baltimore's Inner Harbor, easily the city's most picturesque area. A one-half-mile brick promenade along the water enables visitors to walk to the many attractions at water's edge.

The Maryland Science Center, set directly on the water, is especially popular with children. Three block-length floors of science exhibits, hands-on displays, and live science demonstrations are featured. The Davis Planetarium boasts 350 projectors and presents multimedia and topical shows. Nearby is one of the world's tallest five-sided buildings, the thirty-two story World Trade Center, designed by I. M. Pei. The "Top of the World" observation deck on the building's 27th floor offers a panoramic view of the harbor.

One of the most spectacular sights at the Inner Harbor is the seven-level National Aquarium, whose unique glass pyramid roofs create dramatic reflections in the water. It is the city's top attraction, boasting over 1.3 million visitors a year as of 2012, and is often rated one of the country's best family attractions. More than 17,000 specimens from more than 750 species are housed in the exhibits, and the Aquarium is crowned by a 64-foot-high model of an Amazon rain forest that looks out over the harbor.

Port Discovery is Baltimore's children's museum and offers interactive exhibits and features a three-story urban tree house.

Visitors to the Inner Harbor may take advantage of the Baltimore Water Taxi, which from mid-April to mid-October shuttles between major points of interest around the harbor. For longer excursions, the Inner Harbor Spirit and the renovated Spirit of Baltimore provide a variety of cruises and sightseeing tours of Baltimore as well.

Among Baltimore's many historical landmarks is the National Park at Fort McHenry, the unusual star-shaped fort that was the site of Baltimore's victory over the British bombardment during the War of 1812, and the inspiration for the U.S. national anthem. The fort's battlements have been carefully preserved. The Flag House and Star-Spangled Banner Museum, built in 1793, preserves the site where Mary Pickersgill sewed the 30-inch by 42-inch flag that flew at Fort McHenry during the War of 1812. A collection of early American art, Federal period furniture, and a unique map of the United States composed of stones from each state are presented.

Homes of several famous Baltimore residents are open to the public. The Babe Ruth Birthplace and Museum offers exhibits commemorating baseball legend Babe Ruth and Maryland baseball history, with numerous photos and memorabilia of Baltimore's major-league teams, the Orioles. The childhood home of Babe Ruth is preserved as it was at the time of his birth in 1895. Continuing the baseball theme is Sports Legends at Camden Yards, which opened to the public in 2005 after a major renovation. The facility houses archives, classrooms, a baseball theater, a baseball-themed restaurant, and a main corridor that resembles a 1920s railroad car. The Benjamin Banneker Historical Park and Museum on Banneker's 142-acre home site commemorates this son of a freed slave and grandson of an African prince.

Edgar Allan Poe lived and wrote in Baltimore from 1832 to 1835. His home on North Amity Street is open to the public. Writer and journalist H. L. Mencken, locally known as the "Sage of Baltimore," lived in Baltimore for more than 68 years until his death in 1956. His nineteenth-century row house overlooking scenic Union Square has been carefully restored with its original furniture and much of Mencken's personal memorabilia. The H. L. Mencken House is part of a seven-museum and park complex collectively known as Baltimore City Life Museums. Other historical buildings around Baltimore include the Baltimore City Hall, Shot Tower, Washington Monument, and the George Peabody Library of Johns Hopkins University.

Baltimore has many public gardens and parks. The largest is Druid Hill Park, at 745 acres one of the country's largest natural city parks. One hundred fifty acres are devoted to the popular Baltimore Zoo, which features a large captive colony of African black-footed penguins. Also in Druid Hill Park is the Conservatory, a remarkable glass pavilion similar in construction to the Victorian-era "Crystal Palace" built in 1888. Known as "The Palm House," the building contains an extensive collection of tropical and desert plants. Other gardens include Cylburn Arboretum, on the grounds of Cylburn Mansion, and Sherwood Gardens, located in the beautifully-landscaped neighborhood of Guildford.

Arts and Culture

Those seeking fine music, theater, and dance performances will not be disappointed in Baltimore, which has seen a renewal of interest in the arts, including new construction or major renovation of existing performing centers. The acoustically impressive Joseph Meyerhoff Symphony Hall is home to the Baltimore Symphony Orchestra. In addition to its classical programs, which include a number of celebrity performers each year, the orchestra presents a Pops series. Summer concert series are held at the Pier Six Pavilion, a unique fabric-covered structure where jazz, country, and classical music, and musical comedy programs are presented by top-name performers. The Eubie Blake National Jazz Institute and Cultural Center, dedicated to the famous Baltimore-born pianist, fosters the development and sponsors performances of community artists. Classes are held at the center in music, dance, and drama. The Creative Alliance at the Patterson showcases a variety of entertainment in a 1930s movie theatre.

Baltimore theater-goers will find dramatic productions to suit every taste. Center Stage produces seven classic and modern plays each year and is among the nation's top regional theaters. Cockpit in Court Summer Theatre offers musicals, comedies, dramas and a children's program each summer on the Community College of Baltimore County Essex campus. The Arena Players is one of the foremost black theater companies on the East Coast, and the Theatre Project is known internationally for its experimental music, drama, and dance.

Baltimore's museums and galleries offer a variety of art and artifacts for viewing. The lifetime collections of Baltimore residents William and Henry Walters are gathered at the Walters Art Museum. Its treasures include more than 30,000 objects from 5,500 years of history-from pre-Dynastic Egypt to twentieth-century Art Nouveau. Particularly resplendent collections are held in ivories, jewelry, enamels, bronzes, illuminated manuscripts and rare books. Baltimore's other major art museum is the Baltimore Museum of Art, designed by John Russell Pope, architect of Washington's National Gallery. The museum's prize holding is the "Cone Collection," a large and valuable collection of paintings and sculpture by such European Post-Impressionist masters as Matisse, Cezanne, Picasso, and Van Gogh. The museum also has important collections of eighteenth- and nineteenth-century American paintings, sculpture, and furniture, art from Africa and Oceania, and the works of Andy Warhol. One of Baltimore's newest museums, the American Visionary Art Museum, combines two historic buildings with modern museum architecture. Said to be the only such institution in the country, the museum was officially designated by the U.S. Congress as "the national museum, education and repository center, the best in self-taught, outsider or visionary artistry." The Contemporary Museum is part of an emerging "arts row" on Centre Street; it suspended operations in 2012 but reopened in 2013.

In the historical former residence of nineteenth-century Baltimore philanthropist Enoch Pratt is the Maryland Historical Society. The Society's Museum and Library of Maryland History are of particular interest to researchers; of general interest are collections of portraits by famous American artists, valuable nineteenth-century silver, furniture from 1720 to 1950, and Francis Scott Key's original manuscript of "The Star-Spangled Banner." Near the heart of industrial South Baltimore, the Baltimore Museum of Industry, housed in the former Platt Oyster Cannery, features recreations of turn-of-the-century machinery, printing, and metalworking workshops, as well as a garment loft.

The B&O Railroad Museum is designed around Mount Clare Station, which was built in 1830 for the Baltimore & Ohio Railroad as the nation's first passenger and freight station. The original 1884 roundhouse, tracks, and turntable have been preserved. Among the more than 130 railroad cars on display here, both originals and replicas, is "Tom Thumb," the first steam locomotive. The Museum has renovated the roundhouse and added exhibits, train rides, visitor facilities, and a museum store. The Baltimore Public Works Museum preserved the history of the city's public works with a collection of more than 2,000 items including early wooden water pipes, water meters, numerous photographs, and an early twentieth-century water-pumping truck. It closed in 2010 due to city budget restraints; the possibility of reopening with private support remained in consideration as of 2013.

The National Great Blacks in Wax Museum is the first of its kind and represents black history and heritage through more than 100 historical wax figures as well as paintings, sculpture, and carvings. The Reginald F. Lewis Museum of Maryland African American History and Culture, located at Inner Harbor, opened to the public in June 2005. Its focus is on the lives, history and culture of African Americans in Maryland. It partnered with the State Board of Education, which adopted a curriculum linked to the museum's programs. The Frederick Douglass–Isaac Myers Maritime Park on the Fells Point Riverfront opened in June 2006. The park is sponsored by the Living Classrooms Foundation and features exhibits and monuments dedicated to the two entrepreneurs, a shipbuilding workshop, a working marine railway, outdoor amphitheater, dockage for historic ships, and other multicultural displays.

Festivals and Holidays

Most of Baltimore's festivals begin in late spring and continue on weekends throughout the fall. The colorful Maryland International Kite Exposition, held on the last Saturday in April, is a competition with homemade kites, judged for their beauty, flight performance, and design. April also rings in Baltimore Green Week, which is celebrated with a week's worth of educational events, workshops, and lectures focused on the environment. In May the highly acclaimed Maryland Film Festival is held, presenting numerous entries in such categories as documentaries, movies by women or children, and animation.

The African American Festival is held for three days in July at M&T Bank Stadium. Artscape is a lively outdoor festival also held in July, showcasing local artistic and musical talent. Baltimore's famous and very popular Showcase of Nations—a series of weekly ethnic festivals held from June through September—celebrates the heritage of many cultures through music, dance, crafts, and international cuisine.

The end of August and beginning of September is the time of the Maryland State Fair, held at the Fairgrounds in nearby Timonium. More than a half million people visit the fair each year. The week-long state fair features livestock, produce, and equestrian competition from Maryland 4-H groups, as well as an amusement midway and horse racing. September also brings the Baltimore Book Festival, a celebration of the literary arts.

In October the Fells Point Fun Festival celebrates the historical waterfront neighborhood with two days of arts and crafts, entertainment, maritime exhibits, neighborhood tours, and music ranging from jazz and blues to Polish polkas. December's Parade of Lighted Boats adds to the festive season, and Big Night Baltimore New Year's Eve Extravaganza offerings include parties at the convention center, ice skating demonstrations, live music, and fireworks at the harbor.

Sports for the Spectator

The National Football League's Baltimore Ravens, named in honor of the Edgar Allan Poe poem, came to the city in 1996 after relocating from Cleveland. The team now plays in the state-of-the-art M&T Bank Stadium and has won two Super Bowl championships, in 2001 and 2013.

Baseball fans come out to watch the American League Baltimore Orioles at Oriole Park at Camden Yards. Architects have praised its distinctive turn-of-the-century style, which is in keeping with its old urban neighborhood. The 48,000-seat stadium incorporates a landmark B&O Railroad warehouse that has been converted to office space for the ball club and the Maryland Stadium Authority.

Another popular warm-weather sport is lacrosse, played by the perennial national contender Johns Hopkins University Blue Jays at Homewood Field; the Lacrosse Museum and National Hall of Fame is located adjacent to Homewood Field. College football and basketball are represented by the University of Maryland Terrapins, Towson University Tigers, Johns Hopkins Blue Jays, and the Naval Academy Midshipmen at nearby stadiums.

Thoroughbred racing, always popular with Maryland horse breeders and followers, can be seen at Pimlico Racecourse, Maryland's oldest racetrack. The famous Preakness Stakes, second jewel in the Triple Crown, is run there in May. In October, on Maryland Million Day, thoroughbreds race at Pimlico Racecourse, and purses total more than $1 million. Maryland's most famous steeplechase is the annual Maryland Hunt Cup, held in Baltimore County.

Baltimore's Major Indoor Soccer League team, the Baltimore Blast, play at the Baltimore Arena; the team's regular season schedule runs from November to March.

Sports for the Participant

Baltimore's proximity to the Chesapeake Bay makes all sorts of water-related activities favorite pastimes of many area residents. Sail- and powerboat regattas are held at the Inner Harbor, nearby Annapolis, and Havre de Grace throughout the summer months. Numerous marinas and yacht clubs dot the bay and river inlets near Baltimore, and local pleasure boats can be seen all along the Chesapeake on a clear day. Fishing, crabbing, and clamdigging are also very popular, even within city limits.

Numerous public and private golf clubs dot the Baltimore area. Art Links Baltimore is a miniature course designed by regional artists and architects. Art Links' 18 holes celebrate the culture of the Baltimore region, incorporating tracks of the B&O Railroad or depicting a crab feast, for example. Tennis courts are available in many of the city's parks, as are bike paths and swimming pools.

Shopping and Dining

Most of the malls in the Baltimore area are located in Baltimore and Anne Arundel counties, close to the city, but many specialized shopping centers can be found within city limits. The twin pavilions of Harborplace and The Gallery offer shops and restaurants at the water's edge. Lexington Market features more than 140 merchants selling fresh seafood, produce, and international delights. Lexington Market is part of Market Center, a bustling and colorful collection of more than 400 diverse shops. One of

the oldest and most luxurious shopping districts in Baltimore is the Charles Street Corridor, where shoppers can find numerous art galleries, jewelers, stationers, furriers, and specialty boutiques; new stores are interspersed with enduring older ones. In the Canton neighborhood of Baltimore, the Shops at Canton Crossing, which opened in 2013, offered shoppers more than 30 stores across the sprawling $105 million development.

As with many other aspects of Baltimore living, restaurant dining is greatly influenced by the city's proximity to the Chesapeake Bay. A wide range of Baltimore restaurants specialize in preparation of crabs, oysters, clams, mussels, and fish from the Bay. Many Baltimore restaurants also reflect the port city's rich ethnic heritage, and diverse international cuisines can be enjoyed throughout the downtown area.

Visitor Information: Baltimore Area Visitors Center, 401 Light Street, Baltimore, MD 21202; telephone (877) 255-8466. Baltimore Area Convention and Visitors Association, 100 Light Street, 12th Floor, Baltimore, MD 21202; telephone (410) 659-7300 or (877) 255-8466; fax (410) 727-2308.

■ Convention Facilities

With its mid-Atlantic coast location and easy access by air, rail, or automobile, Baltimore has long been a strategic choice for convention-holders. The redevelopment of the city's downtown Inner Harbor area has made Baltimore even more attractive to conventioneers, who enjoy the many fine restaurants, retail centers, and cultural attractions on or near the water.

Baltimore's largest meeting facility is the Baltimore Convention Center located between the Inner Harbor and Oriole Park at Camden Yards. An expansion of the facility completed in 1996 tripled its size to more than 1.2 million square feet. A 36,672-square-foot ballroom, 50 meeting rooms, and 300,000 square feet of exhibition space on one level make for an extremely flexible facility. The Convention Center is also one of a growing number across the country to embrace a "green initiative," with focused efforts on recycling and energy-saving measures. The Hilton Baltimore, owned by the city, is the primary hotel facility for the convention center and opened in 2011.

The Baltimore Arena is used primarily for sporting and entertainment events, but can also be used as a meeting facility. The facility has an auditorium with a capacity for 13,000 people, and parking accommodations for 5,000 cars. The Arena can also be curtained down to a 5,000-person capacity with a portable stage house center. Oriole Park at Camden Yards is available for trade shows. Many of Baltimore's downtown hotels also provide meeting facilities. The Baltimore Marriott-Waterfront is a 31-story hotel with 750 guestrooms, 80,000 square feet of total meeting space, exhibition space and 38 meeting rooms.

Convention Information: Baltimore Area Convention and Visitors Association, 100 Light Street, 12th Floor, Baltimore, MD 21202; telephone (410) 659-7300 or (877) 255-8466; fax (410) 727-2308.

■ Transportation

Approaching the City

The Baltimore-Washington International (BWI) Airport, located just 10 miles from downtown Baltimore, has 13 major airlines with non-stop flights to dozens of domestic destinations and seven international destinations, including London.

Major highway links between Baltimore and other cities are Interstate 95, which runs all along the East Coast, and Interstate 70, which crosses through western Maryland to the Midwest. Interstate 395 runs south from Baltimore to Washington and Virginia; Interstate 83 runs north through the city toward central Pennsylvania. All these interstates intersect with Interstate 695, the Baltimore Beltway, which circles the city. Those approaching the central city by car should be aware that most of the streets are one way.

Just north of downtown is the historical, restored Pennsylvania Station, where Amtrak trains pull in and out. For commuters, the Maryland Area Regional Commuter Train Service (MARC) provides weekday service on the most extensive track commuter rail system in the Greater Baltimore region, serving some 8.5 million passengers annually as of 2012. MARC ridership increased across all three lines—Penn, Camden, and Brunswick—in 2012. MARC provides convenient access to both downtown Baltimore and Washington, D.C.

Traveling in the City

Baltimore's highly regarded mass transit system consists of roughly 850 buses, the Metro (subway), light rail, and the Maryland Area Rail Commuter system (MARC). The Metro's 15.5 mile system extends from the Owings Mills corporate and shopping complex in Baltimore County, through the heart of the downtown business, shopping and sightseeing districts to Johns Hopkins Hospital. Baltimore also offers the Charm City Circulator which is comprised of free shuttles intended to reduce gas pollution and congestion. These eco-friendly hybrid electric shuttles travel three routes in Baltimore City with a shuttle arriving every 10 minutes at designated stops.

■ Communications

Newspapers and Magazines

Baltimore is served by one major daily newspaper, *The Baltimore Sun*. The *Daily Record* provides daily business

and legal news, and *The Baltimore Business Journal* and *The Jeffersonian* (Baltimore County) are business weeklies. Weekly newspapers published in Baltimore include *The Baltimore Times* and *Baltimore City Paper*. The *Baltimore Guide* is available online. Quarterly publications include the *Maryland Historical Magazine*.

Television and Radio

Television stations broadcasting from Baltimore include affiliates of ABC, CBS, NBC, Fox, public television, and Warner Brothers. Stations originating in nearby communities are also accessible to Baltimore-area residents, as is cable service.

Baltimore area AM and FM radio stations broadcast programming that ranges from news, religious material, and public broadcasting to music that includes classical, jazz, country, gospel, easy listening, top-40, and contemporary styles.

Media Information: The Baltimore Sun, 501 N. Calvert Street, Baltimore, MD 21278; telephone 410-332-6000 or 888-539-1280.

Baltimore Online

Baltimore Area Convention & Visitors Association. Available baltimore.org

Baltimore City Public School System. Available www.baltimorecityschools.org/

Baltimore County Public Library. Available www.bcpl.info

Baltimore Development Corporation. Available www.baltimoredevelopment.com

Baltimore Sun. Available www.baltimoresun.com

Baltimore Washington Corridor Chamber. Available www.baltwashchamber.org

City of Baltimore home page. Available www.baltimorecity.gov

Economic Alliance of Greater Baltimore. Available www.greaterbaltimore.org

Enoch Pratt Free Library. Available www.prattlibrary.org

Maryland Department of Business & Economic Development. Available www.dbed.maryland.gov

BIBLIOGRAPHY

Bready, James, H., Baseball in Baltimore: The First 100 Years (Baltimore, MD: Johns Hopkins University Press, 1998)

Fein, Isaac M., The Making of an American Jewish Community: The History of Baltimore Jewry from 1773 to 1920 (Philadelphia, PA: Jewish Publication Society of America, 1971)

Stockett, Letitia, Baltimore: A Not Too Serious History (Baltimore, MD: Johns Hopkins University Press, 1997)

Mississippi

The State in Brief

Nickname: Magnolia State

Motto: Virtute et armis (By valor and arms)

Flower: Magnolia

Bird: Mockingbird

Area: 48,432 square miles (2010; U.S. rank 32nd)

Elevation: Ranges from sea level to 806 feet above sea level

Climate: Temperate in north and subtropical in south, with long, hot summers and mild winters

Admitted to Union: December 10, 1817

Capital: Jackson

Head Official: Phil Bryant (R) (until 2016)

Population

1990: 2,573,216
2000: 2,844,658
2010: 2,967,297
2012 estimate: 2,967,620
Percent change, 2000–2010: 4.3%
U.S. rank in 2012: 31st
Percent of residents born in state: 71.4% (2012)
Density: 63.2 people per square mile (2010)
2012 FBI Crime Index Total: 91,692

Racial and Ethnic Characteristics (2012)

White: 1,768,530
Black or African American: 1,101,849
American Indian and Alaska Native: 13,344
Asian: 26,403
Native Hawaiian and Pacific Islander: 345
Hispanic or Latino (may be of any race): 78,634
Other: 57,149

Age Characteristics (2012)

Population under 5 years old: 208,315
Population 5 to 19 years old: 638,424
Percent of population 65 years and over: 12.9%
Median age: 36.0

Vital Statistics

Total number of births (2012–13): 39,348
Total number of deaths (2012–13): 28,976
AIDS cases reported through 2011: 8,538

Economy

Major industries: Manufacturing, electronics, agriculture, food processing, fishing
Unemployment rate (2012): 6.2%
Per capita income (2012): $20,670
Median household income (2012): $38,882
Percentage of persons below poverty level (2012): 22.3%
Income tax rate: 3.0% to 5.0%
Sales tax rate: 7.0%

Biloxi

■ The City in Brief

Founded: 1719, incorporated 1981

Head Official: Mayor A. J. Holloway, Jr. (R) (since 1993; current term expires 2017)

City Population
> 1990: 46,319
> 2000: 50,644
> 2010: 44,054
> 2012 estimate: 44,288
> Percent change, 2000–2010: −13.0%

Metropolitan Statistical Area Population
> 2000: 246,190
> 2010: 248,820
> 2012 estimate: 257,312
> Percent change, 2000–2010: 1.1%
> U.S. rank in 2000: 171st
> U.S. rank in 2010: 186th

Area: 46.53 square miles

Elevation: 20 feet above sea level

Average Annual Temperatures: 68° F

Average Annual Precipitation: 61 inches

Major Economic Sectors: gaming, tourism, military, seafood industry, boat building and repair

Unemployment Rate: 5.1% (2012)

Per Capita Income: $23,271

2012 FBI Crime Index Property: 2,267

Major Colleges and Universities: Mississippi Gulf Coast Community College

Daily Newspaper: *Sun Herald*

■ Introduction

Biloxi, with its 25 miles of white Gulf Coast beaches, is one of the oldest cities in the United States. Historically a sleepy resort town that originally served vacationers from Mobile and New Orleans, it was noted for its oyster and shrimp fisheries. The introduction of legalized gambling at offshore casinos led to the city's renaissance and a booming economy. Biloxi's rich history and cultural attractions also contributed to its becoming one of the new "hot spots" for Southern tourism. However, the devastating impact of Hurricane Katrina in 2005 and the Deepwater Horizon BP oil spill in 2010 was keenly felt, with some 90 percent of buildings in Biloxi affected by the storm, and the spill halting tourism and fishing for months. Recovering into the 2010s was visible but slow, with many acknowledging that Biloxi would never be the same.

■ Geography and Climate

Biloxi is located on a little peninsula between Biloxi Bay and the Mississippi Sound on the Gulf of Mexico. It is 70 miles northeast of New Orleans, 70 miles southwest of Mobile, and 150 miles west of Jacksonville. The city has a moist semitropical climate, and sunny days with frequent cool breezes predominate. From May through September the hot, humid weather can be uncomfortable at times, and afternoon thundershowers are not uncommon. Winter brings primarily warm, clear weather and occasional cold spells lasting no longer than three or four days. Tropical cyclones occur most often during June through November; Hurricane Katrina was one of these, devastating Biloxi on August 29, 2005.

Area: 46.53 square miles

Elevation: 20 feet above sea level

Average Temperatures: 68° F

Average Annual Precipitation: 61 inches

City of Biloxi/biloxi.ms.us

■ History

Many Flags Have Flown over Biloxi

An area across Biloxi Bay from the city, called Old Biloxi, was first visited by French explorer Pierre LeMoyne d'Iberville in 1699. The explorer, who was looking for the mouth of the Mississippi River, was instructed by the King of France to claim the coastal region. D'Iberville sailed into Biloxi Bay with a small group of men and established Fort Maurepas and a similar colony on the east shore, now the site of Ocean Springs. The word Biloxi means "First People" and was the name of a local Native American tribe met by d'Iberville and his men when they explored the land. Since its discovery, eight flags have flown over the city including the French, English, Spanish, West Florida Republic, Mississippi Magnolia, Confederate State, Mississippi State, and that of the United States.

In 1719 Fort Louis was founded on the site of the present-day city, which served as the capital of French colonial Louisiana from 1720 to 1722. In 1783 Biloxi was taken over by the Spanish, who merely collected tariffs, while the area retained its strong French influence. The Spanish maintained their rule until 1810, when a rebellion occurred and the area was seized by American insurgents. At that time, Biloxi became part of the Republic of West Florida. Although petitions for statehood were denied, the Biloxi region became part of the Territory of Orleans (which had been part of the Louisiana Purchase). Two years later, in 1812, Biloxi became part of the Mississippi Territory. In 1814 a British attempt to capture New Orleans failed, but the British remained on nearby Ship Island until 1815. Finally, on December 10, 1817, Mississippi became the 20th state of the United States.

Biloxi Established as a Resort

During the 1820s Biloxi became a popular summer resort for New Orleanians wishing to escape their city's heat and yellow fever epidemics. Biloxi was incorporated officially in 1838. The city grew as families and their servants flocked to the area, which by 1847 had become the most important of the Gulf Coast's resort towns. By the middle of the nineteenth century, even more people came for the ostensible healing powers of the waters, and for the balls, outings, and hunting events that enlivened the social scene.

At the time of the Civil War, Union troops took over nearby Ship Island and carried out a blockade of the gulf. Citizens protected the city from invasion by the Yankees through the threatening appearance of fake cannons, which were really only logs planted in the sand. Mullet fish, called "Biloxi bacon," saved the local populace from starvation in the war years. The first fish cannery opened in 1881, and the city's seafood industry quickly developed. By 1900 Biloxi was termed the "seafood capital of the world." Polish, Austrian, and Acadian French soon came to the city to work in the industry, adding their own cultural influences. Tourism flourished and more hotels were built to accommodate the visitors, many of them from the Midwest, who came to escape the harsh northern winters.

During the early twentieth century, the city grew and new developments included electricity, a street railway system, and telephone service. During the 1920s a paved highway was built along the beach, and more hotels were constructed as tourism increased. In 1928 the world's longest seawall, which spanned 25 miles of Biloxi's coastline, was dedicated. The 1930s saw the decline of the area's seafood industry, but a new boom took place during World War II when Biloxi was chosen to be the site of a new U.S. Air Force base.

Legalized Gambling Revitalizes City

Mid-century saw the construction of a four-lane super-highway and the production of a sand beach, thanks to the use of hydraulic dredges. The development of Edgewater Plaza Shopping Center took place in the early 1960s, and the mall served to draw people from all over the region thereafter. In 1969 Biloxi suffered considerable damage when Hurricane Camille ravaged the entire Gulf Coast area, but the citizens soon rallied and rebuilt their town. A new era began in the city in 1992 with the opening of the first Las Vegas-style gambling casino. The resort casinos with their 24-hour entertainment availability spurred a tremendous growth in both local and tourist populations, and restaurants and other businesses grew accordingly.

Biloxi suffered some damage from Hurricane Georges in 1998 but rallied a year later to celebrate its tricentennial with music fests, sporting events, exhibits, and tours. The city's ninth casino, the Beau Rivage, opened in 1999, further stimulating Biloxi's economy through tourism and gaming revenues. On August 29, 2005, Hurricane Katrina—one of the most catastrophic hurricanes in U.S. history—made landfall in southeast

Louisiana and on the Louisiana-Mississippi border. Biloxi was particularly hard hit, especially the low-lying Point Cadet area. Total damage from Katrina in the region was estimated at $80 billion. Rebuilding efforts had results: as cleanup and reconstruction from Katrina continued into the 2010s, tourists returned to Biloxi and other places on Mississippi's Gulf Coast. Not all buildings or businesses could be saved, however. The Deepwater Horizon BP oil spill in 2010 weakened the city's seafood processing industry. Sandwiched in between the two traumas was a nationwide recession that exacted additional economic damage on the city.

Historical Information: Harrison County Library System, 12135 Old Highway 49, Gulfport, MS 39503; telephone (228) 539-0110.

■ Population Profile

Metropolitan Statistical Area Population

2000: 246,190
2010: 248,820
2012 estimate: 257,312
Percent change, 2000–2010: 1.1%
U.S. rank in 2000: 171st
U.S. rank in 2010: 186th

City Residents

1990: 46,319
2000: 50,644
2010: 44,054
2012 estimate: 44,288
Percent change, 2000–2010: −13.0%

Density: 1,092.3 people per square mile

Racial and ethnic characteristics

White: 31,472
Black or African American: 8,265
American Indian and Alaskan Native: 165
Asian: 2,375
Native Hawaiian and Other Pacific Islander: 0
Hispanic or Latino (may be of any race): 3,479
Other: 2,011

Percent of residents born in state: 46.9%

Age characteristics

Population under 5 years old: 2,686
Population 5 to 9 years old: 2,905
Population 10 to 14 years old: 2,156
Population 15 to 19 years old: 3,408
Population 20 to 24 years old: 4,655
Population 25 to 34 years old: 6,456
Population 35 to 44 years old: 5,228
Population 45 to 54 years old: 6,144

Population 55 to 59 years old: 2,890
Population 60 to 64 years old: 2,291
Population 65 to 74 years old: 2,551
Population 75 to 84 years old: 1,944
Population 85 years and over: 974
Median age: 34.8

Births (2010–11 Metropolitan Area)
Total number: 3,419

Deaths (2010–11 Metropolitan Area)
Total number: 2,079

Money income (2012)
Per capita income: $23,271
Median household income: $37,826
Total households: 17,821

Number of households with income of ...
less than $10,000: 1,378
$10,000 to $14,999: 1,635
$15,000 to $24,999: 3,307
$25,000 to $34,999: 1,968
$35,000 to $49,999: 2,769
$50,000 to $74,999: 2,955
$75,000 to $99,999: 1,648
$100,000 to $149,999: 1,413
$150,000 to $199,999: 465
$200,000 or more: 283

Percent of families below poverty level: 22.9%

FBI Crime Index Property: 2,267

FBI Crime Index Violent: 188

■ Municipal Government

Biloxi has a strong mayor-council form of government, with council members elected by each of seven local districts. The mayor and council members serve four-year terms.

Head Official: Mayor A. J. Holloway, Jr. (R) (since 1993; current term expires 2017)

Total Number of City Employees: 597 (2012)

City Information: City of Biloxi, P.O. Box 429, Biloxi, MS 39533; telephone (228) 435-6254; fax (228) 435-6129; email mayor@biloxi.ms.us

■ Economy

Major Industries and Commercial Activity

Gaming and tourism is Biloxi's most important industry. As of 2013, there were 12 Las Vegas–style casinos in the

region, nine of which were in Biloxi. The casinos featured restaurants, floor shows, and round-the-clock gambling. According to a formula devised when gambling was legalized, 8 percent of gross gaming revenue went to the state and 3.2 percent of gross gaming revenue was distributed among city institutions, including the general fund, the city public safety department, the city school system, the county school system, and the county public safety department. The lure of gaming also bolsters the region's tourism industry in general, as many gamblers visit other area attractions outside the casinos. The city's tourism and gaming industries recovered within two years of Hurricane Katrina, with Biloxi's casino industry reporting an all-time high in income in 2007; the businesses generated $97.3 million in gross gaming revenue. Through 2013, monthly gaming revenue typically vacillated between $60 million and $80 million. In the years following Katrina, rules were altered to allow casinos to rebuild 800-feet ashore; prior to the storm, Mississippi casinos were required to be on floating barges, limiting their size.

The seafood industry suffered both from Hurricane Katrina in 2005 and the Deepwater Horizon BP oil spill in 2010. During the latter event, federal waters were closed to fishermen from May 2010 until April 2011; this amounted to as much as 37 percent of fishing waters being made off-limits to area fishermen. Some seafood processing plants closed or moved elsewhere as a result; 20 seafood processing plants were situated along the Gulf Coast in 2013, with 9 in Biloxi. Vietnamese immigrants have revived the seafood industry by accepting packing plant jobs that most other groups avoided. They built their own boats, opened their own businesses, and became a vibrant part of the seafood and ethnic community in Biloxi. Building boats and producing boat paraphernalia were also big businesses in the area. Ingalls Shipbuilding, based 20 miles east of Biloxi in Pascagoula, employed approximately 11,000 workers as of 2013, more than any other private employer in Mississippi.

Military and federal government installations are another key sector of the area's economy. Keesler Air Force Base is the largest single employer in Biloxi. Keesler is a lead Joint Training installation, instructing not only Air Force, but Army, Navy, Marine Corps, Coast Guard, and other military and civilian federal agency personnel. The 81st Training Wing is host to the Second Air Force, the 403rd Wing (Air Force Reserve), and home of the second largest Air Force medical facility, Keesler Medical Center. The base added a Cyberspace Education and Training program in 2011; the new training program highlighted the recovery of the base in the wake of Hurricane Katrina.

The John C. Stennis Space Center, located 45 miles west of Biloxi, impacts the local economy by employing approximately 5,304 people in the region as of 2012, with 929 of employees residing in Harrison County. Its economic impact on the region within a 50-mile radius was estimated at $654 million. Stennis partnered with the Orbital Science Corporation to test spaceship engines meant to aid transport to the International Space Station. The first test flight launched in April 2013.

Other federal installations in the region are the Naval Construction Battalion Center and National Guard facilities in Gulfport, and the Office of Supervisor of Shipbuilding, Conversion and Repair, located about 30 miles east of Biloxi.

Items and goods produced: seafood products, canned foods, boats, fishing nets

Incentive Programs-New and Existing Companies

Local programs: The Harrison County Development Commission works with companies interested in developing or expanding their business in the county. Its services include the coordination of financial incentives, including tax abatements, as well as assisting in industrial park and Foreign Trade Zone activities. It also manages the Innovation Center, a small business incubator based in Biloxi. The Biloxi Community Development Department offers a renovated building tax exemption to businesses that renovate existing structures in the city's central business district. The Department had to take on greater responsibilities after Hurricane Katrina, when 6,000 homes and business were destroyed in the city. As of 2013, it maintained 26 full-time and 10 part-time employees in service to the city. The Biloxi Chamber of Commerce offers reoccupany grants to encourage small business owners to return to their places of work. Ten $1,000 grants were awarded in 2012, with five available in 2013.

State programs: A tax credit program is offered through the Mississippi Department of Archives & History for the restoration of buildings listed on the National Register of Historic Places or designated as Mississippi Landmarks. As of 2013, the state tax credit stood at 25 percent for restoration of either residential or commercial properties.

Momentum Mississippi was created in 2004 by Governor Haley Barbour as a long-range economic development implementation organization. The 2005 legislation was designed to help existing industries invest in technology and expand; attract high-value, high-technology enterprises; and provide counties and cities throughout Mississippi with the economic development tools to compete. Specifically, Momentum Mississippi identifies and pursues targets in both manufacturing and services, and aligns incentives—including dozens of grants, loans, and tax credits—around these targets. Targeted industries included advanced manufacturing, aerospace, agribusiness, automotive, energy, health care, and shipbuilding. Mississippi was named a top-five state for cost of doing business by *Area Development Magazine* in 2012, and was ranked second in utility costs and permitting speed.

Job training programs: The state of Mississippi provides recruitment, job referral and placement services; customized pre-employment, industry-based, and vendor training; project-specific training; and on-the-job training reimbursement and tax credits for new, expanding, or existing industries. The Workforce Training and Services division of the Mississippi Development Authority administers employee training. The Mississippi Department of Employment's WIN Job Centers provide access to employment, education, training, and economic development services. Other WIN services for employers include a database of qualified job candidates, assistance in writing job descriptions, proficiency testing, labor market data, and information on work opportunity tax credits. The Mississippi Contract Procurement Center, which includes a regional center located in Biloxi, provides information about bid opportunities from federal, state, and local government agencies; it also offers training, marketing assistance, technical support, and counseling.

Development Projects

Rebuilding from Hurricane Katrina in 2005 remained a major driver—both in terms of need and funding—through 2013. Hurricane Katrina drew more than $5 billion in federal funding to the state, with roughly $4.1 billion spent by 2013, more than half of which went to homeowner programs. Coastal areas like Biloxi were prime recipients of these funds, expediting development projects that otherwise would have taken decades. Development initiatives maintained three priorities enunciated in the city's 2009 economic development master plan: reduce storm vulnerability, rebuild storm-damaged areas, and manage northward growth of the city.

Other Katrina-related improvements centered on the Biloxi Small Craft Harbor, the port administration building, the Coliseum Pier, and the Point Cadet Marina. A $400,000 restoration project of the Biloxi Lighthouse, funded by the Federal Emergency Management Agency and the Mississippi Emergency Management Agency, was completed in 2010. An $11 million, 24,000-square-foot Biloxi Lighthouse Visitors Center opened in August 2011. Repairs and improvements were also made to other landmarks such as the Old Brick House, City Hall, The Magnolia Hotel, and many other structures. Total repair costs were estimated at between $355 million and $450 million. All projects were slated for completion by 2016. A state-of-the-art health facility was expected to open in 2014 to replace Gulf Coast Medical Center, which closed permanently in 2008 following damage from Hurricane Katrina three years prior.

Investments in infrastructure at the Gulfport-Biloxi International Airport totaled $287 million between 2005 and 2012, doubling the airport's capacity from 1 million to 2.4 million annual passengers and installing new covered walkways, two hotels, and an air traffic control tower. More than half of the investment was funded privately.

The $45 million Ohr-O'Keefe Museum of Art, designed by Frank Gehry during 1999–2003, opened its first phase in 2011. Construction began in 2004 but was destroyed by Hurricane Katrina in 2005. After the first phase opened in 2011, the related City of Biloxi Center for Ceramics opened the following year, with construction for the John S. and James L. Knight Gallery slated for opening in 2014.

Community Development Block Grant funds from the U.S. Department of Housing and Urban Development provided hundreds of thousands of dollars annually—an estimated $615,779 for 2014—to support development for low- and moderate-income residents around Biloxi. Projects for 2014 included waterline and drainage improvements. City funds supported grants to renovate community buildings for the De L'Epee Deaf Center, South Mississippi AIDS Task Force, Coastal Family Health Center, and the American Red Cross.

Economic Development Information: Mississippi Development Authority, 501 N. West St., PO Box 849, Jackson, MS 39205; telephone (601) 359-3449; fax (601) 359-2832. Biloxi Chamber of Commerce, 11975E Seaway Road, Gulfport, MS 39503; telephone (228) 604-0014; email info@mscoastchamber.com.

Commercial Shipping

Biloxi is located less than one hour from the major cities of New Orleans, Louisiana, and Mobile, Alabama. The Gulfport-Biloxi International Airport is the site of Foreign Trade Zone #92, a 1,000-acre area where foreign goods bound for international destinations can be temporarily stored without incurring an import duty. The airport features a total of 46,000 square feet of cargo space. CSX Corporation is a cargo railroad serving Biloxi. The Mississippi State Port, located at nearby Gulfport, covers 204 acres with nearly 6,000 feet of berthing space. As of 2013, the port averaged two million tons of cargo annually and was the second largest importer of green fruit in the United States, as well as the third busiest container port on the Gulf of Mexico. Liner services were offered by Great White Fleet, Crowley Maritime, and Dole Fresh Fruit Company. A number of industrial parks on the Gulf Coast offer prime waterfront industrial sites on navigable water. Worldwide overnight and local shipping capability is provided by express, courier, and parcel companies that serve the coast region.

Labor Force and Employment Outlook

The success of gaming in Biloxi is responsible for the creation of many new jobs in the area. Some, like those in the hospitality and tourism industries, are directly linked to gaming; others, like those in the construction, medical services, and general retail industries are indirect offshoots of an economy driven by casinos. The rebuilding of Biloxi's gaming and resort industry after Hurricane Katrina was interrupted by a nationwide recession in the late 2000s and the Deepwater Horizon BP oil spill in 2010. Federally funded reconstruction projects buoyed the economy in the interim, as did expansions at Kessler Air Force Base.

The following is a summary of data regarding the 2012 Biloxi labor force:

Size of civilian labor force: 21,166

Number of workers employed in . . .

agriculture and mining: 331
construction: 1,236
manufacturing: 937
wholesale trade: 396
retail trade: 2,243
transportation: 849
information systems: 403
finance: 803
professional administration: 1,352
education and social services: 3,217
arts and leisure: 4,498
other: 761
public administration: 2,028

Average hourly earnings of production workers: $15.41

Unemployment rate: 5.1% (2012)

Employers

Largest employers (2012)	*Number of employees*
Keesler Air Force Base	12,222
Beau Rivage Casino & Resort	2,826
Biloxi Veterans Admin Hospital	1,985
Imperial Palace Casino Resort Spa	1,842
Hard Rock Hotel & Casino Biloxi	966
Margaritaville Casino & Resort	960
Grand Casino Biloxi	808
Palace Casino Resort	763
Biloxi Regional Medical Center	750
Isle Casino	688

Cost of Living

Following the damage that resulted from Hurricane Katrina in 2005, the cost of living in Biloxi remained lower than the national average into the 2010s.

The following is a summary of data regarding several key cost of living factors in the area.

State income tax rate: 3.0% to 5.0%

State sales tax rate: 7.0%

Local income tax rate: None

Local sales tax rate: None

Property tax rate: 109.10 mills (2013)

Economic Information: Biloxi Chamber of Commerce, 11975E Seaway Road, Gulfport, MS 39503; telephone (228) 604-0014; email info@mscoastchamber. com.

■ Education and Research

Elementary and Secondary Schools

The Biloxi Public School District offers a curriculum ranging from remedial education to college-level advanced placement courses, as well as specialized programs in technology or vocational studies. The Mississippi Department of Education gave the district an "A" rating for 2011–12, and North Bay Elementary was honored as a National Blue Ribbon School by the U. S. Department of Education in 2011.

The following is a summary of data regarding the Biloxi Public School District.

Total enrollment: 5,008

Number of facilities

total: 7
elementary schools: 4
junior high schools: 1
high schools: 1
other: 1

Student/teacher ratio: 14.73:1

Teacher salaries

average (statewide): $46,818

Funding per pupil: $9,919

Public Schools Information: Biloxi Public School District; 160 St. Peter Street, Biloxi, MS 39530; telephone (228) 374-1810; fax (228) 374-1764.

Colleges and Universities

Mississippi Gulf Coast Community College (MGCCC) has one campus in Gulfport, and also offers classes in Biloxi through the Keesler Center at Keesler Air Force Base. In 2013 the college opened the Haley Reeves Barbour Maritime Training Academy in Pascagoula, a joint venture with Ingalls Shipbuilding to support apprenticeship training. Also that year, the college announced plans for a nursing simulation complex that would allow it to double enrollment in its associate degree program in nursing. Nearly half the funds for the program were to come from Katrina Community Development Block Grants.

Also, operating out of Keesler Air Force Base is the University of Southern Mississippi–Gulf Coast, which offers a variety of classes for civilians and military personnel. Total enrollment numbered just over 3,000 for 2012. Tulane University's School of Continuing Studies, based in New Orleans, maintains a campus in Biloxi that offers associate's, bachelor's, and master's degree programs. Located in nearby Gulfport is William Carey University's Tradition Campus, within comfortable commuting range of students from Biloxi.

Libraries and Research Centers

The Harrison County Library System maintains four library branches in Biloxi, with its headquarters in Gulfport. Biloxi branches include the Biloxi Public Library, Margaret Sherry Memorial Library, West Biloxi Library, and Woolmarket Library. Biloxi Public Library houses a special collection covering local history and genealogy.

The Gulf Coast Research Laboratory (GCRL), located in Ocean Springs, is administered by the University of Southern Mississippi. It receives less than 25 percent of funds from the state, with the remainder coming from grants, contracts, and self-generated funds. It offers a broad marine science curriculum and collaborates with the local commercial seafood industry to devise efficient methods of harvesting the waters and to develop future ventures, such as aquaculture. After sustaining approximately $50 million in damages to buildings, contents, collections, research, and intellectual property as a result of Katrina's storm surge and winds, the library has recovered and expanded through work on a $40 million facilities project at Cedar Point that included facilities for marine aquaculture, environmental research, and marine education.

Public Library Information: Harrison County Library System, 12135 Old Highway 49, Gulfport, MS 39503; telephone (228) 539-0110.

■ Health Care

Biloxi has two hospitals, while the entire Gulf Coast region has seven general hospitals. Services at the Biloxi Regional Medical Center, which has 198 beds, include a cardiac intensive care unit, an emergency department, an outpatient care center, HIV services, a medical surgical intensive care unit, a neonatal intensive care unit, oncology services, pediatric intensive care, physical rehabilitation, psychiatric care, and a radiation department. The Gulf Coast Medical Center was seriously damaged during Hurricane Katrina in 2005 and closed in

2008. A new state-of-the-art health facility, to be located in North Biloxi, was expected to open by 2014 after a $132 million investment.

The Gulf Coast Veterans Health Care System consists of a 392-bed main campus in Biloxi and four clinics serving Mobile, Alabama, and the Floridian cities of Eglin, Pensacola, and Panama City. Facilities for the blind opened in 2011 with 26 inpatient beds over 63,000 square feet. Outpatient and inpatient mental health facilities opened in 2011 and 2012, respectively, and a community living center with eight 12-bed houses became operational in spring 2012.

Keesler Medical Center is one of the largest Air Force medical facilities in the United States, serving 27,000 military personnel, including more than 8,000 active-duty members. The center also oversees other regional health networks that serve an estimated 80,000 people. Construction projects during 2009–11 included a $50 million inpatient tower and a $10 million radiation oncology center. Keesler Medical Center has the only medical geriatrics center in the Department of Defense; its laboratory provides 25,000 tests annually.

■ Recreation

Sightseeing

Prior to the devastation wrought by Hurricane Katrina, Biloxi's bygone eras were captured in a number of historical structures. Some buildings survived the storm with little damage or were reopened after extensive repairs; others were fully lost.

Visitors to Beauvoir, the last home of Jefferson Davis, only president of the Confederacy, are able to see where he lived, worked, and entertained the notables of his day. The house is set on a 52-acre estate containing museums with Confederate artifacts, two pavilions, and a cemetery with the Tomb of the Unknown Soldier. Beauvoir House and the Jefferson Davis Presidential Library suffered heavy damage from Hurricane Katrina in 2005. Nearly 4,000 artifacts were photographed, inventoried, boxed, and stored in environmental storage. The federal government agreed to pay $2.5 million of the $4.1 million cost to repair Beauvoir House, and in 2008 the mansion was restored to its original form and reopened to the public for daily tours.

French and American architectural styles of the nineteenth century are exhibited in the Old Brick House, overlooking Back Bay. The Old Brick House was seriously damaged by Hurricane Katrina, with most of the south wall gone and the interior exposed. Some $740,000 in repairs were necessary to renovate the structure, which reopened to the public in 2011. The Tullis-Toledano Manor, built in 1856, was one of the area's finest examples of the antebellum style. It was destroyed by Katrina. The Pleasant Reed House was named for its builder, who was born into slavery in 1854 and moved to Biloxi after the Civil War. The Pleasant Reed House was lost in the storm, but the museum's Board of Trustees voted in June 2007 to rebuild it completely. The Redding House is a Colonial Revival home listed on the National Register of Historic Places. The Spanish Captains Quarters and the Old French House, reflecting two distinct architectural styles and cultures that were once powerful in the area, dated to the early 1700s; the Old French House had been a restaurant. Both were destroyed in the storm.

The Biloxi Lighthouse, erected in 1848, has been welcoming sailors since the days of the sailing schooners, and provides a wonderful view of the Gulf Coast area. Unlike so many other structures, Biloxi Lighthouse survived Katrina, a symbolic victory for residents. There was significant damage to its interior brick lining, but despite the storm surge that pressed up against its base, Biloxi Lighthouse endured and became an anchor for the city's rebuilding process. A 24,000-square-foot Biloxi Lighthouse Visitors Center opened in August 2011.

Visitors to the Old Biloxi Cemetery can read the gravestones of the first French settlers. Fort Massachusetts, on the western tip of Ship Island, was inhabited by the Confederate Army and later recaptured by Union Troops, who used it as a prison. On the grounds are a library, a summer cottage, and a Confederate cemetery. Fort Massachusetts, located on West Ship Island some 12 miles off the coast, suffered minimal damage during Katrina. Tours are offered during the spring, summer, and fall.

As of 2013, nine casinos were open in Biloxi, with three others located in surrounding areas. Many are open 24 hours a day, seven days a week and offer Las Vegas–style gaming, entertainment, hotel rooms, retail shops, and other amenities. Biloxi casinos include Beau Rivage, Boomtown, Golden Nugget Biloxi, Grand Biloxi Casino, Hard Rock Hotel and Casino, IP Casino Resort Spa, Jimmy Buffett's Margaritaville Casino & Restaurant, Palace Casino Resort, and Treasure Bay. Nearby casinos are Hollywood Casino and Silver Slipper in Bay St. Louis, and Island View Casino Resort in Gulfport.

Biloxi's Katrina Memorial is located on U.S. Highway 90 in Biloxi's Town Green. The memorial is dedicated to the Gulf Coast victims who died in Hurricane Katrina. Dedicated on February 15, 2006, it stands 12 feet tall—roughly the height of Hurricane Katrina's storm surge at the Town Green. The Memorial contains a tile inlay of a wave and a glass case containing various items from destroyed buildings. A Katrina sculpture project in 2007 created marine wildlife from the city's many standing dead trees. The sculptures were created by local chainsaw artist Dayton Scoggins.

Arts and Culture

Biloxi is home to a diverse collection of museums. The Maritime and Seafood Industry Museum traces Biloxi's

300-year history as the seafood capital of the world. The museum was destroyed by Hurricane Katrina. Ground-breaking for a new museum occurred in February 2013, and that museum was scheduled to open in April 2014. The Ohr-O'Keefe Museum of Art, designed by Frank Gehry, opened its first phase in 2011. Construction began in 2004 but was destroyed by Hurricane Katrina in 2005. After the first phase opened in 2011, the City of Biloxi Center for Ceramics opened the following year, with construction for the John S. and James L. Knight Gallery slated for completion by 2014.

The Saenger Theatre for the Performing Arts is home to the Gulf Coast Opera Theatre, Gulf Coast Symphony Orchestra, Gulf Coast Symphony Youth Orchestra, and KNS Theatre, a non-profit community theater. The Saenger Theatre was damaged by Katrina but reopened in 2010. Biloxi Little Theatre, an all-volunteer community theatre, presents four major productions each year, and Center Stage presents a variety of regular performances, children's theater, and workshops.

The Mardi Gras Museum showcased the splendor of that celebration at the restored antebellum Magnolia Hotel, the oldest hotel structure on the Gulf Coast. Major damage to the Hotel and Museum closed both until restoration efforts completed in 2013.

Moran's Art Studio displayed original works of Joe Moran, George E. Ohr, and Mary and Tommy Moran. The Biloxi gallery was destroyed by Hurricane Katrina, but Moran's Art Studio reopened in nearby Ocean Springs, Mississippi.

Other museums that reopened after Hurricane Katrina in Biloxi's surrounding region include Lynn Meadows Discovery Center in Gulfport. Lynn Meadows has been ranked one of the top 50 children's museums in the United States, was the first children's museum in Mississippi, and was honored as the "Best Attraction for Kids" in Mississippi by *Mississippi Magazine* in 2013. It has presented interactive exhibits on health, history, art, careers, trees, tornadoes, and the shipping industry, among other topics. Children can experience Mississippi in the 1890s in the History Hotel, climb the Super Colossal Climbing Structure, and record themselves reading the daily news.

The GI Museum is a military museum in Ocean Springs. It features more than 16,000 pieces of memorabilia and military artifacts, including soap, razors, cigarettes, helmets, hats, jackets, and coats used in wars from World War I to the War in Iraq. Also included are authentic letters and postcards, canteens, and language guides used by soldiers. There is a special section dedicated to African Americans and women who served their country.

Also in Ocean Springs is the Walter Anderson Museum of Art. Mississippi-born artist, naturalist, and writer Walter Anderson is known for his vivid depictions of animals, people, and plants from the Gulf Coast area. The extensive permanent collection includes drawings, watercolors, oils, ceramics, carvings, and more. The Little Room features murals that were not discovered until Anderson's death. Temporary exhibits also show the works of other significant artists from around the country. The museum complex is comprised of the main museum facility and the Art Education Cottage.

Festivals and Holidays

The Gulf Coast's variety of festivals, many of them centering on water events, have long delighted both hometown crowds and visitors. May brings the Great Biloxi Schooner Races & Blessing of the Fleet, a celebration of the onset of shrimping season that features a street festival, coronation of the Shrimp King and Queen, and a parade of boats. Bay Harborfest in nearby Bay St. Louis, with music, art, and food, also occurs in May, with 2013 its inaugural year. June features the Mississippi Coast Coliseum Summer Fair & Music Festival. A variety of Independence Day celebrations enliven the area in July. September is the time for the Biloxi Seafood Festival. The Highland & Island Scottish Games, held in Gulfport, take place in November. Christmas on the Gulf Coast features Biloxi's Christmas on the Water boat parade and the Lighting of the Fish Net Christmas Tree and parade.

Vietnamese New Year salutes the city's unique ethnic heritage, and French heritage is celebrated at Coast History Week with its French Encampment. Queen Ixolib (Biloxi spelled backwards) presides over the festivities at Mardi Gras, which has been celebrated longer in Biloxi than in New Orleans. March brings the St. Patrick's Day Parade.

Sports for the Spectator

Biloxi's Mississippi Sea Wolves were one of 25 teams in the East Coast Hockey League. On March 30, 2009, the Sea Wolves suspended operations. However, within a few weeks, the team's management announced the establishment of a new professional hockey team, the Mississippi Surge, which began playing in the Southern Professional Hockey League later that year. Fans watch home games at the Mississippi Coast Coliseum & Convention Center, located in Biloxi.

Sports for the Participant

The city of Biloxi maintains 25 traditional parks, 3 sports complexes, 2 community centers, and 2 pools. Many of these facilities were damaged or destroyed by Hurricane Katrina, with repairs continuing into 2013. Damage estimates totaled more than $7 million. The Biloxi Natatorium, one of cities two pools, offers an Olympic-sized indoor-outdoor pool with a retractable top. Golf courses include the renowned Fallen Oak course at Beau Rivage Casino, Bay Breeze Golf Course on Keesler Air Force base, Sunkist Country Club & Golf Course, and Dogwood Hills Golf Course. The Great Biloxi Schooner Races are held in May.

Shopping and Dining

Edgewater Mall is the largest enclosed mall on the Gulf Coast. Totaling more than one million square feet, the mall is anchored by four major retailers, including Dillard's, Belk, Sears, and JCPenney, and is occupied by more than 100 specialty stores. Nearby, more than 60 retailers offer discounted wares at the Gulfport Premium Outlets.

Biloxi's cuisine is an enticing blend of Spanish, French, Cajun, and traditional Southern cuisine. Gumbo, a succulent blend of seafood, okra, celery, scallions, and chopped bell peppers, is the featured item on many restaurants' menus.

Visitor Information: Mississippi Gulf Coast Regional Convention & Visitors Bureau, 2350 Beach Blvd Suite A, Biloxi, MS; telephone (228) 896-6699.

■ Convention Facilities

The Mississippi Coast Coliseum and Convention Center, which opened in 2008, has 400,000 square feet of meeting space and can accommodate up to 4,700 people in a single space, depending on the hall used. The majority of Biloxi's casinos also provide meeting space, with the largest facilities maintained by Beau Rivage (50,000 square feet) and IP Casino Resort Spa (37,600 square feet) as of 2013. There are more than 45 additional meeting facilities, from the Biloxi Civic Center, which has a 15,000-square-foot ballroom, to the more intimate settings of restored homes, such as the Amour Danzar Event Center or Bond Grant House. Some 13,000 hotel rooms support convention center events.

Convention Information: Mississippi Gulf Coast Regional Convention & Visitors Bureau, 2350 Beach Blvd Suite A, Biloxi, MS; telephone (228) 896-6699.

■ Transportation

Approaching the City

Investments in infrastructure at the Gulfport-Biloxi International Airport totaled $287 million between 2005 and 2012, doubling the airport's capacity from one million to 2.4 million annual passengers and installing new covered walkways, two hotels, and an air traffic control tower. More than half of the investment was funded privately.

Airlines serving the facility are American Eagle, Delta, United, US Airways, and Vision Airlines. Amtrak's Sunset Limited rail line operates service running from Los Angeles to Orlando, which includes a stop in Biloxi. Biloxi also has private and public marinas for those who choose to arrive by boat.

Seven Interstates provide access to the Alabama-Mississippi-Louisiana region via Interstate 10, which runs east and west across northern Biloxi. U.S. Highway 90 also runs east and west, but along the beaches of the Gulf. Interstate 110 extends north and south through the city, and U.S. Highways 67 and 15 run north toward central Mississippi.

Traveling in the City

Local bus service is provided by the Coast Transit Authority. The popular Beachcomber Line, serviced by replica trolley buses, runs along U.S. Highway 90. In addition, seven main routes—and the Casino Hopper line—covered the tri-county coastal of Harrison, Jackson, and Hancock counties in 2013. Paratransit services were available, as were curb-to-curb services for senior citizens.

■ Communications

Newspapers and Magazines

The *Sun Herald*, Biloxi's daily paper, is published every morning. Weeklies include *Gulf Pines Catholic* and the *Keesler News*, published at Keesler Air Force Base.

Television and Radio

As of 2013, Biloxi had two television affiliates and three FM and three AM radio stations.

Media Information: The *Sun Herald*, 205 DeBuys Road, Gulfport, MS 39507.

Biloxi Online

Biloxi Chamber of Commerce. Available www. biloxi.org

Biloxi Public Schools. Available www.biloxischools. net

City of Biloxi. Available www.biloxi.ms.us

Harrison County Development Commission. Available www.mscoast.org

Harrison County Library System. Available www. harrison.lib.ms.us

Mississippi Development Authority. Available www. mississippi.org

Mississippi Gulf Coast Regional Convention & Visitors Bureau. Available www.gulfcoast.org

Sun Herald. Available www.sunherald.com

The Buildings of Biloxi: An Architectural Survey (City of Biloxi, 1975)

Husley, Val, *Maritime Biloxi* (Mount Pleasant, SC: Arcadia Publishing, 2000)

McGrath, Barbara Barbieri, *The Storm: Students of Biloxi, Mississippi Remember Hurricane Katrina* (Watertown, MA: Charlesbridge, 2006)

Santa Cruz, Alan J. and Joan C., and Jane B. Shambra, *Biloxi* (Charleston, SC: Arcadia Publishing, 2012)

378   CITIES OF THE UNITED STATES, EIGHTH EDITION

Jackson

■ The City in Brief

Founded: 1821 (incorporated 1833)

Head Official: Mayor Chokwe Lumumba (since 2013; current term expires 2017)

City Population
>1990: 202,062
>2000: 184,256
>2010: 173,514
>2012 estimate: 175,376
>Percent change, 2000–2010: −5.8%
>U.S. rank in 1990: 78th (State rank: 1st)
>U.S. rank in 2000: 127th (State rank: 1st)
>U.S. rank in 2010: 134th (State rank: 1st)

Metropolitan Statistical Area Population
>2000: 525,346
>2010: 539,057
>2012 estimate: 548,945
>Percent change, 2000–2010: 2.6%
>U.S. rank in 2000: 90th
>U.S. rank in 2010: 96th

Area: 106.82 square miles

Elevation: 291 feet above sea level

Average Annual Temperatures: 64.1° F

Average Annual Precipitation: 55.95 inches

Major Economic Sectors: automobiles and related automotive components, fabricated metals, electrical and electronic equipment, food products, wood products, transportation equipment, rubber and plastic products, portable electric tools, welded steel tubing, aircraft parts

Unemployment Rate: 7.4% (2012)

Per Capita Income: $19,013

2012 FBI Crime Index Property: 11,568

Major Colleges and Universities: Jackson State University, University of Mississippi Medical Center, Hinds Community College, Belhaven University, Millsaps College

Daily Newspaper: *The Clarion-Ledger*

■ Introduction

Jackson, Mississippi's capital and largest city, is still essentially a proud Southern city where the living is gracious and activities move at a relaxed pace. But Jackson is also a financial center and a rapidly growing major distribution center, with interstate highways and railroads affording access to all parts of the Sun Belt. A rich history has given the city the opportunity to progress through renovation of historic structures rather than the construction of new edifices. Perhaps more than any other southern capital, Jackson defined the fortunes and served as a beacon for the entirety of the state.

■ Geography and Climate

Standing on the west bank of the Pearl River about 150 miles north of the Gulf of Mexico, Jackson is about 45 miles east of the Mississippi River. The city is the seat of Hinds County, though parts of Jackson are also located in Rankin and Madison counties. The terrain surrounding Jackson is gently rolling; alluvial plains up to three-miles wide extend along the river near Jackson, where some levees have been built on both sides of the river. Jackson receives approximately 55 inches of rainfall per year, but only trace amounts of snow, making it rather wet and significantly humid most of the year. The vicinity enjoys a fairly long warm season with light winds late in the day during summer.

Gil Ford Photography.

Area: 106.82 square miles

Elevation: 291 feet above sea level

Average Temperatures: 64.1° F

Average Annual Precipitation: 55.95 inches

■ History

City Named for "Old Hickory"

The earliest inhabitants of the Jackson area were of the Choctaw and Chickasaw Native American tribes. During the late eighteenth century, a French-Canadian named Louis LeFleur began operating a trading post on a high bluff along the west bank of the Pearl River. The subsequent settlement became known as LeFleur's Bluff. In October 1821 when the Choctaws relinquished their land to the federal government as part of the Treaty of Doak's Stand, it was decided that LeFleur's Bluff was the most suitable location for a seat of government. A November 1821 act of the U.S. Congress established Mississippi's state government at this site, renamed Jackson in honor of General Andrew "Old Hickory" Jackson. The city's development cannot be separated from its role as Mississippi's capital.

In little more than a year, a two-story brick statehouse was ready for the historic opening session of the Mississippi state legislature in December 1822. A second capitol, now

known as the "Old Capitol," opened in 1840; that edifice, now a historical museum, was in turn replaced. Based on the design of the nation's capitol in Washington, Jackson's architecturally splendid New Capitol has, since its dedication in 1903, been the focus of Mississippi's government activities.

Jackson Rebuilds After Fires

The cotton industry had made Jackson the capital of a wealthy state, but during the Civil War, when Union forces occupied Jackson under the command of General George Sherman, the city suffered three major fires. Because brick chimneys were the most visible structures left standing, Jackson earned the nickname "Chimneyville." The City Hall was spared from burning, probably because it was used as a hospital. Jackson residents had to begin slowly rebuilding after 1865. Railroads radiating out from the city contributed to the growth of transportation and trade in Jackson.

While Jackson's population was less than 8,000 people at the close of the century, by 1905 it had nearly doubled. Natural gas fields near the city were opened in the 1930s, providing inexpensive fuel for factories. Abundant energy coupled with existing transportation systems began to attract industries to the Jackson area. Since the 1960s an active program for economic development has stimulated building of many kinds, spurred industrial expansion, and attracted new residents to Jackson.

Modern Jackson

Jackson's lingering reputation as a racially divided city changed in 1997, when Harvey Johnson was elected the city's first African American mayor. He won 70 percent of the vote with a campaign that transcended race. Continuing to reinvent itself as a diverse and progressive city, Jackson made a major foray into the automobile industry by enticing Nissan Motor Company to construct a $930 million automotive plant in 2003. By continued its makeover, as a newly renovated glass-fronted Mississippi Museum of Art relocated to a new space downtown. The King Edward Hotel, a 1923 palazzo-style building, was renovated from 2006 to 2009 after being vacant for four decades. The renovation was one of 23 restoration projects honored by the National Trust for Historic Preservation in 2010.

The city looked to build on this achievements into the 2010s. Chokwe Lumumba succeeded Johnson as mayor in 2013, becoming the second African American mayor in the city's history. And just as Lumumba followed in Johnson's footsteps, the city sought to transfer the success of the Nissan plant and King Edward renovations to other industries and buildings. Long-awaited development of Farish Street remained elusive, but city leaders believed they had a blueprint in place to further progress in the capital.

Historical Information: Mississippi Department of Archives and History, 200 North St., Jackson, MS 39201; telephone (601) 576-6850; email info@mdah.state.ms.us

■ Population Profile

Metropolitan Statistical Area Population

2000: 525,346
2010: 539,057
2012 estimate: 548,945
Percent change, 2000–2010: 2.6%
U.S. rank in 2000: 90th
U.S. rank in 2010: 96th

City Residents

1990: 202,062
2000: 184,256
2010: 173,514
2012 estimate: 175,376
Percent change, 2000–2010: −5.8%
U.S. rank in 1990: 78th (State rank: 1st)
U.S. rank in 2000: 127th (State rank: 1st)
U.S. rank in 2010: 134th (State rank: 1st)

Density: 1,562.5 people per square mile

Racial and ethnic characteristics

White: 31,889
Black or African American: 139,207
American Indian and Alaskan Native: 129
Asian: 749
Native Hawaiian and Other Pacific Islander: 0
Hispanic or Latino (may be of any race): 3,017
Other: 3,402

Percent of residents born in state: 83.2%

Age characteristics

Population under 5 years old: 11,995
Population 5 to 9 years old: 13,477
Population 10 to 14 years old: 13,076
Population 15 to 19 years old: 14,004
Population 20 to 24 years old: 16,173
Population 25 to 34 years old: 26,337
Population 35 to 44 years old: 21,433
Population 45 to 54 years old: 21,076
Population 55 to 59 years old: 11,551
Population 60 to 64 years old: 8,160
Population 65 to 74 years old: 10,171
Population 75 to 84 years old: 4,993
Population 85 years and over: 2,930
Median age: 32.0

Births (2010–11 Metropolitan Area)

Total number: 7,534

Deaths (2010–11 Metropolitan Area)

Total number: 4,551

Money income (2012)

Per capita income: $19,013
Median household income: $32,232
Total households: 61,612

Number of households with income of ...

less than $10,000: 8,899
$10,000 to $14,999: 5,365
$15,000 to $24,999: 10,149
$25,000 to $34,999: 8,413
$35,000 to $49,999: 9,768
$50,000 to $74,999: 9,087
$75,000 to $99,999: 3,836
$100,000 to $149,999: 3,435
$150,000 to $199,999: 1,134
$200,000 or more: 1,526

Percent of families below poverty level: 30.3%

FBI Crime Index Property: 11,568

FBI Crime Index Violent: 1,668

■ Municipal Government

Jackson has operated through a mayor-council form of government since 1985. Its seven councilmen are elected by wards while the mayor is elected at-large for a four-year term.

Head Official: Mayor Chokwe Lumumba (since 2013; current term expires 2017)

Total Number of City Employees: 2,323 (2012)

City Information: City of Jackson, 200 S. President St., Jackson, MS 39201; telephone (601)960-1084; fax (601)960-2193

■ Economy

Major Industries and Commercial Activity

Known as the "Best of the New South," Jackson is a major business force in Mississippi. Its diversity of business and industry and its position as the state capital help insulate the metropolitan area from the economic downturns experienced by other cities. Jackson's success in drawing high-paying industrial operations is attributed to the city's combination of an attractive labor pool and a good quality of life.

There are three banks headquartered in Jackson: Tower Loan, First Commercial Bank, and Trustmark National Bank. Ergon Inc., a network of petroleum-related companies, is headquartered in Jackson, as is Cal-Maine Foods, Inc. Cattle is the primary commodity in Hinds County, though other commodities important to the region are cotton, grains, poultry, and timber. Government jobs, ranging from municipal to federal, employ approximately 45,000 residents in metropolitan Jackson. Manufacturing remains an important economic sector. Construction, distribution and trade, health care, retail, telecommunications, and travel and tourism are also vital to the local economy.

One of the most promising sectors for Jackson is the automobile industry. For years, city officials worked to lure automotive manufacturers to the area by highlighting its assets, namely the availability of large parcels of land, a well-developed energy and utility infrastructure, and low industrial expenses. Nissan Motor Company responded to their efforts, and in 2003 produced the first truck in Jackson's new, $930 million automobile plant. This investment by Nissan helped offset the downturn the Jackson area had incurred with the bankruptcy of WorldCom Incorporated, whose headquarters were in nearby Clinton, Mississippi, as well as the losses it faced in 2004 when Tyson Foods Incorporated announced the closing of its Jackson processing plant. An analysis in 2013 concluded that the plant ultimately led to the direct or indirect creation of 16,000 area jobs, added $2.5 billion annually to state gross domestic product and $1.2 billion to disposable income, and generated some $180 million in local and state tax revenue.

Among the largest manufacturers in Hinds County were: Delphi-Clinton, which produces automotive wiring harness components; Eaton Aerospace, which produces hydraulic pumps for aerospace; and Unified Brands, which produces commercial cooking equipment.

Items and goods produced: automobiles and related automotive components, fabricated metals, electrical and electronic equipment, food products, apparel, wood products, furniture, transportation equipment, rubber and plastic products, portable electric tools, welded steel tubing, aircraft parts

Incentive Programs-New and Existing Companies

Local programs: Founded in 1994, the Greater Jackson Alliance, an alliance consisting of the Claiborne County Economic Development District, Copiah Count Economic Development District, Entergy Mississippi, Hinds County Economic Development Authority, Jackson Muncipal Airport Authority, Madison County Economic Development Authority, Greater Jackson Chamber Partnership, Rankin First Economic Development Authority, Simpson County Development Foundation, and Vicksburg-Warren County Port Commission, markets and promotes the metropolitan Jackson area and encourages economic development through the expansions of existing businesses and industries and locations. The City of Jackson Storefront Improvement Grant Program offers grants for exterior structural improvements to businesses located in designated areas of the city. Its Special Economic Development Grant program provides businesses with up to $50,000 for business investments of $1.5 million, or the creation of at least 30 jobs. Other city programs include the Small Business Disadvantage Development Program, the Minority Business Enterprise Program, Business Outreach, and Brownfields Redevelopment Program. Tax incentives were available for developments that rehabilitated multi-family residential structures, converted commercial buildings to residential use, or renovated historic landmarks.

State programs: A tax credit program is offered through the Mississippi Department of Archives & History for the restoration of buildings listed on the National Register of Historic Places or designated as Mississippi Landmarks. As of 2013, the state tax credit stood at 25 percent for restoration of either residential or commercial properties.

Momentum Mississippi was created in 2004 by Governor Haley Barbour as a long-range economic development implementation organization. The 2005 legislation was designed to help existing industries invest in technology and expand; attract high-value, high-technology enterprises; and provide counties and cities throughout Mississippi with the economic development tools to compete. Specifically, Momentum Mississippi identifies and pursues targets in both manufacturing and services, and aligns incentives—including dozens of grants, loans, and tax credits—around these targets.

Targeted industries included advanced manufacturing, aerospace, agribusiness, automotive, energy, health care, and shipbuilding. Mississippi was named a top-five state for cost of doing business by *Area Development Magazine* in 2012, and was ranked second in utility costs and permitting speed.

Job training programs: The state of Mississippi provides recruitment, job referral and placement services; customized pre-employment, industry-based, and vendor training; project-specific training; and on-the-job training reimbursement and tax credits for new, expanding, or existing industries. The Workforce Training and Services division of the Mississippi Development Authority administers employee training. The Mississippi Department of Employment's WIN Job Centers provide access to employment, education, training, and economic development services. Other WIN services for employers include a database of qualified job candidates, assistance in writing job descriptions, proficiency testing, labor market data, and information on work opportunity tax credits. The Mississippi Contract Procurement Center provides information about bid opportunities from federal, state, and local government agencies; it also offers training, marketing assistance, technical support, and counseling.

Development Projects

By far, the largest development project of the early 2000s was the Nissan Motor Company truck plant. The $930 million facility ultimately led the direct or indirect creation of 16,000 area jobs and added $2.5 billion annually to state gross domestic product.

The King Edward Hotel, listed on the National Register of Historic Places in 1976, was closed for 40 years before a major renovation project during 2006–09. The $90 million restoration finished in December, and the hotel reopened as the Hilton Garden Inn Jackson Downtown with 186 rooms and suites, and 64 luxury apartments. Also included were a restaurant, bar, convenience store, coffee shop, fitness center, swimming pool, business center, retail space, and 7,000 square feet of meeting and event space.

A November 2004 referendum funded construction of the Jackson Convention Center, which opened in 2009, through an increase in hotel and restaurant taxes. The 330,000-square-foot complex ended Jackson's status as the only state capital in the United States without a convention center. However, the absence of an adjoining hotel limited growth of the city's convention industry and remained a central point of future development.

Jackson Square, a prime retail and restaurant development created in 1968, was left largely vacant by 2010. However, the site was refurbished and reopened as Jackson Square Promenade in April 2012, with near complete occupancy in a matter of months.

In 2012 Jackson's Vision 2022 development plan layed out core development initiatives for the decade to follow. Focal points were the expansion of existing health care infrastructure; developing water and sewage infrastructure to handle business and population growth; grow Jackson-Evers International Airport's reputation as a premier desitnation for aerospace industries; create a 1,500-acre lake for flood protection, economic development, and quality of life; utilize local executives to market Jackson as the nation's top business destination; build a convention center hotel in downtown Jackson; establish bicycle and walking trails throughout the area; encourage local business talent; enhance the city's art and cultural institutes; and further education through grassroots efforts.

The develoment of Farish Street in Jackson continues to be an important but elusive development project for the city. Performa Entertainment Real Estate purchased much of the surrounding property but was forced to sell in 2008 after delays and setbacks. Watkins Development, which took over the project at a cost of nearly $2 million, continued early stages of development through 2013, having secured more than $10 million in historic tax credits.

Economic Development Information: Greater Jackson Chamber Partnership, P.O. Box 22548, Jackson, MS 39225; telephone (601) 948-7575.

Commercial Shipping

Equidistant from Memphis to the North, New Orleans to the south, Atlanta to the east, and Dallas to the west, Jackson is advantageously positioned to serve the South's distribution needs. A transportation network of major carriers, regional airlines, major trucking lines, and rail lines operated by the Canadian National Railway and the Kansas City Southern Railway Company assures Jackson's position as a vital provider of the nation's freight service. The Jackson Municipal Airport Authority operates Jackson-Evers International Airport (JIA) and Hawkins Field, both of which handle considerable freight activity. JIA is the site of Foreign Trade Zone #158, where foreign goods bound for international destinations can be temporarily stored without incurring an import duty, as well as the Mississippi Air Cargo Logistics Center. The nearest full-service port is the Port of Vicksburg. The Port is 45 miles west of Jackson and is a U.S. Customs port of entry and foreign trade zone. U.S. Highway 61 can access this port easily. A Commercial Trucking Zone is nearby for land transportation needs.

Labor Force and Employment Outlook

Industrial leaders credit the metropolitan Jackson work force with a demonstrated willingness to adapt to rapidly changing technologies. Job growth in 2012 was 0.7 percent, with professional and business services pacing total growth, followed by education and health services, leisure and hospitality, and financial services.

The following is a summary of data regarding the 2012 Jackson labor force:

Size of civilian labor force: 80,677

Number of workers employed in . . .

agriculture and mining: 252
construction: 3,647
manufacturing: 4,722
wholesale trade: 1,345
retail trade: 8,027
transportation: 3,221
information systems: 1,617
finance: 3,045
professional administration: 5,167
education and social services: 21,058
arts and leisure: 7,384
other: 3,706
public administration: 6,462

Average hourly earnings of production workers: $15.5

Unemployment rate: 7.4% (2012)

Employers

Largest employers (2012)	Number of employees
State of Mississippi	31,556
University of Mississippi Medical Center	8,000
United States Government	5,500
Jackson Public School District	4,814
Baptist Health Systems	2,875
St. Dominic Health Services	2,600
City of Jackson, Mississippi	2,323
Jackson State University	1,667
AT&T	1,300
Central Mississippi Medical Center	1,200

Cost of Living

The following is a summary of data regarding several key cost of living factors in the area.

2013 ACCRA Average House Price: $242,960

2013 ACCRA Cost of Living Index: 90

State income tax rate: 3.0% to 5.0%

State sales tax rate: 7.0%

Local income tax rate: None

Local sales tax rate: None

Property tax rate: 111.08 mills (2013)

Economic Information: Greater Jackson Chamber Partnership, P.O. Box 22548, Jackson, MS 39225; telephone (601) 948-7575.

■ Education and Research

Elementary and Secondary Schools

Public education in Jackson is provided by Jackson Public Schools (JPS), the largest school district in Mississippi. Jackson is notable for being the city where Parents for Public Schools was founded in 1989. The group began a national movement to make public schools truly integrated. JPS offers a number of special programs to meet students' individual needs. Preschool is offered at 25 of the city's 38 elementary schools The Open Doors program serves gifted students at the elementary and high-school levels. Intensive visual and performing arts curriculums are available for middle- and high-school students. The International Baccalaurate program is available to all students beginning in kindergarten. In 2013 students from JPS received more than $12 million in scholarship offers. Public facilities are supplemented by several private and parochial schools that serve the area.

The following is a summary of data regarding the Jackson Public School District.

Total enrollment: 30,366

Number of facilities

total: 60
elementary schools: 38
junior high schools: 13
high schools: 7
other: 2

Student/teacher ratio: 16.15:1

Teacher salaries

average (statewide): $46,818

Funding per pupil: $8,616

Public Schools Information: Jackson Public Schools, PO Box 2338, Jackson, MS 39225-2338; telephone (601) 960-8700

Colleges and Universities

Jackson State University is a public coeducational institution established in 1877. The University of Mississippi Medical Center has schools of medicine, dentistry, nursing, and health-related professions, and a graduate school of medical sciences. Hinds Community College, a two-year public institution serving approximately 32,000 students each year, has a campus in Jackson. Belhaven University, affiliated with the Presbyterian Church, awards bachelor's, master's, and associate's degrees. Millsaps College, a private college affiliated with the United Methodist Church, awards bachelor's and master's degrees. Other Jackson-area colleges include Tougaloo College and the Mississippi College School of Law. Mississippi College's main campus is located in nearby Clinton, Mississippi.

The Ayers agreement, which was a desegregation lawsuit filed in 1975, provided allotted funds that allowed Jackson State University to expand. The settlement, valued entirely at $503.2 million, has provided for the university to add master's and doctoral programs in urban planning. The money also funded a new School of Public Health and School of Engineering. The provisions of the agreement significantly lowered funding beginning in 2012 with a second drop in 2018.

Libraries and Research Centers

The Jackson-Hinds Library System supports 15 branches, eight of which are located in the city of Jackson. Its collection numbers more than 640,000 books, videos, audio cassettes, compact discs, and multimedia kits, in addition to periodicals, microfiche, magazine and newspapers on microfilm, and CD-ROMs. The main library, the Eudora Welty Library, houses a special collection on Mississippi writers and serves as the Capital Area Bar Association's public law library.

Jackson State University maintains a large library holding 400,000 book titles, government documents, and a special Black Studies collection. The University's Center for Economic Development conducts small business research. The University of Mississippi Medical Center is a leader in innovative medical research.

Public Library Information: Jackson-Hinds Library System, c/o Eudora Welty Library, 300 N. State St., Jackson, MS 39201; telephone (601) 968-5811.

■ Health Care

Two of the city's largest health-care facilities are Mississippi Baptist Health Systems and the Central Mississippi Medical Center. A major asset is the University of Mississippi Medical Center. Besides providing instruction in medicine, dentistry, nursing, and health-related professions, the University Medical Center operates the renowned University Hospitals and Clinics, which serve as Jackson's major teaching institutions. It is one of the city's largest employers and included more than 500 physician faculty members as of 2013. The Montgomery Veterans Affairs Medical Center, also a

teaching facility, has an 86-bed Community Living Center, three 150-bed state veterans nursing homes, and an array of clinics serving the veteran population. Other health care institutions in the Jackson area include Brentwood Behavioral HealthCare of Mississippi, Methodist Rehabilitation Center, Mississippi Hospital for Restorative Care, River Oaks Hospital, St. Dominic Hospital, and Woman's Hospital.

■ Recreation

Sightseeing

As the capital of the Magnolia State, Jackson offers visitors several buildings of historical interest. The New Capitol, built in 1903 in the Beaux Arts style of architecture and patterned after the nation's capitol in Washington, is the working seat of Mississippi's government. The restored Old Capitol, which was built in 1833 and served as the government seat for 70 years, is the home of the State Historical Museum. It was temporarily closed due to roof damage from Hurricane Katrina, but was renovated and reopened in 2009. It is the oldest building in the state. The Governor's Mansion was headquarters for Union Generals Grant and Sherman during the Civil War and has been home to all of Mississippi's governors since 1842; it is the second oldest continously occupied governor's residence in the United States. City Hall was one of the few buildings left standing after Union troops set fire to the city.

On 110 acres in the heart of the city, the Jackson Zoological Park houses more than 775 birds, reptiles, and mammals representing more than 120 species from all over the world, including 12 endangered species. A Sumatran tiger exhibit opened in 2010. The zoo drew more than 130,000 visitors in 2013. At Mynelle Gardens, Jackson's botanical gardens, more than a thousand varieties of plants are tended among several distinct gardens situated on seven acres. About 10 miles north of Jackson is the 444-mile historic Natchez Trace Parkway, where a series of Indian paths became a post road. Mississippi Crafts Center, a showcase for folk arts, and pleasant picnic areas are located along the historic drive. It celebrated its 40 anniversary in 2013, having grown from 30 to 400 members during that period. The Mississippi Blues Trail winds its way through the city and offers music lovers several sites marking blues history.

Arts and Culture

With pride in their southern hospitality and culture, Jacksonians have created facilities and assured an atmosphere where the arts flourish. In 2007 a newly renovated Mississippi Museum of Art moved to a location down the street from the Mississippi Arts Center. The 1.2-acre Art Garden at the museum, a second phase of construction, completed in 2011. The Russell C. Davis Planetarium offers a variety of public shows and educational programs, including sky shows and laser light concerts, designed to give students of all ages a better understanding of the universe and space exploration. It is one of the largest and most well equipped planetariums in the South.

The performing arts offer variety to Jackson residents and visitors. New Stage Theatre stages live dramatic performances, as do local colleges and national touring companies. Ballet is hugely popular in Jackson. It is presented locally by Ballet Mississippi, which was established in 1964 as the Jackson Ballet Guild. Every four years Jackson is proud to host the two-week USA International Ballet Competition. The Mississippi Opera, Mississippi Symphony Orchestra, Mississippi Academy of Ancient Music, Jackson Choral Society, and Metropolitan Chamber Orchestra Society offer a full calendar of live music to the region's audiences. Jackson-area nightspots, including the famous Hal & Mal's, feature music for every taste, including reggae, blues, Dixieland, country, jazz, and rock.

Old Capitol Museum, formerly the seat of state government, now exhibits Mississippi's state historical collections. After closing temporarily in 2007 due to roof damage from Hurricane Katrina, it reopened in 2009. Wildlife specimens, aquariums, and ecological exhibits are on display at the Mississippi Museum of Natural Science. The Municipal Art Gallery displays month-long exhibitions of works that are available for sale.

The Mississippi Agriculture and Forestry Museum, spanning 40 acres, depicts the stories of men and women who made their living as farmers and woodsmen. African American culture and African American Mississippi history are featured in the Smith Robertson Museum and Cultural Center. The International Museum of Muslim Cultures is devoted to contributions Muslims have made to the city of Jackson, the state, the nation, and the world. Other Jackson museums of note are the Oaks House Museum, which is the oldest house in the city; the Manship House Museum, a rare example of Gothic Revival architecture in Mississippi closed during 2010 and 2011 for foundation repairs; and the Mississippi Sports Hall of Fame and Museum, which features interactive exhibits and more than 500 televised interviews with famous Mississippi athletes. The Eudora Welty Museum offers visitors a chance to see the writer's home as she lived in it: Welty left her house and collection of thousands of books to the state, and the Welty family donated furniture and art. The garden stretches over a lot of about three-quarters of an acre in the Belhaven neighborhood, where Welty and her family were early residents.

Festivals and Holidays

Jackson hosts one of the nation's largest parades in honor of Dr. Martin Luther King Jr. This two-week celebration in January also features gospel music, a talent show, and live entertainment. Right on its heels is the Dixie National Livestock Show, Parade, and Rodeo; held over three weeks at the Mississippi Fairgrounds, the event also includes a three-day Western Festival, a rodeo dance, and two trade shows. March brings Mal's St. Paddy's Parade & Festival, featuring the local favorite and world-famous Sweet Potato Queens. Spring ushers in the Crossroads Film Festival in April, which highlights films made by or about Mississippi or the South.

Jubilee! JAM, held in downtown Jackson each June, is a celebration of music, arts and crafts, and food. Several events celebrate the nation's independence each July, such as the Old Fashioned 4th of July Celebration at the Mississippi Agriculture & Forestry Museum. August brings LatinFest, a celebration of Latin American culture. September is the month for several cultural festivals, including Celtic Fest and the Farish Street Heritage Festival. Each October features the huge Mississippi State Fair, a 12-day event that attracts more than one-half million visitors.

Trustmark's Red Beans & Rice Celebration, featuring Southern-style food, music, and activities, is also held in the autumn, as are the Halloween Carnival and the Harvest Festival. Numerous musical and theatrical performances, a parade, and tours of architecturally significant buildings contribute to festive Christmas and Kwanzaa seasons.

Sports for the Spectator

College football is a local favorite in Jackson. More than 30,000 spectators turned out for the annual Capital City Classic between the Jackson State University Tigers and the Alcorn State University Braves for 20 years between 1993 and 2013, but the event moved to Alcorn State's home field beginning in 2014. Memorial Stadium, the former home of the game, still played host to other contests, pageants, and events. Smith-Wills Stadium, formerly occupied by several minor league baseball teams in Jackson, is home to the Belhaven University Blazers. The Mississippi Braves, a Double-A affiliate of the Atlanta Braves, play in nearby Pearl, Mississippi.

The National Cutting Horse Association event is at the Mississippi State Fairgrounds, with competition from amateur and professional riders. The Tour LeFleur Bike Race is a regional cycling event with multiple races throughout downtown Jackson. The Sanderson Farms Championship, Mississippi's only regular PGA tour event, is held in Madison, Mississippi, in November.

Sports for the Participant

Taking advantage of its warm climate, many of Jackson's sports facilities emphasize outdoor life. With 56 parks and facilities in the city system, residents and visitors can enjoy facilities ranging from swimming pools to playgrounds to primitive camping. Public and private golf courses, tennis and basketball courts, baseball and soccer fields, jogging and biking routes, nature trails, bowling and roller skating facilities, a go-cart track, and a model airplane field are all available in the area. Sports leagues suited to children include T-ball, baseball, football, and soccer.

An outdoor asset to Jackson only 10 miles northeast of the city center is the 33,000-acre Ross Barnett Reservoir, where water sports-boating, sailing, water skiing, swimming, and fishing-abound, with additional areas designated for camping and picnicking. LeFleur's Bluff State Park offers camping, fishing, picnic spots, hiking trails, and a nine-hole golf course situated on 305 acres.

Shopping and Dining

The central business district offers a variety of stores for shopping pleasure. Highland Village Shopping Center offers a range of upscale boutique shops. MetroCenter Mall in Jackson and Northpark Mall in Ridgeland provide a wide variety of retail outlets. Numerous specialty shopping centers located outside of the major malls offer unique merchandise. Among these are the Chimneyville Crafts Gallery, specializing in crafts made by local artists, and two local outlets featuring the work of members of the Craftsmen's Guild of Mississippi. More than 40 antique dealers operate in the Jackson area.

Dining opportunities in Jackson's some 300 restaurants can suit every taste, from fast food or southern style cuisine, such as southern fried chicken, biscuits, and pecan pie, to fresh Gulf Coast seafood, including shrimp, oysters, and crab. International establishments in the Jackson area feature French, Continental, Greek, Oriental, and Mexican menus.

Visitor Information: Jackson Convention & Visitors Bureau, 111 East Capitol St., Suite 102, Jackson, MS 39201; telephone (601) 960-1891; toll-free (800) 354-7695; fax (601) 960-1827.

■ Convention Facilities

The Jackson Convention Complex was completed in 2009. It includes some 330,000 square feet of exhibit, ballroom, and meeting space. The complex hosted 231 events in 2012 over 295 days, with a total attendance of 141,464 people. It brought in more than $3.4 million in gross income that same year.

The Mississippi Fair Grounds Complex, which is comprised of the Mississippi Coliseum, an all-season arena with 6,500 permanent seats and up to 3,500 additional temporary seats, and the Mississippi Trade Mart, which offers 66,000 square feet of exhibit space and is ideal for professional conventions and exhibits of automobiles and other types of equipment. Thalia Mara Hall, adjacent to the Mississippi Arts Center downtown, offers 8,000 square feet of exhibit space and seating space for 2,500 people. Mississippi Veterans Memorial Stadium has 60,492 seats, while Smith-Wills Stadium, near the Agriculture and

Forestry Museum, can seat 5,200 people. A number of area hotels offer meeting facilities, including the Hilton Jackson & Convention Center with seating up to 1,200 and meeting space of 8,100 square feet, and the Jackson Marriott with 20 meeting rooms totaling 35,000 square feet.

Convention Information: Jackson Convention & Visitors Bureau, 111 East Capitol St., Suite 102, Jackson, MS 39201; telephone (601) 960-1891; toll-free (800) 354-7695; fax (601) 960-1827.

■ Transportation

Approaching the City

Most air passengers arrive in Jackson through Jackson-Evers International Airport. American Eagle, Delta, Southwest, US Airways, and United provide nonstop service to 10 cities. Hawkins Field, located in northwest Jackson and serving Hawkins Industrial Park, accommodates private and company planes. Motor traffic is handled by two primary interstate highways, I-55 running north and south, and I-20 going east and west; a third interstate, I-220, connects I-20 with I-55. Additional approaches to the city are U.S. highways 49, 51, and 80, and state highways 18, 25, and 471. Amtrak and Greyhound-Trailways Bus Lines accommodate rail and bus passengers traveling to Jackson.

Traveling in the City

Jackson's urban mass transit includes 12 fixed bus routes, with paratransit services for passengers with disabilities. Jatran operates every day except Sunday, as well as major holidays. Sixteen new buses were purchased for $4.4 million, with a matching federal grant money, by the city in 2010.

■ Communications

Newspapers and Magazines

The Clarion-Ledger publishes an evening paper seven days a week. Weekly newspapers include the *Jackson Advocate*, Mississippi's oldest African American newspaper; *Mississippi Business Journal*, Mississippi's only statewide business publication; and *Northside Sun*. *The New Southern View* is a quarterly e-magazine featuring articles, local information, and a community calendar for residents of the Greater Jackson metropolitan area. The *Jackson Free Press* provides an alternative news source for the city.

Television and Radio

Jackson has nine television stations, with additional coverage available through cable television service and stations based in surrounding communities. Nine AM and eight FM radio stations broadcast from Jackson.

Media Information: *The Clarion-Ledger,* 201 S. Congress St., Jackson, MS 39201; telephone (601)961-7200; toll-free, in state (877) 850-5343.

Jackson Online

City of Jackson Home Page. Available www.city. jackson.ms.us

The Clarion-Ledger. Available www.clarionledger. com

Greater Jackson Alliance. Available www.metro jacksoneda.com/index.php

Hinds County Economic Development District. Available www.selecthinds.com

Jackson Convention & Visitors Bureau. Available www.visitjackson.com

Jackson-Hinds Library System. Available www. jhlibrary.com

Jackson Public Schools. Available www.jackson.k12. ms.us

Greater Jackson Chamber Partnership. Available www.greaterjacksonpartnership.com

Mississippi Department of Archives and History. Available www.mdah.state.ms.us

BIBLIOGRAPHY

Brown, Jennie, *Medgar Evers* (Los Angeles, CA: Holloway House, 1994)

Brown, Rosellen, *Civil Wars* (New York: Knopf, 1984)

Kimbrough, Julie L., *Jackson, MS: Images of America Series* (Mount Pleasant, SC: Arcadia Publishing, 1998)

Sweet, Grace Britton, *Church Street: The Sugar Hill of Jackson, Mississippi* (Charleston, SC: History Press, 2013)

North Carolina

The State in Brief

Nickname: Tar Heel State; Old North State

Motto: Esse quam videri (To be rather than to seem)

Flower: Dogwood

Bird: Cardinal

Area: 53,819 square miles (2010; U.S. rank 28th)

Elevation: Ranges from sea level to 6,684 feet above sea level

Climate: Warm and mild with abundant rainfall; subtropical in southeast, cooler in the mountains

Admitted to Union: November 21, 1789

Capital: Raleigh

Head Official: Pat McCrory (R) (until 2017)

Population

    1990: 6,628,637
    2000: 8,049,313
    2010: 9,535,483
    2012 estimate: 9,544,249
    Percent change, 2000–2010: 18.5%
    U.S. rank in 2012: 10th
    Percent of residents born in state: 58.1% (2012)
    Density: 196.1 people per square mile (2010)
    2012 FBI Crime Index Total: 363,058

Racial and Ethnic Characteristics (2012)

    White: 6,659,867
    Black or African American: 2,047,092
    American Indian and Alaska Native: 110,171
    Asian: 211,708
    Native Hawaiian and Pacific Islander: 4,424
    Hispanic or Latino (may be of any race): 796,293
    Other: 510,987

Age Characteristics (2012)

    Population under 5 years old: 627,188
    Population 5 to 19 years old: 1,926,792
    Percent of population 65 years and over: 13.1%
    Median age: 37.4

Vital Statistics

    Total number of births (2012–13): 119,932
    Total number of deaths (2012–13): 81,568
    AIDS cases reported through 2011: 21,421

Economy

    Major industries: Trade, manufacturing, agriculture, business and financial services
    Unemployment rate (2012): 6.6%
    Per capita income (2012): $25,285
    Median household income (2012): $46,450
    Percentage of persons below poverty level (2012): 16.8%
    Income tax rate: 6.0% to 7.75%
    Sales tax rate: 4.75%

Asheville

■ The City in Brief

Founded: 1784 (incorporated, 1797

Head Official: Mayor Esther Manheimer (since 2013)

City Population
    1990: 61,607
    2000: 72,883
    2010: 83,393
    2012 estimate: 85,721
    Percent change, 2000–2010: 14.4%
    U.S. rank in 2010: 366th

Metropolitan Statistical Area Population
    2000: 369,171
    2010: 424,858
    2012 estimate: 432,406
    Percent change, 2000–2010: 15.1%
    U.S. rank in 2000: 124th
    U.S. rank in 2010: 117th

Area: Not available

Elevation: 2,140 feet above sea level

Average Annual Temperatures: Not available

Average Annual Precipitation: Not available

Major Economic Sectors: education and health services, government, leisure and hospitality, retail

Unemployment Rate: 5.8% (2012)

Per Capita Income: $25,840

2012 FBI Crime Index Property: 4,910

Major Colleges and Universities: University of North Carolina at Asheville, Warren Wilson College

Daily Newspaper: *Asheville Citizen-Times*

■ Introduction

Asheville has been attracting tourists since the late 1800s, when rail service came to the city. With the spectacular Biltmore Estate continuing to attract visitors to the area, Asheville, North Carolina, is known for its spectacular mountain scenery and friendly North Carolina atmosphere. It is the largest city in western North Carolina and the county seat for Buncombe County, which combine to make it a center of business and cultural activities. Asheville's unique architecture is a mixture of art deco, beaux arts, and neoclassical buildings, which gives Asheville businesses an interesting and quaint setting, surrounded by the spectacular scenery of the Blue Ridge Mountains. All things considered, the Land of Sky has become a great place to live, work, and play.

■ Geography and Climate

Asheville is situated in the Blue Ridge Mountains where the French Broad River and the Swannanoa River join together. The Snowbird Mountains, Great Smoky Mountains, Balsam Mountains, Newfound Mountains, and Nantahala Mountains are southwest of the French Broad River basin. The mountains, including 5,721-foot Mount Pisgah and Grandfather Mountain, attract tourists with their caverns, trails, and abundant wildlife. The area is prone to flooding by the Swannanoa and French Broad Rivers, which has challenged economic development.

Asheville's moderate climate is largely the result of the mountains around it. The median yearly temperature is 55.6 degrees Fahrenheit. Average temperatures in the winter are slightly above freezing, and summer

The Biltmore Estate in Asheville; the home took six years to build, and was completed, under the direction of original owner George Vanderbilt, in 1895. © *The Biltmore Company*

temperatures remain in the low 70 degrees Fahrenheit. Precipitation, averaging about 38 inches annually occurs year round; in winter, it may take the form of freezing rain. In the summer, dramatic thunderstorms are not uncommon. The fall brings mild, dry weather. Snow is relatively infrequent, with an annual average of less than 13 inches.

Area: Not available

Elevation: 2,140 feet above sea level

Average Temperatures: Not available

Average Annual Precipitation: Not available

■ History

The rise of county and city

Asheville's recorded history began in 1784, when William Davidson and his relatives made a settlement among the Blue Ridge Mountains. Nearly six years later, after the settlement had been permanently established, Davidson helped designate the area as Buncombe County, which occurred in December 1791. Settlers began moving into the mountainous region. In 1797, the city of Asheville

was incorporated and named for the governor at the time, Samuel Ashe.

Asheville became a vital Confederate military center during the Civil War. A company of soldiers, known as the Buncombe Rifles, carried a flag made from the silk dresses of Asheville women when it marched on April 18, 1861.

City develops access to the country

After Asheville's official founding, infrastructure development in the city took off. Roads were built along the French Broad River, allowing travel to and from other states, such as Tennessee. Asheville was becoming a resort area for travelers who lived in the cities of the South. The building of a railroad in 1880 expanded Asheville's connections to other parts of the United States for trade and travel. People flocked to the area, looking for a fresh mountain retreat. By 1890, the population of Asheville reached nearly 30,000.

Biltmore becomes a reality

In 1895, Biltmore, the stately home built by the affluent George W. Vanderbilt, became the nation's largest private home. The mansion was constructed in a French design, with gardens and detailed architectural attributes.

During the nearly six years it took to construct Biltmore, a village, known as Biltmore Village, grew up to house hundreds of construction workers. Vanderbilt had purchased 120,000 acres for his mountain retreat. Vanderbilt commissioned Frederick Law Olmsted, the landscape architect who designed New York City's Central Park, to design the gardens. To preserve the natural beauty of Vanderbilt's property, Olmsted created at Biltmore the country's first managed forest.

The new century brings buildings and prosperity

The 1900s brought with it the formation of government and a building boom that added to Asheville's designation as a hub for western North Carolina. City Hall, the Jackson Building, the Asheville Board of Trade, and an opera house became emblems of the city's identity as a credible and culturally interesting town. The Pack Memorial Public Library moved into a new white marble building in 1926; in late 1928, a new brick and limestone courthouse building was dedicated. The city designated lands for parks, and space for resorts and businesses that would attract people to the area for years to come.

When the stock market crashed, Asheville was hit hard. On November 20, 1930, Asheville's Central Bank and Trust Company, major holder of county funds, closed. Massive debt for the city and county loomed, and Asheville struggled with the highest per capita debt of any city in the country. City officials vowed not to default on their debts, and it took until 1977 for the city to repay all the bond debt and to recover financially from the Great Depression.

But there were new developments in the Asheville area. President Franklin D. Roosevelt's Civilian Conservation Corps (CCC) undertook construction of the Great Smoky Mountains National Park and Blue Ridge Parkway, which employed local workers. Two major transportation projects in the 1960s helped place Asheville on the map as a place to live, work, and play. These were the opening of the Asheville-Henderson Airport in 1961 (now Asheville Regional Airport) and the dedication of the Blue Ridge Parkway in 1968.

As manufacturing declined over the next two decades, city officials faced the challenge of revitalizing and reinventing Asheville. The Asheville Area Economic Development Partnership was established in 1987 to champion new developments in the city. By 1995 tourism was the leading industry in Buncombe County, and the nation began to notice the eclectic character of Asheville. From 2000 through 2012, Asheville held a spot as one of the Top 25 Arts Destinations in the annual survey by *American Style* magazine. A variety of travel organizations and publications recognized Asheville as a prime destination for family travel, while others marked the city as one of the best places in the country to retire. Into the 2010s, city officials hoped to draw new business and new residents to the city with a careful balance of development projects that promote diversity in the marketplace and the community.

Historical Information: Preservation Society of Asheville and Buncombe County, 324 Charlotte Street, Asheville, NC 28802; telephone (828) 254-2343.

■ Population Profile

Metropolitan Statistical Area Population
2000: 369,171
2010: 424,858
2012 estimate: 432,406
Percent change, 2000–2010: 15.1%
U.S. rank in 2000: 124th
U.S. rank in 2010: 117th

City Residents
1990: 61,607
2000: 72,883
2010: 83,393
2012 estimate: 85,721
Percent change, 2000–2010: 14.4%
U.S. rank in 2010: 366th

Density: 1,855.9 people per square mile

Racial and ethnic characteristics
White: 70,482
Black or African American: 10,697
American Indian and Alaskan Native: 0
Asian: 2,084
Native Hawaiian and Other Pacific Islander: 0
Hispanic or Latino (may be of any race): 4,434
Other: 2,458

Percent of residents born in state: 46.2%

Age characteristics
Population under 5 years old: 5,298
Population 5 to 9 years old: 3,763
Population 10 to 14 years old: 5,073
Population 15 to 19 years old: 4,517
Population 20 to 24 years old: 7,363
Population 25 to 34 years old: 15,044
Population 35 to 44 years old: 10,043
Population 45 to 54 years old: 10,601
Population 55 to 59 years old: 5,273
Population 60 to 64 years old: 4,464
Population 65 to 74 years old: 7,658
Population 75 to 84 years old: 4,049
Population 85 years and over: 2,575
Median age: 36.6

Births (2010–11 Metropolitan Area)
Total number: 4,384

Deaths (2010–11 Metropolitan Area)

Total number: 4,478

Money income (2012)

Per capita income: $25,840
Median household income: $42,419
Total households: 36,896

Number of households with income of . . .

less than $10,000: 3,587
$10,000 to $14,999: 3,269
$15,000 to $24,999: 4,272
$25,000 to $34,999: 4,419
$35,000 to $49,999: 5,712
$50,000 to $74,999: 7,277
$75,000 to $99,999: 3,437
$100,000 to $149,999: 3,100
$150,000 to $199,999: 755
$200,000 or more: 1,068

Percent of families below poverty level: 20.2%

FBI Crime Index Property: 4,910

FBI Crime Index Violent: 423

■ Municipal Government

The city of Asheville's charter dictates a council-manager form of government. The city manager oversees and carries out daily operations in accordance to laws implemented by city council. The city council consists of the mayor and six council members, who are elected at-large on staggered, four-year terms. The mayor oversees city council meetings and serves as a representative and spokesperson for the city government.

Head Official: Mayor Esther Manheimer (since 2013)

Total Number of City Employees: 1,750 (2013 est.)

City Information: City of Asheville, 70 Court Plaza, P.O. Box 7148, Asheville, NC 28802; telephone (828) 251-1122; email: info@ashevillenc.gov.

■ Economy

Major Industries and Commercial Activity

Traditionally, Asheville has excelled in health care, tourism, and manufacturing. Into the 2010s, health-care and educational services saw the greatest job increases in the metropolitan area. Professional and business services also seemed to be expanding, as did the leisure and hospitality sector. The tourist industry is a major force in attracting new residents. It is not uncommon for visitors, especially retirees, to enjoy Asheville so much that they

move to the area permanently. The largest source of population growth remains people moving to Asheville from other parts of the country. Its status as the largest city in western North Carolina has made it a hub for the surrounding region.

The Economic Development Coalition of Asheville-Buncombe County has been working to attract new and expanding business in five target clusters: advanced manufacturing, health care, science and technology, arts and culture, and knowledge-based entrepreneurs.

Top manufacturers in the area are BorgWagner Turbo Systems; Eaton Corporation; Arvato Digital Services, Thermo Fisher Scientific, Inc.; Kearfott Corp.; and Nypro Asheville.

Items and goods produced: electrical equipment, computers, transportation equipment, beer and wine, plastics, vehicle parts, and health-care products

Incentive Programs-New and Existing Companies

Local programs: Asheville taps into its existing resources to promote economic success in the region. The Asheville Hub plan has been the driving force behind local group collaborations. Asheville Area Chamber of Commerce's Economic Development department offers incentives for new companies, and existing ones that might expand in the area. Under a special discretionary incentive for industrial development, companies in Asheville might qualify for a discount on property tax for up to five years. New and expanding companies that invest a minimum of $1.5 million dollars in new construction, machinery, and equipment in Buncombe County and/or the City of Asheville may be eligible for an economic development incentive grant from Buncombe County and/or the City of Asheville.

State programs: North Carolina, a right-to-work state with a low unionization rate, offers a revenue bond pool program through various banks. Several venture capital funds operate in the state and inquiries can be made through North Carolina's Council for Entrepreneurial Development (CED). Industrial Revenue Bonds issued by the state provide new and expanding businesses the opportunity to provide good employment and wage opportunities for their workers.

The state offers an income tax allocation formula that permits the double weighting of sales in calculating corporate income tax. Additional tax credits offered by the state include those for new markets, renewable energy property investment, job creation, and research and development. A business property tax credit and film incentive tax credit are also available, along with economic development riders and land use incentive grants.

The North Carolina Department of Transportation administers a program that provides for the construction of access roads to industrial sites and road improvements in areas surrounding major corporate installations.

The North Carolina Small Business and Technology Development Center (SBTDC) makes capital available to entrepreneurs and begin building a stronger early-stage investment industry. Financing assistance may be available to qualified businesses under the following programs: traditional bank loans, SBA-guaranteed loans, federal research and development and commercialization funding, equity capital investment, international export financing, the North Carolina Capital Access Program (NC-CAP), and North Carolina Loan Participation Program (NC-LPP). The Asheville office of the SBTDC is affiliated with Western Carolina University and serves Buncombe, Haywood, Henderson, Madison, McDowell, Polk, Rutherford, and Transylvania counties.

Job training programs: NC Workforce, a division of the North Carolina Chamber of Commerce, sponsors the Incumbent Workforce Development Program, which offers grants of up to $25,000 for companies for training and continuing education of existing employees. The Asheville Career Center serves Buncombe County.

State funding allows North Carolina Community Colleges to offer a special customized training program for new, expanding, and existing businesses. The Job Growth Training for new and expanding businesses is available for companies that create at least 12 new production jobs in the state, or to any new or prospective employee referred for training by a participating company. The Productivity Enhancement Training program specifically targets incumbent workers who must regularly update their skills as technology changes. Technology Investment Training and Continuous Improvement Training fill in the gaps to ensure that programs are available for employers and employees as needed. Employees may go through training before or after employment by the company. In Asheville, customized training programs are offered at Asheville-Buncombe Technical Community College.

Another training resource is the City of Asheville Youth Leadership Academy (CAYLA). This program gives area youth the chance to work in city and county offices, where they can learn in the field and prepare for future careers. Students receive hourly pay and $2,000 toward an NC 529 college savings account/fund.

Development Projects

Asheville is continually in the process of improving the city and attracting business. In 2010 the city received the Livable Communities Award from the U.S. Departments of Transportation and Housing and Urban Development. The award was given to 62 cities throughout the nation that demonstrated superior progress in sustainable development. Portions of the $850,000 from the Challenge Grant/TIGER II have gone toward housing, development projects, and transportation throughout

Asheville's riverfront. The Riverfront Redevelopment project, which is spearheaded by the city's Asheville Area Riverfront Redevelopment Commission, includes projects that span the River District of Biltmore Village, East Swannanoa River, and French Broad River.

In 2013 the commission was a primary advisory and advocacy group for the proposed River Arts District Transportation Improvement Project (RADTIP), which focuses on a 2.2-mile stretch of roadway that includes Lyman Street and a portion of Riverside Drive. If adopted and implemented, the project would allow for upgrading and realigning the road. Stormwater control systems would be added, along with special provisions for constructing multiuse trails along the roadway. New sidewalks and other amenities, such as street parking, transit stops, and landscaping would complete the project.

The stretch of road covered under the RADTIP project is part of the larger Wilma Dykeman Riverway, which is another ongoing project in the city. The Wilma Dykeman Riverway Master Plan, a collaborative effort between RiverLink and city of Asheville, aims to improve transportation and economic development in the area. The riverway will provide a 17-mile greenway linking the French Broad and Swannanoa Rivers, connecting north and east parts of the city and providing bicycle and pedestrian access. Property will be redeveloped along the city rivers. To prevent flood damage, the city will attempt to elevate buildings to make them flood-proof, or relocate the buildings out of the designated flood path. Plans also extend to flood-proofing existing historic structures.

Besides making riverway and building improvements, Asheville continues to welcome new business development in the area. In 2013 construction began on the New Belgium Brewing facility. The facility will serve as a brewery and distribution center for the Colorado-based company. When fully operational, the company is expected to employ 140 workers. Construction of the new Sierra Nevada brewery was also underway in 2013. Keeping with the city's goal to promote sustainable design and energy efficient in new development, the new brewery will be LEED certified, with a focus on alternative energy, environmentally conscious construction, reforestation, and river quality monitoring and protection. Southwood Realty Company was in the planning stage of developing a new 224-unit apartment complex called The Palisades. Preliminary plans are for a complex offering one- two-, and three-bedroom apartments at market rates.

Economic Development Information: Asheville Area Chamber of Commerce, 36 Montford Ave., Asheville, NC, 28801; telephone (828) 258-6101.

Commercial Shipping

The Asheville Regional Airport, a hub for domestic flights, is the nearest airport, but shipping needs are better served at nearby other international airports less than an hour-and-a-half away. Greenville Spartanburg Airport is a 40-minute drive away. McGhee Tyson Airport in Alcoa, Tennessee, is 85 miles away, and Charlotte Douglas Airport is 92 miles away from Asheville. There are various trucking companies that go to and from Asheville along Interstate 40 and Interstate 26. The Norfolk Southern railway operates freight lines through Asheville for carrying cargo to different cities, and nearby sea ports such as the Port of Charleston handle water-bound cargo.

Labor Force and Employment Outlook

In 2013 the largest industries for employment in the area were health services and private education, with more than 31,000 employees. The government sector had about 26,000 employees, while leisure and retail each supported more than 23,200 jobs. From 2000 through 2012, health services and private education were the largest growth industries by jobs created, increasing employment by nearly 47 percent. During the same period, employment in professional and business services increased by a little more than 34 percent, while leisure and hospitality employment increased by 26 percent. Manufacturing jobs declined by 33 percent.

In 2011 the Asheville Area Chamber of Commerce and the Economic Development Coalition of Asheville-Buncombe County launched Asheville 5X5, an initiative to create 5,000 new jobs in five years, with a particular focus on the five industry clusters of health care, advanced manufacturing, science and technology, arts and culture, and knowledge-based entrepreneurs. By 2013 the group reported success in attracting 40 new firms to the area and welcoming 3,739 new jobs in new and expanding businesses, including a total of more than 400 new jobs at Linamar Corporation, a leading supplier of engine, transmission, and driveline components.

Major employers in the metropolitan area include Buncombe Country Public Schools, Mission Health System and Hospital, The Biltmore Company, Ingles Markets, Eaton Corporation, and BorgWarner Turbo Systems.

The following is a summary of data regarding the 2012 Asheville labor force:

Size of civilian labor force: 45,261

Number of workers employed in . . .

agriculture and mining: 457
construction: 1,781
manufacturing: 3,217
wholesale trade: 827
retail trade: 4,487
transportation: 707
information systems: 856
finance: 2,057
professional administration: 4,816
education and social services: 12,324
arts and leisure: 6,267

other: 1,901
public administration: 1,226

Average hourly earnings of production workers: $15.8

Unemployment rate: 5.8% (2012)

Employers

Largest employers (Buncombe County, 2013)	*Number of employees*
Buncombe County Public Schools	at least 3,000
Mission Health System and Hospital	at least 3,000
City of Asheville	1,000–2,999
The Biltmore Company	1,000–2,999
Buncombe County Government	1,000–2,999
The Grove Park Inn Resort and Spa	1,000–2,999
Ingles Markets, Inc. (home office)	1,000–2,999
VA Medical Center-Asheville Department of Veterans Affairs	1,000–2,999
CarePartners	750–999
Eaton Corporation— Electrical Division	750–999

Cost of Living

In 2013 the cost of living in Asheville was slightly below the national average.

The following is a summary of data regarding several key cost of living factors in the area.

2013 ACCRA Average House Price: $334,260

2013 ACCRA Cost of Living Index: 102

State income tax rate: 6.0% to 7.75%

State sales tax rate: 4.75%

Local income tax rate: None

Local sales tax rate: 2.25%

Property tax rate: $1.179 per $100 of assessed valuation (2013)

Economic Information: Asheville Area Chamber of Commerce, 36 Montford Ave., Asheville, NC, 28801; telephone (828) 258-6101.

■ Education and Research

Elementary and Secondary Schools

Asheville City Schools hosts nine district schools, five of them being elementary magnet schools with different focuses. The ACS Preschool offers a head start program for women and children from birth through three years old. The City of Ashville Youth Leadership Academy (CAYLA) is an innovative program that helps Asheville High School students acquire paid internships during the summer months. These experiences resulted in increased student involvement in leadership and community service.

There are a number of private and parochial schools in Asheville, including Carolina Day School, Odyssey Community School, Asheville School, Asheville Catholic School, and Nazarene Christian School.

The following is a summary of data regarding the Asheville City Schools.

Total enrollment: 3,872

Number of facilities

    total: 9
    elementary schools: 5
    junior high schools: 1
    high schools: 2
    other: 1

Student/teacher ratio: 11.5:1

Teacher salaries

    average (statewide): $46,850

Funding per pupil: $12,131

Public Schools Information: Asheville City Schools, 85 Mountain St., Asheville, NC 28801; telephone (828) 350-7000.

Colleges and Universities

University of North Carolina (UNC) at Asheville is the area's premier academic institution. It enrolls about 3,700 students annually who study any of 30 majors and graduate with bachelor of arts, bachelor of science, or master of liberal arts degrees. It is the only dedicated liberal arts institution in the UNC System. In 2013 it was ranked the seventh best public liberal arts college in the nation by *U.S. News & Report. Forbes* listed UNC Asheville at number 20 in its annual listing of Best Value Colleges in 2013.

Warren Wilson College is a service-learning college that enrolls less than 1,000 students annually. It has been recognized six times among America's Best Colleges by *U.S. News & World Report.* For 2014 the *Fiske Guide to Colleges* chose Warren Wilson College as one of the nation's 20 "Best Buys" among private colleges and universities. The school incorporates community service and weekly work for the school into the academic curriculum. The school is also known for its efforts in sustainability, with its own working farm. Small classes of an average 14 students provide a more focused, private atmosphere for learning some 48 majors and 28 minor programs. Montreat College is a small private Christian college of about 1,000 students, and offers associate, bachelor, and master degrees.

Asheville-Buncombe Technical Community College, established in 1959, is a two-year college that offers associate degrees, certificates, and diplomas in a variety of studies. The school enrolls more than 10,000 students annually. Other area colleges (near Asheville) include Western Carolina University, an extension of the UNC system that enrolls 9,000 students; Mars Hill College, a private liberal arts college of 1,200 students; and Haywood Community College, which enrolls about 3,000 students annually.

Libraries and Research Centers

Buncombe County Public Libraries has existed for 125 years. There are 11 branch libraries throughout the county. Pack Memorial Library, the main branch, is located in downtown Asheville. The county courthouse houses a law library for public legislative information needs. The Pack Library contains the Foundation Center collection of fundraising and nonprofit management, and the North Carolina Collection chronicles the western part of the state's historical information and literary accomplishments. The collection pays special attention to Asheville and Buncombe County. While the majority of the collection can be seen only at Pack Memorial Library, some images are available on the Internet.

The library system website has 10 photo galleries devoted to online exhibits. The library offers special services to schools, including the Preschool Outreach Program (POP) that brings library materials into eligible preschool classrooms. Also for children, the library conducts a 24-hour story line by phone where children can have stories read to them. Additional programming includes in-library story times for preschoolers and toddlers, a storytelling festival, and special shows in the Pack Memorial Lord Auditorium. The libraries' summer reading programs attracts thousands of children and teen participants.

The University of North Carolina-Asheville's D. Hiden Ramsey Library offers academic resources, including books, and instructional materials for better learning. The library contains more than 385,000 volumes and allows access to two million titles from the Western North Carolina Library Network. Students can also obtain resources through online databases and journals either during library visits or remotely from any location. The databases contain more than 15,000 magazines, journals and newspapers, and about 3,500 scholarly journals.

Public Library Information: Buncombe County Public Libraries, 67 Haywood St., Asheville, NC, 28801; telephone (828) 250-4711; fax (828) 250-4746.

■ Health Care

Mission Health System serves Buncombe County and surrounding areas. It includes Mission Hospital (in Asheville), a facility that also houses the region's Level II trauma center; Mission Children's Hospital (Asheville), with the region's only pediatric intensive care unit; McDowell Hospital (Marion), an acute-care facility that serves McDowell County; and Blue Ridge Regional Hospital (Spruce Pine), a facility serving Mitchell and Yancey counties.

The Charles George VA Medical Center provides health care to more than 100,000 veterans living in the region. CarePartners Health Services has a main campus in Asheville that includes a rehabilitation hospital, outpatient center, hospice, adult daycare services, bereavement services, mobility clinic, and administrative offices. Besides the main campus, there are four additional clinics located throughout the Asheville area. CarePartners also offers an orthotic and prosthetic clinic, and can arrange in-home care for patients.

■ Recreation

Sightseeing

Asheville boasts many cultural and historical sites that date back to the city's origins. The oldest residence in the city, the Smith-McDowell House Museum was once the home of James McConnell Smith plus many other influential citizens. After centuries of many owners, it was restored for reopening in 1981. It has been used as a history museum since then, sharing ground with the Buncombe County Civil War Memorial.

Visitors can spend a long afternoon at the Biltmore Estate is the largest private residence in North America. The 250-room mansion built by George W. Vanderbilt (completed in 1895) was modeled after the sixteenth-century chateaux Blois, Chenonceaux, and Chambord in France's Loire Valley. Tours of the home and gardens and other activities are available throughout the year.

The Thomas Wolfe Memorial State Historic Site, located in downtown Asheville, was the setting of novelist Thomas Wolfe's *Look Homeward, Angel*. Guests can tour the premises and visitor center featuring personal items from Wolfe's life. Young aspiring authors between grades four through eight can participate in writing workshops in the boarding house where Wolfe lived.

Visitors interested in city history can tour the 1.7-mile, bronze-sculpture-lined Asheville Urban Trail, which features 30 pieces of art. For a light-hearted look at the city, visitors can take the LaZoom Comedy Tour, a traveling tour bus with a cast that performs 90-minute shows while traveling throughout Asheville. Those wishing to see the largest freestanding elliptical dome in the nation can visit the Basilica of St. Lawrence, a catholic church designed by Rafael Gustavino and Richard Sharpe Smith.

Arts and Culture

The Asheville Art Museum features permanent collections of twentieth and twenty-first century American pieces, and provides film viewings, exhibitions, and other public programs throughout the year. The Colburn Earth Science Museum houses North Carolina minerals, including the largest amount of the rare mineral, hiddenites, in the world. The museum also offers interactive classes and events.

Pack Place Education, Arts, and Science Center in downtown Asheville was built in 1992 and is comprised of five facilities: the Asheville Art Museum, Colburn Earth Science Museum, The Diana Wortham Theatre; and the YMI Cultural Center. Other notable sites to visit are the Estes-Winn Antique Car Museum at Grovewood Gallery, Biltmore, Museum of the Cherokee Indian, Black Mountain College Museum and Arts Center, and the Grove Arcade.

The Diana Wortham Theatre is a 500-seat theatre that hosts music, theatre, and dance performances by local and touring groups. The YMI Cultural Center began as a community center for African Americans and provides exhibits and cultural programming in collaboration with many local organizations.

The Asheville Choral Society is a chorus of 150 people that has been active for more than 30 years. Asheville Lyric Opera celebrated its fifteenth anniversary in 2013. It is the region's professional opera that performs three elaborate operas during the year. Asheville Symphony Orchestra, under the direction of Daniel Meyer, performs classic works written by Beethoven, Brahms, Mozart, and Rachmaninoff, among the many composers it emulates. The Asheville Community Theater has been performing for guests for more than 65 years. The company performs dramatic, classic, comedic plays, and musicals at the Heston Mainstage Auditorium and 35Below theater.

The Asheville Contemporary Dance Theatre is the first modern dance company in Western North Carolina, and has been known to perform 80 times each year. The group also performs at various festivals in Asheville.

Other notable arts attractions in the area are the Folk Art Center, a hub for southern Appalachian craft demonstrations; and Allanstand, the first craft shop in America.

Festivals and Holidays

Asheville hosts a variety of performing arts festivals that celebrate and preserve the city's origins. The city is also known for its annual Moogfest: The Synthesis of

Technology, Art, and Music, held in April. May features Asheville Beer Week, highlighting several local breweries. The event is so popular that *Forbes* magazine featured Asheville as one of the top Five Beer Cities to Hit This Summer in 2013. Singing on the Mountain, the oldest old-time gospel convention of its kind in Southern Appalachia, takes place in June. Bele Chere is a three-day street festival of music held in July. The Festival of Native Peoples celebrates the region's first inhabitants and features Native American song and dance in July.

The famous Mountain Dance and Folk Festival, which takes place in August, has been a tradition since 1928. It is the longest running folk celebration in the United States and features mountain singers and dancers who draw from the cultures of the area's original settlers. The Mountain Oasis Electronic Music Summit takes place in October.

Harvest House Annual Holiday Craft Show and Sale takes place annually in November, and features ceramics, jewelry, handmade toys, holiday decorations, and other items. The annual Christmas at Biltmore and Candlelight Evenings at Biltmore provide festive holiday entertainment from November through the first week in January.

Sports for the Spectator

The Asheville Tourists are the area's minor league baseball team, affiliated with the Colorado Rockies. The team plays at McCormick Field. The Ashville Grizzlies, a professional football team, play at Memorial Stadium. The team is owned by the Asheville Grizzlies Players Association, a 501 non-profit organization.

Residents can also tune in to local college sports teams, such as the University of Carolina at Asheville Bulldogs and Warren Wilson College Fighting Owls. Nontraditional sports are also found among Asheville's sports scene. The Blue Ridge Rollergirls are a women's flat-track Roller Derby team that play at the Asheville Civic Center.

Sports for the Participant

Asheville's athletic offerings span a variety of sports. Adults can play in volleyball leagues during fall, winter, and summer. Many leagues of coed softball are offered through the city's athletic division. Other league sports include flag football, basketball, hockey, ultimate frisbee, soccer, rugby, lacrosse, and disc golf. Beginning and seasoned bicyclists can participate in Rumble on the River, a geared bike racing series that meets weekly at the Carrier Park Mellowdrome from May to September. Children can participate in youth teams like track and field, cheerleading, and major sports. There are 11 recreation centers throughout the Asheville area.

Asheville has natural features like rivers and mountains that offer an ideal environment for adventurers. Swimming, canoeing, kayaking, and rafting down the French Broad River are popular water sports in the area.

The Blue Ridge Mountains provide a picturesque background when taking a cruise or boating on one of the region's lakes. Horseback riding is also an option for equestrians at Biltmore's 8,000 lush acres and other stables throughout Asheville. The challenging terrain provides a rugged bicycle ride through the Pisgah Mountains and Nantahala Forest. Bike paths extend to scenic paths along Fontana Lake and the Windy Gap Overlook on the Blue Ridge Parkway. Grandfather Mountain allows hikers to explore the home of many wildlife species, including otters, cougars, and bears, while Linville Caverns offer guided tours inside a mountain itself.

Golf courses abound throughout Asheville's hilly landscape. Enthusiasts can golf at various courses, including the Grove Park Inn Resort and Spa Golf Course, which was designed by Donald Ross.

Shopping and Dining

Asheville offers a variety of shopping experiences, from noted brand stores to unique craft shops. The Asheville Mall, located near Interstate 240 and the Biltmore, features more than 100 specialty stores including Eddie Bauer, Victoria's Secret, American Eagle Outfitters, and Foot Locker. Department stores on the property are Belk, Sears, Dillard's, and JCPenney. Biltmore Square Mall is a collection of less than 50 shops, salons, food court, and miscellaneous tenants.

The Biltmore Antiques District is comprised of the 31,000-square-foot Sweeten Creek Antique Mall; Biltmore Lamp and Shade Gallery, which sells antique lamps, and accessories; Village Antiques, a retailer of European items dating back to the seventeenth century, and other stores. Historic Biltmore Village is home to more than 40 shops, galleries, and dining spots found within homes and buildings from the 1900s. Downtown Asheville has more than 150 shops, galleries, and eateries. The Downtown Market is a 42,000-square-foot indoor center featuring artisans, craft makers, musicians, and chefs. Art, jewelry, clothing, and handmade items are displayed for sale, and vendors put on daily demonstrations for visitors.

Dining in Asheville appeals to many tastes as the local scene offers Mediterranean, Asian, German, French, Italian, and vegetarian cuisine, alongside seafood, and barbeque. The area gives space to many farmers' markets that are frequented by chefs trying to bring more flavors to their creations. As a result, more farm-to-table restaurants have sprung up in the city. They are also an example of the area's dedication to its agricultural roots. More than 50 restaurants throughout Asheville serve up locally grown meats and produce, including unique heirloom fruits and vegetables. In 2013 *Southern Living* magazine named Asheville one of the Tastiest Towns in the South.

Visitor Information: Asheville Convention and Visitors Bureau, 36 Montford Ave., Asheville, NC, 28801; telephone (828) 258-6103; fax (828) 254-6054.

■ Convention Facilities

U.S. Cellular Center (formerly the Asheville Civic Center) is the area's premier venue for trade shows and events. The center includes the 2,431-seat Thomas Wolfe Auditorium; the ExploreAsheville.com Arena, which can seat up to 7,200 people; the 25,148-square-foot Exhibition Hall, which can accommodate 2,000 people; and the Banquet Hall, which holds 500 people. The arena has 11 additional meetings rooms in the mezzanine section. In the downtown area, Pack Place has 6,875 square feet of additional meeting space to host casual or upscale occasions for 300 people. North of downtown, the Montford Historic District boasts 11 bed and breakfasts aside from the area's various hotels. Several local inns and hotels offer meeting spaces as well.

Convention Information: Asheville Civic Center, 87 Haywood St., Asheville, NC, 28801; telephone (828) 259-5544.

■ Transportation

Approaching the City

The Asheville Regional Airport is located in Buncombe County. It is situated 10 miles south of Asheville and 8 miles north of Hendersonville. The airport offers service through six major airlines: Allegiant, Delta, US Airways, and United Airlines. Non-stop service is provided to eight major U.S. cities.

Travelers driving can reach Asheville from interstate highways 26, 40, 240, and 26, as well as U.S. Highways 19/23, 25, 25A, 70, and 74. The airport is located adjacent to Interstate 26, so ground travel is convenient. The Blue Ridge Parkway, which stretches 469 miles, is accessible from U.S. Highways 25, 70, 74, and North Carolina Highway 191. Visitors can also arrive in Asheville via Greyhound and Trailways bus lines.

Traveling in the City

The Asheville Transit is public transportation that carries passengers to different points throughout the city. The bus system has 16 routes and runs Monday through Saturday from 6 a.m. until 11:30 p.m. Paratransit services are provided for eligible riders by Mountain Mobility of Buncombe County. Asheville Transit also provides programs to ease the burden of transportation costs for students, employees, and minority-owned and operated businesses. The Emergency Ride Home program helps regular commuters get home in the event of a crisis. The city also has several different taxi services.

■ Communications

Newspapers and Magazines

The *Asheville Citizen-Times,* owned by Gannett Company, Inc., is a daily newspaper covering the Western North Carolina area. *Mountain Xpress* is an independent weekly publication that reports on arts, culture, and politics.

Television and Radio

There are four television stations that serve the Greenville-Spartanburg-Asheville-Anderson area. WLOS-TV Channel 13, an ABC affiliate station, is the primary station in the area, followed by WUNF Channel 33 (PBS programming), which is owned by University of North Carolina. WYCW-TV is a CW affiliate on Channel 62, and WHNS Channel 21 is a FOX affiliate. The area also picks up stations from Upstate South Carolina. Asheville has 14 licensed FM and AM radio stations that play rock, country, news, contemporary, and sports commentary.

Media Information: *Asheville Citizen-Times,* 14 O. Henry Ave., Asheville, NC, 28801; telephone (828) 252-5610; e-mail news@citizen-times.com.

Asheville Online

Asheville Area Chamber of Commerce. Available www.ashevillechamber.org

Asheville Buncombe Library System. Available www.buncombecounty.org/governing/depts/library

Asheville City Schools. Available www.ashevillecityschools.net

Asheville Convention and Visitors Bureau. Available www.ashevillecvb.com

Buncombe County Tourism Development Authority. Available www.exploreasheville.com

City of Asheville. Available www.ashevillenc.gov

The Asheville Citizen-Times. Available www.citizen-times.com

BIBLIOGRAPHY

Harshaw, Lou, *Asheville: Mountain Majesty* (Fairview, NC: Bright Mountain Books, 2007)

Huso, Deborah, *Blue Ridge and Smoky Mountains* (Berkeley, CA: Avalon Travel, 2010)

Charlotte

■ The City in Brief

Founded: circa 1750 (incorporated 1768)

Head Official: Mayor Patrick Cannon (since 2014)

City Population

    1990: 419,558
    2000: 540,828
    2010: 731,424
    2012 estimate: 775,208
    Percent change, 2000–2010: 35.2%
    U.S. rank in 1990: 35th (State rank: 1st)
    U.S. rank in 2000: 33rd (State rank: 1st)
    U.S. rank in 2010: 17th (State rank: 1st)

Metropolitan Statistical Area Population

    2000: 1,499,293
    2010: 1,758,038
    2012 estimate: 1,831,084
    Percent change, 2000–2010: 17.3%
    U.S. rank in 2000: 37th
    U.S. rank in 2010: 33rd

Area: 242.87 square miles

Elevation: Ranges from 730 to 765 feet above sea level

Average Annual Temperatures: 60.1° F

Average Annual Precipitation: 43.1 inches

Major Economic Sectors: trade, transportation, and utilities; healthcare and educational services; financial and business services; manufacturing; leisure and hospitality; government

Unemployment Rate: 7.6% (2012)

Per Capita Income: $30,501

2012 FBI Crime Index Property: 32,587

Major Colleges and Universities: University of North Carolina at Charlotte, Davidson College, Queens University of Charlotte, Johnson C. Smith University

Daily Newspaper: *The Charlotte Observer*

■ Introduction

Charlotte, known as the Queen City, offers a fascinating mix of southern culture and growing business mecca. The city is at the center of one of the largest urban regions in the country and has emerged as a major financial center. An excellent interstate highway system, good railroad access, and an inland port facility are other factors that have made Charlotte a major distribution center of the Southeast and one growing in both national and international importance. Yet even as Charlotte has emerged as a major city of the new South—and of the nation—its people continue to keep a clear vision of what makes a good life. Neighborhood streets are filled with majestic 90-foot water and willow oaks. Uptown's major thoroughfare is lined with trees. Each spring, the entire county is filled with delirious color as dogwoods and azaleas bloom. Just two hours east of the Appalachian Mountains and three hours west of the Atlantic Ocean, life in this comfortable, mid-sized city provides the best of all worlds.

■ Geography and Climate

Charlotte is located in southwestern North Carolina's Piedmont region of rolling hills. The city is about 85 miles south and east of the Appalachian Mountains and about 180 miles northwest of the Atlantic Ocean. Situated near the South Carolina state line, Charlotte is the Mecklenburg county seat.

    Charlotte's moderate climate enjoys a sheltering effect from the mountains; its cool winters seldom bring

© digidreamgrafix/Shutterstock.com

extreme cold temperatures or heavy snowfall, while the city's long, quite warm summer days are mitigated by considerably cooler nights. Summer precipitation falls principally in the form of thundershowers, followed by comparatively drier fall weather. The average annual snow fall is generally less than six inches.

Area: 242.87 square miles

Elevation: Ranges from 730 to 765 feet above sea level

Average Temperatures: 60.1° F

Average Annual Precipitation: 43.1 inches

■ History

Colonists Win King's Favor

The first colonial settlers-German, Scotch-Irish, English, and French Huguenot-in the region that is now Charlotte encountered a friendly, peaceful native tribe, the Catawba. The area's fertile soil brought more settlers and by 1761 the Catawba were restricted to assigned territory in South Carolina. The colonists were aggressive in seeking political advantages. In the mid-1750s, for

example, to win favor with England's King George III, the first settlers to the area named their town Charlotte, after the king's wife, Charlotte Sophia of Mecklenburg-Strelitz (Germany). The town was incorporated in 1768. Their next step was to convince the royal government that they deserved to be a separate county. They diplomatically named their new county Mecklenburg, in honor of the queen.

But their ambitions did not stop there. Thomas Polk, one of the town's first settlers, and his neighbors wanted Charlotte as the county seat. Although there really was not much in Charlotte to justify such a designation, that did not stop these enterprising individuals. They built a log cabin where two Native American trails converged and called it a courthouse, and the existence of that courthouse led to the royal government appointment of Charlotte as the county seat in 1774.

Gold Fever Spurs Boom

Charlotteans' can-do attitude also included a strong streak of stubbornness and independence. It was in Charlotte that the Mecklenburg Declaration of Independence was signed on May 20, 1775, predating the colonies' joint declaration by more than a year. During the Revolutionary War, British General Lord Cornwallis referred to Charlotte as "a damned hornet's nest of rebellion."

From 1781 to 1800 Charlotte added a flour mill and a saw mill to its growing settlement. In 1799, a young boy discovered a 17-pound gold nugget at the Reed Gold Mine, 30 miles east of the city. Soon, mines dotted the area and business in Charlotte boomed. Gold fever lasted until starry-eyed prospectors were lured west by the California Gold Rush of 1849.

City Becomes a Financial and Textile Center

As the importance of the mines diminished, cotton took hold as the town's money producer. The invention of the cotton gin helped to establish Charlotte as a ginning and exchange center, and the town evolved into a textile power. The beginning of the city's development as a major distribution center began in the mid-1880s with the convergence of several railroad lines in Charlotte. After the Civil War, hydroelectric power was developed on the Catawba River near Charlotte. The city began to serve as a textile center in the late nineteenth century, and by 1903, more than half of the nation's textile production was located within a 100-mile radius of Charlotte. The evolution of North Carolina's interstate highway system in the 1900s further paved the way for Charlotte to become the major distribution center that it is today. Charlotte enjoyed great expansion after World War I. The location of a branch of the Federal Reserve Bank in the 1920s also had a major impact, and Charlotte subsequently evolved into a top banking center. In the 1940s Charlotte contributed to military efforts and in the 1950s underwent another period of growth. Charlotte became a banking and distribution center that grew more than 30 percent in the 1970s, profiting from a historic desegregation ruling and a dedication to metropolitan renewal and development.

In the 1990s, large-scale business expansions and relocations created many new jobs and an economy that continued to thrive despite a nationwide recession in the late 2000s. Several factors contributed to the success of the area, including a cost of living below the national average and a graceful blend of historical homes alongside new development. An excellent transportation infrastructure has also contributed to growth. Charlotte is at the center of the largest consolidated rail system in the United States and has been designated as an inland port city. As such, the city has become a major distribution and transportation hub, as well as a major financial center. Bank of America (ranked fifth on the *Fortune* 500 list of America's largest corporations) is headquartered in Charlotte. The city is also the site of a branch of the Federal Reserve. As businesses have grown, so has population of both city and county. Providing services for such a rapidly growing population has been a challenge for local officials, particularly in the areas of public education, a growing number of working poor, and environmental concerns.

Historical Information: The Charlotte Museum of History, 3500 Shamrock Dr., Charlotte, NC 28215; telephone (704) 568-1774.

■ Population Profile

Metropolitan Statistical Area Population
2000: 1,499,293
2010: 1,758,038
2012 estimate: 1,831,084
Percent change, 2000–2010: 17.3%
U.S. rank in 2000: 37th
U.S. rank in 2010: 33rd

City Residents
1990: 419,558
2000: 540,828
2010: 731,424
2012 estimate: 775,208
Percent change, 2000–2010: 35.2%
U.S. rank in 1990: 35th (State rank: 1st)
U.S. rank in 2000: 33rd (State rank: 1st)
U.S. rank in 2010: 17th (State rank: 1st)

Density: 2,457.1 people per square mile

Racial and ethnic characteristics
White: 407,772
Black or African American: 271,441
American Indian and Alaskan Native: 3,597
Asian: 42,313
Native Hawaiian and Other Pacific Islander: 980
Hispanic or Latino (may be of any race): 104,913
Other: 49,105

Percent of residents born in state: 41.9%

Age characteristics
Population under 5 years old: 58,634
Population 5 to 9 years old: 54,215
Population 10 to 14 years old: 50,610
Population 15 to 19 years old: 49,341
Population 20 to 24 years old: 58,234
Population 25 to 34 years old: 136,671
Population 35 to 44 years old: 117,301
Population 45 to 54 years old: 103,295
Population 55 to 59 years old: 45,340
Population 60 to 64 years old: 33,269
Population 65 to 74 years old: 39,814
Population 75 to 84 years old: 19,988
Population 85 years and over: 8,496
Median age: 33.3

Births (2010–11 Metropolitan Area)
Total number: 24,619

Deaths (2010–11 Metropolitan Area)
Total number: 11,581

Money income (2012)

> Per capita income: $30,501
> Median household income: $51,209
> Total households: 292,501

Number of households with income of . . .

> less than $10,000: 21,875
> $10,000 to $14,999: 15,366
> $15,000 to $24,999: 30,789
> $25,000 to $34,999: 32,009
> $35,000 to $49,999: 42,819
> $50,000 to $74,999: 53,467
> $75,000 to $99,999: 32,248
> $100,000 to $149,999: 34,197
> $150,000 to $199,999: 13,418
> $200,000 or more: 16,313

Percent of families below poverty level: 17.8%

FBI Crime Index Property: 32,587

FBI Crime Index Violent: 5,238

■ Municipal Government

Charlotte has a council-manager government with an 11-member city council and a mayor, all of whom are elected officials serving two-year terms. Seven council members are elected to single-member districts and four are elected at large. The mayor presides at city council meetings and serves as the official representative of the city. The day-to-day operations of the city are have the oversight of the professional city manager, a position appointed by the city council.

Head Official: Mayor Patrick Cannon (since 2014)

Total Number of City Employees: 6,000 (2012)

City Information: City of Charlotte, Charlotte-Mecklenburg Government Center, 600 E. Fourth St., Charlotte, NC 28202; telephone (704) 336-7600.

■ Economy

Major Industries and Commercial Activity

Charlotte has a diverse economy with a good balance of industries and businesses ranging from local retail to large international manufacturing companies. Proximity to a wide variety of markets has led to Charlotte's maturation as a financial, distribution, and transportation center for the entire urban region. The city has developed into a major wholesale center. Charlotte is also gaining recognition as a national and international financial center. Bank of America, ranked among the top 25 Fortune *500* companies in 2013, has its headquarters in Charlotte.

Health care and education are also important sectors in the local economy, but manufacturing remains strong as well, with companies producing a wide range of goods, such as furniture, textiles, food, machinery, appliance, and paper products. Government is a significant sector as well. Charlotte is the seat of Mecklenburg County, and several federal departments and organizations have offices within the metropolitan area.

Several factors attract foreign businesses to Charlotte from such countries as Germany, the United Kingdom, Japan, France, Switzerland, Italy, and Canada. These include an inland port facility, a foreign trade zone, and the area's customs and immigration offices. Hundreds of foreign-owned companies have facilities in the Charlotte region, including Siemens Energy (German), Compass Group North America (United Kingdom), and Electrolux (Sweden).

As the subsidiary headquarters for a variety of major national companies, Charlotte's urban region continues to attract sophisticated industries such as microelectronics, metalworking, and vehicle assembly, as well as research and development, technology, and service-oriented international and domestic firms. More than 250 *Fortune* 500 companies have facilities or offices in Charlotte, including Duke Energy, Nucor Corporation, and Sonic Automotive. In recent years, Charlotte has emerged as a magnet for defense-related industries. Companies receiving defense contracts include Curtiss-Wright Flow Control Company and UTC Aerospace Systems, both headquartered in Charlotte.

With an eye toward the future, Charlotte area officials hope to maintain economic diversity while preparing to welcome companies from emerging industries. The Charlotte Chamber of Commerce has identified eight targeted sectors and industries for economic development: biotech, energy, financial services, future technologies, international firms, headquarters, logistics and distribution, and manufacturing.

In 2013 the Charlotte metropolitan area was ranked among the top-40 Best Performing Cities in an annual survey by the Milken Institute and placed at number 11 on the Bloomberg list of Top Boomtowns. That year *Forbes* placed Charlotte as the fourth Fastest Growing City Since Recession and eighth among the Best Cities for Jobs in the metropolitan area category.

Items and goods produced: textiles, home appliances, food and beverages, printing and publishing, machinery, primary and fabricated metals, aircraft parts, computers, paper products

Incentive Programs-New and Existing Companies

Local programs: A variety of incentives, grants, bonds, and other programs are offered by the City of Charlotte and Mecklenburg County to help local businesses. These include the City Brownfield Grant Program, which offers matching funds in the form of reimbursement of eligible expenses with a cap of $20,000 per site for eligible assessment and cleanup activities within the Business Corridor Revitalization Area. Funding for small businesses is available through the Business Equity Loan Program and the Charlotte Community Capital Fund. Short-term financing is available through the Small Business Mobilization Loan program, offering loans between $15,000 and $75,000. A Security Grant Program provides 50 percent reimbursement up to $2,500 for the installation of eligible security improvements.

Several programs are designed to support development related to the city's Business Corridor Revitalization plan. The Business Corridor Fund supports projects to create housing and retail within the city's five priority areas. The Business District Organization Program offers reimbursement for eligible operating expenses for corridor businesses. The Business Investment Program encourages job creation and retention efforts of new and expanding businesses.

The City of Charlotte is a state-designated Urban Progress Zone. This designation provides enhanced economic incentives for businesses in certain industries that inspire the creation of new jobs and investments in business property. Under the terms of the program, these tax credits are available for companies involved in such businesses as aircraft maintenance and repair, air courier services, customer service call centers, information technology and services, manufacturing, research and development, wholesale trade and warehousing, and motorsports facilities and racing teams.

State programs: North Carolina, a right-to-work state with a low unionization rate, offers a revenue bond pool program through various banks. Several venture capital funds operate in the state and inquiries can be made through North Carolina's Council for Entrepreneurial Development (CED). Industrial Revenue Bonds issued by the state provide new and expanding businesses the opportunity to provide good employment and wage opportunities for their workers.

The state offers an income tax allocation formula that permits the double weighting of sales in calculating corporate income tax. Additional tax credits offered by the state include those for new markets, renewable energy property investment, job creation, and research and development. A business property tax credit and film incentive tax credit are also available, along with economic development riders and land use incentive grants.

The North Carolina Department of Transportation administers a program that provides for the construction of access roads to industrial sites and road improvements in areas surrounding major corporate installations.

The North Carolina Small Business and Technology Development Center (SBTDC) makes capital available to entrepreneurs and begin building a stronger early-stage investment industry. Financing assistance may be available to qualified businesses under the following programs: traditional bank loans, SBA-guaranteed loans, federal research and development and commercialization funding, equity capital investment, international export financing, the North Carolina Capital Access Program (NC-CAP), and North Carolina Loan Participation Program (NC-LPP). The Charlotte office of the SBTDC is affiliated with the University of North Carolina Charlotte and serves Anson, Cabarrus, Iredell (southern), Mecklenburg, Montgomery, Rowan, Stanly, and Union counties.

Job training programs: NC Workforce, a division of the North Carolina Chamber of Commerce, sponsors the Incumbent Workforce Development Program, which offers grants of up to $25,000 for companies for training and continuing education of existing employees.

State funding allows North Carolina Community Colleges to offer a special customized training program for new, expanding, and existing businesses. The Job Growth Training for new and expanding businesses is available for companies that create at least 12 new production jobs in the state, or to any new or prospective employee referred for training by a participating company. The Productivity Enhancement Training program specifically targets incumbent workers who must regularly update their skills as technology changes. Technology Investment Training and Continuous Improvement Training fill in the gaps to ensure that programs are available for employers and employees as needed. Employees may go through training before or after employment by the company. In Charlotte, customized training programs are offered through Central Piedmont Community College.

Development Projects

According to the Charlotte Chamber of Commerce, 7,039 new businesses created more than 57,277 jobs for the city from 2003 to 2013. Investments ranged from downtown office towers to regional retail centers, manufacturing facilities, and *Fortune* 500 headquarters. During 2012 Charlotte saw $1.3 billion in business investment from 1,180 firms.

In 2013 the city broke ground for a new Blue Line Extension of the Lynx light rail system. When completed, the 9.3-mile extensions from uptown to the University of North Carolina–Charlotte was to include 11 new stations and double the size of the existing system. The city also broke ground for its CityLYNX Gold Line, which will link Time Warner Cable Arena to Novant Presbyterian Hospital and run from French Street on West Side to Sunnyside Avenue on the East Side. Together, the new links are expected to generate more than seven million square feet of new developments along the affected corridors.

Also in 2013, the city adopted a new Community Investment Plan consisting of an $816-million bond package to fund critical projects across the city. Anticipated projects include the construction of six new police stations and a joint police and fire communications center; a cross-Charlotte multiuse trail from Pineville to the Cabarrus County line; $60 million for an affordable housing strategy that includes housing stock rehabilitation, land-banking programs, and rental subsidies; $133 million for roads, bridges, sidewalks, and traffic control projects; and $120 million for targeted neighborhood improvement investments. These investments are expected to create more than 18,000 jobs and have a $2.2 billion impact on the city.

The city continues to support developments along its five priority business corridors, which include Rozzelles Ferry Road, Beatties Ford Road; North Tryon Street; the Eastland Area; and the Freedom, Wilkinson, Morehead corridor. Proposed projects for these areas include redevelopment of Eastland Mall and the completion of the Stewart Creek Greenway.

Economic Development Information: Charlotte Chamber of Commerce, 330 S. Tryon St., PO Box 32785, Charlotte, NC 28232; telephone (704) 378-1300.

Commercial Shipping

Charlotte Douglas International Airport provides exceptional air service in and out of the city. The Charlotte Air Cargo Center handles more than 127,000 tons of domestic and international cargo per year with service by more than 15 cargo airlines, and cargo lifts by commercial carriers. Charlotte also serves as a major hub for small package express.

Charlotte is at the center of the largest consolidated rail system in the United States. Two major rail systems, Norfolk Southern and CSX Transportation, link 43,200 miles of rail systems between 23 states, Washington D.C., and Canada. About 600 trains pass through the city each week. The railroads, in fact, have enabled Charlotte to gain inland port and port of entry status, although the city is located about 175 miles from the coast. The Charlotte Intermodal Terminal (CIT), operated by the North Carolina State Ports Authority, links Charlotte with the port of Wilmington, Delaware, through a Seaboard Railroad System piggyback ramp operation. CIT is the first fully operational inland container staging and storage facility in the United States operated by a port authority. Greater Charlotte is designated as a foreign trade zone.

With more than 300 trucking companies, motor cargo transport is available for everything from liquid and dry bulk to freight and containers.

Labor Force and Employment Outlook

The work force in both Mecklenburg County and surrounding areas is plentiful. Studies have found North Carolina workers are more productive than other workers in the same industries nationally. Several area educational institutions provide education and training for employees, including classes in technical skills and management development, as well as graduate degree programs.

According to the U.S. Bureau of Labor, the top employment industries for the Charlotte-Gastonia-Rock Hill, NC-SC area in 2013 were trade, transportation, and utilities; professional and business services; government; leisure and hospitality; and education and health services. Top employers in the Charlotte region included Carolinas HealthCare System, Wells Fargo, Charlotte-Mecklenburg Schools, Bank of America, Wal-Mart and Sam's Club stores, and Novant Health.

In April 2013, *Forbes* ranked Charlotte as the eighth Best City for Jobs, and then followed-up by ranking the city as the fourth Best City for Jobs Fall 2013.

The following is a summary of data regarding the 2013 Charlotte labor force:

Size of civilian labor force: 420,039

Number of workers employed in . . .

agriculture and mining: 638
construction: 23,041
manufacturing: 29,277
wholesale trade: 12,388
retail trade: 40,220
transportation: 20,168
information systems: 9,990
finance: 48,904
professional administration: 48,466
education and social services: 70,643
arts and leisure: 39,988
other: 19,581
public administration: 7,421

Average hourly earnings of production workers: $16.29

Unemployment rate: 7.6% (2012)

Employers

Largest employers (2012)	*Number of employees*
Carolina's Healthcare System	32,500
Wells Fargo Company	20,600
Charlotte-Mecklenburg Schools	18,143
Bank of America	15,000
Wal-Mart and Sam's Club Stores	12,200
Novant Health	10,573
Lowe's	8,500
Food Lion LCC	7,734

Duke Energy	7,700
North Carolina State Government	7,684
US Airways	7,060
City of Charlotte	6,000
U.S. Postal Service	5,400

Cost of Living

A cost of living only slightly above the national average, big-city amenities, and broad economic base converge to make Charlotte attractive to new residents.

The following is a summary of data regarding several key cost of living factors in the area.

2013 ACCRA Average House Price: $248,717

2013 ACCRA Cost of Living Index: 95

State income tax rate: 6.0% to 7.75%

State sales tax rate: 4.75%

Local income tax rate: None

Local sales tax rate: 2.5%

Property tax rate: $1.2844 per $100 of assessed valuation (2013)

Economic Information: Charlotte Chamber of Commerce, 330 S. Tryon St., PO Box 32785, Charlotte, NC 28232; telephone (704) 378-1300.

■ Education and Research

Elementary and Secondary Schools

Charlotte is at the forefront of innovation in education. The public school system, which implemented court-ordered busing to achieve desegregation in 1970, is now considered a model for the entire country in terms of race relations.

Charlotte-Mecklenburg Schools is one of the largest school districts in the country. In 2013 there were 160 schools throughout the system, including 37 magnet schools. More than 140,000 students were enrolled throughout the district. In 2013 Providence Spring Elementary School was named as a national Blue Ribbon School. Several of the district's magnet schools have consistently been recognized as top programs by Magnet Schools of America.

A wide range of special programs are available in the system, including an Exceptional Children's program for students with disabilities, English as a Second Language classes, Advancement Via Individual Determination (a college prep program for students in academic middle by GPA), and a wide variety of arts programs.

Besides advanced placement programs, high school students may participate in the College Experience Program of the Central Piedmont Community College, which allows students to earn both high school and college credits. Charlotte-Mecklenburg Schools was the first school district in the state to offer courses in the International Baccalaureate (IB) program.

Education in grades kindergarten through 12 is also provided at more than 50 private schools in the area, including the British American School of Charlotte, Anami Montessori School, Charlotte Latin School, Brisbane Academy Preparatory School, Charlotte Catholic High School, Charlotte Jewish Day School, and Chesterbrook Academy.

The following is a summary of data regarding the Charlotte-Mecklenburg Schools.

Total enrollment: 135,954

Number of facilities
    total: 160
    elementary schools: 89
    junior high schools: 39
    high schools: 28
    other: 4

Student/teacher ratio: 15.9:1

Teacher salaries
    average (statewide): $46,850

Funding per pupil: $8,050

Public Schools Information: Charlotte-Mecklenburg Schools, Board of Education, 600 E. Fourth Street, Charlotte, NC 28202; telephone (980) 343-5139; fax (980) 343-7128.

Colleges and Universities

The University of North Carolina at Charlotte, the fourth largest of the 16 schools in the University of North Carolina system, offers 80 bachelor's degree programs, 63 master's programs, and 21 doctoral degrees through 7 colleges. Enrollment is more than 26,500 students, including approximately 5,000 graduate students. The university has students from about 80 foreign countries and maintains working relationships with colleges and universities throughout the world.

Three local institutions are affiliated with the Presbyterian Church: Davidson College, Queens University of Charlotte, and Johnson C. Smith University. With 1,700 students, Davidson College in northern Mecklenburg County (founded in 1837) is considered one of the most competitive liberal arts and sciences colleges in the nation. The school is especially well-known for foundational programs in medicine, law, international affairs, business, teaching, and religious ministries.

Queens University of Charlotte, founded in 1857 as Queens College, has more than 2,400 students in six colleges and schools: College of Arts and Sciences, McColl School of Business, Knight School of Communications, Cato School of Education, Blair College of Health, and the School of Graduate and Continuing Studies. In 2014 Queens University of Charlotte was listed among the top-20 Best Regional Universities (South) by *U.S. World & News Report* for the second year in a row.

Originally chartered as the Biddle Memorial Institute in 1867, Johnson C. Smith University is one of the oldest historically African American colleges in the country. Enrollment in 2013 was 1,387 students. The school offers 22 undergraduate majors.

Johnson & Wales University–Charlotte Campus offers three colleges: the College of Business, the College of Culinary Arts, and the Hospitality College. Both associate's and bachelor's degrees are available. Many Charlotte residents take advantage of cooking skills classes through the schools Chef's Choice program. The Charlotte campus of Pfeiffer University (main campus in Misenheimer, North Carolina) is the site of the School of Graduate Studies and Center for Professional Advancement.

Central Piedmont Community College (CPCC) offers a central campus site in downtown Charlotte and three other campuses within Charlotte. About 5,600 students are enrolled each year. The school offers associate's degree programs and diploma and certificate programs for more than 100 technical specialties. CPCC offers state-sponsored customized training programs for local employers and employees, along with other workforce training services and courses.

Other area institutions include the Art Institute of Charlotte, Brookstone College of Business, Carolinas College of Health Sciences, ECPI University, King's College, Lee University–Charlotte Center, Montreat College School of Professional and Adult Studies, Strayer University–Charlotte Campus, and the Wake Forest University School of Business.

Libraries and Research Centers

The Public Library of Charlotte and Mecklenburg County is North Carolina's largest system, with a 187,000-square-foot main library, 6 regional libraries, 12 community branch locations, and the ImaginOn library for youth. The library system lends books, CDs, tapes, e-books, videos, and software along with providing many searchable online resources. The total library collection includes more than 1.1 million physical items and more than 12,800 digital items.

The main library downtown contains a large local history and genealogy library, a depository for U.S. government publications, an International Business Library, and the Virtual Library—a computer learning laboratory. ImaginOn is a collaborative venture of the public library and the Children's Theatre of Charlotte to bring stories to life through small theater programs. The

Checkit Outlet in uptown offers area workers and residents the opportunity to request books from any location and pick them up at this convenient spot during their lunch hours.

The collection at University of North Carolina's J. Murrey Atkins Library exceeds one million volumes. The Atkins Library special collections include the Motor Sports Collection, which documents the history of automobile racing in the Southeast; a Rare Books Collection emphasizing American literature; and an Oral History Collection featuring interviews with North Carolina's writers, politicians, businessmen, and other professionals and residents. The Atkins Library has been designated a U. S. Patent and Trademark Depository Library.

The Billy Graham Library displays exhibits on the life and work of the famous evangelist and houses the personal papers of Graham. Official documents of his ministry remain at the Wheaton College in Illinois.

Research centers affiliated with the University of North Carolina at Charlotte focus on applied research and public service. Centers and institutes hosted by the university include the Charlotte Research Institute for optics, e-business technology, precision metrology and bioinformatics; the Urban Institute, for community research and planning; Institute for Social Capital on education and social services; the Center for Optoeletronics and Optical Communications; Center for Precision Metrology; eBusiness Technology Institute; Center for Transportation Policy Studies; the Global Institute for Energy and Environmental Systems; the NC Motorsports and Automotive Research Center; and the Center for Applied Geographic Information Science.

The North Carolina NASA Educator Resource Center is located at the UNC Atkins Library. The University Research Park, located on a 3,200-acre campus near the University of North Carolina at Charlotte, has attracted a combination of regional and national businesses engaged in research, manufacturing, and services. The Electric Power Research Institute has a facility in Charlotte to conduct research and development relating to the generation, delivery, and use of electricity for the benefit of the public.

Public Library Information: Public Library of Charlotte & Mecklenburg County, 310 N. Tryon St., Charlotte, NC 28202-2176; telephone (704) 336-2725.

■ Health Care

The importance of the availability of quality, cost-efficient health care has long been recognized by Charlotte's citizens. Early recognition in the community of future cost problems and cooperative efforts to keep cost increases under control have resulted in reasonable costs, thoughtful use of services by physicians, and efficient hospital management.

Carolinas Medical Centers, operated by Carolinas HealthCare System (CHS), has seven service locations in Charlotte. The flagship Carolinas Medical Center site at Blythe Blvd (with 874 beds) is designated as a Level 1 trauma center and as the official Poison Control Center for the state. It also houses the Levine Children's Hospital at Carolinas Medical Center, providing the region's only 24-hour children's emergency department. For 2014 Levine Children's Hospital was recognized by *U.S. News & World Report* as one of the top-50 children's hospitals in the nation in the specialty areas of cancer care, cardiology and heart surgery, gastroenterology and GI surgery, neonatology, and nephrology.

CMC–Mercy Hospital is home to the specialty Heart Center, Lung Center, Southeast Pain Center, and the Sleep Center. Other Charlotte sites include CMC–Pineville and CMC–University. The CMC–Randolph provides psychiatric care and treatment for substance abuse and behavioral illnesses. The Carolinas Rehabilitation, also operated by CHS, specializes in rehabilitative care after stroke and spinal cord and brain injuries.

Another major hospital system is Novant Health, with three hospitals in Charlotte: Presbyterian Medical Center, Charlotte Orthopedic Hospital, and Hemby Children's Hospital. Novant Health also operates the NH Heart and Vascular Institute, NH Cancer Center, and NH Women's Center. Health services are offered through the Charlotte Dental Society, Mecklenburg County Medical Society, and Mecklenburg County Mental Health Services.

■ Recreation

Sightseeing

History buffs can take in the Hezekiah Alexander Home, built in 1774 and considered the oldest building in Mecklenburg County. Listed on the National Register of Historic Places, the home is furnished with authentic articles from the eighteenth century, and the adjacent Charlotte Museum of History presents a variety of changing exhibits.

The Billy Graham Library, opened in 2007, is part of a 40,000-square-foot museum-like complex on the grounds of the Billy Graham Evangelistic Association built to resemble the dairy farm that was the Graham homestead. The library offers exhibits about the life and work of Billy Graham, a resource center that includes Graham's personal papers, and a restaurant.

Racing enthusiast can enjoy a day at the NASCAR Hall of Fame, which opened in Charlotte in 2010 with about 40,000 square feet of exhibit space displaying the history and heritage of the sport. The Hall of Fame's Belk High Octane Theater presents a film on the history of NASCAR. After checking out the historic cars on Glory Road, visitors can grab a bite to eat at the onsite Buffalo Wild Wings restaurant.

Arts and Culture

Culturally minded residents and visitors in Charlotte can view a wide array of collections at the Mint Museum of Art, founded in 1936, that houses more than 27,000 items including American art, pre-Columbian art, and American and European ceramics by such artists as Winslow Homer, Andrew Wyeth, and Frederic Remington. As the oldest art museum and emerging as a major southern landmark in North Carolina, the museum's building formerly served as the first branch of the U.S. Mint from 1837 to 1861. Other collections include a 6,000-piece costume collection, antique maps, and contemporary American prints. In 1999 its sister museum, the Mint Museum of Craft and Design, opened to present ceramics, glass, jewelry, wood, and metalworks from historical to contemporary times.

The McColl Center for Visual Arts, located in a renovated downtown Associate Reformed Presbyterian Church, was a joint project of Bank of America and the Arts and Science Council. The center houses studios for resident-artists as well as galleries to display their works and classrooms to offer educational programs on contemporary arts. The Levine Museum of the New South features exhibits on post-Civil War Southern history. The permanent exhibits include the award-winning *Cotton Fields to Skyscrapers: Charlotte and the Carolina Piedmont in the New South*. The Harvey B. Gantt Center for African American Arts and Culture opened in 2009. The center displays exhibits by African American artists and sponsors many cultural and educational events throughout the year.

The Arts and Science Council (ASC), organized in 1958, serves all Charlotte-Mecklenburg communities. Arts education throughout the county is sponsored in part by the ASC ArtsTeach program. Primary funding for the arts comes from the ASC annual fund drive, which raises over $10 million each year.

Collectible treasures from around the world are on display at the Farvan International Gallery. There are several galleries located in NoDa, as Charlotte's historic northern district is called. The ArtHouse Center for Creative Expression has fine art, photography, textile art, and sculptures. Lyons Fine Art Consulting (formerly the Center of the Earth Gallery) displays an eclectic collection of contemporary works from both regional and national artists.

Visitors can explore the wonders of science at Discovery Place near Spirit Square, ranked among the 10 most outstanding hands-on science and technology museums in the country, which includes an IMAX Dome Theatre. Located adjacent to Freedom Park, the Charlotte Nature Museum is geared to younger visitors and features nature trails, live animals, classes, a planetarium, and a puppet theater.

A crown jewel of Charlotte's arts scene is the North Carolina Blumenthal Performing Arts Center, which includes Belk Theater, Booth Playhouse, and Stage Door Theater. Resident companies include the Charlotte Symphony Orchestra and the Oratorio Singers of Charlotte (the official orchestra chorus), Opera Carolina, Queen City Theatre Company, The Light Factory (offering exhibits and educational programs on photography and film), On Q Productions, and the Caroline Calouche & Co. dance group. The Community School of the Arts offers programming at the center. The Charlotte Symphony Youth Orchestra and the Charlotte Symphony Jr. Youth Orchestra also play at Blumenthal, among other venues. Carolina Voices, known for their annual Singing Christmas Tree, performs at Oven Auditorium and McGlohon Theatre at Spirit Square.

Two blocks away from Blumenthal is Spirit Square Center for Arts & Education, which houses the 700-seat McGlohon Theatre and the Duke Energy Theater. Spirit Square, opened in 1980, was anchored on the renovation of the First Baptist Church, originally built in 1909. It is considered the keystone of Charlotte's cultural center on North Tryon Street, which includes restaurants, several art galleries, and the public library. More than 500,000 people visit the facility each year to enjoy its four galleries, take classes in such areas as theater, fiber, clay, and dance, and watch performances.

The state-of-the-art Verizon Wireless Amphitheatre at Encore Park showcases world-class concerts, Broadway shows, opera, and ballet; it is an outdoor amphitheater that can accommodate 19,000 people. Theatre Charlotte, the state's oldest community theater, presents more than 2,600 performances productions fueled by more than 500 local volunteers each year. Central Piedmont Community College's (CPCC) Summer Theatre has chased away the summer doldrums with its mostly-musicals schedule for over three decades. Since 1954, the Children's Theatre of Charlotte has produced plays for and by children, and also presents special events and holds classes.

The Bojangles' Coliseum hosts a wide variety of family-oriented entertainment including ice-skating shows and *Sesame Street Live*. Musical acts ranging from U2 to The Wiggles have performed at the Time Warner Cable Arena.

Offerings in theater—as well as the other arts—are enriched in Charlotte because of its many colleges and universities. The University of North Carolina at Charlotte, Davidson College, Queens University of Charlotte, and Johnson C. Smith University all offer a variety of cultural programs for the general public. UNCC is the site of WFAE-FM, Charlotte's National Public Radio affiliate.

Festivals and Holidays

Charlotte residents like to celebrate, and festivals abound almost year-round. The biggest is the three-day Spring Fest, which draws more than 300,000 people uptown to celebrate the rites of spring each April. The annual Queen's Cup Steeplechase is a family event the last Saturday in April at Brooklandwood in nearby Mineral Springs. Among the offerings are food, entertainment by local and nationally known performers, games, art exhibits, and an art competition. Also, during May, the city celebrates the 600 Festival, an auto-racing event tied to the Coca-Cola 600 that includes a parade, fireworks, and unusual competitive events such as a bathtub derby and culminates with a charity ball.

Numerous neighborhoods have festivals and celebrations throughout the summer. In the fall, Festival in the Park, held in Freedom Park, says farewell to summer in a fun-filled four days featuring 175 artists and nearly 1,000 entertainers. The free event has art awards totaling about $4,000. Charlotte SHOUT!, a month-long festival in September, celebrates art, culture, and community through more than 200 performances and events at some 40 venues throughout the city. The annual Greek Yiasou Festival celebrates Charlotte's largest ethnic community, and November's Southern Christmas Show, the largest indoor event in the Carolinas and Virginia, is a holiday crafts show that extends in excess of 10 days at Charlotte's Merchandise Mart. Each year, the Christmas season is launched in Charlotte with the Carolinas' Carousel Parade on Thanksgiving Day.

Sports for the Spectator

The Carolina Panthers, a National Football League expansion team and 2008 NFC South Champions, began play in Charlotte in the 1996 season in Bank of America Stadium, a $187 million, state-of-the-art black and silver 73,778-seat stadium custom built for the team. Bank of America Stadium has also hosted the Atlantic Coast Conference Championship. Local basketball fans were disappointed when the Charlotte Hornets decided to move their National Basketball Association team to New Orleans. However, the expansion Bobcats came to town in 2004. The Bobcats take the court at the Time Warner Cable Arena. The Charlotte Checkers of the American Hockey League also play at the arena. The UNC Charlotte 49ers basketball team plays at Halton Arena.

April brings the annual Queens' Cup Steeplechase at Brooklandwood, about 40 minutes away from downtown Charlotte. Summer ushers in a full season of baseball played by the Charlotte Knights, the city's Triple A minor league team in the Chicago White Sox farm system. Professional golf comes to town during May for the Wells Fargo Championship at Quail Hollow Club; the annual event has raised millions of dollars for local charities, the majority going toward Teach for America Charlotte.

Spring signals the opening of the 167,000-seat Charlotte Motor Speedway, which attracts fans to its NASCAR events, the World of Outlaws World Finals, the Bank of America 500, and the Coca-Cola 600 during Memorial Day weekend, among other races.

Sports for the Participant

For active pursuits, the Mecklenburg County Park and Recreation Department maintains 17,600 acres of parks and 27 recreation centers. The county's 210 parks include a petting zoo, playgrounds, 2 outdoor swimming pools, 2 skateparks, 4 off-leash dog parks, 5 spray-grounds, 12 nature preserves, and 8 fitness centers. There are about 80 public and private golf courses in the area and 17 disc golf sites. Volleyball (including sand) and tennis courts are available at several county park locations, as are softball, baseball, and soccer fields. A BMX bike track (which has hosted national tournaments) is located at the Hornets Nest Park, which sits on 102 acres and also has facilities for baseball, softball, basketball, and volleyball; 10 playgrounds; and a lake with a fishing pier.

For those who prefer water activities, Lake Wylie and Lake Norman are about a 20-minute drive from uptown. Boating, swimming, water skiing, and fishing can be enjoyed in an unspoiled wooded environment. The mountains of North Carolina—the highest east of the Mississippi—are just two hours away by car, and they offer the delights of skiing, backpacking, hiking, and mountain climbing. Thrill seekers can spend a day riding the 13 roller coasters at Carowinds amusement park, which also features the Boomerang Bay waterpark and Planet Snoopy kid's park.

The Golf Club at Ballantyne Hotel and Lodge has been named as one of the "Top 38 Golf resorts in the World" by *PGA Magazine* and as one of the "Top 25 Golf Schools" by *Golf Magazine*. The Spa at Ballantyne offers a 20,000-square-foot European-style space and health facility. Embassy Suites Charlotte-Concord Golf Resort and Spa also has an 18-hole course, the Rocky River Golf Club, and the onsite Spa Botanica.

The U.S. National Whitewater Center attracts professional and amateur athletes to the world's largest manmade whitewater river with Class III–IV rapids. The facility and grounds include 11 miles of trails for hiking, running, and biking and a 5,700-square-foot climbing service. Ropes courses are offered. Amateur kayaking and canoeing competitions are held each year.

The Thunder Road Marathon and Half Marathon events take place in December in downtown. The race serves as a qualifier for the Boston Marathon.

Shopping and Dining

Many shopping experiences are available to Charlotte residents and visitors. SouthPark Mall, Charlotte's most upscale facility, offers 1.5 million square feet of shopping space in one of America's top selling retail centers, featuring stores such as Tiffany & Co., Nordstrom, and Coach. Charlotte Regional Farmers Market features locally grown produce, baked goods, flowers, and crafts from March through December. The North Davidson district is Charlotte's version of New York's SoHo and has been dubbed NoDa by locals; the district counts antique and boutique shops among its eclectic mix.

From an elegant dinner by candlelight to a rollicking night of food with Dixieland jazz, a variety of dining options is offered in the city. Visitors may chose from Chinese, Japanese, Indian, Egyptian, Arabian, Greek, French, Indian or Mexican cuisines, as well as good old down-home Southern cooking. Among the mid-South regional food specialties diners may seek in Charlotte are southern fried chicken, barbecue, country ham, and Brunswick stew—a mixture of chicken, pork, corn, tomatoes, beans, and hot peppers—as well as biscuits and hushpuppies, and pecan pie and banana pudding.

Visitor Information: Charlotte Regional Visitors Authority, 500 S. College Street, Suite 300, Charlotte, NC 28202; telephone (704) 334-2282 or (800) 722-1994.

■ Convention Facilities

Boasting more than 30,000 hotel rooms, Charlotte has become the major business travel center in the Carolinas and a prime meeting and convention center in the Southeast. The Charlotte Convention Center hosts trade shows, conventions, conferences, and expositions. The exhibit space consists of 280,000 square feet of contiguous space that is also divisible into four separate halls. There are 46 meeting rooms with 90,000 square feet of flexible meeting space, a deluxe hotel-quality ballroom measuring 35,000 square feet, and wide, light-filled concourses that converge at the heart of the center, the Grand Hall. The Ovens Auditorium is a 2,600-seat facility where arts-related events and business meetings are held. Hospitality Rooms at Ovens can accommodate receptions for up to 125 people. Cricket Arena, sometimes used to host high school graduations, offers seating for more than 9,600.

Featuring a 9,100 square-foot ballroom along with more than 20,000 square feet of meeting space, the Marriott Charlotte Center City offers a unique atrium for events. The Bank of America Stadium offers packages for special events, meetings, and outings.

The Embassy Suites Charlotte-Concord offers 42,000 square feet of event space, a 28,800-square-foot ballroom, and 26 meeting rooms. The resort offers Spa Botanica and an 18-hole golf course. Ballantyne Hotel and Lodge, also with a golf course and a spa, offers 20,000 square feet of conference space. The U.S. National Whitewater Center has a 500-seat outdoor amphitheater and a 2,400-square-foot conference center. Area hotels offering meeting and ballroom space include the Westin Charlotte and Hilton Charlotte Center City.

Convention Information: Charlotte Regional Visitors Authority, 500 S. College Street, Suite 300, Charlotte, NC 28202; telephone (704) 334-2282 or (800) 722-1994.

■ Transportation

Approaching the City

Charlotte-Douglas International Airport is about 20 minutes from uptown. There are seven domestic airlines and two foreign carriers (Air Canada and Lufthansa Airlines) serving the airport with non-stop service available to 150 cities. Millions of commuters pass through the airport every year. For motor travel to the region, Interstates 77 and 85 intersect in Charlotte and Interstate 40, an important east–west link, is about 30 minutes away. Greyhound bus service is available with a station in Charlotte. Amtrak provides north–south connections to the city, and east–west lines provide access to most of the United States.

Traveling in the City

The Charlotte Department of Transportation (CDOT) maintains the local commuter system. The Charlotte Area Transit System (CATS) serves both the city and county with more than 70 bus and rail routes; the system also offers two vanpool programs, special transportation services for the disabled, and shuttle services. The Gold Rush Trolley also operates loop service in the city. The 10-mile South Corridor line runs parallel to Interstate 77 and South Boulevard from Tremont Avenue to Seventh Street. A 25-year light rail plan includes a vision for an additional four corridor lines, all connecting to Center City Charlotte.

■ Communications

Newspapers and Magazines

The Charlotte Observer is Charlotte's major daily newspaper (morning). Also published in Charlotte is *Sports-Business Journal,* a national tabloid-size glossy weekly that reports on the glitzy and the mundane of sports business. The *Rhino Times,* with weekly editions published in Greensboro and Charlotte, presents entertainment and social news. Other publications originating in the area include the weekly *The Charlotte Post,* serving the African American community; a Charlotte edition of *Creative Loafing,* a weekly arts and entertainment resources; the twice-weekly *The Mecklenburg Times,* featuring financial, legal, and realty news; and the *Charlotte Business Journal.*

Television and Radio

Seven television stations broadcasting from Charlotte include three network affiliates (ABC, CBS, and NBC), a PBS affiliate, and three independent stations (Fox, CW and My Network). Programming from independent and educational stations originating in neighboring cities is also available to Charlotte-area television viewers. Fifteen AM and five FM radio stations are licensed in Charlotte, broadcasting a variety of offerings that include religious and sports programming as well as contemporary, rock and roll, gospel, and country music. UNCC is the site of WFAE-FM, Charlotte's National Public Radio affiliate.

Media Information: The Charlotte Observer, 600 S. Tryon St. Charlotte NC 28202; Telephone (704) 358-5000.

Charlotte Online

Charlotte Center City Home Page. Available www.charlottecentercity.org

Charlotte Chamber of Commerce. Available www.charlottechamber.org

Charlotte-Mecklenburg Schools. Available www.cms.k12.nc.us

Charlotte Observer. Available www.charlotteobserver.com/

Charlotte Regional Visitors Authority. Available www.charlottesgotalot.com

City of Charlotte Home Page. Available www.charmeck.org

Public Library of Charlotte and Mecklenburg County. Available www.cmlibrary.org

BIBLIOGRAPHY

Claiborne, Jack, *The Charlotte Observer: Its Time and Place, 1869-1986* (Chapel Hill, NC: University of North Carolina Press, 1986)

Graves, William, and Heather A. Smith, eds., *Charlotte, NC: The Global Evolution of a New South City* (Athens: University of Georgia Press, 2010)

Rothacker, Rick, *Banktown: The Rise and Struggles of Charlotte's Big Banks* (Winston-Salem, NC: John F. Blair, 2010)

Setzer, Lynn, *Tar Heel History on Foot: Great Walks through 400 years of North Carolina's Fascinating Past* (Chapel Hill, NC: University of North Carolina Press, 2013)

Greensboro

■ The City in Brief

Founded: 1808 (incorporated 1829)

Head Official: Mayor Nancy Vaughan (since 2013)

City Population
    1990: 185,125
    2000: 223,891
    2010: 269,666
    2012 estimate: 277,095
    Percent change, 2000–2010: 20.4%
    U.S. rank in 1990: 88th
    U.S. rank in 2000: 88th (State rank: 3rd)
    U.S. rank in 2010: 69th (State rank: 3rd)

Metropolitan Statistical Area Population
    2000: 643,430
    2010: 723,801
    2012 estimate: 736,065
    Percent change, 2000–2010: 12.5%
    U.S. rank in 2000: 74th
    U.S. rank in 2010: 71st

Area: 116.6 square miles

Elevation: 897 feet above sea level

Average Annual Temperatures: 58.1° F

Average Annual Precipitation: 50.24 inches total precipitation; 3.8 inches of snow

Major Economic Sectors: manufacturing, trade and transportation, healthcare and educational services, professional and business services

Unemployment Rate: 7.1% (2012)

Per Capita Income: $23,912

2012 FBI Crime Index Property: 12,064

Major Colleges and Universities: University of North Carolina at Greensboro, Guilford College, Greensboro College

Daily Newspaper: *News & Record*

■ Introduction

"It is perhaps the most pleasing, the most bewitching county which the continent affords." So wrote J. Hector St. John de Crevecoeur in the 1770s when he bestowed the eighteenth-century equivalent of a quality-of-life award on a Quaker community called New Garden. The community became part of Greensboro in 1808. Today Greensboro is part of a large developing area called the Triad, which is composed of three major cities (Greensboro, High Point, and Winston-Salem). Located between the mountains and the sea in Piedmont, North Carolina, Greensboro has evolved from a small government center in the early 1900s into a major textile and transportation hub. Despite job losses in recent years in the manufacturing industry, the formation of new hubs for commercial travel signals a comeback in jobs and reputation as a center for transportation and shipping needs. The Greensboro government prides itself in involving its residents every step of the way, from getting input on downtown development projects to local festivals. These efforts spurred the Public Technology Institute to award Greensboro the distinction of being a Citizen-Engaged Community for 2010.

■ Geography and Climate

Located in the north-central Piedmont section of North Carolina, near the headwaters of the Haw and Deep rivers, the city is about 25 miles east of Winston-Salem and serves as the Guilford County seat. The cities of Greensboro, Winston-Salem, and High Point make up

© Andre Jenny/Alamy

what is known as the Piedmont Triad, a significant economic region for the area.

Greensboro enjoys a relatively mild climate, partly due to the moderating influence of the mountains southwest of the city. Zero degree winter days are virtually unknown. The average yearly snowfall is only about 9.1 inches. Summer temperatures vary depending on cloud cover and thundershower activity, which itself varies greatly from year to year. There are occasional summer thunderstorms.

Area: 116.6 square miles

Elevation: 897 feet above sea level

Average Temperatures: 58.1° F

Average Annual Precipitation: 50.24 inches total precipitation; 3.8 inches of snow

■ History

City Named for Revolutionary Hero

Greensboro is the county seat of Guilford County, which was founded in 1771 and named after England's first Earl of Guilford, Lord Francis North. Perhaps the first thing

that newcomers notice about Greensboro is how green the city is. They are often surprised to learn that Greensboro is named for a man-not its lush landscape.

They soon hear the story of Nathanael Greene, a Revolutionary War general, who in 1781 played a major role in the colonists' fight for independence at a battlefield called Guilford Courthouse just north of present-day Greensboro. Greene lost the battle to Britain's Lord Charles Cornwallis, but historians credit him with so weakening Cornwallis's army that surrender soon followed.

More than 25 years later, the settlers of Guilford County decided to replace their county seat of Martinville with a more central city. They measured out the exact center of the county, and in 1808, a new 42-acre city was created. It was named Greensborough (meaning town of Greene) to honor Nathanael Greene. By 1895 Greensborough had become Greensboro.

City Rises to the Confederate Call

The city grew slowly at first, but by the mid-1800s the seeds for its future as a textile, insurance, and transportation center had been planted. In 1828 the first steam-powered textile mill opened and in 1850 the first insurance company came to town. In 1851 men began

416

laying railroad tracks. The progressiveness of the county's educational community was showing, too. A log college for men had been operated there since 1767 and in 1837 the first coeducational institution in North Carolina opened. Called the New Garden Boarding School, it continues today as Guilford College.

The founders of the school were Quakers, many of English and Welsh descent, who were among Guilford County's first permanent settlers. Other early arrivals were a group of Germans who settled in the eastern portion of the county, and a number of Pennsylvanians of Scots-Irish descent who traveled south in search of land and opportunity.

The peace-loving nature of the Quakers influenced the area and its development. Quakers established the first Underground Railroad in Greensboro in the 1830s. When the Civil War was at hand, Guilford County citizens voted 2,771 to 113 against a state convention to consider secession from the union, writes local author Gayle Hicks Fripp in her history, *Greensboro: A Chosen Center.* North Carolina eventually became the last state to secede on May 20, 1861, and Guilford County citizens accepted the decision. They turned churches into hospitals and melted church bells for ammunition. For a few days in April 1865, Greensboro was the seat of the Confederate government as President Jefferson Davis contemplated surrender in a meeting with his military leaders.

Transportation and Textiles Spur Growth

The turn of the nineteenth century brought tremendous growth to Greensboro. Much of the prosperity then and now can be traced to one man and the moving of a line. The man was John Motley Morehead, state governor from 1841–1845. He used his influence to curve an east-west line of railroad tracks miles north so it would pass through his hometown of Greensboro. The city soon became known as the Gate City for its busy train station (60 running daily), and ever since, transportation has remained a key to the city's development.

In 1892 two Maryland salesmen, the Cone brothers, chose Greensboro as the site for the first textile-finishing plant in the South. Thus began an enterprise called Cone Mills, which would become one of the largest makers of denim and corduroy in the world. By 1920 Blue Bell was making bib overalls there and Burlington Mills, which later became Burlington Industries, had moved to Greensboro by 1935. Both companies added to the textile industry's influence on the economy.

Modern Era Sees Racial Problems; Skyline Changes

The influence of the insurance industry showed on Greensboro's skyline in 1923, when the city became the site of the tallest building between Atlanta and Washington, D.C. the 17-story Jefferson Standard Building. The 1940s brought people from all over the country to Greensboro. During World War II, the military located an Overseas Replacement Depot in the city in 1944, and more than 300,000 men and women were processed or trained for service there.

In 1960 Greensboro was the site of the first Civil Rights-era sit-in when four African American students refused to accept a lunch-counter color bar; their actions led to the collapse of segregation in the American South.

Economic Diversification Spurs Growth

The next few decades brought economic as well as social change to Greensboro. The opening of the new Piedmont Triad International Airport (PTIA) in 1982 to serve Greensboro and its Triad neighbors set off a spurt of industrial growth there and united the cities more closely than ever. The city quickly became a significant center for trade. During the 1980s and 90s, thousands of manufacturing jobs were lost throughout the region, but downtown revitalization efforts brought new businesses to diversify the economy.

As the city approached its 2008 bicentennial, the continued influx of new businesses and the expansion of existing businesses in a variety of fields translated to an overall general prosperity for the area's workforce and the city as a whole. Though many jobs were lost during a 2007–09 nationwide recession, city officials worked hard to attract businesses in key target industries, including aviation, innovative manufacturing, and specialized business services.

Historical Information: Greensboro Historical Museum, 130 Summit Ave., Greensboro, NC 27401; telephone (336) 373-2043; fax (336) 373-2204.

■ Population Profile

Metropolitan Statistical Area Population
2000: 643,430
2010: 723,801
2012 estimate: 736,065
Percent change, 2000–2010: 12.5%
U.S. rank in 2000: 74th
U.S. rank in 2010: 71st

City Residents
1990: 185,125
2000: 223,891
2010: 269,666
2012 estimate: 277,095
Percent change, 2000–2010: 20.4%
U.S. rank in 1990: 88th
U.S. rank in 2000: 88th (State rank: 3rd)
U.S. rank in 2010: 69th (State rank: 3rd)

Density: 2,131.5 people per square mile

Racial and ethnic characteristics

> White: 131,026
> Black or African American: 118,409
> American Indian and Alaskan Native: 1,161
> Asian: 12,671
> Native Hawaiian and Other Pacific Islander: 65
> Hispanic or Latino (may be of any race): 21,627
> Other: 13,763

Percent of residents born in state: 55.4%

Age characteristics

> Population under 5 years old: 18,216
> Population 5 to 9 years old: 18,813
> Population 10 to 14 years old: 15,969
> Population 15 to 19 years old: 21,084
> Population 20 to 24 years old: 26,942
> Population 25 to 34 years old: 42,178
> Population 35 to 44 years old: 36,156
> Population 45 to 54 years old: 34,439
> Population 55 to 59 years old: 16,023
> Population 60 to 64 years old: 13,964
> Population 65 to 74 years old: 17,157
> Population 75 to 84 years old: 11,716
> Population 85 years and over: 4,438
> Median age: 33.6

Births (2010–11 Metropolitan Area)

> Total number: 8,593

Deaths (2010–11 Metropolitan Area)

> Total number: 6,267

Money income (2012)

> Per capita income: $23,912
> Median household income: $40,323
> Total households: 111,765

Number of households with income of . . .

> less than $10,000: 10,277
> $10,000 to $14,999: 7,474
> $15,000 to $24,999: 16,275
> $25,000 to $34,999: 15,385
> $35,000 to $49,999: 17,311
> $50,000 to $74,999: 18,940
> $75,000 to $99,999: 9,988
> $100,000 to $149,999: 9,456
> $150,000 to $199,999: 3,439
> $200,000 or more: 3,220

Percent of families below poverty level: 19.9%

FBI Crime Index Property: 12,064

FBI Crime Index Violent: 1,555

■ Municipal Government

Greensboro has a council-manager form of government. The council consists of the mayor and eight members, all of whom are elected on a nonpartisan ballot for two-year terms. The mayor and three council members are elected at large, and five council members are elected by districts. The council in turn appoints a city manager to administer government policy.

Head Official: Mayor Nancy Vaughan (since 2013)

Total Number of City Employees: 3,141 (2012)

City Information: City of Greensboro, 300 West Washington Street, Greensboro, NC 27401; telephone (336) 373-CITY.

■ Economy

Major Industries and Commercial Activity

The traditional manufacturing industries—including textiles and tobacco—remain a dominant influence on the local economy, but Greensboro has succeeded in creating a diverse economy. For example, the city has been an insurance center for decades. Mortgage insurance provider United Guaranty Corp, service station equipment producer Gilbarco Veeder-Root, and RF Micro Devices (RFMD) are all headquartered in Greensboro. Honda Aircraft Company chose Greensboro as its world headquarters and the site of a major manufacturing center for HondaJet.

Vicks VapoRub was invented in Greensboro more than 75 years ago. Other familiar products, such as Nyquil nighttime cold medicine, Vicks Formula 44 cough mixture, Vicks cough syrup, and Vicks cough drops have also been produced in Greensboro. Vicks products are now produced by Procter & Gamble, which has major operations in the city. International flavor has been added, courtesy of Fuji Foods of Japan, which located its U.S. manufacturing plant in Greensboro. Sweden's Volvo Trucks North America is headquartered in Greensboro.

The opening of the Piedmont Triad International Airport (PTIA) terminal just west of the city in 1982 set off a building boom along nearby Interstate 40 and the feeder roads to the airport that has not yet shown signs of abating. The corridor is being called the downtown of the Triad, and the chambers of commerce from the three Triad cities have joined forces to attract businesses to the area. PTIA's central location and state-of-the-art facilities make the airport a catalyst for commercial and industrial development.

Items and goods produced: textiles, apparel, tobacco products, chemicals, pharmaceuticals and personal care products, microchips and integrated circuits, fuel dispensing equipment, automotive electronics, aircraft engines and systems

Incentive Programs-New and Existing Companies

Local programs: Both the city of Greensboro and Guilford County have incentive policies available to assist new and expanding businesses. City officials are involved in part in promoting new businesses through the Small and Emerging Business Assistance program and the Minority and Women's Business Enterprise Program. Greensboro is part of a state-designated Urban Progress Zone, where qualified businesses are eligible for a variety of tax incentives. The Greensboro Economic Development Alliance offers assistance through its Existing Industry Services Program, which focuses on growth and development and employment retention for existing Greensboro business.

Downtown Greensboro, Inc. oversees a number of programs and initiatives to help attract new businesses. Financial assistance is provided to qualified businesses through the Retail Grant Program, Facade Improvement Program, Greensboro Community development Fund, and County Small Business Grant Program.

State programs: North Carolina, a right-to-work state with a low unionization rate, offers a revenue bond pool program through various banks. Several venture capital funds operate in the state and inquiries can be made through North Carolina's Council for Entrepreneurial Development (CED). Industrial Revenue Bonds issued by the state provide new and expanding businesses the opportunity to provide good employment and wage opportunities for their workers.

The state offers an income tax allocation formula that permits the double weighting of sales in calculating corporate income tax. Additional tax credits offered by the state include those for new markets, renewable energy property investment, job creation, and research and development. A business property tax credit and film incentive tax credit are also available, along with economic development riders and land use incentive grants.

The North Carolina Department of Transportation administers a program that provides for the construction of access roads to industrial sites and road improvements in areas surrounding major corporate installations.

The North Carolina Small Business and Technology Development Center (SBTDC) makes capital available to entrepreneurs and begin building a stronger early-stage investment industry. Financing assistance may be available to qualified businesses under the following programs: traditional bank loans, SBA-guaranteed loans, federal research and development and commercialization funding, equity capital investment, international export financing, the North Carolina Capital Access Program (NC-CAP), and North Carolina Loan Participation Program (NC-LPP). The Greensboro offices of the SBTDC are affiliated with the North Carolina

Agricultural and Technical State University and the University of North Carolina at Greensboro. These two locations serve Caswell, Guilford, Randolph, and Rockingham Counties.

Job training programs: NC Workforce, a division of the North Carolina Chamber of Commerce, sponsors the Incumbent Workforce Development Program, which offers grants of up to $25,000 for companies for training and continuing education of existing employees. The Greensboro Career Center serves Guilford County.

State funding allows North Carolina Community Colleges to offer a special customized training program for new, expanding, and existing businesses. The Job Growth Training program for new and expanding businesses is available for companies that create at least 12 new production jobs in the state, or to any new or prospective employee referred for training by a participating company. The Productivity Enhancement Training program specifically targets incumbent workers who must regularly update their skills as technology changes. Technology Investment Training and Continuous Improvement Training fill in the gaps to ensure that programs are available for employers and employees as needed. Employees may go through training before or after employment by the company. Greensboro residents and business owners can take customized training classes through Guilford Technical Community College.

Development Projects

The Greensboro Economic Development Alliance manages and supports development projects throughout the community. In the 2010s, the alliance established a development strategy that encourages growth in five targeted industry clusters: aviation, innovative manufacturing, life science, specialized business services, and supply chain and logistics.

In 2010 Downtown Greensboro, Inc., Action Greensboro, the City of Greensboro, and Guilford County officials joined forces to design a comprehensive plan to promote the revitalization of Downtown Greensboro. The plan involved six priority projects: the completion of an approved $7-million greenway, Encouraging connectivity through a comprehensive streetscaping program, providing incentives for quality new mixed-use development, promoting the redevelopment and use of historic buildings, creating a new performing arts center, and supporting the growth of a knowledge community by encouraging colleges and universities to locate programs and facilities downtown.

Throughout 2013, plans continued for the first phase of development of a $40 million downtown Greensboro university campus. This new educational center is expected to include office space, classrooms, and lab space for use by seven colleges and universities: University of North Carolina at Greensboro, North Carolina Agricultural and Technical State University,

Greensboro College, Guilford College, Bennett College, Guilford Technical Community College, and Elon University's law school. The first phase of development could also include faculty offices, an auditorium, and a parking deck. Planners expect the first phase to focus on attracting students in health-care professions, such as nursing and radiology. A second phase of development could include a Global Opportunities Center focusing on exporting and entrepreneurship. A proposed third phase would provide distance learning and shared technology for online courses for degree completion.

In 2013 FFF Enterprises Inc., a California-based biopharmaceutical company, announced plans to build a new 800,000-square-foot facility in Triad Business Park that will serve as its East Coast logistics center. The company is a leading distributer of influenza vaccines, critical care biopharmaceuticals, and other plasma products. Officials expected the project to involve a total investment of about $7.6 million.

Economic Development Information: Greensboro Chamber of Commerce, 342 N. Elm St., Greensboro, NC 27401; telephone (336) 387-8301; fax (336) 275-9299.

Commercial Shipping

Greensboro is a hub for moving freight nationwide by rail or truck. The Piedmont Triad International Airport (PTIA) terminal, located only minutes from downtown, is served by four cargo companies. The airport has convenient access to two major interstates, the east–west Interstate 40 and north–south Interstate 85. These highways provide connections to other major arteries throughout the region and the nation, such as Interstate 77 and Interstate 95. New construction on Interstate 785 will connect with Interstate 73/74 to provide easy access to the city and the airport. There are numerous trucking companies serving the Triad, with at least 60 terminals local to Greensboro.

Norfolk Southern Railway Corporation operates one of the most active intermodal facilities in its 20-state system in Greensboro. Dedicated piggybacks hauling trailers travel out of Greensboro. CSX also offers freight service through the city. The Piedmont Triad Inland Terminal (PTIT) in Greensboro is about 185 miles northwest of the Port of Wilmington, serving the Interstate 40 and Interstate 85 corridors.

Labor Force and Employment Outlook

Greensboro has a growing population from which to draw employees; a motivated and trainable work force; and a respected community college system that provides employee training assistance at no charge through a state program. According to the U.S. Bureau of Labor, trade, transportation, and utilities accounted for the largest number of jobs for the Greensboro–High Point area in

2013. Manufacturing accounted for a significant number of jobs, followed by professional and business services, government, and educational and health services.

The largest employers in Greensboro in 2013 included Cone Health, the U.S. Postal Service, Bank of America, Lorillard Inc., The Volvo Group, and UPS.

The following is a summary of data regarding the 2012 Greensboro labor force:

Size of civilian labor force: 143,818

Number of workers employed in . . .

agriculture and mining: 340
construction: 5,839
manufacturing: 15,414
wholesale trade: 4,815
retail trade: 14,764
transportation: 6,026
information systems: 2,935
finance: 9,664
professional administration: 11,257
education and social services: 32,610
arts and leisure: 14,548
other: 5,409
public administration: 3,386

Average hourly earnings of production workers: $15.34

Unemployment rate: 7.1% (2012)

Employers

Largest employers (2013)	Number of employees
Moses H. Cone Health System	at least 5,000
United States Postal Service	2,500–5,000
Bank of America	1,500–2,500
Lorillard, Inc.	1,500–2,500
The Volvo Group	1,500–2,500
UPS	1,500–2,500
AT&T	1,000–1,500
Gilbarco Veeder-Root	1,000–1,500
Lincoln Financial Group	1,000–1,500
VF Corporation	1,000–1,500
RFMD	1,000–1,500
TE Connectivity	1,000–1,500
TIMCO Aviation Services	1,000–1,500
UnitedHealth Group	1,000–1,500

Cost of Living

The following is a summary of data regarding several key cost of living factors in the area.

State income tax rate: 6.0% to 7.75%

State sales tax rate: 4.75%

Local income tax rate: None

Local sales tax rate: 2.0%

Property tax rate: $0.6325 per $100 of assessed valuation (2013)

Economic Information: Greensboro Chamber of Commerce, 324 N. Elm St., Greensboro, NC 27401; telephone (336)387-8301; fax (336) 275-9299.

■ Education and Research

Elementary and Secondary Schools

The Guilford County Schools (GCS) system was established in 1993 when the former Greensboro, High Point, and Guilford County school systems merged to form the third largest school district in North Carolina. In 2013 the district served more than 72,000 students at 126 schools.

Many special programs are available for students in the district. GCS offers its high school students several options to help them prepare for future careers. The College Tech Prep program is available for students interested in technical occupations and pursuing two-year associates degrees. There are several early/middle college high schools located on local college campuses, offering students an alternative to the traditional high school setting. The Early College Academy programs offer high school seniors a chance to earn college credits while they fulfill their graduation requirements. These students are also eligible for three-year scholarships upon graduation.

The districts sponsors 53 magnet on specialized topics such as communications, cultural arts, and foreign language. Four International Baccalaureate programs are also available. There are three Montessori schools in the district. Weaver Education Center offers vocational/technical training, performing arts, advanced academics, and distance learning programs to all high school students.

Students with autism, cerebral palsy, orthopedic impairments, and severe and profound handicaps can attend GSC's Gateway Education Center, a facility that is world-renowned for its exceptional programs. Meredith Leigh Haynes-Bennie Lee Inman Education Center, Christine Joyner Greene Education Center, and Herbin-Metz Education Center also provide classes for students with special needs. In 2013 there were two community locations for the system's SCALE Program (School/Community Alternative Learning Environments). These sites, serving about 20 students each, offer programs for students under long-term suspension.

Greensboro Academy and Guilford Preparatory Academy are charter schools in Greensboro serving K–8 students. Greensboro has a diverse selection of private schools. There are more than 30 private schools in the county. The nation's first and only liberal, pluralistic Jewish boarding school, the American Hebrew Academy, offers students grades 9 to 12 a rigorous college preparatory curriculum along with Jewish studies courses. Other notable schools in the county include Caldwell Academy, Greensboro Day School, New Garden Friends School, and Our Lady of Grace Catholic School.

The following is a summary of data regarding the Guilford County Schools.

Total enrollment: 73,205

Number of facilities
    total: 129
    elementary schools: 68
    junior high schools: 23
    high schools: 28
    other: 10

Student/teacher ratio: 14.9:1

Teacher salaries
    average (statewide): $46,850

Funding per pupil: $8,684

Public Schools Information: Guilford County Schools, 712 N. Eugene St., Greensboro, NC 27401; telephone (336) 370-8100.

Colleges and Universities

The 200-acre University of North Carolina at Greensboro (UNCG), with more than 17,500 students in 2013, is the largest of the colleges and universities in Greensboro. Founded in 1891 as a women's school, it became coeducational in the fall of 1964. Undergraduate degrees are offered in more than 100 fields. There are also 65 master's programs and 30 doctoral programs.

The city's other state university, North Carolina Agricultural and Technical State University (NC A&T), was founded in 1891 as a land-grant institution offering agricultural and mechanical training to African Americans. In 2013 more than 10,000 students were enrolled at the university. Known for its nationally accredited engineering department, the university offers undergraduate and master's degrees in a half-dozen engineering specialties.

The oldest college in Greensboro, Guilford College is also one of the city's most respected institutions. Founded in 1837 by the Religious Society of Friends, or Quakers, Guilford is the third oldest coeducational institution in the United States. Undergraduate majors are offered in more than three dozen areas, ranging from accounting to criminal justice to women's studies. In 2013 enrollment was about 2,450.

One year after Guilford College was founded, Greensboro College opened its doors, becoming the third college chartered for women in the United States. It became coeducational in 1954. Located in the historic College Hill area, Greensboro College today is a Methodist-affiliated institution with about 1,250 students. The college emphasizes individual attention (student-teacher ratio is 17:1) within a traditional liberal arts framework.

Rounding out the private liberal arts colleges in Greensboro is Bennett College, which opened in 1873 as a school for the children of former slaves and became a women's college in 1926. Bennett is still for women only and is affiliated with the United Methodist Church. Among the most popular areas of study for its approximately 766 students are interdisciplinary studies, biology, and business administration. Unique programs include womanist religious studies, global studies, and Africana women's studies.

A wide variety of opportunities, from career exploration to high-technology business training, are offered through Guilford Technical Community College (GTCC), which has a main campus in nearby Jamestown and satellite campuses in downtown Greensboro. Established in 1958, GTCC is the third largest public two-year college in the state. The Greensboro Wendover Campus offers adult education, continuing education, and a Technical Education Center with classes in architectural technology, civil engineering, green construction technology, paralegal studies, telecommunications, and more. The T. H. Davis Aviation Center of GTCC is in Greensboro, offering pilot training and aviation management programs.

The Greater Greensboro Consortium (GGC) provides the unique opportunity to degree-seeking students of the eight participating institutions in the metropolitan area (Bennett College, Elon College, Greensboro College, Guilford Technical Community College, High Point University, North Carolina Agricultural and Technical State University (A & T), and the University of North Carolina at Greensboro) to take classes at any of the schools that meet specific criteria.

Libraries and Research Centers

The Greensboro Public Library, opened in 1902, consists of a central facility and six branches and has more than 541,000 books and 17,000 serial volumes in its collection, as well as e-books, audio tapes and video tapes, CD ROMs, DVDs, slides, maps, and art prints. All locations have computers with Internet access (about 200 in total), and some provide classes.

Special collections are maintained in the areas of business and management, local history, and genealogy. The Glenwood Branch is home to the Nonprofit

Resource Center, the Greensboro Neighborhood Information Center, and the Multicultural Resources Center. The Kathleen Clay Edwards Family Branch is located in the 98-acre Price Park and includes a bird and butterfly meadow, a reading garden, walking trails, ponds, and wetlands. This location has an extensive collection of nature, gardening, and environmental resources. The newest addition to the system is the McGirt-Horton Branch, a Leadership in Energy and Environmental Design (LEED) facility that opened in 2010. The Greensboro Historical Museum became a division of the public library in 1997.

The University of North Carolina at Greensboro is the home of the 220,000-square-foot Walter Clinton Jackson Library. It maintains more than 3.4 million items featuring 700,000 federal and state documents, and 5,100 serial subscriptions.

Several research centers are based in Greensboro, representing a wide variety of fields and topics. The University of North Carolina Greensboro is classified as a Doctoral/Research-Intensive University by The Carnegie Foundation. Among the centers affiliated with the University of North Carolina at Greensboro are the Center for Drug Design, the Center for Global Business Education and Research, the Center for Health of Vulnerable Populations, the Center for Innovation in Interior Architecture, and the Center for Biotechnology, Genomics and Health Research. The Music Research Institute at UNCG covers topics such as multisensory processing, sound level exposures, the genetic basis of musicality, and biomusic science (exploring the role of music in nature in both human and non-human expressions).

Research centers affiliated with the North Carolina Agricultural and Technical State University include the Center for Advanced Materials and Smart Structures, the Center for Composite Material Research, the Center for Energy Research and Technology, the Center for Human-Machine Studies, and the Interdisciplinary Scientific Environmental Technology Cooperative Science Center (ISET). The Center for Human Machine Studies at NC A&T works in collaboration with the U.S. Army Center for Battlefield Capability Research Office and several other member colleges.

The city also boasts a Center for Creative Leadership that has a variety of programs geared toward the development of leaders in the business world.

Public Library Information: Greensboro Public Library, 219 N. Church St., Greensboro, NC 27401; telephone (336) 373-2471.

■ Health Care

From lifesaving open-heart surgery to the newest diagnostic technologies, Greensboro is a city where advanced medical technology is readily available. The city and surrounding area has specialized and general physicians, representing virtually every specialty and most subspecialties.

The private, not-for-profit, Moses Cone Health System (MCHS) provides most of the health care in the Greensboro area, offering a complete range of medical and surgical services. The largest Greensboro hospital in the system is the Moses H. Cone Memorial Hospital, founded in 1953, which has a national reputation for cardiovascular research. The hospital has a Level II trauma center and offers excellent programs through its Rehabilitation Center, Neuroscience Center, and Heart and Vascular Center. It is a teaching hospital and a referral center.

The Wesley Long Community Hospital, also part of the Cone Health System, is a modern 175-bed hospital. Adjacent to the main building is the Moses Cone regional Cancer Center, which has been designated as a Community Hospital Comprehensive Cancer Center by the American College of Surgeons Commission on Cancer. Wesley Long is also the site of the MCHS Sleep Disorders Center.

The 134-bed Cone Health Women's Hospital of Greensboro is the first freestanding hospital dedicated to women's services in the state. Special departments include a 12-bed Level II neonatal intensive care unit and a 24-bed Level III neonatal intensive care unit. The Behavioral Health Center supplies 80 beds—50 for adults and 30 for adolescents—to assist those with mental health issues.

The MCHS Pediatric Sub-Specialists of Greensboro offer services in pediatric cardiology, endocrinology, gastroenterology, and surgery. Another MCHS hospital, the 110-bed Annie Penn Hospital, provides specialty services such as a cancer center and sleep center and is located 20 miles north of the city.

Kindred Hospital Greensboro, operated by Kindred Healthcare, is a 124-bed acute-care facility specializing in extensive treatment for pulmonary and ventilator-dependent patients. There are 23 beds for long-term care. The hospital also offers inpatient and outpatient surgical services.

■ Recreation

Sightseeing

A tour of Greensboro might begin with Blandwood Mansion, a nineteenth-century Italian villa in downtown Greensboro, which is a National Historic Landmark and former home of Governor John Motley Morehead. Not far from Blandwood is the William Fields House, a Gothic Revival-style structure that is listed on the National Register of Historic Places.

Guilford Courthouse National Military Park, located in North Greensboro, provides a fascinating look at a battle that helped win America's independence. The 220-acre park, which was the first Revolutionary War battleground to be preserved as a national military park, includes a museum and interpretive automobile, bicycle,

and foot trails for retracing the battle. The adjacent eight-acre Tannenbaum Historic Park/Colonial Heritage Center served as a staging area for British troops under Cornwallis's command during the Revolutionary War. Today, the park features a visitor's center, gift shop, and exhibits depicting colonial life.

Castle McCullough, restored gold refinery in nearby Jamestown, is listed on the National Register of Historic Places. Originally built in 1832, the castle is a large granite structure complete with a drawbridge, moat and a 70-foot tower. Tours of the McCulloch Gold Mine may include an opportunity to pan for gold and other gems. The castle hosts a variety of public events and festivals throughout the year.

The International Civil Rights Center and Museum opened in 2010 at the site of the former Woolworth's where four African American men launched a movement by sitting down at the whites-only lunch counter and refused to leave without being served. The focal point of the museum is the historic lunch counter and the original stools where the NC A & T University freshmen Ezell Blair Jr., Franklin McCain, David Richmond, and Joseph McNeil sat down on February 1, 1960. The rest of the museum space contains artifacts and interactive displays that chronicle the history of the Civil Rights Movement.

The Greensboro Children's Museum is an exciting, colorful place with interactive exhibits and activities designed for kids up to age 12 as well as summer camp, programs, and workshops. Fun for the whole family can be had at Celebration Station, featuring miniature golf, water bumper boats, arcade games, batting cages, and more. The North Carolina Tennis Hall of Fame is located in the Harold T. and Mildred F. Southern North Carolina Tennis Center.

Greensboro Science Center is a premier family destination that features an aquarium, a museum, and a zoo. The Carolina SciQuarium is North Carolina's only inland aquarium. Visitors can see a variety of aquatic animals, including penguins, sharks, stingrays, a rare fishing cat, and an anaconda. Animal Discovery Zoological Park offers up-close creature encounters with tigers, meerkats, howler monkeys, lemurs, farm animals, and many more. At the Science Center Museum features several different activity centers, including Prehistoric Passages, complete with fossils and dinosaurs; the Extreme Weather Gallery; HealthQuest, where visitors explore the human body; and the Herpetarium, for an up-close look at numerous snakes and amphibians. The museum also features the state-of-the-art OmniSphere Theater, presenting digital, laser, and 3-D shows on a 40-foot dome ceiling.

Arts and Culture

The energy behind Greensboro's vibrant arts scene is ArtsGreensboro (formerly the United Arts Council), located in the Greensboro Cultural Center at Festival

Park, downtown's performing arts showplace and home base for several visual and performing art organizations as well as art galleries, a sculpture garden, and an outdoor amphitheater. The council serves as the fundraising umbrella for the city's many arts groups. The council funds several organizations and provides support to other groups. It also operates an artists' center, where serious, talented writers, painters, potters, and others may rent inexpensive studio space.

The Greensboro Symphony Orchestra, founded in the 1920s, performs masterworks and pops concerts from September to May at the War Memorial Auditorium in the Greensboro Coliseum Complex and at Dana Auditorium at Guilford College. Since 1980 the Greensboro Opera Company has presented performances by local talent year-round and an annual production featuring international talent in operatic works performed in the original language, also at the War Memorial Auditorium. The Greensboro Ballet, also the home of the School of Greensboro Ballet, offers three performances each season and delights holiday audiences each December with a presentation of *The Nutcracker*. The North Carolina Dance Project holds an annual concert in Greensboro and features two dance troupes that travel throughout the state.

The Greensboro Coliseum hosts a variety of tour events for family entertainment including rock concerts, circuses, Disney shows, and even professional bull riding. Jazz is very popular in Greensboro with nationally known musicians performing in the 1927 vintage Carolina Theatre and in local clubs. The Carolina Theatre is the principal venue for performing arts productions sponsored by City Arts of the Greensboro Parks and Recreation Department. City Arts oversees the Livestock Players Musical Theatre, which features shows by youth from ninth grade through 20 years old. The Livestock Players present Broadway musicals in November, April, and July. The 3rd Stage Theatre is the City Arts for actors and actresses ages 16 and older. Greensboro Children's Theatre performs during the school year.

The City Arts Music Center is home to the Greensboro Concert Band, the Philharmonia of Greensboro, the Gate City Horizons Band, the Choral Society of Greensboro, and the Greensboro Youth Chorus, all of which feature volunteer, nonprofessional musicians from the city.

Theatrical entertainment also abounds in Greensboro. At the Barn Dinner Theatre audiences have enjoyed dinner and a Broadway-style play year-round since 1962. Professional theater in an intimate setting is the specialty of the Broach Theatre in the Old Greensborough Historic District, which produces seven adult plays from February to December. Community Theatre of Greensboro presents five Broadway plays and musicals.

Greensboro's universities and colleges sponsor arts events throughout the year that are open to the public.

The artist's series at Guilford College, for example, brought the Prague Chamber Orchestra to Greensboro, and the UNCG Concert and Lecture Series has sponsored such notables as violinist Isaac Stern and actor Hal Holbrook.

Museum lovers enjoy the Greensboro Historical Museum, which traces the development of Guilford County from Native American times through the present. Special collections include memorabilia of author William Sydney Porter, better known as O. Henry, who grew up in Greensboro, as well as a variety of items and information related to Edward R. Murrow and First Lady Dolley Madison, who lived in Guilford County. The museum also has two restored log homes open for touring on its downtown site and has recreated an 1880s village of Greensboro, showing the city as it might have been when O. Henry left in 1882.

North Carolina Agricultural and Technical State University is the site of a nationally recognized facility, the Mattye Reed African Heritage Center in the Dudley Building, a repository for more than 3,500 artifacts from more than 30 African and Caribbean countries.

Greensboro is not lacking in art galleries. The Center for Visual Arts Gallery provides special exhibits of works by emerging artists. The Weatherspoon Art Museum, on the campus of the University of North Carolina at Greensboro is widely recognized for having one of the most outstanding collections of post-World War II American art in the Southeast. The African American Atelier in the Greensboro Cultural Center features works by local artists and presents six to eight exhibitions per year. North Carolina artists are the focus at the Gallery at Greenhill. The Guilford Native American Art Gallery was the first of its kind in the Southeast.

Arts and Culture Information: ArtsGreensboro, Greensboro Cultural Center, 200 N. Davie St., Ste. 201, Greensboro, NC 27401; telephone (336) 373-7523.

Festivals and Holidays

Many of Greensboro's biggest celebrations focus on music. The nationally acclaimed Eastern Music Festival began in 1962 and brings the world's most promising music students to Greensboro each year for six weeks of intense study with the world's most accomplished musicians. The performers, who spend the summer on the Guilford College campus, present more than 40 concerts from June through August.

St. Patrick's Day brings the Green Party to the downtown area in the form of several bands performing at various venues. Fun Fourth Festival in the downtown National Register Historic District is a street festival that thousands flock to in the inner city to celebrate the Independence Day. Arts and crafts from all over the country take center stage at two events sponsored by the Gilmore Shows' Carolina Craftsmen: the annual Spring Show in April and the Christmas Classic in late November. The Native American Cultural festival is held in November in conjunction with the Guilford Native American Association. African American arts and culture take the spotlight during the African American Heritage Extravaganza in March with dance, music, art exhibits, and food sampling.

September is a busy month for festivals. The Central Carolina Fair is held at the Greensboro Coliseum in September. An annual Greek festival is held at the Greensboro Greek Orthodox Church in September. The annual Ice Cream and Music Fest at the Music Academy of North Carolina (a community music school) is a great family-friendly event.

The November Festival of Lights features strolling carolers and other live music at Hamburger Square. The one-night event ends with a Christmas Tree Lighting and community sing-along.

Sports for the Spectator

When it comes to recreation, Greensboro is a city for all seasons and all sports. From May through August, the United Soccer League's Carolina Dynamo play Macpherson Stadium, which is part of the extensive Bryan Park. The stadium has hosted the NCAA Division III soccer championships in 2004, 2005, and 2008.

The Greensboro Aquatic Center (GAC) was selected to host the USA Swimming's 2013 Speedo Winter Junior National Championships and the USA Swimming's 2014 AT&T Winter National Championships. The GAC is a state-of-the art facility that opened at the Greensboro Coliseum Complex in 2011. The Greensboro Grasshoppers, a Class A farm team of the Miami Marlins, take the field at NewBridge Bank Park, with more than 5,000 seats, party decks, and a children's play area. The Wyndham Championship of the PGA Tour comes to the Forest Oaks Country Club in August.

Sports fans can also find plenty of collegiate sports in the area. The Spartan soccer team takes to the field at the University of North Carolina at Greensboro (UNCG), and winter often brings Carolinians' favorite rivalry, the Atlantic Coast Conference (ACC) basketball tournament at the Greensboro Coliseum. The North Carolina Agricultural and Technical State University basketball team often lands a berth in the NCAA tournament, but the football team also draws crowds to the 21,500-seat Aggie Stadium. Women's sports include basketball and track. UNCG women's soccer, basketball, and tennis teams have been prominent nationally.

Sports for the Participant

One of the highlights of Greensboro is the extensive and continuously expanding parks and recreation system, which includes 170 parks on more than 3,500 acres.

Bicycling routes, fitness and hiking trails, 7 swimming pools and 10 recreation centers are spread throughout the city. Tennis is an especially popular sport in Greensboro, both for players and spectators. The city operates five fully equipped tennis centers. The United States Tennis Association's (USTA) Greensboro January Indoor Junior Championships is played annually at the Simkins Indoor Pavilion in Barber Park in Greensboro. Additional facilities include Lathan Tennis Center and Spencer Love Tennis Center.

The area's many golf aficionados find challenging golf in the 600-acre Bryan Park Golf and Conference Center, as well as at many private golf courses. The park includes two 18-hole championship golf courses, two putting greens, a driving range, and a golf school. Facilities at Bryan Park also include a tennis center, a nature trail, and a wildlife sanctuary. Golf enthusiasts might also visit Grandover Resort, which features two 18-hole golf courses designed by the world-renowned golf architects David Graham and Gary Panks.

The Greensboro Sportsplex has many amenities on its 106,000 square feet of space including eight basketball courts, four state-of-the-art indoor soccer fields, volleyball courts and clubs, and indoor roller hockey. Summer camps and special tournaments are offered.

Another well-used city park is Country Park, a 126-acre facility in northern Greensboro listed as a National Historical Landmark property that includes two stocked fishing lakes; hiking, bicycling, and jogging trails; pedal-boat rentals; and plenty of places for a quiet picnic. It also is the site of the annual Carolina Cup Bicycle Road Race in September sponsored by U.S. Cycling.

Wet 'n Wild Emerald Pointe is the largest water park in the state, with a giant wave pool and other water activities.

Shopping and Dining

North of downtown Greensboro, visitors can stroll through a relaxed neighborhood of unique shops, restaurants, and boutiques housed in elegantly refurbished 1920s vintage buildings at State Street Station. On the city's southwest side, the Four Seasons Town Centre features three levels with more than 200 shops and restaurants. With 95 stores on 75 acres of open-air shopping, the Friendly Center has three department stores, a 16-screen theater, and many national retailers. In the section of downtown called Old Downtown Greensborough, browsers will find more than a dozen antique stores housed in turn-of-the-century storefronts. The Super Flea Market is held about one weekend each month at the Greensboro Coliseum. Hundreds of dealers participate in this event with vendors offering an amazing variety of wares. The city and neighboring communities are also home to dozens of outlet stores. Products manufactured locally, such as clothing and furniture, are especially popular with shoppers.

As for dining, barbecue, hushpuppies, and coleslaw are North Carolina staples, and restaurants serving these local favorites are plentiful in the metropolitan Greensboro area's some 500 eateries. Hungry visitors will also find upscale eateries and a variety of ethnic cuisines.

The locals enjoy going down to the Greensboro Farmers Curb Market year-round for an abundance of fresh produce, baked goods, flowers, and crafts. The market highlights different products on most Saturdays, including herbs, strawberries, and tomatoes when in season.

Visitor Information: Greensboro Area Convention and Visitors Bureau, 2200 Pinecroft Rd., Ste 200, Greensboro, NC 27407; telephone (336) 274-2282; fax (336) 230-1183.

■ Convention Facilities

The city-owned Greensboro Coliseum Complex, the largest facility of its kind in the state, seats 23,500 people in its Coliseum Arena. The War Memorial Auditorium, adjacent to the arena, has 2,400 seats and the smaller Odeon Theater has 300 seats. The special events center has 167,000 square feet of exhibit space that can be partitioned into four smaller halls. A 30,000-square-foot pavilion sits directly next to the special events center.

The largest hotel-convention complex between Washington D.C., and Atlanta, Georgia, is the more than 1,000-room Sheraton Greensboro Hotel at Four Seasons, which includes about 250,000 square feet of meeting space and 100,000 square feet of exhibition space with 75 meeting rooms, located adjacent to the three-level Four Seasons Town Centre mall with more than 200 shops and restaurants and a multi-theater cinema. The hotel's largest meeting area, the 40,000-square-foot Guilford Ballroom, can accommodate in excess of 4,000 people for a banquet or 6,000 people for a meeting with full tradeshow capabilities.

The Greensboro–High Point Marriott Airport hotel, adjacent to Piedmont Triad International Airport, provides a convenient meeting place for groups arriving by air. With 299 guest rooms, the Marriott can accommodate large groups in its 9,925 square feet of meeting space within 20 rooms. Also near the airport is the Embassy Suites Greensboro Airport, with 13,000 square feet of meeting space and 219 suites available. The Greensboro Marriott Downtown has 24,000 square feet of meeting space and 281 guest rooms.

Grandover Resort and Conference Center features 45,000 square feet of meeting space, including a 13,500-square-foot ballroom. Hotel amenities include 247 guest rooms and two championship, 18-hole golf courses designed by David Graham and Gary Panks. There is also an onsite spa.

Also in the heart of downtown is the Biltmore Greensboro Hotel, a charming meeting location for small groups. The inn, which dates to 1895 and originally housed corporate offices for Cone Mills, today is a 24-room hotel furnished with eighteenth-century reproductions. A maximum of about 80 people can be accommodated for meetings.

Most other major hotels offer some type of meeting and/or banquet spaces. Meeting space is available at many other local facilities, including the Carolina Theatre; the 1840s Blandwood Mansion and Carriage House; Brookwood Golf Course; and Castle McCulloch & Crystal Gardens, to name a few. The Conference Center at Bryan Park can handle business or social events in its 22,000-square-foot facility overlooking championship golfing greens.

Convention Information: Greensboro Area Convention and Visitors Bureau, 2200 Pinecroft Rd., Ste 200, Greensboro, NC 27407; telephone (336) 274-2282; fax (336) 230-1183.

■ Transportation

Approaching the City

Greensboro is proud of its convenient and efficient transportation network. The city is located at the intersection of two major interstates, the east–west Interstate 40 and north–south Interstate 85, midway between Charlotte and Raleigh. In addition to cities served directly by Interstates 40 and 85, those highways provide connections to other major arteries throughout the region and the nation, such as Interstates 77 and 95, leading virtually anywhere along the eastern seaboard. Parts of Interstates 73 and 74 were still under construction in 2013; both routes will provide easy access to the city and the airport.

The Piedmont Triad International Airport (PTIA) terminal, located only minutes from downtown, is served by nine airlines, with more than one million enplaned passengers annually. Nonstop service was available to 17 cities. Travelers can also catch the train in Greensboro; Amtrak trains going north and south stop daily at the Greensboro station. Greyhound also has a route through Greensboro.

Traveling in the City

The smooth traffic flow in Greensboro, which often amazes newcomers, gives Greensboro the feel of a smaller city. It is an impression that has been carefully created through years of planning that began when the city developed its transportation plan in the 1950s. As development has taken place over the years since then, planners have kept pace to meet city needs. One key to Greensboro's smooth-flowing traffic is Wendover Avenue, an expressway that takes motorists from Interstate

40 on the west through Greensboro to U.S. Highway 29 on the east in a matter of minutes. Many of the city's other major thoroughfares are four-lane.

Good public transportation is provided by the Greensboro Transit Authority, with 15 routes running Monday through Saturday and 7 Sunday routes. Special bus service for elderly and handicapped persons is provided through Specialized Community Area Transportation (SCAT). The Higher Education Area Transit (HEAT), initiated in 2007, offers college and university transit service for qualified students of six area institutions of higher learning. Express routes are available between schools and select stops along four routes and also include connecting service to the entire Greensboro Transit Authority system.

The Greensboro Department of Transportation has added bike lanes to several thoroughfares in the city in efforts to encourage an alternative, environmentally friendly mode of transportation. The lanes are part of the greater Greensboro Urban Area Bicycle, Pedestrian and Greenway Master Plan (BiPed Plan).

■ Communications

Newspapers and Magazines

Greensboro's major daily (morning) newspaper is the *News & Record*. The paper is distributed throughout the county with special metro sections for local editions. Several weekly or biweekly newspapers are published in Greensboro, including *Carolina Peacemaker,* for the African American community, and *Go Triad*, an arts and entertainment weekly sponsored by the *News & Record* and distributed on Thursdays. *Yes! Weekly* is an alternative serving the Triad with a focus on politics, arts, and culture. The *Rhino Times*, with weekly editions published in Greensboro and Charlotte, presents entertainment and social and community news.

Several magazines and journals are published in Greensboro, including *BIZlife magazine*, covering people and events in the Triad business community; *Carolina Gardener;* and *SportsKidsPlay*, a sports news and events magazine for youth.

Television and Radio

Only three television stations broadcast from Greensboro, including affiliates of CW, TCT (Tri-State Christian Television), and Gannett Broadcasting. Several other stations are based in nearby towns and serve viewers in the entire metropolitan region. Additional stations are available via cable. There are 9 AM and 5 FM stations licensed in Greensboro. NC A&T, Guilford College, and UNC Greensboro all have stations.

Media Information: *News & Record,* 200 East Market Street, Greensboro NC 27401; telephone (336) 373-7000.

Greensboro Online

City of Greensboro home page. Available www. greensboro-nc.gov

County of Guilford home page. Available www. countyweb.co.guilford.nc.us/

Downtown Greensboro. Available www.downtown greensboro.net

GoTriad Online. Available www.gotriad.com

Greensboro Area Convention and Visitors Bureau. Available www.visitgreensboronc.com/

Greensboro Chamber of Commerce. Available www. greensboro.org

Greensboro Historical Museum. Available www. greensborohistory.org

Greensboro Public Library. Available www. greensboro-nc.gov/index.aspx?page=780

Guilford County Schools. Available www.gcsnc.com

News and Record. Available www.news-record.com

BIBLIOGRAPHY

Dunkerly, Robert M. *The Confederate Surrender at Greensboro: The Final Days of the Army of Tennessee, April 1865* (Jefferson, NH: McFarland & Company, Inc., 2013)

Redding, Sarah and Sherry Roberts, eds., *Greensboro: A Portrait of Progress* (Montgomery, AL: Community Communications, 1998)

Wolff, Miles, *Lunch at the 5 & 10* (Chicago, IL: Ivan R. Dee, 1990)

Raleigh

■ The City in Brief

Founded: 1792 (incorporated 1795)

Head Official: Mayor Nancy McFarlane (since 2011); City Manager Ruffin L. Hall (since 2013)

City Population
    1990: 218,859
    2000: 276,093
    2010: 403,892
    2012 estimate: 423,743
    Percent change, 2000–2010: 46.3%
    U.S. rank in 1990: 75th
    U.S. rank in 2000: 73rd (State rank: 2nd)
    U.S. rank in 2010: 43rd (State rank: 2nd)

Metropolitan Statistical Area Population
    2000: 797,071
    2010: 1,130,490
    2012 estimate: 1,188,564
    Percent change, 2000–2010: 41.8%
    U.S. rank in 2000: 59th
    U.S. rank in 2010: 48th

Area: 117.3 square miles

Elevation: 434 feet above sea level

Average Annual Temperatures: 59.6° F

Average Annual Precipitation: 43.05 inches

Major Economic Sectors: business and professional services, health-care and educational services, government, wholesale and retail trade

Unemployment Rate: 6.2% (2012)

Per Capita Income: $29,710

2012 FBI Crime Index Property: 13,779

Major Colleges and Universities: North Carolina State University, Shaw University, Meredith College, St. Augustine's College

Daily Newspaper: *The News and Observer*

■ Introduction

Blessed with beautiful residential areas, expansive parks, and historic buildings, the city of Raleigh exudes southern charm. Raleigh is the largest city in the central North Carolina Research Triangle, which some refer to the Silicon Valley of the East. Research Triangle includes Raleigh, Durham, and Chapel Hill, with Raleigh's North Carolina State University, the University of North Carolina at Chapel Hill, and Duke University in Durham forming the intellectual nucleus of the Research Triangle. Research Triangle Park (RTP) is one of the country's leading centers for high technology research, with more than 170 companies and organizations. Into the twenty-first century, Raleigh has prospered as an education, government, and research and development center. The city has easy access to the ocean and the mountains and a moderate climate that encourages year-round outdoor activities. The city also hosts numerous arts organizations and cultural centers. In all, Raleigh has become a great place to live, work, and play.

■ Geography and Climate

Raleigh is located in the gently rolling pine woods of the central Piedmont section of North Carolina, midway between the Great Smoky Mountains to the west and the Atlantic Ocean to the east, each about a three-hour drive. Together, the cities of Chapel Hill, Durham, and Raleigh are known as the Research Triangle, which is an extremely important economic region for the state. With its proximity to the Atlantic Ocean, the Raleigh-Durham

Raleigh, NC skyline. © iStockPhoto.com/Mlenny

area does receive some occasional severe weather in the form of thunderstorms and hurricanes. Temperatures average around 59.3 degrees in mid-spring and 59.7 degrees in mid-autumn. Snowfall averages 7.5 inches per year.

Area: 117.3 square miles

Elevation: 434 feet above sea level

Average Temperatures: 59.6° F

Average Annual Precipitation: 43.05 inches

■ History

City Named Capital of State

In 1771 a new North Carolina county was created by the state assembly. They named the county Wake, in honor of Margaret Wake, wife of Governor William Tryon. In 1792 the General Assembly purchased 1,000 acres of Wake County and established the city of Raleigh, which was named in honor of Sir Walter Raleigh, to serve as the first permanent state capital. The word "Raleigh" comes from two Anglo-Saxon words meaning "meadow of the

deer," which captures the essence of the city's peaceful setting.

Early Citizens Seen as "Roughnecks"

William Christmas of Franklin County, North Carolina, was hired to create a plan for the new city. Christmas designed a layout with one square mile of perpendicular streets and one-acre lots. Union Square, future home of the State House, lay at the center. Equidistant from it, the planner designated four squares to serve as green space. Even now, the original city boundaries can be recognized by their original names, North, South, East, and West.

Enthusiastic about Christmas's plans, legislators authorized the building of a new courthouse in Raleigh, making it the county seat as well as the capital. During its early days, Raleigh had a questionable reputation because of the bachelors and saloons that dominated the scene. Its citizens were not granted the right to vote until the beginning of the nineteenth century.

Raleigh in the Nineteenth Century

Raleigh grew larger at a slow but steady pace during this time when most of its residents were in the business of agriculture. Eventually towns developed along railroad lines and market centers. In time, small textile and furniture factories grew up. In 1831 the original State House burned down. The legislature agreed that the new State House should be a more durable structure. For this purpose solid granite was quarried in the east side of the county and brought to Raleigh via a specially built rail line. The permanent Executive Mansion was designed by architects Samuel Sloan and Gustavus Bauer, and constructed entirely of North Carolina materials, from the slate roof to the pine balustrade and brick facade. Construction was performed by prison inmates whose names and initials can still be seen in the brick sidewalks surrounding the mansion.

During the Civil War, Raleigh did not experience the tremendous suffering at the hands of Union forces as did many other southern towns and cities. Destruction was narrowly averted when some torch-carrying troops from the 60,000 troops quartered in the city approached the downtown upon hearing of the assassination of President Abraham Lincoln. Their commander, General John A. Logan, turned them back at gunpoint.

City Takes Off After WWII

Raleigh's major growth occurred after World War II ended in 1945. The seeds of the city's modern renaissance were sewn in the 1950s when the state of North Carolina created the world-famous Research Triangle Park west of the city. The park was conceived by Dr. Howard Odom, a University of North Carolina sociologist who envisioned the development as a place for the highly trained graduates of North Carolina's colleges and universities, most of whom were leaving for more promising careers elsewhere. The area boomed as both well-established and new companies found homes at Research Triangle.

Throughout the next few decades, numerous development and redevelopment projects created new jobs and new opportunities for businesses and residents. Major downtown projects included the new Raleigh Civic Center, Fayetteville Street Mall, the First Union Capitol Center, and the Walnut Creek Amphitheatre. Step by step, the city continued to grow into the twenty-first century with a major downtown revitalization program and an influx of businesses and residents.

Following an economic slump during the recession of 2007–09, the city experienced renewed growth in the 2010s as city planners worked to attract new businesses in target industries such as cleantech and advanced manufacturing. In 2013 the U.S. Bureau of Labor Statistics listed Raleigh as eighth in the nation for largest growth increase in private-sector employment since the recession, and 10th for overall increase in private-sector jobs. That year, *Forbes* placed Raleigh as the fourth fastest growing city in America.

Historical Information: North Carolina Department of Cultural Resources, Office of Archives and History,

109 East Jones Street, Raleigh, NC 27699; telephone (919) 807-7300.

■ Population Profile

Metropolitan Statistical Area Population
2000: 797,071
2010: 1,130,490
2012 estimate: 1,188,564
Percent change, 2000–2010: 41.8%
U.S. rank in 2000: 59th
U.S. rank in 2010: 48th

City Residents
1990: 218,859
2000: 276,093
2010: 403,892
2012 estimate: 423,743
Percent change, 2000–2010: 46.3%
U.S. rank in 1990: 75th
U.S. rank in 2000: 73rd (State rank: 2nd)
U.S. rank in 2010: 43rd (State rank: 2nd)

Density: 2,826.3 people per square mile

Racial and ethnic characteristics
White: 255,854
Black or African American: 126,167
American Indian and Alaskan Native: 883
Asian: 20,142
Native Hawaiian and Other Pacific Islander: 79
Hispanic or Latino (may be of any race): 44,083
Other: 20,618

Percent of residents born in state: 46.3%

Age characteristics
Population under 5 years old: 29,031
Population 5 to 9 years old: 28,261
Population 10 to 14 years old: 26,446
Population 15 to 19 years old: 27,586
Population 20 to 24 years old: 42,476
Population 25 to 34 years old: 78,140
Population 35 to 44 years old: 63,715
Population 45 to 54 years old: 52,072
Population 55 to 59 years old: 20,999
Population 60 to 64 years old: 17,831
Population 65 to 74 years old: 21,453
Population 75 to 84 years old: 10,634
Population 85 years and over: 5,099
Median age: 32.4

Births (2010–11 Metropolitan Area)
Total number: 15,559

Deaths (2010–11 Metropolitan Area)
Total number: 5,951

Money income (2012)

Per capita income: $29,710
Median household income: $52,709
Total households: 161,309

Number of households with income of ...

less than $10,000: 10,275
$10,000 to $14,999: 8,295
$15,000 to $24,999: 15,149
$25,000 to $34,999: 18,998
$35,000 to $49,999: 22,808
$50,000 to $74,999: 31,038
$75,000 to $99,999: 19,679
$100,000 to $149,999: 19,525
$150,000 to $199,999: 7,966
$200,000 or more: 7,576

Percent of families below poverty level: 17.3%

FBI Crime Index Property: 13,779

FBI Crime Index Violent: 1,780

■ Municipal Government

Raleigh has a council-manager form of government with a mayor and seven council members. Three members, including the mayor, are elected at large, and five members are elected to represent single-member districts. All officials are elected for two-year terms. The city manager is hired by the council and serves as the chief administrator of most city departments.

Head Official: Mayor Nancy McFarlane (since 2011); City Manager Ruffin L. Hall (since 2013)

Total Number of City Employees: 3,244 (2013)

City Information: City of Raleigh, Municipal Building, 222 W. Hargett St., Raleigh, NC 27601; telephone (919) 996-3000.

■ Economy

Major Industries and Commercial Activity

Although the region felt the pinch of the nation's economic slowdown in the late 2000s, many factors point to Raleigh's continued fiscal health. Numerous high technology and medical corporations have been attracted to the Raleigh-Durham area because of the outstanding educational and research facilities at area universities, such as North Carolina State University, which is home to one of the nation's largest schools of engineering; Duke University; and the University of North Carolina–Chapel Hill. Nearby Research Triangle Park is one of the leading centers for high-technology

research and development in the country. Roughly 170 corporate, academic, and government agencies in the park employ some 39,000 workers.

The city has managed to create a balance between large and small business ventures. Several large corporations are headquartered in Raleigh, including First Citizens Bank, INC Research, Salix Pharmaceuticals, Red Hat Software, and Sensus. However, in 2013, the National Federation of Independent Businesses ranked Raleigh second in the nation in its survey of best places to start a business. *The Business Journals* ranked the Raleigh-Cary area as fourth in the nation in its survey of best cities for small businesses.

The government sector accounts for a significant number of jobs at state, county, and municipal levels. Business and professional services is the leading industry sector in the Raleigh-Cary metropolitan area, followed by health-care and educational services, and trade, transportation, and utilities.

Items and goods produced: pharmaceuticals, electronic equipment, medical diagnostic equipment, computer software, electrical machinery, processed foods, metal products

Incentive Programs-New and Existing Companies

Local programs: The Raleigh Economic Development Partnership oversees a number of programs to assist new and existing businesses with the city, such as the Downtown Loan Pool. The Greater Raleigh Chamber of Commerce helps businesses apply for Article 3J Tax credits, which include a job creation credit and research and development credits. Raleigh has created a designated Urban Progress Zone, where businesses are eligible for enhanced tax credits. The City of Raleigh offers special programs to advise and assist small businesses throughout the city.

State programs: North Carolina, a right-to-work state with a low unionization rate, offers a revenue bond pool program through various banks. Several venture capital funds operate in the state and inquiries can be made through North Carolina's Council for Entrepreneurial Development (CED). Industrial Revenue Bonds issued by the state provide new and expanding businesses the opportunity to provide good employment and wage opportunities for their workers.

The state offers an income tax allocation formula that permits the double weighting of sales in calculating corporate income tax. Additional tax credits offered by the state include those for new markets, renewable energy property investment, job creation, and research and development. A business property tax credit and film incentive tax credit are also available, along with economic development riders and land use incentive grants.

The North Carolina Department of Transportation administers a program that provides for the construction of access roads to industrial sites and road improvements in areas surrounding major corporate installations.

The North Carolina Small Business and Technology Development Center (SBTDC) makes capital available to entrepreneurs and begin building a stronger early-stage investment industry. Financing assistance may be available to qualified businesses under the following programs: traditional bank loans, SBA-guaranteed loans, federal research and development and commercialization funding, equity capital investment, international export financing, the North Carolina Capital Access Program (NC-CAP), and North Carolina Loan Participation Program (NC-LPP). The Raleigh SBTDC is located at North Carolina State University.

Job training programs

NC Workforce, a division of the North Carolina Chamber of Commerce, sponsors the Incumbent Workforce Development Program, which offers grants of up to $25,000 for companies for training and continuing education of existing employees. There are three Wake County Career Centers located in Raleigh.

State funding allows North Carolina Community Colleges to offer a special customized training program for new, expanding, and existing businesses. The Job Growth Training program for new and expanding businesses is available for companies that create at least 12 new production jobs in the state, or to any new or prospective employee referred for training by a participating company. The Productivity Enhancement Training program specifically targets incumbent workers who must regularly update their skills as technology changes. Technology Investment Training and Continuous Improvement Training fill in the gaps to ensure that programs are available for employers and employees as needed. Employees may go through training before or after employment by the company. In Raleigh customized training programs are offered through Wake Technical Community College.

Development Projects

The Raleigh Economic Development Program is funded by the City of Raleigh and administered by the Greater Raleigh Chamber of Commerce. Economic planners from all three organizations have adopted eight target industries for future development: advanced manufacturing, cleantech, corporate headquarters, defense technologies, entrepreneurs, game development, information technologies, and life sciences. The Downtown Raleigh Alliance (DRA) works specifically to promote revitalization efforts in the downtown area. According to a DRA report, five major projects with a total investment of $160 million were completed during 2012. In 2013 projects valued at $371 million were under construction, while

projects involving nearly $504 million were still in the planning stages.

One major project completed in 2012 was the $130 million Green Square project, a mixed-used complex that includes the 80,000-square-foot Nature Research Center, offices for the NC Department of Environment and Natural resources, and a parking garage. Red Hat Tower, the new headquarters for the Linux software company, was completed in 2013.

One planned project in 2013 involves the redevelopment of Union Station into a modernized multimodal transit center. The City of Raleigh is working with the NC Department of Transportation (NCDOT) on the construction of a new passenger train station at 510 West Martin Street. The new $60 million station was to replace the existing Amtrak Station on Cabarrus Street and was expected to open in 2017.

The $60 million, 23-story SkyHouse Raleigh apartment tower broke ground in 2013. This represented the first stage of the larger Edison project, which is expected to include a 13-story office tower and a second apartment complex.

Economic Development Information: Raleigh Economic Development, One Exchange Plaza, Suite 707, Raleigh, NC 27601; telephone (919) 996-2707.

Commercial Shipping

Raleigh-Durham International Airport (RDU) is located 15 miles from downtown Raleigh. There are two cargo areas at the airport—North Cargo and South Cargo. All cargo carrier aircraft facilities are located in the North Cargo area. The South Cargo area handles freight shipped via commercial passenger aircraft. Cargo facilities include processing centers, regional offices and ramp space.

Raleigh is an integral part of Norfolk Southern's rail service linking the east coast to Midwest markets and is in the center of CSX's 27,000-mile network serving 22 states and Canada. Numerous motor freight carriers operate in the area, which has more than 40 motor freight terminals. The city is located within 500 miles of half the population of the United States. The state's 78,000-mile highway network makes the area a highway hub for the Northeast, Mid-Atlantic, and Southeast states, while providing rapid access to Midwest markets.

Labor Force and Employment Outlook

In 2013 the Milken Institute ranked the Raleigh-Cary metropolitan statistical area as third in the nation in a survey of top cities for creating and sustaining jobs and economic growth. That year, both Modis and CIO.com ranked Raleigh among the top 10 cities in the nation for information technology jobs. In addition, the U.S. Bureau of Labor Statistics listed Raleigh eighth in the nation for largest growth increase in private-sector employment since the recession, and 10th for overall increase in private-sector jobs.

According to the U.S. Bureau of Labor Statistics, professional and business services accounted for the largest number of jobs for the Raleigh-Cary metropolitan statistical area at the end of 2013. Trade, transportation, and utilities came in next, followed by government and educational and health services.

The largest employers in 2013 were from the government (municipal, county, and state), education, and health-care sectors. These included the Wake County Public Schools, North Carolina State University, WakeMed Health and Hospitals, and Rex Healthcare.

The following is a summary of data regarding the 2012 Raleigh labor force:

Size of civilian labor force: 229,363

Number of workers employed in . . .

    agriculture and mining: 528
    construction: 11,688
    manufacturing: 16,194
    wholesale trade: 5,387
    retail trade: 23,091
    transportation: 6,165
    information systems: 5,020
    finance: 14,285
    professional administration: 34,617
    education and social services: 46,016
    arts and leisure: 22,455
    other: 11,131
    public administration: 11,342

Average hourly earnings of production workers: $16.03

Unemployment rate: 6.2% (2012)

Employers

Largest employers (Metropolitan area, 2013)

	Number of employees
State of North Carolina	24,083
Wake County Public Schools	17,527
WakeMed Health and Hospitals	8,423
North Carolina State University	8,080
Cisco Systems Inc.	5,500
Rex Healthcare	5,400
Wake County	4,341
North Carolina Department of Health and Human Services	3,879
City of Raleigh	3,244
Affiliated Computer Systems	2,915
North Carolina Department of Commerce	2,884

Cost of Living

The following is a summary of data regarding several key cost of living factors in the area.

2013 ACCRA Average House Price: $227,454

2013 ACCRA Cost of Living Index: 93

State income tax rate: 6.0% to 7.75%

State sales tax rate: 4.75%

Local income tax rate: None

Local sales tax rate: 2.0%

Property tax rate: $.9166 per $100 of assessed valuation (2013)

Economic Information: Raleigh Economic Development, One Exchange Plaza, Suite 707, Raleigh, NC 27601; telephone (919) 996-2707.

■ Education and Research

Elementary and Secondary Schools

The Wake County Public School System is a comprehensive system offering a variety of programs for gifted and talented students while also providing educational options for students with special needs. While there are 170 schools in the district, only 84 are in Raleigh. Students have the option of either attending their neighborhood school or a network of 32 magnet schools, including year-round schools, schools with gifted and talented programs, and schools with other programs, including Montessori, creative arts, extended day, and accelerated studies. Project Enlightenment targets preschool students who may need extra assistance.

Several elementary and middle schools in the system operate on a year-round schedule. Under such a schedule, students in participating schools are organized into four tracks. Each track follows a different schedule so that while three tracks are in school, one track is out on break. The 45/15 schedule means that students attend classes for 45 days and are then on break for 15 days. This multi-track system accommodates up to 33 percent more pupils in a building. Some elementary schools offer enrichment or catch-up programs for students during their scheduled break.

The system also sponsors Early College schools, which allow students to fulfill the requirements for an associate's degree from a local community college at the same time they are satisfying requirements for high school graduation. Students who go on to a four-year college are often able to enter at a junior level. The International Baccalaureate program is also offered through some high schools.

Private school education in Raleigh thrives under many forms, with more than 30 schools in Raleigh including church-related schools, preschools, college preparatory schools, and special institutions for the learning disabled.

The following is a summary of data regarding the Wake County Schools.

Total enrollment: 144,173

Number of facilities
    total: 84
    elementary schools: 51
    junior high schools: 17
    high schools: 13
    other: 3

Student/teacher ratio: 15.8:1

Teacher salaries
    average (statewide): $46,850

Funding per pupil: $7,714

Public Schools Information: Wake County Public School System, 5625 Dillard Drive, Cary, NC 27518; telephone (919) 431-7400.

Colleges and Universities

Higher education plays an important role throughout the Raleigh area. Colleges and universities in the area are consistently ranked among the best in the nation. North Carolina State University is the state's largest university. NCSU offers bachelor's degrees in more than 110 fields, master's degrees in more than 110 fields, and doctorates in 61 fields. The most popular programs are engineering and humanities/social sciences.

Shaw University is the oldest historically African American university in the South. It was established to educate freedmen in theology and interpreting the Bible. Now the school offers several bachelor's programs in a variety of areas and master's degrees in divinity, religious education, curriculum and instruction, and early childhood education.

St. Augustine's College was founded by the Episcopal Church after the Civil War to educate freed slaves. The predominantly African American coeducational liberal arts college offers more than 25 undergraduate majors. The most popular programs are business management, criminal justice, human performance and wellness, and sociology.

William Peace University, a women's college affiliated with the Presbyterian Church, was founded in 1857

and offers bachelor's degrees in 14 majors, including criminal justice, simulation and game design, and political science. Meredith College is a Baptist-affiliated women's liberal arts college that offers its more than 2,000 students 70 undergraduate programs and 4 master's programs.

Wake Technical Community College provides vocational programs and two-year associate degree programs in such areas as business computer programming, automatic robotics technology, criminal justice, hotel and restaurant management, and early childhood education to its nearly 50,000 curriculum and continuing education students. Continuing-education programs include short-term, non-credit classes for job skills development or occupational licensing. The college also offers English as a Second Language, adult high school, GED and basic skills programs. An Occupational Education Division offers training programs for law enforcement, emergency medical service, fire prevention and hospitality professionals.

Libraries and Research Centers

Wake County Public Libraries operates 19 branches and 6 regional libraries within Wake County. There are nine branches in Raleigh. The library has more than 1.4 million volumes, along with thousands of audio materials, videos, serial subscriptions, and e-books. Annual circulation is nearly six million. Special Collections include the Mollie Houston Lee Collection on African American subjects and the North Carolina History Collection. A Nonprofit Resource Center is open to the public at the Cameron Village Regional Library.

The Triangle Research Libraries Network, created in 1977, combines the resources of four major universities—Duke University, North Carolina State University (NCSU), North Carolina Central University (NCCU), and UNC-Chapel Hill (UNCCH). Through this network, nearly 14 million volumes are available to students, researchers, and companies throughout Research Triangle Park. The NCSU libraries in Raleigh include D. H. Hill Library, Design Library, Natural Resources Library, Textiles Library, and the Veterinary Medicine Library. Other resource centers on campus include the African American Cultural Center Reading Room, the College of Education Media Center, and the Mathematics Working Collection.

Research Triangle Park (RTP) near Raleigh-Durham, commonly referred to as the Silicon Valley of the East, is one of the country's leading centers for high technology research. Its 7,000-acre campus is the largest planned research facility in the world. RTP has more than 170 organizations, employing more than 39,000 full-time professionals. Companies range from small start-ups to larger 11,000-plus employee businesses in RTP. Companies with facilities in RTP include RTI International, Dupont, Bayer, GlaxoSmithKline, IBM, and the North Carolina Biotechnology Center. Numerous other companies represent the biotechnology, pharmaceuticals, information technology, and telecommunications industries.

North Carolina State University hosts several research centers, including the Water Resources Research Institute, the Center for Marine Science and Technology, the Institute for Computational Sciences and Engineering, and the Forensic Sciences Institute. NCSU researchers are also involved cooperative projects at the North Carolina Institute for Climate Studies and the North Carolina Sea Grant Program.

North Carolina State University's Centennial Campus Research Park, a 1,334-acre research and technology transfer park sometimes referred to as a *technopolis*, serves as a model for research universities nationwide. This academic village and research center includes both academic and private laboratory spaces; office, retail, and restaurant space; and housing for researchers. More than 100 businesses, government agencies, and university academic units and research programs are represented. The Centennial Biomedical Campus is an extension of the Centennial Campus concept that is anchored by the College of Veterinary Medicine.

Public Library Information: Wake County Public Libraries, 4020 Carya Drive, Raleigh, NC 27610; telephone (919) 250-1205. Triangle Research Libraries Network, CB#3940 Wilson Library, Suite 712, Chapel Hill, NC 27514-8890; telephone (919) 962-8022; fax (919) 962-4452. Research Triangle Park, 12 Davis Drive, Research Triangle Park, NC 27709; telephone (919) 549-8181; fax (919) 549-8246.

■ Health Care

The Raleigh area offers world-class care and state-of-the-art technology in the health field, in part because of the proximity of nearby pharmaceutical, nursing, and medical schools at the University of North Carolina and Duke University at Durham.

WakeMed Health and Hospitals, with headquarters in Raleigh, is Wake County's largest hospital system. The main campus, WakeMed Raleigh, has the only state-designated trauma center in Wake County and the only 24-hour freestanding children's emergency department in the state. The WakeMed Heart Center is a national leader in cardiac disease care. The Raleigh campus also houses the only neurological intensive care unit in the county and is regarded as a leader in care for neurological injuries and illnesses. A Women's Pavilion and Birthplace and WakeMed Children's Center are also located at the Raleigh campus.

Part of the Duke University Health System, Duke Raleigh Hospital (DRH) is a 186-bed acute-care facility. The DRH Cancer Center and DRH Cardiovascular

Center offer exceptional care. Other special departments include the Childbirth Center and Special Care Nursery, Musculoskeletal Center, Diabetes Program, a pain clinic (as part of the Orthopedic Center), an emergency department, and a same day surgery center.

The not-for-profit, 665-bed acute care Rex Hospital is part of the UNC Health Care System. It serves as home to the first and only nationally accredited chest pain center in the Triangle area and has the region's most advanced vascular diagnostics center. The hospitals Cancer Center includes a cancer genetics testing program as well as advanced diagnostic capabilities and oncology care. The Rex Family Birth Center has delivered more babies than any other Wake County hospital. Rex Hospital has specialized clinics for sleep disorders and pain management. The Rex Senior Health Center offers primary care through specialists in geriatric medicine. Rex Wellness Centers also offer primary care services. Rex Home Services offer a variety of care services to homebound patients in the area.

Mental health and addiction treatment programs are the focus of Dorothea Dix Hospital, a regional psychiatric facility sponsored by the state division of mental health. Located within 30 miles of the city are a Veteran's Administration Hospital and Lenox Baker Children's Hospital, as well as North Carolina Memorial Hospital in Chapel Hill.

■ Recreation

Sightseeing

Visitors to Raleigh should start their explorations with a trip to the Capital Area Visitor Center, which provides free brochures, maps, and a film about the city's offerings. Tours are available of the North Carolina Executive Mansion, a masterpiece of Queen Ann Victorian architecture completed in 1891. Historic Oakwood, a neighborhood of restored Victorian homes built between 1870 and 1900, occupies a 20-block area adjacent to the 1876 Oakwood Cemetery. The birthplace of President Andrew Johnson can be viewed at Mordecai Historic Park, which is the site of the Mordecai House, a 200-year-old furnished plantation house. Haywood Hall, a Federal-style house built in 1799, is the oldest residence in the city still on its original site.

A life-sized bronze statue of civil rights leader Martin Luther King Jr. is on view at the Dr. Martin Luther King Jr. Memorial Gardens, which are surrounded by trees, shrubs, and flowering plants. The State Capitol, built between 1833 and 1840, is an excellent preserved example of the Greek Revival style. Tours are also available through the North Carolina State Legislative Building, home of the General Assembly. Built in the 1760s, the Joel Lane House, decorated with furnishings and gardens of the period, is Raleigh's oldest dwelling and one of the sites on the National Register of Historic Places.

Dubbed the Smithsonian of the South, Raleigh is home to a number of museums, including three free state museums. The North Carolina Museum of History displays more than 100,000 artifacts reflecting the history of the state. Holdings include furniture, fashions, crafts, military artifacts, dolls, toys, and period exhibits. Free lectures, films, and demonstrations are presented in its Month of Sundays series. The North Carolina Museum of Natural Sciences has four floors of exhibits, live animals, and the only Acrocanthosaurus dinosaur relic in existence. This museum is the largest museum of natural history in the Southeast. The Raleigh City Museum offers a look at local history.

The North Carolina Museum of Art houses paintings and sculpture representing more than 5,000 years of artistic heritage. It also features the Museum Park Theater, an outdoor amphitheater hosting a popular summer concert series. Marbles Kids Museum is an interactive learning center, so named because kids are encouraged to "use their marbles" (or brains) to learn new things through imagination, discovery, and play. The Wells Fargo IMAX Theatre is also located there.

Sports fans might want to check out the North Carolina Sports Hall of Fame featuring nationally known athletes such as Arnold Palmer and Richard Petty. The Ray Price Legends of Harley Drag Racing Museum is the only one of its kind in the world. It is located on the second floor of the Harley-Davidson dealership.

Eight acres with 6,000 varied plants from almost 50 countries are the highlights of the North Carolina State University's JC Raulston Arboretum, which also features a Victorian gazebo, Japanese garden, and special areas such as water and reading gardens. Tours are available of the five acres of landscaped garden surrounding the WRAL-TV studio, which features more than 2,000 azaleas, trees, and plants.

Arts and Culture

Raleigh's downtown arts district is a collection of galleries clustered in a three-block area around the historic City Market at Moore Square. The district comprises a variety of galleries, including Artspace, Inc., which offers 26,000 square feet of studio and gallery space to working visual and performing artists. Visitors can tour the gallery and studios while the artists are working.

The Gregg Museum of Art and Design on the campus of North Carolina State University features changing exhibits of ceramics, furniture, photography, textiles, drawings, and graphic design. Also on campus is the Crafts Center, the largest campus-based crafts facility of its kind in the Southeast, which features changing exhibitions of local, regional, and national craftspersons. Visual Arts Exchange offers classes, workshops, and exhibits for public viewing. The gallery hosts numerous exhibitions and educational programs annually.

Raleigh's premier music venue is the Walnut Creek Amphitheatre. In its natural setting on 212 acres, the amphitheatre presents big-name rock and pop performers in its 7,000-seat open-air pavilion and to an additional 13,000 people seated on a sloping lawn.

The Duke Energy Center for the Performing Arts is home to the North Carolina Symphony, the first state-supported orchestra in the nation. The orchestra performs its regular season in the Meymandi Concert Hall but also tours statewide. Programming includes solo performances by world-class performers as well as classical, pops, and children's series, outdoor summer programs, and special holiday performances. The center's Fletcher Opera Theater is designed for opera, dance, and theatrical productions, offering performances from the Carolina Ballet and the North Carolina Opera. The Kennedy Theater is an experimental theater home to the theatre company Hot Summer Nights, which performs a variety of shows during the year. The North Carolina Theatre brings touring musicals to its home at the Raleigh Memorial Auditorium. The city's community theater groups include the Raleigh Little Theatre, which has been performing for more than 50 years, and Burning Coal Theatre Company.

Stewart Theatre at NCSU presents a professional series of theater, music, film, and lectures. North Carolina State University presents dance, opera, orchestra, and other cultural events at its student center and at Reynolds Coliseum. Theatrical productions are also offered at NCSU, William Peace University, Meredith College Theatre, and Shaw University Theatre.

The city park system hosts two community arts centers. Pullen Arts Center, located within Pullen Park, offers studio programs in pottery, jewelry-making, painting, printmaking, weaving, and glass arts. A summer art camp, Art4Fun, makes art education fun and accessible for young residents. Special events and gallery exhibits are offered throughout the year. Sertoma Arts Center offers a well-equipped darkroom studio. Programs in music, dance, and fitness are offered along with classes in painting, drawing, and pottery. The city is also the site of the Raleigh Chamber Music Guild, which brings in international guest performers, and the North Carolina Master Chorale.

Festivals and Holidays

Raleigh welcomes spring in May with the Artsplosure Jazz and Arts Festivals, which combines exhibitions, food, and open-air performances. Independence Day in Raleigh can be celebrated in a number of ways. The annual July 4th at the State Capitol celebration includes picnic and patriotic concert on the grounds of the capital. The North Carolina Symphony's annual extravaganza includes a concert and fireworks at Regency Park. In August, attendees can meet, greet, and perhaps eat some of the coolest critters around at Bugfest!, an annual festival at the North Carolina Museum of Natural Sciences. Autumn brings the Pops in the City Park in September with the North Carolina Symphony performing pop music in a picnic setting.

The North Carolina State Fair in mid-October offers craft demonstrations, livestock exhibits and competitions, top-notch concerts, games, rides, side shows, food, and other family-friendly entertainment. The four-day handicrafts and entertainment of the Carolina Christmas Show also takes place at the convention center in early December. November's Raleigh Christmas Parade kicks off the holiday season, which includes December's Holiday Festival at the North Carolina Museum of Art; the Christmas Celebration on the Mall in downtown Raleigh; annual performances of *A Christmas Carol* and *The Nutcracker*; and candlelight tours through a variety of historic homes decked out for the holiday season. First Night Raleigh on December 31 welcomes the new year with performances, visual arts, food, and a midnight countdown downtown.

Sports for the Spectator

Raleigh's state-of-the-art PNC Arena hosts the city's first major league professional franchise, the National Hockey League's Carolina Hurricanes. The Hurricanes won the Stanley Cup in 2006, and were hosts of the NHL All-Star Game in 2011.

Celebrated college sports teams in Raleigh and the Research Triangle area include the North Carolina State University Wolfpack, who play their basketball games at the PNC Arena and their football games at Carter-Finley Stadium. Some local residents also root for the University of North Carolina Tarheels and the Duke University Blue Devils. Sports fans also enjoy athletic events at Raleigh's Shaw University (Bears) and St. Augustine's College (Falcons).

The Wake County Speedway hosts stock car racing on Friday nights from April through September.

Sports for the Participant

Raleigh citizens take pride in their extensive recreational assets. The Raleigh Parks and Recreation Department maintains 9,764 acres of parkland, 850 acres of nature preserves, and 100 miles of greenways. Park facilities include 112 tennis courts, 68 playgrounds, 62 ball fields, 40 staffed facilities, 9 aquatic facilities, and 6 historic sites. Two new senior centers opened in 2012: The Five Points Center for Active Adults and Anne Gordon Center for Active Adults.

Major recreational sites include Pullen Park, a 65-acre inner city children's play facility with an aquatic center, complete with a 50-meter indoor pool. Lake Wheeler offers boating, skiing, fishing, and picnicking. Shelley Lake can accommodate boating as well as bird watching, fishing, nature walks, jogging, and concerts. Falls Lake is a 12,000-acre facility with beaches, boat ramps, fishing, and picnic areas. Jordan Lake features a lakeside recreation area and marina that is the largest summertime home of the bald eagle in the eastern United States. Lake Johnson is a creek-fed lake with forests and a boathouse. The Millbrook Exchange Off-Leash Park is a two-acre facility designed for canine friends of the city.

Shopping and Dining

There are numerous shopping centers serving the Raleigh area. The shopping scene is made more interesting by the variety of local shops featuring original art, crafts, jewelry, children's boutiques, native gem jewelers, and garden shops, as well as burgeoning outlet stores. Antique shops are located all over the city, and settings range from flea markets to upscale import-export emporiums. Among the city's favorite shopping sites are Crabtree Valley Mall, North Hills, Briar Creek Commons, Cameron Village, and Triangle Towne Center. The old mission-style City Market Building and adjacent Moore Square have been transformed into a festive retail district. The State Farmer's Market is also a fun place to shop for fresh produce, crafts items, and plants.

Fayetteville Street Mall near the Duke Energy Center for the Performing Arts offers numerous shops and restaurants and several with outdoor dining options. Beautifully landscaped walks and public art invite window shoppers as well as buyers.

Greater Raleigh offers a wide variety of dining experiences, from steak houses, chain restaurants, and ethnic eateries (featuring French, Middle Eastern, Indian, Mexican, Chinese, Italian, and Japanese food) to down-home cooking. Ambience ranges from casual cafes to big-screen sports bars to elegant dining rooms.

Visitor Information: Greater Raleigh Convention and Visitor's Bureau, 421 Fayetteville Street, Suite 1505, Raleigh, NC 27601; telephone (919) 834-5900; toll-free (800) 849-8499.

■ Convention Facilities

The Raleigh Convention Center can host groups anywhere from 50 to 5,000. The 150,000-square-foot exhibit hall can accommodate 790 booths, or can be divided into three halls. The 32,617-square-foot ballroom can also be partitioned into three separate rooms to accommodate groups of various sizes. The center also features 20 meeting rooms and a 4,100-square-foot, street-level mezzanine that overlooks the exhibit hall.

The Duke Energy Center for the Performing Arts offers five auditoriums with seating ranging from 600 in the Fletcher Opera Theater to 2,277 in the Raleigh Memorial Auditorium. The PNC Arena offers up to 700,000 square feet of space for exhibits or meetings. The North Carolina Fairgrounds offers eight indoor venues for meetings or shows. The McKimmon

Conference and Training Center at North Carolina State University offers several options in banquet, meeting, and classroom facilities.

Most major hotels offer meeting rooms and larger banquet or exhibit spaces. Other unique meeting sites in Raleigh include Artspace, which can handle receptions for 600 people and the Capital City Club, which can accommodate up to 600 people.

Convention Information: Greater Raleigh Convention and Visitor's Bureau, 421 Fayetteville Street, Suite 1505, Raleigh, NC 27601; telephone (919) 834-5900; toll-free (800) 849-8499.

■ Transportation

Approaching the City

Raleigh-Durham International Airport (RDU), located 15 miles from downtown Raleigh, is served by nine major airlines that offer more than 400 daily departures to 40 destinations. Raleigh can also be reached by an extensive network of state highways and roads. With one of the largest state-maintained highway systems in the nation, the Triangle area lies at the intersection of three interstate highways: Interstates 40, 85, and 95. Other major highways serving the area include U.S. Highways 1, 64, 70, and 401. Interstate 540 connects Interstate 40 and U.S. Highway 70, and provides easy access to RDU. The Raleigh Beltline, or Interstate 440, is approximately 21 miles long and circles the city. Carolina Trailways/Greyhound Bus Lines provide service to points in the eastern United States, and Amtrak offers rail service to and from 56 cities at its downtown station.

Traveling in the City

Raleigh is a comfortable city to get around in. The main thoroughfares give easy access to the heart of the city from any direction. Local bus service is provided by Capital Area Transit with 29 routes. The Accessible Raleigh Transportation Program (ART) offers rides for residents with disabilities. The Triangle Transit Authority (TTA) provides intercity service between Raleigh, Durham, and Chapel Hill. The TTA also has routes to the airport and through Research Triangle Park.

■ Communications

Newspapers and Magazines

Raleigh's daily newspaper is *The News and Observer*. *Triangle Business Journal* and *Tech Journal South* are weekly papers serving the business community. *The Triangle Downtowner Magazine* is a free monthly publication focusing on arts, entertainment, and news in the Triangle. The online version contains additional information and is updated more frequently. Nearly 30 magazines are published in Raleigh, including *Raleigh Metro Magazine* and *Carolina Country. TCP Magazine*, published by The Connection Place is a quarterly journal covering Christian ministry, music, and business. *Wake Living* is also published quarterly. The Associated Press has an office in Raleigh.

Television and Radio

There are 11 licensed television stations broadcast directly from Raleigh. News 14 Carolina is the 24-hour cable television news channel for central North Carolina. There are 15 FM and 9 AM radio stations licensed in Raleigh. A wide variety of programming is offered such as top-40, country, classical, religious, Hispanic, and jazz. NCSU, Duke University, and Shaw University all have student sponsored stations.

Media Information: *The News and Observer*, 215 South McDowell Street, PO Box 191, Raleigh, NC 27602; telephone (919) 829-4500.

Raleigh Online

City of Raleigh home page. Available www. raleighnc.gov

Greater Raleigh Convention & Visitors Bureau. Available www.visitraleigh.com

The News and Observer. Available www.news observer.com

Raleigh Chamber of Commerce. Available www. raleighchamber.org

Raleigh Economic Development. Available www. raleigh4u.com

Wake County Public Libraries. Available www. wakegov.com/libraries/Pages/default.aspx

Wake County Public Schools. Available www.wcpss. net

BIBLIOGRAPHY

Grant, Gerald, *Hope and Despair in the American City: Why There Are No Bad Schools in Raleigh* (Cambridge, MA: Harvard University Press, 2009)

Cantor Foundation Gift to the North Carolina Museum of Art (Raleigh: North Carolina Museum of Art, 2010)

Souter, Stormi, and Elizabeth Weichel, *Legendary Locals of Raleigh, North Carolina* (Charleston, SC: Arcadia Publishing, 2013)

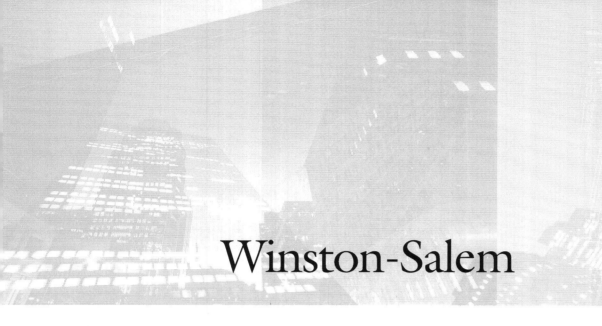

Winston-Salem

■ The City in Brief

Founded: Salem, 1766; Winston, 1849; joined,1913

Head Official: Mayor Allen Joines (since 2001)

City Population
1990: 143,485
2000: 185,776
2010: 229,617
2012 estimate: 234,354
Percent change, 2000–2010: 23.6%
U.S. rank in 1990: 119th
U.S. rank in 2000: 109th
U.S. rank in 2010: 83rd

Metropolitan Statistical Area Population
2000: 421,961
2010: 477,717
2012 estimate: 484,437
Percent change, 2000–2010: 13.2%
U.S. rank in 2000: 106th
U.S. rank in 2010: 105th

Area: 109 square miles

Elevation: 963 feet above sea level

Average Annual Temperatures: January, 40.3° F; July, 66.8° F; annual average, 52.6° F

Average Annual Precipitation: 40 inches of rain; 6.6 inches of snow

Major Economic Sectors: Health care and educational services, professional and business services, trade and transportation, government

Unemployment Rate: 7.2% (2012)

Per Capita Income: $23,849

2012 FBI Crime Index Property: 13,701

Major Colleges and Universities: Wake Forest University, University of North Carolina School of the Arts

Daily Newspaper: *Winston-Salem Journal*

■ Introduction

Winston-Salem, located in North Carolina's Piedmont Triad region, is perhaps best-known as the home of one of America's largest tobacco companies and the origin of the famous Krispy Kreme brand. However, locals know that there is far more to Winston-Salem than cigarettes and donuts. The town is a hub for education, health care, and research, and is home to a number of theaters, festivals, and museums that celebrate the city's colonial heritage. Winston-Salem has an expanding, diversified economy, and the constant influx of new residents means that the city will continue to evolve and grow.

■ Geography and Climate

Winston-Salem is located in the Piedmont Triad region of North Carolina, near Greensboro and High Point. It is situated about halfway between Atlanta, Georgia, and Washington, D.C. The Triad Region is inland, west of Raleigh, and abuts the Southern Virginia border. Winston-Salem has a four-season climate, and the area is particularly renowned for its lovely fall foliage. There is very little precipitation during the mild winter, and summer temperatures tend to be in the 70s.

Area: 109 square miles

Elevation: 963 feet above sea level

Average Temperatures: January, 40.3° F; July, 66.8° F; annual average, 52.6° F

Winston-Salem Dash, visitwinstonsalem.com

Average Annual Precipitation: 40 inches of rain; 6.6 inches of snow

■ History

The history of Winston-Salem has its origins in post-Reformation Europe, when the Moravians, German-speaking Protestants persecuted in Moravia, Bohemia, and Poland, fled to Pennsylvania for religious freedom in 1735. In 1753 Bishop Augustus Spangenberg of Pennsylvania led a party to survey a 100,000-acre tract of land in North Carolina, which he called Der Wachau after an Austrian estate (the anglicized version of the name became Wachovia). Today, the area colonized by the Moravians is known as Historic Bethabara Park. Salem, which means "peace," was so-named in 1766 by Moravian settlers, and quickly became a center for small-scale craft and textile production. The handiwork of the Moravians as potters and cabinet-makers inspired the Piedmont craft movement. The Moravians also left a musical legacy as well; the

sect began the first community orchestras and chamber music ensembles, in addition to building the first organs. In the wake of the Revolutionary War, textile and furniture manufacturing companies sprang up in growing Salem. The Wachovia area, along with Bethlehem, Pennsylvania, was also the spiritual center of the American Moravian church and was a close-knit community throughout much of the nineteenth century.

Nearby Winston was named after a local war hero, Colonel Joseph Winston, in 1849, and that same year Winston and Salem were officially incorporated as part of the newly minted Forsyth County, with Winston as the county seat. The towns of Winston and Salem formally joined in 1913, though people had been referring to them as a unit since around the turn of the twentieth century.

In 1874 R.J Reynolds formed the R.J Reynolds Tobacco Co. in Winston-Salem, which would grow to become the second-largest tobacco company in the United States. In 1911 Wachovia Bank was founded as the first major financial service in the growing town. The tobacco industry, along with textile manufacturing, helped form the identity of Winston-Salem, and its unique position as a shipping center helped the town grow and thrive, becoming North Carolina's fifth-largest city. In 1937 Krispy Kreme made its first donuts in Winston-Salem, creating a brand that expanded through the country. In the 1960s the first expressway through the city was completed, paving the way for new residents and new businesses.

The city experienced some civil unrest sparked by the Civil Rights Movement during the 1960s. However, many city officials and residents continued to embrace diversity within the community and within city organizations. African Americans had been welcomed on city boards since 1881. The first African American police officers were hired in the 1940s, and the first African American firefighters joined the city force in the 1950s. In 1976 Jack Bond became the first African American to hold the position of deputy city manager.

As manufacturing declined into the 1990s, technology moved in. In 1994 the Wake Forest School of Medicine's Department of Physiology and Pharmacology and eight researchers from Winston-Salem State University moved into a former R. J. Reynolds Tobacco Co. warehouse downtown to establish the Piedmont Triad Community Research Center. In 2002 the first major development effort was launched to create an expanded research park, with biotechnologies a targeted industry. The park continued to grow through the beginning of the twenty-first century. In 2013 the park was renamed Wake Forest Innovation Quarter, and a second major development effort was launched with hopes to attract new businesses and create thousands of new jobs.

Historical Information: Wachovia Historical Society, P.O. Box 20803, Winston-Salem, NC 27120-0803; telephone (336) 722-5020.

■ Population Profile

Metropolitan Statistical Area Population
2000: 421,961
2010: 477,717
2012 estimate: 484,437
Percent change, 2000–2010: 13.2%
U.S. rank in 2000: 106th
U.S. rank in 2010: 105th

City Residents
1990: 143,485
2000: 185,776
2010: 229,617
2012 estimate: 234,354
Percent change, 2000–2010: 23.6%
U.S. rank in 1990: 119th
U.S. rank in 2000: 109th
U.S. rank in 2010: 83rd

Density: 1,733.6 people per square mile

Racial and ethnic characteristics
White: 136,932
Black or African American: 83,870
American Indian and Alaskan Native: 122
Asian: 5,192
Native Hawaiian and Other Pacific Islander: 0
Hispanic or Latino (may be of any race): 34,753
Other: 8,238

Percent of residents born in state: 59.2%

Age characteristics
Population under 5 years old: 16,968
Population 5 to 9 years old: 16,601
Population 10 to 14 years old: 14,666
Population 15 to 19 years old: 16,702
Population 20 to 24 years old: 19,832
Population 25 to 34 years old: 34,774
Population 35 to 44 years old: 28,694
Population 45 to 54 years old: 30,812
Population 55 to 59 years old: 13,544
Population 60 to 64 years old: 11,499
Population 65 to 74 years old: 15,740
Population 75 to 84 years old: 10,793
Population 85 years and over: 3,729
Median age: 34.4

Births (2010–11 Metropolitan Area)
Total number: 5,920

Deaths (2010–11 Metropolitan Area)
Total number: 4,003

Money income (2012)
Per capita income: $23,849
Median household income: $39,170
Total households: 90,752

Number of households with income of . . .
less than $10,000: 9,919
$10,000 to $14,999: 6,211
$15,000 to $24,999: 12,482
$25,000 to $34,999: 12,181
$35,000 to $49,999: 14,483
$50,000 to $74,999: 14,260
$75,000 to $99,999: 7,894
$100,000 to $149,999: 7,601
$150,000 to $199,999: 2,293
$200,000 or more: 3,428

Percent of families below poverty level: 23.6%

FBI Crime Index Property: 13,701

FBI Crime Index Violent: 1,556

■ Municipal Government

Winston-Salem operates under a council-manager form of government. The city manager is hired by the city council and is responsible for day-to-day-operations that implement city policies. The mayor presides over meetings of the city council and provides leadership on policy issues. Both the mayor and the eight-person council are elected every four years.

Head Official: Mayor Allen Joines (since 2001)

Total Number of City Employees: 2,660 (2012)

City Information: City of Winston-Salem, 101 N. Main Street, Winston-Salem, NC 27101; telephone (336) 727-8000.

■ Economy

Major Industries and Commercial Activity

Though traditionally known mostly for its tobacco production, Winston-Salem now has a diverse economy built on a foundation of the health care, professional and business services, trade, and transportation. Health care is the dominant industry sector, represented by two of the largest employers, Wake Forest Baptist Medical Center and Novant Health. The financial services sector is significant to the local economy, with companies including Wells Fargo and the *Fortune* 500 BB&T (with headquarters in Winston-Salem).

The manufacturing sector is known for its strong ties to the tobacco industry, with R. J. Reynolds Tobacco Co. (a *Fortune* 500 company) calling the city its home. Winston-Salem is also known as the headquarters for Krispy Kreme. Textile production continues to play a key role, with the Hanes Corporation headquartered in Winston-Salem as well.

Items and goods produced: baked goods, tobacco products, textiles, medical devices, beverages, aerospace parts

Incentive Programs-New and Existing Companies

Local programs: The city of Winston-Salem sponsors a Target Area Business Assistance Program for businesses that locate within one of six distressed areas in the city: the Liberty Street Corridor (Southern and Central segments); Waughtown Street and Sprague Street between Old Lexington Road and Thomasville Road; 100-200 blocks of Kapp Street; Central Business District 1; and Central Business District 2. In order to qualify for city funds, the company must have at least four employees and invest at least two dollars of private funds for each dollar invested by the city. The funds may be used for structural improvements or the purchase of capital equipment. The Brownfields Revolving Loan Fund disburses loans to clean up brownfield areas (property that is environmentally contaminated) in the city. The city also provides long-term, low-interest loans of up 20 percent of project cost for development projects that create new jobs in the city. The Small Business Loan Program helps businesses located in the Winston-Salem Neighborhood Revitalization Strategy Area or in the Hewitt Business Center in Old Salem.

State programs: North Carolina, a right-to-work state with a low unionization rate, offers a revenue bond pool program through various banks. Several venture capital funds operate in the state and inquiries can be made through North Carolina's Council for Entrepreneurial Development (CED). Industrial Revenue Bonds issued by the state provide new and expanding businesses the opportunity to provide good employment and wage opportunities for their workers.

The state offers an income tax allocation formula that permits the double weighting of sales in calculating corporate income tax. Additional tax credits offered by the state include those for new markets, renewable energy property investment, job creation, and research and development. A business property tax credit and film incentive tax credit are also available, along with economic development riders and land use incentive grants.

The North Carolina Department of Transportation administers a program that provides for the construction of access roads to industrial sites and road improvements in areas surrounding major corporate installations.

The North Carolina Small Business and Technology Development Center (SBTDC) makes capital available to entrepreneurs and begin building a stronger early-stage investment industry. Financing assistance may be available to qualified businesses under the following programs: traditional bank loans, SBA-guaranteed loans, federal research and development and commercialization funding, equity capital investment, international export financing, the North Carolina Capital Access Program (NC-CAP), and North Carolina Loan Participation Program (NC-LPP). The Winston-Salem SBTDC is affiliated with Winston-Salem State University and serves Davidson, Davie, Forsyth, northern Iredell, Stokes, Surry, and Yadkin Counties.

Certain areas in Winston-Salem are part of the state-designated Urban Progress Zone. Qualified business may receive state tax credits for job creation and new investment in these distressed areas. State income tax credits of up to $3,750 are available for each new job created, with a minimum of five jobs created during the taxable year. A 7 percent state income tax credit is also available for business property investment.

Job training programs: NC Workforce, a division of the North Carolina Chamber of Commerce, sponsors the Incumbent Workforce Development Program, which offers grants of up to $25,000 for companies for training and continuing education of existing employees. There are three Forsyth County Career Centers located in Raleigh, including one at Forsyth Technical Community College.

State funding allows North Carolina Community Colleges to offer a special customized training program for new, expanding, and existing businesses. The Job Growth Training program for new and expanding businesses is available for companies that create at least 12 new production jobs in the state, or to any new or prospective employee referred for training by a participating company. The Productivity Enhancement Training program specifically targets incumbent workers who must regularly update their skills as technology changes. Technology Investment Training and Continuous Improvement Training fill in the gaps to ensure that programs are available for employers and employees as needed. Employees may go through training before or after employment by the company. In Winston-Salem customized training programs are offered through Forsyth Technical Community College.

Development Projects

One of the biggest economic development projects in the county was introduced in 2013 when Wake Forest University and Wake Forest Baptist Medical Center announced plans for the newly named Wake Forest Innovation Quarter. This research park was previously known as the Piedmont Triad Research Park, but officials decided to rebrand the facility following the launch of the Wake Forest Innovation division of Wake Forest Baptist Hospital in 2012. The hospital owns and operates much of the park. The plans unveiled in 2013 involve an investment of more than $500 million to redevelop existing facilities and build new ones. Officials hope to attract enough new business to expand park residency from about 1,000 employees in 2013 to 10,000 employees by 2017. Inmar Inc., a leader in creating online commerce networks, announced that it would relocate its headquarter to Innovation Quarter in 2014, bringing more than 1,000 employees. Forsyth Technology Community College announced plans to open its new Center for Emerging Technologies in the quarter by the end of 2014, with an investment of $7 million for the new facility.

In 2013 Benton Investment Company began renovating the historic Glade Street YMC to great the Glade and West End, a residential complex of 15 custom-built, single-family homes and seven condominiums. This project involved an investment of $4.5 million. Meanwhile, the Housing Authority of Winston-Salem was working to complete The Oaks at Tenth, a 50-unit apartment community that represented the first phase of the Cleveland Avenue Initiative Master Plan. When completed, The Oaks at Tenth was to consist of affordable one-, two-, and three-bedroom units.

Economic Development Information: Winston-Salem Chamber of Commerce, 411 West Fourth Street, Suite 211, Winston-Salem, NC 27101; telephone (336) 728-9200. Wake Forest Innovation Quarter, 575 N. Patterson Ave., Winston-Salem, NC 27101; telephone (336) 716-8672.

Commercial Shipping

Located midway between Washington D.C. and Atlanta, Georgia, Winston-Salem is well-positioned to be a center of commercial shipping.

Piedmont Triad International Airport is about 25 minutes east of Winston-Salem. The airport is a multimodal facility with terminals operated by several major trucking lines. Air cargo carriers include DHL, FedEx, Mountain Air Cargo, and UPS. Winston-Salem is located within a half-day's trucking to deep-water ports in Wilmington, North Carolina; Morehead City, North Carolina; Charleston, South Carolina; and Norfolk, Virginia. An intermodal facility near the airport offers piggyback services for the three railroads serving Forsyth County: Norfolk Southern, Winston Salem-Southbound (connecting to CSX south of Charlotte), and Tadkin Valley Railroad.

Labor Force and Employment Outlook

According the U.S. Bureau of Labor Statistics, the largest employment industry in Winston-Salem in 2013 was education and health services. Trade, transportation, and utilities was the next largest employment sector, followed by professional and business services, government, and leisure and hospitality. Expansion and development of facilities at Wake Forest Innovation Quarter is expected to attract new companies and create jobs in targeted tech and research fields, including information technology, biomedical engineering, clinical training and development, laboratory services, and nanotechnology.

The following is a summary of data regarding the 2012 Winston-Salem labor force:

Size of civilian labor force: 114,099

Number of workers employed in ...

agriculture and mining: 254
construction: 5,766
manufacturing: 10,852
wholesale trade: 2,701
retail trade: 9,706
transportation: 3,713
information systems: 1,772
finance: 6,184
professional administration: 10,580
education and social services: 30,524
arts and leisure: 10,401
other: 5,019
public administration: 2,341

Average hourly earnings of production workers: $15.49

Unemployment rate: 7.2% (2012)

Employers

Largest employers (2012)	*Number of employees*
Wake Forest Baptist Medical Center	11,750
Novant Health	8,145
Winston-Salem/ Forsyth County School System	6,692
Reynolds American, Inc.	3,000
Wells Fargo	2,800
City of Winston Salem	2,660
Hanesbrands	2,251
BB&T	2,200
Forsyth County	2,029
Wake Forest University (Reynolda Campus)	1,680

Cost of Living

The following is a summary of data regarding several key cost of living factors in the area.

2013 ACCRA Average House Price: $201,308

2013 ACCRA Cost of Living Index: 88

State income tax rate: 6.0% to 7.75%

State sales tax rate: 4.75%

Local income tax rate: None

Local sales tax rate: 2.0%

Property tax rate: $1.2468 per $100 of assessed valuation (2013)

Economic Information: Winston-Salem Business, Inc., 1080 West Fourth Street, Winston-Salem, NC 27101; telephone (336) 723-8955; fax (336) 761-1069.

■ Education and Research

Elementary and Secondary Schools

The Winston-Salem/Forsyth County Public Schools is the fourth-largest district in North Carolina. The district operates under a Schools of Choice plan that allows parents to choose a school for their child within eight elementary zones or six middle school zones. Overall, the district is home to 81 schools, including 15 magnet programs. Fifty-one schools are located within Winston-Salem. The district adopted Common Core Standards for the 2012–13 school year.

The Crosby Scholars Community Partnership is a college access resource for families in Winston-Salem and Forsyth County. Serving around 200 students per year, the program provides workshops and mentoring, in addition to bridge scholarships that address the disparity between the cost of college attendance and other forms of financial assistance.

There are several private independent and parochial schools in Winston-Salem, including Berea Baptist Christian School, Forsyth County Day School, Our Lady of Mercy School, St. John's Lutheran School, and Summit School.

The following is a summary of data regarding the Forsyth County Schools.

Total enrollment: 53,367

Number of facilities

total: 81
elementary schools: 43
junior high schools: 13
high schools: 14
other: 11

Student/teacher ratio: 13.9:1

Teacher salaries

average (statewide): $46,850

Funding per pupil: $8,604

Public Schools Information: Winston-Salem/Forsyth County Schools, 1605 Miller St., Winston-Salem, NC 27103; telephone (336) 727-2816.

Colleges and Universities

Wake Forest University is a major national research institution located in Winston-Salem. The school has a total enrollment of more than 7,432 undergraduate and graduate students in five schools: Wake Forest College (undergraduate college of arts and sciences), WFU School of Business, WFU School of Divinity, WFU School of Law, WFU School of Medicine, and Graduate School of Arts and Sciences. In 2013 *U.S. News and World Report* placed Wake Forest University in a tie for 23rd place on its annual survey of best universities in the nation.

Winston-Salem State University, a historically black institution, enrolls more than 6,000 students annually. The university offers more than 43 undergraduate programs and 10 graduate programs and is particularly well-known for its nursing program and the nation's first bachelor's program in motorsport management.

The University of North Carolina School of the Arts offers programs in dance, design and production, drama, filmmaking, and music. The school offers a full curriculum high school diploma program as well as bachelor's and master's degrees and professional artist certificates. More than 1,000 students enroll each year.

Salem College is a four-year liberal arts college for women. It is the oldest educational institution for women in the nation and enrolls 1,100 students annually. The school offers four undergraduate degrees and two graduate degree programs. Men can attend the schools Fleer Center for Adult Education and may be admitted to the graduate program for teacher education. Other area institutions of higher education include High Point University Graduate Studies and Forsyth Technical Community College.

Libraries and Research Centers

Winston-Salem is served by the Forsyth County Public Library System. The Central Library is located in Winston-Salem and serves as both a federal depository library and a depository of the North Carolina State Publications Clearinghouse. The North Carolina Room provides resources on local history and three meeting spaces. The Central Library also holds special collections of African American Literature and small collections of popular fiction and non-fiction books in Spanish, Japanese, Korean, Chinese, Vietnamese and Russian. Malloy/Jordan East Winston Heritage Center is the second Winston-Salem branch in the Forsyth County system. This center offers a full range of library services, but specializes in resources that reflect an African American perspective. The center sponsors the Shades of Forsyth oral history program and hosts an annual community Kwanzaa celebration. There are eight additional branches in the system.

The Z. Smith Reynolds Library at Wake Forest University has more than 1.4 million volumes in its collection. The library subscribes to more than 5,500 print journals and nearly 30,000 electronic journals. Over 100,000 items are circulated annually. Special collections include rare books, university archives, and the North Carolina Baptist Historical Collection.

Wake Forest University sponsors several research centers, including the Center for Bioethics, Health, and Society; Center for Nanotechnology and Molecular Materials; Center for Molecular Communication and Signaling; and the Translation Science Center, which focuses on the aging process. Winston-Salem University also sponsors several programs that promote research, professional development, and community collaboration in various fields. These include the Maya Angelou Institute for Improvement of Child and family Education, the Center for Innovation in Health Disparities Research, and the Center for Community Safety.

Wake Forest Innovation Quarter is on its way to becoming a leading center for research and development efforts in information technology and biomedical science. The center is primary operated by Wake Forest Baptist Medical Center, working cooperatively with local colleges, universities, and other organizations. The Wake Forest University research departments located within the quarter include the Childress Institute for Pediatric Trauma, the Wake Forest Institute for Regenerative Medicine, Lipid Sciences Research Program, and the Preclinical Transitional Services program, among others. The quarter is also home to the Winston-Salem State University (WSSU) Biomedical Research Infrastructure Center, the North Carolina BioNetwork Pharmaceutical Center, the North Carolina Biotechnology Center, and the Neuroscience Research Institute of North Carolina. Research and development companies within the quarter include Carolina Immunochemistry, Carolina Liquid Chemistries, CleanBlue Technologies, and KeraNetics.

The Moravian Music Foundation is a nonprofit foundation that seeks to preserve the musical heritage of the Moravians, a Protestant sect that came to North Carolina in the eighteenth century. The group maintains an archival collection with 10,000 music manuscripts, first editions, early imprints, and related materials, in addition to the 6,000-volume Peter Memorial Library.

Public Library Information: Forsyth County Central Library, 660 West Fifth Street Winston-Salem, NC 27101; telephone (336) 703-2665; fax (336) 727-2549.

■ Health Care

The Wake Forest Baptist Health (WFBH) Medical Center provides inpatient services for acute care, rehabilitation, and psychiatric care, along with outpatient services and community health centers. The Comprehensive Cancer Center of WFBH is the largest cancer facility in the state. For 2013–14 it was ranked as the best cancer hospital in the state and 12th best in the nation by *U.S. News & World Report*. Brenner Children's Hospital (also affiliated with WFBH) ranked among the top 50 children's hospitals in the nation in pediatric urology, orthopedics, and neonatology. The WFBH Heart Center has been named as a gold-level provider by the American College of Cardiology. Primary care outpatient clinics are available throughout Winston-Salem.

With 921 beds, Novant Health Forsyth Medical Center is the largest hospital in the Novant Health System. The center provides a full-range of emergency services, medical services, surgical services, and rehabilitation and behavioral health services. Centers of excellence include Novant Health Rehabilitation, Maya Angelou Women's Health and Wellness Center, the Heart and Vascular Institute (which is affiliated with the Cleveland Clinic), Derrick L. Davis Cancer Center, Stroke and Neurosciences Center, Orthopedic Center, and Behavioral Health. Novant Health Medical Park

Hospital is a 22-bed hospital that specializes in elective inpatient and outpatient surgeries.

■ Recreation

Sightseeing

From the NASCAR enthusiast to the colonial historian, anyone can find an activity that piques his or her interest when visiting Winston-Salem. Old Salem Museums and Gardens includes the restored Historic Town of Salem and the Museum of Early Southern Decorative. The Historic Town features staff in colonial costume and activities like pottery, sewing, writing with quill pens, fireplace cooking, and painting. The MESDA has furniture, paintings, ceramics, textiles, and metalwork in its six galleries.

The Children's Museum of Winston-Salem, a Science Center and environmental park, features a planetarium, educational programming, and exhibits that focus on anything from the human body to the geography and topography of North Carolina. The Winston Cup Museum highlights R.J. Reynolds Tobacco Company's 33-year sponsorship of the NASCAR Winston Cup Series. The museum has more than 30 racing vehicles, trophies, uniforms, helmets, winner's checks, autographed pictures, and signed original racing posters.

Arts and Culture

The Arts Council of Winston-Salem and Forsyth County was the first locally established arts council in the nation, sparking the nationwide movement for local arts councils. The organization raises funds and advocates for the arts, in addition to sponsoring events and educational cultural programming in the Winston-Salem area. One of the council's most ambitious projects was the opening of the Milton Rhodes Center for the Arts in 2010. The council raised $26 million to renovate a downtown city block and create what is now described as the community's artistic living room. The Rhodes Center is home to two permanent art installations (the Womble Carlyle Gallery and the Eleanor and Egbert Davis Gallery), the Hanesbrand Theatre, and the Sawtooth School for Visual Art.

The Stevens Center of the University of North Carolina School of the Arts was originally built in 1929 as a silent movie theater. Known for its fine acoustics, the Stevens Center plays host for many of the cultural programs of Winston-Salem.

The Piedmont Opera stages two or three productions per year. The Winston-Salem Symphony features classics, pops, and education programs, and performs several shows each season at the Stevens Center. The Twin City Stage (formerly the Little Theatre of Winston-Salem) is a non-profit community theater that stages several productions with amateur actors annually. It is the

longest-running theater in Winston-Salem. Students at the University of North Carolina School of the Arts give several dance recitals per season at the Stevens Center, in both contemporary and classical styles. *The Nutcracker*, performed at Christmas by the students, is an annual highlight.

There are several art museums and galleries in the area as well, most along a cultural corridor called the Reynolda Mile. The Reynolda House Museum of American Art includes works from renowned artists such as Albert Bierstadt, Mary Cassatt, Frederic Church, John Singleton Copley, Thomas Eakins, Jacob Lawrence, Georgia O'Keeffe, and Grant Wood. The Southeastern Center for Contemporary Art (SECCA) awards artist fellowships, plans community programming in the visual arts, and invites artists to work in residence on projects that are of broader benefit to the community. Just down the road from the SECCA is the Charlotte and Philip Hanes Art Gallery, which displays the work of Wake Forest University art students. The Diggs Gallery at Winston-Salem State University is the state's largest African American exhibition space, specializing in art of the African diaspora.

The Moving Images Archive, owned by the School of Film at North Carolina, is a collection of more than 25,000 films, shown at the Stevens Center in conjunction with the Winston-Salem Cinema Society.

Festivals and Holidays

The annual RiverRun International Film Festival is celebrated each April and showcases the work of independent, international, and student filmmakers. May brings the Celtic Festival & Highland Games held in historic Bethabara Park and the Greek Festival at Annunciation Greek Orthodox Church. The Downtown Winston-Salem Summer Music Series sponsors free jazz and blues on Thursday, Friday, and Saturday nights at several locations throughout the city.

The National Black Theatre Festival is held every other August in Winston-Salem and attracts 60,000 people to the six-day affair. In early September, Bookmarks, Winston-Salem's Festival of Books, is held. The Apple Festival in Bethabara Park takes place each year in late September; that same month ARTSfest is held in Winston-Salem's West End, with arts and crafts, live music, specialty food vendors, and children's activities. September also brings FIESTA, the annual street festival sponsored in part by the Hispanic League. Each October, the city hosts the Dixie Classic Fair at the Dixie Classic Fairgrounds with carnival rides, arts and crafts, and musical entertainment.

Sports for the Spectator

The 17,000-seat Bowman Gray Stadium is the home field of Winston-Salem State University Rams football team, in addition to hosting NASCAR's Whelen All-American

Series, Whelen Southern Modified Tour, and K&N Pro Series East. Baseball fans can cheer for the Carolina League (Class A) Winston-Salem Dash, who play home games at BB&T Ballpark. The Wake Forest Demon Deacons participate in a number of sports, including basketball, football, baseball, soccer, tennis, golf, cross-country, field hockey, and volleyball. Wake Forest and Winston-Salem State University play their basketball games at the Lawrence Joel Coliseum.

Sports for the Participant

For golf fans, the Winston-Salem area boasts 262 playable days per year, and well-known courses include Tangle-wood Park (with two courses designed by Robert Trent Jones, Jr.) and Salem Glen, ranked one of the top 10 new courses in the country when it opened in 1997. The City of Winston-Salem operates two public courses—Reynolds Park Golf Course and Winston Lake Golf Course.

Historic Bethabara Park marks the site of a 1753 Moravian settlement. A museum on the grounds features a restored 1788 church, archaeological ruins, and a visitors' center that provides videos, exhibits, and tours of a reconstructed village, a French and Indian War fort, and colonial and medical gardens. The park contains 20 miles of nature trails that are free to the public.

The Winston-Salem Recreation and Parks Department Recreation and Parks Department maintains 74 parks, which include 112 tennis courts, 51 picnic shelters, 47 playgrounds, 43 soccer fields, 47 softball fields, 25 basketball courts, 8 pools, 6 volleyball courts, and a football field. Fishing and boating enthusiasts can pursue their hobbies on nearby Salem Lake, a 365-acre lake that is home to hybrid bass, largemouth bass, catfish, crappie, bream, carp, and white perch. The lake is ringed by a 6.9-mile trail.

Shopping and Dining

Just across the street from the Benton Convention Center is Fourth Street's Restaurant Row, which features local favorites such as Foothills Micro Brewery, Down-town Deli, the 4th Street Filling Station, and Hatch and Harris Pub. No trip to Winston-Salem is complete without a trip to the flagship Krispy Kreme store, where visitors can watch the donuts roll off the assembly line and purchase the variety of their preference. There are more than 500 restaurants in Forsyth County.

The Twin City Quarter, located just a block away from the city's Arts District, is a major destination for antique hounds in the Triad region. The area also boasts a number of unique craft and gallery boutiques. Winston-Salem's largest shopping malls are the 200-store Hanes Mall (the largest regional mall in the Carolinas), the Reynolda Villages, and the Thruway Center.

Visitor Information: Winston-Salem Convention and Visitors Bureau, 200 Brookstown Avenue Winston-

Salem, NC 27101; telephone (336) 728-4200; toll-free (866) 728-4200; fax (336) 721-2202.

■ Convention Facilities

The M.C. Benton Jr. Convention Center boasts 100,000 square feet of meeting space and is connected to a hotel with an additional 70,000 square feet of meeting space. The facility has 18 rooms, with two main ballrooms that can hold up to 3,000 people theater-style, while the exhibition areas can accommodate more than 200 booths. There are more than 25 hotels in the area that have conference accommodations, and planners can also book meeting space in the Bowman Gray Stadium, Dixie Classic Fairgrounds, the Stevens Center, Milton Rhodes Center for the Arts, and the Millennium Center. There are nearly 1,000 hotel rooms in the downtown area.

Convention Information: Winston-Salem Convention and Visitors Bureau, 200 Brookstown Avenue Winston-Salem, NC 27101; telephone (336) 728-4200; toll-free (866) 728-4200; fax (336) 721-2202.

■ Transportation

Approaching the City

Winston-Salem is served by Piedmont Triad International Airport. Six air carriers fly in and out of the facility, and the airport serves about two million passengers annually. The city is accessible via Interstates 40, 77, 73/74, and 85. Amtrak runs rail service through Winston-Salem, with a bus connection to Winston-Salem State University, and Greyhound operates a station in downtown Winston-Salem.

Traveling in the City

Public transportation in the city is run by the Winston-Salem Transit Authority, headquartered at the Clark Campbell Multimodal Transportation Center. There more than 20 fixed daytime routes and 7 night routes. TRANS-Aid provides service for the disabled and the elderly. The Downtown West End Trolley (WET) provides convenient, inexpensive service for commuters and shoppers. Major arteries in the city include Reynolda Road, Main Street, Fourth Street, and Summit Street. The city participates in different events to encourage bicycling, such as Cycling Sundays and an annual Bike to Work Week.

■ Communications

Newspapers and Magazines

The *Winston-Salem Journal* is a daily newspaper covering the Piedmont region. *Winston-Salem Monthly* and *Greensboro/Winston-Salem Business Journal* are both published in the city. All three have online editions.

Television and Radio

There are three licensed television stations broadcasting from Winston-Salem (affiliates of NBC, ABC, and University of North Carolina). Additional stations are received from nearby cities. There are more than 15 licensed radio stations in the area, which include an NPR affiliate, an oldies station, a Spanish-language station, and a local talk radio station.

Media Information: *Winston-Salem Journal*, 418 N. Marshall St., Winston-Salem, NC 27101; telephone (336) 727-7211; toll-free (800) 642-0925.

Winston-Salem Online

City of Winston-Salem home page. Available www. cityofws.org

Forsyth County Public Libraries. Available www. forsyth.cc/library

Winston-Salem Chamber of Commerce. Available www.winstonsalem.com

Winston-Salem Convention & Visitors Bureau. Available www.visitwinstonsalem.com

Winston-Salem/Forsyth County Public Schools. Available www.wsfcs.k12.nc.us

The Winston-Salem Journal. Available www. journalnow.com

BIBLIOGRAPHY

Setzer, Lynn, *Tar Heel History on Foot: Great Walks through 400 years of North Carolina's Fascinating Past* (Chapel Hill, NC: University of North Carolina Press, 2013)

Oklahoma

The State in Brief

Nickname: Sooner State

Motto: Labor omnia vincit (Labor conquers all things)

Flower: Mistletoe

Bird: Scissor-tailed flycatcher

Area: 69,899 square miles (2010; U.S. rank 20th)

Elevation: Ranges from 289 feet to 4,973 feet above sea level

Climate: Temperate and continental, with seasonal extremes

Admitted to Union: November 16, 1907

Capital: Oklahoma City

Head Official: Mary Fallin (R) (until 2015)

Population
1990: 3,145,585
2000: 3,450,654
2010: 3,751,351
2012 estimate: 3,749,005
Percent change, 2000–2010: 8.7%
U.S. rank in 2012: 28th
Percent of residents born in state: 60.9% (2012)
Density: 54.7 people per square mile (2010)
2012 FBI Crime Index Total: 147,645

Racial and Ethnic Characteristics (2012)
White: 2,766,297
Black or African American: 270,993
American Indian and Alaska Native: 261,060
Asian: 65,643
Native Hawaiian and Pacific Islander: 4,271
Hispanic or Latino (may be of any race): 331,057
Other: 380,741

Age Characteristics (2012)
Population under 5 years old: 261,232
Population 5 to 19 years old: 776,169
Percent of population 65 years and over: 13.6%
Median age: 36.3

Vital Statistics
Total number of births (2012–13): 52,504
Total number of deaths (2012–13): 37,225
AIDS cases reported through 2011: 5,837

Economy
Major industries: Agriculture, aerospace, manufacturing, trade and transportation, business and financial services
Unemployment rate (2012): 4.2%
Per capita income (2012): $24,046
Median household income (2012): $44,891
Percentage of persons below poverty level (2012): 16.6%
Income tax rate: 0.5% to 5.0%
Sales tax rate: 4.5%

Oklahoma City

■ The City in Brief

Founded: 1889 (incorporated 1890)

Head Official: Mayor Mick Cornett (R) (since 2004; current term expires 2014)

City Population

    1990: 444,724
    2000: 506,132
    2010: 579,999
    2012 estimate: 599,309
    Percent change, 2000–2010: 14.6%
    U.S. rank in 1990: 29th (State rank: 1st)
    U.S. rank in 2000: 36th (State rank: 1st)
    U.S. rank in 2010: 31st (State rank: 1st)

Metropolitan Statistical Area Population

    2000: 1,095,421
    2010: 1,252,987
    2012 estimate: 1,296,565
    Percent change, 2000–2010: 14.4%
    U.S. rank in 2000: 47th
    U.S. rank in 2010: 44th

Area: 606.99 square miles

Elevation: 1,291 feet above sea level

Average Annual Temperatures: 60.1° F

Average Annual Precipitation: 35.85 inches total precipitation; 9.5 inches of snow

Major Economic Sectors: Aviation and aerospace; bioscience; health care; manufacturing; professional, business, and financial servicse; wholesale and retail; energy

Unemployment Rate: 4.4% (2012)

Per Capita Income: $24,982

2012 FBI Crime Index Property: 35,390

Major Colleges and Universities: University of Oklahoma Health Sciences Center, University of Central Oklahoma, Oklahoma State University–Oklahoma City

Daily Newspaper: *Oklahoman*

■ Introduction

From its birth at high noon on April 22, 1889, Oklahoma City, the state capital of Oklahoma, has grown to become one of the nation's largest cities in terms of area, with residents spread over 621 miles as of 2013. A low unemployment rate, continuing steady economic expansion, and a prime Sun-Belt location are attractive to new businesses. The sunny climate, educational and job opportunities, numerous cultural assets, and recreational attractions entice new residents. After experiencing economic difficulties with the 1980's oil slump and enduring one of the nation's worst terrorist attacks with the 1995 Murrah Federal Building bombing, Oklahoma City continues a vigorous rebound. It consistently ranked among the top cities for business and job growth through the early 2010s and invested in an ambitious remake of its school system and downtown area to complement the rapid growth of area businesses.

■ Geography and Climate

Surrounded by gently rolling prairie and plains along the North Canadian River, Oklahoma City is at the geographic center of the state. With a climate influenced by the Great Plains region, Oklahoma City is one of the sunniest, windiest cities in the country. Summers are long and hot; winters, short and mild. With an average temperature of 60° F, the city sees an amazing 3,000+ hours of sunshine per year. Tornadoes are not uncommon.

© James Blank.

Area: 606.99 square miles

Elevation: 1,291 feet above sea level

Average Temperatures: 60.1° F

Average Annual Precipitation: 35.85 inches total precipitation; 9.5 inches of snow

■ History

Land Run Leads to City's Founding

Inhabited by Plains tribes and sold to the United States by France as a part of the 1803 Louisiana Purchase, much of what is now Oklahoma was subsequently designated as Indian Territory. As such, it was intended to provide a new home for tribes forced by the federal government to abandon their ancestral lands in the southeastern United States. Many of those forced to relocate in the 1830s were from what were called the Five Civilized Tribes-Cherokee, Choctaw, Chickasaw, Creek, and Seminole-who soon set up independent nations in the new territory. After the Civil War, however, the pressure of westward expansion brought railroads into the Indian Territory, where the U.S. government began to declare some land available for white settlement. Prairie land surrounding a Santa Fe railroad single-track boxcar station was designated as a townsite when presidential proclamation opened the central portion of Indian Territory to claims stakers on noon of April 22, 1889. Thousands crossed the borders of the "unassigned lands" at high noon when a cannon was fired. By sunset of that day the land run had produced a tent city of 10,000 people on the townsite, which eventually became Oklahoma City.

The settlement attained official status in 1890, just a few weeks after the western half of Indian Territory was redesignated Oklahoma Territory, named for a Choctaw phrase meaning "red man." Incorporated as Oklahoma City on May 23, 1890, Oklahoma City swiftly became one of the new territory's largest cities. More railroad connections to the city helped make it a center for trade, milling, and meat packing. The Oklahoma and Indian territories merged and were admitted to the union as the state of Oklahoma in 1907. Oklahoma City became the state capital in 1910.

Oil Brings Prosperity

The capital city was flourishing as a financial and manufacturing center when in 1928 an oil field beneath the city proved to be what was then the largest oil strike ever made. Oklahoma City joined neighboring regions in the petroleum industry with vast economic benefits. A gigantic deposit at the Mary Sudik well in Oklahoma City gushed wildly for 11 days in 1930, spewing 10,000 barrels of oil each day in a great geyser and spreading an oily cloud that deposited petroleum as far away as 15 miles. By the time it was closed down, the Mary Sudik well had produced a total of one million barrels of oil.

Future Points Toward Diversity

The end of the oil boom dealt the city a severe blow. During its height in the early 1980s, developers added 5.2 million square feet of office space downtown. When the boom went bust, so did the real estate market. By the 1990s, downtown Oklahoma City was in a decline, with few shopping areas and too much empty office space. While the petroleum industry continues to be a solid part of Oklahoma City's economy in the early 21stcentury, the region has also been involved in the development of the state's other natural resources, such as coal and metals. In addition, the city supports such industries as livestock, agriculture, energy, aviation, and manufacturing.

Oklahoma City made international headlines on April 19, 1995, when a Ryder truck fitted with a homemade oil-and-fertilizer bomb exploded in the Alfred P. Murrah Federal Building, killing 168 men, women, and children, and injuring more than 400 others. In December 1996, the *Wall Street Journal* reported: "Twenty months after the bombing that vaulted it on to front pages around the world, this gutsy city is hoping a rapidly growing economy and a $300 million public-works program will revive one of the nation's sickest downtowns." Feelings of optimism were running high that a dramatic comeback for the city was in the works.

In April 2000 Oklahoma City unveiled its monument to the victims of the bombing. The main component of the memorial is 168 bronze-and-glass chairs, one for each victim, positioned in rows that correspond to the floors of the building where the victims were when the bomb exploded. It is a potent symbol in a city that still continues to grieve a tragedy even as it rebuilds and modernizes its image.

As the twenty-first century dawned, many of the city's efforts at revitalization paid off. Oklahoma won the sweepstakes for the former Seattle SuperSonics franchise

of the National Basketball Association, becoming home to its first major professional sports team in 2008. Economic growth included cutting-edge fields such as bioscience and aerospace, even as energy stalwarts, like Devon Energy, constructed gleaming skyscrapers to define the city's skyline.

Historical Information: Oklahoma Historical Society, Oklahoma Historical Society, 800 Nazih Zuhdi Drive, Oklahoma City, OK 73105; telephone (405) 521-2491

■ Population Profile

Metropolitan Statistical Area Population
2000: 1,095,421
2010: 1,252,987
2012 estimate: 1,296,565
Percent change, 2000–2010: 14.4%
U.S. rank in 2000: 47th
U.S. rank in 2010: 44th

City Residents
1990: 444,724
2000: 506,132
2010: 579,999
2012 estimate: 599,309
Percent change, 2000–2010: 14.6%
U.S. rank in 1990: 29th (State rank: 1st)
U.S. rank in 2000: 36th (State rank: 1st)
U.S. rank in 2010: 31st (State rank: 1st)

Density: 956.4 people per square mile

Racial and ethnic characteristics
White: 404,951
Black or African American: 84,566
American Indian and Alaskan Native: 17,577
Asian: 24,898
Native Hawaiian and Other Pacific Islander: 0
Hispanic or Latino (may be of any race): 104,812
Other: 67,317

Percent of residents born in state: 59.8%

Age characteristics
Population under 5 years old: 48,620
Population 5 to 9 years old: 43,881
Population 10 to 14 years old: 39,990
Population 15 to 19 years old: 35,112
Population 20 to 24 years old: 42,856
Population 25 to 34 years old: 99,875
Population 35 to 44 years old: 77,074
Population 45 to 54 years old: 75,411
Population 55 to 59 years old: 38,674
Population 60 to 64 years old: 30,506
Population 65 to 74 years old: 36,714

Population 75 to 84 years old: 20,645
Population 85 years and over: 9,951
Median age: 33.7

Births (2010–11 Metropolitan Area)

Total number: 18,778

Deaths (2010–11 Metropolitan Area)

Total number: 9,874

Money income (2012)

Per capita income: $24,982
Median household income: $44,519
Total households: 226,306

Number of households with income of . . .

less than $10,000: 19,639
$10,000 to $14,999: 13,749
$15,000 to $24,999: 27,902
$25,000 to $34,999: 28,817
$35,000 to $49,999: 33,887
$50,000 to $74,999: 40,929
$75,000 to $99,999: 23,951
$100,000 to $149,999: 23,693
$150,000 to $199,999: 6,955
$200,000 or more: 6,784

Percent of families below poverty level: 18.7%

FBI Crime Index Property: 35,390

FBI Crime Index Violent: 5,474

■ Municipal Government

Oklahoma City has a council-manager form of government. Its mayor and eight council members are elected to staggered four-year terms. The mayor and council form policy, while appointing a city manager to run the day-to-day business of the city.

Head Official: Mayor Mick Cornett (R) (since 2004; current term expires 2014)

Total Number of City Employees: 4,500 (2012)

City Information: Oklahoma City Hall, 200 N. Walker Ave., Oklahoma City, OK 73102

■ Economy

Major Industries and Commercial Activity

Although in its early days oil dominated the economy, Oklahoma City today hosts a wide range of businesses and employers. Aviation and aerospace; bioscience; the health care industry; manufacturing; professional, business, and financial services; energy; and the wholesale and retail industry all play major roles in the city's economic well-being. The aviation and aerospace industries employ about 38,000 workers, bringing in an estimated $2.36 billion in income and $4.3 billion in goods and services as of 2013. The Mike Monroney Aeronautical Center and Tinker Aerospace Complex are two of Oklahoma City's major drivers in this industry. The Mike Monroney Aeronautical Center is the largest trainer of Air Traffic Controllers in the world and houses the largest concentration of Department of Transportation personnel outside of Washington DC. Tinker manages a 430-acre facility that is Oklahoma's largest single-site employer and generates $4 billion of economic activity statewide each year.

Oklahoma City is home to the headquarters of many Fortune 500 energy companies as well as many large oil companies. Chesapeake Energy and Devon Energy Corporation, both headquartered ni Oklahoma City, are the two largest independent natural gas producers in the world. Renewable energy showed growth in Oklahoma City, too, with the nation ranking among the top-10 cities in the United States for installed wind energy, according to *Wind Today* in 2013. Biotechnology is a relatively new industry in Oklahoma City, and yet it employs more than 40,000 workers, many of whom perform research at the independent Oklahoma Medical Research Foundation. The health care industry is a major economic driver in the city as well, employing more than 60,000 health care sector workers.

Oklahoma City is also the seat of government for the state of Oklahoma as well as Oklahoma County. There are also many regional federal agency offices located in the City. The government sector accounts for more than 20 percent of the Oklahoma City metropolitan area non-agricultural employment. Hospitality was a growth industry in the city, particularly around its Bricktown entertainment district, one of the fastest growing entertainment districts in the nation as of 2013.

The U.S. Bureau of Labor Statistics determined in 2013 that Oklahoma, and only 12 other U.S. cities, had recovered from a national recession during the late 2000s.

Items and goods produced: motor vehicles, food products, steel, electronic devices, computers, oil-well supplies, paper products, rubber tires

Incentive Programs-New and Existing Companies

Local programs: The Greater Oklahoma City Chamber of Commerce Economic Development Division provides full-service expansion and new business services. The Oklahoma City's Development Center offers one-stop shopping for permits, inspections, and building guidelines. The mission of the Oklahoma Small Business Development Center is to provide high quality one-to-one business counseling, economic development assistance, and training to small businesses and prospective small businesses. Since 1984, it has become the state's most comprehensive business assistance network. Many zones and neighborhoods of Oklahoma City have been designated as Federal Empowerment Zones that offer incentives to businesses looking to start-up or relocate. The Oklahoma Strategic Investment Plan (SIP) is yet another incentive fund intended to encourage businesses to expand or locate themselves in Oklahoma City. Companies located in Oklahoma City who hire at least 50 full-time employees, produce an annual payroll of $1.75 million, and meet specified wage requirements are provided with cash payments.

The Downtown Oklahoma City Business Improvement District (BID) is an area where property owners voted for a property assessment to manage and maintain downtown Oklahoma City in a clean, safe, and professional manner, and to purchase services and make improvements that add to those provided by the City. Two local but federal programs are the Small Business Assistance Loan Program, which can loan up to $100,000 for the start-up and expansion of small businesses to be used for acquisition, renovation and construction, the purchase of machinery and equipment, inventory, and working capital, and the Enterprise Community Revolving Loan Fund, which provides loans of up to $200,000 in an attempt to provide small businesses within the Oklahoma City Neighborhood Revitalization Strategy Area with access to capital.

Foreign-Trade Zone #106 is located in Oklahoma City; almost any imported merchandise can be brought into the Zone, for almost any kind of manufacturing or manipulation, duty-free. Federal Historic and State Historic Tax Credits provide attractive incentives for the rehabilitation of historic and older buildings.

State programs: The Oklahoma Quality Jobs Program allows businesses that are creating large numbers of new quality jobs to receive special incentives to locate or expand in Oklahoma. It is an easy-access program that provides direct payment incentives (based on new wages paid) to companies for up to ten years. The Investment/New Jobs Tax Credit Package provides growing manufacturers a significant tax credit based on either an investment in depreciable property or on the addition of full-time-equivalent employees engaged in manufacturing, processing, or aircraft maintenance. The 21st Century Quality Jobs Incentive Program rewards businesses with a highly skilled workforce and provides cash back up to 10 percent on new payroll for up to 10 years; jobs must pay an average wage of $94,418 or 300 percent of the county average, whichever is less, and out-of-state sales must represent at least half of all sales. Other key Oklahoma incentives include a five-year ad-valorem tax exemption, sales tax exemptions, foreign trade zones, financing programs, export assistance, government contracting assistance,

limited industrial access road assistance, New Market Tax Credits, Aerospace Industry Engineer Workforce Tax Credit, OK Community ED Pooled Financing for infrastructure-related construction, CDBG/EDIF, American Indian Land tax credits, and Oklahoma City's new Emerging Technology Fund (ETF).

Job training programs: The city's Office of Workforce Development administers the federal Workforce Investment Act program. Services include skills assessment, basic skills and GED instruction, career planning and counseling, tuition assistance, and job search assistance. Workforce Oklahoma, also created under the federal Workforce Investment Act, is a training and education development system that partners business leaders, educators, and employment professionals to achieve job growth, employee productivity, and employer satisfaction. This system includes a network of statewide offices called Workforce Oklahoma Centers, where employment, education, and training providers integrate a wide range of services that benefit both employers and employees. Customized industrial training programs, at no cost to the employer, are provided by the Oklahoma State Department of Career and Technology Education.

Known nationwide for its excellence, Oklahoma's Career and Technology Education system provides customized employer training and gives Oklahomans of all ages the opportunity to learn advanced technical skills they can put to use in the workforce. The centerpiece of the effort is the Training for Industry Program or TIP, which is offered to new and expanding companies at little or no cost. Career Tech works closely with the business to develop a program that meets the company's needs and prepares their new workforce for success.

The Chamber of Commerce's Greater Grads program supports a career fair to connect graduating students from Oklahoma institutions of learning with Oklahoma employees. It also manages a website with information for graduates about cost of living and available internships through the Chamber's InternOKC program, which matches students with summer internships at companies based in Oklahoma City.

Development Projects

Several cultural, educational, tourist, and sports-related Metropolitan Area Projects (MAPS), from investments totaling more than a quarter billion dollars, were approved and built in Oklahoma City in the late 1990s and into the 2000s. The $30 million Oklahoma City National Memorial and Memorial Museum, a 30,000 square foot memorial park, museum, and anti-terrorism institute, was dedicated on April 19, 2000, five years to the day after a terrorist bombing claimed the lives of 168 people at the Alfred P. Murrah Federal Building downtown. MAPS 3 was approved by voters in 2008 and included improvements running from 2010 to 2017.

In 2010 Oklahoma City began a 180-acre, three-year renovation project of downtown, named Project 180, with a budget of $140 million to improve the downtown streets, sidewalks, parks, and plazas. By 2013, four miles of downtown streets had been redesigned, including 13 new intersections, lights, and crosswalks, as well as the planting of 863. Expansion of hotel accomodations sought to keep pace with urban growth. There were just under 400 hotel rooms in Downtown Oklahoma City in 1999, but that number had quadrupled to more than 2,000 by 2013, with an additional 600 under construction that year.

The city selected a site for a new $250 million convention center in 2013 to replace the aging Cox Business Servicse Convention Center. The Oklahoma City Metropolitan Area Public Schools Trust was approved by voters in 2002 to earmark $470 million for a massive, 100 project, 10-year effort to make Oklahoma City schools a national model for urban education reform. Work on 63 schools had completed by the end of 2012.

The Oklahoma City SkyDance Bridge is a 380-foot-long pedestrian bridge fitted with a 197-foot-tall sculpture that spans Interstate 40 south of the downtown area. Planning for the bridge began in 2008 and construction completed in 2012, serving as a landmark and symbol of the city. The total cost of the bridge was $5.8 million, funded entirely by the city. Science Museum Oklahoma received a $12 million grant from the Reynolds Foundation in 2013 that was to fund an expansion of their existing facility.

The tallest building in Oklahoma City, Devon Energy Center, completed in 2012 after construction began in 2009. The 38th tallest building in the United States—and among the top 200 in the world—the building stands 844-feet tall, with 52 above-ground floors. It serves as the headquarters for Devon Energy and features a restaurant, Vast, located on the 49th floor of the skyscraper.

Economic Development Information: Greater Oklahoma City Chamber of Commerce, 123 Park Avenue, Oklahoma City, OK 73102; telephone (405) 297-8900. Oklahoma Department of Commerce, 900 North Stiles Ave., Oklahoma City, OK 73104; telephone (405) 815-6552 or (800) 879-6552.

Commercial Shipping

Oklahoma City's Will Rogers World Airport, just 10 miles northwest of the city, is designated as a Foreign Trade Zone with general purpose warehouses and a U.S. Customs Port of Entry office. Air freight service is provided by major carriers as well as freight charters. In addition, there are two municipal airports serving the city, Wiley Post and Clarence Page. Rail service is provided by Burlington Northern Santa Fe Railway and Union Pacific.

Freight such as grain, minerals, and steel products are shipped at low cost via the McClellan Kerr River Navigation System, which offers access to the Mississippi River. The Port of Catoosa is only 140 miles from Oklahoma City. There are several motor freight carriers serving city shipping needs. Trucking is made convenient by the city's central location at Interstates 35, 40, 44.

Labor Force and Employment Outlook

Oklahoma City boasts a productive labor force with a strong work ethic. Absenteeism, work stoppages, and turnover levels are below average. During 2012–13 Oklahoma City was named to several publications' lists of best places to find employment or best places for college graduates, including *New Geography, Careerbuilder.com, Forbes,* and *Business Journal.*

The following is a summary of data regarding the 2012 Oklahoma City labor force:

Size of civilian labor force: 301,804

Number of workers employed in . . .

    agriculture and mining: 8,673
    construction: 23,365
    manufacturing: 18,927
    wholesale trade: 8,124
    retail trade: 34,531
    transportation: 13,077
    information systems: 6,179
    finance: 19,233
    professional administration: 28,403
    education and social services: 57,840
    arts and leisure: 27,204
    other: 15,476
    public administration: 19,183

Average hourly earnings of production workers: $15.43

Unemployment rate: 4.4% (2012)

Employers

Largest employers (2012)	*Number of employees*
State of Oklahoma	42,100
Tinker Air Force Base	27,000
OU–Norman Campus	11,650
FAA Mike Monroney Aeronautical Center	7,500
INTEGRIS Health	6,025
The City of Oklahoma City	5,040
OU Health Sciences Center	4,200

Chesapeake Energy	
Corp	4,000
Hobby Lobby Stores	4,000
OG&E Energy	
Group	3,450

Cost of Living

Despite economic growth, Oklahoma City has maintained an attractive cost of living, coming in at a full 3.5 percent below the national average as of 2013.

The following is a summary of data regarding several key cost of living factors in the area.

2013 ACCRA Average House Price: $243,233

2013 ACCRA Cost of Living Index: 89

State income tax rate: 0.5% to 5.0%

State sales tax rate: 4.5%

Local income tax rate: None

Local sales tax rate: 3.875%

Property tax rate: Varies due to city limits that extend into different counties and school districts; as high as 125.13 mills (2013)

Economic Information: Greater Oklahoma City Chamber of Commerce, 123 Park Avenue, Oklahoma City, OK 73102; telephone (405) 297-8900.

■ Education and Research

Elementary and Secondary Schools

Oklahoma City Public Schools is the largest public school district in the state. Some 2,700 children enroll annually in early childhood programs across 52 district cites. In 2012 district graduates received more than $11.7 million in scholarship money, and the district honored three national merit semifinalists. Some 672 students took Advanced Placement Courses, and the district graduated 52 students from its International Baccalaureate program. The Oklahoma City Public Schools Innovations K–12 Virtual Institute offers full K–12 schooling for students in virtual courses.

A major development project, MAP Kids, invested $700 in the development of Oklahoma City Schools during the late 2000s and early 2010s, with $469 million going to construction, $52 million to technology, and $9 million to transportation. Funding was supported through passage of a bond issue.

Many private and parochial schools also serve students in the Oklahoma City area, including the Oklahoma School of Science and Mathematics, a two-year residential public high school for students who are academically gifted in math and science. As of 2013, the district had 13 charter schools.

The following is a summary of data regarding the Oklahoma City Public Schools.

Total enrollment: 42,989

Number of facilities
  total: 83
  elementary schools: 55
  junior high schools: 12
  high schools: 10
  other: 6

Student/teacher ratio: 17.12:1

Teacher salaries
  average (statewide): $49,039

Funding per pupil: $7,386

Public Schools Information: Oklahoma City Public Schools, 900 North Klein, Oklahoma City, OK 73106; telephone (405) 587-0000.

Colleges and Universities

Fifteen college and university campuses and two community colleges, with a combined enrollment of more than 100,000 students, are located in the greater Oklahoma City area. The largest institution is the University of Oklahoma, roughly 20 miles south of Oklahoma City in Norman Oklahoma, which enrolled more than 31,000 students in 2013. The university 101st among all universities nationwide according to *U.S. News & World Report* in 2013; it ranked 47th among all public universities. The University of Oklahoma is home to the National Weather Center. The school's physician assistant program is highly rated, as our its colleges of business, law, medicine, and engineering. Its athletic teams are highly competitive nationally. The University of Oklahoma's Health Sciences Center, based in Oklahoma City, trains doctors, dentists, pharmacists, nurses, and public health students. Other institutions of higher education include Oklahoma State University–Oklahoma City, University of Central Oklahoma, Rose State College, Oklahoma City Community College, Oklahoma City University, and Oklahoma Christian University.

Libraries and Research Centers

The Metropolitan Library System in Oklahoma County has 14 full-service libraries and five extensions libraries that serve the Oklahoma City and Oklahoma County communities. It also maintains outreach collections in nursing homes and retirement centers, and funds a books by mail service for homebound customers. The city opened a new central library in 2004, the 114,130 square foot Downtown Library and Learning Center, a state-of-the-art facility built with more than $24 million in MAPS taxes and library building funds. In addition to traditional library services, the Downtown Library also has a high-tech theater, classrooms, learning center, Oklahoma Literacy Council Services, on-site business assistance from the Small Business Development Center, and college classes through the Downtown College Consortium. Special collections include local history and local black history. A large collection of books on Native Americans, genealogy, and the history of Oklahoma is housed at the Oklahoma Historical Society Archives and Manuscripts Division. Libraries at city colleges and universities and at state offices also offer reference materials on a wide range of topics.

Much of the state's cutting-edge research is conducted at the nearby University of Oklahoma. The Sarkeys Energy Center is a 4-square-block, 7-acre, 100,000-square-foot teaching and energy research complex where faculty, students, and energy industry researchers can explore interdisciplinary energy issues, train future energy researchers and leaders, and enhance national energy security. The Oklahoma Medical Research Foundation is developing into a research institute of national importance, especially in the fields alzheimers, cancer, children's diseases, diabetes, heart disease, and lupus, and claims more than 700 U.S. and international patents. Research centers affiliated with academic institutions in Oklahoma City study state constitutional law and conduct business research and consulting.

Public Library Information: Metropolitan Library System in Oklahoma County, 300 Park Ave., Oklahoma City, OK 73102; telephone (405) 231-8650

■ Health Care

Baptist Medical Center of Oklahoma is the top-rated hospital in the city and state, according to *U.S. News & World Report* rankings in 2013–14. The hospital is ranked as high performing in five major categories: diabetes and endocrinology; gastroenterology and gastreointenstinal surgery; geriatrics; nephrology; and pulmonology. It has a total of 569 beds and admits more than 23,000 patients annually. The facility is accredited by the Commission on Accreditation of Rehabilitation Facilities (CARF). Oklahoma University's Medical Center, a 750-bed facility, sees more than 28,000 patients annually and was rated by *U.S. News & World Report* as a high-performing hospital in 2013–14 for its care of cancer, gynecology, and urology patients. It was rated the second best hospital in the city and state that year. Integris, Oklahoma's largest health system, has hospitals, rehabilitation centers, and clinics in the Oklahoma City area and is based in the capital city. The St. Anthony health-care network includes multiple facilities

throughout Oklahoma, including a main campus in Oklahoma City. The U.S. Department of Veterans Affairs has a 192-bed facility in Oklahoma City.

■ Recreation

Sightseeing
Oklahoma City offers the visitor a full range of sights and activities. Frontier City Theme Park offers more than 50 acres of rides and western shows. The Oklahoma City Zoo, one of the top zoos in the nation, features more than 500 species and 1,900 animals, including a children's zoo, and state-of-the-art primate and lion exhibits. The website 10best.com named the zoo third best in the nation in 2012. The Stockyards City, which celebrated its 100th birthday in 2010, represents one of the largest cattle markets in the world. The State Capitol Building stands out as the only capitol with producing oil wells on the grounds. The 144-acre Martin Park Nature Center offers 3.5 miles of gentle, self-guided hiking trails, and its education center is home to the city's first observation beehive which boasts over 8,000 bees. The Myriad Botanical Gardens features a unique 224-foot Crystal Bridge and a 17-acre outdoor park with a 1.5-acre sunken lake full of Japanese koi. Crystal Bridge, a seven-story enclosed botanical garden, displays an interesting array of more than 1,000 horticultural specimens from all over the world. The tropical atmosphere is enhanced by the roar of water cascading down a 35-foot waterfall. Nature enthusiasts also are drawn to the scenic variety of the 130-acre Will Rogers Park, which includes the Charles E. Sparks Rose Garden, one of the Southwest's outstanding rose gardens, and also features grassy slopes, fresh water ponds, and a conservatory. Also, an arboretum at the park has more than 600 plant and tree species.

Kirkpatrick Planetarium at Science Museum Oklahoma provides views of the heavens, and Celebration Station, a family amusement center, provides family fun. At the Orr Family Farm, attractions include a vintage 1974 carousel, a three-lane Grand Prix Race Track with pedal cars, a Hidden Lake for fishing, and pony rides and hay rides. White Water Bay has more than 25 acres of water rides, slides, pools and activities in a tropical setting.

Guided tours are offered at several attractions, including the Oklahoma Governor's Mansion, the Oklahoma State Capitol, and the 1903 Overholser Mansion, which was the first mansion in Oklahoma City.

For those who enjoy exploring by boat, Oklahoma River Cruises tour a seven-mile stretch of the Oklahoma River. And for those who enjoy exploring on foot, Oklahoma City's Metro Concourse offers a unique way to see downtown. The concourse, an underground tunnel system connecting most of the downtown buildings, is lined with offices, restaurants, and shops. The renovated Bricktown historic site features shops and restaurants, and was one of nation's fastest growing entertainment districts in 2013.

Arts and Culture

Oklahoma City provides year-around enjoyment for the visitor interested in arts and culture. In 2002, with the success of a $40 million Legacy Campaign that included a $14.5 million grant from the Donald W. Reynolds Foundation, the Oklahoma City Museum of Art in the Donald W. Reynolds Visual Arts Center opened. This three-story, 110,000-square-foot facility features 15 galleries, three education rooms, a library/resource center, a store, a cafe, and the 250-seat Noble Theatre. Since relocating to its new facility, the Museum hosts in excess of 130,000 visitors annually. The Museum has been accredited by the American Association of Museums and houses an extensive permanent collection of European, Asian, and American art, featuring such artists as Pierre Auguste Renoir, Gustave Courbet, Maurice de Vlaminck, Mary Cassatt, Thomas Moran, Robert Henri, Ellsworth Kelly, Alexander Calder, Henry Moore, and Frank Stella. The Museum also owns the largest, most comprehensive collection of Dale Chihuly glass in the world, including a 55-foot-tall tower, commissioned for the atrium of the new facility in memory of Eleanor Blake Kirkpatrick.

The Oklahoma City National Memorial and Museum is another popular museum destination for tourists, documenting the events of the April 19, 1995, bombing of the Alfred P. Murrah Federal Building. The Field of Empty Chairs, a reflection pool, and a variety of other monuments pay tribute to the victims, survivors, and rescuers of the attack.

Civic Center Music Hall, serving over 300,000 patrons annually at 250 performances, is home to the Oklahoma City Philharmonic, which performs classical and pop music; a professional ballet company, Oklahoma City Ballet, with an October through April season; the Canterbury Choral Society, a 140-voice chorus that performs the major choral masterworks with full orchestral accompaniment during its three-concert series; Celebrity Attractions, which presents touring Broadway shows; Lyric Theater and Academy, a year-round professional musical theatre company and the only one in Oklahoma; Oklahoma City Repertory Theatre Company; and Oklahoma City Theatre Company.

A variety of works from contemporary playwrights is presented by the Carpenter Square Theatre, and African American productions are offered by the Black Liberated Arts Center, known as Blac Inc. Oklahoma City's oldest community theater, the Jewel Box Theatre, offers performances from August through May.

Many other Oklahoma City area's museums and galleries display a wide variety of art and artifacts. The Harn Homestead & 1889ers Museum and William Fremont Harn Gardens commemorate the land run of 1889 with a restored homestead. Objects and equipment unique to Oklahoma's citizen soldiers from past to present are exhibited at the Forty-Fifth Infantry Division Museum. The history of Oklahoma from prehistoric times to the present is preserved at the Oklahoma History Center.

Science Museum Oklahoma, formerly known as the Omniplex, is a cultural, educational, and recreational center home to Oklahoma's first public-access planetarium, a dome theater which frequently features IMAX movies, aviation and space artifacts, interactive science exhibits, and cultural galleries.

More than 100 Native American tribes are represented by 1,400 artifacts at the Red Earth Museum. The National Cowboy & Western Heritage Center showcases a collection of fine western art by Frederick Remington, Charles Russell, and others, and portraits of western television and movie stars; each June the museum hosts its annual Prix de West Invitational Art Exhibition to showcase the work of the country's finest contemporary western artists. Approximately 2,500 works of art and artifacts comprise the museum's permanent collection.

The history of softball is the focus of the National Softball Hall of Fame and Museum, which also includes a softball library and research center. Turn-of-the-century fire engines are displayed at the Oklahoma State Firefighters Museum. Also in Oklahoma City is the 99's Museum of Women Pilots, American banjo Museum, International Gymnastics Hall of Fame, Oklahoma Museum of Telephone History, and Oklahoma Railway Museum, among others.

Festivals and Holidays

A variety of annual events are held in Oklahoma City, and horses are a prime attraction. Each January the International Finals Rodeo brings the top 15 cowboys and cowgirls in for the Professional Rodeo Association's season finale. The March Oklahoma Youth Expo has more than 7,000 animals for competition and auction. In April the Oklahoma Centennial Horse Show at State Fair Park features Morgans, Arabians, National Show Horses, American Saddlebreds, and a Hackney/Harness division.

Designated as one of the top outdoor festivals in the United States, the Oklahoma City Spring Festival of the Arts at Myriad Gardens and Festival Plaza displays works of art from across the nation in downtown Oklahoma City. Held for ten days during mid-September, the Oklahoma State Fair is one of the largest in the country. Festivities vary from celebrity shows and carnival activities to livestock, arts and crafts, and home economics exhibits. Also in September, Septemberfest at the Governor's Mansion is a celebration of Oklahoma's heritage. The November World Championship Quarter Horse Show is the largest out-of-state visitor attraction held in Oklahoma City, with more than $1 million in prizes handed out over 15 days of competition. Opening Night in downtown Oklahoma City is an annual family New Year's Eve celebration with live country and rock music, magic shows, theater, and fireworks at midnight.

The deadCENTER Film Festival is Oklahoma's largest film festival, started in 2000, and shows more than 100 films over a period of four days in June. Red Earth Native American Cultural Festival in June brings together more than 1,000 American Indian artists across the continent to showcase their works. The Jim Thorpe Native American Games draw more than 2,000 American Indian competitors to the city each June as well. Paseo Arts Festival, which takes place over Memorial Day weekend overtakes the Historic Paseo Arts District with music, dance, and food.

Sports for the Spectator

Oklahoma City is home to National Basketball Association's Oklahoma City Thunder, whose home arena is the renovated Chesapeake Energy Arena. Formerly based in Seattle as the Seattle SuperSonics, the Thunder relocated to Oklahoma City in 2008. The Oklahoma RedHawks are a Triple-A minor league team for Major League Baseball's Houston Astros who play at the Chickasaw Bricktown Ballpark. Hockey is represented by the Oklahoma City Barons, a minor professional ice hockey team in the American Hockey League (AHL) and affiliate of the top-level Edmonton Oilers. The University of Oklahoma Sooners are members of the Big 12 conference and compete nationally in a wide variety of sports on campus in nearby Norman, Oklahoma. The legendary Sooners' football program has won seven national championships. Oklahoma City is home to the Amateur Softball Association, a governing body of the sport. The NCAA Women's College World Series takes place at ASA Hall of Fame Stadium.

Remington Park Racing and Casino features both quarter-horse and thoroughbred racing. Several national and international horse shows and competitions are held each year at State Fair Park, Lazy E Arena, and Heritage Place. The World Championship Quarter Horse Show is held in November at the State Fair Arena, and the International Finals Rodeo takes place in January. The Oklahoma Regatta Festival is in October.

Sports for the Participant

Public recreation opportunities abound in and around Oklahoma City with 154 municipal parks, 5 municipal golf courses, 6 municipal pools, 15 spraygrounds, 2 tennis centers, 3 lakes, and 3 disc golf courses. The area's lakes offer boating, fishing, sailing, and water skiing across more than 14,000 acres of water. Hikers enjoy the city's 76 miles of trails. White Water Bay, a 25-acre water park, provides a wave pool, rapids, and water slides. Lake Hefner is an excellent place for sailing and sailboat racing, and bird watchers treasure its 17-mile shoreline for bird

migrations that make this one of the best locations in Oklahoma. The Oklahoma City Community College Aquatics Center has hosted the U.S. Olympic Festival and is open to the public for classes, state and community competitions, and major national competitions. The Oklahoma City Marathon occurs in late April each year with more than 23,000 participants.

Shopping and Dining

Just a block from the Chesapeake Energy Arena in downtown Oklahoma City is Bricktown, Oklahoma City's newest entertainment, shopping, and dining district. Oklahoma City has a number of enclosed shopping malls, each anchored by major department stores. They include Plaza Mayor, Northpark Mall, Penn Square Mall, and Quail Springs Mall. Upscale shopping is the attraction at 50 Penn Place. Sportsmen throughout the region come to the massive Bass Pro Shops Outdoor World near the I-35 and I-40 Interchange. Choctaw Indian Trading Post features silver and turquoise jewelry, Indian paintings, Kachina dolls, rugs, and blankets. Shepler's is one of the world's largest western stores and catalogs, carrying a vast assortment of boots, jeans, shirts, and hats for the entire family, plus accessories and home decor. Fancy western wear can be found at Tener's Western Outfitters. The Spanish-style Paseo Arts District is the showcase for the works of Oklahoma artists with 20 galleries and studios displaying works of more than 75 artists. Shoppers can immerse themselves in western culture at Stockyards City, a National Register Historic District near downtown that features western shops, restaurants, art galleries, and crafters producing boots, spurs, hats, belt buckles the size of hubcaps, and other western gear.

Oklahoma City restaurants offer menus ranging from the city specialty—Oklahoma-raised beef—to French, Vietnamese, and Japanese cuisine. The specialty of the house at the city's oldest restaurant, Cattlemen's Steakhouse, is calves' brains and eggs. Steaks and barbecue lead the way at Cimarron Steak House, Earl's Rib Palace, and Murphy's Chophouse.

Visitor Information: Oklahoma City Convention & Visitors Bureau, 123 Park Avenue, Oklahoma City, OK 73102; telephone (800) 225-5652; email contact@visitokc.com.

■ Convention Facilities

A sunny climate, abundant hotel space—some 2,000 rooms in Oklahoma City's downtown area alone—and a wide range of leisure, cultural, and recreational opportunities make Oklahoma City attractive to large and small groups of convention-goers.

The Cox Convention Center, located in the city's business district, offers facilities for sports, banquets, concerts, exhibitions, trade shows, and stage performances. Funding for a new convention center, as well as site selection, had occurred by 2013. The Cox Convention Center offers a 32,000-square-foot arena that seats up to 15,000 people, more than 100,000 square feet of exhibit space, nearly 28,000 square feet of meeting rooms, and a ballroom. The Renaissance, a $32 million, 15-story, 258-room, 53-suite luxury hotel is connected to the center via skywalk, and a climate-controlled walkway also connects to the nearby Westin Hotel. Four blocks from the Cox Center is the Civic Center Music Hall, which underwent a $55 million renovation in 2001, with facilities for concerts, lectures, meetings, conventions, and stage shows. It can seat from 100 to 2,500 people, depending on the occasion.

Funded by a one percent sales tax increase, the sleek Chesapeake Energy Arena, opened in 2002 with seating for about 20,000 and facilities to accommodate professional sporting events and national touring concerts. The Oklahoma City Fairgrounds, with more than one million square feet, also offers a 12,500-seat arena, a racetrack, and a baseball stadium. Another convention facility is Frontier City, with picnic pavilions that accommodate 100 to 15,000 people. Groups of up to 550 people can be accommodated at Metro Tech's Business Conference Center. Additional groups can be accommodated in the facility's meeting rooms, auditorium, and amphitheater. Small and medium-sized groups can find meeting and event space at the Clarion Meridian Hotel and Convention Center or the Will Rogers Theater.

Convention Information: Oklahoma City Convention & Visitors Bureau, 123 Park Avenue, Oklahoma City, OK 73102; telephone (800) 225-5652; email contact@visitokc.com.

■ Transportation

Approaching the City

Oklahoma City's Will Rogers World Airport, just 10 miles northwest of the city, is served by five major carriers that serve more than 3.5 million passengers a year and offer nonstop flights to 21 cities in the United States. Located near the center of the United States, Oklahoma City is connected to the east and west coasts and north and south borders of the nation by interstate highways 40, 35, 44, 235, and 240. Numerous state highways and a turnpike system provide easy access to any location in the metropolitan area. Amtrak provides train service and Greyhound/Trailways Bus Lines schedules buses into and out of the city.

As part of the city's "Core to Shore" development plan, engineers planned to reroute an existing portion of Interstate 40 one mile south. The street was to become a new boulevard at ground level to serve as the gateway to downtown. The project was expected to be fully complete by 2016, with progress coming in stages.

Traveling in the City

Oklahoma City boasts more than 14,000 lane miles of roads. Streets in downtown Oklahoma City are generally laid out in an east–west, north–south grid pattern, with numbered streets running east–west. Taxis and buses are available for transportation to all parts of the city. The extensive bus system was upgraded in 2004 with the addition of the new $6.2 million METRO Transit Downtown Transit Center, an air-conditioned transfer center. It serves three million riders annually. As part of the city's downtown revitalization efforts, the Oklahoma Spirit trolley system, with nine trolley replicas, takes visitors around Bricktown and downtown. In warm weather, pedicabs and horse-drawn carriages ferry customers all over Bricktown. Water taxis carry visitors to canal-side restaurants.

■ Communications

Newspapers and Magazines

Oklahoma City has one morning daily newspaper, the *Oklahoman,* and one business newspaper, *The Journal Record.* Weekday circulation for the *Oklahoman* averaged 125,000 in 2013. Several weekly, semiweekly, and bimonthly newspapers are published there, including *The Black Chronicle, The Capitol Hill Beacon,* and *The Sooner Catholic.* Among the magazines and journals published in Oklahoma City are the lifestyle magazine *Oklahoma Living; Oklahoma Today,* focusing on travel, nature, recreation, and American Indian and New West issues; and others focusing on livestock, pharmacy, retailing, and trades.

Television and Radio

Oklahoma City is home to 19 television stations and also has access to various stations that broadcast from nearby towns. Cable television is available throughout the metropolitan area. In addition, Oklahoma City radio provides listeners with 6 licensed AM stations and 17 licensed FM stations.

Media Information: Oklahoman, 9000 North Broadway, Oklahoma City, OK 73114; telephone (877) 987-2737.

Oklahoma City Online

City of Oklahoma City Home Page. Available www.okc.gov

Metropolitan Library System. Available www.mls.lib.ok.us

Oklahoma City Chamber of Commerce. Available www.okcchamber.com

Oklahoma City Convention and Visitors Bureau. Available www.visitokc.com

Oklahoma City Public Schools. Available www. okcps.org

Oklahoma Department of Commerce. Available okcommerce.gov

Oklahoman. Available www.newsok.com

BIBLIOGRAPHY

Andrews Henningfeld, Diane, ed., *The Oklahoma City Bombing*(Detroit: Greenhaven Press, 2012)

Wright, Stuart A., *Patriots, Politics, and the Oklahoma City Bombing* (New York: Cambridge University Press, 2007)

Tulsa

■ The City in Brief

Founded: 1836 (incorporated 1898)

Head Official: Mayor Dewey F. Bartlett, Jr. (since 2009; current term expires 2017)

City Population
> 1990: 367,302
> 2000: 393,049
> 2010: 391,906
> 2012 estimate: 394,098
> Percent change, 2000–2010: −0.3%
> U.S. rank in 1990: 43rd (State rank: 2nd)
> U.S. rank in 2000: 52nd (State rank: 2nd)
> U.S. rank in 2010: 46th (State rank: 2nd)

Metropolitan Statistical Area Population
> 2000: 859,532
> 2010: 937,478
> 2012 estimate: 951,514
> Percent change, 2000–2010: 9.1%
> U.S. rank in 2000: 53rd
> U.S. rank in 2010: 54th

Area: 186.84 square miles

Elevation: 700 feet above sea level

Average Annual Temperatures: 60.8° F

Average Annual Precipitation: 42.42 inches

Major Economic Sectors: aerospace and air transportation, petroleum and natural gas, health care, telecommunications, business and financial services, wholesale and retail trade, manufacturing

Unemployment Rate: 5.1% (2012)

Per Capita Income: $26,410

2012 FBI Crime Index Property: 20,807

Major Colleges and Universities: University of Tulsa, Oral Roberts University

Daily Newspaper: *Tulsa World*

■ Introduction

Tulsa is the second largest city in Oklahoma. From its earliest ranching and oil boom days to the present, Tulsa has recognized the need for economic diversity and has continually taken appropriate steps. Even growth within the energy sector displayed thoughtful diversification with research and production of alternative energy sources. With a history of steady expansion, a unique geographic location as an important shipping port, and wide range of employment opportunities, Tulsa has made itself attractive to new businesses. It is equally enticing to new residents, with its moderate Sun Belt climate, abundant recreational areas, continuing cultivation of the arts, and educational opportunities. The city's ambitious Vision 2025 program funded extensive downtown development and refurbishment into the 2010s, with development that mixed historic preservation and futuristic design.

■ Geography and Climate

Located 90 miles northeast of Oklahoma City and surrounded by gentle hills stretching toward the Ozark foothills, Tulsa lies along the Arkansas River at an elevation of 700 feet, providing a moderate climate and an average daily temperature of 61° F. Winters are generally mild with light snowfall, and the high temperatures of mid- to late-summer are often moderated by low relative humidity and southerly breezes. Tornadoes and windstorms characterize spring and early summer, but sunny days and cool nights prevail throughout the fall. Rainfall is heaviest in the spring.

Area: 186.84 square miles

Elevation: 700 feet above sea level

Average Temperatures: 60.8° F

Average Annual Precipitation: 42.42 inches

■ History

City's Native American Roots

French traders and plains-culture Osage tribes occupied the region now surrounding Tulsa when the United States bought the land from France as part of the Louisiana Purchase in 1803. Soon the federal government sought to remove communities of the Five Civilized Tribes-Cherokee, Choctaw, Chickasaw, Creek, and Seminole-from their traditional lands in the southeastern United States to Indian Territory in what is now Oklahoma. After violent protest, in 1826 the Osages ceded their land in the Tulsa area to the U.S. government, which in turn gave it to exiled Creeks and Cherokees. Many of the Native Americans who were forced to resettle in Oklahoma brought black slaves with them. In 1836 Archie Yahola, a full-blood Creek, presided over the region's first council meeting, held under an oak tree that came to be known as the Council

Oak. The tree still stands in Tulsa's Creek Nation Council Oak Park.

The settlement convened at the Council Oak was first named Tallassee-Lochapoka, for the Alabama regions the Creeks had left behind; eventually it became known as Tulsey-or Tulsee-Town. The name Tulsa became official for the settlement in 1879 with the establishment of the post office, which also marked the beginning of Tulsa as an economic force in the area. When a railroad connection reached Tulsa in 1882, the town began to supply beef and other staples to the East, South, and Midwest. Ranching and farming-mostly by Creeks or Cherokees-flourished. Tulsa grew steadily and became incorporated as a municipality on January 18, 1898.

Oil Spurs White Settlement; Racial Uneasiness Surfaces

In 1901 oil reserves were discovered in Red Fork, across the Arkansas River from Tulsa. Enterprising Tulsans built a toll bridge to connect their city with the oil country, and oil men crossed the river to make Tulsa their home. Despite Indian Territory laws that discouraged white settlement, the region became increasingly open to whites, and Tulsa grew into a business and residential center. Oil gushed again in 1905, this time from the Glenn Pool well. Oil companies built headquarters in Tulsa, bringing families of corporate executives, urban tastes, and money. In 1906 the U.S. Congress passed the Enabling Act, which merged Indian Territory and Oklahoma Territory, achieving statehood for Oklahoma and bringing down the last barriers to settlement of the region. The decade of the 1920s was a tumultuous period for Oklahoma as a whole, with oil wells gushing, whites and Native Americans becoming fabulously wealthy, and the Ku Klux Klan boasting close to 100,000 members statewide. A race riot erupted in Tulsa in 1921 that has been described as one of this country's worst incidents of racial violence. Some 300 people died and 35 city blocks of Tulsa's Greenwood section, known as "the Black Wall Street," were destroyed after a black man was arrested for allegedly assaulting a white woman. In 1997 the Oklahoma state legislature named an 11-member Tulsa Race Riot Commission to unearth the facts behind the incident. In early 2000 the commission recommended direct payments to survivors and victims' descendants, scholarships, a tax checkoff program to fund economic development in the mostly black Greenwood district, and a memorial to the dead.

Modern Economy Diversified

Between 1907 and 1930, Tulsa's population grew by 1,900 percent. By the 1920s Tulsa was being called the Oil Capital of the World. But not content to be an oil capital only, Tulsa continued its expansion into other commercial and industrial areas as well. In fact, several of Tulsa's firms had a part in the U.S. moon-thrust endeavor, Project Apollo. Today, oil retains importance but Tulsa primarily relies on aerospace, telecommunications, energy, and environmental engineering/manufacturing for its industrial base.

Due in large part to planning and intelligent growth, as well as a general demographic shift that has seen continued growth in the southern and southwestern states, Tulsa joins a number of other mid-sized cities enjoying revitalization in the early twenty-first century. Tulsa's strides to prepare itself for the new global economy, in fields such as aerospace, alternative energy, and advanced manufacturing, have consistently ranked it among the top cities nationally for job opportunities, as well as one of the best places to live.

Historical Information: Tulsa Historical Society, 2445 South Peoria, Tulsa, OK 74114; telephone (918) 712-9484.

■ Population Profile

Metropolitan Statistical Area Population
2000: 859,532
2010: 937,478
2012 estimate: 951,514
Percent change, 2000–2010: 9.1%

U.S. rank in 2000: 53rd
U.S. rank in 2010: 54th

City Residents
1990: 367,302
2000: 393,049
2010: 391,906
2012 estimate: 394,098
Percent change, 2000–2010: −0.3%
U.S. rank in 1990: 43rd (State rank: 2nd)
U.S. rank in 2000: 52nd (State rank: 2nd)
U.S. rank in 2010: 46th (State rank: 2nd)

Density: 1,991.9 people per square mile

Racial and ethnic characteristics
White: 262,157
Black or African American: 58,472
American Indian and Alaskan Native: 16,341
Asian: 9,987
Native Hawaiian and Other Pacific Islander: 596
Hispanic or Latino (may be of any race): 58,138
Other: 46,545

Percent of residents born in state: 55%

Age characteristics
Population under 5 years old: 29,534
Population 5 to 9 years old: 26,061
Population 10 to 14 years old: 26,145
Population 15 to 19 years old: 24,768
Population 20 to 24 years old: 31,562
Population 25 to 34 years old: 59,966
Population 35 to 44 years old: 46,454
Population 45 to 54 years old: 53,130
Population 55 to 59 years old: 26,373
Population 60 to 64 years old: 21,159
Population 65 to 74 years old: 25,762
Population 75 to 84 years old: 15,713
Population 85 years and over: 7,471
Median age: 34.8

Births (2010–11 Metropolitan Area)
Total number: 13,581

Deaths (2010–11 Metropolitan Area)
Total number: 8,231

Money income (2012)
Per capita income: $26,410
Median household income: $40,359
Total households: 162,791

Number of households with income of …
less than $10,000: 16,098
$10,000 to $14,999: 11,268
$15,000 to $24,999: 21,937

$25,000 to $34,999: 21,805
$35,000 to $49,999: 25,493
$50,000 to $74,999: 27,761
$75,000 to $99,999: 13,838
$100,000 to $149,999: 12,959
$150,000 to $199,999: 4,982
$200,000 or more: 6,650

Percent of families below poverty level: 20.3%

FBI Crime Index Property: 20,807

FBI Crime Index Violent: 3,949

■ Municipal Government

Incorporated as a municipality on January 18, 1898, Tulsa operates under a mayor-council form of city government. Nine council members are elected to two-year terms, with the mayor serving a four-year term.

Head Official: Mayor Dewey F. Bartlett, Jr. (since 2009; current term expires 2017)

Total Number of City Employees: 3,923 (2013)

City Information: City Hall at One Technology Center, 175 E. 2nd Street, Suite 690, Tulsa, OK 74103; telephone (918)596-2100

■ Economy

Major Industries and Commercial Activity

Tulsa's central location in the United States makes it a desirable place to locate nearly any type of business, from manufacturing to retail, telecommunications, and service-oriented industries. Operating costs generally run well below the national average.

Tulsa was literally the "Oil Capital of the World" from the early 1920s until World War II. By the time companies moved operations closer to offshore production, Tulsa had begun to develop the aircraft and aerospace industry; its more than 20,000 aerospace jobs make it the region's largest industry and generated an economic impact of nearly $2 billion in 2013. The American Airlines Maintenance Repair and Overhaul Division was Tulsa's largest employer in 2012. Tulsa's major industries, in addition to aerospace, are advanced manufacturing, energy, health care, information technology, professional services, and transportation, distribution, and logistics.

The U.S. Bureau of Labor Statistics ranked Tulsa eighth among U.S. cities for manufacturing in 2012. As of 2013, one in nine Tulsa workers was employed by a manufacturing company. The industry generated more than $2.1 billion in economic impact annually. Energy

remained an important sector with nearly 1,000 energy-related companies based in the region; however, the industry has diversified away from fossil fuels and now includes many businesses working to develop alternative forms of energy. Economically, the energy industry generated some $9.6 billion in annual revenue.

In early 1971, Tulsa opened the Tulsa Port of Catoosa on the Verdigris River, thereby becoming a major inland port along the 445-mile McClellan-Kerr Navigation System. More than 50 companies operate from Tulsa's port, and it provides low-cost shipping for such products as oil, coal, fertilizer, and grain to the Mississippi River, and from there on to the Great Lakes or the Gulf of Mexico and around the world. The port has a 2,000-acre industrial park and some 500 acres of terminal facilities. It also includes Foreign Trade Zone 53 and offers year-round service.

Items and goods produced: airplane parts, appliances, metal pipes and pumps, fiber optics, natural gas, alternative energy fueling stations

Incentive Programs-New and Existing Companies

Local programs: Tulsa receives $3–4 million annually in Community Development Block Grant and HOME Funds from the federal government. The local fire department offers up to $8,000 to install sprinklers in public right-of-way areas. The Small Business Capital Formation Tax Credit Act provides up to a 20 percent tax credit of equity investment for qualifying companies, with some limitations. Tax incentive districts provide five to six years of property tax abatement in designated areas for specific development projects.

State programs: The Oklahoma Quality Jobs Program allows businesses that are creating large numbers of new quality jobs to receive special incentives to locate or expand in Oklahoma. It is an easy-access program that provides direct payment incentives (based on new wages paid) to companies for up to ten years. The Investment/New Jobs Tax Credit Package provides growing manufacturers a significant tax credit based on either an investment in depreciable property or on the addition of full-time-equivalent employees engaged in manufacturing, processing, or aircraft maintenance. The 21st Century Quality Jobs Incentive Program rewards businesses with a highly skilled workforce and provides cash back up to 10 percent on new payroll for up to 10 years; jobs must pay an average wage of $94,418 or 300 percent of the county average, whichever is less, and out-of-state sales must represent at least half of all sales. Other key Oklahoma incentives include a five-year ad-valorem tax exemption, sales tax exemptions, foreign trade zones, financing programs, export assistance, government contracting assistance, limited industrial access road assistance, New Market Tax Credits, Aerospace

Industry Engineer Workforce Tax Credit, OK Community ED Pooled Financing for infrastructure-related construction, CDBG/EDIF, American Indian Land tax credits, and Oklahoma City's new Emerging Technology Fund (ETF).

Job training programs: Workforce Oklahoma, also created under the federal Workforce Investment Act, is a training and education development system that partners business leaders, educators, and employment professionals to achieve job growth, employee productivity, and employer satisfaction. This system includes a network of statewide offices called Workforce Oklahoma Centers, where employment, education, and training providers integrate a wide range of services that benefit both employers and employees. Customized industrial training programs, at no cost to the employer, are provided by the Oklahoma State Department of Career and Technology Education.

Known nationwide for its excellence, Oklahoma's Career and Technology Education system provides customized employer training and gives Oklahomans of all ages the opportunity to learn advanced technical skills they can put to use in the workforce. The centerpiece of the effort is the Training for Industry Program or TIP, which is offered to new and expanding companies at little or no cost. Career Tech works closely with the business to develop a program that meets the company's needs and prepares their new workforce for success.

Development Projects

In 2003, Tulsa voters approved "Vision 2025: Foresight 4 Greater Tulsa," a one-cent sales tax increase through 2016 to fund several Tulsa 2025 initiatives. As of 2013, the program had collected more than $526 million, which had supported some 58 projects, including $21 million to support the American Airlines presence. Additional funds supported renovation or building of schools, community colleges, health clinics, the city's convention center, recreation facilities, and city infrastructure. The convention center, which opened in 2010, was the biggest single expenditure to date, with construction costs totaling nearly $189 million. No other single project exceeded $39 million.

The Mayo Hotel, opened in 1925, was purchased with private funds in 2001 for $250,000. A full renovation at a cost of $42 million led to its reopening in 2009 and paved the way for additional downtown renovations. Vision 2025 included funds for a number of minor projects to beautify the downtown area. The Marriot Courtyard Atlas Life secured private investment for renovation of the 12-story historic building and its conversion into a 120-room hotel. A Holiday Inn at Tulsa City Center, also privately funded, was built on 7th Street. The Visual Arts Center at Brady Village utilized $40 million to convert existing warehouse space into studio and performance areas for local non-profit corporations. The city built a $5 million park on the adjacent city block.

A 30-year master plan for the downtown area detailed in 2009 dedicated several hundred million dollars to infrastructure projects related to expansion of commuter rail, maintaining and refurbishing city bridges, and expanding city streets.

Economic Development Information: Metropolitan Tulsa Chamber of Commerce, One West Third St., Suite 100, Tulsa, OK 74103; telephone (918) 585-1201. Oklahoma Department of Commerce, 900 N Stiles Ave., Oklahoma City, OK 73104; telephone 405-815-6552.

Commercial Shipping

The Tulsa Port of Catoosa is an inland port and foreign trade zone along the Arkansas River, with more than 2,000 acres of adjacent industrial parks. The port continued to grow rapidly, with its 2013 total above 2.3 million inbound and outbound tons matching the record pace of the previous year. Improvements at its main dock warehouse, to be completed by 2016, were expected to increase the amount of container traffic handled by the port.

Tulsa International Airport, just nine miles northeast of downtown and only seven miles from the Port of Catoosa, is served by six freight carriers. Total air freight exceeded 56,000 tons in 2012. U.S. Customs offices are located at the airport. There are two mainline rail carriers into the airport: Burlington Northern and Union Pacific. Access to four short line carriers—Sand Springs, Tulsa-Sapulpa Union, St. Louis Southwestern, and SK&O—is also available. More than 50 motor freight carriers serve the area.

Labor Force and Employment Outlook

The local population is generally well-educated and growing. Tulsa workers were found to be above state and national averages in terms of computer and technology skills, experience, and diversity of skills. Professional and managerial talent can be recruited to the area with relative ease. Contributing to this favorable recruiting climate is a large number of students enrolled in and graduating from the region's post-secondary institutions. These assets provide a significant labor supply ready to fill the needs of Tulsa's businesses.

TYPros, the city's organization of young professionals, is the largest of its kind in the nation. Tulsa was named the number-one U.S. city for young entrepreneurs by both *Forbes* and *NerdWallet*. *The Fiscal Times* listed Tulsa as the second best city for young people to find a job in 2012, and *Manpower* ranked the city third nationally for its employment outlook in 2012.

The following is a summary of data regarding the 2012 Tulsa labor force:

Size of civilian labor force: 200,773

Number of workers employed in . . .

agriculture and mining: 3,548
construction: 13,177
manufacturing: 19,803
wholesale trade: 5,493
retail trade: 19,982
transportation: 8,857
information systems: 5,324
finance: 11,995
professional administration: 22,695
education and social services: 38,911
arts and leisure: 20,805
other: 8,622
public administration: 4,735

Average hourly earnings of production workers: $17.6

Unemployment rate: 5.1% (2012)

Employers

Largest employers (2013)	*Number of employees*
American Airlines, Inc.	7,000
Tulsa Public Schools	6,500
St. John Medical Center	6,000
Saint Francis Health System	5,500
City of Tulsa	4,000
Spirit Aerosystems, Inc.	3,000
Caprock Pipeline Company	3,000
AHA Hillcrest Medical Center	2,500
Baker Hughes Oilfield Operations	2,500
Bank of Oklahoma	2,500

Cost of Living

Tulsa's cost of living is 6.1 percent below the national average, even as household income continued to grow in 2013.

The following is a summary of data regarding several key cost of living factors in the area.

2013 ACCRA Average House Price: $192,992

2013 ACCRA Cost of Living Index: 87

State income tax rate: 0.5% to 5.0%

State sales tax rate: 4.5%

Local income tax rate: None

Local sales tax rate: 3.0%

Property tax rate: 126.84 mills (average, 2013)

Economic Information: Metropolitan Tulsa Chamber of Commerce, One West Third St., Suite 100, Tulsa, OK 74103; telephone (918) 585-1201.

■ Education and Research

Elementary and Secondary Schools

The second largest public school system in the state of Oklahoma, Tulsa Public Schools featured a staff with 69 doctorate degrees and more than 1,100 master's degrees as of 2013. The school district's five-year plan, developed in 2011, prioritized review and development of its staff as effective teachers and leaders in order to drive student achievement. The U.S. Department of Education named Tulsa Eisenhower International Elementary School a National Blue Ribbon School of Excellence in 2013. It was one of only six schools in the state, and the only school in the district, to receive the honor. Magnet programs in the district support student learning in fine and performing arts; restaurant, lodging, and health management; scientific and technological utilization; and broadcasting and digital media. The municipal government announced in 2013 its intention to develop an educational program in conjunction with the local aerospace industry to prepare students for skilled labor positions in related manufacturing.

There are more than 20 private religious schools or secular secondary and elementary schools in greater Tulsa.

The following is a summary of data regarding the Tulsa Public Schools.

Total enrollment: 41,501

Number of facilities
total: 79
elementary schools: 54
junior high schools: 14
high schools: 11

Student/teacher ratio: 16.09:1

Teacher salaries
average (statewide): $49,039

Funding per pupil: $8,423

Public Schools Information: Tulsa Public Schools, Education Service Center, 3027 S .New Haven, Tulsa, OK 74114; telephone (918) 746-6800.

Colleges and Universities

Metropolitan Tulsa has four major state and several private institutions of higher learning. Public institutions include Oklahoma State University at Tulsa, the University of Oklahoma at Tulsa, Rogers State University, and Tulsa Community College.

The University of Tulsa, the state's oldest private university, was founded as a school for Indian girls. Today it offers 90 different majors and programs through the doctoral level to its more than 4,300 students. *U.S. News & World Report* ranked the university 86th nationally in 2014. The university's petroleum engineering programs are some of its most well-known academic fields. Oral Roberts University is a Christian-centered liberal arts college that offers more than 100 majors and minors to its students. Major colleges include arts and cultural studies; business; education; nursing; science and engineering; and theology and ministry. It was ranked 54th among regional universities by *U.S. News & World Report* in 2014.

The renowned Spartan School of Aeronautics, one of the oldest continually operating aviation schools in the world, has graduated more than 90,000 in its 85 years of education in the fields of aviation maintenance technology, avionics technology, communications technology, quality control, and aviation. Other kinds of specialized education and training are available at the Tulsa Technology Center, which trains high school juniors and seniors as well as adults. Students in Tulsa also attend several business and trade schools.

Libraries and Research Centers

The Tulsa City-County Library has a Central Library, four regional libraries, 19 branches, and a Genealogy Center. Approximately 415,000 cardholders checked out more than 6 million volumes as of 2013. In addition to its permanent collection of 1.78 million volumes, the library houses more than 150,000 government documents, maps, art reproductions, and audio/videotapes, plus talking and large-print books. Special collections include the Land Office Survey Map Collection and the Shakespeare Collection. The Library's American Indian Resource Center provides cultural, educational, and informational resources, and activities and services honoring American Indian heritage, arts, and achievements. The center provides access to more than 4,000 books and media for adults and children by and about American Indians, including historical and rare materials, new releases, videos and music compact discs.

Thomas Gilcrease Institute of American History and Art Library is home to around 100,000 rare books, manuscripts, other archival material, and special collections, such as the Hispanic documents from the period 1500–1800 and the papers of Cherokee Chief John Ross and Choctaw Chief Peter Pitchlynn. Tulsa has some 30 other libraries offering reference materials on a wide range of topics, many having to do with petroleum. Research centers affiliated with the University of Tulsa conduct projects in such fields as information security and

petroleum engineering, while a center affiliated with Oral Roberts University researches the Holy Spirit, among other topics.

Public Library Information: Tulsa City-County Library, 400 Civic Center, Tulsa, OK 74103; telephone (918) 549-7323.

■ Health Care

Tulsa has more than nine major medical centers in its metropolitan area that offer state-of-the-art services to patients. Treatment and consultation are offered in virtually all fields of medicine, including such specialties as burn care, open-heart surgery, cardiac rehabilitation, genetic counseling, and neonatal intensive care. Hospice and long-term-care facilities are also available.

The largest medical facility in the area is Hillcrest Medical Center, with its 727-bed facility that admits nearly 50,000 patients annually. As of 2013, the 646-bed St. Francis Hospital was undergoing a $200 million expansion. St. John Medical Center, with 547 beds, saw more than 57,000 patients annually. A total of 1,678 physicians serve the community, and major hospitals are supplemented by 138 local clinics and 6 ambulatory surgery centers.

The Oxley Foundation pledged $30 million toward a Tulsa School of Community Health in 2012, to be located in downtown Tulsa. The effort was a joint project in conjunction with the University of Tulsa and the University of Oklahoma–Tulsa. Oklahoma State University's College of Osteopathic Medicine was rated the most popular medical school by *U.S. News & World Report* in 2012.

■ Recreation

Sightseeing

Tulsa boasts one of the nation's largest city-owned parks, the 3,183-acre Mohawk Park. Along with picnic and recreation areas, the park contains the Tulsa Zoo, with its Robert J. LaFortune WildLIFE Trek, Tropical American Rainforest, Children's Zoo, Dave Zucconi Conservation Center. The Tulsa Zoo has emerged as one of the most impressive zoos in the region, with some 3,000 animals representing 128 species. Also in Mohawk Park is the Oxley Nature Center, one of the largest urban nature centers with a variety of habitats from marshland to deep woods. The Tulsa Garden Center features beautiful dogwood and azalea plantings. Nearby is the award-winning Tulsa Rose Garden. Tulsa's oldest landmark is a tree, the Council Oak, which still stands in the Creek Nation Council Oak Park as a memorial to the Lachapokas and Tallassee Creek tribes, the first settlers of what later became Tulsa.

Industrial tours of Tulsa are offered by several facilities, including the American Airlines Maintenance Engineering Base, which overhauls and repairs aircraft. Sightseers may also tour the campus of Oral Roberts University with its unique Prayer Tower. The Blue Dome District, defined by a 1920s gas station and its Art Deco blue dome intended to attract Route-66 travelers, is a cultural and nightlife destination of the city.

Arts and Culture

Long known as a cultural center and leading the state in the number and quality of cultural events, Tulsa offers the visitor year-round entertainment. A blooming arts scene in the historic Greenwood District features numerous stage performances and art galleries. The district is also a hotbed for jazz and blues. In 2004 the county purchased the district's Tulsa Union Depot, a historic train station, and converted it into the new home of the Oklahoma Jazz Hall of Fame. The Hall was created to educate the public about the significant contributions of Oklahoma's jazz musicians. During Greenwood's heyday, such notable jazz and blues performers as Nat "King" Cole, Louis Armstrong, Duke Ellington, Cab Calloway, Dizzy Gillespie, and Lionel Hampton, all visited Tulsa to play at white clubs and then jam afterwards with local musicians on Greenwood Avenue. For performances of theater, dance, and music, the six-level Tulsa Performing Arts Center (or PAC), located in BOK Tower in downtown Tulsa, seats 2,400 people in its music hall and 450 people in the performing theater and sees more than 300,000 visitors annually. Among groups and programs in residence are the Tulsa Symphony Orchestra, Tulsa Ballet, Tulsa Opera, Tulsa Town Hall, Chamber Music Tulsa, Choregus Productions, Theatre Tulsa, Tulsa Oratorio Chorus, and the Broadway series. The Oklahoma Aquarium and Museum is another frequently visited Tulsa attraction. It features thousands of salt and fresh water and mammal species in seven core exhibits.

Among the many museums and galleries in the Tulsa area is the Thomas Gilcrease Museum, which features more than 10,000 works by American artists from colonial times to the present. The centerpiece is the country's most impressive collection of works by famous western artists such as Frederic Remington, Charles Russell, and George Catlin, plus maps, manuscripts, rare books, and prehistoric and modern Indian artifacts. The Tulsa County Historical Society Museum displays photographs, rare books, furniture, and tools representative of Tulsa's early days. Objects of Jewish art, history, ceremony, and everyday life are presented at the Sherwin Miller Museum of Jewish Art. The Philbrook Museum of Art exhibits more than 8,500 works of art, including Chinese jades, paintings of the Italian Renaissance and of nineteenth-century England and America, plus Native American basketry, paintings, and pottery. It is listed among the top art museums in the United States and is also on the National Register of Historic Places. The center is surrounded by several acres of formal gardens. A satellite campus of the museum opened in the Brady Arts District of the city in 2013. The Alexandre Hogue Gallery of Art at Tulsa University showcases traveling art collections as well as works by local artists, including students and instructors. The Tulsa Air and Space Museum and Planetarium promotes Tulsa's rich aviation history. It is home to one of the world's best space theaters.

Arts and Culture Information: VisitTulsa, 1 W. Third St., Suite 100, Tulsa OK 74103; telephone 800-558-3311.

Festivals and Holidays

Mayfest, a celebration of spring held in late May, is Tulsa's most prominent downtown event. The festivities include arts, crafts, music, and food. Rocklahoma, also in late May, is a major and growing three-day, multi-stage rock concert. The Tulsa Powwow, one of the largest Native American powwows in the world, takes place in early June. Highlights include authentic arts and crafts plus ceremonial dances and fancy-dress competitions. Oklahoma's Scottish Festival, SCOTFEST, is In mid-September and includes music, food, and games. The end of September brings the Tulsa State Fair; with more than one million fairgoers, it is one of the largest in the country. The fair includes a rodeo event of the Professional Rodeo Cowboys Association. Tulsa's Oktoberfest, held in Oktoberfest, features German musicians and, of course, beer. For nearly half a century, Tulsa has hosted the U.S. National Arabian and Hal-Arabian Horse Show during two weeks of October, which draws in excess of 10,000 visitors to the city.

Sports for the Spectator

Fans of professional sports will find the Double-A Tulsa Drillers, a farm team of the Colorado Rockies, rounding the bases from April through August at ONEOK Field, which rang in its inaugural season in 2010 with a capacity of 7,833. The Tulsa Oilers of the Central Hockey League take to the ice at the BOK Center. The Tulsa 66ers are a developmental league team of the National Basketball Association, affiliated with their in-state counterpart, the Oklahoma City Thunder. The Tulsa Shock of the Women's National Basketball Association also call the BOK Center home. In collegiate sports, the University of Tulsa Golden Hurricanes field 16 total men and women's athletic teams and compete in NCAA Division I athletics. Football games are played at Skelly Field at H.A. Chapman Stadium, which has a capacity of 30,000. The Oral Roberts University Golden Eagles field 14 athletic teams.

Tulsa's numerous equestrian events include the Longhorn World Championship Rodeo, in which top money-winners on the rodeo circuit compete. Tulsa also plays host to several prestigious golf tours and championships at its challenging Southern Hills Country Club, including the 2007 PGA Championship and 2009 USGA Amateur Championship. Other spectator sports include tennis and horse racing as well as stockcar races.

Sports for the Participant

Public recreation opportunities abound on and around the seven large lakes surrounding Tulsa. The area has become known locally as "Green Country," encompassing thousands of miles of shoreline on Grand Lake, Lake Eufala, Keystone Lake, Lake Tenkiller, and others. In the River Parks system along the Arkansas River in the heart of Tulsa, visitors can enjoy more than 50 miles of hiking/biking trails as well as picnic and playground areas. Turkey Mountain, a favorite of mountain bikers, offers rugged trails for the extreme biker and hiker. Tulsa had 141 city parks as of 2013. Mohawk Park offers bridle trails and a polo field. Other facilities include 92 playgrounds, 186 sports fields, 109 tennis courts, 5 swimming pools, and 4 18-hole golf courses.

Shopping and Dining

From nationally known stores to specialty shops, Tulsa provides shoppers with a wide range of choices. Three large malls serve the metro area, including the largest, Woodland Hills Mall, as well as the Tulsa Promenade. Utica Square is a tree-lined avenue of posh stores and diverse retailers. Just northwest of Utica Square, trendy boutiques and restaurants cater to more Bohemian tastes, while the Brookside area, a little south of the Square, offers still more individualized shopping, with some of Tulsa's best dining. The Cherry Street Historic District has been restored, and many small shops have opened there. Jenks, America, defines itself as the antique capital of Oklahoma, and is near the downtown Jenks neighborhood. Smaller shops featuring Native American crafts and Oklahoma memorabilia abound. Saturday's Flea Market at Expo Square is also a favorite shopping destination.

Dozens of restaurants offer menus ranging from traditional American cuisine to those with an international flavor. Regional specialties include chicken-fried steak, Santa Fe–style Mexican food, and authentic western barbecues.

Visitor Information: VisitTulsa, 1 W. Third St., Suite 100, Tulsa OK 74103; telephone 800-558-3311.

■ Convention Facilities

A moderate climate, abundant hotel space, and a wide range of leisure, cultural, and recreational opportunities make Tulsa attractive to large and small groups of convention-goers. In 2005 ground was broken on the city's most exciting development project in many years,

the BOK Center, featuring a stunning, futuristic design by world-renowned architect Cesar Pelli. The arena, which opened in 2008, offers 19,199 permanent and retractable seats and totals 565,000 square feet. The BOK Center was honored in 2011 with the International Association of Venue Managers' Venue Excellence Award. Renovations at the Cox Business Center, the city's convention center, completed in 2010, revamped a facility that covers more than 300,000 square feet in the heart of the business district and is only six blocks from the Performing Arts Center, which is also available for meetings. It offers an 8,900-seat arena, 102,600-square-foot, column-free exhibit hall, a ballroom, and numerous meeting rooms, all of which are utilized for sports, banquets, concerts, exhibitions, trade shows, and stage performances. Expo Square is home to 400,000 square feet of exhibit space in four main buildings: River Spirit Expo, Exchange Center, Central Park Hall, and the Pavilion. Among the city's other convention facilities are the Downtown Doubletree Hotel, the Doubletree Hotel at Warren Place, Crowne Plaza, Marriott Tulsa Southern Hills, Aloft Tulsan, and the fully renovated Mayo Hotel.

Convention Information: VisitTulsa, 1 W. Third St., Suite 100, Tulsa OK 74103; telephone 800-558-3311.

■ Transportation

Approaching the City

Visitors arriving by air touch down at Tulsa International Airport, just nine miles northeast of downtown— approximately 15 minutes by taxi. As of 2013, the airport was served by six carriers: Allegiant, American, Delta, Southwest, United, and Sun Country. Total passenger service in 2012 exceeded 2.7 million enplanements and deplanements. South of the city is the Richard Lloyd Jones Jr. Airport, a smaller facility serving general aviation traffic.

For those traveling to Tulsa by car, Interstate 44 from the east and south merges with U.S. Highway 75 southwest of the city and U.S. Highway 169 to the northeast. Interstate 44 also intersects with Interstate 244 both to the east and southwest of the city. Four toll expressways radiate from the city, the Red Fork and Crosstown (both are Interstate 244), Cherokee (U.S. Highway 75), and Broken Arrow (U.S. Highway 64/State Highway 51). U.S. Highway 412 crosses through the city from east to west. Greyhound travels into Tulsa with a station on South Detroit. The famous Route 66, a U.S. highway, passes through Tulsa.

Traveling in the City

Tulsa's bus-based mass transit system, Tulsa Transit, has 18 daytime routes, 6 evening routes, and 2 express routes served by the city's 60 buses. The Lift Program offers curb-to-curb transportation for the disabled and the elderly through its 50 available vans. Through the Bike and Bus Program, transport bike racks (for two bikes) are available on every bus, and stationary bike racks are provided at all bus stops for riders to lock their bikes. To make commuting easier, the city also offers a free computerized service matching individuals who drive similar routes daily.

■ Communications

Newspapers and Magazines

Tulsa's morning and Sunday newspaper is the *Tulsa World.* As of 2013, its daily circulation was just under 100,000. In addition, an African American community newspaper, *The Oklahoma Eagle,* two business newspapers, and several suburban and metro area weeklies serve the city. Tulsa also publishes a wide variety of periodicals, including the geophysical journal *The Leading Edge,* the *James Joyce Quarterly,* published by the University of Tulsa, and others covering such topics as science, petroleum, dentistry, and medicine.

Television and Radio

Sixteen television stations broadcast from Tulsa, including affiliates of NBC, PBS, CBS, ABC, and Fox. In addition, Tulsa radio provides listeners with a choice of 6 AM and 13 FM stations broadcasting religious programs, country music, oldies and contemporary hits, talk, and sports.

Media Information: *Tulsa World.* 315 S. Boulder Ave., Tulsa, OK 74103; telephone: 918-582-0921.

Tulsa Online

City of Tulsa. Available www.cityoftulsa.org
Grow Metro Tulsa. Available www.growmetrotulsa.com
Metropolitan Tulsa Chamber of Commerce. Available www.tulsachamber.com
Oklahoma Department of Commerce. Available www.okcommerce.gov
Tulsa City-County Library. Available www.tulsalibrary.org
Tulsa Oklahoma Convention & Visitors Bureau. Available www.visittulsa.com
Tulsa Public Schools. Available www.tulsaschools.org
Tulsa World. Available www.tulsaworld.com

BIBLIOGRAPHY

Bernhardt, William, *Dark Justice*(New York: Ballantine Books, 1999)

Johnson, Hannibal B., *Black Wall Street: From Riot to Renaissance in Tulsa's Historic Greenwood District* (Marion Koogler McNay Art Museum, 1998)

South Carolina

The State in Brief

Nickname: Palmetto State

Motto: Animism opibusque parati (Prepared in mind and resources); Dum spiro spero (While I breathe, I hope)

Flower: Carolina jessamine

Bird: Carolina wren

Area: 32,020 square miles (2010; U.S. rank 40th)

Elevation: Ranges from sea level to 3,560 feet above sea level

Climate: Humid and subtropical, with long, hot summers, short, mild winters, and abundant rainfall

Admitted to Union: May 23, 1788

Capital: Columbia

Head Official: Nikki R. Haley (R) (until 2015)

Population
    1990: 3,486,703
    2000: 4,012,012
    2010: 4,625,364
    2012 estimate: 4,630,351
    Percent change, 2000–2010: 15.3%
    U.S. rank in 2012: 24th
    Percent of residents born in state: 58.8% (2012)
    Density: 153.9 people per square mile (2010)
    2012 FBI Crime Index Total: 206,947

Racial and Ethnic Characteristics (2012)
    White: 3,108,466
    Black or African American: 1,290,704
    American Indian and Alaska Native: 15,122
    Asian: 57,635
    Native Hawaiian and Pacific Islander: 1,791
    Hispanic or Latino (may be of any race): 232,926
    Other: 156,633

Age Characteristics (2012)
    Population under 5 years old: 299,819
    Population 5 to 19 years old: 919,801
    Percent of population 65 years and over: 13.8%
    Median age: 37.9

Vital Statistics
    Total number of births (2012–13): 57,457
    Total number of deaths (2012–13): 42,931
    AIDS cases reported through 2011: 17,022

Economy
    Major industries: Manufacturing, agriculture, services
    Unemployment rate (2012): 6.8%
    Per capita income (2012): $23,906
    Median household income (2012): $44,623
    Percentage of persons below poverty level (2012): 17.6%
    Income tax rate: 0.0% to 7.0%
    Sales tax rate: 6.0%

Charleston

■ The City in Brief

Founded: 1670 (incorporated 1783)

Head Official: Mayor Joseph P. Riley, Jr. (D) (since 1975; current term expires 2016)

City Population
> 1990: 88,256
> 2000: 96,650
> 2010: 120,083
> 2012 estimate: 125,941
> Percent change, 2000–2010: 24.2%
> U.S. rank in 1990: 266th
> U.S. rank in 2000: 272nd (State rank: 2nd)
> U.S. rank in 2010: 209th (State rank: 2nd)

Metropolitan Statistical Area Population
> 2000: 549,033
> 2010: 664,607
> 2012 estimate: 697,439
> Percent change, 2000–2010: 21.1%
> U.S. rank in 2000: 85th
> U.S. rank in 2010: 79th

Area: 97 square miles

Elevation: Ranges from sea level to 20 feet above sea level

Average Annual Temperatures: 65.6° F

Average Annual Precipitation: 51.53 inches

Major Economic Sectors: military, tourism, marine products, fertilizer, rubber products, textiles, aircraft parts, paper, textiles, food products, lumber, metal components, heavy machinery, transportation equipment, furniture

Unemployment Rate: 5.4% (2012)

Per Capita Income: $32,526

2012 FBI Crime Index Property: 3,373

Major Colleges and Universities: College of Charleston, Medical University of South Carolina, Charleston Southern University, The Citadel

Daily Newspaper: *The Post & Courier*

■ Introduction

Charleston, the flagship city of three South Carolina counties, is an important economic and political hub in the state. Charleston owes much to its warm, sunny climate and proximity to the sea. Although the Charleston Naval Base closed in 1996, Charleston still has a large military presence. The Port of Charleston ranks as one of the fastest-growing in the nation, and expansions by Boeing South Carolina have converted the city into an aeronautical hub. Charleston consistenly ranks among the top U.S. and international travel destinations. The city's tourism industry owes much to those who preserve its historic buildings. Cobblestone streets, quaint gardens, historic homes and buildings, mingled with flower stalls and specialty shops, draw tourists to Charleston for a glimpse of a gracious and genteel lifestyle long gone. Visitors appreciate the rich arts and cultural offerings of the city. Waterfront and downtown renovation and new construction blend with historic structures to preserve and further the spirit of the city.

■ Geography and Climate

Prior to 1960, Charleston proper was limited to the South Carolina peninsula bounded on the west and south by the Ashley River, on the east by the Cooper River, and on the southeast by an excellent harbor almost completely landlocked from the Atlantic Ocean. The city

Bob Stefko/Getty Images

has expanded to include other areas, but most residents still think of Charleston as the peninsula. In fact, the physical size of Charleston has increased from approximately 17 square miles in 1975 to 97 square miles. A chain of barrier islands between Charleston's mainland and the Atlantic Ocean adds sandy beaches and marshland to the region's geography. The city of Charleston is the seat of Charleston County. The commercial and geographic region known as the Charleston Region includes three counties—Charleston, Berkeley, and Dorchester. Charleston is also generally considered to be part of the South Carolina Lowcountry, a region that includes the state's coastal counties of Charleston, Beaufort, and Jasper, as well as the coastal islands.

Charleston's proximity to the Atlantic Ocean provides a temperate to subtropical climate. During the winter months temperatures on the peninsula can be as much as 15 degrees warmer than inland because of the ocean's influence. Average annual snowfall is less than one inch. In summer, sea breezes cool the city to a temperature about three degrees below higher country. The summer is Charleston's rainiest season with 41 percent of the annual rainfall occurring in the form of thundershowers and occasional tropical storms. Hurricanes threaten in late summer and early fall. It is estimated that Charleston is affected by hurricanes every 4.62 years. In September 1989 Hurricane Hugo inflicted more than $5 billion in property damage to the region.

Area: 97 square miles

Elevation: Ranges from sea level to 20 feet above sea level

Average Temperatures: 65.6° F

Average Annual Precipitation: 51.53 inches

■ History

Settlement Named for British King

In April 1670, the first English colonists sailed into Charleston harbor. This band of some 150 men and women soon established themselves on what they called Albemarle Point on the Ashley River. Ten years later, the colony was moved to Oyster Point, a peninsula of land between the Ashley and Cooper Rivers, the present site of Charleston. The settlement was named Charles Towne in honor of King Charles II of England, who had granted the land for colonization. The colony began to grow as people arrived first from England and the Caribbean islands. They were followed by Huguenots and Quakers who, along with Scottish, Irish, and Belgian colonists settled the area. The thriving port became known as one of the most religiously tolerant of the colonies. About 5,000 people inhabited the town by 1700, and friendly relations with the area's tribal natives had been established.

City Incorporated Following Revolution

By this time, the town was protected by a formidable wall; situated along the river bluff, it stood five feet thick and was made of brick on a base of palmetto logs and wood planks; on the land side, the wall was made of earth and bordered by a moat. The mere sight of it turned back a frontal attack on the settlement from a combined French-Spanish fleet in 1706. Ships sailed out of the harbor carrying corn, pork, lumber, deerskins, and rice, conveying goods to England and the West Indies. But shipping was threatened when, following a devastating 1713 hurricane and renewed tribal hostility, pirates became bold enough to attack the sea trade. Notable among the pirates was Edward Teach, known as Blackbeard. He seized several ships carrying Charles Towne residents and demanded, and received, ransom. Teach was eventually captured and executed, but residents of Charles Towne had become dissatisfied with the administration of the colony, especially in regard to the protection of the populace. England's Privy Council took over responsibility for the government of South Carolina and appointed the first royal governor in 1720. With the threat of hostile native and pirate attacks effectively quelled by the new administration, Charles Towne residents took down most of the city walls, opened and extended the streets, and built spacious homes with well-tended grounds. The shoreline was developed, and shipping activity was brisk. Left standing was the Battery, a large retaining wall that today overlooks the harbor and Fort Sumter.

Beginning with the Stamp Act of 1765, Charles Towne was seriously torn over conflicts between loyalty to England and resistance to England's imposition of unjust taxes on the colonies. Residents protested the tea tax at a mass meeting held in 1773 and set up the formal governmental structure of South Carolina in July 1774. In September 1775, the last royal governor left the colony and took refuge aboard a British ship in the harbor. Then on June 28, 1776, a British fleet attempted to sail into the harbor at Charles Towne and was repulsed by revolutionary patriots. This victory persuaded the South Carolina delegates to the Continental Congress to sign the Declaration of Independence. Following the Revolution, Charles Towne remained politically troubled. Violence was directed against suspected British sympathizers, and various factions of the town faced each other

with open animosity. Finally, in an attempt to restore order, the city was incorporated under the name of Charleston in 1783. Three years later, the South Carolina General Assembly voted to move the state capital from Charleston to the new city of Columbia. That move was completed in 1790.

The Citadel Founded to Quell Uprisings

Several innovations improved Charleston's economy in the 1790s. The invention of the cotton gin made the cotton business profitable. A method of using tidal force to irrigate rice plantings expanded the possibilities for rice cultivation. New and more efficient rice mills were built. Meanwhile, the shipping industry, no longer forced to comply with British mercantile laws, found new markets for American goods; wagon trade expanded, rolling cotton and other produce into Charleston's King Street for sale. When other regions began to draw trade away from Charleston, the city began construction of the South Carolina Railroad. By 1833, rail service began out of Charleston, but while the railroad did improve the economy, Charleston never again regained its dynamic growth pattern.

In 1822, just as Charleston was beginning to feel economic woes, it also experienced an attempted slave rebellion led by a former slave from the West Indies, Denmark Vesey, a dynamic, well-educated leader. Vesey had laid plans for obtaining weapons and had determined which buildings would be attacked when he was betrayed by two house servants and arrested. After a trial during which he engaged counsel and expertly examined witnesses himself, he was condemned to be hanged along with 36 of his co-conspirators. Others involved in the rebellion were deported. Following this attempted uprising, the Old Citadel was built as an arsenal and staffed by federal troops, and stricter laws governing slaves and their activities were adopted. The Citadel was later staffed by state troops, and in 1843 by a 20-man force that became the first Corps of Cadets of The Citadel.

"Cradle of Secession" Surrenders to Yankees

Unresolved economic and philosophical conflicts between northern and southern states reached a crisis on December 20, 1860, when the South Carolina Secession Convention unanimously voted to adopt the Ordinance of Secession, leading other southern states in an attempt to leave the Union and form their own Confederacy. On April 12, 1861, Confederate batteries fired on Union forces occupying Fort Sumter, an installation off Charleston's coast. The Union forces on the island surrendered, Confederate forces occupied the fort, and one week later President Abraham Lincoln ordered all southern ports blockaded. While preparing for Union attack, Charleston was ravaged by a fire that destroyed 540 acres. Blockade runners were able to slip some supplies past the Union's blockade of Charleston harbor, but as the war continued it brought shortages of all vital supplies, including meat, sugar, and salt. Charleston, the "Cradle of Secession," withstood Union attacks until February 17, 1865, when, with the Confederacy crumbling, hundreds of fires swept through the city. After four years of siege, Charleston succumbed to Union forces, and two months later the Confederacy surrendered.

Navy Yard Helps Stabilize Economy

Following the Civil War, Charleston was powerless. The city lay in ruins, railroads were destroyed, banking capital was depleted, and private capital was scarce. An industry eventually developed around phosphate deposits mined from local rivers and land sites and by 1880 was the most profitable industry in the state. Other commercial concerns recovered or developed, such as lumber mills, locomotive engine manufacturing, cotton presses and mills, breweries, and grist and flour mills. Port trade thrived, and the cotton business revived. Charleston recovered from an 1885 hurricane and an 1886 earthquake only to battle political trade obstacles, industrial competition from other regions, and insect destruction of the cotton industry. By the turn of the century, the city had to look to new industries and new developments for new hope.

In a move that proved to be the single most important gesture affecting the city's economy in the twentieth century, the United States Navy Yard was located at Charleston in 1901. Although other industries established themselves in the area, the military facility fueled the city's economy through two world wars and provided the stability that enabled Charleston to solidify its identity. In the 1920s and 1930s, although the rest of the country was mired in the Great Depression, efforts to preserve and capitalize on Charleston's historic buildings began. Leading the way were wealthy people with well-known names like Doubleday, du Pont, and Whitney, who used Charleston's abandoned rice fields as quail- and duck-hunting preserves, and also began the task of restoring the city's beautiful old mansions. In 1989 Hurricane Hugo, one of the most destructive hurricanes to ever have struck the U.S. mainland, inflicted more than $5 billion in property damage on the region. Citizens quickly repaired the damage, restoring the city to the pristine freshness that still beguiles its 4.6 million annual visitors. Although the U.S. Naval Base in Charleston closed in 1996, a significant U.S. Naval and Air Force presence remains at Joint Base Charleston.

In 2001 the city embarked on a new incentive and growth program dubbed the Charleston Digital Corridor. The Digital Corridor represents efforts to create a technological, knowledge-based economy in the region through a combination of initiatives and business incentives, private business support and member-driven

programming. Every digital corridor company reported an increase in hiring during 2012. In an important boon to local, high-quality job growth, Boeing South Carolina conducted major expansions of area operations during the late 2000s and early 2010s, adding billions to the local economy. Aeronautical development inspired local technical schools to offer courses in related fields as Boeing Dreamliner aircraft rolled off assembly lines.

Economic development sometimes clashed with residents' image of the quaint city. This tension was exemplified by a decision in 2010 to make Charleston a year-round destination for cruise ships. While short-term cruise passengers brought revenue into local tourist attractions, shops, and restaurants, they also brought with them added congestion and long-term concerns over pollution. Debate over the cruise industry and whether its expansion was a boon or burden for the city continued through the 2013.

Historical Information: South Carolina Historical Society Library, Fireproof Building, 100 Meeting Street, Charleston, SC; telephone (803)723-3225. College of Charleston, Avery Research Center for African American History and Culture-Library, 125 Bull Street, Charleston, SC 29401; telephone (843) 953-7609.

■ Population Profile

Metropolitan Statistical Area Population

2000: 549,033
2010: 664,607
2012 estimate: 697,439
Percent change, 2000–2010: 21.1%
U.S. rank in 2000: 85th
U.S. rank in 2010: 79th

City Residents

1990: 88,256
2000: 96,650
2010: 120,083
2012 estimate: 125,941
Percent change, 2000–2010: 24.2%
U.S. rank in 1990: 266th
U.S. rank in 2000: 272nd (State rank: 2nd)
U.S. rank in 2010: 209th (State rank: 2nd)

Density: 1,101.9 people per square mile

Racial and ethnic characteristics

White: 91,468
Black or African American: 29,947
American Indian and Alaskan Native: 134
Asian: 1,209
Native Hawaiian and Other Pacific Islander: 43
Hispanic or Latino (may be of any race): 5,230
Other: 3,140

Percent of residents born in state: 51.3%

Age characteristics

Population under 5 years old: 7,632
Population 5 to 9 years old: 6,309
Population 10 to 14 years old: 5,006
Population 15 to 19 years old: 7,643
Population 20 to 24 years old: 16,329
Population 25 to 34 years old: 23,346
Population 35 to 44 years old: 14,806
Population 45 to 54 years old: 14,374
Population 55 to 59 years old: 7,825
Population 60 to 64 years old: 7,471
Population 65 to 74 years old: 8,520
Population 75 to 84 years old: 4,747
Population 85 years and over: 1,933
Median age: 33.3

Births (2010–11 Metropolitan Area)

Total number: 9,320

Deaths (2010–11 Metropolitan Area)

Total number: 4,798

Money income (2012)

Per capita income: $32,526
Median household income: $50,602
Total households: 52,182

Number of households with income of ...

less than $10,000: 6,114
$10,000 to $14,999: 3,083
$15,000 to $24,999: 5,131
$25,000 to $34,999: 5,025
$35,000 to $49,999: 6,494
$50,000 to $74,999: 8,597
$75,000 to $99,999: 6,168
$100,000 to $149,999: 6,006
$150,000 to $199,999: 2,368
$200,000 or more: 3,196

Percent of families below poverty level: 21.2%

FBI Crime Index Property: 3,373

FBI Crime Index Violent: 296

■ Municipal Government

Charleston is governed by a mayor and a 12-member city council. Council members are elected on a single-member district basis for four-year terms. Every two years, six members are elected.

Head Official: Mayor Joseph P. Riley, Jr. (D) (since 1975; current term expires 2016)

Total Number of City Employees: 1,749 (2012)

City Information: City of Charleston, Media Relations, 50 Broad Street, Charleston, SC 29401; telephone (843) 724-3746.

■ Economy

Major Industries and Commercial Activity

The economy in the Charleston region rests upon several sturdy bases. The military has traditionally been the major industry in the area since 1901 when the Charleston Naval Shipyard was founded. Even after the Naval Base and Shipyard closed in 1996, the military has remained the largest single employer in the Charleston region. The Department of Defense has remained at installations such as the Charleston Naval Weapons Station, Naval Hospital, and the SPAWAR Systems Center. Charleston Air Force Base is the home for the U.S. Air Force's 437th Airlift Wing, adding substantially to the region's economic foundation.

The Port of Charleston, the fourth busiest container port in the United States in 2013, drives an increasing amount of economic activity, with 9 percent growth in fiscal year 2014 alone. Port exansion sought to to create a new 280-acre terminal at the former Navy Base to accommodate more vessels. The first phase of the project was expected to be completed in 2016, with major projects completed by 2018, including the deepending of Charleston Harbor.

Oil, electronics, computers, mining, and health care are also major industries in the Charleston area. Two of the region's largest employers are in the health care industry—Medical University of South Carolina, and Trident Health Systems. Boeing South Carolina made significant expansions in the Charleston area beginning in the late 2000s and into the 2010s, focused mainly on production of the Boeing Dreamliner aircraft. Auxiliary and support facilities for the production and delivery of the aircraft made Charleston a major player in the aircraft manufacturing industry.

Tourism is another significant factor in the area's economy. The Charleston Metro Chamber of Commerce, the nation's oldest chamber of commerce, has long promoted Charleston as a place to visit, and despite wars, fires, hurricanes, and earthquakes, Charleston has preserved and restored hundreds of historic buildings that make it one of the most visited cities in the United States. Visitors enjoy shopping and dining, as well as touring historic plantations, landmarks, and churches. Most visitors come from South Carolina or nearby states, although about 5 percent arrive from international destinations. Charleston's world-famous barrier islands feature outstanding resort facilities in a semi-tropical climate, serving as powerful elements in the area's allure for tourists. Tourism spending totaled $16.5 billion in 2011, a record.

Items and goods produced: marine products, fertilizer, rubber products, textiles, aircraft parts, paper, textiles, food products, lumber, metal components, heavy machinery, transportation equipment, furniture, instruments and chemicals

Incentive Programs-New and Existing Companies

Both the State of South Carolina and the Charleston community offer a number of business incentives designed to provide measurable economic advantages and reduce the cost of start-up operations.

Local programs: The Berkeley-Charleston-Dorchester Council of Governments operates a revolving loan fund offering financing for projects meeting certain criteria. Charleston County operates a Small Busines Enterprise Porgram that encourages participation of local small businesses in bidding for public contracts. Five-year property tax abatements for new manufacturing facilities locating in the tri-county area and an exemption from the county portion of ordinary property taxes for five years on all additions to existing facilities are available under certain circumstances. The Charleston Citywide Local Development Corporation (LDC) offers financial assistance through a number of different loan programs for small businesses.

State programs: The following incentives and financing sources may be available to qualifying companies: Job Development Credit that rebates a portion of new employee's withholding taxes for use to address specific needs of a company; Economic Development Set-Aside Program to improve infrastructure surrounding new or exmpanding businesses; Enterprise Zone Retraining Credit Program to subsidize the cost of retraining workers; Rural Infrastructure Fund to further economic development in remote areas; Port Volume Increase Credit for companies that increase port cargo volume by at least 5 percent; and Tourism Infrastructure Development Grants to complete infrastructure projects that support new tourist developments. Additional credits include a Job Tax Credit, Economic Impact Zone Investment Credit, Corporate Headquarters Credit, and Research and Development Tax Credit. South Carolina's 5 percent corporate income tax is one of the lowest in the region.

Job training programs: The South Carolina Technical College System provides an array of job-training programs throughout the state. The readySC program, established in 1961, trains employees for several industries, including aerospace, automotive, biotech, and call centers. Apprenticeship Carolina, also part of the state's technical college system, provides consulting at no charge to employers and assists employers in training their workforce in technological, health-care, and transportation industries, among others. Trident Technical College

in North Charleston is part of the South Carolina Technical College System and the main facility in the tri-county area.

Development Projects

The South Carolina legislature has mandated additional expansion to the Port of Charleston, including the addition of a sixth container terminal located at the former Charleston Naval Complex. This terminal will accommodate the expanding international container trade and the increasingly larger container ships that arrive in the port. A groundbreaking on the new three-berth, 280-acre container terminal was held in May 2007, and major construction was expected to complete in 2018, the same year that the deepening of the Charleston harbor was slated for completion.

Boeing South Carolina has enjoyed substantial growth during the past decade as a fabricator and assembler of fuselage sections for the Boeing Dreamliner aircraft. In 2009 Boeing annouced it would construct a new Dreamliner assembly and delivery line in North Charleston; the 1.2-million-square-foot facility was completed in 2011, and the first airplane rolled off the assembly line in April 2012. The Boeing South Carolina Deliver Center, a nearly 60-square-foot facility opened the prior year. The Boeing facilities in and around Charleston are one of only three sites in the world to assemble and deliver twin-aisle commercial airliners. Additional Boeing facilities continued to support strong economic development in the Charleston area, including an IT Center of Excellence and an Engineering Design Center planned for 2015.

Charleston's Digital Corridor continues to thrive, placing three of its companies on the list of the *Inc 500* fastest growing companies in 2012. One-hundred percent of companies in the corridor added emloyees in 2012. In 2013 a wind turbine drivetrain test facility was dedicated in Charleston. The project, named the SCE&G Energy Innovation Center, was supported by Clemson University's Restoration and Institute and the namesake energy company, SCE&G. The new testing facility housed the world's most advanced divetrain systems for wind turbines and was funded in part by the U.S. Department of Energy.

Target industries for economic development included advanced security and information technology, aerospace and aviation, biomedical, and energy systems industries.

Economic Development Information: Charleston Regional Development Alliance, 4401 Belle Oaks Drive, Suite 420, Charleston, SC 29405; telephone (843) 767-9300; fax (834) 760-4535; alliance@crda.org.

Commercial Shipping

International trade is a growing sector of the regional economy, and the Port of Charleston is making strides to accommodate that growth. Known as one of the most efficient ports in the world, it handled 723,420 tons of coargo in 2013, with top commodities including agricultural products, consumer good,s machinery, metals, vehicles, chemicals, and clay products. Total value of cargo at the Port of Charleston amounted to more than $63.6 billion in 2012, ranking eighth among all international ports in terms of dollar value. Charleston International Airport's air cargo facilities include a 21,000-square-yard facility and a separate cargo/freight area on the airport's east side. Rail service is provided by CSX and Norfolk Southern. In addition, about 200 motor freight carriers serve the area, which also boasts an efficient highway network.

Labor Force and Employment Outlook

Charleston boasts a plentiful supply of skilled labor. The percentage of Charleston residents that are high school graduates, as well as those with bachelor's degrees, both rank above state and national averages. Advanced degree holders exceed state averages as well. Growth industries included manufacutring, fueled in part by relocation of several Boeing facilities, and professional and business services. The tourism industry remained a steady and growing employer of local residents, too.

The following is a summary of data regarding the 2012 Charleston labor force:

Size of civilian labor force: 68,278

Number of workers employed in . . .

agriculture and mining: 367
construction: 2,788
manufacturing: 3,563
wholesale trade: 1,120
retail trade: 6,578
transportation: 2,197
information systems: 1,513
finance: 3,949
professional administration: 7,351
education and social services: 16,064
arts and leisure: 9,891
other: 3,256
public administration: 3,727

Average hourly earnings of production workers: $19.52

Unemployment rate: 5.4% (2012)

Employers

Largest employers (2012)	*Number of employees*
Joint Base Charleston	22,000
Medical University of South Carolina (MUSC)	13,000
Boeing Charleston	5,900
Charleston County School District	5,300
Roper St. Francis Healthcare	5,100
JEM Restaurant Group	3,000
Trident Health Systems	2,500
College of Charleston	2,400
Charleston County	2,300
WalMart, Inc.	2,300

Cost of Living

The city's cost of living was 6.7 percent above the national average in 2013, due in part to the coveted but limited real estate available in the historic downtown area.

The following is a summary of data regarding several key cost of living factors in the area.

2013 ACCRA Average House Price: $236,573

2013 ACCRA Cost of Living Index: 100

State income tax rate: 0.0% to 7.0%

State sales tax rate: 6.0%

Local income tax rate: None

Local sales tax rate: 2.5%

Property tax rate: 0.2583 mills (2012)

Economic Information: Charleston Metro Chamber of Commerce, 4500 Leeds Avenue, Suite 100, North Charleston, SC 29405; telephone (843) 577-2510; fax (843) 723-4853; mail@charlestonchamber.org.

■ Education and Research

Elementary and Secondary Schools

Most students in the city of Charleston are served by the Charleston County School District, which is further divided into eight constituent districts. As of 2012, the school district's graduation rate was 75.5 percent, an increase from 67 percent just two years prior. Charleston County School District was one of 17 districts awarded a federal Race to the Top Grant, with the eighth-best composite score. The grant, worth $19.4 million, was targeted to increase personalized learning in 19 district schools. Drayton Hall Elementary was named an Apple Distinguished school in 2012, one of seven across the country, for its innovative use of Apple iPads in the classroom.

There are more than 35 private and parochial schools in Charleston County, including the exclusive Charleston

Day School, where children from Charleston's oldest families matriculate, and the nationally known Ashley Hall and Porter-Gaud Schools.

The following is a summary of data regarding the Charleston County School District.

Total enrollment: 43,654

Number of facilities

> total: 77
> elementary schools: 46
> junior high schools: 13
> high schools: 14
> other: 4

Student/teacher ratio: 14.57:1

Teacher salaries

> average (statewide): $49,434

Funding per pupil: $9,824

Public Schools Information: Charleston County School District, Office of Superintendent, 75 Calhoun Street, Charleston, SC 29401; telephone (843) 937-6300.

Colleges and Universities

Charleston's colleges and universities have been ranked among the best in the nation. The Medical University of South Carolina (MUSC), the South's oldest medical school, has six health-related colleges, including a graduate school. MUSC was one of the first medical schools in the country to open its own infirmary for teaching. MUSC employed 1,400 full-time faculty in 2013 to support increasing enrollment. The College of Charleston, founded in 1770, is the oldest institute of higher education in the state and 13th oldest in the nation. The school was incorporated into the South Carolina State College System in 1970 and opened its graduate school in 1992. College of Charleston offers dozens of degree programs across six major schools: Art; Business; Education, Health, and Human Performance; Humanities and Social Sciences; Languages, Cultures, and World Affairs; Sciences and Mathematics; Graduate School; and Honors College. Enrollment was 10,500 students in 2013.

Charleston Southern University (CSU) enrolled about 2,800 students in its College of Arts and Science, ROTC program, and schools of business, education, and nursing. The school offers more than 30 undergraduate degrees and master's degrees in education and business administration. CSU is affiliated with the South Carolina Baptist Convention.

The Citadel, The Military College of South Carolina, a coeducational, liberal arts school with a strict military structure, is also located in Charleston. The Citadel has nineteen academic departments across six schools offering bachelor's and master's degrees. The ROTC Department includes study options in aerospace studies, military science, and naval science. Enrollment at The Citadel is about 3,500 students. In 2013 *U.S. News & World Report* named The Citadel the top public college in the South, the third consecutive honor for the institution. Webster University, a St. Louis-based facility granting master's degrees, offers courses in the Charleston area, including a campus at Joint Base Charleston. Southern Illinois University and Embry-Riddle Aeronautical University also have campuses on the base.

Trident Technical College (TTC) is a two-year institution that emphasizes training in job skills. TTC offers more than 150 programs of study across 12 academic divisions. Enrollment at TTC is about 17,000. Expansion of Boeing South Carolina led TTC to expand its training to include degrees in various fields of aeronautical studies. The Lowcountry Graduate Center (LGC) in North Charleston was created through a partnership with the College of Charleston, The Citadel, and MUSC to offer more students access to graduate-level education. Additional partner schools include Clemson University and the University of South Carolina.

The Charleston School of Law is the city's newest addition to its academic institutions. Opened in August 2004, the law school enrolled 200 students in its first class. It received full accreditation from the American Bar Association in 2011.

There are several other institutes of higher learning in the greater Charleston Region. A satellite campus of Southern Wesleyan University offers accelerated learning programs for working adults. Limestone College offers bachelor's and associate's degrees in several disciplines, including art, science, and business administration. Miller-Motte Technical College, with more than one dozen campuses throughout the Carolinas, offers both certificate and college degree programs. Springfield College offers undergraduate and graduate degrees to about 2,3000 undergraduates and 1,000 graduate students. Voorhees College is a private, historically African American, coeducational, liberal arts school affiliated with the Episcopal Church.

Libraries and Research Centers

The city of Charleston is served by the Charleston County Library, the first public library in the country, with a main library, 10 local branch libraries, 5 regional libraries, and a traveling bookmobile. The main library, four branches, and two regional libraries are located within the city of Charleston. The library system houses about 2.2 million catalogued items including books, magazine subscriptions, compact discs, records, videotapes, films and film strips, cassettes, as well as an excellent collection of Charleston and South Carolina historical and genealogical materials. It maintains a complete business reference library, as well as legal resources pertaining to federal, state, and local law. A special section, The Jerry and Anita Zucker Holocaust Memorial Collection, is housed at the main library in Charleston.

The Avery Research Center for African American History and Culture at the College of Charleston contains manuscripts, photographs, oral histories, newspapers, video and audio tapes, and nearly 4,000 books and other research documents on the African American experience in Charleston and the South Carolina Lowcountry. With such a regional focus, it is considered to be one of the only public access research centers of its kind in the United States.

The University Research Resource Facilities (URRFs) of the Medical University of South Carolina include the Flow Cytometry Facility, the Biomolecular Computing Resource Facility, the Center for Health Economic and Policy Studies, the Gene Targeting and Knockout Mouse Facility, and the X-ray Crystallography Facility. Other facilities are available for research on topics such as mass spectrometry, monoclonal antibodies, nuclear magnetic resonance, and nucleic acid analysis. In 2007 MUSC announced a partnership agreement with Force Protection to establish the Force Protection Center for Brain Research at MUSC. Force Protection is a leading blast and ballistics research and manufacturing firm that specializes in work on armored vehicles. The focus of the Center for Brain Research is on research surrounding the treatment of traumatic brain injuries. During 2011–12 alone, the hospital received more than $230 million in research funding.

Public Library Information: Charleston County Library, 68 Calhoun Street, Charleston, SC 29401; (843) 805-6930.

■ Health Care

Medical University of South Carolina (MUSC) was one of the first medical schools in the nation to open its own teaching infirmary. The MUSC Medical Center, now a leading teaching and research center, had 709 beds and 1,400 full-time faculty as of 2013. Specialists from more than 40 fields are work at the facility. In 2013 *U.S. News & World Report* ranked MUSC as "One of America's Best Hospitals," with six specialty areas ranked in the top 50 in the nation.

The main hospital has the only Level I Trauma Center in coastal South Carolina, served in part by the 24-hour MEDUCARE emergency medical transport service. Special treatment and research programs include the Heart and Vascular Center, the Hollings Cancer Center, and the Transplant Center. The Transplant Center is the only one in the state to offer a full range of transplants, such as heart, kidney, liver, pancreas, corneas, and bone marrow. Charleston is also home to

the MUSC Children's Hospital, a 186-bed facility that features a Level III Neonatal Intensive Care Unit and a Pediatric Intensive Care Unit. *U.S. News & World Report* ranked its pediatriccardiology and heart surgery 15th in the United States, its gastroenterology program within the top 50, and also recognized six physicians at the hosptial on its Top Doctors 2013 list.

The MUSC Institute of Psychiatry features the Center for Drug and Alcohol Program, one of the finest facilities in the nation for treatment and research on substance abuse. The MUSC Storm Eye Institute is known for its research in fields such as intraocular lenses and the study of retinal diseases.

Roper St. Francis Health Care is the next largest health system in the metro Charleston area. Its two hospitals are Bon Secours St. Francis Hospital, specializing in acute care, Roper Hospital, a tertiary care facility, and Mount Pleasant Hospital. Other medical facilities serving the region's health-care needs include the U.S. Naval Clinic Charleston, which serves military personnel; East Cooper Regional Medical Center (140 beds); and Trident Health System (Columbia/HCA), with three medical centers: Trident, Summerville, and Moncks Corner.

■ Recreation

Sightseeing

Visitors to Charleston are greeted with a delightful array of sights and activities year-round. The colonial port city is famous for its horse-drawn carriage tours that take visitors over cobblestone streets through quaint colonial neighborhoods. The historic district consists of more than 2,000 preserved and restored buildings, 73 of which are pre-Revolutionary, 136 date from the 1700s, and 600 from the early 1800s.

Using guide services, boat and motorized trolley tours, or walking or bicycling with directions on audio cassettes, visitors can view Charleston's historic and stately buildings and churches. Opened in 1736, the Dock Street Theatre was one of the nation's first theaters. Later, the Planters Inn, built around the ruins of the theater, was a gathering spot where "Planters Punch" is said to have originated; the hotel was remodeled into the Dock Street Theatre in the mid-1930s. The Dock Street Theater was closed for renovations in 2007; the theater reopened in 2010.

Completed in 1772 by Daniel Heyward, the Heyward-Washington House was the property of Thomas Heyward, delegate to the Continental Congress and signer of the Declaration of Independence; the house is furnished with period furnishings, and visitors may tour the only restored eighteenth-century kitchen open to the public in Charleston. The Aiken-Rhett House, built around 1818, contains some of the finest rooms of the

Greek Revival and rococo styles in the city. Built between 1767 and 1771, the Old Exchange was the site of the election of South Carolina's delegates to the first Continental Congress in 1774. Although its Provost Dungeon was used by the British to confine prisoners during the Revolution, the U.S. Constitution was ratified at the Old Exchange in 1787; the building was later used as a customs house and post office and is now open to the public. The Avery Research Center for African-American History and Culture in the beautifully restored former Avery School preserves and makes public the historical and cultural heritage of South Carolina Lowcountry African Americans. The Cabbage Row section of Church Street was the inspirational setting for Gershwin's *Porgy and Bess* opera.

The oldest church in the city is St. Michael's Episcopal Church, which was completed in 1761. The edifice was designed after St. Martin's-in-the-Field in London; richly ornamented, the church includes a clock and bells operating since 1764. The mother church of the province, St. Philip's Episcopal Church originally stood on the site where St. Michael's Episcopal Church stands today; the present edifice was constructed between 1835 and 1838. St. Philip's churchyard contains the graves of John C. Calhoun, Secretary of War and Vice President of the United States; Edward Rutledge, signer of the Declaration of Independence; Charles Pinckney, signer of the U.S. Constitution; and DuBose Heyward, author of the novel *Porgy*. Construction for the Unitarian Church was begun in 1772, but work was stopped during the Revolution and not completed until 1787; remodeled in 1852, the church is noted for its fan-tracery ceiling and striking stained-glass windows. The Circular Congregational Church was designed by Robert Mills, built in 1806, and destroyed by fire in 1861; 30 years later the original brick was used to erect the present building on the site. The First Baptist Church, also designed by Robert Mills, was completed in 1821; its original congregation founded the Anabaptist Church in 1682 in Kittery, Maine, and, fleeing persecution from the Puritans, settled in colonial Charles Towne. Congregation Beth Elohim, an imposing Greek Revival building dating from 1841, is the oldest synagogue in the United States in continuous use; this synagogue introduced a liberalized ritual using instrumental music during the service for the first time and is recognized as the birthplace of Reform Judaism in the nation.

The first Adam-style house in Charleston, the Joseph Manigault House, was designed by Charleston architect Gabriel Manigault; completed in 1803, the house is a parallelogram with half-moon bows at either end and features French, English, and Charleston-made furniture, as well as a restored garden. The Nathaniel Russell House, built in 1808, is noted for its astonishing flying staircase spirals, oval drawing rooms, and extensive interior detailing, as well as for its fine china, silver, and

furniture. St. John's Lutheran Church, the mother church of the South Carolina Synod of the Lutheran Church in America, is noted for its wrought iron gates and fence; the first church on the site was built in 1759, and the present building dates from 1817. The French Protestant (Huguenot) Church was built in the 1840s; each spring a French liturgy service is held to commemorate the French Huguenots who fled religious persecution and settled in Charleston.

Visitors to Charleston will also enjoy the numerous gardens, parks, and plantations. Rainbow Row, north of the Battery along East Bay Street, is one of Charleston's most famous sections. Throughout the district are walled gardens, noted for their lavish floral displays and lacy ironwork. Charles Towne Landing is the original site of South Carolina's first permanent English settlement; this extensive park features the original colony's history at an interpretive center and reconstructed earthworks and palisade, as well as a replica of a seventeenth-century trading vessel moored in Old Towne Creek. Animals indigenous to South Carolina in 1670 roam in the Animal Forest behind concealed barriers, while the Settlers' Life Area invites visitors to participate in activities typical of early colonists' lives. Fort Sumter, where the Civil War's armed conflict began, is on a man-made island; visitors reach the island, now a National Monument, by boat from the Municipal Marina and Patriots Point. Snee Farm, a country club since 1966, is a remnant of the plantation home of Charles Pinckney, a principal architect and signer of the U.S. Constitution. Boone Hall Plantation, McLeod Plantation on James Island, Drayton Hall, Magnolia Plantation and Middleton Place rice plantation are other area plantations not to be missed.

Ravenel Caw Caw Interpretive Center is a 643-acre park highlighting Charleston's historical, natural and cultural heritage, especially the practice of rice cultivation brought to the country by Africans. Its eight miles of trails and boardwalks meander through marshland, swamp, and oak forest. A famous landmark in Charleston is the Angel Oak; estimated to be about 500 years old, this giant tree has a circumference of 28 feet and a limb spread of 187 feet. James Island County Park allows crabbing and fishing from floating docks along tidal creeks and lagoons, and offers bike paths, pedal boats, kayaks, picnicking, and 50-foot climbing wall. Its Splash Zone Waterpark is open seasonally. North Charleston Wannamaker County Park in North Charleston features family fun and Whirlin' Waters Adventure Waterpark. Other Charleston-area parks include Cypress Gardens and the Audubon Swamp Garden.

Ghost tours to explore the historic and haunted sites of the city are offered by different groups as walking, guided, and self-guided tours. Other tours feature a history of area pirates and the story of Charleston. Carriage tours, van tours, and water and harbor tours are also popular.

Arts and Culture

In 1735 Charleston's Dock Street Theatre opened as the first building in the American colonies to be used for theatrical productions. Renovations to the Dock Street Theater were completed in 2010. Charleston audiences saw the first opera performed in the New World, and by the 1790s the city supported a symphony orchestra. Jenny Lind, Sarah Bernhardt, Adelina Patti, and other internationally known performers brought their talents to Charleston theaters in the nineteenth century. Local playwright and novelist DuBose Heyward collaborated with composer George Gershwin in the 1930s to produce the musical drama *Porgy and Bess*, based on Heyward's novel *Porgy*.

Charleston is home to two ballet companies. The Charleston Ballet Theatre presents numerous public performances each season plus matinees for school children, and the Robert Ivey Ballet performs in Charleston and beyond, giving performances in 21 different countries through 2013. The Charleston Symphony Orchestra, which performs a September-through-May season and also performs masterworks, pops, and children's concerts. The Charleston Symphony Orchestra, as a nonprofit organization, receives funding from the South Carolina Arts Commission, the National Endowment for the Arts, and the city of Charleston. Financial difficulties temporaily halted performances in 2010, but the orchestra returned in 2011 and continued performing through the 2013–14 season. World-famous musicians are brought to Charleston each year by the Charleston Concert Association. Broadway shows, Shakespeare, and eighteenth-century classics are all part of the repertoire of the Footlight Players, who offer six or more plays a season at the Footlight Players Theatre. The Charleston Stage Company is the company-in-residence at the Dock Street Theatre; they have also given performances at the College of Charleston's Sottile Theatre and the American Theater, on King Street.

Museums and galleries in the region display a wide range of art and artifacts. The Charleston Museum, founded in 1773, is the country's first municipal museum; it focuses on South Carolina and the southeast with displays on history, the arts, archaeology, and natural history, and houses a full-scale replica of the Confederate submarine *Hunley*. The Citadel Archives and Museum, located at the entrance to The Citadel, displays items pertaining to the history of the college and its graduates, including two of the largest flags from the Civil War; each Friday at 3:45 p.m. the Citadel Corps of Cadets conducts a dress parade. The American Military Museum displays uniforms and artifacts of soldiers from all U.S. wars. The Confederate Museum, housed in Market Hall, contains flags, uniforms, swords, and other Confederate memorabilia. Patriots Point Naval and Maritime Museum, two miles east of Charleston, is one of the world's largest naval and maritime museums; featured is the USS

Yorktown, a retired aircraft carrier that saw service in World War II, Korea, and Vietnam, as well as the World War II submarine *Clamagore*, and the destroyer *Laffey*, and displays of missiles, guns, mines, and aircraft. Built in 1713, the Powder Magazine, South Carolina's oldest public building, was used during the Revolutionary War as a powder storehouse; it now serves as a historical museum. The Karpeles Manuscript Library Museum, with nine sites across the country, showcases the world's largest private collection of historically significant manuscripts. The Charleston branch includes original manuscripts of Washington Irving's *The Legend of Sleepy Hollow* and rare essays by Edgar Allen Poe. The Old Slave Mart Museum showcases the contributions of African Americans from 1670 to the civil rights movement. The Children's Museum of the Lowcountry has hands-on exhibits appealing to children through 12 years of age.

The South Carolina Aquarium on Charleston Harbor is one of Charleston's most visited attractions. Opened in May 2000, its exhibits showcase more 5,000 aquatic animals from river otters and sharks to loggerhead turtles. Special traveling exhibits are changed annually. Also for kids of all ages is the Edisto Island Serpentarium, a reptile park open in the summer months.

Featuring a fine collection of American paintings, Japanese woodblock prints, and sculpture, the Gibbes Museum of Art also offers an excellent collection of miniature portraits. The portrait gallery in the Council Chamber of the City Hall contains portraits of important leaders, including John Trumbull's portrait of George Washington and Samuel F. B. Morse's portrait of James Monroe. The City Gallery at the Waterfront Park exhibits the work of Charleston-area artists, especially experimental and contemporary work.

Festivals and Holidays

Today the vitality of the arts in Charleston can be deduced from the tremendous success of the Spoleto Festival USA, recognized as the world's most comprehensive arts festival. A version of an annual festival held in Spoleto, Italy, Charleston's Spoleto was brought to the city by Maestro Gian Carlo Menotti in 1977. For three weeks in late spring, Charleston, draped in banners and showered with fireworks, becomes a showplace for music, dance, opera, theater, and the visual arts. Internationally known performers entertain audiences in Charleston's historic churches, theaters, and plantations. Established works and performers are showcased; however, Spoleto is also an exciting opportunity for new artists and new works, and the festival generates a wide variety of activity. An imaginative spinoff to the Spoleto Festival is Piccolo Spoleto (piccolo is Italian for "small"), a festival that runs concurrently with Spoleto and features a full spectrum of artistic events, many of which are free to the public. Children and adults alike enjoy face-painting, jazz concerts, street musicians, organ and chamber music recitals, and street fairs. The festival celebrated its 35th year in 2013.

The city hosts many other events throughout the year. Begun in 1984, the MOJA Arts Festival is held for two weeks in late September and early October; Moja, the Swahili word meaning "the first" or "one," aptly describes this festival, which features the rich heritage of the African continent presented through dance, theater, films, lectures, and music. For one weekend in mid-February, Charleston hosts the Southeastern Wildlife Exposition; the largest show of its kind, the exposition brings more than 500 wildlife artists and artisans to a show of crafts, wildlife arts, and collectibles in Charleston's historic buildings. Also in February is the Lowcountry Blues Bash, a week-long festival featuring authentic blues music in selected clubs, hotels and restaurants. Spring Jam Music Fest, intended to inaugurate the spring, started in 2013 for two days in March. Charleston's International Film Festival runs each year for five days in April; international film makers exhibit their work in restored eighteenth-century theaters and other historic buildings.

The city's architectural heritage is showcased at various times throughout the year. Each March and April the Historic Charleston Foundation sponsors the Festival of Houses and Gardens, a series of walking tours of private homes and gardens in Charleston's historic district; in October the Preservation Society of Charleston sponsors the Fall Candlelight Tour of Homes and Gardens, which includes walking tours of private houses and gardens in the historic district. Tickets for these tours, which are considered the best way to get an intimate view of the city, are highly sought after.

Other Charleston-area festivals include the Lowcountry Oyster Festival in late January; September's Scottish Games and Highland Gathering; and the Christmas in Charleston Festival, with its parade of boats, held every mid-November through mid-January. In April visitors can enjoy a little taste of Louisiana at the Charleston Lowcountry Cajun Festival at James Island County Park, featuring live Zydeco and Cajun music, authentic food, crafts, and activities for children. Also in April is the World Grits Festival in St. George. The Charleston Harbor Fest in May features tours of tall ships, shipyard tours, model ships, and family boatbuilding. The city also hosts a Chanukah celebration for Jewish residents.

Sports for the Spectator

Baseball fans can watch the Charleston RiverDogs, a New York Yankees South Atlantic league, Single-A affiliate, face opponents at Joseph P. Riley, Jr. Park, often referred to as The Joe. Fans of professional ice hockey enjoy the South Carolina Stingrays of the East Coast Hockey League; the team is affliated with the Boston Bruins of the National Hockey League. United Soccer Leagues

Pro, the league immediately below top-level Major League Soccer, is the forte of the Charleston Battery at Blackbaud Stadium on Daniel Island. Collegiate action is provided by teams fielded by the College of Charleston, The Citadel, and Charleston Southern University. The Family Circle Tennis Cup comes to Daniel Island in April.

Sports for the Participant

Almost any sport that can be enjoyed under the sun is found in the Charleston area with its warm sun and sea breezes. Golf, tennis, horseback riding, swimming, sailing, water skiing, snorkeling, clamming, crabbing, fishing, hunting, bird watching—all are available within minutes of the city. Many visitors to the area are attracted by the challenge of its world-famous golf courses, some of which have been designed by celebrated course designers such as Tom Fazio, Gary Player, Jack Nicklaus, and Robert Trent Jones. The area's breathtaking coastal terrain and Lowcountry woodlands offer great golfing. Many of the area's courses are on Isle of Palms, Kiawah, and Seabrook Islands. Charleston's Department of Recreation operates the Tennis Center, which offers lessons, drills, clinics, and league play, as well as sanctioned tournaments. Most of the numerous public and private tennis courts in and around Charleston employ resident professionals. Young people may participate in soccer, football, volleyball, basketball, indoor soccer, and tennis. Softball and soccer leagues are also popular for adults, as is running.

The challenging 10-K Cooper River Bridge Run is held each year in April and attracts nearly 40,000 runners, making it one of the largest 10-K events in the nation. For those who prefer the less strenuous activity of walking, several lovely parks invite strolling. Many of the parks have biking trails, and bicycles may be rented at several locations.

Charleston affords ample opportunity to pursue sports near, in, or on the water. The Charleston County Parks and Recreation Department operates nearly 100 parks covering about 12,000 acres, including Beachwalker Park at the south end of Kiawah Island, Palmetto Islands County Park, Folly Beach County Park, and James Island County Park, for the enjoyment of swimming, as well as bicycling and other sports. The six barrier island beaches have been called the finest in the world. The Santee-Cooper Lake beaches near Moncks Corner and St. Stephen, and the network of inlets, coves, and tidal creeks provide water skiers with seemingly endless waterways.

The public had access to 19 boat landings in the area as of 2013. The Charleston Maritime Center is a deepwater, full-service marina that also offers facilities for special events and festivals. Sailing is the most popular summer sport in Charleston. Regattas are held throughout the season, drawing sailors from the entire southeast coast. Charleston Race Week in the Charleston Harbor in April draws 100 sailboats and crews of 500 sailors to the city each year. Private marinas along the coast provide facilities for both large and small boats. Surf and pier fishing are popular pastimes, and boats heading for deep water are a common sight in Charleston Harbor. Freshwater fishing for the famous land-locked striped bass in the freshwater lakes of the Santee-Cooper is a challenge few anglers can resist, and in season crabbing and shrimping attract even novices.

The opportunity to bag quail, duck, and deer lures hunters to local hunting clubs. For those who hunt with binoculars and cameras, Bull Island, part of the Cape Romain National Wildlife Refuge, is a wintering ground for many species of migratory birds and a nesting area for sea turtles. Drum Island shelters the largest wading bird rookery in the eastern United States.

Shopping and Dining

Two focal points for shopping in Charleston are the historic City Market and King Street. The City Market underwent a three-year, $5.5 million renovation that completed in 2011. King Street, filled with upscale boutiques and antique shops, has welcomed some mainstream stores including the Apple Store, Cynthia Rowley, and Louis Vuitton. For a more unique experience, antiques shoppers in Charleston can choose from dozens of shops with items ranging from crystal, china, and English mahogany furniture to oriental rugs. Charleston Place offers 50,000 square feet of elegant shops. Specialty shops abound, stocked with imported sportswear, resort wear, perfume, fine jewelry, lingerie, housewares, candies, and other items. The Charleston Farmers Market in Marion Square, open Saturdays from April to December, is consistently ranked as a favorite outdoor event by locals. It brims with fresh vegetables, fruit, flowers, and locally prepared foods. Juried arts and crafts are also available, as are a variety of activities and amusements for children. The major malls are Citadel Mall, which contains three major anchors and more than 150 specialty shops, and Northwoods Mall, with more than 130 stores. Fountain Walk, Charleston's newest waterfront destination located at Aquarium Wharf, also has many shops and restaurants.

Eating well has long been a Southern tradition; in Charleston, however, that tradition was honored in homes, not in restaurants. The growth of tourism in the area has spurred development of new, first-rate eating establishments, and now visitors and locals alike reap the benefits: American, Southern, Chinese, Italian, French, Indian, Japanese, German, Greek, and Mexican cuisine are available. In historic Charleston the atmosphere lends a special touch to dining. Along Shem Creek in Mt. Pleasant Mt. Pleasant, SC, several seafood restaurants afford patrons a view of the shrimp boats

moving over the water, while another establishment south of the city is actually built on piers above the ocean. Almost all restaurants, regardless of ambience, feature seafood, a South Carolina staple. The nearby waters provide millions of pounds of seafood in a harvest that includes shrimp, crabs, oysters, mussels, clams, whiting, spot, mullet, red snapper, grouper, king mackerel, flounder, and catfish. Visitors to Charleston can sample the unique blend of continental recipes with African flavors known as Lowcountry cuisine. Lowcountry specialties include famous she-crab soup, Frogmore Stew (shrimp, sausage, and corn), soft shell crab, shrimp and grits, and red rice.

Visitor Information: Charleston Convention and Visitors Bureau, 423 King Street, Charleston SC 29403; telephone (800) 774-0006.

■ Convention Facilities

The largest meeting facility in Charleston is the Charleston Area Convention Center Complex. The center boasts a 77,000 square foot exhibition hall, a 25,000 square foot ballroom, 21 meeting rooms, and the attached 2,300-seat Performing Arts Theater. The 14,000-seat North Charleston Coliseum offers an additional 45,000 square feet of exhibition space and is connected by covered walkway to the convention center. Completing the complex is an adjacent 255-room Embassy Suites hotel which services the ballroom and meeting rooms at the Convention Center. The Gaillard Municipal Auditorium offers about 15,000 square feet of exhibit space, five meeting rooms, and a 2,726-seat theater.

Lodgings in the Charleston area range from small and medium hotels to gleaming full-range hostelries and provide more than 11,300 hotel rooms. Charleston Place hotel boasts a ballroom with a capacity of 1,700 people and 18 other rooms of varying capacities. In the heart of this historic district and adjacent to the City Market and King Street shops, Charleston Place contains a fitness center and a parking garage in addition to its 440 guest rooms. The Riviera at Charleston Place is the hotel's conference center located across the street, featuring 9,000 square feet of space, with an amphitheater, ballroom, and rooftop terrace.

Visitors who value history, luxury, and personal service will not be disappointed in Charleston, where numerous historic buildings have been restored and furnished with reproductions of Charleston antique furniture. These highly individualized accommodations couple old world, international charm with modern, expert, personal attention. For those who prefer to stay in a home when away from home, some 50 bed-and-breakfast accomodations are available. Next to its historic district, Charleston is best known for its nearby pristine barrier islands: Isle of Palms, Sullivan's Island, Folly Beach, Kiawah Island, and Seabrook Island, featuring top-rated resort amenities. Along with beachfront meeting facilities and conference rooms, seaside facilities offer opportunities for world-class golf, tennis, sailing, and fishing, plus secluded beach walks, nature safaris, and fine dining.

Convention Information: Charleston Convention and Visitors Bureau, 423 King Street, Charleston SC 29403; telephone (800) 774-0006. Charleston Area Convention Center Complex, 5000 Coliseum Drive, Charleston, SC 29418; telephone (843) 747-1882.

■ Transportation

Approaching the City

Visitors arriving at Charleston International Airport enjoy air exits, baggage claim area, and ground transportation facilities all on one level for speedy accommodation to and from the terminal complex. The airport is located in North Charleston adjacent to the Charleston Air Force Base and uses airport facilities and runways jointly with the U.S. Air Force. Six commercial airlines (American Airlines, Delta, jetBlue, US Airways, Southwest, and United) offer flights daily. The airport serves more than one million passengers annually through some 20,000 flights. Several private airports in the region accommodate corporate and private aircraft.

For those driving to Charleston, Interstate 26 is the primary artery into the city. Interstates 95, 77, 20, 85, and 40 all link to Interstate 26. U.S. Highway 52, paralleling I-26 west of Charleston, and U.S. Highway 701 both approach Charleston from the north. Interstate 526, the Mark Clark Expressway, is a 19-mile freeway that forms a semicircle across the region from St. John's Island in the west to east of the Cooper River. U. S. Highway 17 also leads into the city, with access facilitated by the eight-lane Arthur Ravenel Jr. Bridge over the Cooper River. Amtrak has a station in North Charleston.

Traveling in the City

The peninsular city of Charleston is laid out in a grid pattern; however, city blocks are not uniform in size or shape. The downtown historic district is bisected by King Street and Meeting Street. In the north, East Bay Street branches off Meeting Street and becomes East Battery Street and Murray Boulevard around the edge of the Battery. Ashley and Rutledge connect with the west end of Murray Boulevard. Major east–west streets are Calhoun, Broad, and Tradd.

Public bus service in Charleston is provided by the Charleston Area Regional Transportation Authority (CARTA) that offers 21 city routes. All CARTA buses include Rack and Ride service for bicyclists, with bike racks available that stow two bicycles at a time. This service is meant to encourage use of several bike lanes that have been added to main roads throughout the city, including one along Highway 61 from Drayton Elementary School to Bee's Ferry and throughout part of the West Ashley Greenway. Paratransit service is available through Tel-A-Ride. The Downtown Area Shuttle (DASH) trolley provides affordable and convenient transportation from the Visitors Center to various points throughout the Historic District. The Mount Pleasant Shuttle provides service from the airport to area hotels. Charleston is easily explored on foot.

■ Communications

Newspapers and Magazines

The Post & Courier, with a daily circulation of about 85,000 in 2012, is the main daily paper (morning) serving the entire Charleston Region and is the oldest daily newspaper in the South. The *Charleston Regional Business Journal* is published twice a month. The *Charleston City Paper* is an alternative weekly including news and entertainment. The *Charleston Jewish Voice* is published ten times a year to a base of about 2,500 households and includes local, national, and international news affecting Jewish communities. *The Catholic Miscellany* is published weekly with subscriptions arriving by mail. Magazines published in Charleston include *Lowcountry Parent Magazine* (monthly), *South Carolina Historical Magazine* (quarterly), and *Charleston Magazine* (a bi-monthly lifestyle and entertainment publication).

Television and Radio

The nine television stations broadcasting from the Charleston Region are mainly network affiliates; additional television viewing is available through cable service. The city's 12 FM and 9 AM radio stations broadcast educational, sports, religious, public, and special interest programming in addition to music ranging from popular and country-western to jazz and classical.

Media Information: *The Post & Courier,* 134 Columbus Street, Charleston, SC 29403; telephone (843) 577-7111.

Charleston Online

Charleston: A National Register of Historic Places Travel Itinerary. Available www.nps.gov/NR/travel/charleston

Charleston Area Convention Center Complex. Available www.charlestonconvention.com

Charleston Area Regional Transportation Authority (CARTA). Available www.ridecarta.com

Charleston Convention and Visitors Bureau. Available www.charlestoncvb.com

Charleston County Library. Available www.ccpl.org

Charleston Metro Chamber of Commerce. Available www.charlestonchamber.net

Charleston Regional Development Alliance. Available www.crda.org

City of Charleston. Available www.charleston-sc.gov

The Post & Courier. Available www.postandcourier.com

BIBLIOGRAPHY

Hynson, Jerry M.*Free Negroes of Charleston, South Carolina 1841–1842* (Lewes, DE: Colonial Roots, 2012)

Jones, Robert A., *Common Blood: The Life and Times of an Immigrant Family in Charleston, South Carolina* (Philadelphia: Xlibris, 2012)

Vlach, John Michael, *Charleston Blacksmith: The Work of Philip Simmons* (Columbia, SC: University of South Carolina Press, 1992)

Columbia

■ The City in Brief

Founded: 1786 (chartered 1805)

Head Official: Mayor Steve Benjamin (D) (since 2010; current term expires 2014)

City Population
> 1990: 110,734
> 2000: 116,278
> 2010: 129,272
> 2012 estimate: 131,303
> Percent change, 2000–2010: 11.2%
> U.S. rank in 1990: 203rd
> U.S. rank in 2000: 198th (State rank: 1st)
> U.S. rank in 2010: 191st (State rank: 1st)

Metropolitan Statistical Area Population
> 2000: 647,158
> 2010: 767,598
> 2012 estimate: 785,641
> Percent change, 2000–2010: 18.6%
> U.S. rank in 2000: 73rd
> U.S. rank in 2010: 70th

Area: 125 square miles

Elevation: Ranges from 200 to 350 feet above sea level

Average Annual Temperatures: 65° F

Average Annual Precipitation: 50.14 inches

Major Economic Sectors: government, health care, academic research, agriculture, advanced manufacturing, insurance

Unemployment Rate: 6.4% (2012)

Per Capita Income: $22,621

Major Colleges and Universities: University of South Carolina, Benedict College, Columbia College

Daily Newspaper: *The State*

■ Introduction

The capital city of South Carolina is a major industrial, cultural, and educational center located in the heart of a fertile farm region. The romance of the nineteenth century is writ large in the buildings and historical markers that grace its broad, tree-lined streets. Chosen as a compromise site for the interests of wealthy low-country planters and fiercely independent small farmers and merchants from the hill country, this city located directly in the center of the state was specifically designed to serve as its seat of government. From the beautifully preserved antebellum architecture, to the riverbanks and swamps, to the State House with its battle-scarred walls and rich interiors, Columbia is an enchanting city. In an effort to diversify its economy away from state and local government jobs, Columbia has sought to transition into a research center, relying in part on the more than $200 million of annual research conducted at the University of South Carolina, located in the heart of the city.

■ Geography and Climate

Columbia is situated near the geographic center of South Carolina, midway between New York City and Miami. Set near the "fall line" dividing the South Carolina Piedmont and Coast Plains, the rolling hills surrounding the city slope from approximately 350 feet above sea level in the city's northernmost part to 200 feet above sea level in the southeast. The Appalachian and Blue Ridge Mountains northwest of the city often delay the approach of cold weather, and the winters are mild with the lowest temperatures extending from November to mid-March. Below-freezing temperatures are experienced during only one-third of the winter days. Nearly every year brings one day with a one-inch snowfall. Temperatures in spring

The South Carolina State House in Columbia. *Lee Barnwell/BigStockPhoto.com*

range from March's occasional cold snap to warm, pleasant days in much of May. Long summers are the norm, and short-lived late afternoon thundershowers a common occurrence. Typically, there are about six days of over-100-degrees weather in summer, but the heat is eased by frequent summer showers. Sunny days and lack of rain characterize Columbia's typically beautiful fall weather.

Area: 125 square miles

Elevation: Ranges from 200 to 350 feet above sea level

Average Temperatures: 65° F

Average Annual Precipitation: 50.14 inches

■ History

Located at the Middle of South Carolina

The city of Columbia was carved out of the countryside by order of the state legislature, which wanted to establish a new capital more centrally situated than Charleston. By that time, the area had been important in the state's development for more than a century. Early settlers were mostly Scots-Irish, German, and English farmers who moved to the hills of northwestern South Carolina, having little in common with the wealthy planters of Charleston. "The Congarees," a frontier fort on the river's west bank, was the head of navigation on the Santee River system. In 1754 a ferry service was initiated to connect the fort with the settlement that was developing on the east bank's higher ground.

The new capital, named Columbia in honor of Christopher Columbus, was set on Taylor's Hill where the Broad and Saluda rivers merge to form the Congaree River. The General Assembly moved to Columbia in 1791. History tells of a visit by George Washington during that year as part of his tour of South Carolina.

Development of America's First "Planned City"

One of the first planned cities in America, Columbia was laid out in a two-mile square surrounding the site of the State House. The city's streets, designed in a grid, were named for heroes of the Revolution and for the state's agricultural products, such as rice, wheat, blossom, and indigo.

By the early 1880s the town had become an agricultural center, and soon the state had become the leading cotton producer in the nation. The first textile mill was introduced in 1832, and saw mills, cotton gins, tanneries, carriage manufacturers, and iron foundries were soon to follow. With the establishment of steamship connections to the Congaree and Santee rivers, many of the city's cotton merchants handled shipments that earlier had moved overland to the port at Charleston. South Carolina College (now the University of South Carolina) was founded in 1801, and the ensuing close relationship between the college, the city, and the legislature endures to the present day.

By mid-century, the local economy was strengthened by growing accessibility to the eastern United States via the railroad. A distinctive style of architecture, known as Columbia Cottage, had emerged. To help assuage the often unpleasant summer heat, builders designed a structure to maximize the effect of natural breezes. The building featured a raised cottage with an enclosed basement above the ground, halls from front to back, windows that reached the floor, and ceilings often 15 feet high.

Civil War Brings Destruction

Columbia, with a population of 8,000, was the site of the First Secession Convention and was instrumental in establishing the Confederacy and keeping it supplied with uniforms, swords, cannonballs, and other supplies over the course of the Civil War. The city was destroyed by the fiery rampage of General William T. Sherman in 1865, which left almost everything in ruins except the university. Reconstruction was a time of great hardship, but by the 1890s the city finally reemerged as a center of agricultural commerce.

Major Fort Important to City

By 1900 large cotton mills had been built and nearly 9,000 people worked in the city's mill district. The period prior to World War I and until the Great Depression of the 1930s was one of prosperity. Trade was growing, banks and hospitals multiplied, and the city became the state's business center. East of the city the U.S. Army built Fort Jackson, presently one of the country's largest infantry training bases. Thanks to a diversified economy, the city survived the Great Depression without as much pain as some other areas of the country. Between 1940 and 1950 the population grew by more than one-third, in part due to Fort Jackson's role in the training of soldiers for World War II.

Economic and Social Progress Made Since Mid-Century

By the post-War 1950s, small and medium-sized factories were developing, and new industries such as electronics, military equipment, textiles, cameras, and structural steel further diversified the economy. During the period of the civil rights struggle in the 1960s, Mayor Lester Bates and a biracial committee of 60 citizens worked together to quietly and systematically encourage the desegregation of the city. By 1963 the university was integrated, and in 1964, 24 African American students entered previously all-white public schools.

The 1970s saw the creation of downtown's Main Street Mall and the completion of Riverbanks Zoological Park. In subsequent years Riverfront Park was developed, the Koger Center for Performing Arts opened, and new interstate highways made the city even more accessible regionally and nationally. Today, development in Columbia has attempted to improve downtown streetscapes and make the area's river system more accessible and enjoyable for residents. Uneven development at the Innovista research facility, a joint venture between the public university and private businesses, offered glimpses of the cutting-edge, high-technology future Columbia continued to seek.

Historical Information: South Carolina Department of Archives and History, Archives and History Center, 8301 Parklane Rd., Columbia, SC 29223; telephone (803) 896-6104. South Carolina Confederate Relic Room and Military Museum, Columbia Mills Building, 301 Gervais Street, Columbia, SC 29201; telephone (803) 737-8095.

■ Population Profile

Metropolitan Statistical Area Population
2000: 647,158
2010: 767,598
2012 estimate: 785,641
Percent change, 2000–2010: 18.6%
U.S. rank in 2000: 73rd
U.S. rank in 2010: 70th

City Residents
1990: 110,734
2000: 116,278
2010: 129,272
2012 estimate: 131,303
Percent change, 2000–2010: 11.2%
U.S. rank in 1990: 203rd
U.S. rank in 2000: 198th (State rank: 1st)
U.S. rank in 2010: 191st (State rank: 1st)

Density: 977.8 people per square mile

Racial and ethnic characteristics
White: 65,433
Black or African American: 56,840
American Indian and Alaskan Native: 0
Asian: 2,752
Native Hawaiian and Other Pacific Islander: 158
Hispanic or Latino (may be of any race): 8,690
Other: 6,120

Percent of residents born in state: 57%

Age characteristics

Population under 5 years old: 7,691
Population 5 to 9 years old: 7,161
Population 10 to 14 years old: 6,680
Population 15 to 19 years old: 15,355
Population 20 to 24 years old: 20,580
Population 25 to 34 years old: 22,410
Population 35 to 44 years old: 13,407
Population 45 to 54 years old: 13,887
Population 55 to 59 years old: 6,973
Population 60 to 64 years old: 4,780
Population 65 to 74 years old: 6,572
Population 75 to 84 years old: 3,566
Population 85 years and over: 2,241
Median age: 28.1

Births (2010–11 Metropolitan Area)

Total number: 9,771

Deaths (2010–11 Metropolitan Area)

Total number: 5,984

Money income (2012)

Per capita income: $22,621
Median household income: $40,501
Total households: 44,324

Number of households with income of ...

less than $10,000: 4,960
$10,000 to $14,999: 3,606
$15,000 to $24,999: 5,842
$25,000 to $34,999: 5,513
$35,000 to $49,999: 6,367
$50,000 to $74,999: 7,182
$75,000 to $99,999: 3,973
$100,000 to $149,999: 3,674
$150,000 to $199,999: 1,360
$200,000 or more: 1,847

Percent of families below poverty level: 23.5%

■ Municipal Government

The city of Columbia has a mayor-council form of government, established in 1950. The mayor is elected at large and there are six council members, four elected from districts and two elected at large; all are elected to staggered four-year terms.

Head Official: Mayor Steve Benjamin (D) (since 2010; current term expires 2014)

Total Number of City Employees: 2,651 (2012)

City Information: Columbia City Hall, 1737 Main Street, PO Box 147, Columbia, SC 29217; telephone (803)545-3000

■ Economy

Major Industries and Commercial Activity

Columbia prides itself on a diverse and stable economy based on jobs in local and state government, manufacturing, and services, and on being the site of the Fort Jackson military base. In recent years, distribution, manufacturing, and research and development have increased that diversity. The city relies on its technology infrastructure, active entrepreneurial community, major research university, and diverse quality of life to attract and keep new business. Columbia serves as a service center for the insurance, telecommunications, computer, and real estate industries. The headquarters of SCANA, a *Fortune* 500 company that supplies energy to the Carolinas and Georgia, is located in nearby Cayce, South Carolina. Dozens of international companies from Australia, France, Italy, Germany, the United Kingdom, Denmark, Japan, South Korea, Belgium, Luxembourg, Taiwan, and Canada have operations in the region. In 2012 the region's largest employers were a mix of healthcare, government, and university sectors.

The University of South Carolina in downtown Columbia bolsters the economy through the expenditures of its more than 31,000 students. In 2013 the University unveiled its Office of Economic Engagement to support economic development in the area through coordination of faculty research and private businesses. Fort Jackson, located within the city's boundaries, employed nearly 3,500 civilians in 2013 and spent more than $700 million annually for salaries, utilities, contracts and other services, much of it in Columbia. It hires local firms for construction work and buys its supplies from local businesses.

Ample rainfall and the temperate climate promote the area's success as an agricultural center. The wholesale trade industry, which began its growth in the years prior to World War I, benefits from the fact that approximately 70 percent of the nation's population and 70 percent of its industrial/commercial power are within 24-hour ground access.

Items and goods produced: electronics, military equipment, marine products, chemicals, processed foods

Incentive Programs-New and Existing Companies

Local programs: The City of Columbia Office of Economic Development stands ready to provide a wide range of services to companies interested in the Columbia region; incentives range from new business tax incentives to site planning. The University of South Carolina technology incubator helps recruit, develop, and launch high-tech companies. Business partnerships between the university and private companies occur through the university's Office of Economic Engagement. It provides office and laboratory space for innovation-focused businesses and startups at the Innovista Research District. The Central SC Alliance is a public/private partnership engaged in the recruitment of capital investment and jobs to the Columbia region.

State programs: The following incentives and financing sources may be available to qualifying companies: Job Development Credit that rebates a portion of new employee's withholding taxes for use to address specific needs of a company; Economic Development Set-Aside Program to improve infrastructure surrounding new or expanding businesses; Enterprise Zone Retraining Credit Program to subsidize the cost of retraining workers; Rural Infrastructure Fund to further economic development in remote areas; Port Volume Increase Credit for companies that increase port cargo volume by at least 5 percent; and Tourism Infrastructure Development Grants to complete infrastructure projects that support new tourist developments. Additional credits include a Job Tax Credit, Economic Impact Zone Investment Credit, Corporate Headquarters Credit, and Research and Development Tax Credit. South Carolina's 5 percent corporate income tax is one of the lowest in the region.

Job training programs: The South Carolina Technical College System provides an array of job-training programs throughout the state. The readySC program, established in 1961, trains employees for several industries, including aerospace, automotive, biotech, and call centers. Apprenticeship Carolina, also part of the state's technical college system, provides consulting at no charge to employers and assists employers in training their workforce in technological, health-care, and transportation industries, among others. In Columbia, the Midlands Education and Business Alliance operates as a not-for-profit in Richland, Lexington, and Fairfield counties, offering pre-employment, internships, and worker training programs to seven area colleges and nine school districts.

Development Projects

Attracting area residents to live and work in Columbia is a main objective of the city's Office of Economic Development. The Three Rivers Greenway is a multi-year, ongoing partnership of city and county governments and other area institutions to develop a 12-mile linear park system for the 90-mile interconnecting Saluda, Congaree, and Broad Rivers. Conceived in 1995, the River Alliance has constructed parks, river walks, an amphitheater, bike lane, running trail, housing communities, and water sport activities along the rivers. As of 2013, some nine-and-one-half miles had been constructed.

In 2006, construction began on Columbia's newest development project, Innovista, a $144 million research park affiliated with the University of South Carolina. The

project sought to tap into the university's research initiatives in nanotechnology, health sciences, Future Fuels, the environment, and information and knowledge technologies, to attract private companies into the complex. However, the project struggled to attract technology companies and create the high-tech jobs promised by the taxpayer investment. Two buildings in the complex, one supporting biomedical research and the other focsued on next-generation energy intiatives, were expected to be completed and filled with tenants by 2014. Construction plans for two additional buildings supported by private investment failed in the wake of a recession during the late 2000s, as well as mismanagement.

South Carolina's former state mental hospital, a 165-acre lot sold to private developers for $15 million in 2010, offered the potential for considerable economic development into the 2020s. Developers planned to convert the former medical campus into a shopping and dining area in four phases through the early 2030s. Once complete, the area was expected to generate $1.2 billion in annual economic activity, as well as $20 million in local tax revenue. Initial criticism of plans to establish several "big box" retailers in the area led to changes that focused development on smaller retailers and independent restaurants. The city was scheduled to contribute millions to support surrounding infrastructure, including improvements to streets and sewers, and a new parking garage.

Economic Development Information: Economic Development Division, Greater Columbia Chamber of Commerce, 930 Richland Street, Columbia, SC 29201; telephone (803) 733-1155; fax (803)733-1149. Office of Economic Development—Columbia; 1201 Main Street, Suite 250, Columbia, SC 29201; telephone (803) 734-2700; fax (803) 734-2702; email development@columbiasc.net.

Commercial Shipping

With the benefit of its location where three major interstate highways cross within its regional boundaries and two rail systems operate, Columbus is positively positioned for businesses that require major transportation access. The Columbia Metropolitan Airport handles more than 168,000 tons of cargo annually. The airport's Foreign Trade Zone #127 is a 108-acre tract with a 40,000 square foot warehouse and office building and an additional 52,000 square feet of multi-tenant space. The U.S. Customs Services offices, Port of Columbia, are also located in this zone along with several Custom House brokers. Columbia is served by nine major motor freight carriers and is the site of United Parcel Service's southeastern regional air cargo hub, ensuring low costs and timely delivery for local industry. Charleston, the second busiest seaport on the east coast, is just 110 miles away.

Labor Force and Employment Outlook

Columbia boasts a large and growing workforce, especially in the 20–40 age group. Many retirees from Fort Jackson choose to stay in the area, adding skill and maturity to the available workforce. Workers are described as efficient and productive, and work stoppages are rare. South Carolina is a right-to-work state and was the country's second least-unionized state as of 2013. According to the Columbia Office of Economic Development, South Carolina's workforce consistently ranked in the top five nationally for productivity.

The following is a summary of data regarding the Columbia labor force:

Size of civilian labor force: 61,313

Number of workers employed in ...

agriculture and mining: 302
construction: 2,020
manufacturing: 2,441
wholesale trade: 1,094
retail trade: 5,646
transportation: 1,148
information systems: 1,188
finance: 4,468
professional administration: 5,721
education and social services: 15,286
arts and leisure: 7,772
other: 2,232
public administration: 4,000

Average hourly earnings of production workers: $15.41

Unemployment rate: 6.4% (2012)

Employers

Largest employers (2012)	*Number of employees*
Palmetto Health	9,000
University of South Carolina	8,717
South Carolina Department of Mental Health	4,917
South Carolina Department of Transportation	4,553
Richland County School District One	4,036
South Carolina Department of Health and Environmental Control	3,445
City of Columbia	2,651
Sisters of Charity Providence Hospital	2,075
Richland County	1,708
Dorn VA Medical Center	1,457

Cost of Living

Columbia maintained a cost of living slightly below the national average in 2013.

The following is a summary of data regarding several key cost of living factors in the area.

2013 ACCRA Average House Price: $216,008

2013 ACCRA Cost of Living Index: 97

State income tax rate: 0.0% to 7.0%

State sales tax rate: 6.0%

Local income tax rate: None

Local sales tax rate: 1.0%

Property tax rate: 0.5023 mills (2012)

Economic Information: Greater Columbia Chamber of Commerce, 930 Richland Street, Columbia, SC 29201; telephone (803) 733-1155; fax (803)733-1149.

■ Education and Research

Elementary and Secondary Schools

Richland County has three school districts: Richland County School Districts One and Two and School District Five of Lexington and Richland Counties. Most students in Columbia are served through Richland County School District One (RDO), with some Columbia schools sponsored by Richland County School District Two (RDT). The system offers Advanced Academic Programs like Mathematics Education for Gifted Secondary School Students in grades 6 to 12 and a more general Advanced Academic Program (AAP) for gifted and talented students in grades 3 to 12. A special High School Scholars program, available to students in grades 9 and 10, includes a curriculum of AAP and advanced placement classes and special requirements for extracurricular activities, fine arts, credits, and community service. Students who successfully complete the requirements of the program receive a special diploma upon graduation. A Middle School Scholars program also exists. Special-needs students receive support from a full continum of special education programs, available from early grades through post-secondary transitional periods.

Palmetto Center for the Arts, part of Richland County School District Two (RDT), is a special magnet school in Columbia. Richland Northeast High School offers three upper-level magnet programs, including one in collaboration with the Palmetto Center for the Arts.

Greater Columbia is home to several private schools, including religious and Montessori schools.

The following is a summary of data regarding the Richland County School District.

Total enrollment: 22,659

Number of facilities

    total: 84

    elementary schools: 46

    junior high schools: 16

    high schools: 12

    other: 10

Student/teacher ratio: 11.39:1

Teacher salaries

    average (statewide): $49,434

Funding per pupil: $11,944

Public Schools Information: Richland County School District One, Stevenson Administration Building, 1616 Richland Street, Columbia, SC 29201; telephone (803) 231-7000. Richland County School District Two, 6831 Brookfield Road, Columbia, SC 29206; telephone (803) 787-1910.

Colleges and Universities

The University of South Carolina (USC) has gained regional recognition for its programs in law, marketing, geography, medicine, marine science, nursing, engineering, business administration, and social work. The Columbia campus of South University offered 324 degree programs to its more than 30,000 students in 2013. The university's Darla Moore School of Business has been ranked consistently as one of the top programs in the nation by *U.S. News & World Report*. As of 2013 the university had an endowment in excess of $500 million.

The independent, Baptist-affiliated Benedict College, a traditionally African American college, offered four-year degrees in 34 majors to its nearly 3,000 students in 2013. Columbia College, a Methodist-affiliated women's liberal arts school, offers bachelor's of arts and science and master's of arts degrees in such areas as public affairs and human relations, business administration, and communications, as well as a coeducational Evening College and Graduate School. Columbia College has consistently been ranked as one of the best regional liberal arts colleges in the South by *U.S. News & World Report*. It attained a ranking of 46th for 2013. Allen University, an African Methodist Episcopal four-year college, offers liberal arts and teacher education. Columbia International University (CIU) is an

evangelical Bible college, graduate, school, and seminary. CIU is also home to the Zwemer Center for Muslim Studies, which provides resources for those seeking to learn more about Islam and for those who expect to minister in Islamic areas of the world. Lutheran Theological Southern Seminary, affiliated with the Evangelical Lutheran Church in America, is one of the oldest Lutheran seminaries in North America.

Midlands Technical College, a two-year multi-campus community college, offers technical and academic training. The Columbia Campus of South University offers associate's and bachelor's programs through its colleges of Arts & Sciences, Business, Health Professions, Nursing and Public Health, and Pharmacy.

Libraries and Research Centers

In addition to its main library, the Richland County Public Library has 10 branches. A fully renovated branch in Eastover reopened in 2013 after $1.6 million in improvements, including a state-of-the-art children's area. The library system circulated more than 5.3 million items in that same year. In addition to print materials, the library's collection includes microforms, audio cassettes/tapes, compact discs, CD-ROM titles, maps, and art reproductions. Its special collections include a local history collection, large print books, and rare and out-of-print books. The library offers many programs for children and adults, including frequent lectures by authors. The library enjoys many programming partnerships with the University of South Carolina (USC), the Historic Columbia Foundation, and the Cultural Council of Richland and Lexington counties. Since 1987 it has co-sponsored the annual A(ugusta) Baker's Dozen—a Celebration of Stories with the College of Library and Information Science Department at USC. The celebration honors Augusta Baker and features well-known, award-winning authors and illustrators of children's books and outstanding storytellers each year.

In partnership with the library of Columbia International University, the Zwemer Center holds more than 5,000 volumes dedicated to Islam, its history, theology, language, and culture, and on Christian understanding of Islam in various contexts. The Center is a community of Christian scholars, teachers, and students devoted to Muslim-Christian relations.

Also located in Columbia is the South Carolina State Library, which houses about 313,000 volumes, more than 2,200 periodical subscriptions, and 621,000 microforms, plus government publications, and audio visual materials. Its special collections include a Grants Research Collection, South Carolina collection, and a Talking Book collection of more than 337,000 items, as well as official state documents. Many state library programs are supported by grants from the U.S Institute of Museum and Library Services. The University of South Carolina campus library system has more than two million volumes, as well special collections such as the Irvin Departemtn of Rare Books and Special Collections, with more than 150,000 items, and the Moving Image Research Collections, with more than 6,000 hours of local television news, commercials, home movies, and other films.

Many of Columbia's research centers are affiliated with USC. More than 100 institutes and centers comprise the university's research effort. Notable among these is the NanoCenter which is engaged in researching the applications of the world's smallest electronic circuits. Others include the Center for Information Technology Implementation Assistance, the Institute for Families in Society, the Future Fuels program, and the Earth Sciences and Resources Institute. There are also several ongoing biomedical research programs at USC. In all, USC obtained $220 in sponsored research awards during 2013.

Public Library Information: Richland County Public Library, 1431 Assembly Street, Columbia, SC 29201; telephone (803) 799-9084. South Carolina State Library, Information and Resource Center, 1500 Senate Street, Columbia, SC 29211; telephone (803) 734-8666.

■ Health Care

The city of Columbia prides itself on being a regional leader in providing quality health-care services. The University of South Carolina School of Medicine adds invaluable research and training resources. The university is one of the few in the country offering a graduate program in genetic counseling. Palmetto Health Alliance is the state's largest and most comprehensive health-care systems; its institutions in Columbia include Palmetto Health Richland, a 649-bed regional community teaching hospital serving all of South Carolina, and Palmetto Health Baptist, with 489 beds. The Palmetto Health South Carolina Cancer Center works in collaboration with researchers at the University of South Carolina and physicians from both Palmetto hospitals to provide comprehensive cancer care programs. The Palmetto Health Heart Hospital, with 124 all-private beds, opened in 2006 as the state's first freestanding hospital dedicated only to heart care. Palmetto Health Children's Hospital, opened in 1983, includes 30 medical subspecialties and treats nearly 80,000 children annually.

The Dorn Veterans Affairs Medical Center complex includes a 216-bed hospital and seven community outpatient clinics located in Anderson, Florence, Greenville, Orangeburg, Rock Hill, Sumter, and Spartanburg. The hospital saw 73,690 patients in 2012.

Other Columbia hospitals are the G. Werber Bryan Psychiatric Hospital for adults; and the Moncrief Army Community Hospital in Fort Jackson, among others. Also serving the health-care needs of Columbia-area residents are Fairfield Memorial Hospital located in Winnsboro; Providence Hospital and the Providence Heart & Vascular Institute, a nationally recognized referral center for the diagnosis, prevention, and treatment of cardiovascular disease; and the 414-bed Lexington Medical Center in West Columbia, offering specialized care for breast cancer and prostate problems, plus advanced cardiac, vascular and pulmonary rehabilitation, outpatient surgery, a state-of-the-art emergency department, outpatient surgery and diagnostics, radiation oncology, radiology, surgery, and physical therapy.

■ Recreation

Sightseeing

Columbia has an interesting array of historical, cultural, and recreational sites to delight both visitors and residents. Consistently rated as one of the top travel attractions in the Southeast, the Riverbanks Zoo and Garden is home to more than 2,000 mammals, reptiles, fish, and invertebrates, representing in excess of 350 species. Animals roam freely in the zoo's unique recreated environments, such as the two-acre African savanna. Visitors can watch the daily feeding of penguins and sea lions. Across the Saluda River from the zoo, the Riverbanks Botanical Garden features 70 acres of woodlands, gardens, historic ruins, and plant collections.

The EdVenture Children's Museum opened to the public in November 2003. The $19.4 million facility is located next to the South Carolina State Museum and features 74,000 square feet of hands-on exhibit space in eight indoor and outdoor galleries, as well as laboratories and other visitor amenities. Special exhibit areas are designed to appeal to very young children, although the museum serves children up to age 12. It receives funding from a mix of donor support, admission receipts, city and county government funding, earned revenue, and educational programming.

The Historic Columbia Foundation conducts bus and walking tours of the city and heritage education programs. An especially popular sight is Governor's Green, a nine-acre complex made up of the 1830 Caldwell-Boylston House, the 1854 Lace House, and Governor's Mansion, home to the state's first family since 1868. Other historic houses are the Hampton-Preston Mansion, an elegant, restored antebellum society home, and the fully restored and furnished boyhood home of Woodrow Wilson. The State Archives has contemporary exhibits and houses the state and county official records. The South Carolina Law Enforcement Officers Hall of Fame traces the history of law enforcement, including the gun collection of Melvin Purvis, the FBI agent who captured John Dillinger. The Robert Mills Historic House and Park, designed by the state's most famous architect, has been refurbished with period pieces and has park gardens covering an entire block.

Arts and Culture

Columbia boasts an active arts environment. The showcase of Columbia's cultural sites is the Ira & Nancy Koger Center for the Arts, an acoustically excellent facility with three-tier seating for 2,254 patrons. The center is home to the South Carolina Philharmonic, Broadway in Columbia, Columbia City Ballet, and the University of South Carolina symphony.

Theater in its many forms is available from the city's robust theater community. The 312-seat Longstreet Theatre, an 1855 Greek Revival structure, is the site for many University of South Carolina–sponsored productions at its theater-in-the-round. Trustus Theatre presents quality alternative productions with a different show each month. The Town Theatre stages Broadway comedies and musicals. The Workshop Theatre offers modern and classical productions by its amateur group. The Chapin Community Theatre performs plays for children as well as musicals and dramatic productions. The South Carolina Shakespeare Company performs in September and October at Finlay Park. Columbia Marionette Theatre is one of only 20 such theaters in the country.

The Columbia Museum of Art is the city's premier museum, maintaining 25 galleries that attract more than 120,000 visitors annually. The museum also offers a hands-on children's gallery and traveling exhibits, as well as European and American works of the eighteenth and nineteenth centuries, decorative arts, and contemporary crafts. The South Carolina State Museum, located in a renovated textile mill, contains a comprehensive array of exhibits on art, natural history, and science and technology. The Mann-Simons Cottage is a fine example of the Columbia Cottage style of architecture and includes an outdoor museum with remnants of other period structures. An excavation of the site that concluded in 2012 uncovered some 60,000 artifacts, many of which are on display inside the house. The Confederate Relic Room and Military Museum contains relics from the Colonial period to the Space Age, with special emphasis on Civil War objects.

The original 1801 campus of the University of South Carolina is today known as the Historic Horseshoe. It has been restored and is open for tours. There visitors will find the McKissick Museum, which features changing exhibitions of art, science, and regional history and folk art; as well as the Baruch Silver Collection, the Mineral Library, and Fluorescent Minerals and Gemstones. The U.S. Army Basic Combat Training Museum at Fort Jackson, formerly the Fort Jackson Museum, details the evolution of training methods throughout U.S. military history. Memorial Park is the site of the South Carolina Vietnam Monument, the largest monument of its type outside Washington, D.C.

Festivals and Holidays

The wearin' of the green is a common sight at the parade, children's areas, and arts and music events that highlight Columbia's St. Patrick's Day Festival in Five Points. The Earth Day festival in Finlay Park brings together environmental booths and traditional festival favorites. Dance, arts and crafts, music, and a road race combine to celebrate spring's Mayfest. The spectacle of decorated boats, a parade, and fireworks light up the July Fourth celebration at Lake Murray. Peanuts galore—roasted, boiled and raw—are the stars of August's South Carolina Peanut Party. Columbia's music festivals include the Three Rivers Music Festival in July. One of the biggest events in Columbia is the ten-day South Carolina State Fair in October, which draws more than one-half million visitors. The fair features agricultural and handicraft displays, rides, and entertainment. Jubilee: Festival of Heritage celebrates African American heritage with crafts, storytelling, music and dance. Vista Lights festival combines walking tours of area homes and musical entertainment with carriage rides through the antique district. The Christmas season is ushered in by December's Christmas Candlelight Tour of Historic Houses, and Lights Before Christmas at the Riverbanks Zoo. The World Beer Festival in January is recognized as one of the premier beer events in the United States.

Sports for the Spectator

The University of South Carolina's Fighting Gamecocks play football at the Williams-Brice Stadium. The university's baseball team won back-to-back NCAA Division I national championships in 2010 and 2011. Male and female intercollegiate sports teams from other local colleges offer sporting opportunities for spectators. The Columbia Inferno, a professional hockey team in the East Coast Hockey League, have been on voluntary leave since 2009. Although they were expected to resume playing when a new arena in Lexington County was completed, the team remained inactive as of 2013. Teams from Major League baseball, National Football League, National Hockey League, and National Basketball Association all play within easy driving distance in nearby Charlotte or Atlanta.

Sports for the Participant

Columbia's mild climate encourages outdoor recreation year-round. Water skiers, campers, windsurfers, fishermen, boating enthusiasts, bikers, and runners enjoy the myriad regional and municipal parks in and around Columbia. Lake Murray boasts 540 miles of scenic shoreline perfect for boaters of all types. Dreher Island State Park on its shores offers RV and primitive camping, fishing, boating and swimming. Columbia's Saluda River, a navigable whitewater river with thrilling rides down the rapids, also offers gentler waters for canoeists and rafters. The 1,445-acre Sesquicentennial State Park offers nature trails, camping and picnic sites, swimming, fishing, and miniature golf. The Congaree National Park and Monument, located 20 miles southeast of the city, is a national monument offering nature walks and self-guided canoe trails affording views of old-growth bottomland hardwood forest.

The City of Columbia maintains nearly 60 parks and green spaces, 55 tennis courts, and 16 pools. Finlay Park in the downtown area is host to many festivals and celebrations. Granby Park is the gateway to the rivers in Columbia. Memorial Park is a tribute to those South Carolinians who served their country. Soccer enthusiasts enjoy the nine fields located at Owens Field Park. Winding along the Congaree River is the Riverfront Park and Historic Columbia Canal. Planned around the city's original 1906 waterworks plant, the park features an old pump house and jogging and bicycle paths. City and county parks offer organized baseball, youth and adult basketball, youth football, soccer, softball, volleyball, racquetball, and roller skating, as well as a variety of other activities. Twenty-two public and private golf courses serve the greater Columbia area. Several local private golf clubs offer special golf packages to visitors. The Charles R. Drew Wellness Center offers indoor swimming, jogging, and weight training. The Strom Thurmond Wellness & Fitness Center, opened in 2003 on the University of South Carolina's campus, offers exceptional facilities to the student body.

Shopping and Dining

Shopping is a many-dimensional affair in a city that offers spacious malls, fashionable boutiques, specialty stores, antique shops, and antique malls. The most popular shopping center is Columbiana Centre, with more than 100 specialty shops. Columbia Place is the region's largest, offering more than 100 specialty stores. Old Mill Antique Mall in West Columbia and City Market Antiques Mall offer out-of-the-ordinary shopping experiences. The Village at Sandhill provides upscale shopping and dining options to residents of northeast Columbia. The State Farmers Market is one of the largest produce markets in the southeast. In 2010 it moved from the Williams-Brice Stadium to West Columbia.

Dining out in Columbia presents myriad possibilities, from the fresh seafood provided by its proximity to the state's Atlantic Coast, to a variety of ethnic cuisines such as Greek, Chinese, Cajun, or Japanese, as well as traditional Southern. Southern cooking favorites may include tasty barbecue, vegetable casseroles, sweet potato pie, biscuits and gravy, red beans and rice, country fried steak, pecan pie, and the ever-popular fried chicken. From simple lunchtime fare to haute cuisine, the area boasts quality restaurant fare. Columbia's Main Street, Five Points, and the Congaree Vista neighborhoods draw visitors to their nightlife.

Visitor Information: Columbia Metropolitan Convention & Visitors Bureau, 1101 Lincoln Street, PO Box 15, Columbia, SC 29202; telephone (803) 545-0000; toll-free (800) 264-4884.

■ Convention Facilities

The Columbia Metropolitan Convention Center opened in summer 2004 in the historic downtown Vista area. It features 142,500 square feet of space including a 25,000-square-foot exhibit hall, 18,000-square-foot ballroom, divisible meeting rooms, and a full banquet kitchen. Columbia's Carolina Coliseum offers 60,000 square feet of exhibit space and seats 12,000 for sporting events. The South Carolina State Fairgrounds accommodates up to 3,000 delegates in 100,000 square feet of space. The Township Auditorium has a stage and seats 3,099 people. Other area meeting facilities include Williams-Brice Stadium, Koger Center for the Arts, and Jamil Shrine Temple. Saluda Shoals Park offers a secluded 10,000-square-foot state-of-the-art facility on the shores of the Saluda River, located minutes from downtown. Columbia provides choice accommodations with more than 7,000 rooms in a variety of hotels and motels.

Convention Information: Columbia Metropolitan Convention & Visitors Bureau, 1101 Lincoln Street, PO Box 15, Columbia, SC 29202; telephone (803) 545-0000; toll-free (800) 264-4884.

■ Transportation

Approaching the City

Columbia is centrally located and easily accessible from cities throughout the state and the nation. Four airlines—American Eagle, Delta, United, and US Airways—serve Columbia Metropolitan Airport, which is located eight miles from downtown. Into the 2010s, the aiport averaged more than 400,000 passengers annually. The decade prior, it underwent a $3.1 million road improvement project and construction of a multilevel parking garage for 1,837 cars, plus an additional 1,668 uncovered spaces. Amtrak offers daily rail departures and arrivals from the Eastern seaboard from New York City to Miami. Three interstate highways, Interstates 20, 26, and 77) crisscross the city of Columbia, with two other major interstates, Interstaets 85 and 95, within an hour's drive. The area also has eight U.S. highways. Columbia is directly linked to Atlanta, GA; Richmond, VA; Jacksonville, FL; and Charlotte, NC, via these roadways. Greyhound/Trailways supplies inter-city bus service.

Traveling in the City

Columbia is an easily navigable city. While rush hour traffic is heavy on I-26 and other major thoroughfares, it most often moves steadily. Central Midlands Transit serves the heart of the Midlands, including Columbia, Cayce, West Columbia, Forest Acres, Arcadia Lakes, Springdale, and the St. Andrews area, with 17 fixed routes. It rebranded itself as the The COMET in 2013. Its services include the trolleys in Downtown Columbia and the DART service (Dial-a-Ride Transit). Several taxi companies provide a fleet of more than 175 cabs.

■ Communications

Newspapers and Magazines

Columbia's daily (morning) newspaper, *The State*, is South Carolina's major paper with a 2013 daily circulation of 87,384 in 26 of 43 South Carolina counties. In addition, the city publishes three weekly newspapers including the *Columbia Star*, which covers human interest and legal news; *Free Times*, Columbia's free alternative weekly paper; and *South Carolina Black News*. Magazines and journals published in Columbia the bimonthly *Columbia Metropolitan Magazine* and magazines directed at farmers.

Television and Radio

Seven television stations broadcast in Columbia, including South Carolina Educational Television. Cable and satellite services are widely available. Six AM and 10 FM radio stations offer music, information, news, call-in talk programs, and religious programming.

Media Information: *The State*, 1401 Shop Road, Columbia, SC 29201; telephone (800) 888-3566

Columbia Online

Central South Carolina Alliance. Available www.centralsc.org

City of Columbia Home Page. Available www.columbiasc.net

Columbia Metropolitan Convention Center. Available www.columbiacvb.com

Greater Columbia Chamber of Commerce. Available www.columbiachamber.com

Richland County Public Library. Available www.richlandlibrary.com

Richland School District One. Available www.richlandone.org

South Carolina State Library. Available www.statelibrary.sc.gov

The State. Available www.thestate.com

BIBLIOGRAPHY

Aboyan, Laura, *Columbia Food: The History of Cuisine in the Famously Hot City* (Charleston, SC: History Press, 2013)

Greenville

■ The City in Brief

Founded: 1797 (chartered 1869)

Head Official: Mayor Knox White (R) (since 1995; current term expires 2015)

City Population
    1990: 58,282
    2000: 56,716
    2010: 58,409
    2012 estimate: 59,955
    Percent change, 2000–2010: 3.0%
    U.S. rank in 2010: 586th

Metropolitan Statistical Area Population
    2000: 559,927
    2010: 636,986
    2012 estimate: 653,498
    Percent change, 2000–2010: 13.8%
    U.S. rank in 2000: 84th
    U.S. rank in 2010: 83rd

Area: 28.78 square miles

Elevation: Not available

Average Annual Temperatures: 59° F

Average Annual Precipitation: 50.45 inches of rain; 1.20 inches of snow

Major Economic Sectors: textiles, manufacturing, services, government

Unemployment Rate: 7.5% (2012)

Per Capita Income: $29,943

2012 FBI Crime Index Property: 3,223

Major Colleges and Universities: University of South Carolina Upstate, Clemson University, Furman University, Bob Jones University

Daily Newspaper: *The Greenville News*

■ Introduction

Situated in northwest South Carolina in the foothills of the Blue Ridge Mountains, Greenville is the seat of Greenville County. The city combines spectacular scenery, including a pedestrian bridge that affords views of a waterfall at the city's center, with Southern charm. Located in the 10-county region known as the Upstate, Greenville's position between Atlanta, Georgia, and North Carolina have made it a stopping point for those wishing to take in the best of the region's sites. Once a stronghold of textile manufacturing, the city experienced plant closures over time. City leaders have pursued progressive policies to attract new businesses to the area, drawn by tax benefits and the prevailing low wages. These policies have spurred significant economic growth in modern manufacturing, which in turn has contributed to a revitalization of the now-thriving downtown area. With tourism also a major economic activity, Greenville has earned its spot as a "must see" destination, for its mountains, waterfalls, and green valleys.

■ Geography and Climate

Located equidistant between Atlanta, Georgia, and the North Carolina border, Greenville sits high up in northwest South Carolina along Interstate 85. The region is tucked away between the Appalachian Mountains, with Sassafras Mountain being the highest point in the state at 3,564 feet. The Reedy River runs through the city, with a cascading waterfall in the center of Greenville. Temperatures during the year are generally mild, averaging 59 degrees Fahrenheit annually. January average temperatures are usually above freezing, but the summer

© Sean Pavone/Shutterstock.com

can get hot and humid, averaging in the upper 90 degrees Fahrenheit.

Area: 28.78 square miles

Elevation: Not available

Average Temperatures: 59° F

Average Annual Precipitation: 50.45 inches of rain; 1.20 inches of snow

■ History

The area that would eventually become settled and known as Greenville was once part of Cherokee Indian territory. In the mid-1700s, Irish settler and Indian trader Richard Pearis acquired the land from the Cherokee. Pearis married a Cherokee woman and established a settlement, which included a house, a trading post, a smokehouse, stables, a dairy, a blacksmith shop, mills, and slave quarters. Most of the small settlement was lost during the Revolutionary War because Pearis was a Loyalist (loyal to the British). After the British were defeated and the Cherokee driven off, the land became

occupied by the Revolutionary War soldiers, mostly of Scots-Irish and English descent. Greenville County was established in 1784. According the South Carolina State Library, Greenville County may have been named to honor Revolutionary War general Nathanael Greene (1742-1786) or an early resident, Isaac Green.

Around the 1790s, the land was purchased by Lemuel Alston (who bought it from previous owner and soldier, Thomas Brandon). Plans were drawn for a town, with government buildings such as a courthouse and jail, designed to be built from logs. In 1815, Alston sold the land and his home to Vardry McBee, who became known as the "Father of Greenville." McBee contributed land for the first four churches and the first academies.

McBee saw, in the region's many streams and rivers, a potential source of water power. He built on the first cotton mills and the Reedy River; the region soon became a center of textile manufacturing. McBee also arranged for the relocation of Furman University from Edgefield to Greenville in 1851. In 1853, he was responsible for the establishment of Greenville's first railroad, the Columbia and Greenville.

In 1831, the town, which was the county seat of Greenville County but was called "Pleasantburg," became known as "Greeneville."

The arrival of the railroad connected Greenville to other cities in the region, which helped the community to grow and prosper. Greenville became a popular escape for Southerners hoping to escape the heat and malaria of the coastal areas some four hours away. When the Civil War broke out, Greenville was not the site of any battles; in fact, there was significant pro-Union sentiment in and around the area, led by prominent citizen Benjamin F. Perry. After the Civil War ended, in June 1865 President Andrew Johnson appointed Perry governor of South Carolina.

Greenville officially became a city in February 1869, signaling more development. The first African American church to be established following the Civil War was in Greenville. Over the next decades, streets, railroads, textile mills, telephone lines, mail service, and a hospital appeared, as did streetcars.

Soon, Greenville became known as "Textile Center of the South." The Great Depression brought textile mill strikes and a plummeting economy, but signs of improvement showed with the building of the Greenville Army Air Base, which opened in 1942 and was renamed Donaldson Air Force Base in 1951.

During the period of civil rights activism of the 1960s, blacks in Greenville, as elsewhere, were required to ride in the back of city buses, were restricted to the balcony of movie theaters, and were prevented from staying at many hotels. Black were even restricted from using the public library. To protest lack of access to the library, activist and Greenville resident Jesse Jackson, with the support of the NAACP, organized a sit-in at Greenville's F.W. Woolworth store. Greenville's protests were peaceful.

In the 1970s, Greenville undertook a revitalization program. Downtown was made more pedestrian-friendly and groundwork was laid for downtown development. By the 1990s, the Peace Center for Performing Arts opened and textile plants were restored into functional buildings. The 2000s brought restoration projects of public fixtures in the city. A baseball field, modeled after Boston's Fenway Park, was erected downtown and opened in 2006. With entertainment and dining fixtures in place downtown by the early 2010s, the city focused development on building residential space in the downtown area. The combination of business, tourist, and residential development worked hand-in-hand, each reinforcing the other as the city center continued to thrive.

Historical Information: City of Greenville, South Carolina, 206 S. Main St., SC 29602; telephone (864) 232-2273.

■ Population Profile

Metropolitan Statistical Area Population
2000: 559,927
2010: 636,986
2012 estimate: 653,498

Percent change, 2000–2010: 13.8%
U.S. rank in 2000: 84th
U.S. rank in 2010: 83rd

City Residents
1990: 58,282
2000: 56,716
2010: 58,409
2012 estimate: 59,955
Percent change, 2000–2010: 3.0%
U.S. rank in 2010: 586th

Density: 1,264.8 people per square mile

Racial and ethnic characteristics
White: 38,340
Black or African American: 18,408
American Indian and Alaskan Native: 100
Asian: 972
Native Hawaiian and Other Pacific Islander: 50
Hispanic or Latino (may be of any race): 3,630
Other: 2,085

Percent of residents born in state: 54.5%

Age characteristics
Population under 5 years old: 4,290
Population 5 to 9 years old: 3,506
Population 10 to 14 years old: 2,846
Population 15 to 19 years old: 4,047
Population 20 to 24 years old: 5,604
Population 25 to 34 years old: 10,896
Population 35 to 44 years old: 7,500
Population 45 to 54 years old: 7,570
Population 55 to 59 years old: 3,677
Population 60 to 64 years old: 3,292
Population 65 to 74 years old: 3,388
Population 75 to 84 years old: 2,078
Population 85 years and over: 1,261
Median age: 33.7

Births (2010–11 Metropolitan Area)
Total number: 9,631

Deaths (2010–11 Metropolitan Area)
Total number: 5,385

Money income (2012)
Per capita income: $29,943
Median household income: $39,308
Total households: 25,539

Number of households with income of ...
less than $10,000: 3,135
$10,000 to $14,999: 2,013
$15,000 to $24,999: 3,385
$25,000 to $34,999: 3,160
$35,000 to $49,999: 3,132

$50,000 to $74,999: 3,956
$75,000 to $99,999: 1,903
$100,000 to $149,999: 2,364
$150,000 to $199,999: 1,050
$200,000 or more: 1,441

Percent of families below poverty level: 20.8%

FBI Crime Index Property: 3,223

FBI Crime Index Violent: 509

■ Municipal Government

Greenville operates through a council-manager form of government, which was established in 1976. The city council consists of a mayor and six council members. Four members are selected from single-member districts, while the mayor and two council members are elected at-large. The city manager, appointed by the council, is responsible for daily operations and administers the annual budget, which is approved by the city council.

Head Official: Mayor Knox White (R) (since 1995; current term expires 2015)

Total Number of City Employees: 946 (2013)

City Information: City of Greenville, South Carolina, 206 S. Main St., Greenville, SC 29602; telephone (864) 233-2273

■ Economy

Major Industries and Commercial Activity

Once known as the "Textile Capital of the World," Greenville has long since been a leader in manufacturing. With beginnings in textile manufacturing, Greenville has grown into a center for corporate headquarters, warehousing, and distribution, and aims to extend into research and development. The business climate features lower prevailing wages and a favorable tax climate, which has made the city attractive to many international businesses. As of 2013, the city was home to more than 40 *Fortune* 500 companies, with more than 20 businesses headquarted in the area. Some 240 international companies also conducted operations in and around the city.

The area is the headquarters of Michelin North America and Bi-Lo LLC grocery chain. The Donaldson Air Force Base, after closing in 1963, became Lockheed Martin Aeronautics. Greenville is also home to a General Electric plant that is the largest turbine manufacturing plant in the world. Other manufacturing companies in Greenville County include Michelin North America, Sealed Air Corp–Cryovac division, Magna Drive Automotive, Mitsubishi Polyester Film, House of Raeford

(Columbia Farms), Honeywell, Milliken & Company, and Nutra Mfg USA.

Current industry includes metalworking, automotive, aviation, call centers, computer and software services, advanced materials, and warehousing/distribution. In 2008, Greenville, like most U.S. cities, experienced the economic downturn, with many business closings and employee layoffs. Businesses that closed include Cox Custom Media, Steel Summit, TelCheck/ TRS Recovery Services, Whitehall Jewelers, and North Star Food Service (Carolinas Facility and Support Office). However, in the face of economic blows due to recession, the city was still rated that year as one of the top-five cities to weather the economic downturn by *Forbes*. Through 2013, target industries remained advanced materials, automotive, aviation/aerospace, and biosciences.

Items and goods produced: Food, tires, maps, digital services, turbines, plastic bags and film, aircraft modification and maintenance, auto body panels, polyester film, poultry, vitamins

Incentive Programs-New and Existing Companies

Local programs: The City of Greenville's Department of Economic Development offers assistance through many different programs. Loans that help cover expenses for acquiring or developing property are offered to developing small businesses. Businesses are encouraged through these programs to act in ways that help local communities thrive. Greenville supports an Accomodations Tax Grant Program for tourism-related events or promotional opportunities. An Anniversary Discount Program rewards businesses for their longevity in the community—those with at least 10 years in Greenville— with tax reductions as high as $10,000. The city also offers smaller programs for historic building restorations.

State programs: The following incentives and financing sources may be available to qualifying companies: Job Development Credit that rebates a portion of new employee's withholding taxes for use to address specific needs of a company; Economic Development Set-Aside Program to improve infrastructure surrounding new or exmpanding businesses; Enterprise Zone Retraining Credit Program to subsidize the cost of retraining workers; Rural Infrastructure Fund to further economic development in remote areas; Port Volume Increase Credit for companies that increase port cargo volume by at least 5 percent; and Tourism Infrastructure Development Grants to complete infrastructure projects that support new tourist developments. Additional credits include a Job Tax Credit, Economic Impact Zone Investment Credit, Corporate Headquarters Credit, and Research and Development Tax Credit. South Carolina's 5 percent corporate income tax is one of the lowest in the region.

Job training programs: The South Carolina Technical College System provides an array of job-training programs throughout the state. The readySC program, established in 1961, trains employees for several industries, including aerospace, automotive, biotech, and call centers. Apprenticeship Carolina, also part of the state's technical college system, provides consulting at no charge to employers and assists employers in training their workforce in technological, health-care, and transportation industries, among others. Greenville Works is a partnership among local, state, and federal organizations to support new and existing businesses through assistance in attracting, selecting, and training the area workforce. Greenville County Workforce Development's business services assist employers with pre-screening of applicants, pre-employment skills assessments, and referrals of quality job seekers.

Development Projects

Greenville has experienced major construction developments and renovations in the 2000s. A renovation on Falls Park on the Reedy River at Greenville's West End district, which included adding a pedestrian bridge, was completed in 2004. The 355-foot long Liberty Bridge is a modern suspension bridge overlooking the park, river, and Reedy River falls. Following the park's completion, more than $100 million of private investment had flowed into the area around the park by 2013.

In 2010 construction began on the Green Avenue Project, part of the city's four-year capital improvement program. The entire master project, expected to be completed in 2015, included Anderson Street, Casey Street, Green Avenue, Lafayette Street, Lincoln Street, McLeod Street, and Nelson Street, all of which would receive infrastructure improvements. The plan also included 40 single-family homes or apartments being constructed. A mixed-use residential development was slated for the corner of University Ridge and Church Street, with 348 residential units. A $20 million renovation of the Peace Center, the city's downtown performing arts center, took place during 2011–12.

Several downtown developments focused on adding dense residential space. An apartment development at the corner of McBee Avenue and Spring Street broke ground in 2013 and was to include 55 luxury apartments. Additional residential construction was underway in 2013 at Rhett Street, a four-level apartment complex, and a 100-unit apartment facility near Flour Field, the city's minor league baseball stadium.

A major development underway downtown included Project One, a 185,000-square-foot mixed-use development under construction in 2013, with a projected cost of $100 million. In addition to retail and restaurant space, the development was to house an MBA program for nearby Clemson University. The first phase of the development opened in 2013 and was fully leased, with a second phase underway at that time.

In 2013 the city secured a site for construction of a new United States Federal Courthouse, but construction was not anticipated for several years.

Economic Development Information: Greenville Area Development Corporation, 233 N. Main St., Suite 250, Greenville, SC 29601; telephone (864) 235-2008.

Commercial Shipping

The Greenville-Spartanburg International Airport is the designated hub for shipping to and from the city. It shares space with a 120,000-square-foot Federal Express facility. The Port of Charleston and Port of Georgetown, both located within four hours of Greenville, serve as container loading facilities for shipping cargo by sea. They are operated by the South Carolina State Ports Authority.

Trucks carry items into or from the city on Interstates 85, 185, and 385, or U.S. Highways 25, 29, 123, and 276. Norfolk-Southern and CSX railroads provide freight and cargo shipping from the Port of Charleston to Greenville.

Labor Force and Employment Outlook

As of 2013, an estimated 30.7 percent of the Greenville labor force held a bachelor's degree or higher, with 10.6 percent having obtained a graduate or professional degree. Growth industries were paced by jobs in business and professional services, followed by manufacturing and trade, transportation, and utilities. Nearly 85,000 college students are enrolled in area universities annually, providing part-time and seasonal employees, as well as a ready workforce for white-collar jobs.

The following is a summary of data regarding the 2012 Greenville labor force:

Size of civilian labor force: 32,320

Number of workers employed in . . .
agriculture and mining: 74
construction: 1,508
manufacturing: 2,821
wholesale trade: 635
retail trade: 2,737
transportation: 1,007
information systems: 803
finance: 2,111
professional administration: 3,658
education and social services: 7,562
arts and leisure: 3,646
other: 1,250
public administration: 707

Average hourly earnings of production workers: $16.37

Unemployment rate: 7.5% (2012)

Employers

Largest employers (Greenville County, 2012)

	Number of employees
Greenville Hospital Systems	10,925
School District of Greenville County	10,850
Greenville Hospital System	4,500
Michelin North America	4,000
GE Energy	3,200
South Carolina State Government	3,036
Fluor Corporation	2,500
Bi-Lo Supermarkets	2,089
Greenville County Government	1,830
United States Government	1,835
Bob Jones University	1,519
Greenville Technical College	1,400

Cost of Living

As of 2013, the cost of living in Greenville remained below the national average, which makes the city an affordable place to live.

The following is a summary of data regarding several key cost of living factors in the area.

2013 ACCRA Average House Price: $204,488

2013 ACCRA Cost of Living Index: 92

State income tax rate: 0.0% to 7.0%

State sales tax rate: 6.0%

Local income tax rate: None

Local sales tax rate: None

Property tax rate: 0.3152 mills (2012)

Economic Information: Greenville Area Development Corporation, 233 N. Main St., Suite 250, Greenville, SC 29601; telephone (864) 235-2008.

■ Education and Research

Elementary and Secondary Schools

Greenville County School District enrolls more than 70,000 students annually, making it the largest school district in the state and 47th largest in the United States. Greenville boasted 13 National Blue Ribbon schools, 9 high schools named to *Newsweek's* "Best High Schools"

list, 21 state-recognized "Palmetto's Finest Schools," and 48 "Red Carpet Schools," given for a family-friendly learning environment. Testing scores for the ACT College Entrance Test consistently outscored state and national averages. SAT scores also outpaced state averages. Some 90 percent of all high school graduates attend college, and 24 National Merit Scholarship Semi Finalists came from the Greenville County School District in 2013–14. The district offers a K-12 International Baccalaureate program at a number of schools and also provides special centers for children who need alternative education, early childhood programs, opportunities to participate in performing arts and special clubs, and various after school sports teams.

The following is a summary of data regarding the Greenville County School District.

Total enrollment: 71,930

Number of facilities
total: 94
elementary schools: 51
junior high schools: 18
high schools: 14
other: 11

Student/teacher ratio: 17.31:1

Teacher salaries
average (statewide): $49,434

Funding per pupil: $7,515

Public Schools Information: Greenville County Schools, 301 E. Camperdown Way, Greenville, SC, 29601; telephone (864) 355-3100; fax (864) 355-1086.

Colleges and Universities

The University of South Carolina, a public four-year university, has a campus that serves Spartanburg and Greenville—University of South Carolina Upstaet—that opened in 1967 as a registered nursing school. It became a four-year university in 1975 and is now the academic center for some 5,500 students each year. The school is also home to the Spartans sports teams.

Clemson University is a four-year university located 30 minutes outside of Greenville in Clemson, South Carolina. It enrolls nearly 21,000 students annually who can choose from about 80 undergraduate and 110 graduate degree programs. The university is home to the Clemson Tigers sports teams and has been consistently ranked one of the best public universities in the nation by *U.S. News and World Report.*

Furman University is a four-year, private liberal arts university five miles north of downtown Greenville. The school enrolls 2,700 students with a student-faculty ratio of 11:1. The university offers majors in several dozen fields, with programs in political science, business, and health sciences the most popular. The university also sponsors internships and study abroad programs to enrich student experiences.

Bob Jones University is a private, four-year Christian university founded in 1927. The school enrolls more than 3,000 students annually who come from across the nation and 40 counties around the world. Aside from the nearly 70 undergraduate and graduate disciplines the university offers, students can major in the Bible, Biblical Counseling, Missionary Aviation, and other religious subjects. The university is accredited by the Transnational Association of Christian Colleges and Schools (TRACS). Bob Jones University also has a collection of artwork on display at the Bob Jones University Museum and Gallery in downtown Greenville. Holmes Bible College is a private seminary in Greenville offering four-year degrees in pastoral, missions, and church music.

Brown Mackie College has a Greenville campus that offers bachelor's degrees, associate's degrees, diplomas, and certificate programs with the goals of preparing students for specialized career paths. There are four main areas of study: nursing; healthcare and wellness; business and technology; and legal studies. The main areas are further subdivided into 15 different career paths.

Virginia College is a two-year college that has had a satellite campus in Greenville since 2008. It offers associate's degrees, and bachelor's degrees. EPCI College of Technology is another career college that offers accelerated bachelor's degrees, and has a campus in Greenville. Strayer University is a career college that offers certificates, associate's degrees, bachelor's, and master's programs to students either at various locations or online.

The University Center of Greenville consists of a network of colleges (Clemson University, Furman University, South Carolina State University, University of South Carolina, and the University of South Carolina Upstate) meant to help Upstate citizens complete their degrees while working regular jobs. It was established in 1987 in part because Greenville was one of the largest cities in the South with no university in the downtown area.

Greenville Technical College is a public two-year college of about 15,000 degree-seeking students, and 15,000 students who are continuing education. The school offers short-term career training for needs of the current workforce, and offers credits that are transferable to four-year colleges.

Libraries and Research Centers

Greenville County Library System was established in 1921, with a collection of only 200 books. As of 2013 it had 11 locations: Hughes Main Library is the flagship, followed by branches at Anderson Road, Augusta Road, Berea, Fountain Inn, Greer, Mauldin, Pelham Road, Simpsonville, Taylors, and Travelers Rest. A bookmobile makes eight stops for people who cannot travel to branches because of location or disability. The library system offers one million book titles, movies, music, Internet resources, and more to the public. The library has a speaker series, seminars, craft groups, language lessons, and groups for children and teens. The library concluded a major 13-year rebuilding program in 2010.

Public Library Information: Greenville County Library System, Hughes Main Library, 25 Heritage Green Place, Greenville, SC, 29601; telephone (864) 242-5000.

■ Health Care

Greenville Memorial Hospital is the leading facility in the Greenville Hospital System. *U.S. News & World Report* ranked Greenville Memorial Hospital second among all hospitals in South Carolina, and first in the Greenville metropolitan area for 2013–14. It has a 24-hour Level I emergency trauma center, children's emergency center, cancer center, and oncology research institute, and sleep center among its many services. Behavioral health services are offered through the Greenville Hospital System, with inpatient services for mental health illnesses available at the Marshall I. Pickens Hospital, an acute-care facility.

The Robert C. Peace Hospital is a 53-bed rehabilitation facility that offers inpatient and outpatient care for orthopedic and neurologic needs. The Hospital has the only CARF-certified Traumatic Brain Injury program, Spinal Cord, Amputee, and Pediatric Specialty Program in the state. It also houses the state's only driver rehabilitation program. The Greenville Hospital System operates four other medical campuses throughout upstate South Carolina.

Bon Secours St. Francis Health System is another large provider of health services in the area, with locations throughout Greenville. St. Francis downtown is a 245-bed, completely private room facility offering a variety of services in various specialties, and a 24-hour Emergency department. St Francis eastside is a 93-bed facility that provides women's services, including a neonatal care unit; orthopedics, imaging and radiology services, and other medical care. St. Francis Institute for Chronic Health at Millennium is the newest addition to the health system that focuses on preventing and managing chronic illnesses. St. Francis also has an outpatient center on the downtown campus, surgery center on the east side, home care provider, and 30-bed hospice center.

■ Recreation

Sightseeing

Many visitors to Greenville pay a visit the historic Falls Park and walk along the $4.5 million, 355-feet-long Liberty Bridge suspended above the Reedy River. The park has been called a "must-see" attraction in the city because of its spectacular view of Reedy River falls.

The Greenville Zoo, a fixture of the city for more than 50 years, covers 40 acres and was awarded with an honorable mention in 2012–13 by the Center for Interactive Learning and Collaboration. The award recognized effotrs to deliver outstanding interactive videoconferencing programs to a K–12 audience. Victoria Valley Vineyards in Cleveland, South Carolina, modeled after a French chateau, hosts tastings of regional wines. The vineyard, which produces Vinitera Wines, offers wine dinners for guests on the 47-acre premises.

Visitors longing to explore the region's past can tour the Upcountry History Museum, operated by Furman University, which includes artifacts and oral histories from fifteen South Carolina counties located in the region.

The natural beauty surrounding downtown Greenville is best enjoyed with a walk or cycle along the Greenville Hospital System's Swamp Rabbit Trail, a 17.5-mile multi-use trail that allows strollers to wind their way along the Reedy River and pass by local businesses and schools.

Arts and Culture

Greenville has a variety of performing arts and cultural venues. The Peace Center for the Performing Arts in downtown Greenville serves the city and surrounding communities and features a 2,100-seat concert hall and a 400-seat theater. The Greenville Symphony Orchestra, 200-singer Greenville Chorale, and acts such as Mannheim Steamroller, Lyle Lovett, and Vince Gill perform there.

The Charter Amphitheatre at Heritage Park, located in Simpsonville, 15 miles southeast of downtown Greenville, opened in 2008 and presents outdoor movies and other entertainment events during the summer months. It features 4,000 reserved seats and 6,000 lawn seats, for a total capacity of roughly 10,000.

Centre Stage, founded in 1983, is a 285-seat theatre just outside the downtown area. It hosts theater performances, art shows, music concerts, films, lectures, and other events. Greenville Little Theater hosts about six shows per year, from traditional plays to modern musicals. The Carolina Ballet Theater, founded in 1972, offers performances of all different genres from traditional ballet to contemporary at the Peace Center.

The Greenville County Museum of Art has three permanent exhibits and hosts temporary shows throughout the year. One notable exhibit, The Southern Collection, displays American art from early times to the modern era. The museum holds the largest public collection of watercolors by famed U.S. artist Andrew Wyeth, and also has a robust collection of works by Jasper Johns. The Bob Jones University Art Gallery and Museum is home to 30 galleries that showcase more than 400 works of art from the thirteenth century forward.

The Children's Museum of the Upstate, which found a site in December 2003 when the former Greenville County Library building was donated for its use, is among the largest children's museums in the United States. It officially opened in 2009 and welcomed nearly 200,000 visitors in 2012, including 20,000 school children from more than 21 counties in Georgia, North Carolina, and South Carolina.

The Shoeless Joe Jackson Museum and Baseball Library is dedicated to one of baseball's most famous ballplayers and one of the city's best-remembered residents.

Festivals and Holidays

Greenville is the site of many festivals and holiday celebrations. Artisphere, the International Arts Festival in Greenville, happens annually in May, and offers multicultural performing and visual arts presentations from all over the world. Aloft, one of the largest hot-air balloon festivals in the Southeast occurs for three days toward the end of May each year.

The Greenville Scottish Games, known as Gallabrae, also take place in May, with events held at various venues in the city. The festival is geared toward the high concentrations of Scots-Irish descendents who live in or around the city. The festival goes for two days, and includes a parade, music, dancing, and athletic competition.

On Thursday evenings from March through August, Piedmont Natural Gas sponsors Downtown Alive, a street party with live music to entertain locals and visitors as they wander city streets. The events attract an estimated 45,000 visitors annually. Wells Fargo Red, White & Blue, presented by AT&T each July 4, is one of the largest fireworks displays in the state.

St. Francis Festival fo Trees runs through December and celebrates the holiday season, as does Roper Mountain Holidays Lights at the Roper Mountain Science Center, which allows visitors to drive through a winding display of holidays lights. The Greenville Poinsettia Christmas Parade has been a downtown staple since the early 1990s.

Sports for the Spectator

Greenville's local baseball team, which began playing at Fluor Field in 2006, is the Greenville Drive, an affiliate of the Boston Red Sox. The city's hockey team, the Greenville Road Warriors, is an East Coast Hockey League affiliate that located in Greenville in 2010. The Road Warriors take the ice at the Bon Secours Wellness Arena in downtown Greenville.

The Greenville Derby Dames, established in 2008, is a women's flat-track roller derby team for the city. The Dames play their home bouts at The Pavilion in Taylors, South Carolina. Residents can also tune into or visit the area's college and university sports teams, like the Furman University Paladins, which participate in NCAA Division

I athletics in the Southern Conference, or the nearby Clemson University Tigers, a member of the Atlantic Coast Conference.

Sports for the Participant

Greenville's City Parks and Recreation Department has 39 parks that span 267 acres of land. Residents and visitors can enjoy scenic views of waterfalls and greenery from Liberty Bridge overlooking Reedy River Falls in Falls Park, or bike or walk along the area's many trails. The largest park is the 122-acre Cleveland Park with tennis courts, softball fields, playgrounds, trails, and picnic facilities. Greenville County manages an additional 55 parks and facilities, including a public ice-skating rink, a 74-acre equestrian park, and the only 50-meter public indoor swimming facility in the state. The parks and recreation department also offers youth and adult league sports programs through its five community centers.

Water sports and boating are available at Lake Jocassee, Lake Keowee, and Lake Hartwell, all within 50 miles of Greenville. Also nearby are Paris Mountain State Park, a 1,540-acre park, and the 3,083-acre Table Rock State Park.

Shopping and Dining

Shopping in Greenville ranges from small shops to big name retailers. Haywood Mall, operated by Simon Mall, offers five department stores—Belk, Dillard's, JCPenney, Macy's, and Sears—in addition to more than 100 mainstream specialty stores. The Mast General Store, a downtown landmark, is a restored 1920s shop and sells items like footwear, cookware, gourmet foods, toys, and a large selection of unique candies. Other unique shops downtown include Art Crossing at Riverplace alongside the Reedy River, where the works of local artists and craftspeople are featured. The Beaded Frog offers a selection of beads and jewelry-making classes, offering semiprecious stones, tools, glass, wood, and other supplies to create personalized pieces.

Many cuisines are featured in Greenville restaurants, including Italian, French, Japanese, Thai, Mexican, Greek, and even Dutch. The downtown area, especially near Main Street, has gained recognition for its culinary sophistication.

Visitor Information: Greenville Convention and Visitors Bureau, Visitors Center, 148 River Street, Suite 222, Greenville, SC 29601; telephone (864) 421-0000.

■ Convention Facilities

The TD Convention Center's 39-acre campus is Greenville's premiere venue for meetings and conventions. It has 280,000 square feet of exhibit space, 60,000 square feet of meeting and conference space, and a 30,000 square foot ballroom that can accommodate groups from 25 to 25,000. The center underwent a $22 million renovation in 2008 that added space and capabilities to host many different types of events under one roof. As of 2013, It had an estimated annual impact of about $50 million for the city.

The $63 million Bon Secours Wellness Arena, formerly the Bi-Lo Center, is operated by the Greenville Arena District Board, a political subdivision of the state of South Carolina. A 10-year, 4.5 million naming rights partnership was finalized with the Bon Secours Health System in 2013. The 17,000-seat Bi-Lo Center is home to concerts, sporting events, and entertainment events. The center consistently has been named one of the top 50 entertainment venues in the world. Noted performers such as Cher, Elton John, Michael Buble, and The Eagles have all performed at the Bi-Lo Center. Sporting events have included wrestling, boxing, monster trucks, NBA basketball, motocross, and hockey. The venue has hosted the Barnum and Bailey Circus, Disney on Ice, and the Lipizzaner Stallions, and may be reserved for trade shows or seminars.

Convention Information: Greenville Convention and Visitors Bureau, Visitors Center, 148 River Street, Suite 222, Greenville, SC 29601; telephone (864) 421-0000.

■ Transportation

Approaching the City

Visitors to Greenville can arrive through the Greenville-Spartanburg International Airport, which is 12 miles from downtown. The airport is served by six airlines—Allegiant, American, Delta, Southwest, United, and US Airways—and continues to grow its passenger service, from 1.27 million passengers in 2010 to more than 1.8 million in 2012. Some 53 non-stop departures are available to 22 U.S. airports on a daily basis. For international travel to Greenville, U.S. Customs, Immigration, and Agriculture operates two inspection stations as the airport capable of handling 250 international passengers per hour. The Greenville Downtown Airport provides general air services; it is the busiest general aviation airport in the state with more than 80,000 annual departures and arrivals.

The Greyhound Bus Line includes stops in Greenville. Amtrak also provides passenger rail service through Greenville on a line that stretches from New York to New Orleans. The city is served by a number of highways. Those arriving by car can take Interstates 85, 185, or 385 to the city, as well as any of four U.S. highways: 25, 29, 123, and 276.

Traveling in the City

The Greenville Transit Authority (GTA) provides bus service through Greenlink, which transports passengers to points throughout the city on 11 fixed routes; all buses have wheelchair and bicycle accommodations. Greenlink expanded service to Easley, South Carolina, and Clemson University in 2013. GAP, a free paratransit service, is also provided by GTA for qualifying disabled individuals. There are also a variety of taxi cab companies throughout the city.

■ Communications

Newspapers and Magazines

The Greenville News, the city's daily newspaper, was established in 1874, and has been owned by Gannett since 1995. As of 2013, its daily circulation hoverd around 50,000, with the Sunday edition reaching an audience nearly twice that size. Launched in February 2010, *Upstate Business Journal* is a weekly publication covering Greenville and Spartanburg county businesses. *GSA Business* is a bi-weekly business resource for Greenville, Spartanburg, and Anderson. *Greenville Business Magazine* is a monthly magazine about business in Greenville.

Television and Radio

Five television stations, affiliates of major network broadcasters, served the Greenville area as of 2013. There were 5 AM and 13 FM stations broadcasting in the area.

Media Information: The *Greenville News,* 305 S. Main St., PO Box 1688, Greenville, SC, 29602; telephone (864) 298-4100.

Greenville Online

City of Greenville. Available www.greenvillesc.gov

Greater Greenville Chamber of Commerce. Available www.greenvillechamber.org

Greenville Area Development Corporation. Available www.greenvilleeconomicdevelopment.com

Greenville Convention and Visitors Bureau. Available www.greenvillecvb.com

Greenville County Library System. Available www.greenvillelibrary.org

Greenville County Schools. Available www.greenville.k12.sc.us

The *Greenville News.* Available www.greenvilleonline.com

BIBLIOGRAPHY

Bainbridge, Judith T., *Academy and College: The History of the Woman's College of Furman University* (Macon, GA: Mercer University Press, 2001)

Baker, Bruce E. and Brian Kelly, eds., *After Slavery: Race, Labor, and Citizenship in the Reconstruction South* (Gainesville, FL: University Press of Florida, 2013)

Tennessee

The State in Brief

Nickname: Volunteer State

Motto: Agriculture and commerce

Flower: Iris

Bird: Mockingbird

Area: 42,144 square miles (2010; U.S. rank 36th)

Elevation: Ranges from 178 feet to 6,643 feet above sea level

Climate: Continental; mild weather with abundant rainfall in the east; hot humid summers in the western region; severe winters in mountains

Admitted to Union: June 1, 1796

Capital: Nashville

Head Official: Bill Haslam (R) (until 2015)

Population

1990: 4,877,185
2000: 5,689,262
2010: 6,346,105
2012 estimate: 6,353,226
Percent change, 2000–2010: 11.5%
U.S. rank in 2012: 17th
Percent of residents born in state: 61.4% (2012)
Density: 153.9 people per square mile (2010)
2012 FBI Crime Index Total: 259,214

Racial and Ethnic Characteristics (2012)

White: 4,982,977
Black or African American: 1,060,494
American Indian and Alaska Native: 15,991
Asian: 92,800
Native Hawaiian and Pacific Islander: 2,765
Hispanic or Latino (may be of any race): 288,582
Other: 198,199

Age Characteristics (2012)

Population under 5 years old: 406,033
Population 5 to 19 years old: 1,263,875
Percent of population 65 years and over: 13.6%
Median age: 38.0

Vital Statistics

Total number of births (2012–13): 79,933
Total number of deaths (2012–13): 60,358
AIDS cases reported through 2011: 15,668

Economy

Major industries: Wholesale and retail trade, services, manufacturing
Unemployment rate (2012): 6.1%
Per capita income (2012): $24,294
Median household income (2012): $44,140
Percentage of persons below poverty level (2012): 17.3%
Income tax rate: State income tax is limited to dividends and interest income only.
Sales tax rate: 7.0%

Chattanooga

■ The City in Brief

Founded: 1838 (chartered 1839)

Head Official: Mayor Andy Berke (since 2013; current term expires 2017)

City Population
>1990: 152,393
>2000: 155,554
>2010: 167,674
>2012 estimate: 171,282
>Percent change, 2000–2010: 7.8%
>U.S. rank in 1990: 113th (State rank: 4th)
>U.S. rank in 2000: 148th (State rank: 4th)
>U.S. rank in 2010: 138th (State rank: 4th)

Metropolitan Statistical Area Population
>2000: 465,161
>2010: 528,143
>2012 estimate: 539,094
>Percent change, 2000–2010: 13.5%
>U.S. rank in 2000: 94th
>U.S. rank in 2010: 97th

Area: 135.2 square miles

Elevation: Ranges from 675 feet above sea level in city to 2,391 feet at Lookout Mountain

Average Annual Temperatures: 60.5° F

Average Annual Precipitation: 54.5 inches

Major Economic Sectors: wholesale and retail trade, services, manufacturing

Unemployment Rate: 7.4% (2012)

Per Capita Income: $24,753

Major Colleges and Universities: University of Tennessee at Chattanooga

Daily Newspaper: *The Chattanooga Times Free Press*

■ Introduction

Located in the heart of the beautiful Tennessee Valley, Chattanooga is a small industrial city rich in history. Near the border of Georgia and Tennessee, it is a population center becoming well known today for its commitment to sustainable economic growth and quality of life. Perhaps nowhere in the country has a city undergone as dramatic an improvement as that experienced by Chattanooga, a city named America's most polluted by the U.S. Department of Health, Education, and Welfare in 1980. The privately-funded Vision 2000 program was initiated in 1982 to revitalize the city's riverfront and downtown by the year 2000. And change, it did. Chattanooga is now one of the cleanest U.S. cities, known especially for its breathtaking beauty and natural attractions. Today's Chattanooga boasts a vital and diverse economy, rich cultural history, and gleaming new downtown attractions loved by residents and visitors alike. Location of a Volkswagen manufacturing facility in Chattanooga opened in 2011, securing the city's manufacturing future.

■ Geography and Climate

Chattanooga is located at the juncture of Tennessee, Alabama, and Georgia, in a valley in southeastern Tennessee between the Appalachian and the Cumberland mountain ranges. The city lies on both banks of the Tennessee River at Moccasin Bend and is bordered by Signal Mountain on the north and Lookout Mountain to the south, with Missionary Ridge running through the eastern section of the city. The mountains shelter the city from major weather systems. The Tennessee Valley Authority's Chickamauga Dam, a hydroelectric dam used for power and flood control, is located north of the downtown area.

View from Lookout Mountain, Chattanooga, TN. © *Zack Frank/Shutterstock.com*

The city has four seasons and a moderate climate, with cool winters and hot summers, and springs and falls characterized by plentiful sunshine and rainfall, mild temperatures, and lush foliage. Extreme cold is rare, and the annual average snowfall is only 4.3 inches.

Area: 135.2 square miles

Elevation: Ranges from 675 feet above sea level in city to 2,391 feet at Lookout Mountain

Average Temperatures: 60.5° F

Average Annual Precipitation: 54.5 inches

■ History

Native Americans Displaced by Early Settlers

In 1663 the British established the colony of Carolina, which included all of the Tennessee country. The French from the Mississippi Valley also claimed the land at that same time. About 1769, a crude structure known as the "Old French Store" was established, most likely on Williams Island, marking the first white settlement in the area. England gained undisputed title to the territory in 1763 at the end of the French and Indian War.

The Chickamaugas, a splinter group of the Cherokee tribe, moved to the South Chickamauga Creek villages in 1777. They resisted white settlement and cooperated with the British during the American Revolution. Frontiersmen destroyed the Chickamauga villages in 1779. Three years later, on the slope of Lookout Mountain, the Native Americans engaged the frontiersmen who had destroyed their villages. This confrontation has become known as the "last battle of the American Revolution." In 1785, the United States government took control of Native American affairs.

Tennessee became the sixteenth state in 1796. At that time Native American lands made up about three-fourths of the region, including the Chattanooga area. Ross's Landing was established in 1816 as a trading post on the banks of the Tennessee River by Chief John Ross, leader of the Cherokee nation. Chattanooga became a center of education and culture for the Native Americans when the Brainerd Mission was created in 1817. Hamilton County was established in 1819 on land north of the Tennessee River. With the Cherokee removal in 1838, the county expanded south of the river to encompass Ross's Landing.

Cherokee removal was part of the 1837-1838 episode known as the "Trail of Tears," one of the most shameful events in American history. As the result of a treaty from a disputed land sale, the Cherokee were driven from their homes in several southeastern states and were assembled at various camps, including Ross's Landing, for expulsion to Oklahoma. Forced on a harsh journey through wilderness and bad weather, more than one-half of the 16,000 Native Americans died along the way or upon arrival, largely because of the strenuous trip.

Railroads Key To Chattanooga's History

The name of Ross's Landing was changed to Chattanooga by the U.S. Post Office in 1838. Although the origin of the city's name is uncertain, some say the name was a Native American expression meaning the "rock that comes to a point," describing Lookout Mountain. Legislation establishing Chattanooga and its boundaries was passed in 1839.

Rail transportation began in Chattanooga in the 1850s. Connections to other cities were constructed by the Western & Atlantic, Nashville & Chattanooga, Memphis & Charleston, and East Tennessee & Georgia Railroads. The city's population stood at approximately 2,500 people at the beginning of the Civil War. Although Chattanoogans supported secession, Hamilton County as a whole voted to remain in the Union. The county became one of the key battlegrounds of the war, as both the Confederate and Union armies attempted to keep possession of this important railway hub.

City Experiences Major Civil War Battles

Union soldiers, under the command of General William Rosecrans, marched into Chattanooga in September of 1863, intent on holding the key railroad center. The Battle of Chickamauga took place on September 19 and 20, 1863, followed by the Battle of Lookout Mountain (which was commanded by General Ulysses S. Grant) on November 24, and the Battle of Missionary Ridge on November 25. Confederate defenses were broken during the last battle and the southerners began their retreat into Georgia. According to Confederate General D. H. Hill, "Chattanooga sealed the fate of the Confederacy."

In November 1863, the nation's first National Cemetery was established in Chattanooga. Of the 12,000 Union soldiers buried at the cemetery, 5,000 are unknown. The cemetery is the site of 31,000 graves of soldiers from every American war and conflict. Most Confederate soldiers were buried at the city's Citizens Cemetery.

Gradual Recovery Follows War

Following the war, the city began to experience economic progress. Disaster struck in March 1867, when the largest flood on record-56.8 feet-washed away the city's only bridge spanning the Tennessee River. Chattanooga remained without a bridge until 1891 when the Walnut Street Bridge was built.

Major events occurring in the nineteenth century include the publishing of the first issue of *The Chattanooga Times* in 1869; creation of the public school system in 1872; a Yellow Fever epidemic in 1878 that claimed 366 lives; the advent of telephone service in 1880; and the introduction of the first electric lights in 1882.

During the late nineteenth century, as the city's rail access increased, so did the push to develop mineral and timber resources. Two industries that still thrive in the community today, manufacturing and tourism, began during that period. In 1899, Chattanooga became the site of the first franchised Coca-Cola bottling plant.

Early in the twentieth century there occurred a boom in downtown construction, and "skyscrapers" of the time, such as the James Building, were erected. The Hamilton County Courthouse, struck by lightning in 1910, was rebuilt, Market Street Bridge was dedicated in 1917, and airport facilities opened at Lovell Field in 1930.

Chattanooga entered the annals of musical history in 1923 when Bessie Smith, who began her career singing for coins on Chattanooga's streets, gained prominence with the release of her recording "Downhearted Blues" by Columbia Records. The city received special notoriety with the popularity of the Glenn Miller Orchestra's big band hit, "Chattanooga Choo-Choo," in 1941.

TVA Crucial to City's Development

The Great Depression struck Chattanooga hard, as it did the rest of the country, and in 1933 the U.S. Congress created the Tennessee Valley Authority (TVA) which proved to be the most successful of all Franklin Roosevelt's New Deal programs. Construction of TVA's most dramatic plan, the Chickamauga Dam, began in 1936. TVA's extensive system of power-producing and flood-control dams created a number of lakes, which are widely used for commercial transportation and recreation. In 1941 the city became the center for all TVA power operations.

Suburbs Grow, Bridges Built

Over time, communities began to develop around the city in areas such as Cameron Hill, Riverview, Lookout Mountain, and Signal Mountain. Although these were primarily enclaves for the wealthy, middle-class communities developed in Brainerd, East Ridge, and Red Bank.

Beginning in the 1950s, the growth of the city necessitated the building of additional bridges to span the Tennessee River. The Wilkes T. Thrasher Bridge across Chickamauga Dam opened in 1955; the Olgiati Bridge was dedicated in 1959; the C. B. Robinson Bridge opened in 1981; and the Veterans Bridge opened in 1984.

The history of local race relations began a new era in 1962 when the Chattanooga and Hamilton County school systems were desegregated. More recently, in 1990 a new city council form of government was mandated by the federal court for the purpose of insuring fair racial representation.

A New City Emerges

From the late 1960s to the early 1980s, Chattanooga was known as America's dirtiest city. By 1982, city residents and leaders were tired of the bad reputation of the city, and an $850 million plan was devised to revitalize the city's downtown and riverfront by the year 2000.

In 1986 the River City Company was formed to promote, encourage, and assist local economic development along 22 miles of river frontage and in the central business district. It was succeeded by a new agency formed in 1993 when River City Company merged with Partners for Economic Progress, forming a public-private economic development agency called RiverValley Partners. Also in 1986, the Chattanooga Neighborhood Enterprise Housing Program was founded to make housing affordable for local residents and to eliminate substandard housing.

In the 1990s, Chattanooga Venture, a community think tank, was begun to introduce new programs for local residents. In 1991 the Target '96 Plan, an environmental initiative-the first of its kind in the country-was established to deal with education, business development, and community action in a comprehensive, coordinated manner. At the end of the century, Chattanooga's focus on sustainable development centers and on creating an environment that would attract and retain companies that provide good jobs in businesses that would continue to grow in the twenty-first century. Today, Chattanooga is realizing those goals with a new focus enhancing its allure for conventioneers, tourists, and Chattanoogans alike through the completion of several major renovation projects throughout the city.

By 2007, the Moccasin Bend Task Force had helped spur riverfront and downtown redevelopment. Private-public partnerships led to the Tennessee Aquarium, the Walnut Street Bridge pedestrian link, and efforts to create affordable housing. The city's resurgence can be seen in the 21st Century Waterfront Project, expanded parks, and the 2010 opening of the BlueCross BlueShield of Tennessee's new $299 million headquarters. Chattanooga is taking steps to recruit industry related to new technology. One such step is the University of Tennessee at Chattanooga's SIM Center that focuses on computational engineering. The city has held onto major employers such as Unum (*Fortune 500* headquarters), BlueCross, and Cigna.

Rebirth of Manufacturing; Speeding into the Future

Chattanooga has, for the most part, been successful in cleaning up its dirty, industrial image of the mid-century as it entered the new century. However, in late 2008 TVA had a major ash spill at its Kingston Fossil Plant, about one and a half hours from Chattanooga. Estimates for full cleanup approached $1 billion, and reports in 2013 suggested that groundwater surrounding the facility may still be polluted.

Nonetheless, the city has made major investments that continue in line with Chattanooga's goals of becoming an economically powerful and sustainable city prepared for the next generation. The opening of a Volkswagen manufacturing plant in 2011 went a long way to secure the economic future of the city, and a steady increase in tourism revenues motivated the state to invest more money in tourism promotion for the state beginning in 2013.

Historical Information: Chattanooga-Hamilton County Bicentennial Library, Local History and Genealogical Collections, 1001 Broad Street, Chattanooga, TN 37402; telephone (423) 757-5310.

■ Population Profile

Metropolitan Statistical Area Population

2000: 465,161
2010: 528,143
2012 estimate: 539,094
Percent change, 2000–2010: 13.5%
U.S. rank in 2000: 94th
U.S. rank in 2010: 97th

City Residents

1990: 152,393
2000: 155,554
2010: 167,674
2012 estimate: 171,282
Percent change, 2000–2010: 7.8%
U.S. rank in 1990: 113th (State rank: 4th)
U.S. rank in 2000: 148th (State rank: 4th)
U.S. rank in 2010: 138th (State rank: 4th)

Density: 1,222.5 people per square mile

Racial and ethnic characteristics

White: 103,821
Black or African American: 58,559
American Indian and Alaskan Native: 336
Asian: 4,227
Native Hawaiian and Other Pacific Islander: 85
Hispanic or Latino (may be of any race): 8,682
Other: 4,254

Percent of residents born in state: 58.5%

Age characteristics

Population under 5 years old: 11,126
Population 5 to 9 years old: 10,378
Population 10 to 14 years old: 8,658
Population 15 to 19 years old: 10,927
Population 20 to 24 years old: 14,539
Population 25 to 34 years old: 26,192
Population 35 to 44 years old: 20,269

Population 45 to 54 years old: 22,013
Population 55 to 59 years old: 11,047
Population 60 to 64 years old: 10,408
Population 65 to 74 years old: 14,332
Population 75 to 84 years old: 7,481
Population 85 years and over: 3,912
Median age: 36.4

Births (2010–11 Metropolitan Area)

Total number: 6,264

Deaths (2010–11 Metropolitan Area)

Total number: 5,078

Money income (2012)

Per capita income: $24,753
Median household income: $37,140
Total households: 69,721

Number of households with income of ...

less than $10,000: 8,583
$10,000 to $14,999: 5,571
$15,000 to $24,999: 9,663
$25,000 to $34,999: 9,526
$35,000 to $49,999: 9,236
$50,000 to $74,999: 11,669
$75,000 to $99,999: 6,674
$100,000 to $149,999: 5,517
$150,000 to $199,999: 1,390
$200,000 or more: 1,892

Percent of families below poverty level: 23.2%

■ Municipal Government

The city of Chattanooga government is a strong mayor form, consisting of a full-time mayor elected at-large and a nine-member city council elected by districts. The mayor and council serve four-year terms. The mayor and all nine council members are elected on the same election cycle.

Head Official: Mayor Andy Berke (since 2013; current term expires 2017)

Total Number of City Employees: 2,274 (2013)

City Information: Chattanooga City Hall, Suite 100, 101 E. 11th Street, Chattanooga, TN 37402; telephone (423)757-5152; website www.chattanooga.gov.

■ Economy

Major Industries and Commercial Activity

Chattanooga is the hub of a thriving economic region located at the crossroads of three states: Alabama, Georgia, and Tennessee. The city has leveraged its

advantages in the beginning of the twenty-first century to create a diverse economy, balancing its industrial past with a growing professional services industry. Among the city's economic advantages are abundant natural resources (chiefly iron and steel), a strong tourism industry, a trained labor force, and a centralized location. An extensive system of highway, air, water, and rail transportation helps make the city a major transportation and distribution center. In addition, the city has a designated Foreign Trade Zone.

One of the nation's oldest manufacturing cities, Chattanooga's employment in that sector decreased in the latter half of the twentieth century, mirroring national trends. However, in the late 2000s, the auto manufacturing industry was revived by Volkswagen's construction of a new plant, which employed nearly 2,500 residents in 2012. In addition, also mirroring national trends, increases have occurred in information, financial activities, and professional and business services. Companies like Unum Group, ranked 260th among the *Fortune* 500 in 2012, and BlueCross/BlueShield of Tennessee continue to maintain their roots in the city. Chattanooga has also experienced a modest growth trend in transportation, trade, and utilities. Its location as a commercial shipping hub attracts several large trucking and shipping companies.

Other major employers, such as McKee Foods Corporation, which makes Little Debbie and Sunbelt snacks, are headquartered in the area. Local hospital systems were also among the city's major employers. Not all economic news was good, however, as Pilgrim's Pride Corporation, formerly a major employer in the city, laid off hundreds of employees during 2013, and Covenant Transport Inc.

The Tennessee Valley Authority (TVA), the Knoxville-based and largest utility in the United States, has a main office in Chattanooga. TVA is a federal corporation that works to develop the natural resources of the Tennessee Valley. Chattanooga is in an enviable position: both electricity and natural gas are readily available at very reasonable rates. Water supplies are also plentiful, and sewage treatment has considerable excess capacity to support industrial expansion. In addition, TVA and its power distributors offer a growth credit program that provides significant savings to new commercial and industrial customers requiring a large capacity.

Items and goods produced: processed foods, iron and steel products, textiles, apparel, cosmetics, pharmaceuticals, clay products, furniture, machinery, paper, petroleum products

Incentive Programs-New and Existing Companies

Local programs: The Chattanooga Chamber of Commerce has staff to help expedite business permitting by facilitating the licensing process. Foreign Trade Zone 134 includes several industrial sites in the area—a total of 5,000 acres—to provide business with an option to eliminate, reduce, or defer customs duties on a range of imports and exports. Chattanooga and Hamilton County governments have tax incentives that include a payment in lieu of tax program for new and expanding businesses. This tax incentive allows qualified businesses to significantly reduce local or personal property taxes for qualifying new investments. The typical qualifying investment must have a value of at least $5 million and create 50 or more jobs with wages equal to or greater than the average wage in Hamilton County. Additional tax abatements may be negotiated on a case-by-case basis for businesses considering relocation to the Chattanooga area.

State programs: Tennessee is a right-to-work state and its overall state and local tax burden is among the lowest of all 50 states. Tennessee has no personal income tax on wages or salaries. The state's Jobs Tax Credit is available to businesses creating 25 new jobs within a three-year period and investing at least 500,000. These qualifying businesses may claim a tax credit of $4,500 per job to offset up to 50 percent of its franchise and excise tax liability for up to 15 years. The credit is available for businesses in a range of industries, especially advanced manufacturing. The Jobs Tax Super Credit allows businesses with a minimum $1 billion investment to claim up to $10,000 per job for six years.

The Industrial Machinery Tax Credit allows companies to write off up to 50 percent of their franchise and excise tax liability by earning up to 10 percent of the cost of industrial machinery in tax credits. Industrial machinery definitions extend to technological equipment such as computers and computer software, systems, and networks.

A headquarters relocation reimbursement offers tax credits to cover relocation costs of businesses. If the credit exceeds the tax liability of a company in the first year, the remainder is given to the company as a cash payment. Companies must provide evidence of relocation expenses, and certain qualifications regarding the size and operations of the headquarters must be met. There are also state sales tax exemptions and reductions for industrial machinery purchases that support manufacturing businesses.

The state's Industrial Access Program utilizes resources in the Tennessee Department of Transportation to undertake roadways projects that support industrial development. Annual funding for these projects is roughly $10 million.

Job training programs: Overall, the city's collaboration with educational institutions, Chattanooga State, a community college, and University of Tennessee at Chattanooga, an engineering school, to develop a base of young workers with specific skills has rejuvenated manufacturing in the area. The Southeast Tennessee Private Industry Council also assists businesses in meeting labor force training needs. The Council strives to provide businesses with a more competent workforce, higher employee productivity, a reduction in employee turnover, lower employee retraining costs, and highly motivated employees. The council works with Chattanooga State Technical Community College on vocational training, and helps new companies combine resources to meet their training needs.

Tennessee's FastTrack Training Program is the state's primary source of financial support for new and expanding business and industry training. FastTrack staff work with businesses to plan, develop, and implement customized training programs. Training may be done in a classroom setting, or on the job. The state also offers free applicant recruitment and screening for Tennessee companies. The Department of Labor and Workforce Development works with companies to find and review ideal employees, and is entirely free of charge. The state's database contains a pool of more than 70,000 potential employees; 62 Tennessee Career Centers across the state manage applicants locally.

Development Projects

By 2010, employees of BlueCross/BlueShield of Tennessee moved to a new, sprawling $299 million campus on Cameron Hill in downtown Chattanooga. Also that year, Alstom Power completed a $300 million investment in a new production facility.

Power is a major economic player in the Chattanooga area, particularly when the Tennessee Valley Authority is consistently recognized nationally and internationally for its energy efforts. As of 2010, TVA was working to finish updates at the Watts Bar plant. The $4.5 billion project was scheduled to complete in 2015 after an initial target completion date of 2012.

Volkswagen completed construction o a $1 billion facility in Chattanooga in 2011. The plant was built on 1,350 acres formerly the site of a government ammunition plant; the Volkswagen facility covers some 2 million square feet. Capable of producing 150,000 cars per year, the plant was expected to generate $12 billion in income growth and add nearly 10,000 jobs—direct and indirect—to the local economy.

Shaw industries, a hardwood flooring company, announced a $40 million expansion at its facility that would also add 25 jobs to the local economy in 2013. Roper Corporation unveiled an $88 million expansion that same year. Like the Roper Corporation, Lodge Manufacturing also makes cookware—primarily cast iron—and planned a $34 million expansion in 2013.

The Block, a mixed use facility with a fitness center, outdoor outfitters retail store, and 16,500-square-foot climbing wall completed in 2013. The Block was one of the largest adaptive reuse projects in the city's history, replacing the old Bijou theater that formerly occupied the area. In April 2013, the city opened Center Park, which added greenspace to a previously vacant lot and also created a "food truck court."

The city's Office of Economic and Community Development included a number of minor projects in its 2013–14 Action Plan to maintain and expand affordable housing for low- and middle-income residents.

Economic Development Information: Chattanooga Area Chamber of Commerce, 811 Broad Street, Chattanooga, TN 37402; telephone (423) 756-2121; fax (423) 267-7242.

Commercial Shipping

While new energy is focused on technology and service sectors, Chattanooga's economy is still tied to the railroad system of the past. As a major freight hub of Norfolk Southern and CSX, more than 70 motor freight lines are certified to transport shipments in the area. Two ports—the Port of Chattanooga and Centre South Riverport—are within city limits. Chattanooga remains an important port as a result of the Tennessee Valley Authority's system of locks and dams, and the Tombigbee waterway, which saves days, miles, and dollars on shipments to and from ports along the Ohio and Mississippi Rivers and the Gulf of Mexico. Air cargo service carriers operate out of Chattanooga Metropolitan Airport, where FedEx feeder operations ship cargo to Memphis. In addition, Chattanooga is located at the crossroads of several major U.S. highways, including Interstates 75, 24, and 59. The city is within one day's drive of nearly one-third of the major U.S. markets and population, and within 140 miles of Nashville, Atlanta, Knoxville, Huntsville, and Birmingham. Chattanooga is the distribution center for the region that includes southeast Tennessee, northwest Georgia, southwest North Carolina, northeast Alabama, and parts of several neighboring states.

Labor Force and Employment Outlook

Chattanooga's work force is said to be distinguished by its pride in individual workmanship. Workers are prepared for specialized professions by the state's excellent industrial training programs. Tennessee is a right-to-work state, and the city's cost of labor remains lower than in many other areas of the United States. Such attributes of the labor force have made Chattanooga attractive to companies looking to invest in new cities. Government, educational and health services, and manufacturing accounted for nearly half of all jobs in the area.

The following is a summary of data regarding the 2012 Chattanooga labor force:

Size of civilian labor force: 84,577

Number of workers employed in . . .
agriculture and mining: 421
construction: 3,779
manufacturing: 9,596
wholesale trade: 1,505
retail trade: 7,927
transportation: 5,016
information systems: 1,637
finance: 6,237
professional administration: 7,600
education and social services: 15,930
arts and leisure: 8,342
other: 3,408
public administration: 2,625

Average hourly earnings of production workers: $15.09

Unemployment rate: 7.4% (2012)

Employers

Largest employers (2012)	Number of employees
Hamilton County Dept. of Education	4,489
BlueCross BlueShield of Tennessee	4,337
Tennessee Valley Authority	4,217
Erlanger Health System	3,447
Memorial Health Care System	3,171
McKee Foods Corporation	2,950
Unum	2,800
Volkswagen Chattanooga	2,487
City of Chattanooga	2,274
Hamilton County Government	1,763

Cost of Living

The following is a summary of data regarding several key cost of living factors in the area.

2013 ACCRA Average House Price: $261,165

2013 ACCRA Cost of Living Index: 94

State income tax rate: State income tax is limited to dividends and interest income only.

State sales tax rate: 7.0%

Local income tax rate: None

Local sales tax rate: 2.25%

Property tax rate: $5.0742 per $100 assessed value (2013)

Economic Information: Chattanooga Area Chamber of Commerce, 811 Broad Street, Chattanooga, TN 37402; telephone (423) 756-2121; fax (423) 267-7242.

■ Education and Research

Elementary and Secondary Schools

The Hamilton County Department of Education is the largest employer in Chattanooga, educating more than 40,000 students in more than 70 schools. The county department was formed in 1997 upon the merger of Chattanooga Public Schools and Hamilton County Schools. Hamilton County schools operate 13 magnet programs that support language arts, mathematics, science, and social studies curriculum. Magnet schools are available as early as kindergarten and continue through high school. Junior ROTC programs exist for the army, air force, and navy. Eligible students with special needs or disabilities have access to an array of special classes, small group instruction, and support for home-bound schooling. Vocational education and training programs are also offered through continuing vocational education of the public school systems.

Chattanooga has a strong tradition of private and parochial elementary and secondary education, including the nationally recognized Girls' Preparatory School, the McCallie School for Boys, and the coeducational Baylor School (a boarding school attracting students from all around the world). More than 11,000 students attend 41 private and parochial schools.

The following is a summary of data regarding the Hamilton County School District.

Total enrollment: 42,589

Number of facilities

  total: 77
  elementary schools: 45
  junior high schools: 12
  high schools: 20

Student/teacher ratio: 14.34:1

Teacher salaries

  average (statewide): $47,043

Funding per pupil: $8,645

Public Schools Information: Hamilton County Department of Education, 3074 Hickory Valley Road, Chattanooga, TN 37421; telephone (423) 209-8400.

Colleges and Universities

The University of Tennessee at Chattanooga (UTC), the second largest campus of the University of Tennessee system with 11,660 students as of 2013, is comprised of a College of

Arts and Sciences, College of Business, College of Engineering and Computer Science, and College of Health, Education, and Professional Studies, a school of Nursing, and a graduate school offering master's degrees, specialist certifications, and doctoral degrees. The university was ranked 49th regionally in 2014 by *U.S. News & World Report*. The University of Tennessee College of Medicine also has a branch in the city, affiliated with Erlanger Health Systems.

Chattanooga State Community College, with more than 20,000 students, is a two-year college offering the following areas of study: business and information technologies; engineering technology; humanities and fine arts; math and sciences; nursing and allied health; social and behavioral sciences; and the Tennessee College of Applied Technology.

Several private colleges operate in the Chattanooga area: Tennessee Temple University, with 11 majors and 20 minors; Southern Adventist University, in nearby Collegedale, TN, with more than 3,000 students; and Covenant College, in Lookout Mountain, GA, with 1,100 students. The University of the South, also known as "Sewanee," is located northwest of Chattanooga. With more than 1,500 students, was ranked 38th among national liberal arts colleges by *U.S. News & World Report* in 2014; it is also recognized for its school of theology.

Libraries and Research Centers

The Chattanooga Public Library system consists of a main downtown library and three branches. Special collections include interviews on Chattanooga and Hamilton County history and genealogy, as well as an index of Chattanooga obituaries that dates to 1897. The library also offers special events, concerts, and programs, including preschool story hours and film festivals.

The University of Tennessee at Chattanooga makes the following research and testing resources available to business and industry: Center of Excellence in Applied Computational Science and Engineering, which provides resources associated with high technology; and Center for Economic Education and its associated Probasco Chair of Free Enterprise, which designs and implements research projects and education programs about basic economic principles. At the university's SimCenter, research professionals, faculty, and students serve government and industry through research in computational engineering. The Tennessee Valley Authority has several research centers in Chattanooga.

Public Library Information: Chattanooga Publicl Library, 1001 Broad Street, Chattanooga, TN 37402; telephone (423) 757-5310; email library@lib.chattanooga.gov.

■ Health Care

Three major health systems are offered to Chattanooga area residents: Erlanger, Memorial, and Parkridge hospitals. Erlanger Baroness Campus, the region's largest and oldest public hospital with 538 beds, offers a full range of health-care services and admits nearly 28,000 patients a year, in addition to the more than 250,000 outpatient visits and 100,000 emergency room visits it receives annually. Erlanger is also the area's primary trauma center, a Level I Trauma Center for adults, and the only provider of tertiary care for the residents of southeastern Tennessee, north Georgia, north Alabama, and western North Carolina. Erlanger hosts a branch of the University of Tennessee College of Medicine. Other branches of the Erlanger Health System include the Children's Hospital at Erlanger, Erlanger Bledsoe Campus, Erlanger East Campus, Erlanger North Campus, and UT Erlanger Physicians Group.

Memorial Hospital, a 365-bed affiliate of the Kentucky-based Sisters of Charity of Nazareth Health System—which has since joined the broader Catholic Health Initiatives network—offers an ambulatory intensive care unit. The 109-bed Siskin Hospital for Physical Rehabilitation offers treatment programs in brain injury, amputation, stroke, spinal cord injury, orthopedics, and major multiple trauma. It specializes in treatment of lymphedema.

Parkridge Medical Center, with 275 beds, is known for its strong open-heart and cardiac services program and bypass surgeries. Parkridge East Hospital (formerly East Ridge Hospital), provides specialty services including a women's center, a sleep disorder center, bariatric surgery services, neonatal intensive care, and a spine and orthopedic center. It opened a Center for Robotic Surgery in 2012 and boasts the most experienced robotic surgery team in the region. Parkridge Valley hospital specializes in behavioral health. Other Chattanooga health care facilities include HealthSouth Chattanooga Rehabilitation Hospital, which offers comprehensive physical rehabilitation services.

■ Recreation

Sightseeing

More than four million people visit Chattanooga annually to explore the city's past, take part in activities, and enjoy the region's unique sights and diversions. The $45 million Tennessee Aquarium, one of the world's largest freshwater aquariums, takes spectators everywhere a river goes—from small mountain streams, to raging currents, to deep reservoirs, to the sea. Displays of thousands of living plants, fish, birds, and other river animals show how water supports life. A $30 million, 60,000-square-foot addition holds 650,000 gallons of water, with ten-foot sharks, stingrays, and barracuda swimming among coral formations. This expansion was part of a $120 million Waterfront Plan, completed in May 2005, that included a $19.5 million expansion to the Hunter Museum of

American Art, and a $3 million renovation and enhancement to the Children's Creative Discovery Museum, as well as other riverside revitalization projects. The story of Chattanooga's rich cultural, historical, and geographical significance is related through chronologically progressive exhibits at Ross's Landing Park and Plaza, which is adjacent to the Aquarium. The $10.5 million Chattanooga History Center was slated to open in the aquarium plaza in 2014.

The Chattanooga Zoo at Warner Park presents a variety of exotic animals and birds, including primates, jaguars, nocturnal animals, and a petting zoo, as well as classes about animal life. In 2013 the zoo was planning a $7 million expansion that included a brand-new habitat for its giraffe population. The Tennessee Valley Railroad Museum offers an impressive collection of classic railroad memorabilia, including a 1911 steam locomotive, a 1917 office car with three bedrooms, a 1926 dining car, a Pullman sleeping car, and a 1929 wooden caboose. Visitors can ride the train on its 40-acre site with its four railroad bridges and a historic tunnel through Missionary Ridge; four-hour roundtrip train rides to historic Chickamauga, Georgia, are also available.

The Chattanooga Choo-Choo is a 30-acre complex offering accommodations in restored Victorian railroad cars, dining options including dinner in an elegant dining car, browsing in unique shops, and touring the entertainment complex via old-fashioned trolley. At Ross's Landing, the sternwheeler *Southern Belle,* which can carry 500 people, conducts excursions up the Tennessee River on its dining and entertainment cruises. Another excursion boat, the *Chattanooga Star,* is an authentic side paddle wheeler that can accommodate up to 145 passengers.

The Lookout Mountain Incline Railway ascends and descends the mountain every half hour with trolley-style railcars, offering panoramic views of the city. One of the steepest railways in the world, its gradient reaches 72.7 percent. The self-guided tour of famous Rock City on Lookout Mountain reveals giant prehistoric rock formations, breathtaking views, and visits to Fairyland Caverns and Mother Goose Village, where fairy tales are celebrated. Ruby Falls-Lookout Mountain Caverns is a cave providing a view of a 145-foot waterfall that is 1,120 feet underground. The Chattanooga Arboretum and Nature Center is an environmental educational facility featuring exhibits such as a wildlife diorama, interactive computer games, and a crawl-in beaver lodge, as well as a 1,400-foot Wetland Boardwalk, and a Wildlife Rehabilitation laboratory. Adjoining Lookout Mountain is Reflection Riding, a 300-acre nature preserve that permits visitors to drive through a grand variety of trees, shrubs, and wildflowers similar to those in an English landscape.

Straddling the Tennessee-Georgia border, the 9,000-acre Chickamauga and Chattanooga National Military Park is the nation's oldest and largest preserved area of Civil War sites. Chickamauga Battlefield offers "living history" programs, the Fuller gun collection, a self-guided tour, and a multimedia presentation on the battle. Lookout Mountain offers free programs, the Craven's House Museum, and magnificent views from Point Park. The National Medal of Honor Museum displays memorabilia, artifacts, equipment, and history about the Medal of Honor. An exciting three-dimensional presentation of Chattanooga's Civil War history is presented at the Battles for Chattanooga Museum, which features 5,000 miniature figures, 650 lights, sound effects, and details of major battles. Signal Point, atop Signal Mountain, is the site where messages were relayed to clear the way for supplies coming down the Tennessee River for Union soldiers during the Civil War.

A number of interesting historical houses and buildings are located around the city. The Brabson House, built in 1857 and later used as a hospital during the 1878 yellow fever epidemic, was destroyed by fire in 1881 and rebuilt in the early 1990s. The John Ross House, a memorial to the man who was the greatest chief of the Cherokee Nation, was built in 1779 by Ross's grandfather. Craven's House, built circa 1854, was the center of action in the Battle of Lookout Mountain, and the 1840s Gordon Lee Mansion served as headquarters to General William Rosecrans in 1863 as well as serving as a soldiers' hospital. After the Confederate evacuation of Chattanooga in 1863, General Braxton Bragg established his headquarters at the Lee & Gordon's Mill.

Other area attractions include views of the underground lake of Lost Sea Adventure, tours of the Jack Daniels Distillery at Lynchburg, and the games and rides at Lake Winni Amusement Park.

Arts and Culture

Chattanooga has an active performing arts community. The Chattanooga Symphony and Opera presents symphony concerts, operas, chamber music, pops programs, young people's concerts and operas, and youth orchestras, with guest artists of international renown at the Tivoli Theatre. The restored Tivoli is a fine example of 1920s baroque elegance. With its ample stage depth and first-rate backstage and rehearsal facilities, the theater is the site of some of the city's major entertainment and cultural events, including touring Broadway productions. The Soldiers and Sailors Memorial Auditorium was built in 1924 and rededicated in 1991 after being refashioned into a theatrical venue with a sloped concert hall with permanent seating. The auditorium is an ideal venue for concerts, theatrical performances, meetings, and conventions.

Founded in 1923 as the Little Theatre of Chattanooga, the Chattanooga Theatre Centre is a 40,000 square-foot facility with a main stage seating 380 and a smaller Circle stage seating 200. The Theatre Center offers a variety of locally produced programs featuring professionally directed local and regional talent in its seven main stage shows, four smaller and more adventurous Circle Series shows, and four youth theater productions each year. The Encore Theatre, the Mountain Opry, and other area and regional theaters offer a variety of locally produced performances year-round.

Chattanooga has a number of dance companies including Ballet Tennessee, Chattanooga Ballet, and Barking Legs Theater. These companies present a variety of programs from the holiday classic *The Nutcracker* to avant garde drama. The Chattanooga Boys Choir, which includes approximately 200 boys in the program each year, and Girls Choir, composed of nearly 150 girls, travel throughout the United States and abroad. Rock and popular concerts are held at Memorial Auditorium.

The Bessie Smith Culture Center includes a 300-seat performance hall, a legacy of the city's "Empress of the Blues," and Chattanooga's African-American History Museum, which contains a library and a collection of artifacts including African art, original sculptures, paintings, musical recordings, and local African American newspapers. The Houston Museum of Decorative Arts is famous for its outstanding collection of American decorative arts assembled by Anna S. Houston, a local antiques dealer. The museum features beautiful pieces of porcelain, glass, furniture, and ceramics. With one of the largest and finest collections of American art in the Southeast, the Hunter Museum of American Art is situated high on a bluff overlooking the Tennessee River. The museum houses masterworks from Thomas Hart Benton, Winslow Homer, and Andrew Wyeth.

The University of Tennessee at Chattanooga (UTC) provides the community with numerous offerings in the cultural and fine arts. The University Theatre presents several stage productions annually while faculty, student, and guest musicians participate in the Cadek Department of Music and Conservatory offerings. The university's Cress Gallery of Art houses visiting exhibitions as well as local and student art work. Patten Performances series, formerly The Dorothy Patten Fine Arts Series, hosts top quality theatrical, concert, and dance presentations.

Festivals and Holidays

Festivals in Chattanooga are an extension of its art and culture. An interesting merger of festival and intellectual pursuits, Chattanooga hosts a variety of "writing conferences," including the Conference on Southern Literature and the Festival of Writers, both sponsored by the Arts & Education Council of Chattanooga. Traditional festivals are also abundant. Held in April, the two-day 4 Bridges Arts Festival celebrates the visual arts. The annual River Roast, held in May, draws thousands to the riverfront and features a barbeque, volleyball tournament, and Mayor's Regatta. One of the recreational highlights in Chattanooga is June's nine-day Riverbend Festival, a musical celebration on the riverfront at Ross's Landing, which draws more than 600,000 people each year to see top-name entertainers. Musical performances on its six stages range from jazz, blues, rock, folk, country, bluegrass, classic and more. At the Southern Brewers Festival in August, microbrewers from across the country offer more than 30 ales and lagers; the event also features music and food. The Bessie Smith Heritage Festival in August is a two-day jazz extravaganza held at the Bessie Smith Performance Hall. Oktoberfest is held for one weekend at the Chattanooga Market and attracts more than 30,000 people. The first weekend in November invites the start of the Head of the Hooch rowing regatta in downtown Chattanooga. The race originally began at the Chattahoochee River in Atlanta, giving it the name the Head of the Hooch. With more than 2,000 boats over two days in 2013, the race was one of the largest regattas in the United States. When the thousands of rowers descend on Chattanooga, other festivities like hot-air balloon rides and a street market also cover the city. The holiday season is highlighted by Christmas on the River, a parade of festively decorated lighted boats on the Tennessee River.

Sports for the Spectator

Chattanooga has a minor league professional team in baseball, the Chattanooga Lookouts, a Double-A Southern League team affiliated with the Los Angeles Dodgers. The Chattanooga Locomotion, an Independent Women's Football League team, also competes in the city. The Lookouts play in the 6,500-seat AT&T Field, while the Locomotion play home games at Red Bank High School. Chattanooga is also home to Chattanooga FC, a semi-professional soccer team of the National Premier Soccer League.

Major collegiate sports entertainment is available through the University of Tennessee at Chattanooga. The university's Mocs compete in NCAA Division I sports, with the exception of football, which competes in Division I-AA in the Southern Conference. Finley Stadium is the home for football and soccer, while McKenzie Arena hosts both the men and women's basketball teams. UTC also fields NCAA Division I teams in cross country, golf, softball, tennis, indoor/outdoor track and field, volleyball, and wrestling.

Sports for the Participant

Surrounded by parks, mountains, and nearly 50,000 acres of rivers and lakes, the Chattanooga area offers recreation opportunities of all kinds. The mountains circling the city feature camping, rock climbing, rappelling, and spelunking. Mountain rivers offer exciting whitewater rafting, kayaking, and canoeing. Paddlers can take a 50-mile trip down the Tennessee River Blueway. Fishing on the Tennessee River is always an attraction, and nearby Lake Chickamauga provides more than 35,000 acres of water for sailing, water skiing, and rowing. Another site for water enthusiasts is the 192 miles of shoreline on Nickajack Lake. The city has its own program, Outdoor Chattanooga, responsible for promoting bicycling for transportation, recreation and active living. *Bicycling* magazine ranked Chattanooga among its top 50 bicycle friendly cities in 2012, praising the city for its ample greenways, including the Tennessee Riverwalk, a 15-mile multiuse path that follows the Tennessee River from downtown to the Chickamauga Dam.

One of the jewels in the Tennessee Riverpark system is Coolidge Park, located on Chattanooga's north shore waterfront. The six-acre park is named in honor of Charles Coolidge, a World War II Medal of Honor recipient. The park boasts a restored Denzel carousel originally built in 1895 for Atlanta's Grant Park; it features 52 intricately painted, hand-carved animals created by students of artisan Bud Ellis at Horsin' Around, a year-round carousel animal carving school in Chattanooga.

More than 200 tennis courts, as well as hundreds of basketball courts, softball and baseball fields, dot city neighborhoods. Chattanooga has dozens of recreation centers and supervised playgrounds to occupy the young set. Around the city, organized team sports include softball, baseball, wrestling, polo, boxing, soccer, rugby, gymnastics, and swimming, while sporting clubs center on hunting, fishing, running, biking, and skiing. In all, the city and county maintain 4,800 acres of park space.

Shopping and Dining

Chattanooga is a shopping mecca for a region covering a 50-mile radius in Tennessee, Alabama, and Georgia. Residents are served by more than 40 shopping centers, including several enclosed major malls. Hamilton Place, with more than 200 stores, is located in southeast Hamilton County. Rehabilitation efforts in the city's downtown have restored its vitality as a popular shopping and dining site. There, Warehouse Row, a $30 million upscale outlet complex, features designer shops located in eight cavernous former turn-of-the-century railroad warehouses. Chattanooga's riverfront area has numerous shops alongside piers, boatslips, and waterfront parks. The East Ridge Flea Market, open on weekends and holidays, is a huge indoor/outdoor market featuring more than 250 vendors selling new and used items, and three restaurants.

Dining experiences in Chattanooga can be as varied as having dinner while walking or cruising along the Tennessee River or while watching a stage production or eating in a former railway dining car. Fine dining and more moderately priced traditional American fare are offered in many areas of the city. Casual eateries include burger joints, delis, buffets and cafeterias, and novelty settings. Ethnic cuisine runs the gamut from Chinese, Italian, and Tex-Mex to Jamaican.

Visitor Information: Chattanooga Area Convention & Visitors Bureau, 736 Market Street, 18th floor,

Chattanooga, TN 37402; telephone (423) 756-8687; toll-free (800) 322-3344.

■ Convention Facilities

Chattanooga offers several facilities designed to hold such diverse events as trade shows, conventions, meetings, banquets, or any other special event. Located in the heart of downtown, the 312,000 square-foot Chattanooga Convention Center offers 100,000 square feet of column-free exhibit space and has a seating capacity of 8,000. It is one of the nation's "greenest" convention centers, including the nation's first farm-to-table catering service. The Tivoli Theatre, which is listed on the National Register of Historic places and was once known as "The Jewel Box of the South," can host meetings and conventions for about 1,800 people. Soldiers & Sailors Memorial Auditorium features two theaters, the larger of which seats 4,843, and an exhibit hall providing 9,600 square feet of display space, suitable for small trade shows. The Chattanoogan Conference Center is a 25,000-square-foot facility with 20 meeting rooms. The Chattanooga Choo-Choo has more than 30,000 square feet of convention space and 12 meeting rooms. For larger groups, McKenzie Arena at the University of Tennessee seats 12,000 people, and can provide 27,000 square feet of exhibit space.

Convention Information: Chattanooga Area Convention & Visitors Bureau, 736 Market Street, 18th floor, Chattanooga, TN 37402; telephone (423) 756-8687; toll-free (800) 322-3344.

■ Transportation

Approaching the City

Three Interstates, 75, 24, and 59, converge near the city. Interstate 75 runs southwest toward the city from Knoxville, and north–northwest from Atlanta; Interstate 59 runs north, then east from Birmingham; and Interstate 24 runs south, then east from Nashville. A variety of tunnels surround the area, woven into the ridges. The city is considered a gateway to the "Deep South," as it is a convenient stop en route to cities such as New Orleans, Orlando, and many other southern destinations. Chattanooga Metropolitan Airport, just 15 minutes from downtown, serves more than 300,000 passengers annually; the terminal was undergoing a renovation during 2013. Greyhound/Trailways Bus Lines provides interstate service. Despite the relatively high level of freight rail activity, and the famous Glenn Miller Orchestra big band song "Chattanooga Choo Choo" of the 1940s, there is no longer passenger rail service in the city for commuters or long-distance travelers. Occasionally, however, the Lookout Mountain Incline Railway is used for commuting by local residents when going up and down the mountain may be dangerous.

Traveling in the City

The three interstate highways are particularly busy during the rush hour to and from work. Major thoroughfares include Hixson Pike, which runs north–south, and Brainerd Road, which runs east–west then turns north into Lee Highway. Ringgold Road is another important east–west route. Riverside Drive curves around many major downtown sites. Staying true to its new sustainable vision, the city and county have developed an extensive greenway system which includes 15 miles of constructed riverwalk beginning downtown, meandering through the historic art district and several parks. The city, through the Chattanooga Area Regional Transportation Authority (CARTA), supports a downtown shuttle fleet of zero-emission electric buses for commuters and visitors wishing to park-and-ride. The buses are manufactured in Chattanooga. CARTA provides regularly scheduled public bus transportation for the area on 19 routes, as of 2013.

■ Communications

Newspapers and Magazines

The *Chattanooga Times Free Press* is the city's only daily morning paper. Average weekday circulation reached nearly 72,000 during 2013. There are several general and special weekly newspapers, among them the *The Chattanooga Pulse,* a weekly alternative newspaper that debuted in 2003. Magazines covering Chattanooga include *Trend,* published quarterly by the Chattanooga Area Chamber of Commerce, and *East Tennessee Business Journal,* published monthly; and *Chattanooga CityScope* and *Chattanooga Magazine,* published quarterly. Chattanooga is generally served by media outlets seeking to reach the four-state region of which Chattanooga is a part: Tennessee, Alabama, Georgia, and North Carolina.

Television and Radio

Eleven television stations, 5 licensed AM stations, and 12 licensed FM stations serve the Chattanooga area, providing a variety of music and talk shows.

Media Information: The *Chattanooga Times Free Press,* 400 E. 11th St., Chattanooga, TN 37403; telephone (423) 756-6900.

Chattanooga Online

Chattanooga Area Chamber of Commerce. Available www.chattanoogachamber.com
Chattanooga Area Convention & Visitors Bureau. Available www.chattanoogafun.com
Chattanooga-Hamilton County Bicentennial Library. Available chattlibrary.org

Chattanooga History Center. Available
chattanoogahistory.org
Chattanooga Regional History Museum. Available
www.chattanoogahistory.com
City of Chattanooga Home Page. Available www.
chattanooga.gov
Chattanooga Times Free Press. Available www.
timesfreepress.com
Hamilton County Department of Education.
Available www.hcde.org

BIBLIOGRAPHY

Ezzell, Tim, *Chattanooga, 1865–1900: A City Set Down
in Dixie* (Knoxville, TN: University of Tennessee
Press, 2013)

Potter, Susanna Henighan, *Moon Spotlight Chattanooga
and Knoxville* (Berkeley, CA: Avalon Travel Publishing, 2010)

Woodworth, Steven E. and Charles D. Grear, eds., *The
Chattanooga Campaign* (Carbondale, IL: Southern
Illinois University Press, 2013)

Knoxville

■ The City in Brief

Founded: 1786 (incorporated 1791)

Head Official: Mayor Madeline Rogero (since 2011; current term expires 2015)

City Population
> 1990: 169,761
> 2000: 173,890
> 2010: 178,874
> 2012 estimate: 182,196
> Percent change, 2000–2010: 2.9%
> U.S. rank in 1990: 101st (State rank: 3rd)
> U.S. rank in 2000: 135th (State rank: 3rd)
> U.S. rank in 2010: 129th (State rank: 3rd)

Metropolitan Statistical Area Population
> 2000: 616,079
> 2010: 698,030
> 2012 estimate: 709,492
> Percent change, 2000–2010: 13.3%
> U.S. rank in 2000: 76th
> U.S. rank in 2010: 75th

Area: 92.7 square miles

Elevation: Approximately 936 feet above sea level

Average Annual Temperatures: 60.0° F

Average Annual Precipitation: 48.2 inches

Major Economic Sectors: wholesale and retail trade, services, government, education

Unemployment Rate: 4.6% (2012)

Per Capita Income: $22,610

2012 FBI Crime Index Property: 12,169

Major Colleges and Universities: University of Tennessee at Knoxville, Knoxville College, Pellissippi State Technical Community College

Daily Newspaper: *The Knoxville News Sentinel*

■ Introduction

Just 30 miles north of the country's most visited national park, Knoxville, Tennessee, has long been known as the "Gateway to the Smokies." The second-oldest city in the state, and the state's first capital, Knoxville is a hallmark of the state's history and is poised to be a standout city among mid-sized cities. The city serves as the corporate hub of east Tennessee and home to the Tennessee Valley Authority (TVA) and the University of Tennessee's main campus. In the last several decades Knoxville has experienced impressive gains, particularly in high-technology industries and related firms. Knoxville's Sunsphere, a remnant of the 1982 World's Fair, remains the towering symbol of Knoxville's past, present, and future as a beacon of energy development. Because of the influence of TVA, the University of Tennessee at Knoxville, and world-famous Oak Ridge, 30 miles away, Knoxville has become known as one of the foremost energy centers in the world. Meanwhile, the greater Knoxville area has won accolades for its "livability"—a combination of qualities that encompasses such factors as economic outlook, climate, cost of living, education, transportation, and the arts. Even as a nationwide recession in the late 2000s slowed the pace of private investment, the city continued its effort to improve streetscapes and add greenways in preparation for the city's continued growth.

■ Geography and Climate

Knoxville is located at the headwaters of the Tennessee River in a broad valley between the Cumberland Mountains to the northwest and the Great Smoky

Gay Street Bridge and Tennessee River, Knoxville, TN. © *Melinda Fawver/Shutterstock.com*

Mountains (a sub range of the Appalachian Mountains) to the southeast. Both mountain ranges modify the type of weather that plains areas at the same latitude experience by slowing and weakening cold winter air from the north and tempering hot summer winds from the west and south. Although in a valley, Knoxville is still over 900 feet above sea level. Downtown Knoxville and the business areas are located mostly on the north bank of the Tennessee River, while the southern portion (often referred to as "South Knoxville") encompasses industrial and other residential areas. Precipitation is usually in the form of rain, and falls primarily during the winter and in late spring, though sudden thunderstorms are also quite common in summertime and provide relief on extremely warm days in the valley. Snowfall averages approximately 12 inches annually, most often in amounts of less than four inches at one time; it rarely stays on the ground for more than a week.

Area: 92.7 square miles

Elevation: Approximately 936 feet above sea level

Average Temperatures: 60.0° F

Average Annual Precipitation: 48.2 inches

■ History

Settlement Becomes Supply Center

Archaeological evidence suggests that the first humans to live in what is now Knoxville were of the Woodland tribe, a group of hunters and trappers driven south from the Great Lakes region by climatic changes, probably about 1000 B.C. Their simple culture eventually gave way to that of the more sophisticated mound builders, whose influence was felt throughout most of the South. By 1761, the year the first white men were known to have explored Knoxville, the mound builders had been displaced by yet another group of Native Americans, the Cherokee.

Early contacts between the white settlers and the Cherokee were fairly cordial, which encouraged colonial expansion into the land west of the Great Smoky Mountains. In 1783 North Carolina's James White and several friends crossed the mountains in search of a place to stake a claim. White later returned to the area with his family, and in 1786 he became Knoxville's first permanent settler when he built a log cabin on a hill overlooking a stream that fed into the Tennessee River. A peace treaty with the Cherokee sparked additional migration into the region, and soon White's cabin was joined by several others. After the pioneers connected their cabins with a stake fence, the settlement took on the name White's Fort. Because of its strategic location, it quickly began serving as a repair and supply center for westbound wagon trains.

In 1790 William Blount, newly appointed governor of the territory south of the Ohio River and superintendent of Indian affairs for the same region, arrived at White's Fort and established his headquarters there. One of his first tasks was to meet with the Cherokee and establish territorial boundaries; this he accomplished almost immediately, purchasing from the Cherokees much of the East Tennessee Valley and opening the area to even more settlers. In 1791, at Blount's suggestion, streets were laid out around White's Fort and a town was incorporated that the governor named Knoxville in honor of the Secretary of War, Major General Henry Knox. By 1792, Knoxville had become the county seat, and it continued to grow steadily as a trading post. When Tennessee was admitted to the Union in 1796, Knoxville even served as the state's first capital, a designation it retained until 1812. Despite its political and economic status, Knoxville at the turn of the century was little more than a rowdy village of taverns and smithies that catered to teamsters, flatboat men, soldiers, and homesteaders on their way west.

City Grows Slowly

Knoxville's first industries were related to its function on the frontier; among the most common were grist mills, sawmills, tanyards, cotton-spinning factories, and wool-carding mills. Because of the transportation difficulties posed by the mountains and unnavigable parts of the Tennessee River, no attempt was made to mine nearby coal, iron, and marble for shipping out of the region. As a result, Knoxville grew rather slowly in comparison with the rest of the state, posting a population of barely more than 2,000 people in 1850. The arrival of the railroad in the 1850s promised change, but the advent of the Civil War put a halt to further development.

A majority of east Tennessee citizens were loyal to the Union before and even during the Civil War, and their opposition to secession made Tennessee the last state to join the Confederate States of America. Alarmed at the thought of so many Union sympathizers in a critical border state, the Confederate Army occupied the city from early 1861 until August 1863, shortly before Union troops arrived and established headquarters there. In November of that same year, Confederate troops tried to recapture Knoxville. After a two-week-long siege, they were eventually repulsed, but victory for the Union forces came at a great cost to Knoxville-railroad shops, factories, virtually all public buildings, and some private homes were either burned to the ground or badly damaged.

The Reconstruction period was a boon to the city as hundreds of former Union soldiers chose to return to Knoxville to settle permanently, bringing with them the business and labor skills so desperately needed to rebuild what had been destroyed during the war. The population swelled to almost 10,000 people in 1870, up from less than 3,000 people in 1860. The rest of the century brought still more development; iron plants, cloth mills, furniture factories, marble quarries, and foundry and machine companies were established, and Knoxville began to emerge as a major southern commercial center.

Economic Problems Abound

Throughout much of the twentieth century, however, Knoxville saw its postwar progress eroded by racial tension, periodic economic downturns, the Great Depression of the 1930s, loss of population to the suburbs, and a series of ineffective city governments. The 1920s provided a brief respite from economic woes as the city benefited from the national boom, but social and political conditions continued to deteriorate when conservative leaders clashed with progressive elements over the best way to tackle Knoxville's problems. Like so many other cities, Knoxville was hit hard by the Great Depression; factories closed, major banks failed, and the optimism of the previous decade faded, leaving in its place a cautiousness that influenced decision-makers for years to come.

Wartime Brings Prosperity

World War II brought prosperity to the area, especially at Alcoa Aluminum, Oak Ridge National Laboratory, the Tennessee Valley Authority, and Rohm & Haas, manufacturers of plexiglass for airplanes. The influx of federal money and jobs led to increased activity in other areas, including construction, service industries, and retail and wholesale trade. But Knoxville failed to capitalize on the wartime gains and instead entered another period of stagnation during the 1950s.

City Celebrates Progressive Spirit

After the mid-1960s, a new generation of progressive business and political leaders worked to make the city more attractive to developers, initiating facelifts for downtown buildings, arranging financing for new projects, cleaning up the riverfront, and demolishing or upgrading substandard housing. The 1982 World's Fair and its theme of "Energy Turns the World" focused even more attention on the city's attempts to stage a comeback. This motto could continue into the twenty-first century, as high-powered staples like the Tennessee Valley Authority (TVA) and the Oak Ridge National Laboratory are consistent leaders in the field of energy. In addition, new industries, especially high-technology ones, have established facilities in the area, and old industries have expanded. Innovation Valley, a Knoxville Chamber of Commerce imitative to target certain business, was named the number-one area for green jobs growth in the

United States in 2013 by the Brookings Institution. This in turn has led to gains in construction, services, and retail trade as thousands of young, well-educated, and affluent workers have followed the high-technology firms to Knoxville.

Historical Information: East Tennessee Historical Society, McClung Historical Collection, 601 S. Gay St., PO Box 1629, TN 37901; telephone (865) 215-8824.

■ Population Profile

Metropolitan Statistical Area Population

2000: 616,079
2010: 698,030
2012 estimate: 709,492
Percent change, 2000–2010: 13.3%
U.S. rank in 2000: 76th
U.S. rank in 2010: 75th

City Residents

1990: 169,761
2000: 173,890
2010: 178,874
2012 estimate: 182,196
Percent change, 2000–2010: 2.9%
U.S. rank in 1990: 101st (State rank: 3rd)
U.S. rank in 2000: 135th (State rank: 3rd)
U.S. rank in 2010: 129th (State rank: 3rd)

Density: 1,815.6 people per square mile

Racial and ethnic characteristics

White: 139,551
Black or African American: 34,605
American Indian and Alaskan Native: 325
Asian: 2,031
Native Hawaiian and Other Pacific Islander: 156
Hispanic or Latino (may be of any race): 5,269
Other: 5,528

Percent of residents born in state: 67.8%

Age characteristics

Population under 5 years old: 11,363
Population 5 to 9 years old: 8,142
Population 10 to 14 years old: 7,496
Population 15 to 19 years old: 10,585
Population 20 to 24 years old: 24,004
Population 25 to 34 years old: 29,775
Population 35 to 44 years old: 21,178
Population 45 to 54 years old: 20,375
Population 55 to 59 years old: 11,014
Population 60 to 64 years old: 9,471
Population 65 to 74 years old: 15,287
Population 75 to 84 years old: 9,524

Population 85 years and over: 3,982
Median age: 34.9

Births (2010–11 Metropolitan Area)

Total number: 8,009

Deaths (2010–11 Metropolitan Area)

Total number: 6,517

Money income (2012)

Per capita income: $22,610
Median household income: $32,632
Total households: 84,221

Number of households with income of . . .

less than $10,000: 11,246
$10,000 to $14,999: 6,082
$15,000 to $24,999: 13,564
$25,000 to $34,999: 14,127
$35,000 to $49,999: 12,567
$50,000 to $74,999: 12,753
$75,000 to $99,999: 6,265
$100,000 to $149,999: 4,598
$150,000 to $199,999: 1,272
$200,000 or more: 1,747

Percent of families below poverty level: 22.4%

FBI Crime Index Property: 12,169

FBI Crime Index Violent: 1,774

■ Municipal Government

Knoxville operates via a mayor-council form of government. The mayor and nine council members are elected to four-year terms. Six council members represent districts, while three are elected at-large. The vice-mayor is elected to a two-year term from among council members.

Head Official: Mayor Madeline Rogero (since 2011; current term expires 2015)

Total Number of City Employees: 2,811 (2012)

City Information: City of Knoxville, 400 Main St., Knoxville, TN 37902; telephone (865)215-2000

■ Economy

Major Industries and Commercial Activity

Knoxville's economy is highly diversified with no one employment sector accounting for any significant portion of the area's total employment. Knoxville is home to the National Transportation Research Center. The city is within one day's drive of three-fourths of the U.S.

population. Because of its central location in the eastern half of the United States, and the intersection of two major interstate highways, many shipping, warehousing, and distribution companies continue to operate in and around the Knoxville area. Location is one important reason why many manufacturing businesses have relocated or expanded in the area. Location is also a factor in the area's booming tourism industry, particularly in nearby Sevier County, where approximately 10 million people annually visit the Great Smoky Mountains National Park—the most visited national park in the United States in 2012—and the many other attractions in Gatlinburg.

Perhaps the most significant factor in Knoxville's economy is the presence of the Tennessee Valley Authority headquarters and the University of Tennessee at Knoxville. The Tennessee Valley Authority (TVA) is a government-owned corporation created in 1933 to provide flood control, fertilizer manufacturing, and electricity to the Tennessee Valley during the Great Depression, and it continues to act as a major utility company today. TVA provides services to most of Tennessee and parts of Alabama, Mississippi, Kentucky, North Carolina, South Carolina, Virginia, West Virginia, and Indiana. The TVA was the government's first regional planning agency and remains the largest. While TVA has generally bolstered Knoxville's economy, a major coal ash spill at their Kingston Fossil Plant in 2008, in which one billion gallons of wet coal ash was spread throughout 300 acres of land and infiltrated the tributaries of the Tennessee River, warranted a clean-up effort that totaled nearly $1 billion, and was still managing groundwater contamination into 2013.

The area also features an unusually high number of incubator facilities, particularly in nearby Oak Ridge—a city whose roots can be traced to the Manhattan Project of the late 1930s and early 1940s. Today, Oak Ridge continues to be a center of technology. The Oak Ridge National Laboratory (ORNL), a major U.S. Department of Energy facility, is known around the world. Scientists and engineers at ORNL labs do research and development work to bring scientific knowledge and technological solutions that strengthen U.S. leadership in the area of science; increase the availability of clean energy; restore and protect the environment; and contribute to national security. These institutions provide unlimited education and training opportunities for area businesses and are active in a cooperative technology transfer program that has successfully spawned many spin-off companies. The Spallation Neutron Source (SNS), based in Oak Ridge, is an accelerator-based neutron source that provides the most intense pulsed neutron beams in the world for scientific and industrial research and development. The $1.5 billion project, completed in 2006, is carried out through the collaboration of six national laboratories, and is based at an 80-acre site at ORNL. The project has applications in the areas of chemistry, physics, biology,

genetics, semiconductors, and aerospace engineering. With projects like these, the Knoxville region has become a world leader in technology.

Through the assistance of the ORNL and University of Tennessee (UT), spin-off companies have been formed. UT, Lockheed Martin Energy Systems, and TVA, have been successful in recruiting national high-technology consortiums. The city itself is very technology-forward, with fiber-optic lines threaded throughout its downtown core. Knoxville's state-of-the-art telecommunications infrastructure is a critical factor in the site selection process of relocating companies and has helped the city attract several telemarketing divisions of large corporations.

Knoxville remains an urban center for mining in the Cumberland range. Knoxville was once known as "The Marble City," for the many quarries providing Tennessee pink marble to much of the country in the early twentieth century. Notable buildings like the National Gallery of Art in Washington D.C. are constructed with Knoxville marble. Zinc and coal mining are carried on in the region. Burley tobacco and a variety of food crops are harvested on farms just outside the city, and livestock and dairy products are also important to the local economy.

Knoxville's stable economy garnered it honors from the Brookings Institution in 2012, which named it one of three cities—along with Pittsburgh and Dallas—to have recovered from a national recession during the late 2000s. The Brookings Institute report showed that the city enjoyed manufacturing growth of 9.9 percent during 2010 and 2011, nearly four times the national average. Such rapid progress placed Knoxville sixth among all cities for manufacturing growth. The only blemish on Knoxville's recent manufacturing record was the multi-stage closing of a Sea Ray Boats plant, which cut 540 jobs in 2009 and an additional 225 in 2012.

Items and goods produced: motor vehicles supplies, manufactured housing, aluminum products, clothing, computer peripherals, electrical equipment, plastics, processed foods

Incentive Programs-New and Existing Companies

Local programs: Knoxville has a Foreign Trade Zone, an inland Port of Entry, and a U.S. Customs Office. The city offers an excise tax credit equal to 1 percent of the purchase, installation, and repair of qualified industrial machinery; it offers the same credit for equipment purchases associated with capital investment of at least $500,000. Net operating losses may be carried forward 15 years, and all capital losses may be claimed during the year incurred. Jobs tax credits of $2,000–3,000 per employee are available for businesses creating at least 25 new full-time jobs and an associated capital investment of at least $500,000. Finished goods inventory in excess of

$30 million may be tax-excluded. Pollution-control equipment is exempt from franchise taxes. Most manufacturing equipment can be purchased tax-free, and credits up to 5.5 percent of state sales tax are available for building materials and associated machinery for expansions or new construction meeting minimum investment requirements. Additional tax incentives are also available.

State programs: Tennessee is a right-to-work state and its overall state and local tax burden is among the lowest of all 50 states. Tennessee has no personal income tax on wages or salaries. The state's Jobs Tax Credit is available to businesses creating 25 new jobs within a three-year period and investing at least 500,000. These qualifying businesses may claim a tax credit of $4,500 per job to offset up to 50 percent of its franchise and excise tax liability for up to 15 years. The credit is available for businesses in a range of industries, especially advanced manufacturing. The Jobs Tax Super Credit allows businesses with a minimum $1 billion investment to claim up to $10,000 per job for six years.

The Industrial Machinery Tax Credit allows companies to write off up to 50 percent of their franchise and excise tax liability by earning up to 10 percent of the cost of industrial machinery in tax credits. Industrial machinery definitions extend to technological equipment such as computers and computer software, systems, and networks.

A headquarters relocation reimbursement offers tax credits to cover relocation costs of businesses. If the credit exceeds the tax liability of a company in the first year, the remainder is given to the company as a cash payment. Companies must provide evidence of relocation expenses, and certain qualifications regarding the size and operations of the headquarters must be met. There are also state sales tax exemptions and reductions for industrial machinery purchases that support manufacturing businesses.

The state's Industrial Access Program utilizes resources in the Tennessee Department of Transportation to undertake roadways projects that support industrial development. Annual funding for these projects is roughly $10 million.

Job training programs: Tennessee's FastTrack Training Program is the state's primary source of financial support for new and expanding business and industry training. FastTrack staff work with businesses to plan, develop, and implement customized training programs. Training may be done in a classroom setting, or on the job. The state also offers free applicant recruitment and screening for Tennessee companies. The Department of Labor and Workforce Development works with companies to find and review ideal employees, and is entirely free of charge. The state's database contains a pool of more than 70,000 potential employees; 62 Tennessee Career Centers across the state manage applicants locally.

The Southeast Tennessee Private Industry Council also assists businesses in meeting labor force training needs. The Council strives to provide businesses with a more competent workforce, higher employee productivity, a reduction in employee turnover, lower employee retraining costs, and highly motivated employees. Pellissippi State Technical Community College, Fountainhead College, and South College offer technical certification programs. Knox County offers a manufacturing skills grant.

Development Projects

In 2006 a 20-year revitalization strategy for redeveloping the South Waterfront was adopted. The plan for the three-mile South Waterfront includes a continuous Riverwalk along the shoreline, several parks and other "windows" to the water, public improvements for streets, sidewalks, bikeways, and parking, and private development that will add new housing units, retail and office space, and entertainment opportunities. In light of a national recession in the late 2000s, developers conceded that demand was not high enough to spur the private investment necessary for the development for several years. Phase I, set to occur between 2008 and 2013, was largely on hold as of 2013; smaller public improvement projects to streets and surrounding areas continued until private investment interest returned.

In 2013 Knoxville Locomotive Works announced a new fabrication and assembly plant in Knoxville to help satisfy new Environmental Protection Agency emission requirements. The $6.6 million facility was expected to create 203 jobs over three years. It was joining several other high-tech firms in Knoxville's Innovation Valley, a Knoxville Chamber of Commerce imitative to target certain business; the Brookings Institution named Innovation Valley the number-one area for green jobs growth in the United States in 2013. Also that year, Leisure Pools revealed plans for $6.2 million corporate headquarters that would bring 240 jobs into the area. Renovations to the city's Medical Arts Building completed in 2013.

A mixed-use facility, with luxury apartments, a hotel, and 45,000-square-feet of retail space, was planned for an old hospital, Baptist Hospital, in south Knoxville. Construction was expected to complete in 2014 or 2015 at an estimated cost of between $125 million and $150 million. University Commons, a retail center located near the University of Tennessee, anticipated opening in fall 2014 with Wal-Mart and Publix as anchor stores. Some 30 additional retailers were expected to lease spaces in the complex. The city purchased six properties, including the historic McClung Warehouses, in July 2013 with plans to sell the buildings to private developers.

Economic Development Information: Knoxville Chamber, 17 Market Square, No. 201, Knoxville, TN 37902; telephone (865)637-4550; website www.knoxvillechamber.com

Commercial Shipping

All major air shipments in Knoxville originate out of McGhee Tyson Airport. A new cargo facility was constructed in the early 1990s, more than doubling the airport's cargo capacity. In 2012 the facility handled more than 7.3 million tons of freight. Rail is another option for those needing to transport freight to and from the Greater Knoxville area. Rail freight service is provided by the Norfolk Southern and the CSX rail systems. More than 100 regular-route, common-carrier truck lines have terminals in Knox County. Many irregular routes and special-contract carriers also supply the area with efficient ground freight services.

Because of navigation improvements made by the Tennessee Valley Authority on the Tennessee River system, Knoxville enjoys barge commerce with other states on the Tennessee, Ohio, and Mississippi Rivers. This interconnected inland water system runs from the Gulf of Mexico to the Great Lakes, allowing shipments on water to such distant points as Houston, Tampa, Pittsburgh, Minneapolis, and Little Rock.

Labor Force and Employment Outlook

The Knoxville area labor force is drawn from a nine-county region in eastern Tennessee. The presence of a variety of instructional centers, combined with the city's proximity to key U.S. markets and the state's commitment to nurturing research and development firms, has made Knoxville a considerable force in the world of high-technology industry. The labor force has one of the lowest turnover and absenteeism rates in the country.

The following is a summary of data regarding the 2012 Knoxville labor force:

Size of civilian labor force: 92,435

Number of workers employed in . . .

agriculture and mining: 50
construction: 6,330
manufacturing: 4,782
wholesale trade: 2,598
retail trade: 12,592
transportation: 3,411
information systems: 2,125
finance: 5,199
professional administration: 9,804
education and social services: 21,394
arts and leisure: 9,668
other: 4,955
public administration: 2,338

Average hourly earnings of production workers: $15.47

Unemployment rate: 4.6% (2012)

Employers

Largest employers (2012)	*Number of employees*
Covenant Health	9,494
Knox County Public Schools	6,891
University of Tennessee, Knoxville	6,400
Wal-Mart Stores	4,668
University of Tennessee Medical Center	3,942
K-VA-T Food Stores	3,924
Tennova Healthcare	3,857
State of Tennessee, Regional Offices	3,528
County of Knox	2,998
City of Knoxville	2,811

Cost of Living

Knoxville is consistently ranked in national publications for its reasonable cost of living and quality of life, an advantage that is a draw for the community and businesses.

The following is a summary of data regarding several key cost of living factors in the area.

2013 ACCRA Average House Price: $259,984

2013 ACCRA Cost of Living Index: 88

State income tax rate: State income tax is limited to dividends and interest income only.

State sales tax rate: 7.0%

Local income tax rate: None

Local sales tax rate: 2.25%

Property tax rate: $2.32 per $100 assessed value (2013)

Economic Information: Knoxville Chamber, 17 Market Square, No. 201, Knoxville, TN 37902; telephone (865) 637-4550.

■ Education and Research

Elementary and Secondary Schools

Knox County Schools are considered models of quality. Knox County's magnet schools offer enhanced arts and science curriculums. In 2013, 10 Knox County schools were designated as Reward Schools, a state program honoring the top 5 percent of schools in Tennessee. The district's four-year graduation rate in 2012 was 90.3

percent, an improvement ver 79.3 percent in 2007. In 2010 the board announced the opening of one of two STEM (science, technology, engineering, mathematics) schools in the state in the historic L&N building in downtown Knoxville.

In addition to the public schools, students in metropolitan Knoxville may attend one of the area's nearly 50 private or parochial schools. Hearing-impaired children from across the state attend the Knoxville-based Tennessee School for the Deaf.

The following is a summary of data regarding the Knox County School District.

Total enrollment: 57,977

Number of facilities

total: 89
elementary schools: 50
junior high schools: 14
high schools: 15
other: 10

Student/teacher ratio: 14.95:1

Teacher salaries

average (statewide): $47,043

Funding per pupil: $7,590

Public Schools Information: Knox County Schools, 912 S. Gay St., Knoxville, TN 37902; telephone (865) 594-1800.

Colleges and Universities

Knoxville is home to several public and private institutions of higher learning. The largest and most influential by far is the main campus of the University of Tennessee at Knoxville (UT), located near downtown. It had an enrollment of nearly 30,000 students as of 2013. The flagship of the statewide university system, it has 13 different schools and colleges, among them a College of Veterinary Medicine. UT offers bachelors, masters, doctoral, and professional degrees in more than 300 fields of study ranging from engineering and business to history and music. Several of the university's programs are highly ranked nationally, including its Physician Executive MBA program, graduate program in printmaking, pharmacy, and nuclear engineering. Overall, *U.S. News & World Report* ranked it 101st among all universities nationwide, public or private. The university works closely with area industries and research centers, including the Tennessee Valley Authority and nearby Oak Ridge National Laboratory, to provide leadership and expertise in a variety of high-technology fields.

The city's other major post-secondary institutions are Knoxville College and Johnson Bible College, both of which provide four-year degrees in liberal arts and sciences. Located nearby are Carson-Newman College and Maryville College. Pellissippi State Technical Community College offers two-year college transfer and technical programs. Fountainhead College of Technology (formerly Tennessee Institute of Electronics) offers students technical training and certification. South College (formerly known as Knoxville Business College) is a regionally-accredited private university offering bachelor's and master's degrees. The Huntington College of Health Sciences is a for-profit university offering programs in health and nutrition via distance education based in Knoxville.

Libraries and Research Centers

The Knox County Public Library system consists of the Central Library downtown (the East Tennessee Historical Center and Lawson McGhee libraries) and 18 branches located throughout Knox County. Its annual circulation is over two million. The system's holdings encompass approximately one million volumes as well as numerous films, videos, compact discs, and other materials. Special interest fields include the history and genealogy of Tennessee, and the city of Knoxville and Knox County archives. The library system offers free Internet access to patrons. The University of Tennessee (UT) at Knoxville and Knoxville College also maintain their own large libraries. Additionally, several Knoxville-area hospitals and city, county, and federal offices maintain libraries.

In addition to the Tennessee Valley Authority and Oak Ridge National Laboratory, the region's two largest research and development facilities, Knoxville is home to several other research centers, most of which are affiliated with the University of Tennessee at Knoxville. In 2010 UT celebrated the 10th anniversary of the opening of nine Research Centers of Excellence in the following areas: information technology research, food safety, neurobiology of brain diseases, diseases of connective tissue, environmental biotechnology, structural biology, vascular biology, genomics and bioinformatics, and advanced materials.

Public Library Information: Knox County Public Library System, Lawson McGhee Library, 500 West Church Avenue, Knoxville, TN 37902-2505; telephone (865) 215-8750.

■ Health Care

Quality, affordable health care is available through the Knoxville's hospital systems, providing every imaginable specialty, including many that are generally not found in communities of this size. An additional six hospitals serve the Knoxville region. The largest hospital in the area is the University of Tennessee Medical Center at Knoxville (UT). UT, a Level 1 Trauma Center, is nationally known for its research programs in heart disease, cancer, and genetics. Pediatrics, intensive care for newborns, and organ transplants are among its expanding services. The UT Medical Center has 515 beds and admits more than 23,000 patients annually, in addition to 14,000 outpatient surgeries and nearly 70,000 emergency room visits. Another of Knoxville's outstanding hospitals is Fort Sanders Regional Medical Center. Fort Sanders features the Patricia Neal Rehabilitation Center, an $8 million facility specializing in treatment for disabled accident or stroke victims. The hospital houses the Thompson Cancer Survival Center, a $20 million regional cancer unit closely affiliated with the prestigious Duke University Cancer Center The facility had 402 beds as of 2013 and is accredited by the Commission on Accreditation of Rehabilitation Facilities.

Another major health system in the area is Tennova Healthcare, associated with the Sisters of Mercy, which operates many hospitals in the area, including six regional hospitals: Physicians Regional Medical Center, Turkey Creek Medical Center, North Knoxville Medical Center, Jefferson Memorial Hospital, LaFollette Medical Center, and Newport Medical Center. It also manages surgery centers, assisted living facilities, and a hospice. Knoxville's East Tennessee Children's Hospital devotes itself exclusively to prenatal and intensive care, pediatrics, and children's surgery. Baptist Hospital of East Tennessee closed in 2008.

■ Recreation

Sightseeing

Aside from the natural beauty of the surrounding Knoxville area, a good place to begin a tour of Knoxville is at Volunteer Landing on the riverfront, the site of the Women's Basketball Hall of Fame, which recounts the first 100 years of women's basketball, and the Gateway Regional Visitor Center, 500,000 square feet of total space showcasing information about the scenic beauty surrounding Knoxville. In the four-county Knoxville area are hundreds of thousands of acres of parks and recreational space, including 800 miles of forests, 800 square miles of trout streams, and seven major Tennessee Valley Authority lakes that provide more than 11,000 miles of shoreline and 1,000 square miles of water surface. Knoxville itself boasts the east-side Chilhowee Park and Tyson Park in the University of Tennessee at Knoxville area, and the Ijams Nature Center, a non-profit regional environmental education center located minutes from downtown Knoxville.

Much of Knoxville's outdoor and tourism activity centers around the Great Smoky Mountains National Park, America's most visited national preserve, with more than nine million visitors annually as of 2013. The Smokies—located 45 minutes from downtown Knoxville and skirted by Gatlinburg, Pigeon Forge, Sevierville, and Townsend—provide both active and passive recreation. The park boasts 800 square miles, 95 percent of which is forested, including 20 percent old-growth forest; 700 miles of trout streams; and more than 800 miles of trails.

Many more miles of trails and trout streams are found in Cherokee National Forest, an hour's drive south of Knoxville. Five whitewater rivers flow through Cherokee National Forest's 640,000 acres. Commercial outfitters will rent equipment or provide guided trips on some of the rivers. There are five state parks located nearby: Big Ridge State Park, Cove Lake State Park, Frozen Head State Park and Natural Area, Norris Dam State Park, and Panther Creek State Park.

The area's lakes, known as the Great Lakes of the South, are a major source of pleasure to residents and visitors. They include Norris Lake to the north, recognized nationwide for its striper fishing, and Melton Hill Lake in Oak Ridge, known for its world-class rowing conditions. The climate stays warm from May through September, and water skiing, sailing, and swimming are popular pastimes.

The site of the 1982 World's Fair has developed into a permanent recreation area in the heart of the city. The 266-foot-tall Sunsphere is still within the park, and is Knoxville's unofficial symbol. Visitors can take in a 365-degree view of Knoxville from 26 stories up on the observation deck of the Sunsphere.

Historical homes are also popular with sightseers. Among the best known in Knoxville are the Armstrong-Lockett House (often called Crescent Bend because of its location in a bend of the Tennessee River), a stately mansion built in 1834 as the centerpiece of a 600-acre farm; Blount Mansion, the oldest frame house west of the Allegheny Mountains (it was built in 1792 by Governor William Blount); the Craighead-Jackson House, a brick home built in 1812 adjacent to Blount Mansion; and Ramsey House, a two-story stone structure built in 1797. James White's Fort, Knoxville's most visited historic site, is still standing on a bluff high above the Tennessee River near downtown; seven log cabins now house pioneer artifacts and furnishings, giving a glimpse into regional life of the past.

Built in 1858, Mabry-Hazen House retains its original furniture. The site is on eight acres atop the highest hill north of the Holston River. It was once a fort-first for Confederate soldiers and then for Union troops. Mark Twain memorialized the home's builder, Joseph A. Mabry, Jr., in *Life on the Mississippi*. The second generation to live in the house was fictionalized in the best seller *Christy,* and the third and last generation at Mabry-Hazen House was featured in *Life Magazine.*

With more than 800 exotic animals, many in their natural habitats, including gorillas, red pandas, and rhinos, the Knoxville Zoo is full of family fun, adventure, and learning. The zoo is nationally known for its work with red pandas, white rhinoceroses, and reptiles. The Knoxville Zoo has been known as the Red Panda Capital of the World, having had great success in breeding and survival of baby Red Pandas. Popular exhibits include Gorilla Valley, Penguin Rock, North American River Otters, and the Cheetah Savannah. Special attractions include the Bird Show, featuring free-flying birds of prey, and camel rides, elephant encounters, and the Wee Play Zoo for children.

The historic Candy Factory Building was built circa 1917. There visitors can see chocolatiers at work at the South's Finest Chocolate Factory, which features more than 100 candies made and sold on the site. Nearby, visitors will encounter a row of beautifully restored Victorian houses. These quaint, brightly hued dwellings were built in the 1920s and are now home to antique and curiosity shops as well as studios and art galleries.

Arts and Culture

Organizations like the Arts Council of Greater Knoxville and the Arts & Culture Alliance support an active arts community. The Tennessee Amphitheater, located in World's Fair Park, is a popular venue and is used for numerous free concerts and productions sponsored by the city of Knoxville and private groups. The Oak Ridge Art Center is also a boon for the cultural climate of the region. It has a studio and a gift shop and displays both local and traveling artists' and photographers' exhibits. Classes are offered in such artistic endeavors as pottery, oil painting, watercolor, drawing, and sculpture.

Knoxville boasts the world-class Knoxville Symphony Orchestra (KSO). KSO, established in 1935, plays several concerts a year to sold-out houses at the magnificent Tennessee Theatre, which reopened in 2005 following an extensive $23.5 million restoration, and at the Civic Auditorium and Coliseum. The orchestra's core group also makes up the Knoxville Chamber Orchestra, which was founded in 1981 and performs a five-concert series in the historic Bijou Theatre.

The Knoxville Opera Company, which has achieved a position of prominence among American opera companies, produces several major operas annually and is a major part of a week-long spring festival in Knoxville. The Civic Music Association brings internationally known musicians to Oak Ridge; their performances alternate with concerts by the Oak Ridge Symphony and Chorus, composed of local musicians and full-time professional directors.

A variety of dance forms are presented to Knoxville audiences by the Appalachian Ballet Company, Circle Modern Dance Company, and the internationally acclaimed Tennessee Children's Dance Ensemble.

The University of Tennessee at Knoxville and Maryville College also serve as cultural centers for the region. UT's Department of Theatre is committed to providing drama education and exposure to outstanding theatrical productions—both to university students seeking a career in theater and to East Tennessee audiences desiring quality dramatic fare. The Ula Love Doughty Carousel Theatre, the Music Hall, and the Clarence Brown Theatre present musical, comedies, dramas and dance performances. Maryville College supports a Playhouse and College-Community Orchestra series.

The Knoxville Civic Auditorium and Coliseum brings to the area the best in professional traveling companies presenting Broadway hits. Local residents can not only view fine theater but also are encouraged to participate at the Oak Ridge Playhouse. The playhouse has a full-time professional director and offers a full season of plays and musicals. Listed on the National Register of Historic Places and honored as the Official State Theatre of Tennessee, "Knoxville's Grand Entertainment Palace" has something for everyone: classical music, vintage films, dance, theater, and stellar performances by today's hottest musicians. The Bijou Theatre Center is another one of Knoxville's oldest buildings and offers musicals, light operas, dances, plays, and can be rented out for any other special event. The Tennessee Stage Company presents the annual Shakespeare on the Square and Knoxville New Play Festival, and was working to add a Tennessee Williams Festival to its repertoire. Other community-based theatre companies abound, such as The Carpet Bag Theatre, Inc., and the Jubilee Community Arts at Laurel Theatre.

Highlighting the history of the Knoxville region are many excellent museums and historic sites. The history of the entire area is the focus at the Museum of East Tennessee History, housed at the East Tennessee Historical Center along with the public library's McClung Historical Collection and the Knox County Archives. The Museum, Historical Collection, and Archives doubled in size upon the completion of a $20 million expansion in 2005. African American history and culture reaching as far back as the 1840s is chronicled at the Beck Cultural Exchange Center in downtown Knoxville. Confederate Memorial Hall, also known as Bleak House, is an antebellum mansion that once served as General Longstreet's headquarters during the siege of Knoxville and is now a museum that houses artifacts, documents, and furniture of the Civil War era. The University of Tennessee at Knoxville's McClung Museum highlights collections of history, anthropology, archaeology, natural history, science, fine arts, and furnishings.

The Knoxville Museum of Art is a dynamic institution providing exciting exhibitions from the surrounding region, the country, and the world. This state-of-the-art facility, located in downtown Knoxville's World's Fair Park, presents an average of 20 traveling exhibitions annually in its four galleries; its permanent collection is drawn from American art of the twentieth century and later. The Arts Council of Greater Knoxville sponsors exhibits and varied galleries at the Candy Factory at World's Fair Park, at the Ewing Gallery of Art and

Architecture, and at the Joseph B. Wolffe Sculpture Gallery. The University of Tennessee Gallery Concourse focuses on the work of local, regional, and national artists.

To the north of Knoxville, Oak Ridge lures visitors with its American Museum of Science and Energy. One of the world's largest energy exhibitions, it features interactive displays, live demonstrations, computer games, and films for all ages.

In nearby Norris, the Museum of Appalachia offers the most authentic and complete documentation of the Appalachian way of life in the world. The museum houses one of the nation's largest collections of pioneer, country, mountain, and contemporary artifacts such as baskets, coverlets, quilts, early animal traps, thousands of tools, and early musical instruments. Enhancing the main display are 35 other authentic log structures-houses, cabins, a school, a church, and barns-all fully furnished with period relics.

Festivals and Holidays

Knoxville presents a variety of popular seasonal activities for residents and visitors. Festivals and holidays highlight the arts, various cultural heritages, and the Civil War. The 17-day Dogwood Arts Festival in April offers more than 350 events. The Dogwood Arts Festival is the largest civic celebration in North America, with more than 8,000 volunteers helping with its staging. This nationally renowned festival includes craft shows, concerts and sporting events, and features 60 miles of marked motor trails in Knoxville to showcase the abundant spring blossoms on the dogwood trees. Merging the arts and Italian culture is the week-long Knoxville Opera's Rossini Festival which, according to the city, "brings a taste of Europe to East Tennessee," also in the spring. The Kumba Festival, in June and July, demonstrates the shared heritage of the African, African American, and African Appalachian communities in diaspora and how integral this heritage is to the culture of East Tennessee. The festival showcases visual arts, folk arts, dance, theater, music, storytelling, games, and food. For more cultural events, visitors can attend food and cultural festivals, like Greekfest, relive a day in the life of the Cherokee Indians at James White's Fort's Cherokee Heritage Day, or visit area Civil War reenactments.

On Labor Day weekend, the Boomsday Festival touts itself as the largest Labor Day weekend fireworks show in the nation, staged on the downtown river front at Neyland Drive. Organizers report dignitaries from Europe and Asia have visited the event, and National Geographic has filmed it for a special. Attendance has been estimated at close to 400,000 guests. The Tennessee Valley Fair runs for 10 days every September. Tennessee Fall Homecoming in October celebrates Appalachian crafts and mountain music. December's Christmas in the City is sponsored jointly by the city of Knoxville and downtown businesses. This two-month long center-city event is a combination of more than 100 activities featuring music, lights, a parade, trees on the rooftops, whimsical window scenes, and memories of Christmases past.

Sports for the Spectator

The Tennessee Smokies, the Double-A minor affiliate of the Chicago Cubs, provide professional baseball for the area; they play at Smokies Baseball Park, located in Sevierville, Tennessee, just 15 miles from downtown Knoxville. The Knoxville Ice Bears, part of the Southern Professional Hockey League, play at the Knoxville Civic Coliseum. Area residents also enthusiastically attend the sporting events of the University of Tennessee at Knoxville. The 102,037-seat Neyland Stadium on the UT campus is the largest collegiate stadium in the South, and the second largest in the country. It underwent $63 million of renovations during 2008–10, which was the third of three renovation phases. The Thompson-Boling Arena, a 24,535-seat basketball arena, is home to the University of Tennessee Volunteers and the Lady Volunteers basketball team and is also one of the largest collegiate basketball arenas in the country. It also hosts a variety of other community events. The Knoxville Rugby Club, also known as the Possums, celebrated their 30th anniversary in 2010. Knoxville is also home to the Hard Knox Roller Girls, an all-female flat-track roller derby league.

Sports for the Participant

Surrounded by the mountains and nestled into the banks of the Tennessee River, residents and visitors have many options for enjoying the beauty of the area. Since it is in a temperate climate zone, outdoor activities are common and accessible throughout the city. Six national parks are located within 90 miles of the city, such as the Smoky Mountains National Park. The Knoxville Greenway Coalition has worked for nearly 20 years on improving the area's park and trail system, which had nearly 42 miles of greenway as of 2013. Rowing on the Tennessee River is also a popular sport. Knoxville city parks contained some 1,854 acres of parks as of 2013. Other facilities included 5 dog parks, 3 municipal golf courses, 4 pools, and 22 tennis facilities, some with as many as 14 courts. At Volunteer Landing Marina, watercraft including houseboats, pontoons, paddleboats, and aqua-cycles can be rented. In March 2005 Knoxville hosted its first Knoxville Marathon, a 26.2-mile run beginning at World's Fair Park and ending at UT's Neyland Stadium, which has continued annually each March as the Covenant Health Knoxville Marathon.

Shopping and Dining

There are more than 150 shopping centers in Knoxville. The city boasts three large shopping malls—Knoxville Center, Windsor Square, and West Town Mall. In the downtown area, there are several areas of retail activity, including Market Square Mall. Knoxville's historic downtown warehouse district, called The Old City, is a bustling area of dining, shopping, and entertainment nestled in restored nineteenth-century brick warehouses. Near the University of Tennessee at Knoxville campus, Cumberland Avenue is noted for its shops. Antiques and boutiques are popular throughout the city. Visitors can also shop the Bearden Antique Mall, the largest and oldest of its kind in Knoxville. University Commons, a retail center located near the University of Tennessee, anticipated opening in fall 2014 with Wal-Mart and Publix as anchor stores. Some 30 additional retailers were expected to lease spaces in the complex.

Visitors and residents alike can sample a broad array of foods at Knoxville-area dining establishments. With more than 600 restaurants, Knoxville offers all sorts of world cuisines. Nonetheless, Southern cooking's popularity is marked by many barbecue and country-style restaurants. Other choices abound, among them continental cuisine and ethnic specialties such as Greek, Italian, Mexican, and Asian.

Visitor Information: Knoxville Convention and Visitors Bureau, 301 S. Gay Street, Knoxville, TN 37902; telephone (800) 727-8045.

■ Convention Facilities

Knoxville played host to the world in 1982 when the city staged a highly successful World's Fair. Today, Knoxville continues to host large gatherings in a variety of settings. Situated within World's Fair Park is the Knoxville Convention Center, a sparkling, technologically-advanced facility boasting a 119,922 square-foot exhibit hall, a 27,300 square-foot divisible ballroom, 14 functional meeting rooms seating attendees in theater style, a lecture hall with seating for 461, and three luxury conference rooms. Opened in July of 2002, the Convention Center is within walking distance of excellent dining, charming shops, and major hotels.

While the Knoxville Convention Center is the area's newest and largest meeting facility, the Knoxville Civic Auditorium and Coliseum has served the community well for many years. It has been the site of political rallies, rock concerts, major theatrical presentations, international circuses, glitzy ice shows, and grueling sports events. Conveniently situated in the downtown area, the Coliseum Convention Hall provides 34,000 square feet of uninterrupted exhibition space, with an additional 11,000 square feet available for storage. Seating capacity in the Convention Hall is 2,200 people. Smaller shows can be accommodated in the 11,130-square-foot Exhibition Hall. The ballroom is a multifunctional area of the Civic Coliseum used for banquets, exhibits, dancing and meetings. It has a seating capacity for meetings of 500 people. The Civic

Auditorium, which seats up to 2,407 people, features two balconies, upholstered seating arranged in tiers, excellent acoustics, and a fully equipped stage.

Unusual meeting spaces include the Lamar House/Bijou Theatre and the Tennessee Theater. Knoxville's fine hotels and motor lodges not only furnish more than 8,000 rooms throughout the county, but also provide additional private meeting rooms.

Convention Information: Knoxville Convention and Visitors Bureau, 301 S. Gay Street, Knoxville, TN 37902; telephone (800) 727-8045.

■ Transportation

Approaching the City

Knoxville's McGhee Tyson Airport, located 12 miles south of downtown, offers more than 120 daily flights, serving more than 1.7 million passengers annually. The airport is also home to an Air National Guard base. The city's other major facility is Island Home Airport, three miles from downtown, which is a base for smaller general aviation traffic and privately-owned planes.

Access to the city via car, truck, or bus is made easy by the fact that two of the nation's busiest interstate highways—Interstate 40 (toward Nashville and Asheville, North Carolina) and Interstate 75 (toward Chattanooga and Lexington, Kentucky)—intersect in Knoxville. Greyhound offers bus service to Knoxville.

Traveling in the City

Interstates 40 and 75 surround the city and are connected via Interstate 275. Public transportation is provided in Knoxville by Knoxville Area Transit (KAT) buses; lift service for the disabled and handicapped is available. KAT routes reach within one-quarter-mile of 90 percent of Knoxville's population, carrying an estimated 3.6 million passengers annually. Colorful trolleys reminiscent of those of the turn of the century provide free service in the downtown area.

■ Communications

Newspapers and Magazines

Knoxville has one daily (morning) newspaper, *The Knoxville News Sentinel. The News Sentinel* rebranded itself, dropping the hyphen between "News" and "Sentinel" in 2002 and became the cornerstone of the KNS Media Group, which helped prepare the news organization for the ongoing transition away from print media sources and toward electronic products. The *Metro Pulse* was a weekly news publication but is now available only online, distributed by the Scripps Interactive Newspapers Group. *Everything Knoxville* is a monthly lifestyle magazine in the area, while *Cityview* caters to the business community.

Other weekly, biweekly, and monthly publications are published in Knoxville, as well as quarterly academic journals on such topics as mental health nursing, education for the gifted, economics, and journalism.

Television and Radio

Twelve television stations operate in Knoxville. Ten AM and 11 FM stations broadcast to listeners from Knoxville, offering programs to suit every taste.

Media Information: Knoxville News Sentinel, 2332 News Sentinel Drive, Knoxville, TN 37921; telephone (865) 523-3131.

Knoxville Online

City of Knoxville Home Page. Available www. cityofknoxville.org

Knox County Public Library System. Available cat. knoxlib.org

Knox County Schools. Available knoxschools.org

Knoxville Area Chamber Partnership. Available www.knoxvillechamber.com

Knoxville News Sentinel. Available www.knoxnews. com

BIBLIOGRAPHY

Agee, James, *A Death In The Family,* (New York: McDowell Oblensky, 1957)

Mahurin, Tasha and Shannon Mahurin, *South Knoxville* (Charleston, SC: Arcadia Publishing, 2012)

Potter, Susanna Henighan, *Moon Spotlight Chattanooga and Knoxville* (Berkeley, CA: Avalon Travel Publishing, 2010)

Memphis

■ The City in Brief

Founded: 1818 (incorporated 1826)

Head Official: Mayor A. C. Wharton, Jr. (since 2009; current term expires 2015)

City Population
    1990: 618,652
    2000: 650,100
    2010: 646,889
    2012 estimate: 655,141
    Percent change, 2000–2010: −0.5%
    U.S. rank in 1990: 18th (State rank: 1st)
    U.S. rank in 2000: 24th (State rank: 1st)
    U.S. rank in 2010: 20th (State rank: 1st)

Metropolitan Statistical Area Population
    2000: 1,135,614
    2010: 1,316,100
    2012 estimate: 1,333,315
    Percent change, 2000–2010: 15.9%
    U.S. rank in 2000: 41st
    U.S. rank in 2010: 41st

Area: 279.3 square miles

Elevation: 331 feet above sea level

Average Annual Temperatures: January, 39.9° F; July, 82.5° F; annual average, 62.3° F

Average Annual Precipitation: 54.65 inches of rain; 5.1 inches of snow

Major Economic Sectors: services, wholesale and retail trade, government

Unemployment Rate: 8.7% (2012)

Per Capita Income: $20,377

2012 FBI Crime Index Property: 41,503

Major Colleges and Universities: The University of Memphis, Rhodes College, LeMoyne-Owen College, University of Tennessee Health Science Center, Christian Brothers University

Daily Newspaper: *The Commercial Appeal*

■ Introduction

Situated on bluffs overlooking the Mississippi River, Memphis historically has served as a commercial and social center for western Tennessee, northern Mississippi, and eastern Arkansas. The list of commercially recorded songs that mention the city of Memphis, Tennessee, numbered more than 1,000 in 2013. While it is the youngest of Tennessee's major cities, Memphis is considered by many to be the true capital of the Mississippi River delta. Nonetheless, the city's rich history includes eighteenth-century French and Spanish forts, colorful riverboat traffic, and an important agricultural commodity: cotton. The city counts barbecue cooking among its contributions to the national culture and calls itself "Home of the Blues" and "Birthplace of Rock 'n Roll," home to famous musicians like Elvis Presley, Jerry Lee Lewis, B.B. King, and Johnny Cash. Memphis boasts a high quality of life enhanced by a pleasant climate and abundant recreational opportunities. Already a distribution hub and headquarters for leaders in services such as hotels and package express, the Memphis area, also known as the "Mid-South," has added a burgeoning health-care industry to its list of economic drivers. Memphis Medical Center and St. Jude Children's Research Hospital are leaders in research and medical care, and the city continues to be an important commercial center. Expanded on these industries, and broadening downtown development, remained a priority in to the 2010s.

David Liu/Getty Images

■ Geography and Climate

Located in southwestern Tennessee on the east bank of the Mississippi River, Memphis is surrounded by slightly rolling countryside. Memphis is in a humid subtropical climate, with four distinct seasons. The area, while subject to frequent changes in weather, experiences few temperature extremes. Precipitation is fairly evenly distributed throughout the year. Summer is usually very hot, and, depending on whether the weather comes from Texas or the Gulf of Mexico, varies between dry and humid. May and October are considered to be particularly pleasant months in Memphis. Memphis receives about four inches of snow each year, but the bigger danger are ice storms which tear down trees and cause power outages. Memphis is also located above a natural aquifer (the "Memphis aquifer") which is estimated to contain more than 100 trillion gallons of soft, pure water.

Area: 279.3 square miles

Elevation: 331 feet above sea level

Average Temperatures: January, 39.9° F; July, 82.5° F; annual average, 62.3° F

Average Annual Precipitation: 54.65 inches of rain; 5.1 inches of snow

■ History

Jackson Helps Found City

Lush wilderness covered the Mississippi River bluffs (now known as the Memphis metropolitan area) when Spanish explorer Hernando De Soto encountered the area's Chickasaw inhabitants in 1541. In 1673, French explorers Louis Joliet and Jacques Marquette explored the region, called the Fourth Chickasaw Bluffs, which in 1682 was claimed for France by Robert Cavelier de La Salle as part of the vast Louisiana Territory. The French established Fort Assumption at the Fourth Chickasaw Bluffs in 1739. As ownership of the region was disputed by various nations, Fort Assumption was followed by the Spanish Fort San Fernando, built on the site in 1795, and the American Fort Adams, erected in 1797. The Chickasaw ceded West Tennessee to the United States in 1818, and the following year John Overton, James Winchester, and Andrew Jackson founded a settlement on the Mississippi River bluffs that they named Memphis, after an ancient Egyptian city on the Nile River.

"King Cotton" Spurs City's Growth

Irish, Scots-Irish, Scottish Highlanders, and German immigrants joined westward-advancing pioneers from the eastern United States in settling the new town, which was incorporated in 1826. They served as gunsmiths and blacksmiths and operated saw mills, cotton mills, and cotton warehouses. The economy of the region was based primarily on the cotton industry, which utilized slave labor, and Memphis became the largest slave market in the mid-South. The necessity of transporting cotton to the marketplace made Memphis the focus of transportation improvements. The Memphis-to-New Orleans steamship line was established on the Mississippi River in 1834; six miles of railroad had been constructed around Memphis by 1842; and four major roads were carved out in the 1850s. In 1857 the Memphis-to-Charleston railroad line linked the Mississippi River to the Atlantic Coast. From 1850 to 1860 Memphis's population more than quintupled, swelling to 33,000 people.

When the economic and social differences between northern and southern states that led Tennessee to secede from the United States and join the Confederacy erupted in war, Memphis served temporarily as Tennessee's state capital. But in 1862 a Confederate fleet near Memphis was defeated by Union forces, which then captured Memphis. At the conflict's conclusion, Tennessee was the first state to rejoin the Union and the following year, in 1867, Memphis was made Shelby County seat. A series of yellow fever epidemics in the 1870s ravaged the city, leaving it deserted and bankrupt; in 1879 its charter was revoked.

Subsequent improvements to the city's sewage and drinking water systems helped reduce the threat of epidemic, trade resumed in Memphis, and its population mounted to almost 65,000 by 1890. The first railroad bridge across the Mississippi south of St. Louis opened in Memphis in 1892, increasing the city's trade opportunities. The following year Memphis regained its city charter, and by the turn of the century the city was once again established as a booming trading center for cotton and lumber.

King Assassinated in City

In the first half of the twentieth century adversities in Memphis-such as the 1937 Mississippi River flood that brought 60,000 refugees into the city-were offset by advances-such as the formation of the Memphis Park Commission, the establishment of colleges, airports, military installations, and municipal utilities, and construction of port improvements. In the 1960s Memphis annexed neighboring areas and was the subject of federal court decisions ordering desegregation of the city's schools, parks, and recreational facilities. The city's sanitation workers, protesting discriminatory labor practices in a 1968 strike, attracted civil-rights leader Martin Luther King Jr. to their cause. On April 4, 1968, King, an advocate of nonviolent protest, was slain by a sniper at a Memphis motel. A steel structure entitled "The Mountaintop" honors King in Memphis's Civic Center Plaza. By 1973 court-ordered busing for school desegregation in Memphis was adopted without major incident, and the 1980 Memphis Jobs Conference, a broad-based economic planning initiative, was praised for its thorough integration of various Memphis sectors.

Economic Growth

Starting in the 1990s, Memphis began a rebirth of entertainment and tourism, as well as a major commercial shipping hub, both industries leading the way in terms of economic vitality. In the 1990s, Beale Street made a comeback as a tourist destination and entertainment district with clubs, offering live music seven days a week. The entertainment district continued to flourish throughout the decade. By the early 2000s, Memphis was welcomed its first top-level professional franchise, the Memphis Grizzlies of the National Basketball Association.

Present-day Memphis boasts renovated historic districts and city landmarks, and a diversified community of residents and workers. Traditional economic mainstays such as cotton, lumber, and distribution mix with services, including overnight package express, insurance, and hospitality, and newer enterprises like agricultural technology and biomedical technology to make Memphis a strong economic community. Its future lay in expanding these industries and attracting new ones, as well as bringing lasting economic viability to all parts of its downtown area. Multi-million renovations to its iconic pyramid, set to unveil in 2014 as a mixed-use facility anchored by Bass Pro Shops, represented positive movement along this path.

Historical Information: West Tennessee Historical Society, Box 111046, Memphis, TN 38111. Center for Southern Folklore, 119 South Main Street, Memphis, TN 38103; telephone (901) 525-3655. Pink Palace Family of Museums, 3050 Central Avenue, Memphis, TN 38111; telephone (901) 636-2362.

■ Population Profile

Metropolitan Statistical Area Population
2000: 1,135,614
2010: 1,316,100
2012 estimate: 1,333,315
Percent change, 2000–2010: 15.9%
U.S. rank in 2000: 41st
U.S. rank in 2010: 41st

City Residents
1990: 618,652
2000: 650,100

2010: 646,889
2012 estimate: 655,141
Percent change, 2000–2010: −0.5%
U.S. rank in 1990: 18th (State rank: 1st)
U.S. rank in 2000: 24th (State rank: 1st)
U.S. rank in 2010: 20th (State rank: 1st)

Density: 2,053.3 people per square mile

Racial and ethnic characteristics

White: 202,136
Black or African American: 413,365
American Indian and Alaskan Native: 2,069
Asian: 9,516
Native Hawaiian and Other Pacific Islander: 406
Hispanic or Latino (may be of any race): 42,954
Other: 27,649

Percent of residents born in state: 64.4%

Age characteristics

Population under 5 years old: 49,384
Population 5 to 9 years old: 43,341
Population 10 to 14 years old: 44,309
Population 15 to 19 years old: 45,923
Population 20 to 24 years old: 57,372
Population 25 to 34 years old: 102,185
Population 35 to 44 years old: 79,956
Population 45 to 54 years old: 83,565
Population 55 to 59 years old: 42,780
Population 60 to 64 years old: 37,144
Population 65 to 74 years old: 38,250
Population 75 to 84 years old: 22,540
Population 85 years and over: 8,392
Median age: 33.2

Births (2010–11 Metropolitan Area)

Total number: 19,393

Deaths (2010–11 Metropolitan Area)

Total number: 10,778

Money income (2012)

Per capita income: $20,377
Median household income: $36,062
Total households: 244,775

Number of households with income of ...

less than $10,000: 31,608
$10,000 to $14,999: 19,491
$15,000 to $24,999: 35,755
$25,000 to $34,999: 32,394
$35,000 to $49,999: 35,903
$50,000 to $74,999: 40,293
$75,000 to $99,999: 20,925
$100,000 to $149,999: 17,450
$150,000 to $199,999: 5,237
$200,000 or more: 5,719

Percent of families below poverty level: 27.3%

FBI Crime Index Property: 41,503

FBI Crime Index Violent: 11,507

■ Municipal Government

Since 1966 Memphis has operated via a mayor-council form of government. The mayor is elected for four-year terms. Thirteen council members serve four-year terms; of them, six are elected as part of combined super districts, and seven are elected by single district. In 2010, efforts to consolidate the Shelby County and Memphis governments into a metropolitan government made it onto the November ballot by referendum, but failed. (A successful 2011 effort to consolidate county and city school districts was implemented in 2013, although some suburban communities planned to separate in 2014.)

Head Official: Mayor A. C. Wharton, Jr. (since 2009; current term expires 2015)

Total Number of City Employees: 7,274 (2012)

City Information: Memphis City Hall, 125 North Main Street, Memphis, TN 38103; telephone (901)576-6007

■ Economy

Major Industries and Commercial Activity

At the center of a major distribution network, Memphis works from a broad economic base as it continues to diversify its employment opportunities. Historically a trading center for cotton and hardwood, Memphis is the headquarters for major trade and transportation, manufacturing, and services companies.

Transportation and logistics is the lifeblood of Memphis, particularly with the location of FedEx. FedEx began its operations in 1973, with 14 small aircraft delivering packages from Memphis International Airport. Today, FedEx averages more than 3.9 million shipments per day, and serves more than 220 countries and territories. The transportation value is high enough to invite the operation of other major companies. For example, Nike, a top manufacturer of athletic shoes and sports apparel, has a major distribution center in Memphis and announced an expansion of the facility in 2013. FedEx has contributed to Memphis's aim of being "America's Aerotropolis," a city based on the success of its airport and location. Meanwhile, retailing of specially-manufactured products has also risen as an important industry in Memphis. AutoZone opened its first Auto Shack in Forrest City, Arkansas, in 1979; the company is now a leading auto parts retailer, with more than 3,400 stores nationwide and is headquartered in Memphis. International Paper, organized in 1878, is the largest paper and forest products company in the world, with operations in more than 40 countries, also headquartered in Memphis. The privately-owned ServiceMaster company moved to Memphis in 2007. The company's services include lawn care and landscape maintenance, termite and pest control, home warranties, disaster response and reconstruction, cleaning and disaster restoration, house cleaning, furniture repair, and home inspection, serving at least 10.5 million homes and businesses each year.

Memphis's economy is diverse. Services centered in Memphis include banking and finance (First Horizon National Corporation); real estate (Belz Enterprises, Boyle Investment Co., and Weston Co.); and nonprofits, including the world's largest waterfowl and wetlands conservation organization (Ducks Unlimited). Science and technology business is very well represented in Memphis; Brother Industries USA, Buckman Laboratories, Medtronic Sofamor Danek, Sharp Manufacturing of America, Smith & Nephew, and Wright Medical Technologies all have headquarters there. Memphis is considered a mid-South retail center and an attractive tourist destination. Its early and continued role as a major cotton market makes agribusiness an economic mainstay in Memphis. Forty percent of the nation's cotton crop is traded in Memphis, home of three of the world's largest cotton dealers: Dunavant Enterprises, Cargill Cotton, and the Allenberg Company. Hilton Worldwide also has an Operations Center in Memphis.

Memphis is also a major location for processors of soybeans, meats, and other foods. Memphis is important in other areas of agribusiness. The city has long been established as a prime marketing center for hardwood, as well as wood and paper products. Enhancing Memphis's position at the center of agribusiness is Agricenter International, an $8 million, 140,000-square-foot exhibition center for agricultural exhibitions, experimentation, and information exchange. It brings together the most technologically advanced methods of farming and farm equipment available in one location. The exhibition hall, where independent farm-related companies (chemical concerns, irrigation businesses, farm management companies, etc.) lease space, is totally computerized, allowing farmers and consumers to ask specific information of the computer and receive specific answers. The facility also includes about 1,000 acres of farmland, 120 acres of field displays, and a 600-seat amphitheater. Agricenter, a nonprofit entity that operates on a management contract with the Shelby County Agricenter Commission, was built amid 2,000 acres of old Shelby County penal farm land, in the eastern section of the county about 30 minutes from downtown Memphis.

Memphis business activities are facilitated by the city's Uniport Association, the transportation arm of the Memphis Chamber of Commerce, which coordinates a Foreign Trade Zone, and river, air, rail, and road transportation services into a top-ranked distribution network.

In the middle of the twentieth century, Memphis was the fourth leading recording center in the world, and the music industry was the third largest employer in the city of Memphis. While the Memphis music industry today has declined as a commercial and creative presence in the music world, the Memphis music legacy is still thriving, particularly in the form of tourism. Tourism in Memphis contributes $3.1 billion to the Memphis economy annually while generating $127 million in state and local taxes, as of 2013. In addition to music and tourism, focus has begun to return to the entertainment industry through film. In the late 1990s Memphis made a name for itself as a center for movie making. Movies filmed there since then include *The Firm, The Client, The People vs. Larry Flynt, A Family Thing, The Rainmaker, Cast Away, 21 Grams, Forty Shades of Blue, Hustle and Flow, Walk the Line, Soul Men, Losers Take All, The Romance of Lonliness, and Tennessee Queer*.

Items and goods produced: chemicals, machinery, clothing, foodstuffs, electronic equipment, pharmaceuticals, cosmetics, ceiling fans, smokeless tobacco, gift wrap, bubble gum

Incentive Programs-New and Existing Companies

Local programs: Local incentives include PILOT (payment-in-lieu-of-tax) real and personal property tax freeze; manufacturing, distribution, and corporate/division headquarters projects may qualify for a PILOT property tax freeze. The Diversity Plan is an optional add-on to the PILOT program, allowing businesses to add one or two years to the end of the pilot program for meeting certain minority or small business hiring or contracting goals. PILOT programs are available from the city of Memphis, including special incentives related to the downtown area, Shelby County, and the Millington Industrial Development Board. Memphis's foreign trade zone provides businesses with reduced duties and processing fees on certain items, as well as expedited movement of goods through customs.

The city's One-Stop-Shop program expedites the regulatory process related to licensing, codes, taxation, utilities, and any other permitting issues. A Fast Track permitting program increases the rapidity of the process even further. The Greater Memphis Chamber of Commerce offers a research team to assist relocating or expanding companies, performing market research and supplying decision-makers with statistical and demographic information. The chamber also maintains a building and land database. The University of Tennessee Center for Industrial Services utilizes the research capabilities of area public universities to help businesses solve technical problems. Memphis Light, Gas and Water gives relocating industrial operations special incentive rates on electric and natural gas supplies. An Industrial Revenue Bond is available from Memphis and Shelby County for manufacturing operations, and development loans provide up to $90,000 for renovations of downtown businesses.

State programs: Tennessee is a right-to-work state and its overall state and local tax burden is among the lowest of all 50 states. Tennessee has no personal income tax on wages or salaries. The state's Jobs Tax Credit is available to businesses creating 25 new jobs within a three-year period and investing at least 500,000. These qualifying businesses may claim a tax credit of $4,500 per job to offset up to 50 percent of its franchise and excise tax liability for up to 15 years. The credit is available for businesses in a range of industries, especially advanced manufacturing. The Jobs Tax Super Credit allows businesses with a minimum $1 billion investment to claim up to $10,000 per job for six years.

The Industrial Machinery Tax Credit allows companies to write off up to 50 percent of their franchise and excise tax liability by earning up to 10 percent of the cost of industrial machinery in tax credits. Industrial machinery definitions extend to technological equipment such as computers and computer software, systems, and networks.

A headquarters relocation reimbursement offers tax credits to cover relocation costs of businesses. If the credit exceeds the tax liability of a company in the first year, the remainder is given to the company as a cash payment. Companies must provide evidence of relocation expenses, and certain qualifications regarding the size and operations of the headquarters must be met. There are also state sales tax exemptions and reductions for industrial machinery purchases that support manufacturing businesses.

The state's Industrial Access Program utilizes resources in the Tennessee Department of Transportation to undertake roadways projects that support industrial development. Annual funding for these projects is roughly $10 million.

Job training programs: Tennessee's FastTrack Training Program is the state's primary source of financial support for new and expanding business and industry training. FastTrack staff work with businesses to plan, develop, and implement customized training programs. Training may be done in a classroom setting, or on the job. The state also offers free applicant recruitment and screening for Tennessee companies. The Department of Labor and Workforce Development works with companies to find and review ideal employees, and is entirely free of charge. The state's database contains a pool of more than 70,000 potential employees; 62 Tennessee Career Centers across the state manage applicants locally.

The FedEx Institute of Technology specializes in conducting interdisciplinary research, producing a digitally savvy workforce, and being an evolving, dynamic resource for businesses in the region. The Mid-South Quality Productivity Center provides training and consulting services.

Development Projects

Memphis has generally been a major hub of business and transportation development, though development slowed in the middle of the 2000s and was worsened by a nationwide recession that followed. Some projects stalled or were abandoned, but not all development ceased. The Pyramid Arena, former home of the Memphis Grizzlies and the University of Memphis Tigers, was leased to Bass Pro Shops Outdoor World, which planned to renovate the iconic property into 220,000 square feet of retail space, including a 190-room hotel, bowling alley, restaurant, aquarium, indoor shooting range, and demonstration arena. Interior work on the nearly $200 million project began in 2012 and was expected to complete in 2014. Development was supported by $41 in Federal Recovery Zone Facility bonds and $27.7 million in Recovery Zone Economic Development bonds.

Development in the health care industry boomed in the late 2000s, getting a boost from major construction by hospitals with more than $1.5 billion in development. Projects ranged from a parking garage at the University of Tennessee Health Science Center to a $450 million University of Tennessee/Baptist Research Park, home to the Regional Biocontainment Laboratory, Memphis Bioworks Foundation offices, and a newly constructed UT College of Pharmacy. At the Le Bonheur Children's Medical Center, a 650,000-square-foot hospital expansion, including a 12-story tower and a new emergency room that opened in December 2010 at an estimated total cost of $327 million. St. Jude Children's Research Hospital alone began a $1 billion expansion in the mid-2000s, which completed all phases by 2013. Medical arts buildings followed construction of major hospital facilities, including a 36,000-square-foot development undertaken in 2013 at a cost of $4 million. These developments have spillover effect on other part of Memphis' economy. Medtronic Inc. celebrated a $65 million expansion of its distribution center in 2010 to allow the medical device company to ship additional products.

Other city developments included $75 million worth of updates and enhancements at Shelby Farms Park in 2010. Already three times larger than New York City's famed Central Park and home to a wide variety of species, from birds to buffalo and everything in between, Shelby Farms Park received new trails, updated playgrounds, and expansion of Patriot Lake. A $15 million federal TIGER IV grant awarded in 2012 to the city was used to add bicycle and walkway paths over the Harahan Bridge and also undertake basic infrastructure maintenance on the city's Main Street. A public-private partnership catalyzed the building of the Beale Street Landing project, a $42 million project still underway in 2013 after a number of setbacks and budget shortfalls. The project was to consist of a public, commercial riverboat landing, park space, and potential restaurant space, including five "islets" on different elevations planted as park space with seating areas and water features, descending toward the river.

Nike broke ground on a 1.3-million-square-foot expansion of its Memphis distribution facility in 2013, nearly doubling the facility's size. Other downtown development projects in 2013 included a $17.6 residential facility, South Junction Apartments, expected to add 197 downtown residences; AHC Geriatric Hospital, a 30-bed facility constructed at a cost of $8.9 million; Memphis Downtown Hilton, a 300-room hotel and parking garage; the three-story Orpheum Performing Arts and Leadership Center; and several interchange, bridge, and road projects in and around the city at a cost of more than $100 and managed by the Tennessee Department of Transportation.

Industries targeted by the Greater Memphis Chamber of Commerce in 2013 included bioscience, green industries, logistics and distribution, manufacturing, corporate office, and music, film, and tourism.

Economic Development Information: The Greater Memphis Chamber, 22 N. Front St., Suite 200, Memphis, TN 38103; telephone (901) 543-3500. Tennessee Department of Economic & Community Development, 312 Rosa L. Parks Avenue, Eleventh Floor, Nashville, TN 37243; telephone (615) 741-1888.

Commercial Shipping

Home to the world headquarters of FedEx, Memphis touts itself as "America's Distribution Center." The area is served by all major truck lines. In excess of 100 terminals offer direct services to all 48 contiguous states, as well as to Canada and Mexico. Eight federal highways, three interstate highways, and seven state highways connect the Memphis trucking industry with both the rest of the nation and with other vital forms of transportation. The presence of five Class I rail systems makes Memphis a center for world distribution in the new economy and one of the largest rail centers in the United States, trailing only Chicago and St. Louis. Memphis is one of only four cities served by five Class I rail systems. The Greater Memphis Chamber reports the Memphis workforce has a higher percentage of logistics workers than any other metropolitan area in the country. Memphis provides access to the world through its Intermodal Gateway Memphis, an international shipping hub.

Memphis's Uniport combines a Foreign Trade Zone with river, air, rail, and road facilities to make Memphis one of the nation's most important distribution centers. The International Port of Memphis is the second largest inland port on the shallow daft portion of the Mississippi

River and the fourth largest inland port in the United States. It is the largest still-water harbor on the Mississippi, handling more than 12 million tons annually.

Memphis International Airport is less than 15 minutes from most business centers in the area and serves major airlines and commuter lines. It is the world's busiest cargo airport because of FedEx, UPS, and other air freight companies that move approximately 4.5 billion pounds of cargo annually, valued at more than $11.9 billion.

Labor Force and Employment Outlook

Memphis boasts a diverse work force, prepared by nationally recognized schools and training programs. Memphis ranks high among business analysts for low taxes, competitive wages, and cost of living. The most specialized skill in the Memphis workforce is logistics, hosting the largest pool of logistics workers in the nation according to the Greater Memphis Chamber of Commerce. Growth industries in 2013 were paced by mining, logging, and construction, followed by financial activities and health services.

The following is a summary of data regarding the 2012 Memphis labor force:

Size of civilian labor force: 321,416

Number of workers employed in . . .
  agriculture and mining: 762
  construction: 13,524
  manufacturing: 21,132
  wholesale trade: 9,645
  retail trade: 31,772
  transportation: 31,436
  information systems: 4,206
  finance: 15,665
  professional administration: 28,830
  education and social services: 61,853
  arts and leisure: 29,572
  other: 14,088
  public administration: 12,498

Average hourly earnings of production workers: $15.38

Unemployment rate: 8.7% (2012)

Employers

Largest employers (2012)	*Number of employees*
FedEx Corp.	30,000
Memphis City Schools	16,119
United States Government	15,375
Methodist Le Bonheur Healthcare	8,700

Tennessee State Government	8,600
Memphis City Government	7,274
Wal-Mart Stores, Inc.	6,000
Shelby County Government	5,971
Shelby County Schools	5,200
Naval Support Activity Mid-South	4,076

Cost of Living

The city of Memphis has a relatively low cost of living, especially in comparison to other major cities across the country.

The following is a summary of data regarding several key cost of living factors in the area.

2013 ACCRA Average House Price: $207,494

2013 ACCRA Cost of Living Index: 85

State income tax rate: State income tax is limited to dividends and interest income only.

State sales tax rate: 7.0%

Local income tax rate: None

Local sales tax rate: 2.25%

Property tax rate: $4.38 per $100 assessed value (2013)

Economic Information: The Greater Memphis Chamber, 22 N. Front St., Suite 200, Memphis, TN 38103; telephone (901) 543-3500.

■ Education and Research

Elementary and Secondary Schools

Historically, Memphis had been served by two school districts: Memphis City Schools (for students within city limits) and Shelby County Schools (for those outside city limits). However, in 2013, the two districts began the first school year as a Unified School District, the biggest school district consolidation in the United States in decades. The new Unified School District served approximately 150,000 students, making it one of the largest in the nation. The annual budget of roughly $1 billion in 2013–14 was approximately $75 million less than the previous budgets of each district combined, resulting in the layoffs of hundreds of teachers and staff. Six suburban municipalities in Shelby County that feared the merger would lower academic standards in their schools planned to break out of the Unified School District in 2014.

Residents of Memphis also supported a network of 38 private elementary and secondary schools as of 2013. Premier among the list are St. Mary's Episcopal School, a school for girls in grades junior kindergarten through graduation, and Memphis University School, an all-boys preparatory school. Both are located within scenic surroundings in the eastern section of Memphis. Others often considered stepping stones to National Merit Scholarships are the Briarcrest Christian School, Presbyterian Day School, and Harding Academy of Memphis. Presbyterian Day School is one of the largest elementary school for boys in the United States, serving 630 students annually as of 2013.

The following is a summary of data regarding the Memphis City School District.

Total enrollment: 111,834

Number of facilities

total: 260
elementary schools: 115
junior high schools: 54
high schools: 52
other: 39

Student/teacher ratio: 15.46:1

Teacher salaries

average (statewide): $47,043

Funding per pupil: $9,499

Public Schools Information: Shelby County Schools, 160 S. Hollywood St., Memphis, TN 38112; telephone (901) 416-5300.

Colleges and Universities

The University of Memphis is the largest college campus in Shelby County, both in size and student enrollment (more than 22,000 as of 2013). The University of Memphis offers bachelor's degrees in more than 50 majors and master's degrees in more than 40 subjects, as well as doctoral degrees. Set on 1,600 acres, its sprawling campus includes a College of Arts and Sciences, Fogelman College of Business and Economics, College of Communication and Fine Arts, College of Education, Herff College of Engineering, University College, Loewenberg School of Nursing, Cecil C. Humphreys School of Law, and Graduate School.

Rhodes College, ranked 54th among national liberal arts colleges by *U.S. News & World Report* in 2013, is the oldest four-year liberal-arts school in the city. Founded in 1848, before the Civil War, in Clarksville, Tennessee, the college was moved to Memphis in 1925 and quartered in ivy-covered Gothic buildings, 13 of which are now listed on the National Register of Historic Places. It enrolls nearly 2,000 students annually.

LeMoyne-Owen College, a four-year liberal-arts college, was founded in 1862 as LeMoyne sought to educate emancipated slaves; it later merged with Owen College and offers majors in 22 areas of study leading to three degrees: bachelor of arts, bachelor of science, and bachelor of business administration. The Memphis College of Art is an independent professional college of artistic study that offers bachelor's and master's of fine arts degrees in a number of visual arts disciplines.

Future doctors, pharmacists, dentists, research academicians, and others interested in the medical field flock to Memphis to attend and graduate from the University of Tennessee Health Science Center. Among the colleges of the system are those of Allied Health Sciences, Dentistry, Graduate Health Sciences, Medicine, Nursing, and Pharmacy. UT is ranked among the largest and most progressive health science centers in the country.

Christian Brothers University is one of only a few private colleges in the nation to offer degrees in mechanical, electrical, civil, and chemical engineering. It was ranked 24th among regional universities by *U.S. News & World Report* in 2013. Vocational schools such as the Southwest Tennessee Community College offer two-year associate's degrees and technical certificates at several area campuses.

Libraries and Research Centers

The Memphis Public Library and Information Center has an annual circulation of more than two million books. Its special collections focus on Memphis history, art and architecture, and business and management. The system maintains 18 branches. Its Central Library, designed by Memphis architect Frank Ricks, is more than twice the size of the previous Main Library. Funding comes primarily from the city, although the library also receives support from the county and its Foundation for the Library program. The University of Memphis Libraries includes the main Ned R. McWherter Library and four branch libraries. The library system has many special collections, such as Confederate history, Lower Mississippi Valley history, and blues and jazz oral histories. The library's Health Information Center is recognized nationally.

There are more than 40 research centers in Memphis. Research activities at the University of Memphis focus on such areas as business and economics, substance addiction, earthquakes, child development, neuropsychology, women, anthropology, ecology, oral history, educational policy, communication disorders, and genomics. Research conducted at centers affiliated with the University of Tennessee Center for Health Science in Memphis focuses on fields such as neuroscience, vascular biology, genomics, and a variety of diseases and disorders. Christian Brothers University supports the

M. K. Gandhi Institute for Nonviolence. St. Jude Children's Research Hospital studies pediatric diseases and abnormalities and was the first pediatric research center designated as a Comprehensive Cancer Center by the National Cancer Institute.

Public Library Information: Memphis Public Library, 3030 Poplar Avenue, Memphis, TN 38111; telephone (901) 415-2700.

■ Health Care

The hospital corridor of Memphis underwent a series of major investments in the late 2000s and early 2010s, as hospitals and related businesses boomed. The Memphis and Shelby County region supports numerous hospitals, including Methodist and Baptist Memorial hospitals, two of the largest private hospitals in the nation, and the internationally recognized St. Jude Children's Research Hospital.

Methodist Hospitals of Memphis includes a 1,321-bed general medical and surgical facility that admits more than 60,000 patients annually. *U.S. News & World Report* ranked the hospital second among all Tennessee facilities in 2013–14, and it also achieved a national ranking in its nephrology care. Methodist operates Le Bonheur Children's Hospital, which is nationally ranked in six specialties. Baptist Memorial Hospital–Memphis had 642 beds as of 2013 and admitted nearly 27,000 patients annually. It received high-performing marks from *U.S. News & World Report* for its care of diabetes and endocrinology in 2013–14.

St. Jude's Children's Research Hospital is one of the nation's top children's cancer hospital, according to *U.S. News & World Report* in 2013–14; it ranked fifth nationally. St. Jude's is a premier research and treatment facility for children with catastrophic diseases, particularly pediatric cancers. According to the hospital, St. Jude has developed protocols that have helped push overall survival rates for childhood cancers from less than 20 percent when the hospital opened in 1962 to more than 80 percent. The institution was conceived and built by the late entertainer Danny Thomas in 1962 as a tribute to St. Jude Thaddeus, patron saint of impossible, hopeless, and difficult causes. Research at St. Jude's has focused on gene therapy, bone marrow transplant, chemotherapy, the biochemistry of normal and cancerous cells, radiation treatment, blood diseases, resistance to therapy, viruses, hereditary diseases, influenza, pediatric AIDS, and the psychological effects of catastrophic diseases.

Shelby County has more than 100 specialty clinics, including the nationally known Campbell Clinic Orthopedics, Semmes-Murphey Neurologic and Spine Institute, and Shea Ear Clinic.

■ Recreation

Sightseeing

Sightseeing in Memphis encompasses historical and modern attractions, from museums of the Victorian era to attractions related to the city's well known, historic music scene. At Chucalissa Archaeological Museum and Village in south Shelby County, it is easy to step back in time and learn about the Indian farmers, craftsmen and artists who lived in the area from 1000 to 1500 A.D. Operated by the University of Memphis, the archaeological site features tours and craft demonstrations by members of the Choctaw tribe.

The city's oldest private museums are located in an area known as Victorian Village, just a few miles east of downtown Memphis. Where once horse-drawn carriages kicked up dust as settlers arrived for afternoons of "calling" on their friends, Victorian Village today is a busy hubbub of tourist buses, cars, and bicycles as thousands come to see what life was like before electricity—when tea was poured from silver pots and ladies wore long, billowing frocks. The two most notable museum houses are the Woodruff-Fontaine House and the Mallory-Neely House. Woodruff-Fontaine, built in 1870, is French Victorian in style; Mallory-Neely was built in 1852. Several blocks away is the Magevney House; it is the oldest and by far the quaintest of the homes-turned-museums. The small white-frame building was built circa 1836. The home is furnished as it would have been in the 1850s.

Memphis's cultural heritage is strongly rooted in the mystical, magical sounds of jazz, blues, and rock and roll. W. C. Handy, the father of the blues, lived in Memphis when he heard bluesy music on Beale Street and then wrote such memorable songs as "The Memphis Blues" and "The Beale Street Blues." Beale Street has been restored and redeveloped, serving as both a center for African American culture and entertainment and as a tourist attraction since 1983. A restaurant and nightclub district, historic Beale Street also contains the renovated Old Daisy Theatre; just across the street is the new Daisy Theatre, a blues and jazz venue for all ages. The Center for Southern Folklore documents Southern traditions through live entertainment, folk art, and photography exhibits.

Sightseers in Memphis also visit the Peabody, the classic hotel in downtown that was originally built in the 1920s and renovated in 1981, and again in 2005. Of interest are the hotel's Italian Renaissance Revival architecture, Art Deco elevator doors, its stained glass work above the lobby bar, its reconstructed 1930s nightclub, and its resident ducks. By a tradition that started as a practical joke, a group of ducks occupies the hotel lobby's baroque fountain from 11 in the morning until 5 in the evening. During their arrival and departure, to the strains of John Phillip Sousa's "King Cotton March," they march over a red carpet unrolled between the fountain and the elevator that rises to the ducks' rooftop quarters. The Peabody's Plantation Roof attracts crowds of several hundred for rooftop parties. It is the very same spot where Paul Whiteman's and Tommy Dorsey's bands were once heard after their familiar radio introduction, "from high atop the Hotel Peabody, overlooking Ole Man River, in beautiful, downtown Memphis, Tennessee."

More than 600,000 people annually visit Memphis's Graceland, home of the late world-famous musician Elvis Presley; the entertainer moved to Memphis at age 12, attended school there, and recorded his first songs at a studio in the city. He made Graceland, built in 1939, his home in 1957. Set on nearly 14 acres of lush grounds, Graceland is open to the public for tours that include glimpses of Presley's exotic Jungle Room, his gold-leafed piano, numerous television sets, and mirrored walls. Graceland's Trophy Building contains the singer's gold and platinum records, his costumes, and other memorabilia; the carport houses Presley's vehicles, including his legendary pink Cadillac. Graceland's Meditation Garden, the Presley family burial site, is also on view, as is the singer's private jet. Visitors can also see Sun Studio, a museum and studio, where Presley and other musical greats got their start.

Another prime Memphis attraction is the mid-river Mud Island. What began as a sandbar in the Mississippi River grew into what is now called Mud Island, which was officially declared to be above the flood stage in 1965. Development of the island eventually resulted in construction of a visitors' center, park, amphitheater, and a spectacular four-block-long riverwalk that is an exact working replica of the Mississippi River. The riverwalk is a scale model showing 1,000 miles of the Mississippi River from Illinois to the Gulf of Mexico, accompanied by models of cities and bridges along the way; office workers and children alike are encouraged to wade in the riverwalk's flowing waters. It is also home to the Mississippi River Museum. Mud Island affords visitors a magnificent view of the Memphis skyline. Another Memphis-style experience is a sightseeing cruise along the Mississippi River aboard riverboat replicas.

Family fun can be had at the Memphis Zoo, located in mid-town Memphis, featuring 3,600 mammals, reptiles, birds, and fish in facilities that include an aquarium and a petting zoo. The zoo is one of the largest and most highly rated zoos in the United States. The zoo is part of greater Overton Park, a 342-acre public park in Midtown Memphis. In addition to the zoo, Overton Park hosts, among other features, the Memphis Brooks Museum of Art; a nine-hole golf course; the Memphis College of Art; Levitt Shell, an outdoor amphitheater; Rainbow Lake; Veterans Plaza, with veteran memorials; and, the Old Forest State Natural Area, an old-growth forest with trails. The Old Forest is on the National Register of Historic Places and includes more than 300 plant varieties; it is open to the public daily without charge.

Arts and Culture

Home to a variety of music genres, from blues to gospel to rock and roll, music is an integral part of Memphis art and culture. Visitors can see some of its most famous memorialized at the Memphis Walk of Fame. While home to notable singers like Elvis Presley, Johnny Cash, Issac Hayes, and B.B. King of the mid-twentieth century, Memphis continues to support music of all sorts. The Memphis Symphony Orchestra is the premier musical group performing in the Memphis area. The University of Memphis and Rhodes College also support musical performances in the city. Live popular music is plentiful in Memphis, where audiences can hear the unique blend of blues, soul, and rock and roll that has been identified as the "Memphis Sound." Jazz, bluegrass, and country music are also found at Memphis nightspots, which thrive on historic Beale Street and at Overton Square. The Gibson Beale Street Showcase is an active manufacturing facility that offers tours plus the Smithsonian Institute's Rock 'n Soul Museum, which showcases the social and cultural history of music in the Mississippi Delta and Memphis.

Touring Broadway productions are presented at the Orpheum Theatre, a lavish turn-of-the-century theater in downtown Memphis. Next door, construction was underway in 2013 on a $15 million Performing Arts and Leadership Centre to allow the Orpheum to host 30 performing arts events annually and serve more than 100,000 students and families. Memphians and mid-South residents enthusiastically support other area theaters, including Theatre Memphis, Germantown Community Theatre, Jewish Community Center, Old Daisy Theatre (located on renovated Beale Street), Playhouse on the Square, and Circuit Playhouse. In addition, the University of Memphis and Rhodes College theater groups mount stage productions. Ballet Memphis and Opera Memphis also perform in the city.

Memphis-area museums and galleries display a range of art and artifacts. The Memphis Brooks Museum of Art exhibits Renaissance pieces, English portraits and landscapes, regional works, and traveling shows. The Art Museum at the University of Memphis features Egyptian and African collections, as well as regional, faculty, and student work. Exhibits are also mounted at the Memphis College of Art. The Dixon Gallery and Gardens showcases French and American impressionist art and 17 acres of landscaped formal gardens. At the Memphis Botanic Garden, 96 acres form the setting for roses, irises, wildflowers, magnolias, lemon trees, banana trees, orchids, and a Japanese garden. Also located in Memphis is the National Ornamental Metal Museum, which displays weapons, model trains, sculpture, furniture, fencing, tools, and utensils. The Memphis Pink Palace Museum and Planetarium, named for the pink marble used in its construction in the 1920s, houses archaeological gems, prehistoric fossils, a Civil War display, regional exhibits, and a highly ranked planetarium; the museum is one of the largest of its kind in the Southeast.

Festivals and Holidays

The Memphis in May International Festival is a month-long series of festive activities offering celebrations to suit every taste. Events include foot races, canoe and kayak races, a triathlon competition, fireworks, and seminars. A main feature of the festival is the International Fair held at Tom Lee Park, each year honoring a different foreign country with exhibitions and demonstrations of arts, crafts, foods, and culture. The festival also hosts the World Championship Barbecue Cooking Contest, which rewards showmanship as well as culinary talent; the Beale Street Music Festival with top-name jazz and blues artists; and the Sunset Symphony, a beloved Memphis in May tradition with orchestral selections including "Ole Man River," and the "1812 Overture," a bombastic symphonic standard by nineteenth-century Russian composer Petr Ilich Tchaikovsky; the concert is played as the sun sets over the Mississippi River.

In late May and early June Carnival Memphis is celebrated with a river pageant, exhibits, parades, and music. Formerly known as the Memphis Cotton Carnival, the carnival annually selects a king and queen to reign over the activities. Elvis Week, held in mid-August, honors the late entertainer Elvis Presley, who made his home in Memphis and inspired intense fan loyalty. During Labor Day weekend in Memphis, historic Beale Street is the center of the Memphis Music and Heritage Festival, which underlines Memphis's claim as the birthplace of blues, soul, and rock music. September is also the month for the Mid-South Fair, featuring one of the largest rodeos east of the Mississippi, and agricultural, commercial, and industrial exhibits and events. October events in Memphis include Bluff City Oktoberfest and the week-long Pink Palace Crafts Fair.

The Indie Memphis Film Festival in the fall is hosted annually. Other festivals, like the Memphis Greek and Italian festivals dot the annual calendar with multicultural music, foods, and crafts.

Sports for the Spectator

Memphis provides sports enthusiasts with a variety of spectator action. The Memphis Grizzlies of the National Basketball Association play at the FedExForum, seating about 18,000 visitors. The FedExForum is also home to the University of Memphis's basketball team, the Tigers. Baseball fans can cheer for the Memphis Redbirds, AAA affiliate of the St. Louis Cardinals, who play at the 12,000-seat AutoZone Park downtown. The Mississippi RiverKings of the Central Hockey League provide professional hockey action. For college football fans, the AutoZone Liberty Bowl and the Southern Heritage Classic are held in Memphis annually. Early each spring, tennis buffs can enjoy the Regions Morgan Keegan Championships. During mid-summer, golfing devotees can watch the FedEx St. Jude Classic, a professional golfing championship held each year at Tournament

Players Club at Southwind and a regular stop on the PGA tour since 1958. Motorsports are increasingly popular in Memphis, and more than 200 events take place at Memphis International Raceway, which has a three-quarter-mile paved oval track, quarter-mile drag strip, and road course. Dog racing is also popular in the Memphis area; fans wager on favorites at Southland Greyhound Park in nearby West Memphis, Arkansas.

Sports for the Participant

Memphis has 167 parks, totaling 3,219 acres; the oldest and most notable is Overton Park, where 342 acres offer picnic areas, sports fields, natural woods hiking, and bicycle trails, combined with a nine-hole golf course, the zoo, and the Memphis Brooks Museum of Art. Within Overton Park is Greensward, three acres of open, grassy area reserved for outdoor recreation. Other large parks are King Riverside, with facilities for golf and tennis; and Audubon, offering water skiing, boating, swimming, and sailing. Memphis offers five municipal 18-hole golf courses and three nine-hole courses, as well as more than 100 public tennis courts. The T. O. Fuller State Park, at the southern city limits, is the only State Park within Memphis. Its 1,138 acres, primarily of forest land, feature a swimming pool, picnic area, nature trails, and 18-hole golf course. In the north end of Shelby County is 13,467-acre Meeman-Shelby Forest State Park. Located parallel to the Mississippi River 15 miles north of the heart of Memphis, Meeman-Shelby offers horseback riding, swimming, fishing, and miles of camping and hiking trails.

Boating, sailing, and water skiing are popular leisure-hour pursuits at dozens of lakes in the Memphis/Shelby County area. The Memphis Yacht Club, located next to Mud Island, accommodates a vast array of member craft, ranging from small houseboats to ocean-going vessels. Visiting craft are also accommodated at the club's dock.

Hunting dogs from all over the United States compete each year in the National Bird Dog Championship just outside Memphis. Climate allows year-round fishing for bass, crappie, trout, bream, and catfish. Lichterman Nature Center, an urban nature center in the heart of metropolitan Memphis, encompasses 65 acres of sanctuary and nature trails and an exhibit center.

Shopping and Dining

Notable among the city's shopping centers and malls is the Main Street Mall, a downtown array of department stores, boutiques, and eating establishments that together form one of the world's largest pedestrian shopping malls. The city's largest enclosed malls include Southland, Hickory Ridge, and Oak Court malls; the region's largest shopping mall is Wolfchase Galleria, with more than 130 stores, in eastern Shelby County. The city's historic Beale Street district contains unusual shops, including A. Schwab Dry Goods Store, a landmark on Beale Street since 1876, where general merchandise is enhanced by the Beale Street

Museum housed in the establishment's basement. Overton Square in the city's midtown features antique shops and art galleries along with cafes and restaurants.

For those who like to combine dining with entertainment, Memphis offers Peabody Place Retail & Entertainment Center, a mixed-use development and historic preservation project. Peabody Place offers sports restaurants and bars, video games, dancing, bowling, billiards, and restaurants. A veritable city within the city, Peabody Place encompasses three blocks of Beale Street, and includes the Peabody Hotel, the Orpheum Center, FedEx Forum, AutoZone Park, plus 80 restaurants; it attracts more than eight million visitors annually. Overton Square and Beale Street boast a concentration of sidewalk cafes, restaurants, and nightclubs that contribute to the range of culinary experiences awaiting diners in Memphis.

Besides European, Asian, and Mexican cuisines, Memphis-area restaurants offer traditional American choices such as steaks and seafood, as well as a number of typically Southern dishes. Regional specialties include main dishes such as fried chicken, catfish, ham hocks, chitlins, and seafood gumbo; side dishes such as turnip greens, sweet potato souffle, black-eyed peas, collard greens, yams, and cornbread; and desserts such as banana pudding, fruit cobblers, pecan pie, strawberry shortcake, and fried pie-a type of portable filled pastry. But Memphis is mainly known for its pork and barbecue masterpieces, ranging from dry ribs—prepared without sauce—to barbecue sandwiches. Memphis is consistently named one of the best barbeque cities in the nation.

Visitor Information: Memphis Convention & Visitors Bureau, 47 Union Avenue, Memphis, TN 38103; telephone (901) 543-5300.

■ Convention Facilities

The advantages of Memphis's meeting sites include accessibility, adequate space, elegant places for overnight visits, leisure sites to visit, and fine dining. Located at the north end of Main Street Mall, the 350,000-square-foot Memphis Cook Convention Center offers 190,000 square feet of exhibition space. The convention center has 31 meeting rooms; an Executive Conference Center; a 125,000 square foot, column-free exhibit hall; a second, 35,000 square foot hall; a 28,000 square-foot ballroom; and the 2,100-seat Cannon Center for the Performing Arts. Other convention locations include the Agricenter International Expo Center, the FedExForum, and the FedEx Institute of Technology at the University of Memphis. The FedEx Institute of Technology is a $23 million, state-of-the-art facility with a 190-seat tiered amphitheater, complemented a presentation theater and meeting rooms. The Agricenter International Expo

Center is the nation's first international technology/ environmental center for agriculture, providing about 140,000 square feet of meeting and exhibition space, an 800-seat amphitheater, meeting rooms, and a 20,000-square-foot Crystal Pavilion.

There were more than 100 hotels Memphis as of 2013. Many hotels and motels throughout the city provide elegantly decorated spots for meetings. Among them are The Peabody, the renovated "grand old lady" famed the world over for its lobby fountain and daily parade of ducks across a red carpet from the hotel's elevators to the fountain; the Holiday Inn Select Downtown, a hotel directly across from The Peabody; Radisson Hotel Memphis Airport; and the Holiday Inn Select Airport. At the Holiday Inn Select, a sprawling, contemporary-styled hotel within minutes of Memphis International Airport, accommodations provide 33,000 square feet of meeting space.

Convention Information: Memphis Convention & Visitors Bureau, 47 Union Avenue, Memphis, TN 38103; telephone (901) 543-5300.

■ Transportation

Approaching the City

Located minutes from downtown, Memphis International Airport is served by international, regional, and commuter airlines. In fiscal year 2012 the airport transported nearly four million passengers domestically and 46,000 internationally, with total airline revenues from these passengers in excess of $510 million. Between 2008 and 2012, the airport underwent nearly $420 million in renovations, which served both passenger and cargo traffic. The Memphis International Airport is the global "SuperHub" of FedEx Express, the largest airline in terms of freight tons flown. The airport is also a secondary hub of Delta Airlines. Other airports in the Memphis area include Millington Regional Jetport, General DeWitt Spain Airport, Charles W. Baker Airport, Arlington Municipal Airport, Olive Branch Airport, and West Memphis Municipal Airport.

Interstate 40 approaches Memphis from North Carolina to the east and California to the west, while Interstate 55 approaches the city from Chicago, Illinois, to the north and New Orleans, Louisiana, to the south. Interstate 240 rings the city. Motor traffic also enters Memphis via U.S. Highways 51, 61, 64, 70, 72, 78, and 79. Amtrak offers passenger train service through Memphis's historic Central Station. Amtrak's daily City of New Orleans trains head northbound to Chicago and southbound to New Orleans.

Traveling in the City

A fleet of more than 200 buses and vans operated by Memphis Area Transit Authority (MATA) meets public mass transportation needs. MATA manages annual ridership of 9.3 million, servicing an estimated 732,000 residents. The Main Street Trolley, utilizing vintage trolley cars, operates along popular downtown thoroughfares and celebrated its 20th anniversary in 2013.

■ Communications

Newspapers and Magazines

Memphis is served by *The Commercial Appeal,* a morning-circulated daily newspaper. Weekday circulation in 2013 was nearly 95,000. Business and local news is reported weekday mornings in *The Daily News,* while the *Tri-State Defender* is published weekly. *Memphis Business Journal* is available in print and online. *Memphis Magazine* is the area's monthly general-interest magazine. *The Memphis Flyer* is a weekly tabloid that discusses the arts, entertainment, and lifestyles, while the *Mid-South Hunting & Fishing News* is a biweekly tabloid covering outdoor recreation. Special-interest publications originating in Memphis focus on such subjects as environmental legislation, poetry, and hunting, and such industries as glass and metal, trucking, rice and cotton growing, and other agricultural concerns.

Television and Radio

Memphis-area television viewers are served by 16 stations: affiliates of major networks, public broadcasting, and independent channels. Eleven AM and 13 FM radio stations present Memphis audiences with a range of programming from classical, jazz, blues, folk, bluegrass, reggae, easy listening, contemporary, and country music to religious, news, public radio, talk-show, agricultural, and educational broadcasts.

Media Information: The Commercial Appeal, 495 Union Avenue, Memphis, TN 38103; telephone (901) 529-2345. *The Daily News,* 193 Jefferson Avenue, Memphis, TN 38103; telephone (901) 523-1561.

Memphis Online

City of Memphis Home Page. Available www. memphistn.gov

The Commercial Appeal. Available www. commercialappeal.com

The Daily News. Available www.memphisdailynews. com

Memphis Convention & Visitors Bureau. Available www.memphistravel.com

Memphis Public Library. Available www. memphislibrary.org

The Greater Memphis Chamber. Available www. memphischamber.com

Unified School District. Available www.scsk12.org

BIBLIOGRAPHY

Faulkner, William, *The Reivers* (New York: Random House, 1962)

Green, Laurie Boush, *Battling the Plantation Mentality: Memphis and the Black Freedom Struggle* (Chapel Hill, NC: University of North Carolina Press, 2007)

Grisham, John, *The Firm* (New York: Doubleday, 1991)

Guralnick, Peter, *Last Train to Memphis: The Rise of Elvis Presley* (Boston, MA: Little, Brown, and Company, 1994)

Potter, Susanna Henighan, *Moon Spotlight Memphis* (Berkeley, CA: Avalon Travel Publishing, 2008)

Nashville

■ The City in Brief

Founded: 1779 (incorporated 1784)

Head Official: Mayor Karl Dean (D) (since 2007; current term expires 2015)

City Population
> 1990: 488,366
> 2000: 545,524
> 2010: 601,222
> 2012 estimate: 623,255
> Percent change, 2000–2010: 10.2%
> U.S. rank in 1990: 25th (State rank: 2nd)
> U.S. rank in 2000: 32nd (State rank: 2nd)
> U.S. rank in 2010: 25th (State rank: 2nd)

Metropolitan Statistical Area Population
> 2000: 1,231,331
> 2010: 1,589,934
> 2012 estimate: 1,645,638
> Percent change, 2000–2010: 29.1%
> U.S. rank in 2000: 39th
> U.S. rank in 2010: 38th

Area: 473 square miles (Nashville-Davidson)

Elevation: 550 feet

Average Annual Temperatures: January, 36.8° F; July, 79.1° F; annual average, 58.9° F

Average Annual Precipitation: 48.11 inches of rain; 10.0 inches of snow

Major Economic Sectors: services, education, wholesale and retail trade, manufacturing

Unemployment Rate: 6.0% (2012)

Per Capita Income: $25,817

2012 FBI Crime Index Property: 26,052

Major Colleges and Universities: Vanderbilt University, Fisk University, Tennessee State University, Belmont University, Lipscomb University

Daily Newspaper: *The Tennessean*

■ Introduction

Nashville is the state capital of Tennessee, the capital of country music, and a thriving location for the music industry in the eastern United States. Nestled in rolling hills in the part of the state known as Middle Tennessee, Nashville is often called the "garden spot of the world." The lush natural vegetation, changing seasons, and mild climate of the area make a pretty picture that is the setting for miles of green neighborhoods, shaded shopping districts, thick forests, and wide-open pastures, all inside the city limits. It is a city large enough to be headquarters for scores of international corporations, yet small enough for the neighborhood banker to call his customers by name. In Nashville, one can hear the Nashville Symphony perform *Pagliacci* at the Schermerhorn Symphony Center one night and see the historic Grand Ole Opry in all its glory the next. They can live in steel and glass high-rise condominiums near the center of the city or in secluded frame farmhouses on rural routes. While Nashville is the second most populated city in the state, the Nashville metropolitan area is the largest in the state. The traditional values of the rural people who settled the area have blended with influences brought by international business, music studios, film crews, gourmet restaurants, university scholars, couture clothiers, and conventioneers to create an unusual blend of lifestyles. Nashville is consistently ranked among top metropolitan areas as a top place to live, work, learn, and visit. The combination of country charm and city savvy makes the Music City attractive to residents and visitors alike.

© Sean Pavone/Shutterstock.com

■ Geography and Climate

The city ranks with Houston, Texas, and Los Angeles, California, as one of the nation's largest cities in terms of area. Situated in the center of middle Tennessee on the Cumberland River, Nashville is rimmed on three sides by an escarpment rising three to four hundred feet. Nashville's climate is moderate, with seasonal variation rarely lapsing into temperature extremes. Nashville's long springs and autumns combined with a diverse array of trees and grasses can make it uncomfortable for allergy sufferers. The Asthma and Allergy Foundation of America consistently ranks Nashville among the worst spring allergy cities. Its humidity is also considered moderate for the Southeast. Precipitation is heaviest in winter and early spring, though when it falls in the form of snow it is seldom disruptive. Tornados occur occasionally. Thunderstorms in Nashville are moderately frequent from March through September, often causing heavy rainfall.

With this heavy rainfall, Nashville is also susceptible to flooding.

Area: 473 square miles (Nashville-Davidson)

Elevation: 550 feet

Average Temperatures: January, 36.8° F; July, 79.1° F; annual average, 58.9° F

Average Annual Precipitation: 48.11 inches of rain; 10.0 inches of snow

■ History

First Settlers Face Perils

The first settlers in the area that now forms Nashville were attracted by the fertile soil, huge trees, plentiful water, and an abundance of animal life. Native Americans such as the Cherokee, Chickasaw, and Shawnee hunted throughout Middle Tennessee in the 1700s, but ongoing fighting over hunting rights kept them from establishing any permanent settlements. The first Europeans to reach the area were French fur traders, who built trading posts in the dense woods. As more and more hunters brought glowing reports back to settlements in the East of the abundant, unoccupied land in the "west," 400 people in

North Carolina eventually decided to band together and move to the area.

On Christmas Eve 1779, they reached the future site of Nashville. The men, women, and children of the James Robertson party (named for the man who would eventually become an early community leader) first survived in primitive camps at the base of what is now the state Capitol Hill. As spring arrived, they spread out to build cabins, the largest group settling on the banks of the Cumberland River in a "fort" of log blockhouses. They christened the community "Nashborough" for North Carolina's General Francis Nash, a hero of the American Revolution. Months later the pioneers found themselves swept up in war as the settlement became a western front for the American Revolution. Incited by the British, the Native Americans in the area turned on the white settlers, which caused most of them to move to safer ground in nearby Kentucky. The 70 people who remained gathered in the fort and managed to hold off their attackers until frontier conditions became less hostile.

In 1784 the community incorporated and changed its name to Nashville, dropping the English "borough" as a result of anti-British sentiment. The years following the war were a time of growth and prosperity. James Robertson helped to establish Davidson Academy, which would later become the University of Nashville. Churches were erected, public buildings developed, doctors' offices opened, and stores began doing business. In 1796 Tennessee became the sixteenth state of the Union.

"The Age of Jackson"

The period in Nashville history between 1820 and 1845 is quite simply known as "The Age of Jackson." Andrew Jackson, a brash, young local lawyer and public prosecutor, was a formidable figure in the new frontier. He first came to national attention as a hero of the Creek (Native American) War. When he trounced the British army in New Orleans at the end of the War of 1812, he was wildly embraced as a national hero. Jackson served in the U.S. House of Representatives and the Senate, and he was eventually elected the seventh president of the United States in 1829. Jackson's popularity gave Nashville considerable prestige, power, and clout in the nation's eye, and the city was made the permanent capital of Tennessee in 1843. State leaders soon commissioned construction of a new state capitol building, an impressive neo-classic structure erected over the next 14 years on the summit of the city's highest hill. Designed by noted nineteenth-century architect William Strickland, the Capitol ushered in an era of unprecedented building and design in Nashville of which Strickland was the uncontested leader. His distinct, clean, classic structures shaped the frontier town into a city, and left a lasting imprint on the community. Many buildings, such as the Capitol and St. Mary's Roman Catholic Church, are still in use today.

The mid-1800s was also an era of unprecedented development for the city. Traffic on the Cumberland River made Nashville a shipping and distribution center. Wealthy businessmen built lavish estates. A medical school was founded. The Adelphi Theater opened with a series of plays by Shakespeare. The first passenger train pulled into the depot. A board of education was established. P. T. Barnum even brought Jenny Lind, the world-renowned singer, to town. By 1860, all the qualities that had made Nashville such a boom town in times of peace also made it a city of strategic importance in times of war. At first a giant supply arsenal for the Confederates, Nashville was soon taken during the Civil War by Union troops who seized control of the railroad and river. They occupied the city for three years. In a last attempt to turn the war around, Southern troops tried to retake the town in December of 1864. The Battle of Nashville was one of the bloodiest confrontations between the North and South, and the last major conflict of the Civil War.

Post-War Rebuilding

It took nearly ten years to pick up the pieces, but Nashville recovered to experience new growth in business and industry. The city became a printing center, an educational center (both Vanderbilt University and Fisk University were established in 1873), and an important distributing and wholesale center. An elegant new hotel, the Maxwell House, opened its doors and began serving a special blend of coffee that President Teddy Roosevelt said was "good to the last drop." One hundred years after Tennessee was admitted to the Union, the city celebrated with a giant Centennial Exposition that attracted visitors from throughout the United States. A wood and stucco replica of the Parthenon built for the fair was such a popular attraction that the city constructed a permanent version that now stands in Centennial Park. The railroad built a magnificent terminal building, Union Station, making Nashville a major railway center and greatly spurring population growth. The city also began to make a name for itself in the music industry with the opening of the Grand Ole Opry, which later grew to prominence as a national music venue.

Development During Twentieth Century

The twentieth century brought business and skyscrapers. The National Life and Accident Company was formed along with Life & Casualty Insurance Company. In the area, local financial institutions blossomed, manufacturing reached all-time highs, and the city's neighborhoods swelled with workers as a result of World War I and World War II. After the wars, Nashville was part of the country's new wave of technology with a new airport, factory automation, and even a local television station. In time, the recording industry became a mainstay of the local economy, and tourism and convention business became big business. By the 1960s, Nashville was infused with a spirit of urban renewal. Surrounding Davidson County had become a fragmented collection of local governments that lacked unified direction. On April 1, 1963, the city voted to consolidate the city and the county to form the first metropolitan form of government in the United States.

The system of metropolitan government streamlined the city's organization and become an effective agent of progress. The city underwent major municipal rehabilitation projects, and renovated the historical district near the old Ft. Nashborough site. Second Avenue, once a row of dilapidated turn-of-the-century warehouses, is now a bustling center of shopping, offices, restaurants, clubs, and apartments. Many historic buildings have been saved from the wrecking ball. The Hermitage Hotel, built in 1910 as a showplace of Tennessee marble floors and staircases, was totally renovated in the 1990s and is once again packed with guests. Renovation has also come to Union Station, the massive railroad house that now towers over Broadway as one of Nashville's premiere hotels. Unprecedented investment in Nashville in the mid-1990s placed the city on the verge of explosive growth as a sports and entertainment venue. Its Bridgestone Arena (formerly Nashville Arena, Gaylord Entertainment Center, and Sommet Center), home of the National Hockey League team the Nashville Predators, has become a major catalyst for urban developmentThe Tennessee Titans of the National Football League gave the city a professional football team just before the turn of the century.

The Twenty-First Century

Nashville has grown to prominence in the music industry generally, while continuing to maintain its title as the capital of the country music scene. Aside from its history in the genre, Nashville is home to the Country Music Hall of Fame and Music Row. Economic development efforts have capitalized on Nashville's identity as "Music City." The $600 million Music City Center, the city's sparkling new convention center, opened in 2013.

Other industries, especially in health care and medicine, have furthered Nashville's economy. Its three *Fortune* 500 companies, as of 2013, all worked in the health-care field. A strong base of health-care providers has continued to attract a network of related fields. Indeed, Nashville entered the twenty-first century as a thriving metropolis with extensive kudos for its quality of life, business climate, diversified economy, and status as a top tourist destination.

Historical Information: Nashville Public Library, The Nashville Room, 615 Church Street, Nashville, TN 37219; telephone (615) 862-5800. Tennessee State Museum Library, 505 Deaderick St., Nashville, TN 37243; telephone (615) 741-2692.

■ Population Profile

Metropolitan Statistical Area Population

2000: 1,231,331
2010: 1,589,934
2012 estimate: 1,645,638
Percent change, 2000–2010: 29.1%
U.S. rank in 2000: 39th
U.S. rank in 2010: 38th

City Residents

1990: 488,366
2000: 545,524
2010: 601,222
2012 estimate: 623,255
Percent change, 2000–2010: 10.2%
U.S. rank in 1990: 25th (State rank: 2nd)
U.S. rank in 2000: 32nd (State rank: 2nd)
U.S. rank in 2010: 25th (State rank: 2nd)

Density: 1,265.4 people per square mile

Racial and ethnic characteristics

White: 377,215
Black or African American: 178,796
American Indian and Alaskan Native: 1,151
Asian: 21,226
Native Hawaiian and Other Pacific Islander: 82
Hispanic or Latino (may be of any race): 63,142
Other: 44,785

Percent of residents born in state: 52.5%

Age characteristics

Population under 5 years old: 44,264
Population 5 to 9 years old: 41,749
Population 10 to 14 years old: 30,696
Population 15 to 19 years old: 36,783
Population 20 to 24 years old: 51,474
Population 25 to 34 years old: 119,570
Population 35 to 44 years old: 85,232
Population 45 to 54 years old: 79,794
Population 55 to 59 years old: 36,388
Population 60 to 64 years old: 32,315
Population 65 to 74 years old: 36,116
Population 75 to 84 years old: 21,115
Population 85 years and over: 7,759
Median age: 33.6

Births (2010–11 Metropolitan Area)

Total number: 21,555

Deaths (2010–11 Metropolitan Area)

Total number: 11,688

Money income (2012)

Per capita income: $25,817

Median household income: $44,271
Total households: 246,103

Number of households with income of . . .

less than $10,000: 21,829
$10,000 to $14,999: 16,522
$15,000 to $24,999: 29,769
$25,000 to $34,999: 29,570
$35,000 to $49,999: 38,374
$50,000 to $74,999: 45,641
$75,000 to $99,999: 25,324
$100,000 to $149,999: 22,276
$150,000 to $199,999: 8,323
$200,000 or more: 8,475

Percent of families below poverty level: 19.9%

FBI Crime Index Property: 26,052

FBI Crime Index Violent: 7,550

■ Municipal Government

Since 1963, when Nashville merged with surrounding Davidson County, Nashville has operated via a consolidated metropolitan mayor-council government. Voters elect 40 council members to the Metropolitan Council, 35 of which serve separate districts, while five are elected at large.

Head Official: Mayor Karl Dean (D) (since 2007; current term expires 2015)

Total Number of City Employees: 9,155 (2013)

City Information: City of Nashville, 1 Public Square, Metropolitan Courthouse, Nashville, TN 37210; telephone; (615)862-5000

■ Economy

Major Industries and Commercial Activity

Economic diversity permeates Nashville's economy, adding to its strength as a community. The city is a great "neighborhood" of private and public business and industry, where people are as likely to go to work each morning in banks, hospitals, or government offices as to drive trucks, punch cash registers, or work on assembly lines. The area has benefited from low unemployment, consistent job growth, heavy outside investment and expansion, and a broadening of the labor force. Small businesses thrived in Nashville, with roughly 17,000 of the area's 36,000 businesses employing between one and four people as of 2013.

Of all of the products manufactured in the city, music is what makes Nashville most famous. *Rolling Stone* named Nashville the "Best Music Scence" in the country

in 2011. The local recording industry and its offshoots have not only brought worldwide recognition to what was once a sedate southern city, but they have also pumped billions of dollars into the local economy, created a thriving entertainment business scene ranked behind only New York and Los Angeles, and given the city a distinctly cosmopolitan flavor. Major record labels—Universal Music, Sony Music Entertainment, and Warner Music Group—as well as numerous independent labels, have offices in Nashville, mostly on Music Row. There are approximately 200 recording studios in Nashville. Nashville music, which includes country, pop, gospel, and rock, generates more than one-billion dollars in record sales each year. Celebrity spottings are frequent as musicians and stars conduct business in the city.

As a result, spinoff industries have flourished: booking agencies, music publishing companies, promotional firms, recording studios, trade publications, and performance rights associations such as BMI, Broadcast Music, Inc. As Nashville remains a center for the music industry, it continues to draw support businesses and industry to the area. Local music-related advertising firms (especially jingle houses) bring in vast revenues; a burgeoning radio, television, and film industry has enticed some of the country's top producers, directors, and production houses to set up shop in Nashville. The music industry in Nashville is also responsible for a good chunk of the city's tourism activity. Nashville's musical performances bring in more than revenue, however. They draw millions of people to the city each year as well, who also stay at hotels, dine at restaurants, and enjoy the city's other attractions.

While the city is renowned for its music recording industry and tourism, it is actually health care that leads the way in Nashville's economy. More than 250 health-care companies operate in the Nashville area, including the headquarters of HCA Holdings, Vanguard Health Systems, and Community Health Systems, all *Fortune* 500 companies in 2013. Among those 250, some 16 were pubically traded companies as of 2013, with a combined employment of 400,000 and global revenue of $70 billion. In the Nashville area, all health-care companies combined to generate 210,000 jobs and $13 billion in personal income.

Nashville reaps significant benefits from Interstate 840, a limited-access highway that forms another outer ring of roadway around the city completed in the mid-2000s. The new highway has already influenced business location decisions in Middle Tennessee. Companies such as Big Idea Productions, Louisiana-Pacific, Clarcor, and Asurion moved their headquarters to the Nashville area in the mid-2000s. A major private investment in Nashville marked Dell Computer's first U.S. expansion outside of Central Texas. In fall of 2000, Dell opened new manufacturing and office facilities in Nashville, and has since increased its Tennessee workforce from approximately 200 to 2,500 in 2013.

Advanced manufacturing has been drawn to the area by low labor costs and Nashville's central location for the eastern half of the United States. Major manufacturing companies in 2013 were Nissan North America, Electrolux, Dell, Bridgestone, Tyson, Trane Company, General Motors, Hemlock Semiconductor, A.O. Smith Water Products Co., and General Mills/Pillsbury. Non health-care companies with corporate headquarters in Nashville included the aforementioned Nissan North America, Dollar General, Mars Petcare, Caterpillar Financial, Asurion, Tractor Supply, and Jackson National Life. As the city's largest employer, Vanderbilt University remains an economic and intellectual powerhouse in the community.

Items and goods produced: automotive products, trucks, automotive parts, clothing, shoes, lawnmowers, bicycles, telecommunications equipment, pet food, computers

Incentive Programs-New and Existing Companies

Local programs: The Fast Track Permitting and One-Stop Business Assistance Program helps new and expanding businesses avoid delays by expediting their dealings with local, state, and federal government offices regarding regulatory permits, and by assisting with any problems they may have in the process. The Payment in Lieu of Tax (PILOT) program offers qualifying businesses a property tax freeze or reduction on projects involving a large capital investment or creating large numbers of new jobs. Requests for PILOT assistance are considered on a case-by-case basis by the city and county. Industrial Revenue Bonds are available to eligible companies for land, building, or equipment purchases. The Nashville region has three general-purpose foreign trade zones and a number of sub-zones designated for specific company usages. Tax Increment Financing (TIF) is also available: TIF financing allows the cost of infrastructure and the costs of assembly, relocation, demolition, and development of a site within a designated redevelopment district to be financed through future increases in property taxes generated by the development itself. The Commercial Real Estate Database provides site location services for interested businesses, at which time relocation assistance may be provided. Also, due to its location in the Tennessee Valley and Tennessee Valley Authority jurisdiction, the TVA also provides some assistance. The TVA enhanced growth credit provides substantial credit on power bills to certain companies expanding in the area. A special economic development loan fund provides loans for up to $2 million to purchase fixed assets depending on job creation and capital investment.

State programs: Tennessee is a right-to-work state and its overall state and local tax burden is among the lowest of all 50 states. Tennessee has no personal income tax on wages or salaries. The state's Jobs Tax Credit is available to businesses creating 25 new jobs within a three-year period and investing at least 500,000. These qualifying businesses may claim a tax credit of $4,500 per job to offset up to 50 percent of its franchise and excise tax liability for up to 15 years. The credit is available for businesses in a range of industries, especially advanced manufacturing. The Jobs Tax Super Credit allows businesses with a minimum $1 billion investment to claim up to $10,000 per job for six years.

The Industrial Machinery Tax Credit allows companies to write off up to 50 percent of their franchise and excise tax liability by earning up to 10 percent of the cost of industrial machinery in tax credits. Industrial machinery definitions extend to technological equipment such as computers and computer software, systems, and networks.

A headquarters relocation reimbursement offers tax credits to cover relocation costs of businesses. If the credit exceeds the tax liability of a company in the first year, the remainder is given to the company as a cash payment. Companies must provide evidence of relocation expenses, and certain qualifications regarding the size and operations of the headquarters must be met. There are also state sales tax exemptions and reductions for industrial machinery purchases that support manufacturing businesses.

The state's Industrial Access Program utilizes resources in the Tennessee Department of Transportation to undertake roadways projects that support industrial development. Annual funding for these projects is roughly $10 million.

Job training programs: Tennessee's FastTrack Training Program is the state's primary source of financial support for new and expanding business and industry training. FastTrack staff work with businesses to plan, develop, and implement customized training programs. Training may be done in a classroom setting, or on the job. The state also offers free applicant recruitment and screening for Tennessee companies. The Department of Labor and Workforce Development works with companies to find and review ideal employees, and is entirely free of charge. The state's database contains a pool of more than 70,000 potential employees; 62 Tennessee Career Centers across the state manage applicants locally.

Development Projects

Growth in business development has been instrumental in bringing development projects to the city. Nashville's aggressive Partnership 2010 program was responsible for a flurry of business activity in the early part of the new century, including company relocations, expansions, and new corporations. It responded with a new program, Partnership 2020, to carry it into the next decade.

In 2010 construction crews broke ground on a new convention center, the Music City Center. Designed by

Atlanta-based TVA Design, in collaboration with Nashville's Tuck Hinton Architects and Moody-Nolan Architects, construction began with the removal of 200,000 cubic yards of rock and soil from the 16-acre site. Afterward, three years of construction by more than 7,300 led to facility's completion in May 2013. The project cost some $598 million, which city officials believed represented an investment in the future of the downtown area. Unique features of the building included its roof, covered with 14 types of vegetation to limit stormwater runoff, clean air, and conserve energy.

The old convention center was set to be demolished, with plans to build in its place a $230 million, 28-story office tower revealed in late 2013. The ground-level floor was to house retail and entertainment spaces. Total office space was expected to measure between 480,000 and 840,000 square feet, depending on final decisions made in response to market demand. Also planned for the building was a National Museum of African Ameircan Music, set to occupy 69,000 square feet in the new construction.

North of downtown, city planners voted in favor of construction of a new ballpark for the Nashville Sounds, the Triple-A affiliate of the Milwaukee Brewers. Plans were for a $37 million ballpark with an additional $28 spent on land acquistion and interest costs. Located near the Bicentennial Capitol Mall State Park at the historic Sulpher Dell site, the development was to be supported by a $60 million residential and commercial development funded by the team. Property tax revenue from that development, in addition to the stadium lease deal, was expected to help the city recoup the cost of initial investment.

Swiss bank UBS announced in August 2013 its intentions to invest $36.5 million in the Nashville area and create 1,000 jobs by 2018 through establishment of a shared services center in Nashville. The proposed Nashville Business Solutions Center expanded the company's footprint in the Nashville area, where it already employed 200 citizens.

Economic Development Information: Nashville Area Chamber of Commerce, 211 Commerce Street #100, Nashville, TN 37201; telephone (615) 743-3000.

Commercial Shipping

Nashville's central location has made it one of the busiest transportation centers in the Mid-South. More than 80 miles of interstate highways weave in and out of the city, making Nashville a vital link to every corner of the region. The bulk of local transportation services are designed to move freight. For high priority or overnight deliveries Nashvillians often turn to the rapidly expanding air freight industry. The Nashville Air Cargo Link is designated as foreign trade zone and is an all-cargo complex serving the Nashville International Airport. As of 2013, cargo services were offered by American, Delta, Federal Express, Southwest, United, and US Airways. The airport is within five minutes of Interstate 40.

While air freight has been critical, Nashville's strength as a distribution center for the Southeast still lies in the traditional and highly competitive industries of trucking, rail freight, and river barge. Millions of tons of goods are moved through the city each year via truck by more than motor freight lines serving the area; an estimated 87 percent of all freight was moved by truck in 2013. Nashville has become a regional headquarters for the trucking industry primarily because of its tight, efficient network of accessible interstate highways, its conveniently centralized location, and the fact that local terminals provide easy break-bulk distribution and specialized services for products such as produce (refrigeration), gasoline, and hazardous waste.

Since the turn of the century, Nashville has historically been considered the hub of railway activity for the Southeast. CSX Transportation and Norfolk Southern both operate Class I railroads. Most railways in Tennessee run north–south, with a spur running to Memphis to the west and Knoxville to the east.

The Cumberland River, an artery of the Ohio River that weaves in and out of the Nashville Metropolitan area, links the city to points on the Mississippi River and the Gulf of Mexico coast. There are three public terminals in Nashville for loading and unloading freight. Additional private facilities are available. The distance to Gulf ports was cut by 563 miles in the mid-1980s when the United States Army Corps of Engineers opened its $1.8 billion Tennessee-Tombigbee Waterway, connecting the Tennessee River in northern Alabama with the Tombigbee River of southern Alabama 234 miles away. This ambitious man-made water route connected Nashville to the port of Mobile, resulting in an estimated savings of millions in shipping costs.

Labor Force and Employment Outlook

Nashville experienced significant economic expansion in the early half of the twenty-first century, to the extent that employers in certain sectors, such as skilled production, have been experiencing labor shortages. Population growth continues, however, especially in suburban Nashville, which offers a long-term solution to the labor supply problem. With the influx of expansions and new businesses, and in concert with Nashville's diverse and stable economy and growing population, continued economic expansion is predicted. The population of Nashville was generally more educated than both state and national averages. Projections suggest that Nashville would add an additional 151,000 jobs between 2009 and 2019, with significant internal migration from surrounding areas, and from out of state, necessary to fill the gap, which was exacerbated by the retirement of the Baby Boomers generation throughout the 2010s.

The following is a summary of data regarding the 2012 Nashville labor force:

Size of civilian labor force: 337,180

Number of workers employed in . . .

agriculture and mining: 925
construction: 17,392
manufacturing: 21,471
wholesale trade: 8,322
retail trade: 35,864
transportation: 12,375
information systems: 9,321
finance: 20,251
professional administration: 34,783
education and social services: 76,130
arts and leisure: 38,153
other: 16,167
public administration: 14,495

Average hourly earnings of production workers: $16.37

Unemployment rate: 6.0% (2012)

Employers

Largest employers (2013)	*Number of employees*
Vanderbilt University and Medical Center	22,930
State of Tennessee	18,210
Metro Nashville–Davidson Co. Government and Public Schools	18,088
U.S. Government	12,407
Nissan North America Inc.	8,150
HCA	7,000
Saint Thomas Health Services	6,350
Ranstad	3,495
Shoney's Inc.	3,000
The Kroger Company	2,753

Cost of Living

The cost of living in Nashville was significantly below average in comparison to other major U.S. cities.

The following is a summary of data regarding several key cost of living factors in the area.

2013 ACCRA Average House Price: $206,600

2013 ACCRA Cost of Living Index: 87

State income tax rate: State income tax is limited to dividends and interest income only.

State sales tax rate: 7.0%

Local income tax rate: None

Local sales tax rate: 2.25%

Property tax rate: $4.516 per $100 of assessed value (2013)

Economic Information: Nashville Area Chamber of Commerce, 211 Commerce Street #100, Nashville, TN 37201; telephone (615) 743-3000.

■ Education and Research

Elementary and Secondary Schools

In 1855 Nashville became the first southern city to establish a public school system. A program started in Nashville in 1963 became the prototype for Head Start. That same year, Metropolitan Nashville Public Schools formed when the city and Davidson County governments were consolidated. A nine-member elected board and its appointed director of schools are responsible for the running of the public schools. The schools offer diverse educational opportunities recognized statewide for their innovation. There are programs in Nashville for the gifted, the handicapped, and the foreign student who wants to catch up. In 2006 the district began redesigning certain high schools into smaller learning communities, known as "The Academies of Nashville." The Academies allow students to learn through a specific career or theme to personalize the learning experience. There were three academy high schools as of 2013. Enrollment in magnet schools, design centers, and other specialized programs are available in the system.

Numerous school-age children in Davidson County attend private schools. There were 62 preparatory academies, church-affiliated, and alternative schools operating in the area as of 2013, focusing on specific academic and religious needs. A number of widely renowned preparatory schools are found on this list.

Of the four schools in Tennessee recognized as Blue Ribbon Schools of Excellence by the U.S. Department of Education in 2013, two were in Nashville: Holy Rosary Academy and Meigs Middle Magnet School.

The following is a summary of data regarding the Davidson County School District.

Total enrollment: 78,782

Number of facilities

total: 157
elementary schools: 77
junior high schools: 50

high schools: 24

other: 6

Student/teacher ratio: 14.26:1

Teacher salaries

average (statewide): $47,043

Funding per pupil: $9,800

Public Schools Information: Nashville Metropolitan Schools, 2601 Bransford Avenue, Nashville, TN 37204; telephone (615) 259-4636.

Colleges and Universities

The most famous school in Nashville is Vanderbilt University, alma mater of a diverse array of successful politicians and musicians. The private, independent institution of the Vanderbilt family—one of the most prominent and wealthiest families in American history—is highly competitive, maintains impeccable standards, and prides itself on what it calls a "quality liberal arts" undergraduate program. In addition, the school is widely known for its advanced academic offerings in medicine, law, business, nursing, divinity, and education. *U.S. News & World Report,* in a 2013 study of U.S. universities, ranked Vanderbilt University 17th among all universities nationwide. The campus welcomes nearly 13,000 students annually but maintains a student–faculty ratio of 8:1. In addition, the academically rigorous university is competitive at the highest levels of collegiate athletics.

The first predominantly African American institution in the country to be awarded university status, Fisk University is also located in Nashville. Fisk, alma mater of social critic and NAACP co-founder W. E. B. DuBois, is a four-year, private school ranked among the top 150 liberal arts colleges in the nation. Nashville's Meharry Medical College, established to train African American physicians, provides instruction in medical science, public health, and dental surgery. Nashville's largest state-operated university, Tennessee State University, is also a historically black college. The university offers undergraduate and graduate programs in arts and sciences, agriculture, health professions, business, education, engineering and technology, nursing, and public administration.

Belmont University, a private, four-year Baptist school located near downtown's Music Row, offers some 70 undergraduate degree programs as well as graduate programs in accountancy, business administration, education, English, music, nursing, occupational therapy, physical therapy, and sport administration. Belmont's notable Mike Curb College offers majors in Audio Engineering Technology and Music Business, and a specialization in Entertainment and Music Business is offered within the University's M.B.A. program. Students across the country seeking a career in the record industry

have enrolled in specialized courses ranging from record promotion to studio engineering. Belmont was the seventh-ranked regional university in the South according to *U.S. News & World Report* in 2013. Lipscomb University, founded as Nashville Bible School in 1891 by David Lipscomb and James A. Harding, was renamed Lipscomb University in 1918. Lipscomb, ranked 20th among regional universities, offers nearly 50 majors leading to bachelor's degrees in arts, business administration, education, science, and nursing, and 25 graduate degrees in addition to three doctorate programs.

Libraries and Research Centers

The Nashville Public Library boasts more than 740,000 books, 19,000 books on tape, and 4,000 music CDs across its 20 branches. The main library also holds recordings, videotapes, and maps. Its special collections include government documents, business, ornithology, genealogy, and oral and regional history. A new Main Library of approximately 300,000 square feet, quadruple the size of the library it replaced, completed in 2001; it faces the Tennessee State Capitol building. Special services of the library include a talking library for the visually impaired and library services for the deaf and hard of hearing.

Special libraries in the Nashville area include two at Cheekwood Botanical Garden and Museum of Art. The Botanical Gardens Library specializes in works on environmental studies, garden design, horticulture, landscape architecture, plant science, wildflowers, arranging, and botanical illustration. The art museum library collects works on art, art history, decorative arts, contemporary U.S. artists, and photography.

The Sarah Cannon Research Institute, which focuses on cancer treatment, is an industry leader in clinical trials located in Nashville. The institute considers itself one of the largest, community-based research programs in the nation, conducting clinical trials in ten therapeutic areas through its affiliation with a network of hundreds of physicians. Many research facilities in the city are linked to the academic community. Fisk University supports research on computing and molecular spectroscopy. Meharry Medical College's research activities focus on health sciences, and the college has a research center devoted to the study and treatment of sickle cell disease. The Glenmary Research Center Research centers affiliated with Tennessee State University conduct studies in such areas as agriculture and the environment, information systems, business and economics, health, and education. Vanderbilt University is quite active in the research sector, promoting research through more than 120 centers and institutes devoted to a wide variety of subjects in such fields as sociology and culture, medicine, and science.

Public Library Information: Nashville Public Library, The Nashville Room, 615 Church Street, Nashville, TN 37219; telephone (615) 862-5800.

Health Care

Nashville boasts nearly 250 health-care companies. Nashville is home to HCA Holdings, Vanguard Health Systems, and Community Health Systems, all *Fortune* 500 companies in 2013. Centennial Medical Center, operated by HCA, is recognized for its work in cardiology, stroke, orthopedics, and breast cancer management. Skyline Medical Center is a 295-bed hospital overlooking downtown Nashville, notable for its treatment of stroke, back and neck surgery, and spinal fusion. Southern Hills Medical Center is a smaller, community hospital with a full range of heart, oncology, orthopedic, and neurology services and 101 total beds.

Baptist Hospital is the Nashville region's largest not-for-profit medical center, with more than 425 beds. It offers a number of specialty units, including the Mandrell Heart Center. St. Thomas Hospital, with 395 staffed beds, was founded by the Daughters of Charity and is nationally recognized for its heart and cancer units. *U.S. News & World Report* ranked the hospital as high-performing in five specialties in its 2013–14 rankings. Meharry Medical College has been a leading producer of African American physicians and dentists since its founding in 1876. The Nashville Campus of the U.S. Department of Veterans Affairs is available to service men and women.

The Vanderbilt University Medical Center, which adjoins the university's campus near downtown Nashville, is one of the most noted research, training, and health-care facilities in the country. The main hospital boasts 909 beds, ultra-modern surgical units, a labor and delivery area designed around the birthing room concept, a comprehensive burn center, and a coronary care wing. The hospital was nationally ranked in 11 specialties by *U.S. News & World Report* in 2013–14, including sixth in urology, eighth in ear, nose, and throat, and ninth in pulmonology. Vanderbilt Children's Hospital offers comprehensive pediatric care, boasting nine nationally ranked specialties, including the fourth-ranked care for urology according to *U.S. News & World Report* in 2013–14. For adults and children who need immediate medical attention because of accident or sudden illness, Vanderbilt University also operates a helicopter ambulance service called "Life Flight," which quickly moves patients within a 150-mile radius of the city to the hospital.

Recreation

Sightseeing

A roster full of sports, a road laid with music, the unspoiled countryside, a city full of history, and an endless choice of attractions have made Nashville one of the most popular vacation spots in the nation. Nashville is consistently ranked among top cities for affordable and enjoyable getaways and attracted more than 11 million visitors annually, as of 2013. Foremost among the city's historical attractions is The Hermitage, home of the seventh president of the United States, Andrew Jackson. The beautiful 1821 plantation house sits nestled in rolling farmland on the eastern edge of the city. The mansion has been a national shrine since the years shortly following Jackson's death there in 1845. Its vintage rooms display original pieces such as the Jackson family's furniture, china, paintings, clothes, letters, books, and wallpaper. Also on the grounds are the president's official carriage, his wife's flower garden, and both of their tombs.

Beautiful Belle Meade Plantation on the west side of the city is also open to the public. The restored antebellum farm has been called "Queen of the Tennessee Plantations." The mansion itself, built in 1853, displays period furniture and decor, while the mammoth stables on the grounds provide a glimpse of one of the most famous thoroughbred horse farms of that time.

Perched on a hill in the center of the downtown area is the Tennessee State Capitol Building, a renowned architectural monument constructed in 1859. Adjacent to the building is a Bicentennial Mall State Park, a 19-acre urban park designed to complement the Capitol building. The park is a walkable space with geyser fountains and sculptural columns and pieces that incorporate a timeline of Tennessee history. Also open for tours is Belmont Mansion, an 1850s Italianate villa on the Belmont University campus, recognized as one of the most elaborate and unusual houses in the South. Cheekwood Botanical Garden and Museum of Art is a horticulturalist's delight. The sprawling complex, nestled in Nashville's prime residential area, showcases 55 acres of lush gardens, including a color garden, water garden, seasons garden, and the woodland sculpture trail. The huge Georgian mansion houses a permanent display of twentieth-century American art, and American and English decorative arts.

The Metro Board of Parks and Recreation manages Centennial Park, famous for its full-size replica of the ancient Greek temple to the goddess Athena, the Parthenon. Sitting in the midst of the busy central city near Vanderbilt University, the Parthenon was originally built as part of Tennessee's Centennial Exposition of 1897, but it has remained one of the most popular places in town for a century. The city maintains impressive gardens around the structure, which houses rotating art exhibits in a permanent gallery. Just down the street in the heart of the historical district is Riverfront Park, home to historic Fort Nashborough. Here the public can stroll along the banks of the Cumberland River or listen to concerts under the stars. The Tennessee Fox Trot Carousel by artist Red Grooms is housed in Riverfront Park. The 36 "horses" are actually characters depicting the state's history and culture.

The Nashville Zoo at Grassmere featured more than 2,500 animals from around the world in 2012, including 400 different species; it also presented educational programs to more than 60,000 students, who were among the zoo's nearly 800,000 visitors that year. The Adventure Science Center offers unique health and science programs, hands-on exhibitions, live animal shows, and the Sudekum Planetarium.

The Grand Ole Opry, America's oldest and most cherished live country music show, is one of the most popular attractions in the city. Fans from all over the world pack the 4,400-seat Opry House each weekend to see top stars of traditional and country music. Begun in 1925 as the WSM Barn Dance, the Opry is still broadcast over WSM Radio to points all along the Eastern seaboard, providing audiences with a rare behind-the-scenes look at a tradition that literally launched popular country music. The Opry House, built in 1974 at a cost of $22 million, is said to be one of the most acoustically perfect auditoriums in the country; another is the famed Ryman Auditorium, home of the Opry from 1943 to 1974, which was renovated and is used as a performance venue for concerts and plays. The Opryland complex also includes the impressive Gaylord Opryland Resort & Convention Center.

The Opry is only the beginning of the many symbols that make Nashville the home of country music. As a result of the connection, many popular tourist sites involve country music, such as the Country Music Hall of Fame and Museum and the Belcourt Theatre, once home to the Grand Ole Opry. Numerous music clubs and honky-tonk bars can be found in downtown Nashville, especially the area of Lower Broadway, Second Avenue, and Printer's Alley, also known as "the District." Visitors can also visit Nashville's Music City Walk of Fame, located at the Music Mile. Inductees are announced and honored at a special ceremony with a permanent platinum-and-granite, star-and-guitar sidewalk marker. The markers can be seen across the street from the Country Music Hall of Fame and Museum, between the Schermerhorn Symphony Center and Bridgestone Arena and adjacent the Nashville Music Garden. This area is considered the base of the Music Mile in downtown Nashville. The Music Mile is roughly a one-mile stretch connecting downtown to Music Row via the Music Row Roundabout. The Roundabout, site of the Musica sculpture and adjacent to Owen Bradley Park, serves as a gateway to the music industry that has collected on 16th and 17th Avenues South.

Arts and Culture

Nashville may be the home of country music, but the city does not limit itself to this genre. Taking center stage in the area of performing arts, the Nashville Symphony Orchestra has a reputation as one of the leading city orchestras in the Southeast. From 1980 until 2006, the symphony regularly performed on the stage of the Tennessee Performing Arts Center (TPAC), the first state-funded facility of its kind in the nation, which is still home to the Nashville Ballet, the Nashville Opera, and the Tennessee Repertory Theatre. Built in a cantilevered style that allows large auditoriums to be column-free, TPAC three acoustically advanced theaters with expansion capabilities for nearly any kind or size of production imaginable. In September 2006, however, the Schermerhorn Symphony Center opened as the new home of the orchestra. The Schermerhorn Center is named in honor of the late Maestro Kenneth Schermerhorn, who led the Nashville Symphony for 22 years.

One of the oldest companies in town is the Nashville Children's Theater, a group that has been entertaining the area's children and young adults for six decades. Started by the Junior League as a strictly volunteer organization, the Children's Theater is partially funded by the metropolitan government and stages its shows in facilities especially built for the group by the city of Nashville. Nashville is also home to the American Negro Playwright Theatre and the Darkhorse Theatre. The Circle Players is a volunteer community theater group in operation since 1949.

In the area of visual arts, Nashville is a city-wide gallery of creativity. Cheekwood is the area's foremost cultural arts center and its most physically impressive gallery as well. Part of a 55-acre complex that once formed the estate of prominent Nashville businessman Leslie Cheek, the fine arts center is housed in a magnificent 60-room Georgian mansion that sits high atop a hill overlooking most of West Nashville. The Carl Van Vechten Gallery at Fisk University houses more than 100 pieces from the collection of Alfred Stieglitz. Donated to Fisk in 1949 by Stieglitz's widow, noted artist Georgia O'Keeffe, the collection includes works by Cezanne, Picasso, Renoir, Toulouse-Lautrec, and O'Keeffe. The seat of Tennessee's government overlooks a plaza of government office buildings that house parts of the State Museum, a collection of more than 2,000 historical objects from the city's past. The museum includes 15,000 square feet of artifacts from the period in Tennessee history between 1840 and 1865. As it did in mid-nineteenth-century life, the Civil War dominates the collection: battle flags, pistols, and portraits of the war's most colorful personalities are displayed alongside period silver, sewing handiwork, furniture, and photographs. A vast collection of permanent and traveling exhibits is on display at the Frist Center for the Visual Arts downtown, which opened in 2001.

In downtown Nashville, the heart of the country music business beats on a single square mile of city streets known to the world as Music Row. A hodgepodge of contemporary office buildings and renovated houses, Music Row houses complexes belonging to all the major record labels and many individual recording artists. The

Country Music Hall of Fame and Museum houses one of the country's finest collections of country music artifacts and memorabilia. The Hall of Fame moved from its home on Music Row to a new state-of-the-art downtown facility in 2001. Admission includes a visit to RCA Studio B, the oldest surviving recording studio in Nashville, where Elvis Presley, Dolly Parton, Charlie Pride and other music greats recorded their hits.

A discussion of arts and culture in Nashville would not be complete without a reference to the variety of live music locals and residents can see and hear any night of the week. Visitors can find themselves in bars like the famous Bluebird Cafe. This particular cafe is known for its tribute to songwriters, where three or four songwriters would play "in the round" taking turns singing and telling stories about songs they have written.

Festivals and Holidays

Nashville's musical heritage is the focus of many of the city's festivals, including Tin Pan South in March and the Gospel Music Association's Gospel Week in April , as well as the Country Music Association (CMA) Music Festival, formerly known as Fan Fair, held in June. The CMA Music Festival lasts four days, featuring performances by country music stars, autograph signings, and other festival activities. From May to August, the Tennessee Jazz & Blues Society concert series livens up the grounds of Belle Meade Plantation and the Hermitage. The annual three-day African Street Festival in September celebrates the culture of Africa. The festival features exotic food and daily stage shows showcasing poetry, rap, reggae, blues, jazz, gospel, rhythm and blues, and drama. Oktoberfest is held, naturally, in October. Also in the fall, the Tennessee State Fair provides residents and visitors nine days to enjoy rides, exhibits, rodeos, tractor pulls, and numerous other shows and attractions. Country music does not go away for long; in November the Country Music Association hosts its annual awards show, held at Bridgestone Arena and televised nationally to millions of viewers.

The winter holidays are celebrated in a series of events taking place throughout November and December. Highlights are A Country Christmas at Gaylord Opryland, and Victorian Celebrations at Belle Meade Plantation. The Season of Celebration at Cheekwood Botanical Garden and Museum of Art allows visitors to share the magic of the season with fabulous holiday decorations, Christmas trees, and multicultural exhibits during November and December.

Sports for the Spectator

In 2006 the Tennessee Titans began playing football at LP Field. LP Field seats nearly 69,000 spectators in the open-air, natural-grass venue. In addition to hosting the National Football League team, LP field is the site of the Tennessee State University Tigers and home of the

postseason college football game, the Franklin American Mortgage Music City Bowl. The Bridgestone Arena is home to the National Hockey League's Nashville Predators. The Tennessee Sports Hall of Fame is also located in the Bridgestone Arena.

Each spring and summer, crowds turn out in record numbers at Herschel Greer Stadium to cheer on the Nashville Sounds, the local Triple-A affiliate of the Milwaukee Brewers. Plans to build a new stadium north of downtown received approval in 2013. In college action, fall brings Southeastern Conference football with the Commodores of Vanderbilt University. The university also boasts outstanding basketball and tennis teams. Across town, Tennessee State University's Tigers have consistently been a powerhouse in football. The school is also famous for its internationally recognized track team, the Tiger Belles, which has produced Olympic runners like Wilma Rudolph.

NASCAR stock-car racing takes off at the Nashville Superspeedway, where top drivers compete. Special events are also held throughout the year at the speedway. Each May, Percy Warner Park is the site for what Nashville sports writers call the city's "Rite of Spring," the Iroquois Memorial Steeplechase, two- to three-mile amateur races that pit the area's top riders and ponies in a benefit run for Vanderbilt Children's Hospital. The Iroquois Steeplechase takes place at Percy Warner Park.

Sports for the Participant

Two major lakes flank the city of Nashville: Old Hickory to the north and Percy Priest to the east, maintained by the U.S. Army Corps of Engineers. They offer miles of peaceful, accessible shoreline to the entire Middle Tennessee region for fishing, water skiing, sailing, and boating. In addition, there are 30,000 acres of inland lakes in the Nashville area. Just a short drive from downtown, these man-made wonders are favorite weekend spots for local outdoor enthusiasts. A series of public docks houses nearly every kind of freshwater craft, and campgrounds are plentiful. The 385-acre Nashville Shores, with more than 2,500 feet of white sandy beach and three miles of lakefront, is Nashville's largest water playground. Here families can enjoy waterslides, a waterfall, pools, a pond, a young children's play area, parasailing, jet skiing, and banana boat rides.

Nashville is an angler's dream and fishing enthusiasts seek out the crystal-clear reservoirs that lie beneath Nashville area dams. Although most popular in the spring and summer, fishing is excellent year-round. The Harpeth River, which meanders through the western part of Davidson County, provides a peaceful look at the quiet countryside for canoers, while a little further west the Buffalo River, one of the few designated "wild" rivers in the nation, provides the challenge of white water.

Nashville has more than 12,000 acres of city, state, and federal parks in or near its borders, providing a full range of activities for people of all ages. The Metro Board of Parks and Recreation operates 108 parks and playgrounds. There are seven municipal golf courses in addition to dozens of privately operated facilities. Percy and Edwin Warner Parks provide 2,684 acres of woods and meadows that dominate the southwestern side of Nashville; more than 500,000 people visit the parks annually. Other parks in the area include Centennial Park, Shelby Park, and Radnor Lake State National Park. For runners, the annual Country Music Marathon is available in April.

Shopping and Dining

Visitors and locals alike can enjoy the many shopping opportunities in Nashville. Shopping in Nashville includes unique choices that reflect the local attractions. For instance, shoppers seeking musical recordings might visit Ernest Tubb Record Shops, where radio's "Midnite Jamboree" is broadcast live on Saturday nights. Cowboy boots and western clothing are featured in several Nashville-area establishments, such as Robert's Western World, by day a shop and by night a musical free-for-all. On the banks of the Cumberland River, The District is a trendy shopping scene housed in Victorian-era buildings. Shoppers interested in collectibles frequent the city's many antiques malls, or attend the Flea Market at the Nashville Expo Center, a monthly gathering of hundreds of traders considered among the top-10 flea markets in the country. CoolSprings Galleria, one of the city's largest shopping centers, also houses a variety of eating establishments; other area malls include RiverGate, and Bellevue Center. Exclusive shops are found at the Mall at Green Hills. More than 100 stores can be found at Opry Mills, an outlet center across from the Opryland Hotel covering 1.2 million square feet. This shopping, dining, and entertainment complex features top designers and manufacturers, theme restaurants, and entertainment venues including an IMAX theater.

Nashville restaurants offer diners a wide range of cuisines, including continental, oriental, Mexican, French, Italian, and German menus, as well as traditional choices of steaks and seafood. Regional specialties (and often music) are showcased at several Nashville-area establishments that feature entrees such as fried chicken, catfish, barbecue, and country ham; side dishes such as okra, turnip greens, black-eyed peas, yams, cornbread, beans and rice, and biscuits; and desserts such as chess pie, fudge pie, and fruit cobblers. While a center for barbeque nationally, Nashville ranks behind its in-state competitor, Memphis.

Visitor Information: Nashville Convention and Visitors Bureau, One Nashville Place, 150 Fourth Avenue North, Suite G-250, Nashville, TN 37219; telephone (800) 657-6910.

■ Convention Facilities

Convention business and tourism form one of the Nashville area's most important industries, launched primarily by the growth of country music and entertainment. The city is served by more than 25,000 hotel rooms and thousands of square feet of exhibit and meeting space. The city's new convention center, the Music City Center, opened in 2013 after a nearly $600 million investment. The facility has more than 350,000 square feet of exhibit space and the largest ballroom in the state at nearly 58,000 square feet. It has an additional 18,000-square-foot ballroom, 60 additional meeting rooms, and an 1,800-space parking garage. A prominent and unique feature of the new center includes a four-acre, vegetation-covered roof.

The city's Municipal Auditorium seats more than 9,600 people. For conventions and trade shows, the exhibit floor contains 63,000 square feet of space. The Bridgestone Arena offers 43,000 square feet of exhibition and meeting space. LP Field offers a total of 200,000 square feet of space on the club levels for special events and functions; one side features sweeping vistas of downtown Nashville. Parts of the Tennessee Performing Arts Center and the Tennessee Expo Center are also available for sizable events.

One of the most versatile convention-oriented hotels in Nashville is the Gaylord Opryland Resort & Convention Center, offering more than 600,000 square feet of meeting and exhibit space. Its Ryman Exhibit Hall is the largest in-hotel exhibit facility in the world, at nearly 263,000 square feet. The elegant, white-columned facility is located on 30 acres of rolling Tennessee countryside just 8 miles east of downtown Nashville. It is approximately five minutes from the airport and close to shopping, restaurants, and attractions, with the Grand Ole Opry House next door.

Two miles west of the center city, the Loews Vanderbilt Hotel rises next to Vanderbilt University in the middle of one of Nashville's busiest areas of commercial office development. Promoting itself as an "executive-class" hotel, the Vanderbilt has more than 24,000 square feet of flexible meeting space.

Convention Information: Nashville Convention and Visitors Bureau, One Nashville Place, 150 Fourth Avenue North, Suite G-250, Nashville, TN 37219; telephone (800) 657-6910.

■ Transportation

Approaching the City

East of the city, the Nashville International Airport, located just eight miles from the central business district, is approximately a 12-minute ride away. Passengers landing in Nashville may choose from any number of commercial vehicles to take them to their destinations. There is an airport limousine service available along with metered taxicabs, Metro Transit Authority buses, shuttle service to downtown hotels, and car rental agencies with representatives in the lobby of the terminal building. As of 2013, the airport handled more than 10 million passengers annually, taking people to more than 50 markets non-stop on some 380 daily flights. The John C. Tune Airport (JWN) is a general aviation airport on 400 acres of land in west Nashville that serves corporate and personal aircraft users, with particular emphasis on the business community.

Six major highways intersect in the heart of Nashville: Interstate 65 leads northward to the industrialized cities of Chicago, Indianapolis, and Pittsburgh; Interstate 40 takes travelers to the cities of Richmond, Washington, D.C., and Philadelphia, plus the Carolina ports to the east, and to Dallas, Oklahoma, and farther west; Interstate 24 extends to Atlanta and Florida; Interstate 65 reaches Birmingham, New Orleans, and the Gulf; and Interstate 24 extends to St. Louis and Kansas City, the Midwestern heartland.

The inner-city loop, Interstate 265, encircles the downtown area to facilitate a smooth flow of interstate traffic, while an extensive outer loop, Interstate 440, rings the city. Interstate 840 circles the city at a 30-mile radius.

Traveling in the City

Within Nashville, visitors usually travel by cab, rental or private car, or public bus. The Metropolitan Transit Authority (MTA) provides a large network of bus service both in the downtown area and outlying suburbs. MTA buses covered 52 routes as of 2013, including many neighborhood park-and-ride lots designed especially for commuters. Trolleys running around downtown and the Music Valley area are a fun way to see the city. In 2010, the city opened a new, free bus service downtown called the Music City Circuit, with various colored bus lines that serve a variety of downtown destinations, including Bridgestone Arena, Schermerhorn Symphony Center, Ryman Auditorium, Tennessee Performing Arts Center (TPAC), Farmers' Market, Country Music Hall of Fame, Historic Second Avenue, Frist Center for the Visual Arts, Bicentennial Mall, Gulch bars and restaurants, the Richard H. Fulton Complex, downtown hotels and other downtown attractions and landmarks. Suburban rail service, the Music City Star, began in 2006. The rail service runs between Nashville and Lebanon, Tennessee, approximately 32 miles with six stops.

■ Communications

Newspapers and Magazines

The Tennessean is Nashville's two daily papers. The *Tennessean* had a weekday circulation just over 100,000 as of 2013. *The City Paper* is free daily published online. *NashvillePost.com* is another online newspaper, focused on business and politics but also competing with dailies to publish breaking local news. Weekly newspapers include *Nashville Scene* (the alternative paper), *The Nashville Pride* (focusing on community development), *Nashville Business Journal*, and *The Tennessee Tribune*, which serves the African American community. Professional periodicals published in Nashville serve the furniture, insurance, banking, logging, agriculture, and paper industries, and the music and education fields. Numerous directories and newsletters are published in Nashville.

Television and Radio

Nashville-area television viewers are served by 15 stations, such as affiliates of PBS, ABC, NBC, CBS, and Fox. Nashville is also home to cable networks Country Music Television (CMT) and Great American Country (GAC). CMT's "Top 20 Countdown" and "CMT Insider" are taped in their Nashville studios. Nine licensed AM and 12 FM radio stations in Nashville offer educational, cultural, religious, and foreign language programming, as well as rock and roll, gospel, blues, jazz, and country music.

Media Information: *The Tennessean*, 1100 Broadway, Nashville, TN 37203; telephone (615) 259-8000.

Nashville Online

Metropolitan Government of Nashville and Davidson County. Available www.nashville.gov

Metropolitan Nashville Public Schools. Available www.mnps.org/site3.aspx

Nashville Area Chamber of Commerce (including JobsLink). Available www.nashvillechamber.com

Nashville Convention and Visitors Bureau. Available www.nashvillecvb.com

The Nashville Digest. Available www.nashvilledigest.com

Nashville Public Library. Available www.library.nashville.org

The Tennessean. Available www.tennessean.com

BIBLIOGRAPHY

Bobrick, Benson, *The Battle of Nashville: General George H. Thomas and the Most Decisive Battle of the Civil War* (New York: Alfred A. Knopf, 2010)

Chapman, Marshall, *They Came to Nashville* (Nashville: Country Music Foundation Press: Vanderbilt University Press, 2010)

Goodstein, Anita S., *Nashville, 1789–1860: From Frontier to City* (Gainesville, FL: University Press of Florida, 1989)

Havighurst, Craig, *Air Castle of the South: WSM and the Making of Music City* (Urbana, IL: University of Illinois Press, 2007)

Squire, James D., *The Secrets of the Hopewell Box: Stolen Elections, Southern Politics, and a City's Coming of Age* (New York: Times Books/Random House, 1996)

Texas

The State in Brief

Nickname: Lone Star State

Motto: Friendship

Flower: Bluebonnet

Bird: Mockingbird

Area: 268,596 square miles (2010; U.S. rank 2nd)

Elevation: Ranges from sea level to 8,749 feet above sea level

Climate: Semi-arid in western region and central plains; subtropical on coastal plains; continental in the panhandle

Admitted to Union: December 29, 1845

Capital: Austin

Head Official: Rick Perry (R) (until 2015)

Population

1990: 16,986,510
2000: 20,851,820
2010: 25,145,561
2012 estimate: 25,208,897
Percent change, 2000–2010: 20.6%
U.S. rank in 2012: 2nd
Percent of residents born in state: 60.5% (2012)
Density: 96.3 people per square mile (2010)
2012 FBI Crime Index Total: 982,535

Racial and Ethnic Characteristics (2012)

White: 18,670,767
Black or African American: 2,972,834
American Indian and Alaska Native: 127,794
Asian: 979,385
Native Hawaiian and Pacific Islander: 20,671
Hispanic or Latino (may be of any race): 9,479,670
Other: 2,437,446

Age Characteristics (2012)

Population under 5 years old: 1,928,842
Population 5 to 19 years old: 5,676,141
Percent of population 65 years and over: 10.5%
Median age: 33.6

Vital Statistics

Total number of births (2012–13): 381,897
Total number of deaths (2012–13): 173,852
AIDS cases reported through 2011: 86,106

Economy

Major industries: Energy, agriculture, manufacturing, trade, services
Unemployment rate (2012): 5.0%
Per capita income (2012): $25,809
Median household income (2012): $51,563
Percentage of persons below poverty level (2012): 17.4%
Income tax rate: None
Sales tax rate: 6.25%

Austin

■ The City in Brief

Founded: 1835 (incorporated 1839)

Head Official: Mayor Lee Leffingwell (since 2009; current term expires 2014)

City Population
> 1990: 472,020
> 2000: 656,562
> 2010: 790,390
> 2012 estimate: 842,595
> Percent change, 2000–2010: 20.4%
> U.S. rank in 1990: 27th (State rank: 5th)
> U.S. rank in 2000: 22nd (State rank: 4th)
> U.S. rank in 2010: 14th (State rank: 4th)

Metropolitan Statistical Area Population
> 2000: 1,249,763
> 2010: 1,716,289
> 2012 estimate: 1,834,303
> Percent change, 2000–2010: 37.3%
> U.S. rank in 2000: 40th
> U.S. rank in 2010: 35th

Area: 258.43 square miles

Elevation: Ranges from 425 feet to 1,000 feet above sea level

Average Annual Temperatures: January, 50.2° F; July, 84.2° F; annual average, 68.5° F

Average Annual Precipitation: 33.65 inches of rain

Major Economic Sectors: services, government, wholesale and retail trade

Unemployment Rate: 5.4% (2012)

Per Capita Income: $31,130

2012 FBI Crime Index Property: 43,472

Major Colleges and Universities: University of Texas at Austin, St. Edward's University, Houston-Tillotson College

Daily Newspaper: *Austin American-Statesman*

■ Introduction

Nestled in the Texas Hill Country, Austin strikes a balance between nature, education, the arts, and commerce. Austin, the Texas state capital, the Travis County seat, and the cultural and economic center of the Austin-Round Rock metropolitan area, is fueled by an entrepreneurial attitude that has resulted in the city's appearance at the top of numerous business and cultural lists. Austin is the fourth largest city in Texas and one of the most populous cities in the United States. Austin is known for its quality of life and is home to one of the largest universities in the world, which enables companies to attract and retain the very best talent. Austin consistently remains among the top in lists in national publications as one of the best cities in the country to live, work, and play, no matter what the age. Residents have found good jobs, easy living, and excellent health-care facilities. By 2013, Austin was on its way to becoming a Majority-Minority city, meaning no ethnic or demographic group existed as a majority of the city's population.

■ Geography and Climate

Austin is located in south central Texas, where the Colorado River crosses the Balcones Escarpment, separating the Texas Hill Country from the black-land prairies to the east. Austin was once known as the city of the "Violet Crown" for the wintertime violet glow of color across the hills just after sunset. The Colorado River flows through the heart of the city, creating a series of sparkling lakes that stretch for more than 100 miles. Dams in the

© Ian Dagnall Commercial Collection/Alamy

river create several artificial lakes within the city limits, such as Lady Bird Lake, Lake Austin, and Lake Walter e. Long. Mount Bonnell, a natural limestone formation, prominently overlooks Lake Austin. Austin is located at the intersection of several climate regions, making it a green oasis with a variable climate, sometimes characterized by desert conditions, and other times tropical. Generally, however, Austin's climate is humid subtropical with prevailing southerly winds. Summers are hot; winters are mild, with only occasional brief cold spells. Most precipitation falls in the form of rain in late spring and early fall. Snow is rare; Austin may experience several winters in succession with no measurable amount, but may suffer from an ice storm about two times a year. The sun is usually shining in this city, where temperatures drop below 45 degrees Fahrenheit only about 88 days a year.

Area: 258.43 square miles

Elevation: Ranges from 425 feet to 1,000 feet above sea level

Average Temperatures: January, 50.2° F; July, 84.2° F; annual average, 68.5° F

Average Annual Precipitation: 33.65 inches of rain

■ History

City Named State Capital

Lured to the area by tales of seven magnificent cities of gold, Spanish explorers first passed through what is now Austin during the 1530s. But instead of gold, they encountered several hostile Native American tribes; for many years, reports of the natives' viciousness (which included charges of cannibalism) discouraged further expeditions and restricted colonization. Spain nevertheless retained control of the region for nearly 300 years, withdrawing after Mexico gained its independence in 1821.

All of eastern Texas then experienced a boom as hundreds of settlers sought permission to establish colonies in the "new" territory. One of these early settlements was the village of Waterloo, founded in 1835 on the north bank of the Colorado River. In 1839 Mirabeau B. Lamar, vice-president of the Republic of Texas, recommended that Waterloo be chosen as the capital, noting among its assets its central location, elevation, mild climate, and freedom from the fevers that plagued residents of the republic's coastal areas. Despite stiff competition from those whose preference was Houston, Lamar's proposal was eventually accepted, and Waterloo was incorporated as Austin in 1839 and renamed in honor of Stephen F. Austin, "Father of Texas." Austin remained the capital when Texas was annexed by the United States in 1845.

Civil Strife in Texas and the Nation

During the 1850s the country's regional conflicts mounted and Texans were fractured into three distinct camps: those who advocated supporting northern policies, those who wished to ally themselves with secessionist southern states, and those who urged the reestablishment of the independent Republic of Texas. Although Travis County citizens voted strongly against secession, Texas as a whole sided with the South when the Civil War erupted. Austin's contributions to the war effort included the manufacture of arms and ammunition and the mustering of the Austin City Light Infantry and a cavalry regiment known as Terry's Texas Rangers after its leader, B. F. Terry.

Despite some political strife following the Civil War, Reconstruction brought prosperity to Austin. The coming of the Houston & Texas Central Railroad in 1871—and the International-Great Northern five years later—provided stimulus to the city's growth and commerce.

Modern Development Linked to University

Austin's development received further assistance when, in 1883, the University of Texas at Austin held its first classes. In its early decades, the school was rich in real estate but poor in cash. The discovery of oil on university land in 1924 led to enormous wealth which, along with private donations and federal assistance, has made the University of Texas at Austin one of the best-endowed schools in the country. Much of Austin's growth and development in the twentieth century was linked to the University of Texas at Austin. Its presence lent a cosmopolitan air to the city; visitors who expected to see cowboy boots and hats in abundance were usually disappointed because Austin was the least "Texan" of all the cities in the state. Besides making Austin a bastion of liberalism and tolerance, the university attracted much high-technology industry and fostered the city's image as the arts capital of Texas.

As the state's arts capital, it was no surprise that the 1970s also saw Austin's emergence in the national music scene, with artists such as Willie Nelson and venues such as the Armadillo World Headquarters. Austin further developed into a major city in the 1980s and emerged as a center for technology and business. As home to development centers for many technology corporations in semiconductors and software in the high-tech 1990s, the city adopted the nickname "Silicon Hills."

Austin in the Twenty-First Century

In 2000 the resident of the Governor's Mansion moved from Austin into the White House. After a protracted recount effort centered on Florida ballots, George W. Bush resigned as Texas governor in December 2000 to accept his new post as the 43rd president of the United States, which he would hold for two terms.

The recession of the early 2000s hit technology companies especially hard. As a result of its over-reliance on the high technology industry, Austin suffered an economic slump, losing jobs along with public and private revenues. The economy's road toward recovery coincided with the implementation of Opportunity Austin, an initiative launched in 2004 to rejuvenate the industries of existing companies and to diversify into such segments as automotive, biomedicine and pharmaceuticals, and corporate and regional headquarters.

Today, the Austin area is home to many companies, including the headquarters of major corporations such as Whole Foods Market, Freescale Semiconductor, Forestar Group, and Dell. Austin is increasingly developing a reputation as the place to be for startups and entrepreneurs. Notably, social networking giant Twitter started in Austin in 2007 at the South by Southwest Festival. While Austin means business, the city has maintained an easygoing and fun side to the city, fostering the arts and creativity. Austin promotes itself as the "Live Music Capital of the World," a reference to the many musicians and live music venues in the area. In 2012 Austin, with an unemployment rate of 5 percent, saw home sales hit a six-year high. The year ended with increased sales volume, stable prices, and strong demand.

Historical Information: Austin History Center, 9th and Guadalupe, PO Box 2287, Austin, TX 78768-2287; telephone (512) 974-7480.

■ Population Profile

Metropolitan Statistical Area Population
2000: 1,249,763
2010: 1,716,289
2012 estimate: 1,834,303
Percent change, 2000–2010: 37.3%
U.S. rank in 2000: 40th
U.S. rank in 2010: 35th

City Residents
1990: 472,020
2000: 656,562
2010: 790,390
2012 estimate: 842,595
Percent change, 2000–2010: 20.4%
U.S. rank in 1990: 27th (State rank: 5th)
U.S. rank in 2000: 22nd (State rank: 4th)
U.S. rank in 2010: 14th (State rank: 4th)

Density: 2,653.2 people per square mile

Racial and ethnic characteristics
White: 647,851
Black or African American: 65,431

American Indian and Alaskan Native: 5,272
Asian: 54,084
Native Hawaiian and Other Pacific Islander: 776
Hispanic or Latino (may be of any race): 286,850
Other: 69,181

Percent of residents born in state: 53.5%

Age characteristics

Population under 5 years old: 58,339
Population 5 to 9 years old: 59,193
Population 10 to 14 years old: 41,720
Population 15 to 19 years old: 49,709
Population 20 to 24 years old: 85,165
Population 25 to 34 years old: 178,982
Population 35 to 44 years old: 131,702
Population 45 to 54 years old: 99,080
Population 55 to 59 years old: 43,643
Population 60 to 64 years old: 33,963
Population 65 to 74 years old: 35,260
Population 75 to 84 years old: 17,804
Population 85 years and over: 8,035
Median age: 31.7

Births (2010–11 Metropolitan Area)

Total number: 25,973

Deaths (2010–11 Metropolitan Area)

Total number: 7,888

Money income (2012)

Per capita income: $31,130
Median household income: $51,668
Total households: 327,971

Number of households with income of ...

less than $10,000: 27,327
$10,000 to $14,999: 16,821
$15,000 to $24,999: 32,751
$25,000 to $34,999: 34,575
$35,000 to $49,999: 48,399
$50,000 to $74,999: 56,321
$75,000 to $99,999: 37,168
$100,000 to $149,999: 40,207
$150,000 to $199,999: 16,267
$200,000 or more: 18,135

Percent of families below poverty level: 20.1%

FBI Crime Index Property: 43,472

FBI Crime Index Violent: 3,405

■ Municipal Government

Austin, chartered in 1839, operates via a council-manager form of government. The mayor and six council members

appoint the city manager, who is the chief administrator for the city. The city manager earns a salary of $301,544. The highest paid city employee is the General Manager of the Department of Energy, who earns $311,173 per year. Each council member is elected at large to serve staggered three-year terms. Term limits allow the mayor and council members to serve in their respective seat for a maximum of six years, or two consecutive terms.

With the passage of Propositions 1–3 in 2012, several changes to the Austin City Council were scheduled to take place beginning with the November 2014 election. The Austin City Council was to expand from 7 to 11 members, elections to move from May to November in even-numbered years, council terms to lengthen from three to four years, and 10 geographic districts to be established for City Council representation, with the mandate that a Council Member live within the district that he or she represents. The Mayor is still elected citywide.

Head Official: Mayor Lee Leffingwell (since 2009; current term expires June 2014)

Total Number of City Employees: 13,202 (2013)

City Information: City of Austin, PO Box 1088, Austin, TX 78767; telephone (512)974-2000

■ Economy

Major Industries and Commercial Activity

Austin's economy in the late twentieth and early twenty-first century has focused on attracting and cultivating high-technology companies. Austin's role as a center for high technology made it particularly vulnerable to the recession that struck the nation's economy in the early 2000s. For three consecutive years, Austin suffered layoffs and job reductions; even the city government slashed 1,000 jobs.

In the wake of the economic downtown, a regional strategy aimed to create 72,000 regional jobs and increase regional payroll by $2.9 billion. To implement the strategy, the regional business community committed to invest $14.4 million. The program exceeded expectations. Nearly 200,000 new jobs were created, increasing regional payroll to $9.9 billion by 2013. The success of the program was extended with the announcement of Opportunity Austin 3.0. This five-year plan (2014–18) prioritized economic diversification to proactively strengthen the economy and keep the Greater Austin region attractive to entrepreneurs.

An offshoot of Austin's leadership in the semiconductor and software industries is the wireless segment. With a developed infrastructure of telecommunication, transportation, electric, and water capacities, Austin is a leading site for wireless technologies. Austin offers more free wireless spots—including its city parks—per capita than most cities in the nation. Moreover, the University of Texas at Austin is the most wireless university in the country. Qualcomm Corp. constructed a computer chip design center in Austin in 2004, the same year that Verizon Wireless selected Austin as the first city for the launch of its Broadband Access 3G Network, a high-speed wireless Internet access service. Other wireless companies with a presence in Austin include AT&T Wireless Corp., Dell Inc., Intel Corp., and T-Mobile. Austin has a wireless network throughout the central downtown area. The network is comprised of 28 access points located on various buildings and traffic lights.

Drawing on the same expertise in high technology and innovation, the city has ventured into the biomedical and pharmaceuticals industry. The University of Texas at Austin is a primary asset in this arena. It has world-class programs in bioengineering, nanotechnology, bioinformatics, and pharmaceutical research, and is a leader in the number of science and engineering doctoral degrees it awards. Austin ranks high in patent activity—a measure of innovation. The city is home to several biotechnology and pharmaceutical companies, including Apogent Technologies Inc., Luminex Corp., and TOPAZ Technologies Inc.

Austin has a history of success in attracting regional office and national headquarters of major companies. Dell Inc. is not only based in Austin, it is one of the area's largest employers. A diverse array of companies also have elected to make Austin their headquarters: Hoover's Inc. (business/market intelligence), National Instruments Corp. (industrial automation), Schlotzsky's Inc. (sandwich chain), and Whole Foods Market Inc. (natural foods chain).

In the late 2000s, a number of companies established or expanded their Austin headquarters, including Apple Computer (technology and administrative support center), Blizzard Entertainment (PC-based gaming), Borland Software Corp. (software developer/publisher), Education Finance Partners (loan services), Otis Spunkmeyer (snack food manufacturer), Time Warner Cable (media and communications), Total Emersion (game software developer), and United Teacher Associates Insurance (insurance). Samsung Electronics announced a $3.6 billion project to boost the company's payroll by 500 permanent positions in 2010, with another $4 billion investment following in 2012.

The city also serves as divisional or regional headquarters for such companies as 3M Co. (conglomerate well-known for adhesives), Progressive Corp. (insurance), and Waste Management Inc. (garbage collection). In 2010 Facebook accepted a grant to build a downtown office in Austin.

In 2012 the City's economic development efforts resulted in executed contracts with Apple, HID Global, and Visa, resulting in 4,705 new full-time jobs and capital investment of $345.7 million. The City also launched a public/private Family Business Loan Program for small businesses and assisted in the startup of 45 new small businesses. In 2012 the *Business Journal* named Austin the Best city for Small Business. Social networking tool Twitter got its start in Austin. Austin's role in the music and film industries has grown during the 2000s.

Items and goods produced: computers, computer peripherals, software, electronic instruments, semiconductors, biotechnology, pharmaceuticals, business equipment, video games

Incentive Programs-New and Existing Companies

Local programs: The city of Austin offers tax abatements, enterprise zone exemptions, public utility incentives, and financing programs for qualified new and existing companies. The economic development staff of the Greater Austin Chamber of Commerce provides ongoing assistance to relocating companies, from initial inquiry to full employment. Chamber staff can act as area-wide resources for community presentations, initial interface with company employees, spousal employment assistance, residential real estate brokers/tours, special mortgage and banking programs, child care/elder care, and cultural acclimation. The chamber lists a number of local programs by county, including: foreign trade zone eligibility, free port exemptions, industrial foundation programs, reinvestment zones, and training programs.

State programs: Texas is a right-to-work state. The Texas economy performed better than that of any other state during a nationwide recession of the late 2000s. It is believed that this success is due in part to the state's pro-business climate, of which economic incentives are an important part.

The Texas Enterprise Zone Programs offer tax abatement at the local level and refunds of state sales and use taxes under certain circumstances to businesses operating in enterprise zone areas. The Texas Enterprise Zone Program allows local communities to partner with the State of Texas to promote job creation and capital investment in targeted areas of the state that meet specific economic criteria. Designated projects are eligible to apply for state sales and use tax refunds on qualified expenditures. The state of Texas targets many of its incentive programs toward smaller and rural communities. The Rural Municipal Finance Program is a loan program created by the Texas Agricultural Finance Authority (TAFA) to stimulate economic activity in rural Texas. The Texas Enterprise Fund can be used to provide deal-closing money for companies relocating to and investing in Texas. As of 2013, awards had ranged from $194,000 to $50 million. The Texas Emerging Technology Fund, a $200 million fund created by the Texas Legislature in 2005, is available to companies seeking to commercialize new technologies. The program provides grants for early-stage investments in new, technology-based, private entrepreneurial entities that collaborate with public or private institutions of higher education.

Texas is one of the few states with no individual income tax, a very attractive environment for transferring employees. There is also no corporate income tax. The Texas Enterprise Zone Program provides for eligible designated projects to apply for state sales and use tax refunds on purchases of all taxable items purchased for use at the qualified business site related to the project or activity. Special tax exemptions are made for manufacturing machinery, equipment, replacement parts, and accessories that have a useful life of more than six months. Texas businesses are also exempt from paying state sales and use tax on labor for constructing new facilities, electricity, and natural gas used in manufacturing, processing, or fabrication. Tax-Exempt Industrial Revenue Bonds are designed to provide tax-exempt financing of up to $20 million per project to finance land and depreciable property for eligible industrial or manufacturing projects.

The Texas Capital Fund Infrastructure and Real Estate Development programs are designed to provide no interest loans of up to $750,000 to non-entitlement communities. The program funds real estate developments (acquisitions, construction, and/or rehabilitation) to assist a business, which commits to creating or retaining permanent jobs, primarily for low- and moderate-income persons.

Job training programs: The Texas Workforce Commission (TWC) provides workforce development assistance to employers and jobseekers across the state through a network of 28 workforce boards. Apprenticeship training is designed to prepare individuals for occupations in skilled trades and crafts and combines structured on-the-job training—supervised by experienced workers—with related classroom instruction.

The Austin Community College developed the Robotics and Automated Manufacturing program to produce skilled technicians for highly automated industries, such as automotive manufacturing, an industry targeted by the city for growth.

The Greater Austin Chamber of Commerce and the city of Austin founded the Capital Area Training Foundation (CATF), now known as Skillpoint Alliance, as an industry-led, non-profit organization dedicated to establishing long-term education and workforce development solutions. Skillpoint Alliance offers free developmental courses, such as computer and construction training, industry-led professional development programs for teachers, and a yearly College and Career Fair for high school students. Each of these opportunities is meant to provide a "skillpoint" to help participants reach the next level in education or a career path.

Goodwill Industries of Central Texas provides job training services through a City of Austin-funded network of 11 strategic partners to help prepare Austin-area residents to enter or reenter the job market. Services include pre-employment training in computer, applications skills, resume, and interviewing skills; job search assistance including job leads; support services, including vouchers for work clothing, tools, and transportation; and training and certification in industry trades.

Development Projects

Buildings in Austin are generally spread out and relatively low, due to a restriction that preserves the view of the Texas State Capitol building from various locations around Austin (known as the "Capitol View Corridor"). However, new high rises and skyscrapers began to fill the Austin skyline after a boom that started around 2007. In particular, the city began to provide greater incentives for increasing residential density in the urban core.

Developers responded and high rises became vogue; the Austin 360 Condominiums Tower, a residential skyscraper, was finished in 2008, with 44 floors, 430 homes, and over 14,000 square feet of retail space. The 360 Condominium building, once the tallest in Austin, was surpassed in 2009 by the city's current tallest building, the 59-story Austonian. The 700 foot tall high rise condominium building is one of the tallest in the western United States.

In the culture and recreation arena, Austin continued to develop projects to improve the quality of life for residents and visitors. The Jack S. Blanton Museum of Art opened at the University of Texas at Austin in April 2006. The Blanton is considered the largest university art museum in the country and the third largest museum in the state. The Mexican-American Cultural Center, a 126,000-square-foot facility dedicated to Mexican-American cultural arts and heritage had its grand opening in September 2007. Construction finished in 2008 on the Lozano Long Center for the Performing Arts. The famous PBS program "Austin City Limits" finished a new 2,750 seat venue, the Moody Theater, in downtown Austin in 2011.

Development projects under construction in 2014 included The Waller Creek Tunnel Project, a storm water bypass tunnel from Waterloo Park to Lady Bird Lake near Waller Beach. The project was to allow denser development in a very desirable area of downtown and divert floodwaters that create erosion problems and safety concerns. A 1,012-room JW Marriott Hotel on the northeast corner of Congress Avenue and 2nd Street had an estimated completion date of Spring 2015. More than 20 other major projects were in the planning stage as of early 2014. They included Foundation Communities, a 135-unit efficiency-style apartment building at the southwest corner of 11th & Trinity, and the Mexic-Arte Museum, designed by Mexican architect Fernando Romero. There were also plans to build a new $350 million Fairmont Hotel east of the Austin Convention Center, with 50 stories and 1,031 rooms.

Economic Development Information: Greater Austin Chamber of Commerce, 210 Barton Springs Rd., Ste. 400, Austin, TX 78704; telephone (512) 478-9383; fax (512) 478-6389.

Commercial Shipping

Austin-Bergstrom International Airport has a 338,000-square-foot cargo port and handles over 250 million pounds of freight annually. The airport's air cargo carriers included FedEx, DHL Express, Baron Aviation Service, Inc., and UPS. Austin's busy Port of Entry is served by three brokers: LE Coppersmith Inc., Robert F. Barnes, and UPS Supply Chain Solutions Inc. Austin is home to 24 truck lines and four truck terminals. Major Interstates 35 and 90 provide shipping routes. Freight also travels to and from the city via the Burlington Northern Santa Fe Railway, Union Pacific Railroad, Georgetown Railroad, and Austin Area Terminal Railroad.

Labor Force and Employment Outlook

Austin boasts a high quality labor force, based in large part on its highly trained, young population. The region's seven colleges and universities, particularly the University of Texas at Austin, produce highly skilled, innovative graduates seeking entry into the workforce. Generally, Austin is home to a higher percentage of college graduates than the national percentage of college graduates. As a result of these and other factors, Austin is frequently ranked as one of the best metro areas in which to locate a business. In 2013 it ranked 10th in *Forbes*' listing of the Best Cities for Jobs. In 2012 it had claimed the number-one position. Employment growth in 2012 was estimated at 3.7 percent.

The following is a summary of data regarding the 2012 Austin labor force:

Size of civilian labor force: 477,963

Number of workers employed in . . .

agriculture and mining: 2,210
construction: 31,313
manufacturing: 33,260
wholesale trade: 8,438
retail trade: 46,032
transportation: 10,925
information systems: 11,684
finance: 30,072
professional administration: 69,291
education and social services: 92,601
arts and leisure: 52,941
other: 22,965
public administration: 28,071

Average hourly earnings of production workers: $15.85

Unemployment rate: 5.4% (2012)

Employers

Largest employers (2013)	Number of employees
State of Texas	69,777
University of Texas at Austin	5,313
Dell Computer	14,000
City of Austin	12,000
Federal Government	11,991
Seton Healthcare Network	11,500
AISD	10,672
IBM	6,239
St. David's Healthcare	6,600
Freescale Semiconductor	5,000
AT&T	3,450
Apple	3,000
AMD	2,933
Applied Materials	2,250
National Instruments	2,200
Girling Health Care	1,952
Flextronics	1,875
Time Warner Cable	1,765
Whole Foods Grocery	1,694

Cost of Living

Austin is often lauded for its high quality of life and moderate cost of living. The following is a summary of several key cost of living factors for the Austin area.

2013 ACCRA Average House Price: $229,786

2013 ACCRA Cost of Living Index: 92

State income tax rate: None

State sales tax rate: 6.25%

Local income tax rate: None

Local sales tax rate: 2.0%

Property tax rate: 0.136686 mills (2013)

Economic Information: Greater Austin Chamber of Commerce, 210 Barton Springs Rd., Ste. 400, Austin, TX 78704; telephone (512) 478-9383; fax (512) 478-6389. Texas Workforce Commission, 101 E. 15th St., Rm. 651, Austin, TX 78778-0001; telephone (512) 463-2236; email customers@twc.state.tx.us. Opportunity Austin, Greater Austin Chamber of Commerce; telephone (512) 322-5615.

■ Education and Research

Elementary and Secondary Schools

The Austin Independent School District (AISD), the largest public school system in the metro Austin area, is ranked among the nation's top 10 public education systems by national publications. In addition to high quality general education public schools, the district's magnet schools, such as the Science Academy and the Liberal Arts Academy, serve outstanding students throughout the district. Austin students also benefit from the number of successful businesses in the city. Through the Austin Partners in Education program, every school in Austin partners with one or more businesses and organizations that donate millions of dollars in cash and in-kind resources such as school supplies, lab and technology equipment, and landscape materials to support AISD schools and programs.

The Catholic Diocese of Austin maintains a unified school system of 23 schools ranging from pre-K to 12th grade that collectively educate over 5,000 students across Central Texas. All of the diocesan schools follow an accreditation process prescribed by the Texas Catholic Conference, approved by the Texas Education Agency, and directed by the diocesan superintendent's office.

As of 2014, the number of charter schools serving the Austin area had grown to 35. These flexible and sometimes experimental schools can appeal to special skills, like gymnastics or technology, as well as offering opportunities for self-directed and experiential learning. Both the San Antonio-based Resource Center for Charter Schools and the Texas Charter Schools Association provide information on charter schools.

The following is a summary of data regarding the Austin Independent School District.

Total enrollment: 85,697

Number of facilities

    total: 124
    elementary schools: 71
    junior high schools: 21
    high schools: 19
    other: 13

Student/teacher ratio: 14.06:1

Teacher salaries

    average (statewide): $48,261

Funding per pupil: $9,432

Public Schools Information: Austin Independent School District, 1111 W. Sixth Street, Austin, TX 78703; telephone (512) 414-1700.

Colleges and Universities

Austin's population is highly educated; nearly 90 percent of the adult population has a high school diploma, nearly 40 percent have a bachelor's degree, and about 13 percent have obtained a graduate degree. When it comes to higher education, Austin has a proud tradition. The city

had barely been established when the Congress of the Republic of Texas mandated establishment of a "university of the first class."

Today, the University of Texas at Austin is joined by several other institutions of higher education in the metropolitan area but continues to be the most popular and most recognized. In 2013 the University of Texas at Austin was listed as the fifth largest public university by enrollment, serving 52,076 students.

Austin's educational bent is a major attraction for businesses. The University of Texas at Austin has a well-deserved reputation as one of the top research institutions in the country. Its network of research and resources creates a stimulating environment for businesses, and companies benefit from a highly trained workforce.

In 2013 the university ranked 26th among the world's top 100 universities. In 2013 the annual *U.S. News & World Report* ranking placed the university 46th in academic reputation among the top national universities and 16th among public schools.

The area's other institutions of higher education include the Art Institute of Austin, Austin Community College, Concordia University at Austin, Huston-Tillotson College, St. Edward's University, Southwestern University at Georgetown, Texas State University at San Marcos, and Episcopal and Presbyterian seminaries. Several branch campuses are also located in Austin. The unique Action School of Business, a Master of Business Administration program affiliated with Hardin-Simmons University, offers a competitive curriculum for entrepreneurs.

Libraries and Research Centers

Best-selling author and Austin resident James Michener once commented, "The libraries in Austin—you can't imagine how good they are."

On February 16, 1926, the Austin Public Library opened in a rented room at 819 Congress Avenue with 500 donated volumes. Since then it has grown to include 20 branches, the John Henry Faulk Central Library, the Austin History Center, and Recycled Reads used bookstore. The collection includes 1,480,479 items systemwide. More than 494,000 people are registered card holders. Customers visited the Austin Public Library 3.5 million times in 2012 and checked out a total of 4.7 million items. In addition, 20.4 million virtual visits were made to Austin Public Library's website during that period.

In 2006, Austin voters approved a proposition to build a new Central Library. In 2008 the city council selected Lake/Flato Architects and Shepley Bulfinch Richardson to design the Library. The groundbreaking took place on May 30, 2013. The projected opening of the New Central Library was in 2016.

Each of the colleges and universities has its own library whose collection reflects that institution's research interests and curriculum. Austin is also home to numerous special libraries that preserve the records of businesses, research firms, associations, and governmental agencies; the Lyndon Baines Johnson Library and Museum houses the 36th president's papers and other memorabilia. At least 80 research centers affiliated with the University of Texas at Austin sponsor investigations into everything from classical archaeology to artificial intelligence. Other of the city's notable research centers are Sematech, a consortium of U.S. semiconductor producers and the U.S. government in existence for over 25 years, and the National Wildflower Research Center, brainchild of former first lady Lady Bird Johnson, whose facilities are open for tours.

Public Library Information: Austin Public Library (Faulk Central Library), 800 Guadalupe, Austin, TX 78701; telephone (512) 974-7400.

■ Health Care

Austin offers the best that modern medicine can supply and serves as a base for innovative technologies such as remote telecommunications uplinks and telephonic monitoring systems that carry health services into outlying areas or extend it to the home.

Austin is served by 33 hospitals with a total of over 2,500 beds. In 2013 *U.S. News & World Report* listed the following five, in order, as among the best: Seton Medical Center, University Medical Center Brackenridge, Seton Medical Center Williamson; and, tied for fourth, Seton Northwest Hospital and St. David's Medical Center.

Of those, St. David's HealthCare is the region's leading hospital system, with hospitals throughout Central Texas. It is the fifth largest private employer in the Austin area, with more than 7,900 employees and $3.1 billion in annual gross revenues.

Seton Medical Center Austin is Austin's largest acute care center and the only hospital in Central Texas that performs heart transplants. It is one of four hospitals in the Seton network.

Using the latest in medical technology, these facilities provide an array of specialized services such as neonatal care, organ transplants, oncology, and in-vitro fertilization. Seven hospitals specialize in mental health services, including chemical dependency treatment and counseling, and several also offer health classes and fitness centers for both individual and corporate clients. Families who are experiencing traumatic injury or illness with a child can also find a supportive environment within the Children's Hospital of Austin at the Parent's Place.

The community's Ronald McDonald House, located near Children's Hospital of Austin, and Seton League House, located near Seton Medical Center, each provide families with comfortable, affordable accommodations, regardless of which hospital cares for the patient. In an effort to accommodate more families, a second Ronald McDonald House was opened in 2008. Heart to Heart Hospice Austin and its affiliate in Williamson County provide comprehensive in-home services for those with terminal illnesses.

■ Recreation

Sightseeing

Austin beckons the tourist with its carefully maintained natural beauty, historic buildings, art museums and galleries, and vibrant night life. On a walking tour of the downtown area, highlights include the Texas State Capitol, a pink granite structure with a magnificent rotunda, and the antebellum Greek Revival Governor's Mansion. Early Texas history is reflected in the French Legation, a French provincial cottage built in 1841 for the French Charge d'Affaires to the Republic of Texas. Visitors may take guided tours of all three attractions.

The Lyndon Baines Johnson Library and Museum holds the presidential papers of the former president. It also has a scale replica of the Oval Office during his presidency. A First Lady's Gallery is devoted to the work of Lady Bird Johnson.

The State Cemetery, considered the Arlington of Texas, is the final resting place of many notable historical figures. The Umlauf Sculpture Garden and Museum displays over 130 sculptures, drawings, and paintings by Charles Umlauf.

Both the curious and the lover of wildlife may appreciate seeing the largest colony of urban bats in North America. More than one million Mexican free-tailed bats—the namesake of the Austin Ice Bats hockey team—live under the Congress Avenue Bridge between mid-March and early November.

The Second Street District consists of several new residential projects, restaurants, coffee shops, record stores, upscale boutiques and museums, and the Austin City Hall.

Other facets of Austin's past and present are reflected in the landmarks on the University of Texas at Austin campus. In addition to several museums, notable sights include the Center for American History, containing the most extensive collection of Texas history ever assembled; 1893 Littlefield House; and one of only five Gutenberg Bibles in the United States. The Center for American History at The University of Texas at Austin is home to the UT Videogame Archive. The archive focuses on the importance of preserving the history of game development and highlighting the influence of Texas-based developers.

Zilker Park, the city's largest, is a popular destination for Austinites wanting to go for a swim, take a canoe ride, play soccer with friends, or just stroll through the gardens. Just a few minutes from downtown, it features

Barton Springs, fed by natural spring water, as well as a nature center, a fanciful playground, several specialized gardens, a miniature train, large picnic and play areas, and a theater. Wild Basin Wilderness Preserve's 227 acres offer hiking and educational opportunities. Also within the city limits is the 744-acre McKinney Falls State Park.

Lady Bird Lake in downtown Austin is also considered one of the city's best recreational spots. The Lady Bird Lake Hike and Bike Trail, is a 10.1-mile path bordering the lake. The Lady Bird Johnson Wildflower Center pays homage to Lady Bird's devotion to native landscaping and preservation. Visitors can explore where planting areas, wildflower meadows, exhibits and an observation tower.

At night, visitors can see parts of the city illuminated by the Austin Moonlight Towers, collectively listed on the National Register of Historic Places. Once popular in American cities in the late 1800s, Austin is the only city in the world known to continue to operate these towers. Seventeen of the 31 original 150-foot-tall towers remain.

Arts and Culture

Austin is hailed as the "Live Music Capital of the World," and has nearly 200 live music venues located mainly in the Sixth Street entertainment district or the Warehouse District. The PBS television program "Austin City Limits" has brought the city nationwide attention as a major center for progressive country music, popularized by such entertainers as Willie Nelson, a native Austinite. This is only part of a cultural scene that includes private theaters, two ballet companies, a symphony orchestra, an opera company, dozens of film theaters, and numerous art galleries and museums. The University of Texas Cultural Entertainment Committee hosts a constant stream of visiting entertainers, many of whom perform at the lavish University of Texas at Austin Performing Arts Center, comprised of Bass Concert Hall, Hogg Auditorium, Bates Recital Hall, B. Iden Payne Theatre, McCullough Theatre, and Oscar G. Brockett Theatre. The Long Center for Performing Arts, which is home to opera, symphony and ballet, has also become a cultural staple of Austin. The Long Center serves over 250 performing groups including the Austin Symphony, Ballet Austin, and the Austin Lyric Opera. Other classical groups in the city include Chorus Austin and the Austin Civic Orchestra. For performers, the Austin International Folk Dancers are a nonprofit that have been teaching cultural dance to Austinites for more than 50 years.

Aficionados of the stage may choose from traditional or more avant-garde fare presented by Austin's independent theater companies. The Paramount Theatre, a restored 1915 vaudeville house, hosts traveling and children's productions. Repertory venues include Live Oak Theater and Zachary Scott Theatre. The city supports Shakespearean productions and a children's troupe. Musical theater is the forte of the Gilbert and Sullivan Society, which stages an annual "grand production" and free monthly musicales. Satirical performances are staged by Esther's Follies.

Austin claims to be home to the highest number of artists per capita of any city in Texas and offers a wide variety of art galleries. Among Austin's galleries and museums is the Elisabet Ney Museum, which displays the work of the state's first important sculptress in her former home. One of the world's largest collections of Latin American art is on display at the two locations of the Huntington Art Gallery on the University of Texas at Austin campus, while the Jack S. Blanton Museum of Art at the university has a large collection of Old Master paintings and drawings.

Austin's other museums celebrate Texas history and some of its notable citizens. For instance, the General Land Office Building, where William Sydney Porter, better known as O. Henry, once worked, was used as the setting for one of his stories and is open for tours. The O. Henry Home and Museum exhibits the writer's personal effects and, on the first Sunday of May, is the site of the O. Henry Pun-Off. The collections of the Daughters of the Republic of Texas are on view at the Republic of Texas Museum. The George Washington Carver Museum and Cultural Art Center is Texas's first African American history museum. The Lyndon B. Johnson Presidential Library and Museum maintains a collection of the late president's documents and displays memorabilia and a re-creation of his White House Oval Office. The state's natural history is the focus of the Texas Memorial Museum. Old and young alike enjoy Discovery Hall, a hands-on science museum, and the Austin Children's Museum.

Festivals and Holidays

Austin hosts several major events throughout the year, the largest of which are centered on the arts.

The South by Southwest (SXSW) music, film, and media festival is an internationally acclaimed, 10-day extravaganza held each March. SXSW is the highest revenue-producing special event for the Austin economy. It was estimated that 2013 festival was responsible for injecting more than $218 million into the Austin economy. The festival offers 9 days of industry conferences, a 4-day trade show, a 6-night music festival featuring more than 2,200 bands, and a 9-day film festival with more than 400 screenings. While it is one of the largest music and film festivals in the nation, SXSW has also generated great interest by technology entrepreneurs.

Spring brings the Old Settler's Music Festival, the Austin International Poetry Festival, and the Austin Fine Arts Festival. The Austin City Limits Music Festival, an extension of the popular "Austin City Limits" television show, has been held in Zilker Park each September since its 2002 debut. The following month is the Austin Film

Festival, a showcase of commercial and independent films. Festivals with an ethnic flavor include the Carnival Brasiliero, a celebration of Brazilian culture and music held each February, and Cinco de Mayo (May 5th) and Diez y Seis (September 16th), which honor Mexican Independence.

The Star of Texas Fair & Rodeo takes place over two weeks in March at the Travis County Exposition Center, which is also the site of the Republic of Texas Biker Rally in June.

Numerous holiday celebrations, including Chuy's Christmas Parade, enliven the winter. In December, The Trail of Lights and 5K run offers more than 50 displays and exhibits with three lighted tunnels and over 100 trees wrapped in lights.

Other music festivals include the Urban Music Festival and the Fun Fun Fun Fest.

Sports for the Spectator

It has been noted that Austin is the largest city in the United State without a major professional sports franchise. The Texas Stars of the American Hockey League, and affiliate of the Dallas Stars of the National Hockey League, moved to the area in 2009, where they play at Cedar Park Center. Cedar Park Center is also home to the Austin Toros, an NBA Development League basketball team. The Round Rock Express, a Triple-A baseball affiliate of the Texas Rangers, began play in the nearby city of Round Rock after relocating there from Mississippi in 2000. The Austin Turfcats, an indoor football team of the Southern Indoor Football League, came to the city in 2009. Spectators can watch the Dallas Cowboys at their preseason football training camp at St. Edward's University in July and August. Professional basketball fans can view the National Basketball Association's San Antonio Spurs train at the University of Texas at Austin Rec Center.

In 2012 Austin hosted its first United States Formula One Grand Prix race. The most obvious physical impact is the addition of the state-of-the art, $400 million dollar complex erected at the Circuit of the Americas, a 375-acre motorsports and entertainment complex. In addition to being the first purpose-built Grand Prix facility in the United States, the complex houses a 40,000-square-foot conference/media center, a 5,500 square foot medical center, and a 14,000-person capacity amphitheater, the largest of its kind in Texas.

While professional sports may be lacking, sports fans are not. In college action, the city is gripped with football fever each fall as the University of Texas at Austin Longhorns take on the Big 12 Conference at Memorial Stadium. While football is the Longhorns' specialty, university athletes engage in a full range of other sports as well, including volleyball, baseball, basketball, cross country, golf, track, tennis, swimming, rowing, diving, and women's soccer.

Sports for the Participant

With over 200 parks and playgrounds totaling over 16,600 acres, numerous municipal golf courses and more than 50 miles of hiking and biking trails, amateur athletes can delight in Austin's extensive sports facilities. The 150-mile chain that makes up Highland Lakes offers opportunities for swimming, canoeing, fishing, and boating. With 32 golf courses, Austin has earned a reputation as one of the best tennis and golf environments in the nation. Annual sporting events invite residents and visitors to put their best foot forward.

The AT&T Austin Marathon, a 26.2-mile race, is held in February. Texas's largest footrace, the Capitol 10,000, takes place in April and attracts approximately 10,000 runners on a 10K course between Congress Avenue and Auditorium Shores, one of the largest in the nation. Triathlons are also available, like the Capital of Texas Triathlon on Lady Bird Lake on Memorial Day weekend. The Longhorn Ironman features a 1.2-mile, one-loop swim in Decker Lake, followed by a scenic one-loop, 56-mile bike ride passing through rolling Texas farmlands, and ending with a three-loop half-marathon.

Austin is also the hometown of several cycling groups. The city is well known as one of the most bicycle friendly in the nation, for both commuters and enthusiasts.

Shopping and Dining

The infusion of wealthy high-tech, film, and music professionals into Austin has turned it into a retail boom town. Austin offers residents and visitors a variety of shopping experiences. Downtown, for example, the streets around the capitol and other government buildings feature a wide array of upscale shops. One of the city's liveliest areas for both shopping and other forms of entertainment is Old Pecan Street, also known as Sixth Street, a seven-block strip of renovated Victorian and native stone buildings. Sporting more than 70 shops, restaurants, and clubs, Old Pecan Street displays a Bourbon Street flair in the evening. Adjacent to the University of Texas at Austin campus—especially along a street known as "The Drag"—are dozens of small clothing boutiques and bookstores; on weekends, sidewalk vendors sell handcrafted items. More traditional mall shopping is common in the fast-growing northern part of the city. SoCo is a shopping district stretching down South Congress Avenue from Downtown. The district has shops, restaurants, and popular music venues. On the first Thursday of each month, merchants keep their doors open until 10 p.m. Shopping can also be found in the Second Street District.

Austin offers a diverse array of fine dining restaurants. The city's restaurants feature everything from down-home Texas barbecue to the most elegant continental cuisine. Mexican restaurants are particularly abundant, and Asian restaurants have been proliferating.

Visitor Information: Austin Convention & Visitors Bureau, 301 Congress Ave., Ste. 200, Austin, TX 78701; telephone (512) 474-5171; toll-free (800) 926-2282; email visitorcenter@austintexas.org.

■ Convention Facilities

With its mild climate, many restaurants and live entertainment, strong business environment, and proximity to other Texas cities, Austin offers convention planners an attractive package. Its facilities include more than 30,000 hotel rooms city-wide (6,500 in downtown) and 900,000 square feet of high-tech, highly desirable meeting space right in the heart of downtown.

The Austin Convention Center boasts 246,000 square feet of contiguous, column-free exhibit space, five halls, and 54 meeting rooms, with a total of 881,400 square feet of space stretched over six city blocks. At 43,300 square feet of space, its Grand Ballroom is the largest ballroom in Texas.

The Long Center for the Performing Arts offers a grand performance hall with seating for 2,400, as well as a smaller theater to accommodate conventions and receptions. The Travis County Exposition Center is located just 15 minutes from the downtown area. The Performing Arts Center and the Frank Erwin Center on the University of Texas at Austin campus offer a variety of large meeting and performance spaces, while a number of hotels can provide banquet and meeting rooms for smaller gatherings.

Convention Information: Austin Convention & Visitors Bureau, 301 Congress Ave., Ste. 200, Austin, TX 78701; telephone (512) 474-5171; toll-free (800) 926-2282; email visitorcenter@austintexas.org. Austin Convention Center, 500 East Cesar Chavez Street, Austin TX 78701; telephone (512) 404-4000.

■ Transportation

Approaching the City

Located about eight miles from downtown, the Austin-Bergstrom International Airport (airport code AUS) offers nonstop flights to 36 destinations, including New York, Chicago, Washington DC, Atlanta, Phoenix, Los Angeles, and Detroit. During 2012, the airport set an all-time record with 9.4 million passengers. The airport is served by 11 airlines including Alaska Airlines, Branson Airlines, American, Continental, Delta, Frontier, JetBlue, Southwest, United, and US Airways. The airport has a Family Viewing Area near the east runway with one acre set aside for viewing plane takeoffs and approaches. Showcasing the city's diverse music scene, the airport features live music each afternoon on one of several stages throughout the airport. The Airport Flyer

bus and Metro Bus service offer transportation to the downtown area.

Amtrak Rail offers the Texas Eagle, traveling daily between Chicago and San Antonio, with stops in Austin and Dallas and other major cities.

Drivers approach Austin via Interstate 35, which runs north–south through the city and links it with Dallas and San Antonio, and Interstate Highway, running east–west along the southern edge of the city. Austin is also accessed via U.S. Highways 79, 90, 183, and 290. In 2006 Austin opened its first tollway system, State Highway 130. Rail riders can board Amtrak's Texas Eagle line (from Chicago to San Antonio) or its Sunset Limited line (Orlando to Los Angeles).

Traveling in the City

Austin is bisected by Interstates 10 and 35, and is also served by U.S. Highways 79, 90, 183, and 290. Two other main roads, Loop 360 and Route 1, run north–south. The city is easy to explore by car and parking is plentiful. Austin is a bike friendly city and has a silver rating from the League of American Bicyclists. Austin is also home to a car-sharing program, Car2Go, which opened with a fleet of Smart microcars in 2010. Cars can be accessed on-demand or booked 24 hours in advance.

Capital Metropolitan Transportation Authority provides the city's bus service. Each day, an average of 130,000 one-way passengers ride the system; it stops at more than 3,000 points throughout central Texas. The downtown area is served by the Armadillo Express trolleys known as 'Dillos, which offer free service to such places as the State Capitol and the University of Texas at Austin. Students and visitors to the University of Texas campus enjoy their own shuttle bus system. Visitors should note that only vehicles with special permits are allowed to drive through or park on the University of Texas at Austin campus.

■ Communications

Newspapers and Magazines

Austin's major daily newspaper is the *Austin American-Statesman,* a morning paper. *The Daily Texan* is the student newspaper of the University of Texas at Austin. Weekly publications include the *Austin Chronicle,* a free tabloid that publishes entertainment listings, and the *Austin Business Journal,* which reports on local commerce. *Texas Monthly* is a major regional magazine that chronicles state politics and culture. Also among the more than 80 newspapers and periodicals published in Austin are *Southwestern Historical Quarterly,* published by the Texas State Historical Association; *El Mundo; El Norte; Borderlands: Texas Poetry Review; Community Impact Newspaper;* and *Southwestern Musician. The*

Texas Tribune is an online publication focused on Texas and Austin politics.

Television and Radio

Eight television stations broadcast in Austin: one independent and affiliates of ABC, CBS, Fox, NBC, PBS, CW, and Univision. Access to dozens of cable channels is also available.

The number and variety of the radio stations reflect Austinites' passion for music. Forty-nine AM and FM stations offer everything from contemporary and Christian music to talk radio. KUT is one of the leading public radio stations in all of Texas.

Media Information: *Austin American-Statesman,* 305 S. Congress Ave., PO Box 670, Austin, TX 78767; telephone (512) 445-4040; toll-free (800) 445-9898; email circulation@statesman.com

Austin Online

Austin American-Statesman. Available www. statesman.com

Austin Convention & Visitors Bureau. Available www.austintexas.org

Austin Independent School District. Available www. austinisd.org

Austin Public Library. Available www.ci.austin.tx. us/library

City of Austin Home Page. Available www.ci.austin. tx.uswww.cityofaustin.org

Greater Austin Chamber of Commerce. Available www.austinchamber.org

Texas Workforce Commission. Available www.twc. state.tx.us

BIBLIOGRAPHY

Cantrell, Gregg, *Stephen F. Austin: Empresario of Texas* (New Haven, CT: Yale University Press, 1999)

Cuate, Melodie A., *Journey to the Alamo* (Lubbock, TX: Texas Tech University Press, 2006)

Cuban, Larry, *As Good as It Gets: What School Reform Brought to Austin* (Cambridge: Harvard University Press, 2010)

Douglass, Curan, *Austin Natural and Historic* (Austin, TX: Eakin Press, 2001)

Kerr, Jeffrey Stuart, *Seat of Empire: The Embattled Birth of Austin, Texas* (Lubbock, TX: Texas Tech University Press, 2013)

McDonald, Jason, *Racial Dynamics in Early Twentieth-Century Austin, Texas* (Lanham, MD: Lexington Books, 2012)

Dallas

■ The City in Brief

Founded: 1841 (incorporated 1871)

Head Official: Mayor Mike Rawlings (since 2011; current term expires 2015)

City Population

1990: 1,007,618
2000: 1,188,580
2010: 1,197,816
2012 estimate: 1,241,108
Percent change, 2000–2010: 0.8%
U.S. rank in 1990: 8th (State rank: 2nd)
U.S. rank in 2000: 12th (State rank: 2nd)
U.S. rank in 2010: 9th (State rank: 3nd)

Metropolitan Statistical Area Population

2000: 5,161,544
2010: 6,371,773
2012 estimate: 6,647,496
Percent change, 2000–2010: 22%
U.S. rank in 2000: 5th
U.S. rank in 2010: 4th

Area: 342.54 square miles

Elevation: Ranges from 500 to 800 feet above sea level

Average Annual Temperatures: January, 44.1° F; July, 85.0° F; annual average, 65.5° F

Average Annual Precipitation: 34.73 inches of rain; 2.6 inches of snow

Major Economic Sectors: professional, scientific and technical services, finance and insurance, trade, utilities

Unemployment Rate: 6.1% (2012)

Per Capita Income: $26,032

2012 FBI Crime Index Property: 54,300

Major Colleges and Universities: Southern Methodist University, University of Dallas, University of Texas at Dallas, Dallas Baptist University

Daily Newspaper: *Dallas Morning News*

■ Introduction

Nestled in the rolling prairies of north-central Texas, Dallas is a sophisticated, bustling metropolis that has earned its reputation in the marketplace of the world. Dallas, county seat of Dallas County, is separated from its Fort Worth neighbor by less than 30 miles, leading many to link the two cities and their surrounding suburbs as one of the largest "metroplexes" in the United States, although each retains a distinctive identity. The Dallas/Fort Worth area is larger than the states of Rhode Island and Connecticut combined and encompasses about 25 percent of all Texas residents. Basking in the glow of the nation's Sun Belt, Dallas has attracted people and businesses from colder regions for a number of years. According to a 2012 report by the Manhattan Institute, the city has also become a destination for people migrating from California in search of a better life. In 2013 *Forbes* ranked Dallas as one of America's best cities for good jobs. The steady influx of people combined with successful economic development has caused Dallas to grow in size and global importance, growing its status as a leader in culture, industry, fashion, transportation, finance, and commerce.

■ Geography and Climate

Dallas is located in north-central Texas, 70 miles south of the Oklahoma border, 174 miles west of Louisiana, and approximately 250 miles north of the Gulf of Mexico. The city is situated on the rolling plains near the headwaters of the Trinity River in an area known as the black-land prairies, midway between the Piney Woods of east Texas

Brandon Seidel/Shutterstock.com

and the Great Plains. The general area has an unusual concentration of man-made lakes. Within a 100-mile radius of the city, there are more than 60 lakes and over 50,000 acres of public parkland. Its climate is humid and subtropical, characterized by hot summers and mild winters, with snowfall rare. Summer temperatures often exceed 100 degrees Fahrenheit and are among the hottest in the United States. The rainy season occurs in April and May; July and August are the driest summer months.

Area: 342.54 square miles

Elevation: Ranges from 500 to 800 feet above sea level

Average Temperatures: January, 44.1° F; July, 85.0° F; annual average, 65.5° F

Average Annual Precipitation: 34.73 inches of rain; 2.6 inches of snow

■ History

Bryan Designs Town

Since its pioneer days, Dallas has grown from a fledgling frontier trading post to a bustling city of more than one million people. Dallas was founded in 1841 when a

bachelor lawyer from Tennessee, John Neely Bryan, settled on a small bluff above the Trinity River to open a trading post and lay claim to free land. The area, where three forks of the river merge, was part of a large government land grant, Peters Colony. Bryan decided the location was ideal for a town. He quickly sketched a plan, designating a courthouse square and 20 streets around it. He planned for his settlement to become the northernmost port on the river, which stretched to the Gulf of Mexico, but the unpredictable, too-shallow Trinity thwarted efforts at navigation.

Without a navigable river, an ocean harbor or plentiful natural resources, Dallas had little reason to thrive. Fortunately, Bryan's town was close to a shallow spot in the river often used by Native Americans and early traders as a natural crossing, and the Republic of Texas was already surveying two "national highways," both of which were to pass nearby. As a result, farmers, tradesmen, and artisans were attracted to the small community.

In 1849 Dallas County was created and named after George Mifflin Dallas, supporter of the annexation of Texas and vice president of the United States under James Knox Polk. The city of Dallas is thought to be named after either the vice president or his brother, Alexander James Dallas, a commander of the U.S. Navy's Gulf of Mexico squadron.

Railroad Spurs Growth

Although the Civil War never actually reached Dallas, its effect on the town was significant. Dallas became a food-producer and Texas a recruitment center for the Confederacy. In 1872 when the railroad line from Houston reached Dallas, the town claimed 3,000 inhabitants, and in 1873, the east-west line of the Texas & Pacific Railroad was completed through Dallas, making it the first railroad crossing town in the state. The railroads made Dallas a major distribution center and the home of merchants, bankers, insurance companies, and developers. By 1890 Dallas was the largest city in Texas, with a population of more than 38,000 people.

Economy Forms Around Oil

In 1920, the Trinity River, a source of some early central city flooding, was re-channeled westward as part of an ambitious construction project of the U.S. Army Corps of Engineers. Farming gained importance in the early twentieth century and Dallas was the largest cotton trading center in the nation. The city's position as a regional financial center was enhanced when a branch of the Federal Reserve Bank opened in 1914. Dallas attracted oil company headquarters, partly because Dallas banks were willing to finance exploration and production. Manufacturing arrived as companies were formed to produce supplies for the petroleum industry and, later, for the defense effort in World War II.

City Experiences Tragedies

No city is without its share of fires (Dallas' worst destroyed most of its business district in 1860), floods, other tragedies, and infamous citizens. The notorious thieves Bonnie Parker and Clyde Barrow were Depression-era Dallas residents who captured the imagination and property of a large segment of the American public before their deaths in 1934. But Dallas' greatest trauma came on November 22, 1963, when President John F. Kennedy was assassinated in a cavalcade through the Dallas streets. Harsh world attention was focused on the city and its leaders. As a result, Goals for Dallas, a private planning program that helped promote a climate of involvement, openness, and sensitivity, was formed.

Dallas Becomes a Thriving Metropolis

While much of the nation suffered an economic recession during the late 1970s and early 1980s, Dallas enjoyed unprecedented growth. As northern factories were idled, a rush to the "Sun Belt" created new businesses, industry, and jobs in Dallas. The downtown skyline changed rapidly as construction boomed. In 1984 Dallas was the site of the Republican National Convention, and many saw the occasion as a chance for the city to erase some lingering negative memories in the minds of the American public. In the 1980s Dallas witnessed a real estate bust that drove prices so low that in time many thriving businesses began

to move in and take advantage of the bargain real estate. By 1990 Dallas ranked first in the country for the number of its new or expanded corporate facilities. In the mid-1990s Dallas ranked as Texas's second largest city, next to Houston, and the eighth largest in the United States. In the late 1990s, the telecom industry boomed in the city, becoming Texas' own Silicon Valley. Closing in on the twenty-first century, the city continued to thrive with a healthy and diversified economy and ranked high in the nation in convention activity, as an insurance and oil industry center, in concentration of corporate headquarters, in manufacturing, and in electronics and other high-technology industries.

Modern Dallas: A Global City

After national economic downturns in the early part of the new century and terror attacks of September 11th affected the area's core industries in technology and oil, Texas was primed for growth again by the mid-2000s.

Important to this effort was the rejuvenation of downtown Dallas. The city built an innovative light rail system and created the Dallas Arts District and the West End Historic District. It also continued renovation and upgrading of downtown hotels, which has been a driving force in this renaissance. Dallas touts itself as the number one visitor destination in Texas, both for tourists and for convention goers.

In 2010, the city became home to the nation's 13th official presidential library, named after Texan President George W. Bush. The city's national importance is equally met by a growing importance in the global marketplace. Home to the world's third busiest airport and a plethora of *Fortune* 500 companies, *Forbes* has called the city a world capital of the future.

Abundant job growth in many business sectors, coupled with a rapidly growing population and a strong global economy put Dallas in a position for a continually bright future.

Historical Information: Dallas Historical Society, G.B. Dealey Library, Hall of State, Fair Park, PO Box 150038, Dallas, TX 75315; telephone (214) 421-4500.

■ Population Profile

Metropolitan Statistical Area Population

2000: 5,161,544
2010: 6,371,773
2012 estimate: 6,647,496
Percent change, 2000–2010: 22%
U.S. rank in 2000: 5th
U.S. rank in 2010: 4th

City Residents

1990: 1,007,618
2000: 1,188,580

2010: 1,197,816
2012 estimate: 1,241,108
Percent change, 2000–2010: 0.8%
U.S. rank in 1990: 8th (State rank: 2nd)
U.S. rank in 2000: 12th (State rank: 2nd)
U.S. rank in 2010: 9th (State rank: 3nd)

Density: 3,517.6 people per square mile

Racial and ethnic characteristics

White: 738,525
Black or African American: 309,069
American Indian and Alaskan Native: 2,858
Asian: 40,222
Native Hawaiian and Other Pacific Islander: 915
Hispanic or Latino (may be of any race): 514,026
Other: 149,519

Percent of residents born in state: 55.5%

Age characteristics

Population under 5 years old: 100,561
Population 5 to 9 years old: 90,615
Population 10 to 14 years old: 81,893
Population 15 to 19 years old: 73,820
Population 20 to 24 years old: 97,121
Population 25 to 34 years old: 231,183
Population 35 to 44 years old: 175,262
Population 45 to 54 years old: 153,962
Population 55 to 59 years old: 61,990
Population 60 to 64 years old: 58,072
Population 65 to 74 years old: 65,684
Population 75 to 84 years old: 34,076
Population 85 years and over: 16,869
Median age: 32.4

Births (2010–11 Metropolitan Area)

Total number: 99,733

Deaths (2010–11 Metropolitan Area)

Total number: 36,229

Money income (2012)

Per capita income: $26,032
Median household income: $41,745
Total households: 456,781

Number of households with income of …

less than $10,000: 43,830
$10,000 to $14,999: 30,862
$15,000 to $24,999: 58,926
$25,000 to $34,999: 59,790
$35,000 to $49,999: 66,792
$50,000 to $74,999: 78,223
$75,000 to $99,999: 38,040
$100,000 to $149,999: 39,540
$150,000 to $199,999: 16,365
$200,000 or more: 24,413

Percent of families below poverty level: 24.2%

FBI Crime Index Property: 54,300

FBI Crime Index Violent: 8,380

■ Municipal Government

Dallas is the third largest city in the country with the council-manager form of government. Citizens adopted this form of municipal government in 1931. The system divides responsibility between a policy-making council and the administration of a city manager. The Dallas City Council is comprised of 15 members elected by voters in non-partisan elections. Fourteen are elected from single-member districts, while the mayor is elected at-large. In the early 2000s the efficiency of this system was questioned, especially by members of the press. A 2005 referendum proposed changing the city charter to increase the power of the mayor, but Dallas voters rejected the new plan.

Head Official: Mayor Mike Rawlings (since 2011; current term expires 2015)

Total Number of City Employees: 12,592 (2012)

City Information: Dallas City Hall, 1500 Marilla Street, Dallas, TX 75201; telephone (214)670-3302; website www.dallascityhall.com

■ Economy

Major Industries and Commercial Activity

In 2009 Dallas/Fort Worth reportedly produced about 34 percent of all the goods and services in Texas, just one sign of Dallas' economic significance. Dallas boasts a broadly diverse business climate, with services, financial, insurance, and real-estate sectors in the lead. Technological industries are also prominent in the Dallas area. According to the Greater Dallas Chamber of Commerce, the Dallas/Fort Worth Metroplex is home to about 50 percent of the state's high-tech workers and about 8 percent of the nation's total high-tech workers. Texas Instruments, a major manufacturer of microchips, employs over 10,000 people in Dallas. Other major industries include energy, defense, life sciences, semiconductors, telecommunications, transportation, and processing. Dallas is home to the headquarters of over 20 companies who frequent the *Fortune* 500 list, including AT&T, Texas Instruments, Southwest Airlines, Dean Foods, Energy Future Holdings, Tenet Healthcare, and ACS. The Dallas area is also home to multinational oil and gas giant Exxon Mobil, one of the largest publicly traded companies in the world (rarely falling out of first or second place), which makes its home in nearby Irving.

The number of headquarters listed represents one of the highest numbers of *Fortune* 500 companies clustered in one city. In addition to global and national headquarters, Dallas is the site of many regional headquarters offices. Further, over 10 privately held companies with at least $1 billion in annual revenue are headquartered in the area. The city is home to 15 billionaires, making it among the top 10 cities worldwide with the most billionaires.

Dubbed the "Silicon Prairie," Dallas is among the country's largest employment centers for high technology. Dallas is known as a center for telecommunications manufacturing. The Telecom Corridor is an area in Richardson, Texas, a northern suburb of Dallas. Its nickname is in recognition of the proliferation of telecommunications companies in a small section of the community. The area is a strip about three miles long on U.S. Highway 75, north of Interstate 635; Nortel, Ericsson, Alcatel, Tellabs, AT&T, and other telecom companies call the area home. While affected by the burst of the dot-com bubble in 2001, the Telecom Corridor recovered in the middle of the decade and has been steady through the recessions of the late 2000s. Dallas was ranked among the top 10 sustainable metropolitan areas by *Site Selection* magazine in 2010.

Items and goods produced: chemicals and allied products, electronic components, parts for defense and airline industries, machinery, transportation equipment, and food products

Incentive Programs-New and Existing Companies

Local programs: Many Dallas area communities have enacted ad valorem tax abatement ordinances authorized to grant up to 100 percent abatement for up to 10 years for economic development projects. Businesses may also qualify for a tax credit and an eight-year limitation on the appraised value of a property if it is in a qualified reinvestment zone, usually defined by school districts. Industrial development bonds and sales tax for economic development are also available programs. Tax Increment Finance Districts (TIFs) are designated areas targeted for development, redevelopment, and improvements. Increases in tax revenues from new development and higher real estate values are paid into TIF funds to finance improvements. Public Improvement Districts (PIDs) are created at the request of property owners in the district, who pay a supplemental tax used for services beyond existing city services, such as marketing, security, landscaping, and other improvements. Dallas Regional Momentum is a program dedicated to encouraging corporate relocation to the Dallas area. The Momentum Awards, awarded annually by the Chamber of Commerce since 2003, give a cash prize to companies that have demonstrated job growth and contribute positively to the economic growth of the city.

State programs: Texas is a right-to-work state. The Texas economy has performed better than that of any other state during the recent economic downturn. It is believed that this success is due in part to the states pro-business climate, of which economic incentives are an important part.

The Texas Enterprise Zone Programs offer tax abatement at the local level, and refunds of state sales and use taxes under certain circumstances to businesses operating in enterprise zone areas. The Texas Enterprise Zone Program allows local communities to partner with the State of Texas to promote job creation and capital investment in targeted areas of the state that meet specific economic criteria. Designated projects are eligible to apply for state sales and use tax refunds on qualified expenditures. The state of Texas targets many of its incentive programs toward smaller and rural communities. The Rural Municipal Finance Program is a loan program created by the Texas Agricultural Finance Authority (TAFA) to stimulate economic activity in rural Texas. The Texas Enterprise Fund can be used to provide deal-closing money for companies relocating to and investing in Texas. As of 2014, awards have ranged from $194,000 to $50 million. The Texas Emerging Technology Fund, a $200 million fund created by the Texas Legislature in 2005, is available to companies who seek to commercialize new technologies. The program provides grants for early-stage investments in new, technology-based, private entrepreneurial entities that collaborate with public or private institutions of higher education.

Texas is one of the few states with no individual income tax, a very attractive environment for transferring employees. There is also no corporate income tax. Texas Enterprise Zone Program provides for eligible designated projects to apply for state sales and use tax refunds on purchases of all taxable items purchased for use at the qualified business site related to the project or activity. Special tax exemptions are made for manufacturing machinery, equipment, replacement parts, and accessories that have a useful life of more than six months. Texas businesses are also exempt from paying state sales and use tax on labor for constructing new facilities, electricity and natural gas used in manufacturing, processing, or fabrication. Tax-Exempt Industrial Revenue Bonds are designed to provide tax-exempt financing up to $20 million per project to finance land and depreciable property for eligible industrial or manufacturing projects.

The Texas Capital Fund Infrastructure and Real Estate Development programs are designed to provide no interest loans of up to $750,000 to non-entitlement communities. The program funds real estate developments (acquisitions, construction, and/or rehabilitation) to assist a business, which commits to creating or retaining permanent jobs, primarily for low and moderate-income persons.

Job training programs: The Skills Development Fund, in collaboration with community and technical colleges, provides customized job training for local businesses to be provided to individuals expected to become future employees. The program is administered through the Texas Workforce Commission. The Greater Dallas Chamber promotes economic opportunities for all through a series of seminars and training sessions. Leadership Dallas is a program that trains business leaders in community responsibility through discussion of issues, consideration of options, and first-hand exploration of the needs and concerns of the Greater Dallas Region.

Development Projects

Despite setbacks due to a national recession in the late 2000s, downtown Dallas experienced more than $2 billion in investments between 2003 and 2013, with another $1 billion in the planning stages. At least two dozen developments are planned, including new hotel space, apartments, and remodeled office skyscrapers.

The Downtown Dallas cityscape was enhanced in 2012 with the completion of Museum Tower, a $200 million dollar, 42-story complex that has been described as a "shaft of light." The Spire, in development as of 2014, is an 11.3-acre downtown Dallas development that offers 128,000 square feet of retail, 1.7 million square feet of office space, and 337 residential units. The project is just south of the Dallas Arts District, among the hottest new development areas of any downtown in America.

The Trinity River Corridor Project is a flood protection project that covers 20 miles or approximately 10,000 acres of land bordering the Trinity riveer. The $2 billion project will transform the river into Dallas' greatest park. The entire corridor, including commercial and residential opportunity areas outside the park greenbelt, includes over 40,000 acres with recreation activities within the river's levees and redevelopment areas outside the levees.

The Dallas/Fort Worth (DFW) Airport has invested $2.7 billion into its capital development plan in the 2000s, which included a two-million-square-foot international terminal with an integrated Grand Hyatt Hotel and Skylink, which is reportedly the world's largest airport train system. Airfield, roadway, and airport infrastructure support projects make up the rest of the program. Expansion of the third largest airport in the world is ongoing, with plans announced in 2009 for an additional $3 billion makeover, including four revamped terminals.

Among the city's Tax Increment Finance Districts (TIFs) is the City Center TIF at the historic center of downtown Dallas. With its designation as a development area slated to continue until 2035, City Center TIF projects focus on streetscaping, lighting, acquisition and restoration of historic buildings, façade improvements, and others. The Mercantile Redevelopment Project, centered around the Mercantile Tower and accompanying office buildings, was completed and opened in 2009 with three upscale apartment buildings.

Economic Development Information: Greater Dallas Chamber, Economic Development, 700 North Pearl Street, Suite 1200, Dallas, TX 75201; telephone (214) 746-6600. City of Dallas Economic Development, 1500 Marilla Street, 5C South, Dallas, TX 75201; telephone (214) 670-1685.

Commercial Shipping

A major mid-continent gateway to the world, the Dallas/ Fort Worth International Airport's international cargo shipments are part of the reason why Dallas is one of the largest inland ports in the country. The airport handles nearly 640,000 tons of cargo yearly. More than 15 international cargo carriers use the airport for shipping, with Asia counting for almost half of all air cargo trade within the airport's catchment area. According to the local chamber of commerce, one of the city's geographic advantages is that it is equidistant to North America's five largest business centers: New York, Chicago, Los Angeles, Mexico City, and Toronto. As a result, more than 50 million people can be reached from the Dallas area by overnight truck or rail, and 98 percent of the U.S. population can be reached within 48 hours. In addition to its excellent airport services, interstate highways, and railroad connections, Dallas maintains its edge as a leading distribution center of the Southwest with a healthy trucking industry, whose carriers offer direct service to major points in the United States.

Labor Force and Employment Outlook

As of 2013, the Dallas/Fort Worth metropolitan area had the fifth largest labor force in the United States. Just over 31 percent of the population had at least a bachelor's degree, which is above the national average.

Dallas' job market has grown slightly faster than that of the nation in the 2010s. The expansion of the professional and business sector and the leisure and hospitality services sector aided the state's improving economy, along with solid growth in health and educational services. Professionals are moving back to the urban center to take advantage of the educational and health-care opportunities as well as professional business services that Dallas provides.

The Dallas area entered the twenty-first century experiencing some of the highest economic expansion in the nation. According to *Forbes*, in 2012 Dallas ranked eighth in the nation for best places for business and careers. *Forbes* reported that the job outlook in Dallas is strong, with 2.9 percent annual growth expected through 2014.

The following is a summary of data regarding the 2012 Dallas labor force:

Size of civilian labor force: 628,591

Number of workers employed in . . .
agriculture and mining: 4,150
construction: 58,059

manufacturing: 47,661
wholesale trade: 14,265
retail trade: 60,196
transportation: 27,793
information systems: 12,444
finance: 53,772
professional administration: 84,087
education and social services: 101,274
arts and leisure: 59,844
other: 31,908
public administration: 12,243

Average hourly earnings of production workers: $15.01

Unemployment rate: 6.1% (2012)

Employers

Largest employers (2013)	*Number of employees*
Wal-Mart Stores, Inc.	34,698
American Airlines	24,700
Bank of America	20,000
Texas Health Resources	19,230
Baylor Health Care System	17,097
AT&T	15,800
Lockheed Martin Aeronautics	14,126
JPMorgan Chase	13,500
HCA North Texas Division	12,000
Kroger Food Stores	10,097
Texas Instruments Inc	9,100
Raytheon Co. Defense	8,700
Target	8,674
United Parcel Service	8,555
J.C. Penney Co.	7,964
Southwest Airlines	7,022
Bell Helicopter	6,883

Cost of Living

The Dallas/Fort Worth area has some of the lowest cost of living among the top 20 metropolitan areas. This, along with the option of maintaining a metropolitan or suburban lifestyle, has made the Dallas area a desirable place to live. The following is a summary of several key cost of living factors for the Dallas area.

2013 ACCRA Average House Price: $208,970

2013 ACCRA Cost of Living Index: 96

State income tax rate: None

State sales tax rate: 6.25%

Local income tax rate: None

Local sales tax rate: 2.0%

Property tax rate: 0.797 mills (2013)

Economic Information: The Greater Dallas Chamber of Commerce, 700 North Pearl Street, Suite 1200, Dallas, TX 75201; telephone (214) 746-6600.

■ Education and Research

Elementary and Secondary Schools

The Dallas Independent School District is among the 20 largest school district in the nation, covering 384 square miles and 13 municipalities. The school district serves more than 157,000 students in pre-kindergarten through the 12th grade in 220 schools, employing nearly 20,000 teachers and administrators. It is home to 2 of the top 10 public high schools in the nation, according to *Newsweek, U.S. News & World Report,* and the *Washington Post.* Among them is the School for the Talented & Gifted, one of the district's magnet schools. The students it serves are a diverse group, speaking collectively over 70 languages in their homes.

The Diocese of Dallas educates more than 15,000 students in seven Catholic high schools, three diocesan and four private, and 37 Catholic elementary schools, parochial and private. The schools promote Gospel awareness, personal responsibility, assimilation of cultures, creativity within the individual, maximizing personal gifts, civic concern, and positive societal values.

Dallas has more than 60 public charter schools and a large selection of independent private schools. Among the notable are The Episcopal School of Dallas with 1,000 students in its pre-school through 12th grade program, and the Greenhill School, whose mission is to encourage excellence and openness in learning. Single-sex schools include St. Mark's School of Texas, an independent school for boys in grades 1 through 12 and its sister school, The Hockaday School for girls. Founded in 1993, Yavneh Academy is a Jewish Orthodox high school for girls and boys.

The following is a summary of data regarding the Dallas Independent School District.

Total enrollment: 157,162

Number of facilities
total: 223
elementary schools: 149
junior high schools: 34
high schools: 32
other: 8

Student/teacher ratio: 14.74:1

Teacher salaries

average (statewide): $48,261

Funding per pupil: $9,561

Public Schools Information: Dallas Independent School District, 3700 Ross Avenue, Dallas, TX 75204; telephone (972) 925-3700.

Colleges and Universities

Southern Methodist University (SMU) is a private university in University Park, an independent city that is entirely surrounded by the city of Dallas. SMU educates about 11,000 students annually, about 40 percent of which are graduate students. SMU is frequently cited on national lists, particularly for the quality of its graduate business school.

The University of Texas at Dallas is located in Richardson and consists of seven schools, with a combined enrollment of nearly 20,000 in 2012. In downtown Dallas a unique consortium of educational institutions exists in a former department store building on Main Street. The Universities Center at Dallas is operated by the Federation of North Texas Area Universities and offers undergraduate and graduate courses by seven partner institutions including Texas A&M University–Commerce, Texas Woman's University, University of North Texas, University of Texas at Arlington, University of Texas at Dallas, and Dallas County Community College District.

The Dallas County Community College District educates more than 83,000 credit and non-credit students and operates seven campuses in Dallas County, each offering two-year programs in a variety of fields.

Other Dallas colleges include the University of Texas Southwestern Medical Center educating 3,520 students annually; Dallas Christian College, offering biblical and theological study; Louise Herrington School of Nursing of Baylor University; and Baylor College of Dentistry. Other institutions offering biblical or religious studies or programs from a religious perspective include The Criswell College, Dallas Theological Seminary, Holy Trinity Seminary, Dallas Baptist University, Paul Quinn College, and the University of Dallas.

Libraries and Research Centers

The Dallas Public Library system consists of a central library and 30 service points throughout the city that circulate over eight million items a year. The system has over 2.6 million volumes and serials and a large collection of government documents. The library also maintains a historical section that contains an extensive collection of books, letters, and historical documents of Texas, Dallas, and Dallas black history. The Dallas Public Library in Downtown Dallas has one of the original copies of the Declaration of Independence, printed on July 4, 1776, and William Shakespeare's First Folio of Comedies, Histories, and Tragedies on permanent display at the library. The library's Children's Center is one of the largest in the country. Recent innovations include the very first library inside a shopping mall.

Southern Methodist University's library has more than 2.5 million volumes, with special collections on Western Americana and Texana. It also includes Bridwell Library, which has a large collection of rare theological books. Most of the other area universities and colleges also operate their own libraries. In 2008, Southern Methodist University was selected as the site of the George W. Bush Presidential Library, which broke ground in 2010 and opened on April 25, 2013. The presidential complex includes a library, museum, and policy institute. It holds over 29,000 cubic feet (70 million pages) of textual materials, over 1,200 cubic feet of audiovisual materials, including 46,000 audio and video tapes and 375,000 still photographs, and over 80 terabytes of electronic records, including over 200 million email messages created or received using the White House email system.

Dallas has a number of research centers, many affiliated with local colleges, universities, and hospitals. For example, at Baylor University, research is carried out on bone marrow transplantation, biomedicine, and sports science. The Urban Solutions Center, operated by Texas A&M, researches urban solutions for agricultural problems. The University of Texas Southwestern Medical Center at Dallas conducts more than 3,500 research projects each year at a cost of more than $350 million. The school has four active Nobel laureates on the faculty, more than any other medical school in the nation, and also boasts three-fourths of Texas's medical members of the National Academy of Sciences. The Institute of Biomedical Sciences and Technology conducts interdisciplinary projects with a focus on cures for disease and enhancing health and quality of life.

Public Library Information: Dallas Public Library, 1515 Young Street, Dallas, TX 75201; telephone (214) 670-1400; fax (214) 670-1752. George W. Bush Presidential Library and Museum, 2943 SMU Boulevard, Dallas, TX 75205; telephone (214) 346-1650; fax (214) 346-1699.

■ Health Care

The Dallas area has an extensive network of 90 public and private hospitals, with over 15,000 beds and 11,000 physicians.

Baylor Health Care System's University Medical Center at Dallas—consistently ranked by *U.S. News & World Report* as among the best hospitals in the United States—offers many areas of specialty. The Kimberly H.

Courtwright and Joseph W. Summers Institute of Metabolic Disease at the center provides comprehensive diagnostic and treatment services to children and adults suffering from metabolic diseases. Baylor Dallas has several specialty centers that focus on diabetes: The Ruth Collins Diabetes Center, The Professional Diabetes Educator Program, and the Louise Gartner Center for Hyperbaric Medicine.

Parkland Memorial Hospital, a public hospital operated by the Dallas County Hospital District, is the major trauma center for North Texas and the principal teaching hospital for the University of Texas Southwestern Medical Center. Parkland, also considered among the top 25 hospitals in the country, offers specialized care in its pediatric trauma and burn centers. It is the busiest maternity hospital in the United States.

The Dallas Craniofacial Center at Medical City Children's Hospital is one of the world's leading medical centers for treatment of children with craniofacial birth defects and facial trauma. A member of the National Association of Epilepsy Centers, The Center for Epilepsy at Medical City treats adult and pediatric patients with complex neurological disorders. Methodist Dallas Transplant Institute is one of the largest and most active transplant centers in the southwestern United States. Other major medical facilities in Dallas include Presbyterian Hospital of Dallas, Veterans Affairs Medical Center, and St. Paul Medical Center.

■ Recreation

Sightseeing

Dallas is rich in entertainment opportunities, as is evidenced by its slogan of "Live Large, Think Big." Whether one's preference runs to culture, sports, nightlife, or family fare, the Metroplex—including Fort Worth, Arlington, Irving, Grand Prairie, the "Mid-Cities," and many suburbs—has plenty to offer.

Beginning in downtown Dallas, visitors can see Dallas founder John Neely Bryan's log cabin at Founder's Plaza, wander through the city's historic districts, enjoy a shopping excursion among the shops and stores located in the underground network of downtown office buildings, or seek out merchandise at Neiman-Marcus department store, which maintains a unique fifth-floor museum.

Other downtown Dallas attractions include the beautifully restored Majestic Theatre, the chimes in the bell tower, Thanks-Giving Square, the marvelous bronze steers of Pioneer Plaza, the bargains at Farmers Market, the observation deck on top of the 50-story Reunion Tower, and the ice rinks at Plaza of the Americas complex and at downtown's West End (open December through March). The Sixth Floor Museum commemorates the life of John F. Kennedy. It is located in the former Texas School Book Depository building, which was central to the assassination and death of the president in 1963.

Fair Park is a 277-acre entertainment, cultural, and recreational complex located on the site of the Texas Centennial Exposition of 1936 and home each year to the State Fair of Texas, the country's largest. Visitors are greeted by "Big Tex," a 55-foot tall statue that has become a cultural icon of Dallas and Texas. The original statue was destroyed by fire in 2012 but was replaced by a new "Big Tex" in 2013. Fair Park includes the Cotton Bowl Stadium, a 3,400-seat Music Hall, a 7,200-seat coliseum, a 4,000-seat open-air Band Shell, Starplex Amphitheatre, six major exhibit buildings, livestock facilities, a permanent Midway amusement park, the technologically advanced TI Founders IMAX Theater, and nine museums including the Museum of Natural History, African American Museum, Texas Hall of State, Dallas Horticulture Center, Dallas Aquarium, The Science Place I and II, and Age of Steam Railroad Museum. Fair Park houses one of the largest collections of art-deco structures in the world. More than seven million people visit Fair Park events each year, with 3.5 million visiting during the State Fair of Texas each fall.

Six Flags over Texas in nearby Arlington is a 205-acre theme park that includes more than 100 rides, shows, concerts, games, and restaurants. Six Flags, themed for the six nations that have governed Texas, is open for special events during the holidays. Fossil Rim Wildlife Center in Glen Rose, southwest of Dallas, is dedicated to conservation of endangered species. Programs focus on conservation, management of natural resources, and public education. Most of the animals are free to roam the 1,500 acres of savannah and woodlands, offering visitors a rare chance to see and learn about how species live in the wild.

The Dallas Zoo features more than 2,000 animals, including many rare and endangered species. At 95 acres, it is the largest zoological park in Texas. The zoo's entrance features a 67-foot-tall giraffe, the tallest statue in Texas. The 25-acre Wilds of Africa exhibit features a mile-long monorail, nature trail, African plaza, gorilla conservation center, and lots of animals in their natural habitats. Giants of the Savanna is the only multi-species zoo exhibit in the United States to mix elephants and other species in the same habitat. The Zoo's Monorail Safari takes visitors on a one-mile tour through the six habitats.

The Dallas Nature Center has 4.5 miles of hiking trails and picnic areas amid a variety of native wildflowers. Dallas Arboretum and Botanical Garden has 66 acres of gardens plus the historic DeGolyer Mansion and features the largest public selection of azaleas in the United States.

Old City Park, now known as Dallas Hertiage Village, is a living history museum portraying life in North Texas from 1840 to 1910. The museum features 38 historic structures, including a working Civil War era farm, a traditional Jewish household, Victorian homes, a school, a church, and commercial buildings.

Deep Ellum, a former industrial neighborhood and center of the Dallas jazz scene is home to avant-garde culture in the form of a variety of restaurants, nightclubs, galleries, and shops.

Arts and Culture

In the laste 1970s, Dallas civic leaders envisioned consolidating and exanding the city's cultural institutions in a single downtown location. With the opening of the Dallas Museum of Art in 1984, the formation of the Dallas Arts District was underway. The museum has 370,000 square feet of space on an 8.9-acre site in the Arts District. Its collections include works by renowned American and European artists; the Crow Collection of Asian Art features more than 600 paintings, objects, and architectural pieces from China, Japan, India, and Southeast Asia.

The district expanded in 1989 with the Morton H. Meyerson Symphony Center, designed by Pritzker Prize winning architect I. M. Pei. The center is home to the Dallas Symphony Orchestra (DSO). Acclaimed as one of the world's premier orchestras, it presents numerous subscription concerts, pops concerts, youth concerts, and free park concerts. Classical music is also provided by the Dallas Chamber Orchestra, the Dallas Classic Guitar Society, and the Greater Dallas Youth Orchestra.

The Nasher Sculpture Center opened in 2003. The Center is a 54,000-square-foot building and outdoor sculpture garden featuring the art collection of philanthropist and collector Ray Nasher and his late wife, Patsy. Considered by many to be of the foremost private or public collections of twentieth-century sculpture in the world, it consists of more than 300 pieces by artists such as Matisse, Picasso, Rodin, and others.

The Booker T. Washington High School for the Performing and Visual Arts opened a new addition in 2008. In 2009 the Dallas Opera moved into its permanent location, the newly constructed Winspear Opera House. Three operettas in English are performed each year by the Lyric Opera.

The AT&T Performing Arts Center also opened in 2009. The Center presents a variety of programs year-round in its indoor and outdoor performance venues, including the Lexus Broadway Series and contemporary dance and music, as well as other touring and community performances. The Center also provides performance space for local performing arts organizations, including The Dallas Theater Center, a professional company offering live drama and children's theater.

With the openings of Dallas City Performance Hall, Klyde Warren Park, and The Perot Museum of Nature and Science in 2012, the development of the 60-acre arts district, the largest urban arts district in the country, was complete.

The Music Hall at Fair Park is home of the Dallas Summer Musicals and hosts annual shows during the State Fair each October. The Grapevine Opry is a popular site for country music performances. One of Dallas's oldest dance troupes, Anita N. Martinez Ballet Folklorico, is particularly active during Dance for the Planet festivals. Dallas Black Dance Theatre is a contemporary modern dance company that performs modern, jazz, ethnic, and spiritual works by nationally and internationally known choreographers.

The Dallas Aquarium at Fair Park features electric eels, moon jellyfish, and endangered green sea turtles among the 5,000 aquatic animals from around the world. Also at Fair Park, the Dallas Museum of Natural History contains native-habitat displays of animals—including a hall housing tremendous dinosaur fossils—and minerals, birds, and plants, a photographic gallery, and changing exhibits. Other Fair Park museums include: Hall of State, built in 1936 and home to the Dallas Historical Society; The Science Place, featuring science exhibits, a planetarium, and IMAX theater; The Age of Steam Railroad Museum, a collection of railroad locomotives; the African American Museum; Texas Discovery Gardens, which are botanical gardens; and the Women's Museum.

The Biblical Arts Center features early Christian architecture, Biblical and secular art, a 30-minute light-and-sound presentation of the "Miracle at Pentecost" mural, and an atrium gallery that displays a replica of the garden tomb of Christ. The cultures and lifestyles of indigenous people from all over the world are depicted at the International Museum of Cultures, where exhibits include pottery, habitat displays, and scenes of everyday life.

The Dallas Firefighters Museum permits visitors to walk through Dallas's oldest in-service fire station, which houses "Old Tige," a turn-of-the-century steam pumper, and a variety of antique fire-fighting equipment. The Dallas Holocaust Museum/Center for Education and Tolerance includes a museum, library, and educational institute. As of 2014 it was housed in a temporary location and plans were underway for a permanent location in the historic West End area of downtown Dallas. The American Museum of the Miniature Arts features displays of international dolls and toys.

Festivals and Holidays

Dallas starts off its year with New Year's celebrations and continues strong throughout the year with numerous festivals featuring art, music, food, fun, and more. The Wildflower! Arts & Music Festival is held every May and features national, regional, and local entertainment. It draws over 50,000 people each year. The Shakespeare Festival is held each summer and features Camp Shakespeare and Festival Workshops for kids. ArtFest is held each year in Fair Park, a celebration of art, food and drink, and good times.

Dallas Farmers Market is the scene of seasonal festivals, and the great State Fair of Texas is held each year at Fair Park from late September through mid-October. Additionally, one of the largest wine festivals in the Southwest is Grapefest, held in Grapevine, Texas, a suburb of Dallas. Food festivals include the Addison Oktoberfest. Billed as the largest Oktoberfest celebration on the planet, it attracts more than 75,000 people. The four-day event offers all sorts of German-themed events including a yodeling contest, Dachshund races, a German spelling bee, and barrel rolling. The Greek Food Festival has been an annual event for almost 60 years. There is also a Japanese Fall Festival and Santa Fe Days on the Square, a celebration of authentic Native American food.

Sports for the Spectator

Dallas sports fans can follow their local favorites at the professional or college level. The Dallas Cowboys, a professional football team known widely as "America's Team," is financially one of the most valuable sports franchises in the world. Football historians have recognized the Cowboys as the most successful franchise in National Football League history. In 2009 the Cowboys relocated to the new state-of-the-art Cowboys Stadium in nearby Arlington. The stadium, completed at a cost of $1.3 billion, is the largest domed stadium in the world. The stadium features a retractable roof, an 11,520-square-foot high-definition television, and seating for up to 100,000 spectators. The project was privately funded by the team's famous owner, Jerry Jones.

The American Airlines Center is home to National Basketball Association's Dallas Mavericks, also boasting their share of success, as well as the Dallas Stars of the National Hockey League. The Texas Rangers play Major League Baseball from April through October at Ameriquest Field in Arlington. The Rangers enjoyed success in 2010 when they advanced to the World Series. Major League Soccer's FC Dallas (formerly the Dallas Burn) play at Pizza Hut Park, a 115-acre facility featuring a 20,000-plus-seat soccer stadium. Real championship cowboys compete at the Mesquite Championship Rodeo at Resistol Arena from April to September in Mesquite, Texas. In May, the TPC at Four Seasons Resort in Irving, Texas hosts the annual Byron Nelson Golf Classic, one of the major events on the professional golf tour.

College and university sports fans follow the Southern Methodist University Mustang teams and the Texas Christian University Horned Frogs. The AT&T Cotton Bowl Football Classic each year pits two of the nation's best college teams against each other and is played at the new Cowboys Stadium.

Sports for the Participant

The city of Dallas has more than 21,000 acres of parks and 17 lakes, with nearly 62 miles of jogging and biking paths. Residents and visitors can find almost every kind of recreation in one or more of the municipal facilities. The system's 406 neighborhood, community, and regional parks offer 258 tennis courts, 146 soccer fields, 226 pools, 47 recreation centers, 6 golf courses, and a variety of other fields, shelters, play areas, and recreational facilities.

Sixty lakes and reservoirs lie within a 100-mile radius of Dallas. The largest within the city is Lake Ray Hubbard, with more than 20,000 acres and a public marina. The Dallas Nature Center features 633 acres of preserved wilderness and mesquite prairie, including six miles of hiking trails. Lake Tawakoni State Park, 50 miles east of Dallas, covers 376 rolling, wooded acres on the shores of a large reservoir, and provides a variety of recreational activities, including catfish and bass fishing.

Shopping and Dining

Dallas offers visitors a unique blend of Southwestern warmth, cosmopolitan flair, Old West charm and modern sophistication. One of the wholesale and retail centers of the nation, Dallas has more shopping centers per capita than any major American city. Valley View Center is one of the city's largest shopping centers with more than 175 merchants occupying 1.5 million square feet of space. NorthPark Mall is home to more than 160 stores. The Galleria Dallas features more than 200 stores, including high-end retailers like Tiffany & Co., Gianni Versace, Gucci, Louis Vuitton, Nordstrom and others; the mall also features an ice skating rink inspired by the Galleria Vittorio Emanuele in Milan, Italy.

More than three million antique and bargain hunters visit Traders Village in Grand Prairie, Texas, each year. Spread over 120 acres, more than 2,500 dealers set up shop each weekend in the open-air bargain hunters' paradise.

Dallas, with four times more restaurants per person than New York City, can serve up Texas beef or French cuisine, fiery Texas chili, or a variety of ethnic specialties. TexMex fare is supplemented by the ethnic dishes of Greece, Mexico, Germany, Japan, China, Vietnam, India, and Italy at fine restaurants and eateries. Although some restaurants specialize in traditional southern cooking, this fare is mostly served at home in Dallas. Dallas boasts the invention of the frozen margarita, a popular cocktail made of tequila, lime juice, sugar, and salt. It is also home to high-end dining. Topping the Zagat list is the The French Room at the Adolphus Hotel, which the Zagat Survey ranked as the top restaurant in Texas and one of the best in the United States.

Visitor Information: Dallas Convention and Visitors Bureau, 325 North St. Paul Street, Suite 700, Dallas, TX 75201; telephone (214) 571-1000; fax (214) 571-1008.

■ Convention Facilities

Dallas ranks among the top cities in the nation in convention and meeting attendees. With more than

65,000 hotel rooms available in a variety of hotels throughout the city, the Dallas metro area is the top visitor destination in the state. The city's convenient location in the central United States makes Dallas no more than a three-hour flight from either coast. Major hotels with meeting facilities include the Adam's Mark, Hilton Anatole, the Adolphus, the Doubletree Hotel, the Hyatt Regency, the Hotel Crescent Court, and the Fairmont Hotel.

Visitors to Dallas have available to them other fine convention facilities. The Kay Bailey Hutchison Convention Center is a colossal facility located in the heart of downtown Dallas. Many of its lobbies and concourses are decorated with terrazzo images telling the story of Dallas and its diverse inhabitants. It has more than one million square feet of exhibit space, a 9,816-seat arena, a 1,750-seat theater, 96 meeting rooms, and a pair of ballrooms. It has hosted volleyball tournaments, USA Gymnastics events, cheerleading, weightlifting, and of course hundreds of conventions and trade shows. It was the first convention center in the United States to offer free wireless Internet and now includes a fiber-optic transmission system that allows audio/visual broadcasts to be shared from anywhere.

Convention Information: Dallas Convention & Visitors Bureau, 325 North St. Paul Street, Suite 700, Dallas, TX 75201; telephone (214) 571-1000; fax (214) 571-1008. Dallas Convention Center, 650 South Griffin Street Dallas, TX 75202; telephone (214) 939-2750; fax (214) 939-2795.

■ Transportation

Approaching the City

Most visitors to Dallas arrive via the Dallas/Fort Worth International (DFW) Airport, located approximately 17 miles from the downtown areas of both cities and served by 16 airlines. One of the largest airports in the world, DFW is four hours or less by air from nearly every major North American market, with direct service to more than 184 nonstop destinations worldwide.

Prior to construction of DFW Airport, Dallas' principal airfield was the city-owned Love Field. Today, Dallas Love Field (DAL) is both a general aviation and commercial air facility, with Southwest Airlines principally serving other Texas cities and adjacent states. Delta also has operations at Love Field. Dallas Executive Airport and many smaller municipal airports serve the metropolis. Hosting over seven million passengers a year, the terminal is undergoing a modernization project expected to complete in 2014. The remodel includes a new concourse with 20 gates and an expanded baggage claim area. Rental cars, airport shuttles, taxis and Dallas Area Rapid Transit (DART) buses all provide transportation to and from the airport, which is located seven miles northwest

of the downtown central business district. The airport also features the Love Field Conference Center with state-of-the-art business amenities, catering, and meeting rooms.

The Dallas area is served by four major highways: Interstate 20 (east–west); Interstate 35 (north–south); Interstate 30 (northeast–west); and Interstate 45 (south). All Dallas highways are connected by a twelve-lane loop—LBJ Freeway (Interstate 635) —that encircles the city. Loop 12 is situated primarily within the city limits of Dallas. A third loop circles the Dallas central business district. Amtrak provides train service to Chicago, San Antonio, and Los Angeles.

Traveling in the City

Travel throughout the Dallas area relies heavily on the intricate system of highways that surround the city. Dallas Area Rapid Transit (DART) moves more than 200,000 passengers per day across a 700-square-mile service area of 13 cities with rail, bus, paratransit, light rail system, HOV lane, and rideshare services. DART serves DFW International Airport, Love Field, and Fort Worth via the Trinity Railway Express's (TRE) commuter rail system, which links downtown Fort Worth, downtown Dallas, and DFW Airport. DART operates one of the busiest light rail systems in the nation and is continuing to expand. In 2009 an additional line was added, and several phases of expansion were expected to continue through 2013.

■ Communications

Newspapers and Magazines

Dallas is served by one daily newspaper, *The Dallas Morning News*. Other Dallas staples include the weekly *Dallas Observer*, *Dallas Business Journal*, and *North Texas Journal*. Residents are able to subscribe to a variety of suburban and neighborhood papers, and numerous magazines, such as *D Magazine*. Other publications of the city include the *Auto Revista*, *Daily Commercial Record*, *Dallas Voice*, *Texas Catholic*, and *Texas Jewish Post*.

Television and Radio

As the fifth largest media market, Dallas-area residents are entertained and informed by nearly 20 commercial and public television stations. Other stations are available through cable subscription. North Texas's PBS station, KERA, is one of the most watched public television stations in the nation. The numerous radio stations serving Dallas broadcast a variety of program formats, including all-news and country, rock, and classical music.

The Dallas Communications Complex, a multimillion-dollar film production center developed by Dallas real estate magnate Trammell Crow, includes a 15,000-

square-foot soundstage and has been the site for the filming of several major motion pictures and television specials.

Media Information: *The Dallas Morning News,* PO Box 655237, Dallas, TX 75265; telephone (800) 925-1500.

Dallas Online

City of Dallas Home Page. Available www. dallascityhall.com

Dallas Convention & Visitors Bureau. Available www.dallascvb.com

Dallas Independent School District. Available www. dallasisd.org

The Dallas Morning News. Available www. dallasnews.com

Dallas Observer. Available www.dallasobserver.com

Dallas Public Library. Available dallaslibrary.org

The Greater Dallas Chamber. Available www.gdc.org

BIBLIOGRAPHY

Aron, Jaime, *Dallas Cowboys: The Complete Illustrated History* (Minneapolis: MBI, 2010)

Duty, Michael W., *Dallas & Fort Worth: A Pictorial Celebration* (New York: Sterling Publishing Company, 2007)

Govenar, Alan B., *Deep Ellum: The Other Side of Dallas* (College Station, TX: Texas A&M University Press, 2013)

Harris, Cliff, *Tales from the Dallas Cowboys* (Champaign, IL: Sports Pub., 2006)

El Paso

■ The City in Brief

Founded: 1598 (incorporated 1873)

Head Official: Mayor Oscar Leeser (since 2014; current term expires 2017)

City Population
>1990: 515,342
>2000: 563,662
>2010: 649,121
>2012 estimate: 672,534
>Percent change, 2000–2010: 15.2%
>U.S. rank in 1990: 22nd
>U.S. rank in 2000: 22nd (State rank: 5th)
>U.S. rank in 2010: 19th (State rank: 6th)

Metropolitan Statistical Area Population
>2000: 682,966
>2010: 800,647
>2012 estimate: 827,398
>Percent change, 2000–2010: 17.2%
>U.S. rank in 2000: 69th
>U.S. rank in 2010: 66th

Area: 249 square miles

Elevation: Average 3,762 feet above sea level

Average Annual Temperatures: January, 45.1° F; July, 83.3° F; annual average, 64.7° F

Average Annual Precipitation: 9.43 inches of rain; 5.3 inches of snow

Major Economic Sectors: agriculture, clothing, oil, retail, military

Unemployment Rate: 4.6% (2012)

Per Capita Income: $19,090

2012 FBI Crime Index Property: 16,411

Major Colleges and Universities: University of Texas at El Paso, El Paso Community College, New Mexico State University, and Texas Tech University Health Sciences Center

Daily Newspaper: *El Paso Times*

■ Introduction

The county seat of El Paso County, El Paso is located on the far western edge of Texas on the north bank of the Rio Grande, near the intersection of Texas, New Mexico, and Mexico. The sixth largest city in Texas, El Paso is the 22nd largest city in the United States and one of the country's fastest-growing metropolitan areas. At Mexico's border, El Paso and its Mexican sister city, Ciudad Juárez (in Chihuahua, Mexico), have downtowns that are within walking distance from one another. The fertile valley and surrounding mountains of El Paso del Norte (the Pass of the North), christened by Don Juan de Oñate in 1598, was the first all-weather pass through the Rockies. El Paso is a major transportation hub and is known for its cutting-edge medical facilities, top educational institutions, year-round recreation, vibrant cultural and entertainment life, and favorable cost of living. Additionally, one of the U.S. Army's largest installations, Fort Bliss, has made El Paso its home for over 150 years. El Paso boasts a diverse population, with a majority of its residents speaking both English and Spanish. El Paso attracts new residents with its favorable weather, tax rates, comparably low cost of living, and multiple educational opportunities. Despite the vicious drug cartel war that has turned Juárez, just across the border, into one of the deadliest cities in the world, in 2013, for the third time in a row, El Paso received the "lowest crime rate ranking" of cities with

Frontpage/Shutterstock.com

more than 500,000 people in the annual City Crime Rankings by CQ Press.

■ Geography and Climate

Located in the westernmost corner of Texas, El Paso resides in the Chihuahuan Desert at the confluence of Texas, New Mexico, and Mexico, nestled between the Franklin Mountains and the Rio Grande. With only about 9 inches of precipitation per year, a summer high of 95 degrees and mild winter temperatures, El Paso residents enjoy sun about 300 days of the year. Rainfall generally occurs during the summer from July through September, when weather conditions cause thunderstorms, some severe enough to produce flash flooding and hail, across the region.

Area: 249 square miles

Elevation: Average 3,762 feet above sea level

Average Temperatures: January, 45.1° F; July, 83.3° F; annual average, 64.7° F

Average Annual Precipitation: 9.43 inches of rain; 5.3 inches of snow

■ History

Spanish Lay Claim over a Vast Land

Inhabited for centuries by various Indian groups, El Paso saw its first Europeans when Spaniards passed through in the mid-1500s. During 1540 to 1542, an expedition under Francisco Vázquez de Coronado explored the area now known as the American Southwest. These earliest Spanish explorers saw on their approach from the Rio Grande two mountain ranges rising from the desert, with a deep chasm between. They named the site "El Paso del Norte," or "the Pass of the North." The Rodríguez-Sánchez expedition in 1581 was the first party of Spaniards to explore the Pass of the North, bringing about the beginning of El Paso's modern history. Further expeditions followed, culminating in an April 30, 1598 ceremony near the site of present-day San Elizario in which expedition leader Juan de Oñate took formal possession of the territory drained by the Rio del Norte (now the Rio Grande). Called "La Toma," (the claiming) this act brought Spanish civilization to the Pass of the North, laying the foundation for more than two centuries of Spanish rule.

Population of the area grew when the Pueblo Indian Revolt of 1680 sent Spanish colonists and Tigua Indians of New Mexico southward in search of safety. By 1682, five settlements were thriving on the south bank of the Rio Grande. By the middle of the eighteenth century, approximately 5,000 people populated the El Paso area; among them were Spaniards, *mestizos,* and Indians. The region became known for its vineyards, with residents producing wine and brandy. In 1789, the presidio of San Elizario was founded to defend the El Paso settlements against encroaching Apaches.

Spanish Rule Ends, Tensions Begin

With Mexico's independence from Spain in 1821, the entire El Paso area became part of Mexico. Agriculture and commerce flourished, but the unpredictable levels of the Rio Grande made for difficulties with crops, fields, and structures frequently damaged by the rising water levels. In the 1830s, the river flooded much of the lower Rio Grande valley, creating a new channel and displacing several towns.

May 1846 saw more difficulties as hostilities erupted between the United States and Mexico. During the Mexican War, Col. Alexander Doniphan and a force of American volunteers defeated Mexican fighters at the battle of Brazito, entering El Paso del Norte. The Treaty of Guadalupe Hidalgo on February 2, 1848, ended the dispute and again changed the boundary between the two nations, bringing El Paso territory under the blanket of the United States.

El Paso's settlements grew in 1849 as easterners rushed west in search of gold. Lines between Mexico and the United States were revised yet again; this time the three Mexican towns of Ysleta, Socorro, and San Elizario ended up on the United States side of the line. The military post of Fort Bliss was established in 1858; one year later pioneer Anson Mills completed his plat of the town of El Paso. The name "El Paso" brought about confusion with the Mexican town across the Rio Grande, El Paso del Norte, so the Mexican town's name was changed to Ciudad Juárez in 1888.

During the Civil War, El Paso's alliance was to the South, though the Union presided and local Southern sympathizers eventually received pardons. In 1877, Texans and Mexicans became embroiled in a bitter civil war, the Salt War of San Elizario, which lasted six months.

A Modern City Emerges

A rail system was established through the area in 1881-82, which transformed the village into a lively frontier community with a growing population. El Paso's early years are tinted by a colorful reputation from its many saloons, brothels, and high crime. By 1890 citizens were demanding reform, and by 1905 El Paso ordinances banned gambling and prostitution. At the turn of the century El Paso's frontier image was fading and its fresh start as a modern city began. The population grew from 15,906 in 1900 to 77,560 in just 25 years. Refugees of the Mexican Revolution contributed to the city's growth,

as did burgeoning commercial, industrial, agricultural, and transportation business, along with El Paso's strategic location as a gateway to Mexico. Meanwhile, prohibition in the United States boosted the city's tourism as neighboring residents flocked to El Paso to cross the border for drinking and gambling in Juárez.

In the latter half of the nineteenth century, commercial developments in El Paso expanded. The Kansas City Smelting and Refining Company constructed a large smelter at El Paso in 1887, becoming the American Smelting and Refining Company (ASARCO) in 1899. The completion of Elephant Butte Dam in 1916 in New Mexico ensured a steady water supply for agricultural development in the area and helped cotton to become the predominant local crop. Standard Oil Company of Texas (now Chevron USA), Texaco, and Phelps Dodge located major refineries in El Paso in 1928 and 1929. In 1930 census reports showed 102,421 residents in El Paso, though the city's growth began to slow soon after with the census reporting only 96,810 residents in 1940. After the war, development brought new residents and the 1950 census once again showed growth, with 130,003 people living in El Paso. Fort Bliss grew as well in the 1940s and 1950s. The 1960 census saw a doubling of residents; steady growth continued and by 1970 the population was 339,615. El Paso's population grew again when the city absorbed the Mexican town of Isleta, stretching the reaches of the metropolitan area even further. By the mid-1980s, Fort Bliss' military personnel and family members made up nearly a quarter of the city's population. Petroleum, textiles, tourism, metals, cement, and food processing became major industries by the 1980s.

Struggles at the Turn of the Century

Throughout the 1990s, El Paso's economy suffered from competition with low labor rates from abroad and the closure of its main copper smelter, ASARCO, in 1999. El Paso has also developed the unpleasant distinction of being one of the main entry points for drug smuggling into the United States, an attribute that has plagued the area for decades.

The North American Free Trade Agreement (NAFTA) passage helped local service and transportation firms to expand their businesses, especially when used in conjunction with El Paso's Foreign Trade Zone (FTZ) 68, which encompasses over 2,500 acres in 17 non-contiguous sites. FTZ 68 is the lowest cost and second highest volume general purpose FTZ in the United States. In 2013 it was ranked second in the Top 25 Foreign Trade Zones by *Global Trade* magazine.

Since El Paso is sensitive to changes in Mexico's economy and U.S. and Mexican relations, the devaluation of the Mexican peso in the 1990s and the border traffic controls instituted after the September 11, 2001, terrorist attacks both affected El Paso's economy. The area continues to recover from these incidences, and ill reputation. Nonetheless, the El Paso of today consists of a rich mix of history, culture, a strong military presence, and the excitement of an international border town.

Historical Information: Texas State Historical Association, 1 University Station D0901, Austin, TX 78712-0332; telephone (512) 471-1525; fax (512) 471-1551.

■ Population Profile

Metropolitan Statistical Area Population

2000: 682,966
2010: 800,647
2012 estimate: 827,398
Percent change, 2000–2010: 17.2%
U.S. rank in 2000: 69th
U.S. rank in 2010: 66th

City Residents

1990: 515,342
2000: 563,662
2010: 649,121
2012 estimate: 672,534
Percent change, 2000–2010: 15.2%
U.S. rank in 1990: 22nd
U.S. rank in 2000: 22nd (State rank: 5th)
U.S. rank in 2010: 19th (State rank: 6th)

Density: 2,543.2 people per square mile

Racial and ethnic characteristics

White: 563,281
Black or African American: 25,380
American Indian and Alaskan Native: 3,785
Asian: 8,582
Native Hawaiian and Other Pacific Islander: 1,066
Hispanic or Latino (may be of any race): 532,185
Other: 70,440

Percent of residents born in state: 56.4%

Age characteristics

Population under 5 years old: 51,521
Population 5 to 9 years old: 53,458
Population 10 to 14 years old: 52,526
Population 15 to 19 years old: 54,654
Population 20 to 24 years old: 52,663
Population 25 to 34 years old: 92,977
Population 35 to 44 years old: 85,255
Population 45 to 54 years old: 83,567
Population 55 to 59 years old: 37,248
Population 60 to 64 years old: 29,824
Population 65 to 74 years old: 42,478
Population 75 to 84 years old: 26,272
Population 85 years and over: 10,091
Median age: 32.2

Births (2010–11 Metropolitan Area)

Total number: 13,862

Deaths (2010–11 Metropolitan Area)

Total number: 4,572

Money income (2012)

Per capita income: $19,090
Median household income: $40,920
Total households: 216,792

Number of households with income of . . .

less than $10,000: 21,396
$10,000 to $14,999: 16,299
$15,000 to $24,999: 30,036
$25,000 to $34,999: 26,221
$35,000 to $49,999: 33,572
$50,000 to $74,999: 36,707
$75,000 to $99,999: 20,761
$100,000 to $149,999: 19,996
$150,000 to $199,999: 6,521
$200,000 or more: 5,283

Percent of families below poverty level: 21.9%

FBI Crime Index Property: 16,411

FBI Crime Index Violent: 2,859

■ Municipal Government

El Paso operates under a council-manager form of government, begun in 2004. Previously, El Paso was one of the last strong mayor holdouts in the state of Texas. The mayor presides over the elected council, which hires a professional manager to carry out its directives and oversee the delivery of public services. The mayor is elected every four years; the eight council members are also elected and serve staggered four-year terms. The city manager oversees operations. Residents, who are appointed by the council or the mayor, serve as volunteers on a variety of boards and commissions that help to steer the direction of municipal issues.

Head Official: Mayor Oscar Leeser (since 2014; current term expires 2017)

Total Number of City Employees: 5,772 (2012)

City Information: City of El Paso, 2 Civic Center Plaza, El Paso, TX, 79901; telephone (915)541-4000.

■ Economy

Major Industries and Commercial Activity

After the departure of ASARCO, a major copper smelting operation and important element of El Paso's economy, the city suffered a minor slump in economic activity in the early 2000s. Once a major copper refining area, chief manufacturing industries in El Paso now include food production, clothing, construction materials, electronic and medical equipment, and plastics. Cotton, fruit, vegetables, livestock, and pecans are also produced in the area. Several large companies, including Eureka, Leviton, Hoover, Boeing, and Delphi, have offices in the area. In 2013 *Fortune* 500 company Western Refinery, an oil refinery, was still headquartered in El Paso, with its major operations on 555 acres of land near the city. El Paso was once home to El Paso Natural Gas, which moved to Houston in the 1990s, and Petro Stopping Centers, another *Fortune* 500, until it was acquired by TravelCenters of America in 2007. Helen of Troy Limited, a NASDAQ-listed company and manufacturer of personal care electrical products, is headquartered in El Paso. The company manufactures products under recognizable brands licensed from Vidal Sassoon, Revlon, Dr. Scholl's, Sunbeam, Health o meter, Sea Breeze, and Vitapoint. Other major headquarters include Spira Footwear and Fred Loya Insurance.

El Paso is an important entry point to the United States from Mexico, with four separate international points of entry, and this gateway has led to increased business opportunities. With El Paso's attractive climate and natural beauty, tourism and trade with neighboring Ciudad Juárez, Mexico, have brought economic stability. The maquila industry, which is centered just across the border in Mexico and assembles foreign goods for export, plays a role in attracting companies to El Paso. Maquila, or maquiladora, refers to manufacturing in another country The maquiladoras became attractive to U.S. firms due to the availability of more affordable labor across the border, in addition to favorable custom and trade laws.

Education is also a driving force in El Paso's economy. El Paso's three large school districts are among the largest employers in the area, employing more than 19,000 people between them. In addition, the University of Texas at El Paso (UTEP) is a major employer in the city. The city capitalizes on the local educated workforce to develop their technology industry. Specifically, El Paso offers a unique test bed for developing a diverse range of water-related policy and technology due to its geographic properties. El Paso sits on a complex system of underground aquifers, which contain both fresh and brackish water that span the boundaries of three states and two nations. As a result, desalination, alternative energy technologies, filtration methods, and industrial pumps and motors are developed in the area.

Call center operations constitute a number of the top business employers in El Paso. There are 22 call centers employing over 12,000 people. The largest of these in terms of employees are EchoStar, West Telemarketing, and Verizon.

Finally, the military installation of Fort Bliss is a major contributor to El Paso's economy, and has been instrumental in El Paso for over 150 years. Fort Bliss began as a Calvary post in 1848. Today, Fort Bliss is the site of the United States Army's Air Defense Center and produces approximately $80 million in products and services annually, with about $60 million of those products and services purchased locally. Fort Bliss's total economic impact on the area has been estimated at more than $1 billion, with an expected 37,000 soldiers stationed in the area by 2012. In addition to the military, the federal government has a strong presence in El Paso to manage its status and unique issues as a border region. The Immigration and Naturalization Service (INS), the Drug Enforcement Agency (DEA), and the U.S. Customs Service all have agency operations in El Paso to regulate traffic and goods through ports of entry from Mexico.

Situated on the border of two nations and three states, El Paso's location presents unique opportunities. El Paso and Ciudad Juárez comprise the largest metropolitan area on the border between the United States and Mexico. Into the future, the region is focused business development and relocation of military, defense, homeland security, health and life science, clean technologies, and automotive manufacturing, engineering, and research.

Items and goods produced: petroleum, metals, medical devices, plastics, machinery, automotive parts, food, defense-related goods, tourism, boots

Incentive Programs-New and Existing Companies

El Paso's economy is impacted significantly by the Mexican government's Maquiladora Program. Established in 1965, the program was created to help alleviate unemployment on the U.S.-Mexico border by allowing non-Mexican companies to establish manufacturing operations in Mexico to produce goods for exportation. El Paso's sister city Ciudad Juárez has more than 340 such plants employing approximately 210,000 workers, many of them El Paso residents. Many of the maquiladora plants established in Ciudad Juárez are owned by *Fortune* 500 companies operating in telecommunications, manufacturing of medical supplies, consumer appliances, electronics, and automotive parts. The Texas Workforce Commission (TWC) provides assistance to new companies in screening and pre-qualifying applicants for employment to the client's specifications. TWC is also the agency for the Federal Targeted Job Tax Credits Program. The state of Texas targets many of its incentive programs toward smaller and rural communities. Generally, this assists the economy, but also makes the city's economy sensitive to political issues in Mexico, such as the major issues of drug and gang violence in the border regions.

Local programs: The City of El Paso gives consideration for tax abatements for projects within specified

Strategic Redevelopment Zones. The Tax Abatement Policy is organized to stimulate capital investment needed for residential, retail, commercial, and industrial redevelopment within the zones. The city also provides green building grants and multifamily housing incentives. In addition, downtown development incentives are aplenty. The façade improvement program provides up to $10,000 in grant funds for façade improvements to encourage renovation and rehabilitation of the exterior of buildings in the downtown area. Development permit fees may be reduced in the tax increment reinvestment zones (TIRZs), and tax exemption is available for historic properties. The city also has the Green Building Grant Program, designed to encourage development of energy efficient buildings. The program provides grants for achieving LEED certification for new construction or major renovations of commercial or mixed-use developments. Grant awards start at $50,000 and increase up to $200,000. For certain downtown areas, grant awards double to a maximum of $400,000.

The El Paso Regional Economic Development Corporation also provides certain incentives for the El Paso region (including Ciudad Juárez and southern New Mexico). Tax exemptions are available on property and on inventory. Import duty reduction assistance is available. Grants are provided for job creation. El Paso Electric, a local utility, also began offering energy efficiency and alternative energy incentives in the late 2000s.

State programs: Texas is a right-to-work state. The Texas economy has performed better than that of any other state during the recent economic downturn. It is believed that this success is due in part to the states pro-business climate, of which economic incentives are an important part.

The Texas Enterprise Zone Programs offer tax abatement at the local level, and refunds of state sales and use taxes under certain circumstances to businesses operating in enterprise zone areas. The Texas Enterprise Zone Program allows local communities to partner with the State of Texas to promote job creation and capital investment in targeted areas of the state that meet specific economic criteria. Designated projects are eligible to apply for state sales and use tax refunds on qualified expenditures. The state of Texas targets many of its incentive programs toward smaller and rural communities. The Rural Municipal Finance Program is a loan program created by the Texas Agricultural Finance Authority (TAFA) to stimulate economic activity in rural Texas. The Texas Enterprise Fund can be used to provide deal-closing money for companies relocating to and investing in Texas. The Texas Emerging Technology Fund, a $200 million fund created by the Texas Legislature in 2005, is available to companies who seek to commercialize new technologies. The program provides grants for early-stage investments in new, technology-based, private entrepreneurial entities that collaborate with public or private institutions of higher education.

Texas is one of the few states with no individual income tax, a very attractive environment for transferring employees. There is also no corporate income tax. Texas Enterprise Zone Program provides for eligible designated projects to apply for state sales and use tax refunds on purchases of all taxable items purchased for use at the qualified business site related to the project or activity. Special tax exemptions are made for manufacturing machinery, equipment, replacement parts, and accessories that have a useful life of more than six months. Texas businesses are also exempt from paying state sales and use tax on labor for constructing new facilities, electricity and natural gas used in manufacturing, processing, or fabrication. Tax-Exempt Industrial Revenue Bonds are designed to provide tax-exempt financing up to $20 million per project to finance land and depreciable property for eligible industrial or manufacturing projects.

The Texas Capital Fund Infrastructure and Real Estate Development programs are designed to provide no interest loans of up to $750,000 to non-entitlement communities. The program funds real estate developments (acquisitions, construction, and/or rehabilitation) to assist a business, which commits to creating or retaining permanent jobs, primarily for low and moderate-income persons.

Job training programs: The Greater El Paso Chamber Foundation and a coalition of El Paso workforce development agencies partnered to develop The Center for Workforce Preparedness. The Center houses several agencies and projects, and helps custom-train workers for local businesses. The Upper Rio Grande Work organization (also known as Workforce Solutions) provides help with recruitment, job fairs, locating tax incentive programs, researching labor and employment laws, labor market details, and other services. On-the-Job Training allows participants to work for an employer, receive payment, and develop the skills necessary to continue working. The program provides reimbursement to the employer for up to half of the wages paid for a maximum of three months. The Advanced Technology Center at El Paso Community College provides workforce training for local industry. The College also administers programs through the Workforce Development Center, the Career Training Center, and other centers throughout its four campuses.

The Texas Workforce Commission administers the Skills Development Fund, which helps Texas community and technical colleges finance customized job-training programs for local businesses. Qualifying companies are allowed, through the Texas Skills Development Fund, up to $1,200 per trainee and are limited to $500,000 per project. The state's Self-Sufficiency Fund is a job-training program that is specifically designed for individuals that receive Temporary Assistance for Needy Families (TANF) money. The fund makes grants available to eligible public colleges or to eligible private, non-profit organizations to provide customized job training and training support services for specific employers. The goal of the Fund is to assist TANF recipients become independent of government financial assistance.

Development Projects

The city of El Paso has been involved in about $440 million in extensive improvement projects since 2000, when a plan for specific "Quality of Life Capital Improvements" was approved to span a 10-year period, with additional transportation projects to be prioritized and completed between 2011 and 2017. Under the plan, new zoo facilities were completed, and a new $6.65 million History Museum building opened in 2007. New fire stations and various improvements to city parks and libraries were also completed.

The effect of Fort Bliss on El Paso is also evident in development. In 2009 the base was in the midst of a $4.1 billion expansion to accommodate an additional 28,000 soldiers and 53,000 family members expected to relocate to the area by 2012, when the base population peaked at about 37,000 soldiers. The expansion, started in 2007, has turned East Fort Bliss into a small city. The expansion includes infrastructure, new office buildings, barracks, new dining facilities, a mini mall, a dental facility, and a future medical clinic, in addition to renovations of the main post.

Unexpected heavy rainstorms in the summer of 2006 decimated large portions of the El Paso downtown area, necessitating a large-scale rebuilding effort. Streets in the downtown area, including Franklin Avenue, Mesa Street, Mills Avenue, Oregon Street, Stanton Street, and Santa Fe Street, were rebuilt. In late 2006 initial plans were approved for the Downtown 2015 Land-Use Plan, a long-term, large-scale redevelopment plan for the downtown area, with five separate zones designated for redevelopment in order to make downtown the commercial heart of the city.

In 2013 improvements to Downtown El Paso included approval of an additional $4.5 million by city council for improvements to the 62,000-square-foot Luther Building, which is being renovated to make room for city offices. The San Jacinto Plaza was also under renovation. Improvements include more shade trees, sidewalk benches, and an outdoor cafe with an adjacent seating area. Chess and game tables will be added as well as a horseshoe pit. Also included will be a "splash deck" with interactive water features, an arroyo that runs underneath a walkway in the southeastern quadrant, and a central stage overlooking the reflecting pool/sculpture area in the center of the park. The El Paso Chihuahuas are the newest Triple-A baseball team in the country. The team broke ground on a new 11,500-seat stadium scheduled for completion in spring 2014.

The $500 million Border Highway West extension project is scheduled to begin in 2015. The nine-mile project would create a tolled expressway from downtown El Paso, where Loop 375 currently ends, north and west to a point just south of Interstate 10 at Paisano intersection near Sunland Park.

As of 2013, projected development projects also included new plans for the Franklin Mountains State Park entrance on El Paso's far Northwest Side, which will include a new hiking and wildlife underpass. Future retail developments include a 14.9-acre shopping center at the corner of South Desert Boulevard and Redd Road, and a potential new "big box" development at the corner of Paseo Del Norte Boulevard and North Desert Boulevard.

Economic Development Information: City of El Paso Department of Economic Development, 2 Civic Center Plaza, El Paso, TX 79901; telephone (915) 533-4284; fax (915) 541-1316.

Commercial Shipping

According to the U.S. Department of Transportation, El Paso is the nation's "fifth busiest land border gateway by value for imports and exports transported across the border by highways, railroads, and pipelines." Over $40 billion in merchandise trade passes through El Paso annually, or 7 percent of the national total. The combined land ports of Laredo, El Paso, and Hidalgo, all in Texas, handle trade valued at $170 billion. Trucks carry most of the freight passing through the city, followed by rail. The Union Pacific Railway provides intermodal and other services to Los Angeles, Chicago, and Dallas. The Burlington Northern Santa Fe Railroad also travels to Los Angeles and Chicago. In addition, oil products are delivered from Western's El Paso refinery by truck, rail, and pipeline. There are three product pipelines out of El Paso. Plains Pipeline operates a line to Belen and Albuquerque, New Mexico, and a line to Ciudad Juárez. Kinder Morgan operates a line from El Paso to Tucson and Phoenix, Arizona. Western ships on all of these pipeline systems.

El Paso's position as an international gateway means it is a major thoroughfare for imports and exports. In 2012 total El Paso exports were $29 billion. Mexico, Germany, Japan, Spain, and China are the leading sources of foreign direct investment. El Paso's Foreign Trade Zone did business with over 40 countries.

Labor Force and Employment Outlook

In the mid-1990s, half of El Paso's 50,000 manufacturing jobs were in the apparel and textile industry. Due to the devaluation of the Mexican peso in that decade, several large apparel manufacturers relocated over the border to Mexico, taking jobs with them. Growth in other areas have attempted to make up for this decline, however, as El Paso's job growth continues to rise after a rocky beginning to the twenty-first century. Still, El Paso's unemployment rate remains higher than the national average. Nonetheless, El Paso's labor force has shown a steady growth over the past decade. International trade in the region, stimulated by the North American Free Trade Act (NAFTA) and the Mexican Maquiladora Program, has helped ensure El Paso's success in the global economy. Jobs in globalization and information technology are helping to revitalize the area's economy after its past dependency on ever-reducing manufacturing jobs.

In 2012 El Paso had a younger, more robust workforce population relative to Texas, New Mexico, and the nation. The median age in the Greater El Paso region was just 31.1 years, versus 33.5 years in Texas, 35.8 years in New Mexico, and 36.9 years in the nation. This demographic appeals to firms seeking access to younger talent.

The following is a summary of data regarding the 2012 El Paso labor force:

Size of civilian labor force: 288,300

Number of workers employed in . . .

agriculture and mining: 1,763
construction: 14,788
manufacturing: 18,332
wholesale trade: 7,529
retail trade: 32,941
transportation: 16,562
information systems: 5,805
finance: 14,205
professional administration: 23,853
education and social services: 69,871
arts and leisure: 24,203
other: 12,262
public administration: 20,433

Average hourly earnings of production workers: $12.56

Unemployment rate: 4.6% (2012)

Employers

Largest private employers (2012)

	Number of employees
T&T Staff Management LP	5,020
University Medical Center	2,455
Dish Network	1,800
Alorica	1,755
Texas Tech University Health Sciences Center	1,546
GC Services	1,526
Del Sol Medical Center	1,400
RM Personnel	1,368
Automatic Data Processing, Inc.	1,200
El Paso Electric Corporation	1,000
Visiting Nurse Association of El Paso	900
Las Palmas Medical Center	850
West Customer Management Group	800
Redcats USA Inc.	800
Union Pacific Railroad Co. Inc.	750
Western Refining	700
Datamark	600
Coca-Cola Enterprises	500

Cost of Living

El Paso's cost of living, as well as its housing prices, were below the national average as of 2013. Meanwhile, household incomes have increased.

The following is a summary of data regarding several key cost of living factors in the area.

2013 ACCRA Average House Price: $238,259

2013 ACCRA Cost of Living Index: 93

State income tax rate: None

State sales tax rate: 6.25%

Local income tax rate: None

Local sales tax rate: 2.0%

Property tax rate: 0.678378 mills (2013)

Economic Information: Office of Economic Development, City of El Paso, 2 Civic Center Plaza, 1st Floor, El Paso, TX 79901; telephone (915) 533-4284; fax (915) 541-1316.

■ Education and Research

Elementary and Secondary Schools

El Paso County is served by nine school districts. Of those nine, El Paso city public schools are divided into three districts: the El Paso Independent School District, Ysleta Independent School District, and Socorro Independent School District.

The El Paso Independent School District (EPISD) is the largest, educating about 64,000 students on 94 campuses. It is the 10th largest district in Texas and the

61st largest district in the United States. About 80 percent of the students are Hispanic/Latino. The EPISD offers magnet and alternative programs, including The Academy of International Business and Public Affairs at Bowie High; Silva Health Magnet's curriculum, which focuses on health and sciences; and Connecting Worlds/ Mundos Unidos, which focuses on bilingual education.

The Ysleta Independent School District (YISD) is the second largest in the area, educating about 44,000 students. The district has 62 campuses and employs 8,000 administrators, teachers and support staff. There are 37 elementary schools, 7 high, 11 middle, 3 pre-kindergarten, and 6 special campuses. The district was named a national Broad Prize finalist for two consecutive years in 2010 and 2011. The Broad Prize is awarded to urban school districts that demonstrate the greatest overall performance and improvement in student achievement while reducing achievement gaps among low-income and minority students. In addition, 10 campuses have been designated as National Blue Ribbon Schools.

Though large in its own right, the Socorro Independent School District is the smallest district of the three but one of the fastest growing school districts in the state. The district educates about 44,000 students. In 2013 the district had 45 campuses, including 5 comprehensive high schools, 1 ninth grade academy, 9 middle schools, 6 pre-kindergarten schools, 20 elementary schools, and 4 specialty campuses. More than 90 percent of students are of Hispanic origin. The district been named a two-time Broad Prize finalist and has earned TEA Recognized status three years in a row. The Student Activities Complex includes an 11,000-seat stadium, and the adjacent Aquatic Center, also open throughout the year, has indoor and outdoor pools. The district is one of the fastest-growing in Texas.

More than 25 parochial and 50 private schools educate El Paso students. The Catholic Diocese of El Paso maintains 11 schools serving more than 4,000 students. Many of El Paso's private schools have received national awards: Loretto Academy for girls and St. Clement's Episcopal Parish School are both recipients of the Blue Ribbon award, a prestigious standing for high-performing schools. Other private schools offer technical programs, specialized programs, or mechanical education.

The following is a summary of data regarding the El Paso Independent School District.

Total enrollment: 64,330

Number of facilities

> total: 94
> elementary schools: 58
> junior high schools: 17
> high schools: 13
> other: 6

Student/teacher ratio: 14.62:1

Teacher salaries

> average (statewide): $48,261

Funding per pupil: $8,297

Public Schools Information: El Paso Independent School District, 6531 Boeing Drive, El Paso, TX 79925; telephone (915) 230-2000.

Colleges and Universities

El Paso higher education institutions offer undergraduate and graduate degrees in engineering, business, science, education, health sciences, and liberal arts as well as associate degrees and certification programs in technology.

The University of Texas at El Paso (UTEP), known as Texas Western College until 1967, prides itself on its status as the only major research university in the country with the majority of its students being predominately Mexican American. Its location is quite close to the Mexican border, in the Chihuahuan Desert. UTEP is the second oldest member of the University of Texas system. From its humble beginnings in 1914 as a small mining school, UTEP is now a recognized institution with an enrollment of about 22,000. UTEP ranks in the top five among schools awarding undergraduate degrees to Hispanics. *Hispanic Business Magazine* has ranked it as the top graduate engineering school for Hispanics. It is the only such university to be classified RU/H, research universities with high research activity, by the Carnegie Foundation.

Other colleges include branch campuses of the Texas Tech University Health Sciences Center and College of Architecture. Texas Tech University's Health Sciences Center at El Paso confers degrees in medicine, nursing, pharmacy, and in biomedical and allied health sciences. In nearby Las Cruces, New Mexico, New Mexico State University's five campuses educate more than 23,000 students, many of whom are El Paso residents. Another regional educational institution, Howard Payne University operates an extension campus in the city. In addition, several two-year colleges exist, including El Paso Community College, International Business College, Western Technical College, and the Doña Ana Branch Community College (actually part of the New Mexico State University system). The University of Phoenix, Park University, and Webster University operate campuses in El Paso.

Libraries and Research Centers

The El Paso Public Library was the first public library in the state of Texas. Now, the main branch is a 110,000-square-foot learning center, with a 250-seat auditorium and computer labs and classrooms. The system operates a main library, 13 branches, a bookmobile, and a literacy center. The main library also features the Border Heritage collection of manuscripts. Throughout the 2000s, many of the libraries underwent renovations, and its newest library opened in 2010.

The University of Texas at El Paso (UTEP) Library houses over 1.2 million books, 1 million microforms, and 200,000 government documents in its 6-floor, 275,000-square-foot facility. The library sits atop a hill with a view of the Mexican border and is built in the Bhutanese style of architecture, like many of the university's structures. Other libraries include the Texas Tech University Health Sciences Library at El Paso and the El Paso Community College library system.

The University of Texas at El Paso's research expenditures exceeded $76 million in 2013. The National Institutes of Health awarded UTEP and the University of Texas Houston Health Science Center more than $4 million to establish the Hispanic Health Disparities Research Center at the UTEP campus, which seeks to build the capacity for researchers to reduce health disparities in Hispanic and other minorities. The Border Biomedical Research Center is a preeminent institute focusing on health and biomedical issues affecting the people of the El Paso/Juárez region of the Texas-Mexico border. It is housed in a new $45 million, 140,000-square-foot Bioscience Research Building. Other research centers at UTEP include the Center for Environmental Resource Management, the Center for Transportation Infrastructure Systems, the Institute for Manufacturing and Materials Management, the Materials Research & Technology Institute, and the W.M. Keck Border Biomedical Manufacturing and Engineering Laboratory. Recently opened research centers include the Paso del Norte Research and Business Development Complex. It houses four new research facilities focusing on policy and economic development, economic forecasting, science, and entrepreneur development.

Public Library Information: El Paso Public Library, 501 N. Oregon, El Paso, TX; telephone (915) 543-5401.

■ Health Care

El Paso's 9 hospitals, with approximately 2,200 beds total, serve the general public and the military in El Paso and bordering areas of Mexico. The Las Palmas Regional Healthcare System's facilities include the Las Palmas Medical Center and Heart Institute hospital, the new Emergency Room and Intensive Care Unit, the Rehabilitation Hospital, the Life Care Center, the Regional Oncology and Wound Management Center, the Diabetes Treatment Center, and the Del Sol Medical Center. Specialties include women's and children's services, oncology, heart health, and surgical services. The system's Rehabilitation Hospital is a 40-bed center specializing in treatment of strokes, spinal cord injuries, and other orthopedic or neurological diagnosis.

The Sierra Providence Health Network operates three hospitals consisting of two acute care hospitals (Sierra Medical Center and Providence Memorial Hospital) and a physical rehabilitation hospital (Sierra Providence Physical Rehabilitation Hospital), with a total of 927 beds. Other centers include The Children's Hospital at Providence and the Sierra Providence Eastside Hospital.

The University Medical Center of El Paso, formerly known as Thomason Hospital, is the city's only not-for-profit, community-owned hospital and health-care system and a regional referral center for patients in need of specialty care. It is the only El Paso hospital ever to be named one of America's Top 100 hospitals. Located directly on the U.S.-Mexico border, the center has affiliation agreements with virtually all of the region's educational institutions, including the Texas Tech University School of Medicine, which designated the center as its primary teaching site. It is home to the region's only Level 1 trauma center, and is designated to treat the President of the United States, should he require care while travelling in the region. The center also runs neighborhood C.A.R.E.S. clinics, which are primary care centers.

The William Beaumont Army Medical Center specializes in trauma care and is one of the largest U.S. Army general hospitals in the country.

■ Recreation

Sightseeing

The El Paso area's attractions celebrate the region's rich history and culture, as well as its natural resources of the Franklin Mountains and the Rio Grande. El Paso natural assets are perfect for the outdoor enthusiast. The Franklin Mountains provide a stunning backdrop to hiking, rock climbing, picnicking, or even concert-going at the McKelligon Amphitheatre. Visitors unafraid of heights would enjoy the Wyler Aerial Tramway at Franklin Mountains State Park, which features an aerial cable car situated above rugged mountain and rock formations on the east side of the Franklin Mountains. Another interesting feature are the Kilbourne and Hunt holes, craters (formally known as "maars") formed by old volcanic activity without a mountainous rim, located west of the Franklin Mountains. El Paso is also within several hours drive of other notable natural western landmarks, such as the Hueco Tanks (a low mountain area containing water-holding depressions in the boulders and rock faces), Guadalupe Mountains National Park, and White Sands National Monument.

Magoffin Home State Historic Site is a 1.5-acre park and homage to pioneer Joseph Magoffin. The centerpiece of the park is the Magoffin Home, built in 1875 by Magoffin. The 19-room adobe home, built in the

Territorial style of architecture, showcases period style with mid-Victorian wood trim and original appointments. Guided tours offer a glimpse into the life of the Magoffin family, who occupied the home until its sale to the city of El Paso in 1976.

The Chamizal National Memorial is part of the National Parks system. Established to commemorate diplomatic relations between Mexico and the United States in 1963, Chamizal honors the peaceful settlement of a century-long boundary dispute between neighboring counties. Visitors can learn about this historic event at the Chamizal Museum or through interpretive performances at the indoor theatre. The Los Paisanos Gallery features the work of local and international artists in a variety of media; the gallery also hosts traveling museum exhibits.

Downtown El Paso's "Museum Row" includes the Museum of Art, El Paso Museum of History, and Insights El Paso Science Center. The El Paso Museum of Art is a celebrated fine arts museum housing a permanent collection of more than 5,000 works of art, including the Samuel H. Kress Collection of European art from the thirteenth through eighteenth centuries, American art from the nineteenth and twentieth centuries, Mexican colonial art, and contemporary art from the southwestern United States and Mexico. Temporary exhibitions, educational programs, lectures, and concerts are part of the museum's yearly event schedule. The Museum of History showcases the colorful people who shaped El Paso's history. Insights El Paso Science Center, a privately funded institute, features 60 hands-on exhibits that teach visitors about all aspects of science. Temporary exhibits, classes, and a "Museum on Wheels" round out Insights' offerings to the community.

The Museum of Archaeology at Wilderness Park showcases prehistoric artifacts from the Southwest, including pottery, stone objects, basketry, weavings, and figurines. Exhibits tell the story of El Paso and the region's first inhabitants. The museum's 15 acres feature walking trails and gardens that highlight more than 250 native plants.

The Fort Bliss Museum resides at a reconstructed site of the original Fort. Adobe walls shelter from the heat of the summer as well as create warmth in the winter. Displays include photographs, maps, and personal items. One block south of the museum is the new Air Defense/ Artillery Museum, showcasing the history of air defense equipment. The National Border Patrol Museum highlights the work of those who tirelessly patrol the U.S./ Mexico border in El Paso. The El Paso Holocaust Museum and Study Center chronicles events of the Holocaust and memorializes those who suffered.

The Mission Trail offers visitors a glimpse into the El Paso of the past. One of the oldest roads in the country, the Mission Trail dates back more than 400 years. Along the route are three missions, one of which is the oldest building in Texas.

Arts and Culture

The city's Museums and Cultural Affairs Department (MCAD) has been working to bring art and cultural events to residents since 1978, helped by the blending of cultures in this border town. The MCAD supports local art organizations through funding, grants programs, and educational programs. The Cultural Affairs division sponsors programs including Alfresco Fridays, presenting free summer outdoor concerts at various city locations; Music Under the Stars World Festival, which offers free outdoor music from around the world on summer evenings at Chamizal National Memorial; and the Galleries program, which sponsors art exhibits at City Hall and the El Paso Regional Airport.

The Abraham Chavez Theatre, adjacent to the El Paso Convention & Performing Arts Center, hosts both the El Paso Opera and the El Paso Symphony Orchestra performances. The El Paso Opera brings full-scale, professional opera to the area in addition to several educational outreach programs. Established in the 1930s, the El Paso Symphony Orchestra is the longest continu-ously-running symphony orchestra in Texas, offering a full classical and special events season.

The El Paso Playhouse presents a year-round season of plays and a monthly Dinner Theatre performance. The Adair Margo Art Gallery on E. Yandell exhibits the work of regional, U.S., and foreign fine artists. The Ballet Folklorico Paso del Norte highlights Mexican folklore through traditional dance. The El Paso Kids-N-Co was founded in 1988 to provide a place for young thespians both to perform and to develop an appreciation of theater. It stages four large-scale productions per year, in addition to smaller seasonal plays.

Festivals and Holidays

The events calendar begins with January's El Paso Chamber Music Festival, featuring performances throughout the month of January at a variety of venues throughout the city. The Southwestern International Livestock Show and Rodeo (in its 84th year in 2013) happens at the El Paso County Coliseum and fairgrounds in January or February. Over two weekends in late February and early March, the Siglo de Oro Drama Festival is held in the Chamizal National Memorial Theatre. This annual celebration honors Spain's Golden Age with professional and collegiate performing groups from Spain, Mexico, the United States, and South America. Presentations are often performed in Spanish.

Spring events include the city's semi-annual arts and crafts fair called Art in the Park, held over a weekend in late May at Memorial Park.

Summer events include the annual Independence Day Parades, one each on the city's west and east sides. The popular "Music Under the Stars" series is free and brings both local and international performers to the Chamizal National Memorial on summer Sundays. The

Downtown Street Festival follows in downtown El Paso, with four stages featuring live performances and more than 100 booths featuring arts, crafts, food, and drink. The KLAQ "Taste of El Paso" happens mid-August at Western Playland. In addition to sampling the wares of local restaurants, visitors can enjoy rides and live entertainment. The St. Nicholas Greek Festival celebrates Greek food, music, and culture in late August at the Greek Orthodox Church.

On Labor Day weekend the Fiesta de las Flores (in its 59th year in 2013) is held at the El Paso County Coliseum and includes games, food, arts and crafts, a car show, a children's area, and a variety of entertainment options. Mexican Independence Day is celebrated mid-September at Chamizal National Memorial, and honors Mexico's independence through song and dance.

In September, the annual Chamizal Festival (entering its 39th year in 2013) celebrates the many cultural influences in the El Paso region through traditional arts and music with workshops, performances, demonstrations, and displays. Throughout October, the month-long "Celebration of Our Mountains" features events such as hikes, field trips, driving tours, nature walks, bike rides, and other activities that celebrate the Franklin Mountains. Thanksgiving Day events in El Paso include the Las Palmas Del Sol Sun Bowl Parade in downtown El Paso, and the Thanksgiving Day 5K run and 3K walk benefiting youth and teen programs at the YMCA.

For a month during late November through December, sports fans enjoy a variety of festivities related to the Hyundai Sun Bowl football game on December 31. Events include a parade, a New Year's Eve party, a 5K run, sports skills camps, and more. Visitors and residents enjoy the El Paso/Juárez Trolley Company's Christmas Light Tour, which circuits through the area's best-known seasonal sights at San Jacinto Plaza, the University of Texas at El Paso campus, Rim Road, Scenic Drive, and Eastwood.

Sports for the Spectator

While there are no major professional sports teams, the El Paso region abounds with opportunities for sports fans to watch their favorite activities. The El Paso Chihuahuas is the newest Triple-A baseball team in the country and will compete in El Paso's new downtown ballpark as an affiliate of the San Diego Padres starting in the Spring of 2014. In 2013 The El Paso Diablos, an independent minor league baseball team since 2005, played their final game at Cohen Stadium.

The Chivas El Paso Patriots play soccer as a Premier Development League (PDL) team, the fourth tier of the United Soccer Leagues pyramid. They play at Patriot Stadium, completed in 2005. The El Paso Scorpions professional rugby team has been playing since 1979 and has won 12 Rio Grande Union Championships. Their home is the 5,000 seat Dudley field, the original home of the El Paso Diablos. The El Paso Rhinos, a Junior A Tier III ice hockey team, play in the Western States Hockey League.

The University of Texas at El Paso's athletics include the Miners football, soccer, track, tennis, and men's and women's basketball. El Paso hosts the annual Hyundai Sun Bowl, one of the oldest annual college football bowl games in the country (along with the Sugar Bowl and Orange Bowl).

Sports for the Participant

El Paso's Parks & Recreation Department maintains some 175 park sites with 2,372 acres throughout the city. These parks provide 12 recreation centers, 14 city pools (8 indoor and 6 outdoor), sports and fitness programming, and senior centers. In El Paso County, Ascarate Park is the largest public-use recreational park at 448 total acres. Ascarate Park is home to a golf course, an aquatic center, and an amusement park.

Franklin Mountains State Park is the largest urban park in the nation, with 24,247 acres spanning approximately 37 miles within the city limits of El Paso. Under construction as of 2013 was a trail network that will encompass 118 miles of hiking trail, with 51 miles slated for use for both hikers and mountain bikers, and 22 miles open for hiking, mountain biking, and horseback riding. The Wyler Aerial Tramway offers riders an exhilarating four-minute gondola ride offering unmatched views of the Franklin Mountains. The park's natural rock formations invite rock climbers to the area, as well as outdoor enthusiasts who can enjoy picnic sites, shelters, and grills.

The park, 32 miles northeast of the city in El Paso County, offers some of the best rock climbing opportunities in the area. Named for its natural rock formations, the park's rock basins, or *huecos,* have furnished a supply of trapped rain water to travelers to the region for thousands of years. The park also features rock paintings from hunters and foragers from thousands of years ago, as well as from tribes of the not-so-distant past, including Apaches, Kiowas, and earlier groups. The pictographs include more than 200 paintings of faces left behind by the prehistoric Jornada Mogollon Culture. The park is the site of the last Indian battle in the county.

The Butterfield Trail golf course is designed at a par 72 over 175 acres of natural areas, featuring over 55 feet of elevation changes. With a course designed by Tom Fazio, Butterfield Trail was recognized by *Golfweek* magazine as the third-best municipal (public) course in the country in 2010. During the summer months, Wet N' Wild Waterworld in nearby Anthony, Texas, and Western Playland Amusement Park in El Paso offer family fun and adventure. Polo was often played at the Tarahumara Polo Club until it closed in 2007.

Shopping and Dining

El Paso's main shopping malls are Bassett Place Mall, Sunland Park Mall, Las Palmas Market Place, and Cielo

Vista Mall. Sunland Park is located on the west side of the city and offers four anchors and a variety of popular shops and restaurants. Bassett Center has three department stores and more than 80 specialty shops. On the east side of the city, Cielo Vista Mall features 5 department stores and more than 140 specialty shops. The Mission Trail Harvest Market is a program administered by the city in partnership with the Ysleta del Sur Pueblo Indian Tribe and the Texas Cooperative Extension. Open from June through October, the Market brings farm-fresh goods and handmade crafts for sale to the community. The Market operates at Zaragosa and Socorro Road, across from the Ysleta Mission. Bargain hunters can go to the Fox Plaza, oldest and largest swap meet in El Paso. Various *mercados* (markets) offer unique Southwest goods, as well as a variety of imported goods, such as the open-air Mercado de la Mesilla or The Pink Store. With over 12 manufacturers and retailers of boots, El Paso claims the title of "Boot Capital of the World."

While El Paso may have been known in the past as a place for steaks and traditional and often simple Mexican fare such as enchiladas, today's El Paso restaurants serve a variety of ethnic cuisines that reflect an even bigger variety of cultural influences. Dining in El Paso is a cultural blend drawing from Native Americans, Spanish Colonists, Mexican neighbors and residents, as well as Easterners drawn south for warmer climes. Ethnic and international restaurants include Chinese, Korean, German, Italian, and Middle Eastern, but the majority of El Paso's restaurants are steak houses, barbecue places, and Mexican restaurants. Highly popular in El Paso fare is the chile pepper, which is used in everything from eggs and *chorizo* (spicy sausage), to steaks, salsas, and sauces, and even on its own stuffed with cheese or meat and baked as *chiles rellenos*.

Visitor Information: El Paso Convention and Visitors Bureau, One Civic Center Plaza, El Paso, TX 79901; telephone (800) 351-6024; email info@elpasocvb.com.

■ Convention Facilities

The El Paso Convention & Performing Arts Center's Judson F. Williams Convention Center features three halls, 80,000 square feet of exhibit space, and 14,900 square feet of meeting space in 17 meeting rooms. Its Mt. Franklin Lobby offers 23,300 square feet of additional exhibit space. The Abraham Chavez Theatre, adjacent to the Center features an 800-square-foot meeting room and theatre seating for 2,500 people. The Plaza Theatre offers eating for 2,200 guests in two theatres, the Big Historic and the Philanthropy theatres. McKelligon Canyon Amphitheatre and Pavilion, nestled in the Franklin Mountains, offers another unique venue surrounded on three sides by dramatic canyon walls. McKelligon seats 1,503 in the amphitheatre and up to 300 in the pavilion.

Across the street from the Convention Center, the Camino Real El Paso has 19 meeting rooms and 36,000 square feet of meeting space that can accommodate groups of up to 1,300. Listed in the National Historic Register, the Camino Real El Paso was established in 1912 and boasts crystal chandeliers, a Tiffany cut-glass dome, and "the most photographed grand staircase in the Southwest." Other El Paso hotels, including the El Paso Suites Hotel and The Academy Hotel, offer 7,000 rooms total throughout the city.

Convention Information: El Paso Convention and Visitors Bureau, One Civic Center Plaza, El Paso, TX 79901; telephone (800) 351-6024; email info@elpasocvb.com.

■ Transportation

Approaching the City

The El Paso International Airport offers passenger services and air cargo services and is the gateway to West Texas, southern New Mexico, and northern Mexico. El Paso International Airport offers non-stop flights to more than a dozen cities and is served by five major airlines: American, Delta, Southwest, United, and US Airways. It provides an average of 136 daily arrivals and departures, serving about 3 million passengers annually. In the 2000s, $60 million was invested in an ongoing expansion effort. Once a thriving Air Force Base, Biggs Army Airfield lies adjacent to the El Paso International Airport and boasts the 10th longest runway in the United States, at 2.5 miles. Now part of Fort Bliss, the airfield is used for Army exercises and refueling. The Horizon Airport, also located in the city, is a public-use, privately owned airport for general aviation.

Two major highways transport drivers in, out, and through El Paso: Interstate 10 runs east and west, and U.S. Highway 54 runs north and south; Highway 375 loops around the outskirts of the city, through Fort Bliss, and close to downtown. Several bus lines offer service to and from El Paso. Amtrak provides passenger rail service west to California and east as far as Florida through its historic Union Depot. El Paso shares four international bridges and one railbridge with Ciudad Juárez, Mexico. In 2009 the New Mexico Department of Transportation's Park and Ride began operating a commuter bus service from El Paso to nearby Las Cruces, New Mexico.

Traveling in the City

The Franklin Mountains literally split the city of El Paso down the middle, creating what El Pasoans call the city's east and west sides. Northeast El Paso is connected to West El Paso by Woodrow Bean Transmountain Drive. The Rio Grande flows along the city's southern edge. The city is laid out around these two natural features. Sun

Metro provides bus and trolley service throughout the city, seven days a week.

■ Communications

Newspapers and Magazines

El Paso's major daily newspaper is the *El Paso Times*. The city's first Spanish language daily, *El Diario de El Paso*, was founded in 2005 and has a daily circulation over 20,000. *The Prospector* is a weekly newspaper published by the University of Texas at El Paso; *NOVA Quarterly* is also published by the university.

Television and Radio

El Paso is served by 10 full-powered television stations, of which four are affiliated with the major commercial networks, two with public broadcasting, and one with Spanish-language Univision. The city's 10 AM and 17 FM radio stations broadcast a variety of programs, from sports to talk, religious to rock, and country to Hispanic programming.

Media Information: *El Paso Times*, PO Box 20, El Paso, TX 79999; telephone (915) 546-6200.

El Paso Online

City of El Paso. Available www.ci.el-paso.tx.us
County of El Paso. Available www.co.el-paso.tx.us

El Paso Convention and Visitors Bureau. Available www.visitelpaso.com
El Paso Independent School District. Available www.episd.org
El Paso International Airport. Available www.elpasointernationalairport.com
El Paso Public Library. Available www.elpasolibrary.org
El Paso Scene. Available www.epscene.com
El Paso Times. Available www.elpasotimes.com
Fort Bliss. Available www.bliss.army.mil
Texas State Historical Association. Available www.tshaonline.org
University of Texas at El Paso. Available www.utep.edu

BIBLIOGRAPHY

Eaves, Megan, *Insiders' Guide to El Paso* (Guilford, CT: Insiders' Guide, 2010)

Haskins, Don, *Glory Road: My Story of the 1966 NCAA Basketball Championship and How One Team Triumphed Against the Odds and Changed America Forever* (New York: Hyperion, 2006)

Levario, Miguel Antonio, *Militarizing the Border: When Mexicans Became the Enemy* (College Station, TX: Texas A&M University Press, 2012)

Timmons, W.H. ed., *Four Centuries at the Pass* (El Paso, TX: Guynes Printing, 1980)

Fort Worth

■ The City in Brief

Founded: 1849 (incorporated 1873)

Head Official: Betsy Price (since 2011; current term expires 2015)

City Population
1990: 447,619
2000: 534,694
2010: 741,206
2012 estimate: 782,027
Percent change, 2000–2010: 38.6%
U.S. rank in 1990: 28th (State rank: 6th)
U.S. rank in 2000: 27th (State rank: 6th)
U.S. rank in 2010: 16th (State rank: 5th)

Metropolitan Statistical Area Population
2000: 5,221,801
2010: 6,371,773
2012 estimate: 6,647,496
Percent change, 2000–2010: 22%
U.S. rank in 2000: 5th
U.S. rank in 2010: 4th

Area: 292.5 square miles

Elevation: Ranges from 500 to 800 feet above sea level

Average Annual Temperatures: January, 44.1° F; July, 85.0° F; annual average, 65.5° F

Average Annual Precipitation: 34.73 inches of rain; 2.6 inches of snow

Major Economic Sectors: services, wholesale and retail trade, manufacturing

Unemployment Rate: 6.3% (2012)

Per Capita Income: $23,449

2012 FBI Crime Index Property: 32,514

Major Colleges and Universities: University of Texas at Arlington, Texas Christian University, Texas Wesleyan College

Daily Newspaper: *Fort Worth Star-Telegram*

■ Introduction

Fort Worth, western anchor city of the Dallas/Fort Worth Metroplex, identifies itself as "Where the West Begins." In the generally metropolitan area, Fort Worth touts itself as the "City of Cowboys and Culture." Proud of its colorful western heritage and rowdy past, the city carefully preserves its history even as it plans for the future. Within its downtown, cowboys, cattle auctions, and horse-drawn carriages coexist with cultural centers and modern office towers. Glass and steel skyscrapers housing headquarters of aviation, aerospace, and high-technology companies share sidewalks with renovated historic districts such as the Fort Worth Stockyards National Historic District and downtown's Sundance Square. The city is both an anchor of the Dallas/Fort Worth Metroplex and the Fort Worth-Arlington metropolitan area. Much like the way the West began, in recent years Fort Worth has been a boom town for business, tourists, and residents alike.

■ Geography and Climate

Fort Worth is located in the rolling hills of the Great Plains region of north-central Texas. It is the seat of Tarrant County and the major city in the western half of the Fort Worth/Dallas Metroplex. Fort Worth is 30 miles from Dallas and separated from it by the Dallas/Fort Worth International Airport and several smaller central cities, such as Irving, Arlington, and Grand Prairie. The Clear and West forks of the Trinity River join near the center of Fort Worth and Lake Worth, Eagle Mountain Lake, Benbrook, and Arlington Lakes form parts of its

© James Blank

northwest and southern borders. The city is part of the Cross Timbers region, the boundary between the more heavily forested eastern regions and the almost treeless Great Plains.

Fort Worth's climate is continental and humid subtropical, characterized by wide variations in annual weather conditions: long, hot summers; and short, mild winters. For more than 150 years Fort Worth was the only major city in the United States that had never had a fatal tornado. The city's luck ran out in March 2000 when a spectacular tornado tore through residential neighborhoods and the downtown area. Five people died in the storms, which caused an estimated $450 million in damage.

Area: 292.5 square miles

Elevation: Ranges from 500 to 800 feet above sea level

Average Temperatures: January, 44.1° F; July, 85.0° F; annual average, 65.5° F

Average Annual Precipitation: 34.73 inches of rain; 2.6 inches of snow

■ History

"Cowtown" a Trading Center

Fort Worth's wild and wooly past began in 1849 when Major Ripley Arnold led a small detachment of U.S. Dragoons to the banks of the Trinity River and established an outpost to protect early settlers from Native American attack. The garrison was named for General William Worth, a Mexican War hero. It was more of an encampment than a fort, but after several years the natives ceased their opposition to the settlement. When the soldiers left, the settler stayed, and in 1860 Fort Worth was chosen to serve as Tarrant County seat.

Its location on the Old Chisholm Trail, the route along which ranchers drove their herds, helped establish Fort Worth as a trading and cattle center and earned it the nickname "Cowtown." Cowboys took full advantage of their last brush with civilization before the long drive north from Fort Worth. They stocked up on provisions from local merchants, visited the town's colorful saloons for a bit of gambling and carousing, then galloped northward with their cattle.

Problems Accompanied Prosperity

Post-Civil War reconstruction brought many disillusioned Confederates to Texas in search of jobs and new beginnings. Commerce grew along with the population. Yankees wanted meat, and Texas had a ready supply. During this time rumors grew of a panther that stalked and slept on the city streets at night. A Dallas newspaper ran a story claiming that Fort Worth was so drowsy, a panther was found sleeping on Main Street. Fort Worth citizens good-naturedly dubbed their hometown "Panther City," and many local merchants and sports teams adopted the animal in their logos.

The Texas & Pacific Railroad arrived in Fort Worth in 1876, causing a boom in the cattle industry and in wholesale trade. The city was the westernmost railhead and became a transit point for cattle shipment. With the boom times came some problems. Crime was rampant and certain sections of town, such as Hell's Half Acre, were off-limits for proper citizens. Cowboys were joined by a motley assortment of buffalo hunters, gunmen, adventurers, and crooks. Butch Cassidy and the Sundance Kid were said to roam the streets of Fort Worth between robberies.

Boom Town is Tamed

During the 1880s and 1890s, an influx of home-seekers helped quiet the rowdy streets and create a more stable community. More railroads led to more industry. Meat packing companies, a brewing company, more newspapers, and a stronger banking system arrived. Community leaders modernized the fire department, started a municipal water system, built sanitary sewers, and paved streets. Free public schools were legalized in Texas and colleges were founded. By then most major religious denominations were represented with congregations in the city. Fort Worth women organized teas, dances, dinners, and cakewalks to raise funds for a public library. In 1907, the Texas Legislature helped tame the town by outlawing gambling.

During the early days of the twentieth century, Fort Worth became the meat packing center of the Southwest. Nearly all West Texas cattle stopped there for sale or reshipment. Merchants were delighted to discover that when ranchers brought their cattle to market, they also brought their wives to shop in Fort Worth's stores.

Oil/Aviation Spur Economy

In 1917, oil was discovered in West Texas on McCleskey Farm about 90 miles west of Fort Worth. The gusher meant another boom for the city and helped meet the fuel demand created by World War I. Five refineries were built by 1920 and the city became a center for oil operators. Oil-rich ranchers and farmers moved to Fort Worth and built luxurious homes and towering office buildings.

During World War I three flying fields were established near Fort Worth, all eventually taken over by the U.S. government. In 1927, an airport opened and the aviation industry began. During World War II, B-24 bombers were manufactured at the Convair Plant in Fort Worth, while bomber pilots trained at the nearby Tarrant Field (renamed Carswell Air Force Base in 1948). The opening of Dallas/Fort Worth International Airport in 1974 ushered in a new era of aviation history. At the time it was built, the airport was the largest in the world. The aviation/aerospace industry remains an important factor in Fort Worth's economy today.

Not Just Dallas

Fort Worth is considered one of the most cost effective places to live among metropolitan areas in the West and South Central United States. In 2012 the North Central Texas Council of Governments ranked Fort Worth the fastest-growing city in North Texas. In 2011 the city ranked seventh on the list of "Top U.S. Downtowns" by Livability.com.

Fort Worth benefits from the Dallas/Fort Worth metroplex, while also carving out a future for itself. Even despite the metroplex being one of the top five metropolitan areas in the nation, Fort Worth is, by itself, among the top 20 largest cities in the nation. Oil continues to be prominent in the modern Fort Worth economy. In 2007 advances in horizontal drilling technology made vast natural gas reserves in the Barnett Shale, directly under the city, available, which helped residents receive royalty checks for their mineral rights.

Business, however, does not surpass Fort Worth's old-world charm. The National Trust for Historic Preservation listed Fort Worth among America's Dozen Distinctive Destinations. With a vibrant cultural life, continuing development, and expanding economy in high-tech industries, Fort Worth forecasts a vibrant future.

Historical Information: Fort Worth Public Library, Genealogy and Local History Department, 500 W. 3rd Street, Fort Worth, TX 76102; telephone (817) 871-7740.

■ Population Profile

Metropolitan Statistical Area Population

2000: 5,221,801
2010: 6,371,773

2012 estimate: 6,647,496
Percent change, 2000–2010: 22%
U.S. rank in 2000: 5th
U.S. rank in 2010: 4th

City Residents

1990: 447,619
2000: 534,694
2010: 741,206
2012 estimate: 782,027
Percent change, 2000–2010: 38.6%
U.S. rank in 1990: 28th (State rank: 6th)
U.S. rank in 2000: 27th (State rank: 6th)
U.S. rank in 2010: 16th (State rank: 5th)

Density: 2,181.2 people per square mile

Racial and ethnic characteristics

White: 531,430
Black or African American: 148,245
American Indian and Alaskan Native: 3,094
Asian: 32,330
Native Hawaiian and Other Pacific Islander: 2,004
Hispanic or Latino (may be of any race): 263,593
Other: 64,924

Percent of residents born in state: 55.6%

Age characteristics

Population under 5 years old: 67,138
Population 5 to 9 years old: 62,322
Population 10 to 14 years old: 63,950
Population 15 to 19 years old: 55,107
Population 20 to 24 years old: 52,542
Population 25 to 34 years old: 129,415
Population 35 to 44 years old: 113,102
Population 45 to 54 years old: 96,743
Population 55 to 59 years old: 37,525
Population 60 to 64 years old: 34,571
Population 65 to 74 years old: 41,010
Population 75 to 84 years old: 19,365
Population 85 years and over: 9,237
Median age: 31.9

Births (2010–11 Metropolitan Area)

Total number: 99,733

Deaths (2010–11 Metropolitan Area)

Total number: 36,229

Money income (2012)

Per capita income: $23,449
Median household income: $50,129
Total households: 264,584

Number of households with income of ...

less than $10,000: 20,837
$10,000 to $14,999: 15,204
$15,000 to $24,999: 30,725
$25,000 to $34,999: 28,809
$35,000 to $49,999: 36,380
$50,000 to $74,999: 50,419
$75,000 to $99,999: 33,289
$100,000 to $149,999: 31,018
$150,000 to $199,999: 9,462
$200,000 or more: 8,441

Percent of families below poverty level: 19.5%

FBI Crime Index Property: 32,514

FBI Crime Index Violent: 4,524

■ Municipal Government

Fort Worth has used a council-manager form of government since 1924. This consists of a mayor elected and an eight-member council, who are all elected for two-year terms. Council members represent their respective districts, while the mayor is elected at-large. Together, the council appoints a city manager. The city is the seat of Tarrant County.

Head Official: Betsy Price (since 2011; current term expires 2015)

Total Number of City Employees: 6.646 (2013)

City Information: City of Fort Worth, 1000 Throckmorton Street, Fort Worth, TX 76102; telephone (817) 392-2255.

■ Economy

Major Industries and Commercial Activity

Fort Worth has traditionally been a diverse center of manufacturing, and the city demonstrated strong economic growth since the 1980s. Between 1990 and 1996, defense downsizing resulted in the loss of 44,000 jobs in the Fort Worth area. That development set Fort Worth's economic diversification effort into motion. A plan was adopted called "Strategy 2000, Diversifying Fort Worth's Future," which had as its goal the creation of a healthy, diverse, less defense-dependent economy supported by business development, emerging technologies, international trade, and a world class workforce. Tech Fort Worth, an off-shoot of "Strategy 2000," is a business incubator that works with the Fort Worth Business Assistance Center to foster new start-up companies. Tech Fort Worth opened a new facility in 2004 with over 160,000 feet of office space, laboratories, and conference rooms. Fort Worth has thrived with this investment, becoming one of the most diverse high-tech manufacturing locations in Texas. The city is home to a variety of high-tech corporations including Lockheed Martin, Bell Helicopter, and Motorola.

An economic slowdown in the sector accounted for job losses for the first time in many years between 2001 and 2003. Since then, however, health-care, finance, telecommunications, education, tourism, retail trade, and services sectors all experienced significant growth. In 2013 three *Fortune* 500 companies—AMR/American Airlines, RadioShack, and D.R. Horton—were located in Fort Worth, and an additional 20 were located in the surrounding area. Fort Worth is consistently ranked among the top places in the nation to work, live, and do business by *Money, Fortune, Site Selection,* and *Newsweek* magazines. Emerging economic sectors in the new century include semiconductor manufacturing, communications equipment manufacturing, corporate offices, and distribution.

Tourism is also an important contributor to the local economy. According to the Fort Worth Convention and Visitors Bureau, over 5.5 million visitors go to Fort Worth annually, who spent over a billion dollars in the city and even more in the surrounding areas.

In 2013 the city announced completion of a 1.1-million-square-foot distribution center by the online retailer Amazon; a new 470,000-square-foot factory by Motorola Mobility and Flextronics that will assemble the Moto X, the first smartphone assembled in the United States; a new 788,000-square-foot e-commerce distribution center being constructed by Wal-Mart; and a 120,000-square-foot headquarters and manufacturing facility for NGC Renewables, a manufacturer of wind turbine equipment.

Items and goods produced: aircraft, communication equipment, electronic equipment, machinery, refrigeration equipment, containers, clothing, food products, pharmaceuticals, computers, clothing, grain, leather

Incentive Programs-New and Existing Companies

Local programs: Like many other cities, Fort Worth offers many incentive programs to develop and redevelop the city, with the usual tax incentives, development assistance, and the availability of loans and grants. Fort Worth utilizes Tax Increment Finance (TIF) districts: Downtown, the Speedway, Riverfront, Southside/Medical District, North Tarrant Parkway, Lancaster, the Trinity River Vision, Lone Star, Southwest Parkway, and East Berry Renaissance. There are two Enterprise Zones in Fort Worth, with fee waivers, tax refunds, and other assistance provided by both the city and state. The city, on a case-by-case basis, gives consideration to the granting of property tax incentives to eligible residential, commercial, and industrial development projects. It is the objective of the city of Fort Worth to encourage applications from projects that (a) are located in

enterprise zones or other designated target areas; or (b) result in a development with little or no additional cost to the city; or (c) result in 1,000 or more new jobs, with a commitment to hire Fort Worth and inner-city residents. Fort Worth has two state-designated Urban Enterprise Zones in addition to its Foreign Trade Zones, which provide special customs procedures to manufacturers engaged in international trade.

State programs: Texas is a right-to-work state. The Texas economy has performed better than that of any other state during the recent economic downturn. It is believed that this success is due in part to the states pro-business climate, of which economic incentives are an important part.

The Texas Enterprise Zone Programs offer tax abatement at the local level, and refunds of state sales and use taxes under certain circumstances to businesses operating in enterprise zone areas. The Texas Enterprise Zone Program allows local communities to partner with the State of Texas to promote job creation and capital investment in targeted areas of the state that meet specific economic criteria. Designated projects are eligible to apply for state sales and use tax refunds on qualified expenditures. The state of Texas targets many of its incentive programs toward smaller and rural communities. The Rural Municipal Finance Program is a loan program created by the Texas Agricultural Finance Authority (TAFA) to stimulate economic activity in rural Texas. The Texas Enterprise Fund can be used to provide deal-closing money for companies relocating to and investing in Texas. The Texas Emerging Technology Fund, a $200 million fund created by the Texas Legislature in 2005, is available to companies who seek to commercialize new technologies. The program provides grants for early-stage investments in new, technology-based, private entrepreneurial entities that collaborate with public or private institutions of higher education.

Texas is one of the few states with no individual income tax, a very attractive environment for transferring employees. There is also no corporate income tax. Texas Enterprise Zone Program provides for eligible designated projects to apply for state sales and use tax refunds on purchases of all taxable items purchased for use at the qualified business site related to the project or activity. Special tax exemptions are made for manufacturing machinery, equipment, replacement parts, and accessories that have a useful life of more than six months. Texas businesses are also exempt from paying state sales and use tax on labor for constructing new facilities, electricity and natural gas used in manufacturing, processing, or fabrication. Tax-Exempt Industrial Revenue Bonds are designed to provide tax-exempt financing up to $20 million per project to finance land and depreciable property for eligible industrial or manufacturing projects.

The Texas Capital Fund Infrastructure and Real Estate Development programs are designed to provide no interest loans of up to $750,000 to non-entitlement communities. The program funds real estate developments (acquisitions, construction, and/or rehabilitation) to assist a business, which commits to creating or retaining permanent jobs, primarily for low and moderate-income persons.

Job training programs: The state of Texas provides training funds through its Smart Jobs program, which offers matching funds for training employees who will work for new and expanding Texas companies that pay at or above the state average wage. Job training funds are made available through the federal Workforce Investment Act (WIA). Employers using WIA participants can be reimbursed for up to 50 percent of the cost of training new employees. Fort Worth Works is a program run by the city to help both employers and job seekers by coordinating job fairs and placement agencies, and eliminating barriers to low-income workers. The Texas Department of Commerce has a work force incentive program for industrial start-up training and funding. Local state-supported educational institutions provide the training. The Texas Skills Development Fund, run by the Texas Workforce Commission, also allows employers to obtain funding of up to $500,000 for projects that will contribute towards an increased skill-set among its workforce.

Development Projects

In 2010, Lone Star in Sundance Square, a 21,000-square-foot entertainment multiplex combining music and live entertainment via six new venues under one roof opened in downtown Fort Worth.

In 2013 the Fort Worth city council approved a 10-year tax abatement for Carolina Beverage Group as an enticement for the company to expand its manufacturing facilities in North Texas. It is estimated the company will bring $41 million in capital investment and 225 full-time jobs to the area by December 2018.

The Interstate 35W improvement project spans 10 miles in Fort Worth and includes a section that is currently ranked as the state's most congested roadway. The improvements will double capacity and add two managed toll lanes in each direction. The $1.6 billion project is scheduled for completion in 2017. The Chisholm Trail Parkway is a 27.6-mile toll road that will extend from downtown Fort Worth south to Cleburne. More than 40 years in the making, the project is expected to open to traffic in 2014.

The master plan for the Trinity River seeks to connect every neighborhood in the city to the Trinity River corridor with new recreational amenities, improved infrastructure, environmental enhancements, and event programming. The projects include the urban waterfront communities of Panther Island and Central City. Ultimately, the project will double the size of downtown

and generate more than $600 million in economic development.

Economic Development Information: Fort Worth Chamber of Commerce, 777 Taylor Street, Suite 900, Fort Worth, TX 76102-4997; telephone (817) 336-2491. Fort Worth Economic Development Office, Office of the City Manager, Third Floor City Hall, 1000 Throckmorton, Fort Worth, TX 76102; telephone (817) 871-6103.

Commercial Shipping

A major mid-continent gateway to the world, the Dallas/Fort Worth International Airport's international cargo shipments is part of the reason the airport is one of the largest inland ports in the country. The airport handles nearly 640,000 U.S. tons of cargo yearly. More than 15 international cargo carriers use the airport for shipping, with Asia counting for almost half of all air cargo trade within the airport's catchment area and expanding.

A major rail center for more than 100 years, Fort Worth is home base for one of the nation's largest railroads, BNSF Railway. Union Pacific is Texas's biggest railroad, serving all of its major cities and its gulf ports. Also located in Fort Worth is Tower 55, the busiest railroad intersection in the United States, where several railroads share crossing with Union Pacific.

According to the local chamber of commerce, one of the city's geographic advantages is that it is equidistant to North America's five largest business centers: New York, Chicago, Los Angeles, Mexico City, and Toronto. As a result, more than 50 million people can be reached from the Dallas-Fort Worth area by overnight by truck or rail and 98 percent of the U.S. population can be reached within 48 hours.

In addition to its excellent airport services, interstate highways, and railroad connections, Dallas maintains its edge as a leading distribution center of the Southwest with a healthy trucking industry whose carriers offer direct service to major points in the United States.

Labor Force and Employment Outlook

In 2012 Fort Worth was ranked fourth on the list of "Best Large Cities in U.S. for Jobs" by NewGeography.com. Between 2001 and 2013, Fort Worth's employment expanded 16 percent, with unemployment rates continuing to trend lower. Fort Worth benefits greatly from being part of the Dallas/Fort Worth metroplex, which is one of the most densely populated destinations for *Fortune* 500 companies in the nation. With a diversified economy, a variety of large and successful businesses, employment has remained steady, even through the recession.

The following is a summary of data regarding the 2012 Fort Worth labor force:

Size of civilian labor force: 378,778

Number of workers employed in...

agriculture and mining: 5,008
construction: 26,639
manufacturing: 40,053
wholesale trade: 8,599
retail trade: 37,310
transportation: 24,660
information systems: 7,104
finance: 25,805
professional administration: 35,557
education and social services: 69,541
arts and leisure: 30,793
other: 17,974
public administration: 12,458

Average hourly earnings of production workers: $15.8

Unemployment rate: 6.3% (2012)

Employers

Largest employers (2012)	*Number of employees*
AMR/American Airlines	22,169
Texas Health Resources	18,866
Lockheed Martin	14,988
NAS Fort Worth JRB	11,350
Fort Worth ISD	11,000
Arlington ISD	8,126
University of Texas Arlington	6,239
City of Fort Worth	6,195
JPS Health Network	4,872
Cook Children's Health Care System	4,826
Tarrant County Government	4,173
Texas Health Harris Methodist Hospital	3,968
Bell Helicopter Textron	3,820
Fidelity	3,700
Keller ISD	3,600
Alcon Laboratories	3,346
Genco ATC	3,315

Cost of Living

The cost of living in Fort Worth is low compared to other major cities in the United States.

The following is a summary of data regarding several key cost of living factors in the area.

2013 ACCRA Average House Price: $207,687

2013 ACCRA Cost of Living Index: 95

State income tax rate: None

State sales tax rate: 6.25%

Local income tax rate: None

Local sales tax rate: 2.0%

Property tax rate: 2.82% of assessed value (2013)

Economic Information: Fort Worth Chamber of Commerce, 777 Taylor Street, Suite 900, Fort Worth, TX 76102-4997; telephone (817) 336-2491.

■ Education and Research

Elementary and Secondary Schools

The Fort Worth Independent School District (FWISD) is the largest of the 20 school districts in Tarrant County, and the fifth largest in the state. The district serves about 80,000 students in 83 elementary schools, 28 middle schools and 6th grade centers, 14 high schools, and 17 special campuses. Specific programs aimed at increasing performance include TEAM FWISD, a mentoring program designed to increase the number of high-need students graduating from high school by pairing them with adult mentors. The FWISD's Vital Link program, which places 12-year-old students in workplace situations to show them the link between classroom learning and workplace needs, is nationally recognized. The Adopt-A-School program seeks to build partnerships between schools in the district and community businesses and faith-based organizations.

The FWISD's Chairs for Teaching Excellence program to recognize teaching excellence in a variety of disciplines, is based on the university-level teaching chair concept and is unique in the nation at the public school level. Another feature of the system is a high school for medical professionals. Middle and elementary schools offer preparatory, Montessori, and baccalaureate education. The FWISD is one of only a few schools in the nation to hold the Kennedy Center Imagination Celebration, the national children's arts festival program. In Fort Worth the Imagination Celebration has operated on a year-round basis for over 20 years.

Over 200 private and parochial schools serve Fort Worth and Tarrant County, including special schools for the learning disabled. In 2013 the Roman Catholic Diocese of Fort Worth maintained 20 schools, including 16 elementary and 4 high schools serving a total student body of 6,360. About 90 percent of the students are Catholic. African Americans account for 5 percent, whites 54 percent, Asians 9 percent, and Hispanics 26 percent.

The following is a summary of data regarding the Fort Worth Independent School District.

Total enrollment: 81,651

Number of facilities

    total: 142

    elementary schools: 83

    junior high schools: 28

    high schools: 14

    other: 17

Student/teacher ratio: 15.91:1

Teacher salaries

    average (statewide): $48,261

Funding per pupil: $9,105

Public Schools Information: Fort Worth Independent School District, 100 North University Dr., Fort Worth, TX 76107-1360; telephone (817) 871-2000; email web@fortworthisd.net.

Colleges and Universities

More than 60 Metroplex area universities and colleges enroll over 325,000 students annually and graduate more than 35,000. The Fort Worth area boasts eight major colleges and universities. The University of North Texas, in nearby Denton, is the area's largest research university, with an enrollment of over 36,000. The college is consistently listed among "America's 100 Best College Buys" by Institutional Research & Evaluation Inc. UNT has a graduate level health science center located in Fort Worth. The University of Texas at Arlington (UTA) has more than 32,000 students enrolled in its schools of business, engineering, liberal arts, science, architecture, nursing, social work, and education. UTA is known for programs in high technology applied research. It is the second largest component of the UT system, and out of its 125,000 alumni, over 88,000 live in the North Texas area. The School of Urban and Public Affairs has been listed among the nation's best graduate schools of public affairs in the *U.S. News & World Report* list multiple times.

Located in downtown Fort Worth, Texas Christian University (TCU) educates nearly 9,000 students. It specializes in a liberal arts education and offers research-oriented doctoral programs in chemistry, divinity, English, history, physics, and psychology. Texas Wesleyan University has more than 2,500 students in its schools of business, education, fine arts, sciences, and humanities. The city's other colleges are Tarrant County Junior College (on several campuses and with a total enrollment of over 40,000), Texas Women's University, Southwestern Baptist Theological Seminary, and Arlington Baptist College. There are some 30 other colleges and universities within a 50-mile radius, including technical, business, and nursing schools.

Libraries and Research Centers

The Fort Worth Public Library system has been open for over 100 years. It consists of a central library and 14 other locations. The total system holdings number over 2 million items, including more than 2,000 periodical subscriptions. Special collections include bookplates, early children's books, books in Spanish and Vietnamese, genealogy, earth science, popular sheet music, government documents, and oral history. The newest branch, the Ella M. Shamblee Branch Library, houses an expanded collection of books, media, periodicals, and online resources, in addition to an art gallery and a special Fort Worth African American Heritage digital display. Nearly 30 special libraries are located in Fort Worth, affiliated with local businesses, art museums, hospitals and colleges, and U.S. government agencies. Among them are the Lockheed Martin Fort Worth Company Research Library and the National Archives Southwest Region collection of inactive records of U.S. government agencies in the Southwest.

The University of Texas at Arlington executes advanced research in a number of areas, notably at its Automation and Robotics Research Institute, and its Nanotechnology Research & Teaching Facility. The University of North Texas Health Science Center supports several research centers dealing with such topics as substance abuse and wound healing. Texas Christian University operates an Institute of Behavioral Research and the Center for Texas Studies.

Public Library Information: Fort Worth Public Library, 500 W. 3rd Street, Fort Worth, TX 76102-7305; telephone (817) 871-7701.

■ Health Care

Even health care is more affordable in Fort Worth than the national average, where patients can be treated at a number of high-quality hospitals, in the city and in the metroplex. The Southside Medical District, located south of Fort Worth's Central Business District, encompasses approximately 1,400 acres and includes the area's major hospitals, medical institutions, and support services. Fort Worth is home to 20 hospitals, including general care facilities, a children's medical center, urgent care center, emergency clinics, a cardiac center, and an osteopathic hospital. Harris Methodist Fort Worth Hospital, with more than 600 beds, is the largest hospital in the city and features emergency service, a CareFlite helicopter, open-heart surgery facilities, kidney transplant procedures and a rehabilitation program for head and spinal cord injuries.

JPS Health Network/John Peter Smith Hospital expanded in the late 2000s, adding new beds, operating suites, and a new emergency department. The Plaza Medical Center of Fort Worth similarly underwent $57 million renovation that included a new critical cardiac care center and expanded emergency room. Among the services of All Saints Episcopal Hospital are wellness and fitness programs, a cardiac rehabilitation unit, and the largest freestanding center for radiation cancer therapy in the Southwest. Other health care facilities in Fort Worth are Rehabilitation Hospital, which offers programs for the brain-injured and those with other physical disabilities, and Cook-Fort Worth Children's Medical Center, which specializes in pediatrics. Oceans Healthcare, a Louisiana health care company, planned to expand its operations in North Texas in 2013, starting with a 45-bed specialty hospital in Fort Worth.

■ Recreation

Sightseeing

Fort Worth and the metroplex rank high on the list of U.S. tourist destinations. Many attractions are located in the city or within the mid-cities region of the Dallas/Fort Worth area, including Arlington, Grand Prairie, and Irving. Tourists have a wide range of diversions from which to choose.

The Stockyards National Historic District is a multiblock historic district featuring specialty shops, rodeos, saloons, and livestock auctions. Twice daily in the Stockyards, authentic cowhands drive the Fort Worth Herd, a group of Texas longhorn steer, down Exchange Avenue. Billy Bob's Texas in the Stockyards is the world's largest honky tonk bar/entertainment center and can accommodate a crowd of 6,000 people to hear top western entertainers, play pool and video games, and shop. Sundance Square is another historic district of red-bricked streets, shops, and restaurants. Visitors to Fort Worth can walk through historic Van Zandt Cottage, Thistle Hill mansion, or the Eddleman McFarland House, an elegant Victorian residence. Tourists can also tour downtown Fort Worth and Sundance Square in a carriage. Fort Worth Water Garden Park is an impressive four blocks of concrete-terraced waterfalls, fountains, pools, and gardens. Trinity Trail, expanded throughout the late 2000s, consists of 32 miles of paved trails for walking, biking, or rollerblading, winding from North-side Drive to Foster Park. The Tarantula Steam excursion train takes passengers between Grapevine and the Stock-yards. Stockyards Station also includes retail and dining facilities, plus a children's carnival.

The Fort Worth Zoo is home to 5,000 exotic animals. The Fort Worth Zoo has been named as a top zoo in the nation by *Family Life* magazine, the *Los Angeles Times, USA Today,* and *Southern Living.* Nearby Log Cabin Village features 1850s-era restored cabins, a working grist mill, and pioneer craft demonstrations. Noble Planetarium in the Museum of Science and History features a Texas sky show that changes monthly. Fort Worth Nature Center and Refuge in Lake Worth is a 3,600-acre habitat and National Natural Landmark. It is also the largest city-owned nature center in the United States. The Fort Worth Botanic Garden, including the Japanese Garden, contains acres of plants, and a pagoda, teahouse, and meditation garden. It is the oldest botanical garden in Texas. The Forest Park Miniature Railroad takes visitors on a 40-minute trip from Forest Park to Trinity Park and back. Hurricane Harbor in Arlington is a family-oriented water park. Six Flags over Texas is a large amusement park complex in Arlington. Visitors can also tour such varied businesses as American Airlines Flight Academy, Mrs. Baird's Bakery, or the Bandera Hat Company.

Arts and Culture

Cowboys and culture mix in Fort Worth. Community and commercial groups are generous and cooperative in their support of the arts. The city offers cultural experiences ranging from fine opera and ballet to knee-slapping country hoedowns. Its museums house the art and artifacts of European masters and Texas cattlemen. Fort Worth has 109 acres of museum space, second in the nation behind Washington D.C. for the most accredited museums within walking distance from each other.

The beautiful Nancy Lee and Perry R. Bass Perfor-mance Hall, a $67 million facility that opened in 1998, is the first-ever home of the Fort Worth Symphony, Texas Ballet Theater, and the Fort Worth Opera, as well as the Van Cliburn International Piano Competition. The 2,054-seat performance hall is located in Sundance Square; it makes a grand impression with its pair of 48-foot angels gracing the entrance. Bass Hall is listed among the top 10 opera halls in the world.

Casa Manana, a theater-in-the-round under a geodesic dome, seats 1,800 people and features Broad-way touring productions, a children's playhouse series, and produces its own shows featuring local talent. The Rose Marine Theater is home to the Latin Arts Association of Fort Worth, the only Hispanic theater company in the city, and presents theater, film, and live music series. Other thriving Fort Worth-area theaters include StageWest, Circle Theatre, Jubilee, and the avant-garde group Hip Pocket. A number of area community orchestra and professional ensembles present classical music concerts throughout the year. The Scott Theatre hosts the Fort Worth Theatre, special film productions, and cultural activities. Hyena's Comedy Club features national acts; "Four Day Weekend" improvisational comedy show is Fort Worth's longest running show.

Fort Worth's museums and galleries also offer variety. The Kimbell Art Museum was designed by Louis Kahn and houses collections of classical and prehistoric art, and western European and early twentieth century paintings. The Amon Carter Museum, named for the late Fort Worth newspaper magnate whose foundation supports it, contains a collection of nineteenth- and early twentieth-century Western and American paintings and American photographs. Twentieth-century multimedia art including sculpture, photography, and painting are displayed at the Modern Art Museum of Fort Worth. The Sid Richardson Museum in Sundance Square displays 60 paintings by artists of the American West such as Frederic Remington and Charles Russell.

The American Airlines C.R. Smith Museum is devoted to the history of commercial aviation, having over 1,000 items in its collection, including a restored DC-3 airplane. Fire Station No. 1 is the city's earliest fire house and contains an exhibit entitled "150 Years of Fort Worth." The Texas Cowboy Hall of Fame and National Cowboys of Color Museum and Hall of Fame pay tribute to the people who built Texas. The National Cowgirl Museum and Hall of Fame, the only one of its kind in the world, opened a new home in the city's Cultural District in 2002. The Fort Worth Museum of Science and History normally houses the Omni Theater and Museum School, the Noble Planetarium, and 35,000 square feet of exhibits, including the Hall of Medical Science, Man and His Possessions, Antique Calculators and Computer Technology, Geology, and Texas History, which moved to a new 133,000 square foot facility in 2009. The history of the ranching industry in Texas is traced through film, photographs, and memorabilia at the Cattle Raiser's Museum, which later became part of the Museum of Science and History in 2009.

Tours are available at the Bureau of Engraving and Printing's Visitor Center, allowing the public to watch the printing of paper currency. The Pate Museum of Transportation, located on a ranch near Cresson, maintains a collection of varying modes of transportation including antique, classic, and special interest cars, airplanes, railroad cars, and space exhibits. On the campus of Southwestern Baptist Theological Seminary, the Tandy Archaeological Museum houses a collection of biblical artifacts. The Texas Civil War Museum is home to a large collection of uniforms, weapons, and flags from both North and the South. It is the largest Civil War museum west of the Mississippi River.

Festivals and Holidays

In January/February the Fort Worth Stock Show and Rodeo is held over two weeks at the Will Rogers Memorial Coliseum and includes an indoor rodeo, exhibits, arts and crafts, rides, and a carnival midway. Cowtown Goes Green is Fort Worth's unique, western-style St. Patrick's Day celebration. The festival is held in the National Historic Stockyards District and features a parade, cattle drive, pub crawl, arts and crafts sales, and Irish music. For four days in April, Fort Worth's Main Street becomes a marketplace of food, arts and crafts, and live entertainment during the Main St. Fort Worth Arts Festival.

The arrival of spring is observed with Mayfest activities, games, sports, and arts and crafts in Trinity Park. The Van Cliburn International Piano Competition is held at the Bell Performance Center every four years. At the Quanah Parker Comanche Pow Wow & Honor Dance, Fort Worth's frontier past is highlighted with re-enactors showing off the skills and equipment needed in the days of the old West, along with Comanche dancers performing traditional dances. In June and the beginning of July is the American Paint Horse Association World Championship Show & Sale at the Will Rogers Memorial Center. Pioneer Days in September commemorates the early days of the cattle industry with a fiddler's contest, fajita cook-off, parade, and footrace. Also in September, the Fort Worth Alliance Air Show at Alliance Airport is a family-oriented event conceived as a tribute to Fort Worth's aviation industry. Oktoberfest features music, dance, and food events to raise money for symphonic activities. The Red Steagall Cowboy Gathering & Western Swing Festival fills the Stockyard District with music, rodeo and cowboy poetry in October. November and December are filled with holiday observances including the Zoobilee of Lights and the Christmas Parade of Lights.

Sports for the Spectator

Fort Worth professional sports fans follow the professional teams of the metroplex: Texas Rangers of Major League Baseball, Dallas Cowboys of the National Football League, Dallas Mavericks of the National Basketball Association, and the Dallas Stars of the National Hockey League. None of these is based in Fort Worth, but all are close enough to claim fans. The Texas Brahmas are in the Central Hockey League and play at the NYTEX Sports Centre in nearby North Richland. College fans in Fort Worth pay close attention to the Texas Christian University Horned Frogs and the Texas Wesleyan University Rams, both of which compete in major collegiate sports. In professional golf, the Crowne Plaza Invitational at Colonial and the HP Byron Nelson Classic are held in May. The Texas Motor Speedway, also known as the Great American Speedway, is a 1.5-mile NASCAR oval track with a seating capacity of 155,000 (plus 53,000 more in the infield). The second largest sports facility in the country, it schedules three major racing weekends a year.

Sports for the Participant

Fort Worth boasts about 10,000 acres of park, with an additional 100,000 acres of lakes. Six large lakes within 25 miles of downtown provide Fort Worth residents with ample opportunities for water sports and recreation. Burger's Lake is a 30-acre recreational park with a swimming lake, sandy beaches, and picnic grounds. Heritage Park Boat & Recreation Center bills itself as "a one-hour vacation in the heart of Fort Worth."

Fort Worth maintains over 200 developed city parks with more than 10,000 acres, 98 public tennis courts, 3 bicycle trails, 6 public golf courses, 20 community centers, and 20 municipal pools.

Shopping and Dining

Fort Worth boasts one of the most beautiful and vibrant downtown areas in Texas. The centerpiece of the revitalized downtown is the Sundance Square entertainment and shopping district, a 20-block area filled with historic buildings, movie theaters, live theaters, nightclubs, coffee houses, art galleries and, of course, shopping in a 40-store mall with an indoor skating rink. Other popular shopping areas are Hulen Mall, the Fort Worth Outlet Square, University Park Village, Stockyards Station, the Camp Bowie Boulevard shops, and Ridgmar Mall in west Forth Worth.

Restaurants are plentiful in Fort Worth, offering everything from Continental, Texas Ranch, New American, and ethnic cuisines. The historic districts in particular, such as The Stockyards and Sundance Square, abound in restaurants and saloons. Texas beef, chili, and Tex-Mex are specialties. At Ellington's Southern Table in Sundance Square, diners' plates are piled high with Southern specialties like pot roast, chicken-fried steak, fried catfish, and liver and onions.

Visitor Information: Fort Worth Convention and Visitors Bureau, 415 Throckmorton, Fort Worth, TX 76102; telephone (817) 336-8791 or (800) 433-5747.

■ Convention Facilities

The Fort Worth Convention Center in downtown Fort Worth is the city's major facility. The Fort Worth Convention Center spans 14 blocks of the city's Central Business District. The center has 253,226 square feet of exhibit space, 41 meeting rooms, a 28,160 square foot ballroom, a 3,000-seat theater, and a 14,000-seat arena. The Fort Worth Water Gardens are directly across the street and Sundance Square is only five blocks away. Visitors can take advantage of the free trolley, "Molly the Trolley," to access restaurants, attractions, and shopping. The Center is surrounded by first-class hotels including the Sheraton, Hilton, Renaissance, Embassy Suites, and Courtyard by Marriott. Opened in 2009 adjacent to the Fort Worth Convention Center, the Omni Fort Worth Hotel offers 68,000 square feet of meeting space in addition to luxurious guest rooms. The Ashton Hotel, an elegant boutique hotel fully renovated from two buildings that are listed on the National Register of Historical Places, has 4,863 square feet of meeting space. In all, Fort Worth has over 13,000 rooms, about 2,500 of which are in downtown Fort Worth. The Metroplex area, including the Dallas/Fort Worth Airport, boasts even more convention facilities and is one of the top business meeting destinations in the country.

The American Airlines Training & Conference Center is located five minutes from the Dallas/Fort Worth International Airport. Will Rogers Memorial Center is located in the museum district within walking distance of museums such as the Kimbell, Amon Carter, Modern Art, and the Science and History museums. The Botanic and Japanese Gardens are also nearby. The center contains 100,000 square feet of exhibit space, a 6,000-seat coliseum, a 3,000-seat auditorium, an equestrian center with 2,000-seat arena, and meeting/banquet facilities. The Bass Performance Hall can host events for as many as 500 people in the lobby to well over 2,000 people in the auditorium.

Convention Information: Fort Worth Convention and Visitors Bureau, 415 Throckmorton, Fort Worth, TX 76102; telephone (817) 336-8791 or (800) 433-5747.

■ Transportation

Approaching the City

The Dallas/Fort Worth International Airport (DFW) is located approximately 17 miles from the downtown areas of both cities. Served by 16 passenger airlines, it is one of the largest airports in the world. DFW is four hours or less by air from nearly every major North American market, with direct service to more than 165,184 non-stop destinations worldwide.

Alliance Airport, the world's first master-planned industrial-use airport, is located 20 miles north of the city. Owned by the City of Fort Worth and managed by privately-held Alliance Air Services, it is used by such companies as FedEx, the Drug Enforcement Agency, and Bell Helicopter. Meachum Airport is Fort Worth's leading private aviation airport. The growing Sprinks airport hosts several area flight schools.

Four interstate highways serve Dallas/Fort Worth: Interstate 20 (east–west), Interstate 35 (north–south), Interstate 30 (northeast–west), and Interstate 45 (south).

Intercity passenger service to Fort Worth is available on Amtrak train lines. The Trinity Railway Express, a commuter rail line, connects downtown Dallas, downtown Fort Worth, DFW airport, and the Fort Worth Intermodal Transportation Center, which houses the largest hub for the T and Amtrak trains. In 2013 the line served an average of 180,000 riders per month.

Traveling in the City

Typical commutes for persons working and living in the Fort Worth area are 15–30 minutes. Commutes between Dallas and Fort Worth areas are usually 30–45 minutes. The Fort Worth mass transportation system is called "The T," and includes more than 130 vehicles that travel more than 50 routes. Additionally, there is a trolley service that transports visitors from the downtown area to the

Stockyards National Historic District, the Fort Worth Cultural District, and the Fort Worth Zoo.

■ Communications

Newspapers and Magazines

Fort Worth's daily newspaper is the morning *Fort Worth Star-Telegram*. It also publishes a major Spanish-language newspaper for the entire metroplex known as *La Estrella*. Fort Worth residents also have access to Dallas media. To the north of Dallas and Fort Worth, the *Denton Record-Chronicle* primarily covers news for the city of Denton and Denton County. Other newspapers and magazines focus on horses or cattle, including *Christian Ranchman,* which covers Cowboys for Christ events; several others deal with nurseries, gardening, and religious topics. Two airline in-flight magazines are published in Fort Worth, in addition to *Fort Worth, Texas* magazine.

Television and Radio

Due to their proximity, Fort Worth and Dallas share a number of television and radio stations with other metroplex cities. There are nine network television stations and six independent. Five AM and six FM radio stations broadcast from the city, including two Hispanic stations and one owned by Texas Christian University. Eighty AM and FM signals are available to listeners in Fort Worth.

Media Information: *Fort Worth Star-Telegram,* Capital Cities/ABC, Inc., 400 W. 7th St., Fort Worth, TX 76102; telephone (817) 390-7400.

Fort Worth Online

> City of Fort Worth Home Page. Available www. fortworthgov.org
>
> Fort Worth Chamber of Commerce. Available www. fortworthcoc.org
>
> Fort Worth Convention and Visitors Bureau. Available www.fortworth.com
>
> Fort Worth Independent School District. Available www.fortworthisd.org
>
> Fort Worth Public Library. Available www. fortworthgov.org/Library/
>
> *Fort Worth Star-Telegram.* Available www.star-telegram.com

BIBLIOGRAPHY

Duty, Michael W., *Dallas & Fort Worth: A Pictorial Celebration* (New York: Sterling Publishing Company, 2007)

Jodidio, Philip, *Tadao Ando: Modern Art Museum of Fort Worth* (New York: Rizzoli; Fort Worth: in association with the Modern Art Museum of Fort Worth, 2008)

Nichols, Mike, *Lost Fort Worth* (Charleston, SC: The History Press, 2014)

Roark, Carol and Byrd Williams, *Fort Worth's Legendary Landmarks* (Fort Worth, TX: Texas Christian University Press, 1997)

Houston

■ The City in Brief

Founded: 1836 (incorporated 1837)

Head Official: Mayor Annise D. Parker (since 2010; current term expires 2014)

City Population
> 1990: 1,654,348
> 2000: 1,953,631
> 2010: 2,099,451
> 2012 estimate: 2,161,686
> Percent change, 2000–2010: 7.5%
> U.S. rank in 1990: 4th (State rank: 1st)
> U.S. rank in 2000: 6th (State rank: 1st)
> U.S. rank in 2010: 4th (State rank: 1st)

Metropolitan Statistical Area Population
> 2000: 4,177,646
> 2010: 5,946,800
> 2012 estimate: 6,204,161
> Percent change, 2000–2010: 42.3%
> U.S. rank in 2000: 8th
> U.S. rank in 2010: 6th

Area: 601.69 square miles

Elevation: Ranges from sea level to about 50 feet above sea level

Average Annual Temperatures: January, 51.8° F; July, 83.6° F; annual average, 68.8° F

Average Annual Precipitation: 47.84 inches; 0.4 inches of snow

Major Economic Sectors: services, finance/insurance/real estate, trade, government

Unemployment Rate: 6.1% (2012)

Per Capita Income: $26,235

2012 FBI Crime Index Property: 107,678

Major Colleges and Universities: Rice University, University of Houston, Texas Southern University

Daily Newspaper: *Houston Chronicle*

■ Introduction

One of the largest cities in the United States and the largest city in the state of Texas, Houston is the county seat of Harris County and the economic center of the Houston-Sugar Land-Bayton metropolitan area. During the late 1970s Houston epitomized opulence, glitter, and opportunity. The city's major industry, petrochemicals, rode the crest of a boom "in the oilpatch," as Houstonians say. Get-rich-quick growth became a predominant feature across the sprawling landscape of the city. By 1982, however, a national recession, coupled with a wildly fluctuating oil market and devaluation of the Mexican peso, changed Houston's outlook from boom to bust. Unemployment and the local economy reached depression levels by 1985, prompting a painful retrenchment. Houston's recovery and subsequent expansion are the result of the growth of energy, independent industry, and diversification. Optimism is back in Houston as the city looks to new opportunities in high-technology and service industries. As a result of the boom, and despite the bust, Houston's consolidated metropolitan area now exceeds 8,700 square miles and the population has more than doubled from the 1960 level. By 2013 Houston was the nation's fourth largest city, not including the estimated 5.5 million people in the metropolitan area. Houston is second only to New York as the city with the most *Fortune* 500 companies. Houston is consistently ranked among national publications as a top place for business, a great city for young professionals, among the best cities to find a job, and among the best U.S. cities to live, work, and play. In 2010 Houston was recognized as

Albert Cheng/Shutterstock.com

one of the top cities surviving a national recession in the late 2000s; the city reported the largest five-year employment gain in the country. Houston consistently ranks first in U-Haul's annual national migration trend report, "The U-Haul Top 50 U.S. Destination Cities." In 2012 Houston also posted one of the lowest overall costs of living among the 29 metropolitan areas with more than two million residents. In the new century, Houston is looking up again and approaching the future with confidence.

■ Geography and Climate

Houston lies near the Gulf of Mexico and sprawls westward from the shores of Galveston Bay on the coastal prairie of eastern Texas. Major waterways include the San Jacinto River, part of which is encompassed by the man-made Houston Ship Channel, and an intricate network of meandering creeks and bayous, the largest of which are Buffalo Bayou and Bray's Bayou. The Long Point-Eureka Heights Fault System runs through the center of the city. The Houston area has over 150 confirmed, active faults—estimated to be close to 300—with an aggregate length of up to 310 miles. While there

have been no significant earthquakes in Houston's known history, researchers do not discount that major quakes have occurred in the past and could occur in the future. The faults may also contribute to land in some communities southeast of Houston sinking, reportedly because water has been pumped out from the ground for many years or because of slowly creeping slips along fault lines. The region is classified as temperate to subtropical grassland and forest. The low-lying, sprawling city sits on a flat terrain, which has made flooding a recurring problem for Houstonians. Smog is a major environmental issue in Houston; the American Lung Association has rated the metropolitan area's ozone level among the ten worst in the United States.

The climate is humid and semitropical in the summertime, with an average annual temperature of about 69 degrees. Houston's winters are mild, although freezing sometimes occurs, and its summers are potent. Heat comes from the Mexican deserts, while the humidity comes from the Gulf. Springtime "supercell" thunderstorms sometimes form tornadoes in the area. Snowfall is uncommon, although in the late 2000s, Houston received snow in three consecutive winters. The threat of severe weather, especially hurricanes that form when northern cold fronts collide with moisture-laden

Gulf coast weather systems, is taken seriously by the local population. Houston has been directly hit by two hurricanes in the last forty years, Carla in 1960 and Alicia in 1983, and has been threatened by many others. With Alicia, Houston became the nation's largest city to have endured the passage of a hurricane's eye directly over its downtown area.

Area: 601.69 square miles

Elevation: Ranges from sea level to about 50 feet above sea level

Average Temperatures: January, 51.8° F; July, 83.6° F; annual average, 68.8° F

Average Annual Precipitation: 47.84 inches; 0.4 inches of snow

■ History

Early Days Full of Perils

Inhabited by cannibals, visited by Spanish explorers and missionaries, a base for pirates, former capital of a fledgling nation, and site of a battle that ultimately added millions of acres to the United States-all of this can be said for the rich and varied history of the Houston area.

Amerinds, descended from the early races of mankind that crossed into North America via the Bering land bridge, are known to have occupied the southwestern United States many thousands of years before Christ. As these tribal groups fanned out across North and South America over thousands of years, a primitive culture evolved along what is now the upper Texas coast. The first recorded meetings between Europeans and the native populations of eastern Texas are found in fifteenth- and sixteenth-century accounts of Spanish explorers. These accounts are not particularly pleasant, for the natives of the Gulf Coast region that one day became Houston were notorious cannibals of the small Atakapan and Karankawa tribes. These were ferocious tribal groups, described by the Spaniards as bloodthirsty and barbaric.

The Europeans chose to move on, and despite Galveston Bay's relative attraction as a safe harbor, the upper Gulf Coast of Texas remained largely unsettled by the Spanish, who came to control virtually all of the American Southwest by the early eighteenth century. The area now known as Houston remained a malarial coastal prairie, dotted by marshes and bayous, and home to a few remaining Karankawa.

In the aftermath of the War of 1812, various Caribbean buccaneers, notably Jean Lafitte, established short-lived settlements on Galveston Island, just south of present-day Houston. Local legends persisting to this day in Houston's southeastern suburbs along Galveston Bay tell of buried pirate treasure, placed there by the crafty Lafitte.

War Breaks Out With Santa Ana

By the 1820s settlers from the United States were moving into Texas, then owned by the newly independent nation of Mexico. It was in Mexico's interest at the time to allow these settlements. Later, as the American emigrant population grew, so did Mexico's troubles in Texas. By the 1830s the former Americans, calling themselves Texicans, were eager to form their own government and felt abused by dictates from Mexico City. Disputes emerged as a full-blown war with the Mexican government of General Antonio López de Santa Anna in 1836.

That year the area now encompassed by Houston came foursquare onto the national stage. In April, following the massacres of Texas troops at San Antonio's Alamo, General Sam Houston, leading the main body of the Texas resistance, intercepted a courier and learned of military dispositions planned by Santa Anna, the "Napoleon of the West." Houston, stalling for time, veered away from the superior Mexican force until, at the San Jacinto River near present-day Houston, he used the intercepted information to deploy his small army in an advantageous position. The two armies fought a light skirmish on April 20. Santa Anna, accused by historians of having become contemptuous of Houston, bided his time before pressing home the attack. On the afternoon of April 21, while the Mexican troops prepared for what they expected would be a major engagement the next morning, Houston attacked. By the end of the day, the future of Texas was sealed as Santa Anna lost and Houston won.

Houston Incorporated

In August a settlement named for the hero of San Jacinto began to take shape along the Buffalo Bayou. By the end of the year, even as the town was still being laid out, Sam Houston, by then the first president of the Republic of Texas, moved his capital from Columbia to the town named in his honor. Houston was incorporated in 1837. The capital remained there until 1839, when the town of Austin became Texas's permanent seat of government.

Oil, Port, and Space Center Spur Development

As a settlement, Houston grew slowly but steadily in the mid-nineteenth century. By 1870, with 9,000 citizens, it was the third largest city in Texas behind San Antonio and Galveston. Located 50 miles inland, Houston lagged behind the two larger cities as a transportation center, although even then it was a major steamboat and rail terminus. Houston was mainly a distribution center, and manufacturing of paper products made use of the abundant lumber in the nearby pine forests of east Texas.

Three events, spread out over the first 60 years of the twentieth century, transformed the quiet community into the Southwest's largest metropolis. The first was the discovery of oil at Spindletop, near Houston, in 1901.

Vast fortunes were made in the oil business, and Houston quickly began to accumulate the financial power it had once seen displayed by its neighbor to the south—Galveston—known in the nineteenth century as the "Wall Street of the South." The second major development came in 1914, when a colossal project began to reshape the Buffalo Bayou into a ship channel, navigable by more than shallow draft riverboats.

The combination of the new port with Houston's position as a major petrochemical center enabled the city to surpass San Antonio's population in the 1930s, becoming the largest city in what was then the nation's largest state. After World War II the petrochemical industry and Houston grew even more rapidly, but Houston remained a large city with a small-town flavor.

A third major development changed that small-town flavor in 1961, when the National Aeronautics and Space Administration chose Houston as the site of its new Manned Spacecraft Center. Suddenly, the quiet little city was home to oil tycoons and glamorous astronauts, world-famous surgeons, and a professional baseball team called the Astros. Eight years later the electric phrase, "Houston, Tranquility Base here, the Eagle has landed," made the city's name the first human word spoken from the surface of a heavenly body other than Earth.

Oil-Dependency Hurts Economy

When the Arab Oil Embargo of 1973 precipitated a world energy crisis, oil prices rose and earnings doubled and tripled, and so did stock in Houston. New towers of commerce, many designed by world-class architects such as Philip Johnson and I. M. Pei, rose up to forever change the face of Houston's central business district. Companies expanded, venture capital looked for ways to spend new-found wealth, and Houston's population shot up as northern industrial workers, eager for a share of the opportunity, flocked to the city.

In the late twentieth century, Houston became in many ways a one-industry town, with both oil and chemical production feeding one another through the petroleum distillation process. By the mid-1980s Houston was the headquarters for 8 of the 10 largest energy companies, and some 5,000 businesses related to energy were located either in Houston or within 100 miles of the city. The chemical industry in Houston accounted for almost 50 percent of the total U.S. production capacity by 1987, with more than 200 refining and processing plants in the Houston area. But by then the oil market had slumped.

The Enron Scandal

Since the heady days of the oil boom, Houston's importance on the national scene has been largely economic. Reacting to the oil slump, civic and industrial leaders, intent on decreasing the city's reliance on the ups and downs of oil, were determined to build on Houston's strengths. One of those strengths was major companies,

like the multinational Enron. In 2001, Tropical Storm Allison caused some of the worst flooding in the city's history, but it would be the collapse of Enron, later that year, that would make national news. The Houston-based oil company collapsed, marking the third-largest bankruptcy in U.S. history. Before its bankruptcy in late 2001, Enron employed approximately 22,000 people and was one of the world's leading electricity, natural gas, communications, and pulp and paper companies, with claimed revenues of nearly $101 billion in 2000. Investigation would reveal that the numbers were doctored, and trust in American corporations has declined since.

Into the twenty-first century, out of mutual interest, closer ties between the leaders of Houston's three major industries—oil, medicine, and aerospace—were forged in concert with city government and an aggressive chamber of commerce in order to diversify its economy. The goal of diversification has proven successful, and Houston can count technology, finance, insurance, real estate, and manufacturing among the industries in which it plays a leadership role. Houston also consistently maintains one of the country's strongest housing markets, even despite the recessions of the 2000s.

Hurricane Havoc in the 2000s

In 2005 Houston became the makeshift shelter for over 150,000 people fleeing New Orleans and other coastal cities in anticipation of Hurricane Katrina. One month later, over two million Houston residents had to evacuate the city themselves due to the approaching Hurricane Rita, reportedly making history as the largest urban evacuation ever in the United States. By 2010 the surge of evacuees had netted the Houston area an additional 35,000 residents.

Historical Information: The Heritage Society Research Library, 1100 Bagby, Houston, TX 77002; telephone (713) 655-1912; fax (713) 655-9249; email info@heritagesociety.org. Houston Public Library, Texas and Local History Department, 500 McKinney St., Houston, TX 77002; telephone (832) 393-1658.

■ Population Profile

Metropolitan Statistical Area Population
2000: 4,177,646
2010: 5,946,800
2012 estimate: 6,204,161
Percent change, 2000–2010: 42.3%
U.S. rank in 2000: 8th
U.S. rank in 2010: 6th

City Residents
1990: 1,654,348
2000: 1,953,631
2010: 2,099,451

2012 estimate: 2,161,686
Percent change, 2000–2010: 7.5%
U.S. rank in 1990: 4th (State rank: 1st)
U.S. rank in 2000: 6th (State rank: 1st)
U.S. rank in 2010: 4th (State rank: 1st)

Density: 3,501.5 people per square mile

Racial and ethnic characteristics

White: 1,247,112
Black or African American: 508,366
American Indian and Alaskan Native: 8,144
Asian: 141,213
Native Hawaiian and Other Pacific Islander: 1,157
Hispanic or Latino (may be of any race): 938,882
Other: 255,694

Percent of residents born in state: 53.1%

Age characteristics

Population under 5 years old: 169,085
Population 5 to 9 years old: 158,339
Population 10 to 14 years old: 144,211
Population 15 to 19 years old: 138,408
Population 20 to 24 years old: 170,600
Population 25 to 34 years old: 382,834
Population 35 to 44 years old: 304,286
Population 45 to 54 years old: 268,954
Population 55 to 59 years old: 120,949
Population 60 to 64 years old: 96,925
Population 65 to 74 years old: 120,754
Population 75 to 84 years old: 63,113
Population 85 years and over: 23,228
Median age: 32.5

Births (2010–11 Metropolitan Area)

Total number: 97,795

Deaths (2010–11 Metropolitan Area)

Total number: 33,432

Money income (2012)

Per capita income: $26,235
Median household income: $43,792
Total households: 770,098

Number of households with income of . . .

less than $10,000: 72,533
$10,000 to $14,999: 51,851
$15,000 to $24,999: 99,022
$25,000 to $34,999: 93,294
$35,000 to $49,999: 108,171
$50,000 to $74,999: 121,839
$75,000 to $99,999: 76,115
$100,000 to $149,999: 74,717
$150,000 to $199,999: 30,644
$200,000 or more: 41,912

Percent of families below poverty level: 23.5%

FBI Crime Index Property: 107,678

FBI Crime Index Violent: 21,610

■ Municipal Government

Houston, the Harris County seat, has a strong mayor form of government. The mayor, a 14-member city council, and city controller are elected concurrently to two-year terms. The mayor and council members can be elected up to three consecutive terms. The council consists of representatives from nine districts, as well as five at-large members. The mayor serves as the chief executive, the council as the legislature, and the controller as the financial manager. All elections are non-partisan.

Head Official: Mayor Annise D. Parker (since 2010; current term expires 2014)

Total Number of City Employees: 21,000 (2013)

City Information: City of Houston, 900 Bagby, PO Box 1562, Houston, TX 77251-1562; telephone (713) 837-0311

■ Economy

Major Industries and Commercial Activity

While energy is the main driver, the city continues to be an important site for businesses in the Southwest, generally. In 2013 Houston was home to 25 companies on the *Fortune* 500 list, ranking third behind New York, with 67, and Chicago, with 29. Overall, Houston benefits from an increasingly diversified economy. Energy—oil, natural gas, and, with growing importance throughout the 2000s, renewable energies—defense, aerospace, and medical industries lead the way.

The energy industry has been the primary factor in the Houston economy since oil was first discovered in the region in 1901. Even during the oil and gas bust era of the 1980s, the Enron scandal, and the recessions of the early and late 2000s, expertise, technology, and resources remain in the area, providing the crucial base required to meet current national and international market demands while laying the groundwork for future growth. In 2012 according to the U.S. Bureau of Labor Statistics, the Houston metropolitan area held 27.3 percent of the nation's jobs in oil and gas extraction and 10.8 percent of jobs in support activities for mining.

Houston is home to major U.S. energy firms in every segment, including exploration, production, oil field service and supply, and development.

In 2013 Houston counted more than 3,700 energy-related firms within the Houston metropolitan statistical area. Five of the six major multinational energy companies have major operations in Houston; ConocoPhilips and Marathon Oil are headquartered in the city, which is also home to the major national operations of Exxon-Mobil, Shell Oil, and BP. The nine refineries in the Houston region produce 2.3 million barrels of crude oil per calendar day—approximately 50 percent of the state's total production and 13.8 percent of the total U.S. capacity.

The logistics for moving much of the nation's petroleum and natural gas across the country are controlled from Houston. Sixteen of the nation's 20 largest U.S. interstate oil pipeline companies have a presence in the Houston region, controlling 47 percent of all U.S. oil pipeline capacity. Seventeen of the nation's top 20 natural gas transmission companies control 64 percent of total U.S. pipeline capacity. Given the existence of these firms, and the technically trained and experienced work force, Houston no doubt will remain the center of the energy industry in the United States.

During the last decades of the twentieth century, Houston's dependence on the upstream energy industry made it particularly vulnerable to economic downturns determined by energy prices, the national economy, and the value of the dollar against foreign currencies. In order to insulate itself from further economic distress, the city began diversifying into downstream energy (refining and chemicals manufacturing), as well as industries unrelated to the energy sector.

Houston is also a world leader in the chemical industry, with nearly 40 percent of the nation's capacity for producing the basic chemicals that are used by downstream chemical operations. The Houston area is home to 405 chemical plants employing roughly 36,000 people. With an extensive infrastructure that includes the world's most elaborate pipeline network, Houston is a key production center for derivatives and specialty chemicals. It also has two of the nation's four largest oil refineries. Nearly every major chemical company operates a plant near Houston, including BASF AG, Bayer Corp., Chevron Phillips Chemical Co., E. I. du Pont de Nemours Co., ExxonMobil Chemical Co., and Shell Chemical LP.

Through more than a quarter century of manned space flight, Houston has played an important role in space exploration. The Johnson Space Center of the National Aeronautics & Space Administration (NASA) is the focal point of the U.S. manned space flight program. It has primary responsibility for the research, design, development, and testing of the space shuttle, and also selects and trains astronauts and controls manned space flights. Opened in 1962, the 1,620-acre Johnson complex is an international powerhouse of technological development, employing approximately 15,000 engineers, scientists, and administrative personnel. In addition, the national defense industry is an important factor in the Houston economy, with growing importance in a

globalized society. Major defense contractor Halliburton is headquartered in Houston.

The Texas Medical Center located in southeast Houston maintains one of the highest densities of clinical facilities for patient care, basic science, and medical research in the world. Nearly 50 medicine-related institutions call this area of the city home, the latest being the addition of the University of Texas Medical Branch at Galveston in 2010. Financial services are also a key component to Houston's economy. A number of major financial corporations are headquartered in the city, including American National Insurance Co., and AIG Retirement Services. Situated near the center of a twenty-county coastal prairie agricultural region, Houston is a major international agribusiness center emphasizing the marketing, processing, packaging, and distribution of agricultural commodities. The city also has a strong presence in computer software, electronics, engineering, and nanotechnology.

Items and goods produced: computer software, containers, processed foods, petrochemicals, steel, industrial gases, oil and gas field equipment, synthetic rubber, cement

Incentive Programs-New and Existing Companies

Local programs: The city of Houston and surrounding communities promote business through a number of programs. Many cities and counties in the region offer tax abatement agreements that exempt part of the increased value in real or personal property from taxation for a period not to exceed 10 years. In addition, companies locating in Houston's Foreign Trade Zone can delay payment of U.S. Customs import duties until their goods and merchandise actually enter U.S. commerce.

Brownfield abatements encourage the redevelopment of brownfields, areas where environmental contamination exists in the soil, surface water, or ground water. The city also attracts investments in Tax Increment Reinvestment Zones. These zones usually cover portions of the inner city, raw land in suburban fringe areas, or a major activity center under decline. Several types of incentives are offered to businesses investing capital and creating new jobs in these areas, and can include capital costs, financing costs, real property assembly, relocation costs, professional services, and administrative costs.

Houston is also a very entrepreneurial city, maintaining a strong early-stage financing investor network via the Houston Angel Network, not to mention a plethora of local venture capital firms.

State programs: Texas is a right-to-work state. The Texas economy has performed better than that of any other state during the recent economic downturn. It is believed that this success is due in part to the states pro-business climate, of which economic incentives are an important part.

The Texas Enterprise Zone Programs offer tax abatement at the local level, and refunds of state sales and use taxes under certain circumstances to businesses operating in enterprise zone areas. The Texas Enterprise Zone Program allows local communities to partner with the State of Texas to promote job creation and capital investment in targeted areas of the state that meet specific economic criteria. Designated projects are eligible to apply for state sales and use tax refunds on qualified expenditures. The state of Texas targets many of its incentive programs toward smaller and rural communities. The Rural Municipal Finance Program is a loan program created by the Texas Agricultural Finance Authority (TAFA) to stimulate economic activity in rural Texas. The Texas Enterprise Fund can be used to provide deal-closing money for companies relocating to and investing in Texas. The Texas Emerging Technology Fund, a $200 million fund created by the Texas Legislature in 2005, is available to companies who seek to commercialize new technologies. The program provides grants for early-stage investments in new, technology-based, private entrepreneurial entities that collaborate with public or private institutions of higher education.

Texas is one of the few states with no individual income tax, a very attractive environment for transferring employees. There is also no corporate income tax. Texas Enterprise Zone Program provides for eligible designated projects to apply for state sales and use tax refunds on purchases of all taxable items purchased for use at the qualified business site related to the project or activity. Special tax exemptions are made for manufacturing machinery, equipment, replacement parts, and accessories that have a useful life of more than six months. Texas businesses are also exempt from paying state sales and use tax on labor for constructing new facilities, electricity and natural gas used in manufacturing, processing, or fabrication. Tax-Exempt Industrial Revenue Bonds are designed to provide tax-exempt financing up to $20 million per project to finance land and depreciable property for eligible industrial or manufacturing projects.

The Texas Capital Fund Infrastructure and Real Estate Development programs are designed to provide no interest loans of up to $750,000 to non-entitlement communities. The program funds real estate developments (acquisitions, construction, and/or rehabilitation) to assist a business, which commits to creating or retaining permanent jobs, primarily for low and moderate-income persons.

Job training programs: The Texas Workforce Commission (TWC) provides workforce development assistance to employers and jobseekers across the state through a network of 28 workforce boards. Programs for employers include recruitment, retention, training and retraining, and outplacement services for employees. TWC also administers the Skills Development Fund, a program that assists public community and technical colleges create customized job training for local businesses.

The Houston Community College System (HCC) is the city's leading vehicle for ongoing training and business development. With six regional colleges, HCC has quality, cost-effective training programs conveniently located throughout the Houston area. HCC staff members also can customize training programs to meet a company's specific needs and conduct those classes on site. The HCC Workforce Development Division oversees over 60 degree and certificate programs, including accounting, biotechnology, computer science technology, international business, and real estate.

Development Projects

Houston is well known for liberal land use policies, notably lacking a zoning code, a common staple of modern planned cities. As a result, Houston enjoys lower real estate prices, increased availability of affordable housing, lower population concentration, and, some argue, more opportunities for entrepreneurs. While there have been some benefits gained by a more lax development policy, others argue that it has resulted in a sprawl town. Houston has been known to be a congested city with poor air quality due to the necessity of automobiles.

The renewal of downtown Houston began in the mid-1990s. By 2014, the city experienced more than $5.5 billion in development of buildings, parks and infrastructure. Recently completed projects include One Park Place, a 346-unit high rise apartment building overlooking the 12-acre park Discovery Green; GreenStreet, a $170 million mixed-use entertainment, retail and office complex; BG Group Place, a 47-story, one-million-square-foot office tower; Hess Tower, a 29-story, 844,763-square-foot office tower; the new Houston Ballet Center for Dance; and a new state-of-the-art Tellepsen Family Downtown YMCA. In the planning stages is a new downtown skyscraper for Chevron's growing Houston workforce. The energy giant plans to build a 50-story tower with 1.7 million square feet at 1600 Louisiana St. at Pease. The project is scheduled for completion in 2016. The company said the buildings will comprise an "urban campus with indoor and outdoor common areas, enhanced dining facilities, a fitness center, training and conference facilities, and additional parking."

The city's 2014–18 capital improvement plan calls for the appropriation of $5. 54 billion for the city's enterprise and public improvement programs. Of that amount, $3.01 billion is targeted for projects in the enterprise fund programs—Houston Airport System and the Combined Utility System.

Economic Development Information: Greater Houston Partnership, 1200 Smith, Ste. 700, Houston, TX 77002; telephone (713) 844-3600; fax (713) 844-0200; email ghp@houston.org.

Commercial Shipping

Houston's location, equidistant from the East and West Coasts, makes it an ideal distribution point for shippers sending goods to the U.S. West and Midwest. Two major passenger/air cargo airports, Bush Intercontinental Airport and William P. Hobby Airport, serve the region in addition to a vast network of interstate highways and railroads.

The Port of Houston is a 25-mile-long complex of diversified public and private facilities located just a few hours' sailing time from the Gulf of Mexico. More than 200 million tons of cargo pass through the port annually. In 2013 the port was ranked first in the United States in foreign waterborne tonnage (17 consecutive years); first in U.S. imports (21 consecutive years); first in U.S. export tonnage (4 consecutive years) and second in the U.S. in total tonnage (21 consecutive years).

This complex is served by the port authority, over 100 steamship lines, and more than 150 private industrial companies. The port is also the site of Foreign Trade Zone 84, at which foreign goods can be temporarily stored or processed without an import duty. Two major railroads and more than 150 trucking lines connect the port to the rest of the continental United States, Canada, and Mexico. Major commodities traded at the port include chemicals, petroleum and petroleum products, machinery, motor vehicles, and iron and steel.

Houston is one of the nation's busiest rail centers, with 12 mainline tracks going through the city from which an average of 700,000 rail cars depart and arrive each year. In addition to links with the three airports, the Port of Houston, and local highways, the rail system is linked with the local trucking industry by six intermodal terminals. The Houston area is served by more than 1,100 trucking firms.

Labor Force and Employment Outlook

The Houston metro area is home to more than 2.7 million jobs, of which roughly 2.2 million are in the service industries.

The Texas Workforce Commission reports that Houston led the state in job growth in 2013. While the city accounts for about 23 percent of the state's population, it captured almost 35 percent of the 276,400 jobs created in 2012. The largest sector is trade, transportation, and utilities which accounts for almost 550,000 jobs in the Houston area. Professional and business services is second with 390,000, followed by government (375,000), education and health (350,000), and leisure and hospitality (266,000). The fastest growing sectors were construction, leisure and hospitality, and education and health services. The commission projects that the service industry will also be one of the fastest growing sectors throughout the early twenty-first century, second only to professional occupations.

Houston lags just behind the national rate for high school graduates; however, its concentration of college graduates slightly exceeds the national average. The city is frequently listed by national publications as one of the best cities to begin a career. Houstonians have also retained very specific skill sets due to the vast amount of energy companies in the region. Diversification of these skills has also become evident.

The following is a summary of data regarding the 2012 Houston labor force:

Size of civilian labor force: 1,111,051

Number of workers employed in . . .

agriculture and mining: 25,866
construction: 99,019
manufacturing: 92,939
wholesale trade: 31,491
retail trade: 109,000
transportation: 54,529
information systems: 13,747
finance: 57,051
professional administration: 140,563
education and social services: 193,361
arts and leisure: 93,231
other: 63,375
public administration: 25,842

Average hourly earnings of production workers: $18.24

Unemployment rate: 6.1% (2012)

Employers

Largest employers (2013)	Number of employees
Wal-Mart Stores	30,500
ExxonMobil	21,500
Memorial Hermann Healthcare System	19,500
The University of Texas M.D. Anderson Cancer Center	17,000
United Airlines, Inc.	17,000
Schlumberger Limited	15,500
Shell Oil Company	13,000
The Methodist Hospital	13,000
Kroger Company	12,000
National Oilwell Varco	10,000
BP America	9.537
University of Texas Medical Branch	9,318
Baylor College of Medicine	9,232
HP	9,000
ARAMARK Corp.	8,500

Chevron	8,000
Pappas Restaurants, Inc.	8,000
HCA	7,855

Cost of Living

Historically, the cost of living has ranked lower in Houston than in most major U.S. cities because residents pay no state or local income tax. Housing in general is extremely attractive and relatively affordable in Houston.

The following is a summary of data regarding several key cost of living factors in the area.

2013 ACCRA Average House Price: $247,637

2013 ACCRA Cost of Living Index: 97

State income tax rate: None

State sales tax rate: 6.25%

Local income tax rate: None

Local sales tax rate: 2.0%

Property tax rate: $0.63850 per $100 assessed valuation (2013)

Economic Information: Greater Houston Partnership, 1200 Smith, Ste. 700, Houston, TX 77002; telephone (713) 844-3600; fax (713) 844-0200; email ghp@houston.org. Texas Workforce Commission, 101 E. 15th St., Rm. 651, Austin, TX 78778-0001; telephone (512) 463-2236; email customers@twc.state.tx.us.

■ Education and Research

Elementary and Secondary Schools

About 17 school districts serve the region, but it is the Houston Independent School District (HISD) that is the largest in Texas and the seventh largest in the United States. In 2013 the district served more than 200,000 students in 282 schools. There were 6 early childhood schools, 164 elementary, 40 middle, 44 high, and 26 combined/other. More than 60 percent of the students are Hispanic, 26 percent African American, 3.3 percent Asian, and 8.0 percent White.

In 2012 HISD was named a finalist for the prestigious Broad Prize for Urban Education, receiving high marks for its progress in narrowing the achievement gap. Also in 2012, voters approved a $1.89 billion school construction bond—the largest in the history of Texas—by a 69 percent margin. Special programs include the Houston Academy for International Studies and International Baccalaureate programs at the elementary and secondary level.

In 2013 the city had more than 300 private schools, both parochial and secular, serving over 53,000 students.

The Archdiocese of Galveston-Houston is the largest private school system in Texas, serving over 17,000 students in 50 primary schools and 9 high schools. There are more than 30 charter schools, including one operated by the University of Houston that serves 130 kindergarten through fifth grade students. There are nearly 100 independent private schools.

The following is a summary of data regarding the Houston Independent School District.

Total enrollment: 204,245

Number of facilities
total: 282
elementary schools: 170
junior high schools: 40
high schools: 44
other: 26

Student/teacher ratio: 17.29:1

Teacher salaries
average (statewide): $48,261

Funding per pupil: $8,984

Public Schools Information: Houston Independent School District, 4400 West 18th Street; Houston, TX 77092-8501; telephone (713) 556-6005.

Colleges and Universities

Houston's nearly 300,000 college students make it one of the nation's leading academic centers and college towns, as well as one of the best places for young professionals to start their careers. More than 60 degree-granting public colleges, universities, and institutes dot the Houston landscape. The oldest is Rice University, a top tier undergraduate university consistently ranked among the best national universities by publications like *U.S. News & World Report*. Rice is highly selective, serving about 7,000 students; its endowment per student is fifth highest in the nation, and the school has been called a "new ivy" league school in the new century by *Newsweek*. The largest in the area is the University of Houston, with three campuses in the immediate Houston area. Around 75 percent of its alumni remain in the Houston area after graduation, and the institution ranked among the top five for all national universities in terms of diversity, according to the *U.S. News & World Report* rankings. Other major educational centers include Texas Southern University, University of St. Thomas, and Houston Baptist University. The city also has three law schools and abundant medical training, including the Baylor College of Medicine and the University of Texas–Houston Health Science Center. The Houston Community College System is one of the state's largest.

Libraries and Research Centers

Houston has two major public library systems: the Houston Public Library system and the Harris County Public Library system. In addition to the central Houston Public Library downtown, a 333,000-square-foot facility with holdings of 4,200,301 volumes, the Houston Public Library system encompasses 38 branches along with the Clayton Library for Genealogical Research and the Parent Resource Library in the Children's Museum of Houston. Its collections include the Greenberg Collection, Texas and Local History Collection, and U.S. Government Documents. The system also includes the Houston Metropolitan Research Center, a cooperative project formed in 1976 with Rice University, Texas Southern University, and the University of Houston. Housed in the Julia Ideson Building, this collection makes available the documentary, oral, and visual evidence of Houston's past, including African American, Mexican American, architectural, photographic, jazz music, and oral history components.

The Harris County Public Library maintains 26 branches and over 2 million items in its collection. Specialized libraries and research centers in Houston range from numerous medical and legal facilities to a library run by the American Brahman Breeders Association.

NASA's Johnson Space Center coordinates a great deal of development and design work for the U.S. Space Station. The University of Houston's 24 research entities include the Texas Learning & Computation Center, the Institute for Space Systems Operations, the Environmental Institute of Houston, Center for Materials Chemistry, Center for Public Policy, and Center for Immigration Research. Rice University conducts more than $70 million in grant research annually in such fields as computing, nanotechnology, laser technology, robotics, groundwater management, toxic chemical clean-up, global warming, material science, astronomy, space physics, and biomedical engineering.

The Houston Advanced Research Center combines the facilities of nine major universities in translating scientific advances into practical applications.

As the largest medical complex in the world, the Texas Medical Center is an internationally recognized community of healing, learning, and discovery. In 2012 the Center had 54 member institutions that employed 5,700 researchers with a research budget of $3.4 billion. The center is home to a 400,000-square-foot research complex for biomedical research and education in stem-cell research. Baylor College houses a major center for AIDS research.

Public Library Information: Harris County Public Library, 8080 El Rio, Houston, TX 77054; telephone (713) 749-9000. Houston Public Library, 500 McKinney St., Houston, TX 77002; telephone (832) 393-1313.

■ Health Care

With 95 hospitals within the metropolitan area, Houston is a world leader in medicine and boasts the world's largest medical complex. Approximately 5.2 million patients—more than 10,000 of them foreign—are treated each year in the internationally renowned Texas Medical Center alone, a centralized facility begun in 1943. As the largest medical complex in the world, the Texas Medical Center is an internationally recognized community of healing, learning and discovery. In 2012 the Center had 54 member institutions and employed 106,000 people, including 5,000 physicians and 15,000 nurses. The Center maintains 45.8 million square feet of space among all campuses, comprising 1,345 acres of land and 290 buildings. More than 170,000 surgeries are performed annually at its facilities. Its total operating budget was $15 billion. Among its member institutions are Texas Children's Hospital, Methodist Hospital, and St. Luke's Episcopal Hospital, as well as the M. D. Anderson Cancer Center, which has been ranked as the best hospital for cancer treatment by *U.S. News & World Report* (among top 10 appearances in other specialties) and is consistently ranked in the publication's annual best hospitals list. The Texas Heart Institute at St. Luke's Episcopal Hospital has performed more cardiac procedures than any other institution in the world. Houston's medical community is known for its major contributions in the areas of cardiac care, cancer research and therapy, trauma care, and innovative medical treatment. Two of Houston's other major hospitals include the Menninger Clinic and TIRR: The Institute for Rehabilitation & Research. The Texas Medical Center is known throughout the world for the quality of patient care, teaching, research and prevention of illness and injury.

■ Recreation

Sightseeing

As the nation's sixth largest city, Houston offers a wide selection of recreational opportunities, ranging from professional football, basketball, and baseball to permanent companies in opera, ballet, theater, and symphony. Houston's retail offerings are world class, with several major shopping malls and urban entertainment centers. With mild annual temperatures, abundant lakes, rivers, and wildlife areas, and more than 400 parks, Houston is also very much an outdoor city.

A principal point of interest is the Johnson Space Center, which offers self-guided public tours every day except Christmas. A unit of the National Aeronautics & Space Administration (NASA), the center features a museum, tours of the Mission Control Center, and viewing of samples returned from the Moon. Space Center Houston allows visitors to "experience" manned

Texas: Houston

space flight through the "Blast Off Theater," explore shuttle and Skylab facilities, and operate the simulator.

The historically minded may be interested in the San Jacinto Battleground State Historical Park, the world's tallest masonry structure. It houses documents, art, and memorabilia, and is a permanent berth for the battleship USS *Texas,* a veteran of both world wars and the only surviving dreadnought of its class.

Hermann Park includes the Houston Zoo, Miller Outdoor Theatre, the Houston Museum of Natural Science, and the first desegregated public golf course in the nation. Among other parks offering sightseeing opportunities are Memorial Park Conservancy, featuring an arboretum, herb gardens, and a botanical hall; Sam Houston Park, with seven historical buildings located downtown; and Tranquility Park, in the downtown area. In the Harris County Park system attractions include Armand Bayou Nature Center, with its wilderness preserve, nature trails, working turn-of-the-century farm, and scenic Armand Bayou boat tours; Mercer Arboretum, featuring gardens, a wilderness preserve, and nature trails; and Bay Area Park, featuring a marsh walkway. Moody Gardens on Galveston Island features a tropical setting with white sand beaches, penguins, and a discovery pyramid. The Beer Can House, a unique attraction, is constructed of over 50,000 beer cans.

Arts and Culture

Houston ranks second only to New York City by number of theater seats in a concentrated downtown area. Moreover, it is one of only a handful of cities in the country to feature permanent dance, theater, symphony, and opera companies that operate year-round. The Wortham Theater Center, a $75 million complex housing the Houston Grand Opera and the Houston Ballet, is the centerpiece of Houston's vital cultural community. That community is supported by a 1 percent hotel tax dedicated to the city's arts, which have become nationally prominent. The city also features Jesse H. Jones Hall for the Performing Arts, home of the Houston Symphony and Society for the Performing Arts; the Hobby Center for the Performing Arts, the home of Theatre Under the Stars; and the Alley Theatre, one of the oldest resident professional theater companies in the nation.

Other famed theater groups include Stages Repertory, Main Street Theater, A.D. Players, De Camera of Houston, Theatre Lab Houston, Opera in the Heights, and the Ensemble Theatre, one of the nation's most respected African American theaters.

The Houston Symphony was formed in 1913 and performs more than 200 concerts each year in Jesse H. Jones Hall for the Performing Arts, plus summer concerts in Miller Theatre. Among other musical groups are the acclaimed Houston Grand Opera; the Houston Opera Studio, an international apprenticeship center; the Houston Youth Symphony; and the orchestras of four local universities.

The Houston Ballet, a professional company, performs at home and abroad. The company's new Center for Dance held its grand opening in 2011. The $46.6 million facility features nine dance studios, a Dance Lab that seats 175 for presentations as well as rehearsals, and artistic, administrative and support facilities. It is the largest professional dance facility of its kind in the United States. Other dance companies include the Delia Stewart Dance Company, Allegro Dance Group, Chrysalis Dance Company, City Ballet of Houston, Cookie Joe's Jazz Company, and Several Dancers Core.

With 15 world-class museums, Houston is the fourth largest museum district in the nation. The Houston Museum of Natural Science, located near Hermann Park, features the Burke Baker Planetarium, the Wortham IMAX Theatre, and the Cockrell Butterfly Center, as well as exhibits in space science, geography, oceanography, medical science, and Texas wildlife. The Museum of Fine Arts–Houston, one of the largest museums in the United States, houses more than 27,000 works from antiquities to the present and has over 2.5 million visitors annually. It also features the Bayou Bend Collection of American decorative arts, housed in the historic home of local philanthropist Ima Hogg and surrounded by 14 acres of gardens. Houston also boasts the world-famous Menil Collection, 15,000 pieces representing twentieth-century, medieval, and Byzantine art, antiquities, and tribal art. The Contemporary Arts Museum exhibits modern works and is free to the public.

Other facilities include Children's Museum of Houston, Holocaust Museum Houston, ArtCar Museum, National Museum of Funeral History, Buffalo Soldiers National Museum, American Cowboy Museum, the Moody Mansion & Museum, The Health Museum, Museum of Printing History, and the Byzantine Fresco Chapel Museum, repository for the only intact Byzantine frescoes in the Western Hemisphere. Among the area's galleries are Farish Gallery and Rice University Art Gallery, both on the Rice University campus, and the Blaffer Gallery, on the University of Houston campus.

Arts and Culture Information: Greater Houston Convention & Visitors Bureau, 901 Bagby, Ste. 100, Houston, TX 77002; telephone (713) 437-5200; toll-free (800) 4-HOUSTON.

Festivals and Holidays

Houston celebrates with countless festivals throughout the year. A Grande Parade and Gala is held downtown each January in honor of Martin Luther King Jr. The late-winter Houston Livestock Show & Rodeo commands Reliant Stadium and draws a crowd in excess of 1.8 million over three weeks. April brings the Houston International Festival, a multicultural event spanning 20 city blocks and attracting more than one million visitors across 10 days of performances, art expositions, and open-air markets. The Texas Renaissance Festival is held for eight themed weekends in October and November, while later in November Houston gathers for the H-E-B Holiday Parade on Thanksgiving Day. In December Moody Gardens presents a Festival of Lights, the Heritage Society holds a Christmas Candlelight Tour, and lighted boats are displayed in the Christmas Boat Parade on Clear Lake.

Ethnic celebrations are held throughout the year. They include the Greek Festival, Bayou City Cajun Festival, Japan Festival, Asian/Pacific American Heritage Festival, Cinco de Mayo Celebration, Scottish Highland Games & Celtic Festival, Fiestas Patrias, Houston Turkish Festival, Festa Italiana, and the Texas Championship Pow Wow. Texans' love of a variety of cuisines is apparent from Houston's numerous food celebrations, such as the University of Houston Chili Cook-Off, Bayou Boil, and the Pasadena Strawberry Festival, held 20 minutes southeast of Houston. Celebrations of arts are nearly as frequent. Spring brings the Dance Salad Festival, which presents dancers from the Americas, Europe, Asia, and Africa, followed by the Houston International Film Festival. ArtHouston, Houston International Jazz Festival, Houston Shakespeare Festival, and Trader's Village Bluegrass Festival are held in succession between mid-summer and early autumn.

Some events celebrate the unusual, and others are held just for fun. The Houston Comedy Festival features 20 performances across 8 days in April. Galveston Island hosts the FeatherFest, a birding celebration coinciding with the annual spring migration of nearly 300 species. Each May corporate and community teams race 40-foot dragon boats in the Dragon Boat Festival. RE/MAX Ballunar Festival Liftoff, presented by the Johnson Space Center each August, features a weekend of hot-air ballooning, sky-diving exhibitions, and food and entertainment. The U.S. Air Force Thunderbirds and the Navy's Blue Angels thrill spectators with aerial acrobatics each October in the Wings Over Houston Airshow.

Sports for the Spectator

Fans in Houston have the option of watching professional and collegiate sports. After losing the Oilers to Tennessee in 1996, Houston regained a National Football League (NFL) franchise when the Houston Texans took the field in 2002. Their home is the 69,500-seat Reliant Stadium, featuring the world's first retractable roof in the NFL; several others have since been built. Reliant also hosted Super Bowl XXXVII in 2004, at which the New England Patriots beat the Carolina Panthers. The Houston Astros, a franchise of the National League of Major League Baseball, play home games at Minute Maid Park, named after the major Houston company. The Toyota Center opened in September 2003 and is home to the Houston Rockets of the National Basketball Association; the Houston Comets, of the Women's National Basketball Association; and the Houston Aeros, of the American Hockey League. Houston Energy, a franchise of the Women's Professional Football League, play their home games at The Rig at Pearland High School.

Collegiate teams participate in most major sports by Houston-area academic institutions. Football is particularly notable, with Rice University in Conference USA, the University of Houston in the American Conference, Texas Southern University in the Southwest Athletic Conference, and Houston Baptist University, which competes as an independent. Horse racing can be enjoyed at Sam Houston Race Park, while dogs race at Gulf Greyhound Park. More than 150 of the world's best golfers vie for a $5 million purse in the Shell Houston Open golf tournament each April. The Houston Golf Association has been conducting PGA Tour events since 1946, making Houston's tournament the 10th oldest on the schedule.

Sports for the Participant

Harris County and the City of Houston's 350 developed parks and 200 green spaces embrace 38,945 acres. They offer such attractions for the recreation-minded as eight golf courses (plus dozens of non-municipal public and private courses), 39 swimming pools, 81 tennis centers, 174 baseball/softball fields, over 200 athletic fields and courts, 100 miles of hiking and cycling trails, and Lake Houston. Cullen Park, one of the largest municipal parks in the nation, boasts a velodrome equipped for Olympic cycling events. A driving range is available at Memorial Park, fishing is enjoyed at Eisenhower Park, and a three-story man-made mountain graces Herman Brown Park. Harris County parks include Clear Lake Park, with boating and fishing; Alexander Deussen Park, with boating, fishing, and camping on Lake Houston; Bear Creek Park, with an aviary on Addicks Reservoir lands; Bay Area Park, with canoeing; and Tom Bass Regional Park, offering fishing. Houston lies within an hour of 70 miles of Gulf Coast beaches; deep-sea fishing on the Gulf is available through charter companies.

Annual events invite participants of all athletic levels. In March the Guaranty Bank Tour de Houston attracts competitors in a 20- or 40-mile bike race. For many, the Tour de Houston is a warm-up for the BP MS 150 Bike Tour. Held each April, it is the largest non-profit sporting event in Texas, drawing 12,000 riders and raising more than $47 million in the last two decades to combat multiple sclerosis. The Buffalo Bayou Regatta, Texas's largest canoe and kayak race, is held each October.

Shopping and Dining

The 375 stores and restaurants of The Galleria, one of the largest shopping centers in the nation, are visited by more than 20 million shoppers each year. The complex spans 2.4 million square feet of space, housing 400 fine stores and restaurants, two high-rise hotels, and three office towers. Katy Mills Mall houses 175 retail outlets in 1.3 million square feet of space. Uptown Park is a European-style shopping center featuring unique wares. The largest market on the Texas Gulf Coast is Traders Village, a collection that attracts over 4 million visitors each year. Early 2005 brought the grand opening of Market Square Market, an outdoor marketplace held each Saturday in historic Market Square Park. Antiques and collectibles shoppers seek out the Houston Flea Market, while those seeking Western gear head to Stelzig of Texas and The Hat Store.

With more than 6,100 restaurants and 600 bars and nightclubs in the Houston area to choose from, diners can enjoy a great variety of menus and cuisines. Gulf seafood, such as oysters, shrimp, lobster, and fish, is a regional specialty; other regional specialties include Texas beef, barbecue, Southwestern mesquite-grilled food, Tex-Mex and Mexican fare, and traditional Southern dishes like catfish and chicken-fried steak. Ethnic and international establishments in the Houston area offer the cuisine of 35 countries, including France, Italy, Spain, Greece, Morocco, and India.

Visitor Information: Greater Houston Convention & Visitors Bureau, 901 Bagby, Ste. 100, Houston, TX 77002; telephone (713) 437-5200; toll-free (800) 4-HOUSTON.

■ Convention Facilities

Houston is one of the state's top tourist and meeting destinations. The $165 million expansion of the George R. Brown Convention Center was completed in late 2003. Encompassing 1.8 million square feet in total, the center nearly doubled its exhibition space to 862,500 square feet and now features 117 meeting rooms. Adjacent to the Brown Convention Center is the Hilton Americas-Houston. In addition to more than 1,200 guest rooms, this convention hotel offers 91,000 square feet of flexible meeting space, including 26,000- and 40,000-square-foot ballrooms and 30 meeting rooms. A second convention center hotel, the Marriott Marquis, broke ground in 2014, with a grand opening scheduled for 2016. The new facility will have 1,000 rooms and attached 1,800-car garage, retail shops, and a Texas-shaped "lazy river" pool. A skybridge will connect the hotel to the GRB's north end.

Reliant Center, home to the Houston Texans, offers 1.4 million square feet of convention and meeting space. Reliant Park is also a major convention center; together, the two major convention centers offer nearly 4 million square feet of meeting and exhibit space.

Convention Information: Greater Houston Convention & Visitors Bureau, 901 Bagby, Ste. 100, Houston, TX 77002; telephone (713) 437-5200; toll-free (800) 4-HOUSTON.

■ Transportation

Approaching the City

With two major airports and several regional air facilities, Houston ranks as a central transportation hub. The George Bush Intercontinental Airport is ranked as the eighth busiest in the United States and among the top 20 busiest airports worldwide. It has a $24 billion impact on the Houston economy, and flies to 182 domestic and international destinations. Passenger service is provided by all major domestic and international carriers at the George Bush Intercontinental Airport on the north side of the city, and by most major domestic carriers at the more centrally located William P. Hobby Airport about seven miles south of downtown. Ellington Field serves approximately 80,000 private and corporate passengers each year.

Houston is the crossroads for Interstates 10 and 45. Other major highways serving Houston are Loop 610, U.S. highways 59, 290 and 90, Texas highways 288 and 225, Hardy Toll Road, Sam Houston Tollway, and the Grand Parkway (Texas 99). Visitors can now arrive in Houston via the ocean, as Norwegian Cruise Lines offers service from the Port of Houston. Amtrak passenger rail service to Houston is available via *The Sunset*, connecting Los Angeles and New Orleans. Greyhound and Kerrville Bus Company offer regular motor coach service.

Traveling in the City

Automobiles constitute one of Houston's principal transportation headaches, although an ambitious transit program offers the hope of unsnarling some of the major traffic problems. An extensive commuter bus system operated by the Metropolitan Transit Authority of Harris County (METRO) provides service in the inner city and most outlying areas with a fleet of 1,661 buses covering 1,285 square miles of service area. In 2004 METRO began operating a light rail system. The line started with a 7.5 mile route through downtown Houston but was scheduled to expand to 80 miles by 2025.

■ Communications

Newspapers and Magazines

Houston's major daily, the *Houston Chronicle*, is joined by four smaller-circulation dailies and by the weeklies *Houston Business Journal* and *Houston Press,* an alternative paper. Campus newspapers include the *Daily Cougar* (University of Houston), the *Thresher* (Rice University), and the *UHCLidian* (University of Houston–Clear Lake).

Television and Radio

Dozens of television stations can be watched in the Houston area, including the city's broadcasts of five network affiliates, a public broadcasting affiliate that was the nation's first public broadcasting television station, and two independents. The nearly fifty AM and FM radio stations available in the city broadcast programming ranging from news, Spanish-language, and Christian talk shows to top 40, polka, rhythm and blues, jazz, and country music, university, and public radio.

Media Information: *Houston Chronicle,* 801 Texas Ave., Houston, TX 77002; telephone (713) 220-2700.

Houston Online

City of Houston Home Page. Available www. houstontx.gov

Greater Houston Convention & Visitors Bureau. Available www.visithoustontexas.com

Greater Houston Partnership. Available www. houston.org

Harris County Public Library. Available www.hcpl. lib.tx.us

The Heritage Society. Available www. heritagesociety.org

Houston Chronicle. Available www.chron.com

Houston Independent School District. Available www.houstonisd.org

Houston Public Library. Available www. houstonlibrary.org

NASA Johnson Space Center. Available www.nasa. gov/centers/johnson/home/index.html

Texas Workforce Commission. Available www.twc. state.tx.us

BIBLIOGRAPHY

Brennan, Marcia, *A Modern Patronage: de Menil Gifts to American and European Museums* (Houston, TX: Menil Foundation, 2007)

James, Marquis, *The Raven: A Biography of Sam Houston* (Norwalk, CT: Easton Press, 1988)

McMurtry, Larry, *Terms of Endearment* (New York: Simon & Schuster, 1975)

Roth, Mitchel P., *Houston Blue: The Story of the Houston Police Department* (Denton, TX: University of North Texas Press, 2012)

Strom, Steven, *Houston Lost and Unbuilt* (Austin: University of Texas Press, 2010)

Winningham, Geoff, and Alan Reinhart, *A Place of Dreams: Houston, An American City* (Houston, TX: Rice University, 1986)

San Antonio

■ The City in Brief

Founded: 1718 (incorporated 1809)

Head Official: Mayor Julián Castro (since 2009; term expires 2015)

City Population
  1990: 976,514
  2000: 1,144,646
  2010: 1,327,407
  2012 estimate: 1,383,194
  Percent change, 2000–2010: 16%
  U.S. rank in 1990: 10th (State rank: 3rd)
  U.S. rank in 2000: 13th (State rank: 3rd)
  U.S. rank in 2010: 7th (State rank: 2nd)

Metropolitan Statistical Area Population
  2000: 1,592,383
  2010: 2,142,508
  2012 estimate: 2,234,003
  Percent change, 2000–2010: 34.5%
  U.S. rank in 2000: 29th
  U.S. rank in 2010: 25th

Area: 407.6 square miles

Elevation: Approximately 701 feet above sea level

Average Annual Temperatures: January, 50.3° F; July, 84.3° F; annual average, 68.7° F

Average Annual Precipitation: 32.92 inches of rain; 0.7 inches of snow

Major Economic Sectors: services, wholesale and retail trade, government

Unemployment Rate: 5.2% (2012)

Per Capita Income: $22,233

2012 FBI Crime Index Property: 82,668

Major Colleges and Universities: University of Texas at San Antonio, St. Mary's University, San Antonio College

Daily Newspaper: *Express-News*

■ Introduction

San Antonio, the Alamo City, is often regarded as the "Heart of Texas." This Southwest town's illustrious past and its cosmopolitan present have come to symbolize the rich heritage of the state. The second largest city in the state of Texas and among the most populous in the nation, San Antonio retains its small-town flavor while serving as the headquarters for five of the country's major military installations and *Fortune* 500 companies. In addition to government services, the city's largest industry, trade, high-technology services, and tourism make up a strong economy. Visitors by the millions are drawn to the city's romantic, meandering River Walk, the beauty of eighteenth-century Spanish missions, and of course, the historic site where Davey Crockett, Jim Bowie, William Travis, and 185 others made their last stand in the name of freedom from Mexico. In addition, San Antonio represents the center of Tejano culture and big Texas tourism. The coexistence of the old and new is one reason San Antonio is viewed as an attractive place to live and visit. In 2012 San Antonio was named an All-America City by the National Civic League.

■ Geography and Climate

Commonly known as "the place where the sunshine spends the winter," San Antonio is situated in south central Texas between the Edwards Plateau to the northwest and the Gulf Coastal Plains to the southeast. The city sits on the Balcones Escarpment, a large, inactive fault line, over 700 feet above sea level. Along the fault line is the Edwards Aquifer, a major artesian aquifer

Natalia Bratslavsky/Shutterstock.com

serving as the primary drinking water supply to the city. The city's gently rolling terrain is dotted with oak trees, mesquite, and cacti, which flourish under the clear or partly cloudy skies that prevail more than 60 percent of the time.

Although San Antonio lies 140 miles from the Gulf of Mexico, the seat of Bexar County, pronounced "bear," is still close enough to experience the warm, muggy air of a semitropical climate. During the winter, temperatures drop below the freezing mark an average of only 20 days and only bring measurable snowfall once every three to four years; precipitation is mostly in the form of light rain or drizzle. Annual rainfall is about 33 inches, enough for production of most crops. May and September see the most rainfall building to thunderstorms with winds from the southeast. The city's proximity to the Gulf of Mexico, however, can bring San Antonio some severe tropical storms. Summers are hot; in fact, federal studies of weather patterns rank San Antonio as the fourth hottest city in the nation because of the average 111 days each year that temperatures reach 90 degrees or higher.

Area: 407.6 square miles

Elevation: Approximately 701 feet above sea level

Average Temperatures: January, 50.3° F; July, 84.3° F; annual average, 68.7° F

Average Annual Precipitation: 32.92 inches of rain; 0.7 inches of snow

■ History

Alamo Dominates Early History

Crossing six miles of city blocks, the San Antonio River is the focus of the city, just as it has been ever since the surrounding valley drew wandering Coahuitecan tribes seeking respite from the heat. Members of the Payaya tribe who camped on the river's banks named the region Yanaguana, or "Place of Restful Waters." But written records of these tribes' presence are minimal, and it was not until 1691 that the first visit to the river valley was made by a European. That year, on June 13, a day devoted to Saint Anthony of Padua on the Roman Catholic calendar, the river was christened by a Spanish official exploring the region. After he moved on, it was not until 1709 that a second party of Spaniards encountered the river while searching for a site for a new mission. They returned to the area in 1718 to found Mission San Antonio de Valero and Villa de Bexar, the outpost established to govern the Texas province. The mission eventually became the most famous of all Spanish missions established throughout the American Southwest. Although its crude huts were destroyed in 1724 by a hurricane, they were rebuilt on the site where its remains now stand. The mission's nickname became the Alamo; in Spanish, the word "alamo" means cottonwood, and writings by settlers of the period note the region's groves of trees, its water supply, and its mild climate reminiscent of their home country.

Six missions in all were founded around San Antonio, with a goal of converting the native population to Roman Catholicism. A presidio, or fort, was established near each mission, with soldiers to protect the missionaries and, when necessary, to add force to the missionary argument. The system was designed to create new Spanish subjects out of the natives, enabling Spain to hold onto the vast territories it claimed in North America. Historians blame the eventual failure of the mission system on epidemics that reduced the population, periodic raids by Apaches and Comanches, and cultural differences resulting in feuds among friars, soldiers, and colonists. Mission San Antonio was secularized (removed from Church control) in 1793, and the city was incorporated in 1809.

From 1810 to 1821, San Antonio, which served as the seat of the Spanish government in Texas, was the site of several major battles in Mexico's fight for independence from Spain. Anglo-American colonization began with 300 families brought to Texas by Stephen F. Austin, whose father envisioned a settlement with ties to neither Spain nor Mexico. By 1835, the settlers' resentment of Mexico had grown into an armed revolt. Mexico's first attempt to quell the rebellion was defeated. In revenge, Mexican dictator Antonio López de Santa Anna brought with him an army of 5,000 men to attack San Antonio's defenders, a force of fewer than 200 Texans fighting from inside the fortified Alamo. Among those within its walls who held off Santa Anna's troops for 13 days beginning in February 1836, were frontiersman Davey Crockett, soldier Jim Bowie, and Lieutenant Colonel William Travis, who vowed to neither surrender nor retreat.

Statehood's Aftermath

The "Victory or Death" dedication of the Alamo's defenders, who ultimately perished when their call for reinforcements went unanswered, inspired other insurgents throughout Texas to take up arms against Mexico. Forty-six days after the Alamo fell-to the battle cry "Remember the Alamo!"-Sam Houston's Texans defeated Santa Anna at San Jacinto, and the Republic of Texas was established. The battles and uncertainties, however, did not end until 1845 when Texas became the twenty-eighth U.S. state. The ensuing period brought an influx of German settlers to San Antonio, which increased the population from about 800 to 8,000 people. Texas, aligned with the Confederacy in the Civil War, maintained its rough frontier atmosphere until 1877, when the railroad linked the isolated region with the rest of the nation.

The City in the Twentieth Century

A regional cattle industry evolved, and San Antonio's progress was further enhanced with the advent of gas lights, telephones, and electricity. When the city entered the twentieth century, it was a melting pot of German and Hispanic influence, and its population swelled with newcomers from urban America. Between 1870 and 1920 San Antonio grew to 161,000 people, making it Texas's largest city. Shortly after the turn of the century, "Aeroplane No. 1," a Wright brothers-type aircraft, flew over Fort Sam Houston and marked the debut of military aviation as an economic force in the region. Downtown businesses flourished, and the coming of the automobile fed the growth of newer surrounding communities.

World War I solidified San Antonio's position as a military command center; 70,000 troops trained there in 1917 and 1918. The war also diminished the status of the city's German community, leading to the resurgence of the Hispanic population, which was growing due to the influx of hundreds of thousands of Mexicans into Texas. San Antonio's Great Flood of 1921 left destruction in its wake, but by 1929 the city's adobe structures were complemented by skyscrapers, the most notable being the Tower Life Building, at one time the tallest office building in the state. San Antonio's Conservation Society became a vigorous presence in the preservation of the city's historical treasures, including the river around which it is built.

The onset of World War II meant intensive military activity for San Antonio. Lackland Air Force Base, for instance, trained more than one third of the war's air cadets. Expansion of the military complex led to tremendous postwar growth for the city and its environs. The 1968 HemisFair celebration placed an international spotlight on the city, attracting thousands of visitors, including some who decided to make the thriving Sun Belt community their home. By the 1970s the city's population numbered well over 700,000 people, of which more than half were Hispanic. Demand for more services and housing increased, yet language and cultural barriers had created pockets of poverty and ethnic tensions. Politics reflected the city's changing mood, and in 1975 Lila Cockrell became the first woman mayor of San Antonio. Eventually the Hispanic majority concentrated its new political force in the person of Councilman Henry Cisneros, elected in 1981 as the country's first Mexican-American mayor of a major city. San Antonio entered the 1980s as a national example of growing Latin influence in politics. The 1990 groundbreaking for the Alamodome, a $170 million domed stadium which served as the home to the NBA Spurs and was the city's first venue for major conventions and special events, marked the beginning of a progressive decade for the city. The city saw further growth, with the completion of such projects as the expansion of the Henry B. Gonzalez Convention Center, which helped bring the city's annual convention attendance to 500,000, and the 2002 completion of the SBC Center (now the AT&T Center), a new home for the Spurs, the city's professional basketball team.

In 2005 Hurricane Katrina devastated much of the Gulf Coast; although not directly affected, the city did welcome and assist 30,000 evacuees as well as set up a Hurricane Relief Fund. Visitors to the city are often there under more fortunate circumstances: to take in the popular historic sights of the American Southwest in a growing metropolitan area.

The Mission Trails project, which will make the area's historic missions more easily accessible, got approval on design plans for its final two phases in 2010. In addition to historic ambience, San Antonio's famous River Walk has made it a modern tourist hotbed. The River Walk is a network of walkways along the banks of the San Antonio River, one story beneath downtown San Antonio, Texas. An additional 1.3 miles were added in 2009, called the Museum Reach section. Lined by bars, shops and restaurants, the River Walk is a unique, landscaped pedestrian walkway, separated from the hustle and bustle of cars and adding to San Antonio's charm.

San Antonio's multifaceted allure brings nearly 22 million visitors to the city per year. Like much of Texas, San Antonio has been consistently recognized as one of the best places to buy real estate, one of the best places to retire, one of the most recession-proof economies, and one of the best places to start a career in the twenty-first century.

Historical Information: San Antonio Conservation Society, 418 Villita Street, San Antonio, TX 78205; telephone (210) 224-5711.

■ Population Profile

Metropolitan Statistical Area Population

2000: 1,592,383
2010: 2,142,508
2012 estimate: 2,234,003
Percent change, 2000–2010: 34.5%
U.S. rank in 2000: 29th
U.S. rank in 2010: 25th

City Residents

1990: 976,514
2000: 1,144,646
2010: 1,327,407
2012 estimate: 1,383,194
Percent change, 2000–2010: 16%
U.S. rank in 1990: 10th (State rank: 3rd)

U.S. rank in 2000: 13th (State rank: 3rd)
U.S. rank in 2010: 7th (State rank: 2nd)

Density: 2,879.8 people per square mile

Racial and ethnic characteristics

White: 1,022,508
Black or African American: 96,310
American Indian and Alaskan Native: 12,033
Asian: 32,699
Native Hawaiian and Other Pacific Islander: 2,582
Hispanic or Latino (may be of any race): 879,226
Other: 217,062

Percent of residents born in state: 65.1%

Age characteristics

Population under 5 years old: 100,191
Population 5 to 9 years old: 102,012
Population 10 to 14 years old: 99,138
Population 15 to 19 years old: 99,598
Population 20 to 24 years old: 115,454
Population 25 to 34 years old: 210,039
Population 35 to 44 years old: 176,280
Population 45 to 54 years old: 183,024
Population 55 to 59 years old: 77,489
Population 60 to 64 years old: 65,431
Population 65 to 74 years old: 85,165
Population 75 to 84 years old: 50,096
Population 85 years and over: 19,277
Median age: 33.2

Births (2010–11 Metropolitan Area)

Total number: 31,812

Deaths (2010–11 Metropolitan Area)

Total number: 14,326

Money income (2012)

Per capita income: $22,233
Median household income: $45,074
Total households: 476,131

Number of households with income of . . .

less than $10,000: 44,824
$10,000 to $14,999: 27,575
$15,000 to $24,999: 59,698
$25,000 to $34,999: 56,507
$35,000 to $49,999: 72,135
$50,000 to $74,999: 88,165
$75,000 to $99,999: 51,199
$100,000 to $149,999: 47,838
$150,000 to $199,999: 14,951
$200,000 or more: 13,239

Percent of families below poverty level: 20.4%

FBI Crime Index Property: 82,668

FBI Crime Index Violent: 6,943

■ Municipal Government

San Antonio, the Bexar County seat, is administered by a council-manager form of city government. City council members are elected from 10 districts, and the mayor is elected at-large. All members of council serve a maximum of four, two-year terms. The mayor and city council appoint the city manager. At age 36, Mayor Julián Castro's election in 2009 made him the youngest mayor of a top American city.

Head Official: Mayor Julián Castro (since 2009; term expires 2015)

Total Number of City Employees: 10,386 (2012)

City Information: City of San Antonio, PO Box 839966, San Antonio, TX 78283; telephone (210)207-7060; fax (210)207-4168

■ Economy

Major Industries and Commercial Activity

As San Antonio entered the twenty-first century, its economy, like many Texan cities, saw years of steady growth, despite a national recession. San Antonio has been able to do this through a diversified economy focused on government, tourism, and health care. Major energy companies affect the economy, with renewed interest, in the late 2000s, in shale drilling for natural gas. In addition, the service and manufacturing industries gained importance in the 2000s. In 2009 *BusinessWeek* ranked San Antonio the strongest U.S. metropolitan economy based on job growth, employment, economic growth, and home prices. That same year, The Brookings Institution ranked San Antonio as the best performing economy in the recession.

San Antonio is home to one of the largest military concentrations in the United States. According to the city economic development department, the defense industry in San Antonio employs over 89,000 and provides a $5.25 billion annual impact to the city's economy. The large concentration of government workers in San Antonio is due mainly to the location of several major military bases in the area: Lackland Air Force Base, Randolph Air Force Base, and one Army post, Fort Sam Houston. The Army's Camp Bullis and Camp Stanley training centers are located nearby, but outside the city. From the days its first mission and accompanying presidio military post were founded in 1718, San Antonio has been regarded as an area of strategic importance. By the end of World War II, the city had become the location for the nerve center of the nation's defense network, and it remains the headquarters for the largest military establishment in the United States. In 2001 another of San Antonio's military bases-Kelly-closed and was redeveloped as KellyUSA, a commercial port. The port's name

was again changed and is now referred to as Port San Antonio, focusing on the mission of transforming the former Kelly Air Force Base to benefit economic growth in the city. As part of redevelopment of the port the East Kelly Railport, a $35 million, 6-acre project, was opened in 2007. The East Kelly Railport was seen as a step towards the goal of turning the port into a global distribution hub. In 2002, Brooks Air Force Base was renamed Brooks City-Base when the property was conveyed to the Brooks Development Authority as part of a unique project between local, state, and federal government. The mission of the authority is to redevelop the property into a science, business, and technology center. Meanwhile, the Air Force continues to be its largest tenant.

In addition to the large military presence, San Antonio's tourism industry is one of its most prominent features. In a survey by the Tourism Division of Texas, 5 of the top 10 tourist draws in the state were in San Antonio, with the Alamo and the River Walk in the number one and two spots, respectively. The attractions of the Alamo City, as San Antonio is known, appeal to tourists from across the country. *Yellowpages.com* rated San Antonio's River Walk the best free attraction in the Southwest. Over 10 million people visit San Antonio annually, resulting in over $8 billion of economic impact on the city's economy annually.

The service sector is the largest and fastest growing sector of the economy, largely because of increased demand for health-care and business services, and San Antonio's sound tourism industry. San Antonio's highly regarded medical industry includes the 900-acre South Texas Medical Center, which is a conglomerate of various hospitals, clinics, and research and higher educational institutions. Medical industry employees account for nearly 15 percent of all employees in the San Antonio area. Manufacturing actually grew in San Antonio in the 2000s. It is no surprise that in 2013, *Forbes* cited San Antonio as one of the nation's top cities for middle-class jobs.

In 2013 the city announced a $4 million investment by Southwest Airlines, the addition of Xenex Healthcare Services, Inc., to its growing bioscience and healthcare community, and new investment of $6 million by NBTY, Inc., the largest vertically integrated vitamin manufacturer in the United States.

Items and goods produced: processed foods, airplane parts, storage batteries, steel forms, structural steel, food handling equipment, semiconductors, rolled aluminum sheet, cement

Incentive Programs-New and Existing Companies

Local programs: San Antonio prides itself for a business-friendly climate that welcomes new company relocations, expansions and start-up ventures. Helping the cause is the San Antonio Economic Development Foundation, a not-for-profit organization, founded and supported by the business community of San Antonio for the purpose of recruiting new manufacturing, office, research and development, warehousing, and distribution operations to San Antonio. The staff provides factual information on the community from which a business can make an informed decision on establishing or relocating a new facility in San Antonio.

The City of San Antonio's Economic Development Department (EDD) helps relocating, expanding, and start-up businesses. Through the city's Incentive Score-card System EDD staff awards incentives to projects achieving qualifying scores during the application process. EDD offers a variety of financial incentives to encourage business and residential development, including tax and fee incentives, financing, regulatory reductions, and workforce development assistance, and provides customized, one-on-one service. Programs like the Economic Development Incentive Fund provide financial incentives in the form of grants or loans to attract and retain certain businesses. In 2013 the city reported that 5,670 total new and/or retained jobs and $809 million in investments were logged in fiscal year 2012. The EDD also launched the Mentor Protégé and Bonding Assistance Programs in 2012 in collaboration with the Alamo Colleges. Programs include seminars and individual counseling, in addition to the mentor-protégé matching component.

The city can also set up new businesses with a "briefing team," a group of professionals assigned to assist business owners streamline the business development, construction, or renovation process. Historic tax exemptions are available. A special Health Facilities Development Corporation (HFDC) can issue tax-exempt bonds for non-profit organizations towards the development of health care facilities.

State programs: Texas is a right-to-work state. The Texas economy has performed better than that of any other state during the recent economic downturn. It is believed that this success is due in part to the states pro-business climate, of which economic incentives are an important part.

The Texas Enterprise Zone Programs offer tax abatement at the local level, and refunds of state sales and use taxes under certain circumstances to businesses operating in enterprise zone areas. The Texas Enterprise Zone Program allows local communities to partner with the State of Texas to promote job creation and capital investment in targeted areas of the state that meet specific economic criteria. Designated projects are eligible to apply for state sales and use tax refunds on qualified expenditures. The state of Texas targets many of its incentive programs toward smaller and rural communities. The Rural Municipal Finance Program is a loan program created by the Texas Agricultural Finance Authority (TAFA) to stimulate economic activity in rural

Texas. The Texas Enterprise Fund can be used to provide deal-closing money for companies relocating to and investing in Texas. The Texas Emerging Technology Fund, a $200 million fund created by the Texas Legislature in 2005, is available to companies who seek to commercialize new technologies. The program provides grants for early-stage investments in new, technology-based, private entrepreneurial entities that collaborate with public or private institutions of higher education.

Texas is one of the few states with no individual income tax, a very attractive environment for transferring employees. There is also no corporate income tax. Texas Enterprise Zone Program provides for eligible designated projects to apply for state sales and use tax refunds on purchases of all taxable items purchased for use at the qualified business site related to the project or activity. Special tax exemptions are made for manufacturing machinery, equipment, replacement parts, and accessories that have a useful life of more than six months. Texas businesses are also exempt from paying state sales and use tax on labor for constructing new facilities, electricity and natural gas used in manufacturing, processing, or fabrication. Tax-Exempt Industrial Revenue Bonds are designed to provide tax-exempt financing up to $20 million per project to finance land and depreciable property for eligible industrial or manufacturing projects.

The Texas Capital Fund Infrastructure and Real Estate Development programs are designed to provide no interest loans of up to $750,000 to non-entitlement communities. The program funds real estate developments (acquisitions, construction, and/or rehabilitation) to assist a business, which commits to creating or retaining permanent jobs, primarily for low and moderate-income persons.

Job training programs: The Alamo WorkSource Board serves as the governing board for the regional workforce system and assists businesses in employee recruitment, screening, assessment, and customized training. Also, the State's Skills Development Fund has $25 million available to fund training programs designed by employers in partnership with local community colleges. The Texas Workforce Commission (TWC) provides funds for training via local colleges and in partnership with local businesses.

Development Projects

Unlike most large cities in the United States, San Antonio is not completely surrounded by independent suburban cities. Instead, the city manages the extraterritorial land surrounding the city with an aggressive annexation policy. The city generally opposes the creation of other municipalities surrounding it, preferring instead to annex. Nearly three-fourths of its current land area has been annexed since 1960. Nonetheless, residential development in San Antonio remain some of the most affordable, while cost of living remains significantly lower than most of the country.

At the end of 2010, major construction on a new terminal, Terminal B, at the San Antonio International Airport was completed. Parking and roadway construction was also completed at this time. In 2013, construction started on improvements to the Airport's Terminal A to bring it in line with the state-of-the art Terminal B.

The River Walk is also a place of frequent development. In 2009 the new $72 million Museum Reach section of the River Walk was opened, adding 1.3 miles to the popular destination. Hotels, like the $30 million Embassy Suites completed in 2010, and restaurants are frequently developed along the infamous walk. The city celebrated the completion of the Mission Reach Trails leg in 2013. At a cost of $7.75 million, this final leg, funded by a combination of hotel tax revenue, city bond money, and state and federal matching dollars, consists of 8 miles of reclaimed waterways connecting downtown to the historic Spanish missions located south of city center.

Universities were expanding in the 2000s. Texas A&M University–San Antonio topped off the first building of its permanent campus. The existing 54,096-square-foot Multipurpose Building that houses the library, bookstore, student services offices, classrooms, faculty and administrative offices, and food services will be joined in the summer of 2014 by two new structures at a cost of $75 million. A new four-story academic building will cover 186,000 square feet, with classrooms, lecture halls, administrative offices, and a 400-seat auditorium. The 23,000-square-foot Patriots' Casa will serve student veterans, who make up about 10 percent of the student body.

In May 2012, voters overwhelmingly approved a $596 million bond program, the largest in San Antonio's history. The five-year program targets 140 projects including streets, bridges, sidewalks, drainage and flood control, parks, recreation and open space, library, museum and cultural arts facilities, and public safety facilities. This bond program complements the 2007 voter-approved $550 million Bond Program, providing over $1 billion in investments to the city's capital infrastructure.

The city's innovative SA2020 program is a nonprofit organization that coordinates the efforts of individuals, the private sector, government, and nonprofit organizations in creating development goals for San Antonio. The mission of SA2020 is to catalyze the San Antonio community into focused action to achieve the shared goals that will transform San Antonio into a world-class city by the year 2020.

Economic Development Information: San Antonio Economic Development Foundation, 602 East Commerce Street, San Antonio, TX 78205; telephone (210) 226-1394; toll-free (800) 552-3333; fax (210) 223-3386; email edf@sanantonioedf.com. City of San Antonio Economic Development Department, PO Box 839966, San Antonio, TX 78283-3966; telephone (210) 207-8080; fax (210) 207-8151.

Commercial Shipping

Positioned on airline, highway, and railroad routes to Mexico, San Antonio is also the center of a 47-county agribusiness market area for crops grown elsewhere in the state of Texas. San Antonio firms handle processing, packaging, and nationwide distribution of vegetables, pecans, watermelons, and citrus fruits. Livestock, poultry and poultry products, and dairy products also pass through San Antonio.

San Antonio's Port San Antonio (formerly KellyUSA) is a major logistics port. It has 290,000 square feet of warehouse space available, 11,500-foot heavy-duty runway, and the East Kelly Railport has 720,000 square feet of transload and distribution space. Port San Antonio is directly linked by three interchanges with Interstate 90 to Interstates 35, 10, and 37, and is located on two major rail lines. San Antonio International Airport provides direct and non-stop service to all major hubs with an average 260 scheduled departures and arrivals daily via more than 15 cargo carriers. Dallas and Houston are 50 minutes away by air, and Mexico City is one-and-a-half hours away. Stinson Municipal Airport handles general aviation traffic and acts as a reliever airpost for San Antonio International Airport.

Two freight railroads (Burlington Northern Santa Fe and Union-Pacific System) serve the area, providing service to Mexico and linking San Antonio with St. Louis. The city of San Antonio operates a general purpose Foreign Trade Zone (FTZ) under the supervision of the U.S. Customs Service. Sometimes referred to as "free ports," FTZs are secured areas that officially fall outside U.S. Customs territory. FTZs help U.S.-based businesses cut costs, improve cash flow, and increase return on investment by deferring, reducing, or altogether eliminating duties and excise taxes if the final product is exported from the zone. The City of Antonio also has an active International Relations office. The department's goal is to create wealth in the area by establishing San Antonio's global presence through trade and foreign direct investment.

Labor Force and Employment Outlook

San Antonio's economy saw unprecedented growth in the 1990s and has remained strong in recent years. The remarkable strength of San Antonio's job market can be attributed to its economic diversity and a skilled workforce that appeals to relocating companies and local industries. San Antonio weathered a national economic downturn in the late 2000s better than most U.S. cities. San Antonio's metropolitan workforce in 2012 was 1.03 million, an increase of over 12,000 compared to 2011. Manufacturing, education and health services, as well as leisure and hospitality industries led the employment sectors. In 2012 the unemployment rate in San Antonio was 7.3 percent, compared to 7.9 percent in Texas and 8.7 percent in the United States. The median age in the city was 33; San Antonio is frequently cited in national publications as a great place for young professionals to start their careers.

The following is a summary of data regarding the 2012 San Antonio labor force:

Size of civilian labor force: 663,056

Number of workers employed in . . .

  agriculture and mining: 4,324
  construction: 46,200
  manufacturing: 35,294
  wholesale trade: 14,292
  retail trade: 70,942
  transportation: 25,607
  information systems: 11,657
  finance: 54,906
  professional administration: 65,708
  education and social services: 141,435
  arts and leisure: 68,965
  other: 34,220
  public administration: 29,716

Average hourly earnings of production workers: $15

Unemployment rate: 5.2% (2012)

Employers

Largest employers (2012)	*Number of employees*
Lackland Air Force Base	37,097
Fort Sam Houston– U.S. Army	32,000
H-E-B Grocery Co.	20,000
USAA Capital Corp.	17,000
Northside I.S.D.	12,751
City of San Antonio	11,731
Randolph Air Force Base	11,068
North East I.S.D.	10,522
Methodist Healthcare System	8,000
San Antonio I.S.D.	7,374
Bill Miller Bar-B-Q	4,190
Cullen / Frost Bankers	3,982
Valero Energy	3,777
Rackspace	3,300
Southwest Research Institute	3,046
Toyota Motor Manufacturing	2,900
Clear Channel Communications, Inc.	2,800
KCI	2,000

Cost of Living

San Antonio's cost of living is one of the lowest among large American cities, and remained below the national average in 2013.

The following is a summary of data regarding several key cost of living factors in the area.

2013 ACCRA Average House Price: $224,392

2013 ACCRA Cost of Living Index: 86

State income tax rate: None

State sales tax rate: 6.25%

Local income tax rate: None

Local sales tax rate: 1.875%

Property tax rate: $0.565690 per $100 of assessed valuation (2013)

Economic Information: San Antonio Economic Development Foundation, 602 East Commerce Street San Antonio, TX 78205; telephone (210) 226-1394; toll-free (800) 552-3333; fax (210) 223-3386. City of San Antonio, Economic Development Department, PO Box 839966, San Antonio, TX 78283; telephone (210) 207-8080.

■ Education and Research

Elementary and Secondary Schools

Unlike many school systems elsewhere, the San Antonio area's 19 school districts (the largest of which is the Northside Independent School District) function as separate, independent entities. Each has its own superintendent, its own elected board of education, and its own taxing authority. The Texas Education Agency in Austin oversees all districts, but they function apart from city or county jurisdiction. The Northside school district was named as one of five finalists for a Broad Prize for Urban Education—an award given annually to one school district that best exemplifies improvement in student achievement while successfully bringing together students of different ethnic and class backgrounds.

The San Antonio Independent School District (SAISD) allows parents to choose from traditional classroom settings, magnet programs, and internal charters that specialize in a particular theme or subject matter. Specialized high schools include the Business Careers High School, Jay Science & Engineering Academy High School, and Health Careers High School, which provide curriculums focused on specific fields of study. Another such school is Communication Arts High School (CAHS), which provides a specialized curriculum that focuses on learning exceptional communication skills. The system has four non-traditional schools and 13 secondary schools hosting magnet programs. More than 91 percent of the students are Hispanic/Latino. African Americans make up just over 6 percent of the student body, and whites just under 2 percent. More than 93 percent of the students come from economically disadvantaged households.

In 2012 San Antonio made a commitment to pre-kindergarten education when voters increased a sales tax to fund full-day pre-kindergarten classes for eligible four-year-olds. The goal of the program is to close the achievement gap by at least 10 percent on reading and math assessments.

The Archdiocese of San Antonio has a total of 44 elementary and secondary schools, with an enrollment of 14,303 students from three-years-old through high school. In 2013 more than 700 students graduated from Catholic high schools in the Archdiocese of San Antonio. The system boasts a zero percent drop-out rate and a 98.8 percent graduation rate.

The following is a summary of data regarding the Northside Independent School District.

Total enrollment: 95,581

Number of facilities
    total: 115
    elementary schools: 73
    junior high schools: 19
    high schools: 15
    other: 8

Student/teacher ratio: 15.63:1

Teacher salaries
    average (statewide): $48,261

Funding per pupil: $9,042

Public Schools Information: Northside Independent School District, 5900 Evers Road, San Antonio, TX 78238; telephone (210) 397-8500.

Colleges and Universities

San Antonio's institutions of higher learning include the University of Texas system. The University of Texas at San Antonio (UTSA), which is comprised of Colleges of Business, Education and Human Development, Engineering, Liberal and Fine Arts, Sciences, Public Policy, Honors College, a school of Architecture, and Graduate School, offers over 125 degree programs and is the second largest University of Texas component after UT at Austin. At the University of Texas Health Science

Center, students pursue degrees in medicine, dentistry, and nursing, and receive training at affiliated teaching hospitals. Texas A&M University–San Antonio, a state university, established a permanent campus in San Antonio in 2009 that served more than 3,500 students in 2013.

Trinity University, a private school founded by Presbyterians that offers its students degrees in the liberal arts and the sciences, has been repeatedly selected by *U.S. News & World Report* as one of the best colleges in the West. St. Mary's University, a private Catholic institution, is particularly known for its law and business schools. University of the Incarnate Word, also a private Catholic school, is known for its nursing curriculum. Our Lady of the Lake University is a private Catholic institution that emphasizes minority programs, particularly for Hispanics. Oblate School of Theology is a private Catholic college serving men and women seeking graduate study in theology.

San Antonio College, one of the major junior colleges in Texas, has an average enrollment of more than 22,000 students and is among the largest single-campus two-year colleges in the United States. St. Philip's College, a two-year public facility that focuses its curriculum on restaurant management, data processing, and health-related fields as well as arts and sciences, was founded in 1898 and is one of the oldest and most diverse community colleges in the country. San Antonio's Universidad Nacional Autonoma de Mexico (National Autonomous University of Mexico) offers Hispanic-oriented courses and is the only U.S. branch of UNAM's home campus in Mexico City, Mexico. Palo Alto College, a two-year college in San Antonio's south side, has added programs in Academic Computing Technology, Aviation Management, Criminal Justice, Environmental Technology, Electrical Mechanical Technology, Health Professions, Logistics, Nursing, Teacher Assistant, and Turfgrass Management.

Libraries and Research Centers

The San Antonio Public Library operates the San Antonio Central Library and 22 branch libraries across the city. The Central Library at 600 Soledad Street has received national attention for its unique design and color ("enchilada red"). The library was designed by Ricardo Legorreta Arquitectos of Mexico City. The library collection encompasses over two million items. The Central Library houses the Texana/Genealogy and Latino reference collections, showcasing the history, culture, and art of the region. The Central Library also features an art gallery with exhibits that change periodically. The Central Library is six stories high plus a basement level; the entire third floor is devoted to children 3 and under. Children have their own "KidsCat" computer catalog and a spacious story and craft room.

San Antonio's numerous research centers include those supported by the University of Texas in the fields of archaeology, environmental resources, neuroscience, women's studies, biotechnology, culture and community, aging, music, and bioengineering; UT's Health Science Center has many additional research centers, devoted to areas of the medical field. Others include the Texas Public Policy Foundation and the Mexican-American Cultural Center, which seeks the harmonious integration of Hispanic and North American cultures in a manner consistent with democratic and Christian precepts. The U.S. Army Institute of Surgical Research is affiliated with the U.S. Army Medical Research and Material Command and collated with Brooke Army Medical Center. The institute includes a burn center where approximately 300 patients are admitted annually and a trauma division that admits over 1,300 annually. San Antonio's Southwest Research Institute occupies 1,200 acres and has a staff of over 3,000 studying many topics such as automation, robotics, space sciences, and fuels and lubricants. The Southwest Research Institute has consistently earned numerous *R&D* 100 awards since 1971. The awards listed each year in *R&D* magazine are given in recognition of developments regarded as the top 100 most significant technical accomplishments.

Public Library Information: San Antonio Public Library, 600 Soledad Street, San Antonio, Texas 78205; telephone (210) 207-2500.

■ Health Care

As of 2013, the 900-acre South Texas Medical Center (STMC) was comprised of over 75 medically related institutions, including more than 45 clinics, 12 major hospitals, a higher education institution, and countless small practices, offices, and non-medical businesses. Facilities include the prestigious University of Health Science Center at San Antonio. Total investment in facilities and equipment is valued at $2.679 billion. STMC is recognized worldwide by medical and health care professionals for the impact of its advanced research, patient diagnosis, treatment and rehabilitation, degree programs, and state-of-the-art physical structures. The Medical Center area has expanded to include multiple office buildings, hotels, apartments, restaurants, and shops. And there are approximately 290 acres of foundation land that still await future development

The San Antonio area also has numerous medical facilities outside the boundaries of the South Texas Medical Center, including over two dozen general hospitals, two state hospitals, two children's psychiatric hospitals, and two Department of Defense hospitals: Brooke Army Medical Center at Fort Sam Houston, one of the Army's largest and considered a premier burn treatment facility, and Wilford Hall Medical Center, the Air Force's largest medical facility, at Lackland Air Force Base.

■ Recreation

Sightseeing

San Antonio has so much to do, even other Texas cities defer to the tourist appeal of the Alamo City. A 2010 study funded by the Greater Houston Convention and Visitors Bureau found that San Antonio is the choice city when it comes to destinations with things to do at a reasonable cost. The survey found that San Antonio's River Walk, the Alamo, and SeaWorld are the top attractions for travelers nationwide.

San Antonio's most popular tourist destinations are the Alamo and the Paseo del Rio, or River Walk. The River Walk is a one-and-a-half-mile winding waterway of landscaped cobblestone paths and bridges set 20 feet below street level. The result of a downtown urban revitalization project, the River Walk is lined with cafes, shops, galleries, restaurants, and nightclubs. A visitor can sample the flavor of Mexico or relive the birth of Texas by simply enjoying the scenery, day or night. Tree-lined footpaths are lighted at night, creating a romantic ambience. For those who want more than a waterside view, boats cruise the 21 blocks at 10-minute intervals.

Mission San Antonio de Valero, the Alamo, was the first of five missions established in San Antonio and dates back to 1718 and is located downtown near the river. The chapel's facade represents what is left of the site where nearly 200 Texans died in their fight for independence from Mexico. The four other missions are all part of the San Antonio Missions National Park, a 10-mile Mission Trail that begins at the Alamo, located at street level between Commerce and Houston Streets on Alamo Plaza.

A walking tour from the town's center will take in a number of other attractions. Among them are La Villita, the "little town," adjacent to the River Walk on Alamo Street and across from the Convention Center, where former adobe houses along cobblestone walkways now contain shops, galleries, and a museum; Market Square with its Farmers Market and El Mercado area, with its specialty shops and weekend arts demonstrations; HemisFair Park, site of San Antonio's World's Fair in 1968 and now the center of downtown entertainment; and the King William Historic Area, a 25-block area that had been San Antonio's most elegant residential area, near downtown on the river's south banks.

Now a National Historic District, La Villita was the city's earliest settlement, devolving into a slum by the 1930s. After extensive renovation, it is now home to artists and craftspeople. Market Square is billed as the home of chili, and chili stands draw numerous visitors. The square is also host to a number of citywide festivals throughout the year. Each morning in the Farmers Market section of Market Square, fresh produce is sold directly to consumers. And in El Mercado, patterned after a Mexican market, there are several specialty shops. Inside the 92-acre HemisFair Plaza stands the Tower of the

Americas, where an observation deck provides a panoramic view of the city from 750 feet up. The King William Historic Area serves as a reminder of the city's German heritage, and its stately mansions date to the 1800s. In the King William Historic Area, the Steves Homestead, an 1876 mansion with a slate mansard roof and 13-inch think limestone walls houses Victorian antiques and is open to the public.

The colorful flora and fauna of the Japanese Tea Gardens located at the northwestern edge of 343-acre Brackenridge Park offer a change of pace to visitors. The Sunken Garden Theatre here features Sunday afternoon concerts in the summertime. The main entrance to the park is about two miles from downtown. Inside the park are a bike trail, picnic area, polo field, golf course, carousel, a miniature railroad, riding stables, and paddle boats. The San Antonio Zoo, where exotic animals roam in barless cages, is also located in Brackenridge Park. The 35-acre Zoo is particularly notable for having one of the nation's largest animal collections (3,500 animals representing 750 different species) and its endangered animals, including snow leopards, Sumatran tigers, and white rhinos. One of the newer additions to the Zoo is its Kronkosky's Tiny Tot Nature Spot, designed to connect children aged five and younger with the natural world. Across from the zoo's main entrance is the Skyride, where cable cars afford a panoramic view of the city's skyline. Nearby is Splashtown waterpark, which features water slides and south Texas's largest wave pool.

The military bases of San Antonio are also tourist destinations, but public access can vary. Group tours are welcomed, but advance reservations are advised at all posts except Fort Sam Houston, which is open to the public without restriction. Established in 1876 at its present location, historic Fort Sam Houston was the site of the first military airplane flight. Located here are the Army Medical Department Museum, which traces the history of the U.S. Army medical department with its collection of U.S. Army uniforms, medical equipment, and POW memorabilia; the Fort Sam Houston Museum, which houses a collection of military memorabilia; and the Post Chapel, built in 1917 and dedicated by President Taft. Birds and small animals roam the quadrangle grounds, where the centerpiece is the clock tower. Brooks Air Force Base, now known as Brooks City-Base, permits the public to tour the Hangar 9/Edward H. White Museum, the oldest in the Air Force, which contains capsules used by the first space monkeys. A History and Traditions Museum at Lackland Air Force Base contains combat aircraft parts. Randolph Air Force Base features the Taj Mahal offices of the 12th Flying Wing. The rotunda of the white structure displays aviation memorabilia.

San Antonio is also home to other exciting attractions including Sea World San Antonio, the world's largest marine life showplace and home of The Steel Eel exhibit, the Southwest's first hypercoaster; and Six Flags Fiesta Texas, a $100 million showplace park with live musical productions and world-class rides, including the Rattler, a classic wooden roller coaster, and Superman: Krypton Coaster, the largest steel roller coaster in the region. Fiesta Texas has a million-gallon wave pool shaped like the state of Texas. Other sites of note in the San Antonio area include San Fernando Cathedral, where the remains of Alamo heroes are thought to be held in a marble coffin on display; Spanish Governor's Palace, called the "most beautiful building in San Antonio" by the National Geographic Society, a national historic landmark dating from 1749 that once served as offices for the Spanish Province of Texas; San Antonio Botanical Gardens, emphasizing native Texas vegetation and incorporating a biblical garden, a children's garden, and a conservatory featuring tropical and exotic plants; and Jose Antonio Navarro State Historical Park, the former home of the prominent Texan who participated in the convention to ratify Texas as a state.

Arts and Culture

When actress Sarah Bernhardt performed in San Antonio's Grand Opera House, built in 1886, she called the city "the art center of Texas." While San Antonio attracts well-known performers, it is perhaps better known for opening its cultural doors to the public through colorful festivals that celebrate the blending of its Anglo-Hispanic heritage. The San Antonio Performing Arts Association, founded in 1976, functions as the city's presenter agency.

The Majestic Performing Arts Center, a relic of the days of "movie palaces," has been restored and is home to the San Antonio Symphony, which enjoys a reputation as one of the best in the country. Its repertoire ranges from pops to classical. The Majestic Theater plays host to many of the city's premier events, ranging from traveling Broadway companies to ballet performances to classical music concerts. Not simply a theater or a museum, the Carver Community Cultural Center is a showcase for African American artists while also providing entertainment with broad cultural appeal. Music, literature, art, drama and dance, and a major film festival, all with a Hispanic flavor, are combined at the Guadalupe Cultural Arts Center, where local, national, and international presentations are offered. Grand Opera is performed by the San Antonio Opera Company. The Chamber Arts Ensemble and the Texas Bach Choir, the only one of its kind in the state, round out San Antonio's musical options.

Flamenco dancing is offered at the Arneson River Theatre, a unique venue spanning both sides of the river. The Mexican Cultural Institute showcases folkloric dance as well as theater.

Among the city's museums and galleries is the San Antonio Museum of Art, one of the largest museums in the Southwest and home to the Nelson A. Rockefeller Center for Latin American Art, featuring a 2,500-piece collection dating as far back as 500 B.C.; notable works include a portrait of a Mayan nobleman from A.D. 700–900. The Lenora and Walter F. Brown Asian Art Wing is home to the largest center for Asian art in the southern United States. Witte Museum, located at one of the Brackenridge Park entrances, presents local and natural history exhibits and special children's exhibits. Marion Koogler McNay Art Museum is a former private mansion that now houses modern art. The folk history of Texas unfolds through a multimedia exhibit using 36 screens at the Institute of Texan Cultures. Oddities and western memorabilia are the focus at the Buckhorn Saloon and Museum, housed in a renovated 1881 saloon.

Other special collections and contemporary and historical exhibits are on display at the Mexican Cultural Institute; HemisFair Plaza, featuring art from Mexico and South America; and the Buckhorn Museum containing curiosities such as a two-headed calf and a lamb with eight legs. The Buckhorn is also home of the old Former Texas Rangers Association's Texas Ranger Museum. Other new attractions directly across from the Alamo are the Guinness World Records Museum; Ripley's Haunted Adventure, a multi-million dollar haunted house; and the Plaza Wax Museum. The San Antonio IMAX Theatre at Rivercenter shows a 48-minute docudrama depicting the famous battle at the Alamo. Images shown on a huge screen and magnetic surround sound makes viewers feel that they are there in the thick of battle.

Festivals and Holidays

For 10 days in mid-April, from dawn to well past dusk, San Antonio celebrates the Fiesta San Antonio. Featuring more than 100 events illustrative of the city's gastronomic, ethnic and western history, Fiesta starts out with an oyster bake and culminates in colorful spectacles. Along the way revelers enjoy the crowning of King Antonio, a giant block party known as A Night in Old San Antonio, fireworks, musical productions, fashion shows, and the Battle of the Flowers parade, in which 7,000 participants honor the Queen of the Order of the Alamo and her court. Flickering torches light up the Fiesta Flambeau parade; other activities include street dancing, a carnival, and concerts. Fiesta events have multiplied over the years, and they now attract some 3.5 million people annually.

San Antonio hosts a number of other celebrations and festivals throughout the year. The San Antonio River takes the spotlight in January when River Walk Mud Festival revolves around the annual draining of the river for maintenance. Championship rodeo competitors display their skills during February's San Antonio Stock Show and Rodeo, a 16-day western roundup that begins with a downtown parade. In March the San Antonio River is renamed the River Shannon and is dyed green for the St. Patrick's Day celebration, when Irish music and

entertainment prevail. The Starving Artists Show in early April brings professionals and amateurs to La Villita, a historic arts village, to sell their creations. The Cinco de Mayo events during the weekend nearest May 5 celebrate a historic Mexican military victory through mariachi music, folkloric dancing, and parades. Tejano music, described as a mixture of Mexican and German, is celebrated and studied at the annual Tejano Conjunto Festival in May. The beat of Latin music and dance fills the air in the outdoor Arneson River Theatre in June, kicking off the Fiesta Noche del Rio, which runs on weekends through the summer. San Antonio's Contemporary Art Month, held in July, is the only month-long contemporary arts festival in the nation, attracting private studios, foundations, galleries and institutions, as well as local, national, and international artists. September's FotoSeptiembre USA is one of the three largest photography festivals in the country. Oktoberfest and the River Art Group Show by major state artists enliven the month of October. The Christmas season has a Mexican flair led by the four-day Fiestas Navidenas in Market Square and Las Posadas, a reenactment of the Holy Family's search for an inn during which children go door-to-door seeking shelter. The River Walk itself becomes a festival of lights known as the Fiesta de las Luminarias.

Sports for the Spectator

The San Antonio Spurs of the National Basketball Association, the Silver Stars of the Women's National Basketball Association, and the San Antonio Rampage of the American Hockey League play their home games at the AT&T Center, which opened in October of 2002. The Center is a state-of-the-art 18,500 seat arena. The facility is 730,000 square feet, with four concourses, 56 suites, a practice facility, and restaurants. San Antonio's baseball team, the Missions of the Texas League, play at the Nelson Wolff Municipal Stadium. The Missions are a Double-A affiliate of the San Diego Padres of Major League Baseball. Major league pari-mutuel live and televised horse racing is offered at Retama Park year-round. Two rugby teams, the Alamo City and San Antonio rugby football clubs, call the city home.

For college football fans, the city's Alamodome football stadium is home to the annual U.S. Army All American Bowl, showcasing the nation's top high school players in an East versus West matchup. In addition, the University of Texas at San Antonio Roadrunner football program debuted its inaugural season in 2011 at the 65,000-seat Alamodome. The city council approved a contract extension allowing UTSA to play its home football games in the Alamodome through 2035.

The San Antonio Scorpions, a professional soccer team, made its debut in the North American Soccer League in 2012. That same year, Toyota announced its sponsorship of the Scorpions' new home, the 8,000-seat Toyota Field.

Sports for the Participant

The mild climate of San Antonio lends itself to a multitude of outdoor sport activities, many tied to the network of 210 city-owned parks administered by the city Department of Parks and Recreation. San Pedro Springs Park, the city's oldest, includes the McFarlin Tennis Center. Some 140 tennis courts in various locations augment the McFarlin Tennis Center. Brackenridge Park is San Antonio's showplace, with more than 300 acres of ballfields, horseback riding trails, bike paths, and scenic walkways through intricate gardens. Outside of the city lies Friedrich Park, where wilderness trails offer a peaceful challenge to hikers. The city operates 25 public swimming pools throughout San Antonio, including a year-round indoor Natatorium where competitions take place.

Bordered by the Texas Hill Country, San Antonio provides ready access to a number of recreation areas where hunting and water sports are popular activities. Fifteen lakes are within 150 miles of the city, and the Guadalupe River north of San Antonio is a favorite spot for canoeing, tubing, and white water rafting. Lake McQueeney, 25 miles from the city, attracts weekenders for boating and swimming. Corpus Christi and other Gulf Coast towns provide seacoast attractions about 140 miles from San Antonio. Natural bridge Caverns are located nearby between San Antonio and New Braunfels, off Interstate 35, exit 175. Here you can tour spectacular caverns or climb and "zip" from the tallest climbing tower in Texas, while the less adventurous pan for gems and minerals. Natural Bridge Wildlife Ranch, located in the same area, is a Texas-style African safari with some 50 species of Animals from all over the world roaming freely. The Vietnam War Memorial is located at Veterans Memorial Plaza. Also not to be missed is the marker for the Old Spanish Trail which linked cities of Spanish conquest and settlement.

With more than 300 days of sunshine each year, San Antonio is becoming a major golf destination. More than 40 courses (including military and private) and a championship course at the Hyatt Regency Hill Country Resort are the lure. Opening in 2010 were the PGA Tournament Players Club's J.W. Marriott Hotel and two championship golf courses. Citizens are also fond of bowling—more than 26 commercial and military bowling centers dot the city. It was a San Antonio firm, Columbia Industries, that introduced polyester resin into the manufacture of bowling balls in 1960.

Shopping and Dining

Local shopping and dining can be found along San Antonio's River Walk. In addition, one of the most exciting shopping, dining, and entertainment venues in San Antonio is Sunset Station, housed in the restored 1902 South Pacific Railroad depot near the convention center. Market Square downtown houses a large specialty shopping area, as well as a Mexican-style market featuring crafts, apparel, pottery, and jewelry. La Villita, a historic art district, has various arts and crafts shops as well as restaurants. Southwest School of Art and Craft, on the grounds of a former cloistered convent, sells the works of local artists and operates a restaurant in a beautiful historic setting. Many other art galleries feature Latin American and Native American artworks. Souvenir shops offer the latest in Western wear, including hand-crafted leather boots and ten-gallon hats. Antique stores feature authentic and reproduction items, including miniature replica Civil War and Texas Revolution toy soldiers and fine furniture and jewelry that may once have belonged to turn-of-the-century settlers. For those who wish to make a day of it, many antique stores can be found along the main streets of nearby charming towns such as Comfort, Boerne, Fredericksburg, Castroville, New Braunfels, Gruene, and Leon Springs. In addition, the San Antonio area has 10 major shopping malls.

In 2013, 18 hotels and 8 restaurants received Four-Diamond recognition from AAA Texas. Downtown dining ranges from ethnic cuisine to barbecue. Many restaurants feature some Tex-Mex dishes on their menus, and a number of restaurants specialize in south-of-the-border food. An emerging style of cooking, called New Southwestern, incorporates local produce and game. Italian, Greek, and German restaurants are well represented, as are delicatessens.

Visitor Information: San Antonio Convention & Visitors Bureau, 203 S. St. Mary's St., Suite 200, San Antonio, 78205; telephone (210) 207-6700.

■ Convention Facilities

San Antonio's Henry B. Gonzalez Convention Center, in the heart of San Antonio's historic district along the River Walk, is the city's largest convention facility. Built in 1968 and expanded in 2010, the center has 203,000 square feet of meeting space that is divisible in 67 ways, four exhibit halls offering a total of approximately 440,000 square feet of contiguous display space, and three ballrooms. The convention center complex also features the Lila Cockrell Theatre, a performance art theater offering seating for more than 2,500. In 2013 the theatre hosted 81 events. The Alamodome and more than 13,000 of the City's downtown hotel rooms are within walking distance. In 2012 the City Council allocated $304 million to expand the center. Scheduled for completion in 2016, the expansion will take the City's convention center from the 23rd largest to 8th largest in the country.

The Alamodome, a $186 million state-of-the-art facility that can be used to host large conventions as well as trade shows and other events, opened in 1993.

Featuring a Southwestern color scheme, the Alamodome has 160,000 gross square feet of contiguous floor space and configurations for groups of up to 77,000 people. The Alamodome is within walking distance of the Henry B. Gonzalez Convention Center and HemisFair Park, the River Walk, the Alamo, and more than 9,000 hotel rooms. In 2013 the Alamodome hosted more than 943,000 visitors over 143 event days.

San Antonio's alternate meeting facility is the Municipal Auditorium and Conference Center, an opulent structure dating to 1926 and lovingly restored with attention to historical detail after a 1979 fire. Its main auditorium offers seating for nearly 5,000. The lobby and two small wings on the main level and approximately 23,000 square feet on the lower level provide additional space for meetings, exhibits, and banquets.

Convention Information: San Antonio Convention and Visitors Bureau, 203 S. St. Mary's St., Suite 200, San Antonio, TX 78205; telephone (210) 207-6700.

■ Transportation

Approaching the City

San Antonio International Airport, a modern facility located 13 miles from the downtown River Walk, is served by 13 major carriers flying domestic and international routes, including nonstop flights to 30 destinations. The airport has an average of 260 daily departures and arrivals and serves over 7 million passengers annually. Primary domestic destinations include Dallas/Fort Worth and Houston, New York, Chicago, Washington D.C., Las Vegas, Los Angeles, Atlanta, Baltimore, and Phoenix; primary international destinations include Mexico City, Monterrey, Cancun, and Cozumel. Its terminal was described as "one of the most beautiful in years" by the American Institute of Architects. Traveling from the airport downtown by taxi takes about 15 minutes during normal traffic. Express limousine service runs to major hotels, and buses depart every half-hour. Stinson Field, also operated by the city Aviation Department, handles general aviation traffic. Amtrak carries rail passengers to San Antonio from points all around the country. Entering San Antonio by road is comparatively easy; the loop design of San Antonio freeways and their connecting highways enable a motorist to reach the central district from any direction.

Traveling in the City

The centerpiece of San Antonio's transportation network is its VIA Metropolitan Transit Service. This service enables visitors to experience the major attractions without a car and commuters can enjoy a near perfect on-time record. VIA's buses cover 106 routes; special vehicles serve the handicapped and elderly. To ease the flow of cars into downtown, VIA operates a number of park-and-ride locations from which commuters can catch an express bus to the business area. There are also special schedules for major events. In the downtown area, VIA Streetcars with wooden slats and brass railings cover four routes and function as a shuttle to many major attraction and major stores.

San Antonio can be reached in 30 minutes or less by car from any point in Bexar County. The San Antonio's "hub and spoke" expressway arrangement, where all highways radiate from the central business district, makes all parts of the city easily accessible. San Antonio is also frequently recognized as a bike friendly city.

■ Communications

Newspapers and Magazines

San Antonio's major daily (morning) newspaper is the *San Antonio Express-News*, serving the city since 1865. San Antonio has numerous community newspapers, among them the *San Antonio Register*, which serves the African American community, *Conexion*, a weekly serving the Hispanic community, and specialty papers such as *San Antonio Business Journal* for the business community. Several local newspapers, including *Brooks Discovery, Fort Sam Houston News Leader, Kelly USA Observer, Lackland Talespinner, Medical Patriot,* and *Randolph Wingspread,* serve the military community. Additionally, the official trade magazine of the U.S. Air Force, *Airman,* is published here. Other publications include medical newspapers and magazines, magazines that are geared towards families, and magazines that provide information on local events, entertainment, shopping, and dining.

Television and Radio

While San Antonio boasts one of the most populous regions in the country, its television market is much less popular for a city its size. Part of this is due to low population density in the outskirts of the city, and the proximity to Austin truncating the service area. Eight television stations broadcast from San Antonio: four network affiliates, one public, one independent broadcasting religious and educational programming, one station affiliated with Telemundo, and another with Univision. Additional stations are available via cable. About 28 FM and 20 AM radio stations are available in the San Antonio area, offering a wide variety of formats, from national public radio to Spanish-language programming. Latin stations in the area play regional Mexican, Tejano, or contemporary pop.

Media Information: Express-News, PO Box 2171, San Antonio, TX 78297; telephone (210) 250-3000.

San Antonio Online

City of San Antonio Home Page. Available www.ci.sat.tx.us

Greater San Antonio Chamber of Commerce. Available www.sachamber.org

San Antonio Convention & Visitors Bureau. Available www.sanantoniocvb.com

San Antonio Economic Development Foundation. Available www.sanantonioedf.com

San Antonio Express-News. Available www.expressnews.com

San Antonio Public Library. Available www.sat.lib.tx.us

BIBLIOGRAPHY

Atwell, Wendy Weil, *The River Spectacular: Light, Sound, Color and Craft on the San Antonio River* (San Antonio: Maverick Pub. Co., 2010)

Brown, Amy K. Austin, *San Antonio & the Texas Hill Country* (Woodstock, VT: Countryman Press, 2007)

Harrigan, Stephen, *The Gates of the Alamo* (New York: Alfred A. Knopf, 2000)

Scott, Bob, and Robert Scott, *After the Alamo* (Plano, TX: Republic of Texas Press, 1999)

Virginia

The State in Brief

Nickname: Old Dominion

Motto: Sic semper tyrannis (Thus always to tyrants)

Flower: Dogwood

Bird: Cardinal

Area: 42,775 square miles (2010; U.S. rank 35th)

Elevation: Ranges from sea level to 5,729 feet above sea level

Climate: Mild, cooler in mountains; rainfall evenly distributed throughout the year

Admitted to Union: June 25, 1788

Capital: Richmond

Head Official: Terry McAuliffe (D) (until 2018)

Population

1990: 6,187,358
2000: 7,078,515
2010: 8,001,024
2012 estimate: 8,014,955
Percent change, 2000–2010: 13.0%
U.S. rank in 2012: 12th
Percent of residents born in state: 49.8% (2012)
Density: 202.6 people per square mile (2010)
2012 FBI Crime Index Total: 192,549

Racial and Ethnic Characteristics (2012)

White: 5,575,445
Black or African American: 1,561,042
American Indian and Alaska Native: 25,205
Asian: 443,460
Native Hawaiian and Pacific Islander: 5,438
Hispanic or Latino (may be of any race): 631,669
Other: 404,365

Age Characteristics (2012)

Population under 5 years old: 507,701
Population 5 to 19 years old: 1,576,313
Percent of population 65 years and over: 12.3%
Median age: 37.4

Vital Statistics

Total number of births (2012–13): 103,284
Total number of deaths (2012–13): 60,916
AIDS cases reported through 2011: 20,710

Economy

Major industries: Agriculture, wholesale and retail trade, health care, services
Unemployment rate (2012): 4.5%
Per capita income (2012): $33,326
Median household income (2012): $63,636
Percentage of persons below poverty level (2012): 11.1%
Income tax rate: 2.0% to 5.75%
Sales tax rate: 5.0%

Chesapeake

■ The City in Brief

Founded: 1963

Head Official: Mayor Alan Krasnoff (since 2008; current term expires 2016)

City Population
  1990: 151,976
  2000: 199,184
  2010: 222,209
  2012 estimate: 228,417
  Percent change, 2000–2010: 11.6%
  U.S. rank in 1990: 117th
  U.S. rank in 2000: 90th
  U.S. rank in 2010: 91st (State rank: 3rd)

Metropolitan Statistical Area Population
  2000: 1,551,351
  2010: 1,671,683
  2012 estimate: 1,693,567
  Percent change, 2000–2010: 7.8%
  U.S. rank in 2000: 33rd
  U.S. rank in 2010: 36th

Area: 353 square miles

Elevation: 15 feet above sea level

Average Annual Temperatures: January, 32.30° F; July, 86.80° F

Average Annual Precipitation: 45.74 inches

Major Economic Sectors: industrial/communications, knowledge services, military, health care, retail

Unemployment Rate: 4.4% (2012)

Per Capita Income: $28,373

2012 FBI Crime Index Property: 6,292

Major Colleges and Universities: College of William and Mary, Old Dominion University, Christopher Newport University, Hampton University, Norfolk State University

Daily Newspaper: *The Virginian-Pilot*

■ Introduction

Originally the "Land of the Chesapeake," which the Chesapeake Indians called home, the city of Chesapeake in the heart of Virginia's Tidewater region is today a thriving metropolis that combines cutting edge technologies, a highly educated workforce, and an important port with the bliss of living in a maritime clime. Recreational opportunities abound, with Chesapeake's proximity to the Atlantic Intracoastal Waterway and the Great Dismal Swamp National Wildlife Refuge, and the enjoyments of its own wonderful City Park. Even though the city was not founded until 1963, Chesapeake has a colonial history that dates back to the early seventeenth century; it was also the site of an important Revolutionary battle. Broadband and wireless technologies, health-care technologies, biotechnology, and nanotechnology all find a place in Chesapeake's varied economic land-scape. Chesapeake also has two important research centers within 10 miles of each other—the Thomas Jefferson National Accelerator Facility (Jefferson Lab) and the NASA Langley Research Center. Part of the Hampton Roads metropolitan statistical area, Chesapeake shares the resources and amenities of its sister cities, such as Norfolk, Virginia Beach, Portsmouth, Suffolk, Newport News, and Williamsburg. A deep history, thriving economy, rich culture, and lively nightlife, all located in an astounding landscape surrounded by water have won Chesapeake numerous accolades and was named among "America's Best Cities" in 2011 and 2012 by *Bloomberg Businessweek*.

Intracoastal Waterway's Great Bridge. © *Jeff Greenberg "0 people images" / Alamy*

■ Geography and Climate

The city of Chesapeake is situated on 353 square miles of land. The latitude of Chesapeake is 36.818 degrees north; the longitude is -76.275 degrees west. Chesapeake is adjacent to Portsmouth and Norfolk, Virginia, to the north; Virginia Beach to the south; Currituck County and Camden County, North Carolina, to the south; and Suffolk, Virginia, to the west. The northeastern part of the Great Dismal Swamp is located in Chesapeake. Chesapeake is found in the Hampton Roads region. The water area known as Hampton Roads is one of the world's largest natural harbors and incorporates the mouths of the Elizabeth River and James River with several smaller rivers. Chesapeake experiences consistently mild weather with four distinct seasons. Annual precipitation averages 45.74 inches. Rainfall in is fairly evenly distributed throughout the year. In winter, there are only traces of snowfall.

Area: 353 square miles

Elevation: 15 feet above sea level

Average Temperatures: January, 32.30° F; July, 86.80° F

Average Annual Precipitation: 45.74 inches

■ History

The city of Chesapeake was founded in 1963 as a merger between Norfolk County and the city of South Norfolk. However, the area has a longer history. The area of Norfolk County had originally been called "the Land of the Chesapeake" because it was where the Chesapeake Indians had made their home. The first English settlement began around 1620 along the banks of the Elizabeth River. Norfolk County was founded in 1636.

In December 1775, in the early part of the Revolutionary War, British Royal Governor Lord Dunmore moved his forces from Norfolk to Great Bridge (in what is now the center of Chesapeake), where he and his men awaited the American troops. On December 9, 1775, the historic Battle of Great Bridge was fought. In this brief but decisive battle, the Americans soundly defeated Lord Dunmore's forces.

In 1763, George Washington had an idea for building a canal near what became Chesapeake when he visited the area. In 1793, work began on the Dismal Swamp Canal. Progress on building the canal was slow because it was dug completely by hand. The canal opened in 1805. However, when the Albemarle and Chesapeake Canal was completed in 1858, the Dismal Swamp Canal suffered. The Dismal Swamp Canal is now on the National Register of Historic Places. It is the oldest operating artificial waterway in the country.

The Region Flourishes

No battles of the Civil War were fought in what is now Chesapeake. When the war was over, Norfolk County capitalized on its abundant natural resources, including coastal location, miles of riverfront, deep-water harbors, and fertile, level farmland, to recover quickly.

At the turn of the 20th century, the northern part of Norfolk County near the developing city of Norfolk began to grow as the suburb of South Norfolk. By 1900, South Norfolk had its own waterworks, public schools, and a post office. Improved transportation from two rail lines led to further development, and allowed South Norfolk to incorporate as an independent town in 1919 and a city of the first class, independent of Norfolk County, in 1950.

A City is Born

During the 1950's, parts of both Norfolk County and South Norfolk were annexed by neighboring cities, affecting approximately 50,000 residents and 30 square miles of land. In 1961, city and county officials came up with a merger agreement to address the situation. On February 13, 1962, citizens of both the city of South Norfolk and Norfolk County approved the merger in a special election. In June 1962 the citizens voted again and chose the name "Chesapeake" for the new city, to honor its heritage as the historic land of the Chesapeake. The merger became effective January 1, 1963.

Chesapeake's population has grown from approximately 78,000 in 1963 to more than 225,000 in 2013. Chesapeake's varied neighborhoods provide its citizens with excellent schools, recreational and cultural facilities, and strong city leadership as the city continues to grow. The publication *24/7 Wallstreet* named Chesapeake among the "Best Run Cities in America" in 2012, and both *Parenting Magazine* and *Money Magazine* honored the city among their lists of best places to live in 2010 and 2011.

Historical Information: Chesapeake Economic Development Department, 676 Independence Parkway, Suite 200, Chesapeake, VA 23320; telephone (757) 382-8040; fax (757) 382-8050.

■ Population Profile

Metropolitan Statistical Area Population
    2000: 1,551,351
    2010: 1,671,683
    2012 estimate: 1,693,567
    Percent change, 2000–2010: 7.8%
    U.S. rank in 2000: 33rd
    U.S. rank in 2010: 36th

City Residents
    1990: 151,976
    2000: 199,184
    2010: 222,209
    2012 estimate: 228,417
    Percent change, 2000–2010: 11.6%
    U.S. rank in 1990: 117th
    U.S. rank in 2000: 90th
    U.S. rank in 2010: 91st (State rank: 3rd)

Density: 652.0 people per square mile

Racial and ethnic characteristics
    White: 143,877
    Black or African American: 67,827
    American Indian and Alaskan Native: 681
    Asian: 7,209
    Native Hawaiian and Other Pacific Islander: 103
    Hispanic or Latino (may be of any race): 10,997
    Other: 8,720

Percent of residents born in state: 53.8%

Age characteristics
    Population under 5 years old: 14,277
    Population 5 to 9 years old: 16,391
    Population 10 to 14 years old: 15,732
    Population 15 to 19 years old: 16,411
    Population 20 to 24 years old: 15,440
    Population 25 to 34 years old: 30,566
    Population 35 to 44 years old: 30,196
    Population 45 to 54 years old: 36,665
    Population 55 to 59 years old: 15,567
    Population 60 to 64 years old: 11,841
    Population 65 to 74 years old: 14,897
    Population 75 to 84 years old: 7,454
    Population 85 years and over: 2,980
    Median age: 36.7

Births (2010–11 Metropolitan Area)
    Total number: 22,692

Deaths (2010–11 Metropolitan Area)
    Total number: 12,648

Money income (2012)
    Per capita income: $28,373
    Median household income: $68,750
    Total households: 78,867

Number of households with income of ...
    less than $10,000: 3,278
    $10,000 to $14,999: 2,922

$15,000 to $24,999: 5,552
$25,000 to $34,999: 6,937
$35,000 to $49,999: 9,086
$50,000 to $74,999: 15,374
$75,000 to $99,999: 13,323
$100,000 to $149,999: 14,019
$150,000 to $199,999: 5,168
$200,000 or more: 3,208

Percent of families below poverty level: 8.9%

FBI Crime Index Property: 6,292

FBI Crime Index Violent: 839

■ Municipal Government

Chesapeake has a council-manager form of government. Chesapeake has eight council members and a mayor elected at large for four-year terms, which means that members represent the entire city rather than specific districts. The city council sets policy, approves the budget, and sets the tax rate. Members also hire the city manager, who is responsible for the day-to-day administration of the city. The city manager prepares a budget, recruits and hires most of the government's staff, and carries out the council's policies. The city manager may recommend policy decisions, but he or she is bound by the action of the council.

Head Official: Mayor Alan Krasnoff (since 2008; current term expires 2016)

Total Number of City Employees: 3,550 (2012)

City Information: City of Chesapeake, 306 Cedar Road, Chesapeake, VA 23322; telephone (757) 382-2489.

■ Economy

Major Industries and Commercial Activity

The largest existing economic sectors in the greater Chesapeake area include professional business services and technologies; health care; maritime, logistics, and transportation; defense technologies, services, and support; manufacturing and construction; leisure and hospitality; knowledge services; and retail development. New target industries for 2013 included energy products and services, health-care technologies, and advanced manufacturing.

With two national research laboratories calling Chesapeake and its metropolitan area home, it's no surprise that these regions boast one of the highest per capita concentrations of engineers and scientists in the country. NASA Langley Research Center in Hampton employs several thousand civil service and contract employees with a focus on research in aeronautics. The Applied Research Center at the Thomas Jefferson National Accelerator Facility in Newport News provided residence to ten high-tech business start-ups and venture capital firms as of 2013. These include Virginia's Center for Innovative Technology, the Virginia Philpott Manufacturing Extension Partnership, and the Hampton Roads Research Partnership. Such cutting-edge technologies as robotics, nanotechnology, and photonics have a foothold in Chesapeake. It is also a center for broadband and wireless technologies, media and information services, and biotechnology. Chesapeake resided in the top ten-percent of U.S. metropolitan areas for technology employment as of 2013. Chesapeake also had more highly educated workers and research and development expenditures than places like Charlotte, North Carolina, as well as that state's Research Triangle area.

The Chesapeake metropolitan area is among the 100 largest in the nation. Some 70 international companies from 18 countries operate in Chesapeake, lured by the aforementioned advancements in telecommunications infrastructure, among the city's other quality-of-life benefits. Many of the region's largest employers are based in Chesapeake, including Canon Information Technology Services, Capital One, Cox Communications, Dollar Tree, which is a *Fortune* 500 company with its corporate headquarters in Chesapeake, General Dynamics Information Technology, HSBC Private Label Corporation, Sentara Healthcare, and QVC Chesapeake.

Five military facilities in Chesapeake and another seven in Hampton Roads both contributed to the economy.

Items and goods produced: electronics and communications equipment, plastics and chemical processing, aerospace and aviation, software, electro-medical equipment, automotive parts and equipment

Incentive Programs-New and Existing Companies

Local programs: Chesapeake's Department of Economic Development assists companies with business retention, permits, site selection, workforce services and training, networking, and information resources. Incentives offered in the Chesapeake area include the South Norfolk Hub Zone, which encourages development of historically underutilized business zones, referred to as HUBZones. The local program is part of the U.S. Small Business Administration. The South Norfolk Borough of Chesapeake was designated a technology zone by the Chesapeake city council in 2010, offering incentives to new business that locate within the area. Incentives in the technology zone include exemption from building code fees, zoning fees, land-use fees, and building permit fees, among others, for up to 10 years. There are 1,000 acres of industrial property designated as a foreign trade zone—Foreign Trade Zone 20—within Chesapeake, allowing companies to ship and receive goods internationally duty-free.

State programs: Virginia is a right-to-work state, advertising itself as the northernmost right-to-work state in the nation. The State General Assembly has kept Virginia's taxes on industry very competitive by maintaining relatively moderate corporate income tax rates and by eliminating many tax irritants, resulting in modest tax bills for business and industry. While this alone constitutes an attractive incentive for new and existing businesses, the State of Virginia further offers Governor's Opportunity Funds, which allow the Governor to secure business locations or expansion projects with matching funds from the local community; Virginia Investment Partnership Grant Funds, supporting large employers with businesses established for a minimum of five years in Virginia; property tax exemptions; sales and use tax exemptions; enterprise zones; technology zones; and foreign trade zones. Virginia has a State Historic Rehabilitation Tax Credit Program, as does the federal government. The state's Virginia Small Business Financing Authority provides small businesses with access to capital for growth and expansion efforts. The Virginia Economic Development Incentive Grant is a discretionary performance incentive designed to assist and encourage business investment that creates new employment in the state. Specifically, it targets businesses looking to relocate headquarters or others significant service-sector or administrative jobs in the state.

Job training programs: The state's Virginia Jobs Investment Program offers customized recruiting and training assistance for expanding companies that need to hire more workers. The program seeks to lower human development costs to state businesses. Chesapeake's public schools offer a unique program in which students are guaranteed to employers. Businesses that hire workers within five years of their high school graduation are guaranteed competent employee work performance—if the worker is unable to perform the work due to an educational deficiency in the areas of reading, writing, or math, the school system retrains the worker to company specifications with no added cost to the employer.

In the Hampton Roads area, Opportunity, Inc. provides employers and job seekers with necessary networks and resources in an effort to achieve their mission of "strengthening the localized talent pool of workers to match private sector investments in technology, capital, and product improvement." Acting under the auspices of the Hampton Roads Workforce Development Board, the agency offers workshops, links to online tools and access to a statewide collection of strategic partners. The Hampton Roads Chamber of Commerce also supports the workforce program to keep local employers abreast of labor market trends, employment best practices, and workforce resources.

Development Projects

Investment in Chesapeake grew dramatically in 2011 and 2012, reaching $163.7 million and $204 million, respectively. Private investment created some 1,152 new jobs during that period. The largest private investment came from The Walsh Group, which spent $133.9 million on construction of a Federal Bureau of Investigation regional headquarters in 2012, creating 100 area jobs upon completion. The regional headquarters was a three-story, 135,000-square-foot facility that was also certified as a LEED building for its environmentally conscious design. In terms of job creation, Xerox led the way with 450 new jobs. Additional development projects by private industry included $11.9 million by Capital One and $7.8 million by the Enviva Port of Chesapeake.

The South Norfolk Jordan Bridge, spanning the Elizabeth River, opened in October 2012 as a privately funded development to replace an 80-year-old drawbridge that closed in 2008. Built at a cost of $142 million, the bridge collects revenue exclusively from the E-Z Pass automated system; no manned or unmanned toll booths were created. For its part, the city broke ground on a new four-lane, 95-foot-high bridge, the Dominion Boulevard Bridge, in 2012 to replace the two-lane Steel Bridge constructed in 1962. Expected to complete in 2016, the bridge was being built a cost of $345 million. Additionally city infrastructure projects included the Poindexter Streetscape project, completed in 2013, and the Portsmouth Boulevard project set to begin in 2014 and continue into 2015.

Sumitomo Machinery Corporation of America, which has had a presence in Chesapeake since the 1980s, announced a $12 million project to increase manufacturing capabilities at its Cavalier Industrial Park location. Expected to complete in 2015, the project was set to transform the Chesapeake manufacturing facility from an assembly and distribution center into an assembly and manufacturing center. Some 50 jobs were expected to be added as part of the development.

Economic Development Information: Chesapeake Economic Development Department, 676 Independence Parkway, Suite 200, Chesapeake, VA 23320; telephone (757) 382-8040; fax (757) 382-8050.

Commercial Shipping

With its central location on the eastern coast of the United States, Chesapeake is a major shipping center. The city offers 120 miles of commercial waterfront and 12 miles of draft channels. Its port is the largest intermodal facility on the eastern seaboard and one of the top coal exporters worldwide. The Port of Virginia handles more than one million containers per year and links to more than 250 ports in at least 100 locations overseas. Its economic impact in 2013 was estimated at 343,000 jobs and $41 billion in revenue. Engineers estimate that by 2030 the port will handle an annual load of three million containers, in part because it offers the deepest shipping channels (50 feet) on the East Coast. With the rapid growth of the port's activity, the Virginia Port Authority determined that an additional 60 million square feet of industrial space would be needed in the next 25 years. The study called for the construction of an intermodal park of 3,500 acres to accommodate the port's growth. Shipping terminals currently include Norfolk International Terminal, Portsmouth Marine Terminal, Newport News Marine Terminals, and Virginia Inland Port.

In addition to its status as a marine shipping center, Chesapeake also is home to more than 100 motor carriers. Being a transportation hub for the region, Chesapeake is linked to one of the most modern interstate and state highway systems in the nation. Rail service is provided by Norfolk Southern and CSX.

Air freight service is available at Norfolk International Airport, where airlines and air cargo carriers processed 70 million pounds of freight annually as of 2013.

Labor Force and Employment Outlook

Despite the general economic slowdown of the rest of the country in recent years, Chesapeake has continued to see job growth and retention of its regional labor force. The concentration of high-technology jobs has led Chesapeake to claim one of the most highly educated and technologically advanced workforces in the United States. Some 85 percent of high school graduates in Chesapeake attend two- or four-year colleges. The labor force is supplemented by some 17,000 exiting military personnel and 40,000 military spouses. About 8,500 students graduated from area colleges annually as of 2013.

Virginia is the northernmost right-to-work state. Labor costs in Chesapeake have continually been competitive nationally, especially because Virginia state laws contain employer costs in the areas of workers' compensation and unemployment insurance. Actual wage and salary rates are also competitive, which, combined with an affordable cost of living, make Chesapeake a desirable location for businesses and employees.

The following is a summary of data regarding the 2012 Chesapeake labor force:

Size of civilian labor force: 114,570

Number of workers employed in . . .

agriculture and mining: 505
construction: 7,665
manufacturing: 9,036
wholesale trade: 3,009
retail trade: 13,381
transportation: 5,041

information systems: 2,414
finance: 5,761
professional administration: 12,259
education and social services: 22,963
arts and leisure: 8,620
other: 5,121
public administration: 9,829

Average hourly earnings of production workers: $Not available

Unemployment rate: 4.4% (2012)

Employers

Largest employers (2012)	*Number of employees*
City of Chesapeake Public Schools	5,729
City of Chesapeake	3,550
Chesapeake Regional Medical Center	2,300
Cox Communications	1,600
Sentara Home Care Services	1,100
General Dynamics Information Technology	780
Dolalr Tree Stores, Inc.	660
Capital One	650
Xerox	600
Canon Information Technology Service, Inc.	550
Oceaneering International	360

Cost of Living

Cost of living in the Chesapeake metropolitan area hovered around the national average in 2013.

The following is a summary of data regarding several key cost of living factors in the area.

State income tax rate: 2.0% to 5.75%

State sales tax rate: 5%

Local income tax rate: None

Local sales tax rate: 1%

Property tax rate: $1.05 per $100 of assessed value (2013)

Economic Information: Chesapeake Economic Development Department, 676 Independence Parkway, Suite 200, Chesapeake, VA 23320; telephone (757) 382-8040; fax (757) 382-8050. City of Chesapeake, 306

Cedar Road, Chesapeake, VA 23322; telephone (757) 382-2489.

■ Education and Research

Elementary and Secondary Schools

Chesapeake Public Schools are regularly ranked among the top public schools in both Virginia and the country. In 2013 all of its public schools received Standards of Learning accreditation from the Virginia Department of Education. There are two special programs in the district for students: Chesapeake Alternative School and Chesapeake Center for Science and Technology. The city's Technology Academy open in Chesapeake in 2008; it earned the distinction of being named a Governor's STEM Academy in 2012. International Baccalaureate programs are available. The drop-out rate of the school system was only 1.26 percent in 2011.

The district's 2010–20 Proposed Capital Improvement Plan focused on improving education through the planning and maintenance of system facilities, with a 2014–18 budget of more than $273 million. The funds were to replace roofs, mechanical systems, and other large maintenance projects. It also was to renovate existing facilities, plan for future new or expanded facilities, and purchase land.

There are also around 70 private secondary schools in the Chesapeake area, including those with and without religious affiliation. Saint Patrick Catholic School in Norfolk was named a Blue Ribbon School of Excellence by the U.S. Department of Education in 2013.

The following is a summary of data regarding the Chesapeake City Public Schools.

Total enrollment: 39,748

Number of facilities
 total: 47
 elementary schools: 28
 junior high schools: 10
 high schools: 7
 other: 2

Student/teacher ratio: 19.22:1

Teacher salaries
 average (statewide): $51,559

Funding per pupil: $10,114

Public Schools Information: Chesapeake Public Schools, 312 Cedar Road, Chesapeake, VA 23322; telephone (757) 547-1033.

Colleges and Universities

There are several four-year colleges and universities in the Chesapeake region. Located in Williamsburg, the College of William and Mary is America's second-oldest college, chartered in 1693 by King William III and Queen Mary II of England. With an enrollment of 8,258 in 2013, it was named by *U.S. News & World Report* as the 32nd-best university nationally. Old Dominion University in Norfolk, with a 2013 enrollment of nearly 25,000, is a public research university established in 1930 as the Norfolk Division of the College of William and Mary. It became an independent institution in 1962 and currently offers popular degree bachelor's programs in the fields of business and health professions, among many others. Christopher Newport University, located in Newport News, is a public liberal arts college that offered more than 80 undergraduate and graduate programs of study to its 5,186 students in 2013. It also has ties to William and Mary, being established in 1960 as a two-year school of the College of William and Mary. It became a four-year college in 1971 and a university in 1992. Hampton University in Hampton is a private, non-sectarian, co-educational, historically black university that enrolled just under 5,000 students in 2013. Norfolk State University in Norfolk was founded in 1935 and is a public, historically black university, offering both undergraduate and graduate degrees to more than 7,000 students. Regent University in Virginia Beach was established in 1978 by M. G. "Pat" Robertson. It is a Christian university. Eastern Virginia Medical School in Norfolk, established in 1973, is the only school of medicine founded by a grassroots effort of the local community.

Community colleges and trade schools include: Aviation Institute of Maintenance; Centura College; Tidewater Community College; ECPI College of Technology; Thomas Nelson Community College; Paul D. Camp Community College; and Strayer University, which offers bachelor's degrees as well as associate's degrees.

Libraries and Research Centers

The Chesapeake Public Library System has a central library and six branches. The central library contains the most comprehensive collection and serves as the reference resource center, including computerized information services. Branch libraries contain current and popular books, as well as a basic reference collection, newspapers, magazines, videos, DVDs, CDs, and a computerized information service. The Wallace Room in the central library serves as a reference resource of non-circulating genealogical and local history materials. It is supported by the Norfolk County Historical Society of Chesapeake.

Chesapeake has two national research laboratories within 10 miles of each other: the Thomas Jefferson National Accelerator Facility (Jefferson Lab), a Department of Energy national laboratory for nuclear physics research; and NASA Langley Research Center, which conducts research in aeronautics, earth sciences, space technology, and structures and materials. The Chrysler

Library at the Chrysler Museum of Art is one of the largest art reference libraries in the Southeast.

Public Library Information: Chesapeake Public Library System, 298 Cedar Road, Chesapeake, VA 23322-5598; telephone (757) 410-7100.

■ Health Care

Twenty-one general hospitals and medical centers serve the area, including Chesapeake Regional Medical Center, which includes Chesapeake General Hospital, a 310-bed facility that admits nearly 17,000 patients annually and also treats 189,000 through outpatient services. Specialties of the facility include bariatric surgery, breast cancer, other cancers, cardiology, digestive disease, gastroenterology, neuroscience, and orthopedic surgery. Sentara Norfolk General Hospital is the top-ranked hospital in the state, according to *U.S. News & World Report* in 2013–14, and admits almost 25,000 patients annually to its 491-bed hospital. The facility was nationally ranked in cardiology and heart surgery, as well as nephrology. It was high performing in an additionally eight specialties. Sentara also operates facilities in Virginia Beach, the Sentara Princess Anne Hospital, with 160 beds, and the Virginia Beach General Hospital, which was a 234-bed facility. The Naval Medical Center in Portsmouth is a general medical and surgical hospital with 274 beds and is operated by the Bureau of Medicine and Surgery within the U.S. Department of the Navy. The Jones Institute for Reproductive Medicine, the Diabetes Institute Foundation, and the Children's Hospital of the King's Daughters are also located in the Chesapeake area.

■ Recreation

Sightseeing

Chesapeake is a popular vacation spot, offering the draw of historical landmarks, beaches, and a plethora of attractions. Located in the beautiful Hampton Roads region, some of Chesapeake's main attractions are water-related. Chesapeake has close access to the Atlantic Intracoastal Waterway, which extends for about 3,000 miles along the Atlantic Ocean and Gulf of Mexico coasts. Thousands of boats ply the Intracoastal Waterway passing through the Dismal Swamp Canal and the Albemarle Chesapeake Canal annually. The waterway links the Chesapeake Bay to North Carolina's sounds, providing an important East Coast connection between Boston and Key West, Florida. Whether visitors are sailing or watching from the shore, they can enjoy the sights along this historic waterway. Parks at Deep Creek and Great Bridge provide excellent observation points. The Great Bridge Lock Park has bleachers to allow spectators to view the many yachts that transit the lock.

There is also a playground and a boat ramp. Deep Creek Lock Park is heavily wooded, with a pedestrian bridge and elevated walkway system to cross a tidal inlet and marsh area. Other features include foot trails that wind through the woods. The Dismal Swamp Canal Trail is used by horse owners, bicyclists, walkers, joggers, and boat owners. The trail runs 8.5 miles along the Dismal Swamp Canal. It is a nature and history lover's delight. The Great Dismal Swamp National Wildlife Refuge was established in 1973; it consists of more than 112,000 acres of forested wetlands in southeastern Virginia and northeastern North Carolina. The 3,100-acre Lake Drummond lies at the center of the swamp. The refuge is home to white tailed deer and black bear. Birding is popular as in excess of 200 species of birds have been identified on the refuge. The Chesapeake City Park is a 90-acre site that has 60 acres of open space with the remainder being rows of reforested pine trees.

Also for the nature lover, the Chesapeake Arboretum has 48 acres dedicated to promoting horticulture and environmental awareness. One of Virginia's finest trail systems meanders through a mature hardwood forest with many varieties of native plants and trees. The Arboretum headquarters is an eighteenth-century farmhouse with theme gardens that include a fragrance and antique rose garden. The farmhouse was built in 1730 with an addition built in 1822.

Located at the Chesapeake Municipal Center is the Chesapeake Planetarium, where visitors can explore the wonders of the universe. Free public programs including telescope observations are offered each week. It celebrated its 50th anniversary in 2013. The Chesapeake Veterans' Memorial commemorates the service and sacrifice of Chesapeake citizens who have served or are serving in the military. The memorial is located on the municipal grounds and is made up of a marble structure and more than 1,000 individual memorial pavers.

Cuffeytown-Longridge is the site of the oldest continuous community of Free-Born Africans in Virginia. Cuffeytown-Longridge history has been traced back to the eighteenth century. The community encompasses an area that contains many historic sites including Gabriel Chapel African Methodist Episcopal Zion Church, founded in 1866. Cuffeytown Road was named to commemorate the service of the Cuffeytown 13, a group of African Virginia Union Army Civil War Veterans who served in the 19th, 5th, and 36th U.S. Colored Infantries. These veterans are buried in the Cuffeytown History Cemetery. The Bells Mill Historical Research and Restoration Society sponsors tours of Cuffeytown and 20 other historical sites. The J.J. Moore Visitor, Archives, and Family Life Center is the only visitor center in Virginia with an Afro-Union and Afro-Virginian repository theme. The archives room has a historical collection that serves as a repository of documents, pictures, and records of more than 140 years of Cuffeytown, Gabriel

Chapel Church, and Afro-Union, Afro-Virginian, and Afro-Norfolk County military, political, and educational histories.

Chesapeake is also home to a number of stops on the Virginia Civil War Trails, including Dismal Swamp Canal, Deep Creek, Great Bridge, Glencoe, Pleasant Grove Baptist Church Cemetery, Seven Patriot Heroes, and Gabriel Chapel and Cuffeytown Cemetery.

Two important museum complexes within close reach of Chesapeake include the National Maritime Center in Norfolk and the Mariners' Museum in Newport News. The National Maritime Center consists of Nauticus, the battleship *Wisconsin*, the Hampton Roads Naval Museum (HRNM), and Cruise Norfolk. Nauticus is a maritime-themed science center featuring interactive theaters, hands-on exhibits, aquaria, digital high-definition films, and many educational programs. Special exhibits are provided in part by NOAA at Nauticus, the result of a partnership between the center and the National Oceanic and Atmospheric Administration. An NOAA Education Resource Center is located on the third floor of Nauticus, offering access to free NOAA educational materials. The U.S.S. *Wisconsin* is one of the largest and last battleships ever built by the U.S. Navy. The HRNM highlights more than 200 years of naval history and houses more than 50 exhibits that interpret the history of the U.S. Navy in Hampton Roads. The Cruise Norfolk Terminal is the only homeport passenger terminal for Virginia with more than 100,000 passengers sailing to the Caribbean each year.

The Mariners' Museum is one of the largest international maritime history museums complete with prized artifacts celebrating the spirit of seafaring adventure. Visitors can explore more than 60,000 square feet of gallery space with rare figureheads, handcrafted ship models, Civil War ironclad U.S.S. *Monitor* artifacts, paintings, and small craft from around the world. In 2007 the U.S.S. *Monitor* Center opened. A $30 million addition to the Mariners' Museum, the *Monitor* Center represents one of the nation's premier Civil War attractions. Visitors enjoy a high-definition battle theater, can walk on a full-scale replica of the *Monitor*, enjoy exciting interactive exhibits, experience a wide array of educational programs for school children, adults, families and scholars, and walk down a mock dock between a wooden sailing frigate and the C.S.S. *Virginia*.

Also close to Chesapeake is the Virginia Zoological Park in Norfolk, located on 53 acres along the Lafayette River. The zoo is home to 400 animals ranging from elephants, Siberian tigers, and monkeys to reptiles and birds. A ten-acre Okavango African habitat, a reptile and nocturnal gallery, a barnyard, and botanical gardens are just some of the features of the zoo. Other nearby attractions include Busch Gardens, Colonial Williamsburg, the Jamestown and Yorktown areas, and Naval Station Norfolk.

The Children's Museum of Virginia in Portsmouth is the state's largest children's museum, which provides 72,000 square feet of exhibit space. The museum features dozens of interactive exhibits and a planetarium, as well as an antique toy and model train collection, one of the largest on the East Coast. It reopened in 2011 after $13 million renovations during 2010.

Arts and Culture

Chesapeake is minutes away from outstanding professional theater, opera, dance troupes, symphony, and museums. In Norfolk the Chrysler Museum of Art is a fine collection of art and two historic houses. Represented artists include Andy Warhol, Louis Tiffany, and Paul Gauguin. Adjacent to the galleries and included in admission are the Moses Myers House, residence of Norfolk's first Jewish citizen, and the Willoughby-Baylor House. The Moses Myers House offers visitors a chance to view life as it was for a wealthy citizen in the late Federal period. The Portlock Galleries at SoNo in Chesapeake is a collection of artist working studios, shops, and galleries. Portlock Galleries hosts local and traveling art exhibits, art education for area schools, and summer art camps.

The Virginia Symphony in Norfolk serves the community of Hampton Roads and is one of the nation's leading regional symphony orchestras. The Virginia Opera stages four productions annually at the Harrison Opera House in Norfolk. The Virginia Stage Company is Southeastern Virginia's premier professional theater company, performing from May to September at Well's Theatre in Norfolk. The Sandler Center for the Performing Arts, located in Virginia Beach, opened in 2007 as one of nation's most acoustically sound venues for the arts.

Festivals and Holidays

In May the annual Chesapeake Jubilee takes place in City Park, featuring music, 4-H, crafts, educational exhibits, rides, fireworks, and food. In June the American Indian Festival is held, featuring American Indian storytelling, traditional dancing, and demonstrations, as well as a great selection of Native American jewelry, crafts, and food vendors. In September in City Park the Virginia Symphony Orchestra features a "Symphony under the Stars" performance, complete with wine tasting, fireworks, and the popular Tidewater Pipes & Drums with the Sheriff's Pipe Band. From March through May are a number of events associated with the Virginia Arts Festival. Other festivals and events are held in nearby cities and towns, which Chesapeakers and visitors alike can enjoy.

Sports for the Spectator

There are a number of professional sports for the spectator to enjoy in the Chesapeake region. The Norfolk

Tides, Triple-A affiliate of the Baltimore Orioles, play at Norfolk's Harbor Park, which can seat roughly 12,000 spectators. The Hampton Roads Piranhas are a United Soccer Leagues women's team that plays at the Virginia Beach Sportsplex. The Chesapeake Bayhawks compete in Major League Lacrosse and play at Navy-Marine Corps Memorial Stadium.

Sports for the Participant

Chesapeake has plenty of opportunities for sports and recreation, including golf, tennis, water sports, camping, horseback riding, and more. There are more than 30 miles of waterways in Chesapeake and three public and three commercial boat ramps. In addition, the wide, clean beaches of Virginia Beach are just minutes away, and North Carolina's Outer Banks are within easy reach.

Residents and visitors can enjoy themselves at Chesapeake's 67 parks and play areas. One of these is the 763-acre Northwest River Park, which was developed as a natural recreation area incorporating camping, an extensive trail system, picnic shelters, play areas, an equestrian area for horse owners, and fully-equipped rental cabins. There is fishing, miniature golf, the Marjorie Rein Memorial Walkway, and plenty of open areas. Rental boats and canoes are available. A fragrance garden for the visually impaired and a classroom building are located at the north end. The lake stretches almost to the southern activity area on the banks of the Northwest River. The city also supports a major skate park and three dog parks.

Chesapeake features two courses, the Chesapeake Golf Club and Cahoon Plantation Golf Club. The Chesapeake Golf Club is in a beautiful woodland setting. It is a 6,278-yard semi-private golf course featuring rolling fairways, challenging doglegs, and some of the best greens in the Tidewater area. The Isles Golf Links at Cahoon Plantation was inspired by the great links style courses of the British Isles and features more than 3,500 yards of golf. Golfers can enjoy the smoothest, greenest playing surface available on the only bent grass golf course from tee to fairway to green in the Williamsburg, Virginia Beach, and Outer Banks of North Carolina corridor.

Shopping and Dining

Shoppers can find both necessities and whimsies in Chesapeake's more than six million square feet of retail space. Townplace at Greenbrier has more than 170,000 square feet of restaurants, retails shops, walkways, and an outdoor entertainment center. The shopping center also offers a Summer Series each year, providing visitors with concerts as well as an art show. There are also two malls, nearly 50 strip shopping centers, chic boutiques, funky stores, and unique shopping districts. From fashion to art to antiques to department and outlets, shoppers are close to it all in Chesapeake. The Chesapeake Square Mall features more than 130 stores, including Macy's, JCPenney, Sears, Burlington Coat Factory, and a 101,000-square-foot Target. Greenbrier Mall has more than 120 stores, including Dillard's, Macy's, Sears, JCPenney, and specialty stores offering jewelry, home furnishing and accessories, men's and ladies apparel, hair and beauty, music, restaurants, movie theaters, gift stores and more. Antique Alley, located at S. Military Highway and Canal Drive, is an eclectic group of stores offering antique collectables, furnishings, glassware and stained glass, pottery, jewelry, tools, shabby chic, and many more treasures. The area also hosts auctions and flea markets.

There are more than 2,000 restaurants within a fifteen-mile radius of Chesapeake. Chesapeake Bay and Atlantic Ocean seafood is a specialty in this maritime region. Other cuisines include Asian, Italian, French, Mediterranean, Middle Eastern, Indian, and Mexican.

Visitor Information: Chesapeake Convention & Visitors Bureau, 860 Greenbrier Circle, Suite 101, Chesapeake, VA 23320; telephone (757) 502-4898; toll-free (888) 889-5551; fax (757) 502-8016.

■ Convention Facilities

Chesapeake Conference Center is a conference and meeting center in the dynamic Hampton Roads metropolitan area. It offers 23,700 square feet of meeting and banquet space, and can seat groups with 10 to 2,000 guests. There are nine meeting/banquet rooms designed for maximum flexibility, and space for up to 200 exhibit booths. The Chesapeake Conference Center is within walking distance of hundreds of accommodations.

Many area hotels also offer meeting space. The Norfolk Marriott Chesapeake offers 12,000 square feet of meeting space, nine meeting rooms, and a Grand Ballroom that seats 800. The Hilton Garden Inn Chesapeake-Greenbrier has around 1,400 square feet of meeting space and three conference rooms. The Hampton Inn & Suites Chesapeake has 1,100 square feet of meeting space and two meeting rooms. SpringHill Suites Chesapeake Greenbrier has about 980 square feet of meeting space and one meeting room. Several other hotels have meeting spaces of fewer than 1,000 square feet.

In addition, Cahoon Plantation features a 1,100-square-foot meeting room and a 500-square-foot conference room. The Chesapeake Arboretum has 10,000 square feet for outdoor tables and seating for 30. Historic Williamson Farmhouse can accommodate 150 with tents.

Convention Information: Chesapeake Convention & Visitors Bureau, 860 Greenbrier Circle, Suite 101, Chesapeake, VA 23320; telephone (757) 502-4898; toll-free (888) 889-5551; fax (757) 502-8016.

■ Transportation

Approaching the City

Norfolk International Airport is a 20 minute drive from Chesapeake. The airport offers direct flights from Air-Tran, American, Delta, Southwest, United, and US Airways to 21 cities. In 2012 the airport served nearly 3.3 million passengers, making it the 68th largest primary airport in the United States. Chesapeake Regional and Hampton Roads airports provide corporate flight service within the city.

Being a transportation hub for the region, Chesapeake is linked to one of the most modern interstate and state highway systems in the nation. Interstate Highway 64 originates in Chesapeake; Interstates 264, 464, and 664 also serve the city. U.S. Route 58 connects Chesapeake to the principal north–south highways on the East Coast, Interstates 95 and 85. U.S. Route 13 connects the city to Virginia's Eastern Shore. The Chesapeake Expressway (Route 168) links Interstate 64 to North Carolina and the Outer Banks.

Amtrak provides passenger rail service, and Greyhound provides bus service.

Traveling in the City

Public transportation is provided by Hampton Roads Transit (HRT). HRT serves seven cities: Norfolk, Virginia Beach, Chesapeake, Hampton, Newport News, Portsmouth, and Suffolk. In Chesapeake HRT operates ten routes. Daily ridership across routes in all cities averaged between 50,000 and 60,000 in 2013.

Hampton Road Transit's "The Tide" is a 7.4-mile light-rail line that runs straight into the heart of downtown Norfolk, starting at the Eastern Virginia Medical Center. It opened in 2013.

■ Communications

Newspapers and Magazines

The Virginian-Pilot serves both southeast Virginia and northeastern North Carolina. As of 2013, its circulation averaged 350,000 on weekdays and 470,000 on weekends. *The Chesapeake Angler* is a monthly fishing magazine published since 1997.

Television and Radio

Three television stations broadcast from Chesapeake, but the city receives broadcasts from Norfolk, Portsmouth, Virginia Beach, and elsewhere. One AM and three FM radio stations broadcast from Chesapeake.

Media Information: *The Virginian-Pilot,* 150 W. Brambleton Avenue, Norfolk, VA 23510; telephone (757) 446-9000.

Chesapeake Online

Chesapeake Conventions & Visitors Bureau. Available www.visitchesapeake.com

Chesapeake Public Library System. Available www.chesapeake.lib.va.us

Chesapeake Public Schools. Available www.cpschools.com

City of Chesapeake. Available www.cityofchesapeake.net

Hampton Roads Chamber of Commerce. Available www.hamptonroadschamber.com

The Virginian-Pilot. Available pilotonline.com

BIBLIOGRAPHY

Berman, Eleanor, *Away for the Weekend: Mid-Atlantic: Great Getaways within 250 miles from Washington, D.C. in Delaware, Maryland, Virginia, West Virginia, Pennsylvania, New Jersey* (New York: Three Rivers Press, 2002)

Ernst, Howard R., *Chesapeake Bay Blues: Science, Politics, and the Struggle to Save the Bay* (Lanham, MD: Rowman & Littlefield Publishers, 2003)

Eshelman, Ralph E., Scott S. Sheads, and Donald R. Hickey, *The War of 1812 in the Chesapeake: A Reference Guide to Historic Sites in Maryland, Virginia, and the District of Columbia* (Baltimore, MD: Johns Hopkins University Press, 2010)

Norfolk

■ The City in Brief

Founded: 1682 (incorporated 1705)

Head Official: Mayor Paul D. Fraim (since 1994; current term expires 2014); City Manager Marcus D. Jones (since 2011)

City Population
  1990: 261,250
  2000: 234,403
  2010: 242,803
  2012 estimate: 245,782
  Percent change, 2000–2010: 3.6%
  U.S. rank in 1990: 75th (State rank: 2nd)
  U.S. rank in 2000: 72nd (State rank: 2nd)
  U.S. rank in 2010: 78th (State rank: 2nd)

Metropolitan Statistical Area Population
  2000: 1,551,351
  2010: 1,671,683
  2012 estimate: 1,693,567
  Percent change, 2000–2010: 7.8%
  U.S. rank in 2000: 33rd
  U.S. rank in 2010: 36th

Area: 53.73 square miles

Elevation: 13 feet above sea level

Average Annual Temperatures: January, 40.1° F; July, 79.1° F; annual average, 59.6° F

Average Annual Precipitation: 45.74 inches of rain; 7.8 inches of snow

Major Economic Sectors: Government, health care, research, trade, transportation, services

Unemployment Rate: 6.8% (2012)

Per Capita Income: $24,191

2012 FBI Crime Index Property: 11,391

Major Colleges and Universities: Old Dominion University, Norfolk State University, Virginia Wesleyan College, Eastern Virginia Medical School, Troy State University, Tidewater Community College

Daily Newspaper: *The Virginian-Pilot*

■ Introduction

Norfolk is one of the world's largest and busiest port cities, and is also home to the world's largest naval base, Naval Station Norfolk. Water is central to the past, present and future of Norfolk, where the infamous *Merrimac* sea vessel was converted to the ironclad *Virginia*. The National Maritime Center recognizes the waterlogged character of this culturally and historically rich community. The city boasts 144 miles of shorelines along its lakes, rivers, and bay, and seven miles of Chesapeake Bay. Norfolk is also the site of the North American headquarters of the North Atlantic Treaty Organization (NATO). But the serious side of business in Norfolk is tempered with a wide variety of recreational, educational, and cultural opportunities that draw visitors, new residents, and new businesses. Norfolk's development in the first decades of the twenty-first century was astoundingly rapid, with some $2 billion invested in 2012 alone. In 2013 the city inaugurated "The Tide," a light-rail transit system, becoming the smallest U.S. city to have its own light rail.

■ Geography and Climate

Norfolk, nearly surrounded by the waters of the Chesapeake Bay, is located near the southern border of Virginia, 18 miles west of the Atlantic Ocean and about 200 miles southeast of Washington, D.C. Immediately north is Chesapeake Bay and west is Hampton Roads, the

Marina and Harbor at dusk, Norfolk, VA. *DenGuyliStockPhoto.com*

natural channel through which the waters of the James River and its tributaries flow into the mouth of the Chesapeake Bay. Norfolk is situated at the mouth of the James, Elizabeth, and Nansemond rivers. Within the city the land is low and level.

Norfolk is fortunate in that it is south of the average path of storms originating in the higher latitudes. It is also north of the usual tracks of hurricanes and other tropical storms. The city usually has mild winters and sunny, warm autumns and springs. The long hot summers are often interrupted by cool periods as a result of the

northeasterly winds off the Atlantic Ocean. Waves of extreme cold are rare, and often winters have no measurable snow. All in all, the National Weather Service has ranked Norfolk's climate as "one of the most desirable in the nation."

Area: 53.73 square miles

Elevation: 13 feet above sea level

Average Temperatures: January, 40.1° F; July, 79.1° F; annual average, 59.6° F

Average Annual Precipitation: 45.74 inches of rain; 7.8 inches of snow

■ History

In the Beginning

Beginning in about 9500 B.C., the area that is now Norfolk was called Skicoak and was ruled by the Chesipean Indians. But by the time the first Europeans reached the area, the tribe members had been driven out or killed by Chief Powhatan, after one of his advisors told Powhatan that in a dream he had seen the Powhatan Confederacy destroyed by strangers from the East. Powhatan thought this was a sign he should destroy the Chesipeans, even though they were a peaceful people.

In the 1560s settlers arrived from Spain, briefly living along the York River in a Jesuit community called Ajacan. Initially, the plan was to convert the Indians, but when the native people attacked the settlement in 1571, the Spanish abandoned Ajacan. The English were the next to test the area as a colony site, establishing Roanoke Settlement in 1585 under the guidance of Sir Walter Raleigh. The initial group of colonists abandoned Roanoke the next year and was followed by a second group in 1587. This second settlement disappeared without a trace by 1590 in one of the enduring mysteries of early recorded American history.

In 1624 Virginia became a Royal Colony when King James I of England granted 500 acres of land in what is now the Ocean View section of Norfolk to Thomas Willoughby. Twelve years later King Charles I of England gave Willoughby 200 additional acres, and this also became part of the original town of Norfolk.

In 1670, the British government directed the "building of storehouses to receive imported merchandise...and tobacco for export." This marked the beginning of Norfolk's importance as a port city. In 1673 the Virginia House of Burgesses called for the construction of Half Moone fort at the site of what is now Town Point Park.

City Prospers, Then Faces Destruction and Rebuilding

In 1682 England decreed that the "Towne of Lower Norfolk County" be established. The town was incorporated in 1705 and rechartered as a borough in 1736. For several decades the building of homes, farms, and businesses continued throughout the area, and Norfolk developed into a center for West Indies trade and the shipping of export products from the plantations of Virginia and the Carolinas. By 1775, Norfolk was known as the most prosperous city in Virginia.

The city served as a center for Tory forces during the American Revolution. On New Year's Day 1776, English ships under Royal Governor Lord Dunmore opened fire on the city, continuing their assault for eleven hours. High winds whipped up the flames and two-thirds of the city was destroyed by fire or cannonballs. By month's end the patriot colonists had torched the rest of the city to prevent the sheltering of Lord Dunmore and his forces. Every building in the city was destroyed by fire or cannonballs except Saint Paul's Church; a British cannonball remains in the wall of the church as testimony to the conflict. After the war, the citizens rallied and the city was rebuilt. In time it became a major shipbuilding and maritime center. In 1810 the U.S. government constructed a new fort at the site of dilapidated old Fort Norfolk. At that time the city's population stood at about 9,000 people.

Ports, Forts and Exports

The nineteenth century brought more troubles for the city. A major fire in 1804 destroyed 300 houses, warehouses, and stores. The population, which had been growing steadily, actually declined from more than 9,000 people in 1810 to 8,478 people by 1820.

Conveniently situated on the water and philosophically allied with the agitating Confederate states, Norfolk in 1821 became the embarkation point for African and African American individuals being sent back to Africa. Norfolk native Joseph Jenkins Roberts went on to become the first president of the Republic of Liberia after being deported. Virginia seceded from the Union in 1861, with the Norfolk Navy Yard assuming a critical role as vessels docked there were burned or scuttled, including the famed Merrimac. It was in the Navy Yard that the Merrimac was rebuilt as an ironclad vessel renamed the Virginia, which went on to engage in the first ironclad battle against the Monitor. In May 1862, early in the Civil War, Norfolk was captured by Union forces. The troops ransacked the houses of the citizenry and forced passengers on local ferries to trample on the Confederate flag.

At the end of the Civil War, Norfolk buildings were in ruins and the city's foreign trade was nonexistent. At that time, the population stood at about 19,000 citizens. But within 20 years the city experienced a turnaround and three-story brick buildings lined the streets of Norfolk, which by then had thriving hotels and a large farmers' market. Steamships visited the port regularly and rail service connected it with other parts of the country. The 1880 population had grown to 21,966 residents.

And the Pendulum Swings: Prosperity, Then Depression Times

In 1907 the Jamestown Exposition, held to celebrate the 300-year history of that nearby city, led to Norfolk's building several downtown hotels and office buildings. Visitors came from every state and dignitaries traveled from around the world to take part in the seven-month run of the event.

Norfolk's tremendous military growth began during World War I. In 1917 the land that was the site of the Jamestown Exposition became the U.S. Naval Operating Base and Training Station, which was later renamed Naval Station Norfolk. It was during this time that Norfolk was nationally recognized for leading the country in Navy recruitment. Between 1910 and 1920 the city's population grew from around 67,000 people to nearly 116,000 people as the city also experienced an influx of workers at numerous new private manufacturing plants.

Prosperity declined after the heady war years, when Norfolk handled much of the coal that came by train from West Virginia to be shipped elsewhere. In 1922 Norfolk helped establish solid economic ground for itself by building a $5 million grain elevator and terminal. It also built a $500,000 farmers' market and annexed 27 square miles of nearby land, which included the Navy base area and the Ocean View resort district. Because of large-scale naval operations, the city did not suffer as much from the Great Depression as some others, and by 1940 the population stood at more than 144,000 residents.

New Development Follows War Years

With the coming of World War II, Norfolk once again saw thousands of workers descend on the city and the region, where more than 100 ships and landing craft were built during the war. The war years saw a rapid increase in the development of individual residences and apartment buildings, and the city struggled to deal with over-crowding. Between 1940 and 1944 the population practically doubled. That period also saw the expansion of furniture manufacturing, fertilizer plants, and other industries.

In the years after World War II, Norfolk began a campaign to annex neighboring counties. Slums were cleared and public housing was constructed. In addition, hundreds of acres of land in the downtown were razed and rebuilt. Much of this redevelopment was spurred by the SCOPE Convention and Cultural Center. This facility includes the Chrysler Museum and Chrysler Hall, named in honor of automobile mogul Walter P. Chrysler, who donated his extensive art collection to the city.

In 1950 construction began on the first non-defense public housing project near Oak Leaf Park. Four additional projects began the next year. In 1952 the Elizabeth River Tunnel between Norfolk and Ports-mouth was completed, and a second tunnel followed 10 years later. By then the Hampton Roads Bridge-Tunnel linking Norfolk to the nearby city of Hampton was also built. Also in 1952 the city became home to Supreme Allied Command Atlantic, the western arm of the North Atlantic Treaty Organization and the only international command in the western hemisphere. The Norfolk International Terminals were built in 1966. Virginia's third medical college, the Eastern Virginia Medical School, was built in Norfolk in 1973.

During the next decade old buildings were razed and the Waterside Festival Marketplace, Town Point Park, and a number of condominiums were built along Norfolk's waterfront. Between 1950 and 1980 the population grew from 213,513 people to nearly 267,000 people. The 1980s saw development in the city that included the National Maritime Center, a new baseball stadium, and the construction of the Ghent Square neighborhood containing restored upscale residences. The World Trade Center was built in Norfolk in 1983.

The year 1989 saw the beginning of changes for municipal government in the city. Since 1918 the city was served by a city manager-city council model in which five city council members were elected at large. This system replaced a single-member five-ward system that had previously been in place. In 1989 the city reestablished the single-member representative ward system but expanded the number to seven, with five wards and two superwards. A mayor had been appointed from within the council. But 2006 marked the first at-large election for city mayor.

Norfolk continued its long tradition of self-renewal with ambitious building projects in the downtown area, new residential developments along the water, and revitalization efforts within the abundance of varied historical neighborhoods. Total annual investment in the city during the early 2010s averaged over $1 billion and reflected an array of public, private, and public-private partenership projects. The city's light-rail system began operations in 2013, providing a glimpse into the future of a rapidly growing city. While Norfolk was the smallest U.S. city with a light-rail system at the time, its rapid growth suggested it may not hold that title indefinitely.

Historical Information: The Norfolk Historical Society, 227 W Freemason St., Norfolk, VA 23510; telephone (757) 640-1720.

■ Population Profile

Metropolitan Statistical Area Population

    2000: 1,551,351
    2010: 1,671,683
    2012 estimate: 1,693,567
    Percent change, 2000–2010: 7.8%
    U.S. rank in 2000: 33rd
    U.S. rank in 2010: 36th

City Residents

    1990: 261,250
    2000: 234,403
    2010: 242,803
    2012 estimate: 245,782
    Percent change, 2000–2010: 3.6%
    U.S. rank in 1990: 75th (State rank: 2nd)

U.S. rank in 2000: 72nd (State rank: 2nd)
U.S. rank in 2010: 78th (State rank: 2nd)

Density: 4,486.3 people per square mile

Racial and ethnic characteristics

White: 117,707
Black or African American: 104,236
American Indian and Alaskan Native: 995
Asian: 6,662
Native Hawaiian and Other Pacific Islander: 492
Hispanic or Latino (may be of any race): 17,623
Other: 15,690

Percent of residents born in state: 49.1%

Age characteristics

Population under 5 years old: 16,866
Population 5 to 9 years old: 14,877
Population 10 to 14 years old: 12,381
Population 15 to 19 years old: 18,134
Population 20 to 24 years old: 36,510
Population 25 to 34 years old: 44,232
Population 35 to 44 years old: 27,068
Population 45 to 54 years old: 28,406
Population 55 to 59 years old: 12,860
Population 60 to 64 years old: 10,897
Population 65 to 74 years old: 12,410
Population 75 to 84 years old: 7,470
Population 85 years and over: 3,671
Median age: 29.6

Births (2010–11 Metropolitan Area)

Total number: 22,692

Deaths (2010–11 Metropolitan Area)

Total number: 12,648

Money income (2012)

Per capita income: $24,191
Median household income: $43,708
Total households: 85,626

Number of households with income of ...

less than $10,000: 7,966
$10,000 to $14,999: 5,077
$15,000 to $24,999: 10,355
$25,000 to $34,999: 10,969
$35,000 to $49,999: 14,049
$50,000 to $74,999: 16,619
$75,000 to $99,999: 7,946
$100,000 to $149,999: 7,812
$150,000 to $199,999: 2,794
$200,000 or more: 2,039

Percent of families below poverty level: 18.9%

FBI Crime Index Property: 11,391

FBI Crime Index Violent: 1,332

■ Municipal Government

Norfolk operates under a mayor-council-city manager form of government. There are seven council members, with 5 elected from single wards and two from super-wards. All council members serve four-year terms, with staggered elections every two years. The mayor is elected at large to a four-year term. The council appoints a city manager.

Head Official: Mayor Paul D. Fraim (since 1994; current term expires 2014); City Manager Marcus D. Jones (since 2011)

Total Number of City Employees: 4,079 (2012)

City Information: Mayor's Office, City of Norfolk, 810 Union St., Suite 1001, Norfolk, VA 23510; telephone (757) 664-4679.

■ Economy

Major Industries and Commercial Activity

Norfolk's largest industry was in the military, which should come as no surprise given that Norfolk is home to the largest naval base in the world, Naval Station Norfolk. It also serves as home to the headquarters of the Fifth Naval District of the Atlantic Fleet and the Second Fleet, and it houses the district headquarters of the Coast Guard. In addition to the thousands of U.S. Navy personnel stationed in Norfolk, many local citizens also work in naval operations. An astounding 29,000 military veterans were living in Norfolk in 2013. In the 2011 fiscal year, the direct economic impact of the military sector rose to a whopping $14.9 billion.

Only health care employed trailed that of the government sector, with health care employing more than 20,000 residents as of 2013. While hospitals composed the most visible sign of the industry's presence, some 35 companies performing research and development in the area brought in $150 million annually in funding to national research centers studying bioelectrics and proteomics, as well as research parks and business incubaters like Innovation Research Park and the Hampton Institute.

Norfolk also serves as the business and financial center of the Hampton Roads region of Virginia. Shipbuilding and shipping are a vital part of Norfolk's economy. As a major seaport through which millions of tons of cargo pass each year, it handles such commodities as tobacco, cotton, timber, coal, truck crops, and grain. Over 95 percent of the world's leading shipping lines utilize the Port of Hampton Roads, which linked Virginia to nearly 400 porst in 100 different countries as of 2013.

The port's 50-foot-deep channels are the deepest on the U.S. East Coast. The port is home to Carnival cruise lines. Norfolk is also corporate headquarters of the Norfolk Southern Railway, one of North America's principal Class I railroads and was a *Fortune* 500 company in 2013. The rail system handles some 30 percent of all cargo coming into or out of the Port of Hampton Roads.

The Hampton Roads region is home to two other *Fortune* 500 headquarters: Smithfood Foods and Dollar Tree, as well as a former member, Amerigroup, last listed in 2012. Norfolk is also corporate headquarters for Landmark Media Enterprises, one of the country's largest privately owned media companies with ownership of several daily newspapers, local television stations, specialty publications, and The Weather Channel. Some 180 international companies operate in Norfolk, most headquarter in Germany and Japan.

Items and goods produced: chemicals, fertilizer, textiles, automobiles, ships, military and law enforcement equipment, agricultural machinery, seafood, and peanut oil

Incentive Programs-New and Existing Companies

Local programs: Incentives offered include the South Norfolk Hub Zone, which encourages development of historically underutilized business zones, referred to as HUBZones. The local program is part of the U.S. Small Business Administration. The Commercial Façade Improvement Program awards grants to certain commercial corridors in Norfolk to encourage private investment by matching funds for aesthetic improvements to commercial properties. Enterrpise zone incentives from local and state authorities are available. New Market Tax Credits program, administered by the city, allows taxpayers to claim credits against federal income tax for qualified equity investments in designated Community Development Entities. The Tax Abatement Program allows businesses not to pay taxes on improvements to commercial, residential, or industrial structures.

State programs: Virginia is a right-to-work state, advertising itself as the northernmost right-to-work state in the nation. The State General Assembly has kept Virginia's taxes on industry very competitive by maintaining relatively moderate corporate income tax rates and by eliminating many tax irritants, resulting in modest tax bills for business and industry. While this alone constitutes an attractive incentive for new and existing businesses, the State of Virginia further offers Governor's Opportunity Funds, which allow the Governor to secure business locations or expansion projects with matching funds from the local community; Virginia Investment Partnership Grant Funds, supporting large employers with businesses established for a minimum of five years in Virginia; property tax exemptions; sales and use tax exemptions; enterprise zones; technology zones; and

foreign trade zones. Virginia has a State Historic Rehabilitation Tax Credit Program, as does the federal government. The state's Virginia Small Business Financing Authority provides small businesses with access to capital for growth and expansion efforts. The Virginia Economic Development Incentive Grant is a discretionary performance incentive designed to assist and encourage business investment that creates new employment in the state. Specifically, it targets businesses looking to relocate headquarters or others significant service-sector or administrative jobs in the state.

Job training programs: The state's Virginia Jobs Investment Program offers customized recruiting and training assistance for expanding companies that need to hire more workers. The program seeks to lower human development costs to state businesses. In the Hampton Roads area, Opportunity, Inc. provides employers and job seekers with necessary networks and resources in an effort to achieve their mission of "strengthening the localized talent pool of workers to match private sector investments in technology, capital, and product improvement." Acting under the auspices of the Hampton Roads Workforce Development Board, the agency offers workshops, links to online tools and access to a statewide collection of strategic partners. The Hampton Roads Chamber of Commerce also supports the workforce program to keep local employers abreast of labor market trends, employment best practices, and workforce resources.

Development Projects

Development projects have exploded in the Norfolk metropolitan area since the mid-2000s, continuing through the 2010s. An estimated $2 billion in development took place during 2012 alone. Hampton Road Transit's "The Tide," a $317 million investment, is a 7.4-mile light-rail line that runs straight into the heart of downtown Norfolk, starting at the Eastern Virginia Medical Center. It opened in 2012 and averaged 4,650 daily riders in its first year. The rail project spurred an estimated $500 in surrounding developments, including the $180 million Wells Fargo Center, a 250-square-foot office facility that also has apartments and retail space, which opened in 2007.

A number of other transportation-related projects also were underway in the 2010s, including a massive $1.9 billion development at Elizabeth Rivers Crossings, which sought to implement modifications to local interchanges and dig a new two-lane tunnel under the Elizabeth River, adjacent to the existing Midtown Tunnel. A $3 million, 3,500-square-foot Amtrak station opened in 2012 to serve passenger traffic to Richmond and Washington, D.C., and beyond. Harbor Park was a planned multi-modal passenger station to connect bus, ferry, and light-rail traffic. An additional bus transfer station in the St. Paul's area, a $5.5 million project, was under consideration in 2013. Construction began in 2012 and was supported by $87 million in state funding. A connecting interstate highway branch from Interstate 574 to port terminals began construction in 2013 at a cost of $170 million.

Construction of the Norfolk Consolidated Courthouse Complex was expected to complete in 2015 with a final price tag of $123. The new complex was to house the General District, Circuit and Juvenile, and Domestic Relations Courts. The building was to be a LEED-certified building for its environmentally conscious design. Another municipal building, Colonel Samuel L. Slover Memorial Main Library was being constructed next to Seaboard Building housing the main library. The Slover Library was set to add 70,000 additional square feet of space for meetings, as well as a technology center. The new building was expected to open in 2014 at a cost of $64.

Sentara Healthcare, one of the city's leading employers, completed $20.5 million in renovations to its surgery ward and emergency care department in 2010, then followed with a $126 million investment to expand its main hospital by 40 percent to 506,000 total square feet in 2012. The project was scheduled for completion in 2014. Also in 2012, Bon Secours Depaul Medical Center began adding 105,000 to its facility; the Renova Center, Lake Taylor Transitional Care Hospital, and St. Mary's Home for Disabled Children were other expanding health facilities in the area.

Arts were also enjoying a throng of investment. The Chrysler Museum of Art was working to add 10,000 square feet of gallery space to its facility by 2014, and Norfolk Collegiate Center for the Arts completed in 2013, a new facility with a 425-seat theater built at a cost of $8.5 million.

Economic Development Information: Department of Development, City of Norfolk, 500 East Main St., Suite 1500, Norfolk, VA 23510; telephone (757) 664-4338.

Commercial Shipping

The Norfolk International Terminals of the Port of Virginia offer fourteen container cranes, including the largest class of crane in the world. Exports of coal, food products, tobacco, and the majority of grain from the United States pass through the port of Norfolk. Annually, the Port of Virginia manages more than 70 million tons of cargo, as of 2012. That year, the Port of Virginia ranked third behind New York and Savannah, Georgia, for marketshare among East Coast terminals. The Norfolk International Terminal is a Foreign Trade Zone. Several freight forwarder and custom broker services are available. Norfolk is also home to Lambert Point Docks, which covers 117 acres and is a major trans-shipment point for coal.

Air freight service is available at Norfolk International Airport, where airlines and air cargo carriers processed 70 million pounds of freight annually as of 2013. Railroad freight carriers include the Norfolk Southern and CSX railroads. Direct-service trains serve the airport and port areas. More than 150 trucking companies serve the city's shipping needs in and out of the three terminals of the Port of Virginia every day.

Labor Force and Employment Outlook

The Chamber of Commerce has noted that the local workforce is numerous but unprepared for the new employment opportunities offered by the community's companies. Efforts have been underway to enlist the support of Hampton Roads employers in advocating for classes and degree programs that are tailored more closely to the needs of local industries; at the same time, the city continues to focus on attracting technological, medical and industrial companies to entice graduates of the region's universities to stay and work locally. Growth occupations in 2012 were personal care aide, veterinary technologists and technicians, carpenters, physical therapist assistants, and software developers. The city had some 14,731 residents with post-graduate degrees, and another 23,437 with bachelor's degrees.

The following is a summary of data regarding the 2012 Norfolk labor force:

Size of civilian labor force: 116,544

Number of workers employed in ...

  agriculture and mining: 225
  construction: 8,016
  manufacturing: 6,389
  wholesale trade: 1,569
  retail trade: 12,917
  transportation: 4,931
  information systems: 1,627
  finance: 5,090
  professional administration: 11,420
  education and social services: 22,889
  arts and leisure: 10,894
  other: 5,488
  public administration: 10,419

Average hourly earnings of production workers: $17.57

Unemployment rate: 6.8% (2012)

Employers

Largest employers (2012)	*Number of employees*
U.S. Department of Defense	
Sentara Healthcare	
Norfolk City School Board	

City of Norfolk
Old Dominion
  University
Children's Hospital
  of the King's
  Daughters
Norshipco
Norfolk State
  University
Eastern Virginia
  Medical School
Portfolio Recovery
  Association

Cost of Living

The following is a summary of data regarding several key cost of living factors in the area.

2013 ACCRA Average House Price: $268,961

2013 ACCRA Cost of Living Index: 100

State income tax rate: 2.0% to 5.75%

State sales tax rate: 5%

Local income tax rate: None

Local sales tax rate: 1%

Property tax rate: $1.15 per $100 of assessed value (2013)

Economic Information: Hampton Roads Chamber of Commerce, 500 East Main St., Suite 700, Norfolk, VA 23501; telephone (757) 622-2312; fax (757) 622-5563.

■ Education and Research

Elementary and Secondary Schools

Norfolk Public Schools offer many special programs, such as gifted and special education programs and also utilize community-based education to reify the academic concepts being taught in classes. Special programs offered for high school students include the studies in military science, medical and health professions, engineering, the arts, and the International Baccalaureate program. Special programs in world studies, technology, communications, the arts, and languages are available at the middle school level. Vocational programs for students with disabilities are offered through the NPS Technical and Vocational Center, Norfolk Skills Center, and Madison Career Center.

The area is also host to a variety of specialized education programs, from private religious schools, to Headstart programs, to technical and vocational schools. Saint Patrick Catholic School in Norfolk was named a Blue Ribbon School of Excellence by the U.S. Department of Education in 2013.

The following is a summary of data regarding the Norfolk City Public Schools.

Total enrollment: 33,787

Number of facilities

total: 50
elementary schools: 33
junior high schools: 8
high schools: 5
other: 4

Student/teacher ratio: 16.24:1

Teacher salaries

average (statewide): $51,559

Funding per pupil: $9,939

Public Schools Information: Norfolk Public Schools, 800 E. City Hall Avenue, Norfolk, VA 23510; telephone (757) 628-3931.

Colleges and Universities

Norfolk is home to a number of institutions of higher learning that span the spectrum of vocational specialty schools, community colleges, and colleges or universities. Old Dominion University, founded in 1930 as a division of the College of William and Mary, is a public coeducational school and a sea- and space-grant institution with a combined undergraduate and graduate enrollment of about 25,000 students. From baccalaureate to doctoral programs, Old Dominion grants degrees in education, liberal arts, business and public administration, sciences, health sciences, engineering, and technology. The university capitalizes on its proximity to the naval base and the NASA's Wallops Flight Facility, creating fieldwork experiences that contribute to those industries. Old Dominion has been classified as a Doctoral Research University–Extensive by the Carnegie Foundation.

Virginia Wesleyan College, with 1,431 students, is a private liberal arts college that emphasizes the value of gaining real-world experience through internships, field work, study abroad, and community service. The college offers baccalaureate degrees in various divisions of the humanities, natural sciences and mathematics, and the social sciences.

Norfolk State University is one of the largest predominantly African American institutions in the United States, with an enrollment of more than 7,000 students. It has undergraduate schools in business, education, liberal arts, social work, and science and technology, as well as graduate departments. The most popular majors are business, nursing, psychology, biology, and music education.

The Eastern Virginia Medical School is a public institution with its main campus at Norfolk's Eastern Virginia Medical Center. Its enrollment, including medical residents, was 6,801 in 2013. The school does not own a teaching hospital but works in partnership with several local hospitals and clinics, including Sentara Norfolk General Hospital and the Children's Hospital of the King's Daughters. The schools includes 365 clinical faculty and 30 health professions faculty.

The Joint Forces Staff College (JFSC) in Norfolk is a division of the National Defense University of Washington, D.C. JFSC offers courses in joint, multinational, and interagency operational-level planning and warfighting for military and national security leaders.

Tidewater Community College is a two-year college offering career and technical education programs as well as college transfer programs. With nearly 45,000 enrolled each year, it is the 11th two-year college in the nation, as of 2013. Campuses are located in Norfolk, Portsmouth, Virginia Beach, and Chesapeake. Visual arts centers are located around the region, as is the college's Advanced Technology Center, Regional Health Professions Center, Regional Automotive Center, and Center for Military and Veterans Education. The college has 11 accredited programs and is the 17th-largest degree-producer among two-year colleges.

Libraries and Research Centers

The more than 100-year-old Norfolk Public Library system nearly one million books and subscribes to more than 1,000 periodicals. It serves patrons through the SloverMemorial main library, a new $64 million facility to open in 2014, 11 branches, and a bookmobile with Internet-access computers. The Treasure Truck provides free books to children at local preschools, daycare centers, and other locations. The library has special sections on African American literature, business, juvenile literature, and local history. The Norfolk Public Library is a government depository library for selected documents.

The city's Chrysler Museum of Art houses the Jean Outland Chrysler Library, containing more than 106,000 unique and rare volumes of books relating to the history of art, with special emphasis on Western European and American painting, drawing, sculpture, Art Nouveau decorative arts, textiles, glass, art history, and photography. The library's archives are home to many treasures, not the least of which is Mark Twain's original typescript of a speech he delivered at the Tricentennial Exposition of 1907 in Jamestown.

MacArthur Memorial Library and Archives has special collections on the life of American General Douglas MacArthur, who is buried nearby, and on American wars in the first half of the twentieth century. MacArthur Memorial is a nonlending research library with more than 2 million documents, 80,000 photographs, 111 films, and numerous sound recordings,

newspapers, rare books, and microfilms. The U.S. Navy's Submarine Force Library and Museum is the official repository for the records and history of the force. It has 6,000 volumes and more than 2.5 million documents and photographs focusing on submarine development, salvage, and history. The Ike Skelton Library at Joint Forces Staff College, with 144,000 volumes and 450 periodical and newspaper titles, is primarily for military personnel. Civilians may gain access to library resources, including the Federal Depository Collection, through advance permission. Civilian visitors may only borrow books through interlibrary loan.

The Edward E. Brickell Medical Sciences Library at Eastern Virginia Medical School (EVMS) is a state-of-the-art facility that houses the original Moorman Memorial Library collection and a computer lab giving students access to a wealth of digital resources. Special collections at the library include the Historical Collection, featuring old and rare books on medical history, and the St. Jude Collection, which also contains classical books on medicine.

There are also college libraries at Virginia Wesleyan College, Norfolk State University, and Old Dominion University. Norfolk Psychiatric Center maintains a medical library. The Norfolk Law Library provides legal reference material to the public, lawyers and the courts.

Old Dominion University is home to a diverse collection of research facilities, including the Center for Advanced Ship Repair and Maintenance, Center for Coastal Physical Oceanography, Dental Hygiene Research Center, Laser & Plasma Engineering Institute, and Center for Global Business and Executive Education, among others. Old Dominion University's Office of Research acts as a clearinghouse for research efforts centralized at the university. The Norfolk area is also the site of two NASA-affiliated centers: NASA Langley Research Center and NASA Wallops Island Flight Facility.

Research programs through Eastern Virginia Medical School include the Jones Institute for Reproductive Medicine, Leroy T. Canoles Jr. Cancer Research Center, and Strelitz Diabetes Center-Research. The National Center for Collaboration in Medical Modeling and Simulation is research center dedicated to improving patient care by advancing the quality and quantity of medical modeling and simulation-based training and education for students and practitioners.

The Center for Materials Research at Norfolk State University works with support from NASA, the U.S. Department of Energy, and Los Alamos National Laboratory. Marine and naval research facilities abound within Naval Station Norfolk, including a laboratory that focuses on specific medical issues related to service in a submarine.

Public Library Information: Norfolk Public Library, 235 East Plume Street, Norfolk, VA 23510; telephone

(757) 664-7323. Old Dominion University, Office of Research, 4111 Monarch Way, Suite 203, Norfolk, VA 23529; telephone (757) 683-3460.

■ Health Care

Norfolk is the site of Virginia's only free-standing, full-service pediatric hospital, Children's Hospital of the King's Daughters. The emergency room serves more than 47,000 children annually, and the 206-bed facility serves more than 5,400 children as inpatients each year, with in excess of 200,000 children receiving outpatient services. Staffed with educators, therapists and social workers in addition to pediatric medical specialists, the hospital specializes in the treatment of cancer, neonatal medicine, infectious diseases, orthopedics, and craniofacial and urological reconstructive surgery.

Sentara Norfolk General Hospital is one of the top-ranked hospitals in the state, according to *U.S. News & World Report* in 2013–14, and admits almost 25,000 patients annually to its 491-bed hospital. The facility was nationally ranked in cardiology and heart surgery, as well as nephrology. It was high performing in an additionally eight specialties. Sentara also operates facilities in Virginia Beach, the Sentara Princess Anne Hospital, with 160 beds, and the Virginia Beach General Hospital, which was a 234-bed facility. The Sentara Leigh Hospital is a 238-bed hospital featuring private rooms and specializing in orthopedic, gynecological, general, and urological services.

Bon Secours Health System also offers a number of facilities in Norfolk and the surrounding area. Bon Secours DePaul Medical Center is a 238-bed acute-care facility that includes the Midwifery Center, the Center for Birth, a Cancer Center, the Joint and Spine Center, the Wound Care and Hyperbaric Oxygen Center, and additional programs for hearing/balance, sleep disorders, cardiac care, and epilepsy. Province Place of DePaul is an assisted living residence on-campus at the Bon Secours DePaul Medical Center. In 2013 the hospital treated more than 46,000 emergency room patients and admitted nearly 8,000.

Lake Taylor Hospital is a 293-bed transitional care and chronic disease facility. Inpatient behavioral health and substance abuse services for adolescents are available through the Norfolk Psychiatric Center on Kempsville Road.

The Norfolk area and its major medical facilities are supported by dozens of specialized clinics, hundreds of private medical practitioners and a number of alternative treatment providers. The Naval Medical Center in Portsmouth is a general medical and surgical hospital with 274 beds and is operated by the Bureau of Medicine and Surgery within the U.S. Department of the Navy.

■ Recreation

Sightseeing

Visitors to Norfolk can observe giant aircraft carriers and guided-missile cruisers juxtaposed with sailboats and pedestrian ferries in the city's busy harbor. As home to the world's largest naval base, Naval Station Norfolk, the port has many significant U.S. Marine, U.S. Coast Guard, and NATO facilities as well. The *Spirit of Norfolk* passenger ship offers lunch and dinner cruises along Norfolk's scenic and historic waterfront. Sightseeing harbor cruises are also provided Norfolk's own tall-sailing ship *American Rover* and the Mississippi-style paddle-wheeler *Carrie B.* Trolley tours to the city's major historic and cultural attractions are offered daily from the Waterside complex. Tour buses also make trips to Naval Station Norfolk, home port to more than 100 ships of the Atlantic fleet. The Norfolk Cruise Port opened in 2007 and is served by Carinval cruise lines, which offers cruises to the Bahamas, as well as sea-faring "cruises to nowhere."

The National Maritime Center is home to four main attractions. Nauticus, a 120,000 square foot science center with a nautical theme, celebrates the region's rich maritime heritage. It offers interactive exhibits, a shark tank, a weather forecasting lab, a giant-screen theater, and hands-on displays for all ages, as well as traveling exhibits. Special exhibits are provided in part by NOAA at Nauticus, the result of a partnership between the center and the National Oceanic and Atmospheric Administration. An NOAA Education Resource Center is located on the third floor of Nauticus, offering access to free NOAA educational materials. Hampton Roads Naval Museum introduces tourists to more than two centuries of naval history through ship models, works of art, and artifacts from sunken ships. Docked outside is the 1933 tugboat *Huntington,* which houses a tugboat museum that salutes the "Workhorses of the Waterways." One of the largest and last battleships ever built by the U.S. Navy, USS *Wisconsin,* is also moored next to Nauticus. Visitors can take self-guided tours across the decks of this World War II vessel. Waterside Festival Marketplace is adjacent to Nauticus, offering restaurants and nightclubs for visitors.

Strollers through Town Point Park can stop by the Armed Forces Memorial, which has on display descriptions of life during wartime taken from letters written home by U.S. service people who were killed in wars, from the American Revolution to the Persian Gulf War. The region's military history is further reflected in Fort Norfolk, with brick and earthwork buildings dating back to 1810. It is surrounded by a wall and ramparts built to protect the structure against invasion by the British.

Nearby is the picturesque Freemason district, Norfolk's oldest existing neighborhood. There visitors can walk along cobblestone streets, following the Cannonball Trail through 400 years of recorded history, including a stop at the Norfolk History Museum at Willoughby-Baylor House. This 1794 Federal townhouse was opened as a museum in 2005 in partnership with the Chrysler Museum of Art. The nearby Moses Myers House is also open for tours. Freemason Street Baptist Church, the cannonball-studded wall of St. Paul's Episcopal Church and the Confederate Memorial. Norfolk's Freemason District is also part of the Civil War Trails system, linking more than 200 Civil War sites around and beyond the city. Included in Norfolk is the Black Soldiers Memorial, which stands as the only monument in the South specifically dedicated in recognition of the service given by African Americans during the Civil War.

The Ghent district, Norfolk's first planned community, is a combination of restored houses, galleries, boutiques, restaurants, and antique shops. The Hermitage Museum and Gardens are housed in a wooded setting on the Lafayette River on a 12-acre estate. Within the splendid English Tudor home are displays of European ceramics and paintings, German hand-painted glass *objets d'art*, ivory carvings, Persian rugs, and ritual bronzes and ceramic tomb figures from China.

For more than a century the Virginia Zoological Park has provided a look into the lives of many kinds of animals, which number more than 400 and range from white rhinos to red-ruffed lemurs spread out over 53 acres. The zoo grounds are divided into habitats of animals from various continents in large enclosures that encourage natural behaviors. On a path that features interactive exhibits about African river deltas and other ecological zones, visitors encounter many interesting animals and sights, including a unique dismal swamp exhibit. The Norfolk Botanical Gardens encompasses 155 acres of colorful flower gardens. A few of the themed gardens are the Annette Kagan Healing Garden, the Colonial Herb Garden, the Enchanted Forest, the Fragrance Garden, Turner Sculpture Garden, and the Hummingbird Garden. Signature gardens include the Bicentennial Rose Garden, Bristow Butterfly Garden, Kaufman Hydrangea Garden, the Virginia Native Plant Garden, and the World of Wonders—A Children's Adventure Garden. Boat trips are available through the garden's waterways with their brilliant exotic blooms.

Arts and Culture

The Chrysler Museum of Art contains a collection of original works from many time periods and geographic areas; it broke ground on an expansion in 2012, set to finish in 2014. The American Painting and Sculpture collection contains a selection of colonial and folk art offerings along with examples of American Impressionism. The European Painting and Sculpture collection features Italian Renaissance, Baroque, Dutch, and French works from such masters as Rubens, de Clerck, and Renoir. The showpiece exhibit may be a magnificent 8,000-piece glass collection featuring wonderful Tiffany

and Lalique displays. The d'Art Center is home to 43 visual artists who both create and sell their works on-site; visitors can tour the studios to watch painters, sculptors, potters, and jewelry makers at work.

Military museums abound in Norfolk, including The National Maritime Center and the Hampton Roads Naval Museum. The latter incorporates 234 years of Hampton Roads naval history and operates the living history experience aboard the USS *Wisconsin*.

Downtown Norfolk provides a number of opportunities to see what life was like in the early days of the city, including the Hermitage Museum and Gardens, featuring a Tudor home from 1908, and the Hunter House Victorian Museum, built in 1894 by architect W. D. Wentworth.

Norfolk boasts the oldest theater designed, developed, financed, and operated entirely by African Americans—the Attucks Theatre, named for the African American man who fell as the first casualty of the American Revolution. The theater has recently been renovated after being closed in the mid 1950s, with the aim of again hosting luminaries of the caliber of Duke Ellington and Nat King Cole.

Norfolk's premiere performing arts center is Chrysler Hall, which annually stages the Broadway at Chrysler Hall series, touring productions of musicals and plays, and a star-studded roster of musical and spoken-word performers. Harrison Opera House is home to the well-respected Virginia Opera, which offers four productions annually in addition to other dance, music and theatrical works. The opera building also houses the Virginia Opera's Education and Outreach Program, sending resident artists into the public schools to awaken students to the joys, passions and tragedies that are opera. The Virginia Stage Company professional theater produces six major shows yearly, as well as smaller shows and children's theater activities at the historic and elegant Wells Theater. Several small, local theater groups also operate in the Norfolk region, including the Generic Theater (off-beat theater), the Little Theatre of Norfolk (one of the nation's oldest community theaters), and the Hurrah Players (family theater starring aspiring performers).

Ballet Virginia was created in 1961 to promote regional ballet, train young dancers, and provide a creative center for the performing arts. Ballet Virginia Academy is home to a professional faculty offering classes in classical ballet, modern dance, tap, jazz, yoga, and character dance.

The Virginia Symphony Orchestra performs more than 140 concerts each year, from classical to pops. The group also offers young people's concerts. Under the direction of JoAnn Falletta, the symphony has recorded five CDs for national release, performed *Peter and the Wolf* for airing on National Public Radio, and played at both the Kennedy Center and Carnegie Hall. The

Virginia Symphony also lends orchestral support to the Virginia Opera.

The Virginia Chorale has, since 1984, been the commonwealth's only fully professional choral group, performing music from all time periods and particularly skilled in *a cappella* renditions. The Chorale offers Masters Classes and the Young Singers Project as part of their outreach and education endeavors.

The Governor's School for the Arts, at home in Norfolk, plays a pivotal role in keeping the arts alive in the Hampton Roads area. Art education programs are offered in dance, vocal and instrumental music, theater, and visual arts, with a number of student productions performed to further develop the artists and showcase their burgeoning talents.

The Norfolk Commission on the Arts and Humanities, established in 1978, provides support for local arts organizations.

Festivals and Holidays

Norfolk celebrates St. Patrick's Day on March 17 with the Greening of Ghent, which includes a parade and party in the Ghent neighborhood. April's events include the International Azalea Festival at the Botanical Gardens, and the Virginia International Tattoo, a spectacle of music featuring drill teams, massed pipe and drum corps, gymnasts, and folk dancers. The Tattoo is part of Virginia's Arts Festival, a month-long celebration of the arts (from April through May) that includes classical music, jazz, and chamber music events, as well as dance and visual arts exhibitions that take place at venues throughout the region. The Virginia Beer Festival in mid-May is part of the broader Arts Festival.

In June the Norfolk Harborfest celebrates the region's rich nautical heritage. June also supports the AT&T Bayou Boogaloo and Cajun Festival, which includes cajun food and music. The Bayou Ball is an evening component of the festival with more food and music, as well as the opportunity to meet New Orleans artists and purchase their artwork. Independence Day brings the Great American Picnic and Celebration, which ends with a spectacular fireworks display. The weekend Norfolk Jazz Festival takes place at Town Point Park in mid-July.

In September is the Norfolk Seafood and Beach Music Festival, and the Mid-Autumn Moon Festival. A one day Children's Festival comes to Town Point Park in early October. October breezes also bring the Great Chesapeake Bay Schooner Race, a three-day race designed to increase awareness of the fragile ecosystem contained in the Bay. The race concludes at Town Point Park, where the racing vessels line up and create a backdrop for the AT&T Town Point Virginia Wine Festival. At this event, more than 25 Virginia wineries provide samplings; also featured are gourmet foods, specialty crafts, and live musical entertainment. The

holidays are welcomed with the Grand Illumination Parade and its associated events that take place in downtown Norfolk and nearby Portsmouth, including a progressive dinner termed "Wine and Dine."

Sports for the Spectator

Norfolk fans watch the puck drop to start the games of the Norfolk Admirals, an American Hockey League team and affiliate of the National Hockey League's Anaheim Ducks. The Admirals play at Norfolk Scope Arena. The Norfolk Tides, Triple-A affiliate of the Baltimore Orioles, play at Norfolk's Harbor Park, which can seat roughly 12,000 spectators. The Hampton Roads Piranhas are a United Soccer Leagues women's team that plays at the Virginia Beach Sportsplex. Rugby fans can enjoy Norfolk Blues rugby team matches; the highly successful club has been playing in the Norfolk area since 1978. The nearby Chesapeake Bayhawks compete in Major League Lacrosse and play at Navy-Marine Corps Memorial Stadium.

Norfolk State University varsity teams (Spartans) compete in the Mid-Eastern Athletic Conference, while Old Dominion's men's and women's teams are part of Conference USA. The Virginia Wesleyan Marlins play basketball in Division III of the NCAA and entertain fans with a selection of varsity and club sports.

Sports for the Participant

Surrounded by all that water, it's natural that the Norfolk area entices avid rowers, sea kayakers, swimmers, jet skiers and windsurfers. Fishing can become a religion for some, with access to Chesapeake species such as speckled trout, flounder, bluefish, rockfish, and more. A number of private companies run charters out of the Chesapeake Bay area. The City of Norfolk Police Department coordinates the Police Athletic League, or PAL, which gives local youth a chance to participate in volleyball, boxing, basketball, football, girls' softball and track events. Golfers can go 18 holes on any of two public golf courses: Lake Wright Golf Course and Ocean View Golf Course. Nearby Virginia Beach is home to even more public and private courses, including Stumpy Lake Golf Course. The Tidewater Tennis Center and Northside Park, where many local tournaments are held, are but two of more than a dozen tennis courts in the city. Northside Park is also home to Imagination Island, the largest community-built playground in the state.

The city sponsors over 10 recreation centers, 3 indoor pools, and 3 seasonal outdoor pools. Three beaches are maintained through the city: Community Beach Park, Sarah Constance Beach Park, and Ocean View Beach Park. There are 11 designated dog parks throughout the city park system. Barraud Park is home to the Norfolk Recreational Boxing Program, and Northside Skate plaza is open from March through December.

Venturing outside of Norfolk, there are spectacular hikes in Shenandoah National Park in the Blue Ridge Mountains approximately 2.5 hours northwest of the Tidewater region. The Old Rag Summit Ridge Trail is often recommended, as is the section of the Appalachian Trail that meanders through the park.

Shopping and Dining

MacArthur Center, a regional shopping mall, is within walking distance of the local convention center. The $300 million complex offers more than one million square feet of shops, restaurants and entertainment centers, with Nordstrom and Dillard's as its anchor stores. It also boasts a 70-foot atrium and 18-screen movie theater. The Selden Arcade & Gallery downtown in the city's financial district was recently refurbished and renovated and now offers not only clothing shops, bookstores, and jewelry shops but also two city-run art galleries. The upscale Ghent shopping district is known for its home furnishings, boutiques, and clothing shops. The Gallery at Military Circle is a mega-mall that offers department stores and a cinema. JANAF Shopping Yard, the largest regional shopping center, offers bargains on clothing, sports equipment, and home furnishings in more than 100 stores. For an eclectic mix of retailers, restaurateurs and entertainers, the Waterside Festival Marketplace is located right on the water, with ferries and boat tours departing from the premises. Granby Row has an array of art galleries and specialty shops.

Norfolk's southern location means that diners can get quality soul food, including ribs, fried chicken, collard greens, biscuits, and other delectables. The community is home to an astonishing number of establishments serving Italian food, with northern Italian cuisine coming on strong at present. Southwestern and Mexican restaurants are also plentiful, with a couple of spots dedicated to the art of tapas. Diners can catch a taste of fresh seafood at a number of places along the waterfront and beyond. Being a port city with a constant international influence, Norfolk eateries cater to a broad variety of other tastes as well, including French, Mediterranean, Cajun/Creole, German, Caribbean, Indian, Greek, Irish, Chinese, Thai, Japanese, and American fare. Granby Street has been nicknamed "Restaurant Row" for its wide variety of dining options.

Visitor Information: Norfolk Convention and Visitors Bureau, 232 E. Main Street, Norfolk, VA 23510; telephone (757) 664-6620 or (800) 368-3097.

■ Convention Facilities

Norfolk is an impressive destination for conventions and meetings, boasting 5,400 hotel rooms scattered citywide and a whopping 263,370 square feet of function space. The Half Moone Cruise and Celebration Center offers five different spaces able to accommodate 50 to 1,500 guests. The 80,000-square-foot facility is a neighbor of the Nauticus and the Battleship *Wisconsin* on the Elizabeth River. Just blocks from Norfolk's waterfront is also the Waterside Convention Connection, a joint project of the Waterside Convention Center, the Waterside Festival Marketplace, and the Scope Arena. These combined entities offer 121,000 square feet of function space, 55 meeting rooms, 1,000 first-class rooms for lodging and a large exhibit hall that can accommodate up to 2,400 guests for a reception, 2,000 people in a theater set-up, and 1,400 for a banquet. The dome-shaped Scope Arena offers 85,000 feet of meeting space as well as event seating capacity of up to 12,600. The Ted Constant Convocation Center at Old Dominion University provides a 9,100-square-foot hospitality room that can be divided into five smaller meeting or exhibit rooms. Other meeting suites are available for group events, as is the 7,319-fixed-seat arena.

The Harrison Opera House, Attucks Theater, and Chrysler Hall all offer spaces for meetings and special events. Several local restaurants and hotels also offer reserved spaces for meetings and conventions, creating a unique experience with a definite Norfolk flavor, as do some of the major attraction sites, such as the Norfolk Botanical Gardens and the Virginia Zoological Park.

Convention Information: Norfolk Convention and Visitors Bureau, 232 E. Main Street, Norfolk, VA 23510; telephone (757) 664-6620 or (800) 368-3097.

■ Transportation

Approaching the City

The easiest way by car to the city is by Interstates 64 and 264. From the south, Interstate 95 connects to State Route 58 and then to Interstate 264. From the north, Interstate 95 connects to Interstate 295 and then to Interstate 64. The 17-mile-long Chesapeake Bay Bridge-Tunnel links the Norfolk region to the Delmarva Peninsula and the Paddlewheel Ferry, a natural gas-powered pedestrian ferry that provides service between Norfolk's Waterside and Portsmouth. Pleasure craft can travel on the Atlantic Intracoastal Waterway from Norfolk all the way down to Miami, Florida, on a protected inland channel. Greyhound provides bus service to the city and train travel is offered by Amtrak.

Norfolk International Airport is a 20 minute drive from Chesapeake. The airport offers direct flights from AirTran, American, Delta, Southwest, United, and US Airways to 21 cities. In 2012 the airport served nearly 3.3 million passengers, making it the 68th largest primary airport in the United States. Chesapeake Regional and Hampton Roads airports provide corporate flight service within the city.

Traveling in the City

Interstates 64 and 564 run north–south through the city, and Interstate 264 runs east–west. State Highway 460, known locally as St. Paul's Boulevard, runs north–south through the downtown, while State Highway 58, known as Brambleton Avenue, runs east–west. Other main downtown streets running north–south are Boush Street, Church Street, and Tidewater Avenue. Waterside Drive and Water St. run east–west along the riverfront.

Hampton Roads Transit provides public transportation regionally, connecting Norfolk with Virginia Beach, Hampton, Newport News, Suffolk, Portsmouth, and Chesapeake. There are 24 routes within the city of Norfolk. Some buses are equipped with bike racks. Daily ridership across routes in all cities averaged between 50,000 and 60,000 in 2013. Handi-Ride service, for disabled travelers, is available by reservation at sites within three-quarters of a mile of regularly scheduled bus routes. Hampton Road Transit's "The Tide" is a 7.4-mile light-rail line that runs straight into the heart of downtown Norfolk, starting at the Eastern Virginia Medical Center. It opened in 2013.

The Paddlewheel Ferries between Portsmouth and Waterside run every 30 minutes during the week with 15-minute service available at some weekend hours. Passengers who are traveling within the cities for work or leisure may board with bicycles.

■ Communications

Newspapers and Magazines

The Virginian-Pilot serves both southeast Virginia and northeastern North Carolina. As of 2013, its circulation averaged 350,000 on weekdays and 470,000 on weekends. The city is also home to several military newspapers. *The Flagship* primarily serves the families of the Naval Base with weekly a paper. *Soundings* is an independent weekly covering all military branches. *The Jet Observer*, distributed free at Naval Air Station Oceana (Virginia Beach), is published in Norfolk. *The Mace & Crown* is the newspaper of Old Dominion University. The weekly *New Journal and Guide* serves the African American community.

Television and Radio

Norfolk is served by about five television stations and is home to 11 FM radio stations and 5 AM stations, spanning public, religious, and music formats.

Media Information: *The Virginian-Pilot,* 150 W. Brambleton Avenue, Norfolk, VA 23510; telephone (757) 446-9000.

Norfolk Online

City of Norfolk. Available www.norfolk.gov
Hampton Roads Chamber of Commerce. Available www.hamptonroadschamber.com
Naval Station Norfolk. Available www.navy.mil/local/nsn
Norfolk Convention and Visitors Bureau. Available www.visitnorfolktoday.com
Norfolk Public Library system. Available www.npl.lib.va.us
Norfolk Public Schools. Available www.nps.k12.va.us
The Virginian-Pilot. Available hamptonroads.com

BIBLIOGRAPHY

Berent, Irwin Mark, *Norfolk, Virginia: Evolution of a City in Maps* (Norfolk, VA: Norfolk History Publishers, 2013)

Berman, Eleanor, *Away for the Weekend: Mid-Atlantic* (New York: Three Rivers Press, 2002)

Flanders, Alan B., *Bluejackets on the Elizabeth: A Maritime History of Portsmouth & Norfolk, Virginia from the Colonial Period to the Present* (Portsmouth, VA: Portsmouth Naval Shipyard Museum, 1998)

Parramore, Thomas C., Peter C. Stewart (Contributor), and Tommy L. Bogger (Contributor), *Norfolk: The First Four Centuries* (Charlottesville, VA: University Press of Virginia, 1994)

Wright, Renee, *Virginia Beach, Richmond, and Tidewater Virginia including Williamsburg, Norfolk, and Jamestown* (Woodstock, VT: Countryman Press, 2010)

Richmond

■ The City in Brief

Founded: 1742 (incorporated, 1782)

Head Official: Mayor Dwight C. Jones (D) (since 2009; term expires 2017)

City Population
> 1990: 202,798
> 2000: 197,790
> 2010: 204,214
> 2012 estimate: 210,309
> Percent change, 2000–2010: 3.2%
> U.S. rank in 1990: 76th (State rank: 3rd)
> U.S. rank in 2000: 105th (State rank: 4th)
> U.S. rank in 2010: 104th (State rank: 5th)

Metropolitan Statistical Area Population
> 2000: 1,055,683
> 2010: 1,258,251
> 2012 estimate: 1,280,678
> Percent change, 2000–2010: 19.2%
> U.S. rank in 2000: 46th
> U.S. rank in 2010: 43rd

Area: 62.55 square miles

Elevation: Ranges from 9 to approximately 312 feet above sea level

Average Annual Temperatures: January, 36.4° F; July, 77.9° F; annual average, 57.6° F

Average Annual Precipitation: 43.91 inches of rain; 13.8 inches of snow

Major Economic Sectors: government, tobacco, education, health and social services, retail trade

Unemployment Rate: 7.1% (2012)

Per Capita Income: $24,973

2012 FBI Crime Index Property: 9,103

Major Colleges and Universities: Virginia Commonwealth University, University of Richmond, Virginia Union University, J. Sargeant Reynolds Community College, ECPI Technical College

Daily Newspaper: *Richmond Times-Dispatch*

■ Introduction

The capital of Virginia, Richmond is steeped in a history that spans more than 400 years, dating back to 1607 when Jamestown colonists identified the site. During the Revolutionary War era, it was the locale of several important conventions at which such notables as Thomas Jefferson and Patrick Henry sounded the call for freedom and determined the course of a fledgling nation. Later, Richmond proudly served as the capital of the Confederate States of America. Contemporary Richmond and its booming metropolitan area, which also encompasses the counties of Chesterfield, Hanover, and Henrico, are regarded as a prime example of the ideal "New South" community—one that successfully blends its heritage with modern social and industrial development. Richmond's dedication to maintaining and restoring historic structures makes it clear that Richmond still avidly champions its roots. Many high-end, mixed-use development projects of the 2010s were renovations of historic factory buildings. The city's strategic location in the middle of the eastern seaboard puts it within 500 miles of nearly half the U.S. population and only 100 miles from the nation's capital. Combining this asset with a mild climate, gently rolling terrain, and a wealth of cultural and recreational attractions has made Richmond another Sun Belt city on the move, and all indications of a promising future.

Virginia State Capitol. *Dave Newman/Shutterstock.com*

■ Geography and Climate

Richmond is located at the head of the navigable part of the James River between Virginia's coastal plains and the Piedmont, beyond which are the Blue Ridge Mountains. The open waters of Chesapeake Bay and the Atlantic Ocean to the east and the mountain barrier to the west are responsible for the region's warm, humid summers and generally mild winters. Precipitation, mostly in the form of rain, is distributed fairly evenly throughout the year, though dry spells lasting several weeks are especially common in the fall. Snow usually accumulates in amounts of less than fourteen inches and remains on the ground only one or two days.

The James River occasionally floods low-lying areas, but the Richmond flood wall, completed in the 1990s, goes a long way toward minimizing damage in those areas. Hurricanes and tropical storms have been the cause of most flooding during the summer and fall, particularly Hurricanes Connie and Diane in 1955, Hurricane Camille in August 1969, Hurricane Agnes in June 1972, Hurricane Isabel in September 2003, Tropical Depression Ernesto in August 2004, and Hurricane Irene in 2011.

Area: 62.55 square miles

Elevation: Ranges from 9 to approximately 312 feet above sea level

Average Temperatures: January, 36.4° F; July, 77.9° F; annual average, 57.6° F

Average Annual Precipitation: 43.91 inches of rain; 13.8 inches of snow

■ History

Conflicts Prevent Settlement

On May 21, 1607, one week after Captain John Smith and his party landed at Jamestown, a group led by Captain Christopher Newport set out from camp to explore the James River. Within a week, their travels took them to some falls and a small island where on May 27 they set up a cross. This marked the "discovery" of Richmond, though three decades would pass before another Englishman established a permanent post on the site; the area had already long been home to Powhatan tribes.

During their first few years in the New World, the English colonists devoted most of their energies to securing the stockade at Jamestown. Their arrival had displaced many of the Algonquin and other Native Americans in the region and, as a result, the newcomers often found themselves engaged in violent battles with the indigenous tribes. Temporary truces brought occasional respite from the hostilities, but it still proved difficult to entice settlers to homestead outside the stockade. Several attempts to colonize a site near the falls on the James River failed due to repeated conflicts with angry Algonquins.

The Founding of Richmond

In 1637, however, Thomas Stegg set up a trading post at the spot where the river became navigable; he was later granted some additional land around the falls. After a sudden native uprising in 1644, some Jamestown settlers built a fort near Stegg's claim and offered freedom from taxation to anyone willing to establish a home there. Few people took the settlers up on their offer until after 1670 when, upon the death of Stegg's son, the family holdings (which had expanded to include property on both sides of the river) passed to William Byrd I, a nephew. Byrd received certain additional privileges in return for inducing able-bodied men to homestead in the area, and at last the post began to grow, eventually becoming a trading center for furs, tobacco, and other products.

The year 1737 marked the official laying out of the town of Richmond and its founding as the central marketplace for inland Virginia. Despite the fact that it served as host to three historic political conventions in the pre-Revolutionary War years, including the one at which Patrick Henry closed his impassioned speech with the memorable "Give me liberty or give me death," the town grew very slowly throughout most of the rest of the eighteenth century, even after it was named the capital of Virginia in 1779. Following the Revolutionary War, however, Richmond entered an era of rapid growth. In 1782 it was officially incorporated as a city. By 1790 it boasted a population of 3,761 people, up from only 684 people ten years earlier.

City Made Confederate Capital

By the time of the Civil War, Richmond was one of the major commercial and industrial centers of the country. It prospered as a port city. In addition, America's first iron and brick supplies were manufactured in Richmond, and the first-discovered coal veins in America were mined in neighboring Chesterfield County. Tobacco processing and flour milling also emerged as regional industrial powers. Shortly after Virginia seceded from the Union in April 1861, Richmond was made the capital of the Confederacy in acknowledgment of its preeminent economic and political position.

The Civil War left the city in ruins. Besieged for nearly four years by Union troops but never taken in battle, Richmond was very nearly destroyed in April 1865 by Confederate troops who set fire to tobacco and cotton warehouses as they fled the city. After the war, Richmond began the slow task of rebuilding its bankrupt economy. The old industries, tobacco and iron in particular, once again surfaced as the dominant forces, remaining so throughout the early 1900s. Banking also emerged as an important factor on the local scene as Richmond became one of the South's leading financial centers.

A City Divided and Finally United

Both world wars sparked industrial expansion in Richmond, leading to a diversification that has made the area prosperous for many years. Racial tensions surfaced during the 1950s with the development of a strategy of "massive resistance" during which Virginia politicians and leaders were encouraged to prevent desegregation of schools in the wake of the *Brown vs. the Board of Education* ruling. The NAACP filed numerous suits and the federal government ordered integration of a number of Virginia counties and municipalities; in response, the Virginia governor ordered many schools to close rather than comply. Richmond fought integration until 1970, when a district court judge devised a busing strategy to integrate the schools. Sixteen years later, the same judge approved a neighborhood schools system that effectively ended the city's struggles in regard to segregation.

The 1980s were marked by concerted efforts to foster cooperation and growth to benefit the entire metropolitan area. Those efforts transformed Richmond into not only a manufacturing center of note, but also a hub for research, federal and state government, banking, transportation, trade, and health care. The city showed a commitment to preserving the best of its nearly 400-year past while carefully crafting a future that includes continued economic development. This synthesis was possibly reflected best in the development agency Richmond Renaissance, which acted as a bridge between the corporate, governmental, and African American communities as they began to work toward a common goal of a vital, thriving city in the "New South." In 1996 the tennis player and Richmond native Arthur Ashe became the first African American to be honored with a statue on the city's Monument Avenue.

The year 2004 brought a change in city government as Richmond residents elected their first mayor since 1948. The city had established a council-manager form of government, by which city council had chosen a mayor from its own nine members to serve a largely ceremonial role. The new mayor-council form was inaugurated with the election of L. Douglas Wilder, who was previously known as the first African-American elected governor in the state and the nation.

Into the 2010s, Richmond continued the revitalized of its downtown area. Historic buildings are found throughout the city, but many abandoned factories represented an eyesore more than a landmark. Mixed-use development projects were changing that, converting the cavernous spaces into apartments, restaurants, and retail areas. The continuing growth of the biomedical industry was pushed forward by private research centers and the sprawling medical campus of Virginia Commonwealth University.

Historical Information: Library of Virginia, 800 E. Broad Street, Richmond, VA 23219; telephone (804) 692-3500.

■ Population Profile

Metropolitan Statistical Area Population

2000: 1,055,683
2010: 1,258,251
2012 estimate: 1,280,678
Percent change, 2000–2010: 19.2%
U.S. rank in 2000: 46th
U.S. rank in 2010: 43rd

City Residents

1990: 202,798
2000: 197,790
2010: 204,214
2012 estimate: 210,309
Percent change, 2000–2010: 3.2%
U.S. rank in 1990: 76th (State rank: 3rd)
U.S. rank in 2000: 105th (State rank: 4th)
U.S. rank in 2010: 104th (State rank: 5th)

Density: 3,414.7 people per square mile

Racial and ethnic characteristics

White: 91,110
Black or African American: 103,831
American Indian and Alaskan Native: 1,123
Asian: 3,887
Native Hawaiian and Other Pacific Islander: 72
Hispanic or Latino (may be of any race): 13,410
Other: 10,286

Percent of residents born in state: 63.1%

Age characteristics

Population under 5 years old: 14,214
Population 5 to 9 years old: 12,135
Population 10 to 14 years old: 9,363
Population 15 to 19 years old: 14,673
Population 20 to 24 years old: 23,394
Population 25 to 34 years old: 38,783
Population 35 to 44 years old: 24,295
Population 45 to 54 years old: 25,687
Population 55 to 59 years old: 13,061
Population 60 to 64 years old: 10,893
Population 65 to 74 years old: 12,608
Population 75 to 84 years old: 6,604
Population 85 years and over: 4,599
Median age: 32.3

Births (2010–11 Metropolitan Area)

Total number: 15,340

Deaths (2010–11 Metropolitan Area)

Total number: 9,821

Money income (2012)

Per capita income: $24,973
Median household income: $40,001
Total households: 83,747

Number of households with income of ...

less than $10,000: 11,083
$10,000 to $14,999: 6,460
$15,000 to $24,999: 10,698
$25,000 to $34,999: 9,646
$35,000 to $49,999: 12,621
$50,000 to $74,999: 13,231
$75,000 to $99,999: 8,047
$100,000 to $149,999: 6,453
$150,000 to $199,999: 2,536
$200,000 or more: 2,972

Percent of families below poverty level: 26.4%

FBI Crime Index Property: 9,103

FBI Crime Index Violent: 1,348

■ Municipal Government

The city of Richmond operates under the mayor-council form of government, with council members serving part-time, two-year terms and each representing one of nine districts in the city. A mayor is elected at large through a majority of votes in at least five of the nine council districts. The mayor serves a full-time, four-year term. The council elects a vice-mayor and assistant vice-mayor from among its own ranks. The city was formerly governed by a council-manager system and in 2004 elected its first mayor in almost 60 years.

Head Officials: Mayor Dwight C. Jones (D) (since 2009; term expires 2017)

Total Number of City Employees: 4,385 (2012)

City Information: City of Richmond, 900 East Broad Street, Richmond, VA 23219; telephone (804) 646-7000.

■ Economy

Major Industries and Commercial Activity

The Richmond area has a strong and diverse manufacturing base that has helped the community remain resilient during economic recessions and even the Great Depression. Other factors that have contributed to this economic stability include the city's location as a commercial and distribution center, a concentration of federal and state agencies, the headquarters of major corporations and bank-holding companies, numerous

health facilities, and the concentration of educational institutions in the area.

The Richmond metropolitan area has been a historically favorable location for international companies and commerce, with more than150 firms located in the area representing 26 countries and employing nearly 18,000 people as of 2013. Richmond has also become a major East Coast distribution center and customer service center. In 2013 Richmond was home to six *Fortune* 500 companies—Altria Group, Dominion Resources, Car-Max, Genworth Financial, Owens and Minor, and MeadWestvaco—and another four *Fortune* 1000 companies—Brink's, Markel, Universal, and NewMarket. The concentration of *Fortune* 1000 companies placed Richmond second among all cities with fewer than 1.5 million residents, trailing only Bridgeport, Connecticut.

The life sciences sector of industry in Richmond, which includes careers in bioscience, pharmaceutical manufacturing, medical device and equipment manufacturing, and healthcare service industries, is also a booming industry. The Virginia Biotechnology Research Park is located in downtown Richmond, and its 67 companies, laboratories, and research centers employ more than 2,500 scientists, engineers, and researchers.

Richmond, as headquarters of the Fifth Federal Reserve District, is a financial nerve center for an industrially strong and diverse region that consists of Maryland, Virginia, West Virginia, North Carolina, South Carolina, and the District of Columbia. Banking has always been a significant employment factor in the Richmond area, and liberalization of banking laws has increased the centralization of headquarters activity in the Richmond area by many of the state's large and regionally oriented banks. Insurance is also a strong industry in the Richmond area.

Philip Morris, which began in tobacco production, has been a part of Richmond's business community since 1929. Richmond's $200 million Philip Morris Manufacturing Center, a 200-acre site, is one of the largest and most modern facilities of its kind in the world. The company made another major investment in the area through construction of the Philip Morris Center for Research Technology, a $350 million facility that opened in the Virginia BioTechnology Research Park in 2007. In 2009 Philip Morris's consolidation of all its cigarette manufacturing into South Richmond and its decision to move the headquarters of its sister companies, U.S. Smokeless Tobacco and John Middleton Co., to Richmond have made Richmond the most important tobacco center in the nation.

Other industries represented in Richmond include creative and knowledge-based services. Target industries in 2013 were health and life sciences; supply-chain management; advanced manufacturing; finance and insurance; professional and creative services; food and beverage; data centers; and corporate headquarters.

Items and goods produced: tobacco products, toiletries, processed foods, aluminum, chemicals, textiles, paper, printing, over-the-counter pharmaceuticals

Incentive Programs-New and Existing Companies

Local programs: Richmond's Department of Economic & Community Development offers numerous incentives for businesses located in the city. Financing for small companies is available through the James River Development Corporation, the Crater Development Company, REDC Community Capital Group Inc., the Virginia Small Business Financing Authority, and other firms. Dominion Virginia Power offers a variety of rate options to lower operating costs for commercial and industrial businesses. The Business Expansion Incentive Fund is available through the Chesterfield County Economic Development Department. The Defense Production Zone legislation allows a locality to establihs a zone dedicated to meeting the need of national defense, which offers permit and tax incentives for up to 20 years. In addition to the state's enterprise zone incentives, Richmond's Local Enterprise Zone Program, also in Chesterfield and Henrico, and offers Enterprise Zone incentives, tax abatements, grants, and rebates. At the Richmond International Airport, Foreign Trade Zone 207 allows for imported goods to be held in the zone and exempted from U.S. Customs duties until they've crossed the zone barrier into use in the United States. This provides generous opportunities for international businesses to invest, develop, or expand using Foreign Trade Zone benefits. The City of Richmond also offers infrastructure improvement incentives.

State programs: Virginia is a right-to-work state, advertising itself as the northernmost right-to-work state in the nation. The State General Assembly has kept Virginia's taxes on industry very competitive by maintaining relatively moderate corporate income tax rates and by eliminating many tax irritants, resulting in modest tax bills for business and industry. While this alone constitutes an attractive incentive for new and existing businesses, the State of Virginia further offers Governor's Opportunity Funds, which allow the Governor to secure business locations or expansion projects with matching funds from the local community; Virginia Investment Partnership Grant Funds, supporting large employers with businesses established for a minimum of five years in Virginia; property tax exemptions; sales and use tax exemptions; enterprise zones; technology zones; and foreign trade zones. Virginia has a State Historic Rehabilitation Tax Credit Program, as does the federal government. The state's Virginia Small Business Financing Authority provides small businesses with access to capital for growth and expansion efforts. The Virginia Economic Development Incentive Grant is a discretionary performance incentive designed to assist and encourage business investment that creates new employment in the state. Specifically, it targets businesses looking to relocate headquarters or others significant service-sector or administrative jobs in the state.

Job training programs: The state's Virginia Jobs Investment Program offers customized recruiting and training assistance for expanding companies that need to hire more workers. The program seeks to lower human development costs to state businesses. Two community colleges, J. Sargeant Reynolds Community College and John Tyler Community College, have joined forces to create the Community College Workforce Alliance (CCWA). The CCWA supports economic development and provides workforce development in both the private and public sectors. Employers can potentially receive a tax credit for sending their employees through professional development with CCWA. The Capital Area Training Consortium, with an office in Richmond, is an official Employment and Training Agency providing career assessment, counseling, training, re-training, and job search assistance. Community members with disabilities can access job training and support services via the Department of Rehabilitative Services, while older job seekers may find assistance through the Capital Area Agency on Aging.

Development Projects

Downtown Richmond enjoyed $1.2 billion worth of investment in development projects during 2012, spanning 47 projects and mixing both private and public investment. Major projects included conversion of The Locks, four historic buildings undergoing total renovation to create 174 apartments and 6,000 square feet of retail space during 2012 and 2013. The $34.5 million investment was privately funded. Another private, high-end project was the Lofts at Canal Walk, which utilized $22 million in financial support to build 130 loft apartments. The two projects exemplified more than one dozen similar development efforts underway in 2012 and 2013. Between 2003 and 2012, the Manchester area of Richmond enjoyed more than $225 million of total investment across 35 development projects that created more than 1,500 residences and 300,000 square feet of commercial space.

Transportation development projects by the city included a third phase of Main Street Station development, which began in 2013 and was expected to complete in 2015. The final, $72.3 million project was to retrofit, upgrade, and expand existing platforms to allow train traffic to increase from 6 to more than 32 trains per day. The development also included stabilization of the structure and total replacement of its roof, as well as improvements to the surrounding Franklin Street area. An estimated 80,000 square feet of retail space was also set to become available in interior of the buildling.

Completed in 2013, the Virginia Commonwealth University McGlothlin Medical Education Center represented a nearly $160 million investment by the university to construct a 200,000-square-foot educational facility that would allow the educational institution to expand its medical class from 750 to 1,000 students. Virginia Commonwealth spent $160 million to consolidate its outpatient pediatric clincis into a single facility, the Children's Hospital of Richmond Pavilion. The city's premier college also spent $7 million renovating the seventh floor of the research aspect of its Pauley Heart Center and $12 million renovating the third floor of its Massey Cancer Center Lab.

Health Diagnostics Laboratory, a Richmond biotechnology firm, constructed a 212,000-square-foot building in the Virginia Biotechnology Reseach Park during 2012–13. The $24 million project supported the company's addition of some 400 employees.

Federally funded Community Development Block Grant funding totaled $30 million in Richmond for the fiscal year 2012–13.

Economic Development Information: Greater Richmond Partnership, 901 East Byrd Street, Richmond, VA 23219; telephone (804) 643-3227; toll-free (800) 229-6332. City of Richmond Office of Economic and Community Development, Main Street Station, 1500 E. Main St., Suite 400 Richmond, VA 23219; telephone (804) 646-5633.

Commercial Shipping

Richmond has its own port, owned by the municipal government and offering direct container ship service to northern Europe, the United Kingdom, Canada, Iceland, Mexico, the Mediterranean, the Caribbean, and South America. The Port of Richmond is located four miles south of Richmond's Central Business District and offers services such as stevedoring, supply chain services, export packaging and transfer, and warehouse and inland distribution services. The port is equipped for heavy lifting and can handle a range of cargo, from livestock to breakbulk. Some of its major imports and exports include pharmaceuticals, machinery, consumer goods, produce, steel, and vehicles, just to name a few. U.S. Customs and Border Protection offices are onsite.

Four dedicated air cargo airline service the Richmond International Airport, which is located 10 minutes from the downtown area. The airport handles an average of more than 100 million pounds of cargo annually, making it one of the busiest air cargo facilities in the nation. Charter cargo flights are also available. The airport is a Foreign Trade Zone with U.S. Customs inspection on-site and can hold cargo in 142,000 square feet of warehouse space.

Richmond is crisscrossed by north–south and east–west interstates and railroads, making it an ideal United Parcel Service (UPS) district hub and FedEx regional hub. There are more than forty courier service companies and 100 motor freight companies and brokers that serve the area. Couriers include scheduled and rush, local, intrastate, and interstate. Freight companies include specialists in liquid or dry bulk, heavy hauling, and overdimensional loads. The Richmond area is within a day's drive of 50 percent of the U.S. population, 55 percent of the nation's manufacturing facilities, and 60 percent of the country's corporate headquarters. A 750-mile radius encompasses almost three-fifths of the population and two-thirds of the nation's manufacturing facilities.

Two rail lines converge in Richmond: the Norfolk Southern and CSX. CSX covers 21,000 miles across 23 states and extends its reach to Canada. CSX provides direct service to and from the Port of Richmond along with international terminal services, domestic container shipping, domestic ocean-liner services, and more. Northern Southern provides service via local switch.

Labor Force and Employment Outlook

Generally speaking, a positive labor-management relationship enhances the Richmond work ethic. As the northernmost right-to-work state, Virginia unionization rates are low, about 2.6 percent as of 2011. Strikes are rare, and Richmond enjoys one of the lowest work-stoppage records in the nation. As of 2013, Virginia Commonwealth University was the state's largest university, adding a significant number of college-educated laborers into the workforce annually.

As of 2013 health care and social assistance employed the largest number of people in the Richmond area, followed by retail trade. Nearly 40 percent of all residents in the metropolitan area had at least a two-year college degree, while more than 30 percent had a four-year degree or beyond.

The following is a summary of data regarding the 2012 Richmond labor force:

Size of civilian labor force: 110,026

Number of workers employed in . . .

agriculture and mining: 146
construction: 5,103
manufacturing: 6,331
wholesale trade: 1,494
retail trade: 10,471
transportation: 3,838
information systems: 2,003
finance: 8,230
professional administration: 12,736
education and social services: 25,057
arts and leisure: 11,520
other: 5,018
public administration: 5,614

Average hourly earnings of production workers: $17.41

Unemployment rate: 7.1% (2012)

Employers

Largest employers (2012)	*Number of employees*
Capital One Financial Corp.	9,995
Virginia Commonwealth University Health System	7,935
HCA Virginia Health System	7,236
Bon Secours Richmond Health System	5,991
Wal-Mart Stores Inc.	5,462
Dominion Resources Inc.	5,378
Altria Group Inc.	4,110
SunTrust Banks	4,100
DuPont	3,084
Wells Fargo & Co.	2,851

Cost of Living

Richmond's cost of living was slightly above the national average in 2013.

The following is a summary of data regarding several key cost of living factors in the area.

2013 ACCRA Average House Price: $244,000

2013 ACCRA Cost of Living Index: 101

State income tax rate: 2.0% to 5.75%

State sales tax rate: 4.3%

Local income tax rate: None

Local sales tax rate: 1%

Property tax rate: $1.20 per $100 assessed value (2011)

Economic Information: Greater Richmond Chamber of Commerce, 600 East Main St., Suite 700, Richmond, VA 23219; telephone (804) 648-1234.

■ Education and Research

Elementary and Secondary Schools

The Richmond Public Schools, one of four major systems in the area has earned a reputation for innovative and highly successful new programs. The district also offers three specialty high schools: Franklin Military Academy, a public military school that is noteworthy for being the first military school in a public school system in the nation; the Open High School, which offers academic strategies to reach alternative learners; and Richmond Community, which provides a focused curriculum to prepare gifted students for college while emphasizing outreach to economically and socially disadvantaged youth. The Amelia Street school serves students with exceptional needs, and two programs serve students with exceptional needs—the REAL School (Richmond Educational Alternative for Learning), which offers middle school programming for children with learning disabilities or special emotional needs, and Thirteen Acres, located at Carver Elementary School.

All four public school systems in the Richmond area have one joint educational venture, the Center for Science, Mathematics, and Technology located in the Henrico County Public System. It is believed to be the only such regional center in the country supported completely by local funds, and it is one of the early examples of regional cooperation in the Richmond area.

Richmond also offers numerous alternative institutions for Richmond area students, including private college-preparatory schools and schools for exceptional children.

The following is a summary of data regarding the Richmond City Public Schools.

Total enrollment: 23,454

Number of facilities

total: 44
elementary schools: 28
junior high schools: 8
high schools: 5
other: 3

Student/teacher ratio: 18.64:1

Teacher salaries

average (statewide): $51,559

Funding per pupil: $12,613

Public Schools Information: Richmond Public Schools, 301 North Ninth Street, Richmond, VA 23219; telephone (804) 780-7710.

Colleges and Universities

Virginia Commonwealth University (VCU), with two downtown Richmond campuses, is the state's largest urban public university; it enrolls nearly 32,000 students. VCU is the home of the Medical College of Virginia and additionally offers 223 baccalaureate, master's, doctoral and certificate degree programs in 13 schools and one liberal arts college. In 2013 *U.S. News & World Report* ranked VCU amon the top 170 universities natioanlly. Well-known programs include its studies in education, medicine, business, and engineering. Additionally, VCU has a campus in Qatar focusing on arts programs.

The University of Richmond is one of the largest private colleges in Virginia and one of the most academically challenging schools in the country, ranking 25th among national liberal arts colleges according to *U.S. News & World Report* in 2013. It began in 1830 as Richmond College, a college of liberal arts and sciences for men. Around this nucleus have been added the School of Arts and Sciences, the Jepson School of Leadership Studies (the first school of its kind in the nation), and the E. Claiborne Robins School of Business. The school opened the T. C. Williams School of Law in 1870, making it one of the oldest law schools in the state. The university offers its enrollment of more than 3,000 undergraduates a menu of baccalaureate degrees in some 60 major areas of study. It is also well known for its study-abroad and international studies programs, which give students the opportunity to make use of 75 direct exchange programs in 30 different countries.

Virginia Union University was founded in 1865 by the Baptist Church to give educational opportunities to African Americans. It offers its diverse student body undergraduate liberal arts, sciences, education, and business courses, as well as graduate courses in theology. The liberal arts foundation is augmented by specialized programs, such as a dual-degree engineering program, offered in conjunction with the University of Michigan, the University of Iowa, and Howard University in Washington, D.C.

Union Presbyterian Seminary is one of the top theological institutions in the nation. It is recognized for its rigorous academic program and its pioneering work in field education and student-in-ministry experiences, with a student body of roughly 300. A seminary of the Presbyterian Church (USA), Union Theological offers doctor of ministry, master of divinity, master of theology, and doctor of philosophy degrees. The Presbyterian School of Christian Education, a graduate school, is the only one of 11 theological institutions of the Presbyterian Church to specialize solely in the discipline of Christian education. The Baptist Theological Seminary at Richmond, which officially opened in 1991, offers a Master of Divinity degree and a Doctor of Ministry.

J. Sargeant Reynolds Community College, founded in 1972, operates three campuses: one in downtown Richmond, another in Henrico County, and the western campus in Goochland County. It offers programs in liberal arts and sciences, engineering, education, and business administration as well as technical vocation training in a number of fields. The school offers two-year occupational or technical degree programs and certificate programs, and has enrolled more than 300,000 students in credit courses since it opened.

John Tyler Community College, with more than 50 career and technical programs, operates a main campus in Chesterfield County and two auxiliary campuses. Also offering higher educational opportunities in metro Richmond are Randolph-Macon College, Virginia State University (in nearby Petersburg), and Richard Bland College.

Libraries and Research Centers

Libraries abound in Richmond. There is the Library of Virginia, with more than 1.7 million books, periodicals, government publications and microforms specializing in Virginian, Southern and Confederate history, and genealogy. The Richmond Public Library system has a main library plus eight branches containing more than 800,000 books, periodicals, and audio- and videocassettes. The main library maintains the city records and archives. City approval for $7 million in library improvements was put to work during the next several years, with renovations on two branches and the main library completed in 2010. The Henrico County Public Library system has more than 500,000 books, videocassettes, periodicals, and art prints. It was given a four-star rating by *Library Journal* in 2013. Many other libraries are operated by area universities, colleges, and museums. The Virginia Department for the Blind and Vision Impaired is a member of the National Library Service for the Visually and Physically Handicapped, a Library of Congress network. As the seat of government in Virginia, Richmond is naturally home to the primary branch of the Virginia State Law Library, containing comprehensive legal materials for use by defendants, inmates, attorneys, the courts and the general public.

Virginia Commonwealth University Libraries contain more than 2 million print volumes, 50,000 serial titles, and hundreds of work stations. The Tompkins-McCaw Library at the Medical College of Virginia Campus of VCU contains the largest collection of medical materials in the state. The James Branch Cabell Library at the Monroe Park Campus contains over 30,000 volumes in special collections on subjects such as Virginia history and literature, popular culture and graphic arts, comic arts, and artist's books. VCU also maintains a Community Health Education Center.

The William Smith Morton Library at Union Theological Seminary contains more than 315,000 volumes, with an accrual rate of some 5,000 volumes per year. The library receives in excess of 600 print periodicals and 6,000 electronic journals. As a major research library, special collections include the libraries of Dr. George Gunn (Scottish history, literature, and theology), Dr. H. H. Rowley (Old Testament), Dr. Gotthold Muller (nineteenth and twentieth century German theology and philosophy with Reformed and Lutheran writings), and Dr. Thomas F. Torrance (patristic, Calvin, and other Reformed materials). As of 2013, the library was cataloging the Hugh McElrath hymnal and sacred music collection.

In general, VCU is the primary academic research headquarters of the city, primarily in the biological and health sciences. Research centers and institutes include the Mid-Atlantic Addiction Technology Transfer Center, the Clinical Research Center for Periodontal Diseases, the Institute for Drug and Alcohol Studies, the Pauley Heart Center, Massey Cancer Center, the VCU Reanimation Engineering Shock Center, the Virginia Center for Urban Development, the Mid-Atlantic Twin Registry, the Center for Judaic Studies, and the Virginia Center on Aging. Total research funding awards received by the university were in excess of $247 million in 2013, and averaged more than $255 million annually in the preceding three years.

Virginia BioTechnology Research Park was home to 67 biotechnology, bioscience, and other related companies and research institutions in 2013, helping make Virginia an East Coast technology leader. More than 2,500 scientists, researchers, engineers and technicians work in fields that include drug development, medical diagnostics, biomedical engineering, forensics and environmental analysis. The United Network for Organ Sharing is based at the park, which is also home to the Virginia Office of the Chief Medical Examiner, Virginia Department of Agriculture and Consumer Services, Boehringer Ingelheim Chemicals, and Philip Morris, USA, among others.

Public Library Information: Richmond Public Library, 101 East Franklin Street, Richmond, VA 23219; telephone (804) 646-7223. Virginia BioTechnology Research Park, 800 E. Leigh St., Richmond, VA 23219; telephone (804) 828-5390; fax (804) 828-8566.

■ Health Care

The Richmond region has obvious credentials to support its claim as one of the best medical and health-service areas in the country. It boasts more than 3,500 physicians and 21 specialty and acute-care hospitals with some 4,000 staffed beds. HCA Virginia Health System operates nine hospitals and medical centers in Greater Richmond: Chippenham Hospital, Hanover Emergency Center, Henrico Doctors' Hospital, John Rnadolph Medical Center, Johnston-Willis Hospital, Parham Doctors' Hospital, Retreat Doctors' Hospital Spotsslyvania Regional Medical Center, and West Creek Emergency Center.

Chippenham Hospital has 466 beds and specializes in heart care at its Levinson Heart Hospital on campus. Also on campus is the Tucker Pavilion, which provides emotioanl and mental health services. The emergency room is a Level III trauma center, and Chippenham also has central Virginia's only pediatric emergency room staffed around-the-clock with pediatric nurses and physicians. Johnston-Willis Hospital is a 292-bed facility specializing in cancer care with its Thomas Johns Cancer Center. It houses the first Gamma Knife Center in Richmond. Henrico Doctors' Hospital is another of the

system's largest facilities, with 340 beds and specialties of stroke and heart care, and women's health.

Bon Secours Richmond Health System, a not-for-profit Catholic system, operates four hospitals in the area and numerous outpatient service sites. St Mary's Hospital was honored by *U.S. News & World Report* in 2013–14 with two high-performing rankings for its gastroenterology and GI surgery, as well as nephrology. It was ranked 13th among all hospitals in Virginia by the same publication. St. Mary's has a total of 391 beds and admitted more than 22,000 patients in 2013.

Largest among the area's major health-care institutions is the Virginia Commonwealth University Health System, one of the largest medical schools in the nation and home to one of the nation's oldest transplant programs. The Medical College of Virginia Hospitals (MCV) is the teaching component of the VCU system, providing a real-life laboratory for teaching, research, community service, and health-care delivery at the centerpiece of the health sciences campus of Virginia Commonwealth University. The VCU Medical Center was ranked the top hospital in Virginia according to *U.S. News & World Report* in 2013–14, with nationally ranked specialties of nephrology and orthopedics. Additionally, the 747-bed hospital garnered high-performing marks in eight other specialties.

■ Recreation

Sightseeing

Richmond boasts more than 100 attractions of interest to visitors. Among them are homes and other buildings from all eras of the city's history, as well as battlegrounds and cemeteries. A great place to start is with the Canal Walk along the James River in downtown Richmond, where visitors can meander for 1.25 miles by foot or ride a tour boat past 22 historical markers, statues and points of interest. One of those points of interest is the Civil War Visitor Center along the Canal Walk. Housed in the former Tredegar Iron Works, the Civil War Visitor Center contains three floors of exhibits and interpretive displays recollecting Richmond's role in the Civil War, and provides an introduction to the National Battlefield Park in Richmond.

A convenient next stop along the Canal Walk is Brown's Island, a historic city park often used for outdoor concerts, picnics, biking, and Frisbee. Belle Isle is accessible via the footbridge under the Lee Bridge near the Tredegar Iron Works building. The site served as a camp for Union prisoners of war but is now a popular recreation spot for Richmond residents. More canal history is reflected by the Kanawha Canal Locks, where Reynolds Metals Company has preserved two locks that were built in 1854. The magnificent stone locks were part of the nation's first canal system, as originally planned by George Washington to carry river traffic around the falls.

The Floodwall along the James River, built to minimize damage from storm-induced rising waters, has become a work of art in its own right with the Floodwall Picture Gallery of murals. A walking tour can transition from the Floodwall into the Shockoe Bottom District, where a variety of historic structures remain and have been restored post-flood. The focal point in Capital Square's 12-acre park-like setting is the Virginia State Capitol, which has served as the seat of state government since 1788. Thomas Jefferson designed the central portion of the classic building, the first of its kind in America. Inside, French sculptor Houdon's life-size statue of George Washington stands in the Rotunda.

Visitors can find many examples of residential life in early Richmond, including Scotchtown, which was the Hanover County home that Patrick Henry occupied during the years of his Revolutionary War activities. The restored house and grounds are a national historic landmark. City-owned and recently restored as a museum, John Marshall's sturdy but unpretentious brick house (1790) honors the third Chief Justice of the U.S. Supreme Court who lived in Richmond. Built in 1813 and frequently remodeled, the Governor's Mansion is the oldest executive mansion in the United States in continuous use for its original purpose. It has been furnished with fine antiques by a Virginia citizens group. Dabbs House is a pre-Civil War dwelling that was used by General Robert E. Lee as headquarters during the "Seven Days Battle" in 1862. It is now Henrico eastern division police headquarters. This White House of the Confederacy served as the residence of Jefferson Davis during the Civil War. The Maggie Walker National Historic Site, now a museum, was the home of the African American woman who became the nation's first woman of any race to found a bank and become its president.

The late-Victorian estate Maymont, located in the heart of Richmond, has more than 100 acres featuring a Victorian home and decorative arts, formal Japanese and Italian gardens, a unique arboretum, a nature center with an outdoor wildlife habitat (native Virginia species), a demonstration farm, and a working carriage collection. Maymont's Robins Nature and Visitors Center features a 20-foot waterfall and exhibits describing the history and power of the James River.

Agecroft Hall, a medieval manor house moved to Richmond from England during the 1920s, is perched above the James River much as it originally overlooked the Irwell River. The house was built in England about the time Columbus was planning his voyage in 1492 to the New World. It is now a museum house open to the public and features an Elizabethan Knot garden. Also shipped to Richmond from England during the 1920s were portions of the sixteenth-century English house, Warwick Priory. Situated in Windsor Farms, a fashionable residential area, it was originally a private home but is now a museum known as Virginia House.

Sightseers can visit several other kinds of historic buildings in Richmond. At Hanover Courthouse, a young Patrick Henry successfully argued his first major case. St. John's Church in Richmond's Church Hill district, built in 1741, is famous as the site of Henry's impassioned "Give me liberty or give me death" speech. Finally, the Egyptian Building, erected in 1845 and still in use, is the Medical College of Virginia's first building. Its Egyptian Revival architecture is regarded as the finest of its kind in the country. The Egyptian motif extends to the fence, which has posts shaped like mummy cases.

History buffs may also find places of interest elsewhere in and around the Richmond area. Flowerdew Hundred Plantation is the site of an excavated, seventeenth-century English settlement in Prince George County, location of the first windmill in English North America. A visitor's center in the former plantation schoolhouse features films and archaeological exhibits. Chickahominy Bluff, Cold Harbor, Malvern Hill, Fort Harrison, and Drewry's Bluff have special interpretive facilities. Hollywood Cemetery (named for its holly trees) is the burial place of U.S. presidents James Monroe and John Tyler, Confederate president Jefferson Davis, General J. E. B. Stuart, and 1,800 Confederate soldiers, along with members of prominent Richmond families. Illustrious Chief Justice John Marshall and the infamous Elizabeth Van Lew, a Yankee spy during the Civil War, are both buried at Shockoe Cemetery.

Atop the 18-story City Hall is an observation deck from which visitors can obtain a sweeping view of Richmond and its environs. A map is available to help identify the visible landmarks in a panorama that covers four centuries of the city's history.

Plantation homes dating from the seventeenth century fan out on all sides of Richmond. Of special interest are the elegant James River Plantations to the east. Other Richmond area plantations include Belle Air (c. 1670); Berkeley (ancestral home of two U.S. presidents and the site of the first Thanksgiving in 1619); Evelynton (ancestral home of the Ruffin family); Sherwood Forest (home of President John Tyler); Shirley (home of the Carter family since 1723); Tuckahoe Plantation (the most complete plantation layout in North America, dating from the eighteenth century); Westover (c. 1730; home of William Byrd II, founder of Richmond); and Wilton (built in 1750 by William Randolph II and moved to Richmond in 1933).

Self-guided automobile tours, bus tours, walking tours, individual tours, and riverboat paddlewheel cruises (as far downriver as Shirley Plantation) are also available.

Visitors and residents alike find relaxation and meaning along the statue-studded length of Monument Avenue. Robert E. Lee, "Stonewall" Jackson, J. E. B. Stuart, Jefferson Davis, Bill "Mr. Bojangles" Robinson, Arthur Ashe, and Matthew Moury each command major focal points. One of the grand boulevards of the world,

Monument Avenue provides a good site for an easy-paced stroll, and it is closed off once a year for one of the city's largest street festivals.

Arts and Culture

A driving and energetic force in the Richmond arts and culture scene is the Arts Council of Richmond, which sponsors festivals and art exhibits throughout the year. The Arts Council has established partnerships with all Richmond Public Schools in an effort to extend the performing and visual art experience to students of all ages.

The Richmond CenterStage Performing Arts Complex opened its doors in downtown Richmond in the fall of 2009. The space is 179,000 square feet with an education facility and three performance spaces. Its cornerstone is the historic and fully renovated Carpenter Theater, which is home to the Richmond Symphony and offers local ballet and opera, as well as Broadway shows and other productions of national acclaim.

The Virginia Opera Association, based in Norfolk, performs an expanded number of productions each season at the Carpenter Theater. The opera company operates a nationally-recognized In-School Touring Program to bring opera to the students, then brings the students to the opera with special Student Nights and Student Matinees. The Richmond Symphony and the Richmond Philharmonic remain dynamic musical entities in the area. The Richmond Symphony's Masterworks Series focuses on the classics and brings the world's great soloists to the city, while programs such as Genworth Financial Symphony Pops concerts broaden the appeal of the traditional symphonic repertoire. The Richmond Philharmonic, a member-run orchestra, has entertained Richmond for more than 30 years and performs four or five concerts per season.

Richmond is also home to a number of community orchestras and choruses, school and university musical organizations, and a growing number of other musical groups. The Richmond Concert Band's annual Fourth of July performance in Dogwood Dell of Tchaikovsky's *1812 Overture* is a Richmond tradition. Other musical groups include the Richmond chapter of the Sweet Adelines, Richmond Chamber Players, the Richmond Renaissance Singers, and many others. Outdoor performances are frequently presented at parks and public sites around the city.

Theater of all sorts is plentiful. Besides Carpenter Center, Richmond's Landmark Theater plays host to musical groups of national prominence in an opulent structure equipped with a magnificent Wurlitzer theater organ.

Theater IV, the Children's Theater of Virginia, and Barksdale Theatre combined to form the Virginia Repertory Theatre in 2012. The company offers a Broadway Series, an Off-Broadway Series, and a Family Playhouse, one of the nation's second largest children's theaters. For a more off-beat or contemporary theater experience, the Firehouse Theatre Project offers productions of off-Broadway and original works never before seen in the Richmond area. The Richmond Triangle Players push the envelope even more, in theater that explores alternative themes.

Theatre VCU, Virginia Commonwealth University's student theater group, performs dramas, comedies, and musicals in the university's Shafer Street Playhouse and in the Raymond Hodges Theatre in VCU's Performing Arts Center. Virginia Union University Players perform in the university's Wall Auditorium. The Randolph-Macon Drama Guild presents four plays a season in the college's old Chapel Theater. Other theater groups include Chamberlayne Actors Theatre and the Henrico Theatre Company.

Richmond also has three ballet companies: the Richmond Ballet, the Concert Ballet of Virginia, and the Latin Ballet of Virginia, which performs at the Cultural Arts Center of Glen Allen. The Richmond Ballet's interpretation of *The Nutcracker* is an annual Christmas classic that has been playing to sold-out audiences for years. The Richmond Ballet is a professional ballet company, maintaining dancers on full-time seasonal contracts. Accompanied by the Richmond Symphony, it provides the best dance training in the state and attracts dancers from across the United States and abroad, with an impressive repertoire and touring schedule throughout the state and nation. The Concert Ballet of Virginia holds four repertoire programs per season featuring Virginia composers, choreographers, musicians, and dancers. The Latin Ballet of Richmond fuses Latin dance styles with ballet to evoke the passionate cultures and histories of Spain and Latin America. The company educates and attracts diverse participants and audiences through its outreach activities and performances.

The Virginia Museum of Fine Arts reopened in May 2010 after a $150 million expansion that increased gallery space by 50 percent. The museum has long had a national reputation for creative and innovative arts programming, dating back to its founding in 1936 as the nation's first state-supported art museum. The museum achieved an international reputation with the 1985 opening of the West Wing, which houses collections of nineteenth- and twentieth-century decorative arts, contemporary paintings and sculptures, and various eighteenth-, nineteenth-, and twentieth-century British, French, and American works of art. Expansions birthed both the James W. and Frances G. McGlothlin Wing whose focal point is the Louis B. and J. Harwood Cochrane Atrium, which provides a bird's eye view of the surrounding neighborhood. The museum houses more than 30 permanent galleries, as well as collections that are broad and varied: French Impressionists, Indian sculpture, medieval tapestries, French Romantics, American art of all periods, and the largest collection outside Russia of the Russian Imperial jewels crafted by Peter Carl Fabergé.

Another museum that has focused international attention on Richmond is the Science Museum of Virginia. The museum's $7 million Ethyl IMAX Dome and Planetarium is equipped with Digistar 1, the world's first computer graphics planetarium projection system. Information on the 6,772 stars visible from earth and the 55 known major objects in the solar system is programmed in the computer's memory. The Science Museum also owns the Virginia Aviation Museum on the east side of Richmond. The Science Museum includes exhibits on local industry and technology, as well as an in-depth look at ecosystems.

There are many other Richmond-area museums, all distinctive in character. Among them is the Chesterfield County Museum, which houses murals and displays depicting the county's history through the Revolutionary and Civil wars and into modern times. Among its artifacts, the Museum of the Confederacy displays the sword and uniform worn by Lee when he surrendered at Appomattox. The uniform coat worn by J. E. B. Stuart when he was felled is displayed at the Virginia Historical Society Museum, visible bullet hole and all. The Virginia Fire and Police Museum, dating to the early 1800s, uses window bars, a possible gallows, and fire poles to tell the story of its history as a jail and a police station. Memorabilia of Edgar Allan Poe is displayed in the Poe Museum; the eighteenth-century stone structure is believed to be the oldest in the city. The Virginia E. Randolph Museum, a Henrico County cottage, is dedicated in memory of Virginia E. Randolph, an African American woman who was a pioneer educator and humanitarian. The Black History Museum and Cultural Center of Virginia was founded in 1981 to preserve the oral, visual, and written records that commemorate the lives and accomplishments of African Americans in Virginia and to serve as a cultural and educational center for exhibitions, performances, and displays. It announced in 2013 that it would move to the Leigh Street Armory, supported by a 500,000 donation from Dominion Resources, Inc.

The Valentine Richmond History Center is devoted to the life and history of Richmond. It also houses one of the largest textile collections in the South. The Children's Museum of Richmond, established in 1981, introduces young people to the arts and humanities through participation in exhibits, workshops, and special programs.

Galleries include the Virginia Commonwealth University's Anderson Gallery and the 1708 Gallery. The University of Richmond features exhibitions in Marsh Art Gallery in the Modlin Fine Arts Center. Nonprofit galleries include the Weinstein Jewish Community Center, the Richmond Public Library, the Westover Hills Branch Library, and many bank spaces and commercial galleries.

Festivals and Holidays

February is time for the Maymont Flower and Garden Show. The month also includes a great indoor activity—the Virginia Wine Expo, with more than 35 events spread across six days to highlight Virginia wine and food. John Tyler Community College hosts an annual Literary Festival in March. The Church Hill Irish festival usually takes place the weekend after St. Patrick's Day. The Strawberry Hill Horse Races take place in April, as does Historic Garden Week. Arts in the Park, the Greek Festival, and the Camptown Races are available in May.

A summer-long Festival of the Arts is sponsored by the city Department of Parks, Recreation, and Community Facilities, with most events staged at the Dogwood Dell amphitheater in Byrd Park. The Richmond Jazz Festival occurs in August with three days of live music from national and international jazz bands. Also in August is the Down Home Family Reunion, celebrating the African American family. The 2nd Street Festival, celebrating African American history, takes place in Jackson Ward in October.

The State Fair of Virginia, a 12-day event, is held in late September and early October. The Central Virginia Celtic Festival and Highland Games is a two-day event in October. Also in October is the Richmond Folk Festival, which attracts more than 200,000 visitors to downtown Richmond to celebrate various American cultures. November ushers in the Anthem Richmond Marathon. The Grand Illumination and Christmas Parade is a popular event in December. The Capital City Kwanzaa Festival is also held in December.

Sports for the Spectator

Richmond's ball park, The Diamond, is now home to the Richmond Flying Squirrels who replaced the Richmond Braves a year after they relocated. The team is a Double-A affiliate of the National League's San Francisco Giants. The Richmond Coliseum is an air-conditioned dome that also hosts stage shows, concerts, college basketball, professional basketball and hockey games, ice shows, the circus, and professional wrestling matches. The Richmond Kickers compete in the United Soccer Leagues.

Richmond hosts the Round-Robin World's Largest Softball Tournament each Memorial Day weekend, with teams from across the United States, Canada, and Iceland participating. Virginia Commonwealth University supports both men's and women's NCAA Division I sports teams. The men's basketball program has achieved national prominence.

The Richmond International Raceway is the only three-quarter-mile track of its kind on the NASCAR circuit. The raceway is host to two Nationwide Series and two Sprint Cup Series events.

Sports for the Participant

The Anthem Richmond Marathon each November features comfortable temperatures, a scenic route, and an enthusiastic crowd along the entire 26.2 mile route.

When Richmond residents want to get out, the James River is the destination of choice. Kayaking and rafting instruction and trips are available, and fishing is also a popular pastime. Attractions along the James also include James River Park, one of the few wilderness parks in the United States that has an urban setting. The 550-acre James River Park is just a tiny segment of what may be the largest amount of park space in any urban area of the country with over 24,000 acres of local, state, and national park land in and around the Richmond metropolitan area. The Pony Pasture loop trail is recommended as an easy, one-hour hike that passes through wetlands and meadows. Pocahontas State Park and Forest, south of the river in Chesterfield County, and several lakes surrounding the Richmond area offer myriad outdoor activities as well.

Golfers can haul their clubs to any of a vast array of local and area courses, including the 18-hole Belmont Golf Course and the 27 holes of family golfing at the Hollows Golf Club just west of Richmond in Montpelier. First Tee of Richmond has an 18-hole course as well as a short par-three course for beginners. Private and public tennis facilities are also available, most notably the Arthur Ashe Junior Athletic Center. The city maintains eight outdoor and two indoor pools. Gillies Creek Park and Bryan Park have disc golf courses.

Shopping and Dining

Richmond's downtown area offers shoppers a wide variety of stores from which to choose. Shockoe Slip, a cobble-stoned riverfront area that used to serve as a cotton and tobacco trading district, is now a focus for nightlife, restaurants, shops, offices, and apartments. The Carytown section of Richmond, a nine-block area with more than 250 unique and colorful shops and another 25 restaurants. The "On the Avenues" shopping area at the juncture of Libbie and Grove Avenues is a collection of 45 specialty shops intermingled with Victorian residences and sidewalk cafes, creating a boutique shopping experience. The 300-year-old 17th Street Farmers' Market supplies regional and organic foods to locals and tourists, along with an open-air community experience of conversation and music with neighbors. A variety of more mainstream malls are sprinkled throughout Richmond, including The Shops at Willow Lawn, Regency Square Mall, River Road Shopping Center, and Chesterfield Towne Center. Just outside the city are outlet malls that attract numerous bargain-hunters, and Richmond is within easy distance of the renowned Williamsburg Pottery Factory.

Richmond has cultivated an increasingly international flavor as a city, and its varied menu of restaurants is evidence. There are more than 400 restaurants in the city. Lemaire at Jefferson Hotel, considered to be one of the most romantic restaurants in the city. Barbecue and soul-food eateries have a strong presence, with Italian and seafood spots running a close second. There are several microbreweries in the area, including the Legend Brewing Company. Other restaurant specialties include Argentinean, steaks, British, cheese and wine, Chinese, continental, French, German, Greek, Indian, international, Irish-American, Japanese, Vietnamese, Mexican-American, organic, Polynesian, regional specialties, southern cooking, and tea rooms.

Visitor Information: Richmond Metropolitan Convention & Visitors Bureau, 401 N. 3rd St., Richmond, VA 23219; telephone (800) 370-9004.

■ Convention Facilities

The Greater Richmond Convention Center (GRCC) is Virginia's largest exhibition and meeting facility, with 700,000 total square feet of room. Adjacent to the Richmond Marriott Hotel and close to sports venues, GRCC accommodations include 178,159 square feet of exhibit space, 32 meeting rooms and a Grand Ballroom that spans 30,550 square feet. Within a short walk or trolley ride are one-third of the area's hotel rooms. The center is just blocks off Interstate 95 and within easy access of the Richmond International Airport.

Other convention and meeting facilities include the Richmond Coliseum, which offers a total of 50,000 square feet of exhibition space under a giant circular dome and is capable of seating up to 13,359 persons; Richmond's Landmark Theater; the Fairgrounds; Dogwood Dell Amphitheater; and Richmond CenterStage. More than 40 hotels have extensive meeting facilities, several of which are located downtown.

Convention Information: Richmond Metropolitan Convention & Visitors Bureau, 401 N. 3rd St., Richmond, VA 23219; telephone (800) 370-9004.

■ Transportation

Approaching the City

Seven airlines make more than 100,000 takeoffs and landings annually at Richmond International Airport (RIA), which is located 10 minutes, via Interstate 64, from the center city. Airlines include American Airlines, Delta, US Airways, Continental, United, AirTran, and Jet Blue. The airport offers complete executive and general aviation services. More than 3 million passengers are estimated to pass through RIA in any given year. As an alternative to the busier RIA, general and corporate aviation services are also available at the Hanover and Chesterfield County Airports.

Crisscrossing the metropolitan area are major north–south and east–west interstates. Interstate 95 provides roadway access up and down the East Coast. Interstate 64 is a major corridor from St. Louis to the port of

Hampton Roads. Interstate 295 connects with Interstate 95 to the north and south of Richmond. Greyhound/ Trailways has a terminal in the city.

Rail passenger service is provided by Amtrak, serving the East Coast and points west with northbound and southbound trains daily. Amtrak's Main Street Station downtown originally opened in 1901 and was undergoing renovations in 2013.

Traveling in the City

Within the city, the average commute time is about 24 minutes, a testament to the Richmond area's well-planned and well-maintained network of expressways, cross-town arteries, and streets that make the use of private vehicles convenient. The Greater Richmond Transit Company (GRTC) operates a fleet of 154 buses and transit vehicles on a radial network of 40 routes across Richmond and Henrico County. GRTC offers specialized services such as CARE and C-Van to provide access to riders with mobility issues, while the Ridefinders program matches carpool and vanpool candidates. From June through November, a trolley system connects sites in the different areas of downtown.

■ Communications

Newspapers and Magazines

Richmond's daily newspaper is the morning *Richmond Times-Dispatch,* which has an average daily circulation above 100,000. *Style Weekly* is an alternative paper for the city. The *Richmond Free Press* and the *Richmond Voice* are free weeklies serving the African American community. The monthly magazine, *Virginia Jewish Life,* is published in Richmond. The weekly *Presbyterian Outlook* is distributed through paid subscriptions, as is the *Religious Herald,* the weekly news journal of the Baptist General Association of Virginia. *Richmond Parents Monthly* and *Fifty Plus* are free publications. The local universities each publish their own collegiate newspaper. Several other magazines and journals are published in Richmond, including *Richmond Magazine,* a lifestyle magazine and *Virginia Business,* a comprehensive state-wide business journal.

Television and Radio

Nine television stations broadcast from Richmond, including major network affiliates and public broadcasting channels. There are 8 AM and 14 FM radio stations broadcasting from Richmond, featuring public radio, adult contemporary, sports, religious content, and others.

Media Information: *Richmond Times-Dispatch,* 300 E. Franklin Street, Richmond, VA 23219; telephone (804)649-6000; toll-free (800) 468-3382.

Richmond Online

City of Richmond home page. Available www.ci. richmond.va.us

Greater Richmond Chamber of Commerce. Available www.grcc.com

Richmond Economic Development Authority. Available www.yesrichmondva.com

Richmond Metropolitan Convention & Visitors Bureau. Available www.visitrichmond.com

Richmond Public Library. Available www. richmondpubliclibrary.org

Richmond Public Schools. Available web.richmond. k12.va.us

Richmond Times-Dispatch. Available www2. timesdispatch.com

Venture Richmond. Available www. venturerichmond.com

BIBLIOGRAPHY

Davis, William C., ed., *Virginia at War, 1862* (Lexington, KY: University Press of Kentucky, 2007)

Furguson, Ernest B., *Ashes of Glory: Richmond at War* (New York: Alfred A. Knopf, 1996)

Wright, Renee, *Virginia Beach, Richmond, and Tidewater Virginia including Williamsburg, Norfolk, and Jamestown* (Woodstock, VT: Countryman Press, 2010)

Virginia Beach

■ The City in Brief

Founded: 1906 (city formed by merger with Princess Anne County, 1963)

Head Official: Mayor William D. Sessoms, Jr. (since January 2009; current term expires 2016)

City Population
1990: 393,089
2000: 425,257
2010: 437,994
2012 estimate: 447,021
Percent change, 2000–2010: 3%
U.S. rank in 1990: 37th (State rank: 1st)
U.S. rank in 2000: 38th (State rank: 1st)
U.S. rank in 2010: 39th (State rank: 1st)

Metropolitan Statistical Area Population
2000: 1,569,541
2010: 1,671,683
2012 estimate: 1,693,567
Percent change, 2000–2010: 6.5%
U.S. rank in 2000: 33rd
U.S. rank in 2010: 36th

Area: 248 square miles

Elevation: Sea level to 12 feet above sea level

Average Annual Temperatures: 59.6° F

Average Annual Precipitation: 45.74 inches

Major Economic Sectors: services, wholesale and retail trade, government

Unemployment Rate: 4.0% (2012)

Per Capita Income: $30,924

2012 FBI Crime Index Property: 11,717

Major Colleges and Universities: Old Dominion University, Norfolk State University, ODU Virginia Beach Center, Virginia Wesleyan College, Regent University, Tidewater Community College

Daily Newspaper: *The Virginian-Pilot*

■ Introduction

Although mention of Virginia Beach often evokes wistful visions of its 28 generous miles of public beach and 30 beautiful miles of shoreline, the city of Virginia Beach is much more than just a dreamy tourist hot spot. As part of a seven-city metropolitan area called Hampton Roads, Virginia Beach boasts a strong economy that has garnered it much national recognition. The city's location, temperate climate, quality labor force, economic stability, competitive taxes, and good transportation system have attracted a growing number of national and international firms that have relocated their corporate headquarters to the area. The city's economy is strengthened by a strong tourist and convention industry, four major military bases, stable real estate, construction, retail and wholesale trade, and distribution. History buff, entrepreneur, culture-lover, or nature enthusiast, Virginia Beach offers something for everyone; the city generated a record $1.28 billion in revenue during 2012.

■ Geography and Climate

Virginia Beach is located on the ocean in the mid-Atlantic region in the southeastern corner of Virginia, with the Atlantic Ocean on the east and the Chesapeake Bay on the north. It is part of the area known as Hampton Roads. In the early 1600s the world's largest natural harbor—where the Chesapeake Bay meets the James River—provided easy access to the colony of Virginia. An English nobleman named Henry Wriothesley, the third

AP Images/Jay Bernas

Earl of Southampton, financed early expeditions to Virginia. In his honor the harbor was named Earl of Southampton's Roadstead. Eventually it was shortened to Hampton Roads. Today, a bridge-tunnel spans the great harbor linking the peninsula cities of Hampton, Newport News, and Williamsburg, the town of Poquoson, and the counties of Gloucester, James City, and York with the Southside cities of Virginia Beach, Chesapeake, Norfolk, Portsmouth, Suffolk, Franklin, and the counties of Isle of Wight and Southampton. This eastern coastal plain region is also referred to as the Tidewater region.

The area experiences four moderate seasons without climactic extremes, in which the warm spring leads to hazy, hot summer days, and warm muggy nights that turn into the bright sunny days and cool crisp nights of autumn and the colder days of winter. The area has an average snowfall of 2.5 inches annually, with snows typically melting within 24 hours.

Area: 248 square miles

Elevation: Sea level to 12 feet above sea level

Average Temperatures: 59.6° F

Average Annual Precipitation: 45.74 inches

■ History

British Land at Cape Henry

In spring of 1607 Captain John Smith and his band of explorers landed at Cape Henry at the northern tip of what is now Virginia Beach. Around them they saw expanses of white sand, rolling dunes, and pine forests. A few days later, they sailed up the James River to establish the New World's first permanent settlement at Jamestown.

Cape Henry, where the Chesapeake Bay meets the Atlantic Ocean, soon became a pathway for British merchant ships that traversed the treacherous seas to reach America. In 1720, the governor of Virginia requested that a lighthouse be built to increase safety. The kings of England refused until 1774. The

Revolutionary War halted construction of the lighthouse, and it was not completed until 1791. A new tower was erected in 1881, but the old one lived on to become Virginia Beach's official symbol in 1962. Cape Henry played a critical role in the Revolution, for it was there the French fleet, led by Admiral Compte De Grasse, stopped the British fleet.

Resort Town Built on Rail Line

Virginia Beach's history as a resort town began in 1880 when a clubhouse was built on the ocean. In 1883, with the help of northern capitalists, a corporation was formed to build a railroad from the busy port of Norfolk to the ocean front. An elaborate hotel that occupied two ocean front blocks, the Princess Anne Hotel, marked the birth of Virginia Beach. The hotel had rail tracks running almost into the lobby for the unloading of steamer trunks. In addition to sunbathing and swimming in the ocean, visitors could soak in salt and freshwater tubs, and enjoy the casino, dance halls, and saltwater pools of nearby Seaside Park.

Two of Hampton Roads' oldest cities, Norfolk and Portsmouth, experienced two centuries of moderate growth following the colonization of the New World, and grew significantly during the twentieth century due to the massive military build-up in support of World War II. Until the 1980s, Norfolk was the most populated city in the region.

Annexation Brings Tremendous Growth

The popularity of Virginia Beach's beachfront, which according to the *Guinness Book of Records* is the largest pleasure beach in the world, extends to the present. Since the building of the boardwalk and the Cavalier Hotel in the late 1920s, the city experienced tremendous growth both as a resort and as a center of industry for the East Coast. Before World War II, the total combined population of the city and county was fewer than 20,000 people. In 1963, by annexing adjacent Princess Anne County, a small resort community became a city of 125,000 people that had grown from an original 1,600 acres to 172,800 acres. With more land for development, Virginia Beach soon surpassed Norfolk as the region's most populated city. With a growth rate of nearly 50 percent between 1980 and 1990, Virginia Beach became the largest city in Virginia.

While this explosive growth rate slowed the following decades, Virginia Beach remained the state's largest city. Downtown development projects and a burgeoning tourism industry attributed to economic growth in the early 2000s. These projects supported incoming businesses and sought to retain the 24,000 college graduates and exiting servicemen living in the city each year. The $350 million Town Center project, which continued in advanced phases through 2013, was a mixed-use facility that represented everything Virginia Beach hoped to keep

and grow with its mix of office space, high-end apartments, and luxurious retail shopping.

Historical Information: Princess Anne County/ Virginia Beach Historical Society, 2040 Potters Road, Virginia Beach, VA 23454; telephone (757) 491-3490.

■ Population Profile

Metropolitan Statistical Area Population
2000: 1,569,541
2010: 1,671,683
2012 estimate: 1,693,567
Percent change, 2000–2010: 6.5%
U.S. rank in 2000: 33rd
U.S. rank in 2010: 36th

City Residents
1990: 393,089
2000: 425,257
2010: 437,994
2012 estimate: 447,021
Percent change, 2000–2010: 3%
U.S. rank in 1990: 37th (State rank: 1st)
U.S. rank in 2000: 38th (State rank: 1st)
U.S. rank in 2010: 39th (State rank: 1st)

Density: 1,758.9 people per square mile

Racial and ethnic characteristics
White: 303,805
Black or African American: 86,078
American Indian and Alaskan Native: 976
Asian: 28,845
Native Hawaiian and Other Pacific Islander: 347
Hispanic or Latino (may be of any race): 32,159
Other: 26,970

Percent of residents born in state: 40.1%

Age characteristics
Population under 5 years old: 29,454
Population 5 to 9 years old: 27,338
Population 10 to 14 years old: 29,376
Population 15 to 19 years old: 29,247
Population 20 to 24 years old: 36,239
Population 25 to 34 years old: 72,501
Population 35 to 44 years old: 58,556
Population 45 to 54 years old: 63,562
Population 55 to 59 years old: 28,791
Population 60 to 64 years old: 21,299
Population 65 to 74 years old: 29,473
Population 75 to 84 years old: 15,533
Population 85 years and over: 5,652
Median age: 34.9

Births (2010–11 Metropolitan Area)
Total number: 22,692

Deaths (2010–11 Metropolitan Area)

Total number: 12,648

Money income (2012)

Per capita income: $30,924
Median household income: $65,169
Total households: 164,066

Number of households with income of . . .

less than $10,000: 6,658
$10,000 to $14,999: 4,877
$15,000 to $24,999: 10,805
$25,000 to $34,999: 14,042
$35,000 to $49,999: 23,122
$50,000 to $74,999: 34,617
$75,000 to $99,999: 24,079
$100,000 to $149,999: 27,729
$150,000 to $199,999: 10,628
$200,000 or more: 7,509

Percent of families below poverty level: 8.3%

FBI Crime Index Property: 11,717

FBI Crime Index Violent: 758

■ Municipal Government

The city operates under a council-manager form of government. There are 11 members in the city council; each serves a four-year term. Eight members must live in their specific district, although the public votes for all council members; three council members and the mayor are elected at large. Staggered city council elections are held every two years. The mayor is elected to a four-year term. The city manager is appointed by the council.

Head Official: Mayor William D. Sessoms, Jr. (since January 2009; current term expires 2016)

Total Number of City Employees: 6,903 (2013)

City Information: City of Virginia Beach, Citizen Services (VB 311), 2508 Princess Anne Rd., Bldg 30, Virginia Beach, VA 23456; telephone (757) 385-3111.

■ Economy

Major Industries and Commercial Activity

Virginia Beach has a diverse economy based on various-major sectors: agribusiness, industry, construction and real estate, defense and military services, retail and wholesale trade, and tourism, conventions, and meetings. Many international corporations have established headquarters in the region, and rapid population growth—from 84,215 people in 1960 to nearly 450,000 in 2012—has allowed retail sales to flourish, while also providing a large labor pool. Open land for industrial development and high-quality office space continue to attract new industry.

Agribusiness contributes substantially to the local economy. A 2012 study by the University of Virginia estimated that agribusiness employed roughly 820 people in the Virginia Beach area and was responsible for more than $60 million of direct and indirect output, with a total economic impact of some $120 million. Principal products included swine, soybeans, corn, horticultural specialties, wheat, vegetables, horse breeding, and dairy products.

The Virginia Beach metropolitan area has military bases representing all branches of the armed forces. The city is also home to a number of defense-related firms that support the largest active-duty population in the nation They have had a tremendous economic impact on the region, with an estimated $8.3 billion in salary earned among the 93,000 military personnel stationed in the metropolitan area. Defense-related activities and spending accounted for more than 40 percent of the total economy, with over $35 billion in gross regional product. The bases included Oceana Naval Air Station, the largest master jet base in the United States; Naval Amphibious Base Little Creek; Fort Story, which conducts amphibious training operations; and Dam Neck, a training base for combat direction and control systems. Businesses serving soldiers, sailors, and their families employ even more area residents.

The 2012 season was record-setting for the Virginia Beach area, which totaled $1.28 billion in revenue, representing a four-percent increase over the prior year's totals. The tourism industry supported more than 12,000 local jobs and created more than $100 million in local tax revenue.

Business and industry takes place in seven major business corridors, including the Airport Industrial Park and the Corporate Landing Business Park. Distribution and transportation for businesses benefits greatly from the fact that Virginia Beach is within 750 miles of three-fourths of the country's industrial activity and two-thirds of its population. An integrated system of highway, air, rail, and sea services provides easy access to national and international markets.

Items and goods produced: power tools, gears, industrial abrasives, furniture, recreational products, machinery, agricultural products, beer

Incentive Programs-New and Existing Companies

Local programs: Virginia Beach offers several incentives to reduce the costs of relocating and expanding a facility within the city. The Virginia Beach Department of Economic Development (DED) prepares customized in-depth research packages for prospects, conducts tours of facilities, helps new industry begin operations and aids existing businesses in their growth, advises on the availability of Industrial Development Bonds and conventional funding, and assists in the development of office parks. DED also helps to expedite the permit process for developments under construction, and provides engineering and landscape assistance at no charge. The Department of Economic Development assists firms in identifying and securing conventional financing. The Virginia Beach Development Authority encourages relocation of businesses to Virginia Beach and also expansion of those currently located there by providing Economic Development Investment Program funds to qualifying businesses and issuing tax-exempt industrial development bonds covering the cost of land, buildings, machinery, and equipment to eligible manufacturing facilities. For non-manufacturers, the Virginia Small Business Financing Authority provides long-term fixed asset financing at rates below those of conventional sources for financing land, buildings and capital equipment. Virginia Beach is the only city in Virginia with no machinery and tools tax.

State programs: Virginia is a right-to-work state, advertising itself as the northernmost right-to-work state in the nation. The State General Assembly has kept Virginia's taxes on industry very competitive by maintaining relatively moderate corporate income tax rates and by eliminating many tax irritants, resulting in modest tax bills for business and industry. While this alone constitutes an attractive incentive for new and existing businesses, the State of Virginia further offers Governor's Opportunity Funds, which allow the Governor to secure business locations or expansion projects with matching funds from the local community; Virginia Investment Partnership Grant Funds, supporting large employers with businesses established for a minimum of five years in Virginia; property tax exemptions; sales and use tax exemptions; enterprise zones; technology zones; and foreign trade zones. Virginia has a State Historic Rehabilitation Tax Credit Program, as does the federal government. The state's Virginia Small Business Financing Authority provides small businesses with access to capital for growth and expansion efforts. The Virginia Economic Development Incentive Grant is a discretionary performance incentive designed to assist and encourage business investment that creates new employment in the state. Specifically, it targets businesses looking to relocate headquarters or others significant service-sector or administrative jobs in the state.

Job training programs: The state's Virginia Jobs Investment Program offers customized recruiting and training assistance for expanding companies that need to hire more workers. The program seeks to lower human development costs to state businesses. In the Hampton Roads area, Opportunity, Inc. provides employers and job seekers with necessary networks and resources in an effort to achieve their mission of "strengthening the localized talent pool of workers to match private sector investments in technology, capital, and product improvement." Acting under the auspices of the Hampton Roads Workforce Development Board, the agency offers workshops, links to online tools and access to a statewide collection of strategic partners. The Hampton Roads Chamber of Commerce also supports the workforce program to keep local employers abreast of labor market trends, employment best practices, and workforce resources.

The Advanced Technology Center, a partnership between Tidewater Community College and Virginia Beach City Public Schools, offers industry-certified training to both high school students and adults. The Virginia Workplace Readiness Skills program also teaches high school students skills they will need to take part in the workforce. GrowSmart is an initiative of the Department of Economic Development that started in July 2011 to facilitate greater strategic alliances with existing workforce development efforts that reach as far down as kindgergarten, working to incrase reading and mentoring.

Development Projects

The Virginia Beach Department of Economic Development includes the City of Virginia Beach Development Authority, whose goal is to facilitate expansion of the city's tax base and employment opportunities by increasing business development and expansion. In 2012 the department succeeded in attracting more than 2,200 jobs and $260 million in new capital investment.

Virginia Beach's largest development project is Town Center of Virginia Beach, a massive, $350 million mixed-use development project encompassing 17 blocks in the downtown area. The first three phases of the Town Center development plan completed by 2010, including major hotels, parking structures, and retail, office, and residential spaces. This also included completion of the Sandler Center for the Performing Arts, which opened in 2007. Phase IV included a 14-story, $89 million office and apartment complex known as Main Street Tower. The 794,000-square-foot project was to include 288 apartments and a nearly 1,000-care parking garage. It was expected to open in 2014. At full capacity, Town Center was to have a living and working population of more than 24,000.

Proposed projects included the Virginia Beach Arena, an 18,500-seat arena proposed by entertainment producers Comcast-Spectacor and Live Nation in 2013. The potential public-private partnership was estimated to generate 1,200 new jobs and have an annual economic impact just under $100 million. The private partners agreed to accept a 25-year lease of the facility if construction went forward.

"The Tide," Norfolk's light-rail transit system that opened in 2013, drew insterest from the Virginia Beach government. In 2013 officials commissioned a feasibility study regarding an extension and connection to the existing 7.4-mile system to contain the Virginia Beach Oceanfront. The extension would utilize an inactive portion of existing track owned by Norfolk Southern.

Economic Development Information: Virginia Beach Department of Economic Development, 222 Central Park Ave., Ste. 1000, Virginia Beach, VA 23462; telephone (757) 385-6464.

Commercial Shipping

The Port of Virginia, with three area terminals, offers fourteen container cranes, including the largest class of crane in the world. Exports of coal, food products, tobacco, and the majority of grain from the United States pass through the port. Annually, the Port of Virginia manages more than 70 million tons of cargo, as of 2012. That year, the Port of Virginia ranked third behind New York and Savannah, Georgia, for marketshare among East Coast terminals. Several freight forwarder and custom broker services are available.

Air freight service is available at Norfolk International Airport, where airlines and air cargo carriers processed 70 million pounds of freight annually as of 2013. Also serving the Hampton Roads area is the Newport News/Williamsburg International Airport, less than an hour away. Railroad freight carriers include the Norfolk Southern and CSX railroads. Direct-service trains serve the airport and port areas. More than 150 trucking companies serve the city's shipping needs in and out of the three terminals of the Port of Virginia every day.

Labor Force and Employment Outlook

In terms of major occupations, the Hampton Roads area population, including that of Virginia Beach, exhibits a balanced proportion of managerial, professional, technical, and support personnel in a variety of businesses and industries. Some 12,000 college students graduate from area universities annually, complemented by an equal number exiting military service. Military spouses number roughly 30,000. As of 2012, professional, technical enterprise, and support management positions accounted for the highest percentage of jobs, followed closely by retail trade, as well as health care and food services. Historically, the Virginia Beach unemployment rate has generally been less than that of the surrounding metropolitan area.

The following is a summary of data regarding the 2012 Virginia Beach labor force:

Size of civilian labor force: 226,729

Number of workers employed in . . .

agriculture and mining: 646
construction: 13,898
manufacturing: 13,570
wholesale trade: 4,799
retail trade: 24,548
transportation: 7,640
information systems: 4,550
finance: 15,919
professional administration: 26,258
education and social services: 44,857
arts and leisure: 22,899
other: 10,743
public administration: 21,465

Average hourly earnings of production workers: $17.57

Unemployment rate: 4.0% (2012)

Employers

Largest employers (2013)	*Number of employees*
City of Virginia Beach and Schools	17,804
Naval Air Station Oceana/Dam Neck	7,427
Sentara Healthcare	5,189
Joint Expeditionary Base Little Creek	4,688
Farm Fresh	4,000
Lynnhaven Mall	2,600
Navy Exchange Service Command	2,450
GEICO	2,300
STIHL Inc.	2,067
Amerigroup	1,850

Cost of Living

The following is a summary of data regarding several key cost of living factors in the area.

2013 ACCRA Average House Price: $268,961

2013 ACCRA Cost of Living Index: 100

State income tax rate: 2.0% to 5.75%

State sales tax rate: 5%

Local income tax rate: None

Local sales tax rate: 1%

Property tax rate: $0.93 per $100 of assessed valuation (2013); assessment ratio = 100% for residential

Economic Information: Virginia Beach Department of Economic Development, 222 Central Park Ave., Ste. 1000, Virginia Beach, VA 23462; telephone (757) 385-6464.

■ Education and Research

Elementary and Secondary Schools

The Virginia Beach City Public Schools is one of the largest systems in the Commonwealth. A number of special curriculum programs are offered for both special needs and advanced students. As of 2013, Virginia Beach City Public Schools were one of seven Virginia districts honored by the College Board by being named to its AP District Honor Roll. Arts are a strong offering in the district, with the National Association of Music Merchants Foundation naming the district one of only 307 districts nationwide to qualify among the "Best Communities for Music Education in America" in 2013.

Kemps Landing Magnet Schools was one of two schools in the state to earn the 2013 Governor's Award of Educational Excellence, and John B. Dey, Kingston, and Red Mill elementary schools were given the 2013 Board of Education Distinguished Achievement Awards. The district's graduating class in 2013 earned more than $32 million in college scholarships.

The Adult Learning Center offers educational services for students over the age of 18 who are retiring to school or are non-English speaking adults. Students enrolled in alternative educational programs are eligible for participation in a special team-building and problem-solving Ropes and Initiatives Course. The Virginia Workforce Readiness Program provides vocational education and skills for high school students. The school system sponsors the Virginia Beach City Public Schools Planetarium.

There are several private, parochial, and military schools in the city enrolling students in all grades.

The following is a summary of data regarding the Virginia Beach City Public Schools.

Total enrollment: 71,185

Number of facilities
    total: 86
    elementary schools: 56
    junior high schools: 14
    high schools: 11
    other: 5

Student/teacher ratio: 18.09:1

Teacher salaries
    average (statewide): $51,559

Funding per pupil: $10,311

Public Schools Information: Virginia Beach City Public Schools, 2512 George Mason Drive, PO Box 6038, Virginia Beach, VA 23456-0038; telephone (757) 263-1000.

Colleges and Universities

Old Dominion University, founded in 1930 as a division of the College of William and Mary, is a public coeducational school and a sea- and space-grant institution with a combined undergraduate and graduate enrollment of about 25,000 students. From baccalaureate to doctoral programs, Old Dominion grants degrees in education, liberal arts, business and public administration, sciences, health sciences, engineering, and technology. The university capitalizes on its proximity to the naval base and the NASA's Wallops Flight Facility, creating fieldwork experiences that contribute to those industries. Old Dominion has been classified as a Doctoral Research University–Extensive by the Carnegie Foundation.

Norfolk State University is one of the largest predominantly African American institutions in the United States, with an enrollment of more than 7,000 students. It has undergraduate schools in business, education, liberal arts, social work, and science and technology, as well as graduate departments. The most popular majors are business, nursing, psychology, biology, and music education.

The Old Dominion University Virginia Beach Center offers select graduate and undergraduate degree, certificate, and continuing-education programs in traditional, distance, and hybrid learning formats. While there are three area centers, the Virginia Beach Center offers doctorates in English, master's degrees nursing, public health, business administration, education, accounting, and engineering management, in addition to others, and bacherlor's degrees in more than one dozen fields. The Center also is a headquarters for the Institute for Learning Retirement, Virginia Tidewater Consortium-Educational Opportunity Center, and programming from Norfolk State University.

Virginia Wesleyan College, with 1,431 students, is a private liberal arts college that emphasizes the value of gaining real-world experience through internships, field work, study abroad, and community service. The college offers baccalaureate degrees in various divisions of the humanities, natural sciences and mathematics, and the social sciences. Regent University in Virginia Beach was established in 1978 by M. G. "Pat" Robertson. It is a Christian university.

Tidewater Community College is a two-year college offering career and technical education programs as well as college transfer programs. With nearly 45,000 enrolled each year, it is the 11th two-year college in the nation, as of 2013. Campuses are located in Norfolk, Portsmouth, Virginia Beach, and Chesapeake. Visual arts centers are located around the region, as is the college's Advanced Technology Center, Regional Health Professions Center, Regional Automotive Center, and Center for Military and Veterans Education. The college has 11 accredited programs and is the 17th-largest degree-producer among two-year colleges.

Libraries and Research Centers

Virginia Beach Public Libraries encompass the central library and eight branch libraries, as well as a Municipal Reference Library, the Wahab Public Law Library, and a Library for the Blind and Physically Handicapped. The library system circulated more than 3.6 million items annually as of 2011, and also managed more than 700,000 annual hits on its website.

The Regent University Library contains more than 300,000 printed volumes; 593,000 microform items; 11,000 video and audio recordings; 116 article databases; 151,000 electronic books and downloadable audio books; and 55,000 full-text journal titles via article databases.

The Hampton Roads Agricultural Research and Extension Center in Virginia Beach is affiliated with Virginia Tech. A Master Gardener program is offered through the extension. The Edgar Cayce Association for Research and Enlightenment is also located within the city. A number of research facilities are located on the campus of Old Dominion University, Eastern Virginia Medical School, and Norfolk State University, all in nearby Norfolk.

Public Library Information: Virginia Beach Central Library, 4100 Virginia Beach Blvd., Virginia Beach, VA 23452; telephone (757) 385-0150.

■ Health Care

Sentara Healthcare, a not-for-profit health care provider in southeastern Virginia, operates numerous hospitals in the Hampton Roads area, with two of them in Virginia Beach. Sentara Virginia Beach General Hospital is a 234-bed facility that ranked as a high-performing hospital in three specialties according to *U.S. News & World Report* in 2013–14. The hospital features the region's only Level III Trauma and also houses the system's Heart Center. Other facilities associated with the hospital include the Coastal Cancer Center and Accredited Sleep Disorders Center. Sentara Princess Anne Hospital is a general medical and surgical hospital with 160 beds. Rehabilitation services are provided by Sentara Therapy Center. Virginia Beach Psychiatric Center is a freestanding hospital that offers psychiatric and substance abuse services for children, adolescents, and adults.

■ Recreation

Sightseeing

Virginia Beach is home to many interesting historical landmarks and recreational areas. The First Landing Cross marks the spot where America's first permanent English settlers, the Jamestown colonists, reached the

New World in 1607. The Old Cape Henry Lighthouse at Fort Story, built in 1791, is open for tours. The Old Coast Guard Station, one of the first life-saving stations in the United States, is one of several such stations along the East Coast that are still open to the public. Located in a 1903 former Coast Guard Station, the Old Coast Guard Station displays photographs, nautical artifacts, scrimshaw, ship models, and other marine memorabilia about the Life-Saving Service. Veterans are saluted by the Tidewater Veterans Memorial, complete with a flag display and waterfall. The Norwegian Lady statue, a gift from the people of Moss, Norway, commemorates the wreck of the Norwegian bark *Dictator* off the city's coastline.

Local historical houses include the Adam Thoroughgood House, built in the mid-1600s, which may be the oldest remaining brick house in America; the Lynnhaven House, one of America's best-preserved eighteenth-century middle class dwellings; Francis Land House and Historic Site, built in 1732, which is the largest and finest gambrel-roofed house in Virginia; and Upper Wolfsnare, a beautifully restored 1759 house that is a Virginia Landmark Home. The Princess Anne Courthouse, built in 1824, and the beautifully landscaped Municipal Building are among the 28 major buildings that house the executive offices of the local government.

The Virginia Aquarium & Marine Science Center's more than 800,000 gallons of aquaria and over 300 species, including hands-on exhibits that offer visitors the opportunity to explore the depths of the Atlantic Ocean, walk under the waves of the Chesapeake Bay, view the life of a saltwater marsh, and stroll through a coastal plains river. A 3-D IMAX theater, nature trail, and traveling exhibits add to the fun. Ocean Breeze Waterpark has 16 waterslides and a one-million-gallon Runaway Bay wave pool. The Virginia Beach Farmer's Market, open every day of the year, offers 17,000 square feet of food stalls, craft items, and a country-style restaurant. In the warm months the Market has educational programs for students and Friday Night Hoedowns. Guided tours are available at the Christian Broadcasting Network Center, which includes Regent University and state-of-the-art broadcasting facilities where the popular religious program "The 700 Club" is taped.

The Association for Research and Enlightenment Library and Conference Center documents the life work of Edgar Cayce, world-renowned psychic, through exhibits, lectures, and extrasensory perception testing. The center also has a meditation garden and labyrinth for peaceful contemplation.

Within one hour's drive of the city are many attractions for culture-lovers and history buffs alike. The Virginia Air & Space Center and Hampton Roads History Center, located in historic Hampton, are housed in a nine-story wonder of a building on the waterfront that combines super modern and traditional architectural styles. Visitors can view vintage aircraft suspended from the ceiling, the Apollo 12 Command Module with a three-billion-year-old moon rock, plus an authentic Chesapeake Bay deadrise workboat. Based on the theme, "From the Sea to the Stars," this $30 million building reviews Hampton Roads' seafood and shipbuilding history, and its role as a military defense post and pioneer in aviation and space exploration. The museum also features a 300-seat 3-D IMAX theater, which shows aviation and space exploration films; and a restored 1920 merry-go-round.

The Military Aviation museum in Virginia Beach is another must-see tourist destination for airplane-lovers, with one of the largest military aircraft collections in the nation. The aircraft are not merely for display; many are flown at regional air shows and local flight demonstrations.

Located between Virginia Beach and Williamsburg is the Mariners' Museum in Newport News, which invites visitors to reflect on the lore of the sea and maritime exploration over the past 3,000 years. The museum's galleries contain a unique collection of more than 35,000 figureheads, paintings, small craft, ship models, and other marine artifacts. In addition, the museum offers demonstrations by costumed interpreters, films, and a five-mile nature trail around picturesque Lake Murray. The nearby Peninsula Fine Arts Center provides changing monthly exhibits, a children's art center and adult classes, and the Virginia War Museum traces U.S. military history from the Revolution to the first Gulf War.

Just one hour west of Virginia Beach, Williamsburg's Colonial Williamsburg helps tourists make the journey back to the early days of our nation. Visions of our colonial ancestors abound in the 173-acre Historic Area, which features more than 30 buildings and craftsmen in eighteenth-century attire practicing industries of the era. Also in the area is Busch Gardens Williamsburg, where visitors can step back in time to life in old England, Scotland, Germany, Italy, and Ireland, while enjoying thrill rides, live shows, and animal attractions. The Williamsburg Pottery Factory has been offering bargain prices for over 60 years, and the water park Water Country USA contains one of the longest flume rides in the country. A trip to Yorktown allows one to look over the site of the 1781 battle that ended the Revolutionary War, and visitors to historic Jamestown can see full-sized replicas of three 1607 ships, re-creations of the colonists' fort, and a Powhatan village.

Arts and Culture

The City of Virginia Beach Office of Cultural Affairs directs the Virginia Beach Arts and Humanities Commission. The Virginia Museum of Contemporary Art celebrates the work of both American artists and artists from around the world. The Artists Gallery in Virginia Beach is a working marketplace for the visual arts that provides views of the actual process of artistic creation. Many of the art works are for sale.

The Sandler Center for the Performing Arts, opened in November 2007, features a 1,300-seat Performance Theatre, a 2,400 square-foot Studio Theatre/Rehearsal Space, and an Outdoor Performance Plaza to accommodate 400 guests. It is an impressive space to view live music, with the farthest seat from the stage a mere 100 feet away. Resident companies include the Virginia Symphony Orchestra, which has also performed at Regent University Theater in Virginia Beach and at venues in Norfolk and Williamsburg. Sharing the stage at Sandler are the Virginia Musical Theater, offering four Broadway shows each year, and the Virginia Beach Chorale, the oldest continuous performing arts group in Virginia Beach, offering two concert series, one in spring and one in December. The Hurrah Players children's theatre group offers special summer camps as well as year-round classes.

The Virginia Beach Amphitheater is a 20,000-seat venue hosting major musical acts from April through October. As a resort town, Virginia Beach also offers a wide range of jazz, blues, reggae, and rock at the many local nightclubs and dance halls. Virginia Opera performs in the Harrison Opera House and to thousands of school children every year. The Tidewater Winds, a concert band in the Souza tradition, performs all over the Hampton Roads area. The Little Theatre of Virginia Beach is a community theater that produces five shows and a summer musical per year.

Festivals and Holidays

In January the Pavilion plays host to the Virginia Flower and Garden Expo. The Mid-Atlantic Sports and Boat Show in February is one of the largest indoor boat shows in the state. March includes the Shamrock Marathon SportsFest. The Historic Garden Week Tour, International Azalea Festival, Atlantic Coast Kite Festival and Mid-Atlantic Home & Garden Show happen in April. May brings in the Patriotic Festival, Big Flea Market, Pungo Strawberry Festival, and Verizon Wireless American Beach Music Festival. It also features the K-9 Karnival, which includes demonstrations and athletic competitions centered on man's best friend. June has the Annual Boardwalk Art Show and Hardee's Latin Fest. July features a huge Fourth of July Celebration and the Mid-Atlantic Hermit Crab Challenge. Labor Day weekend brings the Verizon Wireless American Music Festival and the Virginia Beach Rock 'n' Roll Marathon.

The Neptune Festival in September is the main festival of the year. It attracts more than one million spectators and features parades, an air show, a triathlon, art and crafts exhibits, wine tastings, live entertainment, a sand sculpting contest and more. October brings the city's Brewfest. The Virginia Beach Christmas Market and Holiday Parade at the Beach happen in late November; and December's Holiday Lights at the Beach, annual *Nutcracker* program, and New Year's Rock Around the Clock ends the year.

Sports for the Spectator

Athletic stars come to the city for the Shamrock Marathon SportsFest, which takes place each March. Rudee Inlet is the site every August of the Coastal Edge East Coast Surfing Championships. The Virginia Beach Oceanfront hosts several beach volleyball events each year and is the finish line for the annual Rock 'n' Roll Marathon.

Sports lovers in the Hampton Roads region attend the baseball games of the Norfolk Tides baseball team, a Triple-A minor league affiliate of the Baltimore Orioles who play at the Riverfront's Harbor Park. The Norfolk Admirals, an affiliate of the American Hockey League Tampa Bay Lighting, play at Norfolk Scope Arena. The Virginia Beach Piranhas, the name of both the women's USL soccer team, play at the Virginia Beach Sportsplex. NCAA teams from Old Dominion, Norfolk State, and Virginia Wesleyan are also popular with students and locals. The USA Field Hockey National Training Center at Virginia Beach hosts a number of national and international events.

Sports for the Participant

Virginia Beach's greatest asset is the 38 miles of golden shoreline that has attracted visitors for more than a century. The city's three-mile-long boardwalk, with a parallel bike track, is enhanced with teak benches, lampposts, and colorful flags. The city's most popular beaches are the Resort Area, North End, Back Bay, Croatan, Sandbridge, and Chesapeake beaches.

The Virginia Beach Fishing Center offers half-day or full-day offshore sport fishing, as well as wreck fishing, and deep-sea fishing is available from Lynnhaven Seafood & Marina. Freshwater fishing is enjoyed at Back Bay or Lake Smith, and pier fishing is possible at several sites around the city. Sightseeing, scuba diving and whale watching cruises can also be booked with the many charter boats at the Marina. Kayak rentals and tours of the area are offered by multiple companies.

Mount Trashmore is a mountain of compacted layers of soil and solid waste within the city that has been transformed into a 165-acre park with bicycle trails, playgrounds, skateboard ramps, picnic facilities, and two lakes. A registered National Landmark, First Landing State Park offers more than 20 miles of hiking and biking trails through its 2,888 acres. Back Bay National Wildlife Refuge has 9,000 acres of beach, woodland, and marsh,

where whistling swans, peregrine falcons, and bald eagles can be spotted in the wintertime. Hiking trails exist at First Landing and False Cape State Parks. Camping is permitted at False Cape State Park among the maritime forests and ocean dunes. The park also boasts six miles of unspoiled beaches. Virginia Beach's jet observation parks permit spectators to watch the U.S. Navy's most advanced aircraft take off and land from Ocean Naval Air Station.

Virginia Beach boasts numerous public tennis courts, anchored by the Owl Creek Municipal Tennis Center. The resort area's other recreational offerings include boogie-boarding, windsurfing, jet skiing, parasailing, miniature golf, volleyball, softball tournaments, bowling, and roller skating. Most recreational equipment, including bicycles, can be rented near the beach. The city's 265 parks, encompassing more than 4,000 acres, offer such features as playgrounds, ball fields, dog parks, and picnic areas. The city operates seven recreation centers. Mild weather year-round makes golf a tremendous draw for visitors. There are five municipally operated golf courses, including the prestigious Virginia Beach National; many other public and private courses dot the region.

Shopping and Dining

Numerous off-price outlets, such as the Great American Outlet Mall and Loehmann's Plaza, make Virginia Beach a shopper's delight. The Town Center spans 17 blocks dedicated to shopping, which ranges from major department stores to small boutiques, and restaurants. There are traditional malls, such as Lynnhaven, one of the largest malls on the east coast, boasting more than 180 stores and 1.35 million-square-feet of retail space; Pembroke Mall, with large department stores and specialty shops; the various Hilltop locations and La Promenade; as well as the boardwalk and resort area's souvenir shops, surf shops, boutiques, and craft shops. The Virginia Beach Farmers Market is open year round.

Seafood in a wide variety of forms is the star of the culinary show in Virginia Beach. The oyster and the blue crab are local delicacies, and flounder, scallops, and numerous other varieties of fish tempt the palate at local restaurants. Ethnic dishes run the gamut from fajitas, to sushi, to Cajun jambalaya or fettuccine alfredo. Oceanfront cafes offer scenic dining opportunities, and eating establishments range from elegant to casual. The Town Center development is becoming a hub for restaurants as well, with large national chain restaurants like P. F. Chang's and The Cheesecake Factory.

Visitor Information: Virginia Beach Convention and Visitors Bureau, Visitors Center, 2100 Parks Avenue, Virginia Beach, VA 23451; telephone (800) 822-3224.

■ Convention Facilities

The city's primary convention facility is the Virginia Beach Convention Center, an environmentally-friendly convention space that is both a Virginia Green certified facility and an Energy Star Partner, making it a perfect location for green events. It has more than150,000 square feet of column-free exhibition space, 29,000 square feet of meeting space, and a ballroom of over 31,000 square feet. Plans to build a major hotel next to the convention, under discussion since the mid-2000s, were formally rejected by the city in 2012, meaning new proposals likely would be forthcoming. The $17.5 million Verizon Wireless Virginia Beach Amphitheatre is a 93-acre site that accommodates seating for about 20,000 people, with 7,500 seats in a covered pavilion and room for about 12,500 on the surrounding lawn. The Cavalier Hotel offers 25 function areas, providing space for groups of twenty to 2,000. The Founders Inn & Spa houses 25,000 square feet of conference space, including twenty function rooms, a ballroom, and an amphitheater, all of which can accommodate groups from 10 to 1,400. Several other major hotels offer meeting and banquet spaces. Grand Affairs is a full-service banquet facility offering five ballrooms. Smaller groups may meet at the Virginia Museum of Contemporary Art or the Virginia Aquarium and Marine Science Center.

Convention Information: Virginia Beach Convention Center, 1000 19th Street, Virginia Beach, VA 23451; telephone (757) 385-2000.

■ Transportation

Approaching the City

Norfolk International Airport is a 20 minute drive from Chesapeake. The airport offers direct flights from Air-Tran, American, Delta, Southwest, United, and US Airways to 21 cities. In 2012 the airport served nearly 3.3 million passengers, making it the 68th largest primary airport in the United States. Chesapeake Regional and Hampton Roads airports provide corporate flight service within the city. Newport News/Williamsburg International Airport handles roughly one million passengers annually.

Interstate 264 and U.S. Highway 58 approach the city from the west; Interstate 64 and U.S. Highway 460 merge with these two routes to enter the city. From the north and south convenient routes are U.S. Highway 60, which goes directly into the city, and U.S. Highway 17. Interstates 64 and 264 connect the city directly to the Hampton Roads region. The part of Interstate 264 that enters directly into Virginia Beach is formerly known as the Virginia Beach-Norfolk Expressway.

The Chesapeake Bay Bridge-Tunnel connects Virginia Beach with Virginia's eastern shore. The Hampton Roads Bridge-Tunnel links the southside of Hampton Roads with the peninsula cities of Newport News and Hampton. The Merrimac-Monitor Memorial Bridge Tunnel connects the south side and peninsula via the James River.

Bus service is provided by the Greyhound Bus Line and Amtrak provides rail service and connections to numerous Eastern and Southern points from nearby both Virginia Beach and nearby Newport News. Virginia Beach can be reached by water from the Atlantic Ocean or via the Intercoastal Waterway.

Traveling in the City

The VB Wave, a three-route trolley system, services residents and visitors throughout the summertime, extending from the resort area to shopping malls to points of local cultural and historic importance. Hampton Roads Transit provides public transportation regionally, connecting Virginia Beach with Norfolk, Hampton, Newport News, Suffolk, Portsmouth, and Chesapeake. There were 19 routes within the city of Virginia Beach as of 2013. Some buses are equipped with bike racks. Handi-Ride service, for disabled travelers, is available by reservation at sites within three-quarters of a mile of regularly scheduled bus routes.

■ Communications

Newspapers and Magazines

The Virginian-Pilot serves both southeast Virginia and northeastern North Carolina. As of 2013, its circulation averaged 350,000 on weekdays and 470,000 on weekends. Also published in Virginia Beach are the monthly subscription magazine *Tidewater Parent* and the free monthly magazine *Tidewater Women,* which is published in Virginia Beach and distributed in Virginia Beach, Norfolk, Chesapeake, Portsmouth, and Suffolk.

Television and Radio

Virginia Beach is served by cable television and by stations broadcasting from the surrounding Hampton Roads area. The Christian Broadcasting Network (CBN), headed by Pat Robertson, has a headquarters and a main television studio in Virginia Beach. CBN is known worldwide for broadcasts of The 700 Club and CBN Newswatch. One AM and six FM radio stations are broadcast out of Virginia Beach.

Media Information: The Virginian-Pilot, 150 W. Brambleton Avenue, Norfolk, VA 23510; telephone (757) 446-9000.

Virginia Beach Online

    City of Virginia Beach home page. Available www.vbgov.com

    Virginia Beach City Public Schools. Available www.vbschools.com

    Virginia Beach Department of Economic Development. Available www.yesvirginiabeach.com

    Virginia Beach Public Library. Available www.vbgov.com/libraries

    Virginia Beach Convention and Visitors Bureau. Available www.visitvirginiabeach.com

BIBLIOGRAPHY

Callis, Ann Hanbury, *Vintage North End Virginia Beach: An Illustrated History* (Atglen, PA: Schiffer Publishing Ltd, 2012)

Jackson, Katherine, *Walking Virginia Beach* (Helena, MT: Falcon Publishing Co., 1999)

Wright, Renee, *Virginia Beach, Richmond, and Tidewater Virginia including Williamsburg, Norfolk, and Jamestown* (Woodstock, VT: Countryman Press, 2010)

Williamsburg

■ The City in Brief

Founded: 1699

Head Official: Mayor Clyde Haulman (R) (since 2010; current term expires 2014)

City Population
   1990: 11,530
   2000: 11,992
   2010: 14,068
   2012 estimate: 15,167
   Percent change, 2000–2010: 17.25%%

James City County Population
   2000: 48,102
   2010: 67,009
   2012 estimate: 68,967
   Percent change, 2000–2010: 39.3%

Area: Not available

Elevation: Not available

Average Annual Temperatures: 58.2° F

Average Annual Precipitation: Not available

Major Economic Sectors: services, retail, education, hospitality

Unemployment Rate: 13.4% (2012)

Per Capita Income: $23,007

2012 FBI Crime Index Property: 259

Major Colleges and Universities: College of William & Mary

Daily Newspaper: *Richmond Times Dispatch*

■ Introduction

Part of America's Historic Triangle, Williamsburg evolved from a meager settlement into a center of politics and education. The city, which was filled with historic homes and buildings long after the American Revolution, was restored starting in the late 1920s, and became the largest living history attraction. It also became the largest employer in the area, partially due to Williamsburg's small size. The other largest employer, the College of William and Mary, complements Williamsburg with its focus on research and its status as the nation's second oldest university next to Harvard. Colonial Williamsburg continues to thrive despite the national recession. The College of William and Mary is diversifying the area's business climate as it has begun to explore research and development. New creative businesses in the city's arts and culture district, established in 2011, have begun adding a new chapter to the city's rich history.

■ Geography and Climate

Williamsburg is located in the southeast part of Virginia, referred to as the Hampton Roads region, about equidistant between Richmond and Norfolk along Interstate 64/U.S. Highway 60. The city spans about nine square miles, 39.5 percent of which is designated green space, and is 6 to 90 feet above sea level. Williamsburg has four seasons that often present mild temperatures. Summer averages have been in the 60-degree range, and winter averages have been in the lower 30-degree range. The average yearly temperature is 58.2 degrees Fahrenheit. Rainfall generally occurs year round.

Area: Not available

Elevation: Not available

Average Temperatures: 58.2° F

Average Annual Precipitation: Not available

Governor's Palace, historic Colonial Williamsburg. *Laurie Fundukian*

■ History

Captain John Smith and his party landed in the New World in 1607 to find that the area was already occupied by the Powhatan tribe. During their first few years in the new settlement they called Jamestown, the English colonists spent the majority of their efforts securing the fort. Since the area they had discovered was already occupied by Native Americans, Smith and his men many times fought with the opposing tribes. The battles deterred them from attempting to settle outside the original fort.

Williamsburg was officially founded in 1699, and was named after King William III of England. The governor, Francis Nicholson, put together plans to make the city one of the largest British colonies. Jamestown was the original state capital, and became a large legislative force. The city quickly became a significant political and educational center, with the College of William and Mary having already been established six years before in 1693. Future American

presidents Thomas Jefferson, James Monroe, and John Tyler were educated at the College of William and Mary.

After independence from Britain was won in 1776, the state capital relocated to Richmond, Virginia. No longer a governmental hub, Williamsburg reverted to becoming a humble center for education, and an ideal setting for peaceful plantations. In 1926, a reverend named W.A.R. Goodwin partnered with John D. Rockefeller, Jr., to restore the city, and construction began soon after. The Colonial Williamsburg Foundation came into being, and the largest historical attraction in the United States was born. Colonial Williamsburg welcomes thousands of visitors annually, and continues to educate through tours and demonstrations. Diversification away from the tourist industry, which slumped during a nationwide recession in the late 2000s, was an economic priority moving forward and best evidenced by the city's establishment of an arts and culture district in 2011, which sought to attract creative industries to the city's downtown area.

Historical Information: City of Williamsburg, Municipal Building, 401 Lafayette St., Williamsburg, VA, 23185; telephone (757) 220-6100.

■ Population Profile

James City County Population

2000: 48,102
2010: 67,009
2012 estimate: 68,967
Percent change, 2000–2010: 39.3%

City Residents

1990: 11,530
2000: 11,992
2010: 14,068
2012 estimate: 15,167
Percent change, 2000–2010: 17.25%%

Density: 1,559.3 people per square mile

Racial and ethnic characteristics

White: 10,407
Black or African American: 1,968
American Indian and Alaskan Native: 38
Asian: 808
Native Hawaiian and Other Pacific Islander: 5
Hispanic or Latino (may be of any race): 941
Other: 842

Percent of residents born in state: 37.9%

Age characteristics

Population under 5 years old: 433
Population 5 to 9 years old: 366
Population 10 to 14 years old: 364
Population 15 to 19 years old: 2,337
Population 20 to 24 years old: 3,887
Population 25 to 34 years old: 1,624
Population 35 to 44 years old: 922
Population 45 to 54 years old: 1,053
Population 55 to 59 years old: 549
Population 60 to 64 years old: 654
Population 65 to 74 years old: 1,071
Population 75 to 84 years old: 603
Population 85 years and over: 205
Median age: 24.0

Births (2010–11 Metropolitan Area)

Total number: 22,692

Deaths (2010–11 Metropolitan Area)

Total number: 12,648

Money income (2012)

Per capita income: $23,007

Median household income: $50,865
Total households: 4,281

Number of households with income of ...

less than $10,000: 463
$10,000 to $14,999: 97
$15,000 to $24,999: 295
$25,000 to $34,999: 530
$35,000 to $49,999: 715
$50,000 to $74,999: 814
$75,000 to $99,999: 469
$100,000 to $149,999: 433
$150,000 to $199,999: 218
$200,000 or more: 247

Percent of families below poverty level: 18.4%

FBI Crime Index Property: 259

FBI Crime Index Violent: 20

■ Municipal Government

The council-manager government in Williamsburg includes a five-member city council, which appoints a mayor and vice-mayor from among their ranks. All members are elected at-large, and serve staggered, four-year terms. The mayor acts as the head of government, while the city manager carries out legislation put in place by city council.

Head Official: Mayor Clyde Haulman (R) (since 2010; current term expires 2014)

Total Number of City Employees: 188 (2013)

City Information: City of Williamsburg, Municipal Building, 401 Lafayette St., Williamsburg, VA, 23185; telephone (757) 220-6100.

■ Economy

Major Industries and Commercial Activity

The Williamsburg business climate is dominated by industries including professional and business services, retail, construction, and leisure and hospitality. More than 700 area businesses are in the retail, food services, and hospitality categories. Williamsburg is largely supported by education and tourism, with the College of William and Mary, and the Colonial Williamsburg Foundation leading the area's economic strength. The College of William and Mary was established in 1693 and employs more than 1,000 people, making it the city's largest employer. The college is a large source of the area's research and development capabilities, which are centered in New Town's Discovery Business Park.

Colonial Williamsburg has attracted visitors since its inception in 1932 after Reverend Dr. W.A.R. Goodwin (along with John D. Rockefeller, Jr.) began preserving historic buildings throughout the city in 1926. The Colonial Williamsburg Foundation, the founding and supportive arm of the tourist attraction, is a top employer along with the College of William and Mary. The foundation received more than $63 million in financial support in 2012 from more than 100,000 donors across the country. The foundation's endowment exceeded $735 million that year.

Other businesses that have a major presence in the area are Busch Gardens, TowneBank, Riverside Health System, Sentara Healthcare, and Smithfield Foods. Manufacturing company Buntrock Industries, which makes casting shell equipment, is headquartered in Williamsburg. The National Center for State Courts is also located in Williamsburg. Some 47 new businesses opened in Williamsburg in 2012.

Items and goods produced: Wax injection equipment, boilers, hydrogen torches, metal alloys, health products, foods, furniture, colonial collectible items, clothing, arts, and crafts

Incentive Programs-New and Existing Companies

Local programs: The Williamsburg Economic Development Authority matches grants up to $1,500 for small businesses trying to create or improve their online presence. Incentives are also offered to businesses via tax exempt bonds to construct or expand facilities. The Sign Grant Program awards up to $2,000 for businesses to match efforts to replace nonconforming signage. Tax incentives in the city's Arts and Cultural District, defined in 2011, are also available.

State programs: Virginia is a right-to-work state, advertising itself as the northernmost right-to-work state in the nation. The State General Assembly has kept Virginia's taxes on industry very competitive by maintaining relatively moderate corporate income tax rates and by eliminating many tax irritants, resulting in modest tax bills for business and industry. While this alone constitutes an attractive incentive for new and existing businesses, the State of Virginia further offers Governor's Opportunity Funds, which allow the Governor to secure business locations or expansion projects with matching funds from the local community; Virginia Investment Partnership Grant Funds, supporting large employers with businesses established for a minimum of five years in Virginia; property tax exemptions; sales and use tax exemptions; enterprise zones; technology zones; and foreign trade zones. Virginia has a State Historic Rehabilitation Tax Credit Program, as does the federal government. The state's Virginia Small Business Financing Authority provides small businesses with access to

capital for growth and expansion efforts. The Virginia Economic Development Incentive Grant is a discretionary performance incentive designed to assist and encourage business investment that creates new employment in the state. Specifically, it targets businesses looking to relocate headquarters or others significant service-sector or administrative jobs in the state.

Job training programs: The state's Virginia Jobs Investment Program offers customized recruiting and training assistance for expanding companies that need to hire more workers. The program seeks to lower human development costs to state businesses. Thomas Nelson Community College in Hampton joins with local businesses to provide apprenticeship experiences to students in a variety of trades, including welding, teaching, and pipefitting. Businesses are eligible to receive tax breaks if participating in the training program. The program is offered through the Virginia Registered Apprenticeship training system, and apprenticeship programs usually have a duration of one to six years. Workforce Investment Act Career development workshops are offered through Thomas Nelson Community College.

Development Projects

The City of Williamsburg's economic development plan, adopted in 2012, focused on recovering from a nationwide recession in the late 2000s that significantly impacted the city's tourism market, and by extension many of its related businesses. The city began a demolition program in 2007 to rid the city of underutilized buildings and clear the way for new development. The effort, which provided public assistance to property owners to demolish buildings, won the 2012 Virginia Economic Development Association's Community Economic Development Award.

In 2011 the city council created an Arts and Cultural District to create specific incentives for creative industries to locate in certain parts of the city where vacancy rates exceeded 20 percent. Six businesses created 35 new jobs had moved into the area as of 2012. The city also revised its zoning laws to further encourage business development in the area. Annual new business starts in Williamsburg averaged 53 between 2010 and 2012, exceeding starts during the recessionary years of 2007–09, which averaged only 27.

The midtown area of Williamsburg enjoyed several investments in 2012, including a 6,600-square-foot retail development on Richmond Road and renovations to Solutionz Inc.'s commercial space on Mt. Vernon Avenue. Downtown developments include the construction of 10,600 square feet of retail space known as Tribe Square in 2011 and an additional 7,000 square feet of commercial space for the Cook Building in 2012.

The College of William and Mary's Capital Plan, running from 2012 to 2018, totaled more than $426 million, with major investments in the third phase of construction for its Integrated Science Center, renovations to Tucker and Tyler halls, multiple phases of a new Arts Complex, a IT Data Center, and major renovations to three other halls: Jones, Morton, and Washington.

Economic Development Information: City of Williamsburg Office of Economic Development, 401 Lafayette Street, Williamsburg, VA 23185; telephone (757) 220-6120.

Commercial Shipping

There are three major international airports within an hour of Williamsburg that can be used for cargo shipping: Newport News/Williamsburg International Airport, Norfolk International Airport, and Richmond International Airport. Many all-cargo flights leave from these airports every day via Airborne Express, Federal Express, United Parcel Service, and United States Postal Service carriers. There are more than 150 nearby motor freight carrier companies that go to and from warehouses, distribution centers, and marine ports. Williamsburg is near three sea ports, all part of the Port of Virginia: Newport News Marine Terminal, Portsmouth Marine Terminal, and Norfolk International Terminal. CSX Transportation provides commercial rail service in the region and connects to other national destinations.

Labor Force and Employment Outlook

Williamsburg is a small city, and many workers commute into the city from nearby towns. The College of William and Mary graduates thousands of educated students prepared for the workforce each year. The Williamsburg-James City County School System offers a transitional educational program that places high school seniors as employees with local businesses.

The following is a summary of data regarding the 2012 Williamsburg labor force:

Size of civilian labor force: 6,155

Number of workers employed in . . .

    agriculture and mining: 0
    construction: 272
    manufacturing: 162
    wholesale trade: 85
    retail trade: 567
    transportation: 52
    information systems: 48
    finance: 257
    professional administration: 460
    education and social services: 2,145
    arts and leisure: 1,121
    other: 221
    public administration: 273

Average hourly earnings of production workers: $16.08

Unemployment rate: 13.4% (2012)

Employers

Largest employers (2013)	Number of employees
College of William & Mary	at least 1,000
Colonial Williamsburg Foundation	at least 1,000
Colonial Williamsburg Company	at least 1,000
W-JCC Schools	250 to 499
Aramark	250 to 499
City of Williamsburg	250 to 499
Red Lobster & The Olive Garden	100 to 249
Walsingham Academy	100 to 249
National Center for State Courts	100 to 249
Outback Steakhouse	50 to 99

Cost of Living

The following is a summary of data regarding several key cost of living factors in the area.

State income tax rate: 2.0% to 5.75%

State sales tax rate: 5%

Local income tax rate: None

Local sales tax rate: 1%

Property tax rate: $0.77 per $100 of assessed value (2013)

Economic Information: City of Williamsburg Office of Economic Development, 401 Lafayette Street, Williamsburg, VA 23185; telephone (757) 220-6120.

■ Education and Research

Elementary and Secondary Schools

Williamsburg-James City County Public Schools has nine elementary schools, three middle schools, and three high schools. James River Elementary School is an authorized International Baccalaureate School for students from kindergarten to fifth grade. The district also offers GED and adult education programming, including a testing center. A program for high school students behind in their studies allows them to work for their GED with focused preparatory courses. In 2012 the district had 22 commended students as recognized by the National Merit Scholarship Program.

Independent schools in the area are Williamsburg Christian Academy, Walsingham Academy, and Walnut Hills Baptist Church Learning Center.

The following is a summary of data regarding the Williamsburg-James City Public Schools.

Total enrollment: 10,857

Number of facilities

    total: 15
    elementary schools: 9
    junior high schools: 3
    high schools: 3

Student/teacher ratio: 16.61:1

Teacher salaries

    average (statewide): $51,559

Funding per pupil: $10,843

Public Schools Information: Williamsburg-James City County Public Schools, 117 Ironbound Road, Williamsburg, VA. 23185; telephone (757) 603-6400.

Colleges and Universities

The College of William and Mary is a four-year university. It is the second oldest college in the United States, having been established by King William III and Queen Mary II of England in 1673. The school has two campuses, one in Williamsburg and one in Gloucester Point, which houses the Virginia Institute of Marine Science. Presidents Thomas Jefferson, James Monroe, and John Tyler attended the College of William and Mary.

Christopher Newport University, located in Newport News, is a public liberal arts college that offered more than 80 undergraduate and graduate programs of study to its 5,186 students in 2013. It also has ties to William and Mary, being established in 1960 as a two-year school of the College of William and Mary. It became a four-year college in 1971 and a university in 1992. Hampton University in Hampton is a private, non-sectarian, co-educational, historically black university that enrolled just under 5,000 students in 2013.

Old Dominion University is a large public university in Norfolk, Virginia. Originally begun in 1930 as a division of the College of William and Mary, it officially became a university in 1969 and has a combined undergraduate and graduate enrollment of about 25,000 students. From baccalaureate to doctoral programs, Old Dominion grants degrees in education, liberal arts, business and public administration, sciences, health sciences, engineering, and technology.

Other universities an hour away are Virginia Commonwealth University, and Virginia Union University in Richmond. Thomas Nelson Community College offers two-year degrees.

Libraries and Research Centers

The Williamsburg Regional Library has two branches: The Williamsburg Library, and the James City County Library. The Williamsburg Library has a collection of 150,000 items that spans 40,000 square feet. Besides its many volumes, the library houses a theatre, art gallery, and even meetings rooms that can be used for programming. The James City County Library, the smaller of the two, has 100,000 volumes and is 35,000 square feet in size. The library contains a computer literacy center for families, meeting rooms, and electronic resources.

The John D. Rockefeller, Jr., Library in Colonial Williamsburg has been the site of historical manuscripts, archaeological drawings, and rare works from early America since it opened in 1997. The collection concentrates on eighteenth century history and culture, and largely focuses on the American Revolutionary War. The library also contains a photography archive. By 2009, the library had acquired the William Ashley certificate of freedom and estate papers, 1845-1915; the John Tadlock bill of sale for a slave girl, from August 1, 1795; and the Jonathan Ela Account Book, 1776-1824, among other original documents. Besides being on display at the library, images of these acquisitions are also available online.

The College of William and Mary has multiple libraries including the 400,000-volume Wolf Law Library, and the Earl Gregg Swem Library. The Earl Gregg Swem Library houses the university archives, rare books collection, Chief Justice Warren E. Burger collection, and other rare manuscripts.

Public Library Information: The Williamsburg Regional Library, 7770 Croaker Rd., Williamsburg, VA, 23188; telephone (757)259-4040; fax (757) 259-7798

■ Health Care

Williamsburg offers a wide choice of medical treatment facilities to its residents. Sentara Williamsburg Regional Medical Center is a 145-bed hospital with a 24-hour emergency room center. Sentara Healthcare also operates hospitals in nine other cities throughout Virginia. Sentara Norfolk General Hospital, located in its namesake city, was ranked by *U.S. News and World Report* as one of the top hospitals in Virginia. Sentara's Williamsburg facility was ranked third regionally. Riverside Doctors Hospital of Williamsburg opened in 2013 and is a two-story, 100,000-square-foot facility located on 25 acres. The hospital has a 12-room emergency department, 40 private rooms, 33 surgical rooms, and 7 intensive care rooms. Eastern State Hospital is psychiatric health facility in Williamsburg that was the first psychiatric hospital in the Americas, founded in1773.

■ Recreation

Sightseeing

The city's largest and best known attraction is Colonial Williamsburg, a re-enactment of seventeenth century life in the nation's earliest settlements. Nestled within Colonial Williamsburg's 301 acres is historic Jamestown Settlement, the site of America's first permanent settlement that was established in 1607. Jamestown features replicas of three British ships, Powhatan village, the colonists' fort, and other exhibits narrated by costumed interpreters. Visitors can tour Yorktown Battlefield, the birthplace of America's independence, to see buildings, cannons, and monuments that commemorate Britain's last stand at Surrender Field. The Yorktown Victory Center museum serves as a glimpse into military, and civilian life during the American Revolution. Colonial Williamsburg also hosts programs such as walking tours, arts performances, political speeches, craft demonstrations, military parades, and African-American historical programs that are performed by actors. Visitors can also witness rare breeds of live animals from olden times, such as Leicester Longwool Sheep, American Cream Draft Horses, American Milking Red Devons, and English Game Fowls. Haunted ghost walks in Colonial Williamsburg are led by costumed guides who bring old legends to life throughout town.

Williamsburg is home to many original residences, including Berkeley Plantation on the James River. Guests can explore the expansive gardens and terraces that once decorated the plantation, which was the headquarters of General McClellan during the Civil War, and the site of the first Thanksgiving. Bassett Hall is an eighteenth century house on 585 acres, and was once the dwelling of John D. Rockefeller, Jr. It is open to visitors with passes to Colonial Williamsburg.

The Mariners' Museum, located in nearby Newport News, contains a unique collection of more than 35,000 figureheads, paintings, small craft, ship models, and other marine artifacts. In addition, the museum offers demonstrations by costumed interpreters, films, and a five-mile nature trail around picturesque Lake Murray.

Busch Gardens, owned by SeaWorld Parks and Entertainment, is an amusement park in the Williamsburg area. During the summer months, guests can enjoy Water Country USA, Busch Gardens' water park. The park is home to a 23,000-square-foot wave pool, lazy river, and more than 35 other wet attractions. Strange illusions are on display at Ripley's Believe it or Not! Museum in Williamsburg. The museum features art made from normal objects, strange hobby collections, interactive displays, and a 4-D theater.

Williamsburg AleWerks, which opened in 2006, is one of the youngest attractions in the city. The brewery offers year-round tours of facilities where its seasonal beers are made.

Arts and Culture

Williamsburg's rich historical background is attributed to its wealth of cultural and arts organizations. The Williamsburg Players is the city's oldest continuous community theatre act. Established in 1984, the Williamsburg Symphonia was originally meant to perform educational shows for children. The Symphonia evolved into performing classical music concerts for the entire public.

Williamsburg also boasts plenty of art and photography galleries and numerous museums. The most significant history museum in the city is Colonial Williamsburg, which features hundreds of restored buildings and reminders of early settlement life. Notable museums on the premises include the DeWitt Wallace Decorative Arts Museum, and the Abbey Aldrich Rockefeller Folk Art Museum.

The Virginia Arts Festival performs in Williamsburg in May, and features chamber music, jazz, and dance acts. The College of William and Mary's Virginia Shakespeare Festival features the comedies and tragedies of Shakespeare, which are performed during the summer months. Riverwalk Landing in Yorktown is a popular venue for seasonal performances, as well as Lake Matoaka Amphitheatre on the campus of William and Mary.

Festivals and Holidays

The Colonial Williamsburg Garden Symposium, held annually in late April, is a conference for gardeners to learn more about their craft. The symposium usually happens close to Historic Garden Week, which highlights local plantations, in late April. Jamestown Landing Day, also in May, celebrates the founding of Jamestown with replicas of ships and historical demonstrations. The Virginia Beer Festival, which features beers from around the world, takes place in May at Town Point Park in nearby Norfolk. Rhythms on the Riverwalk is a five-week concert series in Historic Yorktown. The Williamsburg Scottish Festival, which features live music and traditional Scottish food, happens in September. Colonial Williamsburg hosts a Veterans Day celebration every November. Fireworks and candles light up historic Colonial Williamsburg for the famed Grand Illumination the first Sunday in December each year. First Night Williamsburg is the New Years Eve festival hosted in Downtown Williamsburg, and the College of William and Mary.

Sports for the Spectator

Williamsburg has no professional sports teams but is home to the College of William and Mary Tribe athletics. The Tribe has men's and women's basketball, cross county, golf, gymnastics, swimming and diving, tennis, and track and field teams, as well as men's football, and other sports. Football can be watched at Zable Stadium at Cary Field, and basketball games can be seen at Kaplan Arena at William and Mary Hall. Local high school sports teams are the Lafayette Rams, Bruton Panthers, and Warhill Lions. Residents can also travel to Richmond or other nearby cities to watch professional teams play.

Sports for the Participant

Golfing is a popular pastime in Williamsburg, which boasts eight courses among its wooded features. The Kingsmill Resort is home to courses designed by golfing greats Arnold Palmer and Pete Dye. The resort has been listed among the 75 Best Golf Resorts in North America by *Golf Digest*. Other notable courses are Kiskiack Golf Club, Stonehouse Golf Course, and Williamsburg National Golf Course.

Williamsburg maintains nine parks, playgrounds, tennis courts, and a dog park. The Quarterpath Park Pool is available for recreational swimming. Residents can participate in a variety of athletic programs through the City of Williamsburg Parks and Recreation Departments. League sports offered are basketball, softball, tennis, and volleyball. Youth athletic programs and summer camps are also offered. Williamsburg hosts the Run for the Dream Half-Marathon annually, which also includes an eight-kilometer run and a fun-run.

Shopping and Dining

Many of the shopping areas in Williamsburg feature items that are unique to the Colonial era, such as quilts, home décor, jewelry, and patriotic mementos. Merchants Square in Colonial Williamsburg is the area's first shopping center, having been established in 1927. It features a variety of bookstores, clothing shops, specialty stores, and restaurants. Riverwalk Landing at Yorktown features more than 10 specialty stores, cafes, and restaurants near the beach. New Town is a mixed-use development that spans 365 acres in Williamsburg. Besides being an important hub for the College of William and Mary, it houses many mainstream stores including Ann Taylor Loft, Footlocker, Bath and Body Works, and White House Black Market. Those who want an alternative shopping experience can visit the Williamsburg Antique Mall, a 45,000-square-foot center that contains 400 booths of unique finds. Other area shopping sites include the shops at High Street, and Williamsburg Premium Outlets, which features an array of outlet stores including Coach, Cole Haan, Michael Kors, and Hugo Boss.

Dining in Williamsburg spans a variety of traditions, including American, Japanese, Chinese, Italian, French, and Southern foods. Visitors can choose from many unique restaurants, including local favorite Captain George's, which hosts a buffet-style haunted dinner theater.

Visitor Information: The Greater Williamsburg Chamber and Tourism Alliance, 421 North Boundary St., Williamsburg, VA, 23187; telephone (757) 229-6511.

■ Convention Facilities

There is no main convention center in Williamsburg; instead, the College of William and Mary facilities and numerous hotels serve the purpose of accommodating groups. Kaplan Arena at William and Mary Hall is a multi-purpose venue that can accommodate 8,973 seated guests, and 10,175 guests for concerts. The space is ideal for hosting trade shows, full-stage events, graduations, athletic events, and so forth. The largest hotel in the area is the Williamsburg Marriott Hotel, which has 45,000 square feet of total meeting space consisting of 45 meetings rooms. The President's Ballroom, the largest meeting space, is 12,672 square feet and can seat 1,657 attendees. The rejuvenated Williamsburg Lodge in Colonial Williamsburg offers 29,000 square feet of meeting space, and can hold 1,300 people at theater-style capacity. There are 17 available meeting rooms, and four guesthouses featuring 30 hotel rooms each. Other area hotels with significant meeting space are the Lexington George Washington Inn and Conference Center, Crown Plaza Williamsburg Hotel and Conference Center, the Fort Magruder Hotel and Conference Center, and Kingsmill George Washington Inn and Conference Center. Area hotels have more than 5,000 guest rooms to accommodate visitors.

Convention Information: The Greater Williamsburg Chamber and Tourism Alliance, P.O. Box 3495, 421 North Boundary St., Williamsburg, VA, 23187; telephone (757)229-6511

■ Transportation

Approaching the City

The closest full-service airport that serves the region is the Newport News/Williamsburg International Airport, located 20 minutes outside Williamsburg. It is served by Allegiant, Apple Vacations, Delta, Frontier, US Airways, and People Express airlines, which travel non-stop to multiple destinations every day. The airport also accommodates corporate and general aviation air craft carriers. The airport serves more than one million passengers annually. Norfolk International Airport and Richmond International Airport are located some 45 minutes from Williamsburg on either side of the city. The Williamsburg-Jamestown Airport, though only two miles from the city, is a small airport that offers maintenance services, and private service for small light-frame planes. For visitors arriving by car, Williamsburg can be reached by Interstates 64 and 85, which are the two major highways.

Williamsburg Transportation Center is a full-service hub for travelers going to and from the city. Located a mere four blocks from Colonial Williamsburg, the center houses Amtrak offices, bus and car rental offices, waiting rooms and vending machines. Companies such as Amtrak, Greyhound, Trailways Bus Lines, Williamsburg Area Transport buses, Colonial Rent-a-Car, Yellow Cab of Williamsburg, Historic Taxi, and Williamsburg Taxi Service operate though the station.

Traveling in the City

Williamsburg Area Transport provides bus transportation to visitors and residents. There are nine bus routes throughout the city. Williamsburg Area Transport offers service for people with disabilities, as well as many other organizations in the city. Williamsburg Trolley runs every half hour from early afternoon until evening, stopping at High Street, Merchants Square, New Town, and Richmond Road.

■ Communications

Newspapers and Magazines

The Virginia Gazette is Williamsburg's major newspaper, and is published twice during the week. The nearest major daily newspaper is the *Richmond Times Dispatch.* Colonial Williamsburg publishes its own history journal, *Colonial Williamsburg,* which is published quarterly. Other research-oriented publications include the *William and Mary Quarterly,* and the *Bill of Rights Journal. Ideation Magazine* is a scholarly publication that highlights artistic and research endeavors within the College of William and Mary that is published twice a year. The college also prints the *Journal of Women and the Law,* a publication which promotes debate about gender issues within the legal realm.

Television and Radio

Residents can tune into many television stations within the Hampton Roads region. Cable and satellite television service is widely available. Radio listeners can listen to AM/FM radio stations throughout the city that play contemporary music, sports commentary, classical, and religious programming.

Media Information: *The Virginia Gazette,* 216 Ironbound Rd., Williamsburg, VA, 23188; telephone (757) 220-1736; fax (757) 220-1736.

Williamsburg Online

The Virginia Gazette. Available www.vagazette.com
Greater Williamsburg Chamber and Tourism Alliance. Available www.williamsburgcc.com
Williamsburg Area Convention and Visitors Bureau. Available www.visitwilliamsburg.com
Williamsburg-James City County Public Schools. Available www.edline.net/pages/WJCC
Williamsburg Regional Library. Available www.wrl.org
City of Williamsburg Available www.williamsburgva.gov

BIBLIOGRAPHY

Monroe, Lisa Oliver, *Williamsburg with Jamestown and Yorktown, America's Historic Triangle* (New York: Channel Lake Inc, 2010)

Wright, Renee, *Virginia Beach, Richmond, and Tidewater Virginia including Williamsburg, Norfolk, and Jamestown* (Woodstock, VT: Countryman Press, 2010)

Washington, D.C.

■ The City in Brief

Founded: 1790 (authorized by Congressional act)

Head Official: Mayor Vincent Gray (D) (since 2011; current term expires 2015)

City Population

    1990: 607,000
    2000: 572,059
    2010: 601,723
    2012 estimate: 632,323
    Percent change, 2000–2010: 5.2%
    U.S. rank in 1990: 19th
    U.S. rank in 2000: 21st
    U.S. rank in 2010: 24th

Metropolitan Statistical Area Population

    2000: 4,796,183
    2010: 5,582,170
    2012 estimate: 5,804,333
    Percent change, 2000–2010: 16.4%
    U.S. rank in 2000: 7th
    U.S. rank in 2010: 7th

Area: 68.3 square miles

Elevation: Ranges from 40 to 410 feet above sea level

Average Annual Temperatures: 54.0° F

Average Annual Precipitation: 39.73 inches

Major Economic Sectors: government, health and education services, hospitality, wholesale and retail trade

Unemployment Rate: 7.1% (2012)

Per Capita Income: $44,670

2012 FBI Crime Index Property: 29,264

Major Colleges and Universities: Georgetown University, Howard University, American University, Catholic University of America, George Washington University

Daily Newspaper: *The Washington Post; The Washington Times*

■ Introduction

During the nineteenth century, Washington, D.C., the capital of the United States, was considered so unbearably warm and humid during the summer months that foreign diplomats received hardship pay for serving there. Now, the district holds a worldwide reputation as a cosmopolitan city rich in museums, monuments, and culture—and crackling with political power. From the hill where the U.S. Capitol sits to Embassy Row, home to much of the foreign diplomatic corps in Washington, the wide avenues hum with the business of America.

Heavy industry never took hold in the region, and outside the downtown government district and the upscale northwest quarter of the city, poverty still grips many residents. City officials have worked hard to change that, tailoring comprehensive development projects to specific parts of the city. Residents from the surrounding suburbs commute on one of the nation's busiest subway systems, and the population living within the District continued to expand rapidly through the 2010s. Despite of the city's burgeoning population and fast-paced life, Washingtonians pride themselves on retaining almost southern-style hospitality. In the words of Frederick Douglass, "Wherever the American citizen may be a stranger, he is at home here."

■ Geography and Climate

Located on the Potomac River between the Blue Ridge Mountains and the Atlantic Ocean, Washington is known

The White House, Washington, D.C. *Jeremy R. Smith Sr./Shutterstock.com*

for its hot, humid summers, pleasant springs and autumns, and mild winters with seasonal snowfall averaging about 15 inches. Carved from south-central Maryland, Washington is bordered on three sides by that state and sits across the Potomac River from Virginia on its fourth side. The District is also divided by the Anacostia River and Rock Creek. One fourth of the District is park land. The city is divided artificially into four quadrants: northeast, northwest, southeast, and southwest.

Area: 68.3 square miles

Elevation: Ranges from 40 to 410 feet above sea level

Average Temperatures: 54.0° F

Average Annual Precipitation: 39.73 inches

■ History

George Washington Chooses Capital's Site
When the U.S. Congress sought a new capital for the young United States in the late eighteenth century, it chose an obscure piece of undeveloped swampland on the Potomac River. This unlikely location was a compromise. Southern politicians resisted placement of the capital too far north in New York or New England. For all representatives—northern and southern alike—Philadelphia, the capital in 1783, was deemed too close to potentially volatile constituents, especially one band of angry soldiers who had disrupted a Congressional session earlier that year to demand back pay. Determining the new capital's exact location was left to President George Washington, who had known the area since boyhood. The diamond-shaped district he carved out included parts of Maryland and Virginia. President Washington modestly referred to the city that came to bear his name as the Federal City.

Early Days of Future Capital
In 1571 Pedro Menendez, a Spanish admiral who founded St. Augustine and was governor of Spain's Florida territories, was the first European to explore the future capital region. The area became a trading center for British settlers who dealt with Native Americans of the region. The Potomac River, one of the few native place names to survive from the colonial period, means "trading place" in the Algonquin language. Later, white landowners in the region made huge profits growing tobacco.

When the area was selected as the new capital site in 1790, Congress had almost no money to spend on its future home. Virginia and Maryland contributed small sums to erect public buildings, but President Washington was left to barter for property with tobacco-growing landowners in the area. Meanwhile, the task of creating the look of a capital city worthy of the new nation fell to Pierre L'Enfant, a French architect and engineer also selected by President Washington, who eventually persuaded tobacco planters to sell their land cheaply. At the time, L'Enfant's vision of boulevards 400-feet wide and one-mile long lined by great buildings seemed like a waste of real estate to the property owners.

Nonetheless, the first temporary buildings of the new capital were ready in 1800, and in May of that year, the government left Philadelphia. One year later, Thomas Jefferson became the first U.S. president inaugurated in Washington. But L'Enfant's vision of what Washington should be remained for decades just a vision. Today's grand Pennsylvania Avenue was an unpaved road from the U.S. Capitol to the White House and a muddy path on the other side of the White House during the first half of the nineteenth century. Americans and foreign diplomats assigned to the city dreaded its dull cultural life and oppressive summers. Few houses and plenty of open space separated official buildings.

War's Impact on the City

The War of 1812 made life in Washington even more unpleasant, as British forces stormed the city in 1814, burning the President's House—later rebuilt, painted white, and forever after known as the White House—as well as the partially completed U.S. Capitol and other federal buildings. By the 1860s Washington's population had grown to 75,000 people. As the geographic border between the North and South, the District of Columbia acutely felt the mounting tension between factions at the approach of the Civil War. President Abraham Lincoln's 1861 inauguration was completed under a heavily armed phalanx of soldiers ready to repel an attack by the South. Washington was the headquarters for Union troops during the four-year war, and several times during the bloody conflict Confederate troops nearly took the capital, defeated only by bad luck or faulty military intelligence.

Government Buildings Proliferate

Gradually, Washington architects filled in the blanks left by L'Enfant. The Mall—a vast tree-lined park stretching out from the U.S. Capitol—sprouted other government buildings and the Smithsonian museums. Tributes to some of the nation's great men were built: the Washington Monument, the Lincoln Memorial, and the Jefferson Memorial. The population of the city jumped during World War I as the civil service rapidly expanded, and again during the Great Depression of the 1930s

when working for the government was the most secure employment. Many current government buildings date from the 1930s when President Franklin D. Roosevelt's Works Progress Administration erected offices for the Internal Revenue, Commerce, and other federal departments.

Washington during the 1960s reflected the social upheaval and turbulence experienced throughout the nation. The 1963 "March on Washington for Jobs and Freedom" showed America at its best and most righteous. It was there that Martin Luther King Jr. delivered his inspirational "I have a dream" speech to 200,000 citizens. But when King was assassinated in Memphis, Tennessee, in 1968, violent riots rocked the capital. Recovering from the damage during the last half of the 1970s and into the 1980s, the capital enjoyed an economic rebirth with major commercial projects downtown and in some neighborhoods.

Behind the glitter and glamour attendant upon conducting one of the world's most powerful governments, though, lay a district plagued by many problems. In the 1990s Washington, D.C., suffered from virtual insolvency, a crumbling infrastructure, and significant population loss. Since 1995 Washington, D.C., has operated under a federal control board to manage spending. The board stripped the local school board of most of its powers and eliminated thousands of jobs. Anthony Williams, appointed the city's first independent chief financial officer, managed to reverse years of fiscal mismanagement and turned a runaway budget deficit into a steadily growing surplus. He also hired highly qualified people, held them accountable, and streamlined agencies under his control. In 1999 Williams was elected mayor; by that time Washington, D.C., had come a long way toward reversing its decline. Williams continued to place emphasis on the city's economy, housing, health care, education, and public safety.

Never was the nation's reverence for its capital city more reaffirmed than in the wake of the tragic September 11, 2001, terrorist attacks that shook New York and Washington, D.C. One of several hijacked planes was crashed into the massive, fortress-like Pentagon Building, claiming the lives of more than 120 people. It is widely believed that another hijacked aircraft, which eventually was forced down by heroic passengers in Pennsylvania, was bound for the Capitol Building. Residents were somberly reminded of the city's prominence as the greatest seat of political power on the planet.

In the later 2000s and into the 2010s, the city made inroads to diversify its economy away from jobs in the federal government and those dependent upon it. The necessity to do so was made abundantly clear after deep cuts in the federal budget, known as sequestration, that took place in 2013 and reverberated into 2014. Attracting high-technology jobs was a priority of the municipal government. The real estate market, for both homes and offices, drove significant development and allowed the city to pursue its goal of becoming the nation's "greenest" city by the 2030s. Efforts at elimination of poverty focused on improving student performance and preparing young adults for the modern work environment.

Historical Information: Historical Society of Washington, D.C., City Museum of Washington, D.C., 801 K Street, NW, Washington, DC 20001; telephone (202) 249-3955; email info@historydc.org.

■ Population Profile

Metropolitan Statistical Area Population

2000: 4,796,183
2010: 5,582,170
2012 estimate: 5,804,333
Percent change, 2000–2010: 16.4%
U.S. rank in 2000: 7th
U.S. rank in 2010: 7th

City Residents

1990: 607,000
2000: 572,059
2010: 601,723
2012 estimate: 632,323
Percent change, 2000–2010: 5.2%
U.S. rank in 1990: 19th
U.S. rank in 2000: 21st
U.S. rank in 2010: 24th

Density: 9,856.5 people per square mile

Racial and ethnic characteristics

White: 247,079
Black or African American: 311,415
American Indian and Alaskan Native: 2,018
Asian: 21,923
Native Hawaiian and Other Pacific Islander: 105
Hispanic or Latino (may be of any race): 59,076
Other: 36,237

Percent of residents born in state: 37.6%

Age characteristics

Population under 5 years old: 35,966
Population 5 to 9 years old: 28,017
Population 10 to 14 years old: 24,659
Population 15 to 19 years old: 40,170
Population 20 to 24 years old: 61,368
Population 25 to 34 years old: 132,832
Population 35 to 44 years old: 83,042
Population 45 to 54 years old: 75,963
Population 55 to 59 years old: 34,634
Population 60 to 64 years old: 31,824
Population 65 to 74 years old: 38,243
Population 75 to 84 years old: 21,830

Population 85 years and over: 10,229
Median age: 33.7

Births (2010–11 Metropolitan Area)

Total number: 78,603

Deaths (2010–11 Metropolitan Area)

Total number: 30,368

Money income (2012)

Per capita income: $44,670
Median household income: $64,610
Total households: 261,567

Number of households with income of . . .

less than $10,000: 27,198
$10,000 to $14,999: 12,420
$15,000 to $24,999: 20,368
$25,000 to $34,999: 18,542
$35,000 to $49,999: 27,558
$50,000 to $74,999: 38,940
$75,000 to $99,999: 28,151
$100,000 to $149,999: 38,709
$150,000 to $199,999: 19,122
$200,000 or more: 30,559

Percent of families below poverty level: 18.8%

FBI Crime Index Property: 29,264

FBI Crime Index Violent: 7,448

■ Municipal Government

Washington won the right to govern itself in 1975. Until then, Congress had complete jurisdiction over the District. Now Washington is led by a mayor and 13 city council members, all of whom serve four-year terms. Eight city council members represent separate wards while five, including a chairman, are elected at large. District voters also elect a non-voting delegate to the U.S. Congress.

Head Official: Mayor Vincent Gray (D) (since 2011; current term expires 2015)

Total Number of City Employees: 27,209 (2012)

City Information: Council of the District of Columbia, 1350 Pennsylvania Avenue, NW, Washington, D.C. 20004; telephone (202)724-8000

■ Economy

Major Industries and Commercial Activity

Key sectors driving the economy continued to be the federal government, technology, construction, international business, health and education services, and hospitality. People often think of Washington, D.C., as a "company town" where most people work for the federal government. However, by the early twenty-first century, federal government employment was below peak levels of the late 1960s due to gradual downsizing and streamlining, including the effects of forced federal spending cuts known as sequestration that took place in 2013 and continued into 2014.

By contrast, private sector jobs have increased dramatically, especially in the service sector. Still, many employees work for companies who rely on government contracts. As one of the largest consumers of technological equipment and service in the world, the federal government stimulates business through purchases, research and development funding, and grant and loan programs. As a result, Washington is a magnet for growth industries, such as paper products, telecommunications, information and computer firms, and many service industries, especially tourism and hospitality firms.

There are hundreds publishing and printing companies in the district to produce the vast array of electronic and paper documents generated by the federal government. In addition, the city houses more than 1,000 national associations' headquarters and lobby groups who maintain a presence to attempt to shape and influence the legislative process on their behalf.

The Capital City has an inventory of more than 100 million square feet of office space. Between 2010 and 2012 alone, some $2.8 billion in office development took place. A key to office development has been the growth of the Metrorail subway stations. As of 2012 the Metrorail system included 106.3 miles of track and 86 operating stations, a key factor in convenient and efficient business travel. Commercial projects typically have followed the opening of new subway stops. Many new buildings are connected directly to the stations through underground tunnels that also serve retail stores and restaurants.

The District's "Great Streets" program, an initiative of Mayor Gray, invests in revitalizing 11 major street corridors to create new opportunities for housing, retail, and office projects. By 2013, major improvements had been made to Howard Theatre, H Street, and Georgia Avenue and Petworth.

Items and goods produced: printed and published documents; telecommunications equipment

Incentive Programs-New and Existing Companies

Local programs: The DC Department of Small & Local Business Development (DSLBD) offers site visits, counseling, classes, and workshops to support small and local business enterprises. It also manages a certified business enterprise microloan program to provide small businesses with up to $25,000 in start-up capital. The

program operates in conjunction with the Washington Area Community Investment Fund. DSLBD partners with Kauffman FastTrac for the FastTrac DC initiative, which works to translate local business ideas into reality. FastTrac DC features three training programs to support different business stages and industries: NewVenture, GrowthVenture, and TechVenture. The D.C. Chamber of Commerce also supports a Business Resource Center that also offers training and consulting for area businesses.

The DC Enterprise Zone (DCEZ) was created for in 1997, providing up to $1.2 billion in federal tax credits, deductions, exemptions, and conclusions. Included among these was tax-exempt bond financing, exclusion of capital gains from DCEZ assets, employee and work opportunity tax credits, and a welfare-to-work tax credit. The city also sponsored Work Opportunity Tax Credits, making D.C.-area business eligible for up to $9,000 of credits over two years for hiring an employee that previously qualified as a "long-term family assistance recipient." A separate tax credit of $2,400 is available for the hiring of economically disadvantaged persons in the area. DC Tech Incentives provides credits and exemptions for qualifying high-tech companies; the program formerly was known as NET 2000.

Job training programs: The D.C. Department of Employment Services contracts with private companies to provide customized training programs through the D.C. Private Industry Council, the federal Workforce Investment Act (WIA, formerly Job Training Partnership Act), the Youth Employment Act, the Training and Retraining for Employment Program, the On-The-Job Training program, and through the One-Stop Career Center approach now in effect in several states and supported in part by the Department of Labor. Contracts have encompassed such areas as shop training, technical training, basic education areas, office skills, legal research, food service, tourism, art-related occupations, industrial maintenance, mail handling, bank tellering, health care, child care, truck driving, construction industry retraining, and brick and masonry training. The city initiated a workforce intermediary program in 2011 to support hiring in hospitality, retail, and construction sectors, in large part to recover jobs lost during economic recession in the late 2000s. The "Raise DC" effort, sponsored by the city government, partnered with local business and community leaders to establish procedures to better prepare young residents to enter the local workforce. The D.C. Department of Employment Services also provides a variety of tax credits and wage reimbursements to qualified employers.

Development Projects

Washington, D.C., adopted a new comprehensive development plan in 2006 that has served as the basis for ongoing development projects and city improvements. Rapid population growth during the 2010s fueled significant construction in both housing and commercial building, with some 4,900 housing units added between 2010 and 2012, with another 2,000 units rehabilitated. Guiding construction decisions was the Sustainable DC Initiative, which sought to make the capital the nation's leader in green building development by 2032. An estimated 37-square-feet per capita of Leadership in Energy & Environmental Design (LEED)–certified construction took place in the District during 2012 alone. That year, employment in real estate and construction was at its highest level in more than two decades.

Part of the city's development involved comprehensive development of small geographic areas, referred to as Small Area Plans. Locations within a Small Area Plan made up 45 percent of new housing developments between 2010 and 2012, despite representing only 10 percent of the city's geographic area. They also accounted for 21 percent of the city's new office space, 61 percent of new medical offices, and 27 percent of new retail outlets.

Transit-oriented development was exemplified by "The Avenue" development on Square 54, completed in 2011. The development, located directly above the Foggy Bottom Metrorail stop, used $213 million in private investment from Boston Properties to construct 400,000 square feet of new office space, 335 new residences, and 80,000 square feet of retail space. Eighty percent of all new housing and 91 percent of all new office space built between 2010 and 2012 was within one-half mile of a Metrorail station.

In addition to new construction and revitalization projects, the District worked to preserve some of its oldest structures, distributing a total of $650,000 to low- and moderate-income homeowners to maintain and improve their historic structures between 2010 and 2012. During that same time period, the city designated 41 properties as historic landmarks.

Future development visions focused on a continuation and growth of sustainable construction and refurbishment, a diversification away from reliance on growth in federal employment, a reduction in retail leakage caused by an absence of sufficient retail within District limits, and enhanced efforts to prepare the local workforce for employment.

Economic Development Information: Washington, DC Economic Partnership, 1495 F Street, NW, Washington, D.C. 20004; telephone (202) 661-8670; DC Chamber of Commerce, 506 9th Street, NW, Washington, DC 20004; telephone (202) 347-7201.

Commercial Shipping

Ronald Reagan National Airport, Dulles International Airport, and Baltimore/Washington International Airport handle the bulk of air freight in the area and provide comprehensive cargo service to domestic and international destinations. For shipping, Washington, D.C., mainly utilizes large port facilities in Baltimore, Maryland, and in both Alexandria and Norfolk, Virginia, although there are also smaller ports on the Anacostia and Potomac Rivers.

Labor Force and Employment Outlook

The D.C. Department of Employment Services Office of Market Research and Information issues reports identifying high-demand and emerging occupations. Employment projections for 2010–20 suggested the highest gains in goods-producing industries, such as construction, and professional and business services, including management and technical consulting, and security services. A decrease in information services—especially newspaper, periodical, and book publishing—was expected, as were slight gains in financial and other service-sector jobs. In the near term, an increase in computer and scientific design was expected to pace job growth.

The following is a summary of data regarding the 2012 Washington, D.C., area labor force:

Size of civilian labor force: 352,623

Number of workers employed in . . .

   agriculture and mining: 158
   construction: 10,185
   manufacturing: 3,682
   wholesale trade: 1,997
   retail trade: 15,018
   transportation: 11,115
   information systems: 12,962
   finance: 16,881
   professional administration: 67,604
   education and social services: 61,209
   arts and leisure: 28,413
   other: 28,506
   public administration: 54,640

Average hourly earnings of production workers: $18.26

Unemployment rate: 7.1% (2012)

Employers

Largest employers (2012)	*Number of employees*
MedStar Health	15,773
Marriot International	15,000
Science Applications International Corporation	15,000
Northrop Grumman	14,451
Booz Allen Hamilton	13,900
University of Maryland at College Park	13,451

Inova Health System	12,963
Verizon	
Communications	12,600
Lockheed Martin	11,000
Safeway	9,432

Cost of Living

Housing costs in Washington, D.C., are higher than U.S. averages due primarily to the fact that approximately two-thirds of all land is either owned or controlled by the federal government, foreign embassies, and other non-profit organizations, which renders that land and property tax-exempt. New high-rise residential developments continued to appear throughout the 2010s.

The following is a summary of data regarding several key cost of living factors in the area.

2013 ACCRA Average House Price: $772,186

2013 ACCRA Cost of Living Index: 141

State income tax rate: Not applicable

State sales tax rate: Not applicable

Local income tax rate: 4.0% to 8.95%

Local sales tax rate: 6.0%

Property tax rate: $0.85 per $100 of assessed valuation (2013)

Economic Information: Washington, DC Economic Partnership, 1495 F Street, NW, Washington, D.C. 20004; telephone (202) 661-8670. District of Columbia Department of Employment Services, 4058 Minnesota Avenue, NE, Washington, D.C. 20019; telephone (202) 724-7000; email does@dc.gov.

■ Education and Research

Elementary and Secondary Schools

The District of Columbia's public school system is among the largest in the country. The school system is guided by a strategic plan covering the years 2012–17. The plan seeks to align curriculums with Common Core State Standards to improve proficiency rates in both reading and math, setting a goal of increasing 2010–11 proficiency rates of 43 percent to 70 percent by the end of the 2016–17 school year. Additionally, the plan placed as a goal an increase in four-year high-school graduation rates, from 53 percent (2010–11) to 75 percent (2016–17). To achieve this goal, the district implemented policies to increase early communication for students struggling at each grade level.

Dozens of private and parochial schools operate in the district with varied curriculums. Numerous major private schools, including several of national renown,

operate as traditional, parochial, and alternative/arts schools.

The following is a summary of data regarding the District of Columbia Public Schools.

Total enrollment: 44,199

Number of facilities

total: 129
elementary schools: 58
junior high schools: 34
high schools: 17
other: 20

Student/teacher ratio: 11.7:1

Teacher salaries

average (statewide): $Not available

Funding per pupil: $18,475

Public Schools Information: District of Columbia Public Schools, 1200 First Street, NE, Washington, D.C. 20002; telephone (202) 442-5885.

Colleges and Universities

Washington, D.C., is home to 17 colleges and universities. Georgetown University has one of the largest and most well known schools of international affairs, as well as law. Among its other accolades, Georgetown was ranked 20th on *US News & World Report's* list of top U.S. universities in 2013. Howard University is the alma mater of many prominent African Americans. Nearby in Baltimore, Johns Hopkins University is the nation's oldest research university. Other major institutions are American, Catholic, Gallaudet, George Washington, Corcoran College of Art and Design, Trinity, and the University of the District of Columbia. Several licensed trade and technical schools also operate in the district, including the ITT Technical Institute and the Harrison Center for Career Education.

Libraries and Research Centers

The Library of Congress is the nation's oldest federal cultural institution and serves as the research arm of Congress, responding to more than 700,000 Congressional requests in fiscal year 2012 alone. It is also the largest library in the world, with more than 151 million items as of 2013, including 34.5 million cataloged books in more than 470 languages, 3.4 million audio materials, 13.6 million photographs, 5.5 million maps, and 68 million manuscripts. The library maintains a permanent staff of roughly 3,300.

With Internet research becoming increasingly important, the Library of Congress has made many of its materials available online. Some 1.7 million unique visitors made their way to the library's website in fiscal year 2012, amounting to 87 million total visits and more than one-half billion page views. Primary-source documents catalogued online numbered about 37.6 million.

Founded in 1896, the District of Columbia Public Library system has 25 branches, as well as the main Martin Luther King Memorial Library. The Library Building Program guides the renovation and expansion of city library buildings, including green building initiatives. By 2013, the program had successfully renovated or rebuilt 14 libraries. Library construction projects in various stages of development during 2013 included branches in West End and Woodridge neighborhoods. Among the several special collections of the library system is Washingtoniana, which specializes in local history and celebrated its 100th anniversary in 2005. The Black Studies Center, founded in 1972, holds 15,000 volumes focusing on the African American experience in the United States.

There are nearly 600 special libraries in the District, including those maintained by foreign embassies, colleges and universities, and the Smithsonian Institution. The Smithsonian Institution Libraries alone consisted of 20 branches holding more than 1.5 million books and manuscripts as of 2013.

Public Library Information: District of Columbia Public Library, Martin Luther King Memorial Library, 901 G Street, NW, Washington, D.C. 20001; telephone (202) 727-0321. Library of Congress, 101 Independence Avenue, SE, Washington, D.C. 20540; telephone (202) 707-5000.

■ Health Care

The District of Columbia boasts one of the finest health-care systems in the country. Its 20 hospitals, many of which are affiliated with major medical schools and research centers, include hospitals at Georgetown, Howard, and George Washington universities. The city offers state-of-the-art specialty hospitals for women, children, and veterans; world-renowned centers for neuroscientific research and the study of fertility, pregnancy, and development; and nationally recognized services for trauma, cancer, heart disease, and organ transplants. Beginning in 2010, the District of Columbia Department of Health, which monitors the city's health concerns and provides assistance to the underserved, initiated the Live Well DC! program to encourage healthy lifestyle practices among all District residents. Its educational website served thousands of visitors annually. Also nearby in Baltimore, Maryland, is The Johns Hopkins Hospital and Health Systems, supported by the university's school of medicine and one of the most renowned medical-care and research facilities in the world. In 2013 the institution was named the nation's best hospital according to *U.S. News & World Report* for

the 22nd time in 23 years; it ranked in the top 10 for 15 specialty categories and claimed the number-one national rank for ear, nose, and throat; geriatrics; neurology and neurosurgery; rheumatology; and urology.

■ Recreation

Sightseeing

As a city with tremendous history as a worldwide capital, and also a place where news and historic events take place nearly every day, Washington, D.C., is one of the most popular tourist destinations for U.S. families, serious researchers, and foreign travelers. Visitors to Washington can choose from some 66 museums and more than 150 historical sites—many of them free of charge. Any tour of Washington starts on the Mall, the long strip of open park land between Capitol Hill and the Lincoln Memorial. Tours of the U.S. Capitol building are given Monday through Saturday, and visitors can receive admittance cards from their elected representatives to visit the House or Senate chambers, when in session. In the middle of the Mall, surrounded by American flags, stands the 555-foot-tall Washington Monument, completed in 1888. For many years, an elevator ride to the top provided the best—and highest—view of the District of Columbia. However, an August 2011 earthquake damaged the monument, closing access to the public until spring 2014 to allow $15 million in external and internal repairs. The president's residence, the White House, is the oldest public building in Washington and is open for tours Tuesday through Saturday. The majestic Lincoln Memorial, on the west end of the Mall, was finished in 1922. Here the 19-foot-high statue of Lincoln looks out over the Reflecting Pool, which mirrors the Washington Monument dramatically at dusk. Located between the Washington Monument and Lincoln Memorial is the World War II Memorial. Opened in April 2004, the memorial honors the 16 million who served in the war. In a special commemorative area of the memorial, a field of 4,000 gold stars sculpted on the Freedom Wall commemorates the more than 400,000 who sacrificed their lives during World War II. The Martin Luther King Jr. Memorial, which features a 30-foot stone statue of the civil rights leader emerging from a larger boulder, was dedicated in August 2011 and lies on a four-acre site along the Tidal Basin.

Just outside the Mall, the Jefferson Memorial, at the foot of the Tidal Basin, is a popular spot to view the city's famous cherry blossoms in the spring. The Vietnam Veteran's Memorial provides a moving experience for the millions of people who observe the names of the war dead with which it is inscribed. The Bureau of Engraving and Printing shows how it provides the nation with currency and stamps. The National Archives Museum offers daily tours and displays copies of the Declaration of

Independence, the U.S. Constitution, and the Bill of Rights, plus other key documents in U.S. history. The Library of Congress, besides being one of the nation's premier research facilities, also hosts concerts and literary programs. Sessions at the Supreme Court Building, near the U.S. Capitol, are always open to the public. Lafayette Park, across from the White House, is notable for frequent civil demonstrations on current issues, in addition to its statue honoring Andrew Jackson. Elsewhere in central Washington, costumed guides at the Frederick Douglass National Historic Site—home to Douglass's residence Cedar Hill—explain the life of the former slave, statesman, and civil rights activist. Ford's Theater, where Lincoln was shot, and the Petersen House, where he died, retain their 1860s style and are open to the public. The U.S. National Arboretum and Dumbarton Oaks on the edge of Georgetown display a breathtaking variety of plant life.

Sixteen miles outside the city, in Mount Vernon, Virginia, George Washington's Mount Vernon Estate and Gardens sits on 500 acres overlooking the Potomac River. Another of America's most revered monuments is the Arlington National Cemetery in nearby Arlington, Virginia. The 600-acre site bears thousands of simple white crosses to honor the nation's war dead, as well as the gravesites of other prominent citizens that include President John F. Kennedy, boxer Joe Louis, and the Tomb of the Unknowns.

Arts and Culture

Washington, D.C., is a cultural as well as governmental center. It boasts a higher concentration of museums and art galleries than any other city in the nation. The District of Columbia regularly attracts performers as diverse as touring Broadway shows and major rock and jazz acts to its opulent theaters and concert halls.

Much of Washington's cultural life is based in the John F. Kennedy Center for the Performing Arts, home of the National Symphony Orchestra and the Washington Opera, and host to almost daily performances by world-famous artists. The Kennedy Center presents more than 2,000 performances a year before more than two million guests. Each December the Kennedy Center Honors, a national celebration of the arts, recognizes the talents and achievements of the world's greatest performing artists. The Arena Stage and the National Theater all offer major stage shows, including dramas and musicals. Other local theater groups include the Shakespeare Theatre, Theater J, Source Theater, Wooly Mammoth Theatre Company, Studio Theatre, GALA Hispanic Theater, and scores more around the Washington, D.C., area. The Washington Ballet presents a varied repertoire, and the District of Columbia's African Heritage Dancers and Drummers present special children's programs. Young audiences enjoy special performances presented at the Kennedy Center Lab. Special events are also offered at the D.C.

Armory. Many college-affiliated groups offer theatrical performances.

Washington, D.C.'s many museums and galleries provide a feast of viewing variety. The museums operated by the Smithsonian Institution, often called "America's Attic," contain everything from a 50-foot section of the legendary American highway Route 66 to the original Kermit the Frog hand puppet, from Charles Lindbergh's historic trans-Atlantic solo plane, *The Spirit of St. Louis,* to Archie Bunker's armchair from the television series *All in the Family.* Most Smithsonian museums, which would take weeks to fully navigate, are located on or just off the Mall and include the National Air and Space Museum (with eight million annual visitors, the United States' most visited museum), Arts and Industries Building, Freer Gallery of Art, Hirshhorn Museum and Sculpture Garden (modern and contemporary art), National Museum of Natural History, National Museum of American History, Arthur M. Sackler Gallery of Asian Art, and the National Museum of African Art. The National Portrait Gallery and the National Museum of American Art reopened in July 2006 as a collective museum under the name of the Donald W. Reynolds Center for American Art and Portraiture. The National Museum of African American History and Culture was established by Congress in 2003 as the 19th Smithsonian Institution museum; a museum site was selected in January 2006, and construction was expected to be completed in 2015. The Smithsonian's National Zoological Park is set on 160 acres in Rock Creek Park and is home to about 2,000 animals of nearly 400 different species.

Other museums in the city include the International Spy Museum, National Museum of the Marine Corps, United States Holocaust Memorial Museum, Corcoran Gallery of Art (specializing in American art), Art Museum of the Americas, National Museum of Women in the Arts, and the National Building Museum. A planned science-fiction museum—covering literature, television, film, and music—was scheduled to open in 2017.

Festivals and Holidays

Washington, D.C.'s biggest and best-known celebration is the National Cherry Blossom Festival, stretching from late March to early April to coincide with the blooming of the trees. Started in 1927 to commemorate the planting of 3,000 Japanese cherry trees that were a gift from the mayor of Tokyo in 1912, the festival now runs roughly three weeks. Special events include a major parade, a Japanese lantern lighting ceremony and street festival with more than 80 exhibitors, and a Smithsonian Kite Festival held near the Washington Monument. Some 1.5 million people venture to the District annually to join in the festivities.

Other exciting annual events include January's antique and fine art event, the Washington Winter Show;

the Chinese New Year's celebration in February; the St. Patrick's Day Parade along Constitution Avenue in March; the White House Easter Egg Roll, the White House Spring Garden Tour, and Filmfest DC in April; the National Cinco de Mayo Festival in May; the National Capital Barbecue Battle in June; the Smithsonian's Folklife Festival in late June through early July; a massive July Fourth celebration; the Kennedy Center Prelude Festival in September to kick off the arts season; the Marine Corps Marathon in October, the November Washington Craft Show; and the lighting of the national Christmas tree outside the White House in December.

Sports for the Spectator

Plagued by controversy that almost squashed the deal, Washington, D.C., was finally able to convince taxpayers and Major League Baseball that it was the right place for the new home of Major League Baseball's struggling Montreal Expos franchise. The Washington Nationals began play in 2005 and brought big-league baseball back to the city for the first time since the old Washington Senators left town some 30 years prior. A new $400 million ballpark was opened for the 2008 season. Washington is home to four other top-level professional sports teams. The Washington Redskins, the true sporting passion of Washingtonians, face National Football League opponents at FedExField in Landover, Maryland. The Washington Capitals of the National Hockey League, the Washington Wizards of the National Basketball Association, and the Washington Mystics of the Women's National Basketball Association play at the Verizon Center (formerly the MCI Center). Georgetown University's basketball team has earned a national reputation for outstanding performance and is a perennial contender in the NCAA Division I tournament each March.

Sports for the Participant

Washington, D.C., offers a wide selection of participant sports. The city's close proximity to rivers, bays, and the Atlantic Ocean make a variety of water sports within reach, particularly boating, sailing, fishing, canoeing, scuba diving, and windsurfing. A true oasis in the city and one of its most treasured resources is Rock Creek Park, operated by the National Park Service and featuring more than 25 miles of trails for hiking among its 2,100 acres. In all, the city maintains more than 300 parks, including 90 playgrounds and gardens, 67 community recreation centers, 51 public swimming pools and aquatic centers, and more than 100 basketball and tennis courts. Every resident of the District, regardless of location, lives within two miles of a city-maintained recreation center.

Shopping and Dining

Avid shoppers can lose themselves in the proliferation of urban malls in downtown Washington, D.C. Perhaps the most legendary is Union Station, a historic urban shopping center with marble floors, 210,000 square feet of upscale shopping, 50,000 square feet of restaurant space, a full schedule of events and exhibitions, and nearly 33 million visitors a year. In keeping with the city's efforts toward sustainable development, Union Station announced in 2013 that it all of its electricity was generated by wind power. The glass-roofed Old Post Office Pavilion, once a working post office, is now home to retail concerns, restaurants, and offices and has been ranked as the one of the most popular destinations in the District.

A different kind of shopping experience is found in Georgetown, where unique boutiques and specialty stores are housed in historic townhouses, mostly along Wisconsin Avenue and M Street; elegant stores abound at The Shops At Georgetown Park. Mazza Gallerie is a three-story enclosed mall filled with elite shops, stylish boutiques, and a new state-of-the-art movie theater. Washington's Eastern Market, in the southeast section of the city, has been a farmer's market since 1873 with fresh fruit, vegetables, poultry, and sausage for sale. Weekends at the market are packed with even more options as the market hosts hundreds of local artists and artisans.

Restaurants in Washington reflect the influence of the many foreign cultures present in the capital. The city has seen an explosion of culinary creativity on the local restaurant scene. Top-ranked restaurants in 2013, according to *Washingtonian Magazine,* included The Inn at Little Washington, Komi, and CityZen. Many of the most interesting establishments are clustered in the Georgetown and Dupont Circle areas and in urban malls downtown. Capital Grille, located between the White House and the Capitol Building, is one of the best places to spot high-powered politicos gathered for lunch, drinks, or dinner.

Visitor Information: Destination DC, 901 Seventh Street, NW, Fourth Floor, Washington, D.C. 20001; telephone (202) 789-7000; fax (202) 789-7037.

■ Convention Facilities

In 2008 the Washington DC Convention and Tourism Corporation rebranded itself as Destination DC to promote Washington as a tourist and business destination; available facilities and amenities for conventions have grown to meet new demand. In 2013 there were 623 special-event venues in the District and nearly 30,000 hotel rooms. The 2.3-million-square-foot Walter E. Washington Convention Center opened in 2003 in the heart of downtown, with total of 703,000 square feet of exhibit space covering six city blocks. Capable of hosting as many as 42,000 attendees, the center also boasts a $4 million art collection.

In further development of the Washington Convention Center, an agreement was reached in 2007 with Marriott International to build a convention center headquarters hotel. Open in 2014, the new Marriott Marquis hotel included 105,000 square feet of meeting space and 1,126 rooms. The addition of both the convention center and hotel, two state-of-the-art facilities, along with the city's proximity to the nation's government, powerbase, and riches of cultural and tourist destinations, Washington, D.C., should continue to be one of the great magnets for the United States' lucrative convention business well into the twenty-first century.

While the old convention center was razed in 2004 to make way for the new development, The D.C. Armory, with nearly 70,000 square feet of exhibit space, offers alternative space for somewhat smaller gatherings. The Armory can also provide sports or theater seating for up to 10,000, with 8,000 parking spaces available to accommodate visitors. The greater Washington area also provides more than 100,000 additional hotel rooms; and many hotels offer meeting space, such as the Shoreham Omni Hotel (more than 100,000 square feet), the Capital Hilton (30,000 square feet), and the Grand Hyatt Washington (43,000 square feet).

Convention Information: Destination DC, 901 Seventh Street, NW, Fourth Floor, Washington, D.C. 20001; telephone (202) 789-7000; fax (202) 789-7037.

■ Transportation

Approaching the City

Washington is served by three major international airports. The closest, Ronald Reagan National Airport—across the Potomac in Virginia—is minutes from downtown Washington by car or the Metrorail subway system. Dulles International is about 20 miles west of the District of Columbia in Virginia. Baltimore/Washington International is 20 miles northeast of the city in Maryland.

Travelers driving to Washington by car must cross the Capital Beltway, also known as Interstate 495, which circles the city and connects it with Maryland and Virginia. Interstates 295, 395, and 66 also run between the District of Columbia and surrounding areas.

Continuous daily trains connect New York's Pennsylvania Station to Washington's Union Station, which is in sight of the Capitol, and daily trains connect Washington, D.C., with more than 500 cities around the United States.

Traveling in the City

Travel in the District of Columbia, one of the most congested areas in the nation, is made easier by the mass transportation system operated by the Washington Metropolitan Area Transit Authority, which runs the second largest heavy rail transit system, fifth largest paratransit service, and sixth largest bus network in the United States. The award-winning Metrorail system includes 106.3 miles of track and 86 operating stations. The system has stations at Union Station and National Airport. Annual Metrorail ridership in 2012 totaled more than 200 million trips. The annual Cherry Blossom Festival and Washington Nationals baseball games mark the busiest travel days annually, although the 2009 inauguration of U.S. president Barack Obama set several all-time records for ridership.

The approximately 1,500-vehicle Metrobus system has some 325 bus routes covering all major streets in the District and nearly all primary roads in the region, with a total of 11,500 bus stops. Ridership in 2012 totaled 132 million trips. The Transit Authority also operates a door-to-door service called MetroAccess for people with disabilities. In 2012 the transit authority announced a 6-year, $5-billion plan known as Metro Forward to improve the transit experience for passengers. Improvements included renovations to existing infrastructure, as well as new railcars and buses.

The DC Circulator, a downtown Washington bus service, operates on five routes linking major cultural, entertainment, and business sites around the city, including service to the Washington Convention Center. The DC Circulator was a public-private partnership between city authorities and DC Surface Transit, Incorporated. An abundant number of taxis cruise city streets, making it a convenient form of transportation.

■ Communications

Newspapers and Magazines

The capital's major daily newspaper, and one of the most influential newspapers in the country, is the Pulitzer Prize-winning *Washington Post*, which is published daily. The newspaper was sold to Amazon.com founder Jeffrey Bezos in October 2013. *The Washington Post Magazine*, a weekly focusing on Washington personalities and issues affecting the city and its surrounding metropolitan area, is another product of the larger news organization. A smaller newspaper, *The Washington Times* is the more conservative voice in the city. The national daily *USA Today* is another of several newspapers published in the metropolitan area. The monthly *Washingtonian Magazine*, one of hundreds of periodicals published in the District, looks at local politics, lifestyles, culture, and dining. The Washington *Afro American Newspaper* serves the African American Community, and the Washington Blade, a news source for the gay and lesbian community, has been published since 1969.

Television and Radio

Washington has 18 television stations broadcasting in the city; cable and satellite systems are available. The capital is also served by 38 FM and 18 AM radio stations in the city, including several public radio outlets.

Media Information: *Washington Post,* 1150 Fifteenth Street, NW, Washington, D.C. 20071; telephone (202) 334-6000. *Washington Times,* 3600 New York Avenue, NE, Washington, D.C. 20002; telephone (202) 636-3000.

Washington Online

City of Washington, D.C. Home Page. Available www.dc.gov

Cultural Tourism DC. Available www.culturaltourismdc.org

DC Chamber of Commerce. Available www.dcchamber.org

Washington, DC Economic Partnership. Available www.wdcep.com

DC Public Library. Available www.dclibrary.org

Downtown DC. Available www.downtowndc.org

TheInTowner. Available www.intowner.com

Library of Congress. Available www.loc.gov

Washington Business Journal. Available www.bizjournals.com/washington

Washington City Paper. Available www.washingtoncitypaper.com

Washington, D.C. Convention and Visitors Association. Available www.washington.org

Historical Society of Washington, D.C. Available www.historydc.org

DC Pages. Available dcpages.com/Top_Sites/

Washington Post. Available www.washingtonpost.com

Washington Times. Available www.washtimes.com

Washingtonian. Available www.washingtonian.com

BIBLIOGRAPHY

Baldacci, David, *Saving Faith* (New York: Warner Books, 1999)

Eshelman, Ralph E., Scott S. Sheads, and Donald R. Hickey, *The War of 1812 in the Chesapeake: A Reference Guide to Historic Sites in Maryland, Virginia, and the District of Columbia* (Baltimore, MD: Johns Hopkins University Press, 2010)

Gottlieb, Steve, *Washington, DC: Portrait of a City* (Taylor Trade Publishing, 2004)

Holland, Jesse J.*Black Men Built the Capitol: Discovering African-American History in and around Washington, D.C.* (Guilford, CT: Globe Pequot Press, 2007)

Vidal, Gore, *Washington, D.C.* (Boston, MA: Little Brown, 1967)

West Virginia

The State in Brief

Nickname: Mountain State

Motto: Montani semper liberi (Mountaineers are always free)

Flower: Big rhododendron

Bird: Cardinal

Area: 24,230 square miles (2010; U.S. rank 41st)

Elevation: Ranges from 240 feet to 4,861 feet above sea level

Climate: Continental; humid, with hot summers and cool winters, colder in mountains

Admitted to Union: June 20, 1863

Capital: Charleston

Head Official: Earl Ray Tomblin (D) (until 2017)

Population

1990: 1,793,477
2000: 1,808,344
2010: 1,852,994
2012 estimate: 1,850,481
Percent change, 2000–2010: 2.5%
U.S. rank in 2012: 37th
Percent of residents born in state: 70.6% (2012)
Density: 77.1 people per square mile (2010)
2012 FBI Crime Index Total: 49,747

Racial and Ethnic Characteristics (2012)

White: 1,737,369
Black or African American: 58,260
American Indian and Alaska Native: 2,934
Asian: 12,694
Native Hawaiian and Pacific Islander: 531
Hispanic or Latino (may be of any race): 22,026
Other: 38,693

Age Characteristics (2012)

Population under 5 years old: 104,141
Population 5 to 19 years old: 334,577
Percent of population 65 years and over: 16.2%
Median age: 41.3

Vital Statistics

Total number of births (2012–13): 20,408
Total number of deaths (2012–13): 21,424
AIDS cases reported through 2011: 1,909

Economy

Major industries: Energy, manufacturing, wholesale and retail trade
Unemployment rate (2012): 4.3%
Per capita income (2012): $22,482
Median household income (2012): $40,400
Percentage of persons below poverty level (2012): 17.6%
Income tax rate: 3.0% to 6.5%
Sales tax rate: 6.0%

Charleston

■ The City in Brief

Founded: 1794 (incorporated 1818)

Head Official: Mayor Danny Jones (since 2003; current term expires 2015)

City Population
 1990: 57,287
 2000: 53,421
 2010: 51,400
 2012 estimate: 51,153
 Percent change, 2000–2010: −3.8%
 U.S. rank in 1990: 415th (State rank: 1st)
 U.S. rank in 2000: 662nd (State rank: 1st)
 U.S. rank in 2010: 685th (State rank: 1st)

Metropolitan Statistical Area Population
 2000: 309,635
 2010: 304,284
 2012 estimate: 305,091
 Percent change, 2000–2010: −1.7%
 U.S. rank in 2000: 147th
 U.S. rank in 2010: 154th

Area: 32 square miles

Elevation: Ranges from 601 feet to approximately 1,100 feet above sea level

Average Annual Temperatures: January, 33.4° F; July, 73.9° F; annual average, 54.5° F

Average Annual Precipitation: 44.05 inches of rain; 34.0 inches of snow

Major Economic Sectors: services, health care, trade, government, technology research

Unemployment Rate: 4.5% (2012)

Per Capita Income: $35,330

Major Colleges and Universities: West Virginia State University, West Virginia University Institute of Technology, University of Charleston, Marshall University Graduate College

Daily Newspaper: *Charleston Daily Mail; Charleston Gazette*

■ Introduction

Charleston, the capital of West Virginia and seat of Kanawha County, is a regional hub for transportation, finance, retail trade, commerce, government, and health care, and acts as a lively center for arts and recreation while also serving as West Virginia's state capital. A vital urban area, the city also projects a comfortable charm that invites visitors and residents alike; its downtown is active and filled with people in the evening. With its nineteenth-century style brick sidewalks and streets lit by antique reproduction light posts and dotted with wooden benches, the Village District stands as a monument to the modern thinking that has kept the city on track both financially and aesthetically. The Clay Center for the Arts and Sciences opened in 2003, expanding the city's cultural identity. Realizing major plans to develop the city's waterfront remained high on the agenda of its leaders and citizens into the 2010s.

■ Geography and Climate

Charleston is located in a narrow valley in the western Appalachian Mountains at the junction of the Kanawha and Elk rivers. The city is the county seat for Kanawha County. Framed with green hills, the city and neighboring towns have developed along the Kanawha to the east and west, though some residential areas can be found on the surrounding hills and in nearby valleys. The Charleston Metropolitan Statistical Area (MSA), a significant economic zone, covers a five county area that includes Boon, Clay, Lincoln, Putnam, and Kanawha counties.

Capitol Street, Charleston, WV. © *Charleston Convention & Visitors Bureau*

The region's weather is highly changeable, particularly during the winter months when Arctic air may alternate with tropical air. Consequently, sharp temperature contrasts are the rule-even on a day-to-day basis-and total annual snowfall ranges from less than 5 inches to more than 50. Spring temperatures warm rapidly, however, and summers can occasionally be hot, hazy, and humid. Most of Charleston's precipitation falls in the form of rain; the brief, sometimes heavy, thunderstorms of July make it the wettest month of the year. The terrain and air flow patterns combine to make Charleston one of the foggiest cities in the United States.

Area: 32 square miles

Elevation: Ranges from 601 feet to approximately 1,100 feet above sea level

Average Temperatures: January, 33.4° F; July, 73.9° F; annual average, 54.5° F

Average Annual Precipitation: 44.05 inches of rain; 34.0 inches of snow

■ History

Fort Leads to Founding of City

Centuries before the first white frontiersmen explored the area that is now Charleston, the Adena, a Native American tribe, inhabited the Kanawha Valley. The Adenas were mound builders, and one of West Virginia's largest examples of their unique earthworks is located in downtown South Charleston.

The influx of traders and land surveyors-most of whom were Virginians-into the Kanawha Valley region began in the mid-1760s. In 1773, Colonel Thomas Bullitt and a group of surveyors on their way to Kentucky briefly established a camp there. Bullitt again visited the valley in 1775 and, in return for his military service during the French and Indian War, he was allowed to stake a claim of more than 1,000 acres. Upon his death the claim went to his brother, Cuthbert Bullitt, who in turn sold the land to Colonel George Clendenin in 1787.

Just a few weeks after the deal was finalized, the governor of Virginia instructed Clendenin to organize a company of soldiers to protect the Kanawha Valley from native raiding parties. In 1788, the colonel erected a fort on a portion of his land that ran along the river. The completion of this stockade-known officially as Fort Lee but often referred to as Clendenin's Settlement-and the security it represented attracted a number of pioneers to the area in just a few years. So many people had settled there by 1794 that some of the other Clendenin land holdings were divided into lots, and the Virginia Assembly authorized the creation of a town, named Charles Town in honor of George Clendenin's father. (Common usage eventually shortened this to Charleston, the name of record on January 19, 1818, the day the town was officially established.) Drawn by reports of abundant game in the valley, Daniel Boone and his family were among Charleston's early residents, but the region grew so quickly that they soon left for the Kentucky wilderness.

Economy Grows Around Natural Resources

Salt manufacturing was the first industry to gain a foothold in Charleston. In 1797, a salt furnace was constructed in nearby Malden, and by the mid-1800s Kanawha Valley salt was being shipped from Charleston to all parts of the country. Throughout the first half of the century the city also grew in importance as a transportation center, primarily as a point of transfer for east-west travelers who arrived by wagon or on horseback and continued their journey by boat.

The Civil War divided Charleston. Some citizens fought for the Confederacy, but most sided with the Union. The conflict also hastened the decline of the salt trade (which had already reached its peak around 1856) and forced the development of alternative industries, particularly those involving coal, oil, and gas. The city grew rapidly after the war, aided in part by the relocation of West Virginia's capital from Wheeling to Charleston in 1870. The coming of the railroad in 1873 and improved navigation on the Kanawha River opened up coal mining on an even larger scale, and Charleston prospered as a market and wholesale center.

Between 1885 and the beginning of World War I, Charleston grew slowly but steadily, its economy bolstered by increasing demand for the natural resources it processed and sold throughout the country. Around 1913, however, a new era in the city's development began when the first chemical company was established. Others soon followed and were eventually joined by glass manufacturers. With America's entry into the war, some of these new factories switched over to producing munitions, but coal and chemicals continued to attract the most foreign capital and new residents.

In the years since World War I, Charleston has come to rely more and more on the manufacture of synthetic materials as the basis of its industrial economy; during World War II, for example, the Kanawha Valley was a center for synthetic rubber production. Thus, as has been the case since its earliest days as a frontier town, the fortunes of the city are inextricably linked with the demand for the natural resources it has in such abundance.

Charleston, as well as most of West Virginia, was affected by recession in the early 1980s. Moderate growth followed, and between 1985 and 1990 personal income grew due to Charleston's industrial growth. The year 2000 was said to mark a period of potential growth and rebirth for Charleston, spurred in part by Downtown revitalization programs beginning a decade or so before. The 2003 opening of the Clay Center for the Arts and

Sciences proved a commitment to strengthen the city's hold as a center for culture and the arts as well as to provide more opportunities for possible tourists. In 2004 the city also began working with both private business and government authorities on planning for a Riverfront Development Project with the hopes of responsibly maintaining the natural resources of the Kanawha River, as well as adding a development of more recreational and retail opportunities for both residents and tourists. As of 2013, leaders were still planning how to best utilize limited resources and balance various interests in the development of the Riverfront.

Historical Information: West Virginia Department of Education and the Arts, Division of Culture and History, Archives and History Library, 1900 Kanawha Blvd. E., Bldg. 9, Charleston, WV 25305; telephone (304) 558-0230.

■ Population Profile

Metropolitan Statistical Area Population
2000: 309,635
2010: 304,284
2012 estimate: 305,091
Percent change, 2000–2010: −1.7%
U.S. rank in 2000: 147th
U.S. rank in 2010: 154th

City Residents
1990: 57,287
2000: 53,421
2010: 51,400
2012 estimate: 51,153
Percent change, 2000–2010: −3.8%
U.S. rank in 1990: 415th (State rank: 1st)
U.S. rank in 2000: 662nd (State rank: 1st)
U.S. rank in 2010: 685th (State rank: 1st)

Density: 1,033.7 people per square mile

Racial and ethnic characteristics
White: 42,067
Black or African American: 3,857
American Indian and Alaskan Native: 51
Asian: 1,250
Native Hawaiian and Other Pacific Islander: 0
Hispanic or Latino (may be of any race): 909
Other: 3,928

Percent of residents born in state: 71.8%

Age characteristics
Population under 5 years old: 2,493
Population 5 to 9 years old: 2,632
Population 10 to 14 years old: 3,180

Population 15 to 19 years old: 3,264
Population 20 to 24 years old: 2,990
Population 25 to 34 years old: 6,547
Population 35 to 44 years old: 6,021
Population 45 to 54 years old: 7,770
Population 55 to 59 years old: 4,110
Population 60 to 64 years old: 3,178
Population 65 to 74 years old: 4,141
Population 75 to 84 years old: 3,298
Population 85 years and over: 1,529
Median age: 42.1

Births (2010–11 Metropolitan Area)

Total number: 3,287

Deaths (2010–11 Metropolitan Area)

Total number: 3,275

Money income (2012)

Per capita income: $35,330
Median household income: $47,864
Total households: 23,454

Number of households with income of ...

less than $10,000: 2,229
$10,000 to $14,999: 1,912
$15,000 to $24,999: 2,886
$25,000 to $34,999: 2,127
$35,000 to $49,999: 3,060
$50,000 to $74,999: 4,238
$75,000 to $99,999: 2,314
$100,000 to $149,999: 2,341
$150,000 to $199,999: 834
$200,000 or more: 1,513

Percent of families below poverty level: 18.6%

■ Municipal Government

Charleston, the capital of West Virginia and the Kanawha County seat, has a mayor-council form of government. There are 27 council members elected by ward for four-year terms. Twenty-one members represent single-member districts, and six are elected at-large. Both a majority and a minority leader are elected by respective council parties. A president pro-tempore is elected by the entire council. The mayor is elected to a four-year term.

Head Official: Mayor Danny Jones (since 2003; current term expires 2015)

Total Number of City Employees: 785 (2012)

City Information: City of Charleston, 501 Virginia Street, E., Charleston, WV 25301; telephone (304) 348-8000.

■ Economy

Major Industries and Commercial Activity

The Kanawha Valley owes much of its past and future prosperity to its reputation as a transportation and distribution hub. From river port to interstate hub, the sophisticated transportation routes have lured and kept industry in the region when other parts of West Virginia were troubled with the same economic doldrums that affected much of the nation. Insulated from the boom-or-bust coal industry, the Kanawha Valley has relied on its diversity of natural resources and its importance in the eastern and central states' waterways system, moving goods to the Gulf of Mexico via the Ohio and Mississippi rivers. Three interstate highways converging in downtown Charleston provide the extra transportation links that the rivers cannot provide. Moreover, the highways bring Charleston within 500 miles of more than 50 percent of the nation's major market areas and 50 percent of its entire population.

Since 1929, the chemical industry has been an important economic sector in the valley. Union Carbide, a subsidiary of Dow Chemical since 2001, has its headquarters for research and development in South Charleston. Valley residents have been very supportive of the chemical industry, acknowledging that the industry's first priority has always been safety. Likewise, local governments have been involved and have participated in safety and emergency planning. Other Kanawha Valley industries include heavy steel fabricating, glass manufacturing, and energy development.

The state and government serves as a major economic sector for the city in terms of employment. Second in line is health care, with the Charleston Area Medical Center and Thomas Memorial Hospital taking the lead. Health insurance and claims processing companies in the area include the Capital Area Services Company and Wells Fargo Insurance. Manufacturing companies in metropolitan area include Toyota Motor Manufacturing, Walker Machinery Company, and NGK Spark Plugs. The West Virginia American Water Company, the state's largest water supplier, is headquartered in Charleston. Appalachian Power, owned by the American Electric Power of Columbus, Ohio, also has headquarters in Charleston.

A growing economic sector for Charleston is research and technology. In 2007 Expetec Technology Services, Inc., a full-service information technology (IT) franchise with locations in 15 states and Canada, opened a new location in Charleston. In 2010 the state of West Virginia acquired the West Virginia Regional Technology Park in South Charleston, formerly owned by Union Carbide, and planned to revitalize the technology park over the coming decade. One of the first projects was the opening of an Advanced Technology Center in 2013, associated with the Community and Technical College System of West Virginia.

Items and goods produced: chemicals, telecommunications products, publishing, mining equipment, fabricated metal products, automobile parts

Incentive Programs-New and Existing Companies

Local programs: The Charleston Area Alliance is a non-profit economic development corporation serving Metropolitan Charleston. It offers a range of services to companies considering the area for new or expanded operations. Assistance is offered in worker training and education, financing, site selection, and with buildings. Both professional economic development and engineering services are free and confidential. The alliance offers a small business incubator with spaces available to new start-up businesses seeking to open an office in the Charleston area. Available facilities include office space and a number of core business amenities, such as fax and copy machines, Internet access, and telephone service.

State programs: West Virginia's frequent budget surpluses have allowed the state cut business taxes and become increasingly competitive. The state's direct loan program, administered by the West Virginia Economic Development Authority, funds up to 45 percent of business financing with low-interest loans and 5- to 15-year terms. Industrial revenue bonds are available to small manufacturing projects, qualifying projects in Enterprise Communities, and exempt facility projects. A linked deposit loan program gives businesses with fewer than 50 employees and $5 million in annual revenue access to loans at 1 percent above New York Prime rates, up to $250,000. Venture capital funding is provided through the West Virginia Jobs Investment Trust. Tax credits, exemptions, and similar programs include Corporate Headquarters Credit, Economic Opportunity Credit, "Five-for Ten" Program, Manufacturing Investment Credit, Manufacturing Inventory Credit, Strategic R&D Credit, West Virginia Film Industry Investment Act, High-Tech Manufacturing Credit, Aircraft Valuation, High-Technology Business Property Valuation Act, The Freeport Amendment, Manufacturing Sales Tax Exemptions, Special Rates of Electric Power for Industrial Consumers, Research and Development Sales Tax Exemption, Sales Tax Exemption for E-Commerce, Tax Increment Financing, Tourism Matching Advertising Partnership, and Lodging Exemptions.

Job training programs: The Governor's Guaranteed Work Force Program provides training grants of up to $1,000 per employee for companies that create a minimum of 10 new jobs within a 12-month period. WorkKeys Career Readiness Certificates from Workforce West Virginia help match qualified job seekers with employers. The Workforce Investment Act Program offers customized training to employers that hire economically disadvantaged or displaced residents. West Virginia Advance Program operates in conjunction with the state's community and technical colleges to award customized job training to start-up and existing businesses.

Development Projects

In 2009 plans were announced for the Charleston Riverfront Project, funded by a grant from the U.S. Small Business Administration. The project intended to create new public gathering spaces and to beautify the city. While support for the plan remained strong into 2013, a number of obstacles slowed development, including basic infrastructure challenges such as potential road rerouting, which may result in fewer lanes, a concept opposed by some community member.

In 2012 Gestamp, a Spanish automotive company, announced reopening of a South Charleston plant expected to sustain 700 jobs. The investment was expected to reach $100 million by 2017, with 175 jobs available by the end of 2013. Most investments went toward new equipment for the facility. Gestamp signed a 12-year lease on the manufacturing building, with an option to renew the lease for another 12 years.

Charleston's Yeager Airport announced in 2013 that it had received a $700,000 grant from the federal government to attract three airlines in the hope of reopening a service route to Florida. Half the money was intended to market the new route, with the remainder going to cover the expenses of an airline that relocated service to the area, from employee training to hardware purchases. Until 2009, the airport was serviced by an AirTran route to Orlando. While profitable, the route was dropped after Southwest Airlines purchased AirTran in 2012; the route was not part of Southwest's business model.

Charleston's historic downtown is supported by East End Main Street, an active National Main Street Program. As of 2013, improvement projects included public art displays, preservation of historic buildings, façade and sign grants, and free interior design consultations provided by the University of Charleston. Imagine Charleston is an alliance of several organizations supporting downtown development and preservation.

Economic Development Information: Charleston Area Alliance, 1116 Smith Street, Charleston, WV 25301; telephone (304)340-4253 or (800) 792-4326; fax (304) 340-4275.

Commercial Shipping

The Kanawha Valley's transportation systems may be the region's biggest economic asset, since Charleston is the region's hub for air service, river commerce, and highways. The city is an important distribution center because of its extremely sophisticated transportation routes. Charleston was designated a port of entry by the U.S.

Customs Office in 1973 and the business and industrial sectors take advantage of direct shipments from foreign countries. The customs office at Yeager Airport inspects air, barge, rail, and other freight shipments received at locations throughout the region. A fixed-base operator with complete maintenance shop and 24-hour service is located at Yeager. Yeager Airport has four air cargo carriers.

West Virginia had eight freight railroads as of 2011, with more than 2,200 miles of track. Some 93 percent of all rail shipments out of West Virginia carried coal, with the remainder carrying stone, sand, gravel, chemicals, petrol, concrete, and gypsum.

The U.S. Army Corps of Engineers maintains a navigation channel 200 feet wide and 9 feet deep in the Kanawha River-from the mouth at Point Pleasant on the West Virginia-Ohio border to a point 91 miles east at Deepwater, about 40 miles upriver from Charleston. Waterborne commerce has tripled on the Kanawha River since the early 1950s, and the inland port frequently places among the top-10 U.S. inland ports based on tonnage. A U.S. Foreign Trade Zone has been established on the Kanawha River, and companies involved in export businesses can establish subzones at remote warehousing sites in order to provide duty-free storage prior to shipment. Charleston is served by more than 50 motor freight carriers.

Labor Force and Employment Outlook

Due to the strong manufacturing base of Charleston's economy, the city boasts a workforce that is familiar with the machinery, equipment, and processes involved in technologically complex operations. But as the mining and manufacturing sectors shrink in response to national economic trends, services and retail trade are continuing to show significant growth. The area's extensive transportation network, stable workforce, and diverse economy combine to enable companies in the chemical, automotive, health-care, telecommunications, and professional services sectors to thrive. Many West Virginia residents commute from more than 50 miles away due to the scarcity of jobs outside the capital area. As of 2013, some 31.4 percent of the city's labor force resided in another county, above the national average of 26.7 percent.

The following is a summary of data regarding the 2012 Charleston labor force:

Size of civilian labor force: 25,899

Number of workers employed in . . .

agriculture and mining: 603
construction: 1,043
manufacturing: 881
wholesale trade: 354
retail trade: 2,078
transportation: 895

information systems: 705
finance: 1,824
professional administration: 3,344
education and social services: 6,237
arts and leisure: 2,389
other: 1,172
public administration: 2,459

Average hourly earnings of production workers: $17.93

Unemployment rate: 4.5% (2012)

Employers

Largest employers (Kanawha County, 2012)

	Number of employees
Charleston Area Medical Center	6,577
Kanawha County Board of Education	3,978
Herbert J. Thomas Memorial Hospital Association	1,200
West Virginia Department of Highways	1,100
Wal-Mart Associates, Inc.	1,000
The Kroger Company	900
City of Charleston	785
West Virginia Department of Helath and Human Resources	750
U.S. Postal Service	720
TRG Customer Solutions, Inc.	715

Cost of Living

The overall cost of living in Charleston was more than 8 percent below the national average as of 2013. The median home price was $132,400.

The following is a summary of data regarding several key cost of living factors in the area.

State income tax rate: 3.0% to 6.5%

State sales tax rate: 6.0%

Local income tax rate: $104 per year city service fee

Local sales tax rate: 0.005%

Property tax rate: $0.1634 per $100 of assessed valuation (2013)

Economic Information: Charleston Area Alliance, 1116 Smith Street, Charleston, WV 25301; telephone (304)340-4253 or (800) 792-4326; fax (304) 340-4275.

■ Education and Research

Elementary and Secondary Schools

Public education in Charleston is provided by Kanawha County Schools. The district is administered by a five-member board of education and a superintendent who follow policies established by the State Department of Education and the West Virginia Board of Education. The district is the largest in the state of West Virginia.

Some fifth grade students may have an opportunity to attend the West Virginia STARBASE Academy. This Department of Defense Youth Program provides academic enrichment for both public and private schools, focusing on mathematics, science, and technology, with an aerospace theme. STARBASE is a five-day program, which students attend one day each week for five consecutive weeks. Since the program's inception, more than 10,000 Kanawha County students have attended STARBASE.

English as Second Language programs are available, with an estimated 170 students enrolled in the program, representing 28 different countries. Some 500 students in the school district speak a language other than English at home. The district's Work Exploration Program gives special education students career exploration opportunities, including supervision by employment specialists. Eight magnet academies support special programs in the performing arts, criminology, finance and business, international studies, International Baccalaureate programs, cadet and pre-engineering, hospitality and tourism, and Advanced Placement.

The Virtual High School program operated by the county allows students to earn course credits from home. The program is available for high school students and requires them to meet certain qualifications, such as referral by school counselors or administrators, or status as homebound.

Students in Charleston may also attend one of the valley's more than a dozen private Catholic, Christian, and non-denominational schools.

The following is a summary of data regarding the Kanawha County Schools.

Total enrollment: 28,458

Number of facilities

   total: 71
   elementary schools: 44
   junior high schools: 14
   high schools: 8
   other: 5

Student/teacher ratio: 15.4:1

Teacher salaries

   average (statewide): $47,253

Funding per pupil: $11,701

Public Schools Information: Kanawha County Schools, 200 Elizabeth Street, Charleston, WV 25311; telephone (304) 348-7770.

Colleges and Universities

The University of Charleston, a privately endowed institution, has a beautiful campus situated on the Kanawha River across from the State Capitol. It offers undergraduate degrees in 23 academic fields, an; associate's degree in nursing, radiologic science, occupational therapy assistance, and culinary arts; and graduate programs in executive leadership, business administration, forensic accounting, pharmacy, physician assistant, and strategic leadership. Enrollment is about 1,400 students. In 2013, the University of Charleston was listed 19th among regional universities in the South by *U.S. News & World Report.* West Virginia Junior College in Charleston offers associate degree programs.

In the greater Kanawha Valley area there are two state-supported colleges, West Virginia State University and West Virginia University Institute of Technology. There is also a state-supported graduate school, the West Virginia Graduate College of Marshall University. West Virginia State University, eight miles west of Charleston on Interstate 64 in the town of Institute, is a historically black college with an undergraduate enrollment of some 2,553 as of 2013. The college provides a broad spectrum of undergraduate degree programs. Master's degrees are available in biotechnology, media studies, and law enforcement.

West Virginia University Institute of Technology in Montgomery, a regional campus of West Virginia University, offers engineering and other degree programs; enrollment was 1,107 in 2013.

Established in 1969 as the West Virginia Graduate College to aid degree-holders working in the valley in obtaining master's degrees without leaving the community, the Marshall University Graduate College in Huntington offers doctorates in seven areas of study and master's degrees in nearly50 fields. Graduate certificates are also available in a wide variety of topics, such as Appalachian studies, family literacy, Medieval and Renaissance Studies, technology management, and family nurse practitioners.

Libraries and Research Centers

Housed in the former Federal Building in downtown Charleston, the Kanawha County Public Library is the largest public non-university library in West Virginia. With a main library, 10 branches in area communities, and a bookmobile, the system maintains more than 600,000 volumes and holds special history and oral history collections plus government documents. In 2006, the Kanawha County Public Library initiated a $47 million capital campaign to build a new main library and improve existing branch library buildings. The campaign had been put on hold as of 2013.

The Cultural Center in the Capitol Complex houses state archives, a genealogical library, and a general reference library. The Schoenbaum Library of the University of Charleston houses special collections that include the James David Barber Collection on the Presidency, the James Swann Etchings Collection, and the Kendall Vintroux Political Cartoons Collection.

The West Virginia Technology Park seeks to further diversify the local economy to better connect higher education and research investments with business and economic opportunities. The Charleston Area Medical Center Health Education and Research Institute sponsors four research departments: the Centers for Clinical Sciences Research, the Center for Health Services and Outcomes Research, the Center for Cancer Research, and the Clinical Trials Center.

Public Library Information: Kanawha County Public Library, 123 Capitol Street, Charleston, WV 25301-2686; telephone (304) 343-4646.

■ Health Care

Charleston is the hub of West Virginia's health-care system. The area's largest major hospital, the Charleston Area Medical Center (CAMC), is the flagship hospital of the larger CAMC Health System. The non-profit, 838-bed, regional referral center is also the largest teaching hospital in southern West Virginia, serving as the Charleston base for West Virginia University's School of Medicine. CAMC has a leading heart program, one of two kidney transplant centers in the state, and a Level I Trauma Center. In 2013 CAMC was named a high-performing hospital in seven specialties by *U.S. News and World Report.* There are three CAMC locations in Charleston: General Hospital, Memorial Hospital, Women and Children's Hospital. General Hospital is the location for the Trauma Center as well as the Center for Joint Replacement, Facial Surgery Center, Kidney Transplant Center, Medical Rehabilitation Center, Neurosciences Center, and the CAMC Sleep Center. Memorial Hospital is home to the Cancer Services Center, Hemophilia Treatment Center, Prostate Cancer Center, and the CAMC SurgiCare Center. The Women and Children's Hospital has a Level III Neonatal Intensive Care Unit as well as a full array of specialty departments in matters regarding pediatric and women's health issues. The CAMC Health Education and Research Institute, based in Charleston, offers

community health education programs as well as professional education opportunities. CAMC also supports the Teays Valley Hospital with its 70 beds, located in Hurricane, West Virginia.

Thomas Memorial Hospital is a 260-bed, not-for-profit hospital serving South Charleston. In response to growing demand, Thomas Memorial Hospital opened a new six-story building in 2010 that would add private rooms, obstetrics unit, surgical center, satellite gift shop, cafe and kitchen. Other area hospitals include St. Francis Hospital and Boone Memorial Hospital.

■ Recreation

Sightseeing

Charleston's parks, museums, and music and cultural activities provide a variety of enjoyable and stimulating experiences. The state's Cultural Center at the Capitol Complex has a museum, performing arts, film and music festivals, and The Shop, which sells only West Virginia native crafts. The Capitol Complex also offers tours of the Governor's Mansion two days a week. On the State Capitol grounds is a memorial honoring Malden, West Virginia, native Booker T. Washington. Glass factories in the area provide tours to groups. The Clay Center for Arts and Sciences houses the Avampato Discovery Museum and contains four interactive science exploration galleries, the ElectricSky Theater (a planetarium), and the Juliet Museum of Art, with a permanent collection of over 750 pieces. The Haddad Riverfront Park invites residents and visitors with its river views, evening concerts, and plays. The park offers paved paths for runners, walkers, and cyclists, as well as plenty of areas for picnicking, sunbathing, and relaxing.

A variety of historic homes from the late 1800s and early 1900s can be toured in Charleston. The Craik-Patton House, built in 1834 in the Greek Revival style of architecture, is open mid-April through mid-October for tours. The East End Historical District features homes in a variety of architectural styles, including Queen Anne, Victorian, Richardson Romanesque, Georgian, Italianate, and others, mainly built between 1895 and 1925. Victorian Block on Capitol Street features some of the oldest structures on Capitol Street, with homes dating back to 1887. Shrewsbury Street acknowledges sites and buildings that are prominent in West Virginia's African American history.

Formerly the Daniel Boone Hotel, 405 Capitol Street was built in 1929 at a then-extravagant cost of more than $1.2 million. Renovated in the 1990s, the building now houses business offices and is known for its unique 10-story atrium. Also afforded new life in the city is the C&O Railroad Depot, built in 1905. Refurbished in 1987, the Beaux Arts-style brick and terra cotta trimmed depot houses offices and a restaurant.

Charleston is home port to the *P. A. Denny*, a beautiful excursion sternwheeler available for scenic rides on the Kanawha or for rental trips for private groups. In addition, many of the forests, parks and resorts in West Virginia's excellent park system are within a half-day's drive of Kanawha Valley.

Arts and Culture

A well-respected symphony orchestra, a resident chamber-music string quartet, a youth orchestra and visiting chamber-music ensembles ensure a steady diet of live classical music in the Charleston area. The Clay Center for the Arts and Sciences is home to the West Virginia Symphony Orchestra, which performs classical and pops concerts and regularly features guest artists from around the world.

The West Virginia Youth Symphony Orchestra is one of Charleston's special cultural assets, and the group performs extensively in the Kanawha County school system and in schools throughout the state. The Charleston Light Opera Guild provides musical comedy and drama each season at the Guild Theater and the Civic Center Little Theater. Many community singers, actors, and actresses, such as the Charleston Civic Chorus, have formed a close-knit group of talented performers who act, sing, and dance their way through Broadway musicals each year.

The Civic Center in Charleston contains a 13,500-seat coliseum as well as the 750-seat Little Theatre, home for most of Charleston's community theater groups. Municipal Auditorium, part of the Civic Center Complex, hosts programs of traveling musicians sponsored by the Charleston Chamber Music Society, Broadway touring shows, and national recording artists.

Children's Theatre of Charleston introduces many youngsters to the stage. The group produces four plays annually and conducts a performing arts school for its aspiring young actors and actresses. The Kanawha Players—the oldest continuous community theater group in West Virginia—hosts a season of drama and comedy performances each year. From experimental drama and dinner theater settings to more traditional offerings, the Kanawha Players has performed in Charleston since the 1920s, and the group has been designated the official state theater of West Virginia. Using community directors and actors, the group plays to full houses season after season and performs at the workshops in Kanawha City and the Civic Center Little Theatre. Mountain Stage, a West Virginia Public Radio presentation that brings jazz, folk, blues, rock, and classical musicians from around the world to the city is broadcasted live to a national audience from the Cultural Center at the Capitol. Tickets to Sunday performances are available to the public.

Charleston is also home to the Charleston Ballet, which performs three to five ballets each season, and the West Virginia Dance Company. The Kanawha

Valley Friends of Old Time Music and Dance (FOOT-MAD) is a non-profit, volunteer organization dedicated to promoting traditional music and dance programs in Charleston and the Greater Kanawha Valley. The group sponsors concerts and dance events from October through April.

Arts and Culture Information: Charleston Convention and Visitors Bureau, 800 Smith Street, Charleston, WV 25301; telephone (304) 344-5075.

Festivals and Holidays

"Symphony Sunday," held each year in the spring, features an outdoor concert on the campus of the University of Charleston. Another annual event that has become a favorite of West Virginians and thousands of out-of-state visitors is May's Vandalia Gathering. For this event, crowds flock to the Cultural Center and its grounds to see magnificent quilts, traditional folk dancers, and demonstrations of blacksmithing and toy making and to taste treats like corn roasted over open fires. But it is the traditional music that lures most spectators. Banjo pickers, fiddlers, and dulcimer players compete in good-natured contests, and "jam sessions" seem to be going on everywhere. The first Sunday of June, the State Capital Complex features artisans, food, and music at the Rhododendron Art & Craft Show. The annual Fall Fling in September is a festival of traditional music and dance sponsored by the Friends of Old Time Music and Dance (FOOTMAD). The Capital City Art and Craft Show at the Civic Center, held the week prior to Thanksgiving, brings together craftspeople and music and craft events for an exhibition with a holiday theme.

Sports for the Spectator

Charleston has the West Virginia Power, a Single-A affiliate of the Pittsburgh Pirates that plays baseball at Appalachian Power Park. For fans of dog racing, the Tri-State Greyhound Park in Cross Lanes operates six days a week all year long.

Sports for the Participant

In Charleston, recreation can be as simple as a riverside stroll down Kanawha Boulevard when the dogwoods are in bloom or chipping a golf ball around one of several public and private golf courses in the area. Cyclists, hikers, and runners appreciate the miles of wooded trails and paved paths available in nearby parks, and the paved riverfront path at Kanawha Boulevard downtown. Charleston Parks and Recreation maintains seven city parks. Sand volleyball courts are available at Magic Island Park. Tennis courts, holes of golf, and an Olympic size swimming pool are available at Cato Park. There are four other swimming pools in the city. The city also sponsors four community centers that provide a variety of sports opportunities. These—along with a number of private country clubs and sports and fitness facilities—can accommodate many recreational interests.

The Little Coal River Trail System, located minutes from downtown Charleston, is part of the Hatfield-McCoy Trails, a multiuse, 500-mile system of trails for ATVs, bikers, hikers, and horseback riders.

Charleston annually hosts the Charleston Distance Run, one of the oldest road runs in the United States. This rigorous 15-mile course—set along 4 miles on the hills and 11 miles on the flatlands—has tested the mettle of world champions.

The Kanawha Parks and Recreation Commission operates recreational facilities in Kanawha County. The largest, Coonskin Park, has 1,200 wooded acres near Yeager Airport and offers picnic areas, shelters, tennis, swimming, golf, hiking, a modern amphitheater, soccer stadium, and wedding garden. Sandy Brae Golf Course, 20 minutes north of Charleston off Interstate 79, is an 18-hole championship course. Big Bend is a 6,000-yard golf course along the beautiful Coal River at Tornado.

Kanawha State Forest, adjacent to Charleston, is a sprawling, 9,300 acre unspoiled area ideal for picnicking, hiking, fishing, horseback riding, mountain biking and camping, and cross-country skiing in the winter. Some of the best whitewater rafting in the country is available just a short distance from Charleston on the Gauley and New rivers; the area attracts more than 100,000 rafters and kayakers each year.

Shopping and Dining

Opportunities for pleasant shopping and dining experiences are abundant in Charleston. The Charleston Village District features specialty shops for clothing, books, photography, and other unique items in an architecturally interesting setting. The Village District also offers fine dining experiences. Town Center Mall has more than 130 shops and specialties, in addition to its three main anchor stores, JCPenney, Macy's, and Sears. The Shops at Kanawha Mall, 10 minutes from downtown, were being revamped in 2013, following a corporate bankruptcy, which included the conversion of the mall from an indoor to outdoor facility. Other popular shopping locations in and around the city include Nitro Marketplace, Riverwalk Plaza, St. Albans Mall, Capitol Market, and the Shoppes at Trace Fork. A number of hand production glass factories are in the area, where one may observe skilled craftspersons at work and purchase their wares. Quilts and furniture, handcrafted in West Virginia, are available at local specialty stores. Diners in Charleston will find options for casual and fine dining as well as ethnic flavors of Chinese, Greek, Japanese, Indian, Mediterranean, Italian, and Mexican specialties.

Visitor Information: Charleston Convention and Visitors Bureau, 800 Smith Street, Charleston, WV 25301; telephone (304) 344-5075.

■ Convention Facilities

In total, Charleston offers more than 173,300 square feet of meeting space, more than 4,000 hotel rooms, and easy access to shopping, dining, and recreation for visitors. One of the city's main meeting locations, the Charleston Civic Center, is located only one block from the central business district and has more than 100,000 square feet of exhibition space in its Grand Hall, North and South halls, and meeting rooms to accommodate up to 6,000 attendees. The Civic Center Coliseum, a multipurpose facility that offers unobstructed-view seating for 13,500 people for events ranging from concerts and circuses to athletic competitions and horse races. A brick walkway links the Charleston Town Center complex—which consists of the Civic Coliseum, a three-story enclosed mall, the four-star Marriott Hotel, and many restaurants and night clubs—with the renovated Village District. Just two blocks away is the Civic Center Municipal Auditorium with seating for up to 3,400 people and the Little Theater, which seats about 750. The Haddad Riverfront Park is available for special events. The University of Charleston also has facilities for groups of varying size, and all downtown hotels have ample meeting space. The Capitol Conference Center has three event spaces at 1,475 square feet, 925 square feet, and 650 square feet. The Summit Conference Center has seven exhibit/ballrooms, with the largest accommodating about 180 people. Many shops and restaurants are within walking distance of the downtown hotels, and a low crime rate further enhances the appeal of the area for visitors and conventioneers.

Convention Information: Charleston Convention and Visitors Bureau, 800 Smith Street, Charleston, WV 25301; telephone (304) 344-5075.

■ Transportation

Approaching the City

Arriving in Charleston by air, travelers land at Yeager Airport—a facility located 10 minutes from downtown that is a remarkable feat of engineering named for an even more remarkable man. First known as the Kanawha Airport, it was built in the late 1940s by shearing off mountaintops and filling in adjacent valleys. In 1986 the terminal facilities were completely renovated, and the airport was renamed after General Charles S. "Chuck" Yeager, the World War II flying ace and first man to break the sound barrier. Yeager happens to be a native of Lincoln County, located about 30 miles southwest of Charleston. Yeager Airport provides service from five commercial air carriers: American, Delta, United, Spirit, and U.S. Airways Express. The airport has private aviation facilities as well and is home to the 130th Tactical Airlift Group of the West Virginia Air National Guard.

Arriving by car, visitors approach Charleston via three major interstates: Interstates 64, 77, 79, which intersect near downtown. Charleston is one of only about a dozen cities in the nation where three interstates merge. Interstate 64 links the Midwest through Charleston to Virginia's eastern seaboard. Interstate 77 links the Great Lakes area through Columbia, South Carolina, terminating in Cleveland. The West Virginia Turnpike, which originates in Charleston and ends at the Virginia border near Princeton, has been incorporated into the Interstate 77 and 64 systems. Interstate 79 runs from Erie, Pennsylvania, where it connects with the New York throughways, through Pittsburgh, and terminates in Charleston. Amtrak offers rail passenger service, and Greyhound bus service is available.

Traveling in the City

Charleston and the Kanawha Valley have a reputation of being cosmopolitan and compact. For those who live and work in the city, it is 10 minutes to work from most neighborhoods and 15 minutes to the airport. A bus system provided by the Kanawha Valley Regional Transportation Authority (KRT) serves the entire valley from the western end at Nitro to the eastern end as far as Montgomery, 26 miles east of Charleston. There are 21 routes in Charleston. In 2008 the KRT in partnership with the Tri-State Transit Authority opened bus routes between Charleston and Huntington, West Virginia, through a service called Intelligent Transit. The new service gives options to commuters and students, where there previously were not any. Buses in downtown Charleston are designed as replicas of old fashioned trolleys and shuttle passengers between major downtown sites. All buses are handicapped accessible; trolleys, however, are not. An on-demand van transport service is also available for disabled passengers who are not accommodated by fixed routes.

■ Communications

Newspapers and Magazines

Charleston's two daily newspapers are the *Charleston Daily Mail* (afternoon) and *The Charleston Gazette* (morning). While under separate ownership, a joint operating agreement houses the two papers under one roof, and on Sundays they combine efforts to produce the *Sunday Gazette-Mail*. *The State Journal* is weekly business news journal published out of Charleston for statewide distribution. The monthly *Wonderful West Virginia* is published monthly by the state Department of Natural Resources.

Television and Radio

Major network television stations broadcast directly from Charleston, including WCHS (ABC) and WVAH (Fox). Three other stations also broadcast locally. Cable television is available in Charleston, as are several television stations broadcasting from neighboring towns in West Virginia, Kentucky, and Ohio, providing viewers with a full range of options.

Eight FM and four AM stations broadcast directly from the city, although other regional stations can be heard in Charleston. A variety of formats, including country/western, talk radio, sports, adult contemporary, religious, and public radio, are available.

Media Information: Charleston Daily Mail/Charleston Gazette, 1001 Virginia Street East, Charleston, WV 25301; telephone (800) 982-6397.

Charleston Online

Charleston Area Alliance. Available www.charleston alliance.org

Charleston Daily Mail. Available www.charleston dailymail.com

The Charleston Gazette. Available www.wvgazette. com

Charleston West Virginia Convention & Visitors Bureau. Available www.charlestonwv.com

City of Charleston Home Page. Available www. cityofcharleston.org

Kanawha County Public Library. Available www. kanawhalibrary.org

Kanawha County Schools. Available kcs.kana.k12. wv.us

Sunday Gazette-Mail. Available www. sundaygazettemail.com

BIBLIOGRAPHY

Bell, Quentin, Virginia Nicholson, and Alen MacWeeney, *Charleston: A Bloomsbury House and Garden* (London: Francis Lincoln, 1997)

Burns, Shirley Stewart, *Bringing Down the Mountains: the Impact of Mountaintop Removal Surface Coal Mining on Southern West Virginia Communities, 1970–2004* (Morgantown: West Virginia University Press, 2007)

Huntington

■ The City in Brief

Founded: 1871

Head Official: Mayor Steve Wolfe (since 2013; current term expires 2017)

City Population
> 1990: 54,844
> 2000: 51,475
> 2010: 49,138
> 2012 estimate: 49,309
> Percent change, 2000–2010: –4.5%
> U.S. rank in 1990: 450th (State rank: 2nd)
> U.S. rank in 2000: 696th (State rank: 2nd)
> U.S. rank in 2010: Not available (State rank: 2nd)

Metropolitan Statistical Area Population
> 2000: 288,649
> 2010: 287,702
> 2012 estimate: 286,603
> Percent change, 2000–2010: –0.3%
> U.S. rank in 2000: 151st
> U.S. rank in 2010: 161st

Area: 16 square miles

Elevation: Averages 570 feet above sea level

Average Annual Temperatures: January, 32.7° F; July, 75.3° F; annual average, 55.0° F

Average Annual Precipitation: 42.31 inches of rain; 26.2 inches of snow

Major Economic Sectors: energy, health care, manufacturing, transportation, wholesale and retail trade

Unemployment Rate: 4.5% (2012)

Per Capita Income: $19,520

Major Colleges and Universities: Marshall University, Marshall Community and Technical College, Huntington Junior College

Daily Newspaper: *The Herald-Dispatch*

■ Introduction

Huntington is the largest city in the Tri-State Region, located just across the Ohio River from Ohio and across the Big Sandy River from Kentucky. The city retains the charm of an earlier time, with century-old homes, historic districts, and nineteenth-century preserved villages. It also looks to the future by encouraging business creation in technology and biotechnology, and a world-class university contributes research, creative arts, and cultural events to the city.

■ Geography and Climate

Huntington is located on the flood plain of the Ohio River, which acts as its northern border, and also sits at the foothills of the Appalachian Mountains. It is the county seat of Cabell County, but parts of the city are also in Wayne County. Because of the proximity to the river, flooding has been a problem during heavy rains. Huntington is less than an hour away by car from Charleston, West Virginia's capitol. The other two cities in the Tri-State area are Ashland, Kentucky and Ironton, Ohio. Huntington is in a continental temperate zone, with warm and humid summers, and cold winters without arctic fronts.

Area: 16 square miles

Elevation: Averages 570 feet above sea level

Average Temperatures: January, 32.7° F; July, 75.3° F; annual average, 55.0° F

Photograph by David Fatellah. Cabell-Huntington Convention and Visitors Bureau. Reproduced by permission.

Average Annual Precipitation: 42.31 inches of rain; 26.2 inches of snow

■ History

Native Tribes are First Inhabitants

The first known inhabitants of the Ohio River Valley were the Adena people, also known as the "mound builders" because of the artifact-laden mounds they built, some over 2000 years ago. Since the 1500s, different Native American tribes lived in the Ohio Valley and in the area now called Huntington, such as the Hurons, but the area was also used as hunting grounds by the larger Shawnee of Ohio and the Iroquois Confederacy from New York. There was much fighting in the region between the British and Native Americans in the 1760s and 1770s, resulting in battles and massacres of entire villages. As more settlers entered the region after the American Revolution, the Mingo and Shawnee tribes were forced to move further inland.

War and Railroads

In 1837 Marshall Academy, the forerunner of Marshall University, was created in the town of Barboursville. Named after U.S. Supreme Court Chief Justice John Marshall, it started as a subscription school, and after being closed during the Civil War it reopened as the State Normal School of Marshall College to train teachers.

Inhabitants of Cabell County during the Civil War were divided about their allegiances. The Border Rangers were a local pro-South militia formed in 1860, but the county's representative to the Virginia secession convention of 1861 voted to remain in the Union. While Virginia seceded, Cabell County voted to stay in the Union, with the exception of the town of Guyandotte, now part of Huntington. The Battle at Barboursville in 1861 was the first battle in the county, won by the Confederacy. The town was eventually captured by Union forces, which then burned most of Guyandotte to the ground. It was due to the area's Union leanings that caused the State of West Virginia to be created in 1862.

Huntington, originally called Halderby's Landing, was named after Collis P. Huntington, a railroad baron who was a major partner in the Central Pacific Railroad, and who bought out the Chesapeake & Ohio Railway. In 1869 he began construction of the western terminus to the C & O, connecting the Ohio River and trains from the Midwest to the Atlantic Seaboard. The city was incorporated in 1871 by the West Virginia State

Legislature. In 1873, the first locomotive arrived from Richmond to the celebration of the entire community. The railroad was the city's largest employer for a century, until eventually becoming part of CSX in the 1970s.

A Glimpse of Modern Life

In 1884 the Ohio River overflowed its banks, flooding the city and causing major damage. Huntington became the seat of Cabell County in 1887, just after the first electric streetlights were installed. Electric streetcars became a fixture in the city soon afterwards. Just west of Huntington, Central City was incorporated in 1893. Central City started as just a few farms but grew as manufacturers, such as glass and chain factories, entered the area, and in 1909 Central City was annexed by Huntington. The same year, construction of Ritter Park was begun, which was completed in 1913, and the park continues to be a valued part of Huntington today.

Again in 1913 the river flooded Huntington, causing serious damage. However, it was not as bad as the flood to come. The "Great Flood of 1937" left 6,000 residents homeless and the region devastated. The disaster caused the U.S. Army Corps of Engineers to build a 15-mile flood wall to protect the town, which it continues to do today.

Readily available raw materials, cheap coal power, and connections to major markets by the railroad caused Huntington to grow into the industrial hub of the area. Steel producers and fabricators blossomed along with manufacturers of railcars and railroad equipment. Huntington is still known for its glassworks and pigment production.

Huntington Today

In 1970 tragedy struck the city when a plane carrying 75 passengers, including the entire Marshall University football team, crashed in rain and fog on approach to Tri-State Airport. The crash was the worst aviation disaster in the country that year. In 2006 a feature film based on the event, *We Are Marshall,* starred actor Matthew McConaughey; much of the filming was done in Huntington.

West Virginia's economy has had its ups and downs. At first, mechanization in mining increased the unemployment rate when fewer workers were needed. In the 1970s, when energy prices were high, the coal industry and state profited. When energy prices dropped in the 1980s it was a devastating blow to the entire state, affecting all the mining communities and all business sectors beyond. Huntington suffered from factory closures and a declining population.

Today's Huntington is still a center of manufacturing and shipping, especially of the region's coal and petroleum. In the future, however, the city may become a regional center for health care and technology, as the community becomes more educated and as the economic leaders search for new paths out of the nationwide recession of 2008 and 2009.

Historical Information: The City of Huntington, City Hall, 800 5th Avenue, Huntington, WV 25701; telephone (304) 696-5530.

■ Population Profile

Metropolitan Statistical Area Population

2000: 288,649
2010: 287,702
2012 estimate: 286,603
Percent change, 2000–2010: −0.3%
U.S. rank in 2000: 151st
U.S. rank in 2010: 161st

City Residents

1990: 54,844
2000: 51,475
2010: 49,138
2012 estimate: 49,309
Percent change, 2000–2010: −4.5%
U.S. rank in 1990: 450th (State rank: 2nd)
U.S. rank in 2000: 696th (State rank: 2nd)
U.S. rank in 2010: Not available (State rank: 2nd)

Density: 1,376.7 people per square mile

Racial and ethnic characteristics

White: 43,221
Black or African American: 3,893
American Indian and Alaskan Native: 105
Asian: 337
Native Hawaiian and Other Pacific Islander: 26
Hispanic or Latino (may be of any race): 582
Other: 1,727

Percent of residents born in state: 73.7%

Age characteristics

Population under 5 years old: 2,390
Population 5 to 9 years old: 2,151
Population 10 to 14 years old: 2,535
Population 15 to 19 years old: 3,914
Population 20 to 24 years old: 5,826
Population 25 to 34 years old: 7,690
Population 35 to 44 years old: 5,601
Population 45 to 54 years old: 5,718
Population 55 to 59 years old: 3,550
Population 60 to 64 years old: 2,920
Population 65 to 74 years old: 3,364
Population 75 to 84 years old: 2,665
Population 85 years and over: 985
Median age: 35.4

Births (2010–11 Metropolitan Area)

Total number: 3,287

Deaths (2010–11 Metropolitan Area)

Total number: 3,275

Money income (2012)

Per capita income: $19,520
Median household income: $28,201
Total households: 21,353

Number of households with income of . . .

less than $10,000: 4,020
$10,000 to $14,999: 2,642
$15,000 to $24,999: 3,207
$25,000 to $34,999: 2,434
$35,000 to $49,999: 2,936
$50,000 to $74,999: 3,011
$75,000 to $99,999: 1,434
$100,000 to $149,999: 936
$150,000 to $199,999: 287
$200,000 or more: 446

Percent of families below poverty level: 30.8%

■ Municipal Government

The Huntington City Council has eleven members, one from each of the nine municipal election districts and two members elected at-large. The mayor and council members are elected for four-year terms in November, with primaries held in May.

Head Official: Mayor Steve Wolfe (since 2013; current term expires 2017)

Total Number of City Employees: 358 (2013 est.)

City Information: The City of Huntington, City Hall, 800 5th Avenue, Huntington, WV 25701; telephone (304) 696-5530.

■ Economy

Major Industries and Commercial Activity

Huntington and Cabell County have long been known for their strong manufacturing base, although now health care and education make up the largest percentage of jobs. Steel and glass were industries that grew in the city's Industrial Revolution origins, as did the transportation sector, which is the town's origin. New industries, such as biotechnology and research, are being lured to the area with economic incentives. The health-care industry in the area continues to grow, with health-care organizations among the area's top employers. The state remains a major producer of oil, natural gas, and coal.

Items and goods produced: steel, glass, medical devices, railroad equipment, petroleum, natural gas

Incentive Programs-New and Existing Companies

Local programs: A variety of incentive programs are available to companies who establish new businesses in the Huntington area with a certain level of capital investment and jobs created. These include free land programs, relocation grants, financing of equipment, rent breaks, and others. Many of these are provided by the Huntington Area Development Council. If a business locates in the Huntington/Ironton Empowerment Zone, it may be eligible for such incentives as federal wage credits and bond financing.

State programs: West Virginia's frequent budget surpluses have allowed the state cut business taxes and become increasingly competitive. The state's direct loan program, administered by the West Virginia Economic Development Authority, funds up to 45 percent of business financing with low-interest loans and 5- to 15-year terms. Industrial revenue bonds are available to small manufacturing projects, qualifying projects in Enterprise Communities, and exempt facility projects. A linked deposit loan program gives businesses with fewer than 50 employees and $5 million in annual revenue access to loans at 1 percent above New York Prime rates, up to $250,000. Venture capital funding is provided through the West Virginia Jobs Investment Trust. Tax credits, exemptions, and similar programs include Corporate Headquarters Credit, Economic Opportunity Credit, "Five-for Ten" Program, Manufacturing Investment Credit, Manufacturing Inventory Credit, Strategic R&D Credit, West Virginia Film Industry Investment Act, High-Tech Manufacturing Credit, Aircraft Valuation, High-Technology Business Property Valuation Act, The Freeport Amendment, Manufacturing Sales Tax Exemptions, Special Rates of Electric Power for Industrial Consumers, Research and Development Sales Tax Exemption, Sales Tax Exemption for E-Commerce, Tax Increment Financing, Tourism Matching Advertising Partnership, and Lodging Exemptions.

Job training programs: The Governor's Guaranteed Work Force Program provides training grants of up to $1,000 per employee for companies that create a minimum of 10 new jobs within a 12-month period. WorkKeys Career Readiness Certificates from Workforce West Virginia help match qualified job seekers with employers. The Workforce Investment Act Program offers customized training to employers that hire economically disadvantaged or displaced residents. West Virginia Advance Program operates in conjunction with the state's community and technical colleges to award customized job training to start-up and existing businesses.

Development Projects

The Huntington Area Development Council (HADCO) has been an important factor in economic growth in recent years. Since 1992, when HADCO was created, the region has seen the creation of over 10,000 new jobs. In addition, over 2.8 million square feet of building space has been leased, sold or built; 30 new companies have announced locations in Cabell and Wayne Counties, and there has been over $260 million in new capital investment. In 2006 HADCO was recognized as the best economic development organization in the South by the Southern Economic Development Council.

In 2013 HADCO announced that Allevard Sogefi, an Italian Company in nearby Prichard, West Virginia, was adding 250 jobs as part of a $20 million expansion. The company manufactures parts for automobile engines used by a number of motor companies.

In 2009 construction completed on the Marshall University Forensic Science Center addition, a three-story, 15,000-square-foot project completed at a cost of $4.2 million. The facility includes HADCO's Biotech Incubator labs, as well as classrooms and other laboratories. Some $1 million in funding for the project came from HADCO. Additional funding came in the form of grants from Verizon West Virginia and Benedum, who combined to provide $250,000 of additional financial support.

Also that year, Marshall University completed a $30 million, 123,000-square-foot student recreation center, completed with a climbing wall, juice bar, racquetball courts, basketball courts, fitness center, group exercise room, and three-lane jogging track. The following year, Marshall completed construction on the $9 million Erickson Alumni Center and Foundation Hall. The 33,000-square-foot building has four floors and spaces designed for conferences and events, in addition to housing offices for the Marshall University Foundation.

Alcon, a medical device manufacturer, opened a new facility in the HADCO Business Park in 2011. The expansion allowed Alcon to maintain its facility's status as the world's largest intraocular lens manufacturing site. The two-year project created more than 350 new jobs in the area and added 101,000 square feet of space.

A municipal bond issue supported construction of five area schools between 2006 and 2010.

Economic Development Information: Huntington Area Development Council, 916 Fifth Avenue, Suite 400, Huntington, WV 25701; telephone (304)525-1161; fax (304)525-1163; email hadco@hadco.org. Huntington Regional Chamber of Commerce, 1108 3rd Avenue, Huntington, WV 25701; telephone (304) 525-5131; fax (304) 525-5158.

Commercial Shipping

Huntington's central location in the heart of the Tri-State region of West Virginia, Ohio, and Kentucky affords it a convenient midway point between Pittsburgh, Pennsylvania, and Louisville, Kentucky. Products and people move through the Tri-State region's efficient transportation network that includes the Tri-State Airport; an interstate highway system that links the area to East Coast, Southern, and Midwestern markets; an advanced rail network; and the largest tonnage barge port on the Ohio River. The Tri-State Airport is a FedEx regional hub. In addition, Huntington is within a 24-hour drive of approximately 44 percent of the nation's industrial market and 37 percent of the consumer market.

The Port of Huntington-Tristate is the largest inland river port in the United States and one of the top ten largest ports in the nation by shipping weight. The port area covers 100 miles along the Ohio River, 90 miles along the Kanawha River, and 9 miles on the Big Sandy River. Many docks are under private ownership. The Huntington region, including the port area, is served by CSX and Norfolk Southern and by 14 motor freight companies.

Labor Force and Employment Outlook

The outlook for the Huntington area looks bright, despite the city's stable and sometimes declining population. HADCO's development plans and joint ventures with Marshall University offer the promise of bringing new technology and biotech firms to the area to replace a loss of manufacturing jobs. As of 2013, HADCO and its partners had created more than 10,000 new jobs and over $260 million in new investments. As of 2012, the highest area salaries were in management positions, followed by business and finance, construction and extraction, and education.

The following is a summary of data regarding the 2012 Huntington labor force:

Size of civilian labor force: 22,696

Number of workers employed in . . .
   agriculture and mining: 125
   construction: 1,185
   manufacturing: 1,058
   wholesale trade: 426
   retail trade: 3,036
   transportation: 632
   information systems: 536
   finance: 854
   professional administration: 1,975
   education and social services: 6,057
   arts and leisure: 3,000
   other: 997
   public administration: 861

Average hourly earnings of production workers: $17.22

Unemployment rate: 4.5% (2012)

Employers

Largest employers (2013)	*Number of employees*
St. Mary's Medical Center	2,600
Cabell Huntington Hospital	2,300
Marshall University	2,000
CSX, Huntington Division	1,100
VA Medical Center	1,078
Special Metals	996
University Physicians & Surgeons	850
Marathon	800
U.S. Army Corps o Engineers	775
Wal-Mart	750

Cost of Living

The cost of living in Huntington is some 13.7 percent below the national average, with the median home price only $96,900.

The following is a summary of data regarding several key cost of living factors in the area.

State income tax rate: 3.0% to 6.5%

State sales tax rate: 6.0%

Local income tax rate: $156 per year city service fee

Local sales tax rate: 1.0%

Property tax rate: 1.6994 mills (2013)

Economic Information: Huntington Area Development Council, 916 Fifth Avenue, Suite 400, Huntington, WV 25701; telephone (304)525-1161; fax (304)525-1163; email hadco@hadco.org.

■ Education and Research

Elementary and Secondary Schools

In 2006 Cabell County voters approved a 15-year $60.4 million school bond levy that added three new middle schools and two elementary schools to the Cabell County Schools. By 2010, construction had completed on all five schools. Also that year, two consortiums of Cabell County schools, one of elementary schools and the other of secondary, were awarded Innovation Zone Planning grants by the state to raise the level of academic achievement in the schools through learning communities and the exploration of different teaching and learning styles.

The Cabell County Career Technology Center, sponsored by the county school board, offers adult basic education classes as well as career programs in auto mechanics, graphic design and commercial art, heating and air condition, hospitality management, drafting, welding, and interior design, among others. The center also operates the School of Practical Nursing, which is a Licensed Practical Nursing Program for adults.

Advanced Placement courses are available in a range of subjects at Cabell County High Schools. As of 2012, the graduation rate was 83.6 percent. Some 48.6 percent of students qualify as low income. The attendance rate was 95.8 percent, and the dropout rate was 4.2 percent.

There were five private and parochial schools serving Huntington and Cabell County in 2013.

The following is a summary of data regarding the Cabell County Schools.

Total enrollment: 12,700

Number of facilities

total: 27
elementary schools: 19
junior high schools: 5
high schools: 2
other: 1

Student/teacher ratio: 14.4:1

Teacher salaries

average (statewide): $47,253

Funding per pupil: $11,592

Public Schools Information: Cabell County Schools, 2850 Fifth Avenue, Huntington, WV 25702; telephone (304) 528-5000; fax (304) 528-5080.

Colleges and Universities

Huntington is home to three colleges and universities. Marshall University (MU) is the area's largest university and was ranked by *U.S. News & World Report* as one of top 40 regional universities in the South in 2013. With enrollment at 13,708 students, it offers 2 associate degree programs, 68 baccalaureate programs, and 52 graduate programs in programs spanning business, fine arts, education, liberal arts, science, journalism, and medicine. The Marshall University Campus is constantly evolving. In 2009 Marshall University opened a new student recreation center, and in 2010 the school opened the Marshall University Erickson Alumni Center and Foundation Hall, a state-of-the-art facility for conferences and events. Marshall University operates the Joan C. Edwards School of Medicine.

Also in the region, the Marshall Community and Technical College in 2010 became the Mountwest Community and Technical College. It is a two-year institute offering associates degrees in numerous areas of study including allied health, business, graphic design and communications, and information and manufacturing technologies. Certificate programs are also available in such fields as medical transcription, paramedic science, police science, public library technology, culinary arts, and accounting.

Huntington Junior College is located in the downtown area and offers eight associate degree programs in the business and health professions. Diploma programs are also available in dental assisting, medical assisting, and professional office administration. Many classes are available online.

The Ashland Community and Technical College and the Ohio University Southern Campus are also regional options for higher education.

Libraries and Research Centers

The Cabell County Public Library system operates a main library in Huntington and seven branches in neighboring towns. Over 100 years old, it was the first library system in the state to have a computerized catalog and circulation system. The main branch is home to a local history and genealogy room, and three social services agencies: The Tri-State Literacy Council, the Adult Learning Center, and the Information and Referral Services. The library also hosts the Sub-Regional Library for the Blind and/or Physically Handicapped. The Cabell County Library offers a wide array of e-books and audiobooks for download.

The John Deaver Drinko Library on the main campus at Marshall University opened in 1998. The library holds over 180,000 book volumes and has a 24-hour reading room and computer lab. The Special Collection Department at Morrow Library, also on the main campus of Marshall, includes the West Virginia Collection of regional history and the Rosanna Alexander Blake Library of Confederate History. The Morrow library is also a selective depository for U.S. government documents.

Marshall University has several prominent research centers. The Center for Business and Economic Research investigates promoting regional economic growth. The Center for Environmental, Geotechnical and Applied Sciences researches environmental management and technology using geo-science. The Robert C. Byrd Center for Rural Health runs rural health programs across the state and the Center of Biomedical Research Excellence focuses on cancer research. Others include the West Virginia Autism Training Center and the West Virginia Prevention Resource Center. In 2009, construction was completed on a new addition to Marshall's Forensic Science Center, including bio-tech incubator laboratories and classrooms. The Huntington VA Medical Center houses state-of-the-art research laboratories and support facilities.

Public Library Information: Cabell County Public Library; 455 9th Street Plaza, Huntington, WV 25701; telephone (304) 528-5700.

■ Health Care

The Tri-State area has eight hospitals that serve the community, with a total of over 1,300 beds and the largest private physician practice in the state. The largest hospital in the area and second largest in the state is St. Mary's Medical Center. With 375 beds and centers in cardiac care, neuroscience, diabetes, and cancer treatment, St. Mary's is a teaching hospital for Marshall University Joan C. Edwards School of Medicine and programs in nursing, medical imaging, and respiratory care that are also associated with Marshall University. St. Mary's Regional Cancer Center is sponsored in part by the Research and Education Program of the Duke Comprehensive Cancer Center. St Mary's also hosts a specialized neuroscience unit and a Level II Trauma Center.

Cabell Huntington Hospital, a 303-bed referral center, opened the 50,000 square-foot Edwards Comprehensive Cancer Center in 2005 and the five-story North Patient Tower in 2007. The hospital is also home to West Virginia's only Burn Intensive Care Unit, a Neonatal Intensive Care Unit, a Level II trauma Center, and a Joint Replacement Center. The hospital also hosts the Regional Pain Management Center. It is also a teaching hospital affiliated with Marshall University.

The Huntington VA Medical Center serves veterans with an 80-bed acute care and surgical hospital and four outpatient clinics. The VA is also a teaching hospital for Marshall University Joan C. Edwards School of Medicine.

Valley Health operates general health care centers and public health programs at locations in the area, including some school-based health services and a special Black Lung Care program at several locations. Valley Health Huntington offers family practice, internal medicine, and pediatric primary care services as well as operating an urgent care center. Women's Place, Valley Health Diagnostics Lab, Valley Health Pharmacy, and Valley Health Youth and Pediatrics are all located in Huntington. HealthSouth operates two centers in the area: the Rehabilitation Hospital of Huntington, with 52 beds, and the Cabell-Huntington Outpatient Surgery Center. The Prestera Center provides outpatient mental health services for adults, children, and families, and has inpatient substance abuse and psychiatric facilities. Mildred Mitchell-Bateman Hospital is an adult inpatient psychiatric facility. The locally owned River Park Hospital provides inpatient psychiatric services for both adults and adolescents. Genesis HealthCare runs Heritage Center, an eldercare and rehabilitation center.

In 2008, a report from the Center for Disease Control labeled Huntington as the unhealthiest city in America, with more than half of the adult population overweight and numerous other community health problems related to diabetes, dental hygiene, and smoking. This is perhaps why the health industry is one of the largest area employers. The city received national attention when celebrity chef Jamie Oliver made it his test subject for his healthy food campaign "Food Revolution." Jamie's Kitchen in Huntington exists to educate the community on eating healthy and preparing meals at home. In 2013 Huntington ranked third among all U.S. cities for obesity.

■ Recreation

Sightseeing

Huntington has a range of attractions for the history buff, the arts lover, and families. A number of the city's historic buildings are open to the public and available for tours. The Jenkins Plantation Museum is a brick mansion built in 1835 and is part of the Civil War Discovery Trail. Featured are tours, reenactments and special events. The Madie Caroll House, run by the Huntington Park District, was floated into town on a barge in 1810 and survived an attack by federal troops in 1861. The building was home to the Caroll family, existed as an inn, and was the first house of Catholic worship in Cabell County. The Cabell County Courthouse was built in 1901 and is on the National Register of Historic Places. Heritage Village, across from Riverfront Park, consists of the restored original B&O Railway station and Huntington's first bank, reportedly robbed by Jessie James in 1975. On display are a period locomotive and Pullman car, and shops and restaurants draw visitors.

Heritage Farm Museum and Village displays Appalachian farm culture by preserving 16 buildings from the 1800s, including a schoolhouse, blacksmith shop, meeting hall, a mill, and barns. Collections of farm equipment, a petting zoo, a country store, and four bed and breakfasts are part of the attractions. The Rose Garden at Ritter Park has existed for over 70 years and features more than 2,000 rose bushes. Blenko Glass Company is home to artisans creating handmade glassware, which can be viewed from an observation area. Camden Park, West Virginia's only amusement park, has been in existence since 1903 but is still going strong with 12 major rides, a Kiddieland area with nine rides, and a Midway full of games and food. The Mardi Gras Casino and Resort is in nearby Cross Lanes and features Greyhound racing, slot machines, and video gambling.

Arts and Culture

The 5th Avenue Theater Company, a non-profit production company, specializes in musicals and theater for children and families. The company performs in the historic Jean Carlo Stephenson Auditorium in Huntington's City Hall. For over 70 years, the Joan C. Edwards Performing Arts Center at Marshall University has hosted plays, films, musicians, dance companies, and other touring productions through the Marshall Artists Series. Students from Marshall's Department of Theater also put on productions at the University's venues. Huntington Outdoor Theatre presents musicals every July in the Ritter Park Amphitheater. Huntington Dance Theatre performs and teaches ballet and modern dance. In nearby Ashland, Kentucky, the 1,400-seat Paramount Arts Center presents plays, music, and dance performances from national and local groups.

The Huntington Symphony Orchestra presents an average of six classical and three pops performances each season, with classical performances presented at Jean Carlo Stephenson Auditorium and pops shows at Harris Riverfront Park in the summer. Marshall University's many ensembles showcase jazz, chamber, orchestral, and choral music. The Greater Huntington Park and Recreation District hosts music performances at Ritter Amphitheater.

Huntington's several museums and galleries appeal to a wide variety of tastes. The Huntington Museum of Art has a broad collection of nineteenth- and twentieth-century paintings, drawings, sculpture, glass, silver, folk art, and firearms. Attached to the Museum of Art is the C. Fred Edwards Conservatory, West Virginia's only plant conservatory and home to sub-tropical native plants and seasonal displays. The Huntington Railroad Museum in Ritter Park is home to two locomotives and two cabooses; free tours are available by arrangement. The Birke Art Gallery at Marshall University displays student and professional art. The Museum of Radio and Technology features radios from the 1920s through the 1950s, military radio technology, and vintage computers. Benjy's Harley-Davidson Motorcycle Museum, located in a Harley dealership, shows off an amazing collection of antique and modern motorcycles.

Festivals and Holidays

In March, Huntington's Park District holds a St. Patrick's Day Celebration with live music, Irish food, and fun for kids. At Easter time, an Egg Hunt goes on in Ritter Park. For decades, the Huntington Dogwood Arts and Crafts Festival took place in April at the Big Sandy Superstore Arena. It was cancelled in 2013 due to a lack of vendor interest. The city celebrates West Virginia Day, June 20th, with entertainment, food, and crafts. Also in June, Jazz-MU-Tazz, Marshall University's jazz festival, features plenty of free music outdoors, and Old Central City Days has the area's streets busy with flea markets and historic tours. The Fourth of July brings fireworks and music to Riverfront Park. The Cabell County Fair takes place for four days at the end of July. Begun in 2005, the West Virginia Hot Dog Festival on the last Saturday in July celebrates the unusual number of hot dog restaurants in the Huntington area and raises money for the area's children. Food is first billing in September's ChiliFest, which is also the state's chili championship. September also brings the Hilltop Festival to the Huntington Museum of Art and the Pilot Club of Huntington

Antique Show and Sale. In October comes the Grecian Festival at St. George Greek Orthodox Church and the West Virginia Pumpkin Festival. Guyandotte Civil War Days in November brings re-enactors together to commemorate the raid on the town in 1861 with period music, history tours, and craft displays. The Lions Tri-State Arts and Crafts Festival happens in December at the Big Sandy Superstore Arena.

Sports for the Spectator

Fans of Marshall University's Thundering Herd sports program enjoy watching football, baseball, and men's and women's basketball. Other sports at Marshall include volleyball, soccer, golf, tennis, and swimming. Regional college and local high school football and basketball are also enjoyed by residents.

Sports for the Participant

The Greater Huntington Park District offers 15 parks with many sports facilities and a dog park. The Ritter Park Tennis Center has 11 hard courts with 4 indoor courts and a pro shop. Veterans Memorial Field House was home to indoor soccer, inline hockey, and basketball games until it was demolished in 2012. There were plans to replace it with new sports facilities. Softball fields, basketball courts, pools and other amenities serve the community. The Park District coordinates an active softball community league. Huntington's YMCA provides many recreational activities, including an indoor pool. An 18-hole golf course is at the Esquire Country Club in nearby Barboursville. There are one private and five public golf courses in the city. The city maintains three public pools. Hiking trails, camping, boating and fishing are available activities in the three nearby state parks: Virginia Point Park, East Lynn Lake and Dam, and Beach Fork Lake and State Park.

Shopping and Dining

Huntington's several shopping areas range from the historic to the modern. Old Central City features antique shops and is close to the Railroad Museum and Heritage Farm. Pullman Square has attracted numerous specialty shops and national chains. The Huntington Mall has about 130 stores, including clothing, book, electronics and jewelry retailers.

Dining choices at local restaurants vary and are plentiful. For casual eating, Huntington is well-known for its hot dog/root beer stands and "Huntington-style" hot dogs, such as those offered at the Frostop Drive-In, Stewart's Original, Sam's, and Bowincal. The hot dog's sauce, of which Stewart's claims to have invented, makes the difference. Jim's Steak and Spaghetti House is a Huntington institution, in business for over 60 years and still operated by the original owner. Buddy's All-American Bar-B-Que has killer wings famous on the Marshall University campus. For more refined dining,

fine Italian, American, seafood, Indian, and Mexican food are available. Two restaurants in historic buildings are Savannah's, serving traditional southern food in a 1903 Victorian mansion, and Boston Beanery, at the old B&O Railroad station.

Visitor Information: Cabell-Huntington Convention and Visitor's Bureau, 210 11th St. Huntington, WV 25701; telephone (304) 525-7333; toll-free (800) 635-6329.

■ Convention Facilities

The Big Sandy Superstore Arena and Conference Center offers more than 100,000 square feet of exhibition, conference, meeting and ballroom facilities, as well as an on-site caterer and videoconferencing equipment. Marshall University's Memorial Student Center can be rented for conferences; its recital halls and the Joan C. Edwards Playhouse make interesting venues for meetings or conferences. The University can also provide housing at its Twin Towers Residence Hall and the newer Marshall Commons suites residence hall. Until 2012, Veterans Memorial Field House, able to seat up to 5,964 people, was the city's largest convention venue. It was demolished in 2012. The site had 20,000 square feet of exhibition space and hosted to concerts, rodeos, circuses, and sporting events. Heritage Farm Museum and Village has banquet space available. The Jean Stephenson Auditorium at City Hall can seat 1,985 people. Several area hotels have exhibition and conference space. Savannah's Restaurant and Wesvanawha can also host large parties and events.

Convention Information: Cabell-Huntington Convention and Visitor's Bureau, 210 11th St. Huntington, WV 25701; telephone (304) 525-7333; toll-free (800) 635-6329.

■ Transportation

Approaching the City

The Tri-State Airport is located only nine miles from Huntington, and is served by US Airways and Allegiant Air, making connections to Charlotte, North Carolina; Orlando and St. Petersburg, Florida; and seasonally to Myrtle Beach, South Carolina. In nearby Charleston, West Virginia, Charles Yeager Airport provides service from additional carriers. Tri-State and Yeager airports offer private aviation facilities as well.

Interstate 64 runs along the south side of Huntington, heading east to the capitol, Charleston, and west to Lexington, Kentucky. Interstate 77 intersects with Interstate 64 to the east of Huntington. West

Virginia Route 60 runs right through Huntington's downtown.

Intercity passenger service to Huntington is available on Amtrak's Cardinal Line, running from New York City to Chicago, Illinois. There is also an Amtrak station in nearby Ashland, Kentucky. Greyhound Bus Lines offers regular service to downtown.

Traveling in the City

The Tri-State Transit Authority (TTA) runs 16 routes, all connected at the TTA Center on 4th Avenue. There is a special shuttle service between Marshall University and Pullman Square. Bus service is available primarily on weekdays. Three evening and Saturday routes are offered but with limited stops. There is no Sunday service. Buses and vans are accessible for those with disabilities. The TTA connects Huntington with Milton, Barboursville, Ceredo and Kenova, making stops in Ohio and Kentucky. In 2008, the TTA in partnership with the Kanawha Valley Regional Transportation Authority opened bus routes between Huntington and Charleston, West Virginia, through a service called Intelligent Transit. The service gives options to commuters and students, where there previously were none. Yellow Cabs are available for hire and Top Hat Pedal Cab has bicycle-powered rickshaws that drive passengers around downtown Huntington.

■ Communications

Newspapers and Magazines

Huntington's daily newspaper is *The Herald-Dispatch*. *Huntington Quarterly* is a full-color magazine that features articles about the community and city.

Television and Radio

Huntington is home to five television stations, including one public television broadcast. The city also receives broadcasts from Charleston, West Virginia; Ashland, Kentucky; and Portsmouth, Ohio. Cable service is provided through Comcast and Suddenlink. There are 16 FM and AM radio stations broadcast from the Huntington area.

Media Information: *The Herald-Dispatch*, 946 5th Ave., Huntington, WV 25701; telephone (304) 526-4000.

Huntington Online

Cabell County Public Library. Available cabell.lib.wv.us

Cabell County Schools. Available boe.cabe.k12.wv.us

Cabell-Huntington Convention and Visitors Bureau. Available www.wvvisit.org

City of Huntington Home Page. Available www.cityofhuntington.com

The Herald-Dispatch. Available www.herald-dispatch.com

Huntington Area Development Council. Available www.hadco.org

Huntington Regional Chamber of Commerce. Available www.huntingtonchamber.org

BIBLIOGRAPHY

Pekar, Harvey, *Huntington, West Virginia "On the Fly"* (New York: Village Trade Paperbacks, 2011)

Rice, Otis K., *West Virginia: A History* (Lexington, KY: The University of Kentucky Press, 1985)

Cumulative Index

The 219 cities featured in *Cities of the United States*, Volume 1: *The South*, Volume 2: *The West*, Volume 3: *The Midwest*, and Volume 4: *The Northeast*, along with names of individuals, organizations, historical events, etc., are designated in this Cumulative Index by name of the appropriate regional volume, or volumes, followed by the page number(s) on which the term appears in that volume.

Waterbury, VT **Northeast:** 547

Waterbury, CT **Northeast:** 60

Watkins Glen, NY **Northeast:** 394

Wayne, Anthony **Midwest:** 89–90, 245, 486, 521, 533–534

Wayne, Anthony **Northeast:** 410, 414

Wayne, Anthony **South:** 109

Wayne State University **Midwest:** 243, 247, 250–253, 256

Weiser, ID **West:** 346

Wellesley, MA **Northeast:** 171

Welty, Eudora **South:** 385–386

West Hartford, CT **Northeast:** 31, 65

West Memphis, AR **South:** 562

West Springfield, MA **Northeast:** 168–169

Western Connecticut State University **Northeast:** 20–22

Western Dakota Tech **Midwest:** 563, 568

Western Michigan University **Midwest:** 264

Westinghouse, George **West:** 298

Wethersfield, CT **Northeast:** 13, 50

Whistler, James Abbott McNeill **Midwest:** 238

Wichita, KS **Midwest:** 217

Wilkes-Barre, PA **Northeast:** 465, 471–472

William J. Clinton Presidential Center **South:** 75, 82–83

Williams, Tennessee **South:** 142

Williams, William Carlos **Northeast:** 300, 306

Williamsburg, VA **South:** 680, 725

Wilmington, DE **South:** 97, 107, 408

Wilson, Woodrow **South:** 504

Windsor Locks, CT **Northeast:** 23, 35, 66

Windsor, Ontario **Midwest:** 241, 249, 252, 255

Winston-Salem, NL **South:** 441

Winthrop, John **Northeast:** 140

Winthrop, MA **Northeast:** 129

Wolfsonian Museum **South:** 152

Wood, Grant **Midwest:** 143, 148, 158

Wood, Grant **South:** 448

Woodstock, VT **Northeast:** 551

Worcester, MA **Northeast:** 179

Works Progress Administration **South:** 7, 161, 737

Works Progress Administration **West:** 55

Worthing, SD **Midwest:** 577

Wright Brothers **Midwest:** 108, 197, 527

Wright, Frank Lloyd **Northeast:** 201, 222, 344, 371

Wright-Patterson Air Force Base **Midwest:** 519, 522–524, 526, 529

X

Xerox Corporation **Northeast:** 379

Y

Yellowstone National Park **West:** 349, 371, 374, 378, 403, 630, 635

Young, Brigham **West:** 323, 418, 537, 539, 542–545, 547–548, 553, 629